Conversational Artificial Intelligence

Scrivener Publishing
100 Cummings Center, Suite 541J
Beverly, MA 01915-6106

Publishers at Scrivener
Martin Scrivener (martin@scrivenerpublishing.com)
Phillip Carmical (pcarmical@scrivenerpublishing.com)

Conversational Artificial Intelligence

Edited by
Romil Rawat
Rajesh Kumar Chakrawarti
Sanjaya Kumar Sarangi
Piyush Vyas
Mary Sowjanya Alamanda
Kotagiri Srividya
and
Krishnan Sakthidasan Sankaran

Scrivener
Publishing

WILEY

This edition first published 2024 by John Wiley & Sons, Inc., 111 River Street, Hoboken, NJ 07030, USA and Scrivener Publishing LLC, 100 Cummings Center, Suite 541J, Beverly, MA 01915, USA
© 2024 Scrivener Publishing LLC
For more information about Scrivener publications please visit www.scrivenerpublishing.com.

Wiley Global Headquarters
111 River Street, Hoboken, NJ 07030, USA

For details of our global editorial offices, customer services, and more information about Wiley products visit us at www.wiley.com.

Library of Congress Cataloging-in-Publication Data

ISBN 9781394200566

Cover images: Machine Learning AI: Semisatch | Dreamstime.com, AI Chess: Maxuser2 | Dreamstime.com, AI Monitoring MachineL Ekkasit919 | Dreamstime.com
Cover design by Kris Hackerott

Set in size of 11pt and Minion Pro by Manila Typesetting Company, Makati, Philippines

Printed in the USA

10 9 8 7 6 5 4 3 2 1

Contents

Preface

The book talks about how conversational artificial intelligence (AI) models, like chatbots, may help IT departments work more efficiently by offering solutions like self-service chatbots that let users change their passwords and do other user identification procedures. The use of chatbots, or artificial conversation systems, is growing, although not all of their security issues have been resolved. The term "conversational AI" refers to a group of technologies that allow computers and other devices to create speech- and automated messaging applications. This enables human-like interaction between humans and robots. One of the many chatbots available today with speech recognition and the ability to respond to challenging inquiries is Alexa. As demand for AI assistants rises, voice recognition technologies are becoming increasingly crucial. Hackers and other harmful software are naturally drawn to chatbot technology since it is responsible for obtaining and safeguarding sensitive information. Businesses have included conversational chatbots and automatic response software on their websites and social media platforms despite the increased threat of cyberattacks. Platforms like Facebook, WhatsApp, and WeChat frequently deploy chatbots in their customer service operations. While conversational AI will probably improve company processes, hackers may also use it to reroute their cyberattacks. AI systems already possess a plethora of knowledge about people, which helps them better grasp the kinds of arguments that each individual respond to, When coupled with extraordinary human-like conversational abilities, it is a recipe for disaster. Possible results include phishing attacks, spam calls, and fraudulent endeavours. In order to serve clients via a spoken or written interface, conversational AI integrates natural language processing with conventional software such as chatbots, voice assistants, or an interactive speech recognition system. Customers are helped by conversational chatbots, which are an intriguing development since they make the customer service sector relatively self-sufficient and react to their inquiries quickly and accurately. A well-automated chatbot may drastically reduce personnel demands, but building one takes time. The importance of voice recognition systems is increasing as AI assistants like Alexa gain popularity. Thanks to advancements in artificial intelligence, chatbots in the business sphere may now communicate with clients in a sophisticated and technical way. Contrary to popular belief, the proliferation of sensitive data in these chatbots has led to grave security problems. Threats are one-off occurrences like malware or DDOS attacks.

A Glance View on Cloud Infrastructures Security and Solutions

Srinivasa Rao Gundu[1], Charanarur Panem[2]* and J. Vijaylaxmi[3]

*[1]Department of Computer Science, Government Degree College-Sitaphalmandi,
Hyderabad, Telangana, India*
*[2]School of Cyber Security and Digital Forensic, National Forensic Sciences University,
Goa Campus, Goa, India*
[3]PVKK Degree & PG College, Anantapur, Andhra Pradesh, India

Abstract

Clients may benefit from cutting-edge cloud computing solutions created and offered in a cost-effective way by firms. In terms of cloud computing, the most serious problem is security, which serves as a significant disincentive to individuals from embracing the technology in the first place. Making cloud computing secure, particularly when it comes to the underlying infrastructure, is essential. The domain of cloud infrastructure security has been subjected to a number of different research programs; nonetheless, certain gaps remain unresolved, and new challenges continue to emerge. This article provides an in-depth analysis of security issues that might arise at various levels of the cloud architecture hierarchy. Specifically, it focuses on the most significant infrastructure-related challenges that might have an impact on the cloud computing business model in the near future.

This chapter also discusses the several literature-based approaches to dealing with the different security challenges at each level that are now accessible. To assist in the resolution of the challenges, a list of the obstacles that have still to be conquered is presented. It has been discovered that numerous cloud characteristics such as flexibility, elasticity, and multi-tenancy create new problems at each infrastructure level after conducting an examination of the existing challenges. According to research, a variety of security threats, including lack of availability, unauthorized usage, data loss, and privacy violations, have the greatest effect across all levels of infrastructure. Multi-tenancy, in particular, has been proven to have the largest effect on infrastructure at all levels, even the most basic. The study comes to a close with a number of suggestions for further research.

Keywords: Cloud computing, secure cloud infrastructure, application security, network security, host security, data security

**Corresponding author*: panem.charanarur_goa@nfsu.ac.in

Romil Rawat, Rajesh Kumar Chakrawarti, Sanjaya Kumar Sarangi, Piyush Vyas, Mary Sowjanya Alamanda, Kotagiri Srividya and Krishnan Sakthidasan Sankaran (eds.) Conversational Artificial Intelligence, (1–16) © 2024 Scrivener Publishing LLC

1.1   Introduction

Models for offering cloud computing services include the ones listed below as examples:

When it comes to providing cloud services, there are three fundamental models to consider, each of which is becoming more established and common with each passing generation. For this, there are many various approaches to consider, including software as a service, platform as a service, and infrastructure as a service (to name a few). A few of these strategies include software development, platform and infrastructure as a service, and cloud computing, among others (IaaS). In contrast to these three major models [1], an SPI model is a combination of them and may be characterized as follows:

In order to get access to programs that are hosted on service provider infrastructure, users must connect to them over the Internet. This is referred to as software as a service (also known as SaaS for short) or cloud computing, depending on who you ask. These strategies assist the customers of software offered under the SaaS business model, who are typically end users who subscribe to readily available programs. The SaaS model has also been associated with a pay and use feature that would allow the end users to access software through a web browser without having to deal with the headaches of installation, maintenance, or making a significant upfront payment [2]. Some of the popular SaaS apps include Sales force, Google Apps, and Google Docs.

User awareness is an important component of SaaS security from a security viewpoint. However, the SaaS provider must hold on to a set of security conditions in order to ensure that users adhere to the essential security protocols while using the service. Things like multi-factor authentication, complicated passwords, and password retention are examples of these requirements. An additional component that SaaS providers should have in place is the adoption of security measures to secure customers' data and to guarantee that it is available for permitted usage at all times [3].

In computing, the phrase Platform as a Service refers to a collection of software and development tools that are stored on the servers of a service provider and are available from any location on the Internet. It provides developers with a platform on which they may construct their apps without having to worry about the underlying mechanics of the service they are relying on for support. It also makes it easier to manage the software development life cycle, from planning to maintenance, in an efficient and effective way, thanks to the PaaS architecture.

The platform also makes use of programming languages such as VC++, Python, Java, etc. to allow users to construct their own apps on top of it. Many developers and programmers now depend on Platform as a Service (PaaS) firms such as WordPress, Go Daddy, and Amazon Web Services to build their websites and host their online applications. Security, according to the PaaS paradigm, is a shared responsibility that must be handled by both developers and service providers in equal measure. Example: When developing applications, developers must follow security standards and best practices to guarantee that the applications are safe and secure. A programmer, for example, must certify that the software is free of flaws and vulnerabilities [4] before exposing it to the general public.

Aspects of this process that are equally important include the detection and correction of any security flaws that attackers may exploit in order to get access to and compromise users' data. For developers, the dependability of PaaS technology, on the other hand, is critical in order to provide a safe and secure environment for application development. For example, several programming environments, such as C++, are well-known for having poor memory management, which enables attackers to conduct a variety of assaults against their victims, including stack overflows.

A lack of sufficient authentication in some relational database management systems (RDBMSs), such as Oracle, may also be exploited by attackers. Oracle, for example, allows users who have been granted admin permissions at the operating system level to access the database without the need for a username and password [5].

A kind of cloud computing paradigm in which a cloud computing service provider keeps the resources that are only shared with contractual customers that pay a per-use charge to the cloud computing service provider is known as Infrastructure as a Service (IaaS). In particular, one of the key benefits of the Equipment as a Service model is that it removes the need for a significant initial investment in computer infrastructure such as networking devices, computer processors and storage capacity, and servers. The technology may also be used to quickly and cost-effectively increase or reduce the amount of computer resources available to a user. In this day and age, with the proliferation of cloud delivery systems, it may be challenging to determine the boundaries of one's security responsibilities. Security is the responsibility of both cloud service providers (CSPs) and the clients that use their services. As seen in Illustration 5, the duties of cloud computing service delivery models are outlined. Cloud computing services include infrastructure as a service (IaaS) offerings such as Amazon Web Services, Cisco Meta-cloud, Microsoft Azure, and Google Compute Engine (GCE). It is important to note that customer-facing infrastructure is critical in terms of security since it acts as the first line of defense for the system's perimeter.

In this environment, attackers may use a variety of strategies to target the infrastructure, including denial of service (DoS) attacks and malware distribution campaigns. The majority of the time, the security of a PaaS solution is the responsibility of the service provider.

Cloud Models and Architectures: An introduction determining the kind of cloud an institution should use is the first and most important stage in cloud deployment, as this will allow for a more smooth installation process to take place. During the cloud deployment process, the second and final step is known as deployment. According to the authors, institutions who have failed to execute a deployment plan have done so as a result of selecting the incorrect kind of cloud infrastructure. In order to prevent failure, organizations must first assess their data before deciding on the kind of cloud infrastructure to use. While many consumers consider security when signing up for cloud services, many do not because they have a misconception of the efficiency of the protection given by cloud services in and of itself. When it comes to keeping their data secure, many businesses that use cloud computing depend only on the security measures employed by cloud service providers. This may provide hostile actors the ability to exploit client-side vulnerabilities in order to attack the systems of one or more tenants as a result of the situation [6].

To mention a few examples, public cloud, private cloud, community cloud, and hybrid cloud are all concepts that are being explored.

Public cloud is often referred to as an external cloud in some areas, as is the case with the Amazon Web Services (AWS) public cloud. This kind of cloud is accessible to all users or large groups of users through the Internet, with cloud service providers retaining control over the environment. Customers may access any data that are made accessible on the network using this service, which is managed by the service provider. A cost-effective and scalable means of implementing information technology solutions is made feasible via the usage of public cloud computing. Because of the Internet connection, a variety of security dangers are introduced into the system, including denial-of-service (DoS) attacks, malware, ransomware, and advanced persistent threat (APT) assaults [7, 8].

Cloud inside an organization: The private cloud, also known as the internal cloud, is a kind of cloud that is used within an organization. This category's emphasis is focused on a single user, group, or institution at the time of writing. Although the cost of private clouds is more than the cost of public clouds, they are more secure than public clouds. The fact that a private cloud is housed behind an enterprise's firewall allows users within the organization to access it via the company's intranet. Privatized clouds, in contrast to public cloud computing, are less secure since less money and experience is directed on the development of services and systems, much alone the protection of data in the private cloud. Consequently, some components may become vulnerable, allowing hostile actors to conduct attacks against these vulnerable components by exploiting the weaknesses of these vulnerable components [8].

The community cloud provides assistance for a variety of communities with common interests, such as missions, rules, security needs, and regulatory compliance difficulties, among other things. Depending on the circumstances, institutions or a third party may be in charge of managing it on-site or off-site. When compared to the standard cloud, the community cloud offers stronger privacy, security, and policy compliance protections. The degree of security in a community cloud environment is determined by the quantity of security awareness present in the community, as well as the importance of security to the activities of the community as a whole. The cloud storage of sensitive data from a government agency may endanger national security if the material is made available to the public, as has happened in the past. It follows as a result that security measures should be included in cloud computing environments [9].

Hybrid Cloud: Due to the diverse variety of needs that an institution has, this kind of cloud deployment is required. It combines two or more models in order to deliver cloud-based computing services (public, private, or community). Enterprises may use private clouds to store sensitive data or apps in a secure environment while hosting non-sensitive data or applications in a public cloud environment. Because of the federation of clouds with a diverse set of incompatible security measures, cloud hybridization, on the other hand, generates a host of security challenges. A consequence of this is that attackers uncover vulnerabilities in one or more clouds with the intent of getting access to the whole infrastructure.

1.2   Methodology

In this research, the results were gathered through a review of the available literature. How to Plan and Organize the Review Process: The following are the three sub-phases of this phase: acquiring the research goals, establishing the research questions, and choosing the search technique to be employed in the study are all included in this phase.

The Investigation's Goals and Objectives
The following are the key aims of the research:

1. The goal of this project is to provide a new taxonomy for safe cloud architecture based on the current state-of-the-art literature.
2. To provide an in-depth review of a wide range of issues and solutions that are used in cloud infrastructure at various degrees of complexity.
3. To draw attention to the disadvantages and dangers of the presently available solutions with respect to the research challenges and upcoming possibilities.

Take a look at the following questions:
Accordingly, the research explores if it is possible to answer two critical issues, which are listed below, in order to fulfill the goals.
Answer Question 1: What are some of the most well-known challenges in cloud computing architecture, as well as the proposed remedies at different levels of abstraction?
In your opinion, what is the security dangers associated with cloud that might prevent it from being more extensively used?

Various Methods of Obtaining Information
Academia's digital resources, such as the ACM Digital Library, Arxiv, and a few more relevant international conferences, were employed to pull related works for this research from a variety of academic digital resources. It was also possible to find relevant worldwide conferences via Springer, IEEE Explore, Science Direct, ACM Digital Library, Arxiv, and a few more relevant international conferences through other sources.

It is believed that they are adequate for covering the most recent and credible literature on cloud infrastructure challenges as well current security solutions, according to the study's authors who conducted the research. In the period between 2011 and 2020, an extensive study of the literature was conducted. For the purpose of obtaining reliable search results, this research searched large libraries using a combination of various search phrases that were generated using a reduplicate technique in order to increase the number of relevant studies found in the results (optimal results). The terms "Application Security" and "Network Security" were also among the most frequently used. These keywords were used to split the study into various categories, which allowed researchers to connect the relevant studies with the proper cloud infrastructure tiers, which comprised application, network, and host tiers as well as data and data infrastructure tiers, among others. In order to accomplish this approach, it is required to collect keywords and topics from the abstracts of the studies that emphasize the contributions of the study [10] that are relevant to the research.

1.3   Literature Review

Over the course of the previous decade, a number of survey studies have been published in which the security risks connected with the cloud computing environment have been explored. When it comes to cloud security, the great majority of the information that has been evaluated has made a substantial contribution to the management of these problems.

One such study looked at the most often found cloud security flaws and discovered a number of them. They also offered a number of additional solutions to security challenges that arise in cloud architecture, each of which was meant to be sensitive to the personal data of individual users. Data transfer through the cloud is subject to considerable security risks, according to a research done. Participants in this survey were provided practical advice on how to deal with potential dangers over the course of the survey. The results of a study included a taxonomy and survey of cloud services, which were organized by cloud infrastructure providers and revenue.

A service taxonomy was created, which encompasses themes such as computers, networking, databases, storage, analytics, and machine learning, among other things, as well as additional topics. Regarding functionality, the computing, networking, and storage services provided by all cloud suppliers are of a high quality, and they are commonly recognized as the backbone of the cloud computing architecture.

According to a survey, cloud computing firms face a number of security issues. The cloud client, the cloud service provider, and the owner of the data stored in the cloud were all involved in this process. An investigation of various communication and storage options in the crypto cloud was also conducted as part of the project. Researchers conducting studies into the causes and consequences of different cyberattacks have access to the most up-to-date information.

Many data protection issues that may develop in a multi-tenant cloud computing system were examined and solutions were provided in a study published by the researchers. While this poll focused more on data privacy than security, the prior survey was concerned with both concerns at once.

A research gave a full definition of cloud computing, as well as the many different levels of cloud architecture that can be found in the cloud computing environment. Part of the research included a comparison of three service models (including SaaS, PaaS, and IaaS), as well as three deployment methodologies, as part of the overall research design (private, public, and community). It was determined that both private and public clouds have information security needs; thus, the writers looked into it. A few of the most urgent difficulties and restrictions related with cloud computing in terms of security were also covered during this session.

According to a study published in the journal, one of the many different types of vulnerabilities that often occur in cloud computing systems is the inability to recognize the flaws. To this research, the author's contribution consisted in the categorization of different sorts of threats in accordance with the accessibility of cloud-based service resources. It was necessary to create this category in response to the extensive description and extent of the multiple dangers that were faced.

There are several concerns about the security of cloud computing infrastructure. Four critical levels of consideration should be taken into account while designing and executing cloud infrastructure security: the data level, the application level, the network level, and the host level (or the host itself) (or the physical location of the cloud infrastructure).

First and foremost, security refers to the protection of programs when they are using hardware and software resources in order to prevent others from gaining control of them. Among the most serious dangers at this level are distributed denial of service (DDoS) assaults on software programs, which are becoming more common.

Second, network-level security is concerned with network protection via the use of a virtual firewall, the creation of a demilitarized zone (DMZ), and data in transit protection procedures. Information about various kinds of firewalls should be monitored, collated, and preserved for future reference in order to achieve this goal.

Third, the degree of security refers to the protection that is offered for the host itself rather than for the virtual machine when a virtual server, hypervisor, or virtual machine is used in conjunction with another virtual machine. Obtaining information from system log files is required for the purpose of knowing when and where applications have been recorded in order to make these determinations. When it comes to defending cloud infrastructure, it is critical to look at the primary CIA components at each level of the organizational hierarchy. As cloud-based systems gain in popularity, the security dangers connected with their use are becoming better recognized. However, despite its many benefits, cloud computing is susceptible to a broad variety of security risks and assaults. The cloud computing infrastructure is always under assault, and attackers are constantly on the search for security flaws. The parts that follow discuss security issues that might arise at various levels of cloud architecture, as well as how to solve them.

Fourth is data-level difficulties: At this level of complexity, issues such as data breaches, data loss, data segregation, virtualization, confidentiality, integrity, and availability may all be discovered.

In terms of application-specific options, there are a plethora of options accessible.

The authors have presented an ECC-based multi-server authentication approach that is specific to the MCC context and does not need any pairing on the part of the users. While saving time and money, this method also maintains the benefits of more expensive pairing systems, such as safe mutual authentication, anonymity, and scalability, without necessitating the use of extra resources. This is shown theoretically by the formal security model, which illustrates the robustness of the method in practice.

The Open Stack platform was used as a reference by the authors in order to develop a number of models for information and resource sharing among tenants in an IaaS cloud environment, which were then evaluated. A tenant is encouraged to interact with the IT resources of other tenants in a regulated manner by using the models provided. Network access to virtual machines (VMs) must be regulated, however, in order to prevent malicious software from moving data in an uncontrolled way from the virtual machine.

According to the results, unique access control architecture for cloud computing that addresses cloud security and privacy challenges has been created. In order to construct the suggested system, the notion of dynamic trustworthiness served as its foundation. An access control system based on dynamic trustworthiness is used to, among other things, minimize the probability of undesirable behavior and ensure that only authorized users have access to cloud resources. The results reveal that the system recognizes potentially dangerous actions in order to prevent unlawful access, which would improve cloud computing security and, as a consequence, raise user confidence in the system, according to the researchers.

A hybrid access control framework, called iHAC, was presented by the authors, which allows type enforcement and role-based access control to be utilized in combination with other access control techniques. As a result, the architecture recommended is universally applicable to IaaS cloud systems and allows for the implementation of extremely flexible access control settings. An access control mechanism based on the Virtual Machine

Manager (VMM) was also created, which allows the VM's actions to be confined to the underlying resources at a finer level of detail. It has been shown in these researches that the implementation of the iHAC framework aids in the selection of real-world access control choices while imposing an acceptable performance cost on the system under examination.

In another research, it was shown that dynamic access control may be utilized to handle the many security threats that can arise in a cloud setting. Through the use of this technique, it is feasible to safeguard cloud data by taking into consideration the interrelationship between the requestor, the data that are being sought, and the action that will be taken on those data. The demands of the user were taken into account as well while offering dynamic access control. A first attempt at putting the anticipated method into action was all that was achieved as a consequence of the ultimate outcome.

Network-level solutions such as SNORT, an intrusion detection system for cloud computing, were offered by the authors under the Network-Level Solutions section as a network-level solution to prevent DoS and DDoS assaults. Such an attack floods the server with unnecessary packets, rendering it unusable for genuine users.

In order to recognize and prevent DDoS assaults, the suggested system takes use of certain criteria that have been set in advance of implementation. The authors outlined a strategy along the same lines, and they showed a mechanism for recognizing and filtering diverse DDoS assaults in cloud-based systems. When constructing this strategy, it is vital to use both the GARCH model and an artificial neural network to get the best results (ANN). When the actual value of variances is compared to a specified value of variances, Garch is used to calculate the value of variances and find any probable anomalies in real-world traffic. After values that are less than a certain threshold are eliminated, the ANN is used to categorize traffic into two categories: normal traffic and anomalous traffic. Normal traffic is defined as traffic that is less than a certain threshold.

Following the publication of a new article, users may randomly encrypt and push data blocks in a peer-to-peer network based on Blockchain by using a technique detailed in the study. In certain circumstances, the existence of several data centers and users in a distributed cloud might complicate the placement of file block copies, which can lead to performance issues. As a result, it seems that the Blockchain technique is the most favorable in terms of file security and network transmission time, respectively.

Another research presented a dynamic proof to aid in public audibility in the case of data corruption by combining irretrievability methods with communication-efficient recovery strategies in the event of data corruption.

The suggested technique might be used in storage to decrease the effect of modifications on data that are stored in a different place from the one being modified. Therefore, any effort to update will have only a little influence on the actual codeword symbols. In the event of a server failure, a dependable data reformatting technique may be used to restore data integrity.

Using the domain name system as a springboard, the authors developed a thorough list of all the different kinds of DNS assaults. Firewall use is the most common approach to DNS strategy, and this is considered to be one of the best practices in establishing DNS servers, according to the authors of this paper. There is an additional layer of security provided by the dynamic DNS firewall and carefully created signatures.

OpenPipe software-as-a-service was invented by researchers and then used by the industry (SaaS). Hybrid control mode was used to implement it, with the top level being a software-defined network (SDN) controller and the bottom level being local controllers, using the hybrid control mode. SDN's separation of the control plane from the data plane was expected to provide a number of advantages, including network virtualization and programmability. OpenPipe was shown in a laboratory environment. Certificates, higher-level-based authentication, and other encryption-based measures have been demonstrated to be successful in protecting cloud computing environments against unauthorized access, according to the findings of the study (e.g., symmetric and asymmetric key algorithms).

They suggested a Bayesian network-based weighted attack route modeling approach to model attack pathways in order to get a better understanding of how they operate. Moreover, they presented an enhanced technique for determining the most direct and least expensive attack vector from a large number of sources, which was based on the use of key nodes and critical edges. Apart from determining the most direct path between two points of interest, the algorithm also dismantles any links that may exist between routes of equal significance.

When it comes to data, there are several alternatives, but one of the most essential is the necessity to place a strong focus on data security and privacy as we migrate from traditional computer models to the Internet-based cloud computing paradigm. It is possible that data loss or leakage may have a substantial impact on a company's bottom line and will cause customers to lose confidence in the company's product or service. In a recent research, the auditing procedure in a cloud computing environment was examined in more detail. When it comes to data auditing, it is necessary to check for a range of characteristics, including confidentiality, integrity, remanence, provenance, and lineage, among other things. In accordance with the research, each of these concerns has a set of basic procedures that, with the exception of data remanence, is still a hot topic in public cloud services and may be able to meet the data auditing requirements of cloud service users.

It is the responsibility of a third-party auditor to ensure that client data stored on a cloud storage server is correct and complete. This was the theme on which the authors focused. It has been discovered that an improved Chameleon Authentication Tree, a technique for dynamic data updates, has been devised. By demonstrating that their enhanced auditing protocol is immune to assaults such as replay, replace, and forge, the researchers were able to further demonstrate the security of the protocol.

A categorization method based on a range of criteria has been devised as a result of the outcomes of a research. The parameters were selected by examining a range of various aspects of the problem. It is meant to give varied degrees of protection depending on the kind of material utilized and the degree of accessibility. In accordance with the authors' findings, data security may be offered at various degrees of protection, depending on the amount of protection required. Security precautions for storage may be implemented depending on the data set that has been classed as dimensions in the database and can be enforced accordingly.

Secure data classification is the name given by the authors to a cloud computing strategy based on safe data categorization and classification. Using TLS, AES, and SHA cryptographic methods, which are chosen depending on the kind of classified data, minimizes the total time necessary to protect data. The results of the inquiry reveal that the proposed model has been thoroughly tested and is both reliable and effective.

They came up with a privacy-preserving paradigm for outsourced categorization, which they used as a case study for cloud computing (POCC). When training a POCC model utilizing encrypted data that have been distributed across many sources, the evaluator may be certain that the model's classification accuracy and dependability will not suffer. The authors utilized Gentry's approach to create the world's first entirely homomorphism encryption system, which they used to protect sensitive data throughout the development process.

1.4   Open Challenges

The National Science Foundation says cloud computing research is still in its infancy, despite the widespread use of the technology by companies and sectors. Most cloud infrastructure gaps have not yet been closed, and new issues are always on the horizon. The following subsections give an overview of the most critical open issues that require further investigation.

Hypervisor security: the security of cloud computing is jeopardized if the hypervisor is compromised. It has the potential to do serious harm to the whole network. Because of the dynamic nature of the cloud, traditional methods of detection and prevention are no longer useful. These technologies are critical for distinguishing between normal and aberrant cloud computing behaviors. In addition, any recommended treatment must be executed as quickly as feasible in order to prevent damaging the cloud infrastructure or interfering with routine operations [11].

A third-party auditing firm: Data loss and erasure due to hardware–software failures and/or human mistake have been highlighted as worries regarding the integrity of cloud-based information storage systems expand in popularity and reach. Expert integrity verification services should be provided by a third-party auditor who is independent of the firm. Public cloud information auditing requires that private information of a client not be given to any public verifier throughout the process. As a consequence, a new privacy-related main concern has emerged: the risk of third-party auditors accessing private data. Researchers are always looking for ways to keep cloud storage safe and secure.

When a security breach occurs, the system must be able to function normally again. It is described as the extent to which data, software, and hardware are made accessible to authorized users in answer to their requests. It is the framework's ability to perform duties at any hour of the day or night that is considered system availability. Three of the cloud environment's most confusing challenges have been data protection, availability, and security.

When data are destroyed, reformatted, or redistributed to a new user, it is known as data remanence. As a result, the privacy of erased files is at risk. Computer forensics and other methods may be used to identify data remanence. Data recovery software may also be used to recover data that have been accidentally deleted from a computer. There has been little to no effort by cloud providers to address the issue of data remanence, despite the fact that it is one of the most pressing issues.

It was falsely claimed that IaaS's suggested security measures would secure the network, however this was not the case. Some assaults are insurmountable by a standard firewall, but not all of them. Cloud computing is getting more risky because of the enormous number of assaults that have been recorded as a result of the DNS hit. Because of the lack of investigation into the problem of reusing IP addresses, serious data and system breaches have occurred, endangering customers' privacy and data security.

IaaS security cannot be strengthened by traditional access control and identity management systems, because of the obvious cloud-specific properties. Computer security in the modern world requires the usage of cutting-edge technology like Blockchain and computational intelligence.

The great majority of authentication methods are both time-consuming and difficult to implement. Compared to more conventional techniques, existing research used simulation to evaluate their ideas with a little quantity of data, rudimentary resources, and a small number of users. Ultimately, though, the cloud is a complex system with a large number of users and a variety of other variables. A greater effort should be made to design approaches that address all of these limitations. The cloud service provider, on the other hand, does not offer a platform that enables for simultaneous usage of different user interfaces for authentication.

1.5   Recommendations

The following are some proposals based on the present challenges:

Context-aware solutions are necessary in order to avoid any potential harm to the cloud infrastructure. These solutions must be able to identify new and changing attack patterns and react quickly in order to prevent any potential harm to the cloud infrastructure. Consider both the client's preferences and the extent of the client's security understanding while creating these solutions.

The following aspects should be taken into consideration while developing third-party auditing solutions for third parties: Performing third-party audits without having access to the examined data ensures that the privacy of the data is always protected. It is advised that the data be divided up and encrypted in a cloud storage system to guarantee that they are kept hidden at all times.

Detecting process whether or not the stored data has been tampered with and alerting the user of the results, this is performed at the request of the client. Data are available upon request. The manner in which data are stored has an effect on how easily accessible information is to consumers. As indicated in the following points, a variety of ways may be used to assure data availability, and it is possible that these strategies will be the topic of future study in the area of cloud infrastructure security: In order to ensure data security, backups must be kept on an individual user basis, or in a widely scattered network environment. This means that if the storage component fails or degrades, the user will not be forced to delete all of his or her data. A frequent updating of backups is required so that the user may always access the most up-to-date versions of the data stored on the system. Data loss prevention (DLP) solutions assist in the prevention of data breaches as well as the reduction of physical damage to data center equipment and infrastructure, according to the company. Many technologies rely on third-party cloud-based secure storage to keep their data safe and secure and to prevent it from being lost or stolen. Many data loss protection programs include features such as monitoring, threat blocking, and forensic analysis, among others. Object storage makes use of sophisticated erasure coding techniques in order to assure data availability and integrity. It is described here how to combine data with parity data before breaking and distributing it throughout a storage area using the technique of "erasure coded" data.

Residual Data: As seen in the following table, several solutions may be utilized to either remove or minimize the quantity of residual data that are there. In certain circles, sterilization is referred to as "purging", and it refers to the process of eliminating sensitive data from a storage system in order to prevent it from being recovered via the use of a recognized method or technology. Encryption is a very effective means of keeping your data safe and secure.

Network Security Measures: The following are some ideas for securing your network against cyberattacks. Secure communication protocols such as HTTPS and TLS (Transport Layer Security) must be used to protect cloud internal communications (Transport Layer Security). There are several ways to identify and prevent hazardous network intrusions using HTTP request anomaly detection. You may easily get your hands on these solutions.

Two critical parts of operating a successful company are access control and identity management. In any future research on access control and identity management, the following security issues should be included. Access key authentication should be the only method of gaining access to the cloud. All assets and business systems in the cloud should be organized and classified in order to ensure that SOM in the cloud includes the following:

(A)   Situation awareness, as well as
(B)   Safe operation and maintenance, which incorporates unified ID authentication, as well as
(C)   Unified account management, as well as
(D)   SSO, or single sign-on, is already standard practice in many cloud environments, including AWS. One way to utilize SSO is to use it in combination with Blockchain-based self-sovereign identity management systems. A standard and private means of storing and maintaining credentials will be available to customers as a consequence of this update.

Security: Because of the complexity of the resources, the huge number of users, and the varied nature of the cloud, it is vital to utilize time-saving authentication mechanisms. Also required are authentication methods for various types of user interface authentications, which must be in place. According to some experts, Blockchain technology may be leveraged to produce more secure authentication techniques in the near future.

Every company is moving towards adopting a conversational chatbot [12, 13] to communicate with clients as a result of the changing times. This revolution will advance every sector of the economy thanks to artificial intelligence [14–16]. By 2030, billions of client inquiries will be generated automatically by chatbots and virtual agents. Because chatbot technology collects and safeguards sensitive data, it inevitably attracts [17–21] hackers [22–26] and other malicious [27–29] software. Businesses have used conversational chatbots and automatic response technologies on their websites and social media platforms despite the increased threat of cyberattacks [30]. We anticipate that chatbots will be widely used in customer care roles on messaging platforms like Facebook, WhatsApp, and WeChat. Threats are one-time occurrences like virus attacks and DDOS attacks (Distributed Denial of Service) [30]. Targeted attacks on businesses are common, and they routinely lock employees up.

1.6   Conclusion

There are many benefits to using a cloud computing service, but they are outweighed by concerns about security and privacy, which experts say are major hurdles to the mainstream use of cloud computing services. As a first step in promoting cloud adoption and use, cloud users should be aware of the risks, dangers, and vulnerabilities that may arise from their use of the cloud. Several distinct levels of abstraction were examined in order to better understand the difficulties and limitations of cloud computing architecture in this research (Application, Network, Host, and Data). There are a variety of existing ideas that might help resolve these issues. Below, you can find detailed instructions on how to use these approaches. Since the cloud is a public service that can be accessed by any user, many present problems remain unsolved, and new ones are constantly emerging. Following that, the research focuses on a variety of methods for fixing cloud infrastructure security vulnerabilities, which are explored in further detail below.

Acknowledgments

It is with great gratitude that we, the writers of this book chapter, like to convey our gratitude to the late Mr. Panem Nadipi Chennaih for his assistance and creation of this book chapter, which is in his honor.

References

1. Sethi, R., Emerging technique in libraries: Cloud computing. *2015 4th International Symposium on Emerging Trends and Technologies in Libraries and Information Services*, pp. 29–31, 2015, doi: 10.1109/ETTLIS.2015.7048167.
2. Patel, J. and Chouhan, A., An approach to introduce basics of Salesforce.com: A cloud service provider. *2016 International Conference on Communication and Electronics Systems (ICCES)*, pp. 1–8, 2016, doi: 10.1109/CESYS.2016.7889991.
3. Deshmukh, S.N. and Khandagale, H.P., A system for application deployment automation on cloud environment. *2017 Innovations in Power and Advanced Computing Technologies (i-PACT)*, pp. 1–4, 2017, doi: 10.1109/IPACT.2017.8245025.
4. Liu, Y., Design and implement a safe method for isolating memory based on Xen cloud environment. *2016 7th IEEE International Conference on Software Engineering and Service Science (ICSESS)*, pp. 804–807, 2016, doi: 10.1109/ICSESS.2016.7883189.
5. Baraković, S. and Husić, J.B., Short and sweet: Cloud computing and its security. *2016 XI International Symposium on Telecommunications (BIHTEL)*, pp. 1–5, 2016, doi: 10.1109/BIHTEL.2016.7775725.
6. Marchiori, M., Little big data: Shaping minds for the Cloud. *2016 Intl IEEE Conferences on Ubiquitous Intelligence & Computing, Advanced and Trusted Computing, Scalable Computing and Communications, Cloud and Big Data Computing, Internet of People, and Smart World Congress (UIC/ATC/ScalCom/CBDCom/IoP/SmartWorld)*, pp. 745–752, 2016, doi: 10.1109/UIC-ATC-ScalCom-CBDCom-IoP-SmartWorld.2016.0120.
7. Rudas, I.J., Cloud computing in education. *2012 IEEE 10th International Conference on Emerging eLearning Technologies and Applications (ICETA)*, pp. 327–327, 2012, doi: 10.1109/ICETA.2012.6418311.
8. Morioka, E. and Sharbaf, M.S., Digital forensics research on cloud computing: An investigation of cloud forensics solutions. *2016 IEEE Symposium on Technologies for Homeland Security (HST)*, pp. 1–6, 2016, doi: 10.1109/THS.2016.7568909.

9. Abuzagia, K.M., Cloud computing techniques: Strategies and applications for education. *2017 Joint International Conference on Information and Communication Technologies for Education and Training and International Conference on Computing in Arabic (ICCA-TICET)*, pp. 1–14, 2017, doi: 10.1109/ICCA-TICET.2017.8095301.

10. Bărbulescu, M. *et al.*, Energy efficiency in cloud computing and distributed systems. *2013 RoEduNet International Conference 12th Edition: Networking in Education and Research*, pp. 1–5, 2013, doi: 10.1109/RoEduNet.2013.6714197.

11. Li, Y., Shen, Y., Liu, Y., Utilizing content delivery network in Cloud computing. *2012 International Conference on Computational Problem-Solving (ICCP)*, pp. 137–143, 2012, doi: 10.1109/ICCPS.2012.6383505.

12. Rawat, R., Oki, O.A., Sankaran, K.S., Olasupo, O., Ebong, G.N., Ajagbe, S.A., A new solution for cyber security in big data using machine learning approach, in: *Mobile Computing and Sustainable Informatics: Proceedings of ICMCSI 2023*, Springer Nature Singapore, Singapore, pp. 495–505, 2023.

13. Rawat, R., Chakrawarti, R.K., Raj, A., Mani, G., Chidambarathanu, K., Bhardwaj, R., Association rule learning for threat analysis using traffic analysis and packet filtering approach. *Int. J. Inf. Technol.*, 1–11, 2023.

14. Rawat, R., Logical concept mapping and social media analytics relating to cyber criminal activities for ontology creation. *Int. J. Inf. Technol.*, 15, 2, 893–903, 2023.

15. Rawat, R., Mahor, V., Álvarez, J.D., Ch, F., Cognitive systems for dark web cyber delinquent association malignant data crawling: A review, in: *Handbook of Research on War Policies, Strategies, and Cyber Wars*, pp. 45–63, 2023.

16. Rawat, R., Chakrawarti, R.K., Vyas, P., Gonzáles, J.L.A., Sikarwar, R., Bhardwaj, R., Intelligent fog computing surveillance system for crime and vulnerability identification and tracing. *Int. J. Inf. Secur. Priv. (IJISP)*, 17, 1, 1–25, 2023.

17. Rawat, R., Sowjanya, A.M., Patel, S.I., Jaiswal, V., Khan, I., Balaram, A. (Eds.), *Using Machine Intelligence: Autonomous Vehicles Volume 1*, John Wiley & Sons, 2022.

18. Rawat, R., Mahor, V., Díaz-Álvarez, J., Chávez, F., Rooted learning model at fog computing analysis for crime incident surveillance, in: *2022 International Conference on Smart Generation Computing, Communication and Networking (SMART GENCON)*, 2022, December, IEEE, pp. 1–9.

19. Rawat, R. and Shrivastav, S.K., SQL injection attack detection using SVM. *Int. J. Comput. Appl.*, 42, 13, 1–4, 2012.

20. Rawat, R., Bhardwaj, P., Kaur, U., Telang, S., Chouhan, M., Sankaran, K.S., *Smart vehicles for communication, Volume 2*, John Wiley & Sons, 2023.

21. Mahor, V., Bijrothiya, S., Rawat, R., Kumar, A., Garg, B., Pachlasiya, K., IoT and artificial intelligence techniques for public safety and security, in: *Smart Urban Computing Applications*, p. 111, 2023.

22. Mahor, V., Pachlasiya, K., Garg, B., Chouhan, M., Telang, S., Rawat, R., Mobile operating system (android) vulnerability analysis using machine learning, in: *Proceedings of International Conference on Network Security and Blockchain Technology: ICNSBT 2021*, 2022, June, Springer Nature Singapore, Singapore, pp. 159–169.

23. Rawat, R., Garg, B., Pachlasiya, K., Mahor, V., Telang, S., Chouhan, M., Mishra, R., SCNTA: Monitoring of network availability and activity for identification of anomalies using machine learning approaches. *Int. J. Inf. Technol. Web Eng. (IJITWE)*, 17, 1, 1–19, 2022.

24. Mahor, V., Garg, B., Telang, S., Pachlasiya, K., Chouhan, M., Rawat, R., Cyber threat phylogeny assessment and vulnerabilities representation at thermal power station, in: *Proceedings of International Conference on Network Security and Blockchain Technology: ICNSBT 2021*, 2022, June, Springer Nature Singapore, Singapore, pp. 28–39.

25. Rawat, R., Gupta, S., Sivaranjani, S., CU, O.K., Kuliha, M., Sankaran, K.S., Malevolent information crawling mechanism for forming structured illegal organisations in hidden networks. *Int. J. Cyber Warf. Terror. (IJCWT)*, *12*, 1, 1–14, 2022.

26. Rawat, R., Rimal, Y.N., William, P., Dahima, S., Gupta, S., Sankaran, K.S., Malware threat affecting financial organization analysis using machine learning approach. *Int. J. Inf. Technol. Web Eng. (IJITWE)*, *17*, 1, 1–20, 2022.

27. Rawat, R., Mahor, V., Chouhan, M., Pachlasiya, K., Telang, S., Garg, B., Systematic literature review (SLR) on social media and the digital transformation of drug trafficking on darkweb, in: *International Conference on Network Security and Blockchain Technology*, Springer, Singapore, pp. 181–205, 2022.

28. Rawat, R., Ayodele Oki, O., Sankaran, S., Florez, H., Ajagbe, S.A., Techniques for predicting dark web events focused on the delivery of illicit products and ordered crime. *Int. J. Electr. Comput. Eng. (IJECE)*, 13, 5, 5354–5365, Oct. 2023, doi: 10.11591/ijece.v13i5.pp5354-5365.

29. Rawat, R., Garg, B., Mahor, V., Telang, S., Pachlasiya, K., Chouhan, M., Organ trafficking on the dark web—The data security and privacy concern in healthcare systems, in: *Internet of Healthcare Things: Machine Learning for Security and Privacy*, pp. 189–216, 2022.

30. Vyas, P., Vyas, G., Chauhan, A., Rawat, R., Telang, S., Gottumukkala, M., Anonymous trading on the dark online marketplace: An exploratory study, in: *Using Computational Intelligence for the Dark Web and Illicit Behavior Detection*, pp. 272–289, IGI Global, 2022.

2

Artificial Intelligence Effectiveness for Conversational Agents in Healthcare Security

Ahmad Mateen Buttar[1]* and Abdul Hyee[2]

[1]University of Agriculture Faisalabad, Faisalabad, Pakistan
[2]University of Agriculture, Faisalabad, Pakistan

Abstract

Artificial intelligence (AI) is increasingly being used in healthcare security. Informal agents in healthcare are used to promote and prevent health, as well as to interact with other new technologies to give patients with in-home care. Because of the increased demand for health services and the expanding potential of AI, informal agents have been developed to assist a number of health-related tasks, such as behavior modification, treatment support and services, and health monitoring support. Chatbots powered by artificial intelligence may serve as conversational agents capable of improving health, delivering information, and possibly effecting behavior change. To foresee their acceptability, it is vital to analyze the motivation for employing health chatbots. The computerization of these activities might allow doctors to put a spotlight on extra tricky responsibilities even as mounting community admission to healthcare services. Assembling the facts, a full appraisal of the suitability, worth, and effectiveness of these causes in healthcare is necessary. Future research may then concentrate on areas for improvement and the prospect of long-term adoption. The reason of this research was to see whether people were willing to communicate with AI-powered health chatbots.

Objective: The purpose of this thorough research is to assess the efficacy and usability of AI-powered conversational bots in healthcare security.

Keywords: Security, acceptability, Artificial Intelligence, bot, chatbot, conversational agents, healthcare

2.1 Introduction

AI technologies are growing in trade, culture, and healthcare. These skills can revolutionize patient care, management, and medical organizations. Multiple studies have proven that AI can perform and surpass human healthcare tasks like virus identification. Algorithms surpass radiologists in recognizing lethal tumors and advise researchers on building experimental cohorts. AI will not restore people to important medical practice areas for several years [1]. Alan Turing (1950) pioneered AI. The "Turing test" shows that a computer can perform human-level cognitive tasks. In the 1980s and 1990s, AI was popular.

---

*Corresponding author: ahmedmatin@hotmail.com

Romil Rawat, Rajesh Kumar Chakrawarti, Sanjaya Kumar Sarangi, Piyush Vyas, Mary Sowjanya Alamanda, Kotagiri Srividya and Krishnan Sakthidasan Sankaran (eds.) Conversational Artificial Intelligence, (17–30) © 2024 Scrivener Publishing LLC

Furry specialized systems, networks of Bayesian, neural networks of AI, and intelligent systems of hybrid nature have been utilized healthcare research. Most AI in 2016 research reserves went to other regions' healthcare requirements, such as practical and physical AI in medicine [2]. Practical elements include requests and neural network-based therapy outcome tracking, robots in surgery, intelligent prostheses for the crippled, and a developed mind. AI provides advantages over traditional analytics and verdict-creation methods. Learning algorithms improve in accuracy and efficiency as they work with training figures, allowing people to make tremendous advances in diagnosis, treatment techniques, cure irregularities, and patient outcomes. At Partners Healthcare's 2018 Forum (WMIF) on AI, renowned academics and clinical faculty members presented the 12 healthcare technologies and vicinities likely to collide with AI in the next decade [3].

2.2   Types of AI Relevance to Healthcare

Quite a few specific AI technologies for healthcare are described separately and in depth here.

2.2.1   Machine Learning (ML)—Neural Networks and Deep Learning

ML creates accurate copies of data and "learns" by building models. Machine learning is a common AI. 63% of US companies using AI, according to a 2018 Deloitte poll of 1,100 CEOs, use machine learning. Here are some alternatives. It is a common AI technique.

Classical machine learning is used in healthcare to predict which action approaches are likely to work on how each patient differs and the different scenarios of treatment.

Because machine learning and accuracy are widely used in medicine, applications need a training data set in which erratic products (like disease onset) are recognized by direct learning [4].

2.2.2   Rule-Based Expert System

In the 1980s, "if–then" expert systems were the most important AI technology, and they were widely used in business. They were used for "clinical verdict prop up" for decades [5] and still are. Many EHR sources have limitations.

2.2.3   Robotic Process Automation

This approach executed pre-programmed digital activities for directive goals, such as connecting information systems, as if they were user policy. They are cheaper, easier to produce, and more transparent than other AI. RPA refers to server-based programs before robots [6]. It simulates a semi-intelligent user by merging workflow, business rules, and "presentation layer". They are used in healthcare for prior permission, updating patient information, and billing. They can be utilized with figure acknowledgment to extract data from faxes for transactional systems [7].

2.3 The Future of AI in Healthcare

Consider the prospect's AI-powered healthcare solutions. Machine learning is fueling the emergence of precision medicine, a highly sought-after innovation in treatment. The rapid AI growth for imaging manipulation refers to radiology and pathology images that will be analyzed by the computer system. Recognition of text and speech is being utilized for comments of patient and healthcare record preservation.

AI technologies will augment human doctors' time-consuming patient care, not replace them. Human doctors may proceed toward tasks and goals that entail compassion, pushing, and big-picture integration. Those that refuse to collaborate with AI may lose their employment.

2.4 Ways of Artificial Intelligence that Will Impact Hearlthcare

The healthcare industry faces sweeping changes. Chronic illness, cancer, radiography, and risk estimate all offer opportunities for technology to improve patient care.

As payment systems evolve, customers want more from healthcare providers, and available data grow exponentially, AI will promote excellence across the care continuum.

AI can improve analytics and clinical decision-making. As learning algorithms interact with training data, they may become more particular and precise, allowing for better diagnosis, treatment procedures, and inequity resolution [8].

2.4.1 Unifying Mind and Machine Using BCIs

According to some sources, using computers to communicate is not new. However, edifice straight links between machines and the human brain without keyboards or bugs show cutting-edge study field applications for specific illnesses.

Due to neurological disorders and nervous system traumas, patients' abilities to talk, move, and engage with others may be lost. AI-enhanced brain–computer interfaces (BCIs) may restore these experiences to those who dread losing them.

2.4.2 Radiology's Next Generation

MRI, CT, and x-ray machines provide noninvasive views of the human body. The majority of analytic techniques still rely on biopsied hankie samples, which can reveal hidden sickness.

Experts expect that next-generation radiological technologies will be accurate enough to postpone the need for tissue samples in some circumstances.

2.4.3 Developing the Immunotherapy Treatment

Immunotherapy is one of the most promising cancer treatments. Patients can combat cancer with their immune system. Oncologists lack a reliable method for determining which patients will benefit from immunotherapy.

The capacity of machine learning algorithms to merge massively disparate data sets may shed light on novel genetically tailored treatment options.

2.4.4 Tracking Health with Personal and Portable Devices

Nearly all customers have access to health-tracking devices. Health associated data are produced from smartphones with the activity of trackers to wearables that can sense heartbeat 24/7.

AI will be needed to glean insights from this vast data trove.

Patients have more faith in their doctors than in Facebook, which could ease concerns about contributing data to large-scale research projects.

2.5 AI Models

2.5.1 Artificial Neural Network

ANNs are biologically inspired computational tools. ANNs are networks of massively linked computer processors called "neurons" [9]. Artificial neural networks can do data processing and perform illustration calculations. Their ability to learn from precedents, assess non-linear data, manage complicated information, and explain replica application to independent data makes them an excellent analytical tool in medicine. McCulloch and Pitts (1943) created the first artificial neuron [10]. Frank Rosenblatt created the Perceptron in 1958. The multilayer feed-forward Perceptron is the most acclaimed variant of the core Perceptron network. These networks have a layer for an input, one or more hidden layers/intermediate, and a layer for an output, each tightly linked with a distinct layer. Each neuron link has a mathematical weight. A neural network 'learns' by altering weights. ANNs' ability to learn from their data in a training environment is crucial. The use of multilayer feed-forward Perceptrons lacked an effective learning mechanism until Paul Werbos (1974) devised 'back propagation learning' [11]. Hopfield networks, RBF, and SOFM are well-known network diagrams [12]. ANNs have real-world uses. Their ability to recognize and differentiate blueprints has piqued scientists' interest, and they are linked to medical issues. As we realize that analysis, treatment, and forecasting result in many clinical settings reliant on diverse clinical, biological, and pathological communication, there is a growing desire for logical tools like ANNs that can employ sophisticated relationships surrounded by these patches as explained in Figure 2.1.

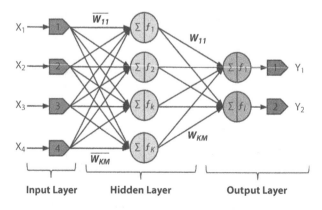

Figure 2.1 Multilayered feed-forward artificial neuron network.

Baxt was the first to uncover the medicinal component of ANNs. Baxt built a neural network mock-up that correctly identifies sensitive myocardial infarction to legitimize his work in the future [13]. ANNs are employed in all medical professions.

2.5.2   Zero Trust Technology Application for AI Medical Research

AI has infiltrated many aspects of human life. One of them is the health department. According to Frost and Sullivan, AI has the potential to get better patient outcomes by 30% to 40% while plummeting healthcare expenditures by up to 50% (Hsieh, 2017a) [14]. AI and machine learning have the potential to enhance healthcare and reduce costs.

For example:

- Cholecystitis can be identified before symptoms appear by using a neural network to analyze risk-related data [15].
- Two IBM Watson Health customers claim that they can reduce medical system explorations by 70%.
- A team from Massachusetts General Hospital (MGH) and Computer Science and AI Laboratory (CSAIL) produced a deep learning replica that can predict breast cancer up to 5 years in the future based on a mammogram.

Artificial intelligence is effective, but it needs a lot of data to learn. In 2019, over 12,000 biomedical research articles addressed AI and machine learning [16], but only 40 reported an FDA sanction. Because medicine requires high-reliability technology, input data should be modest. The sound in the images may make benign spy cells seem malignant. Judgment and fitting require a lot of training data. Developers cannot access these sensitive data at once.

The zero belief may assist you to deal with this difficulty. Its ideology is:

- ❖ Zero Trust has three steps:
- ❖ Use least-privileged access and assume breach.
- ❖ Use free access to verify
- ❖ Confirm clearly, utilize least-privileged access, and assume breach.

There are three phases to implementing Zero Trust:

On a hardware level
Network microsegmentation is implemented. It is necessary to employ network equipment such as switches, firewalls, or an extra gateway device. As a consequence, a person's assets or collection of assets is mentioned in the area of their sheltering network.

Software
The software-defined outskirts are constructed. The software-defined perimeter is constructed at this moment. For this aim, IBN and SDN are commonly utilized. As a result, the access is configured at the request level. This gateway founded a sheltered link flanked by the consumer and the resource.

Organizational
Administrators develop and distribute the tasks and permissions assigned to users at this level.

Skills may be acquired and added along the Zero Trust route to "unlock" a chain of advantages ranging from reduced cyberthreat and increased user familiarity to lower IT expenses and improved digital collaboration. As a result, the knowledge is successfully exploited or brings in the following areas:

The Internet of Things: This model includes the most important parts for the core ideas, such as device access control, visibility and psychiatry, automated safety, data control, user control, workload, and so on.

Supply chain management: The Zero Trust movement is aimed at permitting important supply chain administration aspects such as sustainability, fraud, phoney materials and goods, and poor practice that might undermine organizations' reputations [17].
Federal government agency in the United States: The United States is continually exposed to more complex and vengeful cyberattacks that endanger government-owned institutions, the private zone, and, eventually, the public's safety and solitude. According to the US government, using the Zero Trust method will aid in addressing the challenges that have emerged [18].

The Zero Trust paradigm, among other things, is particularly effective in medical research. The application of contact based on roles, in particular, as a consequence of the second principle. This is great for medical research since it enables algorithm developers to assess the performance of their algorithms without having access to specific data situations.
UCSF has built a zero-trust platform for AI research in medicine with the help of Microsoft, Intel, and Fortanix. This podium's name is BeeKeeper AI. The concept is that no one, including the algorithm's owner, the data's owner, or the stage, has admittance to what is more, the data or the algorithm. BeeKeeper AI makes the subsequent functionalities available: tools and procedures for healthcare that facilitate data set generation, labeling, segmentation, and annotation operations; encryption of critical data for their defense using protected Enclave technology; arbitration between data stewards and algorithm developers; and cosseted cloud storage that reduces the danger of loss of control and "reshoring". This strategy helps developers to decrease project costs, time, and effort by working with largely organized data sets. They do not have to fret about breaking the decree, recovering data, or creating data sets with certain properties. Both software and hardware technologies were used to construct the platform. Beekeeper AI may be accessible through Azure Confidential Computing, as seen in Figure 2.2. The Azure Kubernetes Service hosts hidden compute nodes (AKS). Azure Attestation provides confidence with the diagnostic provider. The diagnostic vendor does not have access to hospital data because, as seen in Figure 2.2, the architecture separates sensitive patient information while processing specified universal data on the cloud using Azure components.
At this level, network micro-segmentation is performed. This requires the use of network devices such as a switch, firewall, or another gateway.
Hardware supporting the virtual machines includes Intel CPUs with Software Guard Extensions (SGX) technology. Intel SGX encrypts and cuts off algorithms and data into

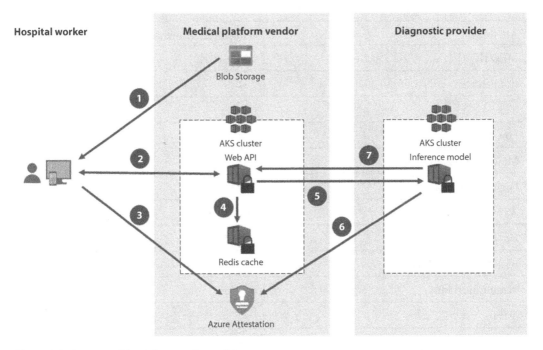

Figure 2.2 Azure confidential computing architecture.

enclaves, which are limited portions of the CPU and memory. The Fortanix software is in charge of encryption and worker processor management.

BeeKeeper AI works in many phases [19]: after receiving an encrypted algorithm from the owner, the algorithm is wrapped in a secure computing container.

2.6   Compare E-Cohort Findings on Wearables and AI in Healthcare

Portable biometric monitoring devices (BMDs) allow high-frequency, outside-the-hospital patient health monitoring. When combined with AI, BMDs' hundreds of data points could inform decisions, forecast outcomes of patient, and help care providers choose the top medication for their patients (AI). As illustrated in Table 2.1, two technology revolts have spawned a wide diversity of digital and AI-based healthcare solutions.

2.6.1   Results

2.6.1.1   Participant Characteristics

Between May and June 2018, 1183 chronic disease patients supplied information, 861 (73%) of them women (Table 2.1) (SD = 14.5). Average age: 49.7 years; 121 diabetics, 77 asthmatics, 367 rheumatologists, 234 neurologists, and 107 cancer patients. A total of 641 members (54%) had several conditions (mean = 2.5, SD = 2.4); 590 (50%) individuals reported utilizing tools for their health; 190 (16%) used online meeting tools, 246 (21%) used wellness

Table 2.1 Comparing E-cohort findings on wearables and AI in healthcare.

Attributes	Unrefined information	Data filtering
MED [IQR]	50 [38–62]	56 [43–67]
(%) Female	861 (73)	641 (54)
n (%).		
Low ed	62 (5.4)	115 (9.6)
Middle school/equivalent	135 (11.2)	667 (56.3)
High school diploma	184 (15.7)	163 (13.6)
AS	266 (22.6)	104 (8.6)
Diploma or degree	536 (45.2)	134 (11.1)
IQR-Med conditions	2 [1–3]	2 [1–3]
% multimorbidity	649 (55)	703 (59)
N (%)		
Asthma	77 (6)	72 (6)
COPD	23 (1)	35 (3)
Other lung disease	111 (9)	118 (10)
Diabetes	121 (10)	192 (16)
Thyroid health	128 (11)	128 (11)
HiBP	137 (12)	190 (16)
Dyslipidemia	54 (5)	88 (7)
Other cardiac-related disorders	111 (9)	143 (12)
Kidney illnesses	79 (7)	101 (8)
Rheumatologic	367 (31)	373 (31)
Conditional systems	113 (10)	80 (7)
Digestive health	169 (14)	132 (11)
Brain disorders	234 (20)	252 (21)
Cancer	107 (9)	108 (9)
Depression	77 (6)	76 (6)
Years since first IQR disease	14 [6–26]	16 [7–29]
N (%) had used as tools	590 (50)	604 (51)

(*Continued*)

Table 2.1 Comparing E-cohort findings on wearables and AI in healthcare. (*Continued*)

Attributes	Unrefined information	Data filtering
Types of tools used, *n* (%)		
Apps for health	246 (21)	273 (24)
Fitness wearables	61(5)	58 (5)
Health internet services and doctors' wearables	50 (4)	49 (4)
Apps for health	190 (16)	188 (16)

wearables, and 61 (5%) used medically prescribed wearables (such as continuous glucose monitoring tools) (1183 contributors).

After calibration on age-specific sex limits and learning echelon using data of a nationwide poll revealing French residents at least self-reporting one continuous circumstance, weighted statistics were generated.

2.7   Ethical Concerns of AI in Healthcare

✓ Physicians seeking diagnostic or therapeutic guidance from AI analysis must understand how the findings were achieved before recommending them to patients.

✓ Given the complexities of AI programs, researchers and doctors must improve their communication skills.

✓ The healthcare system may confront new issues as a result of AI. The benefits of publicly financed healthcare vs. private healthcare are now being debated. Artificial intelligence would be available to those who can afford it in a privatized healthcare system. To summarize, an existing uneven healthcare system would exacerbate the divide between the rich and the poor.

✓ Despite the fact that the enormous number of health records in public healthcare may surpass the cost of AI, its implementation into the medical system is still years away.

✓ The use of massive volumes of data from electronic health records may jeopardize patient anonymity. Misinformation may proliferate on websites that use problematic AI.

2.8   Future in Healthcare

• The atmosphere for AI in healthcare has been prepared by technological breakthroughs. Medical workers should be informed on the usage of AI.

• In order for AI to attain its full potential, healthcare leadership must be standardized across all nations.

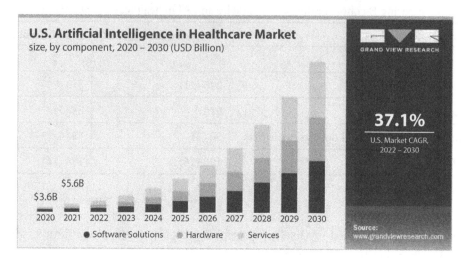

Figure 2.3 Artificial Intelligence in Healthcare Market Size Report, 2030.

- Artificial intelligence will become a useful resource in healthcare provided caution and ethical issues are exercised.

Artificial intelligence has the potential to become the 21st-century stethoscope, which is possible with tight cooperation between the medical community and technologists.

As seen in Figure 2.3, AI is becoming more important in the healthcare industry.

Conversational agents are artificial communication [20–23] systems that are gaining popularity, but not all of their security [24–27] issues have been satisfactorily addressed. Chatbots are used by people to help with a variety of tasks, including shopping, bank communication, meal delivery, healthcare, and automobiles. However, it adds a new security [28–32] risk and generates significant security issues [33–35] that must be resolved. Determining the key processes in the methods used to create security [36]-related chatbots is necessary for identifying the underlying issues. Security risks and vulnerabilities [37] are growing as a result of several causes. They are all thoroughly examined, and security [38] techniques to lessen security flaws are offered. Modern chatbots use machine learning and natural language processing instead of rule-based algorithms. These methods take their cues from conversations, which may contain sensitive information.

2.9   Conclusion

The future of AI in healthcare and medicine seems bright, with endless development opportunities for healthcare service companies. Artificial intelligence has several uses in healthcare, ranging from medical consultation digitalization and automated record management to less invasive robotic surgery and telemedicine services. AI technology is critical in accelerating digital processes throughout care services. There are several AI practices that can address a broad range of therapeutic difficulties. Medical AI technology, on the other hand, has not been overtaken by excitement, despite past anticipation. The main explanation for this is the doctors' stance toward the expertise used in decision-making. Contrary to popular belief, there is no difficulty in accepting the biochemical effects of an auto-analyzer or the visuals shaped by appealing timbre imaging. Nonetheless, it is the responsibility of researchers working in this subject to show the feasibility of these approaches in practice. Additional randomized controlled studies are obligatory to determine the usefulness of AI systems in medicine. Medical AI may play a critical role in aiding doctors to offer better healthcare in the 21st century. There is some misgiving that these tactics will improve as well asynchronize the "medical intelligence" of the scene clinician.

References

1. Mintz, Y. and Brodie, R., Introduction to artificial intelligence in medicine. *Minim Invasive Ther. Allied Technol.*, 28, 73–81, 2019.
2. Hamlet, P. and Tremblay, J., Artificial intelligence in medicine. *Metabolism*, 69S, S36–40, 2017.
3. Lee, S.I., Celik, S., Logsdon, B.A. *et al.*, A machine learning approach to integrate big data for precision medicine in acute myeloid leukemia. *Nat. Commun.*, 9, 42, 2018.
4. Fakoor, R., Ladhak, F., Nazi, A., Huber, M., Using deep learning to enhance cancer diagnosis and classification. *A conference presentation The 30th International Conference on Machine Learning*, 2013.
5. Vial, A., Stirling, D., Field, M. *et al.*, The role of deep learning and radiomic feature extraction in cancer-specific predictive modelling: A review. *Transl. Cancer Res.*, 7, 803–16, 2018.
6. Hussain, A., Malik, A., Halim, M.U., Ali, A.M., The use of robotics in surgery: A review. *Int. J. Clin. Pract.*, 68, 1376–82, 2014.
7. Berg, S., *Nudge theory explored to boost medication adherence*, American Medical Association, Chicago, 2018.
8. Steimann, F., On the use and usefulness of fuzzy sets in medical AI. *Artif. Intell. Med.*, 21, 131–7, 2001.
9. McCulloch, W.S. and Pitts, W., A logical calculus of the ideas imminent in nervous activity. *Bull. Math Biophys.*, 5, 115–33, 1943.
10. Hopfield, J.J., Neural networks and physical systems with emergent collective computational abilities. *Proc. Natl. Acad. Sci. U. S. A.*, 79, 2554–8, 1982.
11. Park, J. and Sandberg, I.W., Universal approximation using radial-basis-functionnetworks. *Neural Comput.*, 3, 246–57, 1991.
12. Carpenter, G.A. and Grossberg, S., The ART of adaptive pattern recognition by a self-organizing neural network. *Computer*, 21, 77–88, 1988.
13. Baxt, W.G. and Skora, J., Prospective validation of artificial neural network trained to identify acute myocardial infarction. *Lancet*, 347, 12–5, 1996.
14. Ahuja, A.S., The impact of artificial intelligence in medicine on the future role of the physician. *PeerJ*, 7, e7702, 2019. https://doi.org/10.7717/peerj.7702.
15. Lazarenko, V.A. and Antonov, A.E., Diagnosis and prediction of cholecystitis development on the basis of neural network analysis of risk factors. *Research'n Pract. Med. J.*, 4, 4, 67–72, 2017. https://doi.org/10.17709/2409-2231-2017-4-4-7.
16. Benjamens, S., Dhunnoo, P., Meskó, B., The state of artificial intelligence-based FDA-approved medical devices and algorithms: An online database. *NPJ Digit. Med.*, 3, 1, 1–8, 2020. https://doi.org/10.1038/s41746-020-00324-0.
17. Topol, E.J., Steinhubl, S.R., Torkamani, A., Digital medical tools and sensors. *JAMA*, 313, 353–354, 2015.
18. Steinhubl, S.R., Muse, E.D., Topol, E.J., Can mobile health technologies transform health care? *JAMA*, 310, 2395–2396, 2013.

19. Gawad, J. and Bonde, C., Artificial intelligence: Future of Medicine and healthcare. *Biochem. Ind. J.*, 11, 2, 113, 2017.

20. Rawat, R., Oki, O.A., Sankaran, K.S., Olasupo, O., Ebong, G.N., Ajagbe, S.A., A new solution for cyber security in big data using machine learning approach, in: *Mobile Computing and Sustainable Informatics: Proceedings of ICMCSI 2023*, Springer Nature Singapore, Singapore, pp. 495–505, 2023.

21. Rawat, R., Chakrawarti, R.K., Raj, A., Mani, G., Chidambarathanu, K., Bhardwaj, R., Association rule learning for threat analysis using traffic analysis and packet filtering approach. *Int. J. Inf. Technol.*, 1–11, 2023.

22. Rawat, R., Logical concept mapping and social media analytics relating to cyber criminal activities for ontology creation. *Int. J. Inf. Technol.*, 15, 2, 893–903, 2023.

23. Rawat, R., Mahor, V., Álvarez, J.D., Ch, F., Cognitive systems for dark web cyber delinquent association malignant data crawling: A review, in: *Handbook of Research on War Policies, Strategies, and Cyber Wars*, pp. 45–63, 2023.

24. Rawat, R., Chakrawarti, R.K., Vyas, P., Gonzáles, J.L.A., Sikarwar, R., Bhardwaj, R., Intelligent fog computing surveillance system for crime and vulnerability identification and tracing. *Int. J. Inf. Secur. Priv. (IJISP)*, 17, 1, 1–25, 2023.

25. Rawat, R., Sowjanya, A.M., Patel, S.I., Jaiswal, V., Khan, I., Balaram, A. (Eds.), *Using Machine Intelligence: Autonomous Vehicles Volume 1*, John Wiley & Sons, 2022.

26. Rawat, R., Mahor, V., Díaz-Álvarez, J., Chávez, F., Rooted learning model at fog computing analysis for crime incident surveillance, in: *2022 International Conference on Smart Generation Computing, Communication and Networking (SMART GENCON)*, 2022, December, IEEE, pp. 1–9.

27. Rawat, R. and Shrivastav, S.K., SQL injection attack detection using SVM. *Int. J. Comput. Appl.*, 42, 13, 1–4, 2012.

28. Rawat, R., Bhardwaj, P., Kaur, U., Telang, S., Chouhan, M., Sankaran, K.S., *Smart vehicles for communication, Volume 2*, John Wiley & Sons, 2023.

29. Mahor, V., Bijrothiya, S., Rawat, R., Kumar, A., Garg, B., Pachlasiya, K., IoT and artificial intelligence techniques for public safety and security, in: *Smart Urban Computing Applications*, p. 111, 2023.

30. Mahor, V., Pachlasiya, K., Garg, B., Chouhan, M., Telang, S., Rawat, R., Mobile operating system (android) vulnerability analysis using machine learning, in: *Proceedings of International Conference on Network Security and Blockchain Technology: ICNSBT 2021*, 2022, June, Springer Nature Singapore, Singapore, pp. 159–169.

31. Rawat, R., Garg, B., Pachlasiya, K., Mahor, V., Telang, S., Chouhan, M., Mishra, R., SCNTA: Monitoring of network availability and activity for identification of anomalies using machine learning approaches. *Int. J. Inf. Technol. Web Eng. (IJITWE)*, 17, 1, 1–19, 2022.

32. Mahor, V., Garg, B., Telang, S., Pachlasiya, K., Chouhan, M., Rawat, R., Cyber threat phylogeny assessment and vulnerabilities representation at thermal power station, in: *Proceedings of International Conference on Network Security and Blockchain Technology: ICNSBT 2021*, 2022, June, Springer Nature Singapore, Singapore, pp. 28–39.

33. Rawat, R., Gupta, S., Sivaranjani, S., CU, O.K., Kuliha, M., Sankaran, K.S., Malevolent information crawling mechanism for forming structured illegal organisations in hidden networks. *Int. J. Cyber Warf. Terror. (IJCWT)*, 12, 1, 1–14, 2022.

34. Rawat, R., Rimal, Y.N., William, P., Dahima, S., Gupta, S., Sankaran, K.S., Malware threat affecting financial organization analysis using machine learning approach. *Int. J. Inf. Technol. Web Eng. (IJITWE)*, 17, 1, 1–20, 2022.

35. Rawat, R., Mahor, V., Chouhan, M., Pachlasiya, K., Telang, S., Garg, B., Systematic literature review (SLR) on social media and the digital transformation of drug trafficking on darkweb, in:

International Conference on Network Security and Blockchain Technology, Springer, Singapore, pp. 181–205, 2022.

36. Rawat, R., Ayodele Oki, O., Sankaran, S., Florez, H., Ajagbe, S.A., Techniques for predicting dark web events focused on the delivery of illicit products and ordered crime. *Int. J. Electr. Comput. Eng. (IJECE)*, 13, 5, 5354–5365, Oct. 2023, doi: 10.11591/ijece.v13i5.pp5354-5365.

37. Rawat, R., Garg, B., Mahor, V., Telang, S., Pachlasiya, K., Chouhan, M., Organ trafficking on the dark web—The data security and privacy concern in healthcare systems, in: *Internet of Healthcare Things: Machine Learning for Security and Privacy*, pp. 189–216, 2022.

38. Vyas, P., Vyas, G., Chauhan, A., Rawat, R., Telang, S., Gottumukkala, M., Anonymous trading on the dark online marketplace: An exploratory study, in: *Using Computational Intelligence for the Dark Web and Illicit Behavior Detection*, pp. 272–289, IGI Global, 2022.

Conversational AI: Security Features, Applications, and Future Scope at Cloud Platform

Ahmad Mateen Buttar[1]*, Faisal Shahzad[2] and Uzma Jamil[3]

[1]University of Agriculture Faisalabad, Faisalabad, Pakistan
[2]University of Agriculture, Faisalabad, Pakistan
[3]Government College University, Faisalabad, Pakistan

Abstract

Cloud computing is gaining popularity day by day due to its features like stability, ease of manageability, and flexibility, but at the same time, there are serious concerns about the security of data. It sparked the development of brand-new IOT and AI-based business models and hastened technology adoption. IOT devices and big data not only increased the volume of data but also enhanced the complexity, leading to being more prone to hacking and privacy compromises. More smart and intelligent models need to be introduced to handle these security issues; this is where AI comes in. Conversational AI technologies like chatbots and virtual assistants use big data, machine learning, and natural language processing to simulate human interaction. They understand speech and text inputs and translate them into several languages. Data collecting is necessary for conversational AI to reply to user inquiries. The method is prone to privacy and security breaches. Security measures are required at three levels, i.e., data storage, processing, and transmission. Traditional device centric security systems are not sufficient and need to evolve to data-centric protection solutions, in which security aspects need to be focused at all the three levels. AI can help to automate the process of dynamic threat detection, reaction, and future avoidance. Many organizations are still resistant to adopt cloud computing due to security concerns, despite all complexities and overheads of managing on-premises data centers. The paper discusses the available cloud models, related privacy and security issues, and barriers perceived in migrating applications to cloud and finally proposes an advanced security model for cloud-based conversational AI applications.

Keywords: Cloud computing, data, security issues, cloud, AI-based business models, centric security systems, advanced security model

*Corresponding author: ahmedmatin@hotmail.com

Romil Rawat, Rajesh Kumar Chakrawarti, Sanjaya Kumar Sarangi, Piyush Vyas, Mary Sowjanya Alamanda, Kotagiri Srividya and Krishnan Sakthidasan Sankaran (eds.) Conversational Artificial Intelligence, (31–58) © 2024 Scrivener Publishing LLC

3.1   Introduction

Today's technology demands secure data. They had restricted access to critical data [1]. It affects the business's smooth running and short-, medium-, and long-term viability.

Despite the technology's benefits, it can increase IT-related hazards. With more attacks, it is tougher to discover and analyze them. A company needs investigative security and information security experts. Wireless networks must be secure since they use radio waves to transmit data.

A shared and multitenant strategy is utilized to provide cloud computing services. AWS and/or Google Cloud Platform use a multitenant strategy. This is used to safely and economically allocate resources among cloud tenants (companies, organizations, etc.) and applications. Virtualization can isolate tenants. A cloud architecture has clients, servers, apps, and other parts. Cloud computing also includes the Hadoop Distributed File System (HDFS) and/or the Google File System (GFS). Most data on discs are objects or blocks. By isolating storage management from physical storage, these file systems boost capacity. Figure 3.1 explains the Cloud Model and the architecture for cloud computing.

- **Servers**: Networked PCs with virtual machines.
- **Virtualization**: Virtualization abstract servers, storage, and networking as logical resources.
- **Storage**: SANs, NASs, and other networked storage systems; backup and archiving services.
- **Management**: Tools for configuring, maintaining, and tracking cloud server, network, and storage components.
- **Security**: Factors that ensure data availability, confidentiality, and integrity.
- **Services**: For purposes of both backup and recovery.

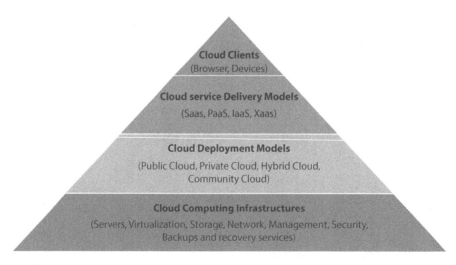

Figure 3.1 Cloud computing architecture.

3.2   How Does Conversational Artificial Intelligence (AI) Work?

Applications like chatbots or virtual assistants fall under the category of conversational artificial intelligence (AI). They mimic human interactions, recognize speech and text input, and translate their meaning into several languages using big data, machine learning, and natural language processing.

3.3   The Conversational AI Components

Natural language processing (NLP) and machine learning are combined in conversational AI. These NLP methods work in tandem with machine learning to continuously refine the AI system. Thanks to its core building blocks, conversational AI can analyze, comprehend, and intuitively produce responses.

Reinforcement learning, output creation, input analysis, and input generation are the four components of NLP. Unstructured data are made machine-readable, and the best course of action is determined after it has been assessed. Fundamental ML algorithms improve the response's accuracy over time as they learn. Here is a breakdown of these four NLP stages:

- **Input generation:** Through a website or application, users provide information. Text or speech can be used as the input format.
- **Input analysis:** When a conversational AI solver gets text-based input, it uses natural language understanding (NLU) to analyze the meaning of the input and infer its intent. automatic voice recognition (ASR) and natural language understanding (NLU) are integrated to analyze the data when the input is speech, though.
- **Dialogue management:** At this point, natural language generation (NLG), a component of NLP, is used to generate a response.
- **Reinforcement learning:** Finally, by improving responses, machine learning algorithms retain accuracy over time.

A conversational AI development approach is built around FAQs. They aid in identifying the customer's primary requirements and issues, which in turn helps the support team handle fewer calls. If your product does not already have a list of commonly asked questions, consult your customer success team to come up with a list of pertinent inquiries that your conversational AI can assist you with.

Suppose you are a bank. Your initial list of frequently asked questions might look like this:

- How can I get to my account?
- Where can I locate my account number and order code?
- Will my debit card delivered soon?
- How can I activate my debit card?
- How I get a check?
- How do I get in touch with a local banker?

The list of inquiries is something you may always expand over time. Therefore, to prototype the conversational AI development process, start with a limited number of queries.

The six main components of a typical dialogue system are speech recognition (ASR), language understanding (SLU), dialogue management (DM), natural language generation (NLG), synthesis (TTS), and knowledge base as shown in Figure 3.2 below. A typical dialogue system's structure is:

A. **Knowledge Base:** There are two knowledge bases. Both the online knowledge base and the local knowledge base, which include all the information and facts based on each model, including dialogues, are the first. Modal ASR datasets for image bodies, video, and chart models, as well as some user information and fitting systems.

B. **Graphics Model:** The input model and graphics model take frames from the video that was captured, and the graphics model then uses those frames to analyze the video and image in real time. In order to evaluate these frames and images and provide findings, it then sends them to graphical models and apps running on cloud servers.

C. **Gesture Model:** Using cameras and Kinect, the gesture model interprets human body motions and facial expressions on the input model. The signal model and cloud server programmers are then sent all the data so they may evaluate the frames and images and provide result.

D. **ASR Model:** The speech recognition model interprets what the user says into the device's microphone and converts it into text using the input model, the ASR model, and the cloud servers' microphone in real time. The text is subsequently forwarded to cloud servers' programmers for analysis, which returns the results.

E. **Interaction Model:** This essential model accepts the input model's data, processes the data supplied to each model in line with the actions done by each model, and then provides the outcome. It is used to arrive at a choice.

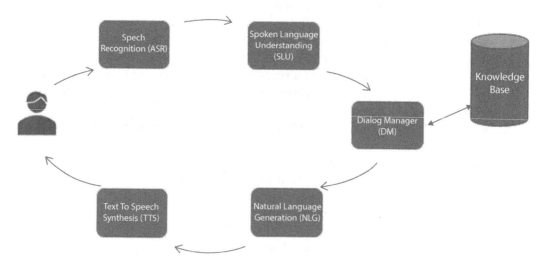

Figure 3.2 The general dialogue system's structure.

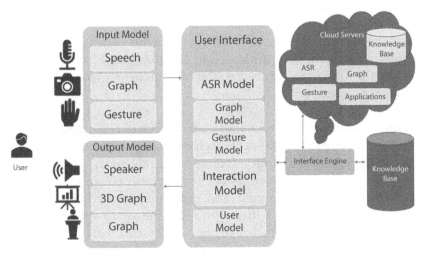

Figure 3.3 The structure of the next-generation of virtual personal assistants.

    F.   **Inference Engine:** Inferences are made by the inference engine and inter-action model using a variety of facts and inferences. Before coming up with a solution, they compile and organize all the facts and principles.

    G. **User Model:** This model includes every bit of data pertaining to the sys-tem's users. Personal data including names, ages, interests, knowledge, objectives, and dislikes of users, as well as information about their actions and interactions with the system, may fall under this category. Asking users questions and saving their responses in the knowledge base is how all the data are gathered.

    H. **Input Template:** All data-gathering input devices, barring the microphone, camera, and Kinect, are managed by this template. Prior to receiving data, the interaction model also integrates intelligence algorithms to govern the input data.

    I.   **Output Model:** This model receives the final option from the interaction model along with a description and, based on the option, chooses the optimal output device to display the result, such as Graph, speaker, or 3D Graph as shown in Figure 3.3.

3.4   Uses of Conversational AI

People usually consider online chatbots and voice assistants for omnichannel customer support when they think about conversational AI. Numerous analytics are included into the backend code of the majority of conversational AI systems, which helps to ensure discussions that feel human.

    Experts believe that current conversational AI applications are inadequate because they concentrate on a very small number of jobs. Theoretically, strong AI centers on a consciousness that is similar to that of a human being and is capable of carrying out a variety of jobs and resolving a variety of issues.

Conversational AI is a very successful business technology that aids businesses in increasing their profitability, despite its specific niche. Although conversational AI most frequently takes the form of an AI chatbot, there are numerous alternative industrial use cases. Here are a few instances:

- **Online customer support:** Online chatbots replace real people throughout the client experience. They give clients individualized advice, cross-sell products or suggest sizes, and they address frequently asked questions (FAQs) about shipping and our view of user engagement on websites and social media platforms. Voice assistants and virtual assistants in general, chat bots on e-commerce sites with virtual agents, and messaging apps like Slack and Facebook Messenger might all revolutionize the work that is done.
- **Accessibility:** Lowering entry barriers will make organizations more accessible, especially for those who use assistive technology. For these populations, conversation AI technologies like text-to-voice dictation and speech translation are frequently employed.
- **HR procedures:** Using conversational AI, several HR procedures, including B, employee training, onboarding procedures, and updating employee information, can be made more efficient.
- **Healthcare:** Conversational AI can increase operational efficiency and speed up administrative processes like claim processing, which will result in more affordable and accessible healthcare for patients.
- **Device for the Internet of Things (IoT):** A minimum of one Internet of Things (IoT) device is already present in the majority of homes, which includes Alexa to smartphones and smart watches. These devices employ automatic speech recognition to talk to the users. Applications like Google Home, Apple Siri, and Amazon Alexa are all well-known.
- **Computer software:** Conversational AI, like B, simplifies a variety of tasks in a desktop context. Automatic search is when you use the spell checker on Google.

Even while the majority of chatbots and AI apps available today only have basic problem-solving capabilities, they can speed up and increase the profitability of contacts with recurring customers, freeing up human resources to concentrate on more client engagements. Applications using conversational AI have generally done a good job at simulating human contact, which has led to high user satisfaction rates.

A chatbot is a piece of computer software that can intelligently communicate with users via text or speech, typically in the form of quick exchanges. The best design concept can be found by evaluating the strategy using the usability heuristic and Messenger platform cues [2]. Then, a bank's intelligent chatbot system will react correctly to user demands. A chatbot system in banking is a computer software designed to mimic an intelligent conversation with human users about any banking-related questions using audio or textual cues. This intelligent machine will have mental processes akin to those of humans. This system will lessen the staff's workload. It responds to users quickly and accurately. Chatbots are one of the most basic and well-known examples of intelligent human–computer interaction (HCI). Chatbots improve greatly when simple calculators, dictionaries, or even games are added as productivity tools. The chatbot can also open programmers, set alarms, create memos and notes, and open programs on-demand on the user's PC or mobile device [3]. Before chatbots, only bots existed. The advent of chat services marked the beginning of a new technological era. Chatbots are virtual chat agents that can text with anyone. Today, a number of cloud-based technologies, such as Microsoft Bot Framework, IBM Watson, Kore, AWS Lambda, Microsoft Azure Bot Service, Chatfuel, Heroku, and more, can be used to create chatbots. Artificial intelligence, natural language processing, service conversion, programming, etc. are only a few of the methods that have disadvantages. In contrast, banking chatbots are a crucial component of FinTech. Chatbots can gradually supplement or take over the work of banking and financial workers by integrating different AI technologies. It can decrease personnel expenses for financial organizations while simultaneously enhancing consumer convenience, job productivity, and service quality. However, trust, data security, and privacy are major issues for customers looking for financial services. AI technology is a component of chatbots that may expose users to unexpected security concerns if a program is ill-conceived, misused, or malevolent. This document describes and prepares a Chatbot Security Control Procedure (CSCP) to safeguard customer information and the protection of personal data [4]. Because chatbots can be trained to connect even more intimately with people and have their interactions "humanized," or made to seem more human, they can be used in banks. Chatbot systems can be secured with two-factor authentication and encryption, just like the majority of websites and apps. Design simply facilitates data flow, according to a new study of studies on mobile health services. In order to give users reliable clinical services, a chatbot with a pre-set health framework can filter and analyze data in a health information system (SIS). Chatbot-based systems provide consumers with interactive access to the information they want in addition to generic information, in contrast to the present mobile health systems. The progress of science and technology is then discussed in [5]. The Facebook Messenger Security Robot provides the chatbot structure needed to assist consumers in getting detection information from cameras as Internet Protocol cameras become more commonly utilized and popular (Sbot) can be followed via day and night. To build an Sbot, a system is developed that comprises of a network of cameras, a human detection server (HDS), and an Sbot server. Real-time human recognition, the Sbot connecting with the HDS via the Facebook Messenger network, and updating the information captured by the security cameras are all components of the system [5]. Users may virtually access and control their home appliances from any location with the help of a Raspberry Pi, a Facebook chatbot, and Google Maps. This enables the experimental use of smart home automation. This technique demonstrates how simple it is for users to communicate and submit commands over Facebook Messenger. The advantage is that you can use any device with an Internet connection to browse Facebook and control your home appliance. Additional capabilities relating to machine learning, voice controls, and natural language processing can be included to keep things operating smoothly (NLP). This enables a better method of comprehending user input [6]. Similar to [7], the use of chatbots has been expanding quickly recently across a variety of industries, including health, marketing, education, support systems, cultural heritage, entertainment, and more. This category includes the student-centered online learning platform, which acts as a model for managing communication and giving students the proper responses. It plans to create a system that can recognize questions, use domain ontologies and natural language processing techniques, and provide students with the appropriate responses using chatbots [7]. Hacking is more valuable than ever with the spread of information technology in many spheres of life. In a similar vein, chatbots can be hacked. A networking chatbot should be set up as a detecting activity for collective and contextual security assaults. One of the most popular applications in user support and many other fields is intelligent chatbot service. This service has a lot of advantages for users, but it also has hazards for businesses. The possible downsides of chatbots are revealed by a description of the features and layout of a typical chatbot service. Intelligent chatbots are already widely used in consumer web services and will continue to be so. Some distinct evolutions, such audio or video chatbots, are already being tested even though they are not yet widely used. Although this technology, which is primarily a tool for communication, offers many benefits, it can also pose new IT-related risks for companies that use it [8]. This service has a lot of advantages for users, but it also has hazards for businesses. The architecture and functionality of a typical chatbot service are described in detail, highlighting the possible dangers of chatbots. The use of intelligent chatbots in consumer web services has become commonplace and will remain so. Although they are not yet commonplace, some discrete evolutions, such audio or video chatbots, are already being tested. This technology has many advantages beyond communication devices, but it can also present more hazards connected to IT for businesses that adopt it. The ability to recognize and analyze cyberattacks is becoming more difficult as the quantity of such attacks rises. To address problems involving information security, a company needs people who can handle investigative security and have in-depth understanding. A chatbot needs to have enough intelligence to believe a trustworthy internet security program. Creating a SOC (security operations center), identifying incidents, using the right security technologies to analyze evidence intelligently, and either addressing the issue on your own or notifying the proper authorities are all examples of such investigations [9].

3.5 Advantages of Conversational AI

Conversational AI is a practical option for many business activities. Here are some instances of how conversational AI could be useful:

3.5.1 Cost-Effectiveness

A customer service desk can be quite expensive, especially if you want to answer questions beyond normal business hours. Providing customer support through a conversational interface can shrink business costs, especially for small and medium-sized businesses.

3.5.2 Enhanced Sale and Customer Engagement

Conversational AI tools provide real-time information quickly. This prompt assistance improved customer experience that leads to his satisfaction. The customer will be more loyal and shall give more referrals.

3.5.3   Scalability

Additionally, because the infrastructure required to enable it can be installed more quickly and affordably than new hiring, conversational AI is incredibly scalable. This is particularly useful when a product is being introduced to a new market or when there are unexpected short-term demand spikes, such as those that occur around the holidays.

3.5.4   Detect and Prevent Cyberattacks Through AI

Cyberattacks are becoming more sophisticated and harder to detect, making robust cyber security measures essential for organizations. However, AI can modify and improve cloud security services in some ways.

    i.   AI can help identify patterns in data that may indicate a cyberattack attempt. For example, if there is a sudden spike in activity from a specific IP address, AI can flag it as suspicious and trigger an investigation.

    ii.   AI can also be used to monitor employee behavior. If an employee suddenly starts accessing confidential data that they do not normally work with, it could be a sign that they are trying to steal information from the company.

    iii.   Additionally, you can use AI to create virtual firewalls that can block traffic from known malicious IP addresses. This can help prevent cyberattacks before they reach your network.

3.5.5   Businesses Benefit from Automated Response Work

An automated response is a process that allows a computer system to automatically respond to a cyberattack. This can be accomplished by identifying the attack and then acting to neutralize it.

Organizations can gain from automated response by cutting down on the time and expense required to respond to an attack. By logging what occurred during an attack, automated response can also aid in the prevention of subsequent attacks.

In a nutshell, artificial intelligence (AI) is the capacity of machines to carry out tasks that typically demand human intelligence, such as decision-making and pattern recognition. This can be accomplished using a variety of methods, including machine learning (ML) and natural language processing (NLP).

- Benefits of using AI for cloud security services include:
- Identifying risks that would otherwise go unnoticed.
- Automating threat response processes.
- Better performance of security operations.
- Ability to reduce the cost of security operations.

3.6   Challenges with Conversational Artificial Intelligence

The commercial use of conversational AI is still in its early stages, and firms have only just begun to do so extensively. As with every new technological advancement, the migration to conversational AI applications comes with a number of challenges like input language, privacy and security, and user apprehensions.

Additionally, chatbots are not always trained to reply to a range of user demands. In this situation, it is crucial to offer a different channel of communication in order to react to these complicated requests because the end user finds it frustrating when they receive a response that is erroneous or partial. Users ought to have access to a human corporate representative in these situations.

Finally, conversational AI can reduce the number of staff members needed for a certain role and streamline workflow inside an organization. This can spur socioeconomic activity, which might prompt a reaction from the corporation.

3.7   Risks Associated with Conversational AI

Although cloud security services that use artificial intelligence are growing in popularity, there are some risks associated with this technology.

- One concern is that AI can provide hackers with new ways to assault systems. For instance, if a thief creates a software that can mimic human behavior, they may be able to get through security precautions intended to spot illicit conduct. Another issue is that AI-driven security systems might make errors and deny access to information or resources to authorized individuals. For companies that depend on the cloud for essential operations, this might result in major issues.
- Lastly, there is a chance that cybercriminals may utilize AI to build "backdoors" into systems that would provide them covert access to private information. It is important to remember that, despite the presence of these risks, AI-based security solutions have the potential to greatly improve the security of data stored in the cloud.

The various distributed denial of service (DDoS) attack types that potentially jeopardize cloud-based conversational AI applications are listed in Table 3.2 [61].

Due to its multi-tenant framework, a distributed denial of service attack might have an impact on the accessibility or availability of cloud services.

With two primary goals in mind, it is applied to the different cooperative systems [62].

It aims to prevent legitimate users from accessing the resource by overwhelming server resources like CPU time or network bandwidth, and to hide the identities of attackers or bad users. The Table 3.1 shows about the Risk associated with Conversational AI.

Cross-site scripting (XSS) attacks: Most cloud-based XSS attacks target online social networks (OSN) like Twitter, LinkedIn, Facebook, and others with multimedia web apps. During an XSS attack, the attacker installs illegal JavaScript on the OSN's web server. This is done by getting the user's or handler's login credentials as well as session tokens and/or bank account details. Large-scale XSS attacks can cause cookie theft, account takeover, fraud, and DOS attacks. Gupta must deal with this assault because he and his colleagues

Table 3.1 Risks associated with conversational AI [10].

Source	Associated risks	Description
[11]	Identity issues and spoofing	1. If an attacker can spoof a chatbot as a real user, they can access a user's personal information. 2. An attacker has the ability to alter the chatbot system interface or perform data injection.
	Unintentional bad behavior	A lack of intelligence, ludicrous or inappropriate reactions, a propensity for making poor decisions, an inability to think clearly, and a lack of spontaneity or naturalness are all indicators of involuntary misbehavior.
[12]	Malware attack	The end user, the chatbot customer site, or the chatbot provider site may all be compromised by malware. Attacks that entail input/output manipulation, the exfiltration of private data, and identity theft are conceivable in each of the three scenarios.
	Attack through distributed denial of service (DDoS)	The availability of the chatbot might be affected by a DDoS, even if the chatbot's customer service is completely operational, because of the large traffic that is arriving to the chatbot provider's server.
	Social engineering attacks	Harmful chatbots can be made by cybercriminals and black hat hackers with the intention of socially engineering victims into clicking on links, downloading malicious files, or disclosing private information.
	Input or string manipulation	False text chatbots can be inserted into real communications by hackers.
	Monitoring issues	Keep an eye on the accessibility of the attendance figures. The fact that chatbots operate on an open system and make both agents and chatbots accountable for their actions is their most important feature. Businesses will be more susceptible to data breaches and even manipulation without these tools.
[11]	Utilizing third-party services	The use of chatbots to target services offered by third parties is one of these issues. Secondly, attacks against third-party services that chatbots rely on to function may result in the bot ceasing to function or giving users inaccurate information. Requiring chatbots to use certain public sources of information, for instance, may be done.

(Continued)

Table 3.1 Risks associated with conversational AI [10]. (*Continued*)

Source	Associated risks	Description
[13]	Manipulating template	The chatbot answer pattern can be changed after being given to the chatbot service. All conversations with chatbots must be secure for the highest level of safety. Only encrypted channels should be used with chatbots, and chatbot conversations should be encrypted.
[11]	Security of communication layer	Data are transmitted using HTTP via an encrypted connection using Transport Layer Security (TLS) or Secure Sockets Layer (SSL).
[14]	Partition or split user input sentences	Users should not be required to utilize proper language and syntax when speaking with chatbots. It is essential to consider crystal-clear disclaimers and possible signs of human participation if the chatbot is unable to deliver explicit instructions.
[21, 23]	WS-security	A major standard that deals with web services security.
[45, 49]	Phishing attack	The threat to the attacker is that they will trick the victim into visiting a bogus Web page and asking them for their login credentials (either through spoof emails or DNS assaults).
[46]	Wrapping attack	There is some risk involved when using an XML-based signature for integrity protection or authentication.
[17, 20]	Injection attack	The idea is to infiltrate the cloud system via a malicious virtual machine or service implementation.
[17]	IP spoofing	Unauthorized access to someone's login information entails some danger.
[31]	Tampering	Network-based data transfer or persistent data modification without authorization.
[21, 24, 47, 49]	Physical protection	There is a danger that humans or natural disasters will harm the hardware components regardless of how much internal software and policy security is offered.
[16, 19, 25, 49]	Security of WLANs	Message manipulation, identity theft, and network eavesdropping have all increased in frequency as a result of WLAN openness' susceptibility.

(*Continued*)

Table 3.1 Risks associated with conversational AI [10]. (*Continued*)

Source	Associated risks	Description
[31, 47, 52]	Direct attacking method	Instead of trying to decrypt the encryption key, it immediately decodes the cypher text.
[34, 39, 55]	Replay attack	A specific type of network assault known as a replay attack involves the deliberate or fraudulent delaying or replaying of an authorized data transaction.
[23, 49]	Attack by a man in the middle	The attacker makes numerous connections with the victims during this kind of active eavesdropping and relays communications between them.
[25, 30, 36]	Reflexion assault	This technique can be used to compromise a challenge-response authentication system that uses the same protocol in both directions.
[28, 30]	Repudiation	The chance that a user might engage in illegal activity in a system without adequate oversight.
[29]	Information disclosure	Unauthorized cloud user reads and accesses a file from a tenant's workflow.
[49]	Continuity of service	An adversary takes over a tenant's virtual machine and shuts down the web server of another tenant.
[47]	Enhancement of privilege	A malicious party hijacks a tenant's virtual machine and brings down another tenant's web server.
[51]	Lack of trust	As more companies provide cloud services, consumers become pickier, finding it challenging to select the best and most suitable vendors from a wide range of choices.
[59, 60]	Interleaving attack	To gain access to the trusted system, an attacker gets past all system defenses.
[20, 41]	Quickness of attack	Lack of a deadline poses the risk of the procedure not knowing when a step is complete, which could result in problems.
[18, 40, 49]	Self-adaptive storage resource management	Schedule data transfer and distribution, use prediction matrices for performance via remotely accessible storage services, and apply dynamic control for huge size data are all important to sustain optimization of sensitive data that are constantly monitored.

(*Continued*)

Table 3.1 Risks associated with conversational AI [10]. (*Continued*)

Source	Associated risks	Description
[15, 17, 42]	Client monitoring and security	The different client types and their respective access privileges must be known to the storage service.
[22, 47, 49, 56]	Completeness	The requirement that, in order to grant access based on the approved access levels, a data service provider must supply a user with all the information to which they are entitled or permitted.
[30, 42]	Service Level Agreements (SLAs) with gaps	Customers may have problems as a result of vendor lock-in, poor security measures, unavailable data, hidden charges, and ambiguous infrastructure.
[30]	Lack of perceived reliability	Risk associated with not being able to determine with certainty whether availability refers to a single server or to multiple servers.
[32]	Auditing	It entails looking at authorization and authentication data to make sure they follow established security conventions and recommendations.
[29, 30]	Back door	It is a technique for breaking into a network by using a "back door," such a modem, to bypass the network's security measures.
[47]	Rollback assault	The malicious service provider keeps providing the user with the outdated information even after the data owner upgrades it to the current version.
[54]	Fairness	After receiving confirmation from a peer, a malicious party may decide to keep quiet in order to acquire certain advantages during the data transfer process.
[38, 44, 48]	Data loss or leakage	In order to sell the data to interested parties, a supplier could maintain extra copies of the information in an unethical way.
[33, 35, 44]	Attack on a computer network (CAN)	Information disruption, denial, degradation, or destruction operations are actions that affect, deny, degrade, or destroy information. Along with the devices themselves, networks and computers have users.

(*Continued*)

Table 3.1 Risks associated with conversational AI [10]. (*Continued*)

Source	Associated risks	Description
[49]	TCP-based hijacking	The IP address of a trusted client is hijacked and communication is made in a way that it seems with a trustworthy client.
[52, 58]	Using social engineering	In such sort of attacks, social skills are used to collect personal information like PIN, CNIC, etc.
[57]	Container diving	Recovering data that have been left behind by a person or organization.
[24, 47, 57]	Login guessing	The most often used user authentication method is this one. Theft of passwords is a common and effective attack tactic.
[37, 53]	Ransomware and trojan horses	They cloak dangerous code within host software that seems to be helpful.
[41, 49, 52]	Denial of service attack	The availability of the system is ruined.
[26, 27]	Data security	Sensitive data for each business are kept within its perimeter, according to rules for access control and physical, logical, and human security.
[17, 18]	Network security	To avoid losing important data, every network data transfer must be protected, and any information breach must be avoided.
[43, 47]	Data locality	The customer might not be aware of the location of their data storage.
[35, 50]	Data reliability	Data integrity in a distributed system must be ensured by an efficient and fail-safe management of transactions between various data sources.

Table 3.2 Attacks that use distributed denial of service (DDoS).

Source	Type of DDoS Attack	Description	Impacted cloud computing layer
	Smurf attack	Attacker sends many ICMP echo requests. The victim's IP address is used as the source and the broadcast IP address is used as the destination. The victim would receive broadcasted addresses.	IaaS
	Death assault PING	Attacker sends an IP packet larger than 65,535 bytes. Handling a large packet may affect the victim's workstation and cloud resources.	PaaS and IaaS
	Attack using IP spoofing	An attacker can modify packet headers when an IP packet's source field contains a real or unreachable IP address. Because the server may adjust the real user machine in response to a legitimate user computer or cannot finish the transaction due to an inaccessible IP address, server resources are disturbed.	PaaS
	Attack due to buffer overflow	Attacker sends executable code to victim to exploit buffer overflow. The attacker will access the victim's computer. The infected PC may be used to launch a cloud-based DDoS attack or destroy a victim's computer.	SaaS
	Teardrop assault	The "Teardrop.c" application is used by attackers to deliver unauthorized IP fragment overlays within TCP packet headers. The victim's computer will therefore crash while the cloud system is being rebuilt.	PaaS and IaaS
	Land assault	Using "Land.c," attackers send fake TCP SYN packets with the victim's IP address. When the computer accepts the request, the system crashes.	PaaS and IaaS
	SYN flood assault	When an attacker sends several packets to the server but is unable to complete the 3-way handshake, it happens. It can prevent servers from answering legitimate queries. The server is taking its time in this instance to process every packet. Similar to sending packets using a bogus IP address, SYN flooding is another approach.	IaaS and PaaS

(Continued)

Table 3.2 Attacks that use distributed denial of service (DDoS). (*Continued*)

Source	Type of DDoS attack	Description	Impacted cloud computing layer
[63]	Botnet-based	Esraa Alomari *et al.* published a study on botnet-based DDoS assaults and their impact on the application layer, namely, the web server. The botnet-based application layer DDoS assault limits resources, makes cash, and upsets customers. The attack aims to: a. Neglect the victim in some way. b. The personal covert purpose of this assault is to deny any destination system access to the required computer resources or to reduce service performance. This assault is therefore being carried out in reprisal. c. The other goal of this attack is to improve its reputation among hackers. This kind of attack could also be carried out with the intention of making money, infringing on privacy and taking advantage of the data and information that is available. d. By looking for indications of botnet control activity and command, Timothy Strayer *et al.* proposed a way to identify botnet attacks. They looked at flow metrics such as packet timing, burst duration, and bandwidth. In addition, the author has developed an architecture that divides traffic that is not likely to be a botnet fragment from the remaining traffic before classifying the remaining traffic into a collection or group. The architecture then connects the likely traffic patterns to identify shared or common communications that point to the existence or activity of a botnet.	

designed an XSS-secure architecture to prevent XSS worms from the OSN cloud web application. The framework has two uses.

- **Training mode**: This mode generates safe JavaScript code for web page templates.
- **Detection mode**: Offline mode employs sanitizer detection. This option detects JS code and unsafe variables.

Cloud virtual machines use Java-created framework to protect privacy and security. A simulation of sensing as a service:

> The concept of sensing as a service is introduced in Reference [64]. Sensors are what ties the Internet of Things and the smart city together, despite their distinct backgrounds. To preserve the privacy of the sensor data, the owner of the sensor may impose restrictions on things like who has access to what information. Additionally, sensitive information like position data needs to be implicitly changed in order to make sensor data anonymous.

3.7.1   5D-Model for Discretion

In Reference [65], the authors discuss a few privacy concerns with respect to smart cities. The idea of a smart city can be used as a guide for protecting people's privacy. The study suggests a 5D model for a smart city's privacy. Identity, query, location, footprint, and owner are the five dimensions.

3.7.2   User Consciousness

Reference [66] provides a thorough explanation of privacy protection measures. User knowledge and authorization are required before data distribution may happen.

3.7.3   RFID Protects Privacy and Security

Physical and cryptographic measures are both necessary for RFID privacy protection [67]. Physical measures can be used to block and disable tags while not in use, including kill codes, Faraday cages, and blocker tags. There are proposed cryptographic techniques for lowering privacy threats. The suggested cryptographic techniques include encryption, hash lock, randomized id, and efficient identification.

3.7.4   Data Aggregation

Another way to safeguard someone's privacy is by data aggregation [68]. A cloud can be used for application-specific data analysis.

3.7.5   Stakeholder Model

Security and privacy framework proposes a stakeholder model of a smart city that addresses privacy issues from the viewpoint of the stakeholder [69]. Sources of privacy protection include user permission, freedom of choice and control, and anonymity technology [70]. Individual users and non-consumers, device manufacturers, IoT cloud service and platform providers, third-party application developers, government and regulatory organizations, and device makers are the main parties accountable for user privacy protection.

3.7.6 2 × 2 Framework

A 2 × 2 methodology suggested in Reference [71] makes predictions about which data applications and technologies are most likely to cause privacy problems. A 2 × 2 framework is used to depict the four different sorts of data sensitivities that individuals have. These four categories are personal information used for services, personal information used for surveillance, impersonal information used for services, and impersonal information used for surveillance. The writers have described how a technology might go from being innocent to becoming sensitive.

3.7.7 Framework for Mobile Cloud

A significant contributor to privacy leaks is the over-gathering of data from smartphones [72]. The act of using smartphone applications to capture more user data than they can handle is known as data overcollection. The authors illustrate mobile device data over-collection scenarios and suggest a mobile-cloud architecture as a remedy to stop data over-collection.

3.7.8 Changes to Pseudonyms in Intelligent Transportation Systems

An attacker could use this information from an intelligent transportation system to keep track of a vehicle's movements in order to carry out their harmful intentions. Reference [73] offers a solution to this problem that requires regular pseudonym changes in order to maintain location secrecy.

3.7.9 Homomorphic Encryption

Homomorphic encryption is a wonderful choice in the e-health sector for safeguarding the privacy of patient health data stored in the cloud [74].

3.7.10 Three-Layer Model

The where, who, and what paradigm for location-based services has reportedly been presented, according to Reference [75]. The three-layer concept proposed by Reference provides user-friendly technology while safeguarding user privacy.

3.7.11 Linear Algebra

A solution based on linear algebra has been put out by the authors of Reference [76]. They compute determinants, eigenvalues, eigenvectors, inner products, and two-party protocols. While maintaining the privacy of the inputs, these techniques generate the output results.

3.7.12 Continuous Streaming Data

Traditional security methods can only manage static data; they are insufficient for handling dynamic data. Due to the enormous volume of data being generated, maintaining privacy with continuously streaming data may be difficult.

3.7.13 DBMS Defense Against Insider Threats

Database management systems can be protected from external threats by firewalls, password schemes, penetration testing, and other safeguards, but it could be challenging to keep track of internal user intentions [77]. Setting up policies is one way to defend oneself against insider attacks, according to the authors of this study. In their suggested paradigm, the authors impose database audits, access control, and encryption. These limits are being put in place to safeguard the database management system from dangerous insider attacks.

3.7.14 Transaction Data Anonymization

The tiers of the medium-stored transaction logs are many. Data that transfer across levels are revealed to an IT manager. An innovative technique-based method that allows mining tools to analyze anonymous transaction data has been put out by the authors of Reference [78].

3.7.15 D-Mash Model

Data as a Service (DaaS) is an emerging topic of research because of its benefits [79]. Due to the two risks associated with DaaS—hackers and compromised data privacy—businesses steer clear of it. D-Mash is one of the privacy models that have been recommended to stop privacy leaks. It is also known as a data mash-up. This paradigm allows data vendors to include their relevant data as needed while maintaining data privacy [80].

3.7.16 A Safe Cryptosystem Based on Lattice

A system is recommended in References for healthcare in smart cities. A notion for cloud-based communication between doctors and patients has been put out by the authors. Because it is designed for confined nodes of smart cities, the system has lower computation and communication expenses than other currently employed systems [10].

3.8 Proposed Model for Conversational AI in Cloud Platform

In the above proposed model in Figure 3.4, text, gesture, and speech are just a few of the communication models that the user might employ to interact with the system. The system will recognize the user using artificial intelligence, and after authentication, the user will interact with the system. The system will analyze the data in encrypted form and respond to the user appropriately if the input activity is authentic. If the input activity cannot be identified, the system will analyze previous data and ask the user further questions in an effort to

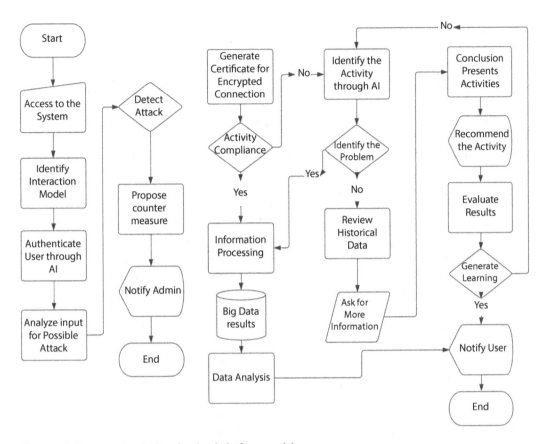

Figure 3.4 Conversational AI in the cloud platform model.

understand the problem. In the event that further evaluation of the data based on history and input questions is required, the system will offer potential outputs based on the processing, evaluate those outputs, and notify the user of the newly learned result. If the system detects an attack based on the pattern of input or through other AI-based trained models, it will notify the administrator and stop the operation. The proposed paradigm will enable secure communication between the user and the system.

Large data [81–83] volumes are necessary for conversational AI [84, 85] to continue to advance. A virtual agent [86, 87] improves at responding to queries and automating requests with each client engagement. However, no actual customer information [88, 89] from chat logs is used to train the model for future development. Chat logs are only used to keep tabs on the virtual agent and see if there are any questions it is unable to answer. If so, the virtual agent is subsequently trained to be able to answer that particular question using a different set of synthetic training data. By removing the client entirely from the security [89–92] equation, keeping the conversation log data and the synthetic training data apart enables more flexibility. Additionally, we have shown that the precision [93–95] of prediction from simulated training data actually beats that from real chat logs [96], negating the need to involve a client [97] and obtain their consent before training the model. Make sure the automated chats are reliable and secure [98]. Create AI chatbots that adhere to the most recent guidelines, rules, and standards. Control access [99] using several alternatives for authorization and authentication. Control security and make sure your client feels comfortable enough to contact you.

3.9   Conclusion

Conversational solutions that can meet privacy goals by reducing the gathering and retention of potentially sensitive user data need to be protected by an AI-based framework. The benefits of conversational AI like cost saving, increased sales and customer engagement, scalability, automation of processes, and detection and prevention of cyberattacks through AI urge organizations to adopt conversational AI based models but still they are reluctant to adopt due to security concerns. The underlying privacy issues and challenges are briefly discussed in this study. We may anticipate that conversational AI will have more sophisticated hardware (such as multiple sensors) and software (such as face and sound identification algorithms) in the near future. The challenges with conversational AI like interpreting the true meanings of input raw data can be improved with more and more sophisticated and AI-based devices that will suppress the noise and sense the emotions of human in the current context of the conversation; the more the people will get educated, the more they will handle the devices intelligently and their concerns with their privacy and security can be addressed with more smart AI-based devices with better AI datasets and least specific user data storages; likewise, the apprehension of users' personal data shall be addressed with the introduction of more secure models that are more human like intelligence, interaction, and interpretation skills. With the advancement in AI, with more and more smart quality checks to address security at different levels, the conversational AI models will improve, and as a result, the adoption of conversational AI will increase. Therefore, a privacy quantification is required so that individuals can choose whether or not to disclose their personal data with conversational AI platforms.

3.10   Future Work

Artificial intelligence is expected to continue to have an impact on how cloud security services are delivered in the future. AI-based systems are getting better and can now identify more sophisticated threats. As they become more widely available and fairly priced, more businesses will be able to utilize them. Future organizations seeking to protect their data and applications from assaults are anticipated to find AI to be even more essential [23].

The blockchain is one of the most recent and cutting-edge developments in computer science. It is a disruptive, digital, and decentralized technology. The information or data included in each block of the chain is not under the jurisdiction of a single centralized authority. Different types of blockchains store different types of data or information inside their blocks. Many people use this new technology to validate transactions using digital currency. This technique can be used to verify everyone in the block's legitimacy even when there is no centralized authority. This technology could be applied to the proposed model to strengthen it even more [61].

References

1. Hendriana, Y. and Hardi, R., Remote control system as serial communications mobile using a microcontroller, in: *2016 International Conference on Information Technology Systems and Innovation, ICITSI 2016 - Proceedings*, 2017, doi: 10.1109/ICITSI.2016.7858212.
2. Nielsen, J. and Molich, R., Heuristic evaluation of user interfaces, in: *Conference on Human Factors in Computing Systems - Proceedings*, 1990, doi: 10.1145/97243.97281.
3. Khanna, A., Pandey, B., Vashishta, K., Kalia, K., Pradeepkumar, B., Das, T., A study of today's A.I. through Chatbots and rediscovery of machine intelligence. *Int. J. u- e-Service, Sci. Technol.*, 8, 7, 277–284, Jul. 2015, doi: 10.14257/ijunesst.2015.8.7.28.
4. Lai, S.T., Leu, F.Y., Lin, J.W., A banking Chatbot security control procedure for protecting user data security and privacy, in: *Lecture Notes on Data Engineering and Communications Technologies*, 2019.
5. Van Cuong, T. and Tan, T.M., Design and implementation of chatbot framework for network security cameras, in: *Proceedings of 2019 International Conference on System Science and Engineering, ICSSE 2019*, 2019, doi: 10.1109/ICSSE.2019.8823516.
6. Parthornratt, T., Kitsawat, D., Putthapipat, P., Koronjaruwat, P., A smart home automation via facebook Chatbot and Raspberry Pi, in: *2018 2nd International Conference on Engineering Innovation, ICEI 2018*, 2018, doi: 10.1109/ICEI18.2018.8448761.
7. Clarizia, F., Colace, F., Lombardi, M., Pascale, F., Santaniello, D., Chatbot: An education support system for student, in: *Lecture Notes in Computer Science (including subseries Lecture Notes in Artificial Intelligence and Lecture Notes in Bioinformatics)*, 2018, doi: 10.1007/978-3-030-01689-0_23.
8. Gondaliya, K., Butakov, S., Zavarsky, P., SLA as a mechanism to manage risks related to chatbot services, in: *Proceedings - 2020 IEEE 6th Intl Conference on Big Data Security on Cloud, BigDataSecurity 2020, 2020 IEEE Intl Conference on High Performance and Smart Computing, HPSC 2020 and 2020 IEEE Intl Conference on Intelligent Data and Security, IDS 2020*, 2020, doi: 10.1109/BigDataSecurity-HPSC-IDS49724.2020.00050.
9. Perera, V.H., Senarathne, A.N., Rupasinghe, L., Intelligent SOC Chatbot for Security Operation Center, in: *2019 International Conference on Advancements in Computing (ICAC)*, pp. 340–345, 2019, doi: 10.1109/ICAC49085.2019.9103388.
10. Tahirkheli, A., I, Shiraz, M., Hayat, B., Idrees, M., Sajid, A., Ullah, R., Ayub, N., Kim, K., A survey on modern cloud computing security over smart city networks: Threats, vulnerabilities, consequences,countermeasures, and challenges. *Electronics*, 10, 1811, 2021, https://doi.org/10.3390/electronics10151811, https://www.mdpi.com/journal/electronics.
11. Schlesinger, A., O'Hara, K.P., Taylor, A.S., Let's talk about race: Identity, chatbots, and AI, in: *Conference on Human Factors in Computing Systems - Proceedings*, 2018, doi: 10.1145/3173574.3173889.
12. Nuruzzaman, M. and Hussain, O.K., A Survey on Chatbot implementation in customer service industry through deep neural networks, in: *Proceedings - 2018 IEEE 15th International Conference on e-Business Engineering, ICEBE 2018*, 2018, doi: 10.1109/ICEBE.2018.00019.
13. D'Silva, G.M., Thakare, S., More, S., Kuriakose, J., Real world smart chatbot for customer care using a software as a service (SaaS) architecture, in: *Proceedings of the International Conference on IoT in Social, Mobile, Analytics and Cloud, I-SMAC 2017*, 2017, doi: 10.1109/I-SMAC.2017.8058261.
14. Hidayatin, L. and Rahutomo, F., Query expansion evaluation for Chatbot application, in: *Proceedings of ICAITI 2018 - 1st International Conference on Applied Information Technology and Innovation: Toward A New Paradigm for the Design of Assistive Technology in Smart Home Care*, 2018, doi: 10.1109/ICAITI.2018.8686762.

15. Choudhary, A. and Bhadada, R., Emerging threats in cloud computing, in: *Proceedings of the International Conference on Emerging Technology Trends in Electronics Communication and Networking*, Surat, India, 7–8 February 2020, Springer, Berlin/Heidelberg, Germany, 2020.

16. Gretzel, U., Sigala, M., Xiang, Z., Koo, C., Smart tourism: Foundations and developments. *Electron. Mark.*, 25, 179–188, 2015.

17. Shepard, D.P., Bhatti, J.A., Humphreys, T.E., Fansler, A.A., Evaluation of smart grid and civilian UAV vulnerability to GPS spoofing attacks, in: *Proceedings of the 25th International Technical Meeting of The Satellite Division of the Institute of Navigation (ION GNSS)*, Nashville, TN, USA, 17–21 September 2012, pp. 3591–3605.

18. Tari, Z., Security and privacy in cloud computing. *IEEE Cloud Comput.*, 1, 54–57, 2014.

19. Edwards, L., Privacy, security and data protection in smart cities: A critical EU law perspective. *Eur. Data Prot. L. Rev.*, 2, 28, 2016.

20. Fortino, G., Russo, W., Savaglio, C., Shen, W., Zhou, M., Agent-oriented cooperative smart objects: From IoT system design to implementation. *IEEE Trans. Syst. Man, Cybern. Syst.*, 48, 1939–1956, 2017.

21. Qureshi, K.N., Abdullah, A.H., Ullah, G., Sensor based vehicle environment perception information system, in: *Proceedings of the 4 IEEE International Conference on Ubiquitous Intelligence and Computing/International Conference on Autonomic and Trusted Computing/International Conference on Scalable Computing and Communications and Its Associated Workshops*, Bali, Indonesia, 9–12 December 2014.

22. Han, G., Jiang, J., Shu, L., Niu, J., Chao, H.C., Management and applications of trust in wireless sensor networks: A survey. *J. Comput. Syst. Sci.*, 80, 602–617, 2014.

23. Aliero, M.S., Qureshi, K.N., Pasha, M.F., Ghani, I., Yauri, R.A., Systematic review analysis on SQLIA detection and prevention approaches. *Wirel. Pers. Commun.*, 112, 2297–2333, 2020.

24. Chakrabarty, S. and Engels, D.W., A secure IoT architecture for Smart Cities, in: *Proceedings of the 2016 13th IEEE Annual Consumer Communications & Networking Conference (CCNC)*, Las Vegas, NV, USA, 9–12 January 2016.

25. Khan, Z., Pervez, Z., Ghafoor, A., Towards cloud based smart cities data security and privacy management, in: *Proceedings of the 2014 IEEE/ACM 7th International Conference on Utility and Cloud Computing*, London, UK, 8–11 December 2014.

26. Arafati, M., Dagher, G.G., Fung, B.C., Hung, P.C., D-mash: A framework for privacy-preserving data-as-a-service mashups, in: *Proceedings of the IEEE 7th International Conference on Cloud Computing (CLOUD)*, Anchorage, AK, USA, 27 June–2 July 2014.

27. Xiao, Y., Jia, Y., Liu, C., Cheng, X., Yu, J., Lv, W., Edge computing security: State of the art and challenges. *Proc. IEEE*, 107, 1608–1631, 2019.

28. Tabrizchi, H. and Rafsanjani, M.K., A survey on security challenges in cloud computing: Issues, threats, and solutions. *J. Supercomput.*, 76, 9493–9532, 2020.

29. Dorri, A., Kanhere, S.S., Jurdak, R., Gauravaram, P., Blockchain for IoT security and privacy: The case study of a smart home, in: *Proceedings of the 2017 IEEE international conference on pervasive computing and communications workshops (PerCom workshops)*, Kona, HI, USA, 13–17 March 2017.

30. Kaaniche, N. and Laurent, M., Data security and privacy preservation in cloud storage environments based on cryptographic mechanisms. *Comput. Commun.*, 111, 120–141, 2017.

31. Verginadis, Y., Michalas, A., Gouvas, P., Schiefer, G., Hübsch, G., Paraskakis, I., Paasword: A holistic data privacy and security by design framework for cloud services. *J. Grid Comput.*, 15, 219–234, 2017.

32. Shakeel, P.M., Baskar, S., Dhulipala, V.S., Mishra, S., Jaber, M.M., Maintaining security and privacy in health care system using learning based deep-Q-networks. *J. Med. Syst.*, 42, 186, 2018.

33. Gong, Y., Zhang, C., Fang, Y., Sun, J., Protecting location privacy for task allocation in ad hoc mobile cloud computing. *IEEE Trans. Emerg. Top. Comput.*, 6, 110–121, 2015.

34. Elhoseny, M., Abdelaziz, A., Salama, A.S., Riad, A.M., Muhammad, K., Sangaiah, A.K., A hybrid model of internet of things and cloud computing to manage big data in health services applications. *Future Gener. Comput. Syst.*, 86, 1383–1394, 2018.

35. Xue, K., Hong, J., Ma, Y., Wei, D.S., Hong, P., Yu, N., Fog-aided verifiable privacy preserving access control for latency-sensitive data sharing in vehicular cloud computing. *IEEE Netw.*, 32, 7–13, 2018.

36. Tian, H., Nan, F., Chang, C.C., Huang, Y., Lu, J., Du, Y., Privacy-preserving public auditing for secure data storage in fog-to-cloud computing. *J. Netw. Comput. Appl.*, 127, 59–69, 2019.

37. Hasson, F., Keeney, S., McKenna, H., Research guidelines for the Delphi survey technique. *J. Adv. Nurs.*, 32, 1008–1015, 2000.

38. Liu, L.S., Shih, P.C., Hayes, G.R., Barriers to the adoption and use of personal health record systems, in: *Proceedings of the 2011 iConference*, Seattle, WA, USA, 8–11 Febuary 2011, pp. 363–370.

39. Bahga, A. and Madisetti, V.K., A cloud-based approach for interoperable electronic health records (EHRs). *IEEE J. Biomed. Health Inf.*, 17, 894–906, 2013.

40. Qiu, M., Gai, K., Thuraisingham, B., Tao, L., Zhao, H., Proactive user-centric secure data scheme using attribute-based semantic access controls for mobile clouds in financial industry. *Future Gener. Comput. Syst.*, 80, 421–429, 2018.

41. Alshehri, S., Radziszowski, S.P., Raj, R.K., Secure access for healthcare data in the cloud using ciphertext-policy attribute-based encryption. *Proceedings of the IEEE 28th International Conference on Data Engineering, ICDE 2012*, Arlington, VA, USA, 1–5 April 2012.

42. Athena, J., Sumathy, V., Kumar, K., An identity attribute–Based encryption using elliptic curve digital signature for patient health record maintenance. *Int. J. Commun. Syst.*, 31, e3439, 2018.

43. Seol, K., Kim, Y.G., Lee, E., Seo, Y.D., Baik, D.K., Privacy-preserving attribute-based access control model for XML-based electronic health record system. *IEEE Access*, 6, 9114–9128, 2018.

44. Lindsay, J.R., Demystifying the quantum threat: Infrastructure, institutions, and intelligence advantage. *Secur. Stud.*, 29, 335–361, 2020.

45. Khan, N. and Al-Yasiri, A., Cloud security threats and techniques to strengthen cloud computing adoption framework, in: *Cyber Security and Threats: Concepts, Methodologies, Tools, and Applications*, pp. 268–285, IGI Global, Hershey, PA, USA, 2018.

46. Chen, M., Zhang, Y., Hu, L., Taleb, T., Sheng, Z., Cloud-based wireless network: Virtualized, reconfigurable, smart wireless network to enable 5G technologies. *Mob. Netw. Appl.*, 20, 704–712, 2015.

47. Pérez-Martínez, P.A. and Solanas, A., W3-privacy: The three dimensions of user privacy in LBS, in: *Proceedings of the 12th ACM Int'l. Symp. Mobile Ad Hoc Networking and Computing*, Paris, France, 16–19 May 2011.

48. David, B., Dowsley, R., van de Graaf, J., Marques, D., Nascimento, A.C., Pinto, A.C., Unconditionally secure, universally composable privacy preserving linear algebra. *IEEE Trans. Inf. Forensics Secur.*, 11, 59–73, 2016.

49. Chourabi, H., Nam, T., Walker, S., Gil-Garcia, J.R., Mellouli, S., Nahon, K., Pardo, T.A., Scholl, H.J., Understanding smart cities: An integrative framework, in: *Proceedings of the 45th Hawaii International Conference on System Sciences*, Maui, HI USA, 4–7 January 2012.

50. Smith, M.L., Viktor Mayer-Schönberger, Delete: The virtue of forgetting in the digital age. *Identity Inf. Soc*, 2, 369–373, 2009.

51. Djigal, H., Jun, F., Lu, J., Secure framework for future smart city, in: *Proceedings of the 2017 IEEE 4th International Conference on Cyber Security and Cloud Computing (CSCloud)*, New York, NY, USA, 26–28 June 2017.

52. Gubbi, J., Buyya, R., Marusic, S., Palaniswami, M., Internet of things (IoT): A vision, architectural elements, and future directions. *Future Gener. Comput. Syst.*, 29, 1645–1660, 2013.

53. Farzandipour, M., Sadoughi, F., Ahmadi, M., Karimi, I., Security requirements and solutions in electronic health records: Lessons learned from a comparative study. *J. Med. Syst.*, 34, 629–642, 2010.

54. Xiao, Z. and Xiao, Y., Security and privacy in cloud computing. *IEEE Commun. Surv. Tutorials*, 15, 843–859, 2013.

55. Kumar, J.S. and Patel, D.R.A., survey on internet of things: Security and privacy issues. *Int. J. Comput. Appl.*, 90, 20–26, 2014.

56. Barth, S. and de Jong, M.D., The privacy paradox–Investigating discrepancies between expressed privacy concerns and actual online behavior–A systematic literature review. *Telemat. Inform.*, 34, 1038–1058, 2017.

57. Khatoun, R. and Zeadally, S., Cybersecurity and privacy solutions in smart cities. *IEEE Commun. Mag.*, 55, 51–59, 2017.

58. Spiekermann, S. and Cranor, L.F., Engineering privacy. *IEEE Trans. Software Eng.*, 35, 67–82, 2009.

59. Chaudhary, R., Jindal, A., Aujla, G.S., Kumar, N., Das, A.K., Saxena, N., LSCSH: Lattice-based secure cryptosystem for smart healthcare in smart cities environment. *IEEE Commun. Mag.*, 56, 24–32, 2018.

60. Perera, C., Ranjan, R., Wang, L., Khan, S.U., Zomaya, A.Y., Big data privacy in the internet of things era. *IT Prof.*, 17, 32–39, 2015.

61. Singh, S., Jeong, Y.S., Park, J.H., A survey on cloud computing security: Issues, threats, and solutions. *J. Netw. Comput. Appl.*, 75, 200–222, 2016.

62. Badve, B. B. G. O. P., Taxonomy of DoS and DDoS attacks and desirable defense mechanism in a cloud computing environment. *Neural Comput. Appl.*, 28, 12, 3655–3682, 2017.

63. Strayer, W.T., Lapsely, D., Walsh, R., Livadas, C., Botnet detection based on network behavior, in: *Botnet Detection*, Advances in Information Security, vol. 36, W. Lee, C. Wang, D. Dagon (eds.), Springer, Boston, MA, 2008.

64. Perera, C., Zaslavsky, A., Christen, P., Georgakopoulos, D., Sensing as a service model for smart cities supported by internet of things. *Trans. Emerging Telecommun. Technol.*, 25, 81–93, 2014.

65. Martínez-Ballesté, A., Pérez-Martínez, P.A., Solanas, A., The pursuit of citizens' privacy: A privacy-aware smart city is possible. *IEEE Commun. Mag.*, 51, 136–141, 2013.

66. Xiao, Z. and Xiao, Y., Security and privacy in cloud computing. *IEEE Commun. Surv. Tutorials*, 15, 843–859, 2013.

67. Qureshi, K.N., Abdullah, A.H., Ullah, G., Sensor based Vehicle Environment Perception Information System, in: *Proceedings of the 4 IEEE International Conference on Ubiquitous Intelligence and Computing/International Conference on Autonomic and Trusted Computing/International Conference on Scalable Computing and Communications and Its Associated Workshops*, Bali, Indonesia, 9–12 December 2014.

68. Cheon, J.H. and Kim, J., A hybrid scheme of public-key encryption and somewhat homomorphic encryption. *IEEE Trans. Inf. Forensics Secur.*, 10, 1052–1063, 2015.

69. Arafati, M., Dagher, G.G., Fung, B.C., Hung, P.C., D-mash: A framework for privacy-preserving data-as-a-service mashups, in: *Proceedings of the IEEE 7th International Conference on Cloud Computing (CLOUD)*, Anchorage, AK, USA, 27 June–2 July 2014.

70. Zaman, A., Obimbo, C., Dara, R.A., Information disclosure, security, and data quality, in: *Proceedings of the International Conference on Industrial, Engineering and Other Applications of Applied Intelligent Systems*, Montreal, QC, Canada, 25–28 June 2018.

71. Van Zoonen, L., Privacy concerns in smart cities. *Gov. Inf. Q.*, 33, 472–480, 2016.

72. Li, Y., Dai, W., Ming, Z., Qiu, M., Privacy protection for preventing data over-collection in smart city. *IEEE Trans. Comput.*, 65, 1339–1350, 2016.

73. Farzandipour, M., Sadoughi, F., Ahmadi, M., Karimi, I., Security requirements and solutions in electronic health records: Lessons learned from a comparative study. *J. Med. Syst.*, 34, 629–642, 2010.

74. Schaffers, H., Komninos, N., Pallot, M., Trousse, B., Nilsson, M., Oliveira, A., Smart cities and the future internet: Towards cooperation frameworks for open innovation, in: *The Future Internet Assembly*, pp. 431–446, Springer, Berlin/Heidelberg, Germany, 2011.

75. Bratterud, A., Happe, A., Duncan, R.A.K., Enhancing cloud security and privacy: The Unikernel solution, in: *Proceedings of the Eighth International Conference on Cloud Computing, GRIDs, and Virtualization*, Athens, Greece, 19–23 February 2017.

76. Balani, Z. and Varol, H., Cloud computing security challenges and threats, in: *Proceedings of the 2020 8th International Symposium on Digital Forensics and Security (ISDFS)*, Belrut, Lebanon, 1–2 June 2020.

77. Chakrabarty, S. and Engels, D.W., A secure IoT architecture for Smart Cities, in: *Proceedings of the 2016 13th IEEE Annual Consumer Communications & Networking Conference (CCNC)*, Las Vegas, NV, USA, 9–12 January 2016.

78. Dorri, A., Kanhere, S.S., Jurdak, R., Gauravaram, P., Blockchain for IoT security and privacy: The case study of a smart home, in: *Proceedings of the 2017 IEEE international conference on pervasive computing and communications workshops (PerCom workshops)*, Kona, HI, USA, 13–17 March 2017.

79. Kumar, J.S. and Patel, D.R.A., Survey on internet of things: Security and privacy issues. *Int. J. Comput. Appl.*, 90, 20–26, 2014.

80. Spiekermann, S. and Cranor, L.F., Engineering privacy. *IEEE Trans. Software Eng.*, 35, 67–82, 2009.

81. Rawat, R., Rimal, Y.N., William, P., Dahima, S., Gupta, S., Sankaran, K.S., Malware threat affecting financial organization analysis using machine learning approach. *Int. J. Inf. Technol. Web Eng. (IJITWE)*, 17, 1, 1–20, 2022.

82. Rawat, R., Mahor, V., Chouhan, M., Pachlasiya, K., Telang, S., Garg, B., Systematic literature review (SLR) on social media and the digital transformation of drug trafficking on darkweb, in: *International Conference on Network Security and Blockchain Technology*, Springer, Singapore, pp. 181–205, 2022.

83. Rawat, R., Ayodele Oki, O., Sankaran, S., Florez, H., Ajagbe, S.A., Techniques for predicting dark web events focused on the delivery of illicit products and ordered crime. *Int. J. Electr. Comput. Eng. (IJECE)*, 13, 5, 5354–5365, Oct. 2023, doi: 10.11591/ijece.v13i5.pp5354-5365.

84. Rawat, R., Garg, B., Mahor, V., Telang, S., Pachlasiya, K., Chouhan, M., Organ trafficking on the dark web—The data security and privacy concern in healthcare systems, in: *Internet of Healthcare Things: Machine Learning for Security and Privacy*, pp. 189–216, 2022.

85. Vyas, P., Vyas, G., Chauhan, A., Rawat, R., Telang, S., Gottumukkala, M., Anonymous trading on the dark online marketplace: An exploratory study, in: *Using Computational Intelligence for the Dark Web and Illicit Behavior Detection*, pp. 272–289, IGI Global, 2022.

86. Rawat, R., Oki, O.A., Sankaran, K.S., Olasupo, O., Ebong, G.N., Ajagbe, S.A., A new solution for cyber security in big data using machine learning approach, in: *Mobile Computing and Sustainable Informatics: Proceedings of ICMCSI 2023*, Springer Nature Singapore, Singapore, pp. 495–505, 2023.

87. Rawat, R., Chakrawarti, R.K., Raj, A., Mani, G., Chidambarathanu, K., Bhardwaj, R., Association rule learning for threat analysis using traffic analysis and packet filtering approach. *Int. J. Inf. Technol.*, 1–11, 2023.

88. Rawat, R., Logical concept mapping and social media analytics relating to cyber criminal activities for ontology creation. *Int. J. Inf. Technol.*, 15, 2, 893–903, 2023.

89. Rawat, R., Mahor, V., Álvarez, J.D., Ch, F., Cognitive systems for dark web cyber delinquent association malignant data crawling: A review, in: *Handbook of Research on War Policies, Strategies, and Cyber Wars*, pp. 45–63, 2023.

90. Rawat, R., Chakrawarti, R.K., Vyas, P., Gonzáles, J.L.A., Sikarwar, R., Bhardwaj, R., Intelligent fog computing surveillance system for crime and vulnerability identification and tracing. *Int. J. Inf. Secur. Priv. (IJISP)*, 17, 1, 1–25, 2023.

91. Rawat, R., Sowjanya, A.M., Patel, S.I., Jaiswal, V., Khan, I., Balaram, A. (Eds.), *Using Machine Intelligence: Autonomous Vehicles Volume 1*, John Wiley & Sons, 2022.

92. Rawat, R., Mahor, V., Díaz-Álvarez, J., Chávez, F., Rooted learning model at fog computing analysis for crime incident surveillance, in: *2022 International Conference on Smart Generation Computing, Communication and Networking (SMART GENCON)*, 2022, December, IEEE, pp. 1–9.

93. Rawat, R. and Shrivastav, S.K., SQL injection attack detection using SVM. *Int. J. Comput. Appl.*, 42, 13, 1–4, 2012.

94. Rawat, R., Bhardwaj, P., Kaur, U., Telang, S., Chouhan, M., Sankaran, K.S., *Smart vehicles for communication, volume 2*, John Wiley & Sons, 2023.

95. Mahor, V., Bijrothiya, S., Rawat, R., Kumar, A., Garg, B., Pachlasiya, K., IoT and artificial intelligence techniques for public safety and security, in: *Smart Urban Computing Applications*, p. 111, 2023.

96. Mahor, V., Pachlasiya, K., Garg, B., Chouhan, M., Telang, S., Rawat, R., Mobile operating system (android) vulnerability analysis using machine learning, in: *Proceedings of International Conference on Network Security and Blockchain Technology: ICNSBT 2021*, 2022, June, Springer Nature Singapore, Singapore, pp. 159–169.

97. Rawat, R., Garg, B., Pachlasiya, K., Mahor, V., Telang, S., Chouhan, M., Mishra, R., SCNTA: Monitoring of network availability and activity for identification of anomalies using machine learning approaches. *Int. J. Inf. Technol. Web Eng. (IJITWE)*, 17, 1, 1–19, 2022.

98. Mahor, V., Garg, B., Telang, S., Pachlasiya, K., Chouhan, M., Rawat, R., Cyber threat phylogeny assessment and vulnerabilities representation at thermal power station, in: *Proceedings of International Conference on Network Security and Blockchain Technology: ICNSBT 2021*, 2022, June, Springer Nature Singapore, Singapore, pp. 28–39.

99. Rawat, R., Gupta, S., Sivaranjani, S., CU, O.K., Kuliha, M., Sankaran, K.S., Malevolent information crawling mechanism for forming structured illegal organisations in hidden networks. *Int. J. Cyber Warf. Terror. (IJCWT)*, 12, 1, 1–14, 2022.

4

Unsupervised BERT-Based Granular Sentiment Analysis of Literary Work

N. Shyamala Devi* and K. Sharmila

*Department of Computer Science, Vels Institute of Science, Technology & Advanced Studies,
Chennai, India*

Abstract

Data mining is an important domain that is essential to many industries irrespective of the information they hold. However, modern times entail the need to extract relevant information from immense volumes of data that may be unstructured or structured. Sentiment analysis is a subfield of the mining process and involves the extraction of the perspectives established from individuals or collective entities. The existing methodologies have highlighted various classifiers and combinational processing methods to analyze the sentiments of different platforms. Nonetheless, the proposed methodology pivots to identify the sentiment on the literary work of Shakespeare. The play Hamlet is a popular piece of study, and the extraction of relative sentiments involved is accomplished through natural language processing methods. The sentiments identified in the dialogues of the play are recognized through fine-grained text analysis and implemented through a sequence of phases to preprocess, extract, and vectorize the features involved. An unsupervised training and classification method through the BERT machine learning is then applied to the literary work to label and further classify the data into sectorized clusters.

Keywords: Natural language processing (NLP), BERT, vectorize, sentiment analysis

4.1 Introduction

This chapter proposes a methodology to identify the sentiment analysis of a literary work of Shakespeare using a natural language processing (NLP) tool, the BERT classifier. The computational study of sentiment analysis is used to determine the text features of Shakespeare's Hamlet. The emotional complexity of the dialogue conversation is fine-grained with its character count, word count, and word frequency and is evaluated for the text. The first phase of the approach is to preprocess the text content of the play using NLP preprocessing tools such as stop word removal, special character removal, tokenization, lemmatization, and text embedding using the TF-IDF (Term Frequency–Inverse Document Frequency) Vectorizer. A survey of digital literary works, computational linguistics analytics, deep learning, neurocognitive poet, and computational analysis

---
*Corresponding author: shyamadevi@gmail.com

Romil Rawat, Rajesh Kumar Chakrawarti, Sanjaya Kumar Sarangi, Piyush Vyas, Mary Sowjanya Alamanda, Kotagiri Srividya and Krishnan Sakthidasan Sankaran (eds.) *Conversational Artificial Intelligence*, (59–70) © 2024 Scrivener Publishing LLC

modeling of narratives or poems still provide a variety of obstacles. The ability of computers to assess the psychological information included in written or spoken texts, also known as sentiment analysis, is a critical subject. While sentiment analysis has advanced significantly, there are still obstacles to be overcome when discussing poetic texts like Shakespeare's play. One such problem is the ability to forecast aesthetic feelings using the Vader sentiment analyzer. It is encouraging to see early attempts at quantifying things such as the narration of words, the most beautiful lines of poetry, or the "appropriateness" of poetic allegories, but progress is hampered by the lack of specialized sentiment analyzer tools and empirical data that can be used to evaluate these measures of descriptive accuracy and predictive validity. The machine modeling of the emotional aspects of a given figure or character described in natural language text and the responsive relationships between characters (or character-to-character analysis) are two unique aspects of sentiment analysis that are discussed in this chapter, which aims to suggest a straightforward heuristic method for calculating emotive conversation of fictional characters. The vectorized text is analyzed for sentiment using Vader lexicon. Then, it is classified using the machine learning BERT classifier.

4.2   Related Works

Examples of how the NLP technique is used to generate various automated analyses of the literary work carried out, such as summarization, identifying the lexical information, and sentiment analysis, are as follows:

1. The NLP technique is used in identifying the lexical structure of the literary work of the writer [1].
2. The NLP tool is used to generate a literary corpus from various books, literary works, and stories of Spanish historical events [2].
3. The data augmentation technique of NLP is used to summarize the literary work in a structured manner.
4. The NLP technique is used to discuss racism and racial (in)justice in a historical/literary work.
5. The NLP technique is used to judge the allegorical behavior of the most popular literary works using an accurate machine learning technique [3].

4.3   Text Extraction

The Shakespeare play Hamlet is web scraped using the Beautiful Soup library from the online library book. It discusses tragedy and explores the different themes depicted in the play such as friendship, madness, and revenge. The extracted text data reveal the conversation between Bernardo and Francisco. The dialogue of the text data is displayed in Figure 4.1.

```
SNO  CHARACTER                                                  DIALOGUE
1.0    BERNARDO                                              Who's there?
2.0   FRANCISCO        Nay, answer me: stand, and unfold yourself.
4.0    BERNARDO                                       Long live the king!
5.0   FRANCISCO                                                 Bernardo?
6.0    BERNARDO                                                        He.
7.0   FRANCISCO              You come most carefully upon your hour.
8.0    BERNARDO       'Tis now struck twelve; get thee to bed, Franc...
9.0   FRANCISCO   For this relief much thanks: 'tis bitter cold,...
11.0   BERNARDO                            Have you had quiet guard?
12.0  FRANCISCO                                  Not a mouse stirring.
13.0   BERNARDO   Well, good night.If you do meet Horatio and Ma...
14.0  FRANCISCO         I think I hear them. Stand, ho! Who's there?
18.0    HORATIO                            Friends to this ground.
19.0  MARCELLUS                         And liegemen to the Dane.
20.0  FRANCISCO                               Give you good night.
21.0  MARCELLUS   O, farewell, honest soldier:Who hath relieved ...
22.0  FRANCISCO        Bernardo has my place.Give you good night.
23.0  MARCELLUS                                  ExitHolla! Bernardo!
```

Figure 4.1 Shakespeare's Hamlet play dataset.

4.4   Data Preprocessing

In reality, the information gleaned from literary works is unstructured, raw data. After obtaining the data, we must use Python's Natural Language Toolkit (NLTK) tool library to preprocess all of the tweets, such as deleting stop words, regular expressions, and hash tags, among other things. The data are then cleaned up during a preprocessing step so that it may be used for additional analysis. Additional preprocessing is required in order to apply machine knowledge or deep learning algorithms to text input. Numerous techniques can be used to convert text data into model-ready formats. The data preprocessing phases listed below are applied to news items and headlines. We also provide information on the various word vector formats that we used for our research.

4.1 Stop Word Removal: This aims to remove stop words from the given text data. Stop words (especially the most often used keywords in a language that do not provide much context) can be managed and sieved from the text because they are more communal and retain fewer pertinent material. Stop words, such as the conjunctions "and," "or," and "but," the prepositions "of," "in," "from," and "to," and the articles "a," "an," and "the," function more as word connectors in sentences. A vital first step in NLP is the removal of stop words as part of data preprocessing since stop words that are less relevant might take up a lot of system time. The NLTK software program used to get rid of stop words is shown in Figure 4.2.

4.2 Punctuation Removal: In everyday speech, punctuation provides the grammatical context for a statement. Commas and other punctuations may not be the best tools for understanding a phrase's meaning. In Figure 4.2, a process for deleting punctuation is shown.

4.3 Labeling the data: The Vader sentiment analyzer library is used to tag the twitter data with positive and negative sentiments after a preprocessing step. Data are classified as having a positive or negative sentiment based on judgments of polarity and subjectivity. A combined score for polarity and subjectivity is

	DIALOGUE	text_lower	text_wo_punct
5	Who's there?	who's there?	whos there
6	Nay, answer me: stand, and unfold yourself.	nay, answer me: stand, and unfold yourself.	nay answer me stand and unfold yourself
8	Long live the king!	long live the king!	long live the king
9	Bernardo?	bernardo?	bernardo
10	He.	he.	he

	DIALOGUE	text_lower	text_wo_punct	text_wo_stop
5	Who's there?	who's there?	whos there	whos
6	Nay, answer me: stand, and unfold yourself.	nay, answer me: stand, and unfold yourself	nay answer me stand and unfold yourself	nay answer stand unfold
8	Long live the king!	long live the king!	long live the king	long live king
9	Bernardo?	bernardo?	bernardo	bernardo
10	He.	he.	he	

	DIALOGUE	text_lower	text_wo_punct	text_wo_stop	text_lemmatized
5	Who's there?	who's there?	whos there	whos	who
6	Nay, answer me: stand, and unfold yourself.	nay, answer me: stand, and unfold yourself.	nay answer me stand and unfold yourself	nay answer stand unfold	nay answer stand unfold
8	Long live the king!	long live the king!	long live the king	long live king	long live king
9	Bernardo?	bernardo?	bernardo	bernardo	bernardo
10	He.	he.	he		

	DIALOGUE	text_lower	text_wo_punct	text_wo_stop	text_lemmatized	text_tokenize
5	Who's there?	who's there?	whos there	whos	who	[who]
6	Nay, answer me: stand, and unfold yourself.	nay, answer me: stand, and unfold yourself.	nay answer me stand and unfold yourself	nay answer stand unfold	nay answer stand unfold	[nay, answer, stand, unfold]
8	Long live the king!	long live the king!	long live the king	long live king	long live king	[long, live, king]
9	Bernardo?	bernardo?	bernardo	bernardo	bernardo	[bernardo]
10	He.	he.	he			[]

Figure 4.2 Text preprocessing.

	DIALOGUE	text_lower	text_wo_punct	text_wo_stop	text_lemmatized	text_tokenize	Subjectivity	Polarity	Analysis
5	Who's there?	who's there?	whos there	whos	who	[who]	0.00	0.000000	-1
6	Nay, answer me: stand, and unfold yourself.	nay, answer me: stand, and unfold yourself.	nay answer me stand and unfold yourself	nay answer stand unfold	nay answer stand unfold	[nay, answer, stand, unfold]	0.00	0.000000	-1
8	Long live the king!	long live the king!	long live the king	long live king	long live king	[long, live, king]	0.45	0.043182	1
9	Bernardo?	bernardo?	bernardo	bernardo	bernardo	[bernardo]	0.00	0.000000	-1
10	He.	he.	he			[]	0.00	0.000000	-1

	DIALOGUE	text_lower	text_wo_punct	text_wo_stop	text_lemmatized	text_tokenize	Subjectivity	Polarity	Analysis
8	Long live the king!	long live the king!	long live the king	long live king	long live king	[long, live, king]	0.45	0.043182	1
17	Well, good night.If you do meet Horatio and Ma...	well, good night.if you do meet horatio and ma...	well good nightif you do meet horatio and marc...	well good nightif meet horatio marcellusthe ri...	well good nightif meet horatio marcellusthe ri...	[well, good, nightif, meet, horatio, marcellus...	0.60	0.700000	1
24	Give you good night.	give you good night.	give you good night	give good night	give good night	[give, good, night]	0.60	0.700000	1
25	O, farewell, honest soldier:Who hath relieved ...	o, farewell, honest soldier:who hath relieved ...	o farewell honest soldierwho hath relieved you	farewell honest soldierwho hath relieved	farewell honest soldierwho hath relieved	[farewell, honest, soldierwho, hath, relieved]	0.90	0.600000	1
26	Bernardo has my place.Give you good night.	bernardo has my place.give you good night.	bernardo has my placegive you good night	bernardo placegive good night	bernardo placegive good night	[bernardo, placegive, good, night]	0.60	0.700000	1

Figure 4.3 Text sentiment.

considered negative if it is less than 0.040 and positive if it is greater than 0.040 because sentiment scores are calculated based on a threshold.

4.4 Text lemmatization: Text lemmatization is a process of converting the inflected words into meaningful forms. In literary works, most of the words are mentioned in short forms but do not reveal the correct meaning. The NLTK lemmatizer converts the misspelled words to meaningful words.

4.5   Sentiment Analysis on Literary Works

The Vader sentiment analysis maps the lexical feature of text data to emotional intensity called the sentiment core. The sentiment analysis of literary works is performed with the aid of a Vader sentiment analyzer; the play's dialogue's substance is examined for sentiment. The text's polarity is analyzed to identify its positive, negative, and neutral tone. The sentiment analysis retrieves the overall sentiment portrayed in the Shakespeare play. Created with the polarity value, the text data are forecasted, and using Matplot, a bar graph for positive, negative, and neutral sentiment is plotted and can be seen in Figure 4.4.

4.6   TF-IDF Vectorizer

To excerpt features from the text using the Scikit learn package, we employed the TF-IDF Vectorizer in our code. A literary set of textual data is transformed into a matrix of TF-IDF features. The TF-IDF will be used in some reports in place of raw frequency [4] instances of tokens in an effort to lessen the impact of tokens [6–8] that appear frequently in specific entities. The vectorizer [9] is mentioned as TF-IDF. The machine learning method converts text into numerical values in order to make predictions. In most cases, it is possible to calculate the weight of each paragraph in a document. The word "frequency" is used to quantify how often a word appears in a text. A technique for figuring out the frequency of frequent and unusual terms in a specific document is called inverse document frequency, or IDF. By separating the

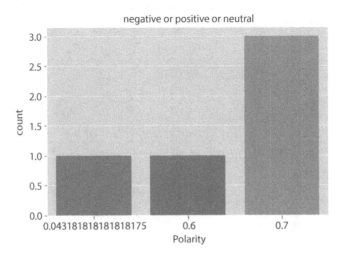

Figure 4.4 Polarity-based sentiment analysis.

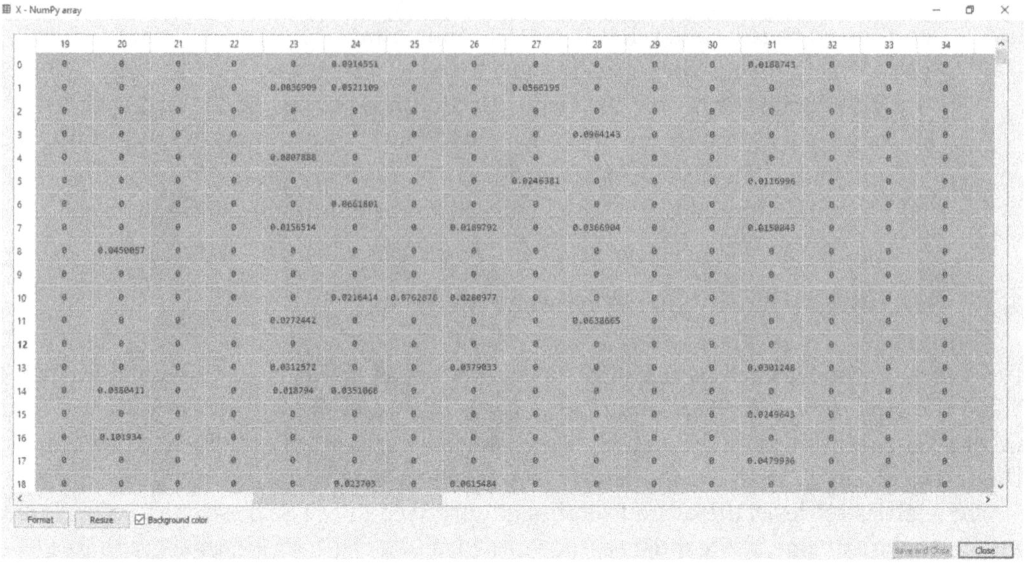

Figure 4.5 TF-IDF vectorization.

total number of documents by the number of documents that include the phrase, the IDF result is determined from the training corpus. Figure 4.5 displays the TF-IDF vector's output.

4.7   Fine-Grained Sentiment Analysis on Literary Data

By using the NLTK toolkit to extract the text's fundamental properties, the text data are fine-grained. The text's character count is first determined, and then in Figures 4.6 and 4.7, the positive and negative emotion of the conversation is shown. Following the Char_count function and taking into account both positive and negative emotion, the normal word count is determined. The average word lengths for positive and negative emotion are established, which paints a perfect picture of the average word length in the conversation dialogue. In order to analyze a tweet's sentiment, its polarity is utilized to classify it as either positive or negative. The tweets' polarity is displayed in Figure 4.7. The

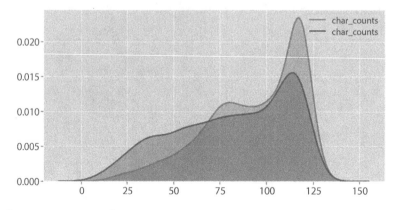

Figure 4.6 Char_count positive and negative sentiment.

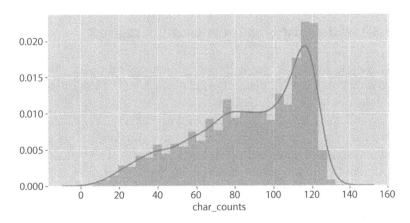

Figure 4.7 Literary char_count.

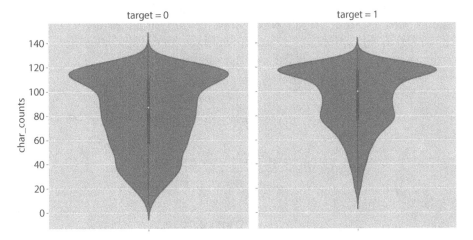

Figure 4.8 Violin plot of sentiment.

Figure 4.9 Literary word cloud.

sentiment of the dialogue is assessed by the polarity and given a rating of 1 for positive and −1 for negative. The violin plot is visualized for the positive and negative sentiment of the dialogue and is shown in Figure 4.8. The word cloud of the play dialogue is plotted to identify the most frequently used words and to identify the overall sentiment of the play. It is shown in Figure 4.9.

4.8   BERT Classifier for Unsupervised Learning

The sentiment analysis model shown in Figure 4.3 successfully recognizes sentiment in microblogging, captures the semantic characteristics and rules of emotional growth, and supports contextual themes by giving recommendations added business value. That is the goal: to display appropriate and relevant adverts, etc., one must first understand user intentions.

Classification Metrics: This method categorizes opinions on literary data. It describes the following measures for evaluating the overall effectiveness of all machine learning models. The proportion of tweets accurately predicted by the version across all tweets is known as accuracy. The percentage of anti-vaccination tweets that can be reasonably predicted by the version over all anti-vaccination forecasts is known as precision, which is also known as fine predictive value. Recall (also known as sensitivity) is the proportion of the story about the literary work that can be reasonably predicted by extrapolating the version over all literary works of Shakespeare. Accuracy could not be the most important statistic because the information is unbalanced; as a result, we used the F1 rating as our primary metric. We also discussed the region below the receiver working feature curve (AUC), which is constructed entirely from genuine positive and false-positive rates [5].

$$\text{F1 score} = 2 \times \frac{\text{precision} \times \text{Recall}}{\text{precision} + \text{Recall}} \tag{4.1}$$

$$\text{Accuracy} = \frac{\text{true positive} + \text{true negative}}{\text{total no. of predictions}} \tag{4.2}$$

$$\text{Precision} = \frac{\text{true positive}}{\text{true positive} + \text{false positive}} \tag{4.3}$$

$$\text{Recall} = \frac{\text{true positive}}{\text{true positive} + \text{false negative}} \tag{4.4}$$

For pre-training purposes, BERT is applied to the Shakespeare play to identify the sentiment of the play and to analyze the emotions for the reader. The output of the BERT classifier is displayed in Figure 4.10.

```
begin training using onecycle policy with max lr of 0.0002...
Epoch 1/3
108/108 [==============================] - 133s 1s/step - loss: 0.3352 - accuracy: 0.8590 - val_loss: 0.4615 - val_accuracy: 0.8228
Epoch 2/3
108/108 [==============================] - 133s 1s/step - loss: 0.3115 - accuracy: 0.8748 - val_loss: 0.5920 - val_accuracy: 0.7480
Epoch 3/3
108/108 [==============================] - 133s 1s/step - loss: 0.1731 - accuracy: 0.9365 - val_loss: 0.5802 - val_accuracy: 0.8346
<tensorflow.python.keras.callbacks.History at 0x7f35389ed5c0>
```

Figure 4.10 Accuracy of the BERT classifier on literary work.

On several platforms [10, 11], harmful [12–15] software assaults [16, 17] and cyber threats [18–21] are on the rise, with serious repercussions for people and organisations. Finding automated machine-learning methods to proactively guard against malware [22, 23] has become essential. Transformers, a class of attention-based deep learning methods, have lately demonstrated outstanding results in resolving various problems, primarily those connected to Natural Language Processing (NLP) [24, 25] work. The use of a transformer [26] architecture to automatically identify malicious [27] software is suggested at AI Models. MalBERT [28] is a model built on BERT (Bidirectional Encoder Representations from Transformers), which conducts static analysis on the source code of Android applications using preprocessed features to characterise existing malware and categorise it into various representative malware categories obtained by Transformer-based models for malicious software detection.

4.9 Conclusion

The sentiment of Shakespeare's literary work is identified with the help of the NLTK tool and the BERT classifier. The text dialogue is preprocessed using the NLTK tool and the sentiment is analyzed with the Vader lexicon analyzer. The BERT classifier outperforms and analyzes the unsupervised data with 83% accuracy. Future work should identify the named entity recognition and topic modeling of the literary work in order for the reader to know the most discussed topic of the literary work before reading it.

References

1. Vetulani, Z., Witkowska, M., Kubis, M., NLP Tools for Lexical structure studies of the literary output of a writer. Case study: Literary works of Tadeusz Boy-Żeleński and Julia Hartwig, in: *Human Language Technology. Challenges for Computer Science and Linguistics. LTC 2019*, Lecture Notes in Computer Science, vol. 13212, Z. Vetulani, P. Paroubek, M. Kubis (eds.), Springer, Cham, 2022, https://doi.org/10.1007/978-3-031-05328-3_17.
2. Moreno-Jiménez, L.G., Torres-Moreno, J.M. *et al.*, MegaLite: A new Spanish literature corpus for NLP tasks, in: *Computing Conference*, 2021.
3. Balyan, R., McCarthy, K.S., McNamara, D.S., Combining machine learning and natural language processing to assess literary text comprehension, in: *Proceedings of the 10th International Conference on Educational Data Mining (EDM)*, Wuhan, China International Educational Data Mining Society, 2017.
4. Khurana, D., Koli, A., Khatter, K., Singh, S., Natural language processing: State of the art, current trends and challenges. *Multimed. Tools Appl.*, 82, 3, 3713–3744, Jul. 2022. doi: 10.1007/s11042-022-13428-4.
5. Christiansen, M.H. and Chater, N., Connectionist natural language processing: The state of the art. *Cogn. Sci.*, 23, 4, 417–437, Oct. 1999. doi: 10.1207/s15516709cog2304_2.
6. Sadler, M. and Onodera, N.O., Japanese discourse markers: Synchronic and diachronic discourse analysis. *Japanese Lang. Lit.*, 40, 1, 105, Apr. 2006. doi: 10.2307/30197999.
7. Raxmatullayev, N.N., Environment of bukhara literature in the anthology 'Muzakkir Ul-As'hob. *Curr. Res. J. of Philological Sci.*, 03, 05, 38–41, May 2022. doi: 10.37547/philological-crjps-03-05-09.

8. Nasirova, S.A., Religious affairs management system in ancient China (linguistic analysis in Diachronic aspect). *Builders of Future*, 02, 02, 288–297, May 2022. doi: 10.37547/builders-v2-i2-44.

9. Alexander V., K., A real gift' (on the edition of 'Anthology on the literature of Transbaikalia'). *Scholarly Notes Transbaikal State Univ.*, 16, 2, 183–187, May 2021. doi: 10.21209/2658-7114-2021-16-2-183-187.

10. Rawat, R., Rimal, Y.N., William, P., Dahima, S., Gupta, S., Sankaran, K.S., Malware threat affecting financial organization analysis using machine learning approach. *Int. J. Inf. Technol. Web Eng. (IJITWE)*, 17, 1, 1–20, 2022.

11. Rawat, R., Mahor, V., Chouhan, M., Pachlasiya, K., Telang, S., Garg, B., Systematic literature review (SLR) on social media and the digital transformation of drug trafficking on darkweb, in: *International Conference on Network Security and Blockchain Technology*, Springer, Singapore, pp. 181–205, 2022.

12. Rawat, R., Ayodele Oki, O., Sankaran, S., Florez, H., Ajagbe, S.A., Techniques for predicting dark web events focused on the delivery of illicit products and ordered crime. *Int. J. Electr. Comput. Eng. (IJECE)*, 13, 5, 5354–5365, Oct. 2023, doi: 10.11591/ijece.v13i5.pp5354-5365.

13. Rawat, R., Garg, B., Mahor, V., Telang, S., Pachlasiya, K., Chouhan, M., Organ trafficking on the dark web—The data security and privacy concern in healthcare systems, in: *Internet of Healthcare Things: Machine Learning for Security and Privacy*, pp. 189–216, 2022.

14. Vyas, P., Vyas, G., Chauhan, A., Rawat, R., Telang, S., Gottumukkala, M., Anonymous trading on the dark online marketplace: An exploratory study, in: *Using Computational Intelligence for the Dark Web and Illicit Behavior Detection*, pp. 272–289, IGI Global, 2022.

15. Rawat, R., Oki, O.A., Sankaran, K.S., Olasupo, O., Ebong, G.N., Ajagbe, S.A., A new solution for cyber security in big data using machine learning approach, in: *Mobile Computing and Sustainable Informatics: Proceedings of ICMCSI 2023*, Springer Nature Singapore, Singapore, pp. 495–505, 2023.

16. Rawat, R., Chakrawarti, R.K., Raj, A., Mani, G., Chidambarathanu, K., Bhardwaj, R., Association rule learning for threat analysis using traffic analysis and packet filtering approach. *Int. J. Inf. Technol.*, 1–11, 2023.

17. Rawat, R., Logical concept mapping and social media analytics relating to cyber criminal activities for ontology creation. *Int. J. Inf. Technol.*, 15, 2, 893–903, 2023.

18. Rawat, R., Mahor, V., Álvarez, J.D., Ch, F., Cognitive systems for dark web cyber delinquent association malignant data crawling: A review, in: *Handbook of Research on War Policies, Strategies, and Cyber Wars*, pp. 45–63, 2023.

19. Rawat, R., Chakrawarti, R.K., Vyas, P., Gonzáles, J.L.A., Sikarwar, R., Bhardwaj, R., Intelligent fog computing surveillance system for crime and vulnerability identification and tracing. *Int. J. Inf. Secur. Priv. (IJISP)*, 17, 1, 1–25, 2023.

20. Rawat, R., Sowjanya, A.M., Patel, S.I., Jaiswal, V., Khan, I., Balaram, A. (Eds.), *Using Machine Intelligence: Autonomous Vehicles Volume 1*, John Wiley & Sons, 2022.

21. Rawat, R., Mahor, V., Díaz-Álvarez, J., Chávez, F., Rooted learning model at fog computing analysis for crime incident surveillance, in: *2022 International Conference on Smart Generation Computing, Communication and Networking (SMART GENCON)*, 2022, December, IEEE, pp. 1–9.

22. Rawat, R. and Shrivastav, S.K., SQL injection attack detection using SVM. *Int. J. Comput. Appl.*, 42, 13, 1–4, 2012.

23. Rawat, R., Bhardwaj, P., Kaur, U., Telang, S., Chouhan, M., Sankaran, K.S., *Smart vehicles for communication, volume 2*, John Wiley & Sons, 2023.

24. Mahor, V., Bijrothiya, S., Rawat, R., Kumar, A., Garg, B., Pachlasiya, K., IoT and artificial intelligence techniques for public safety and security, in: *Smart Urban Computing Applications*, p. 111, 2023.
25. Mahor, V., Pachlasiya, K., Garg, B., Chouhan, M., Telang, S., Rawat, R., Mobile operating system (android) vulnerability analysis using machine learning, in: *Proceedings of International Conference on Network Security and Blockchain Technology: ICNSBT 2021*, 2022, June, Springer Nature Singapore, Singapore, pp. 159–169.
26. Rawat, R., Garg, B., Pachlasiya, K., Mahor, V., Telang, S., Chouhan, M., Mishra, R., SCNTA: Monitoring of network availability and activity for identification of anomalies using machine learning approaches. *Int. J. Inf. Technol. Web Eng. (IJITWE)*, 17, 1, 1–19, 2022.
27. Mahor, V., Garg, B., Telang, S., Pachlasiya, K., Chouhan, M., Rawat, R., Cyber threat phylogeny assessment and vulnerabilities representation at thermal power station, in: *Proceedings of International Conference on Network Security and Blockchain Technology: ICNSBT 2021*, 2022, June, Springer Nature Singapore, Singapore, pp. 28–39.
28. Rawat, R., Gupta, S., Sivaranjani, S., CU, O.K., Kuliha, M., Sankaran, K.S., Malevolent information crawling mechanism for forming structured illegal organisations in hidden networks. *Int. J. Cyber Warf. Terror. (IJCWT)*, 12, 1, 1–14, 2022.

5

Extracting and Analyzing Factors to Identify the Malicious Conversational AI Bots on Twitter

Gitika Vyas[1]*, Piyush Vyas[1], Prathamesh Muzumdar[2],
Anitha Chennamaneni[1], Anand Rajavat[3] and Romil Rawat[4]

[1]Computer Information Systems, Texas A&M University-Central Texas, Killeen, Texas, USA
[2]University of South Florida, Florida, USA
[3]Department of Computer Science Engineering, Director, Shri Vaishnav Institute of Information Technology, Shri Vaishnav Vidyapeeth Vishwavidyalaya, Indore, India
[4]Department of Computer Science, Shri Vaishnav Vidyapeeth Vishwavidyalaya, Indore, India

Abstract

On social media, many third-party vendors utilize Conversational Artificial Intelligence (CAI) to use social bots to spread marketing campaigns and to increase followers, thereby opening the door for malicious bots to compromise the security on social media, especially on Twitter where the posts are concise, making it hard to distinguish between human written posts and bot-generated tweets. Thus, such malicious bots on Twitter can break into user accounts, spread misinformation, breach account data, and market advertising spam. Hence, this chapter aims to conduct a detailed exploratory study to identify the crucial Twitter account features that help to detect malicious bots. Machine learning-based techniques such as information gain, correlation, and chi-square feature selections are used in this chapter to select the top feature set by comparing all three techniques. Twitter account data provided by Kaggle.com, which are publicly available, have been used. The finding suggests that Twitter account age, tweet replies, number of user mentions, friends count, favorites counts, listed count, account verification status, followers count, number of users who liked a tweet, default profile, bot description, and retweet count are the factors that can help to identify and detect the malicious bots on social media.

Keywords: Conversational artificial intelligence, malicious bots, social media, twitter, feature selection

5.1 Introduction

The world is evolving technologically, and the Alpha generation, which will amount to 2.2 billion by 2024, is an integral part of it. As of October 2022, the count of internet users has reached 5.07 billion and, in parallel, social media operators have reached 4.74 billion. With the onset of a digitally savvy era, user-friendly social interactions are geared toward the

Corresponding author: gitika.dadhich@gmail.com

Romil Rawat, Rajesh Kumar Chakrawarti, Sanjaya Kumar Sarangi, Piyush Vyas, Mary Sowjanya Alamanda, Kotagiri Srividya and Krishnan Sakthidasan Sankaran (eds.) *Conversational Artificial Intelligence*, (71–84) © 2024 Scrivener Publishing LLC

adaptation of artificial intelligence (AI) inventions, empowering to-and-fro conversations between devices and humans. Online conversations were made easy with the introduction of social bots, emphasizing 2016 as the "Year of the Bot" with the massive unveiling of over 30,000 chatbots on Facebook Messenger itself. According to Ref., around 3.25 billion people were engaged with AI-based technologies in 2019, and the numbers can rise up to 8.4 billion by 2024. The aforementioned figures indicate the increasing vastness and social involvement of artificial intelligence, and thus, it is the need of the hour that technocrats and researchers should further emphasize the analysis of such fast-flaring techniques and their wide impacts.

The introduction of social networks was meant to link the masses, but the rise of unethical social bots escalated societal destabilization and thought manipulation; the politically controversial 2016 US presidential election is the perfect example of social media bot's influential intrusion over people. Software that is framed to have automated interaction with humans is called a social bot. These social bots contribute actively on the internet mostly on networking sites like Twitter in the form of text messages or tweets. There is a boost in artificial intelligent integrated systems nowadays as AI-enabled bots tend to be more capable and adaptive to learning and can improvise themselves due to their high intellect [1]. Purposely, they were designed to expedite tasks in an efficient way but with the inclusion of AI technologies, the advanced social bots are inclined more towards promoting malicious activities by imitating humans, dissemination of illicit information, airing abusive language, manipulating public opinion on social networking sites, and more. It was reported that there was a huge increase in the percentage of malicious bots starting from 18% and jumping to 45% from the year 2019 to 2022, respectively, which signals the growth of adulteration and deceiving activities by the bots.

The above growing percentages show that social media sites like Twitter are becoming an epicenter of misleading news and the advanced social bots engaged with these platforms can exacerbate the fake views, likes, and even re-tweets of automated accounts. Thus, detection of such malicious activity vectorizing bots is the paramount issue to delve into, and presenting appropriate solutions is crucial. Thus, this chapter aims to conduct a detailed exploratory study to identify the crucial Twitter account features that help to detect or distinguish malicious bot accounts from human accounts through utilizing machine learning-based techniques such as information gain, correlation, and chi-square feature selections.

Existing studies such as [2–5] have focused on detecting the bots on Twitter utilizing machine learning and deep learning but have not emphasized on the importance of the Twitter account features. Thus, this chapter complimenting the efforts of existing studies by providing the key important features that can foster the efforts to detect malicious AI bots on the microblogging platforms like Twitter. Therefore, our systematically identified features will be a great contribution to the literature on CAI detection and will save time during the detection task because optimal feature identification is the preliminary and important task during any machine learning and deep learning model training.

The chapter is organized as follows: first, we present the literature review of existing studies on CAI bot detection on social media platforms such as Twitter; second, we present the detailed methodology (from data collection to feature selection) adopted in this chapter to identify the important key features; and third, we present our results and discuss the findings.

5.2   Literature Review

There has been relevant literature available in the area of CAI on social media; however, there is a paucity of existing literature focusing on the detection of malicious bots on Twitter. Thus, we have explored existing studies related to CAI on social media as well as on Twitter.

A.   Social Media and CAI

CAI in general has many applications on social media, such as [6], focused on the challenges in the utilization of conversational AI for emotion prediction within the African society. The Convolutional Neural Network-based model that utilized speech and image data discovered that results are not sufficient to detect the emotions in African Black faces. Moreover, the detection of abuse against the conversational AI-based text and female voice chatbots was performed using the BERT model by. The interactions between the three different AI bots—Alana v2, CarbonBot, and ELIZA—and the users were analyzed, and it was found that there is a variety of abuse towards the bots, mainly sexual nuances.

Artificial intelligence has played a vital role in enhancing the basic bots into highly equipped bots. Lombardi *et al.* have done a survey-based study to emphasize over-the-period evolutions attained from the simple bots to the sophisticated AI ones. The AI technologies like natural language and its conversion as well as pretending to be human methodologies support social bots to interact with humans. Since bots can behave maliciously and pacifying this problem is a crucial task, it was suggested to target legitimate bot usage. Also, although there is an advancement in the detection of malicious bots, there is a scope to tighten up more. Furthermore, AI bots are gaining attention due to their impact on social manipulation. The weakening of democracies around the globe is the consequence of the remolding of public attitudes due to the opposing and offensive divisive viewpoints over the social media platforms by these bots. Forrester *et al.* particularly emphasize detecting Russian bots' intrusion in deluging and airing controversial Canadian issues and draining the strength of their democracy. Mapping of the Russian bots' interference was mapped on the BEND (build, engage, neutralize, distract) framework, and evidence that bots were active influencers in boosting and increasing outrageous perspective to the public was found.

One of the utmost necessities to train any model is the accumulation of an abundant amount of real-world data. Building a chatbot follows the same work, and for this purpose, a web crawler is developed [7], to fetch numerous conversation records in the JavaScript Object Notation (JSON) file type, over social networks like Reddit, YouTube, and Twitter. It was observed that the proposed web crawler was successful in obtaining conversational data from the mentioned social media platforms. Balaji and Yuvaraj [1] developed a chatbot by integrating a machine learning algorithm named bidirectional neural network and using the Reddit dataset for conversational training of the bot. With the aim of implementing a multi-agent conversational system, identifying the emotional condition of users, and offering solutions to the problems, this chatbot is built. Overall, these chatbots can be customized and trained to behave like humans and work in the direction of the mentioned aims.

B. AI Bots and Twitter

Social bots are widely spreading illicit activities and applications. Moreover, artificial intelligence has made it smooth to mimic human behavior for these bots. The threats related to these are the very base of Pastor-Galindo *et al.* to analyze social bots on Twitter and characterize them. The Botometer tool was used to distinguish bots and categorize them accordingly. It was observed that among the three highlighted categories—Likely Humans (unautomated users), Likely Semi-Bots (partially automated), and Likely Bots (Totally automated)—the Likely bots were easier to reach. Additionally, although the semi-automated bots did not profusely spread but can grab interest and propagate more retweets, they are more alarming than the fully automated bots.

On online social networks (OSNs) automated accounts known as bots are promulgating. They can conduct malicious activities, manipulate opinions and discussions, and even use fake followers on platforms like Twitter and Facebook. In [3], two methodologies based on Natural Language Processing—the feature extraction approach and the deep learning architecture based on bidirectional LSTM—are applied to efficiently detect human Twitter users from the bot operated. It was witnessed that the proposed approaches conquer the previously conducted ones.

Twitter is a powerful place for public opinions to get easily manipulated and driven. Most of the credit for these manipulative tasks either in the political or in the ideological area goes to automated accounts—bots. By utilizing the PAN 2019 Bots and Gender Profiling dataset [8] and applying Recurrent Neural Networks, specifically Long Short-Term Memory (LSTM) and Bidirectional Encoder Representations from Transformers (BERT) models, Kenyeres and Kovács have designed the bot detection models. The depiction of findings projects that the pre-trained model can enhance the efficiency of deep learning-based bot detection models and can compete with machine learning-based approaches.

The traffic on the internet is mostly congested with bots, which can be categorized as good or bad. Web crawlers and chatbots fall under the category of good bot while bots that undertake malicious activities are part of bad bots. The automated accounts on Twitter are controlled by software bound by certain terms. Ramalingaiah *et al.* [5] compared the proposed Bag of bots' word model with different supervised machine learning techniques and revealed that the concept of Bag of words helped the introduced classifier to outperform others in the process of bot detection.

Using the Twitter posts dataset, da Silva *et al.* [9] investigated the capability of Conversational AI to investigate offensive language. The Hybrid Dictionary Model applied concluded that the Conversational AI systems are not apt enough to highlight unethical behavior or language even though this is the topic of concern.

5.3   Methods

A. Data Collection

Relevant data comprising thousands of tweets have been collected. We have collected data from Refs. [10]. The data have real-time tweets for distinct events posted by human users and artificial bots. The data are publicly available and have two classes, i.e., human and bots. Data contain many anomalies such as missing records and multilingualism. We have removed observations that have missing records and do not belong to the English language. After this preliminary scrutinization, we have obtained 1955 observations in the training set of the entire data where label 1 indicates the Bot entries that are 916 in the count, and label 0 indicates the 1039 human entries. Below is an example of a Bot tweet by user "AttentiveBot" wherein it cited many unified resource locators (short URLs) to drive the traffic on Twitter:

> "*@tattakatan_h hello, because your account is protected I need to follow you in order to look for tweets by the people you follow. Thank you!', '@jjbuss: https://t.co/1RNGeVM9Ag', '@ JonahLupton: https://t.co/ctVQh4ZtR9', '@AlexHow39710200: https://t.co/WLGgaIaJ2m', '@jorenschoon: https://t.co/bLBD9JADjq', ...*"

B. Data Features Definitions
In total, we have used 22 features from the dataset including label (bot) wherein we have 21 independent features and 1 dependent feature. Figure 5.1 shows the description of all the features.

C. Data Preprocessing
Usually, publicly available datasets have many irregularities such as missing and redundant records, extreme values, and outliers. Thus, data preprocessing is an important step before analyzing it. Therefore, we have performed missing value detection and imputation, outlier detection, and data transformation tasks before selecting the important features that are important to detect malicious tweet bots on Twitter.

Variable	Description
Followers Count	This implies the count of followers a Twitter account presently has.
Friends Count	This implies the count of accounts followed by a user.
Verified	This implies whether a user account is verified or not. This is often denoted by the Blue tick beside the account name.
Status count	Total count of the tweets posted by a user.
Default Profile background	This is denoted bt Boolean values for whether the account holder has a default profile background or not.
Default Profile Picture	This is denoted by Boolean values for whether the account holder has a default profile picture or not.
Tweets as Favorite Count	The total number of tweets liked/loved by a user.
Account age	Total number of days a Twitter account has been activated (account creation date-date of the last tweet created)
Average tweets per day	Statys count/account age – average count of a tweet posted by a user.
Null Url	Whether there is a URL present or not. It's a Boolean value.
Name Bot	Boolean values of - whether the "Bot" sting is present in an account name or not.
Description Bot	Boolean values of - whether the "Bot" sting is present in a Description of an account of not.
Screen name bot	Boolean values of - whether the "Bot" sting is present in a Twitter handle of an account or not.
Favorite Count	This implies a total number of users who liked/loved a tweet.
Retweet Count	Count of a tweet reposted.
In reply	Boolean value to show whether a tweet is a replying tweet to someone.
In-reply count	Total tweets posted to reply to someone.
Total User mentions	The total number of account holders mentioned in tweets.
The Listed Count	Counting of – how many users have added an account to a list.
Modified hour	The time in an hour a tweet posted.
Extended profile	Boolean value for whether a user has an extended profile or not.
Bot	Boolean value for – whether a tweet is posted by a bot or a human.

Figure 5.1 Variable/feature description.

D.   Missing Value Imputation

Our dataset is in the comma-separated (CSV) file that we have further converted into tabular format (structured) to work upon. In the table, data are arranged in rows and columns and that is where important values can be missing. Missing values has a distinct form and a value can be missed from a row or a column of a data table. For example, missing values can be in the form of special symbols (%, NAN, NULL, N/A.., /) or simple blank spaces (no entry in a cell of a table). Such missing records should be tracked and treated irrespective of their various forms; this surely helps to mitigate the problems while using the data.

There can be various reasons to experience missing values in the dataset such as a flaw in the data collection method, unavailability of data, and changes in the problem domain while collecting the data [11].

Treating missing values is important because the training of supervised or unsupervised machine learning techniques often requires data in the form of tables (row and columns). Structured data without missing values help improve the machine learning technique's performance. Hence, over a period, finding and treating missing values became an essential step for the practitioners and such values were usually replaced by statistical numeric values, thus known as missing value imputation. The straightforwardness and simplistic nature of statistical methods have shown prominent results for the missing value imputation. Such statistical techniques usually work upon the known data values of the dataset and calculate the relevant data values to fill the missing spots. Among all statistical techniques, mean value imputation is the most popular one, wherein a mean value is filled in place of missing data. This is achieved by calculating the simple mean of all presented values in a feature and then filling in the missing cells. Mathematically, "It is the deterministic degenerate form of the linear function with no auxiliary features" [12].

E.   Outlier Detection and Log Transformation

Nowadays, enormous volumes of data are usually collected from a variety of sources, including scientific data, data from networked systems, and social networks, thanks to the technological revolution. Real-world data are imperfect, lacking quality values, and comprising inaccuracies or outliers. Therefore, it will be crucial to have access to trustworthy data to make any prediction, and machine learning techniques are sensitive to high-value data. In a dataset, data points that are far from other closely tied data points are considered outliers. A data point can be a factual piece of information or a discrete unit of information. A data collecting error may have led to the outlier, or it may simply be a sign that the data are deviating from the norm. With applications such as computer security, finance, and medical research, outlier identification is an intriguing machine learning problem [13].

In other words, it is essential to distinguish normal data points/records and abnormal data points. An abnormal data point that usually lies far away from normal data points is known as an outlier. Thus, to enhance the quality of the data and obtain a more consistent outcome from machine learning, outlier identification, also known as anomaly detection, is necessary [13].

Transforming the data is a crucial step during the machine learning training, and utilization of mathematical formulations such as log transformation make it achievable. During log transformation, each feature value is replaced by the logarithmic form of those values (i.e., x is replaced by log(x)). Commonly, log base 2 is used for data transformation.

Smaller values of a feature may be overpowered by larger ones if we have a very wide range of data (extreme values). The idea is that taking the log of the data can restore symmetry to the data [14]. Hence, it is possible to normally distribute the data by taking the log of each feature. For example, if a user has a follower count of 99,999 and another user has 50, then, in this case, the high follower count impacts the data distribution and so do the prediction results.

F.   Features Selection Techniques

To get the best set of features from the collected dataset, we often use feature selection techniques. Herein, this chapter used filter-based feature selection methods such as information gain, chi-square, and correlation coefficient. Filter-based approaches capture the inherent characteristics of the features assessed by univariate statistics. Using filter-based techniques while working with high-dimensional data is quick and computationally more affordable.

The information gain method helps to select the most appropriate features for the prediction task where the aim is to reduce the entropy (disorder) among the transformed features. The high value of information gain indicates strong predictability of the dependent feature through an independent feature. The chi-square test is the statistical method to get the optimum independent features to predict the dependent feature, wherein the high chi-square value indicates how well an independent feature can help to explain or predict the dependent feature (i.e., the higher the chi-square value, the more dependent feature is dependent on the independent feature). Thus, a high chi-square-value independent feature was selected for further ML training. Additionally, the relationship between two or more features is measured via correlation. We can predict one feature based on another through correlation measures. There is a high chance that the target feature may have a strong correlation with the independent features; thus, correlation may be used to select features. Independent features should also be uncorrelated among themselves while being associated with the dependent feature. We can anticipate one feature from another if the two are associated. Moreover, if two independent features are linked or correlated, the ML training only actually requires one of them as the other does not provide any new information or insight related to the dependent feature.

5.4   Results and Discussion

As an experimental setup, we have used the weka data mining/machine learning tool. Weka provides the implementation of several supervised and unsupervised machine learning techniques. We can also customize our machine learning models using weka scripts. We utilized and explored the application of weka software for implementing all three (i.e., information gain, correlation, and chi-square) feature selection techniques under the select attribute tab. Furthermore, the machine configuration was 12 GB random access memory (RAM), an I5 processor, and one CPU environment, considered to perform this work. We have performed two experiments utilizing the aforementioned setup. First, as shown in Figure 5.2, we have selected the final set of features without removing the extreme values and outliers; second, as shown in Figure 5.3, we have selected the final set of features after treating the extreme values and outliers. The reason for utilizing two experiments is to showcase the importance and benefits of using outlier and extreme value treatment. We will

Chi-squared Ranking Filter		Correlation Ranking Filter		Information Gain Ranking Fil
Ranked attributes:		anked attributes:		nked attributes:
944.7353	11 acc_age	0.6628	11 acc_age	.4029	11 acc_age
925.1366	6 In_reply	0.50015	17 verified	.38359	6 In_reply
670.4795	9 total_usrmention	0.39975	18 default_profile	.27178	9 total_usrmention
633.334	2 friends_count	0.39933	16 descbot	.26401	2 friends_count
557.0762	4 favourites_count	0.37881	8 fav_count	.22825	17 verified
514.084	3 listedcount	0.34715	9 total_usrmention	.22785	4 favourites_count
489.044	17 verified	0.33669	7 retweet_count	.22135	3 listedcount
483.9537	1 followers_count	0.28597	14 screennamebot	.21505	1 followers_count
382.6747	8 fav_count	0.26985	15 namebot	.15084	8 fav_count
312.4081	18 default_profile	0.22172	13 null_url	.13446	16 descbot
311.7509	16 descbot	0.21802	6 In_reply	.11826	18 default_profile
289.8756	7 retweet_count	0.21339	20 has_extended_profile	.10991	7 retweet_count
191.0126	12 tweets_per_day	0.15998	3 listedcount	.0779	12 tweets_per_day
159.8788	14 screennamebot	0.15836	1 followers_count	.06972	14 screennamebot
142.359	15 namebot	0.15411	12 tweets_per_day	.06292	15 namebot
119.5667	5 statuses_count	0.1157	21 in_reply_data	.04565	5 statuses_count
96.1093	13 null_url	0.11349	19 default_profile_image	.03577	13 null_url
89.0175	20 has_extended_profile	0.08194	4 favourites_count	.03482	20 has_extended_profile
26.1708	21 in_reply_data	0.06288	5 statuses_count	.00992	21 in_reply_data
25.1813	19 default_profile_image	0.06003	2 friends_count	.00953	19 default_profile_image
0	10 modified_hour	0.00595	10 modified_hour		10 modified_hour

Figure 5.2 Experiment 1—Feature selection without outliers and extreme value treatment.

Chi-squared Ranking Filter		Correlation Ranking Filter		Information Gain Ranking Filter	
Ranked attributes:		0.60898	6 In_reply	Ranked attributes:	
944.7353	11 acc_age	0.54837	9 total_usrmention	0.4029	11 acc_age
925.1366	6 In_reply	0.50981	4 favourites_count	0.38359	6 In_reply
670.4795	9 total_usrmention	0.50015	17 verified	0.27178	9 total_usrmention
633.334	2 friends_count	0.48513	1 followers_count	0.26401	2 friends_count
557.0762	4 favourites_count	0.47944	2 friends_count	0.22825	17 verified
514.084	3 listedcount	0.47402	11 acc_age	0.22785	4 favourites_count
489.044	17 verified	0.39975	18 default_profile	0.22135	3 listedcount
483.9537	1 followers_count	0.39933	16 descbot	0.21505	1 followers_count
382.6747	8 fav_count	0.39153	8 fav_count	0.15084	8 fav_count
312.4081	18 default_profile	0.3754	3 listedcount	0.13446	16 descbot
311.7509	16 descbot	0.32501	7 retweet_count	0.11826	18 default_profile
289.8756	7 retweet_count	0.28597	14 screennamebot	0.10991	7 retweet_count
191.0126	12 tweets_per_day	0.26985	15 namebot	0.0779	12 tweets_per_day
159.8788	14 screennamebot	0.22172	13 null_url	0.06972	14 screennamebot
142.359	15 namebot	0.21339	20 has_extended_profile	0.06292	15 namebot
119.5667	5 statuses_count	0.21268	12 tweets_per_day	0.04565	5 statuses_count
96.1093	13 null_url	0.1157	21 in_reply_data	0.03577	13 null_url
89.0175	20 has_extended_profile	0.11349	19 default_profile_image	0.03482	20 has_extended_profile
26.1708	21 in_reply_data	0.07785	5 statuses_count	0.00992	21 in_reply_data
25.1813	19 default_profile_image	0.00734	10 modified_hour	0.00953	19 default_profile_image
0	10 modified_hour			0	10 modified_hour

Figure 5.3 Experiment 2—Feature selection with outliers and extreme value treatment.

discuss this later in this section. Before performing any experiments, we removed missing values and replaced/imputed the corresponding mean values as discussed in the Methods section. However, we a few missing observations in the entire collected data.

Although we have performed two experiments to get the final set of features or not to skip any important feature, we did not have any major changes in the result of both the experiments except for the Friends count feature that was lower ranked in the correlation-based method for experiment 1 and further jumped into the top 10 in experiment 2 after elimination of outliers and extreme values.

It is always highly suggested to use extreme values and outliers' treatment before the feature selection task.

Table 5.1 shows the final set of the top 12 selected features after treating the outliers and extreme values. Thus, these 12 are the features/factors that can be considered to detect malicious social bots on Twitter. These 12 features are commonly selected by all three methods (i.e., information gain, correlation, and chi-square) and are hence selected as final features.

The internet is the most essential part of one's daily life yet the most vulnerable to breaching someone's data and compromising security measures. Social media presence has become a necessity nowadays. Thus, one needs to consider many security practices to maintain the confidentiality, integrity, and authenticity of personal data. Moreover, social media is not different from other new technologies in that it is subject to abuse of one's personal data and identity. Scientists have created a social bot to help users resolve their problems, but as every coin has two sides, malicious bots were created to cause harm and fall under the

Table 5.1 Top 12 common independent features.

Independent features
Acc_age
In_reply
Total_usermenton
Friends_count
Favourites_counts
Listed count
Verified
Followers_count
Fav_count
Default_profile
Descbot
Retweet_count

dark side of social bots. These bots spread rumors, spam, viruses, false information, slander, and sometimes just noise to deceive users and affect social media debate. This might harm society on many different levels. For instance, bots may pledge support for a political candidate, endangering democracy by affecting the results of elections. These types of abuse have already been seen: during the 2010 U.S. midterm elections, social bots were used to help some politicians and malign their rivals by sending out thousands of tweets linked to websites that published false information [15].

Around the time of the 2010 Massachusetts special election, a similar incident was reported. These kinds of campaigns are sometimes known as Twitter bombs or Astroturf. Establishing the validity of the content being promoted is only part of the issue; this was a problem before social bots became popular and continues to be outside the purview of algorithmic approaches. Bots pose a fresh problem because they can create the misleading appearance that a certain piece of information is widely accepted and supported, regardless of its reality, exerting influence over those who can be easily swayed. A bot could gain tremendous influence thanks to our weaknesses [16].

Intelligent bots can create personalities that seem like loyal followers, making them more difficult to identify by both humans and screening algorithms. They are lucrative commodities on the market for fake social media followers, and accusations of buying followers have affected several well-known politicians in the US and other countries. Journalists, analysts, and researchers are reporting more instances of the potential risks posed by social bots. These include the unjustified effects on market stability that the widespread use of bots may have. There have been suggestions that Twitter signals can be used to forecast the stock market, and there is mounting proof that market participants are attentive to and quick to respond to information from social media. For instance, on April 23, 2013, the Syrian Electronic Army hacked the Twitter account of the Associate Press and spread a story that claimed President Obama had been injured in a terrorist attack on the White House. The stock market immediately crashed because of this. The largest one-day point loss in history happened on May 6, 2010, when the Dow Jones fell over 1,000 points (about 9%) in a matter of minutes. The role of high-frequency trading bots was revealed after a 5-month inquiry, although it is still unknown if these bots had access to data from the social web [17].

Twitter [18, 19] actively and systematically combats spam and harmful [20–23] automation. Instead of waiting until we get a report, we are increasingly focusing on proactively detecting [24, 25] problematic accounts and behaviours. The goal is to create machine learning techniques that can automatically detect [26–29] networks of spam [30–32] or automated accounts and take appropriate action. With less reliance on reactive reporting, we can combat large-scale attempts to control conversations on Twitter across languages and time zones. Monitoring profiles in a synchronised, mass manner is a typical example of spammy [33] and automated behaviour. Our automatic detection [34] algorithms frequently effectively identify accounts involved in these activities soon after the behaviour starts (and delete them from our active user stats). But in the past, we didn't take enough steps to demonstrate how our discoveries [35] and actions had an impact. Because of this, we have started updating account metrics almost instantly. For instance, when we take action on an account [36], the number of followers it has or the number of likes or Retweets it receives will be accurately updated.

5.5   Conclusion and Future Direction

In sum, malicious bots can have adverse effects on society and one's life; therefore, the presented work is one of the initiatives to identify those factors that affect the proliferation of malicious bots on Twitter. Twitter account age, tweet replies, number of user mentions, friends count, favorites counts, listed count, account verification status, followers count, number of users who liked a tweet, default profile, bot description, and retweet count are the factors that can help to identify and detect the malicious bots on social media. As a future work, we will extend this work by automating the process of malicious social bot detection on social media through implementing supervised machine learning and deep learning techniques utilizing identified factors of this work.

References

1. Balaji, M. and Yuvaraj, N., Intelligent chatbot model to enhance the emotion detection in social media using bi-directional recurrent neural network. *J. Physics: Conf. Ser.*, 1362, 1, 12039, 2019.
2. Kouvela, M., Dimitriadis, I., Vakali, A., Bot-detective: An explainable Twitter bot detection service with crowdsourcing functionalities, in: *Proceedings of the 12th International Conference on Management of Digital EcoSystems*, pp. 55–63, 2020.
3. Ilias, L. and Roussaki, I., Detecting malicious activity in Twitter using deep learning techniques. *Appl. Soft Comput.*, 107, 107360, 2021. doi: https://doi.org/10.1016/j.asoc.2021.107360.
4. Rodríguez-Ruiz, J., Mata-Sánchez, J., II, Monroy, R., Loyola-González, O., López-Cuevas, A., A one-class classification approach for bot detection on Twitter. *Comput. & Secur.*, 91, 101715, 2020. doi: https://doi.org/10.1016/j.cose.2020.101715.
5. Ramalingaiah, A., Hussaini, S., Chaudhari, S., Twitter bot detection using supervised machine learning. *J. Physics: Conf. Ser.*, 1950, 1, 12006, 2021.
6. Teye, M.T., Missah, Y.M., Ahene, E., Frimpong, T., Evaluation of conversational agents: Understanding culture, context and environment in emotion detection. *IEEE Access*, 10, 24976–24984, 2022.
7. Patil, A.P. *et al.*, Optimized web-crawling of conversational data from social media and context-based filtering, in: *Proceedings of the Workshop on Joint NLP Modelling for Conversational AI@ ICON 2020*, pp. 33–39, 2020.
8. Rangel, F. and Rosso, P., Overview of the 7th author profiling task at PAN 2019: Bots and gender profiling in twitter, in: *Proceedings of the CEUR Workshop, Lugano, Switzerland*, pp. 1–36, 2019.
9. da Silva, D.A. *et al.*, Could a conversational AI identify offensive language? *Information*, 12, 10, 418, 2021.
10. Ferrara, E., Varol, O., Davis, C., Menczer, F., Flammini, A., The rise of social bots. *Commun. ACM*, 59, 7, 96–104, Jun. 2016. doi: 10.1145/2818717.
11. Witten, I.H. and Frank, E., Data mining: Practical machine learning tools and techniques with Java implementations. *ACM Sigmod Record*, 31, 1, 76–77, 2002.
12. Kalton, G. and Kasprzyk, D., Imputing for missing survey responses, in: *Proceedings of the Section on Survey Research Methods, American Statistical Association*, vol. 22, p. 31, 1982.
13. Myat, K.M. and Mar Win, S.S., Analysis of outlier detection on structured data, in: *WCSE 2020: 2020 10th International Workshop on Computer Science and Engineering*, Feb. 2020, pp. 527–532, doi: 10.18178/WCSE.2020.02.004.
14. Metcalf, L. and Casey, W., Introduction to data analysis, in: *Cybersecurity And Applied Mathematics*, L. Metcalf and W. Casey (Eds.), pp. 43–65, Syngress, Boston, 2016.

15. Ratkiewicz, J., Conover, M.D., Meiss, M., Goncalves, B., Flammini, A., Menczer, F., Detecting and tracking political abuse in social media, in: *Fifth International AAAI Conference on Weblogs and Social Media*, 2011.

16. Aiello, L.M., Deplano, M., Schifanella, R., Ruffo, G., People are strange when you're a stranger: Impact and influence of bots on social networks, in: *Proceedings of the International AAAI Conference on Web and Social Media*, vol. 6, pp. 10–17, 2012.

17. Hwang, T., Pearce, I., Nanis, M., Socialbots: Voices from the fronts. *Interactions*, 19, 2, 38–45, 2012.

18. Mahor, V., Bijrothiya, S., Rawat, R., Kumar, A., Garg, B., Pachlasiya, K., IoT and artificial intelligence techniques for public safety and security, in: *Smart Urban Computing Applications*, p. 111, 2023.

19. Mahor, V., Pachlasiya, K., Garg, B., Chouhan, M., Telang, S., Rawat, R., Mobile operating system (Android) vulnerability analysis using machine learning, in: *Proceedings of International Conference on Network Security and Blockchain Technology: ICNSBT 2021*, 2022, June, Springer Nature Singapore, Singapore, pp. 159–169.

20. Rawat, R., Garg, B., Pachlasiya, K., Mahor, V., Telang, S., Chouhan, M., Mishra, R., SCNTA: Monitoring of network availability and activity for identification of anomalies using machine learning approaches. *Int. J. Inf. Technol. Web Eng. (IJITWE)*, 17, 1, 1–19, 2022.

21. Rawat, R., Rimal, Y.N., William, P., Dahima, S., Gupta, S., Sankaran, K.S., Malware threat affecting financial organization analysis using machine learning approach. *Int. J. Inf. Technol. Web Eng. (IJITWE)*, 17, 1, 1–20, 2022.

22. Rawat, R., Mahor, V., Chouhan, M., Pachlasiya, K., Telang, S., Garg, B., Systematic literature review (SLR) on social media and the digital transformation of drug trafficking on darkweb, in: *International Conference on Network Security and Blockchain Technology*, Springer, Singapore, pp. 181–205, 2022.

23. Rawat, R., Ayodele Oki, O., Sankaran, S., Florez, H., Ajagbe, S.A., Techniques for predicting dark web events focused on the delivery of illicit products and ordered crime. *Int. J. Electr. Comput. Eng. (IJECE)*, 13, 5, 5354–5365, Oct. 2023, doi: 10.11591/ijece.v13i5.pp5354-5365.

24. Rawat, R., Garg, B., Mahor, V., Telang, S., Pachlasiya, K., Chouhan, M., Organ trafficking on the dark web—The data security and privacy concern in healthcare systems, in: *Internet of Healthcare Things: Machine Learning for Security and Privacy*, pp. 189–216, 2022.

25. Vyas, P., Vyas, G., Chauhan, A., Rawat, R., Telang, S., Gottumukkala, M., Anonymous trading on the dark online marketplace: An exploratory study, in: *Using Computational Intelligence for the Dark Web and Illicit Behavior Detection*, pp. 272–289, IGI Global, 2022.

26. Rawat, R., Oki, O.A., Sankaran, K.S., Olasupo, O., Ebong, G.N., Ajagbe, S.A., A new solution for cyber security in big data using machine learning approach, in: *Mobile Computing and Sustainable Informatics: Proceedings of ICMCSI 2023*, Springer Nature Singapore, Singapore, pp. 495–505, 2023.

27. Rawat, R., Chakrawarti, R.K., Raj, A., Mani, G., Chidambarathanu, K., Bhardwaj, R., Association rule learning for threat analysis using traffic analysis and packet filtering approach. *Int. J. Inf. Technol.*, 1–11, 2023.

28. Rawat, R., Logical concept mapping and social media analytics relating to cyber criminal activities for ontology creation. *Int. J. Inf. Technol.*, 15, 2, 893–903, 2023.

29. Rawat, R., Mahor, V., Álvarez, J.D., Ch, F., Cognitive systems for dark web cyber delinquent association malignant data crawling: A review, in: *Handbook of Research on War Policies, Strategies, and Cyber Wars*, pp. 45–63, 2023.

30. Rawat, R., Chakrawarti, R.K., Vyas, P., Gonzáles, J.L.A., Sikarwar, R., Bhardwaj, R., Intelligent fog computing surveillance system for crime and vulnerability identification and tracing. *Int. J. Inf. Secur. Priv. (IJISP)*, 17, 1, 1–25, 2023.

31. Rawat, R., Sowjanya, A.M., Patel, S.I., Jaiswal, V., Khan, I., Balaram, A. (Eds.), *Using Machine Intelligence: Autonomous Vehicles Volume 1*, John Wiley & Sons, 2022.

32. Rawat, R., Mahor, V., Díaz-Álvarez, J., Chávez, F., Rooted learning model at fog computing analysis for crime incident surveillance, in: *2022 International Conference on Smart Generation Computing, Communication and Networking (SMART GENCON)*, 2022, December, pp. 1–9, IEEE.

33. Rawat, R. and Shrivastav, S.K., SQL injection attack detection using SVM. *Int. J. Comput. Appl.*, *42*, 13, 1–4, 2012.

34. Rawat, R., Bhardwaj, P., Kaur, U., Telang, S., Chouhan, M., Sankaran, K.S., *Smart vehicles for communication, volume 2*, John Wiley & Sons, 2023.

35. Mahor, V., Garg, B., Telang, S., Pachlasiya, K., Chouhan, M., Rawat, R., Cyber threat phylogeny assessment and vulnerabilities representation at thermal power station, in: *Proceedings of International Conference on Network Security and Blockchain Technology: ICNSBT 2021*, 2022, June, Springer Nature Singapore, Singapore, pp. 28–39.

36. Rawat, R., Gupta, S., Sivaranjani, S., Cu, O.K., Kuliha, M., Sankaran, K.S., Malevolent information crawling mechanism for forming structured illegal organisations in hidden networks. *Int. J. Cyber Warf. Terror. (IJCWT)*, *12*, 1, 1–14, 2022.

6

Evolution and Adoption of Conversational Artificial Intelligence in the Banking Industry

Neha Aggarwal* and Kriti Bhaswar Singh

Department of Commerce and Financial Studies, Central University of Jharkhand, Ranchi, India

Abstract

Banks and other financial institutions are transforming their client interactions and are now transitioning from traditional banking to conversational banking through automated dialogues with the aid of conversational chatbots. Fintech start-ups like Facebook and Amazon and payment banks such as *Paytm* and *Airtel* are becoming more prominent, giving stiff competition to traditional banks. More than any other industry, banks are investing in AI to support regulatory compliance and risk management. Modern consumers are more tech-savvy and expect banks to provide smooth interactions by providing services at their fingertips. Artificial intelligence (AI) is changing how financial products and service information and advice are provided to banking customers. Using messaging apps, web chat, and voice channels, conversational AI automates customer and business interactions through chatbots or speech-based assistants. When it comes to striking the right balance between implementation costs and customer satisfaction advantages, financial service organizations have not quite gotten there yet.

Keywords: Artificial intelligence, banking, financial sector, conversational chatbots, customer experience, risk and fraud

6.1 Introduction

Banks are known as the heart and soul of an economy as they play a very crucial role in the growth and development of an economy. Indian banks are coming forward to implement AI-based tools for cost reduction and to identify debtors with a high propensity to default, flag high-risk cases, provide customers with a personal financial manager, and detect macroeconomic developments. One of the early users of AI is the banking industry. The technology is being explored and used by banks in a variety of ways, just like other sectors.

Artificial intelligence has completely changed the banking sector by providing services around-the-clock to beat the competition and improve consumer relations. According to *Fintech India* research conducted by PwC in 2017, the world spent $5.1 billion on AI apps, an increase from $4 billion in 2015. According to the research firm *Gartner*,

---

Corresponding author: aggarwal.neha178@gmail.com

Romil Rawat, Rajesh Kumar Chakrawarti, Sanjaya Kumar Sarangi, Piyush Vyas, Mary Sowjanya Alamanda, Kotagiri Srividya and Krishnan Sakthidasan Sankaran (eds.) Conversational Artificial Intelligence, (85–94) © 2024 Scrivener Publishing LLC

the usage of conversational AI has increased by 270% over the last 4 years (a clear sign that growth will occur in the future). Artificial intelligence (AI), in contrast to human or natural intelligence, refers to the ability of robots to exhibit intelligent behavior through imitating and learning from human behaviors to find solutions to challenging issues. It has changed the overall interaction interface between a user and a service provider bank. Customer service, conversational interfaces, and online sales are just a few of the use cases for conversational AI chatbots that can be used in any department or sector. For any organization, user experience is what makes it a hit or a flop. According to the study by *Juniper Research*, 90% of bank-related interactions will be automated through chatbots as customers are replacing visiting banks with better digital experiences. Since its launch in 2014, Alexa, possibly the most well-known social chatbot, has drawn more than 660 million users worldwide.

The idea of chatbots [2–4] is not brand new because they have been applied in numerous contexts since their invention in the 1950s. Chatbots can be rule-based or AI-based. Rule-based [5, 6] chatbots are conventional forms where interaction occurs for a very short period as their responses as per the commands are already scripted and the keywords are scanned [7] and are less flexible; any new query asked by the customer is answered and thus the bot needs to be fed with new details. As chatbots advance, they begin to communicate more and attempt to comprehend problems and find solutions like that of human intellect. This new development is known as conversational AI. It makes an effort to decipher what a user is requesting. The user experience has improved 10 times above what was previously possible with chatbots that were old tech with limited responses. Conversational AI (artificial intelligence) refers to the technology that communicates with customers using natural language processing and machine learning, basically the ability of a machine to think and learn. Systems like chatbots and virtual assistants essentially replicate human speech and behavior to engage users and make choices more quickly. One of the most well-known conversational AI tools is the chatbot. The interaction can take place via text or speech. However, a chatbot and conversational AI vary fundamentally from one another. A chatbot is a rule-based system with pre-defined solutions. Chatbots only offer one-time responses and are less versatile than conversational tools, which primarily use a dialogue system similar to how people converse with one another. They engage in multi-turn conversations, discern the intent, and then make amends.

The nature of financial data is highly varied and intricate. It can be structured, unstructured, publicly available if disclosed by the firms or not, and can have low to high frequency. Data can be sourced from paid platforms such as Bloomberg, Datastream, etc. or freely available, such as data from government websites and stock markets, and economic data from World Bank. Additionally, it may relate to pricing, transactions, and indices that are made available weekly, monthly, quarterly, or annually. It also includes non-financial data that also have a significant role in making business decisions, and here, AI/ML plays a role. Financial data come in many different forms, such as Fundamental data (balance sheet items, income statement items, or macro variable factors), Market data (dividend rates, coupon prices, quotes, interest rates, prices, yields for bonds, and volatility), and Analytics (news sentiments, credit ratings, earning expectations of a shareholder, and credit rating of the companies), which make decisions based on processing data that are fundamental or market, and alternative data, i.e., data from various non-financial sources and complement the other three forms of data (images of products, bills, etc., google searches, chats, tweets, and metadata). By automating tasks and managing financial processes, AI can contribute to cost savings and speed up improvements. To smooth the decisions involved in trading on the stock market, trading algorithms can be specified. Bond ratings and investment decisions that are solely based on an analysis of the balance sheet, income statement, and fundamental market data can be determined more quickly by observing patterns. Financial data are based on statistics and facts rather than judgments that can be influenced by emotion. If properly programmed, they can also reduce human error. These days, working with massive amounts of data is easy because of the availability of technology-based tools. One can run statistical models and can make business decisions such as investing, trading, creating credit risk modeling, and so on based on the output generated.

Based on their evolution, Gao (2019) [1] divided conversational tools into three categories: chatbots, task-oriented dialogue agents, and question-answering agents. AI has covered a long way, from answering a pre-defined set of questions to solving complex tasks using deep semantics. Conversational AI is often referred to as a dialogue system in science. In contrast to conversational AI, which uses technology to store human behavior and make decisions following it, dialogue systems are rule-specific. The CPS (talks/turns per session), or the typical conversations between a user and chatbot, is used by the study to identify various AI-based applications. The question–answer dialogue system makes an effort to comprehend the purpose of a user's query and to make it clear with the least amount of CPS. While a top-level chatbot expands the conversation to keep the user engaged and solve the inquiry, a task-oriented chatbot seeks to comprehend the user's ultimate purpose and address the query with the least amount of dialogue delivery.

Organization of Chapter

The rest of the chapter is divided into five sections. Sections 6.2 and 6.3 discuss the importance of AI with reference to various businesses, including banking, e-commerce, financial industry, and AI as a foundation for these industries. This is followed by a discussion on the use of conversational AI in everyday businesses in Section 6.4. Section 6.5 concludes the chapter.

6.2   Significance of Artificial Intelligence

Customers need not take a day off from their work to visit their bank. Nowadays, banks are even using technology to offer credit online by making the data widely accessible. This makes the lending process more convenient for banks and customers since customers do not need to visit branches to complete it. This is also useful for clients who take minor loans as processing it conventionally could lead to large operational costs. The way we live has changed because of technology. Banks now can examine loan portfolios on real-time basis, which earlier was reviewed on either a monthly or quarterly basis. Even an industry can evaluate the unstructured form of data that is available through a user's social media account and can approach it in that way only. Technological-based tools can even be useful in identifying transactions that are suspicious based on your past transaction history and alerting the user of the same. Thus, fraud detection has become easy and fast. *MeitY* (Ministry of Electronics and Information Technology) is now working towards digitalizing all the property-related documents for the further processing of home loans to smoothen the loan approval verifications.

AI-based tools make it simple for people to manage their finances. Customers can check account balances, send money, and even prevent a card from being used just by asking your app, eliminating the need for complicated navigation menus. Additionally, it enables the proactive sending of bill payment reminders or announcements of extraordinary savings rates. Eighty-seven percent of businesses that have used AI are doing so to enhance email marketing. Even the use of AI in surveillance is widespread, spanning 75 nations.

6.3 Conversational AI in the Indian Banking Industry

Industries are increasingly using chatbots to connect with their customers and give them a personalized experience. Banks are actively participating since they arguably lower the operational expense of routine customer visits. These AI-based chatbots were typically employed by banks to offer basic services including handling consumer complaints, custom financial decisions, tracking transactions, fraud detection, and more. Many websites have chatbots because they appear whenever someone visits to look for information. For instance, if one visits https://www.isme.in/ for more assistance, a chatbot named *Riya* appears for admission-related queries. The official Government of India chatbot, *MyGov Corona Helpdesk,* was created with the same goal in mind to solve the queries of the citizens during the pandemic.

One of the areas that support an economy is the banking industry. By offering fundamental services like account opening, checking balance, obtaining monthly statements, moving cash, paying utility bills, issuing chequebooks, and much more online and more conveniently, banks have grown more efficient as a result of the introduction of technology and moving towards conversational banking from conventional banking with the help of chatbots by automating conversation between customers and the bank as customer interaction is of high importance in banks. *HDFC Bank* became the first Indian bank that introduced a banking chatbot powered by artificial intelligence (AI) named *"Electronic Virtual Assistant (EVA)"* for customer support. *EVA* is known as the largest AI-powered chatbot as it has been upgraded to regional languages to also cover customers geographically. Banks are working towards converting their mundane tasks digitally. Conversational chatbots help banks to interact with customers through text messages, voice, or both to improve customer experience and improve response rate.

According to the *PWC report,* a well-designed chatbot can work relentlessly around the clock, 24 hours a day, 365 days a year, and can deal with customers without holding them up for long, has an intuitive user interface, and can complete routine tasks quickly and efficiently. Table 6.1 summarizes four key areas in which AI is being used by the financial industry.

6.4 Conversational AI in Use in Various Companies

Our daily lives have already been impacted by AI. We use artificial intelligence from the moment we wake up in a variety of ways, from unlocking our phones using face

Table 6.1 Usage of artificial intelligence in the financial industry categorized in four key areas.

Client-centered front office applications	Banking operations-centered back office applications	Investment management	Regulatory compliance
i. Credit scoring	i. Capital optimization	i. Trade execution	i. Regulatory technology
ii. Insurance policies	ii. Model risk management	ii. Portfolio management	ii. Macro-prudential surveillance
iii. Client-facing chat	iii. Stress testing		iii. Data quality assurance
iv. Know your custom (eKYC)	iv. Fraud detection		iv. Supervisory technology

recognition to displaying the items or news that are pertinent to us based on our check-in history. When mail is received, spam filters are also powered by AI, which separates undesirable or dangerous mail based on the content. Siri, Cortana, or Alexa uses natural language processing (NLP) to interact with the user. Smart devices in our homes understand the temperature needed to cool down by learning and retaining information and act accordingly.

AI is used in the E-commerce industry to anticipate sales by giving recommendations to the user based on their search history, preferences, and interests and thus increase engagement with their customers. This leads to an increase in brand loyalty. Even many shopping websites now have the feature of visual searches by uploading images of the product needed and the AI tool shows the recommended products matching their query. Businesses have AI-powered assistants such as chatbots to improve the user experience while buying a product online that works on NLP (natural language processing) to

---

Conversational AI in practice by various companies:

Amazon: An e-commerce giant platform, Amazon has *Alexa* that employs artificial intelligence for many purposes in addition to its voice-activated assistant, including emailing products to potential consumers before they contemplate buying them. They gather a lot of information about consumer behavior. With the use of predictive analytics, they are confident in their ability to foresee what consumers will desire and need before they can acquire it.

L'Oreal: One of the top manufacturers of cosmetics and hair care products and one of the leading salon businesses in the world has adopted *Mya System,* an AI-powered recruiting tool that simplifies the hiring and onboarding procedures. It communicates with candidates via chat or email as well as social media sites like Facebook and Skype. It answers any questions a candidate may have and aids in employee retention by keeping them interested in the company. According to *L'Oreal,* it receives more than 1 million applications annually. *Mya* successfully engages 92% of candidates and has a satisfaction rating that is very close to 100%.

Jio Mart: Indian E-commerce giant Jio Mart tied up with WhatsApp to provide customer support. It offers suggestions and customized discounts and deals with and even solves the queries of customers in real time. One can also keep a track of the products ordered.

Axis AHA! is a one-touch virtual banking assistant that streamlines financial transfers, bill payments, account information, card management, and much more, and was introduced in 2018. Utilizing artificial intelligence and machine learning provides consumers with contextual dialogue assistance, completes transactions, and addresses their banking-related inquiries.

smoothen the conversations and make them more personal and humane with the users and establish a personalized and real-time engagement between the buyer and the seller, which improves the purchasing experience. From the seller's point of view, AI-based tools help in stocking up the particular products that are in demand so that the e-commerce platform can meet up the expectations of the customer. By 2025, the world-wide AI market is projected by market research company *Tractica* to generate $118.6 billion in sales.

Conversational AI in contact centers: Earlier, to deal with the grievances of a customer, human interaction is very much needed. This is can now be handled with the help of conversational chatbots. They have become one of the most popular channels for dealing with human queries as these are available 24/7. For instance, to get any information related to your bank account, card details, monthly bill payments, and complaint registration, chatbots are used. The first and largest AI-powered banking chatbot in India is *EVA (Electronic Virtual Assistant)* introduced by *HDFC Bank*. Almost all the banks nowadays have their chatbots, such as *Axis Aha!* at *Axis Bank*, *AMY* for *HSBC Bank*, *Yes ROBOT* for *Yes Bank*, and more. Businesses can deploy a conversational chatbot to cut their customer service costs by up to 30%, according to Chatbots Magazine.

In the financial sector, cyberattacks [8–12] are getting more and more serious. Conversational Artificial intelligence [13, 14] is being used by the banking industry to build cyber protection [15, 16] systems in an effort to reduce unauthorised [17] access and cyberattacks [18–20]. Banks are aware of the danger posed by cybercrime [21] and the importance of cybersecurity [22, 23] for long-term development. The banking sector is now going through a significant technological change. Understanding how emerging technologies like artificial intelligence (AI) [24] affect banks' cybersecurity becomes crucial. Cybercriminals [25] sent out phishing emails [26], in particular, with dangerous attachments. These emails were sent to several middle management staff members as well as the top executives of various companies. Phishing [23] emails that purport to be from the financial sector have been distributed. The emails include notes that seem to provide some advice on the bank payments. A transaction file that is malware-infected [24, 25] is attached to the email's message.

6.5   Conclusion

Businesses use AI-based tools to improve customer experience and the efficiency of the organization and the staff, enhancing business productivity and customer engagement. Such tools became popular in businesses as they reduce the organization's cost, time, and energy by efficiently utilizing the resources with minimum wastage. Their usage has grown tremendously in various sectors such as banks, e-commerce, fintech firms, etc. More than any other industry, banks are investing in AI to support regulatory compliance and risk management. However, there are still a lot of flaws in chatbots, whether they are speech- or text-based, and rule- or AI-based, and they still need a ton of extra information. To reduce these errors, more development and improvement are required in this field. Banks, which are the main users of chatbots, must manage the risk because a chatbot's failure might cause the economy to become unbalanced. Also, the linguistic barrier needs to be dealt with cautiously and many banks are working towards this improvement as *EVA (HDFC Bank)* has now been upgraded to a regional language as well. *Canara Bank* has unveiled the *Kannada* talking robot *MITRA*, which resolves customer inquiries in their regional language. There are numerous opportunities for AI to be applied in India's banking industry. Regarding acceptance, knowledge, and problems with security and information risks, it is experiencing numerous difficulties. In order to compete with other fintech companies, banks will need to overcome these obstacles and empower themselves.

References

1. Gao, J., Galley, M., Li, L., Neural approaches to conversational AI. *Found. Trends Inf. Retr.*, 13, 2–3, 127–298, 2019. https://doi.org/10.1561/1500000074.
2. Haque, S., Eberhart, Z., Bansal, A., McMillan, C., Semantic similarity metrics for evaluating source code summarization. *IEEE International Conference on Program Comprehension*, pp. 36–47, 2022-March, https://doi.org/10.1145/nnnnnnn.nnnnnnn.
3. https://www.ibm.com/cloud/learn/conversational-ai (accessed on 02.12.22).
4. https://www.artificial-solutions.com/conversational-ai-banking-financial-services (accessed on 02.12.22).
5. https://www.isme.in/the-trend-of-banks-banking-on-chatbots/ (accessed on 03.12.22).
6. https://www.hdfcbank.com/htdocs/common/eva/index.html (accessed on 08.12.22).
7. https://www.icicibank.com/offers/killer-chatbot-offer.page (accessed on 08.12.22).
8. Mahor, V., Bijrothiya, S., Rawat, R., Kumar, A., Garg, B., Pachlasiya, K., IoT and artificial intelligence techniques for public safety and security, in: *Smart Urban Computing Applications*, p. 111, 2023.
9. Mahor, V., Pachlasiya, K., Garg, B., Chouhan, M., Telang, S., Rawat, R., Mobile operating system (Android) vulnerability analysis using machine learning, in: *Proceedings of International Conference on Network Security and Blockchain Technology: ICNSBT 2021*, pp. 159–169, Springer Nature Singapore, Singapore, 2022, June.
10. Rawat, R., Garg, B., Pachlasiya, K., Mahor, V., Telang, S., Chouhan, M., Mishra, R., SCNTA: Monitoring of network availability and activity for identification of anomalies using machine learning approaches. *Int. J. Inf. Technol. Web Eng. (IJITWE)*, 17, 1, 1–19, 2022.
11. Rawat, R., Rimal, Y.N., William, P., Dahima, S., Gupta, S., Sankaran, K.S., Malware threat affecting financial organization analysis using machine learning approach. *Int. J. Inf. Technol. Web Eng. (IJITWE)*, 17, 1, 1–20, 2022.
12. Rawat, R., Mahor, V., Chouhan, M., Pachlasiya, K., Telang, S., Garg, B., Systematic literature review (SLR) on social media and the digital transformation of drug trafficking on darkweb, in: *International Conference on Network Security and Blockchain Technology*, pp. 181–205, Springer, Singapore, 2022.
13. Rawat, R., Ayodele Oki, O., Sankaran, S., Florez, H., Ajagbe, S.A., Techniques for predicting dark web events focused on the delivery of illicit products and ordered crime. *Int. J. Electr. Comput. Eng. (IJECE)*, 13, 5, 5354–5365, Oct. 2023, doi: 10.11591/ijece.v13i5.pp5354-5365.
14. Rawat, R., Garg, B., Mahor, V., Telang, S., Pachlasiya, K., Chouhan, M., Organ trafficking on the dark web—The data security and privacy concern in healthcare systems, in: *Internet of Healthcare Things: Machine Learning for Security and Privacy*, pp. 189–216, 2022.
15. Vyas, P., Vyas, G., Chauhan, A., Rawat, R., Telang, S., Gottumukkala, M., Anonymous trading on the dark online marketplace: An exploratory study, in: *Using Computational Intelligence for the Dark Web and Illicit Behavior Detection*, pp. 272–289, IGI Global, 2022.

16. Rawat, R., Oki, O.A., Sankaran, K.S., Olasupo, O., Ebong, G.N., Ajagbe, S.A., A new solution for cyber security in big data using machine learning approach, in: *Mobile Computing and Sustainable Informatics: Proceedings of ICMCSI 2023*, pp. 495–505, Springer Nature Singapore, Singapore, 2023.

17. Rawat, R., Chakrawarti, R.K., Raj, A., Mani, G., Chidambarathanu, K., Bhardwaj, R., Association rule learning for threat analysis using traffic analysis and packet filtering approach. *Int. J. Inf. Technol.*, 1–11, 2023.

18. Rawat, R., Logical concept mapping and social media analytics relating to cyber criminal activities for ontology creation. *Int. J. Inf. Technol.*, 15, 2, 893–903, 2023.

19. Rawat, R., Mahor, V., Álvarez, J.D., Ch, F., Cognitive systems for dark web cyber delinquent association malignant data crawling: A review, in: *Handbook of Research on War Policies, Strategies, and Cyber Wars*, pp. 45–63, 2023.

20. Rawat, R., Chakrawarti, R.K., Vyas, P., Gonzáles, J.L.A., Sikarwar, R., Bhardwaj, R., Intelligent fog computing surveillance system for crime and vulnerability identification and tracing. *Int. J. Inf. Secur. Priv. (IJISP)*, 17, 1, 1–25, 2023.

21. Rawat, R., Sowjanya, A.M., Patel, S.I., Jaiswal, V., Khan, I., Balaram, A. (Eds.), *Using Machine Intelligence: Autonomous Vehicles Volume 1*, John Wiley & Sons, 2022.

22. Rawat, R., Mahor, V., Díaz-Álvarez, J., Chávez, F., Rooted learning model at fog computing analysis for crime incident surveillance, in: *2022 International Conference on Smart Generation Computing, Communication and Networking (SMART GENCON)*, pp. 1–9, IEEE, 2022, December.

23. Rawat, R. and Shrivastav, S.K., SQL injection attack Detection using SVM. *Int. J. Comput. Appl.*, 42, 13, 1–4, 2012.

24. Rawat, R., Bhardwaj, P., Kaur, U., Telang, S., Chouhan, M., Sankaran, K.S., *Smart vehicles for communication, volume 2*, John Wiley & Sons, 2023.

25. Mahor, V., Garg, B., Telang, S., Pachlasiya, K., Chouhan, M., Rawat, R., Cyber threat phylogeny assessment and vulnerabilities representation at thermal power station, in: *Proceedings of International Conference on Network Security and Blockchain Technology: ICNSBT 2021*, pp. 28–39, Springer Nature Singapore, Singapore, 2022, June.

26. Rawat, R., Gupta, S., Sivaranjani, S., Cu, O.K., Kuliha, M., Sankaran, K.S., Malevolent information crawling mechanism for forming structured illegal organisations in hidden networks. *Int. J. Cyber Warf. Terror. (IJCWT)*, 12, 1, 1–14, 2022.

7

Chatbots: Meaning, History, Vulnerabilities, and Possible Defense

Divya Nair

School of Education and Research, MIT Art, Design and Technology University, Hadapsar, Maharashtra, India

Abstract

Intelligent agents and interactive technology have influenced every aspect of our day-to-day activities. Chatbots are one such program based on artificial intelligence that has added value to the fields of marketing, entertainment, education, and other influential industries. Personal assistants like Alexa are used by the masses for a variety of tasks that range from the creation of a simple to-do list, up to booking a hotel and more complicated and personalized tasks. However, these human-like ability systems can be a free pass for cybercriminals for executing a variety of attacks by exploiting the vulnerabilities of the chatbots. The malicious chatbots have the ability to steal vital information from the customer without his or her awareness. This chapter focuses on presenting the possible chatbot vulnerabilities along with its possible defenses. The chapter outlines the meaning and history of chatbots initially followed by a discussion on the variety of vulnerabilities that can be accessed by the hackers and further exploited in the form of a disastrous attack. DDOS, access control, phishing, etc. are discussed with examples. Towards the end, an attempt is made to list out possible practical solutions of the chatbot vulnerabilities.

Keywords: Interactive technology, chatbots, personal assistants, human-like ability systems, cybercriminals, malicious chatbots, vulnerabilities, attack

7.1 Understanding Chatbots

The idea of making machines efficient enough to interact like humans is not an old one. However, with time and the recent advances in artificial intelligence (AI) and natural language processing (NLP), conversational systems have made a great advancement in every field and aspect of our day-to-day life. A classic case of an interesting AI implication is a chatbot-mediated human–computer communication. Chatbots can be referred to as software packages that mimic humanoid conversations or discussions by using pre-programmed directives or NLP. By way of explanation, the method in which the conversations are regulated through a chatbot can classify them specifically as a rule-based chatbot or an AI

Email: divya.nair@mituniversity.edu.in

Romil Rawat, Rajesh Kumar Chakrawarti, Sanjaya Kumar Sarangi, Piyush Vyas, Mary Sowjanya Alamanda, Kotagiri Srividya and Krishnan Sakthidasan Sankaran (eds.) Conversational Artificial Intelligence, (95–106) © 2024 Scrivener Publishing LLC

chatbot. This means that all chatbots are not AI-based chatbots. To elaborate this further, let us consider the examples presented in Figures 7.1 and 7.2.

Figure 7.1 is a classic example of a rule-based chatbot. Here, the user can initiate a conversation only on the basis of the specific options made available to him via the bot. In this case, the user needs to select among the four options listed in front of him that deals with admission, fee payment, cancellation, and refund. This means that if a user is interested to know about the credit transfer of courses, then he will not be able to initiate a conversation with the bot as it does not offer this option due to the pre-programming directives embedded in it. These bots are also called normal chatbots or button-based bots. They work on pattern recognition [8] and cannot provide responses apart from the fixed set of rules that are part of their programing.

Figure 7.2 displays a hypothetical example of an AI chatbot. These bots utilize machine learning (ML) and NLP for mimicking human interactions by focusing on the user's intent. Natural language processing utilizes the knowledge and practice of human text-based or voice-based language in assembling and creating methods that will allow computers and machines in comprehending and operating expressions for performing desired tasks in a natural way. Natural language understanding (NLU) extracts meaning from natural language and infers user intention [3]. Users can direct the conversations in an AI chatbot. The AI chatbot is able to provide a reply to different variations of the query by identifying the intent. Let us take an example for better clarification. A customer wishes to know the timings of your book store. There can be a variety of ways he may frame his question. He may ask:

- What are the timings of your book store?
- At what time do you guys open?
- What time do you open the shop?

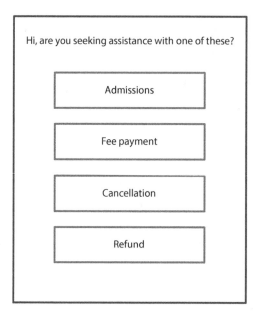

Figure 7.1 Example of a rule-based chatbot.

Figure 7.2 Example of an AI chatbot.

- What time do you shut the shop?
- Can I visit on weekends?
- Can I pay a visit to your store at 9 PM on Monday?
- Does your book store have a weekly off?
- Can I come on Sunday to your store?

The intent of all the above-mentioned questions is the same. By utilizing the past customer experiences backed with the powerful pillars of ML and NLP, the AI chatbot will provide the correct answer based on the intent irrespective of the way the question has been phrased. In this case, the AI chatbot might reply, "We are open from Monday to Saturday from 10 AM to 6 PM. Sunday is a weekly off for us." Thus, the AI bots are more refined and personalized as compared to the rule-based chatbots [6].

7.2   History of Chatbots

The timeline of some of the most popular chatbots is presented in Figure 7.3. The history of chatbots starts with an amazing personality. Alan Turing probed on the possibility whether machines can think [9]. In 1950, he proposed the idea of the Imitation Game, widely known as the Turing Test today. The basic objective of this test is to see whether a machine can be intelligent enough to outsmart a human into thinking that they are having a conversation with another human contestant and not a machine [9]. In the initial test there were two contenders, one was a human and the other was a machine. There was an evaluator who

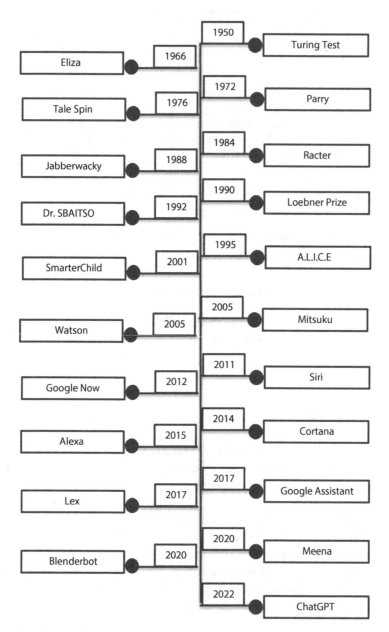

Figure 7.3 Timeline of some of the most popular chatbots.

would ask a series of questions to both the participants. Based on the responses of the participants, the evaluator would then identify which out of the two was a machine and who was a human. If the machine was successful in tricking the evaluator into making an incorrect decision, the machine was considered to be intelligent [9]. The recent modification of this test is based on one participant and the evaluator needs to make a decision of it being a human or a machine.

Alan Turing's work motivated Joseph Weizenbaum to design ELIZA, the first chatbot in 1966 [11]. ELIZA functioned by identifying keywords or expressions from the input given by the humans to replicate an answer based on some preprogramed directions [11]. For example, if a human mentions, "I had an uneventful day at school today," ELIZA will catch hold of the keyword "school" and will reply as, "Share more details about your school life." This type of a response will trick the human into thinking that he is having a conversation with another fellow human, even though this thinking of his is far away from the actual truth.

In 1972, Kenneth Colby created the chatbot called Parry [1]. This chatbot was developed to impersonate the traits of a paranoid patient. In comparison to ELIZA, it was an advanced bot [1]. James Meehan in 1976 created the first chatbot that could narrate stories called Tale-Spin. In 1984, William Chamberlain and Thomas Etter created another story-telling chatbot named Racter [2]. This chatbot provided a conversation experience that was more attention grabbing. The response was usually in the form of a poetry [2]. In 1988, Rollo Carpenter developed a chatbot called Jabberwacky that held the capability of mimicking human speech in a realistic fashion.

In 1990, Hugh Loebner initiated a yearly contest for chatbots, namely, the Loebner Prize. This contest awarded the chatbots that successfully passed the Turing Test. PC therapist III developed by Joseph Weintraub was the first winner of this contest in 1991. A.L.I.C.E. developed by Richard Wallace won this contest three times and Kuki formerly known as MITSUKU developed by Steve Worswick won this contest five times. This contest was discontinued from the year 2020.

Sound Blaster Acting Intelligent Text to Speech Operator that is Dr. SBAITSO was a speech built chatbot invented by creative labs for MS-DOS in 1992. It imitated the reactions of an expert from the psychology field. The research domain of chatbots experienced a revolution with the entry of Artificial Linguistic Internet Computer Entity alias A.L.I.C.E. [5]. It was an Artificial Intelligence Markup Language [AIML] personality program that was regarded as the most human chatbot and was successful in tricking the judges of the Turing test not once but thrice [10]. The intelligence of A.L.I.C.E. revolves around approximately 41,000 categories. These are involved in building associations among the query, i.e., patterns, and the solution, i.e., template. These are collected in a structure called graph master that creates a storage pattern and matches it with the algorithm [10].

In 2001, SmarterChild chatbot was introduced. This chatbot was capable of blending the old or previous information to initiate conversations with humans that could potentially relieve them from lonesomeness. In 2005, Steve Worswick developed the MITSUKU chatbot by employing the AIML commands for basic discussions. This chatbot was linked to various social media platforms [5]. It is a good learner as it improves and responds as per previous experiences. It also holds the potential of being a great analyzer. As an example, if we consider a situation where the user may ask, are all snakes poisonous? The chatbot will look into the characteristics of snakes and will give no as a reply.

In 2005, Thomas Watson put forth a chatbot that held expertise in answering difficult questions by utilizing NLP and the technology of cognitive computing. Watson's chatbot answered the questions posed to it by following a series of steps. The first stage dealt with the analysis of the questions posed. Here, the chatbot comprehended the meaning along with the similarities of words and phrases that formed a part of the question. In the second stage, a series of answers will be generated through a process of primary searching. This will be extended by the collection of supporting and non-supporting evidence for every answer that was listed in the second stage. Scores will be given to every response here. A decision will be made in the final stage by Watson based on the ranks given by considering the scores given to all the responses.

Siri is an intelligent voice bot of Apple that works as a personal assistant and an information guide. Siri performs a wide range of activities ranging from email, messages, reminders, information search, entertainment, controlling settings of devices, etc. Siri was launched in 2011. In 2012, Google Now came into the spotlight. This was later on modified with Google Assistant in 2017. Microsoft introduced the digital assistant Cortana in 2014. It is useful for high-speed information access; it allows better connectivity with others and will also help the user to manage things as per their priority and preferences [7].

> Hey Alexa, play the happy birthday song.
> Hey Alexa, switch on the lights.
> Hey Alexa, book my flight tickets.

Most of the users who are owners of Alexa will be accustomed to these types of commands. Amazon's Alexa was developed in 2015. It is a personal assistant that is capable of executing a variety of tasks efficiently.

In 2017, Amazon introduced Lex. It is powered by advanced AI and NLP features. It easily comprehends the intent, focuses on the utterance, and moves from prompt, slot towards ultimate task fulfilment.

Meena, a chatbot by Google, came into picture in the year 2020. It is a multipurpose, highly adaptable and open-domain chatbot. Since it is trained on a large number of data based on social media conversations, a realistic human touch is seen while interacting with this chatbot. Blenderbot is a highly skilled chatbot introduced by Facebook with advanced memory abilities. This chatbot brings together a combination of interactive skills like compassion, responsiveness, understanding, and persona together in a single structure.

In November 2022, ChatGPT was launched by OpenAI. It identifies text linkages from the net and also gets assistance from humans for producing a more impactful conversation. The basic standout feature is that you can ask almost anything to this chatbot. In the trial period, few users asked ChatGPT to pen down a poem. It accomplished this task successfully. The developers have however warned the users about the possibility of getting incorrect responses from this chatbot.

In this section, an attempt was made to highlight some of the most popular chatbots. Moving ahead, now the focus will shift onto the vulnerabilities and security issues with chatbots.

7.3 Vulnerabilities and Security Concerns of Chatbots

Let us consider a situation. There is an old man who lives alone. He goes to the bank and withdraws his lifelong savings in cash for some urgent work. There was a thief who witnessed this from a distance. The old man was unaware that he was being followed. The thief now knew the exact address of the old man's house. He also realized that the old man was living all alone in an isolated area. At night, when the old man was sleeping, the thief entered the house and was successful in stealing the money. This hypothetical example leads us towards three important concepts in cybersecurity, namely, vulnerability, threat, and attack.

Old age, living alone, and isolated place where no one could come for help [vulnerability] is a defect that was exploited by the thief [threat], leading to the ultimate robbery [attack]. Considering these terminologies from the cybersecurity point of view, we can define threat as all the aspects that possess the probability of interfering and disturbing the operations, performance, availability, and reliability of a network or system. Vulnerability can be elaborated as an intrinsic loophole of your network or system that makes it an at-risk target for a threat. Exploitation of this vulnerability leads to an attack.

The chatbot is always connected to the internet. Every conversation that you have with the bot is stored in its system and this itself opens an array of issues pertaining to security and possible attacks. This is especially true for the chatbots that are specifically used as personal assistants by most of the users. Thus, safety is always a concern when we exchange information using an online channel. The information inputted by the user via the chatbot can have major vulnerabilities during the transferring and processing stages of the message.

Hackers or cybercriminals can mask themselves as a genuine chatbot application and steal vital information as soon as the user provides a response to the conversation. One classic example of this can be a phishing attack. In this type of an attack, emails and links that seem to have an authentic origin is delivered to users. These links in reality are malware packages or virus-infected programs that navigate sensitive data to the attackers as soon as the user accesses the link.

When phishing is mediated through messages, it is called smishing. The Apple chatbot scam is a good elaboration of such attacks. In this scam, the smishing attack is initiated by messages that pretend to come from an Apple chatbot. The message is addressed to a person called Christopher. The intention of the cybercriminal is to give a feeling to the user that the message is delivered to the wrong person by some error. The message details out an address and sends a link that appears authentic. On visiting the link, the user will get the opportunity to win the latest version of iPhone, free of cost as part of a prelaunch trial. There are high chances that many people will fall for this trap due to their curiosity or greed.

As soon as the user clicks on the link, a malicious bot that gives an appearance of a genuine Apple chatbot opens. A series of conversations is initiated. You are asked to enter your name and address for verification purpose. This verification is not a difficult task for the user to bypass as these details are already mentioned in the text message that was delivered to him. This is followed by a general survey comprising of six questions on an average. Some of the questions that are part of this survey will be related to your address, name, age, city, number of members in your family, and a general enquiry of Apple products.

An information verification prompt pops up with a comment section of users who were past participants in this trial offer. This is again fake but is put forth to convince the victim about the authenticity of this irresistible offer. After a few seconds, the victim is declared a winner. This is again followed by a confirmatory message. The user is directed to enter an email address followed by a minimal courier charge that ranges between one to two euros. If you agree to pay the courier charges, you will end up on a website that has proper hypertext transfer protocol (https) credentials that looks genuinely authentic. Through the credit card payment, the victim gives away sensitive data of the card number, pin, etc. to the attacker and this is the final stage where the attack can be termed to be successful. This can lead to a massive loss to the victim on an immediate basis or in the near future. This attack can be extended by the hacker to send similar messages from the hacked account to the victim's friends or families.

Another vulnerability that can be exploited by the cybercriminals is carelessness from the victim's side. Let us consider a case where you have accidentally misplaced your phone somewhere. A stranger gets hold of your phone. He gets an immediate access to the information stored in your phone as you have not locked your phone by a password or any biometric credential. A similar situation can occur if the user has not locked the chatbot window for avoiding unauthorized access. If the bot window is open, all the sensitive and personal data can be leaked out very easily to the cybercriminals. This can take a serious form if this is followed by a denial of service attack (DDOS) or a ransomware attack.

The services and resources become unavailable in a DDOS attack. For example, consider a case where the attackers are successful in crashing the system of a highly acclaimed healthcare chatbot by releasing a set of multiple requests. On successful execution, the attackers deny the services of this chatbot to the users as well as the medical firm. This chatbot has personal information about the patients, their medical history, and the treatment they are taking. This is a serious breach to personal privacy and can be misused by the attackers in multiple ways. An immediate extension of a DDOS attack is a ransomware demand. This can lead to serious financial damage. Similarly, firms that are dependent on chatbots for providing an array of services to their customers will have a disastrous fate if a DDOS attack is executed on their bots.

It is important to note that every chatbot does not use an encrypted security during the conversations. This increases the chance of a man in the middle type of an attack. In such attacks, the hacker eavesdrops on the conversation between the victim and the chatbot and takes control of the information at the proper junction of time. Consider this, a malicious chatbot can be projected by the cybercriminals to be genuine. In simple words, the malicious chatbot might appear to have a genuine source. Once the user starts interacting with it, the bot may lead the conversation in a way where the users are prompted to share sensitive information. The attacker who is eavesdropping the conversation will get access to the sensitive data that can be exploited in different ways by them.

Similarly, the bot can also lead to the installation of malwares and spywares in the system through the medium of conversations. For example, the chatbot might pose a question about your favorite brand of cosmetics. Over a period of time, when the user gets in a natural flow of conversation with the chatbot pertaining to the cosmetic brand, the malicious chatbot might start sharing links of some new offers associated with the said brand. There are high possibilities that the victim will get tricked and will share details that can lead to a successful execution of the man in the middle type of an attack.

Apart from this, conversations exchanged between the chatbot and user is generally stored for training purposes. These conversations are important as it helps in improving the accuracy of responses, understanding the intent, and enhancing the overall performance of the bot. This training cannot be executed on machine learning algorithms and NLP tools if the data are encrypted. This situation is a vulnerability that can be well exploited to execute a cybercrime.

A lot of pre-programming is involved while making a chatbot. As discussed in the introductory section, NLP and AI are used to make the chatbot conversations realistic and as natural as possible. An interesting threat can be the execution of a Trojan attack in the learning model itself [4]. A logical set of words will be used as triggers that lead to the generation of abusive responses [4]. Example, a word as simple as market might trigger a racist response from the chatbot.

The voice command fingerprinting attack can allow a cybercriminal to use the victim's voice instructions to overhear and steal the encrypted information exchanged between a smart home device and the cloud [4]. Chatbots hosted on a third-party app are also a vulnerability that can be utilized by the attackers to their benefit. Apart from this, zero day attacks on chatbots are also a threat that cannot be ignored.

7.4   Possible Defense Strategies

In the previous section, a detailed discussion on the possible vulnerabilities of chatbots was put forth. Now, an attempt will be made to list out the possible strategies through which such problems can be avoided.

User authentication is one of the strategies that increases the security level of chatbots. However, this authentication is not seen in every case. For example, if you are communicating with a chatbot that deals with your financial transactions, it will ask you to authenticate the details for confirming your identity before going ahead with the transaction. However, if your conversation with the chatbot is on some general command like to switch on the camera of your house, it will not ask for any user verification details. Any person who has access to the chatbot or has a voice that very closely resembles the user's voice can take benefit of this situation and can be a virtual spy without the knowledge of the victim. Thus, it is essential that irrespective of the conversation that is being exchanged between the bot and the user, the authentication step is made mandatory as a measure of extra security for avoiding cybercrimes.

The degree of this security can be improved further by using a more elaborate two-step authentication.

Automatic deletion of sensitive messages after a period of time can be a possible solution. This type of a setting can ensure that the data transmitted through the conversation are deleted permanently both from the user's end and from the chatbot's cloud network. This can minimize the risk of potential data leakage and increase the security level.

The developers need to implement certain benchmarks during the chatbot engineering process. Check for possible vulnerabilities and patch the same right at the beginning or in the subsequent updates of the chatbots. Similarly, the chatbots should also be trained for detecting any unusual behavior for preventing a possible cyberattack.

Threats [12–15] and vulnerabilities [16, 17] are the two main types of chatbot security issues [18, 19]. A chatbot might threaten [20, 21] users by impersonating others, tampering with data, and stealing personal information. As long as they are not sufficiently mitigated, a system's vulnerabilities can lead to its penetration. Threats [22] are often one-off occurrences like virus assaults [23], phishing scams, or distributed denial of service (DDoS) [24] attacks. Systems can become susceptible and exposed to attacks when they are not effectively maintained, have bad code, lack protection, or are the result of human error [25]. Long-term problems like vulnerabilities [26] must be continually addressed. Should you want to employ chatbots, there are security [27] measures you can take to make them more secure [28, 29]. In that regard, the procedure is comparable to any other system that introduces sensitive data. The degree of security [30] of your chatbot can be affected by what you do when you're on offence.

7.5   Conclusion

From a simple thought of whether computers can think and converse like humans, to the implementation of the same, chatbots have certainly made great progress. Chatbot is an excellent medium for accomplishing enormous tasks in a simplistic manner. However, every technology comes with its own set of challenges. Cyberattacks are becoming increasingly more sophisticated and potent. Chatbots have its own sets of vulnerabilities that can be easily exploited by the attackers. Thus, it is equally important to come up with preventive and sophisticated strategies to combat such attacks in the future.

References

1. Colby, K.M., Weber, S., Hilf, F.D., Artificial paranoia. *Artif. Intell.*, 2, 1, 1–25, 1971, https://doi.org/10.1016/0004-3702(71)90002-6.
2. Skrebeca, J., Kalniete, P., Goldbergs, J., Pitkevica, L., Tihomirova, D., Romanovs, A., Modern development trends of Chatbots using artificial intelligence (AI). *2021 62nd International Scientific Conference on Information Technology and Management Science of Riga Technical University (ITMS)*, pp. 1–6, 2021, doi: 10.1109/ITMS52826.2021.9615258.
3. Jung, S., Semantic vector learning for natural language understanding. *Comput. Speech Lang.*, 56, 130–145, 2019, https://doi.org/10.1016/j.csl.2018.12.008.
4. Kennedy, S., Li, H., Wang, C., Liu, H., Wang, B., Sun, W., I can hear your Alexa: Voice command fingerprinting on smart home speakers. *2019 IEEE Conference on Communications and Network Security (CNS)*, pp. 232–240, 2019, https://doi.org/10.1109/CNS.2019.8802686.
5. Maher, S., Kayte, S., Nimbhore, S., Chatbots & its techniques using AI: An review. *Int. J. Res. Appl. Sci. Eng. Technol.*, 8, 12, Art. 4363, 2020, https://easychair.org/publications/preprint/GTmK.
6. Nirala, K.K., Singh, N.K., Purani, V.S., A survey on providing customer and public administration based services using AI: Chatbot. *Multimed. Tools Appl.*, 81, 16, 22215–22246, 2022, https://doi.org/10.1007/s11042-021-11458-y.
7. Paul, Z., Cortana-intelligent personal digital assistant: A review. *Int. J. Adv. Res. Comput. Sci.*, 8, 7, 55–57, 2017, https://doi.org/10.26483/ijarcs.v8i7.4225.
8. Singh, J., Joesph, M.H., Jabbar, K.B.A., Rule-based chabot for student enquiries. *J. Phys. Conf. Ser.*, 1228, 1, 012060, 2019, https://doi.org/10.1088/1742-6596/1228/1/012060.
9. Turing, A.M., I.—Computing machinery and intelligence. *Mind*, LIX, 236, 433–460, 1950, https://doi.org/10.1093/mind/LIX.236.433.
10. Wallace, R.S., The Anatomy of A.L.I.C.E, in: *Parsing the Turing Test: Philosophical and Methodological Issues in the Quest for the Thinking Computer*, R. Epstein, G. Roberts, G. Beber (Eds.), pp. 181–210, Springer, Netherlands, 2009, https://doi.org/10.1007/978-1-4020-6710-5_13.
11. Weizenbaum, J., ELIZA—A computer program for the study of natural language communication between man and machine. *Commun. ACM*, 9, 1, 36–45, 1966, https://doi.org/10.1145/365153.365168.
12. Mahor, V., Bijrothiya, S., Rawat, R., Kumar, A., Garg, B., Pachlasiya, K., IoT and artificial intelligence techniques for public safety and security, in: *Smart Urban Computing Applications*, p. 111, 2023.
13. Mahor, V., Pachlasiya, K., Garg, B., Chouhan, M., Telang, S., Rawat, R., Mobile operating system (Android) vulnerability analysis using machine learning, in: *Proceedings of International*

Conference on Network Security and Blockchain Technology: ICNSBT 2021, pp. 159–169, Springer Nature Singapore, Singapore, 2022, June.

14. Rawat, R., Garg, B., Pachlasiya, K., Mahor, V., Telang, S., Chouhan, M., Mishra, R., SCNTA: Monitoring of network availability and activity for identification of anomalies using machine learning approaches. *Int. J. Inf. Technol. Web Eng. (IJITWE)*, 17, 1, 1–19, 2022.

15. Rawat, R., Rimal, Y.N., William, P., Dahima, S., Gupta, S., Sankaran, K.S., Malware threat affecting financial organization analysis using machine learning approach. *Int. J. Inf. Technol. Web Eng. (IJITWE)*, 17, 1, 1–20, 2022.

16. Rawat, R., Mahor, V., Chouhan, M., Pachlasiya, K., Telang, S., Garg, B., Systematic literature review (SLR) on social media and the digital transformation of drug trafficking on darkweb, in: *International Conference on Network Security and Blockchain Technology*, pp. 181–205, Springer, Singapore, 2022.

17. Rawat, R., Ayodele Oki, O., Sankaran, S., Florez, H., Ajagbe, S.A., Techniques for predicting dark web events focused on the delivery of illicit products and ordered crime. *Int. J. Electr. Comput. Eng. (IJECE)*, 13, 5, 5354–5365, Oct. 2023, doi: 10.11591/ijece.v13i5.pp5354-5365.

18. Rawat, R., Garg, B., Mahor, V., Telang, S., Pachlasiya, K., Chouhan, M., Organ trafficking on the dark web—The data security and privacy concern in healthcare systems, in: *Internet of Healthcare Things: Machine Learning for Security and Privacy*, pp. 189–216, 2022.

19. Vyas, P., Vyas, G., Chauhan, A., Rawat, R., Telang, S., Gottumukkala, M., Anonymous trading on the dark online marketplace: An exploratory study, in: *Using Computational Intelligence for the Dark Web and Illicit Behavior Detection*, pp. 272–289, IGI Global, 2022.

20. Rawat, R., Oki, O.A., Sankaran, K.S., Olasupo, O., Ebong, G.N., Ajagbe, S.A., A new solution for cyber security in big data using machine learning approach, in: *Mobile Computing and Sustainable Informatics: Proceedings of ICMCSI 2023*, pp. 495–505, Springer Nature Singapore, Singapore, 2023.

21. Rawat, R., Chakrawarti, R.K., Raj, A., Mani, G., Chidambarathanu, K., Bhardwaj, R., Association rule learning for threat analysis using traffic analysis and packet filtering approach. *Int. J. Inf. Technol.*, 1–11, 2023.

22. Rawat, R., Logical concept mapping and social media analytics relating to cyber criminal activities for ontology creation. *Int. J. Inf. Technol.*, 15, 2, 893–903, 2023.

23. Rawat, R., Mahor, V., Álvarez, J.D., Ch, F., Cognitive systems for dark web cyber delinquent association malignant data crawling: A review, in: *Handbook of Research on War Policies, Strategies, and Cyber Wars*, pp. 45–63, 2023.

24. Rawat, R., Chakrawarti, R.K., Vyas, P., Gonzáles, J.L.A., Sikarwar, R., Bhardwaj, R., Intelligent fog computing surveillance system for crime and vulnerability identification and tracing. *Int. J. Inf. Secur. Priv. (IJISP)*, 17, 1, 1–25, 2023.

25. Rawat, R., Sowjanya, A.M., Patel, S.I., Jaiswal, V., Khan, I., Balaram, A. (Eds.), *Using Machine Intelligence: Autonomous Vehicles Volume 1*, John Wiley & Sons, 2022.

26. Rawat, R., Mahor, V., Díaz-Álvarez, J., Chávez, F., Rooted learning model at fog computing analysis for crime incident surveillance, in: *2022 International Conference on Smart Generation Computing, Communication and Networking (SMART GENCON)*, pp. 1–9, IEEE, 2022, December.

27. Rawat, R. and Shrivastav, S.K., SQL injection attack detection using SVM. *Int. J. Comput. Appl.*, 42, 13, 1–4, 2012.

28. Rawat, R., Bhardwaj, P., Kaur, U., Telang, S., Chouhan, M., Sankaran, K.S., *Smart vehicles for communication, volume 2*, John Wiley & Sons, 2023.

29. Mahor, V., Garg, B., Telang, S., Pachlasiya, K., Chouhan, M., Rawat, R., Cyber threat phylogeny assessment and vulnerabilities representation at thermal power station, in: *Proceedings*

of International Conference on Network Security and Blockchain Technology: ICNSBT 2021, pp. 28–39, Springer Nature Singapore, Singapore, 2022, June.

30. Rawat, R., Gupta, S., Sivaranjani, S., Cu, O.K., Kuliha, M., Sankaran, K.S., Malevolent information crawling mechanism for forming structured illegal organisations in hidden networks. *Int. J. Cyber Warf. Terror. (IJCWT)*, *12*, 1, 1–14, 2022.

8

Conversational Chatbot-Based Security Threats for Business and Educational Platforms and Their Counter Measures

Hriakumar Pallathadka[1]*, Domenic T. Sanchez[2], Larry B. Peconcillo, Jr.[2], Malik Jawarneh[3], Julie Anne T. Godinez[4] and John V. De Vera[5]

[1]Manipur International University, Manipur, India
[2]Cebu Technological University-NEC, Cebu City, Philippines
[3]Faculty of Computing Sciences, Gulf College, Al-Khuwair, Oman
[4]Cebu Technological University-CCMSC, Cebu City, Philippines
[5]Cebu Technological University-Main Campus, Cebu City, Philippines

Abstract

A chatbot, also called a chatterbot or a conversational agent, is a piece of software that is powered by artificial intelligence and can have a smart conversation with one or more human users at any time and from anywhere. They are computer programs that can understand and respond to input in natural language, just like a real person would. With the help of artificial intelligence (AI) technology, it is now possible to come up with ways to build computer programs that mimic the way people think when they are trying to solve problems. Chatbots are an important part of the study of artificial intelligence because they help users get information and help them finish tasks by using advanced AI techniques. Chatbots are used in almost every type of business to answer customer service questions. This lets human workers focus on other tasks, which leads to a rise in productivity and a drop in costs in the long run. A chatbot can be used in business for much more than just customer service. It can be used to generate leads and follow up on those leads, among other things. They could be used to do things like grocery shopping, booking hotels, and setting up meetings automatically. They could also be hired for more creative jobs like artificial teaching, selling products, and working at help desks in big libraries and other places. Chatbots have security issues to be addressed before they flourish in all businesses. Chatbot suffers from security attacks like DDOS attack, MITM attack, etc. Intrusion detection plays a vital role in maintaining confidentiality, integrity, and availability in chatbot communication.

Keywords: Conversational AI, chatbot, chatbot in education, machine learning, security threats, intrusion detection, prevention, attacks

*Corresponding author: harikumar@miu.edu.in

Romil Rawat, Rajesh Kumar Chakrawarti, Sanjaya Kumar Sarangi, Piyush Vyas, Mary Sowjanya Alamanda, Kotagiri Srividya and Krishnan Sakthidasan Sankaran (eds.) *Conversational Artificial Intelligence*, (107–126) © 2024 Scrivener Publishing LLC

8.1   Introduction

A chatbot, also known as a chatterbot or a conversational agent, is a piece of software that is driven by artificial intelligence that is capable of having an intelligent conversation with one or more human users at any time and from any location. They are computer programs that are able to comprehend and react to input in natural language, imitating human interaction in the process. The vast majority of chatbots still depend on text interfaces to communicate with people, despite the fact that certain chatbots are equipped with voice recognition and text-to-speech capabilities.

The purpose of a chatbot is to analyze the user's intent based on the conversational signals that are provided and then provide an appropriate response. Some chatbots make an effort to seem human, while others want to wow users with their superior intellect or one-of-a-kind abilities. There are chatbots that make use of simple approaches, such as matching keywords and phrases against their dataset [1], and there are chatbots that make use of complicated techniques, such as analyzing natural language [2]. Despite the fact that developments are being made in this field, no chatbot has yet deceived its users into believing that it understands natural language and has the capacity to participate in conversation in the same way that humans do. A significant amount of effort is now being spent towards enhancing the conversational abilities of chatbots in order to provide them the ability to engage in conversations that are more humanlike and lifelike.

The development of artificial intelligence (AI) technology has made it feasible to devise methods for constructing computer programs that simulate the intellectual approach that people take to finding solutions to problems. Chatbots are an essential part of the study of artificial intelligence because they act as a conduit for the transfer of information to users and provide assistance to users in the completion of tasks via the use of sophisticated AI techniques. The whole potential of such systems has not yet been examined, nor have they been exploited to the extent that they can realize their full potential.

Virtually every kind of conversational bot accepts queries posed by users in the form of text written in natural language and responds with the most appropriate answer either verbally or in written form. This procedure will go on until the discussion is finally brought to a conclusion. The progression of conversation between real people and chatbots is shown in Figure 8.1. It is essential for a chatbot to have the ability to carry on a continuous discussion with the user using either text or voice. This will only be achievable if the chatbot is able to understand the purpose of the user and respond appropriately.

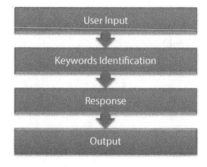

Figure 8.1 Chatbot communication flow.

The knowledge library, the interpretation software, and the conversation engine make up the most important parts of a chatbot [3]. The intelligence of the system is incorporated into the knowledge base, which consists of search phrases and the replies that the system has chosen to be acceptable for those terms. In addition, the knowledge base contains the search terms themselves. Knowledge bases are often built by combining other types of files, such as dat files, text files, database files, and XML files [4]. Through the use of its analyzer and generator components, the interpreter software makes user interaction much more straightforward. The text that is given by a person is read by the analyzer, and it makes judgments about the text based on both its syntax and its semantics. As a pre-processor for user input, it uses a number of different normalization approaches, such as pattern fitting, replacement, and phrase splitting.

After the output of the analyzer has been preprocessed, the conversation engine will attempt to match it with data that are stored in the knowledge base by employing a variety of techniques, including pattern matching, sentence reconstruction, indexing, and so on, in order to determine the appropriate answer. Following the processing of the chat engine's response by the generator, the latter provides a statement that is free of grammatical errors. Figure 8.2 illustrates the common components of a chatbot as well as their interconnections with one another.

However, as the operator's user base expands, it becomes more difficult to give individualized care to each and every one of the operator's customers. In the event that the operator has difficulty comprehending the query, they could deliver an incorrect response. It will not take long for the person in charge of such a system to get worn out and disinterested due to the need that they maintain continual surveillance. Efficiency and production are both negatively impacted by the fact that the task is repeated. As a result of these complications, there has been a growth in the need for self-sufficient inquiry responders across a range of user interaction domains.

Chatbots are being used in almost all business sectors to answer customer support enquiries. This allows human employees to concentrate on other tasks, which eventually leads to an increase in productivity and a reduction in expenses. The use of a chatbot in business goes well beyond the realm of ordinary customer service and into other domains, such as the generation of leads and the fulfilment of those leads. They might be used to automate mundane tasks such as grocery shopping, booking hotels, and organizing meetings. Additionally, they could be employed in more creative jobs such as artificial teaching, product sales, and help desks in large libraries and other institutions [5–7].

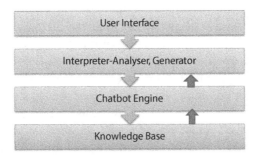

Figure 8.2 Chatbot components.

According to the results of a survey carried out by Oracle in 2016 [8], 80% of the major companies in the world want to use chatbot services for customer interactions by the year 2020. An increase in income may be seen in businesses who include chatbots into their direct consumer marketing efforts.

8.2   Chatbot Applications in Education, Business Management, and Health Sector

8.2.1   Chatbots for Education

The use of intelligent agents, which provide both a human element and a sense of realism to the experience, may prove to be beneficial to the process of education that takes place in a digital environment. The use of a chatbot in an educational environment has the potential to increase the efficiency of online interaction while at the same time mitigating the negative impacts of variables such as time and distance. It is outlined in Ref. [9] how a text-and-voice-enabled AIML chatbot may be used in the classroom, with the emphasis being placed on intelligent pedagogical agents (IPA). The implemented IPA addresses all of these problems by comparing user behavior to preset norms, providing quick feedback, assisting users in locating and correcting mistakes, and routinely updating assessment data for each individual student.

An English Dialogue Companion was created by Huang *et al.* [10] as a tool to make learning English easier for children who are enrolled in elementary school (EDC). The learning companion phase, the discussion phase, and the teaching phase make up the three stages of the design process for the EDC system that are intended to facilitate language acquisition. In their work, Fryer and Carpenter explored a Jabberwacky chatbot that is designed to assist in the process of language acquisition (FLL). According to the authors, students are able to feel more at ease when talking with a chatbot since it maintains their attention throughout the discussion and gives them the opportunity to deliver rapid, constructive comments.

Another well-known chatbot in this field is called Lucy, and it was introduced by Fei and Stephen in Ref. [11]. Lucy is an artificially intelligent online teacher that can hold in-depth conversations with students using the microphones in their computers. These conversations are designed to assist students learn a new language more effectively. T-Bot and Q-Bot are the names of two chatbots that have been introduced by Rodriguez *et al.* [12] with the purpose of educating and evaluating students using free and open-source software such as Moodle and Claroline. Students have the opportunity to engage in fruitful discourse in their mother language while also having access to a search engine for all of their inquiries about their assignments while using T-Bots. Q-Bot is a tool that assists teachers in evaluating their students and also gives students the ability to assess themselves.

A chatbot that is quite similar to the one provided in [6] is described there. This chatbot employs a gamified, structured inquiry-based technique to help students in primary school comprehend basic computer science concepts such as variables and conditionals. It was shown that the levels of involvement, attentiveness, enthusiasm, and curiosity among students greatly increased when chatbots were used as a teaching aid. Academically Productive Talk, often known as APT, is a strategy for developing a conversational agent that may be used to enable online collaborative learning discussions. This is accomplished in line [13].

The agent-based architecture Bazaar, which builds on the Basilica architecture that came before it, was used to establish a unique system for APT-based dynamic collaborative learning aid. Basilica was the architecture that came before Bazaar. It has been shown that using the approach has positive benefits in the classroom.

In the article [14], a framework is presented for the creation of educational chatbots, and an example of their actual application is given to assist young people in gaining knowledge about the many elements that make up urban ecosystems. The findings of the polls indicate that both students and teachers have a favorable perception of the same subject matter.

8.2.2   Healthcare Domain Chatbots

In the healthcare field, there have been reports of research being done using chatbots in an effort to satisfy the requirements of both patients and medical professionals. The sanative chatbot system that was described by Manoj Kumar *et al.* in Ref. [15] is one option for patients to consult when they have questions regarding their therapy. This system places a high priority on delivering pertinent answers to those who are looking for medical help. To do this, it employs a method that mines medical data utilizing both local and worldwide perspectives. In order for this system to offer effective answers to users, user queries need to contain the right medical terminology.

In the article, the author provides in-depth instructions on how to create a chatbot that might be of use to medical students. In order to construct Medchatbot, we relied on the chatbot architecture provided by AIML, and we used the Unified Medical Language System as our primary source of domain knowledge. If MedChatBot were incorporated into a tutoring system, it would make it possible for tutors and students to conduct talks that are more natural.

A chatbot known as Pharmabot: A Pediatric Generic Medicine Consultant was developed by the people behind. This chatbot might potentially serve as a consultant pharmacist and recommend generic pharmaceuticals for children that are suitable, acceptable, and risk-free based on the information provided by the user. The user has to provide some data in order for this functionality to work properly.

8.2.3   E-Commerce Applications

Customers may have a tough time rapidly zeroing in on what they are seeking for since online retailers sometimes supply multiple items, each of which comes with its own set of specifications. The writers of Ref. [7] explain in detail how to develop a chatbot that will improve the overall experience that consumers have when they purchase online. The customer is better able to pick what to buy and the process of making the purchase is streamlined as a result of their brief discussion with the bot. The chatbot makes use of Rivescript in order to get responses to questions posed by users in response to their input.

In addition, Ref. [16] talks about a chatbot called SuperAgent, which was designed especially for online shops. In order to collect huge volumes of e-commerce data, SuperAgent will "crawl" the HTML product pages that are located on the website. An FAQ search engine, a Fact QA module for collecting product facts, a client-ratings-management-focused text QA engine, and a chit-chat engine for replying to inquiries about greetings are the four engines that make up this agent. The Fact QA module gathers product facts.

A chatbot was developed by Amir and his colleagues with the intention of facilitating the sale of products on the internet with little involvement from real people. The consumer provides the chatbot with information, the chatbot evaluates that input to identify who the customer is as a demographic, and then the chatbot uses those data to provide the customer with offers that are specific to them. The WooCommerce platform and the Telegram API both provide information that was already available when this solution was developed.

Another attempt was made by Hemin Joshi and colleagues, who, in Ref. [17], introduced a Cartbot-based e-commerce engine that helps users make and manage purchases made on the site. This was yet another effort that was made. A mobile app for Android smartphones is one component of Cartbot's three-tiered architecture, which also includes a smart agent and an e-commerce engine. Cartbot is an intelligent agent that makes it easier for customers to engage with the engine that powers an online business.

8.2.4   Customer Support

Since the introduction of chatbots into the customer relationship management (CRM) industry, there has been a significant shift in the manner in which companies provide customer care. The authors show how successful the chatbot system is in an automated online customer care environment in the article that they authored [18]. This service provides a greater level of customer satisfaction at lower costs and improved efficiency as a result of a team of intelligent agents based on the AIML programming language. Instead, the authors discuss the possible benefits of using internet-based intelligent agents in customer relationship management [19] (e-CRM). In this piece, we will provide a unified model that we propose to explain how intelligent agents may be used to carry out e-customer relationship management. According to the findings of this study, customer relationship management (CRM) will depend much more on the use of intelligent agents in the not-too-distant future.

The authors of Ref. [20] provide an explanation of how a chatbot may act as a domain-specific information system and present experiments on how to boost accuracy in this respect. The ALICE chatbot served as the basis for the development of the University FAQbot, which was designed to provide assistance to first-year students at the university's information desk. The chatbot has to be able to comprehend the natural language being used by the user, be able to search for information that is relevant to the inquiry, and then respond in the same natural language being used by the user.

Xu et al. [21] have developed a social media conversational agent by using techniques from the field of deep learning. These techniques include long short-term memory (LSTM), sequence to sequence learning, and word embeddings. It is essential to reference this term in your paper. After LSTM has produced a vector representation of the customer's inquiry, it is then able to start providing a response to the question. In order to train the algorithm, 1.6 million tweets were taken from over 160 different companies. The research presented in Ref. [22] demonstrates a method that may be used to develop chatbots as interactive support systems for significant commercial business applications such as e-governance systems. This method has the potential to be used in big commercial business applications. An electronic governance system (IEGS) prototype that already exists is combined with an artificial support entity (ASE). An AIML-based chatbot engine was introduced by the developers so that users of a business program who are not technically savvy would have an easier time using the platform's functionalities.

8.3   Security and Privacy in Chatbot

Data integrity, availability, and confidentiality are the three main security goals that were stated by the National Institute of Standards and Technology (NIST). In order to accomplish these objectives, several mechanisms, including as encryption, authentication, key management, and access control, are used. On the other hand, the security needs for assets connected to the Chatbots are as follows:

1. Confidentiality: The protection of users' personal information is given a high priority in chatbots so that information may flow freely between users. Although TLS [12] and IPsec [13] are used in the transmission of data over the internet, the overall cost of implementing them in IoT systems is prohibitively expensive due to the latter's resource limitations. The most sensitive sections, on the other hand, are those that include identity, communication, storage, and location/tracking [14].

2. Data Integrity: When data are being sent, having its integrity checked guarantees that it will not be altered in any way or become corrupted. In wireless media and network architectures, LLNs are responsible for making large-scale data errors, which data-modification attackers then employ to their advantage. If a checksum or message integrity code (MIC) is included in a packet, the integrity of the packet may be verified and guaranteed [15].

3. Availability: The capacity of a computer or the whole system to provide information and resources when there is a pressing need is what is meant by the phrase "disposability." When there are limited computers and local area networks (LLNs) on a network, it might be difficult to announce their existence. It accomplishes its goals by lending a hand in the conduct of network assaults such as denial of service. Network availability is decreased when more strong security measures are implemented, such as traditional security methods. These procedures are used to increase network and device security. The high overheads that these approaches impose on the constrained devices result in delays in contact, calculation time, transfer time, and battery depletion; all of these factors have an effect on the availability of the network.

4. Authenticity: Objects that involve or interact with humans need to have legal permission to do so and cannot be given access to the property of unauthorized persons; authentication is meant to confirm that the communicating parties are the same. Objects that involve or interact with humans need to have legal permission to do so.

Various security threats in chatbot are shown below in Figure 8.3.

Security Threats
DDOS Attack
Phishing Attack
Man in the Middle Attack
Replay Attack
Sinkhole Attack
Warmhole Attack
Spoofing Attack
Node Jamming Attack
Sybil Attack

Figure 8.3 Security threats.

8.4   Related Work

An improved version of the back propagation (BP) approach is implemented in the cloud-based intrusion detection model that Sun *et al.* developed [23]. This model is the outcome of combining the abilities of the BP algorithm, which are focused on local search, with the PSO algorithm, which are geared toward global optimization. Within the context of momentum and adaptive learning rate, we provide a PSO approach as a means of optimizing the value of BP's initial weight and threshold in order to get the best possible result. As a consequence of this, there is a much-reduced risk of the BP being mired in routine, and the amount of time required for network convergence may be maximized. According to the findings of the research, the proposed model may be used to identify cloud-based intrusions, and it also has a higher average detection rate than other models.

A neural network classifier and key feature selection are used in the network intrusion detection system developed by Seth *et al.* [5]. The binary Grey Wolf Optimization (GWO) algorithm is utilized for key feature selection. Any strategically important node in the network would be an excellent location for the IDS installation. You may be able to rid your dataset of unnecessary characteristics by using GWO. This will, in turn, decrease the size of your dataset, which will, in turn, reduce the amount of time and space required to train your classifier. When doing simulations using the NSL-KDD dataset, we discovered that making use of a feature set that was more condensed resulted in an improvement in the accuracy of the intrusion detection technique.

In 2016, Jaiswal *et al.* [24] were successful in increasing the efficiency of intrusion detection by using a data mining strategy. This allowed them to better protect their network. The activities of the user are monitored by the IDS, which notifies the administrator of any potentially harmful or suspicious behavior. We identify the various invasion types with the help of the KDD Cup dataset, and then we train a KNN classifier to recognize invaders using the ACO method. Measurements are taken to determine how accurate the simulated data are, and a performance indicator known as the false alarm rate (FAR) is computed. This method generates findings that are more accurate than the standard practice that is already in place. These practices are typically recognized as the gold standard in their respective professions. CS is necessary for this position, and it has been shown that CSFCS is a strategy that is both practical and flexible for developing CS.

Principal component analysis was used by Ahmad *et al.* [25] with the intention of reducing the number of characteristics that were deemed to be significant. Following the projection of the characteristics into an eigen space, the characteristics with the highest deviations were selected for further study. Using features with a lower eigen value is one way to increase the sensitivity of a classifier; nevertheless, even if this is done, the features with the highest eigen value will still be used (i.e., eigen values). An optimization strategy is required rather than just picking the features that have the greatest eigen values if the goal is to determine which features, despite being altered, retain the majority of their original characteristics. This is owing to the fact that there is an element of optimization involved in the process of selecting the set of transformed characteristics that ideally isolates the item that is the focus of the study. The genetic algorithm, sometimes known as the GA, is a technique of evolutionary optimization that has been researched for its ability to optimize certain features in order to achieve greater differentiation. Another type of optimization is known as particle swarm optimization, or PSO for short. This type of optimization gets its inspiration from research on the behavior of animals and birds. There are situations when the benefits of PSO are more considerable than those of GA.

Tabatabaefar *et al.* [26] advocate producing two sets of antibodies, one positive and one negative, to differentiate between normal and assault samples as part of their proposal for an AIS-based intrusion detection system. These antibodies would be used to identify abnormal samples. These antibodies would be used in order to differentiate between the two different types of samples. This method speeds up the production of primary detectors by applying the concepts of positive selection and negative selection to the manufacturing process. The conclusion that can be drawn from this is that the detection rate can be enhanced by training state-of-the-art detectors using PSO, which is an older method. In a similar manner, the algorithms that are responsible for producing and training antibodies are continuously building the radii of those antibodies. According to the results of the simulations, the recently created approach achieves a true positive rate of 99.1% while simultaneously maintaining a false positive rate of only 1.9%.

Taking use of the periodicity, volatility, and sensitivity to initial conditions that the chaos operator has, Yang *et al.* [27] have created an improved version of the IPSO approach, which is shorthand for the particle swarm optimization. The particle swarm optimization technique is used to find the optimal values for the penalty factor C and the RBF kernel function parameter g (PSO). As a direct consequence of this, convergence and accuracy are both enhanced. Experiments have shown that the IPSO-SVM intrusion detection model is superior to both the PSO-SVM and the GA-SVM approaches in terms of its overall effectiveness. This assertion is backed up by the higher performance of IPSO-superiority SVMs when compared to both of these models.

Hosseini *et al.* [28] propose a DoS attack intrusion detection system that is based on support vector regression. They also explore how the system may be enhanced by integrating two more methodologies, such as an ant colony and a firefly, respectively. Detailed instructions on how to accomplish this goal are provided. Hosseini and his colleagues emphasize the usefulness of a support vector regression-based intrusion detection system for identifying denial-of-service assaults (2015). It is possible that removing random variables from the equation will make the firefly technique more effective in general. This is due to the fact that the firefly method uses a local search to direct the ants. Utilizing the KDD Cup 99 assessment technique, an exhaustive analysis of the performance of the intrusion detection system was carried out. Our crew has selected 9 of the original 41 available rental homes to look into further. The approach that was recommended has a detection error rate that is just 0.0064%, and it has a success rate of 99.57%.

Kulshestha *et al.* [29] provide an innovative strategy with the intention of finding which feature subset and classifier function most effectively with a particular dataset. If the issue were important enough, the scope of the area in which a solution might be located would need to be rather large. The justification for this may be found in the phrase that comes before this one. The search made use of a powerful meta-heuristic technique called the cuckoo search CS method in order to choose a feature subset and classifier that minimize the dimensionality of the feature vector as well as the rate of classification error. This was done in order to find the optimal solution. By carrying out these steps, we intend to locate the most effective feature subset as well as classifier. Because it improves classification accuracy with a smaller collection of features, the CSFCS has been validated and shown to be correct using a wide variety of datasets. This was done to demonstrate that it is accurate. It was shown that CSFCS has the potential to be used in the manufacturing of CS. It is not necessary to have a complete collection of functions since CSFCS may be simply modified to fulfill certain demands.

A novel method of intrusion detection based on augmented K-means has been developed by Zhao *et al.* [30] in order to meet the one-of-a-kind characteristics of cloud computing as well as the different security needs of the cloud. This idea may be put to use in the development of a clustering algorithm as well as a technique for the widespread detection of intrusions into computer systems. It is able to identify assaults on cloud servers, both those that are predicted and those that are unforeseen. According to the findings of the simulation, using this strategy might potentially hasten the process of intrusion detection while at the same time reducing the rates of both false positives and false negatives.

A strategy that combines data mining with rough sets was presented by Chen *et al.* [31] as a way to improve the detection effectiveness of intrusion detection while simultaneously reducing the number of false alarms that are generated. Comparisons were made between this method of intrusion detection and other traditional ones. After the data have been collected, the first step after that is to organize it, then the values of the obtained variables are normalized, and lastly the nominal variables are processed in a discrete way. In this section, we will discuss how the attributes of the final result set may be used in the Pawlak attribute weight rough set technique to carry out an attribute reduction in a manner that is similar to that of the property up and down approximation set. After attribute reduction has been finished, these rules may be imported into the rule set so that they can be used to generate association rules with a high level of confidence. Experiments show that the detection strategy that utilizes rough sets in conjunction with data mining results in an improvement in detection performance of around 20%. The rate at which new invasions are discovered approximately proportionally grows linearly with the overall number of invasions.

Methods are similar to those that were devised and implemented by Jing *et al.* [32] in order to detect network intrusions. In order to do this, they make use of a constrained Boltzmann machine that has been trained on a suitable deep learning model. Previous research in the subject was examined by our team so that we could determine whether or not it is feasible to use deep learning to network IDS. The technology that is used to identify breaches in a network is now undergoing development to make it more effective via the use of relevance depth learning. The findings of the simulation provide credence to a relevance-based approach to the detection of intrusions in computer networks. Deep learning beats conventional approaches in terms of the average detection rate as well as the rate of false positives when it comes to identifying previously unnoticed intrusions and assaults. Specifically, the average detection rate is lower for assaults and intrusions whose source cannot be determined. The results of the experiments provide evidence that supports the claims made about the robustness and effectiveness of the recently introduced methodology.

The method known as Two Layers Multi-class Detection (TLMD) was used by Yuan *et al.* [33] in order to locate intrusions in adaptive networks. When combined with the C5.0 methodology and the Naive Bayes algorithm, this method enhances the detection rate while simultaneously lowering the number of false alarms. When it comes to data mining, each issue has its own unique challenges, but the TLMD strategy is effective in resolving all of them. Dealing with contiguous features is one of these issues. This issue occurs as a result of the need to cut down on the amount of noise in the training dataset. This challenging situation can be handled by the process. We assess the state-of-the-art algorithms against the recently developed TLMD method by using the detection rate, accuracy, and false alarm rate on the KDD Cup99 benchmark dataset for intrusion detection. This dataset serves as a standard for the detection of intrusions. The innovative TLMD approach seems to still have a low false alarm rate while being applied to an unbalanced dataset, while also having a high detection rate. This is still the case despite the fact that the dataset has certain imbalances in it. This conclusion is consistent with all of the evidence that is currently available.

A risk-based warning prioritization technique was used by Chakir *et al.* [34] while they were carrying out their research. It is possible for the model to determine the severity of the warning based on decision variables such as priority, reliability, and asset value indicators. This improves the capabilities of snort's intrusion detection and guarantees that the security administrator only gets alerts that indicate a true danger. This results in a reduction in both the amount of time spent analyzing false positives and the number of false positives generated. The objective is to prioritize the IDS alerts based on the level of threat they represent to the integrity of the system as a whole. In light of this information, we are in a position to evaluate the significance of each individual IDS alert to the integrity of the system as a whole. When evaluating the model, we use a pattern-matching strategy and utilize the KDD Cup 99 Dataset as our source of information.

Gaikwad *et al.* [35] have developed an innovative intrusion detection system by making use of a technique that is known as ensemble machine learning. Using the Bagging technique of ensembles might prove to be highly beneficial while developing IDS. The REP Tree is used as the foundation for this approach's base class. If the appropriate attributes are selected from the NSL KDD dataset, it is possible to improve classification accuracy while simultaneously reducing the number of false positives. When determining whether or not the new ensemble strategy is successful, many aspects of classification accuracy, the length of time required for model training, and the total number of false positives are taken into consideration. When put into practice, the Bagging ensemble performs mostly well when a REP Tree base class is used. The time necessary to generate the model may be cut down using the Bagging approach, which is one of the possible advantages of using that method. When compared to other approaches to machine learning, the ensemble method delivers an astoundingly low proportion of false positives.

The whole AI community collaborated to produce the KDD Cup 99 dataset, which was then used by Kim *et al.* in their study [36] in order to develop a neural network intrusion detection system using deep learning (DNN IDS). This was done in order to be ready for the future, since the tactics used to attack a network are always evolving over time. It is necessary to clean, convert, and normalize the data in some way before putting it into the DNN model. During the preparation step, the data are initially cleaned before being processed for the analysis stage. When the model is finally constructed, a process referred to as "learning model construction" takes place, during which the DNN technique is applied to the data. In the last step, the performance of the model is evaluated using the whole dataset from the KDD Cup 99. In the end, the accuracy, detection rate, and false alarm rate of the DNN model were calculated in order to determine its detection efficacy. The DNN model has been demonstrated to produce positive results in the field of intrusion detection, and this was ultimately how its detection efficacy was determined. The purpose of this was to evaluate the performance of the detecting system; therefore, it was done.

8.5   Methodology

This article explains how to develop an intrusion detection system by making use of data from chatbots and techniques including machine learning (see Figure 8.4). The NSL KDD data collection is used as its source of input. In order to get started, the CFS-correlation feature selection method is used in the NSL KDD dataset. This method is what is utilized to whittle down the features to just those that are really helpful. The NSL KDD dataset is composed of a total of 41 features. Through the use of the CFS approach, we were able to reduce the number of features to only 8. The malicious software data stored in NSL KDD are categorized and forecasted with the use of machine learning algorithms that are given these 16 criteria.

This is an important attribute-based feature selection evaluation since it takes into account both the features' individual benefits and the degree to which they share similarities

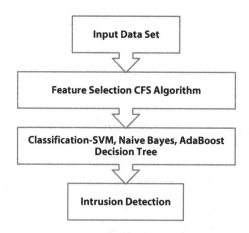

Figure 8.4 Machine learning techniques for design of intrusion detection system for chatbots.

with other options. It is standard procedure [37] to choose qualities that have a strong relationship to the category but a lesser link to each other.

In this section, we will discuss the challenges that come with regression and classification. For the purpose of data classification, SVM searches for and generates a hyperplane, which is a line that divides the data used for training into various groups. After the construction of the hyperplane, which increases the distance that separates the classes, the likelihood of generalizing data that were previously hidden has risen. The SVM is currently the classification technique that is considered to have the highest level of precision in terms of accuracy. As a direct result of this, there is not an overwhelming quantity of data to go through.

When utilizing SVM, no assumptions that are dependent on the data are made (least squares support vector machine), demonstrating that there is a way to improve the effectiveness of data classification in the long term. The two most common types of SVMs are the linear and the non-linear variants. Data that have been organized linearly may be represented on a hyperplane [38].

The theorem of Bayes is the cornerstone of the Bayesian approach to categorization and investigation. The Naive Bayesian Classification techniques, when applied to fundamental bases such as end trees and selected networks, make it feasible to classify enormous datasets. It is possible to utilize the Naive Bayes classification method to express a limited set of features that are reliant on one another. It is possible to calculate the posterior probability of each class by using this procedure. In this study, the academic group that shows the highest potential is used as a standard for measuring achievement.

$$P(c|x) = \frac{P(x|c)P(c)}{P(x)} \tag{8.1}$$

where $P(c|x)$ is the posterior probability of each class given diabetes × attribute

$P(x|c)$ is the likelihood value

$P(c)$ is the prior probability of diabetes class

$P(x)$ is the prior probability of predictor

Each attribute conditionally forgives the subset class

A similar strategy is used by Naive Bayes to predict multiple sorts of probabilities based on various attributes [39].

If the relevance of a particular instance in the dataset is decided by the classifier's prior judgments on comparable cases, then Adaboost's decision tree [40] employs a weighted dataset for each base classification. If they get it wrong when categorizing an instance, then that instance will carry greater weight in succeeding models; however, if they get it correctly, then it will have the same weight as any other instance.

The ultimate conclusion is reached through weighted voting of the fundamental classification, which is decided by the model's weight, which is determined by the misjudgment rate.

$$w_n(x) = sign\left(\sum_{i=1}^{n} \alpha_n w_n(x) \right) \tag{8.2}$$

If the model has a higher classification accuracy, it gets a low weight. If it has a poor classification accuracy, it gets the highest weight. $w_n(x)$ refers to output classifier.

8.6   Results and Discussion

NSL-KDD is designed to fulfill the responsibilities of the cup dataset (KDD99) [41] because of the extensive and current nature of the information it contains. Because the testing data in the NSL-KDD dataset do not include any outliers, the accuracy of the classifier is certain to increase as a direct consequence of this fact. The version of NSL-KDD that is made accessible to the general public may be used by researchers without restriction on their part. There are a total of 41 separate components that make up the whole. Within the NSL-KDD dataset, there are a total of 25,192 test records in addition to 8040 training data test records (100,781 records). In the beginning, we use CFS to determine which characteristics are the most beneficial. The next step consists of naming eight distinguishing features, instances of duplication in the data used for training, and duplicates in the database itself. Table 8.1 shows the eight distinguishing features.

For performance comparison, three parameters, accuracy, sensitivity, and specificity, are used.

Accuracy   = (TP + TN)/(TP + TN + FP + FN)
Sensitivity = TP/(TP + FN)
Specificity = TN/(TN + FP)

Table 8.1 Features selected using the CFS algorithm.

CFS – Best First Search Features
Flag
src_bytes
dst_bytes
Count
srv_serror rate
same_srv_rate
Diff_serv_rate
dst_host_srv_diff_host_rate

where
- TP = True Positive
- TN = True Negative
- FP = False Positive
- FN = False Negative

Results of different machine learning predictors are shown below in Figures 8.5, 8.6, and 8.7. The accuracy of LS SVM is better than that of Naive Bayes and Adaboost algorithms.

This is yet another issue [42, 43] raised by the use of chatbots [44, 45] in hacking [46, 47]. As Educational business rivalry [48, 49] intensifies, it may become necessary to use a chatbot (better known as an "evil bot") [50, 51] to damage the reputation of the competitor in the sector. Tay, a chatbot, was created to imitate users and have real-time conversations with them. Tay, a Twitter bot, was referred to as a conversational understanding experiment. Microsoft claims that Tay becomes more intelligent the more you converse with it.

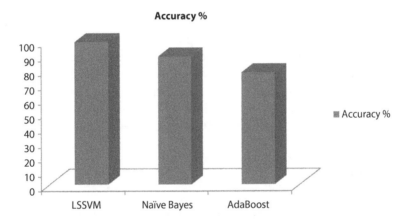

Figure 8.5 Accuracy of machine learning techniques for classification and prediction of the NSL KDD dataset.

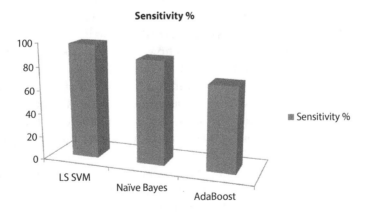

Figure 8.6 Sensitivity of machine learning techniques for classification and prediction of the NSL KDD dataset.

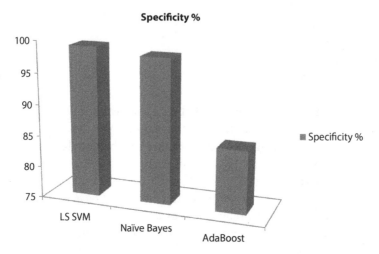

Figure 8.7 Specificity of machine learning techniques for classification and prediction of the NSL KDD dataset.

The bot, however, fell short of expectations and proved to be a blunderbot [52] with offensive language that was both racist and anti-Semitic [53]. There is no doubt that chatbots might be an effective proxy for carrying out cyberattacks [54–57] since they mimic human dialogue. A chatbot on the company's website can be manipulated and managed if a hacker [58] manages to gain control of it. Therefore, the bot would respond with irrelevant [59, 60] information whenever someone interacted with it about questions or information.

8.7   Conclusion

A chatbot is a computer program that is powered by artificial intelligence and is capable of carrying on an intelligent conversation with one or more human users at any time and from any place. It is also known as a chatterbot or a conversational agent. They are computer programs that work in a manner analogous to that of humans in the sense that they are able to grasp and respond to input in natural language. As a result of recent developments in artificial intelligence (AI), it is now possible to write computer programs that can solve issues in a way that is analogous to how humans think about such problems. Researchers in the area of artificial intelligence (AI) have discovered that chatbots, which use cutting-edge AI algorithms to aid users in locating information and accomplishing tasks, are an essential component of the field as a whole. There is not a single sector that does not have at least one company that uses chatbots to handle customer service concerns. This results in higher output as well as a reduction in the costs associated with overhead, which frees up human labor that can be used for other reasons. The benefits that a chatbot may provide to a corporation extend well beyond its use in providing customer service. It may be used for a variety of purposes, including the production of leads and the nurturing of leads. They could be pre-programmed to automatically do tasks like grocery shopping, booking hotels, and arranging meetings, among other things. The creative workforce of the future may be used in a number of non-traditional situations, such as simulated teaching, product sales, and information desks in enormous libraries, among other possible applications. Concerns about security must be answered before businesses will be able to employ chatbots on a widespread scale. Distributed denial of service attacks (also known as DDoS attacks), man-in-the-middle attacks (also known as MITM attacks), and other types of assaults may be launched against chatbot security. Intrusion detection is essential to the protection of users' privacy, as well as the safety and accessibility of conversations that include bots.

References

1. Lokman, A. and Zain, J.M., One-match and all-match categories for keywords matching in Chatbot. *Am. J. Appl. Sci.*, 7, 1406–1411, Oct 2010.
2. A, S. and John, D., Survey on chatbot design techniques in speech conversation systems. *Int. J. Adv. Comput. Sci. Appl.*, 6, 72–80, Oct 2015.
3. Hettige, B. and Karunananda, A.S., First sinhala chatbot in action, in: *Proceedings of the 3rd Annual Sessions of Sri Lanka Association for Artificial Intelligence (SLAAI)*, no. September, pp. 4–10, 2006.
4. Jia, J., CSIEC: A computer assisted English learning chatbot based on textual knowledge and reasoning. *Knowledge-Based Systems-ELSEVIER*, 22, 4, 249–255, 2009.
5. Raghuvanshi, A., Singh, U.K., Panse, Dr. P., Saxena, M., A taxonomy of various building blocks of Internet of Things. *Int. J. Future Gener. Commun. Netw.*, 13, 4, 4397–4404, 2020.
6. Raghuvanshi, A., Singh, U.K., Bulla, C., Saxena, Dr. M., Abadar, K., An investigation on detection of vulnerabilities in Internet of Things. *Eur. J. Mol. Clin. Med.*, 07, 10, 3289–3299, 2020.
7. Raghuvanshi, A., Singh, Dr. U. K., Panse, P., Saxena, M., Veluri, R.K., Internet of Things: Taxonomy of various attacks. *Eur. J. Mol. Clin. Med.*, 7, 10, 3853–3864, 2020.
8. Raghuvanshi, A., Singh, U., Kassanuk, T., Phasinam, K., Internet of Things: Security vulnerabilities and countermeasures. *ECS Trans.*, 107, 1, 15043–15052, 2022, Available: 10.1149/10701.15043ecst.
9. Soliman, M. and Guetl, C., Implementing intelligent pedagogical agents in virtual worlds: Tutoring natural science experiments in OpenWonderland, in: *IEEE Global Engineering Education Conference (EDUCON)*, IEEE, pp. 782–789, mar 2013.
10. Huang, Y.-T., Yang, J.-C., Wu, Y.-C., The development and evaluation of English dialogue companion system, in: *Eighth IEEE International Conference on Advanced Learning Technologies*, IEEE, p. 864–868, 2008.
11. Fei, Y. and Petrina, S., Using learning analytics to understand the design of an intelligent language tutor - Chatbot Lucy. *Int. J. Adv. Comput. Sci. Appl.*, 4, 11, 124–131, 2013.
12. Rodriguez, E., Burguillo, J.C., Rodriguez, D.A., Mikic, F.A., Gonzalez-Moreno, J., Novegil, V., Developing virtual teaching assistants for open e-learning platforms, in: *19th EAEEIE Annual Conference*, IEEE, pp. 193–198, Jun 2008.
13. Dyke, G., Adamson, D., Howley, I., Rose, C.P., Enhancing scientific reasoning and discussion with conversational agents. *IEEE Trans. Learn. Technol.*, 6, 240–247, Jul 2013.
14. Griol, D. and Callejas, Z., An architecture to develop multimodal educative applications with chatbots. *Int. J. Adv. Robotic Syst.*, 10, 1, 2013.
15. Kumar, V. and Keerthana, A., Sanative chatbot for health seekers. *Int. J. of Eng. and Comput. Sci.*, 05, 16022, 16022–16025, 2016.

16. Cui, L., Huang, S., Wei, F., Tan, C., Duan, C., Zhou, M., Super agent: A customer service chatbot for ecommerce websites, in: *Proceedings of ACL 2017, System Demonstrations*, Association for Computational Linguistics, Stroudsburg, PA, USA, pp. 97–102, 2017.

17. Joshi, H., Proposal of chat based automated system for online shopping. *Am. J. Neural Netw. Appl.*, 3, 1, 1, 2017.

18. Kulathunge, C.J., Seneviratne, R. S. M. M. S., Kasthuriarachchi, K.K.J., Perera, B.H.S.H., Automated online customer care system using artificial intelligence. *PNCTM*, 3, 74–78, 2014.

19. Pani, A.K. and Venugopal, P., Implementing e-CRM using intelligent agents on the internet, in: *2008 International Conference on Service Systems and Service Management*, IEEE, pp. 1–6, Jun 2008.

20. Ghose, S. and Barua, J.J., Toward the implementation of a topic specific dialogue based natural language chatbot as an undergraduate advisor, in: *2013 International Conference on Informatics, Electronics and Vision (ICIEV)*, IEEE, pp. 1–5, May 2013.

21. Xu, A., Liu, Z., Guo, Y., Sinha, V., Akkiraju, R., A new chatbot for customer service on social media, in: *Proceedings of the 2017 CHI Conference on Human Factors in Computing Systems - CHI '17*, ACM Press, New York, New York, USA, pp. 3506–3510, 2017.

22. Mahapatra, R.P., Sharma, N., Trivedi, A., Aman, C., Adding interactive interface to E-Government systems using AIML based chatterbots, in: *2012 CSI Sixth International Conference on Software Engineering (CONSEG)*, IEEE, pp. 1–6, Sep 2012.

23. Sun, H., Improved BP algorithm intrusion detection model based on KVM. *IEEE International Conference on Software Engineering and Service Science (ICSESS)*, pp. 442–445, 2016.

24. Jaiswal, S., Saxena, K., Mishra, A., Sahu, S.K., A KNN-ACO approach for intrusion detection using KDDCUP'99 dataset. *IEEE International Conference on Computing for Sustainable Global Development (INDIACom)*, pp. 628–633, 2016.

25. Ahmad, I. and Amin, F., Towards feature subset selection in intrusion detection. *IEEE Joint International Information Technology and Artificial Intelligence Conference*, pp. 68–73, 2014.

26. Tabatabaefar, M., Miriestahbanati, M., Grégoire, J.C., Network intrusion detection through artificial immune system. *IEEE International Systems Conference (SysCon)*, pp. 1–6, 2017.

27. Yang, Q., Fu, H., Zhu, T., An optimization method for parameters of SVM in network intrusion detection system. *IEEE International Conference on Distributed Computing in Sensor Systems (DCOSS)*, pp. 136–142, 2016.

28. Hosseini, Z.S., Chabok, S.J.S.M., Kamel, S.R., DOS intrusion attack detection by using of improved SVR. *IEEE International Congress on Technology, Communication and Knowledge (ICTCK)*, pp. 159–164, 2015.

29. Kulshestha, G., Agarwal, A., Mittal, A., Sahoo, A., Hybrid cuckoo search algorithm for simultaneous feature and classifier selection. *IEEE International Conference on Cognitive Computing and Information Processing (CCIP)*, pp. 1–6, 2015.

30. Zhao, X. and Zhang, W., An anomaly intrusion detection method based on improved k-means of cloud computing. *IEEE International Conference on Instrumentation & Measurement, Computer, Communication and Control (IMCCC)*, pp. 284–288, 2016.

31. Chen, C., Zhou, H., Wu, W., Shen, G., An intrusion detection method combined rough sets and data mining. *IEEE International Conference on Computer Science and Service System (CSSS)*, pp. 1091–1094, 2011.

32. Jing, L. and Bin, W., Network intrusion detection method based on relevance deep learning. *IEEE International Conference on Intelligent Transportation, Big Data & Smart City (ICITBS)*, pp. 237–240, 2016.

33. Yuan, Y., Huo, L., Hogrefe, D., Two layers multi-class detection method for network intrusion detection system. *IEEE Symposium on Computers and Communications (ISCC)*, pp. 767–772, 2017.

34. Chakir, E.M., Moughit, M., Khamlichi, Y.I., An efficient method for evaluating alerts of intrusion detection systems. *IEEE International Conference on Wireless Technologies, Embedded and Intelligent Systems (WITS)*, pp. 1–6, 2017.

35. Gaikwad, D.P. and Thool, R.C., Intrusion detection system using bagging ensemble method of machine learning. *IEEE International Conference on Computing Communication Control and Automation*, pp. 291–295, 2015.

36. Kim, J., Shin, N., Jo, S.Y., Kim, S.H., Method of intrusion detection using deep neural network. *IEEE International Conference on Big Data and Smart Computing (BigComp)*, pp. 313–316, 2017.

37. Aggarwal, M., Performance analysis of different feature selection methods in intrusion detection. *Int. J. Sci. Technol. Res.*, 2.6, 225–231, 2013.

38. Kabir, M.E. and Hu, J., A statistical framework for intrusion detection system. *2014 11th International Conference on Fuzzy Systems and Knowledge Discovery (FSKD)*, pp. 941–946, 2014. doi: 10.1109/FSKD.2014.6980966.

39. Shen, Z., Zhang, Y., Chen, W., A Bayesian classification intrusion detection method based on the fusion of PCA and LDA. *Secur. Commun. Netw.*, 2019, 1–11, 2019. Available: 10.1155/2019/6346708.

40. Raghuvanshi, A., Singh, U., Sajja, G., Pallathadka, H., Asenso, E., Kamal, M. *et al.*, Intrusion detection using machine learning for risk mitigation in IoT-enabled smart irrigation in smart farming. *J. of Food Qual.*, 2022, 1–8, 2022. doi: 10.1155/2022/3955514.

41. Revathi, S. and Malathi, D.S., A detailed analysis on NSL-KDD dataset using various machine learning techniques for intrusion detection. *Int. J. Eng. Res. Technol. (IJERT)*, 2, 12, 1848–1853, December 2013.

42. Mahor, V., Bijrothiya, S., Rawat, R., Kumar, A., Garg, B., Pachlasiya, K., IoT and artificial intelligence techniques for public safety and security, in: *Smart Urban Computing Applications*, p. 111, 2023.

43. Mahor, V., Pachlasiya, K., Garg, B., Chouhan, M., Telang, S., Rawat, R., Mobile operating system (Android) vulnerability analysis using machine learning, in: *Proceedings of International Conference on Network Security and Blockchain Technology: ICNSBT 2021*, pp. 159–169, Springer Nature Singapore, Singapore, 2022, June.

44. Rawat, R., Garg, B., Pachlasiya, K., Mahor, V., Telang, S., Chouhan, M., Mishra, R., SCNTA: Monitoring of network availability and activity for identification of anomalies using machine learning approaches. *Int. J. Inf. Technol. Web Eng. (IJITWE)*, 17, 1, 1–19, 2022.

45. Rawat, R., Rimal, Y.N., William, P., Dahima, S., Gupta, S., Sankaran, K.S., Malware threat affecting financial organization analysis using machine learning approach. *Int. J. Inf. Technol. Web Eng. (IJITWE)*, 17, 1, 1–20, 2022.

46. Rawat, R., Mahor, V., Chouhan, M., Pachlasiya, K., Telang, S., Garg, B., Systematic literature review (SLR) on social media and the digital transformation of drug trafficking on darkweb, in: *International Conference on Network Security and Blockchain Technology*, pp. 181–205, Springer, Singapore, 2022.

47. Rawat, R., Ayodele Oki, O., Sankaran, S., Florez, H., Ajagbe, S.A., Techniques for predicting dark web events focused on the delivery of illicit products and ordered crime. *Int. J. Electr. Comput. Eng. (IJECE)*, 13, 5, 5354–5365, Oct. 2023, doi: 10.11591/ijece.v13i5.pp5354-5365.

48. Rawat, R., Garg, B., Mahor, V., Telang, S., Pachlasiya, K., Chouhan, M., Organ trafficking on the dark web—The data security and privacy concern in healthcare systems, in: *Internet of Healthcare Things: Machine Learning for Security and Privacy*, pp. 189–216, 2022.

49. Vyas, P., Vyas, G., Chauhan, A., Rawat, R., Telang, S., Gottumukkala, M., Anonymous trading on the dark online marketplace: An exploratory study, in: *Using Computational Intelligence for the Dark Web and Illicit Behavior Detection*, pp. 272–289, IGI Global, 2022.

50. Rawat, R., Oki, O.A., Sankaran, K.S., Olasupo, O., Ebong, G.N., Ajagbe, S.A., A new solution for cyber security in big data using machine learning approach, in: *Mobile Computing and Sustainable Informatics: Proceedings of ICMCSI 2023*, pp. 495–505, Springer Nature Singapore, Singapore, 2023.

51. Rawat, R., Chakrawarti, R.K., Raj, A., Mani, G., Chidambarathanu, K., Bhardwaj, R., Association rule learning for threat analysis using traffic analysis and packet filtering approach. *Int. J. Inf. Technol.*, 1–11, 2023.

52. Rawat, R., Logical concept mapping and social media analytics relating to cyber criminal activities for ontology creation. *Int. J. Inf. Technol.*, 15, 2, 893–903, 2023.

53. Rawat, R., Mahor, V., Álvarez, J.D., Ch, F., Cognitive systems for dark web cyber delinquent association malignant data crawling: A review, in: *Handbook of Research on War Policies, Strategies, and Cyber Wars*, pp. 45–63, 2023.

54. Rawat, R., Chakrawarti, R.K., Vyas, P., Gonzáles, J.L.A., Sikarwar, R., Bhardwaj, R., Intelligent fog computing surveillance system for crime and vulnerability identification and tracing. *Int. J. Inf. Secur. Priv. (IJISP)*, 17, 1, 1–25, 2023.

55. Rawat, R., Sowjanya, A.M., Patel, S.I., Jaiswal, V., Khan, I., Balaram, A. (Eds.), *Using Machine Intelligence: Autonomous Vehicles Volume 1*, John Wiley & Sons, 2022.

56. Rawat, R., Mahor, V., Díaz-Álvarez, J., Chávez, F., Rooted learning model at fog computing analysis for crime incident surveillance, in: *2022 International Conference on Smart Generation Computing, Communication and Networking (SMART GENCON)*, pp. 1–9, IEEE, 2022, December.

57. Rawat, R. and Shrivastav, S.K., SQL injection attack detection using SVM. *Int. J. Comput. Appl.*, 42, 13, 1–4, 2012.

58. Rawat, R., Bhardwaj, P., Kaur, U., Telang, S., Chouhan, M., Sankaran, K.S., *Smart vehicles for communication, volume 2*, John Wiley & Sons, 2023.

59. Mahor, V., Garg, B., Telang, S., Pachlasiya, K., Chouhan, M., Rawat, R., Cyber threat phylogeny assessment and vulnerabilities representation at thermal power station, in: *Proceedings of International Conference on Network Security and Blockchain Technology: ICNSBT 2021*, pp. 28–39, Springer Nature Singapore, Singapore, 2022, June.

60. Rawat, R., Gupta, S., Sivaranjani, S., Cu, O.K., Kuliha, M., Sankaran, K.S., Malevolent information crawling mechanism for forming structured illegal organisations in hidden networks. *Int. J. Cyber Warf. Terror. (IJCWT)*, 12, 1, 1–14, 2022.

9

Identification of User Preference Using Human–Computer Interaction Technologies and Design of Customized Reporting for Business Analytics Using Ranking Consistency Index

Martin Aruldoss[1]*, Miranda Lakshmi Travis[2] and Prasanna Venkatesan Venkatasamy[3]

[1]Department of Computer Science, Central University of Tamil Nadu, Thiruvarur, Tamil Nadu, India
[2]PG and Research Department of Computer Science, St. Joseph's College (Autonomous), Cuddalore, Tamil Nadu, India
[3]Dept. of Banking Technology, Pondicherry University, Puducherry, India

Abstract

Business intelligence (BI) provides a comprehensive solution for organizations to make better decisions. Reporting is one of the important functionalities of BI, which provides vital information for decision-making. Due to the extreme growth of information, designing customized reporting according to user level and requirement in an organization is the present challenge of the information analysis system. To develop a well-organized customized reporting, user preference with respect to different criteria (conditions) should be identified. Multi-criteria reporting (MCR) is one of the special kinds of customized reporting that customizes the information according to user preference and criteria. In MCR, preference of information differs from one user to another user and it is identified using Multi-Criteria Decision Making (MCDM) techniques. General Fuzzy TOPSIS (GFTOPSIS) is one of the MCDM techniques, and its working procedure consists of a different number of processes. In GFTOPSIS, the decision matrix is normalized using different kinds of normalization techniques. A better normalization technique gives a better ranking order as well as a better-customized user preference for MCR. This research proposes a metric for Ranking Consistency Index (RCI) to identify a better normalization technique and to improve the user preference.

Keywords: Fuzzy TOPSIS, Ranking Consistency Index, Multi-Criteria Decision Making (MCDM), normalization techniques, multi-criteria reporting, Business Intelligence (BI)

9.1 Introduction

The biggest challenge of business analytics is presenting actionable recommendations to the user requirement. A simple reporting strategy would not be sufficient to handle various

---

*Corresponding author: cudmartin@gmail.com; martin@cutn.ac.in

Romil Rawat, Rajesh Kumar Chakrawarti, Sanjaya Kumar Sarangi, Piyush Vyas, Mary Sowjanya Alamanda, Kotagiri Srividya and Krishnan Sakthidasan Sankaran (eds.) *Conversational Artificial Intelligence*, (127–146) © 2024 Scrivener Publishing LLC

reporting requirements of decision-makers [1]. The recent information growth has led to the necessity of different kinds of reporting based on other conflicting criteria emphasized by decision-makers [2]. The need of decision-makers differs due to change in business trends and information sharing in social media. To meet the customer requirement, multiple conflicting information insights are identified from business analytics. Moreover, presenting or reporting relevant information to the suitable user by building, configuring, consolidating, organizing, formatting, and summarizing in a required form at the right time according to the different conflicting requirements is the present challenge of the information analysis system [3, 4].

Multi-criteria reporting (MCR) is a special kind of customized reporting that customizes the information according to user requirements and conflicting user preferences [5–8]. MCR designs multi-criteria reporting based on user preference concerning detailed information for decision-making. Generally, in MCR, user preference is measured in terms of very low, low, high, very high, moderate, etc.

To identify the user preference, Multi-Criteria Decision Making (MCDM) techniques are applied [9, 10]. This research uses Technique for Order of Preference by Similarity to Ideal Solution (TOPSIS), which is one of the widely applied MCDM techniques [11]. However, the user's preference cannot be determined precisely; hence, Generalized Fuzzy TOPSIS (GFTOPSIS) has been applied to identify the user preference [12]. Different processes are involved in GFTOPSIS [13, 14]. One of the essential processes is the application of the normalization technique that improves the accuracy of the results. Generally, Ranking Consistency Index (RCI) is used to identify the better normalization technique for the TOPSIS method. From the literature, it has been determined that there is a specific metric that has been developed for RCI. This research designs metrics for RCI to identify a better normalization technique to apply in TOPSIS and improve customization for MCR.

The rest of the paper is organized as follows. Section 9.2 describes the literature review, section 9.3 designs the metric for Ranking Consistency Index (RCI) to identify a better normalization technique, section 9.4 describes the experimentation of the RCI metric to identify a user preference to develop the customized reporting, section 9.5 discusses the results obtained for customized reporting for normalization techniques, and section 9.6 concludes the paper with research outcomes.

9.2 Literature Review

MCR is a special kind of reporting that customizes the information based on different criteria (condition). For example, requirements such as the interest of communication, level of responsibility, delivery channels, user context, etc., may be considered. These criteria may have different preferences, such as extremely high, high, very low, low, usual, and so on. These preferences may differ from one person to another person in an organization. MCR customizes the information according to the user preference over criteria (Procurement-notices, 2011). Among the different users in an organization, the most preferred user and intentions of other users are identified according to the requirements to customize the information.

To solve these kinds of multi-criteria problems, MCDM techniques can be applied. These techniques assign weight to conflict criteria by comparing them with one another according to their importance. Then, it identifies the best alternative by a ranking process. Many MCDM techniques are available, and one of the most widely applied techniques is TOPSIS. TOPSIS has a more significant number of contributions carried out for its modifications, extensions, and applications. It solves complex and straightforward multi-criteria problems.

The problem-solving nature of GFTOPSIS resembles the rational human choice of solving the problems. Hence, in this research, GFTOPSIS has been applied to rank the users and identify the user preference. Its working procedure consists of a different number of processes. They are a formulation of decision matrix from the alternatives and criteria (Process-I), normalizing the matrix (Process-II), construction of weighted normalized decision matrix (Process-III), determination of fuzzy positive and fuzzy negative ideal solution (Process-IV), and calculation of separation measure (Process-V). The alternatives are ranked from the Relative Closeness Coefficient (RCC) obtained from the separation measure (Process-VI).

One of the essential critical processes in GFTOPSIS is the application of normalization technique (Process-II). Normalization techniques have a more significant impact on the results of the MCDM methods. The effect of normalization techniques concerning certain conditions of consistent choice of alternatives has been validated [15, 16]. The results of GFTOPSIS have been affected by initial values of normalization techniques [17]. The intention of selection of the normalization technique for GFTOPSIS has limited research contribution. Most of the authors have selected the normalization techniques from the literature, and it is applied without stating the reason.

The different kinds of popularly applied normalization techniques that are considered in this research are linear max normalization, vector normalization, linear max–min normalization, linear sum-based normalization, and so on. From the literature, it is evident that to validate the normalization techniques, the parameters such as normalized ratings, quality of transformation, Relative Closeness Coefficient (RCC), consistency of preference value, and relative data gap in different normalization techniques are considered.

To identify the better normalization technique, Ranking Consistency Index (RCI) has been applied [18]. It is one of the very efficient techniques to identify a better normalization technique. It works based on the consistency of the ranking obtained for alternatives in GFTOPSIS. RCI is used to indicate how well a particular normalization technique produces rankings similar to other normalization techniques [19]. To measure the RCI of a specific normalization technique, the total number of times the method showed similarities/dissimilarities in various extents with other techniques over simulation runs concerning criteria size is considered. Thus, RCI checks the ranking consistency of the normalization techniques. However, the literature also shows that metrics have not been designed for RCI to validate its impact to select the better normalization technique. Hence, it is essential to validate the robustness of normalization techniques using RCI metric to apply in GFTOPSIS.

9.3   Design of Metric for Ranking Consistency Index

This section describes the design of metrics for Ranking Consistency Index (RCI), Computation of Consistency Weight (CW) for RCI, and metric formulation for RCI. The metric for Ranking Consistency Index is designed exclusively to evaluate and rank the normalization techniques. The ranking consistency obtained for a particular normalization technique is validated with the ranking consistency obtained for other normalization techniques. The RCI has calculated the number of times each of the normalization techniques showed similarities and dissimilarities with other normalization techniques. It is named MRCI, which is designed as follows.

Metric Name: Ranking Consistency Index (RCI) metric, **MRCI**

Definition: The RCI metric is denoted by MRCI. It is the ratio of consistency level of normalization technique with other normalization techniques. This metric is applied to find a better normalization technique. The ranking order obtained for a particular normalization technique is checked with the remaining normalization techniques. Then, the obtained value is multiplied by the Consistency Weight (CW) as specified by Chakraborty and Yeh [19].

The normalization technique that has the higher RCI is considered as a better normalization procedure.

Metric formulation: Let the ratio of RCI be denoted by M_{RCI}, and it is calculated using the following equation:

$$
\begin{aligned}
M_{RCI}(NT) = &(((T_{123456} * CW = 1) + (T_{12345} * CW = 4/5) + (T_{12346} * CW = 4/5) \\
&+ (T_{12356} * CW = 4/5) + (T_{12456} * CW = 4/5) + (T_{13456} * CW = 4/5) \\
&+ (T_{1234} * CW = 3/5) + (T_{1235} * CW = 3/5) + (T_{1236} * CW = 3/5) \\
&+ (T_{1245} * CW = 3/5) + (T_{1246} * CW = 3/5) + (T_{1256} * CW = 3/5) \\
&+ (T_{1345} * CW = 3/5) + (T_{1346} * CW = 3/5) + (T_{1356} * CW = 3/5) \\
&+ (T_{1456} * CW = 3/5) + (T_{123} * CW = 2/5) + (T_{124} * CW = 2/5) \\
&+ (T_{125} * CW = 2/5) + (T_{126} * CW = 2/5) + (T_{134} * CW = 2/5) \\
&+ (T_{135} * CW = 2/5) + (T_{136} * CW = 2/5) + (T_{145} * CW = 2/5) \\
&+ (T_{146} * CW = 2/5) + (T_{156} * CW = 2/5) + (T_{12} * CW = 1/5) \\
&+ (T_{13} * CW = 1/5) + (T_{14} * CW = 1/5) + (T_{15} * CW = 1/5) \\
&+ (T_{16} * CW = 1/5) + (TD_{123456} * CW = 0))/TS) / 100
\end{aligned}
\tag{9.1}
$$

where:

$M_{RCI}(NT)$—Ranking Consistency Index of the ith Normalization Technique (six normalization techniques considered for this research)

CW—Consistency Weight

TS—Total number of times the simulation experiment is carried out (*Simulation runs with respect to criteria size)

NT1, NT2, NT3, NT4, NT5, NT6—Selected normalization techniques

T_{123456}—Total number of times NT1, NT2, NT3, NT4, N5, and NT6 produced the same ranking

T_{12345}—Total number of times NT1, NT2, NT3, NT4, and NT5 produced the same ranking

...

...

T_{56}—Total number of times NT5 and NT6 produced the same ranking
TD_{123456}—Total number of times NT1, NT2, NT3, NT4, NT5, and NT6 produced a different ranking

Metric value: Ranking Consistency Index metric M_{RCI} value lies from 0 to 100.
Interpretation: The higher the value of this metric, the better the performance.

*Number of criteria selected to identify a user preference to develop a MCR

M_{RCI} is calculated for each of the normalization techniques. The normalization technique that possesses higher M_{RCI} is considered a better normalization technique. The next section describes simulation experimentation conducted to identify better normalization techniques using the M_{RCI} metric.

9.4 Experimentation

To experiment, in this research, bankruptcy prediction is considered an example. Bankruptcy prediction is conducted in different business domains. In this research, banking is deemed to conduct the bankruptcy prediction. Banking is one of the crucial sectors for the economy and contributes more to national building. A bank may have different stakeholders for its day-to-day operations, like chairman, managing director, deputy managing director, chief general manager, and others. According to various criteria, the stakeholders may have different preference levels over financial distress analysis (or) bankruptcy prediction analysis.

Moreover, all the stakeholders may not have the same kind of information about bankruptcy prediction analysis. Therefore, the study may vary according to the level of decision-making (hierarchy level). Therefore, developing customized reporting about bankruptcy prediction

Table 9.1 List of selected alternatives (users).

Alternative	Name of the alternative	Alternative	Name of the alternative
A1	Chairman	A8	Chief Manager
A2	Managing Director	A9	Manager
A3	Deputy Managing Director	A10	Deputy Manager
A4	Chief General Manager	A11	Assistant Manager
A5	General Manager	A12	Senior Assistant Specialist
A6	Deputy General Manager	A13	Senior Assistant
A7	Regional Manager	A14	Assistant

Table 9.2 List of criteria (financial ratios).

Criteria	Criteria name	Criteria	Criteria name
C1	Working Capital	C6	Total Debt
C2	Total Asset	C7	Equity
C3	Retained Earning	C8	Sales
C4	Earnings Before Interest and Taxes	C9	Cash Ratio
C5	Annual Funds	C10	Current Liabilities
C11	Equity divided by RMA (EQRMA)		

analysis, user preference, and hierarchy status is essential. In this research, by using the RCI metric, a better normalization technique can be identified to apply in fuzzy TOPSIS, which improves the user preference to develop customized reporting. The stakeholders (alternatives) that are selected from the banking domain are described in Table 9.1.

The important alternatives (stakeholders) of the banking domain are described in Table 9.1. They play a vital role in the banking domain and are looking for different levels of information about bankruptcy prediction to make analyses or decisions. The criteria that are applied for this experimentation are selected from the top five bankruptcy models [20–23] that are described in Table 9.2.

The various criteria of bankruptcy prediction considered for this experimentation are described in Table 9.2. Simulation-based experiments are conducted based on multiple problem sizes to identify the similarities and dissimilarities among normalization techniques [18]. Random decision matrices are generated in different sizes from the number of criteria and alternatives with an increment of two (2). Initially, a decision matrix is developed with four (4) criteria and four (4) alternatives to get RCI values for normalization techniques. Further, the decision matrix is generated in 6*6, 8*8, 10*10, and 12*11 with an increment of two (2). From the least size to maximum size, decision matrices are generated to get significant random decision matrices. Next, these decision matrices are normalized using the selected six normalization techniques, and the RCC value is calculated using GFTOPSIS to rank the alternatives. Finally, according to the normalization technique, RCI is computed from these ranks to identify a better normalization technique from equation (9.1).

9.5   Results and Discussion

The random decision matrices are developed with criteria and alternatives in sizes of 4*4, 6*6, 8*8, 10*10, 12*11, and 14*11 to get significant RCI values. These decision matrices are normalized using the selected normalization techniques and from which RCC is calculated to rank alternatives. The respective normalization technique and obtained ranks are described in Table 9.3.

Table 9.3 describes rankings that produced various normalization techniques from the randomly generated decision matrices of sizes 4*4, 6*6, 8*8, 10*10, 12*11, and 14*11. From Table 9.3, the total number of times each of the normalization techniques produced the

Table 9.3 Ranking Consistency Index Metric (M_{RCI}) for normalization techniques.

Ranking Consistency Index Metric (M_{RCI})						
#N/M	M_{RCI} (N1)	M_{RCI} (N2)	M_{RCI} (N3)	M_{RCI} (N4)	M_{RCI} (N5)	M_{RCI} (N6)
4*4	2.8	2.8	4.0	2.8	2.0	2.0
6*6	2.4	0.24	1.8	1.8	1.6	3.2
8*8	1.83	3.2	4.0	3.8	2.4	5.0
10*10	4.6	3.4	3.6	0.8	0.0	3.4
12*11	4.8	5.0	5.8	1.6	1.2	4.6
14*11	1.54	1.83	1.92	1.89	1.54	1.85

#N, Normalization Techniques; M, Matrix Size.

same rankings (T—Total number of times the same ranking is produced by normalization techniques) and different rankings (TD—Total number of times a different ranking is produced by normalization techniques) with respect to different matrix size is calculated. T and TD obtained for the 14*11 matrix size is described in Table 9.4.

From Table 9.4, RCI is calculated for the normalization techniques using T and TD for the matrix size 14*11. From T and TD, RCI is calculated for each of the normalization techniques with respect to different matrix sizes that are described in Table 9.5.

The RCI value obtained for the selected normalization techniques with respect to different matrix sizes (from a number of alternatives and criteria) is described in Table 9.4. The consistency of ranking order (RCI) obtained using these normalization techniques with a different matrix size is represented as a graph that is depicted in Figure 9.1.

The normalization technique that possesses the highest M_{RCI} with different matrix sizes is having more ranking similarities with other normalization techniques. In this analysis, the linear max–min normalization technique is having a higher number of consistency (M_{RCI}) with other normalization techniques. It shows a higher number of RCI with 4*4, 12*11, and 14*11 matrix sizes. In pair with linear max–min normalization, nonmonotonic normalization shows the highest value for RCI with matrix sizes of 6*6 and 8*8. Vector normalization shows the highest value with the matrix size of 10*10. In this analysis, compared to other normalization techniques, linear max–min normalization shows the highest RCI value consistently with 4*4, 12*11, and 14*11 matrix sizes. Based on the M_{RCI}, it is identified that ranking produced by linear max–min matches with other normalization techniques.

In this experimentation, linear max–min normalization shows better results for M_{RCI}. Hence, in GFTOPSIS, linear max–min normalization is applied to calculate the Relative Closeness Coefficient (RCC). Generally, in GFTOPSIS, linear max normalization is applied to develop RCC. From the RCC value, each of the users is given a rank from highest preference to lowest preference. These user preferences are obtained to develop MCR. The RCC value and obtained ranks using GFTOPSIS with linear max normalization and with linear max–min normalization are described in Table 9.6.

The ranks obtained by various users are described in Table 9.6. These ranks are used to decide the user preference to develop the MCR. In GFTOPSIS, with linear max

Table 9.4 Normalization techniques and ranks for decision matrix of size 4*4, 6*6, 8*8, 10*10, and 12*11.

Decision matrix size	Vector	Rank	Linear max	Rank	Linear max min	Rank	Linear sum based	Rank	Gaussian	Rank	Non monotonic	Rank
4*4	0	4	1	1	0.8378	2	1	2	0.2234	3	0.83	2
	0.7268	3	0.6535	3	0.7182	3	0.5847	4	0.0288	4	0.4589	3
	0.9159	2	0.4213	4	0.3799	4	0.4052	3	0.3509	2	0.2552	4
	0.9674	1	1	1	1	1	0.3046	1	0.9748	1	0.9759	2
6*6	0.0029	6	0.5954	3	0.8318	1	1	1	0.4778	4	0	6
	0.6575	5	0.652	2	0.7311	3	0.5954	2	0.1667	6	0.9742	5
	0.8113	4	0.484	5	0.4118	6	0.4259	3	1	1	0.9896	4
	0.8704	3	0.6854	1	0.7593	2	0.3316	4	0.6648	3	0.9953	3
	0.9678	2	0.1968	6	0.4714	5	0.268	5	0.9689	2	0.9983	2
	0.9815	1	0.5385	4	0.6436	4	0.2238	6	0.4349	5	1	1
8*8	0	8	0.6108	3	0.8854	1	1	1	0.5075	6	0	8
	0.6371	7	0.7036	2	0.6878	2	0.5948	2	0.8933	2	0.9505	7
	0.7813	6	0.5615	5	0.4408	6	0.428	3	0.8933	2	0.9783	6
	0.8407	5	0.7282	1	0.5413	4	0.3357	4	0.5113	5	0.9879	5
	0.9276	4	0.2668	6	0.4873	7	0.2741	5	0.6368	4	0.9932	4
	0.9449	3	0.4958	7	0.5809	3	0.2314	6	0.1363	7	0.9963	3

(Continued)

Table 9.4 Normalization techniques and ranks for decision matrix of size 4*4, 6*6, 8*8, 10*10, and 12*11. (*Continued*)

Decision matrix size	Vector	Rank	Linear max	Rank	Linear max min	Rank	Linear sum based	Rank	Gaussian	Rank	Non monotonic	Rank
	0.957	2	0.6108	3	0.3744	8	0.1998	7	0.1117	8	0.9984	2
	0.9883	1	0.4286	8	0.5119	5	0.175	8	0.9066	1	1	1
10*10	0	10	0.6508	4	0.9098	1	1	1	0.495	3	0	10
	0.6234	9	0.7118	1	0.6687	2	0.5929	2	0	10	0.9837	9
	0.7599	8	0.6057	7	0.4372	7	0.4275	3	0	9	0.9927	8
	0.8221	7	0.7045	2	0.5143	5	0.3362	4	0.0928	8	0.9959	7
	0.8941	6	0.4559	10	0.474	8	0.2761	5	0.8543	2	0.9975	6
	0.9198	5	0.5209	9	0.5715	4	0.2341	6	0.3982	4	0.9984	5
	0.9336	4	0.5895	8	0.3099	10	0.2031	7	0.3772	5	0.999	2
	0.9522	3	0.613	6	0.3718	9	0.1791	8	0.2673	6	0.9994	4
	0.9638	2	0.6508	4	0.502	6	0.1599	9	0.8436	1	0.9997	3
	0.9804	1	0.6846	3	0.6296	3	0.1441	10	0.0987	7	1	1
12*11	0.0011	12	0.817	2	0.9406	2	1	1	0.1469	11	0.9837	1
	0.4752	11	0.8252	1	0.9406	2	0.625	2	0.0492	12	0.9465	2
	0.6028	10	0.7934	7	0.9128	6	0.4655	3	0.603	8	0.398	12
	0.653	9	0.8113	5	0.9697	1	0.3761	4	0.8632	2	0.902	3
	0.7215	8	0.7746	10	0.8604	10	0.3162	5	0.7211	6	0.8743	7

(*Continued*)

Table 9.4 Normalization techniques and ranks for decision matrix of size 4*4, 6*6, 8*8, 10*10, and 12*11. (*Continued*)

Decision matrix size	Vector	Rank	Linear max	Rank	Linear max min	Rank	Linear sum based	Rank	Gaussian	Rank	Non monotonic	Rank
	0.7438	7	0.7983	6	0.8861	9	0.2741	6	0.4828	9	0.6077	10
	0.754	6	0.817	2	0.9406	2	0.243	7	0.6226	7	0.8619	9
	0.7778	5	0.793	9	0.9128	6	0.2185	8	0.7857	4	0.8813	6
	0.7865	4	0.817	2	0.9406	2	0.199	9	0.1822	10	0.9232	4
	0.807	3	0.7898	8	0.9059	8	0.1827	10	0.7235	5	0.5933	11
	0.8519	2	0.7389	11	0.5688	11	0.1663	11	0.8385	3	0.8818	5
	0.9041	1	0.6142	12	0.4776	12	0.1517	12	0.9396	1	0.8706	8
14*11	0.1166	14	0.8129	2	0.8354	1	1	1	0.6751	9	0	14
	0.5152	13	0.8132	1	0.8353	2	0.5977	2	0.6752	8	0.0759	13
	0.6283	12	0.7824	8	0.8078	8	0.4366	3	0.6754	7	0.9545	6
	0.6837	11	0.8039	5	0.8267	5	0.3481	4	0.6705	11	0.9697	5
	0.7436	10	0.7686	10	0.7971	10	0.2903	5	0.6379	12	0.7936	11
	0.7678	9	0.7954	7	0.8207	6	0.2499	6	0.7702	6	0.7938	12
	0.7787	8	0.8106	4	0.8337	4	0.2203	7	0.7656	4	0.9918	2
	0.7954	7	0.7822	9	0.8077	9	0.1972	8	0.7123	5	0.9857	4
	0.8051	6	0.8128	3	0.8352	3	0.1789	9	0.675	10	0.9939	1
	0.8253	4	0.794	6	0.8164	7	0.1638	10	0.6309	13	0.9906	3

(*Continued*)

Table 9.4 Normalization techniques and ranks for decision matrix of size 4*4, 6*6, 8*8, 10*10, and 12*11. (*Continued*)

Decision matrix size	Vector	Rank	Linear max	Rank	Linear max min	Rank	Linear sum based	Rank	Gaussian	Rank	Non monotonic	Rank
	0.8188	5	0.6647	12	0.6557	12	0.1586	11	0.2996	14	0.9211	10
	0.8789	2	0.6961	11	0.7189	11	0.1494	12	0.9686	1	0.9212	9
	0.8983	1	0.548	13	0.4736	13	0.1435	13	0.9621	2	0.938	7
	0.8651	3	0.5585	14	0	14	0.1407	14	0.8975	3	0.9324	8

Table 9.5 Calculation of total number of times same and different ranking produced by normalization techniques.

*T, Total number of times the same ranking is produced by normalization techniques. *D, Total number of times a different ranking is produced by normalization techniques. *TD, Total number of times a different ranking is produced by normalization techniques.

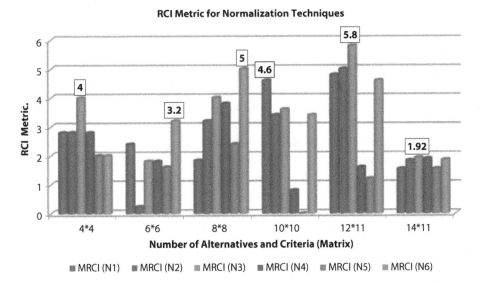

Figure 9.1 RCI metric for normalization techniques. *N1 Vector Normalization, N2 Linear Max Normalization, N3 Linear Max Min Normalization, N4 Linear Sum-based Normalization, N5 Gaussian Normalization, N6 Non Monotonic Normalization.*

Table 9.6 Ranking of alternatives with GFTOPSIS (LM-N) and GFTOPSIS (LMM-N).

Alternatives	GFTOPSIS (LM-N)*	Rank	GFTOPSIS (LMM-N)*	Rank
A1-Chairman	0.7869	7	0.918	1
A2-Managing Director	0.8098	1	0.8145	2
A3-Deputy Managing Dr.	0.7879	6	0.7906	3
A4-Chief General Mgr.	0.7845	8	0.7891	4
A5-General Manager	0.7692	10	0.7313	5
A6-Deputy General Mgr.	0.7952	3	0.7304	6
A7-Regional Mgr.	0.8059	2	0.6894	10
A8-Chief Mgr.	0.791	5	0.7036	9
A9-Manager	0.7912	4	0.7218	8
A10-Deputy Mgr.	0.7711	9	0.7245	7
A11-Assistant Mgr.	0.654	11	0.5895	12
A12-Senior Asst., Spl.	0.6373	13	0.6126	11
A13-Senior Assistant	0.6468	12	0.5472	13
A14-Assistant	0.581	14	0.4925	14

*GFTOPSIS (LM-N), GFTOPSIS with linear max normalization. *GFTOPSIS (LMM-N), GFTOPSIS with linear max–min normalization.

normalization, the chairman receives the seventh rank whereas the same GFTOPSIS with linear max–min normalization receives the first rank. In a similar way, ranks of all the users are validated. For example, A2-Managing Director, A3-Deputy Managing Director, A4-Chief General Manager, A5-General Manager, A6-Deputy General Manager, and others are changed except A14-Assistant. In order to better understand the user preference on MCR, a graph plotted with RCC (obtained using both GFTOPSIS with linear max normalization and GFTOPSIS with linear max–min normalization) and alternatives is represented in Figure 9.2.

The graph in Figure 9.2 indicates the difference in user preference obtained using both of the normalization techniques. In GFTOPSIS (LM-N), most same level of user preference obtained for the first ten (10) banking users expects the last four (4) users, whereas, in GFTOPSIS (LMM-N), a customizable user preference is obtained for all the users. Moreover, each user has a different kind of preference on MCR with GFTOPSIS (LMM-N). In linear max normalization, the normalization value is obtained from the individual performance of each of the criteria and is compared with the maximum performance of the requirements [24]. The best part of linear max normalization is that it transforms outcomes linearly [18].

Moreover, it would not retain the original distribution applied for the criteria, and it will cause performance degradation. In GFTOPSIS (LMM-N), the minimum and maximum performance of the requirements and relative comparison between alternatives are considered to normalize the criteria using linear max–min normalization. The best part of linear max–min normalization is that it thinks both maximum performance and minimum performance of criteria to normalize the decision matrix, which substantially improves the performance of GFTOPSIS compared to linear max normalization.

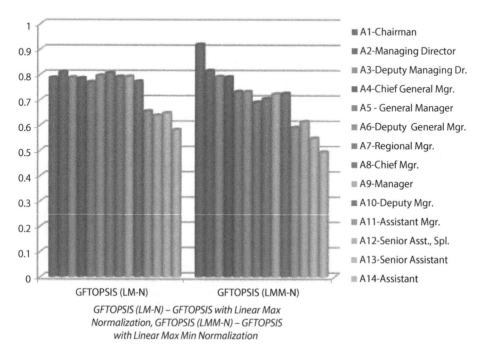

GFTOPSIS (LM-N) – GFTOPSIS with Linear Max Normalization, GFTOPSIS (LMM-N) – GFTOPSIS with Linear Max Min Normalization

Figure 9.2 User preference on MCR with GFTOPSIS (LM-N) and GFTOPSIS (LMM-N).

This kind of customizable user preference is required to develop an MCR for business intelligence. Due to the advancement of social media technologies, an enormous amount of data are generated in every movement. When the analysis is conducted using business intelligence on these massive amounts of data, the user may get different results. These results should be delivered or presented to a particular user/group for decision-making according to their requirement and level in the organization. To submit a customizable report for decision-making, MCR can be applied. GFTOPSIS, with linear max–min normalization, designs the MCR with improved customization according to user preference.

The RCI metric is one of the best ways of identifying the better normalization technique. It works based on the consistency of ranking order obtained using normalization techniques. The ranking order received using a particular normalization has been compared with all other normalization techniques considered for the evaluation. The results obtained using the RCI metric can be applied confidently in generalized fuzzy TOPSIS to identify user preference to design the MCR with better customization. In the RCI metric, the user preference obtained using a particular normalization technique has been compared with all other normalization techniques, which validate the consistency level of each of the normalization techniques. Hence, the results obtained using GFTOPSIS with a normalization technique identified using the RCI metric would give better customization for MCR.

In GFTOPSIS, applying of normalization technique is one of the critical processes. However, other vital, essential, and standard processes in the GFTOPSIS also decide the ranking order for alternatives using the Relative Closeness Coefficient (RCC). The RCC value, the ranking order for other options, the most preferred user, the most minor preferred user, suitable user, average user, and different kinds of users are distinguished to customize the information (high, very high, moderate, normal, low, and very low). When you consider GFTOPSIS processes, applying the weighing method is one of the critical processes, and it has been used to find the weight of the criteria. Similarly, criteria (all standards may not equal importance) selection is another critical process that plays a crucial role in forming the decision matrix. Likewise, GFTOPSIS has a different number of techniques with various levels of importance to decide the ranking order for the alternatives.

Identification of ranking order and user preference using the combination of applying the normalization technique identified using the RCI metric with another process in GFTOPSIS is out of the scope of this research. However, the validation of ranking order with different combinations of the GFTOPSIS process may better understand and influence normalization techniques to customize the user preference for MCR.

In an organization, each user level has various kinds of preferences, requirements, and responsibilities over information. For example, a particular user may be interested in other users' data in certain situations though he is not directly connected with that information. This research designs a multi-criterion reporting within the organizational boundaries to meet different users' preferences and requirements.

Conversational AI [25, 26] has completely changed how companies communicate [27] with their consumers [28, 29]. But it also presents fresh cybersecurity [30–33] difficulties. Businesses [34–36] are increasingly relying on conversational AI for customer service, which raises the risk [37, 38] of cyberattacks [39] directed at these systems. Esse AI has responded to these worries by putting in place a number of cybersecurity [40] precautions. Its AI model was created utilising the potent natural language processing (NLP) [41] and machine learning (ML) tools DialogFlow and TextMagic. With the use of these technologies, the AI assistant can comprehend and analyse consumer requests and then offer wise replies and actions. The AI model [42] may learn and get better over time since it was trained using data from a variety of sources, including customer interactions, and product details towards threat protection [43].

9.6   Conclusion

This research has addressed reporting, which is one of the essential components of business intelligence or e-business. More specifically, it has addressed customization of the reporting component. After conducting the analysis using business intelligence, it is imperative to report it to the respective customizable users according to their requirement. It is one of the objectives of digital transformations followed in e-business technology. The generation of user-specific reports or customized reports is essential for business analytics as well as e-business technology. To improve the user-specific information, it is necessary to understand user preference. The user preference may vary from one user to another user according to different criteria. It has been achieved through MCR. The customization of MCR depends on user preference that other criteria have decided. In this research, using the ranking consistency index, a better normalization technique is identified and applied in GFTOPSIS. Based on the RCC value, the banking users are ranked, and user preference is specified. The experimental results show that the linear max–min normalization tends to give better appreciation compared to linear max normalization. This research has applied an interdisciplinary approach that combines one of the famous operation research techniques, TOPSIS, and business intelligence to develop an MCR for e-business technology. In operations research, many kinds of multi-criteria decision-making techniques have been created. In this research, TOPSIS has been applied to identify user preferences. Instead of TOPSIS, the other MCDM techniques such as AHP (Analytic Hierarchy Process), ELECTRE (Elimination and Expressing Reality), GRA (Gray Relational Analysis), and PROMTHEE (Preference Ranking Organization Method for Enrichment Evaluation) can be applied.

This research has applied RCI to identify the better-performing normalization technique. In GFTOPSIS, normalization is one of the essential processes. However, other necessary processes are required to compute the RCC value, which decides the ranking order of the banking users. Therefore, the influence of normalization concerning other methods should be studied and analyzed. Similarly, identification of better normalization can also be decided by other techniques. Therefore, identifying the different ways of better normalization techniques should be validated with RCI results. This research attempted to design a metric for RCI. It has applied the RCI metric to identify a better normalization technique and improved the customization of user preference concerning the recognized normalization technique.

References

1. Minvielle, E., Fourcade, A., Ricketts, T., Waelli, M., Current developments in delivering customized care: A scoping review. *BMC Health Serv. Res.*, 21, 1, 1–29, 2021.

2. Alles, M.G., Dai, J., Vasarhelyi, M.A., Reporting 4.0: Business reporting for the age of mass customization. *J. Emerg. Technol. Accounting*, 18, 1, 1–15, 2021.

3. Chubinskaya, S., Isic, M.M., Keers, S., Connecting faculty productivity and academic advancement with annual performance assessment by using a customized faculty management system. *J. Faculty Dev.*, 35, 3, 8–15, 2021.

4. Finnaoui, K., Megder, E.H., Ouariti, O.Z., Factors enhancing the use of business intelligence to support organizational learning: A conceptual model. *IEEE 11th Annual Computing and Communication Workshop and Conference (CCWC)*, pp. 0619–0626, 2021.

5. Skobarev, V.Y., Pertseva, E.Y., Ruzmetov, T.V., Preparation of non-financial reporting in modern conditions: Formalization and automation, in: *Industry 4.0*, pp. 289–301, Palgrave Macmillan, Cham, 2021.

6. Sadiku, M.N. and Musa, S.M., Business intelligence, in: *A Primer on Multiple Intelligences*, pp. 177–190, Springer, Cham, 2021.

7. Fischer, T.M. and Baumgartner, K.T., Understanding the reporting of intangibles from a business perspective, in: *Intangibles in the World of Transfer Pricing*, pp. 75–113, Springer, Cham, 2021.

8. Valentinetti, D. and Muñoz, F.F., Internet of Things: Emerging impacts on digital reporting. *J. Bus. Res.*, 131, 549–562, 2021.

9. Rani, A., Multi Criteria Decision Making (MCDM) based preference elicitation framework for life insurance recommendation system. *Turkish J. Comput. Math. Educ. (TURCOMAT)*, 12, 2, 1848–1858, 2021.

10. Patil, M. and Majumdar, B.B., Prioritizing key attributes influencing electric two-wheeler usage: A multi criteria decision making (MCDM) approach–A case study of Hyderabad, India. *Case Stud. Transp. Policy*, 9, 2, 913–929, 2021.

11. Rajak, M. and Shaw, K., Evaluation and selection of mobile health (mHealth) applications using AHP and fuzzy TOPSIS. *Technol. Soc.*, 59, 101186, 2019.

12. Salih, M.M., Zaidan, B.B., Zaidan, A.A., Ahmed, M.A., Survey on fuzzy TOPSIS state-of-the-art between 2007–2017. *Comput. Oper. Res.*, 104, 207–227, 2018.

13. Xian, S. and Guo, H., Novel supplier grading approach based on interval probability hesitant fuzzy linguistic TOPSIS. *Eng. Appl. Artif. Intell.*, 87, 103299, 2020.

14. Marbini, A.H. and Kangi, F., An extension of fuzzy TOPSIS for a group decision making with an application to Tehran stock exchange. *Appl. Soft Comput.*, 52, 1084–1097, 2017.

15. Pavlicic, D., Normalization affects the results of MADM methods. *Yugoslav J. Operations Res.*, 11, 2, 251–265, 2001.

16. Milani, A.S., Shanian, A., Madoliat, R., Nemes, J.A., The effect of normalization norms in multiple attribute decision making models: A case study in gear material selection. *Struct. Multidiscip. Optimization*, 29, 4, 312–318, 2005.

17. Migilinskas, D. and Ustinovichius, L., Normalisation in the selection of construction alternatives. *Int. J. Manag. Decision Making*, 8, 5-6, 623–639, 2007.

18. Chakraborty, S. and Yeh, C.H., A simulation based comparative study of normalization procedures in multiattribute decision making. *6th WSEAS Int. Conf. on Artificial Intelligence, Knowledge Engineering and Data Bases*, vol. 6, pp. 102–109, 2007.

19. Chakraborty, S. and Yeh, C.H., A simulation comparison of normalization procedures for TOPSIS. *International Conference on Computers & Industrial Engineering*, pp. 1815–1820, 2009.

20. Altman, E., I, Financial ratios, discriminant analysis and the prediction of corporate bankruptcy. *J. Finance*, 23, 4, 589–609, 1968.

21. Deakin, E.B., Discriminant analysis of predictors of business failure. *J. Accounting Res.*, 10, 167–179, 1972.

22. Edmister, R.O., An empirical test of financial ratio analysis for small business failure prediction. *J. Financial Quantitative Anal.*, 7, 2, 1477–1493, 1972.

23. Fulmer, J.G., Moon, J.E., Gavin, A.T., Erwin, J.M., A bankruptcy classification model for small firms. *J. Commercial Bank Lending*, 14, 25–37, 1984.

24. Zavadskas, E.K., Zakarevicius, A., Antucheviciene, J., Evaluation of ranking accuracy in multi-criteria decisions. *Informatica*, 17, 4, 601–618, 2006.

25. Mahor, V., Bijrothiya, S., Rawat, R., Kumar, A., Garg, B., Pachlasiya, K., IoT and artificial intelligence techniques for public safety and security, in: *Smart Urban Computing Applications*, p. 111, 2023.

26. Mahor, V., Pachlasiya, K., Garg, B., Chouhan, M., Telang, S., Rawat, R., Mobile operating system (Android) vulnerability analysis using machine learning, in: *Proceedings of International Conference on Network Security and Blockchain Technology: ICNSBT 2021*, pp. 159–169, Springer Nature Singapore, Singapore, 2022, June.

27. Rawat, R., Garg, B., Pachlasiya, K., Mahor, V., Telang, S., Chouhan, M., Mishra, R., SCNTA: Monitoring of network availability and activity for identification of anomalies using machine learning approaches. *Int. J. Inf. Technol. Web Eng. (IJITWE)*, 17, 1, 1–19, 2022.

28. Rawat, R., Rimal, Y.N., William, P., Dahima, S., Gupta, S., Sankaran, K.S., Malware threat affecting financial organization analysis using machine learning approach. *Int. J. Inf. Technol. Web Eng. (IJITWE)*, 17, 1, 1–20, 2022.

29. Rawat, R., Mahor, V., Chouhan, M., Pachlasiya, K., Telang, S., Garg, B., Systematic literature review (SLR) on social media and the digital transformation of drug trafficking on darkweb, in: *International Conference on Network Security and Blockchain Technology*, pp. 181–205, Springer, Singapore, 2022.

30. Rawat, R., Ayodele Oki, O., Sankaran, S., Florez, H., Ajagbe, S.A., Techniques for predicting dark web events focused on the delivery of illicit products and ordered crime. *Int. J. Electr. Comput. Eng. (IJECE)*, 13, 5, 5354–5365, Oct. 2023, doi: 10.11591/ijece.v13i5.pp5354-5365.

31. Rawat, R., Garg, B., Mahor, V., Telang, S., Pachlasiya, K., Chouhan, M., Organ trafficking on the dark web—The data security and privacy concern in healthcare systems, in: *Internet of Healthcare Things: Machine Learning for Security and Privacy*, pp. 189–216, 2022.

32. Vyas, P., Vyas, G., Chauhan, A., Rawat, R., Telang, S., Gottumukkala, M., Anonymous trading on the dark online marketplace: An exploratory study, in: *Using Computational Intelligence for the Dark Web and Illicit Behavior Detection*, pp. 272–289, IGI Global, 2022.

33. Rawat, R., Oki, O.A., Sankaran, K.S., Olasupo, O., Ebong, G.N., Ajagbe, S.A., A new solution for cyber security in big data using machine learning approach, in: *Mobile Computing and Sustainable Informatics: Proceedings of ICMCSI 2023*, pp. 495–505, Springer Nature Singapore, Singapore, 2023.

34. Rawat, R., Chakrawarti, R.K., Raj, A., Mani, G., Chidambarathanu, K., Bhardwaj, R., Association rule learning for threat analysis using traffic analysis and packet filtering approach. *Int. J. Inf. Technol.*, 1–11, 2023.

35. Rawat, R., Logical concept mapping and social media analytics relating to cyber criminal activities for ontology creation. *Int. J. Inf. Technol.*, 15, 2, 893–903, 2023.

36. Rawat, R., Mahor, V., Álvarez, J.D., Ch, F., Cognitive systems for dark web cyber delinquent association malignant data crawling: A review, in: *Handbook of Research on War Policies, Strategies, and Cyber Wars*, pp. 45–63, 2023.

37. Rawat, R., Chakrawarti, R.K., Vyas, P., Gonzáles, J.L.A., Sikarwar, R., Bhardwaj, R., Intelligent fog computing surveillance system for crime and vulnerability identification and tracing. *Int. J. Inf. Secur. Priv. (IJISP)*, 17, 1, 1–25, 2023.

38. Rawat, R., Sowjanya, A.M., Patel, S.I., Jaiswal, V., Khan, I., Balaram, A. (Eds.), *Using Machine Intelligence: Autonomous Vehicles Volume 1*, John Wiley & Sons, 2022.

39. Rawat, R., Mahor, V., Díaz-Álvarez, J., Chávez, F., Rooted learning model at fog computing analysis for crime incident surveillance, in: *2022 International Conference on Smart Generation*

Computing, Communication and Networking (SMART GENCON), pp. 1–9, IEEE, 2022, December.

40. Rawat, R. and Shrivastav, S.K., SQL injection attack detection using SVM. *Int. J. Comput. Appl.*, *42*, 13, 1–4, 2012.

41. Rawat, R., Bhardwaj, P., Kaur, U., Telang, S., Chouhan, M., Sankaran, K.S., *Smart vehicles for communication, volume 2*, John Wiley & Sons, 2023.

42. Mahor, V., Garg, B., Telang, S., Pachlasiya, K., Chouhan, M., Rawat, R., Cyber threat phylogeny assessment and vulnerabilities representation at thermal power station, in: *Proceedings of International Conference on Network Security and Blockchain Technology: ICNSBT 2021*, pp. 28–39, Springer Nature Singapore, Singapore, 2022, June.

43. Rawat, R., Gupta, S., Sivaranjani, S., Cu, O.K., Kuliha, M., Sankaran, K.S., Malevolent information crawling mechanism for forming structured illegal organisations in hidden networks. *Int. J. Cyber Warf. Terror. (IJCWT)*, *12*, 1, 1–14, 2022.

10

Machine Learning for Automatic Speech Recognition

Hrishitva Patel[1]*, Ramakrishnan Raman[2], Malik Jawarneh[3], Arshiya S. Ansari[4], Hriakumar Pallathadka[5] and Domenic T. Sanchez[6]

[1]MS in Computer Science, SUNY Binghamton, New York, USA
[2]Symbiosis Institute of Business Management, Pune & Symbiosis International (Deemed University),
Pune, Maharashtra, India
[3]Faculty of Computing Sciences, Gulf College, Al-Khuwair, Oman
[4]Department of Information Technology, College of Computer and Information Sciences,
Majmaah University, Al-Majmaah, Saudi Arabia
[5]Manipur International University, Manipur, India
[6]Cebu Technological University-NEC, Cebu City, Philippines

Abstract

It is very important to be able to use speech signals correctly so that you can share your feelings, thoughts, and information about the real world, as well as for your day-to-day work. Speech is the most natural way for people to talk to each other verbally. With the help of speech recognition technology, computers can now understand human languages and respond to spoken commands. At the heart of the field of voice recognition is the development of methods and platforms for analyzing spoken and natural language. It is put into the computer these days so that the right processing and rearranging can happen. Over the past 10 years, automatic speech recognizers have gotten much better at what they do. Most studies have looked at the many technologies that are now available to help people who have trouble speaking. Research shows that voice recognition applications for people who have trouble speaking are well within the capabilities of modern technology. However, there is not a lot of work that looks at the human side of things, which is the main thing holding back progress in this field. Concerns have been raised about a number of things that have to do with people. Speech recognition has the most potential to change the lives of people who have trouble talking. This chapter presents a machine learning-based framework for automatic speech recognition. Speech acquisition, speech preprocessing, feature extraction, and classification are the main components of the proposed framework.

Keywords: Automatic speech recognition, deep belief network, ann, knn classifier, accuracy, feature extraction, speech preprocessing

*Corresponding author: hpatel51@binghamton.edu

Romil Rawat, Rajesh Kumar Chakrawarti, Sanjaya Kumar Sarangi, Piyush Vyas, Mary Sowjanya Alamanda, Kotagiri Srividya and Krishnan Sakthidasan Sankaran (eds.) Conversational Artificial Intelligence, (147–168) © 2024 Scrivener Publishing LLC

10.1   Introduction

Speech is generally considered to be the primary and most effective form of natural communication that is used for interpersonal exchanges between people. One of the most intriguing issues that might be asked is whether or not the human voice can be used as a kind of human–machine communication. The researchers' overarching goal has been to create a foolproof system that makes human–machine interaction possible via the use of natural language. This has been their primary focus for the last many years. Since 1950, a large amount of research has been carried out in the field of automatic speech recognition (ASR), and important results have been achieved in this sector in order to produce an improved ASR system. Despite this, the ideal of an ASR system that is perfect in every way has not yet been realized [1].

It is an essential important responsibility to be able to communicate appropriately via speech signal in order to convey feelings, thoughts, and information related to the real world, as well as for day-to-day work. Speech is the most natural way for humans to communicate verbally with one another. The development of speech recognition technology has made it possible for computers to interpret human languages and respond to commands spoken by humans. The development of methods and platforms for the analysis of spoken and natural language is at the heart of the field of voice recognition. These days, it is used as an input to the computer so that the appropriate processing and rearranging may take place. Over the last decade, significant improvements have been made to the performance of automatic speech recognizers. The majority of investigations have investigated the many technologies that are now accessible in order to meet the needs of the population that is articulatory handicapped. Voice recognition applications for articulatory impaired people are well within the capabilities of contemporary technology, according to research. However, there is a significant dearth of work that focuses on human aspects, which is the primary barrier preventing advancement in this domain. There are a number of worries identified that are associated with human factors. Speech recognition has the most potential to make a difference in the lives of those who struggle to communicate verbally [2].

After decades of research, one of the most significant challenges in automatic speech recognition is improving its accuracy for people who have difficulty with their articulation. When creating an automated speech recognition system, one must give careful consideration to the issues of speech class notion, speech representation, feature extraction methods, speech classification, a database, and performance assessment. When you speak to your computer, phone, or app, it recognizes your voice and responds accordingly by taking action and using speech recognition. Speech recognition is utilized in place of any other mode of data entry, such as typing, clicking, or choosing. It is an approach for making technology easier to use while also increasing its overall efficiency. The ability of a computer or piece of software to recognize words and phrases that are spoken by a person and transform them into a format that can be read by a machine is referred to as speech recognition. Deep learning is applicable successfully to recognize speech. This is shown in Figure 10.1.

ASRs that adjust to the speaker use a combination of SI and SD. These systems are meant to recognize the distinctive speech patterns of new speakers as soon as they are brought into the conversation. The vocabulary of an ASR has an impact on its accuracy, complexity, and the amount of time it takes to process information [3]. The more words

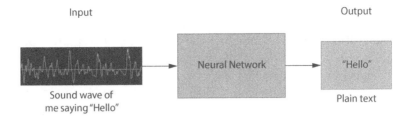

Figure 10.1 Deep learning in speech recognition.

there are in a vocabulary, the more complicated the system becomes, and the longer it takes to teach it new words. The accuracy of the algorithm will suffer when a greater number of terms share pronunciations with other words. It is possible that some applications may call for the use of a high-capacity ASR, such as a speech system that can recognize characters or numbers. Even if a limited vocabulary may be enough for certain tasks, an ASR that is intended to recognize English, for instance, will need a vocabulary that is far greater than that of an ASR that is intended to recognize numbers. Tens of words can be all that is needed to make up a limited vocabulary. Medium-sized vocabularies are generally agreed upon to be those that include several hundred words. It is possible to have a vocabulary that contains thousands upon thousands of different words. Vocabularies that are considered to be extensive often include thousands upon thousands of words. There is a connection between every vocabulary gap and unfamiliar words. An utterance is made up of both independent words and words that are related to one another. Users that depend largely on individual words should stop in a way that is understandable between each statement in order to ensure that a system functions as intended. However, this does not imply that the system will only receive one-word input and will only provide one-word output in any circumstance.

Although these programs may be able to take in a huge body of material, they are only able to do analysis on a single word at a time. Instead, connected words make use of a technique in which words are linked together in such a way that there is little to no pause made between pairings of two or more syllables in the phrase [4]. The technology allows for the simultaneous entry of numerous different words and the processing of all of those words simultaneously. Words and phrases may be broken down into two categories due to the fact that different people have different methods of expressing themselves verbally. Continuous speech and spontaneous speech are the two categories that might be used to describe it. Those who utilize this style of ASR are given the freedom to make remarks that are virtually completely unscripted and in a stream-of-consciousness format. In statements like these, there is no need to use a comma. The method does not make any effort to convert the input into words based on the spaces that are there; rather, it considers the input in its entirety. Conversation that is real and unrehearsed is in a league of its own when it comes to ease of use. The following are some examples of such remarks: errors, yells, laughter, and filler words such as "uh" and "ah." However, this list is not exhaustive [5].

The construction of such a system is challenging since it requires a significant vocabulary. In addition to this, it must be able to differentiate between the sound of actual words and the noise that is occurring around them. There are many additional indicators of ASRs, such as the caliber of the input channel. In order to successfully capture input signals for particular ASRs, an environment devoid of ambient noise is required. It is possible that the incoming voice signal contains data that are unwanted or unnecessary, sometimes known as "noise." There are a number of potential causes for the distorted sound, including background noise such as birds tweeting and poor recording quality. When we utilize numerous programs to adjust the channel of an incoming sound wave, there is a possibility that we can experience sound distortion. A few examples of input signal components that cannot be ignored include things like age, gender, surroundings, and speaking pace. Other examples include an accent. An ASR has to be able to withstand background noise as well as errors in the speech stream it receives. Machine learning is a vital cog in automatic speech recognition [6]. Several machine learning techniques are available to efficiently classify speech-related data [7].

The way a person talks may be altered when they have difficulties with speech production. The disorder that is often referred to as stuttering is among the most common kinds of issues with communicating. People who have speech difficulties sometimes have difficulty articulating their thoughts, despite the fact that they are aware of them. The analysis of speech signals is at the heart of the "voice recognition" study subfield, which was established in the 1980s. Voice processing is one example that may be used to illustrate how digital signal processing can be applied to speech signals. This is due to the fact that speech signals are often interpreted digitally. A component of speech processing is one that is accountable for the collection, management, transportation, transmission, and distribution of auditory signals [5].

The study of speech signals and the various processing techniques used by them is referred to as "voice processing," and it is closely tied to the area of investigating how signals and human language are processed together. Digital voice identification, spoken word conversation systems, text-to-speech, and automated speech recognition are all examples of technologies that fall under the category of speech processing. Speech is another data source that may be derived from its recordings (such as nationality, gender, language identity, or speech recognition). Even if it is true that using one's voice makes it simpler to obtain, manipulate, and transmit information, it is also feasible that there are alternative techniques of interaction with machines that are just as successful. Speech is a natural human ability that is quick, simple, does not need the use of your eyes or hands, and is instinctive. Discussions on processing would be simpler if simple linear correlations were followed between acoustics and articulations, as well as between acoustics and perception. Both the synthesis and identification of automated voices strongly depend on accurate speech transcription. Because of the breakdown in communication, it is hard for people and robots to collaborate effectively. Both human relationships with other people and human connections with machines are negatively impacted when communication breaks down.

10.2   Related Work

Deep Belief Neural Networks (DBNs) were used by the author Jun Ren and colleagues in order to provide a description of the prevalence of dysarthric speech signals in 2017.

The authors decided to go with the DBN model rather of the GMM approach. The DBN system employs a technology that requires a significant amount of processing power in order to recognize human speech. The extraction characteristics are determined using the vocal tract length normalization (VTLN) approach. Training of the GMM-HMM model is accomplished with the assistance of the enhanced MFCC features. We use the speaker-adapted features to train the DNN, along with the derivative and acceleration, so that we may get around the conditional independence postulate that is inherent in the HMMs. According to the findings of the study, DBNs make the detector more resistant to changes in the data associated with speech signals that are caused by varied degrees of dysarthria. The current iteration of this algorithm has a quite high error rate when it comes to creating whole phrases.

In 2014, S. Reza Shahamirietal and colleagues [8] established the best possible combination of MFCC parameters that could be used as dysarthric acoustic features in an Artificial Neural Network that was based on an automatic speech recognition system [8] (ANN). An isolated-word, fixed-length speech-to-text (SI) system is something that individuals who have dysarthria need; thus, researchers are investigating how ANNs may be utilized to assist these patients. The most accurate results are achieved by training speech detectors with the normal 12 coefficient MFCC features rather than the indicated delta and acceleration features. With the speaker-independent ASR system that was recommended, we were able to determine that dysarthric speech is capable of achieving a word recognition rate of 68.38%.

Szczurowska et al. [9], who published their findings in 2006, were able to differentiate between samples of fluent and nonfluent speech and categorize them in accordance with this distinction using neural networks. In the course of the research, eight different speakers who stuttered provided their spectra. Kohonen and Multilayer Perceptron Networks were taught to exploit these traits so that they could more accurately recognize and classify fluent and dysfluent speakers. The optimal neural network, as determined by the authors, consists of 171 input neurons, 53 hidden layer neurons, and 1 output neuron, and it achieves an accuracy of 76.67%.

A method was proposed by Wietlicka et al. [10] in 2009 for automatically recognizing instances of dysfluency in the speech of individuals who stuttered. The dataset that was used in this approach comprised a broad range of data points, such as 59 instances of fluent speech and 59 examples of non-fluent speech, in addition to data points from 8 persons who stutter. In order to analyze speech samples at frequencies ranging from 100 Hz to 10,000 Hz, a total of 21 digital filters with a center frequency of 1/3 octave were used. These aspects of the speech samples were included in the networks as inputs, and they were used to analyze the data. The Multilayer Perceptron (MLP) and Radial Basis Function (RBF) networks are used to differentiate between fluent and nonfluent speech samples and then identify them. The accuracy of data classification across all networks varies from 88.1% to 94.9%. Extensive research has shown that artificial neural networks may be a useful tool for speech analysis, particularly when they are trained on stuttering and other forms of non-fluent speech. The initial use of the neural network made it possible to represent non-fluent speech by highlighting dysfluent portions of the speech and reflecting the syllabic structure of the utterances themselves. This was accomplished by reducing the number of dimensions that were used to store the input signals. The networks performed very well across all types of data, achieving extremely high levels of accuracy, sensitivity, and specificity in their analyses.

The use of neural networks in intelligent speech recognition systems may prove to be beneficial. Understanding the principles that underlie asynchronous signals may also be made easier by the generalization and modeling capabilities of networks, as well as the added complexity that these capabilities provide.

In 2005, Nayak *et al.* [11] developed a method that provides helpful information about the kind of sickness that is present in the speech production system based on the acoustic component of the aberrant speech. Signals that are not stationary are being picked up, and among them might be early warning symptoms of sickness or evidence that a condition is becoming worse over time. It is possible that the symptoms may continue on and on, or they could just appear at random times during the day.

The process of analyzing and diagnosing abnormalities in volume data that has been collected over the course of a number of hours may be strenuous and time-consuming. As a consequence of this, the use of computer-based analytical tools during the course of an entire day may prove to be of considerable assistance in terms of both the diagnostic analysis and the identification of information. In order to diagnose some disorders, the author used an artificial neural network.

Patterns of transformation of the wavelet variety are existing all the time. In modern classification, the coefficients of the discrete wavelet transform (DWT) are used rather often. We are able to classify snippets of speech into one of three categories by using a technique based on neural networks: normal, paralysis, and hyper-function. Continuous wavelet coefficients are used while doing speech analysis. Within the scope of this research project, we present the neural network classifier as a prospective tool that might assist medical professionals in the identification of communication problems associated with the voice. The performance of the classifier is affected by a number of factors, some of which include the size and quality of the training set, the level of intensity of the training, and the input representation parameters. The classifiers that have been developed are effective, with an accuracy ranging from 80% to 85%. Visually analyzing the same signal with a continuous time wavelet modification of the speech signal might provide essential diagnostic information. This analysis can be performed on the same data.

In order to locate an event on the timeline, we now make use of a temporal frame that is only active for a certain amount of time. As it moves through time with the signal, this moving window may do an estimation of the spectral components of the signal in a sequential manner. When applied to signals that include both slowly varying components and quickly changing transient events, the short-time Fourier transform (STFT) does not function well. The FT is the product of a window that is infinitely long and offers very good frequency resolution, but at the sacrifice of temporal details. When your view of time is more limited, you are able to perceive more specifics in the past and the future. Because we are assuming that the windowing would remain stable, the frequency resolution has been reduced. Utilizing the Transform Wavelet approach will allow for the successful resolution of this challenge. There are longer time intervals for lower frequencies, whereas shorter time periods are associated with higher frequencies. It is possible to do analysis and synthesis of the original signal by using the information that is supplied by the transform, which results in a significant reduction in the amount of time required for the calculation.

In 2018, Paria Jamshid Lou *et al.* [12] conducted research on a method that was both straightforward and effective for the automated identification of dysfluency. An autocorrelative neural network best describes this concept (ACNN). This model makes use of a convolutional neural network (CNN), and it improves it at the deepest layer by adding a unique auto-correlation operator. This operator has the potential to capture the "soft copy" dependencies that are typical of speech restoration dysfluencies. Experiments demonstrate that the ACNN model beats the CNN baseline on a dysfluency detection test by 5%, which is extremely close to the result that was previously considered to be the best. This research makes use of the ACNN to identify dysfluency with competitive results, and it does so without relying on any characteristics or representations that were manually designed or otherwise drawn from the output of a preexisting system. Rather, it accomplishes this goal without resorting to either of these methods.

M. Winiewski *et al.* published a suggestion in 2007 on the use of an HMM classifier in order to recognize the prolonged fricative phonemes that are related with speech disorders. Within the scope of this investigation, the HMM classifier is provided with the most common MFCC characteristics that are accessible. This feature supplies an excessive number of parameters; nevertheless, lowering them might result in the loss of essential data, which would in turn diminish the feature's capacity for accurate identification. The K-means approach is used to choose the appropriate feature set from the codebook entries that are currently accessible. If careful attention is paid to the selection of the HMM and the appropriate preparation of input data, it is feasible to achieve maximum identification efficiency while maintaining acceptable computation speeds. This is the case provided that one pays close attention to both of these aspects. The reduction in the size of the codebook is the only way to bring the proportion of acknowledgment down. There is not much of an effect that state count has on political acceptability. During the experiment, it was determined that identification accuracy was around 80%.

Frank Rudzicz proposed a unique method for acoustic-to-articulatory inversion in 2011 [13], which included the use of a nonlinear Hammerstein system. This method has the potential to predict the positions of the acoustic vocal tract. We tracked where in the vocal tract different experimental measures were obtained by using data from the TORGO dysarthric articulation database. This allowed us to monitor where in the vocal tract each measurement was taken. With a confidence level of 95% or higher, it has been shown that this technique, which makes use of adaptive kernel canonical correlation analysis, is much more accurate than mixed density networks when it comes to the majority of the variables that belong to the vocal tract. A fresh strategy for ASR has also been offered, one in which acoustic-based theories are reevaluated in light of the likelihood of their articulatory realizations in the context of task dynamics. This method has been developed in order to improve the accuracy of ASR. Because it takes into account high-level and long-term aspects of voice development, this method has been shown to be much more accurate than hidden Markov models, complex Bayesian networks, and switching Kalman filters.

In 2011, Frank Rudzicz *et al.* [14] applied techniques of lexical and acoustic adaptation in order to correct for articulatory errors made by dysarthric speakers. The use of speaker and pronunciation lexicon adaptation resulted in a reduction in the average number of words containing mistakes of 22.87% (or 42.11% relative), which is a significant amount taking into account the relatively large vocabulary size used in these experiments. After making adjustments to the vocabulary to enhance pronunciation, it was found that both speaker-adapted and speaker-based models underwent changes that were statistically significant. Despite the fact that they seem promising, phonetic articulatory errors are only one component of the greater problem that dysarthric speech presents. The presence of dysarthric vocal features, such as excessive involuntary coughing, articulatory breakdowns, prosodic interruptions, stuttering, and accidental breaks, contributes to the increased difficulty of the part.

Speech assistive technology was developed in 2014 by Caballero-Morales *et al.* for those who have dysarthric speech. The modeling of various pronunciation patterns serves as the basis for our inquiry. The system suggests an approach that blends a number of different paradigms of pronunciation in order to improve its ability to recognize dysarthric speech. When attempting to accomplish this combination, numerous rules and restrictions derived from a variety of language models are used, and the answers of the automatic speech recognition (ASR) system are weighted. A genetic algorithm is used to make predictions on the relative value of each answer (GA). Metamodels, which are derived from discrete hidden Markov models, may be made more user-friendly with the use of GA (HMMs). The GA uses dynamic uniform mutation or crossover to update the candidate weight and structure sets in order to further enhance the outcome of the metamodels. This helps the GA get a better overall result. The method was shown effective via the use of the sustained auditory tools found in the Nemours Dysarthric Speech Repository. These resources were utilized to verify the method by testing it with a more expanded vocabulary. The accuracy of recognition in ASR tests conducted using the recommended technique on these resources was much greater than that attained using traditional metamodels and a typical method of adjusting speakers. A significant statistical discovery was uncovered in this investigation.

In 2014, Elham S. Salama and colleagues proposed a multimodal voice recognition system that might be used in the treatment of speech problems. The procedure that has been proposed improves the dependability of aberrant speech. Due to the fact that it is based on both verbal and visual signals, it may be useful for those who have dysarthria, which is a speech difficulty. The Mel Frequency Cepstral Coefficients of acoustic speech transmissions serve as a means of characterizing these signals (MFCC). The Discrete Cosine Transform (DCT) Coefficients of the visual component are extracted from the region surrounding the lips of the speaker. The Viola-Jones method is one that is used to extract information from the regions of the head and mouth. After that, each of these characteristics of the output is concatenated into a single vector. The classifier known as the hidden Markov model (HMM) is employed in place of a decision logic circuit after the auditory and visual component mix function vector has been obtained. In this particular investigation, we make use of the UA-Speech English server provided by a third party. According to the findings of this research, a multimodal system that makes use of visual elements is superior to a single-modal system and has the potential to increase the accuracy of an experiment by up to 7.91% when utilizing just one speaker and by up to 3% when utilizing both speakers.

The database of the University of Michigan's Aphasia Program (UMAP), which comprises the words and phrases of persons with aphasia, was used by Le *et al.* [15] in their study that was published in 2016 (6 women, 11 men, 14–58 years of age). You may make use of the tablet's inbuilt microphone, which has a sampling rate of 44.1 kilohertz, in order to record audio on the device. By using DNN-HMM with MFCC and LDA features, the authors hoped to improve the automatic speech recognition (ASR) of aphasic speech. Due to the problem of insufficient data, DNN-HMM was unable to provide a result that was encouraging in aphasic speech recognition. The DNN-HMM strategy exhibited a larger error rate (42.9%) than the GMM-HMM approach (39,7%), which may be attributed to the fact that the acoustic model with the recovered features is not as robust as it might be. It is likely that noise distorted the characteristics as the data were being processed at the front end of the system.

The server was located inside the Cantonese Aphasia Bank that Lee *et al.* accessed back in 2016 [16]. For the purpose of compiling this list, a total of 149 native, unimpaired speakers of Cantonese and 104 persons with dependent post-stroke aphasia were interviewed. Each of these individuals offered oral histories, which were then documented for future use. The audio was captured using a digital recorder that had a sampling rate of 44.1 kHz and a head-worn condenser microphone throughout the recording process. They found that the error rate for GMM-HMM was 58.2%, while the error rate for DNN-HMM when employing MFCC and LDA features was 57.8%. According to the findings of the research, acoustic models are not the major contributor to the minimum accuracy, which is characterized by error rates that are only marginally significant.

An autonomous isolated digit recognition system was provided for speakers with very poor intelligibility by Mark Johnson-Hasegawa *et al.* [17] in the year 2006. A number of the symptoms of spastic dysarthria may lead to a reduction in intelligibility in the speaker's speech. Two of the individuals were successful in digitally identifying themselves using HMMs, but the person who had the most obvious tendency to remove consonants from words did not pass the test. On the other hand, two of the individuals were able to effectively recognize digits by using SVM classifiers in conjunction with a predetermined word length, but the third participant, who stutters purposefully and slowly, was unable to do so.

According to the published research, the dynamic temporal warping properties of the HMM provide some robustness against large-scale word-length changes. Additionally, the regularized discriminative error metric that was used to train the SVM provides some robustness against consonant reduction and deletion.

Carlos M. Travieso and colleagues presented in 2017 a novel strategy for the automatic diagnosis of voice disorders using voice biomarkers. Discrete HMM (DHMM) may be converted to a hyperdimensional space using the Fisher evaluator's procedure. The classification issue is solved by using the RBF-SVM after it has been trained with K-fold cross-validation. When we look at three separate datasets related to voice diseases, we get findings that are almost 99% accurate. It has proven possible to identify voice pathologies in prolonged phonations by using linear methods, combinations of linear and nonlinear techniques, as well as continuous speech signals.

The system was trained using data from three different kinds of illnesses: cleft lip and palate, which results in an overly nasal voice; Parkinson's disease, which results in dysarthric expression; and laryngeal abnormalities, which result in dysphonia. According to the findings, the approach that was presented is both sufficient and trustworthy for determining which illnesses are present. In it, a comparison is made between the recommended technique and various forms of classification systems that are commonplace in modern times. To achieve an accurate judgment in the vast majority of situations, we combine RBF-SVM with an HMM-based classifier. Both approaches showed a lower level of accuracy when contrasted with the findings obtained via the use of the DHMM-based transformation. The primary shortcoming of this method is that it cannot improve the sonic quality of voice recordings. This is due to the fact that the researchers conducted their preliminary tests utilizing recordings produced under situations that were not regulated, which resulted in a poor level of accuracy. Recordings of speech carried out in settings free of background noise will serve as the foundation for yet another group of inquiries.

According to a study that was conducted in 2011 by John Labiak *et al.*, the closest neighbor-based approaches offer a method for acoustic modeling that avoids the laborious and heuristic process of training conventional Gaussian mixture-based models. The findings of this study may be utilized to the difficulty of determining a distance metric for a phonetic frame classifier based on k-nearest neighbors (k-NN). Using closest neighbor projections (LMNN) and locality preservation, the standard Euclidean distance is calculated in comparison to two known Mahalanobis distances. The locality-sensitive hashing approach applies approximate nearest neighbor search to get beyond the test time of classification k-NN. The relative degrees of inaccuracy between the different approaches are compared. In this study, we evaluate the effectiveness of using a multilayer perceptron classifier to a baseline Gaussian mixture-based classifier for the task of phonetic frame categorization of speech. K-nearest neighbors (k-NN) classification outperforms Gaussian mixture models but not multilayer perceptron. Using LPP, the recommended system obtains the best k-NN classification performance, while LMNN produces only slightly poorer performance.

Golipour *et al.* [18] predicted that k-NN/SASH phoneme classification algorithms will be competitive with state-of-the-art approaches in 2010. Identification of high-dimensional words and pictures was performed by employing a parallel search approach. SASH's processing time is independent of the data dimension, which is not the case for other search methods. Therefore, the investigator employs both the central and peripheral frames to generate high-dimensional attribute vectors for phonemes that are fixed in length. The k-NN/SASH phoneme classifier is quick, accurate, and able to classify 79.2% of the TIMIT test database correctly. Finally, the GMMHMM monophonic recognizer uses this algorithm's relevance to rescore phoneme lattices it has previously produced for context-independent and context-dependent tasks. Recognizability shifts in both situations may be traced back to the discovery of k-NN/SASH.

Ooi Chia Ai *et al.* applied the speech parameterization methods LPCC and MFCC in 2012. Available data on stuttered events were compared using a recognition system based on repetitions and prolongations. The experimental findings demonstrated that LPCC outperforms MFCC in all cases, including frame length selection, window overlapping percentage, and a value in the first-order high-pass filter. Twenty-one LPCC characteristics are correct to a 94.51% confidence level. The accuracy of 25 MFCC characteristics is 92.55%. This is due to the fact that LPCC is capable of recording excellent data from stuttering events and has a somewhat improved capacity to discern between all stalled events, including repetition and extension. This research also notes that k-NN and LDA may be used as classifiers for repetition and extension. Conventional validation was then used to evaluate k-NN and LDA's respective correctness.

In 2016, Li-Yu Hu and coworkers published their findings. [19] K-nearest neighbor (k-NN) classification is being considered for use in the medical area. This non-parametric classifier is known as K-NN. It has been used as the starting point for several paradigm categorization problems. The distances between the test data and each of the training data are computed to calculate the overall classification performance. From these findings, it is clear that the k-NN classifier's performance depends on the distance variable that is used. Chi-square distance function produced from K-NN works particularly well with categorical, quantitative, and mixed data types in the medical area.

In other words, T. Lakshmi Priya *et al.* Using certain characteristics, a method was proposed in 2012 [20] to improve resilience in a noisy setting. When looking for traits that can be integrated efficiently, the K-NN technique is applied. Each speech signal is classified based on its unique combination of speech and non-speech identification and its classification algorithm, both of which must be improved upon in order to successfully identify endpoints in noisy situations. The identification of a vocal problem is crucial in the field of speech and language. The speaker employs a subjective approach; yet, doing so is challenging and may aggravate patients. Consequently, this study's objective is to facilitate early diagnosis of voice dysfunction. Injury to the speech motor systems is the root cause of dysarthria, a neurological condition. There are pauses in the speaker's pitch, wide swings in volume, tempo shifts, and pauses between sentences. When we use a computer to process our voices, we effectively eliminate this need. The K-NN classifier can tell the difference between typical and dysarthric speech. The effects of several factors on speech/nonspeech categorization in noisy contexts were studied. As it is less complicated and easier to operate than other classifiers, the K-NN recognition method was chosen with an accuracy of 80%.

In 2017, K U Syaliman *et al.* proposed combining local mean-based neighbor k-nearest (LMKNN) with distance weight k-nearest neighbor (DWKNN) to acquire distance weight as a solution to majority voting issues. The k-NN technique is widely used in text classification, pattern recognition, and other machine learning applications. The k-NN is well-liked because of its appealing features, including its simplicity, intuitiveness, and versatility. k-NN's accuracy is shown to be poor compared to other classification techniques.

There are several causes behind k-NN's poor accuracy. One such thing is that the results of using any given method's characteristics in a distance calculation are always the same. The issue may be solved by assigning a value to each data point based on its unique characteristics. Additionally, the k-NN's unreliability is triggered by the fact that new data categories are chosen using a majority voting approach. When the distance between each closest neighbor far exceeds the length of the test data, the majority voting approach is inappropriate since it ignores data proximity. Moreover, the class determination method for new data based on the majority vote and the number of closest neighbors, where the number of nearest neighbors is selected according to the desired degree of success, may result in a Chapter 2 Literature Survey double majority class. While misclassification is a concern, it can be remedied by applying distance weight in choosing new data categories using a voting majority technique. Weights of information length are used to determine data categories. In order to fix these issues, this paper suggests an alternative to the voting majority model in k-NN that makes use of a range weight method.

The weight between datasets may be determined by combining the k-nearest neighbor distance weight (DWKNN) and local k-nearest neighbor (LMKNN) approaches. Accuracy in categorization was enhanced by combining these two approaches. Multiple datasets are used to evaluate the tests' precision in relation to the original k-NN system. Combining LMKNN with DWKNN has been shown to increase k-NN's classification accuracy. This improvement in precision may go as high as 5.16% when applied to the real data. If k = 10, the maximum score is 90.91%, and if k = 1, the minimum is 84.85%.

Empirical proof supporting the effectiveness of K-Nearest Neighbor is offered, and the important factors that affect it are explored by Gustavo E.A.P.A. Batista *et al.* in 2009. Three variables—the number of closest neighbors, the weighting function, and the distance function—are studied. We compared nine different values for k, three different weighting functions, and three different distance measures to see which ones work best with the most typical applications. As a popular distance measure, the Euclidean distance also works well for qualitative characteristics. Datasets often include both qualitative and quantitative features, and it may be difficult to determine how to effectively manage them using a single attribute distance function. For qualitative features, one may use the overlap metric, whereas for quantitative attributes, the usual Euclidean distance would be appropriate. Heterogeneous Euclidean Overlap Metric (HEOM) is the name of this method. One alternative employs the Manhattan distance metric instead of the traditionally used Euclidean distance, which is known as the Heterogeneous Manhattan Overlap Metric.

The lack of access to further data on qualitative characteristics is seen as a weakness of the overlap metric. One way to get through this obstacle is through the Value Difference Metric. The VDM approach uses the classification similarity to quantify the gaps between these values for all of an element's conceivable states. For each characteristic in the training set, this process creates a distance matrix. The statistical sample size is too tiny to be relied upon for each value, and although each numerical attribute value is not unique, there are still an overwhelming number of randomly generated values, making distance calculations very suspect. Because of these issues, using the VDM directly on quantitative qualities is not recommended. The challenge of applying VDM on qualitative qualities may be overcome by resorting to the discretization strategy. A quantitative characteristic may be treated as a qualitative one by being discretized. Because of discretization, valuable quantitative data will be lost. Similar to HEOM, but with a different overlap measure and standardization, is the Heterogeneous Distance Function (HVDM), which employs VDM for qualitative qualities.

The effects of changing the settings on the k-nearest neighbor algorithm's behavior are outlined in this study. The findings of this study support the use of the inverse weighting function. This weighting function outperforms the other two weighting functions statistically, and its penalty for distant neighbors makes for a smooth impact of the parameter k on the algorithm's classification results. According to these findings, the optimal value for k is between 5 and 11 closest neighbors. According to the findings, the inverse weighting function is preferable, with k = 5 demonstrating the best mean performance for HEOM and HMOM, and k = 11 demonstrating the greatest mean performance for HVDM. In addition, there were no significant variations in the results obtained using HEOM, HMOM, and

HVDM for the distance function. Considering that HVDM may only result in classification when qualitative qualities are present, we have limited our analysis to the subset of datasets that have at least one qualitative attribute.

10.3 Methodology

As shown in Figure 10.2, a significant amount of pre-processing is required in order to build a speech recognition system that is accurate. As a consequence of this, the effectiveness and precision of the speech recognition system are both enhanced. Before digging into an analysis of data, it is standard procedure to do some preparatory processing on the data being examined. The process must begin with significant actions such as digitizing, sorting, pre-emphasis scanning, framing, and windowing.

The conversion of analogue data to digital format is the first step in the production of a speech. In digitized speech, a vocal signal is mapped to a series of numbers instead of being represented directly. The amplitude of a digitized signal at certain periods is used to determine when samples of the signal should be obtained in order to create a digital representation of the signal. The sampling rate is an important factor to take into account since it may be used to compute the number of samples taken each second. In order to do an accurate analysis of the waveform, at least two samples from each phase are necessary. One distinct data sample is used for the analysis of each of the positive and negative signal components.

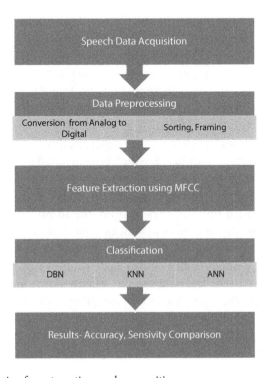

Figure 10.2 Machine learning for automatic speech recognition.

Features are extracted using MFCC (Mel Frequency Cepstral Coefficient). People believe that the structures of the vocal tract, along with other factors such as the tongue, teeth, and so on, are the fundamental contributors to the human voice. This form will ultimately decide the tone that is produced. Once the form has been correctly established, the phoneme that is being created should be expressed in the correct manner. The correct representation of the envelope of the short-term power spectrum, which is an expression of the form of the vocal tract, is within the purview of MFCCs and it is their obligation to fulfil this duty [21].

Given a test sample, the KNN [22] method first employs a subset of neighbors to compute the neighboring degrees of testing and training samples on training sets, and then labels the samples with the K tag of their closest neighbor. This is the fundamental concept that underpins the KNN algorithm. When there are several labels in the closest neighbor's K, the samples are placed in the category that has the majority of those labels. The upgraded version of the approach is used to cluster the training data, the training samples are then dispersed pretty equally, and a new partition clustering-based KNN classification algorithm is created in order to classify the test samples. During the iterative process of developing the new algorithm, make adjustments to the parameters of a dynamic K. A method that accepts as input a constant number, K, for a certain category is used from the very beginning to determine the location of the cluster's center. Pick out K pieces of information from the source papers, where K is the total number of groups. When deciding which cluster each individual item will largely be put in, the degree of similarity across all initial cluster centers will be taken into consideration. Following the examination of each of the practice exams, the K closest neighbor method is used in order to re-categorize the document in question. Carry on in this manner until there are no more changes that need to be made to any of the records.

For each iteration of the nearest k-neighbor search, you will be required to provide two values: the number of clusters to use (K). If the parameter is too small, not enough documents are found to provide an accurate identification; if it is too large, the report is incorrectly assigned to more distant clusters because there are more neighbors in those clusters. If the parameter is too small, not enough documents are found to provide an accurate identification. Include a rescaling of K' in each iteration by modifying the parameter specifying the nearest neighbor to the current value. This will allow the value to be more accurately represented. Each iteration of the clustering procedure adds one to the number of documents in the lowest class size of the cluster, which is designated by the letter K'. This is done to prevent the uneven categorization phenomenon and to ensure that the report is accurately grouped. The K-nearest neighbor algorithm is a basic method for organizing fresh instances in accordance with their degrees of similarity to previously stored data and for preserving older data (e.g., calculation of distance). Therefore, a distance metric is required in order to judge the many scenarios involving "closeness." In order to define an instance, we check for its nearest neighbors and choose the group of neighbors that has the most features with the instance itself. This allows us to narrow down the possible values for the instance's properties. The ranking of the closest neighbor is determined by calculating the distance between the unknown sample and all of the training samples.

Feed-forward networks and feed-backward networks are two types of neural networks that are included in ANN [23]. In feed-forward neural networks, signals can only go in one way, from the input to the output. To put it another way, the output of no layer is fed back into that layer; hence, there are no inputs. Consequently, there are no outputs (loops). The majority of the time, feed-forward NNs are uncomplicated systems that connect inputs to outcomes in a clear manner. Pattern recognition is a common use for them. This kind of administration also goes by the labels' top-down management and bottom-up management, to mention just two of its many aliases. The signals on a network are able to go in either direction after a feedback loop has been established. A feedback network has a dynamic "state" that is always changing up to the point when it reaches equilibrium. They will not move from their current position until the input is altered and a new equilibrium is discovered. The first two names are typically used to describe feedback structures, but the third term is usually used to describe feedback linkages in single-layer organizations.

The DBN is made up of a number of RBMs that have been piled one on top of the other, resulting in a complicated structure that has a great deal of obfuscated layers and a substantial sequence number. The performance of the visual layer in RBMs is constant regardless of the RBM instance being used. The first RBM layer that is created will be referred to as the "visible" layer of the DBN, while succeeding levels will be referred to as the "hidden" layers. In order for participants to be considered for DBN teaching, they will need to finish at least one RBM training session. Following the training of the RBM using example data, the output of the RBM is used as the hidden layer [24]. An RBM was educated with the help of the information that was acquired. After then, the output of the next RBM is enhanced by utilizing the input from the visible layer of the RBM that came before it, and so on and so forth. Deep neural network layer-by-layer training is another name for the outcome of this process (DNN). Because DBN employs unsupervised pre-training and layer-wise greedy during training, the network may be trained to have a greater total number of hidden layers than is possible with other neural network architectures. This is because DBN makes use of layer-wise greedy during training. The DBN techniques cannot work with back-propagation because of their incompatibility. It is simple to make the transition since DBN procedures are taught using RBM exclusively throughout the training process. Neuronal networks are responsible for the job of converting weights in both directions into ones that only go in one way. The more layers of hidden connections that a neural network has, as well as the more training data that it has been exposed to, the better it will perform. Values for the brands that are related to some of the training samples have been acquired with the help of a neural network that has been transformed. The top layer is connected to all of the different sorts of data as well as the total number of neurons in the network. Back-propagation models are used to fine-tune a neural network as a whole while it is being trained. This is done with the help of a neural network. The weights of the neural network have to be determined first before the second phase of training, which is the actual training. This phase comes after the pre-training phase. When employing a neural network, speed that is too great might actually be detrimental to the process. The DBN technique is a trademark structure that puts together the two parts of unsupervised learning. It is used in the deep learning field. Multiple restricted Boltzmann machines, also known as RBMs, are employed in the process of loading this kind of information into the system. This system must develop accurate representations of the data in order for it to be useful for supervised learning. Back-propagation, sometimes known as BP, is a technique that may be learned with this tutorial. It is necessary to use an algorithm in order to categorize the data and evaluate the accuracy of the classification.

10.4   Results

Research in acoustic phonetics, the study of events, and the assessment of automated discourse recognition systems may all benefit from reading speech from the TIMIT [25] corpus. There are 630 speakers of American English who are represented in TIMIT, each reading a phrase pool that is 10 phones broad. These speakers come from eight of the main vernaculars of American English. In addition to a discourse waveform document with a resolution of 16 bits and a frequency of 16 kilobits per second, the TIMIT corpus also contains time-adjusted orthographic, phonetic, and word recordings for each expression. The corpus configuration system was developed in a cooperative effort between MIT, TI, and SRI International (SRI). Before the CD-ROM was created, TI was in charge of the recording, MIT was in charge of the translation, and NIST was in charge of the final certification (NIST). The TIMIT corpus contains data that have all been checked and double checked by human eyes. Determined here are the phonetic and provincial inclusion groupings that will be put to use in testing and in practice. Information that may be accessed using a regular personal computer as well as written instructions are both included in this package. During the rehearsals, around 70% of the 6,300 possible speech signals are used, whereas only 30% are used during the real exams. We record 60 distinct (real-time) discourse signals in genuine contexts for the purpose of validation. Of these, we utilize 70% for training, and we use the remaining 30% for testing. There were a total of 110 conversation signals that were analyzed, and it was determined that 76 of them were reliable and continuous. Seventy percent of the signals were used for training, and 30% were subjected to the test. These vocalizations yielded a total of 375 distinguishing traits when analyzed. In order to start the process of processing the information voice corpus, attribute extraction using AMS is utilized. There are both clean and noisy signals present in the input, and they have been standardized, quantized, and windowed.

Five parameters—accuracy, sensitivity, specificity, precision, and recall—are used in this study to compare the performance of different algorithms. Results are shown in Figures 10.3 to 10.8.

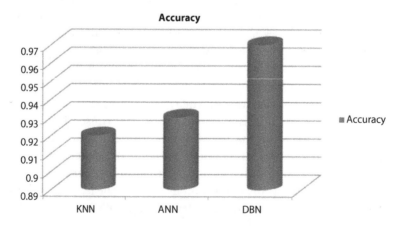

Figure 10.3 Accuracy of classifiers for automatic speech recognition.

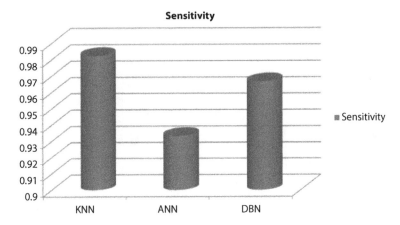

Figure 10.4 Sensitivity of classifiers for automatic speech recognition.

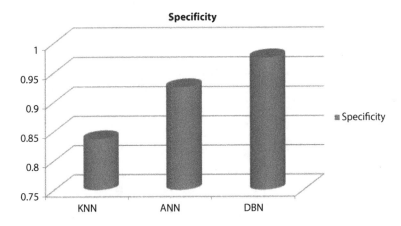

Figure 10.5 Specificity of classifiers for automatic speech recognition.

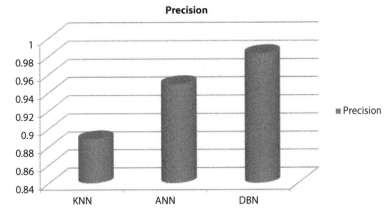

Figure 10.6 Precision of classifiers for automatic speech recognition.

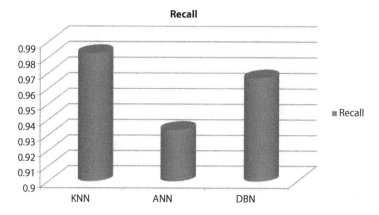

Figure 10.7 Recall of classifiers for automatic speech recognition.

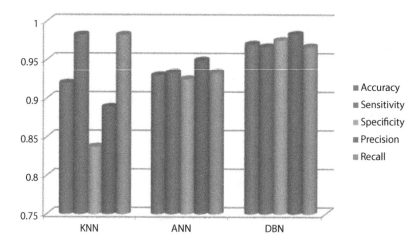

Figure 10.8 Accuracy, specificity, sensitivity, precision, and recall of classifiers for automatic speech recognition.

Accuracy= (TP + TN) / (TP + TN + FP + FN)
Sensitivity = TP/ (TP + FN)
Specificity = TN/ (TN + FP)
Precision = TP/ (TP + FP)
Recall = TP/ (TP + FN)

where
    TP = True Positive
    TN = True Negative
    FP = False Positive
    FN = False Negative

The use of automatic speech recognition (ASR) [26, 27] systems in practical contexts like digital voice assistants, interactive voice response (IVR) [28, 29], and news transcription has permeated our daily lives. For their superior performance, they are depending more and more on deep learning techniques [29, 30]. However, a growing corpus of research on adversarial machine learning has shown significant flaws in these core principles, raising major doubts about the reliability of ASR applications. To regain trust in employing ASR for safety-critical operations, it is necessary to overcome these issues [31–33]. An adversarial attack [34–37] on an ASR model enables the attacker to add a little amount of noise to a speech sample, which can cause the model to accurately transcribe the attacker's desired speech. On examining the traits of ASR models that may defeat targeted adversarial attacks, since this targeted adversarial [38–40] scenario is thought to be more dangerous for an ASR system than introducing noise that results in any random prediction, According to research, hostile [41, 42] instances are expressions of non-robust properties that a deep learning network [43] has learned. The goal is to regularise the ASR model training paradigm in order to teach the model robust features that can withstand such attacks [43, 44].

10.5   Conclusion

Automatic speech recognizers have seen significant improvements in their level of performance during the previous 10 years. The vast majority of research have investigated the different technological aids that are now accessible to those who have difficulties communicating verbally. According to recent research, the use of speech recognition software by those who have difficulty communicating verbally is well within the capability of today's technology. However, there is not a lot of research that looks at the human aspect of things, which is the primary factor that is slowing down advancement in this sector. Concerns have been voiced with regard to a variety of issues that include individuals. People who have problems communicating verbally have the best chance of benefiting from advances in speech recognition technology. A framework for automated voice recognition that is based on machine learning is presented here in this chapter. The key components of the proposed system are referred to as "speech acquisition," "speech preprocessing," "feature extraction," and "classification." Five parameters—accuracy, sensitivity, specificity, precision, and recall—are used in this study to compare the performance of different algorithms. The accuracy of Deep Belief Algorithm is the highest.

References

1. Balaji, V. and Sadashiappa, G., Speech disabilities in adults and the suitable speech recognition software tools – A review. *International Conference on Computing and Network Communications (CoCoNet'15)*, Dec. 16-19, 2015.
2. Jamal, N., Shanta, S., Mahmud, F., Shaabani, M.N.A.H., Automatic speech recognition (ASR) based approach for speech therapy of aphasic patients: A review. *AIP Conference Proceedings*, vol. 1883, p. 020028, 2017, https://doi.org/10.1063/1.5002046 Published Online: 14 September 2017.

3. Cutajar, M., Gatt, E., Grech, I., Casha, O., Micallef, J., Comparative study of automatic speech recognition techniques. *IET Signal Process.*, 7, 1, 25–46, 2013.

4. Akçay, M.B. and Oğuz, K., Speech emotion recognition: Emotional models, databases, features, preprocessing methods, supporting modalities, and classifiers. *Speech Communication*, 116, 56–76, 2020.

5. Wang, Y., Han, K., Wang, D., Exploring monaural features for classification-based speech segregation. *IEEE Trans. Audio, Speech, Lang. Process.*, 21, 2, 270–279, 2013.

6. Hemamalini, V., Rajarajeswari, S., Nachiyappan, S., Sambath, M., Devi, T., Singh, Food quality inspection and grading using efficient image segmentation and machine learning-based system. *J. Of Food Qual.*, 2022, 1–6, 2022, doi: 10.1155/2022/5262294.

7. Prasad, J.V.D., Zamani, A.S., K., A., Naved, M., Pallathadka, H., Sammy, F., Kaliyaperumal, K., Computational technique based on machine learning and image processing for medical image analysis of breast cancer diagnosis. *Secur. Commun. Networks*, 2022, Article ID 1918379, 7, 2022, https://doi.org/10.1155/2022/1918379.

8. Shahamiri, S.R. and Salim, S.S.B., Artificial neural networks as speech recognisers for dysarthric speech: Identifying the best-performing set of MFCC parameters and studying a speaker-independent approach. *Adv. Eng. Inf.*, 28, 102–110, 2014.

9. Szczurowska, I., Kuniszyk-Jozkowiak, W., Smolka, E., The application of Kohonen and multilayer perceptron networks in the speech nonfluency analysis. *Arch. Acoustics*, 31, 205, 2006.

10. Świetlicka, I., Kuniszyk-Jóźkowiak, W., Smołka, E., Artificial neural networks in the disabled speech analysis. *Advances in Intelligent and Soft Computing*, pp. 347–354, 2009.

11. Nayak, J., Bhat, P.S., Acharya, R., Aithal, U.V., Classification and analysis of speech abnormalities. *ITBM-RBM*, 26, 319–327, 2005.

12. Lou, P.J., Anderson, P., Johnson, M., Disfluency detection using auto-correlational neural networks. *Proceedings of the 2018 Conference on Empirical Methods in Natural Language Processing*, Association for Computational Linguistics, Brussels, Belgium, pp. 4610–4619, October 31 - November 4, 2018.

13. Mengistu, K.T. and Rudzicz, F., Adapting acoustic and lexical models to dysarthric speech. *Canadian Conference on Artificial Intelligence*, Springer, 2011.

14. Rudzicz, F., Using articulatory likelihoods in the recognition of dysarthric speech. *Speech Commun.*, 54, 430–444, 2012. Elsevier.

15. Le, D. and Provost, E.M., Improving automatic recognition of aphasic speech with AphasiaBank. *Interspeech*, 2016, 2681–2685, 2016.

16. Lee, T., Liu, Y., Huang, P.-W., Chien, J.-T., Lam, W.K., Yeung, Y.T. *et al.*, Automatic speech recognition for acoustical analysis and assessment of cantonese pathological voice and speech, in: *Acoustics, Speech and Signal Processing (ICASSP), 2016 IEEE International Conference on*, pp. 6475–6479, 2016.

17. Hasegawa-Johnson, M., Gunderson, J., Perlman, A., Huang, T., HMM-based and SVM-based recognition of the speech of talkers with spastic dysarthria. *Acoustics, Speech, and Signal Processing, 1988. ICASSP-88, 1988 International Conference on*, vol. 3, pp. III – III, June 2006.

18. Ai, O.C., M, H., Yaacob, S., Chee, L.S., Classification of speech dysfluencies with MFCC and LPCC features. *Expert Syst. Appl.*, 39, 2157–2165, 2012.

19. Priya, L.T., Raajan, N.R., Raju, N., Preethi, P., Mathini, S., Speech and non-speech identification and classification using KNN algorithm. *International Conference On Modeling Optimization And Computing*, Elsevier Ltd, pp. 1877–7058, 2012.

20. Syaliman, K.U., Nababan, E.B., Sitompul, O.S., Improving the accuracy of k nearest neighbor using local mean based and distance weight. *2nd International Conference on Computing and Applied Informatics 2017 Journal of Physics: Conf. Series*, vol. 978, p. 012047, 2018, doi: 10.1088/1742-6596/978/1/012047.

21. Raufani Aminullah, A., Nasrun, M., Setianingsih, C., Human emotion detection with speech recognition using mel-frequency cepstral coefficient and support vector machine. *2021 International Conference on Artificial Intelligence and Mechatronics Systems (AIMS)*, pp. 1–6, 2021, doi: 10.1109/AIMS52415.2021.9466077.

22. Javid, J., Mughal, M.A., Karim, M., Using kNN algorithm for classification of distribution transformers health index. *2021 International Conference on Innovative Computing (ICIC)*, pp. 1–6, 2021, doi: 10.1109/ICIC53490.2021.9693013.

23. Obeidat, M.A., Mansour, A.M., Al Omaireen, B., Abdallah, J., Khazalah, F., Alaqtash, M., A deep review and analysis of artificial neural network use in power application with further recommendation and future direction. *2021 12th International Renewable Engineering Conference (IREC)*, pp. 1–5, 2021, doi: 10.1109/IREC51415.2021.9427846.

24. Chintada, K.R., Yalla, S.P., Uriti, A., A deep belief network based land cover classification. *2021 Innovations in Power and Advanced Computing Technologies (i-PACT)*, pp. 1–5, 2021, doi: 10.1109/i-PACT52855.2021.9696524.

25. https://paperswithcode.com/dataset/timit.

26. Mahor, V., Bijrothiya, S., Rawat, R., Kumar, A., Garg, B., Pachlasiya, K., IoT and artificial intelligence techniques for public safety and security, in: *Smart Urban Computing Applications*, p. 111, 2023.

27. Mahor, V., Pachlasiya, K., Garg, B., Chouhan, M., Telang, S., Rawat, R., Mobile operating system (Android) vulnerability analysis using machine learning, in: *Proceedings of International Conference on Network Security and Blockchain Technology: ICNSBT 2021*, pp. 159–169, Springer Nature Singapore, Singapore, 2022, June.

28. Rawat, R., Garg, B., Pachlasiya, K., Mahor, V., Telang, S., Chouhan, M., Mishra, R., SCNTA: Monitoring of network availability and activity for identification of anomalies using machine learning approaches. *Int. J. Inf. Technol. Web Eng. (IJITWE)*, 17, 1, 1–19, 2022.

29. Rawat, R., Rimal, Y.N., William, P., Dahima, S., Gupta, S., Sankaran, K.S., Malware threat affecting financial organization analysis using machine learning approach. *Int. J. Inf. Technol. Web Eng. (IJITWE)*, 17, 1, 1–20, 2022.

30. Rawat, R., Mahor, V., Chouhan, M., Pachlasiya, K., Telang, S., Garg, B., Systematic literature review (SLR) on social media and the digital transformation of drug trafficking on darkweb, in: *International Conference on Network Security and Blockchain Technology*, pp. 181–205, Springer, Singapore, 2022.

31. Rawat, R., Ayodele Oki, O., Sankaran, S., Florez, H., Ajagbe, S.A., Techniques for predicting dark web events focused on the delivery of illicit products and ordered crime. *Int. J. Electr. Comput. Eng. (IJECE)*, 13, 5, 5354–5365, Oct. 2023, doi: 10.11591/ijece.v13i5.pp5354-5365.

32. Rawat, R., Garg, B., Mahor, V., Telang, S., Pachlasiya, K., Chouhan, M., Organ trafficking on the dark web—The data security and privacy concern in healthcare systems, in: *Internet of Healthcare Things: Machine Learning for Security and Privacy*, pp. 189–216, 2022.

33. Vyas, P., Vyas, G., Chauhan, A., Rawat, R., Telang, S., Gottumukkala, M., Anonymous trading on the dark online marketplace: An exploratory study, in: *Using Computational Intelligence for the Dark Web and Illicit Behavior Detection*, pp. 272–289, IGI Global, 2022.

34. Rawat, R., Oki, O.A., Sankaran, K.S., Olasupo, O., Ebong, G.N., Ajagbe, S.A., A new solution for cyber security in big data using machine learning approach, in: *Mobile Computing and Sustainable Informatics: Proceedings of ICMCSI 2023*, pp. 495–505, Springer Nature Singapore, Singapore, 2023.

35. Rawat, R., Chakrawarti, R.K., Raj, A., Mani, G., Chidambarathanu, K., Bhardwaj, R., Association rule learning for threat analysis using traffic analysis and packet filtering approach. *Int. J. Inf. Technol.*, 1–11, 2023.

36. Rawat, R., Logical concept mapping and social media analytics relating to cyber criminal activities for ontology creation. *Int. J. Inf. Technol.*, 15, 2, 893–903, 2023.

37. Rawat, R., Mahor, V., Álvarez, J.D., Ch, F., Cognitive systems for dark web cyber delinquent association malignant data crawling: A review, in: *Handbook of Research on War Policies, Strategies, and Cyber Wars*, pp. 45–63, 2023.

38. Rawat, R., Chakrawarti, R.K., Vyas, P., Gonzáles, J.L.A., Sikarwar, R., Bhardwaj, R., Intelligent fog computing surveillance system for crime and vulnerability identification and tracing. *Int. J. Inf. Secur. Priv. (IJISP)*, 17, 1, 1–25, 2023.

39. Rawat, R., Sowjanya, A.M., Patel, S.I., Jaiswal, V., Khan, I., Balaram, A. (Eds.), *Using Machine Intelligence: Autonomous Vehicles Volume 1*, John Wiley & Sons, 2022.

40. Rawat, R., Mahor, V., Díaz-Álvarez, J., Chávez, F., Rooted learning model at fog computing analysis for crime incident surveillance, in: *2022 International Conference on Smart Generation Computing, Communication and Networking (SMART GENCON)*, pp. 1–9, IEEE, 2022, December.

41. Rawat, R. and Shrivastav, S.K., SQL injection attack detection using SVM. *Int. J. Comput. Appl.*, 42, 13, 1–4, 2012.

42. Rawat, R., Bhardwaj, P., Kaur, U., Telang, S., Chouhan, M., Sankaran, K.S., *Smart vehicles for communication, volume 2*, John Wiley & Sons, 2023.

43. Mahor, V., Garg, B., Telang, S., Pachlasiya, K., Chouhan, M., Rawat, R., Cyber threat phylogeny assessment and vulnerabilities representation at thermal power station, in: *Proceedings of International Conference on Network Security and Blockchain Technology: ICNSBT 2021*, pp. 28–39, Springer Nature Singapore, Singapore, 2022, June.

44. Rawat, R., Gupta, S., Sivaranjani, S., Cu, O.K., Kuliha, M., Sankaran, K.S., Malevolent information crawling mechanism for forming structured illegal organisations in hidden networks. *Int. J. Cyber Warf. Terror. (IJCWT)*, 12, 1, 1–14, 2022.

11

Conversational Artificial Intelligence at Industrial Internet of Things

Dhirendra Siddharth[1]*, DilipKumar Jang Bahadur Saini[2], Mummadi Ramchandra[1] and Summathi Loganathan[3]

[1]Sreenidhi Institute of Science and Technology, Hyderabad, Telangana, India
[2]Department of Computer Science and Engineering, Himalayan School of Science & Technology, Swami Rama Himalayan University Uttarakhand, Dehradun, India
[3]Department of Computer Science and Engineering, Thanthai Hans Rover College, Trichy, India

Abstract

The Internet of Things (IoT), which links physical things or devices to the internet, is one of the fundamental technologies influencing the future. The system's usefulness and intelligence may be boosted by merging it with other technology advancements, which is something else it provides for. Due to considerable developments in conversational platforms and frameworks, a number of firms now utilize chatbots. The relevance of IoT and how widespread it is in customer interactions in today's digitally linked world have been made evident to enterprises. Several issues must be handled by IoT systems, including the unified user interface (UI). Applications, services, and settings must be consistently accessible to users across all devices. The quantity of dashboards and applications for each new "IoT object" in the ecosystem could be overwhelming for consumers in a connected world. The businesses' key problems include offering linked devices with cutting-edge smart capabilities for a better user experience and merging user experiences across numerous connected devices.

Keywords: Conversational artificial intelligence, industrial Internet of Things, Internet of Things

11.1 Introduction

The future of website design and development must include conversational AI since chatbots have begun to be embedded into websites, enabling direct client involvement. Chatbots and conversational AI, both of which are taught by algorithms that enable them to learn from prior interactions, require businesses to understand machine learning in order to deploy them. Therefore, in order to effectively administer their websites, firms do not necessarily need to employ sizable staff teams [1]. Instead of forcing users into a pre-defined set of replies that may or may not be appropriate, conversations with these bots are intended to speed up and enhance customer service while also giving

---

*Corresponding author: siddharth.dhirendra1@gmail.com

Romil Rawat, Rajesh Kumar Chakrawarti, Sanjaya Kumar Sarangi, Piyush Vyas, Mary Sowjanya Alamanda, Kotagiri Srividya and Krishnan Sakthidasan Sankaran (eds.) Conversational Artificial Intelligence, (169–184) © 2024 Scrivener Publishing LLC

users choice over what they want from their interactions. Many businesses are adding conversational AI into their website designs in an effort to draw in more customers [2]. By keeping them updated about the items, it also aids in retaining current clients while luring in new ones.

11.1.1   What is Conversational AI?

A class of artificial intelligence called "Conversational AI" enables real-time communication between humans and machines. Its user interface is comparable to that of a human since speech recognition technologies and automated conversations are used. The technologies that make up conversational artificial intelligence include context awareness, machine learning, and natural language processing (NLP). Language distinction, intent interpretation, and voice and text recognition are all capabilities of the technology. Additionally, it responds in a way that is human-like [3]. Conversational AI built on machine learning enables chatbots and other conversational interfaces. Conversational AI may employ natural language processing, machine learning, deep learning, and even video games to deliver a compelling user experience. Conversational commerce, which is gaining popularity in the customer service sector, describes interactions between consumers and their digital counterparts using the appropriate technologies.

11.1.2   What Does Conversational AI Do?

One application of conversational AI is chatbots. The greatest conversational AI chatbots now in use are Google Allo and Amazon's Alexa; both of these AI chatbots are built to respond to requests quickly and logically. Beyond its normal field of application, conversational AI has a variety of uses. It could be included into video games to raise the level of fun (like Halo). Since chatbots have started to be integrated into websites, enabling direct client engagement, conversational AI is a crucial part of the future of website design and development. Today's users utilize a variety of devices, including smart TVs and smartphones, so websites need to maintain visitor attention. Due to the conversational feature, users may do this action from any place and using any device.

11.1.3   How Does Conversational AI Work?

A chatbot may act as the user interface for users to communicate with the website in order to allow conversational AI. Today's chatbots are employed on websites to respond to visitor questions about the site and usually other topics as well. Usually, the user may select a personality for them. As online retailing platforms like Amazon integrate conversational AI into their systems and allow users to make purchases from home using any device at any time, the field of conversational AI is growing in prominence. Conversations with these bots are meant to enhance and accelerate the customer service process by allowing consumers pick what they want from their contacts rather than pushing them into a pre-defined range of responses that may or may not be acceptable. Many businesses are incorporating conversational AI with text to speech components into the design of their websites in an effort to increase their clientele, better communicate with their existing consumers about their services, and attract new ones. Conversational AI, which can be used to make life easier for both the customer and the company, is growing in popularity as more people utilize devices like tablets and smartphones. By removing the need for users to enter information into web forms on devices that are not made for typing out lengthy chats, conversational AI speeds up this process and encourages effective collaboration. Users of websites using AI chatbots feel more valued by the company since they have a voice to express their needs and a sense that the company values them, which improves the user experience all around [4]. The usage of smartphones and tablets more often has accelerated the development of conversational AI. Because more people use mobile devices than PCs when traveling, conversational AI chatbots on these platforms enhance business interactions with customers [5]. The two-way contact between a consumer and a website may be designed to provide better outcomes since occasionally website users prefer personalised information over a pre-set list of solutions or FAQs.

11.2 Technology Components Used in Conversational AI

A variety of technologies are used to run the conversational artificial intelligence. These include the following:

11.2.1 Natural Language Processing (NLP)

Conversational AI uses a language analysis technique called natural language processing (NLP). Languages were previously treated using linguistics, computers, and statistical NLP. Deep learning is improving the capabilities of both NLP processing and conversational AI.

11.2.2 Advanced Dialog Management (ADM)

Natural language processing is used by the ADM to help in response development. The text's aim of conversation management has an impact on the answers. In the end, NLP transforms these replies into a human-readable manner.

11.2.3 Machine Learning (ML)

Machine learning's characteristics, techniques, datasets, and formats often enhance experience (ML). Artificial intelligence is what it is due to this characteristic. The AI-powered system becomes better at spotting trends as input grows.

11.2.4 Automatic Speech Recognition (ASR)

Automatic speech recognition is more commonly referred to as voice recognition (ASR). It uses technology to convert spoken voice into machine- and human-readable plain text.

The technology components stated above are used to recognize, understand, respond to, and learn from user contact.

11.3   Benefits of Conversational AI

Many benefits of conversational AI make it simple to use and might provide organizations cost-effective alternatives. Here are a few of its advantages.

11.3.1   Improved Scalability

Conversational AI may be used by businesses at a cheap cost and with ease. As new companies enter the market, the infrastructure in this industry is continuously developing. It has opened up new markets and decreased the cost of doing business in numerous areas.

11.3.2   Cost-Efficient Technology

It will be expensive to hire a customer support staff, and it will be difficult to provide a 24-hour service. As a consequence, it will be economical for your company to use conversational AI to help your clients. The development of 24/7 services and chatbot training are made possible by conversational AI [6]. Your support team may be able to automate time-consuming procedures and reply to client information requests with the use of conversation driven by artificial intelligence.

11.3.3   Improved User Engagement

Customers must receive ready-to-share real-time information from businesses. Users of your application or website visitors may submit any questions about the goods or services you offer. As a result, an AI-powered chatbot or conversation may be able to hold the audience's attention. Because the conversational AI tool is simpler to use than human staff, users and consumers may interact with the business more effectively and get answers to their questions faster. Lower attrition rates and more income for organizations are results of improved user engagement. Queue-cutting is an option, which improves the client experience. A happy customer could promote your brand and help your business.

11.3.4   Better Accessibility

The availability of your company's products and services will increase as a result of conversational AI. In addition to print media, voice technology may be used to communicate with your customers. If you can use conversational AI to build a tailored experience, you can rapidly locate the information that customers are looking for [7]. You can more actively share ideas with end users if you let businesses cross-market their goods and services to consumers.

11.4   How to Create Conversational AI?

Let us now look at how to develop conversational AI for your business. You spoke about the benefits of using contemporary technology at this wonderful event, which may assist and maintain the conversation with your clients and crucial clientele. Many companies develop chatbots and conversational AI specifically for the office setting. The creation of one's own platform is an option for some people, but it is costly and needs substantial technological expertise [8].

Website Voice is a terrific choice if you want to keep things straightforward while still getting the benefits of user involvement, increased accessibility, a cost-effective platform, and higher scalability [9]. This application may be implemented right away and will give the writing on your website a very appealing voice.

Additionally, you may use these techniques to create conversational AI:

1. **Setting objectives:** To monitor your progress and get better help, you should define your goals at the beginning of the process. Is it your goal to increase website activity and attract loyal visitors? Do you prefer to keep your customer service expenses as low as possible?

2. **Create strategies:** You need to outline the required steps and provide a clear picture of the path visitors will take while interacting with your business online.

3. **Setup the bot or AI:** You must provide details and pose questions in order to train your gadget to operate on its own.

4. **Synchronization of tools:** You must integrate all necessary technology, such as email automation software, lead generation tools, and CRM.

5. **Evaluate and improve:** Once everything is in place, you may maximize business growth by creating KPIs and monitoring results.

11.5 Conversational Platforms and Internet of Things: Relevance and Benefits

Popular and quickly expanding instant messaging (IM) apps like WhatsApp, Facebook Messenger, Snapchat, Line, and Telegram frequently include conversational user interfaces. Compared to other internet programs like social networking sites and email clients, instant messaging services are used by more individuals [10]. Chatbot programs, which are constructed on top of pre-existing platforms, profit on the tremendous popularity of chat-based interfaces. The globalization of chat platforms has boosted the need for a variety of chatbot applications and use cases.

Thanks to advancements in artificial intelligence (AI), particularly in the field of natural language processing, the bar for chatbot effectiveness and standards has also been raised in terms of conversational ease, adaptability, and the ability to allow users to express complex demands using natural language (NLP) [11]. RESTful Web APIs are frequently used by IoT and chatbots because they are so simple to utilize for service delivery.

Here are some of the reasons behind the implementation of chatbots and IoT:

1. For both IoT and Chatbots, developers can utilize an API or service-oriented approach. This implies that the techniques used to develop web API-based applications, such as chatbots, for online services—especially those that employ RESTful designs—should be the same for embedded devices.

2. The design and deployment of chatbots, as well as IoT applications, may be made swift and straightforward utilizing cloud platforms, removing

the need to worry about underlying technologies such as Transport Layer, Storage, and Processing.

3. The use of HTTP RESTful protocols as the only channel for integrating chatbots into IoT systems has become technologically viable and uncomplicated thanks to the establishment of HTTP RESTful standards.

4. The capacity to coordinate chatbot programming within IoT platforms and frameworks is a primary motivator for establishing platforms and frameworks that can do so.

11.5.1   Benefits of Implementing Chatbots with the IoT Interface

The Internet of Things is a collection of smart devices that we utilize in our everyday lives, and by incorporating chatbots into the IoT interface, information and data can be conveyed in a more effective fashion, and this will occur throughout the day as chatbots seldom fatigue.

Smart IoT devices may be operated using plain English without the user needing to recollect elaborate instructions and information essential for establishing intent. The gadgets that customers use on a regular basis may be swiftly added for them to execute various sorts of jobs and submit queries [12].

A chatbot may understand simple phrases or gestures or autocorrect mistakes in the case of a messaging app and may even know popular terminology. Bots can also self-regulate their responses. Therefore, when the chatbot interacts more with the people, it becomes more intuitive and understands the context better. Although the whole command may not be expressed, it may interpret the idea perfectly. Chatbots may boost user desires for more engagement via the IoT interface, for example, if a user receives information from a device regarding anything, he or she may ask it a question in natural language, and a smart chatbot would answer if it has the relevant knowledge. Compared to traditional design interfaces, which have challenges with information abstraction, this has eased interactions with chatbots via IoT.

11.6   Internet of Things Status for Industry

Through sensors, smart equipment, and, like everything else in Industry 4.0, new methods for gathering mountains of data, the Internet of Things (IoT) is quickly becoming more and more applicable in industrial contexts. It improves operations, resource utilization, inventory management, and other areas.

By 2025, $992 billion in investments might be made worldwide in the Industrial Internet of Things (IIoT), according to a new projection by Million Insights. IoT initiatives are being worked on by 85% of businesses, according to a Microsoft survey.

11.6.1   The Impact of IIoT on Operational Effectiveness

The IIoT's quick adoption in the industrial sector is not surprising given how it helps firms optimize their operations through the use of smart equipment, sensors, RFID, and other linked technologies.

According to IDC data, industrial activities were the costliest IoT use cases in 2019. Companies who made the conversion to digital operations saw benefits in overall efficiency of 82%, reported product failures of 49%, and customer satisfaction of 45%, according to a study by the American Society for Quality (ASQ).

In the few sentences that follow, we will concentrate on a few specific instances of how IoT solutions are improving operational performance at diverse organizations.

11.6.2   Evolution of Legacy Systems

One of the key benefits offered by IIoT is the capacity to replace outdated systems. According to McKinsey, the typical plant is 25 years old and uses disconnected machinery that is, on average, 9 years old.

Due to this distance, it is difficult to implement monitoring and controls throughout the whole organization. A practical strategy to enhance current assets is to use integration platforms, a class of cutting-edge technologies that enable manufacturers to connect sensors to vintage equipment. Similar to an adapter for older machinery, these devices gather data given by wired industrial protocols and transfer it via long-range Wi-Fi to a remote-control center [13].

It is also critical to keep in mind that IIoT technology infuses analog processes with intelligence, underscoring the fact that innovation goes beyond the constraints of the instruments themselves. As an illustration, consider the interconnected handhelds and helmets that some businesses have developed to help technicians while they are at work. Through checklists and maintenance procedures, these tools help staff members by lowering the possibility of danger or error while carrying out routine tasks.

11.6.3   Increased Efficiency in Energy

In a Panoramic Power study, 77% of businesses said that their monthly power bills or energy monitoring tools—which only gave them a quick glance at consumption trends—were their main sources of information on energy use. The limitations are altered by IoT, allowing enterprises to install equipment with sensors to monitor energy usage trends.

Today's businesses have unparalleled visibility into their energy usage, and they may employ sensors to check for anomalies, after-hours use, inefficient behaviours, and unforeseen usage trends. The information might be utilized to develop preventative maintenance programs or enhance manufacturing techniques [14].

11.6.4   Intelligent Data Analytics

No industry is now setting the bar for innovation when it comes to data analytics. As industries including manufacturing, oil, utilities, and aerospace swiftly embrace IoT-powered sensors and wireless technologies, the true potential of IIoT is becoming more and more apparent.

The creators of these interconnected gadgets must be able to effectively extract and use the most important data. IoT analytics solutions are becoming more and more necessary as a consequence, and businesses like SAP, Teradata, and SAS are assisting organizations in managing the data flow by offering AI and machine-learning technology [15].

The most recent generation of advanced analytics software centralizes real-time data from all linked systems, from the manufacturing floor to the work site, to break down data silos. Leaders may gather information from a number of touchpoints to gain a comprehensive understanding of how their organization is running. In light of these findings, they could then change their original strategy.

11.6.5 Support Human Workers, Cobots are Connected

Collaborative robots, or "cobots," will be the defining element of the industrial internet of things and will cost $12.4 billion by 2025. There is no error in this. Cobots are distinctive even if the concept of industrial robots is not entirely new. One is that while developing a normal robot, human safety is not the primary priority. Despite the fact that fences commonly separate industrial robots from their human co-workers, safety safeguards are typically in place. Cobots are tiny robots designed to work alongside humans [16]. Cobots are packed with sensors, just like other Internet of Things (IoT) technologies, giving them position, person, and context awareness. Cobots are useful in many settings, such as the operating room and the coffee shop, but they are particularly well-suited for a number of manufacturing vocations, such as:

1. Machine tending
2. Quality assurance testing
3. Finishing tasks like grinding or polishing
4. Packaging and palletizing

11.6.6 Smart Technologies (Digital Twins) are Becoming More Popular

IT teams and data scientists may employ digital twins, which are virtual clones of genuine technology, to perform simulations prior to developing such goods in the real world. An increasing number of industrial organizations are rebuilding their assets digitally using IoT technologies. Businesses may accomplish this by acquiring environmental data, such as temperature, condition, and location, from the sensors on each physical asset and then putting it through numerous scenarios to see how it reacts to change. Due to their ability to aggregate process data, provide accurate insights, and minimize operational inefficiencies, digital twins are becoming more and more popular in the IIoT ecosystem [17]. According to Gartner, 22% of organizations now employ digital twins, and another 43% want to use them during the next 3 years.

11.6.7 The IIoT Landscape is Changing Due to Edge Computing

The organization, processing, and interchange of data produced by networked equipment are being revolutionized by edge computing and the Industrial Internet of Things (IIoT). Cloud computing formerly predominated when it came to managing connected devices and data. However, as more companies deploy IIoT devices and sensors, there will inevitably be a lot more data. Better methods will be needed by businesses to organize, manage, and protect all of those data. Security issues and latency issues result from cloud-based solutions' inability to keep up. Edge computing provides a number of advantages, including the ability to handle local data in IoT devices more effectively [18]. Businesses can monitor data in real time at scale as it does not have to travel as far as it would in a cloud-based architecture.

11.6.8   Adoption Hurdles and Common Pitfalls

Even though many businesses utilize IIoT, more are searching for the best use for this cutting-edge technology. In a poll conducted by PwC's German office, 91% of participants claimed to be going through a digital transformation, while just 7% claimed to be "completely digitized." Experts have cautioned that a corporation may not be able to adopt IIoT technology effectively in a variety of circumstances:

> **Lack of Expertise:** Gartner highlighted that IIoT initiatives are usually surprising since organizations typically fail to identify the right criteria and do not install the technology needed to make constant improvements.
> **Vendors:** Bain & Company underlined that suppliers and customers often do not value the same use cases. For example, clients might be eager to use augmented reality technology for maintenance and training, while suppliers are more focused on promoting predictive maintenance.
> **Security Concerns:** Microsoft reported that 97% of organizations face security vulnerabilities associated with IoT implementation. Given the vast volume of data created by connected IoT devices, manufacturers are anxious about safeguarding internal and customer data from escalating security issues.
> **Unclear ROI:** Finally, enterprises are cautious about whether investment in connected devices and systems will provide meaningful advantages.
>   As we have mentioned in the context of microservices and DevOps, any change without a defined use case and quantifiable set of goals are likely to fail. It is crucial to emphasize that, despite the fact that cobots are growing more and more widespread, businesses are not required to buy a sizable number of them or outfit their equipment with sensors. The same principle applies to the installation of the IIoT.

11.7   Scope of IIoT in Future

As the industrial internet of things (IIoT) expands, businesses of all sizes have a new opportunity to optimize operations, enhance consumer experiences, and realize considerable financial gains.

Companies of all sizes will need to implement predictive maintenance, improved device connectivity, and more affordable access in order to reap the financial rewards of linked buildings. Increased productivity, cost savings, quick action, and early opportunity and problem identification are a few of them [19].

11.7.1   The Effect of IIoT on Research and Development

The IIoT has already altered how companies develop new products. In order to reduce operating expenses, increase productivity, and improve current operations, more than a third of today's organizations have already started using IoT devices, according to Vodafone.

The most current advancements in industrial enterprises' usage of IIoT in the creation of new goods are described in the 2019 IoT Signals report from Microsoft. They do it for this reason:

- **Mass Production and Product Assembly.** Sensors are installed in manufacturing equipment to help businesses determine maintenance needs, project delivery deadlines, etc.
- **Validation and Quality Assurance.** Organizations employing real-time data will assess the batch for dependability and performance quality by sending data to connected equipment at vendor sites.
- **Distribution.** Completed products are delivered to retailers and customers together with inventory management tools.
- **Future Use Cases.** According to Microsoft, industrial IoT-connected hardwired equipment will eventually be more popular among enterprises than Wi-Fi-based alternatives. They add that businesses will begin to apply their validation approach to other product lines and use cases if they develop a repeatable procedure.
- **Testing.** Then, businesses may send those requirements to an overseas supplier for 3D printing a test batch.
- **Development.** Businesses may create new concepts and estimate demand for their goods without wasting physical resources by using 3D modeling software, digital twins, and real-time production and equipment data.

11.8   Work of IIoT with Additional New Innovations

In order to obtain a glimpse into the industrial IoT's future, it is a good idea to start by looking at some of the most popular ideas for 2020.

The following are a few IIoT developments in the field of the industrial Internet of Things:

11.8.1   Manufacturing as a Service with IIoT

IoT as a Service (IoTaaS), like practically everything else in today's cloud-connected world, is becoming more and more well-liked among tech-savvy businesses. The phrase "Internet of Things as a Service" refers to the control, monitoring, and provision of networked devices as a service (IoTaaS). With the help of IoTaaS solutions, customers can quickly build a heterogeneous ecosystem of intelligent "things," which they can utilize to begin gaining real-time insights from all of the linked data sources [20]. A broad range of devices, sensors, and actuators can be supported through the APIs that come with these systems.

Companies may swiftly deploy connected devices in an industrial setting and manage them using IIoT as a service, while a third-party supplier takes care of security, updates, difficult analytics, and other duties.

Thanks to IoTaaS providers, smart manufacturing may be made accessible to a wider variety of organizations, including those with little to no experience with IT, OT, or the cloud. Understanding how their suppliers manage data security is advised for organizations even though it is not required.

By offering this "plug-and-play" option, it is hoped that organizations would be able to save time and money by avoiding the need to, for instance, construct a cloud backend for a specific piece of hardware. Instead, businesses may cut operating costs, promote products more quickly, and put together an entire system in only a few clicks [21].

11.8.2   Cloud and Edge Computing Together

According to the Industrial Internet Consortium, 70% of senior IT executives think that the ability of the industrial IoT to combine data from all linked sources into a single data model is its greatest value (IIC).

As the IIoT expands, more and more data sources are being created. Because of this, many businesses need processing power spread over numerous sites. Organizations require hybrid models to make the best use of these data (cloud edge). These methods enable real-time data analyses and provide scalable, affordable storage alternatives [22].

Here, we take a closer look at this. Simply said, edge computing allows companies to locally and instantaneously adjust data coming from sensors and other devices. Edge computing was developed to address the latency problems that typically plague cloud-based systems, giving companies the ability to avoid delays and lag time that raise safety concerns, result in production failures, and pose a risk of security breaches [23].

However, thanks to the cloud, businesses now have a scalable, economical alternative for long-term data storage. It is also ideal for the historical analysis needed for procedures like demand forecasting, industrial optimization, and supply chain management.

Businesses may create a deep learning model that can be used at the edge thanks to the enormous volumes of data that cloud-based systems manage. For example, AI may be taught to recognize trends and alert customers to cloud-based dangers. The model might then be applied in real-world scenarios to collect information and swiftly detect risks.

11.8.3   Prevention-Based Service

The utilization of data for predictive maintenance is a notion that is new to the IIoT. Early adopters have been utilizing IoT technology for asset management tasks for some time, but its usefulness is expanding as a result of efforts like digital twins, augmented reality, and artificial intelligence. Businesses can now monitor how much energy and equipment are being used, which helps to reduce waste and improve industrial processes, thanks to embedded sensors. Additionally, they may instantly transmit data to the production line from a variety of equipment scattered across several locations, allowing manufacturers to make adjustments straight away.

A "digital twin" is a depiction of anything that is real, be it a process, a physical object, a piece of technology, or anything else. Although the idea of digital twins has existed for some time, technology is progressing. Organizations may now produce real-time digital simulations of events occurring in the real world because of digital twins. Thanks to the use of this technology, businesses are now able to examine a range of situations, remotely analyze physical assets, manage them without ever having to interact with them directly, and take action on data from linked assets [24].

It could be able to offer safer, more accurate maintenance methods using AR and the IoT. By integrating IIoT data from a specific asset with digital instructions and augmented reality apps, front line staff may profit from this cyber-physical relationship.

11.8.4   Equipment, Tool, and Inventory Use in Global Positioning System (GPS)

Another component that offers a peek of the IIoT's future is location-tracking. Although geo-location features have been around for a while, the market is continually growing. Position tracking, which was the primary use of GPS until recently, was inefficient and could only cover a small area of the interior. Organizations may now follow the movement of things on shelves and connect with an ERP system using a range of location monitoring technologies, such as RFID tags. There are also more effective long-range charging methods that allow for remote asset monitoring. Businesses can use additional technologies in conjunction with location-tracking systems. Industrial organizations, for instance, may use AI to monitor environmental and security threats, and GPS-enabled sensors to identify and manage their physical assets.

Construction workers can create a sensory system to find equipment distributed throughout large project sites rather than on GPS. After entering, teams may use an AI-based inside discovery technique based on Wi-Fi or sensors, which may allow for more precise inside placement. This may cut down on the time people or autonomous robots spend attempting to identify a certain machine by utilizing intelligence at the edge [25].

Businesses [26, 27], organisations, and infrastructures are increasingly relying on the Industrial Internet of Things (IIoT) [28–31] and related technologies to enhance their technological and economic advantages [32]. With the use of IIoT, production lines and enterprises may be assisted [33]. However, without effective security [34–37] measures, cyber-attacks [38, 39] on IIoT devices and their strange behaviour might undermine all of IIoT's goals. The security [40] of the overall IIoT system is particularly dependent on the security [41] of edge devices, including sensors, actuators, robots, and controllers. The connection, scalability, and performance of the system are significantly impacted by these devices, which interact closely with other system parts. the interactions in a typical IIoT platform [42] involving edge [43] devices, apps, and the network [44].

11.9   Conclusion

Smart chatbots are the way of the future and integrating them with IoT may deliver benefits that are astonishing. By skipping commas or asking questions that it already knows the answers to, it can work around-the-clock from any location and speed up response times. The turning point of the future has come. Making chatbots instead of using actual people to assist clients makes sense.

As more people utilize gadgets like tablets and smartphones, conversational AI—which can be used to simplify life for both the consumer and the company—is growing in popularity in the customer service sector. Conversational AI streamlines this process by enabling users to communicate effectively rather than filling out online forms on a device that was not designed for typing out lengthy discussions. Using artificial intelligence to interact with website visitors improves the user experience and makes them feel more valued by the firm since consumers are given a voice to express their wants and needs.

References

1. Davenport, T., Guha, A., Grewal, D., Bressgott, T., How artificial intelligence will change the future of marketing. *J. Acad. Mark. Sci.*, 48, 1, 24–42, 2019 Oct 10.
2. De Bruyn, A., Viswanathan, V., Beh, Y., Brock, J., von Wangenheim, F., Artificial intelligence and marketing: Pitfalls and opportunities. *J. Interact. Mark.*, 51, 91–105, 2020 Aug.
3. Montenegro, J.L.Z., da Costa, C.A., da Rosa Righi, R., Survey of conversational agents in health. *Expert Syst. Appl.*, 129, 56–67, 2019 Sep.
4. Siddharth, D., Saini, D.K., Kumar, A., Precision agriculture with technologies for smart farming towards Agriculture 5.0, in: *Unmanned Aerial Vehicles for Internet of Things (IoT): Concepts, Techniques, and Applications*, pp. 247–273, Scrivener Publishing, Beverly, USA, 2021, [Online]. Available: https:// onlinelibrary.wiley.com/doi/abs/10.1002/9781119769170.ch14.
5. Conversational AI market by component (platform and services) type (IVA and chatbots) technology (ML and Deep Learning NLP and ASR) application deployment mode (cloud and on-premises) vertical and region: Global forecast to 2025, [online] Available: https://www.researchandmarkets.com/reports/5136158/conversational-ai-market-by-component-platform.
6. Using conversational AI to decode complex customer interactions, [online] Available: https://www.boost.ai/articles/using-conversational-ai-to-decode-complex-customer-interactions.
7. Wollschlaeger, M., Sauter, T., Jasperneite, J., The future of industrial communication: Automation networks in the era of the Internet of Things and Industry 4.0. *IEEE Ind. Electron. Mag.*, 11, 1, 17–27, Mar. 2017.
8. Ramamurthy, H., Prabhu, B.S., Gadh, R., Madni, A.M., Wireless industrial monitoring and control using a smart sensor platform. *IEEE Sens. J.*, 7, 5, 611–618, 2007.
9. Weking, J., Stöcker, M., Kowalkiewicz, M., Bohm, M., Krcmar, H., Archetypes for Industry 4.0 business model innovations, in: *Proceedings of the 24th Americas Conference on Information Systems*, New Orleans, LA, USA, October 2018.
10. Gera, U.K., Saini, D.K., Singh, P., Siddharth, D., IoT-based UAV platform revolutionized in smart healthcare, in: *Unmanned Aer. Veh. Internet Things*, pp. 277–293, Aug. 2021.
11. Shabandri, B. and Maheshwari, P., Enhancing IoT security and privacy using distributed ledgers with IOTA and the tangle, in: *Proceedings of the 6th International Conference on Signal Processing and Integrated Networks (SPIN)*, Noida, India, 07-08 March 2019, pp. 1069–1075.
12. Xu, L.D. and Viriyasitavat, W., Application of blockchain in collaborative Internet-of-Things services. *IEEE Trans. Comput. Soc. Syst.*, 6, 6, 1295–1305, 2019.
13. Gamble, C., Larsen, P.G., Pierce, K., Woodcock, J., Cyber-physical systems design: Formal foundations, methods and integrated tool chains, in: *3rd FME Workshop on Formal Methods in Software Engineering (FormaliSE)*, pp. 40–46, 2015.
14. Neshenko, N., Bou-Harb, E., Crichigno, J., Kaddoum, G., Ghani, N., Demystifying IoT security: An exhaustive survey on IoT vulnerabilities and a first empirical look on Internet-scale IoT exploitations. *IEEE Commun. Surv. Tutor*, 21, 3, 2702–2733, 3rd Quart. 2019.
15. Delsing, J., Local cloud Internet of Things automation: Technology and business model features of distributed Internet of Things automation solutions. *IEEE Ind. Electron. Mag.*, 11, 4, 8–21, Dec. 2017.
16. Learning-based context-aware resource allocation for edge-computing-empowered industrial IoT. *IEEE Internet Things J.*, 7, 5, 4260–77, May 2020.

17. Sisinni, E. *et al.*, Industrial Internet of Things: Challenges opportunities and directions. *IEEE Trans. Ind. Inform.*, 14, 11, 4724–34, Nov. 2018.

18. Boyes, H., Hallaq, B., Cunningham, J., Watson, T., The industrial Internet of Things (IioT): An analysis framework. *Comput. Ind.*, 101, 1–12, 2018, https://doi.org/10.1016/J.COMPIND.2018.04.015.

19. Carruthers, K., Internet of Things and beyond: Cyber-physical systems, IEEE Internet of Things, 2016, http://iot.ieee.org/newsletter/may-2016/internet-of-things-and-beyond-cyber-physical-systems.html.

20. Radanliev, P., De Roure, D., Van Kleek, M., Ani, U., Burnap, P., Anthi, E., Nurse, J.R.C., Santos, O., Montalvo, R.M., Maddox, L.T., Dynamic real-time risk analytics of uncontrollable states in complex internet of things systems: Cyber risk at the edge. *Environ. Syst. Decis.*, 1, 1–12, 2020, https://doi.org/10.1007/s10669-020-09792-x.

21. Radanliev, P., De Roure, D., Page, K., Nurse, J.R.C., Montalvo, R.M., Santos, O., Maddox, L., Burnap, P., Cyber risk at the edge: Current and future trends on cyber risk analytics and artificial intelligence in the industrial Internet of Things and Industry 40 supply chains. *Cybersecurity*, 3, 13, 1–21, 2020, https://doi.org/10.1186/s42400-020-00052-8.

22. Smart, P., Madaan, A., Hall, W., Where the smart things are: Social machines and the Internet of Things. *Phenomenol. Cogn. Sci.*, 18, 3, 551–575, 2019, https://doi.org/10.1007/s11097-018-9583-x.

23. Du, Z. *et al.*, Federated learning for vehicular Internet of Things: Recent advances and open issues. *IEEE Open J. Comput. Soc.*, 1, 45–61, May 2020.

24. Cao, J. *et al.*, Learning cooperation schemes for mobile edge computing empowered internet of vehicles. *Proc. IEEE Wireless Commun. and Networking Conference (WCNC)*, May 2020, pp. 1–6.

25. Wan, J., Zhang, D., Sun, Y., Lin, K., Zou, C., Cai, H., VCMIA: A novel architecture for integrating vehicular cyber-physical systems and mobile cloud computing. *Mob. Netw. Appl.*, 19, 2, 153–160, 2014, https://doi.org/10.1007/s11036-014-0499-6.31.

26. Mahor, V., Bijrothiya, S., Rawat, R., Kumar, A., Garg, B., Pachlasiya, K., IoT and artificial intelligence techniques for public safety and security, in: *Smart Urban Computing Applications*, p. 111, 2023.

27. Mahor, V., Pachlasiya, K., Garg, B., Chouhan, M., Telang, S., Rawat, R., Mobile operating system (Android) vulnerability analysis using machine learning, in: *Proceedings of International Conference on Network Security and Blockchain Technology: ICNSBT 2021*, pp. 159–169, Springer Nature Singapore, Singapore, 2022, June.

28. Rawat, R., Garg, B., Pachlasiya, K., Mahor, V., Telang, S., Chouhan, M., Mishra, R., SCNTA: Monitoring of network availability and activity for identification of anomalies using machine learning approaches. *Int. J. Inf. Technol. Web Eng. (IJITWE)*, 17, 1, 1–19, 2022.

29. Rawat, R., Rimal, Y.N., William, P., Dahima, S., Gupta, S., Sankaran, K.S., Malware threat affecting financial organization analysis using machine learning approach. *Int. J. Inf. Technol. Web Eng. (IJITWE)*, 17, 1, 1–20, 2022.

30. Rawat, R., Mahor, V., Chouhan, M., Pachlasiya, K., Telang, S., Garg, B., Systematic literature review (SLR) on social media and the digital transformation of drug trafficking on darkweb, in: *International Conference on Network Security and Blockchain Technology*, pp. 181–205, Springer, Singapore, 2022.

31. Rawat, R., Ayodele Oki, O., Sankaran, S., Florez, H., Ajagbe, S.A., Techniques for predicting dark web events focused on the delivery of illicit products and ordered crime. *Int. J. Electr. Comput. Eng. (IJECE)*, 13, 5, 5354–5365, Oct. 2023, doi: 10.11591/ijece.v13i5.pp5354-5365.
32. Rawat, R., Garg, B., Mahor, V., Telang, S., Pachlasiya, K., Chouhan, M., Organ trafficking on the dark web—The data security and privacy concern in healthcare systems, in: *Internet of Healthcare Things: Machine Learning for Security and Privacy*, pp. 189–216, 2022.
33. Vyas, P., Vyas, G., Chauhan, A., Rawat, R., Telang, S., Gottumukkala, M., Anonymous trading on the dark online marketplace: An exploratory study, in: *Using Computational Intelligence for the Dark Web and Illicit Behavior Detection*, pp. 272–289, IGI Global, 2022.
34. Rawat, R., Oki, O.A., Sankaran, K.S., Olasupo, O., Ebong, G.N., Ajagbe, S.A., A new solution for cyber security in big data using machine learning approach, in: *Mobile Computing and Sustainable Informatics: Proceedings of ICMCSI 2023*, pp. 495–505, Springer Nature Singapore, Singapore, 2023.
35. Rawat, R., Chakrawarti, R.K., Raj, A., Mani, G., Chidambarathanu, K., Bhardwaj, R., Association rule learning for threat analysis using traffic analysis and packet filtering approach. *Int. J. Inf. Technol.*, 1–11, 2023.
36. Rawat, R., Logical concept mapping and social media analytics relating to cyber criminal activities for ontology creation. *Int. J. Inf. Technol.*, 15, 2, 893–903, 2023.
37. Rawat, R., Mahor, V., Álvarez, J.D., Ch, F., Cognitive systems for dark web cyber delinquent association malignant data crawling: A review, in: *Handbook of Research on War Policies, Strategies, and Cyber Wars*, pp. 45–63, 2023.
38. Rawat, R., Chakrawarti, R.K., Vyas, P., Gonzáles, J.L.A., Sikarwar, R., Bhardwaj, R., Intelligent fog computing surveillance system for crime and vulnerability identification and tracing. *Int. J. Inf. Secur. Priv. (IJISP)*, 17, 1, 1–25, 2023.
39. Rawat, R., Sowjanya, A.M., Patel, S.I., Jaiswal, V., Khan, I., Balaram, A. (Eds.), *Using Machine Intelligence: Autonomous Vehicles Volume 1*, John Wiley & Sons, 2022.
40. Rawat, R., Mahor, V., Díaz-Álvarez, J., Chávez, F., Rooted learning model at fog computing analysis for crime incident surveillance, in: *2022 International Conference on Smart Generation Computing, Communication and Networking (SMART GENCON)*, pp. 1–9, IEEE, 2022, December.
41. Rawat, R. and Shrivastav, S.K., SQL injection attack detection using SVM. *Int. J. Comput. Appl.*, 42, 13, 1–4, 2012.
42. Rawat, R., Bhardwaj, P., Kaur, U., Telang, S., Chouhan, M., Sankaran, K.S., *Smart vehicles for communication, volume 2*, John Wiley & Sons, 2023.
43. Mahor, V., Garg, B., Telang, S., Pachlasiya, K., Chouhan, M., Rawat, R., Cyber threat phylogeny assessment and vulnerabilities representation at thermal power station, in: *Proceedings of International Conference on Network Security and Blockchain Technology: ICNSBT 2021*, pp. 28–39, Springer Nature Singapore, Singapore, 2022, June.
44. Rawat, R., Gupta, S., Sivaranjani, S., Cu, O.K., Kuliha, M., Sankaran, K.S., Malevolent information crawling mechanism for forming structured illegal organisations in hidden networks. *Int. J. Cyber Warf. Terror. (IJCWT)*, 12, 1, 1–14, 2022.

12

Performance Analysis of Cloud Hypervisor Using Network Package Workloads in Virtualization

J. Mary Ramya Poovizhi* and R. Devi

Schools of Computing Science, Dept. of Computer Science, Vels Institute of Science, Technology and Advanced Studies (VISTAS), (Deemed to be University), Chennai, India

Abstract

AWS (Amazon Web Services), Microsoft Azure, Cloud Zero, Kubernetes, and Google App Engine are cloud computing service providers that can manage client workloads and applications through virtualization and containerization. Computing resources are provided by large data centers that consume large amounts of energy, contributing to global warming. Today's businesses and economies rely heavily on cloud data centers, the world's fastest-growing power users. The latest DCN has two main challenges: scalability and efficiency. A DCN's design directly impacts its scalability, but its power consumption is a significant factor in its cost. If this trend continues, many scientists predict that servers will consume more energy over their lifetime than they cost. Large-scale infrastructure facilities such as clustering, grids, and clouds consisting of thousands of heterogeneous computers present even more significant energy consumption problems. This paper addresses the energy consumption problem of the hypervisor shown in the cloud data center. A single hypervisor does not exhibit the same performance on all platforms as other hypervisors in terms of power and energy consumption. Several vital conclusions presented in this paper will provide system designers and operators of data centers with valuable insights that will assist them in placing workloads and scheduling virtual machines in the most power-aware manner. Researchers in this paper provide insight into power-aware workload placement and VM scheduling for system designers and operators.

Keywords: Amazon Ec2, microsoft Azure, google clouds, virtualization

12.1 Introduction

An extensive system, such as a cloud, a cluster, or a grid, will have numerous nodes involved in network processing. Compared to single systems, these systems perform many modern tasks. Supercomputers and clusters are used for large-scale weather forecasting, space research, testing the strength of encryption, and medical drug development [1, 2]. Grid and

---

Corresponding author: mrp.jamesanto@gmail.com

Romil Rawat, Rajesh Kumar Chakrawarti, Sanjaya Kumar Sarangi, Piyush Vyas, Mary Sowjanya Alamanda, Kotagiri Srividya and Krishnan Sakthidasan Sankaran (eds.) Conversational Artificial Intelligence, (185–198) © 2024 Scrivener Publishing LLC

cloud computing systems are more stable and scalable, have lower acquisition costs, and offer distributed applications (monolithic vs. microservices) over non-distributed methods.

Cloud literature suggests that large heterogeneous IaaS clouds can perform better in energy efficiency, performance, and cost efficiency and identify many open challenges [3, 4]. Here, we describe current techniques taught in existing cloud literature: power management under workload.

Performance and user cost constraints. Mostly, the discussion was done on energy efficiency, but we neglected its performance and cost. However, data centers have so many resource management strategies to increase the performance and energy efficiency of ICT devices. In addition, some notable concerns are mentioned.

As a result of cloud computing, consumers can now access computing resources on a demand and pay-as-you-go basis [5]. It allows users to pay only for the resources that the user used in the time interval. Internet-based computing resources are available based on user needs [6]. Large organizations with hundreds or thousands of employees require servers, storage systems, and applications. All these gadgets and apps require a significant amount of income. To overcome this issue, the cloud provides a wide variety of third-party services by connecting more employees to the cloud field [7]. For example, the cloud offers hardware, storage, software, and apps as computing resources. These facilities are classified into the classifications like SaaS (software as a service), IaaS (infrastructure as a service), and PaaS (platform as a service), as shown in Figure 12.1.

Cloud Platforms

- Cloud-based chatbot [1]: When companies use cloud computing (CC) to implement a chatbot, they implement the resources in the cloud. There are

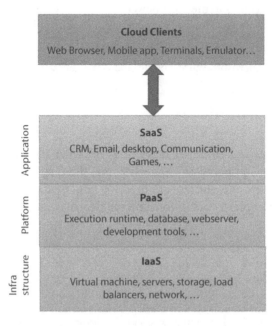

Figure 12.1 The cloud computing stack.

several varieties of CC [2], like inter, hybrid, private, and open clouds. These materials are housed on the service provider's premises via a CC-based chatbot. Thus, businesses may simply access these resources. Individuals have access to these materials from any location at any time.

- On-premises chatbot: In contrast, internal resources are used in an on-premises implementation. The resources may be managed and maintained internally by businesses. They are deployable into the IT infrastructure of businesses [3]. The solution and its associated processes are the exclusive responsibility of the organization.

- Online chatbot: CC-based options streamline the creation of chatbots. They provide many channels and easy connections. Yet, when companies make customer-specific adaptations, they might not have much leeway there. Also, you just pay for what you use in terms of payments. Based on how much is used, there are fees for the service.

- An in-house chatbot: When compared to a traditional system [4], the solution gives companies the option to alter the process. Any client apps that are currently in use by businesses can be integrated into the process as needed. Businesses will benefit from having ongoing internal support and maintenance accessible thanks to the on-premises offering. This reduces or eliminates dependence on the seller.

- Online chatbot: Use caution and security when utilizing the CC-based chatbot system. Cloud suppliers frequently change their policies, which forces organizations to deal with some serious problems. The CC is used to store data in the form of confidential material. Hence, data ownership and privacy must always be a priority for corporations. The privacy of application token access, security keys, customer, partner, and staff data must be guaranteed. Data breaches were a possibility.

- An in-house chatbot: Organizations have superior control over the entire system and the data with on-premise chatbot alternatives. On-premises chatbots are preferred by businesses with strong data and privacy concerns. The financial and government industries, which are heavily restricted, provide significant obstacles to the CC.

Cloud

IaaS: IaaS provides network infrastructure, storage, servers, and other services often housed in data centers. Small businesses may not find viable alternatives due to the high initial cost of these services. A user will pay only for the infrastructure resources he uses and will not charge for the construction and operation of the associated infrastructure. Google Cloud and Amazon EC2 are the most popular IaaS. There will be a predefined virtual machine with a specific size, CPU speed, and RAM, along with some pre-installed applications. IaaS companies often provision resources through virtual machines and storage [8]. A user is billed in an hourly currency (using a pay-as-you-go (PAYG) approach) for her VM/container type specified, based on how long the workload runs. The growth value of IaaS increased in the market by 21.6% in 2019 at 38.9 billion dollars.

PaaS: Platform as a service includes hardware and software that support web servers, programming language, OS, compilers, and databases. A framework for designing, developing, and modifying applications. Programmers need not purchase underlying hardware or software to create software using these services, and you do not have to spend time preparing and configuring your runtime platform. The following are examples of PaaS: web design, online editing, Google App Engine, and compilation tools [9]. According to Gartner research, his PaaS market value was about $19 billion in 2019, up 17.9% from 2018. The growth of PaaS increased by 15.3% in 2019. Overall, PaaS services are offered less frequently than IaaS and SaaS. All three services have the same amount of growth in the market.

AWS Elastic IBM Bluemix, VMware, and Windows Azure Pivotal CF are the most popular PaaS service providers and products. SaaS currently has a larger market share than IaaS. However, according to Gartner's analysis, IaaS will dominate and overgrow.

SaaS: SaaS provides users with server-hosted remote internet access to various software applications (the cloud). This may include e-commerce software, email, banking, or online services [6, 10]. This application-based software has user connections like Facebook, CRM, and online games. They are available online, some for free and some for subscriptions. This is a web-based software where the program resides in a central data center and is sold for users.

Data Center: The data center is used to address the problems of complex scientific and commercial issues in thousands of servers running simultaneously. The technology of virtualization is used to improve system multitasking and concurrency. A single server can run several virtual machines, allowing multiple applications to run. In addition, virtualization technology enables consolidation by shutting down underutilized servers and increasing system utilization (workloads running across fewer hosts). The services provided by data centers do not always belong to the same geographic region [8]. An example of a data center is Amazon EC2; it contains one virtualized data center for 69 zones and 22 areas for each zone. The energy emitted by the data center is large (Figure 12.3).

Role of NLP in Azure

Using Azure Cognitive Service for Language, you can perform natural language processing (NLP) to comprehend and analyze your text. This service provides a web-based Language Studio, REST APIs, and client libraries that make it possible to develop the smart application using the web-based Language Studio. This language service integrates text analytics, and LUIS offers various capabilities. These characteristics may be:

- A preconfigured model indicates that the AI models used by the feature cannot be modified. You provide the data and use the quality output in your apps.
- Flexible means that using our tools, you may train an AI model to match your data perfectly.

Role of NLP in AWS

AWS offers the most extensive and comprehensive collection of artificial intelligence and machine learning (AI/ML) services to clients of all skill levels. These services are linked to vast data sources.

AWS provides various language services based on machine learning for clients that lack ML expertise, want a quicker time to market, or wish to add intelligence to an existing process or application. Using pre-trained APIs for voice, transcription, translation, text analysis, and chatbot capabilities enables businesses to add intelligence to their AI applications [11].

- The Amazon Comprehend service assists users in discovering insights and connections in the text they read.
- The text is translated by Amazon Translate smoothly.
- Amazon Transcribe carries out automated voice recognition.
- As a result of Amazon Lex, chatbots can be developed to interact with consumers to assist them with their daily tasks.
- A computer program called Amazon Polly converts text into voice naturally.

Role of NLP in Google Cloud

Developers use the Natural Language API to take advantage of pre-trained models for analyzing natural language. It comprises sentiment analysis, entity analysis, content categorization, entity sentiment analysis, and syntax analysis, all based on pre-trained models.

AutoML Natural Language, a component of the AutoML product package, allows the creation and deployment of bespoke machine-learning models for natural language with little effort and machine-learning experience.

Type 1 Hypervisors (Bare Metal): Type 1 hypervisors are placed directly on the host hardware. These hypervisors are advantageous for companies because they can access hardware without an operating system or device driver. The approach is also designed to be resistant to OS-level vulnerabilities. Type 1 hypervisors ESXi, Xen, Microsoft Hyper-V, and Oracle VM, operate on PCs [12].

Hyper-V Architecture

Using Microsoft's Hyper-V, it is possible to execute many programs concurrently. The Microsoft Hyper-V virtualization technology is the technology that is used by x64 versions of Windows Server. A hypervisor powers Hyper-V. You may purchase a separate Hyper-V Server package to utilize this hypervisor server. You may also add it to Windows Server as a role or component. Microsoft Hyper-V is not required, regardless of which of these two you select. The hypervisor is the same for all different types of software. Microsoft Hyper-V requires a CPU with virtualization hardware support for it to function. This reduces the size of the codebase and improves performance. It is constructed using micro kernelized hypervisors. This is Figure 12.2. A "parent partition" operating system with capabilities like administration tools and driver downloads for the hardware is one approach to do this [12].

It is significant to note that if Hyper-V is enabled on the host, high-precision, latency-sensitive programs may have execution issues on the host due to Hyper-V. Because virtualization is enabled, both the host and guest operating systems can function on top of the Hyper-V virtualization layer. In contrast to guests, the host OS has direct access to all hardware, enabling hardware-dependent programs to run without difficulty on the host OS.

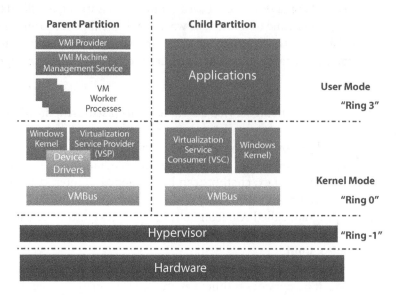

Figure 12.2 Hyper-V architecture.

12.2 A Related Study on Energy Efficiency

Pinheiro *et al*. [13] conducted one of their first studies using power control at the data center level. The authors present strategies for reducing power consumption in heterogeneous clusters of processing nodes. Focusing workloads on as few physical nodes as possible and turning off idle nodes are vital strategies for minimizing power consumption. This strategy requires trade-offs between performance and performance, as workload consolidation can degrade application performance.

Chase *et al*. [14] examined energy-efficient methods for managing identical resources in internet hosting facilities. To allocate the resources efficiently, the resource requirements of each application must be calculated at the current load level and distributed as efficiently as possible. The author countered this problem with an economic framework. The service "provides" support according to quality and quantity. SLAs can be negotiated based on budget and QoS requirements. Balance the cost of using a resource with the value you get from using that resource. Each service requires a specific set of servers.

Network switches change dynamically to adjust the server state as needed. Switching from an idle server to power-saving settings reduces power consumption (sleep mode, hibernation, etc.). The load data contain "noise" because the system is focused on web workloads.

Nathuji and Schwan [15] examined power management strategies in virtual data centers for the first time. The author developed a "soft resource scaling" software for a unique power management technique in addition to scaling hardware and consolidating virtual machines. Due to the restricted range of hardware scalability modes, the authors propose both "hard" and "soft" scaling may result in substantial energy savings.

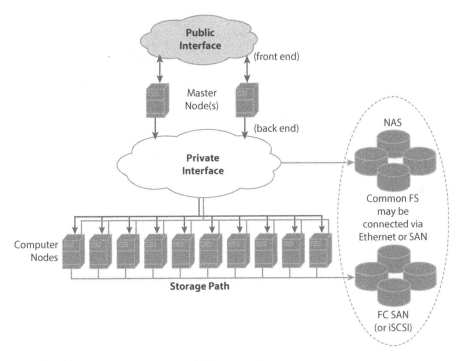

Figure 12.3 Cloud data center view; NAS stands for network area storage.

12.3   Motivation

This research looked at several jobs with quality-of-service requirements (e.g., deadline, priority, and workload). Therefore, selecting a suitable virtual machine from a diverse resource set with minimal energy consumption and a task's met QoS has become a complex scheduling problem.

1. Does a single hypervisor's energy efficiency vary while running multiple programs inside its virtual machines on the same hardware platform? We determine whether various apps or workloads have hypervisor affinity by answering this question.
2. Should we continually upgrade the virtualized environment's hardware to increase energy efficiency? Is there a substantial difference in the energy efficiency of these systems in a virtualized environment?

12.4   Experiment Methodology and Setup

The work was conducted based on workloads, hardware, and hypervisor in the data center. This is an Operating system virtualization based on its critical technologies. The experiment was conducted in data center products on Google Cloud, AWS, and Azure by setting up two virtual machines in each cloud center with a different OS, like windows and ubuntu

Table 12.1 Windows VM.

S. no.	Cloud services	Hypervisor type	Windows configuration
1	Aws	Hyper-V	Windows Server 2016
2	Microsoft Azure	Hyper-V	Windows Server 2016
3	Google Clouds	Hyper-V	Windows Server 2016

Table 12.2 Ubuntu VM.

S. no.	Cloud services	Hypervisor type	Ubuntu configuration
1	Aws	Hyper-V	ubuntu 16.04 LTS AMD server
2	Microsoft Azure	Hyper-V	ubuntu 18.04 AMD server
3	Google Clouds	Hyper-V	ubuntu 18.04 AMD server

in Table 12.1. The energy was analyzed using an energy meter. This work has a minimal workload with a network program run on each cloud data center in Table 12.2.

12.4.1   Work Setup

NetworkX is a Python-based software package designed for the improvement, modification, and examination of the structure, function, and dynamics of complex networks. It analyzes extensive, complex networks represented as graphs with nodes and edges. Using networkX, sophisticated networks may be loaded and stored. We can produce several random and traditional network kinds, assess network structure, construct models, invent new network techniques, and draw networks. The package was installed on each hypervisor, the nodes were created, and the package was executed while running this work; each data center exhibited a different amount of energy.

12.5   Results and Discussion

From the workload, we applied the hypervisor we selected in the data center for power and energy consumption. The chosen data center has its workload capacity and hypervisor with a specific hardware setup. Thus, while running the workload, each hypervisor exhibits different energy efficiency on another platform.

NetworkX

The networkX package contains content like creating a graph edge and graph nodes, examining the elements of the chart or graph, removing parts from the group, using a graph construction, assessing edges and neighbors, directing graph and multigraph, analyzing graphs, and drawing the diagram. Table 12.3 shows an algorithm for details on the graph algorithm.

Table 12.3 An algorithm for details on the graph algorithm.

Algorithms for details on graph algorithms
| ```
import matplotlib.pyplot as pot
G = nxn.petersen_graph()
subax1 = pot.subplot(121)
nxn.draw(G, with_labels=True, font_weight='bold')
subax2 = pot.subplot(122)
nxn.draw_shell(G, nlist=[range(15, 10), range(15)], with_labels=True, font_weight='bold')
pot.show()
# command if you are not using matplotlib in interactive mode.
options = {
   'node_color': 'red',
   'node_size': 50,
   'width': 4,
}
subax1 = pot.subplot(221)
nxn.draw_random(G, **options)
subax2 = pot.subplot(222)
nxn.draw_circular(G, **options)
subax3 = pot.subplot(220)
nxn.draw_spectral(G, **options)
subax4 = pot.subplot(225)
nxn.draw_shell(G, nlist=[range(15,10), range(15)], **options)
G = nxn.dodecahedral_graph()
shells = [[2, 3, 4, 5, 6], [8, 1, 0, 19, 18, 17, 16, 15, 14, 7], [9, 10, 11, 12, 13]]
nxn.draw_shell(G, nlist=shells, **options)
nxn.draw(G)
pot.savefig("path.png")
from networkx. drawing.nx_pydot import write_dot
pos = nxn.nx_agraph.graphviz_layout(G)
nxn.draw(G, pos=pos)
write_dot(G, 'file.dot')
``` |

12.5.1   Observation of Windows

Running the workload on the Hyper-V on Amazon Ec2 bare metal with Windows Server 2016, it exhibits a slightly higher energy than Azure and a slightly lower energy than Google Cloud. The Hyper-V on Azure with Windows 2016 exhibit produced lesser energy conception when compared to the other two. Finally, Google Cloud creates a higher power conception than the other two (Figure 12.4).

12.5.2   Observation on Ubuntu

Running the workload on the Hyper-V on Amazon Ec2 bare metal with ubuntu 16.04 LTS AMD 64 sever, it exhibits a slightly lower energy than the Azure and a slightly higher energy
```

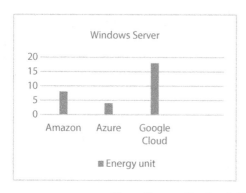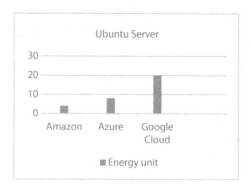

[Power Consumption (x-axis: Workload level,Y-axis: power(watts)]

Figure 12.4 Completion times of varying computation-intensive workloads.

than Google Cloud. The Hyper-V on Azure with ubuntu 18.04 produced more energy conception than Ec2 and less than Google cloud. Finally, Google Cloud has a higher power conception than the other two (Figure 12.4).

Overall Result Analysis
From observation one and observation two, we can arrive at the following conclusions:

a. The hypervisor, hardware, and type of workload are all connected. This prompted design engineers to be careful when choosing hypervisors for virtualized infrastructure and cloud data centers.

b. Objective 1: From Table 12.4, for the observation of windows, the energy calculated for each cloud for running the network workloads shows that Microsoft Azure consumes less energy than the other two, which have a type 1 hypervisor.

c. Objective 2: From Table 12.4, for the observation of ubuntu, the energy calculated for each cloud for running the network workloads shows that Microsoft Azure consumes less energy than the other two, which have a type 1 hypervisor.

d. Thus, the analysis shows that type 1 hypervisors have more advantages than Type 2 hypervisors because Type 2 is built on top of the OS of architecture, is more complicated, and needs more adjustment (Figure 12.5).

Table 12.4 Type 1 hypervisors of cloud platform.

Workload/ VM	Amazon Ec2		Azure		Google Cloud	
	Windows	Ubuntu	Windows	Ubuntu	Windows	Ubuntu
SIMPLE	18	4	4	8	18	20

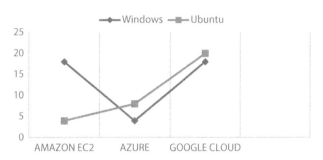

Figure 12.5 Overall comparison of VM.

These days, a lot of businesses [16–18] choose to use cloud-based workplaces [19, 20]. They benefit from the flexibility and financial edge [21, 22] that they would not otherwise have. Additionally, this structure is preferred by the staff as well. They are able to work without being concerned about software [23, 24] and system problems. Anywhere there is an internet connection, they can operate. Because of this, the use of virtual machines (VMs) and, subsequently, hypervisors [25, 26] has increased. The software programmes known as hypervisors assist in allocating resources for virtual computers, such as processing power, RAM, [27, 28] storage, etc. With hypervisors, system administrators can efficiently manage several VMs [29, 30]. The additional safety aspect of hypervisors is their finest feature. This makes it possible for businesses to employ hypervisors without being concerned about data security [31, 32]. Someone accepts requests to construct or utilise virtual machines before they are sent to a server or network. Now imagine someone repeatedly sending queries to the system. A legitimate user can lose out on the authorization and be prevented from accessing the system if all of these requests are denied. Numerous attackers [33, 34] make use of this to clog the hypervisors, create problems, and cause delays. This denial-of-service attack is one to which hypervisors are susceptible.

12.6 Conclusion

A comprehensive understanding of the energy efficiency of different hypervisors on different workloads under other servers can greatly assist data center designers and system operators in several ways, including shifting power, placing virtual machines, designing system capacity, migrations, and scheduling resources. In this work, we experimented with the workload in the different virtual machines in other cloud center platforms. According to the results, there is a difference in response times and memory characteristics between different hypervisors on the same hardware with the same workload on the same machine. It will be possible to test this single-system hypervisor in a cloud environment with even more complicated workloads, and the Type 2 hypervisor will be analyzed even more. Today, there are many open-source commercial hypervisors. These hypervisors can be either Type 1 or Type 2. Type 1 hypervisors run on top of the hardware, while Type 2 hypervisors run inside an operating system (OS).

References

1. Zakarya, M. and Gillam, L., Managing energy, performance and cost in large scale heterogeneous datacenters using migrations. *Futur. Gener. Comput. Syst.*, 93, 529–547, Apr. 2019, doi: 10.1016/J.FUTURE.2018.10.044.

2. Zakaria, M., Energy, performance and cost-efficient datacenters: A survey. *Renew. Sustain. Energy Rev.*, 94, 363–385, Oct. 2018, doi: 10.1016/j.rser.2018.06.005.

3. Zakarya, M. and Gillam, L., Energy efficient computing, clusters, grids and clouds: A taxonomy and survey. *Sustain. Comput. Inf. Syst.*, 14, 13–33, Jun. 2017, doi: 10.1016/J.SUSCOM.2017.03.002.

4. Wei, C., Hu, Z.H., Wang, Y.G., Exact algorithms for energy-efficient virtual machine placement in data centres. *Futur. Gener. Comput. Syst.*, 106, 77–91, May 2020, doi: 10.1016/J.FUTURE.2019.12.043.

5. Katal, A., Dahiya, S., Choudhury, T., Energy efficiency in cloud computing data center: A survey on hardware technologies. *Cluster Comput.*, 25, 1, 675–705, Oct. 2021, doi: 10.1007/S10586-021-03431-Z.

6. Tchana, A., De Palma, N., Safieddine, I., Hagimont, D., Diot, B., Vuillerme, N., Software consolidation as an efficient energy and cost saving solution for a SaaS/PaaS cloud model, in: *Lect. Notes Comput. Sci. (including Subser. Lect. Notes Artif. Intell. Lect. Notes Bioinformatics)*, vol. 9233, pp. 305–316, 2015, doi: 10.1007/978-3-662-48096-0_24/FIGURES/3.

7. Lis, A., Sudolska, A., Pietryka, I., Kozakiewicz, A., Cloud computing and energy efficiency: Mapping the thematic structure of research. *Energies*, 13, 16, 4117, 2020, Aug. 2020, doi: 10.3390/EN13164117.

8. Aldossary, M., Djemame, K., Alzamil, I., Kostopoulos, A., Dimakis, A., Agiatzidou, E., Energy-aware cost prediction and pricing of virtual machines in cloud computing environments. *Futur. Gener. Comput. Syst.*, 93, 442–459, Apr. 2019, doi: 10.1016/J.FUTURE.2018.10.027.

9. Shehabi, A., Smith, S.J., Masanet, E., Koomey, J., Data center growth in the United States: Decoupling the demand for services from electricity use. *Environ. Res. Lett.*, 13, 12, 124030, Dec. 2018, doi: 10.1088/1748-9326/AAEC9C.

10. Kaur, T. and Chabbra, A., Genetic Algorithm Optimized Neural Network for Handwritten Character Recognition. *Int. J. Comput. Appl.*, 119, 24, 975–8887, 2015.

11. Chard, K., Russell, M., Lussier, Y.A., Mendonça, E.A., Silverstein, J.C., A cloud-based Approach to Medical NLP. *AMIA Annu. Symp. Proc.*, 2011, 207, 2011, Accessed: Dec. 24, 2022, Available: /pmc/articles/PMC3243210/.

12. Fayyad-Kazan, H., Perneel, L., Timmerman, M., Benchmarking the performance of microsoft hyper-V server, VMware ESXi and Xen hypervisors. *J. Emerg. Trends Comput. Inf. Sci.*, 4, 12, 922–933, 2013.

13. Chase, J.S., Anderson, D.C., Thakar, P.N., Vahdat, A.M., Doyle, R.P., Managing energy and server resources in hosting centers. *ACM SIGOPS Oper. Syst. Rev.*, 35, 5, 103–116, Oct. 2001, doi: 10.1145/502059.502045.

14. Mootaz Elnozahy, E.N., Kistler, M., Rajamony, R., Energy-efficient server clusters, in: *Lect. Notes Comput. Sci. (including Subser. Lect. Notes Artif. Intell. Lect. Notes Bioinformatics)*, vol. 2325, pp. 179–197, 2003, doi: 10.1007/3-540-36612-1_12/COVER.

15. Khan, A.A. and Zakarya, M., Energy, performance and cost efficient cloud datacentres: A survey. *Comput. Sci. Rev.*, 40, 100390, May 2021, doi: 10.1016/J.COSREV.2021.100390.

16. Mahor, V., Bijrothiya, S., Rawat, R., Kumar, A., Garg, B., Pachlasiya, K., IoT and artificial intelligence techniques for public safety and security, in: *Smart Urban Computing Applications*, p. 111, 2023.

17. Mahor, V., Pachlasiya, K., Garg, B., Chouhan, M., Telang, S., Rawat, R., Mobile operating system (Android) vulnerability analysis using machine learning, in: *Proceedings of International*

Conference on Network Security and Blockchain Technology: ICNSBT 2021, pp. 159–169, Springer Nature Singapore, Singapore, 2022, June.

18. Rawat, R., Garg, B., Pachlasiya, K., Mahor, V., Telang, S., Chouhan, M., Mishra, R., SCNTA: Monitoring of network availability and activity for identification of anomalies using machine learning approaches. *Int. J. Inf. Technol. Web Eng. (IJITWE)*, 17, 1, 1–19, 2022.

19. Rawat, R., Rimal, Y.N., William, P., Dahima, S., Gupta, S., Sankaran, K.S., Malware threat affecting financial organization analysis using machine learning approach. *Int. J. Inf. Technol. Web Eng. (IJITWE)*, 17, 1, 1–20, 2022.

20. Rawat, R., Mahor, V., Chouhan, M., Pachlasiya, K., Telang, S., Garg, B., Systematic literature review (SLR) on social media and the digital transformation of drug trafficking on darkweb, in: *International Conference on Network Security and Blockchain Technology*, pp. 181–205, Springer, Singapore, 2022.

21. Rawat, R., Ayodele Oki, O., Sankaran, S., Florez, H., Ajagbe, S.A., Techniques for predicting dark web events focused on the delivery of illicit products and ordered crime. *Int. J. Electr. Comput. Eng. (IJECE)*, 13, 5, 5354–5365, Oct. 2023, doi: 10.11591/ijece.v13i5.pp5354-5365.

22. Rawat, R., Garg, B., Mahor, V., Telang, S., Pachlasiya, K., Chouhan, M., Organ trafficking on the dark web—The data security and privacy concern in healthcare systems, in: *Internet of Healthcare Things: Machine Learning for Security and Privacy*, pp. 189–216, 2022.

23. Vyas, P., Vyas, G., Chauhan, A., Rawat, R., Telang, S., Gottumukkala, M., Anonymous trading on the dark online marketplace: An exploratory study, in: *Using Computational Intelligence for the Dark Web and Illicit Behavior Detection*, pp. 272–289, IGI Global, 2022.

24. Rawat, R., Oki, O.A., Sankaran, K.S., Olasupo, O., Ebong, G.N., Ajagbe, S.A., A new solution for cyber security in big data using machine learning approach, in: *Mobile Computing and Sustainable Informatics: Proceedings of ICMCSI 2023*, pp. 495–505, Springer Nature Singapore, Singapore, 2023.

25. Rawat, R., Chakrawarti, R.K., Raj, A., Mani, G., Chidambarathanu, K., Bhardwaj, R., Association rule learning for threat analysis using traffic analysis and packet filtering approach. *Int. J. Inf. Technol.*, 1–11, 2023.

26. Rawat, R., Logical concept mapping and social media analytics relating to cyber criminal activities for ontology creation. *Int. J. Inf. Technol.*, 15, 2, 893–903, 2023.

27. Rawat, R., Mahor, V., Álvarez, J.D., Ch, F., Cognitive systems for dark web cyber delinquent association malignant data crawling: A review, in: *Handbook of Research on War Policies, Strategies, and Cyber Wars*, pp. 45–63, 2023.

28. Rawat, R., Chakrawarti, R.K., Vyas, P., Gonzáles, J.L.A., Sikarwar, R., Bhardwaj, R., Intelligent fog computing surveillance system for crime and vulnerability identification and tracing. *Int. J. Inf. Secur. Priv. (IJISP)*, 17, 1, 1–25, 2023.

29. Rawat, R., Sowjanya, A.M., Patel, S.I., Jaiswal, V., Khan, I., Balaram, A. (Eds.), *Using Machine Intelligence: Autonomous Vehicles Volume 1*, John Wiley & Sons, 2022.

30. Rawat, R., Mahor, V., Díaz-Álvarez, J., Chávez, F., Rooted learning model at fog computing analysis for crime incident surveillance, in: *2022 International Conference on Smart Generation Computing, Communication and Networking (SMART GENCON)*, pp. 1–9, IEEE, 2022, December.

31. Rawat, R. and Shrivastav, S.K., SQL injection attack detection using SVM. *Int. J. Comput. Appl.*, 42, 13, 1–4, 2012.

32. Rawat, R., Bhardwaj, P., Kaur, U., Telang, S., Chouhan, M., Sankaran, K.S., *Smart vehicles for communication, volume 2*, John Wiley & Sons, 2023.

33. Mahor, V., Garg, B., Telang, S., Pachlasiya, K., Chouhan, M., Rawat, R., Cyber threat phylogeny assessment and vulnerabilities representation at thermal power station, in: *Proceedings of*

International Conference on Network Security and Blockchain Technology: ICNSBT 2021, pp. 28–39, Springer Nature Singapore, Singapore, 2022, June.

34. Rawat, R., Gupta, S., Sivaranjani, S., CU, O.K., Kuliha, M., Sankaran, K.S., Malevolent information crawling mechanism for forming structured illegal organisations in hidden networks. *Int. J. Cyber Warf. Terror. (IJCWT)*, *12*, 1, 1–14, 2022.

Evaluation of Chabot Text Classification Using Machine Learning

**P. Kumaraguru Diderot[1]*, K. Sakthidasan Sankaran[1], Malik Jawarneh[2],
Hriakumar Pallathadka[3], José Luis Arias-Gonzáles[4] and Domenic T. Sanchez[5]**

[1]Department of ECE, Hindustan Institute of Technology and Science, Chennai, India
[2]Faculty of Computing Sciences, Gulf College, Al-Khuwair, Oman
[3]Manipur International University, Manipur, India
[4]University of British Columbia, Lima, Peru
[5]Cebu Technological University-NEC, Cebu City, Philippines

Abstract

A chatbot is a type of software with artificial intelligence (AI) that is meant to talk like a person, usually over the internet. More and more people use chatbots. Every chatbot is built from the ground up with the main idea that it can have an intelligent conversation with a human user (often through text messages) and respond to their questions in the right way. This chapter gives a detailed literature review of the different ways that chatbot text features can be optimized. In the literature review section, there is also a detailed look at how machine learning techniques can be used to classify texts and group them together. A framework for classifying chatbot text based on machine learning is also shown. The normalization method is used to remove noise during preprocessing. Particle Swarm Optimization is used to improve the features, and KNN, SVM, and Naïve Bayes techniques are used to classify the text.

Keywords: Chatbot text classification, preprocessing, normalization, feature selection, particle swarm optimization

13.1 Introduction

A chatbot is a kind of artificial intelligence (AI) software program that is meant to mimic human conversation, often through the internet. Chatbots are becoming more popular. Every single chatbot is constructed from the ground up based on the essential notion that it is capable of carrying on an intelligent conversation with a human user (often via the use of text messages) and appropriately responding to their inquiries. Since the beginning of computer science, there has been the concept of computers communicating with humans. In point of fact, Alan Turing devised a straightforward test that is now referred to

---
*Corresponding author: diderotpec2007@gmail.com

Romil Rawat, Rajesh Kumar Chakrawarti, Sanjaya Kumar Sarangi, Piyush Vyas, Mary Sowjanya Alamanda, Kotagiri Srividya and Krishnan Sakthidasan Sankaran (eds.) Conversational Artificial Intelligence, (199–218) © 2024 Scrivener Publishing LLC

as the Turing test in the year 1950. In this test, a human judge is tasked with determining whether or not the entity with whom they are interacting via text is in reality a computer program. The scope of this test, on the other hand, is far broader than the normal use of chatbots. The fundamental difference between the two is that chatbots have restricted subject knowledge, but the Turing test presumes that one may speak with the agent about any topic. Because of this, conversational agents may be customized more narrowly as they are developed; for instance, they do not need to know all there is to know about anything in order to help users in doing something as specialized as booking a reservation at a restaurant.

Chatbot designers also keep in mind the more general idea that users often have an end goal in mind when they begin an interaction with a chatbot. This is something that they keep in mind while designing chatbots. As a result, the course of the conversation and its subject matter are susceptible to being steered in this manner in order to promote the end that is sought. As a direct result of this, developers have the opportunity to capitalize on the emergence of predictable patterns of behavior. In 1966, the world's very first conversational agent known as ELIZA was developed. ELIZA was a piece of software that rephrased user input using simple natural language processing (NLP) techniques in order to simulate the work of a psychiatrist [1]. In spite of the fact that it seemed to be straightforward, the program tricked a great number of people into believing that it comprehended the problems that they were experiencing. According to Joseph Weizenbaum, the man who developed ELIZA, his secretary would sometimes ask him to leave the room so that she could have a private conversation with ELIZA [1].

Later on, during the course of several decades, chatbots mostly followed ELIZA's methods. However, there were some tiny advancements made to the field, such as voice synthesis and emotion management. Then, in 2001, ActiveBuddy, Inc., which is now known as Colloquis, presented the world with SmarterChild, a conversational agent that was compatible with both AIM and MSN Messenger. The development of SmarterChild came about as a direct reaction to the rising popularity of instant messaging systems such as SMS, which provide users quick access to information such as current events, weather forecasts, and the results of various sports. The fact that SmarterChild was connected to a knowledge base and provided users with info that was relevant to their needs was the most innovative feature of the program. When the technical limitations of natural language processing finally caught up with them, history unfortunately forgot about the bots that were used on websites of this kind. Conversational bots took a giant leap ahead with the introduction of IBM's Watson AI project, which has been in development since 2006. The agent's primary goal in life was to triumph over two previous Jeopardy champions in a tournament in 2011, and it was successful in achieving this purpose. Because of the game's focus on wordplay and the need for lightning-fast access to huge databases of information, Jeopardy! is attractive from the point of view of natural language processing. Unfortuitously, the previous iteration of this artificial intelligence was only capable of providing one-line responses to questions and was unable to carry on a meaningful conversation with another human person. Then, around the beginning of the 2010s, virtual assistants such as Apple's Siri, Microsoft's Cortana, Google's Google assistant, Amazon's Alexa, and others started to become more popular. The concept of conversation, and more especially discussion with a particular objective in mind, was first presented to the profession of brokering by those individuals. The introduction of

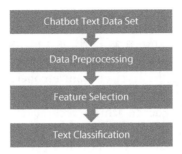

Figure 13.1 Block diagram of chatbot text classification.

the Messenger Platform for Messenger by Facebook in 2016 was a huge step forward for the chatbot industry. This was due to the fact that it allowed companies in industries other than artificial intelligence to create conversational agents using the Messenger platform. A block diagram of chatbot text classification is shown in Figure 13.1. This block diagram consists of components like text acquisition, text preprocessing, feature selection, and classification [2, 3].

This chapter presents a detailed literature survey of various techniques used for optimization of chatbot text features. A detailed review of machine learning techniques for text classification and text clustering is also presented in the literature review section. A machine learning-based chatbot text classification framework is also presented. Preprocessing is performed to remove noise using the normalization method [4]. Features are optimized by Particle Swarm Optimization, and text classification is performed by KNN, SVM, and Naïve Bayes techniques [5, 6].

13.2   Literature Survey

13.2.1   Optimization Techniques for Chatbot Text Feature Selection

Text feature selection that is optimized is necessary because of a number of factors, including but not limited to asymmetric data, positive and negative features, computational complexity, computational time, document size, irrelevant characteristics, and a large dimensionality of the feature space. One such area that has to be addressed is issues with the classification of text in big amounts of data. Using a broad variety of different approaches, one may optimize the selection of text attributes in order to get optimal results. Some of the most well-known examples of these algorithms include the Genetic Algorithm (GA), the Particle Swarm Optimization (PSO), the Ant Colony Optimization (ACO), the Artificial Bee Colony optimization (ABC), the Cat Swarm Optimization (CSO), the Firefly Algorithm (FA), and so on.

Text file clustering was a challenge that Laith Mohammed and his fellow [7] employees were able to overcome (2017). Particle Swarm Optimization (PSO), also known as the harmony search algorithm (HS), and the genetic algorithm are all examples of methods that may be used for feature selection (GA). Each of these methods makes use of a different kind of algorithm for dynamic dimension reduction, as well as a feature weighting technique. The length feature weight approach takes into consideration the frequency with which phrases appear in other publications. This is done while selecting features (LFW). Dynamic dimensionality reduction, often known as DDR, is a method that may improve the efficiency of an algorithm by lowering the minimum number of necessary features, all the while preserving or enhancing the level of feature coherence and information density. The DDR technique was used for the aim of achieving this goal. In addition, the K-means clustering method was used in order to achieve accurate classification of the many textual components.

In order to finish the text feature selection process, Basiri *et al.* [8] made use of a hybrid algorithm that was based on Ant Colony Optimization and the Genetic Approach (ACO-GA) (2009). We employed and analyzed the graph representation, heuristic desirability, pheromone update algorithm, and solution design in order to evaluate ACO. The Reuters dataset was used for the training of the samples. It was found that the ACO-GA technique is superior to the traditional ACO algorithm in terms of successfully using a small feature subset, having a strong search capability, and quickly arriving at a converged state. This was the conclusion reached after comparing the two approaches.

Alghamdi *et al.* [9] have developed a one-of-a-kind fusion method that is based on the trace oriented feature analysis and the Ant Colony Optimization. This method was created for the goal of document categorization. For the purpose of determining whether or not their proposed algorithms were effective, the authors tested them using datasets provided by Reuters and Brown. The experimental results demonstrated that ACO-TOFA was superior than TOFA in terms of performance.

In order to make accurate predictions about cardiovascular illness, Subanya and colleagues [10] provide a novel method for feature selection that is based on the Artificial Bee Colony (ABC) algorithm. They used a support vector machine classifier as a means of determining whether or not their model was accurate. The authors showed that their one-of-a-kind strategy enhanced accuracy in comparison to other feature selection algorithms that had been employed in the past.

Younus and colleagues [11] developed an innovative method for selecting text features that is based on the PSO optimization algorithm. This method was used to classify Arabic text. The suggested system was validated using five different approaches that already existed. The results of the experiments reveal that the proposed algorithm is more accurate than five other techniques that are currently being used.

Ahmad *et al.* [12] provided an innovative feature selection technique for measuring emotional tone that was based on the ACO algorithm. This method was described. In order to evaluate how successful the strategy that was proposed was, the KNN classifier was used. When doing the analysis of the results, a well-known approach for selecting features was used. The results of the experiments demonstrate that the approach that was recommended has a greater level of accuracy.

Zhang *et al.* [13] have created a brand new method for feature selection that builds on the work done by Binary Particle Swarm Optimization (BPSO) and evolutionary technique (EA). The placement of the particles was adjusted once the results of the binary search were analyzed. It was shown that the proposed algorithms are more effective than the Extended Nearest Neighbor, Naïve Bayes, KNN, and Linear Discriminant Analysis approaches, respectively.

Hamdani *et al.* [14] presented a method for choosing characteristics; it was derived from a Genetic Algorithm and included a chromosomal representation with two distinct colors.

The authors used the method as an example. Because this method used both homogeneous and heterogeneous populations, the amount of computing work that needed to be done was cut down significantly. The authors were informed that the strategy that they had proposed had produced the most successful outcomes.

Suguna and colleagues [15] came up with the idea of using a mix of the Artificial Bee Colony (ABC) approach with the independent RSAR in 2011. In order to discover the new subset of characteristics, they used the quick reduct algorithm in their research. They tested the current methods on five distinct machine learning datasets from the University of California, Irvine. They came to the realization that the way that was presented was a more accurate one.

Mohammed Ehsan and colleagues [16] selected text characteristics by using a hybrid algorithm that was based on Ant Colony Optimization and the Genetic Approach (ACO-GA). We employed and analyzed the graph representation, heuristic desirability, pheromone update algorithm, and solution design in order to evaluate ACO. Reuters data are used to train the samples that are used. The ACO-GA approach fared much better than the traditional ACO algorithm when it came to properly selecting a minimal feature subset. In addition to this, it has improved search capabilities and converges at a quicker rate.

Karabulut M. introduced a novel two-stage phrase reduction strategy [17] that made use of IG and Geometric PSO search. The authors have developed a brand new classification algorithm that they term the Fuzzy Unordered Rule Induction Algorithm in order to test the proposed approaches for feature selection (FURIA). The Support Vector Machine, the Naïve Bayes method, and the one that was recommended here were all various text classification algorithms that were reviewed and compared. Throughout the course of their research, they have made use of the Reuters-21578 and OHSUMED document databases. The results of the experiments showed that the recommended algorithm for term reduction obtained a higher level of accuracy than the approaches that are currently considered to be state of the art.

13.2.2   Chatbot Text Classification Using Machine Learning

Bag of Tricks is a technique for classifying texts that was developed by Armand Joulin and his colleagues. In less than 10 minutes, this system that makes use of a multicore CPU has successfully categorized more than a billion different words. The Hashing Tricks method was used since it was found to be the most effective and time-efficient method for mapping ngrams in memory.

Jeremy Howard and colleagues categorized texts by making use of the Universal Language Model Fine-Tuning (ULMFiT). In comparison to other learning strategies, such as state of the art and CoVe (Contextualized Word Vectors), this method has been shown to result in a reduction in the error rate of 22% and 43.9%, respectively. This strategy to transfer learning was not just applicable in any context whatsoever, but also astonishingly straightforward and efficient.

The following is a summary of the classification that Mohit Iyyer *et al.* [18] have provided: Text categorization is achieved by the use of contrasting syntactic and compositional properties. Deep Unordered Compositional Methods is one such example (2015). This strategy was more successful when applied to content that had a wide range of syntactic structures. The dependability improved when words were dropped away. Even though it was trained on data that had a large amount of grammatical variance, the Deep Averaging Network (DAN) performed just as well as more sophisticated neural networks.

RNN-based LSTM models that are able to categorize text in both a discriminative and generative manner were presented by Dani Yogatama *et al.*. Through the use of the learning class embedding, documents were produced one word at a time. In order to model the class, LSTM was used to read the content and create hidden representations of it. The LSTM algorithm makes it possible to process documents as a string of individual words.

Nitish Shirish *et al.*'s research made use of span extraction to achieve unified question answering and text classification. In-the-moment task training was the method that was used to attain this goal. This method created models that were both poor at performing a single task and strong at doing several tasks. The CALR approach was utilized by Anish Acharya and colleagues [19] to get these findings (Cyclically Annealed Learning Rate). The use of low rank matrix factorization has resulted in a reduction in the quantity of necessary storage space. The models had a random compression ratio applied to them, and this was done without any perceptible increase in latency. This approach used an optimization technique known as gradient descent. Knowledge-enhanced document embedding was something that Roberta and her colleagues did in 2019. Word sense embedded vectors were used in this technique in order to circumvent the interpretability issues that are often connected with embedded vectors. Strong quantitative results may be obtained using classifiers that were consistent.

Bidirectional Encoder Representations from Transformers were developed by Wei-Cheng *et al.* for the aim of classifying texts that include a number of different labels (BERT). Controllability at scale for labels, as well as the collection of label dependencies and correlations from a variety of sources, are also additional obstacles that are circumvented by using this methodology.

Vilar E makes use of the algorithm Continuous Bag of Word, abbreviated as CBOW [20]. When compared to the performance of the random initialization method, the overall performance was 10.2% better. The outputs that were supplied by FastText and Word2Vec were of a higher quality than those that were supplied by the GloVe method. The findings of the recent study as well as aims for text categorization were given by Gulin *et al.* [21]. They have presented an overview of the six basics of text classification, which includes document collection and analysis, feature selection and extraction, and the classification model.

Kanika *et al.* [22] proposed a text classification method that makes use of a word weighting system based on the Term Frequency-Inverse Document Frequency Model for the purpose of automating the categorization of news articles. This system is based on the Term Frequency-Inverse Document Frequency Model (TF-IDF). The news documents went through a preprocessing stage as well as a matrix transformation. After that, the total TF-IDF was calculated for each individual document. For the purpose of this study, around 300 distinct kinds were chosen. During the course of their research, they discovered that the proposed algorithm led to an increase in the accuracy of their forecasts.

The classification of documents is an area that might benefit from the use of deep learning techniques, since these methods have the potential to provide both flexibility and incremental advances within a hierarchy. In their 2017 paper, Kowsari *et al.* [23] introduced HDLTex, a Hierarchical Deep Learning strategy that outperformed conventional classification methods for hierarchical classifications in terms of precision. HDLTex was able to achieve this by using a combination of deep learning and hierarchical structures. The unlabeled files went through the same processing as the labeled ones.

Text was categorized successfully by Xiang Zhang *et al.* (2015) thanks to the use of a Character Level Convolution Network [24]. In this scenario, information was merely obtained from unprocessed signals. Because of the scope of this investigation, the utilization of large databases was required. Both the information retrieval system and the tagging of parts of speech have been improved thanks to these updates.

Siwei Lai and colleagues made use of a Recurrent Convolutional Neural Network (RCNN) in their research [25]. In comparison to more traditional methods, this one has a lower level of background noise. In addition to this, we did not consider more broad possible arrangements for the words. The previous techniques of categorizing writing styles, emotions, themes, and taxonomies were enhanced, and new classifications were developed as a result.

A Recurrent Neural Network architecture was used in the research that Pengfei Liu *et al.* carried out, which included text sequence modeling with multitask learning. The semantic vector representation was drawn out using free-form text, and it consists of levels that are common throughout tasks as well as layers that are task-specific. Because the pattern is repeated, even text of varied lengths may be rapidly and easily read. This is because the pattern is consistent.

Pengfei Liu *et al.* were the ones who first introduced the idea of multi-task learning. The dormant feature areas are divided into two different sections, one of which is reserved for private usage and the other of which is reserved for public use. The information that was necessary for a variety of tasks was condensed into a single neuronal layer, where it is now easily available for use in other endeavors.

In 2016, Alexis Conneau, along with other researchers, used a Very Deep Convolutional Network (VD-CNN). Pooling was the approach that was used, along with some minor convolutions. The processing of the text was done on a character-by-character basis, since this is the smallest unit of representation that can be found in text. This structural design was successful because it provided the "benefit of depths." They used the local operators as part of their deep stack.

Rocchio's approach, which was developed by Miao *et al.*, was used in the process of categorizing the publications [26]. They spoke about several approaches to optimizing parameters, and the technique that they established for doing so enables continual fine-tuning of the prototype's relative placement both inside and across document kinds. They have performed tests using the Reuters-21578 dataset, the 20 Newsgroup dataset, and the TDT2 dataset. Their results clearly indicated that the proposed paired strategy was the most effective approach. In addition, the paired strategy developed by Rocchio is contrasted with the SVM method, which has been shown to provide positive outcomes.

Ronghui You *et al.* proposed the use of a hierarchical network with the name HAXMLNet for the purpose of multi-label attention that was both effective and efficient. This paradigm was used in order to achieve goals of simplicity and scaling down. When utilizing this strategy for multi-label classification, performance was improved at the extremities of the spectrum.

Ammar Ismael [27] conducted research in the area of supervised machine learning known as automatic text classification algorithms. We discussed SVM, NB, and k-nearest neighbors among other things (kNN). Among the three techniques, kNN demonstrated the most robust classification skills. In conjunction with TF-IDF, it was used so that enhanced categorization could be achieved. We were able to improve upon several phrases by meticulously designing ideal weights for them using word weighting algorithms, which allowed us to improve upon them.

The Lifelong Machine Learning (LML) technique developed by Muhammad Hassan *et al.* places a primary emphasis on the categorization of texts through the extraction and reuse of knowledge blocks. It was included into a system that was intended to acquire new skills simultaneously across a wide variety of fields. In the field of artificial intelligence, it was often used for application in a number of different learning situations, including reinforcement, unsupervised, and supervised learning. The structure of LML's code fragments made it possible to improve learning for the future based on what had been learnt in the past.

In their study published in 2019, Sahaj Garg and colleagues [28] proposed a novel method that they named Counterfactual Token Fairness (CTF). It was implemented in text classifiers as a measure of fairness, and its purpose was to calculate a specific sort of fairness and characterize its link to cluster fairness. It was determined that a counterfactual token fairness optimization should be performed. It offered separate names for asymmetrical alternative situations that were dichotomous in nature.

Pietramala and colleagues [29] presented the Olex-GA Genetic Algorithm in 2008. This technique is used for rule-based text categorization. The proposed approach for classifying texts made use of a variety of criteria for assessing single binary representations. These criteria included the f-measure and the fitness function, among others. For the sake of their experiments, they have used the OHSUMED and REUTERS-21578 text datasets. It was investigated how the proposed method fared in contrast to many existing text categorization methods such as Naïve Bayes, Ripper, C4.5, and Support Vector Machines. It was shown via testing that it operates quite well with both sorts of data.

13.2.3   Text Clustering Techniques

Clustering texts refer to the process of putting together groups of texts that have similar qualities. Tasks such as classifying and organizing documents, summarizing and organizing corpora, and classifying and navigating through document collections are all examples of applications for this technology. The insufficient amount of data that is readily accessible and the too high dimensionality of the feature space are the two primary shortcomings of text clustering. Text clustering may be broken down into two primary categories: partitioning clustering and hierarchical clustering. Clustering by partitioning is a method that converges quickly, has a linear time complexity, and can be used to datasets that are scalable, simple, and clean. When trying to handle non-convex clusters of varying densities and sizes, dividing clustering may be a challenging process. The phenomenon of "local optimum trapping" occurs often. The results of clustering are very susceptible to the influence of outliers, noise, and initialization. As a direct consequence of this, the high-dimensional regions in between its points are inadequately characterized, and the descriptors of its clusters are lacking. Hierarchical clustering is a common option for problems that include point-to-point relationships because of the inherent flexibility it allows at finer levels of analysis. This is one of the advantages of hierarchical clustering. This method has a number of flaws, such as its inability to retrace steps, its non-linear temporal complexity, the fuzziness of its termination criterion, the expense of dealing with large datasets, and its high dimension. In addition, this method has a number of advantages, such as its high dimension. After the decision has been taken to merge or split, the original data cannot be altered in any way.

Both the Frequent Term-based Clustering Algorithm and the Hierarchical Frequent Term-based Clustering Algorithm were first introduced to the scientific community by Florian Beil and his colleagues [30] in the year 2002. The FTC is not redundant, and it is capable of managing data with a high dimension, a large database, and cluster descriptions. A set of phrases that are used often was employed in order to generate the descriptions of clusters that sound the most natural. The HFTC was able to construct hierarchical clusters that were both intelligible and accessible. Using this strategy, overlapping clusters were also detected.

Aggarwal and others have done a significant amount of research on several text clustering techniques [31]. In a method of clustering that is based on distance, the distance between individual text items was determined by using a similarity function. It accomplished this by increasing the size of the representation of the text, which led to higher results when clustering text that was made up of short portions. Agglomerative and hierarchical clustering methods may be broken down into many basic categories. These categories include single linkage clustering, group-average linkage clustering, and complete linkage clustering. The search engine found it useful to have a structure that naturally resembled a tree evolve over time. The document sets have been merged together to form a single coherent whole. The efficacy of sequential scan searches was significantly increased as a result of the strategy.

Examples of distance-based Partitioning Algorithms include the K-medoid clustering algorithm, the K-means Clustering algorithm, the Crisp K-means algorithm, the Fuzzy K-means algorithm, the Online Spherical K-means algorithm (OSKM), and the Spherical K-means algorithm (SKPM). It was put to productive use in the formation of clusters that were centered on various items. K-medoid was able to identify the document sample that would be most beneficial to employ overall. Intense iteration was required in order to arrive at a point of confluence. The K-means algorithm only required a limited amount of iterations before producing accurate results. Clustering of dynamic text streams was available using OSKM. When working with data that had a high dimension, SKPM optimized the average cosine similarity.

An expectation-maximization technique was developed by Tao Liu *et al.* [32] for the purpose of selecting feature subsets across many clusters. This technique involves the determination of the shortest possible message length as well as the evaluation of the relative importance of each individual feature. The supervised feature selection approach makes it possible to calculate the score of relevance for each phrase by making use of a threshold value that has already been calculated. This technique also makes it easier to estimate the probability that a word is relevant.

Methods for Text Clustering by Using Feature Selection (TCFS) were first reported for the first time by Yanjun Li [33]. The method of text clustering was incorporated with supervised feature selection strategies like CHIR. When the TCFS algorithm has reached its final state, it will have created an acceptable clustering solution as well as a meaningful subset of features at some point in the process.

Wen Zhang *et al.* [34] conducted research on this approach, which included the use of the Minimum Spanning Tree Algorithm to build document clusters via the use of three distinct similarity criteria. Each document is handled as its own node within the network, and connections are made between documents according to the degree of overlap that exists between them. This creates the network.

Jo Taeho outlined a Separate Clustering Algorithm in his presentation [35]. A single cluster is subdivided into many smaller ones. Following the formation of a certain quantity of clusters, it was agreed to come to an end. As soon as that goal was accomplished, the conflict between them ended as well. The Single Pass Algorithm was able to attain exceptional performance with just a moderate amount of complexity in a single pass. It starts with a single cluster, and then, based on the components that are already there, it either generates a new cluster or adds to the one that is already there. The Growing Algorithm began with a base of 100 empty containers as its initial configuration. Over the course of time, every cluster eventually followed its own path and began with a base of zero radius. The variations, the clustering phase, and the beginning phase were the key concerns that were taken into account by the method.

Kusum Kumari and colleagues [36] were successful in solving a number of search and optimization problems by using a population-based algorithm that models the intelligent foraging behavior of honey bees. In order to get the optimal response, the ABC algorithm concurrently investigates many distinct sections of the search space, which is an approach that is both commendable and exploitative. We were able to increase the ABC algorithm's manipulation capabilities by merging chaotic and gradient local search with gbest-guided search equation. This allowed us to find optimal solutions more quickly.

Anand Gupta and his colleagues came up with a novel approach that they called Analog Textual Entailment and Spectral Clustering (ATESC). Logical Text Tiling was used in order to determine the connectedness between the phrases (LTT). Using these ratings, a calculation was made to determine the significance of the sentence, and new sentence fragments were produced. The most essential paragraphs provided the source material for a number of the most crucial statements.

Through the use of Spectral Relaxation, which was developed by Victor Mijangosa, the complexity of graph partitioning was significantly reduced [37]. A distance, which was described as the kernel function, may be said to exist between each point in the vector space. Due to the nature of the matrix space, some analytical techniques, such as principal component analysis and singular value decomposition, are not applicable. They presented a demonstration that showed how a kernel function may be constructed by incorporating a Frobenius-based inner product into a spectrum relaxation.

Zhiqiang Xu and his colleagues created the Spectral technique [38], with the goal of clustering both text and link data (SACTL). The objective functions of the method are straightforward to compute. Because SACTL performed better than the ARI, NMI, and F-measure techniques, in addition to the baseline algorithms, the clustering it produced was very accurate.

13.3   Methodology

This section presents a detailed literature survey of various techniques used for optimization of chatbot text features. A detailed review of machine learning techniques for text classification and text clustering is also presented in the literature review section. A machine learning-based chatbot text classification framework is also presented. Preprocessing is performed to remove noise using the normalization method. Features are optimized by Particle Swarm Optimization, and text classification is performed by KNN, SVM, and Naïve Bayes techniques. It is shown below in Figure 13.2.

We used a method known as Particle Swarm Optimization [39], sometimes abbreviated as PSO, to optimize the parameters of a local enhancement approach in order to increase the contrast and fineness of a picture. This technique is also frequently referred to as PSO. During the time that this approach is being developed and evaluated, a method of image improvement based on genetic algorithms is being used so that the results may be compared. PSO begins by generating a huge number of random choices, after which an iterative procedure is used to whittle the options down until the best possible answer is found. PSO-based image enhancement was shown to be better than GA-based picture enhancement in terms of both the quality of the product that was produced in the end as well as the efficiency with which it was computed, according to the findings of the research. It is necessary to make consistent modifications to the particle displacement while the iteration phase is being carried out, which is one of the potential issues that might arise from using this technique.

The KNN classifier has been used by several research in order to classify their collected data. Pattern recognition employs a huge number of different strategies in order to recognize and organize data. K-Nearest Neighbors (KNN) is a classification approach that is based on the distance between training samples. Learning by events is shown via the KNN algorithm. After the classification step is finished, it is possible to start the calculations by using a locally estimated function. The investigation was carried out by Javid *et al.* [40]. The KNN method of classification is the easiest to put into practice, which makes it ideal for situations in which there is very little information available regarding the distribution of the data. In the realm of pattern recognition, the K-Nearest Neighbor technique is one of the most common approaches utilized. The KNN method has been shown, via extensive study on a broad variety of datasets, to consistently generate outstanding results.

The Nearest Neighbor (NN) rule is the simplest kind of KNN rule, and it is the one that is used when K is equal to 1. In order to use this method, the samples first need to be organized into clusters according to the features they all have in common. You may still use this method to construct an educated estimate based on the features of the sample even if you are unable to correctly categorize the samples that surround the one you are analyzing.

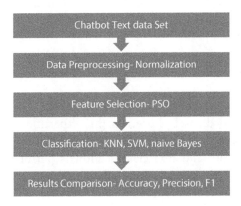

Figure 13.2 Machine learning for chatbot text classification.

By using a training set in conjunction with a query sample, it is feasible to calculate the distance between two different sets of data. Therefore, it is possible to determine the identity of the strange sample by comparing it to its categorization.

A support vector machine (SVM) model is characterized by the fact that each data point is modeled as a point in k-dimensional space (where k is number of features). The value of the feature is determined by adding together the values found at each position. The process of categorization often begins with the selection of an appropriate hyperplane that can effectively partition the classes. Since Vapnik first conceived the SVM, it has captured the interest of scholars from a wide variety of disciplines all around the world. The majority of the time, an SVM classifier will begin by taking a dataset and then utilize that dataset to construct two categories. Following the completion of the classifier's training using the provided training data, a model will be developed to classify the provided test data. There is always a possibility that problems with multiclass classification may arise. To accomplish this task, it will need a large number of binary classifiers. Numerous research have shown that support vector machines (SVMs) offer a higher level of accuracy than other categorization techniques [41]. According to the results of experiments, SVMs perform much better than a variety of other classifiers that are more traditional. The success of the SVM, on the other hand, is highly dependent on the dataset as well as the values that are utilized for the cost and kernel parameters. This approach makes use of a variety of distinct kernel functions, including the following: polynomial, linear, and Gaussian radial basis functions are the three distinct types of this kind of function. (4) It is impossible to avoid having either a sigmoid or a tangent kernel.

When it comes to the process of creating classifier models, the Naïve Bayes method is a basic approach for picking problem occurrence class labels based on feature value vectors. These classifiers are learned not using just one method, but rather a variety of approaches, all of which have a fundamental concept in common. If we just have access to the class variable, then there is no way for us to determine which of the characteristics is more essential than the others [42].

Classifiers based on Naïve Bayes may be taught in supervised learning contexts, and this is possible for several types of probability models. Dealing with the Naïve Bayes model may be done without having to resort to Bayesian probability or any of the other Bayesian techniques by adopting the maximum likelihood strategy for parameter approximation for Naïve Bayes models. Classifiers that are based on the Naïve Bayes theorem combine the Bayes theorem with the "naïve" assumption that all pairs of attributes may be considered independent of one another.

13.4   Results

A question-and-answer [43] dataset is used in this experimental work. Preprocessing is performed to remove noise using the normalization method. Features are optimized by Particle Swarm Optimization, and text classification is performed by KNN, SVM, and Naïve Bayes techniques. This feature selection helps in achieving higher classification accuracy. Results are shown in Figures 13.3 to 13.6.

When doing an analysis of efficiency, the classification accuracy measure, the precision meter, the recall metric, and the F1 score are the most significant metrics to

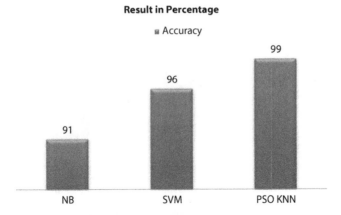

Figure 13.3 Accuracy comparison of classifiers for chatbot text classification.

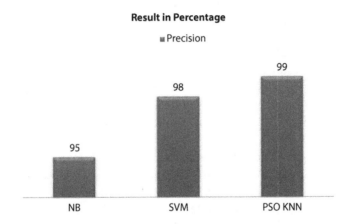

Figure 13.4 Precision comparison of classifiers for chatbot text classification.

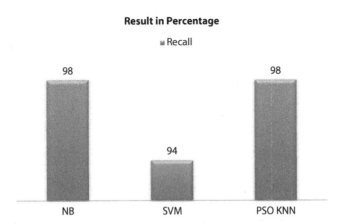

Figure 13.5 Recall comparison of classifiers for chatbot text classification.

Result in Percentage

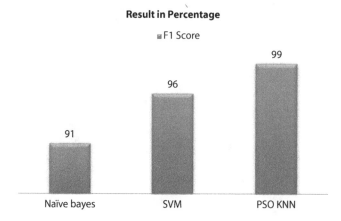

Figure 13.6 F1 score comparison of classifiers for chatbot text classification.

consider. When attempting to explain the performance of the models on test data, a popular representation approach that is utilized is called a confusion matrix. When comparing the efficacy of different machine learning strategies, the confusion matrix is a practical instrument to utilize. The computations of the confusion matrix may provide one of four potential results: True Positive (TP), False Negative (FN), True Negative (TN), or False Positive (FP). When a piece of data is identified by a model as positive and that data really is positive, the result is referred to as a "True Positive." The term "true negative" refers to a situation in which every piece of information has been categorized as unfavorable.

A good example of a false positive is when a piece of information has been incorrectly labeled as having a positive value when, in fact, it has a negative value. One other term for a "false positive" is a "type 1 error," which refers to a typical mistake made during the diagnostic process. In general, false negative denotes the fact that the data quantity is considered to be negative due to the fact that it has a negative value. False negatives are a form of mistake that fall under the category of type 2. With the use of these measures, one is able to evaluate the performance of deep convolutional neural networks in terms of classification, in addition to the performance of other contemporary machine learning and transfer learning approaches.

Accuracy in classification is measured by the proportion of test images generated by the classification models that were successfully assigned to the appropriate category. Even if the categorization is done perfectly each and every time, there is no assurance that it will be accurate. We are able to evaluate the effectiveness of various classification strategies by using this equation.

$$\textbf{Accuracy} = (\textbf{TP} + \textbf{TN}) / (\textbf{TP} + \textbf{TN} + \textbf{FP} + \textbf{FN})$$

To determine what percentage of correctly identified and rejected outcomes the model is able to predict, we divide the total number of recognized results by the total number of identified and rejected outcomes. This gives us the proportion of correctly identified and rejected outcomes. This is how we judge how accurate something is. For the purpose of determining the appropriate ratio of ids, accuracy is absolutely important. It is possible that the accuracy value will fall anywhere between 0 and 1, inclusive. The benefit of using categorization algorithms to make accurate predictions is shown in the emphasis placed on achieving the highest possible level of accuracy. The performance of several categorization techniques may be compared with the help of the following formula:

$$\text{Precision} = TP/ (TP + FP)$$

The recall is calculated by dividing the number of successfully recognized outcomes by the total number of detected and mistakenly rejected outcomes in the sample data. This gives the percentage of outcomes that were correctly recognized. By doing an analysis of the recalls, we will be able to ascertain what percentage of true positives were recognized properly. It is not unheard of for classification schemes to have a recall value of zero. The highest recall value is used as a metric to evaluate the accuracy of predictions made by classification algorithms. The following equation may be used in order to determine the recall value of the various classification strategies.

$$\text{Recall} = TP/ (TP + FN)$$

One of the metrics that is used to measure the effectiveness of machine learning programs is called the F1 score. Take the harmonic mean of the recall and accuracy subscores to generate an F1 score. This is one of the ways to achieve an F1 score. The numbers 0 and 1 are both acceptable alternatives for the F1 variable, which may take on either value. The F1 score provides an indication of how much more accurate the categorization methods are in comparison to the other options. For each of the several classifiers that are accessible, the F1 score may be calculated by using the following formula:

$$\text{F1 Score} = 2TP/ (2TP + FP + FN)$$

For pattern recognition [44–47], text recognition [48, 49], speech recognition, and picture recognition, deep neural networks perform well. However, adversarial instances have the ability to assault [50–52] such networks [53, 54]. Adversarial instances are produced by introducing a negligible amount of noise to a base sample, making the sample undetectable to humans but still being misclassified by the classification algorithm. Although studies have evolved to include the text domain, studies of adversarial [55, 56] instances have traditionally been conducted in the context of pictures. An adversarial [57, 58] example in the context of text is a sample of text in which key words have been modified, causing the sample to be incorrectly classified by a model even though it is identical to the original text in terms of meaning and grammar to humans. There aren't many studies on black box assaults that use text-based adversarial scenarios, though. We suggest the ensemble transfer textfooler [59] technique in this work. This technique creates an ensemble adversarial example [60–62] that concurrently deceives many models before performing a black box assault on an unidentified model. A movie review dataset and TensorFlow as the machine learning library were used in the experiments.

13.5   Conclusion

A piece of artificial intelligence software that is meant to replicate human communication is known as an online chatbot. The use of chatbots is steadily becoming more widespread. The primary objective of any chatbot's development is to enable it to carry on a natural conversation with a human user (typically through text messages), and to provide appropriate responses to the user's inquiries. This is accomplished by giving the chatbot the ability to understand and respond to natural language. This section includes a detailed literature analysis of the many approaches that have been used to enhance chatbot text capabilities. A comprehensive investigation of the ways in which text categorization and grouping may be achieved via the use of machine learning techniques is also included in the literature review. In addition to that, a method for classifying chatbot material that is based on machine learning is described here. A method known as normalization is used during preprocessing in order to filter out undesired background noise. Particle Swarm Optimization is employed to acquire improved features, while KNN, SVM, and Naïve Bayes algorithms are used for text categorization.

References

1. Ali, A.X., Morris, M.R., Wobbrock, J.O., Crowdsourcing similarity judgments for agreement analysis in end-user elicitation studies, in: *The 31st Annual ACM Symposium on User Interface Software and Technology*, pp. 177–188, ACM, 2018.
2. Raghuvanshi, A., Singh, U., Sajja, G., Pallathadka, H., Asenso, E., Kamal, M. *et al.*, Intrusion detection using machine learning for risk mitigation in IoT-enabled smart irrigation in smart farming. *J. Of Food Qual.*, 2022, 1–8, 2022, doi: 10.1155/2022/3955514.
3. Hemamalini, V., Rajarajeswari, S., Nachiyappan, S., Sambath, M., Devi, T., Singh, B., Food quality inspection and grading using efficient image segmentation and machine learning-based system. *J. Of Food Qual.*, 2022, 1–6, 2022, doi: 10.1155/2022/5262294.
4. Prasad, J.V.D., Zamani, A.S., K, A., Naved, M., Pallathadka, H., Sammy, F., Kaliyaperumal, K., Computational technique based on machine learning and image processing for medical image analysis of breast cancer diagnosis. *Secur. Commun. Networks*, 2022, Article ID 1918379, 7, 2022, https://doi.org/10.1155/2022/1918379.
5. Chaudhury, S., Krishna, A.N., Gupta, S., Sankaran, K.S., Khan, S., Sau, K., Sammy, F., Effective image processing and segmentation-based machine learning techniques for diagnosis of breast cancer. *Comput. Math. Methods Med.*, 2022, Article ID 6841334, 6, 2022, https://doi.org/10.1155/2022/6841334.
6. Zamani, A.S., Anand, L., Rane, K.P., Prabhu, P., Buttar, A.M., Pallathadka, H., Dugbakie, B.N., Performance of machine learning and image processing in plant leaf disease detection. *J. Food Qual.*, 2022, Article ID 1598796, 7, 2022. https://doi.org/10.1155/2022/1598796.
7. Abualigah, L.M., Khader, A.T., Al-Betar, M.A., Alomari, O.A., Text feature selection with a robust weight scheme and dynamic dimension reduction to text document clustering. *Expert Syst. Appl.*, 84, 24–36, 2017.
8. Aghdam, M.H., Ghasem-Aghaee, N., Basiri, M.E., Text feature selection using ant colony optimization. *Expert Syst. Appl.*, 36, 3, 6843–6853, 2009.

9. Alghamdi, H.S., Tang, H.L., Alshomrani, S., Hybrid ACO and TOFA feature selection approach for text classification, in: *2012 IEEE Congress on Evolutionary Computation*, IEEE, pp. 1–6, 2012, June.

10. Subanya, B. and Rajalaxmi, R.R., Feature selection using artificial Bee Colony for cardiovascular disease classification. *2014 International Conference on Electronics and Communication Systems (ICECS)*, Coimbatore, pp. 1–6, 2014, doi: 10.1109/ ECS. 2014. 6892729.

11. Younus, Z.S., Mohamad, D., Saba, T., Alkawaz, M.H., Rehman, A., Al-Rodhaan, M., Al-Dhelaan, A., Content-based image retrieval using PSO and k-means clustering algorithm. *Arabian J. Geosci.*, 8, 8, 6211–6224, 2015.

12. Ahmad, S.R., Yusop, N.M.M., Bakar, A.A., Yaakub, M.R., Statistical analysis for validating ACO-KNN algorithm as feature selection in sentiment analysis, in: *AIP Conference Proceedings*, AIP Publishing, vol. 1891, no. 1, p. 020018, 2017, October.

13. Zhang, N., Xiong, J., Zhong, J., Thompson, L., Feature selection method using BPSO-EA with ENN classifier, in: *2018 Eighth International Conference on Information Science and Technology (ICIST)*, IEEE, pp. 364–369, 2018, June.

14. Hamdani, T.M., Won, J.M., Alimi, A.M., Karray, F., Hierarchical genetic algorithm with new evaluation function and bi-coded representation for the selection of features considering their confidence rate. *Appl. Soft Comput.*, 11, 2, 2501–2509, 2011.

15. Suguna, N. and Thanushkodi, K.G., An independent rough set approach hybrid with artificial bee colony algorithm for dimensionality reduction. *Am. J. Appl. Sci.*, 8, 3, 261, 2011.

16. Basiri, M.E. and Nemati, S., A novel hybrid ACO-GA algorithm for text feature selection, in: *2009 IEEE Congress on Evolutionary Computation*, IEEE, pp. 2561–2568, 2009.

17. Karabulut, M., Fuzzy unordered rule induction algorithm in text categorization on top of geometric particle swarm optimization term selection. *Knowl.-Based Syst.*, 54, 288–297, 2013.

18. Iyyer, M., Manjunatha, V., Boyd-Graber, J., Daumé III, H., Deep unordered composition rivals syntactic methods for text classification, in: *Proceedings of the 53rd Annual Meeting of the Association for Computational Linguistics and the 7th International Joint Conference on Natural Language Processing (Volume 1: Long Papers)*, vol. 1, pp. 1681–1691, 2015.

19. Acharya, A., Goel, R., Metallinou, A., Dhillon, I., Online embedding compression for text classification using low rank matrix factorization, in: *Proceedings of the AAAI Conference on Artificial Intelligence*, vol. 33, pp. 6196–6203, 2019.

20. Vilar, E., Word embedding, neural networks and text classification: What is the state-of-the-art? *Junior Manag. Sci.*, 4, 1, 35–62, 2019.

21. Gulin, V.V. and Frolov, A.B., On the classification of text documents taking into account their structural features. *J. Comput. Syst. Sci. Int.*, 55, 3, 394–403, 2016.

22. Kanika, and Sangeeta, Applying machine learning algorithms for news articles categorization: Using SVM and kNN with TF-IDF approach, in: *Smart Computational Strategies: Theoretical and Practical Aspects*, A. Luhach, K. Hawari, I. Mihai, P.A. Hsiung, R. Mishra (eds.), Springer, Singapore, 2019.

23. Kowsari, K., Brown, D.E., Heidarysafa, M., Meimandi, K.J., Gerber, M.S., Barnes, L.E., Hdltex: Hierarchical deep learning for text classification, in: *2017 16th IEEE International Conference on Machine Learning and Applications (ICMLA)*, IEEE, pp. 364–371, 2017.

24. Zhang, X., Zhao, J., LeCun, Y., Character-level convolutional networks for text classification, in: *Advances in Neural Information Processing Systems*, pp. 649–657, 2015.

25. Lai, S., Xu, L., Liu, K., Zhao, J., Recurrent convolutional neural networks for text classification, in: *Twenty-ninth AAAI conference on artificial intelligence*, 2015.

26. Miao, Y.Q. and Kamel, M., Pairwise optimized Rocchio algorithm for text categorization. *Pattern Recognit. Lett.*, 32, 2, 375–382, 2011.

27. Abasi, A.K., Khader, A.T., Al-Betar, M.A., Naim, S., Makhadmeh, S.N., Alyasseri, Z.A.A., A text feature selection technique based on binary multi-verse optimizer for text clustering, in:

2019 IEEE Jordan International Joint Conference on Electrical Engineering and Information Technology (JEEIT), IEEE, pp. 1–6, 2019.

28. Garg, S., Perot, V., Limtiaco, N., Taly, A., Chi, E.H., Beutel, A., Counterfactual fairness in text classification through robustness, in: *Proceedings of the 2019 AAAI/ACM Conference on AI, Ethics, and Society*, ACM, pp. 219–226, 2019.

29. Pietramala, A., Policicchio, V.L., Rullo, P., Sidhu, I., A genetic algorithm for text classification rule induction, in: *Joint European Conference on Machine Learning and Knowledge Discovery in Databases*, pp. 188–203, Berlin, Heidelberg, Springer, 2008, September.

30. Beil, F., Ester, M., Xu, X., Frequent term-based text clustering, in: *Proceedings of the Eighth ACM SIGKDD International Conference on Knowledge Discovery and Data Mining*, ACM, pp. 436–442, 2002.

31. Aggarwal, C.C. and Zhai, C., A survey of text classification algorithms, in: *Mining Text Data*, pp. 163–222, Springer, Boston, MA, 2012.

32. Liu, T., Liu, S., Chen, Z., Ma, W.-Y., An evaluation on feature selection for text clustering, in: *Proceedings of the 20th International Conference on Machine Learning (ICML-03)*, pp. 488–495, 2003.

33. Li, Y., Luo, C., Chung, S.M., Text clustering with feature selection by using statistical data. *IEEE Trans. knowl. Data Eng.*, 20, 5, 641–652, 2008.

34. Zhang, W., Yoshida, T., Tang, X., Wang, Q., Text clustering using frequent itemsets. *Knowl.-Based Syst.*, 23, 5, 379–388, 2010.

35. Jo, T., Text Clustering: Approaches, in: *Text Mining*, pp. 203–224, Springer, Cham, 2019.

36. Bharti, K.K. and Singh, P.K., Chaotic gradient artificial bee colony for text clustering. *Soft Comput.*, 20, 3, 1113–1126, 2016.

37. Mijangos, V., Sierra, G., Montes, A., Sentence level matrix representation for document spectral clustering. *Pattern Recognit. Lett.*, 85, 29–34, 2017.

38. Xu, Z. and Ke, Y., Effective and efficient spectral clustering on text and link data, in: *Proceedings of the 25th ACM International on Conference on Information and Knowledge Management*, ACM, pp. 357–366, 2016.

39. Li, A.-D., Xue, B., Zhang, M., A forward search inspired particle swarm optimization algorithm for feature selection in classification. *2021 IEEE Congress on Evolutionary Computation (CEC)*, pp. 786–793, 2021, doi: 10.1109/CEC45853.2021.9504949.

40. Javid, J., Mughal, M.A., Karim, M., Using kNN algorithm for classification of distribution transformers health index. *2021 International Conference on Innovative Computing (ICIC)*, pp. 1–6, 2021, doi: 10.1109/ICIC53490.2021.9693013.

41. Al-Jumaili, S., Duru, A.D., Uçan, O.N., Covid-19 ultrasound image classification using SVM based on kernels deduced from convolutional neural network. *2021 5th International Symposium on Multidisciplinary Studies and Innovative Technologies (ISMSIT)*, pp. 429–433, 2021, doi: 10.1109/ISMSIT52890.2021.9604551.

42. Li, C., Chen, L., Wu, S., Mo, Y., Chen, L., Application research of naive bayes algorithm based on DIKW in weather website. *2021 IEEE 23rd Int Conf on High Performance Computing & Communications; 7th Int Conf on Data Science & Systems; 19th Int Conf on Smart City; 7th Int Conf on Dependability in Sensor, Cloud & Big Data Systems & Application (HPCC/DSS/SmartCity/DependSys)*, pp. 2253–2257, 2021, doi: 10.1109/HPCC-DSS-SmartCity-DependSys53884.2021.00337.

43. http://www.cs.cmu.edu/~ark/QA-data/.

44. Mahor, V., Bijrothiya, S., Rawat, R., Kumar, A., Garg, B., Pachlasiya, K., IoT and artificial intelligence techniques for public safety and security, in: *Smart Urban Computing Applications*, p. 111, 2023.

45. Mahor, V., Pachlasiya, K., Garg, B., Chouhan, M., Telang, S., Rawat, R., Mobile operating system (Android) vulnerability analysis using machine learning, in: *Proceedings of International Conference on Network Security and Blockchain Technology: ICNSBT 2021*, pp. 159–169, Springer Nature Singapore, Singapore, 2022, June.

46. Rawat, R., Garg, B., Pachlasiya, K., Mahor, V., Telang, S., Chouhan, M., Mishra, R., SCNTA: Monitoring of network availability and activity for identification of anomalies using machine learning approaches. *Int. J. Inf. Technol. Web Eng. (IJITWE)*, 17, 1, 1–19, 2022.

47. Rawat, R., Rimal, Y.N., William, P., Dahima, S., Gupta, S., Sankaran, K.S., Malware threat affecting financial organization analysis using machine learning approach. *Int. J. Inf. Technol. Web Eng. (IJITWE)*, 17, 1, 1–20, 2022.

48. Rawat, R., Mahor, V., Chouhan, M., Pachlasiya, K., Telang, S., Garg, B., Systematic literature review (SLR) on social media and the digital transformation of drug trafficking on darkweb, in: *International Conference on Network Security and Blockchain Technology*, pp. 181–205, Springer, Singapore, 2022.

49. Rawat, R., Ayodele Oki, O., Sankaran, S., Florez, H., Ajagbe, S.A., Techniques for predicting dark web events focused on the delivery of illicit products and ordered crime. *Int. J. Electr. Comput. Eng. (IJECE)*, 13, 5, 5354–5365, Oct. 2023, doi: 10.11591/ijece.v13i5.pp5354-5365.

50. Rawat, R., Garg, B., Mahor, V., Telang, S., Pachlasiya, K., Chouhan, M., Organ trafficking on the dark web—The data security and privacy concern in healthcare systems, in: *Internet of Healthcare Things: Machine Learning for Security and Privacy*, pp. 189–216, 2022.

51. Vyas, P., Vyas, G., Chauhan, A., Rawat, R., Telang, S., Gottumukkala, M., Anonymous trading on the dark online marketplace: An exploratory study, in: *Using Computational Intelligence for the Dark Web and Illicit Behavior Detection*, pp. 272–289, IGI Global, 2022.

52. Rawat, R., Oki, O.A., Sankaran, K.S., Olasupo, O., Ebong, G.N., Ajagbe, S.A., A new solution for cyber security in big data using machine learning approach, in: *Mobile Computing and Sustainable Informatics: Proceedings of ICMCSI 2023*, pp. 495–505, Springer Nature Singapore, Singapore, 2023.

53. Rawat, R., Chakrawarti, R.K., Raj, A., Mani, G., Chidambarathanu, K., Bhardwaj, R., Association rule learning for threat analysis using traffic analysis and packet filtering approach. *Int. J. Inf. Technol.*, 1–11, 2023.

54. Rawat, R., Logical concept mapping and social media analytics relating to cyber criminal activities for ontology creation. *Int. J. Inf. Technol.*, 15, 2, 893–903, 2023.

55. Rawat, R., Mahor, V., Álvarez, J.D., Ch, F., Cognitive systems for dark web cyber delinquent association malignant data crawling: A review, in: *Handbook of Research on War Policies, Strategies, and Cyber Wars*, pp. 45–63, 2023.

56. Rawat, R., Chakrawarti, R.K., Vyas, P., Gonzáles, J.L.A., Sikarwar, R., Bhardwaj, R., Intelligent fog computing surveillance system for crime and vulnerability identification and tracing. *Int. J. Inf. Secur. Priv. (IJISP)*, 17, 1, 1–25, 2023.

57. Rawat, R., Sowjanya, A.M., Patel, S.I., Jaiswal, V., Khan, I., Balaram, A. (Eds.), *Using Machine Intelligence: Autonomous Vehicles Volume 1*, John Wiley & Sons, 2022.

58. Rawat, R., Mahor, V., Díaz-Álvarez, J., Chávez, F., Rooted learning model at fog computing analysis for crime incident surveillance, in: *2022 International Conference on Smart Generation Computing, Communication and Networking (SMART GENCON)*, pp. 1–9, IEEE, 2022, December.

59. Rawat, R. and Shrivastav, S.K., SQL injection attack detection using SVM. *Int. J. Comput. Appl.*, 42, 13, 1–4, 2012.

60. Rawat, R., Bhardwaj, P., Kaur, U., Telang, S., Chouhan, M., Sankaran, K.S., *Smart vehicles for communication, volume 2*, John Wiley & Sons, 2023.

61. Mahor, V., Garg, B., Telang, S., Pachlasiya, K., Chouhan, M., Rawat, R., Cyber threat phylogeny assessment and vulnerabilities representation at thermal power station, in: *Proceedings of International Conference on Network Security and Blockchain Technology: ICNSBT 2021*, pp. 28–39, Springer Nature Singapore, Singapore, 2022, June.
62. Rawat, R., Gupta, S., Sivaranjani, S., Cu, O.K., Kuliha, M., Sankaran, K.S., Malevolent information crawling mechanism for forming structured illegal organisations in hidden networks. *Int. J. Cyber Warf. Terror. (IJCWT)*, *12*, 1, 1–14, 2022.

Enhanced Security in Chatbot

Ambika N.

Dept. of Computer Science and Applications, St. Francis College, Bangalore, India

Abstract

The previous project creates a chatbot based on a blockchain platform. BONIK allows users to securely submit transactions and perform financial tasks like asking for the current balance. BONIK can validate each request against pre-defined access control rules codified in intelligent contracts thanks to the integration with the blockchain. User requests are honored if they are validated. The blockchain platform, chatbot, and dApp (Decentralized Application) are the three main components of this architecture. A blockchain platform is used to connect BONIK's chatbot to several important features and security features. Every financial activity in the system, including balance queries and money transfers, is carried out by this bank, and it is assumed that every user of the system has an account with the bank. Two intelligent contracts in the system provide business logic for handling user requests. The first is provided by the system, which is in charge of user login and registration, and the second is provided by the bank, which stores the business logic for financial transactions. Fabric refers to a smart contract as a chain code, and it can use transactions to invoke it. A user operates a peer to submit a transaction sent to the endorsers. The user receives a response. Docker containers are used to deploy the blockchain platform, with each container acting as one of these entities. A channel into which the chain code is deployed connects these entities. Kafka, which uses two additional orderer nodes to create and disseminate blocks, serves as the foundation for the consensus. Each user receives 10,000 currency units for financial transactions during the initial phase.

The suggestion generates the hash code and attaches the same to provide additional security. The blockchain is generated for the hash code and message. This is authenticated by the server. The work provides 1.84% more security than previous work.

Keywords: Chatbot, artificial intelligence, messenger, interactive software

14.1 Introduction

The term "chatbot," which is an abbreviation for "chat" and "robot," refers to software programs that use artificial intelligence (Ambika N., 2022) (Freiherr, 1980) to reenact in-person conversations or chat interactive software. The chatbot cannot be considered a real-world application because it was developed in a laboratory. It is mostly used for services related to e-commerce, like customer service centers, the Internet, and financial consulting. It has

---

Email: Ambika.nagaraj76@gmail.com

Romil Rawat, Rajesh Kumar Chakrawarti, Sanjaya Kumar Sarangi, Piyush Vyas, Mary Sowjanya Alamanda, Kotagiri Srividya and Krishnan Sakthidasan Sankaran (eds.) Conversational Artificial Intelligence, (219–236) © 2024 Scrivener Publishing LLC

been integrated with apps like Facebook Messenger and Slack that are used for social networking or business communication.

The development and evaluation of intelligent software and hardware, or intelligent agents, are becoming integrated into our day-to-day lives through artificial intelligence. Intelligent agents can perform various activities, from manual labor to complex operations. Although they can imitate human speech and provide users with entertainment, chatbots are not solely designed for this purpose. They are helpful in business, education, information retrieval, and e-commerce applications. The user's social graph spreads contact with the chatbot without leaving the messaging app where it lives, which ensures the user's identity.

Different criteria can be used to classify chatbots: the service provided, the goals, the knowledge domain, the input processing, and response generation method, human assistance, and the construction method. Classification based on the knowledge domain considers the amount of data a chatbot is trained on and the knowledge it can access. While closed-domain chatbots are focused on a specific knowledge domain and may not be able to respond to other questions, open-domain chatbots can talk about general topics and respond appropriately. Classification based on the service provided considers the chatbot's emotional proximity to the user, the amount of intimate interaction, and the task the chatbot is completing. Interpersonal chatbots (Beattie, Edwards, & Edwards, 2020) offer services like restaurant reservations, flight reservations, and FAQ bots and fall under the communication domain. Messenger, Slack, and WhatsApp are intrapersonal chatbots in the user's personal space. They are the user's companions and have a human-like understanding of the user. All chatbots will require some inter-chatbot communication options as inter-agent chatbots become omnipresent. Like FAQ chatbots, informative chatbots are made to provide users with information that has already been stored or is available from a fixed source. The objective of chat-based and conversational chatbots (Hussain, Ameri Sianaki, & Ababneh, 2019) is to correctly respond to the user's sentence in a human-like manner. Task-based chatbots help people book flights or do other specific tasks. These chatbots are intelligent in terms of asking for information and comprehending user input. The classification based on the input processing and response generation method considers how inputs are processed, and responses are generated. The appropriate responses are generated using one of three models: generative, retrieval-based, and rule-based. The majority of the initial chatbots, as well as many online chatbots, used rule-based model chatbot architecture. They select the system response by recognizing the verbal form of the input text without creating any new text answers using a fixed, predefined set of rules. Based on the current and previous user messages, the generative model produces solutions more efficiently than the other three models.

The previous project (Bhuiyan, et al., 2020) creates a chatbot based on a blockchain platform. BONIK allows users to securely submit transactions and perform financial tasks like asking for the current balance. BONIK can validate each request against pre-defined access control rules codified in intelligent contracts thanks to the integration with the blockchain. User requests are honored if they are validated. The blockchain platform, chatbot, and dApp (Decentralized Application) are the three main components of this architecture. A blockchain platform is used to connect BONIK's chatbot to several important features and security features. Every financial activity in the system, including balance queries and money transfers, is carried out by this bank, and it is assumed that every user of the system has an account with the bank. Two intelligent contracts in the system provide business logic for handling user requests. The first is provided by the system, which is in charge of user login and registration, and the second is provided by the bank, which stores the business logic for financial transactions. Fabric refers to a smart contract as a chain code, and it can use transactions to invoke it. A user operates a peer to submit a transaction sent to the endorsers. The user receives a response. Docker containers are used to deploy the blockchain platform, with each container acting as one of these entities. A channel into which the chain code is deployed connects these entities. Kafka, which uses two additional orderer nodes to create and disseminate blocks, serves as the foundation for the consensus. Each user receives 10,000 currency units for financial transactions during the initial phase.

The suggestion generates the hash code and attaches the same to provide additional security. The blockchain is generated for the hash code and message. This is authenticated by the server. The work provides 1.84% more security than previous work.

The work is divided into nine sections. The architecture of chatbots follows the introduction. The working of chatbots is detailed in section 14.3. Background is narrated in section 14.4. Literature survey is briefed in section 14.5. The proposed work is elaborated in section 14.6. Analysis of the work is explained in section 14.7. Future work is briefed in section 14.8. The work is concluded in section 14.9.

14.2 Architecture of Chatbots

The words "chatting" and "robot" are combined in the term "chatbot." It is a computer program based on artificial intelligence that uses messaging apps and websites to encourage conversations or interactions with real people. There are no time or space restrictions on the types of interactions that can take place between humans and chatbots. These interactions can be spoken or text-based. Both forms of machine-based interaction are skillfully disguised as human agent support, which makes it easier for users to initiate a conversation. The chatbot's primary functions include assisting users in meeting their information-searching requirements, responding to questions, and fostering social connections. Chatbots have been used as company representatives to meet customer needs and provide valuable information.

The first-layer intelligence (Villegas-Ch, Arias-Navarrete, & Palacios-Pacheco, 2020) is in charge of collecting data that put IoT devices first. The campus members have been divided into three groups to segment what each of these devices does, and several interact directly with them. The first group includes those in charge of all campus administration, the second group includes teachers, and the third group, which provides for students, places the most emphasis on this work. The Internet of Things (IoT) devices learn about each group's needs and gather important information about their activities. In the case of the students, the various Internet of Things (IoT) devices and sensor systems collect data from them, such as the amount of time each student spends at the university, the places he frequents, and information about his activities and qualifications. This information is crucial when the AI must decide on an event it analyzes. The computing process, which typically uses public or private clouds, is located in the second layer. The architecture of the intelligent campus is in charge of this layer, which entails sending the data to the cloud for processing or storing it in various databases. Analyzing data is the third layer. An extensive data framework called Hadoop is used to carry out this procedure. Because it is in charge of investigating all data, structured or unstructured, that are stored locally, or in the cloud, this layer is one of the most crucial. Hadoop processes these data and presents them to a chatbot with integrated AI. The analysis layer's high-quality information is continuously consumed by the chatbot, allowing it to learn more deeply and more quickly. Through Hadoop, the chatbot has access to all the information about each student. This information is of high quality, so it ensures that the data about the students' tendencies and progress in each subject are accurate. The chatbot incorporates the analysis data gathered in this layer into its analysis, as well as the data collected directly from user interaction. The knowledge layer uses all the knowledge and displays it through dashboards or control panels and applications that students use. The student uses the campus LMS, the application in which the chatbot is embedded, to consume the data. Every time a student accesses the LMS, the chatbot module starts with the user's identification and begins to interact with several natural language questions. Figure 14.1 represents the same.

The most recent machine learning algorithms (Ayanouz, Abdelhakim, & Benhmed, 2020) make up the natural language processing engine. These algorithms match a user's intent with a list of bot-supported ideals. It takes the user's input, determines its meaning, and then applies it to the chatbot-supported goal: It takes the essential information from a user's query. It can manage the user's actual meaning. An agent in the Feedback Mechanism is in charge of periodically reviewing the user's feedback to determine whether the bot is responding appropriately to the user's dialogues or whether the user is satisfied with the bot's responses. The bot can follow as many happy paths as possible from the conversation thanks to a framework that allows us to improve the user experience. After creating a network with happy trails, this higher-level framework directs the conversation so that the end user is pleased. The bot then learns from interactions and follows the same conversational pattern it used to communicate with another user. This system correctly understands the user's questions, and the knowledge base contains relevant responses. Plugins provide

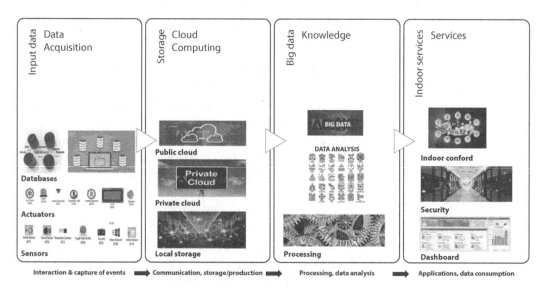

Figure 14.1 Layers of the architecture of a smart campus and its impact on the components of a Chatbot that uses artificial intelligence (Villegas-Ch, Arias-Navarrete, & Palacios-Pacheco, 2020).

innovative chatbot automation components and solution APIs for field workers and HR management chatbots utilized within businesses. A server is in charge of processing the user's request and directing it to the appropriate components. It could develop the front end from several client-facing systems.

14.3   Working of Chatbots

Artificial intelligence and machine learning have galvanized chatbots, a popular new technology with unprecedented business potential. AI chatbots can offer distinct advantages to businesses. They begin by automating customer service and facilitating communications initiated by the company. Chatbots' sophisticated speech recognition and natural language processing capabilities enable them to comprehend convoluted and nuanced conversations and respond to customer requests with depth, compassion, and even humor.

It (Rathnayaka, *et al.*, 2022) used a three-phase structured approach to create the conceptual framework. During this phase, the multilayered relationships between constructs and how they enable it also formulated the BA-based AI chatbot setting. In Phase 2, it added data-driven insights from online mental health support groups to the primary constructs. It produced content that portrayed both the materialization of each build and their connections in online support group environments. Samples of the materialization of each construct were extracted. For this job, it used the PRIME framework. PRIME is a novel collection of machine learning and deep learning algorithms for classification, clustering, association rules, and NLP techniques that gives structure to the unstructured text generated by free-flowing discussions in online mental health support groups. Most of the time, multiple people will talk about various topics during a single conversation. It can tailor the chatbot's conversational capabilities to a specific domain. A cycle of planning, executing, and evaluating the activities in which the user is participating. The conceptual framework was created as a collection of chatbot capabilities that fall into three broad categories. The individualized conversation engine is built on the Rasa chatbot framework and features natural language processing (NLP) modules geared toward the business analyst (BA). The NLP engine has three main parts: response selection, intent and entity extraction, and feature extractor. The user-generated text's preprocessing and representation learning are the responsibility of the feature extractor. User utterances can be annotated with the appropriate entities, and their intended meaning can be determined using intent and entity extraction. The response selector is then used to select a response based on the user's plan and the entities they mention. The goal of the user interface is to get them to schedule the activity regularly. The user receives timely reminders from the chatbot to complete the scheduled task. After the planned action is finished, the user receives a notification with a satisfaction survey. Ecological Momentary Assessment, which aims to address the limitations of the current practice of global retrospective self-reporting at the predefined clinic or hospital visits, is the foundation for remote health monitoring. Recall bias affects the reporting done during these visits, and it misses changes in behavior over time and in different contexts. Figure 14.2 represents the same.

There are several activities at each stage (Caldarini, Jaf, & McGarry, 2022). The first step is to identify appropriate databases of research articles and relevant search terms for the relevant body of literature. The selected databases' research articles on chatbots are then

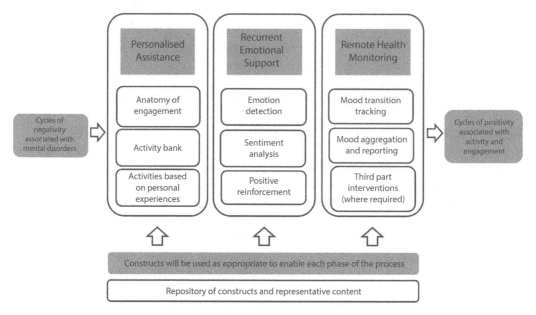

Figure 14.2 Conceptual framework of behavioral activation in an AI-based chatbot. (Rathnayaka, *et al.*, 2022).

gathered. It identified research articles on chatbots by utilizing the databases of three major publishers. IEEE, ScienceDirect, and Springer are these. The purpose of these activities is to gather information about the subject. The analysis of the retrieved articles is the study's second stage. It focuses on categorizing the pieces into groups based on four chatbot characteristics: methods reported in the literature for design, implementation, application, and evaluation.

It assists (Yang & Evans, 2019) in delivering a simulation game in a taught Master's module. The recommendation developed a simulation bot. The chatbot plays the role of a virtual customer who wants to do business with a different company than the one they currently use in this simulation game. Students act as salespeople for the current business; they must communicate with these virtual customers and try to keep them as customers. A reading list bot has been created to help users of new educational software, the digital reading list, learn how to use it. It is based on the information in the list, and students can view these lists. It tells them exactly where, when, and how to access each book in the library. The chatbot will act as a virtual tutor to teach teachers and students how to use the software and, if necessary, teach them how to solve fundamental technical problems on their own.

The widespread use of smartphones and the development of broadband wireless technology have made it possible to live in the social media age that we live in today. In casual conversations, social chatbots can also perform various tasks for users. It must acquire a set of abilities to respond to user requests. The system has a multimodal interface that accepts users' voice, image, and text input. A chat manager in the system directs intake to the appropriate modules, such as core-chat or visual awareness, for understanding and output generation. The chat manager will invoke various skills in response to multiple scenarios, forward the user's request to the appropriate skill components, and receive a response from those components. After that, the chat manager will work with the suitable modules to create an output that fits the current conversation's context. The core component of social chatbots is core-chat. After receiving the user's text input, it generates a text response as the output. It offers social chatbot-like communication capabilities. A social chatbot's ability to create text comments from input images—known as image social commenting—is referred to as its visual awareness. Work has utilized XiaoIce. It recognizes the emotional needs of users and communicates with them like a friend, uplifting, encouraging, and keeping their attention throughout the conversation. Users have reported that having conversations with XiaoIce has improved their outlook, given them emotional support, and made them feel like they are part of a social group. Social chatbots have been able to gain a deeper understanding of their users and better serve them as a result of these conversations, which have contributed to the development of trust and an emotional connection between humans and social chatbots.

14.4   Background

The purpose of this study (DM, Y-TH, & HD, 2021), which combined the trust factor with DeLone and McLean's information systems success (D&M ISS) and expectation confirmation models, was to investigate the factors that influence users' intentions to continue using chatbot services in the banking industry in Vietnam. Users are more likely to be satisfied when they have access to accurate, up-to-date, reliable, and adequate information. Users spend a lot of time and effort on chatbot services to find the information they need to make decisions. As a result, the chatbot systems' information should be precise, straightforward, personalized, and well-presented. The dependability, user-friendliness, response time, and availability of chatbot systems are all reflected in system quality. A chatbot's technical ability to provide users with support with quick, accurate information could be regarded as its system quality. It uses structural equation modeling and gathers 359 questionnaire surveys from actual bank chatbot users. The same is portrayed in Figure 14.3.

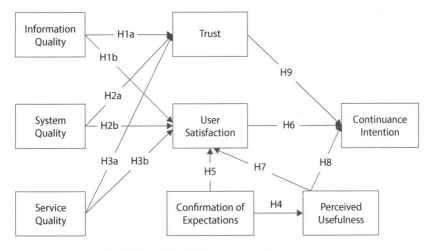

Figure 14.3 System model (DM, Y-TH, & HD, 2021).

14.5   Literature Survey

Software for the financial industry that serves as commerce is a banking chatbot (Lai, Leu, & Lin, 2018) with AI technologies. It needs to pay special attention to its security because it deals with its customers' financial and personal privacy. It could be considered an AI-powered EC application. Banking chatbots must consider EC security measures to safeguard customer data and personal privacy. Design data access security, data usage security, and data transfer security are the three security control operations that security strategies should cover.

The project (Bhuiyan, *et al.*, 2020) creates a chatbot based on a blockchain platform. BONIK allows users to securely submit transactions and perform financial tasks like asking for the current balance. BONIK can validate each request against pre-defined access control rules codified in intelligent contracts thanks to the integration with the blockchain. User requests are honored if they are validated. The blockchain platform, chatbot, and dApp (Decentralized Application) are the three main components of this architecture. A blockchain platform is used to connect BONIK's chatbot to several important features and security features. Every financial activity in the system, including balance queries and money transfers, is carried out by this bank, and it is assumed that every user of the system has an account with the bank. Two intelligent contracts in the system provide business logic for handling user requests. The first is provided by the system, which is in charge of user login and registration, and the second is provided by the bank, which stores the business logic for financial transactions. Fabric refers to a smart contract as a chain code, and it can use transactions to invoke it. A user operates a peer to submit a transaction sent to the endorsers. The user receives a response. Docker containers are used to deploy the blockchain platform, with each container acting as one of these entities. A channel into which the chain code is deployed connects these entities. Kafka, which uses two additional orderer nodes to create and disseminate blocks, serves as the foundation for the consensus. Each user receives 10,000 currency units for financial transactions during the initial phase.

This study (Hill, Ford, & Farreras, 2015) looked at how people communicate differently with an intelligent agent than another human. It compared 100 exchanges with the well-known chatbot Cleverbot to 100 instant messaging conversations across seven dimensions: words per message, words per conversation, messages per conversation, the singularity of each term, the use of profanity, shorthand, and emoticons. One of the most widely used chatbots currently available is Cleverbot. It relies on feedback to communicate and is made to mimic natural conversation by learning from human interaction. A human user types a statement into a synchronous one-to-one online interface that looks like an instant messenger and waits for Cleverbot to respond. This study looked into seven dependent variables. The average number of words per message, the number of messages per conversation, and the number of words per conversation were three variables related to the amount of written content in each conversation. Any single data transmission from the user to their conversational partner was considered a message, regardless of length or content. A single character or emoticon, and communication with multiple sentences, were both considered to be one message. Each transmission of the same word or sentence was counted separately. It used a website made to make custom-banned word lists based on the desired intensity level to compile a list of profane words. A multivariate analysis of variance (MANOVA) was used to look at the seven variables coded from the two corpora.

A medical chatbot (Divya, Indumathi, Ishwarya, Priyasankari, & Devi, 2018) that uses artificial intelligence (Ambika N., 2022) to diagnose a disease and provide basic information about it before consulting a doctor is the concept that has been proposed. The user dialogue has a linear design that goes from symptom extraction to symptom mapping, where it finds the corresponding symptom. It then diagnoses the patient, determining whether it is a major or minor disease. It will refer the patient to the appropriate doctor if it is a significant disease. The user will be identified by the login information stored in the database. It used natural language generation templates to create the state transitions logic. The system took the initiative to communicate with the user and solicit their responses. The bot asks for the user's email address and password to log in, then goes through a loop of symptom extraction states until it has enough information to diagnose. The login information of the user is checked. Then, the symptoms are extracted using the String Searching Algorithm, which finds a substring in the natural language text input that represents the symptoms.

Customers were randomly assigned (Luo, Tong, Fang, & Qu, 2019) to receive sales calls from AI chatbots or human agents. In a between-subject design, each customer only receives one call and is randomly assigned to one of the six experimental conditions. The first condition involves underdogs in the call center—inexperienced human workers whose call report performance in the preceding six months is in the lowest 20 percentile. The second kind of people is proficient workers—those with a previous version in the top 20 percentile. The third requirement is an AI chatbot that does not disclose. The chatbot initiates the sales call in this group without disclosing its machine identity. The fourth condition is an AI chatbot that requires disclosure before speaking. At the start of the conversation with the customer, the chatbot here reveals its machine identity.

The work (Pantano & Pizzi, 2020) used the platform Orbit to gather the patents for the current analysis. The platform provides a query for selecting all patented innovations associated with a particular keyword over a specific period. This method identifies 688 patents from across all international classification categories. The patent number, title, patent abstract, application date, acceptance date, assignees (patent owners), domain, and country were all included in the initial dataset for each patent. The first analysis involved looking into occurrences. Second, built-in algorithms enable the software to extract different topics and phrases and identify idioms and themes prevalent throughout the text corpus. After scanning the entire text corpus, these algorithms sort the most frequently mentioned subjects. It also used WordStat software to examine each patent's content and determine which part of the (online) customer service might be affected. Thirdly, the dendrogram is used to represent the results of the hierarchical cluster analysis and multidimensional scaling carried out during the final analysis. A dendrogram is a tree graph in which the vertical axis represents the items, and the horizontal axis represents the clusters created by each clustering step.

This study (Haristiani, 2019) aims to learn about and examine various forms of chatbot artificial intelligence and the possibility of using them as a medium for language learning. The author's observations of a chatbot-based language learning medium and a literature review of chatbot studies provided the study's data. This study gathered its data through literature reviews of previous studies on chatbots and their applications. An observation report on Gengobot, a chatbot-based language learning platform developed by the author and his team, is also included in this study. The user's message is the first step in the chatbot's fundamental mechanism. After natural language processing processed the message, the chatbot responded by referencing the existing database. The three types of chatbots examined in this study can be divided based on their structure, purpose, and audience. A tree-based chatbot only responds to questions already in the database and has predetermined responses set by the developer.

It created a structured questionnaire following the literature and the use of chatbots in e-retailing (Chen, Le, & Florence, 2021). For this study, existing scales were adapted, modified, and expanded. There were six items on the extrinsic values scale. Using Amazon Mechanical Turk (MTurk), we recruited participants and administered online questionnaires for the primary data collection. Due to its inclusion of diverse respondents in online panels and the interactive nature of the Internet, MTurk was chosen. There were a total of 501 responses to the survey regarding the work. It cleaned up the dataset by excluding cases with missing data and outliers and produced a final sample of 425 valid responses. The hypotheses were tested and looked at using SmartPLS and Statistical Product and Service Solutions (SPSS). SmartPLS provides a path model that can describe the relationships between indicators and variables, thereby reducing model complexity and relationship specifications. To test the hypotheses and investigate the constructs' reliability and validity, SPSS and SmartPLS were used to carry out exploratory factor analysis (EFA) and confirmatory factor analysis (CFA).

The recommendation (Rakhra, *et al.*, 2021) developed an e-commerce engine with a list of products for which a chatbot can search. The customer cannot access the agent's database, which is the foundation for data availability and storage. It will define a natural time frame for each project step and specific software application specifications to determine an acceptable approach. The cascade model is a methodology customarily presented about programming creation. The stages of specification acquisition, analysis, architecture, implementation, and testing are all included in this authoritarian software development model. Each procedure is carried out one at a time. It used the project's outcomes, planning documents, and test plans to calculate its success and progress. Each building ends with the generation of a subsystem or function. New requirements are likely to be discovered and added for each incremental development that builds on the functionality of the previous building, eventually leading to the application's full completion. The best way to gather information for this project is through the electronic questionnaire distribution to the general public. Users can contact the chatbot of the web client, and Google's program lets them talk to the chatbot using a text-based or natural language voice. With Google Assistant integration, users can get rich responses like photos and cards. It makes it easier for users to use and interact with the chatbot because they do not have to use as much paper or effort when speaking to it. The chatbot uses dialog to flow as an engine for understanding language meaning (NLU) to identify entities and attempts in a user's expression. The purpose of operation diagrams is to describe the data-information flow and explain how chatbots work. They show how the machine responds to the actions of users when they communicate with the chatbot. In an explicitly matched user input, the NLU specifies the meaning and existence of the relevant entities.

The work (Cheng & Jiang, 2022) gathered data from customers verified to have participated in chatbot marketing and to be located in the United States. It distributed an anonymous invitation link online, and the researchers recruited participants through a professional research company. There were two separate pilot tests, the first of which had 100 participants and the second of which had 103. It examined the quantitative and qualitative responses in the pretests before the completion and launch of the survey. This research study included 1,800 participants who clicked the survey link; 94 responded. Using the Mplus 7.4 program, a two-step structural equation modeling (SEM) analysis was carried out in this study.

The study (Bharti, *et al.*, 2020) introduces a novel computer program that functions as a personal virtual doctor. It has been purposefully designed and intensively trained to interact with patients like real people. Preventive measures, home remedies, interactive counseling sessions, health tips, and symptoms for the most common diseases in rural India are all provided by this serverless application, which aggregates a doctor's services. It overcomes the bias of machine interaction and creates a user-friendly chat system that makes them feel at ease. The bot's conversation has been framed and designed to mimic human behavior. The application creates an automated conversational chat system using the Dialogflow Conversation API to comprehend the user's natural language. Dialogflow runs on GCP (Google Cloud Platform), which enables applications to scale to hundreds of millions of users and uses Google's expertise in machine learning and its products like Google Cloud Speech-to-Text. An Intent is a set of related expressions made by an end user during a single conversation turn. It generated 255 intents in our conversational design, each of which has been trained with multiple user utterances gathered during user testing. Dialogflow selects the particular actions necessary to carry out the intent. Dialogflow's entities are meaningful characters or lexeme sequences. The bot used our design's input and output contexts to create a contextual conversation flow. It lets the bot know what the user has already asked, what they are requesting next, and how to respond. The chatbot interacts with the user and then provides a helpful response by making use of the intents and entities identified in the user input and the context of the conversation. It guarantees high-quality answers, and data from the National Health Portal are used to build a response database.

The system (Athota, Shukla, Pandey, & Rana, 2020) uses an expert system to answer the questions. Experts in their fields should also register here by providing various details. The chatbot's data are stored as a pattern template in the database. SQL is used to manage the database in this case. The client enters the question as text into the user interface. The user query is received by the user interface and then sent to the chatbot application. The literary experiences pre-processing steps in the chatbot application include tokenization. After that, stop words are removed, and feature extraction is based on n-gram, TF-IDF, and cosine likeness.

14.6 Proposed System

The project (Bhuiyan, *et al.*, 2020) creates a chatbot based on a blockchain platform. BONIK allows users to securely submit transactions and perform financial tasks like asking for the current balance. BONIK can validate each request against pre-defined access control rules codified in intelligent contracts thanks to the integration with the blockchain. User requests are honored if they are validated. The blockchain platform, chatbot, and dApp (Decentralized Application) are the three main components of this architecture.

Table 14.1 Generation of hash code.

Step 1: Input – User id (24 bits), location information (64 bits)
Step 2: Stuff 1's in even position of user id and 0's in odd position to make 64 bits length {at the end of user id}
Step 3: Circular right shift User id bits
Step 4: Circular left shift location information bits
Step 5: Xor user id and information bits (resultant – 64 bits)

A blockchain platform is used to connect BONIK's chatbot to several important features and security features. Every financial activity in the system, including balance queries and money transfers, is carried out by this bank, and it is assumed that every user of the system has an account with the bank. Two intelligent contracts in the system provide business logic for handling user requests. The first is provided by the system, which is in charge of user login and registration, and the second is provided by the bank, which stores the business logic for financial transactions. Fabric refers to a smart contract as a chain code, and it can use transactions to invoke it. A user operates a peer to submit a transaction sent to the endorsers. The user receives a response. Docker containers are used to deploy the blockchain platform, with each container acting as one of these entities. A channel into which the chain code is deployed connects these entities. Kafka, which uses two additional orderer nodes to create and disseminate blocks, serves as the foundation for the consensus. Each user receives 10,000 currency units for financial transactions during the initial phase.

The suggested work generates the hash code using the following data—user id and location information. This code is used in the hash code. It is attached to every message (from the user end). It provides identification to the transaction. The server randomly generates a hash code and attaches it to the message. The blockchain is generated for hash code and message. This message is authenticated by the server. Table 14.1 represents the process of generation of hash code.

14.7   Analysis of the Work

The previous project (Bhuiyan, *et al.*, 2020) creates a chatbot based on a blockchain platform. BONIK allows users to securely submit transactions and perform financial tasks like asking for the current balance. BONIK can validate each request against pre-defined access control rules codified in intelligent contracts thanks to the integration with the blockchain. User requests are honored if they are validated. The blockchain platform, chatbot, and dApp (Decentralized Application) are the three main components of this architecture. A blockchain platform is used to connect BONIK's chatbot to several important features and security features. Every financial activity in the system, including balance queries and money transfers, is carried out by this bank, and it is assumed that every user of the system has an account with the bank. Two intelligent contracts in the system provide business logic for handling user requests. The first is provided by the system, which is in charge of user login and registration, and the second is provided by the bank, which stores the business logic for financial transactions. Fabric refers to a smart contract as a chain code, and it can use transactions to invoke it. A user operates a peer to submit a transaction sent to the endorsers. The user receives a response. Docker containers are used to deploy the blockchain platform, with each container acting as one of these entities. A channel into which the chain code is deployed connects these entities. Kafka, which uses two additional orderer nodes to create and disseminate blocks, serves as the foundation for the consensus. Each user receives 10,000 currency units for financial transactions during the initial phase.

The suggestion generates the hash code and attaches the same to provide additional security. The blockchain is generated for the hash code and message. This is authenticated by the server. The work is simulated using R-programming. Table 14.2 details the parameters used in the work. The work provides 1.84% more security than previous work. Figure 14.4 represents the same.

Table 14.2 Parameters used in the work.

Parameters used in the recommendation	Description
Number of clients assumed	5
User id length	24 bits
Location information length	64 bits
Length of hash code	64 bits
Length of message	250 bits

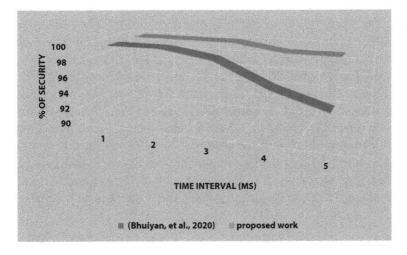

Figure 14.4 Comparison of security in both systems.

14.8   Future Work

Chatbots are conversational agents that enable users to interact with information and services using everyday language. The rapidly expanding body of research on chatbots spans various disciplines, including management and marketing, linguistics and philosophy, psychology and sociology, engineering, design, human–computer interaction, and media and communication science.

- The extensive literature needs to be continuously updated for the broader uses and user groups of chatbots, particularly regarding user motivations and behavior of emerging user groups. It includes information about specific demographics like children, the elderly, and people with special needs, as well as user groups in particular application areas. Because it is necessary to know how the adoption of chatbots may affect groups, organizations, businesses, and society, the implications of chatbot use present several exciting research challenges.

By adopting the Enhance Security (Mahor, Bijrothiya, Rawat, Kumar, Garg, Pachlasiya, 2023; Mahor, Pachlasiya, Garg, Chouhan, Telang, Rawat, 2022; Rawat, Garg, Pachlasiya, Mahor, Telang, Chouhan, Mishra, 2022; Rawat, Rimal, William, Dahima, Gupta, Sankaran, 2022) Framework for Chatbots (Rawat, Mahor, Chouhan, Pachlasiya, Telang, Garg, 2022; Rawat, Ayodele Oki, Sankaran, Florez, Ajagbe, 2023). Using Mac Address Authentication, chatbots may operate at their best, informing consumers about the value of maintaining and protecting customer privacy (Rawat, Garg, Mahor, Telang, Pachlasiya, Chouhan, 2022; Vyas, Vyas, Chauhan, Rawat, Telang, 2022) data. Benefits for customers: The chatbot interaction cannot be resumed if you use a device other than the one that has been registered by the client for access. By filtering the relevant hardware data, this enables the protection of customer chat data. Benefits for the Organisation: Makes it simpler for organisations or businesses to establish legitimate customer identification, making it possible to quickly conduct history and follow-up customer discussions. A project to improve chatbot security is called Security (Rawat, Oki, Sankaran, Olasupo, Ebong, Ajagbe, 2023; Rawat, Chakrawarti, Raj, Mani, Chidambarathanu, Bhardwaj, 2023; Rawat, 2023; Rawat, Mahor, Álvarez, Ch, 2023). Framework On Chatbot Using Mac Address Authentication to Improve Customer Service Quality (Rawat, Chakrawarti, Vyas, Gonzáles, Sikarwar, Bhardwaj, 2023; Rawat, Sowjanya, Patel, Jaiswal, Khan, Balaram, 2022). Before moving on to the next security (Rawat, Mahor, Díaz-Álvarez, Chávez, 2022; Rawat and Shrivastav, 2012) level, the system will perform MAC Address authentication as its initial security (Rawat, Bhardwaj, Kaur, Telang, Chouhan, Sankaran, 2023; Mahor, Garg, Telang, Pachlasiya, Chouhan, Rawat, 2022) check. To communicate with the chatbot, you must register the physical address of the device that owns it. A single device can only be used by one individual and has a single physical address. It is a step towards enhancing chatbot security (Rawat, Gupta, Sivaranjani, Cu, Kuliha, Sankaran, 2022) and educating users about the need to maintain and care for their devices.

14.9   Conclusion

The design of the chatbot layout, interaction mechanisms, and conversational content to manage users' perceptions and responses are all aspects of chatbot user experience and design. User-centered evaluations of chatbots are necessary to obtain insight into users' perceptions and answers, as well as how these are influenced by chatbot design; that is, established methods are used to evaluate user perceptions and responses to chatbots.

The work created a chatbot based on a blockchain platform in the previous project. BONIK allows users to perform financial tasks like asking for the current balance and securely submitting transactions. Because it is integrated with the blockchain, BONIK can validate each request against pre-defined access control rules codified in intelligent contracts. If user requests are validated, they are honored. This architecture consists primarily of the blockchain platform, chatbot, and dApp (Decentralized Application). BONIK's chatbot is connected to several crucial features and security measures via a blockchain platform. This bank handles every financial transaction, including balance inquiries and money transfers. It is assumed that every system user has an account with the bank. The system's two intelligent contracts provide the business logic necessary to respond to user requests. The system, which is in charge of user login and registration, provides the first, and the bank, which stores the business logic for financial transactions, provides the second. Fabric can invoke an intelligent contract through transactions, referring to it as a chain code. To send a trade to the endorsers, a user uses a peer. A response is provided to the user. The blockchain platform is deployed using Docker containers, with each container acting as one of these entities. These entities are connected by a channel through which the chain code is deployed. The consensus is built on top of Kafka, using two additional orderer nodes to create and distribute blocks. Each user receives 10,000 currency units for financial transactions during the initial phase.

The suggestion generates the hash code and attaches the same to provide additional security. The blockchain is generated for the hash code and message. This is authenticated by the server. The work provides 1.84% more security than previous work.

References

Ambika, N., An economical machine learning approach for anomaly detection in IoT environment, in: *Bioinformatics and Medical Applications: Big Data Using Deep Learning Algorithms*, A. Suresh, S. Vimal, Y.H. Robinson, D.K. Ramaswami, R. Udendhran (Eds.), pp. 215–234, Wiley Publications, Hoboken, New Jersey, 2022.

Ambika, N., Enhancing security in IoT instruments using artificial intelligence, in: *IoT and Cloud Computing for Societal Good*, J.K. V., D. S., V. G.-P. (eds.), pp. 259–276, Springer, Cham, 2022.

Athota, L., Shukla, V.K., Pandey, N., Rana, A., Chatbot for healthcare system using artificial intelligence. *8th International Conference on Reliability, Infocom Technologies and Optimization (Trends and Future Directions) (ICRITO)*, Noida, India, IEEE, pp. 619–622, 2020.

Ayanouz, S., Abdelhakim, B.A., Benhmed, M., A smart chatbot architecture based NLP and machine learning for health care assistance. *3rd International Conference on Networking, Information Systems & Security*, Marrakech Morocco, ACM, pp. 1–6, 2020.

Beattie, A., Edwards, A.P., Edwards, C., A bot and a smile: Interpersonal impressions of chatbots and humans using emoji in computer-mediated communication. *Commun. Stud.*, *71*, 3, 409–427, 2020.

Bharti, U., Bajaj, D., Batra, H., Lalit, S., Lalit, S., Gangwani, A., Medbot: Conversational artificial intelligence powered chatbot for delivering tele-health after covid-19. *5th International Conference on Communication and Electronics Systems (ICCES)*, Coimbatore, India, IEEE, pp. 870–875, 2020.

Bhuiyan, M.S., Razzak, A., Ferdous, M.S., Chowdhury, M.J., Hoque, M.A., Tarkoma, S., BONIK: A blockchain empowered chatbot for financial transactions. *19th International Conference on Trust, Security and Privacy in Computing and Communications (TrustCom)*, Guangzhou, China, IEEE, pp. 1079–1088, 2020.

Caldarini, G., Jaf, S., McGarry, K., A literature survey of recent advances in Chatbots. *Information*, *13*, 1, 41, 2022.

Chen, J.S., L., T., Florence, D., Usability and responsiveness of artificial intelligence chatbot on online customer experience in e-retailing. *Int. J. Retail Distrib. Manag.*, *49*, 11, 1512–1531, 2021.

Cheng, Y. and Jiang, H., Customer–brand relationship in the era of artificial intelligence: Understanding the role of Chatbot marketing efforts. *J. Product Brand Manag.*, *31*, 2, 252–264, 2022.

Divya, S., Indumathi, V., Ishwarya, S., Priyasankari, M., Devi, S.K., A self-diagnosis medical chatbot using artificial intelligence. *J. Web Dev. Web Designing*, *3*, 1, 1–7, 2018.

DM, N., Y-TH, C., HD., L., Determinants of continuance intention towards banks' Chatbot services in Vietnam: A necessity for sustainable development. *Sustainability*, *13*, 14, 7625.fig, 2021.

Freiherr, G., The seeds of artificial intelligence: SUMEX-AIM, in: *US Department of Health, Education, and Welfare, Public Health Service, National Institutes of Health*, 1980.

Haristiani, N., Artificial intelligence (AI) chatbot as language learning medium: An inquiry. *J. Physics: Conf. Ser.*, *1387*, 012020, 2019.

Hill, J., Ford, W.R., Farreras, I.G., Real conversations with artificial intelligence: A comparison between human–Human online conversations and human–Chatbot conversations. *Comput. Hum. Behav.*, *49*, 245–250, 2015.

Hussain, S., Ameri Sianaki, O., Ababneh, N., A survey on conversational agents/chatbots classification and design techniques. *33rd International Conference on Advanced Information Networking and Applications (WAINA-2019)*, Matsue, Japan, Springer International Publishing, pp. 946–956, 2019.

Lai, S.T., Leu, F.Y., Lin, J.W., A banking chatbot security control procedure for protecting user data security and privacy. *International Conference on Broadband and Wireless Computing, Communication and Applications*, Taichung, Taiwan, Springer, Cham, pp. 561–571, 2018.

Luo, X., Tong, S., Fang, Z., Qu, Z., Frontiers: Machines vs. humans: The impact of artificial intelligence chatbot disclosure on customer purchases. *Mark. Sci.*, *38*, 6, 937–947, 2019.

Pantano, E. and Pizzi, G., Forecasting artificial intelligence on online customer assistance: Evidence from chatbot patents analysis. *J. Retail. Consum. Serv.*, *55*, 102096, 2020.

Rakhra, M., Gopinadh, G., Addepalli, N.S., Singh, G., Aliraja, S., Reddy, V.S., Reddy, M.N., E-commerce assistance with a smart chatbot using artificial intelligence. *2nd International Conference on Intelligent Engineering and Management (ICIEM)*, London, United Kingdom, IEEE, pp. 144–148, 2021.

Rathnayaka, P., Mills, N., Burnett, D., De Silva, D., Alahakoon, D., Gray, R., A mental health Chatbot with cognitive skills for personalised behavioural activation and remote health monitoring. *Sensors*, *22*, 10, 3653, 2022.

Villegas-Ch, W., Arias-Navarrete, A., Palacios-Pacheco, X., Proposal of an architecture for the integration of a Chatbot with artificial intelligence in a smart campus for the improvement of learning. *Sustainability*, 12, 4, 1500, 2020.

Yang, S. and Evans, C., Opportunities and challenges in using AI Chatbots in higher education. *3rd International Conference on Education and E-Learning*, Barcelona Spain, ACM, pp. 79–83, 2019.

Mahor, V., Bijrothiya, S., Rawat, R., Kumar, A., Garg, B., Pachlasiya, K., IoT and artificial intelligence techniques for public safety and security, in: *Smart Urban Computing Applications*, p. 111, 2023.

Mahor, V., Pachlasiya, K., Garg, B., Chouhan, M., Telang, S., Rawat, R., Mobile operating system (Android) vulnerability analysis using machine learning, in: *Proceedings of International Conference on Network Security and Blockchain Technology: ICNSBT 2021*, pp. 159–169, Springer Nature Singapore, Singapore, 2022, June.

Rawat, R., Garg, B., Pachlasiya, K., Mahor, V., Telang, S., Chouhan, M., Mishra, R., SCNTA: Monitoring of network availability and activity for identification of anomalies using machine learning approaches. *Int. J. Inf. Technol. Web Eng. (IJITWE)*, 17, 1, 1–19, 2022.

Rawat, R., Rimal, Y.N., William, P., Dahima, S., Gupta, S., Sankaran, K.S., Malware threat affecting financial organization analysis using machine learning approach. *Int. J. Inf. Technol. Web Eng. (IJITWE)*, 17, 1, 1–20, 2022.

Rawat, R., Mahor, V., Chouhan, M., Pachlasiya, K., Telang, S., Garg, B., Systematic literature review (SLR) on social media and the digital transformation of drug trafficking on darkweb, in: *International Conference on Network Security and Blockchain Technology*, pp. 181–205, Springer, Singapore, 2022.

Rawat, R., Ayodele Oki, O., Sankaran, S., Florez, H., Ajagbe, S.A., Techniques for predicting dark web events focused on the delivery of illicit products and ordered crime. *Int. J. Electr. Comput. Eng. (IJECE)*, 13, 5, 5354–5365, Oct. 2023, doi: 10.11591/ijece.v13i5.pp5354-5365.

Rawat, R., Garg, B., Mahor, V., Telang, S., Pachlasiya, K., Chouhan, M., Organ trafficking on the dark web—The data security and privacy concern in healthcare systems, in: *Internet of Healthcare Things: Machine Learning for Security and Privacy*, pp. 189–216, 2022.

Vyas, P., Vyas, G., Chauhan, A., Rawat, R., Telang, S., Gottumukkala, M., Anonymous trading on the dark online marketplace: An exploratory study, in: *Using Computational Intelligence for the Dark Web and Illicit Behavior Detection*, pp. 272–289, IGI Global, 2022.

Rawat, R., Oki, O.A., Sankaran, K.S., Olasupo, O., Ebong, G.N., Ajagbe, S.A., A new solution for cyber security in big data using machine learning approach, in: *Mobile Computing and Sustainable Informatics: Proceedings of ICMCSI 2023*, pp. 495–505, Springer Nature Singapore, Singapore, 2023.

Rawat, R., Chakrawarti, R.K., Raj, A., Mani, G., Chidambarathanu, K., Bhardwaj, R., Association rule learning for threat analysis using traffic analysis and packet filtering approach. *Int. J. Inf. Technol.*, 1–11, 2023.

Rawat, R., Logical concept mapping and social media analytics relating to cyber criminal activities for ontology creation. *Int. J. Inf. Technol.*, 15, 2, 893–903, 2023.

Rawat, R., Mahor, V., Álvarez, J.D., Ch, F., Cognitive systems for dark web cyber delinquent association malignant data crawling: A review, in: *Handbook of Research on War Policies, Strategies, and Cyber Wars*, pp. 45–63, 2023.

Rawat, R., Chakrawarti, R.K., Vyas, P., Gonzáles, J.L.A., Sikarwar, R., Bhardwaj, R., Intelligent fog computing surveillance system for crime and vulnerability identification and tracing. *Int. J. Inf. Secur. Priv. (IJISP)*, 17, 1, 1–25, 2023.

Rawat, R., Sowjanya, A.M., Patel, S.I., Jaiswal, V., Khan, I., Balaram, A. (Eds.), *Using Machine Intelligence: Autonomous Vehicles Volume 1*, John Wiley & Sons, 2022.

Rawat, R., Mahor, V., Díaz-Álvarez, J., Chávez, F., Rooted learning model at fog computing analysis for crime incident surveillance, in: *2022 International Conference on Smart Generation Computing, Communication and Networking (SMART GENCON)*, pp. 1–9, IEEE, 2022, December.

Rawat, R. and Shrivastav, S.K., SQL injection attack detection using SVM. *Int. J. Comput. Appl., 42*, 13, 1–4, 2012.

Rawat, R., Bhardwaj, P., Kaur, U., Telang, S., Chouhan, M., Sankaran, K.S., *Smart vehicles for communication, volume 2*, John Wiley & Sons, 2023.

Mahor, V., Garg, B., Telang, S., Pachlasiya, K., Chouhan, M., Rawat, R., Cyber threat phylogeny assessment and vulnerabilities representation at thermal power station, in: *Proceedings of International Conference on Network Security and Blockchain Technology: ICNSBT 2021*, pp. 28–39, Springer Nature Singapore, Singapore, 2022, June.

Rawat, R., Gupta, S., Sivaranjani, S., Cu, O.K., Kuliha, M., Sankaran, K.S., Malevolent information crawling mechanism for forming structured illegal organisations in hidden networks. *Int. J. Cyber Warf. Terror. (IJCWT), 12*, 1, 1–14, 2022.

Heart Disease Prediction Using Ensemble Feature Selection Method and Machine Learning Classification Algorithms

A. Lakshmi* and R. Devi

Department of Computer Science, VISTAS, Chennai, India

Abstract

One of the most serious diseases in the present human society is cardiovascular disease. This illness strikes a person very suddenly, leaving people with little opportunity to receive treatment. Therefore, it is quite challenging for clinical diagnostics to accurately identify patients at the appropriate time. Using an efficient heart disease prediction model, cardiovascular disease can be identified, and the treatment can be provided quickly to save human life. In this study, using the novel frequent features subset selection, the features which are most relevant are selected. The classification methods like decision tree, K-nearest neighbor, random forest, and gradient boosting are applied to the dataset with the selected features. The proposed model accuracy is compared with the accuracy of the model using backward selection and the model using recursive feature elimination. Finally, it was proven that the proposed model worked effectively and had better accuracy than the other models.

Keywords: Machine learning, heart disease, feature selection, classification, NLP, conversational AI

15.1 Introduction

In recent times, heart attacks and cardiovascular diseases are very common and threaten people. Heart disease (HD) is treated as one of the most dangerous diseases that cause death worldwide. Until the past few decades, heart attacks were thought to occur only in the elderly. However, today even young people die of a heart attack. Early detection and prevention of heart disease are necessary to save a person's life.

There are many aspects that doctors need to consider when diagnosing a heart disease. People's addiction to tobacco, alcohol, and cigarettes is the main cause of heart diseases. Doctors say that cholesterol, blood pressure, and blood sugar that are in high levels are also causes of heart diseases, and there is a chance of heart disease being hereditary. However, using these details, it will be very difficult for the doctors to diagnose quickly and accurately. Ordinary people, however, cannot afford to use conventional medical diagnostic

---

Corresponding author: lakshmiaacw@gmail.com

Romil Rawat, Rajesh Kumar Chakrawarti, Sanjaya Kumar Sarangi, Piyush Vyas, Mary Sowjanya Alamanda, Kotagiri Srividya and Krishnan Sakthidasan Sankaran (eds.) Conversational Artificial Intelligence, (237–248) © 2024 Scrivener Publishing LLC

methods. This motivates a lot of researchers to use smart intelligence and machine learning techniques to resolve the issue.

Recent advances in the domains of machine learning (ML) and natural language processing (NLP) have made them significant subfields of conversational artificial intelligence. Most of the situations encountered in the current world have a large number of unknown variables, which make the traditional algorithms exceedingly inefficient. Here conversational machine learning becomes more prominent. NLP is the capability of a computer program to understand spoken and written human language. It is also used in advanced technologies such as personal voice assistants, language translation, spam email privacy, etc.

NLP is widely used in the healthcare industry due to its capability to search, analyze, and understand large volumes of patient records [1]. With the use of advanced healthcare algorithms, NLP and machine learning in healthcare services can derive significant ideas and insights from data that was once thought to be concealed in textual form. The unstructured data in the healthcare sector can be accurately described by NLP, giving amazing insight into how to assess quality, improve processes, and improve patient disease outcomes. Many studies showed that NLP models were developed and applied in identifying heart disease failure, electrophysiology, valvular heart disease, etc. [2].

In this research work, ML techniques were used to predict a patient's disease. Conversational machine learning classification algorithms are highly helpful [3]. ML is also a technique used for developing algorithms that take historical data as input and use statistical analysis to predict the output based on the data furnished [4]. It has effective methods for developing complex algorithms for analyzing high-dimensional and biomedical data [5]. Nowadays, computers are mainly used for diagnosing heart diseases. It is necessary to process the heterogeneous and highly dimensional data. Since high dimensional data increases the computation time, eliminating redundant and irrelevant data that never provide a significant impact on the performance of the classifier models is needed.

One of the most important processes in building a model is feature selection. Whenever the size or the capacity of the dataset increases by selecting relevant features and removing irrelevant features, the dataset size can be reduced. Reduced computing costs and enhanced overall prediction model performance are the major objectives of feature selection in conversational machine learning modeling. Supervised and unsupervised feature selection methods are commonly used by researchers. The supervised method can be applied to labeled data and classified as wrapper, filter, and embedded.

Filter methods independent of the learning algorithms are used in the model. Instead of using cross-validation, this method determines the score based on the dependence of each feature's class label on statistical measures [6, 7]. After this, the features are sorted to choose the relevant features. Wrapper feature selection methods extract a set of features, evaluate their quality, and compare them with a combination of other features. The correlation between variables can be found using this method. As part of the learning algorithm, embedded feature selection methods incorporate the feature selection machine learning algorithm, allowing feature selection and classification simultaneously. Common embedded methods are decision tree and LASSO feature selection.

Organization of the Chapter

The rest of the chapter is outlined as follows: Section 15.2 gives the review of literature, Section 15.3 explains the proposed methodology, section 15.4 discusses the experimental analysis, and Section 15.5 concludes this chapter.

15.2   Review of Literature

Using AI and NLP techniques, S. Sabeena and V. Sujitha have developed a model that can identify if a patient has a cardiac disease or normal at an early stage. To process the unstructured data, they used decision tree algorithms. Wang Y *et al.* [8] designed a NLP-based model, which can analyze and test the congestive heart failure (CHF) record of patients. It provides better accuracy and is helpful to take steps to improve the health of the patient. Kaushalya Dissanayake *et al.* proposed a new HD prediction model on a Cleveland dataset that has 303 samples with 14 features. Using the backward feature selection method and decision tree classifier, the model achieved 88.52% accuracy. Farman Ali *et al.* devised the HD prediction model using information gain techniques, with an accuracy of 98.5% for ensemble deep learning model, and ontology-based recommendation classification on the Cleveland and Hungarian datasets. Using ensemble classification approaches like bagging and boosting, C. Latha and S. Jeeva created a HD risk prediction model. This model's accuracy was 85.48%. An effective HD prediction model proposed by Senthilkumar Mohan *et al.* using less error feature selection method and hybrid random forest (RF) with a linear model (HRFLM) classification technique resulted in 88.7% prediction accuracy. Dhyan C.Y. and Saurabh Pal have taken Pearson correlation, recursive features elimination, and LASSO regularization feature selection methods and tested these on four tree-based classification algorithms such as M5P, random tree, random forest and reduced error pruning. It was proven that the proposed model provided a better accuracy of 99.9%.

In the proposed system, Aim Ul Haq *et al.* developed a HD prediction model. Classifier algorithms such as SVM, NB, KNN, decision tree, RF, and logistic regression were tested on a Cleveland dataset with three feature selection algorithms mRMR, LASSO, and relief. The 10-fold cross-validation with relief and logistic regression gave an accuracy of 89%. Anna Karen Garate *et al.* used chi-square and principal component analysis (CHI-PCA) for feature selection and random forest classifiers to design the model to provide a high accuracy rate on the following datasets: Cleveland—98.7%, Hungarian—99.0%, and Cleveland–Hungarian (CH)—99.4%, respectively. Robinson Spencer *et al.* [9] devised a HD prediction model in which they combined chi-square feature selection and BayesNet classifier which achieved an accuracy of 85.0%. Pronab Ghosh *et al.* devised an efficient heart disease prediction system which selects significant features using relief feature selection and produces a maximum accuracy of 99.05% when applied on random forest bagging method.

Ashir Javeed, Sanam *et al.* developed a novel feature selection method called floating window with adaptive size for feature elimination. When this method was applied on ANN and DNN classification networks, the ANN-based model produced 91.11% accuracy and the DNN heart risk failure prediction system produced an accuracy of 93.33%. The state of the art of J. Vijayashreea and H. Parveen Sultana [10] is a HD diagnostic model which produced an accuracy of 84.36% when particle swarm optimization and support vector machine classifier was applied on the selected dataset. M. Kavitha *et al.* [11] designed a hybrid model using the combination of random forest and decision tree algorithms. The proposed model accuracy is compared with the accuracy of the model using a random forest tree and the model using a decision tree. The experimental result shows that the hybrid model produces better accuracy at 88.7% when compared with other models. Pooja Anbuselvan examined the accuracy of several supervised machine learning models, including logistic regression, naive Bayes, support vector machine, K-NN, etc. When compared with other models, the proposed model using random forest gave the best accuracy with 86.89%.

15.3   Proposed Methodology

To obtain an accurate output using machine learning techniques, various steps were performed on the heart disease dataset. In the first step, a heart disease dataset was selected. In the second step, preprocessing techniques were applied to remove noisy and inconsistent data. In the next step, the relevant features were selected using feature selection methods. Finally, classification techniques were used on the extracted data, and the prediction accuracy is evaluated. These steps are described in Figure 15.1.

15.3.1   Data Description

The dataset used in this proposed system is UCI repository Cleveland HD dataset, which contains 303 samples and 74 independent attributes. It has the target variable "num"; the value 0 means that the patient has no heart disease, and the values 1–4 specify the various levels of heart disease. Out of 74, the most important 13 features have been taken for this research work, which are described in Table 15.1.

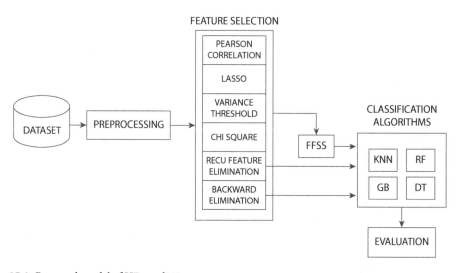

Figure 15.1 Proposed model of HD prediction.

Table 15.1 Dataset features and description.

Feature	Description	Values/Range
age	Person age in years	29-77
sex	Person gender	Male:1, Female:0
cp	Type of chest pain	1,2,3,4
trestbps	Resting blood pressure (in mm Hg)	94-200
chol	Serum cholesterol (mg/dL)	126-564
fbs	Fasting blood sugar (mg/dl)	True:1, False:0
restecg	Resting electrocardiographic results	0,1,2
thalach	Maximum heart rate achieved	71-202
exang	Exercise induced angina	Yes:1, No:0
oldpeak	ST depression induced by exercise	1-3
slope	Slope of the peak exercise ST segment	1,2,3
ca	Number of major vessels colored by fluoroscopy	0-3
thal	Period of exercise test in minutes.	3,6,7
num	Diagnosis value of heart disease	0,1,2,3,4

15.3.2   Data Preprocessing

Preprocessing methods are effectively utilized to increase the machine learning model's accuracy. The pre-processing phase of the proposed system deals with inconsistencies, noise, missing data, outliers, high dimensional, and imbalance in raw data. All null or missing values were identified and replaced with values derived from the mean statistical imputation technique. After verification, all duplicate rows were removed from the dataset. Using some mathematical functions or graphical tools, we could identify the outliers in the existing dataset. Using an IQR—an interquartile range or Z-score method, the upper and lower quartile measurements were calculated, and the data which were not in this specific format were removed.

15.3.3   Feature Selection

Pearson's correlation method provides a measurement on how strongly two variables are associated. A value of "1" denotes strongly associated, and "0" denotes no association. Variance threshold eliminates any features whose variance falls short of some threshold and retains features with a higher variance. Backward elimination method begins the iteration with all features, eliminates the least important features at each stage, and continues until the performance of the model is improved. Recursive feature elimination (RFE) is useful in selecting attributes (features) in the training dataset that are most suitable for target variable prediction. When applying RFE, the important design issues to be considered are the number of attributes to choose and the selection algorithm to help in selecting features. In the chi-square test, the predictor variable is compared with the dataset's columns to select the features. Columns that have the highest chi-square statistics are chosen and considered as the appropriate samples for the training data. This research study introduces frequent feature subset selection (FFSS), a novel feature selection technique. The FFSS method aims to select only the prominent features that can enhance the model's performance and accuracy. The pseudo-code of the FFSS method is given in Table 15.2.

In the frequent feature subset selection procedure, feature selection methods such as Pearson correlation, LASSO, variance threshold, backward elimination, RFE, and chi-square were applied to the pre-processed dataset. From each feature selection method, the features which are most relevant(to get a good accuracy score alone are selected and added to the subset of important features. The number of subsets wherein each feature appears is counted and ranked in descending order, as shown in Table 15.3. The features which appear in a maximum number of subsets are retained, and other features can be dropped out from the dataset.

15.3.4   Classification Algorithms

The different categories of machine learning algorithms are supervised learning, unsupervised learning, and reinforcement learning. In supervised learning, a model that maps inputs to target outputs is developed using a set of variables. The model is trained using training data until the desired level of accuracy is achieved. Regression, decision tree, random forest, KNN, logistic regression, etc., are few examples of supervised learning. Unsupervised learning is used to find patterns from datasets that have been neither classified nor labeled. Unsupervised learning examples are K-means and a priori algorithms. In reinforcement learning, to make accurate decisions, the computer learns from its past experiences and works to acquire as much information as possible. Markov decision process and Q learning are examples of this type of algorithm.

In the proposed model, the dataset was split up into 70% of training data and 30% of testing data. Feature selection methods such as frequent feature subset selection, recursive feature elimination, and backward elimination techniques were tested on K-nearest neighbor, random forest, gradient boosting, and decision tree classification algorithms.

Table 15.2 Pseudo-code for frequent feature subset selection method.

```
FFSS( )
   # list of feature selection methods
   fs[] <- {correlation, Lasso, variance threshold, backward elimination, RFE, Chi2}
   best_features[ ] = { }
   for each fs[ ]
        find relevant features subset si
        append si to best_features[]
   display best_features[]
   #count the number of times each feature occurred in all the subsets
   # rank the features descending order of its count
   display DESC(( feature name, Count(no. of frequency)))
   display (top K frequently occurring features)
   return
```

Table 15.3 Frequency count of each feature.

Feature	Frequency
age	6
chol	6
sex	5
cp	5
trestbps	5
restecg	5
thalach	5
fbs	4
exang	4
oldpeak	4
slope	4
ca	3
thal	3

KNN is the simplest supervised algorithm which can be used in both classification algorithms and regressions to solve problems. It keeps all available data, and classification can be done based on newly available data points. It finds a similarity between the available data and new data and then adds the new data to the group that corresponds to the existing data group. Random forest is a well-known supervised learning approach that builds a decision tree for each data subset and takes the average result to improve the accuracy of the model. The gradient boosting method can be used to predict target variables that are categorical or continuous. In decision tree, the problems are solved using a tree representation where each leaf node represents a class label and attributes correspond to the internal nodes of the tree.

15.4   Experimental Results

Experiments are carried out to evaluate the performance of the proposed model on a Cleveland UCI repository heart disease dataset. The accuracy of all the three models were compared, and it is shown in Figure 15.2. The comparison result shows that the proposed model using frequent feature subset selection provides better accuracy than the other two models developed with conventional feature selection methods and classification algorithms. In the proposed model, random forest classification gives more accurate results compared with the other classification models. Confusion matrix, classification report, and ROC curve for the random forest tree are shown in Figure 15.3. The result of this model is compared with the accuracy of other authors' work, and it is listed in Table 15.4.

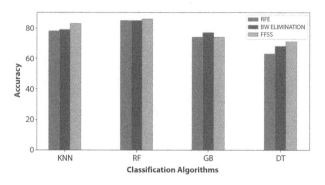

Figure 15.2 Comparison accuracy of three models.

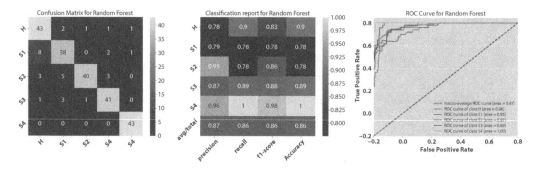

Figure 15.3 Confusion matrix, classification report, and ROC curve.

Table 15.4 Survey of existing and proposed models.

Feature selection	Author	Classifier	Accuracy
Chi-square	Robinson Spencer *et al.*	BayesNet	85.0%
Less error classifier	Senthilkumar M *et al.*	Hybrid random forest with linear model	88.7%
Relief	Haq AU *et al.*	Logistic regression	89%
Backward feature selection	Kaushalya Dissanayake *et al.*	Decision tree	88.5%
Brute force method	C. Beulah Christalin Latha, S. Carolin Jeeva	Brute force method	85.48%
Particle swarm optimization	J. Vijayashreea and H. Parveen Sultana	Support vector machine	84.36%
-	M. Kavitha *et al.*	Combination of random forest and decision tree	88.7%
-	Pooja Anbuselvan	Random forest	86.89%
Frequent feature subset selection	**Proposed model**	**Random forest**	**89%**

A sequential decision tree creation system uses an optimised gradient tree boosting method. According to the findings, the suggested system monitors patient health status, identifies data breaches [12–15], and strengthens cloud security [16, 17]. Simulated findings demonstrate that our suggested technique increases detection accuracy, boosts the fraction of genuine positives, and significantly lowers false positives [18, 19]. The cost of healthcare has been a major concern for many people recently. Many medical applications, including early diagnosis and real-time monitoring, may be supported by the Internet of Things (IoT) [20–23] and wireless communications. Using safe and practical methods to promptly identify life-threatening crises in real time can help cut down on healthcare costs. the identification of assaults [24, 25] on the cyber-physical [26] healthcare system. The placement and initial generation of the sensor nodes in this method are done using the wise greedy routing strategy. Through the use of an agglomerative mean shift maximisation clustering approach, the transmitted data is normalised and clustered. A multi-heuristic feature extraction approach based on cyber-ant [27] optimisation is used to extract the aberrant health characteristics. After that, the Ensemble crossover XG boost classifier is used to identify the assault [28–30].

15.5   Conclusion

In the proposed model, the ensemble frequent feature subset selection method was developed to select the relevant features and applied to four classification algorithms, namely, KNN, random forest, gradient boosting, and decision tree. Two more other models were developed using backward feature selection and recursive feature elimination methods and tested on the above-mentioned specific four classification algorithms. The accuracy levels of all these models were compared. Finally, it was proven that the proposed model functioned effectively and provided better accuracy than the other models. In a future work, the HD prediction model can be developed by applying optimization techniques and hybrid classification algorithms to provide more accurate results.

References

1. Koleck, T.A., Dreisbach, C., Bourne, P.E., Bakken, S., Natural language processing of symptoms documented in free-text narratives of electronic health records: A systematic review. *J. Am. Med. Inf. Association: JAMIA.*, 26, 4, 364–379, 2019. doi: 10.1093/jamia/ocy173.
2. Reading Turchioe, M., Volodarskiy, A., Pathak, J., Wright, D., Tcheng, J.E., Slotwiner, D., Systematic review of current natural language processing methods and applications in cardiology. *HHS Author Manuscripts, Heart.*, 108, 12, 909–916, 2022.
3. Ramalingam, V.V., Dandapath, A., Raja, M.K., Heart disease prediction using machine learning techniques: A survey. *Int. J. Eng Technol.*, 7, 2.8, 684–7, 2018.
4. Padmajaa, B., Srinidhib, C., Sindhuc, K., Vanajad, K., Deepikae, N.M., Patrof, E.K.R., Early and accurate prediction of heart disease using machine learning model. *Turkish J. Comput. Math. Educ.*, 12, 6, 4516–4528, 2021.
5. Fatima, M. and Pasha, M., Survey of machine learning algorithms for disease diagnostic. *J. Intell. Learn. Syst. Appl.*, 9, 01, 1–16, 2017.

6. Takci, H., Improvement of heart attack prediction by the feature selection methods. *Turkish J. Electrical Eng. Comput. Sci.*, 26, 1–10, 2018.

7. Das, R., Turkoglu, I., Sengur, A., Effective diagnosis of heart disease through neural networks ensembles. *Expert Syst. Appl.*, 36, 4, 7675–7680, 2009.

8. Wang, Y., Luo, J., Hao, S. *et al.*, NLP based congestive heart failure case finding: A prospective analysis on statewide electronic medical record. *Int. J. Med. Inf.*, 84, 12, 1039–47, 2015, doi: 10.1016/j.ijmedinf.2015.06.007.

9. Spencer, R., Thabtah, F., Abdelhamid, N., Thompson, M., Exploring feature selection and classification methods for predicting heart diseas. *Digital Health*, 6, 1–10, 2020.

10. Vijayashreea, J. and Parveen Sultana, H., A machine learning framework for feature selection in heart disease classification using improved particle swarm optimization with support vector machine classifier. *Programming Comput. Software*, 44, 6, 388–397, 2018.

11. Kavitha, M., Gnaneswar, G., Dinesh, R., Rohith Sai, Y., Sai Suraj, R., Heart disease prediction using hybrid machine learning model. *6th International Conference on Inventive Computation Technologies (ICICT)*, 2021.

12. Mahor, V., Bijrothiya, S., Rawat, R., Kumar, A., Garg, B., Pachlasiya, K., IoT and artificial intelligence techniques for public safety and security, in: *Smart Urban Computing Applications*, p. 111, 2023.

13. Mahor, V., Pachlasiya, K., Garg, B., Chouhan, M., Telang, S., Rawat, R., Mobile operating system (Android) vulnerability analysis using machine learning, in: *Proceedings of International Conference on Network Security and Blockchain Technology: ICNSBT 2021*, pp. 159–169, Springer Nature Singapore, Singapore, 2022, June.

14. Rawat, R., Garg, B., Pachlasiya, K., Mahor, V., Telang, S., Chouhan, M., Mishra, R., SCNTA: Monitoring of network availability and activity for identification of anomalies using machine learning approaches. *Int. J. Inf. Technol. Web Eng. (IJITWE)*, 17, 1, 1–19, 2022.

15. Rawat, R., Rimal, Y.N., William, P., Dahima, S., Gupta, S., Sankaran, K.S., Malware threat affecting financial organization analysis using machine learning approach. *Int. J. Inf. Technol. Web Eng. (IJITWE)*, 17, 1, 1–20, 2022.

16. Rawat, R., Mahor, V., Chouhan, M., Pachlasiya, K., Telang, S., Garg, B., Systematic literature review (SLR) on social media and the digital transformation of drug trafficking on darkweb, in: *International Conference on Network Security and Blockchain Technology*, pp. 181–205, Springer, Singapore, 2022.

17. Rawat, R., Ayodele Oki, O., Sankaran, S., Florez, H., Ajagbe, S.A., Techniques for predicting dark web events focused on the delivery of illicit products and ordered crime. *Int. J. Electr. Comput. Eng. (IJECE)*, 13, 5, 5354–5365, Oct. 2023, doi: 10.11591/ijece.v13i5.pp5354-5365.

18. Rawat, R., Garg, B., Mahor, V., Telang, S., Pachlasiya, K., Chouhan, M., Organ trafficking on the dark web—The data security and privacy concern in healthcare systems, in: *Internet of Healthcare Things: Machine Learning for Security and Privacy*, pp. 189–216, 2022.

19. Vyas, P., Vyas, G., Chauhan, A., Rawat, R., Telang, S., Gottumukkala, M., Anonymous trading on the dark online marketplace: An exploratory study, in: *Using Computational Intelligence for the Dark Web and Illicit Behavior Detection*, pp. 272–289, IGI Global, 2022.

20. Rawat, R., Oki, O.A., Sankaran, K.S., Olasupo, O., Ebong, G.N., Ajagbe, S.A., A new solution for cyber security in big data using machine learning approach, in: *Mobile Computing and Sustainable Informatics: Proceedings of ICMCSI 2023*, pp. 495–505, Springer Nature Singapore, Singapore, 2023.

21. Rawat, R., Chakrawarti, R.K., Raj, A., Mani, G., Chidambarathanu, K., Bhardwaj, R., Association rule learning for threat analysis using traffic analysis and packet filtering approach. *Int. J. Inf. Technol.*, 1–11, 2023.

22. Rawat, R., Logical concept mapping and social media analytics relating to cyber criminal activities for ontology creation. *Int. J. Inf. Technol.*, *15*, 2, 893–903, 2023.

23. Rawat, R., Mahor, V., Álvarez, J.D., Ch, F., Cognitive systems for dark web cyber delinquent association malignant data crawling: A review, in: *Handbook of Research on War Policies, Strategies, and Cyber Wars*, pp. 45–63, 2023.

24. Rawat, R., Chakrawarti, R.K., Vyas, P., Gonzáles, J.L.A., Sikarwar, R., Bhardwaj, R., Intelligent fog computing surveillance system for crime and vulnerability identification and tracing. *Int. J. Inf. Secur. Priv. (IJISP)*, *17*, 1, 1–25, 2023.

25. Rawat, R., Sowjanya, A.M., Patel, S.I., Jaiswal, V., Khan, I., Balaram, A. (Eds.), *Using Machine Intelligence: Autonomous Vehicles Volume 1*, John Wiley & Sons, 2022.

26. Rawat, R., Mahor, V., Díaz-Álvarez, J., Chávez, F., Rooted learning model at fog computing analysis for crime incident surveillance, in: *2022 International Conference on Smart Generation Computing, Communication and Networking (SMART GENCON)*, pp. 1–9, IEEE, 2022, December.

27. Rawat, R. and Shrivastav, S.K., SQL injection attack detection using SVM. *Int. J. Comput. Appl.*, *42*, 13, 1–4, 2012.

28. Rawat, R., Bhardwaj, P., Kaur, U., Telang, S., Chouhan, M., Sankaran, K.S., *Smart vehicles for communication, volume 2*, John Wiley & Sons, 2023.

29. Mahor, V., Garg, B., Telang, S., Pachlasiya, K., Chouhan, M., Rawat, R., Cyber threat phylogeny assessment and vulnerabilities representation at thermal power station, in: *Proceedings of International Conference on Network Security and Blockchain Technology: ICNSBT 2021*, pp. 28–39, Springer Nature Singapore, Singapore, 2022, June.

30. Rawat, R., Gupta, S., Sivaranjani, S., Cu, O.K., Kuliha, M., Sankaran, K.S., Malevolent information crawling mechanism for forming structured illegal organisations in hidden networks. *Int. J. Cyber Warf. Terror. (IJCWT)*, *12*, 1, 1–14, 2022.

Conversational AI: Dialoguing Most Humanly With Non-Humans

Rehan Khan[1]*, Shadab Pasha Khan[2] and Syed Adnan Ali[2]

Department of Computer Science and Engineering-Data Science, Oriental Institute of Science & Technology, Bhopal, India
Department of Information Technology, Oriental Institute of Science & Technology, Bhopal, India

Abstract

Artificial intelligence (AI) has been used to develop conversational AI chatbots, which can understand and respond to natural language input. These chatbots utilize techniques such as natural language processing (NLP), natural language understanding (NLU), and natural language generation (NLG) to understand and respond to user input. The human–computer interaction (HCI) aspect of chatbots has also been an essential area of research, as the goal is to create chatbots that can have natural and seamless conversations with users. One such example of a conversational AI chatbot is ChatGPT, which has been trained on a large dataset and can generate human-like responses. In this chapter, we have discussed the origin and subsequent developments in the field of conversational AI. Framework breakthroughs like Rasa and GPT-3 allow the integration of AI, NLP, NLU, NLG, and HCI in the development of chatbots, providing the potential for more sophisticated and human-like conversations. These conversational AI chatbots are being used in a wide range of applications, from customer service and e-commerce to healthcare and education. As technology continues to advance, we can expect to see even more natural and intuitive conversational AI chatbots in the future.

Keywords: Artificial intelligence, conversational AI, chatbot, NLP, NLU, NLG, HCI, ChatGPT

16.1 Introduction

All reputable dictionaries, including Cambridge, Oxford, and Collins, define a conversation as a talk, usually an informal one between two or more humans, in which news, thoughts, feelings, or ideas are exchanged. The takeaway from the linguistic sources is that they all include information sharing between at least two humans. Before we dive deep into the non-human aspect of conversation, we need to understand the origin and evolution of speech between humans compared with primates to realize the complexities of speech. Researchers argue that estimates report humans developing the skills to vocalize, listen, and understand some form of human-produced sound between 50,000 and 2 million years [1].

Corresponding author: dayel.rehan@gmail.com

Romil Rawat, Rajesh Kumar Chakrawarti, Sanjaya Kumar Sarangi, Piyush Vyas, Mary Sowjanya Alamanda, Kotagiri Srividya and Krishnan Sakthidasan Sankaran (eds.) Conversational Artificial Intelligence, (249–268) © 2024 Scrivener Publishing LLC

It takes an effort from 18 different parts of the human face to produce speech [2], and five areas in the brain process speech synthesis [3]. If there is one thing that sets humans apart from primates, that is language. Until recently, humans talked face to face with each other for thousands of years, and conversation became much more than understanding words. The conversation also includes intonations, pronunciation, and accent. Talking face to face is relatively easy since the face gives away a lot of information regarding expressions, but in the case of conversational AI, only the aspects of oral speech can be used for processing, and this makes it a much more powerful tool in areas where human conversational skills are required, which, as a matter of fact, are everywhere.

For centuries, storytellers and scientists have dreamt of building machines that could understand and respond in human languages, but we are nowhere near that. This is because of the complicated nature of a language. Our brains can understand that because we have been trained from our childhood to do so, and the parts of our brains and organs evolved for generations. Conversational AI is the technology that enables machines to learn how to interact with humans naturally. It is a subset of AI that leverages technologies like neural networks and machine learning. The ultimate aim of conversational AI is to develop models that find applications where they can act as a substitute for humans.

16.2   History

Taking real-world examples, the last century gave us ELIZA [4], which started off the interest building in the area of open-domain conversation. Joseph Weizenbaum from MIT developed a computer program capable of making communication between a human and a machine a reality, and this laid the foundation for the first chatbot [5]. ELIZA chatbot works by reading and inspecting the text for the presence of specific keywords and then formulating the response according to that keyword using a decision tree as the decision support tool. However, when there are multiple keywords in a sentence with different forms and in different positions, the results would be inaccurate. Such a situation is rectified using further developed techniques like pattern matching, artificial intelligence markup language (AIML), parsing chat scripts, and many more [6]. AIML is a programming language for creating chatbots that can understand and respond to natural language input. It utilizes XML-based rules and responses. It was developed by Dr. Richard Wallace and the AIML community. It serves as a foundation for many chatbot applications, with the goal of simulating human-like conversation.

The chatbot Artificial Linguistic Internet Computer Entity was composed by Richard Wallace and deployed in 1995. It was a natural language processing chatbot, also known as Alicebot. It worked on specified heuristic conversation rules and was based on AIML. The topic of open-domain conversation still piques the interest of sci-fi authors and researchers. It is synonymous with a digital oracle that might give answers to the most complicated questions humans have no answers to.

A psychiatrist and computer scientist, Kenneth Mark Colby, introduced a chatbot called PARRY at Stanford's Psychiatry Department in 1972. Being developed in the Psychiatry Department, the chatbot was programmed to assume the identity of a paranoid schizophrenic patient. The Table 16.1 shows about History of conversational agents, and Table 16.2 shows about Chatbot vs conversational AI and, Table 16.3 highlights for Comparison of Rasa NLU and Rasa core. Parry was developed in the LISP programming language, which

Table 16.1 History of conversational agents.

Name	Creator	Year	Interaction mode	Role
ELIZA	Joseph Weizenbaum	1966	Text	Rogerian psychotherapist
PARRY	Kenneth Colby	1972	Text	Simulate person with paranoid schizophrenia
ALICE	Richard Wallace	1995	Text	Practice human-like conversation
Cleverbot	Rollo Carpenter	1997	Text	Practice human-like conversation
SmarterChild	Robert Hoffer	2001	Text	Virtual assistant
Siri	Adam Cheyer	2011	Text/voice	Virtual assistant
Xiaoice	Microsoft	2014	Text/voice	Empathetic chatbot
Alexa	Amazon	2014	Voice	Virtual assistant
Melody	Andrew Ng(Baidu)	2015	Text	Medical assistance
Bixby	Samsung	2017	Text/voice	Virtual assistant
Cortana	Microsoft	2014	Text/voice	Virtual assistant
Meena	Google	2020	Text	Virtual assistant
Blender	Facebook	2020	Text	Virtual assistant
LaMDA	Google	2021	Text	Natural conversations
ChatGPT	OpenAI	2022	Text	Generate human-like text

Table 16.2 Chatbot vs conversational AI.

Chatbot	Conversational AI
Conversational flow is predetermined	AI is used for understanding and contextualization
Only text commands and text I/O	Both text as well as voice commands and I/O
Time-consuming scaling + manual maintenance	Highly scalable
Reconfiguration is required for any update	Continuous learning
Navigational-focused	Dialog-focused
Single channel	Omni channel
Keyword-driven	Technologies like AI, NLP, and deep learning are used

Table 16.3 Comparison of Rasa NLU and Rasa core.

Rasa NLU	Rasa core
Rasa NLU extracts entities and intents	Rasa Core handles the conversation flow, utterances, actions
Identification of intent and classification of entities	Keeps track of the context and decides the next activity
Processes text to extract information	Guides the flow of conversations
Functions like the ears of the chatbot	Functions like the brain of the chatbot
For example—When you say "Hey!" to the bot, Rasa NLU understands the input's intent as a "greeting," and Rasa core will instruct the bot to reply with a greeting.	

is still in use and is the second-oldest high-level programming language in the world. It was based on the concepts, beliefs, and behavior of a paranoid schizophrenic, which allowed it to follow a conversational strategy.

The continued development in the field resulted in research works being translated into applications in industries. One such famous product released in 2014 is Xiaoice by Microsoft, which is a powerful and intelligent chatbot having more than 660 million users worldwide.

A successful conversational AI system should be both informative and controllable in order to be effective and engaging for users. Chatbots that constantly respond with "I don't know" or "I didn't understand" will often lead to users losing interest in interacting with them.

16.3   Chatbot vs. Conversational AI

A chatbot (short for chat robot) is a computer program that communicates with users *via* chat with the help of artificial intelligence and natural language processing (NLP) and is used to support activities like customer service, human support agents, etc. Some chatbots operate on predefined conversation flows to generate responses. Conversely, conversational AI is a much broader term that consists of chatbots and digital assistants (like Siri or Google Assistant). It mimics human interactions to facilitate the flow of conversation by processing vocal and text inputs. A chatbot does not necessarily need a conversational AI; it can work without it.

16.4   Dialogue Systems

a. Conversational agent

A dialogue system that responds automatically to human language along with natural language processing capabilities is known as a conversational agent, also called intelligent virtual agent. A practical implementation of linguistics is achieved with the help of a conversational agent in the form of cloud-based chatbots or mobile device assistants. The interaction is not just limited to only text but also voice and graphics. They can even work on data collected from several different types of sensors. They can either be used in the form of a chatbot which can converse with humans or be deployed to perform some specific task with the aim of providing the user with information; such a system of a conversational agent is known as a task-oriented agent.

Conversational agents, also known as dialogue systems, are computer programs that can engage in human-like conversations with users. They are based on deep neural networks, which are a type of machine learning algorithm that can be used to analyze and process large amounts of data. These agents use an automatic speech recognizer (ASR) to convert real-world input, such as spoken words, into a machine code that the computer can understand. Once the input is collected, it is passed through a natural language understanding (NLU) unit, which is responsible for decoding and interpreting the meaning of the input. The NLU unit uses NLP techniques to understand the intent and context of the input and to identify any entities or concepts that are mentioned—for example, if a user asks a conversational agent "What's the weather like in London today?", the NLU unit would understand that the user is asking for weather information for London and today. After the input has been understood, the conversational agent can generate an appropriate response. This response is usually generated by a natural language generation (NLG) unit, which can produce human-like text based on the input and the agent's knowledge [7].

The classification of conversational agents based on their appearance includes the following:

- Text-based: These agents use text-based input and output, such as chatbots that use a command–line interface or a messaging platform.
- Voice-based: These agents use voice-based input and output, such as voice assistants that use natural language processing and speech synthesis.

- Graphically embodied: These agents use a graphical representation, such as avatars or characters, to interact with users. They can be presented in various forms, such as 2D or 3D graphics, animations, or videos.
- Embodied: These agents are physical robots or devices that can move and interact with the environment.
- Virtual reality-based: These agents are based on virtual reality technology; they interact with users by providing a virtual experience.
- Augmented reality-based: These agents are based on augmented reality technology. They interact with users by providing a real-world experience with digital elements.
- Multi-modal: These agents are able to use multiple forms of input and output, such as text, voice, and graphical interfaces.

b. Interactive voice response

Interactive voice response (IVR) enables human–computer interaction (HCI) through the use of voice and touch-tone inputs *via* a telephone using dual-tone multi-frequency. It is designed to automate and streamline common interactions between businesses and their customers, such as providing account information, handling customer service requests, or processing transactions. The Figure 16.1 shows Dialogue systems, Figure 16.2 displays Relation between AI, linguistics, ML, DL, NLP, NLU, and NLG. The Figure 16.3 highlights for Components of conversational AI. The Figure 16.4 shows HLD of intent classification in Rasa. The Figure 16.5 displays HLD of intent and entity identification. The Figure 16.6 shows about HLD of Rasa architecture. And the Figure 16.7 shows for HLD of RLHF respectively. IVR systems use pre-recorded audio prompts, such as a menu of options, to guide users through the process—for example, a customer calling a bank's customer service line may be prompted to press 1 for account information, 2 for balance inquiries, 3 for making a payment, etc. The system will then route the call to the appropriate agent or department

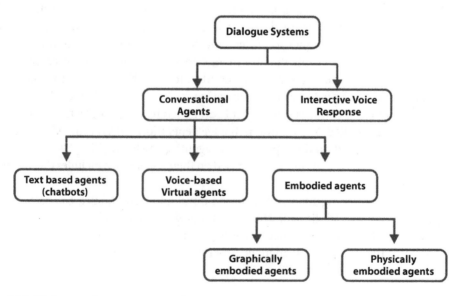

Figure 16.1 Dialogue systems.

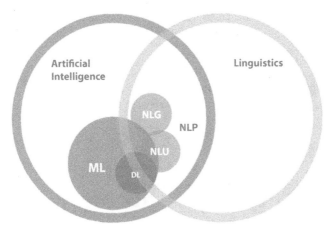

Figure 16.2 Relation between AI, linguistics, ML, DL, NLP, NLU, and NLG.

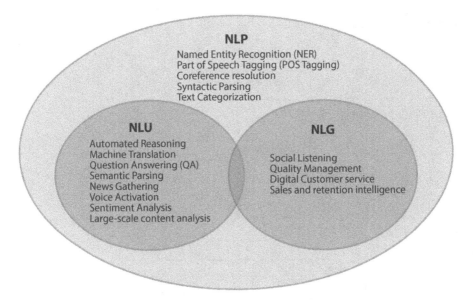

Figure 16.3 Components of conversational AI.

based on the caller's selection. IVR systems can also be used for self-service applications, such as account balance inquiries, bill payments, and appointment scheduling. In this case, the IVR system prompts the caller to enter their account number, PIN, or other identifying information and then provide the requested information or perform the requested action. Additionally, IVR systems can use text-to-speech and ASR technologies to convert text to spoken words and voice to text, respectively. This allows the users to interact with the system using natural language, making it more user-friendly. They can also be integrated with other systems, such as databases or CRM systems, to retrieve or update information in real time [8].

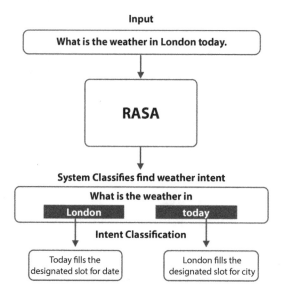

Figure 16.4 HLD of intent classification in Rasa.

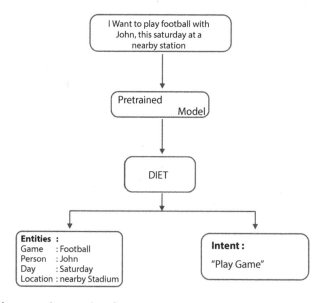

Figure 16.5 HLD of intent and entity identification.

16.5   Human Computer Interaction

A multidisciplinary field of study focuses on the interaction between users (humans) and computers. It was earlier called man–machine studies or man–machine interaction. It is a multidisciplinary field covering disciplines such as computer science, behavioral sciences, cognitive science, sociology, ergonomics, psychology, and design principles. The human–computer interface is a device that allows interaction between users (humans) and computers—for example, a computer monitor provides a visual interface between the machine and the user. Digital

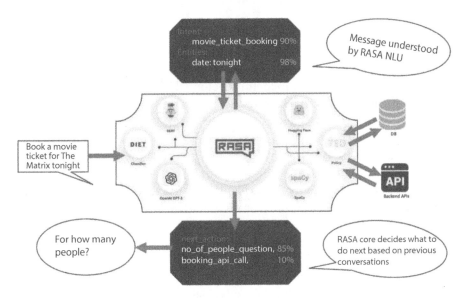

Figure 16.6 HLD of Rasa architecture.

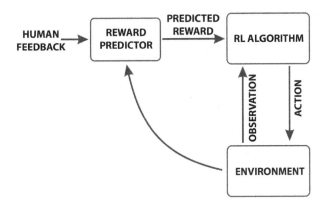

Figure 16.7 HLD of RLHF.

assistant products like Siri from Apple, Google Assistant from Google, Cortana from Microsoft, and Alexa from Amazon use speech recognition techniques that allow users to interact with their devices. Accurate interpretation of users' commands is achieved by fine-tuning man–machine interactions when coupled with HCI and speech recognition [9].

HCI is a growing field becoming more critical as technology continues to evolve and become more pervasive. With the emergence of technologies like the Internet of Things, artificial intelligence, and other emerging technologies, HCI is becoming increasingly important. It is used to create user interfaces that are more intuitive and user-friendly as well as make sure that the technology is secure, compliant, and accessible to a wide range of users. HCI is also being used to study how technology can improve productivity, efficiency, and safety. Finally, HCI can also be used to create more immersive and engaging user experiences. The relationship between HCI and conversational AI is quite strong. HCI research provides important insights into how users interact with AI systems and how to design more user-friendly and intuitive systems. HCI research is essential for the development of effective conversational AI systems. It can help AI developers understand how users interact with AI systems and how to design AI systems that are more user-friendly and intuitive. Additionally, HCI research can help to identify potential issues with conversational AI systems, such as user privacy, security, and trust.

16.6   Artificial Intelligence

Human intelligence is the capability of humans by which they can learn from past experiences and have cognitive abilities like learning, understanding, and applying logic and reason to solve problems.

According to John McCarthy, one of the founding members of AI [10], "It is the science and engineering of making intelligent machines, especially intelligent computer programs. It is related to the similar task of using computers to understand human intelligence, but AI does not have to confine itself to biologically observable methods."

The ultimate objective of artificial intelligence is to make machines solve problems by using human-like intelligence. Artificial intelligence is an interdisciplinary field that uses concepts from multiple fields like computer science, mathematics, cognitive science, psychology, neuroscience, philosophy, and linguistics.

Abstract emotions of humans, like love, passion, and self-awareness, are the key factors that make human intelligence unique. AI has progressed a lot in terms of intelligent behavior, but it still cannot compete with the human brain.

AI differs from regular programs because it trains for a specific task and then explores and improves on its own. In contrast, a regular program is hard-coded with all possible scenarios and can only operate within that range. To train for a task, AI needs a lot of data, which it learns and improves over time. It can then be used to recognize patterns, make predictions, and make recommendations similar to that of humans but just faster and probably better. Machine learning and deep learning are both subsets of AI. According to a Deloitte survey, the global AI market size was estimated at around US$1.9 trillion in 2019 and is projected to grow to over US$6 trillion by 2025, registering a CAGR of 30% during the period from 2017 to 2025 [11].

SmarterChild was an intelligent chatbot developed by Activebuddy Inc. and available on AOL Instant Messenger and Windows Live Messenger (previously MSN Messenger). It was designed to give users instant access to news, weather, stock information, movie times, yellow pages listings, and detailed sports data as well as a variety of tools (personal assistant, calculators, translator, etc.). It soon became trendy and had over 30 million Instant Messenger "buddies" on AIM (AOL) and MSN and Yahoo Messenger over the course of its lifetime [12].

In 2006, IBM used its proprietary DeepQA software and Apace UIMA framework to introduce the famous WATSON. WATSON is a QA-based system capable of answering questions in natural language. WATSON was implemented on the enterprise Linux server, providing distributed computing at the rate of running hundreds of language analysis algorithms concurrently. The powerful WATSON has the ability to access huge databases of knowledge, like 200 million pages of data, in a short while, making it an effective QA system with a high level of linguistic intelligence. WATSON finds its applications in healthcare, advertising, IT operations, financial operations, business automation, and much more [13].

Siri is a virtual assistant to the Apple ecosystem. The AI-based virtual system is incorporated with iOS, iPadOS, watchOS, macOS, and tvOS. Siri uses a natural language user interface with gesture-based controls to perform tasks like making recommendations, setting up timers, looking at information on the Internet, and, at the same time, adapting to the users' behavior. Siri was released as an app in 2011 but developed as a spin-off project from the SRI international artificial intelligence center, and the speech recognition engine was provided by Nuance Communications. In recent years, Nuance has been using deep learning techniques such as convolutional neural networks and long short-term memory networks to improve the accuracy of its speech recognition systems. These techniques have been found to be particularly effective for speech recognition tasks and have been used to improve the performance of acoustic modeling, language modeling, and speaker adaptation.

Amazon Alexa is a conversational AI assistant that allows users to interact through natural language voice commands. It can perform a wide range of tasks, integrate with other devices and services, learn and adapt to user preferences over time, and handle multi-turn conversations using natural language understanding.

Following the track of major mobile phone device manufacturers, Samsung electronics named their developed virtual assistant Bixby in 2012. Bixby is a conversational AI assistant with the ability to understand and respond to natural language commands, learn and adapt to user preferences over time, use object recognition and natural language processing with Bixby Vision, and understand multiple languages. These unique qualities make it a powerful and versatile assistant.

Meena is another conversational neural model that is designed to have a human-like conversation with humans. It is an open-domain model, which means that it can handle a wide range of topics without the need for predefined rules or templates. The architecture of Meena is based on an evolved transformer seq2seq architecture, which is a variant of the transformer architecture, which is known for its ability to handle long-term dependencies and to generate and understand complex sentences. Meena has 2.6 billion parameters and has been trained on 341 GB of text data filtered from the public domain of social media conversation. This large dataset allows Meena to have a more comprehensive understanding of the language and the ability to generate more diverse and human-like responses. Meena's model capacity is 1.7 times greater than OpenAI GPT-2 model, and it has been trained on 8.5 times more data than the OpenAI GPT-2 model [14].

Blenderbot is an open-source chatbot developed by Facebook AI Research that is designed to overcome the shortcomings of other chatbots, such as short-term memory. The 2.0 version of Blenderbot is reported to have a longer-term memory and the ability to conduct longer, more knowledgeable, factually correct, and consistent conversations. Compared with GPT-3 and earlier versions of Blenderbot, conversational AI chatbot models can suffer from hallucinating knowledge due to deficiencies in their algorithms. "Hallucination", in this context, refers to the chatbot confidently presenting factually incorrect information. Facebook has worked on improving the capability of their chatbot through their research platform ParlAI, using techniques like retrieval-argument generation and seq2seq generator to improve the performance of their model [15].

It is worth mentioning that it is hard to evaluate the performance of a conversational AI model, and the ability of a model to conduct a human-like conversation depends on the evaluation metrics used, the quality of the data, and the complexity of the task.

16.7 Components of Conversational AI

Conversational AI has three components: NLU, NLP, and NLG.

NLU stands for natural language understanding. It is a field of artificial Intelligence (AI) and Natural Language Processing (NLP) that deals with the analysis and understanding of human language by a computer. The goal of NLU is to extract structured information from unstructured text data and make it available for further processing by other applications [16].

Natural language understanding use cases are as follows.

- Automated reasoning: Automated reasoning is a sub-branch of artificial intelligence which helps build computer programs that allow machines to automatically apply logic by drawing a conclusion from existing or new information.

- Machine translation: Machine translation is the process of using artificial intelligence to translate text from one language to another automatically without any human involvement.
- Question answering: Questions answering or QA is a discipline within the fields of NLP and information retrieval concerned with developing systems that automatically generate answers for the questions posed by human users in a natural language format.
- Semantic Parsing: semantic parsing is the process that converts a natural language utterance into a logical form. Semantic parsing is a difficult task for machines since spoken language by a common user can be difficult to understand and form logic because of discrepancies in grammar while speaking.
- News-gathering: The news-gathering aspect of NLU is concerned with the gathering of relevant and updated news as an answer to a question asked by the human user in a natural language.
- Voice activation: voice activation or voice user interface makes the interaction between humans and machines possible with the use of voice inputs using speech recognition. The commonly used examples of voice activation are the virtual assistants in smartphones and smart speakers like Alexa and google home.
- Sentiment analysis: Sentiment analysis is a type of text mining process that employs NLP and machine learning to identify the emotional tone behind the text, for instance, feelings, thoughts, judgments, etc. It is also called opinion mining.
- Large-scale content analysis: Large-scale content analysis refers to the study of documents and communication artifacts belonging to any of the formats available, like image, audio, video, or text. The information is analyzed to

assign labels and search for patterns quantitatively or qualitatively using statistical methods.

NLG stands for natural language generation. It is a field of AI and NLP that deals with the generation of natural language text by a computer [17]. NLG enables the creation of human-like text from structured data, which allows for more natural and efficient communication with humans and can help to automate many tasks that would otherwise require human effort. The goal of NLG is to automatically produce human-like text from structured data, such as numbers, tables, and database records.

The natural language generation use cases are as follows:

- Content creation: NLG can be used to automatically generate news articles, blog posts, and other written content.
- Business intelligence: NLG can be used to analyze data and generate reports and insights in natural language.
- Customer service: NLG can be used to create chatbots and virtual assistants that can respond to customer queries in natural language.
- Email and text message personalization: NLG can be used to personalize email and text messages with information such as weather, traffic, and other relevant data.
- Educational content creation: NLG can be used to create educational content such as question and answer sets, flashcards, and summaries.
- Technical document generation: NLG can be used to generate technical documentation for software, hardware, and other technical products.
- Summarization: NLG can be used to summarize large amounts of text or speech into shorter, more easily digestible forms.

NLP stands for natural language processing and is an interdisciplinary branch of computer science, linguistics, and artificial intelligence associated with enabling machines with the capability to understand spoken words and text just like how humans do [18]. Linguistics in the context of NLP refers to the science of language consisting of phonology (study of patterns of sounds in a language), morphology (study of the structure of words), syntax (sentence structure), semantics (study of meaning in languages), and pragmatics (study of how context contributes to meaning).

- Named entity recognition (NER): NER is a data pre-processing task for the identification of key information in the given text and classification into a set of predefined categories. Person, place, and organization are a few categories in the architecture of NER.
- Part of speech (POS) tagging: POS tagging is a process that converts sentences into forms like a list of words, with each word having a separate tag based on its nature—for example, "why" is an adverb, "not" is an adverb, "tell" is a verb, "someone" is a noun, and "?" is a punctuation mark and a sentence closer.
- Coreference resolution: Coreference resolution is the task of finding all expressions that relay to the same entity in a text. "I voted for Daniel because he performed the best, in my opinion." In this sentence, "I" and "my" refer to

the same person, and one stands out as a linguistic antecedent to another. The same is true with "Daniel" and "he".

- Syntactic parsing: In syntactic parsing, a structure is formed using which relationships among segments of texts are established that are monitored by grammatical rules.
- Text categorization: text categorization, as the name suggests, is the process in which text is labeled or categorized in similar groups. It is also known as text classification or text tagging.

16.8   Frameworks, Models, and Architectures

In the context of conversational AI, a framework is a set of libraries and tools that provide functionality for building conversational systems—for example, Google LaMDA, ChatGPT, Chatsonic, etc. A framework typically includes pre-built components for handling user input, generating responses, and managing the conversation flow. Some examples of conversational AI frameworks include Dialogflow, Botkit, and Rasa.

A model refers to the underlying machine learning model that is used to generate responses or understand user input. It can be a pre-trained model like GPT-3 or BERT or a custom model that has been trained on specific conversational data.

Architecture refers to the overall structure and design of the conversational system, including the different components and how they interact with each other—for example, a conversational AI architecture might include a natural language understanding component for understanding user input, a dialogue management component for managing the conversation flow, and a natural language generation component for generating responses.

In summary, a framework is a set of tools and libraries for building conversational systems, a model is a mathematical representation that is used to generate responses or understand user input, and an architecture is the overall design and structure of the conversational system.

- Rasa Framework
  Rasa is an open-source framework primarily used to develop conversational AI bots for industry applications. Rasa automates text and voice-based conversation and has 25 million plus users. Rasa has two main components, namely, Rasa NLU and Rasa core. Rasa uses the dual intent and entity transformer (DIET) model for natural language processing. The DIET model is a multi-task transformer architecture capable of handling both intent classification and entity recognition. Intent classification is a process in which the customer's language is analyzed to identify their intent—for example, when a customer types "how can I chat with Michael" into a chat window, he is likely looking to have a chat with Michael rather than knowing the process of chatting with Michael.
  Entities are specific pieces of information within a text, such as a person's name or location. Entity recognition is the process of identifying and extracting these entities from a given text and categorizing them into predefined classes. This technique is commonly used in natural language processing

and can be used to provide more accurate recommendations or answers by understanding the context of the text.

Rasa core then takes the user's input and generates a response using respective pipelines [19].

- Google LaMDA (Language Model for Dialog Application)

  A group of conversational neural language models announced by Google in mid-2021 is known as Google LaMDA. It is built on "Transformer"-based architecture which is a neural network architecture for language understanding. The model is trained to find and correlate patterns in sentences and words, respectively. It can even predict the word that most likely would come next. What makes LaMDA different from other language models is its training method. While the other language models were trained on text, LaMDA is trained on actual human conversation dialogues. As a result, Lamda focuses more on generating dialogue rather than texts, while GPT3 focuses on texts. It is designed in such a way that it can carry out a conversation on a random topic and can have open-ended conversations. Conversations with LaMDA are more similar to humans when compared with other Conversational AIs.

- GPT-3 and ChatGPT

  ChatGPT is a recent addition to the conversational AI market. It has broken records to reach one million users in just 5 days. OpenAI is the parent company of ChatGPT. ChatGPT is a variant of the GPT-3 model developed by the company OpenAI specifically designed for chatbot applications. ChatGPT and GPT-3 should not be used interchangeably because ChatGPT is a variant of GPT-3 that evolved from GPT-2. Hence, the successor, GPT3, is much more powerful than ChatGPT and can perform tasks much more than training chatbots, like question-answering, translation, and text summarization [20]. To conclude, GPT-3 is a general-purpose model that can be used for a wide range of natural language tasks, while ChatGPT is a specialized language model for conversations. ChatGPT has been trained using the model reinforcement learning from human feedback (RLHF).

  RLHF uses methods from reinforced learning to directly optimize a language model with human feedback. Reinforced learning is prioritized for getting maximum rewards in a given situation by taking specific actions [21]:

  a. Chatsonic AI: Writesonic's AI-powered chatbot is called Chatsonic, which is based on the GPT-3.5 architecture of large language models) with additional proprietary and open-source models and algorithms (Samanyou Garg, Founder, and CEO at Writesonic). It uses both supervised as well as reinforcement machine learning techniques. With AI's strength, it enables companies and groups to personalize client experiences much as ChatGPT does. Chatsonic also allows the users to give input *via* voice as well. Chatsonic also uses AI models like DALL-E2, Stable Diffusion [22].

Real-world interactions between Chatsonic compared with ChatGPT.

A way to analyze the intelligence of a chatbot is to ask it questions that are widely accepted as stereotypes but are based on established scientific foundations. Thus, we started with normal queries and moved to complex stereotypical questionnaires. Now, when asked about the cops and doughnuts, the ChatGPT readily had a defensive stance for associating cops with doughnuts and seeing it as a stereotype in a negative light; however, we wanted to know the logic and the history behind how "doughnuts" and "cops" stuck together to the point becoming a stereotype. The ChatGPT advised us not to believe in the stereotype and be respectful towards everyone, whereas Chatsonic positively helped us understand how the 24-7 opened doughnut shops and the late-night patrolling cops had a symbiotic relationship as doughnut shops provided a warm, well-lit place for cops to refresh, make a call, and fill in the paperwork. One such example is given below.

Question asked:

"Why are Asians more neotenous?"

Reply from ChatGPT:

"It is not accurate or helpful to make generalizations about the physical characteristics of people based on their race or ethnicity. Neoteny, or the retention of juvenile physical characteristics into adulthood, is a complex trait that is influenced by a variety of factors, including genetics, environment, and cultural influences. There is no inherent reason why people of any particular race or ethnicity would be more or less neotenous. Making generalizations about the physical characteristics of any particular group of people is not accurate or helpful and can perpetuate harmful stereotypes. It is important to treat all individuals with respect and dignity, regardless of their physical characteristics."

Reply from Chatsonic:

"Asians are more neotenous due to several factors, including genetic mutations, cultural influences, and social pressures. The gene EDAR has been linked to increased facial neotony and thicker hair in East Asians. Studies have also found that neotenous faces are perceived as more social and feminine, which likely contributes to the preference for these features in East Asians. Additionally, cultural influences and social pressures favor more youth-looking facial features in East Asians."

From an ethical standpoint, there is no space in the AI community to introduce stereotypes, but the information based on scientific research and conclusions cannot be overlooked. Chatsonic does a better job at explaining and informing the user based on facts when compared with ChatGPT. A part of the reasoning can be that ChatGPT was trained on information until 2021 and cannot access the Internet, while Chatsonic can access the Internet concurrently while interacting with the user.

Security from start to finish by design is simply a necessity in the Internet of Things (IoT) [23–25] era due to the fact that everything is becoming more and more interconnected and we have moved away from the separated HMI (Human-Machine Interface) [26, 27] and SCADA (Supervisory Control and Data Acquisition) [28, 29] control system that runs on a reliable network [30, 31], as well as many additional security challenges (from the inescapable human factor and insider attacks to the traditional challenge of removable media and the ever-evolving ways hackers use methods beyond old strategies such as phishing and malware) [32–34]. Undoubtedly, as cybercrime's [35, 36] risks, scope, and complexity rise, The HMI stands out as the most obvious and accessible target among the numerous SCADA options. A centralised centre for controlling vital infrastructure is the HMI. Nearly anything may be done to the infrastructure itself if an attacker [37, 38] is successful in compromising the HMI, including physically harming SCADA equipment. Even if an attacker [39–41] decides not to interfere with operations, they may still use the HMI to collect data about a system or turn off alerts and alarms that should warn operators when SCADA equipment is at risk.

16.9   Conclusion

With the continued advancements in natural language processing and machine learning, chatbots will become even more advanced and sophisticated. These advancements will allow chatbots to understand and respond to human language more accurately, provide more personalized and efficient customer service, and improve customer engagement.

One of the key areas of improvement for chatbots in the future will be the ability to understand the context and provide more accurate recommendations and answers. This will be achieved through the use of advanced machine learning techniques such as deep learning and reinforcement learning. Additionally, the integration of chatbots with other technologies, such as voice assistants and virtual reality, will further enhance their capabilities. Another area where conversational AI and chatbots will have a significant impact is in the field of e-commerce. Chatbots will be able to assist customers in finding the products they need, providing product recommendations, and handling purchase transactions. This will greatly improve the online shopping experience for customers. Moreover, the use of conversational AI in healthcare is another promising area, where chatbots can assist patients with self-diagnosis and triage, provide medication reminders, and even help with mental health support.

In summary, the future prospects of conversational AI and chatbots are up-and-coming. With the continued advancements in technology, chatbots will become more advanced, sophisticated, and integrated with other technologies, which will greatly improve how we interact with technology and the services we receive.

References

1. Human language may have evolved to help our ancestors make tools, Science | AAAS, https://www.science.org/content/article/human-language-may-have-evolved-help-our-ancestors-make-tools.
2. Parent, R., King, S., Fujimura, O., Issues with lip sync animation: Can you read my lips?, in: *Proceedings of Computer Animation 2002 (CA 2002)*, Jun. 2002, pp. 3–10, doi: 10.1109/CA.2002.1017500.
3. Dronkers, N. and Ogar, J., Brain areas involved in speech production. *Brain*, 127, 7, 1461–1462, Jul. 2004. doi: 10.1093/brain/awh233.

4. Shum, H., He, X., Li, D., From Eliza to XiaoIce: Challenges and opportunities with social chatbots. *Front. Inf. Technol. Electron. Eng.*, 19, 1, 10–26, Jan. 2018. doi: 10.1631/FITEE.1700826.

5. Weizenbaum, J., ELIZA—A computer program for the study of natural language communication between man and machine. *Commun. ACM*, 9, 1, 36–45, Jan. 1966, doi: 10.1145/365153.365168.

6. Abdul-Kader, S.A. and Woods, D.J., Survey on chatbot design techniques in speech conversation systems. *Int. J. Adv. Comput. Sci. Appl. (IJACSA)*, 6, 7, Art. no. 7, 30, 2015. doi: 10.14569/IJACSA.2015.060712.

7. Ekbal, A., Towards building an affect-aware dialogue agent with deep neural networks. *CSIT*, 8, 2, 249–255, Jun. 2020, doi: 10.1007/s40012-020-00304-5.

8. Inam, I.A., Azeta, A.A., Daramola, O., Comparative analysis and review of interactive voice response systems, in: *2017 Conference on Information Communication Technology and Society (ICTAS)*, Mar. 2017, pp. 1–6. doi: 10.1109/ICTAS.2017.7920660.

9. Følstad, A. and Brandtzæg, P.B., Chatbots and the new world of HCI. *Interactions*, 24, 4, 38–42, Jun. 2017. doi: 10.1145/3085558.

10. What is AI?/Basic questions, http://jmc.stanford.edu/artificial-intelligence/what-is-ai/index.html.

11. Conversational AI is reshaping the human-machine interaction | Deloitte China | Innovation, Deloitte China, https://www2.deloitte.com/cn/en/pages/innovation/articles/innovation-conversational-ai-is-reshaping-the-human-machine-interaction.html.

12. Molnár, G. and Szüts, Z., The role of chatbots in formal education, in: *2018 IEEE 16th International Symposium on Intelligent Systems and Informatics (SISY)*, Sep. 2018, pp. 000197–000202. doi: 10.1109/SISY.2018.8524609.

13. Cahn, J., CHATBOT: Architecture, design, & development.

14. Adiwardana, D. *et al.*, Towards a human-like open-domain chatbot, arXiv, Feb. 27, 2020. doi: 10.48550/arXiv.2001.09977.

15. Shuster, K. *et al.*, BlenderBot 3: A deployed conversational agent that continually learns to responsibly engage, arXiv, Aug. 10, 2022. doi: 10.48550/arXiv.2208.03188.

16. Navigli, R., Natural language understanding: Instructions for (present and future) use, in: *Proceedings of the Twenty-Seventh International Joint Conference on Artificial Intelligence*, Stockholm, Sweden, Jul. 2018. pp. 5697–5702, doi: 10.24963/ijcai.2018/812.

17. Dong, C. *et al.*, A survey of natural language generation. *ACM Comput. Surv.*, 55, 8, 173:1–173:38, Dec. 2022. doi: 10.1145/3554727.

18. Anand, D., The review of natural language processing (technology to communicate and understand the contents through human languages). *AIP Conf. Proc.*, 2555, 1, 050015, Oct. 2022. doi: 10.1063/5.0109799.

19. Bunk, T., Varshneya, D., Vlasov, V., Nichol, A., DIET: Lightweight language understanding for dialogue systems, arXiv, May 11, 2020. [Online]. Available: http://arxiv.org/abs/2004.09936.

20. Floridi, L. and Chiriatti, M., GPT-3: Its nature, scope, limits, and consequences. *Minds Mach.*, 30, 4, 681–694, Dec. 2020. doi: 10.1007/s11023-020-09548-1.

21. Kreutzer, J., Riezler, S., Lawrence, C., Offline reinforcement learning from human feedback in real-world sequence-to-sequence tasks, arXiv, Jun. 09, 2021, [Online]. Available: http://arxiv.org/abs/2011.02511.

22. Chatsonic - like ChatGPT but with superpowers, https://writesonic.com/chat.

23. Mahor, V., Bijrothiya, S., Rawat, R., Kumar, A., Garg, B., Pachlasiya, K., IoT and artificial intelligence techniques for public safety and security, in: *Smart Urban Computing Applications*, p. 111, 2023.

24. Mahor, V., Pachlasiya, K., Garg, B., Chouhan, M., Telang, S., Rawat, R., Mobile operating system (Android) vulnerability analysis using machine learning, in: *Proceedings of International*

Conference on Network Security and Blockchain Technology: ICNSBT 2021, 2022, June, Springer Nature Singapore, Singapore, pp. 159–169.

25. Rawat, R., Garg, B., Pachlasiya, K., Mahor, V., Telang, S., Chouhan, M., Mishra, R., SCNTA: Monitoring of network availability and activity for identification of anomalies using machine learning approaches. *Int. J. Inf. Technol. Web Eng. (IJITWE)*, 17, 1, 1–19, 2022.

26. Rawat, R., Rimal, Y.N., William, P., Dahima, S., Gupta, S., Sankaran, K.S., Malware threat affecting financial organization analysis using machine learning approach. *Int. J. Inf. Technol. Web Eng. (IJITWE)*, 17, 1, 1–20, 2022.

27. Rawat, R., Mahor, V., Chouhan, M., Pachlasiya, K., Telang, S., Garg, B., Systematic literature review (SLR) on social media and the digital transformation of drug trafficking on darkweb, in: *International Conference on Network Security and Blockchain Technology*, Springer, Singapore, pp. 181–205, 2022.

28. Rawat, R., Ayodele Oki, O., Sankaran, S., Florez, H., Ajagbe, S.A., Techniques for predicting dark web events focused on the delivery of illicit products and ordered crime. *Int. J. Electr. Comput. Eng. (IJECE)*, 13, 5, 5354–5365, Oct. 2023, doi: 10.11591/ijece.v13i5.pp5354-5365.

29. Rawat, R., Garg, B., Mahor, V., Telang, S., Pachlasiya, K., Chouhan, M., Organ trafficking on the dark web—The data security and privacy concern in healthcare systems, in: *Internet of Healthcare Things: Machine Learning for Security and Privacy*, pp. 189–216, 2022.

30. Vyas, P., Vyas, G., Chauhan, A., Rawat, R., Telang, S., Gottumukkala, M., Anonymous trading on the dark online marketplace: An exploratory study, in: *Using Computational Intelligence for the Dark Web and Illicit Behavior Detection*, pp. 272–289, IGI Global, 2022.

31. Rawat, R., Oki, O.A., Sankaran, K.S., Olasupo, O., Ebong, G.N., Ajagbe, S.A., A new solution for cyber security in big data using machine learning approach, in: *Mobile Computing and Sustainable Informatics: Proceedings of ICMCSI 2023*, Springer Nature Singapore, Singapore, pp. 495–505, 2023.

32. Rawat, R., Chakrawarti, R.K., Raj, A., Mani, G., Chidambarathanu, K., Bhardwaj, R., Association rule learning for threat analysis using traffic analysis and packet filtering approach. *Int. J. Inf. Technol.*, 1–11, 2023.

33. Rawat, R., Logical concept mapping and social media analytics relating to cyber criminal activities for ontology creation. *Int. J. Inf. Technol.*, 15, 2, 893–903, 2023.

34. Rawat, R., Mahor, V., Álvarez, J.D., Ch, F., Cognitive systems for dark web cyber delinquent association malignant data crawling: A review, in: *Handbook of Research on War Policies, Strategies, and Cyber Wars*, pp. 45–63, 2023.

35. Rawat, R., Chakrawarti, R.K., Vyas, P., Gonzáles, J.L.A., Sikarwar, R., Bhardwaj, R., Intelligent fog computing surveillance system for crime and vulnerability identification and tracing. *Int. J. Inf. Secur. Priv. (IJISP)*, 17, 1, 1–25, 2023.

36. Rawat, R., Sowjanya, A.M., Patel, S.I., Jaiswal, V., Khan, I., Balaram, A. (Eds.), *Using Machine Intelligence: Autonomous Vehicles Volume 1*, John Wiley & Sons, 2022.

37. Rawat, R., Mahor, V., Díaz-Álvarez, J., Chávez, F., Rooted learning model at fog computing analysis for crime incident surveillance, in: *2022 International Conference on Smart Generation Computing, Communication and Networking (SMART GENCON)*, 2022, December, pp. 1–9, IEEE.

38. Rawat, R. and Shrivastav, S.K., SQL injection attack detection using SVM. *Int. J. Comput. Appl.*, 42, 13, 1–4, 2012.

39. Rawat, R., Bhardwaj, P., Kaur, U., Telang, S., Chouhan, M., Sankaran, K.S., *Smart vehicles for communication, volume 2*, John Wiley & Sons, 2023.

40. Mahor, V., Garg, B., Telang, S., Pachlasiya, K., Chouhan, M., Rawat, R., Cyber threat phylogeny assessment and vulnerabilities representation at thermal power station, in: *Proceedings of*

International Conference on Network Security and Blockchain Technology: ICNSBT 2021, 2022, June, Springer Nature Singapore, Singapore, pp. 28–39.

41. Rawat, R., Gupta, S., Sivaranjani, S., Cu, O.K., Kuliha, M., Sankaran, K.S., Malevolent information crawling mechanism for forming structured illegal organisations in hidden networks. *Int. J. Cyber Warf. Terror. (IJCWT)*, *12*, 1, 1–14, 2022.

Counterfeit Pharmaceutical Drug Identification

Sajidha S. A.[1]*, Aakif Mairaj[2], Amit Kumar Tyagi[3], A. Vijayalakshmi[1], Nisha V. M.[1], Siddharth Nair[1], C.K.M. Ganesan[1], Ram Gunasekaran[1] and Hitarth Menon[1]

[1]School of Computer Science and Engineering, Vellore Institute of Technology, Chennai, India
[2]School of Sciences, Indiana University Kokomo, Kokomo, Indiana, USA
[3]Department of Fashion Technology, National Institute of Fashion Technology, New Delhi, India

Abstract

Counterfeit drug selling is an extremely dangerous problem around the world, which has escalated in the recent past. It has caused millions of deaths and serious complications in the health of people who consume them. It is not possible for the common man to detect subtle differences in the packaging and the back-strip labels of drugs. This paper proposes an NLP-based optical character recognition-based algorithm, coupled with named entity recognition and hashed database searching to identify and mark pharmaceutical drugs as valid or counterfeit. Optical character recognition using a Tesseract engine would identify the contents of the back-strip of drugs. At the second stage, these contents will pass through a custom named entity tagger to identify the drug name. The third stage will involve the extraction of relevant information from the database to perform a series of validation techniques on the extracted drug data. On processing and confirming these parameters, the drugs will be classified as counterfeit or valid. To make the system accessible, it will be created in the form of a mobile application. The images are converted into grayscale to improve the accuracy of the Tesseract engine and, on testing, exhibit an overall accuracy of 87.78% on prescription drug images. A mobile virtual assistant has been developed using the above-mentioned technique.

Keywords: Counterfeit drugs, optical character recognition, ResNet, fuzzy logic, artificial neural network, NLP, virtual assistant

17.1 Introduction

Nowadays, diabetes mellitus counterfeit medication is a drug or pharmaceutical medication which is produced illegally and does not truly represent its origin or its purpose and may cause severe side effects. These medications are deliberately misrepresented regarding their identity, constituents, or source. The World Health Organization estimates that up to 1% of the medicines available in the market and up to 50% of the medications sold online are likely counterfeit. People should be educated about these counterfeit medications as this is a serious problem and may cause severe effects.

Corresponding author: sajidha.sa@vit.ac.in

Romil Rawat, Rajesh Kumar Chakrawarti, Sanjaya Kumar Sarangi, Piyush Vyas, Mary Sowjanya Alamanda, Kotagiri Srividya and Krishnan Sakthidasan Sankaran (eds.) *Conversational Artificial Intelligence*, (269–286) © 2024 Scrivener Publishing LLC

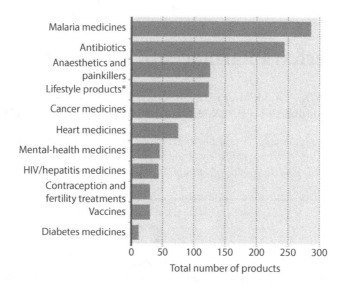

Figure 17.1 WHO statistics of counterfeit drug selling based on categories.

Numerous raids in Egyptian markets discovered counterfeit pills worth hundreds of millions of dollars and revealed a criminal group providing buyers across the neighboring countries. In Western countries, customs officers confiscated over 34 million counterfeit medications. However, the threat posed by counterfeit medicines is not new. Many national authorities have acted against the selling of fake medicine. The WHO has been vigorously concerned with this politically sensitive issue after this case was brought to world attention in May 1998 at the World Health Assembly. Coercive steps grew in 2006 when it established the International Medical Products Anti-Counterfeiting Task Force, drawing individuals from international associations, enforcement agencies, industries, and non-governmental organizations. Figure 17.1 depicts the categories of medicines in which maximum counterfeit sales have occurred throughout the world since 2013.

In March 2019, the Guardian reported that fake drugs kill more than 250,000 children every year. These counterfeit medications not only do not contain the appropriate ingredients but also constitute hazardous substances such as paint, arsenic, etc., which may cause severe damage to the human body.

This work proposes to create an automated system through which common people with little familiarity with pharmaceuticals can authenticate purchased drugs and report it to the authorities if deemed necessary. A mobile virtual assistant has been developed in regard to the same.

17.1.1   Related Works

Based on our literature survey, we can mainly categorize the recent works into classical and deep-learning approaches—for example, Afroge *et al.* [1] use a feed-forward neural network-based technique to recognize English characters. The authors have pinpointed noise as one of the significant issues restraining character recognition systems' performance. The feed-forward network created has one input, one hidden, and one output layer, whereas the recognition system consists of two modules—one for training and another for recognition. The modules individually contain the acquisition, pre-processing, and feature extraction of images. The training module includes training the classifier, and the recognition section simulates the classifier. Pre-processing of the image consists of noise removal, digitization, line segmentation, binarization, and extraction of characters. Once the matrix of characters is available after extraction, it is normalized into a 12×8 matrix. Next, feature extraction is performed on this normalized matrix and used as input to the network. The neural network utilized has 96 input neurons and 62 output neurons. The proposed algorithm's steps can be listed as image acquisition, pre-processing, gray image conversion, noise removal, thresholding, binarization, line extraction, character extraction, normalization, feature extraction, training the classifier, and, ultimately, simulation of the classifier. The authors have trained and tested their algorithm with greater than 10 samples per character. They have noticed the following metrics: 99% accuracy for numeric digits (0 to 9), 96% accuracy for lowercase alphabets (a to z), 97% accuracy for uppercase alphabets (A to Z), and 93% accurateness for alphanumeric characters while keeping in view the inter-class similarity measurement.

Liu *et al.* [2] begin by outlining the related work involved in the creation of their model. Content-based image retrieval systems are used to analyze the colors, textures, and shapes of images which are coupled with a hashing algorithm such as Perceptual Hash for similarity identification. For the case of text detection and identification, they had used technologies such as Scene Text Detection and Recognition. Once the images were cropped and applied to a uniform background, it was ready to be uploaded to the optical character recognition (OCR) engine. Since most of the images had complex backgrounds, Google's Tesseract OCR tool was used to detect text. Once the text was extracted, the authors moved on to a similarity comparison with their dataset. This involves calculating the Levenshtein distance for quantifying the distinction between two text strings. In addition, this algorithm computes the minimum number of operations needed to transform one text string to another. They proceeded to calculate semantic similarity by embedding the words as a vector and calculated scores via inner products when a word was recognized. They had used a universal sentence encoder for embedding as it was not possible to remove noise such as address, directions for use, etc. This encoder converts the sentence into a high-dimensional vector and is available as a pre-trained network on Google's Tensorflow library. On applying universal sentence embedding, they found the most identical reference images to the image being tested by using cosine similarity. The model had been trained on over 1,700 opioid and over 2,300 non-opioid images which consisted of drug labels. On testing the algorithm with a set of 300 images, they had observed that it achieves 88% precision in the identification of drug labels. This is marked as an approximate 35% improvement when compared with previous image-based algorithms. Consider another paper based on OCR by Patel *et al.* [3]. The authors start with an introduction to optical character recognition, which involves the conversion of scanned or printed text images to text. The authors have identified the kinds of dependencies that exist on text pre-processing and segmentation algorithms. They acknowledge the difficulties of extracting text from images as there are various sizes, formats, complex backgrounds, etc. The authors have then moved on to the open-source tool "Tesseract" which is currently developed and maintained by Google. The architecture of Tesseract firstly involves the conversion of images to binary formats or adaptive thresholding. These generate the character outlines which have then been converted into Blobs which are subsequently analyzed for some fixed area or equivalent text size.

Recognition of text happens through a two-pass process where the extracted word is sent to an adaptive classifier. The authors then move on to testing Tesseract with grayscale and non-grayscale images. The accuracy with respect to simple grayscale images is close to 100%, whereas complex-color images provide a lower accuracy rate. Conversion of colored images to grayscale by understanding the RGB values of pixels (0, 0) and (M-1, N-1), namely, the first and the last pixel set, and calculating the mean values of each pixel set with their respective RGB multipliers is used. The results they have obtained support their hypothesis that Tesseract provides a higher accuracy for grayscale images. The authors had conducted an experiment with 20 colored images and have noticed that, for certain images, 100% accuracy is obtained, while for others, the accuracy ranges from 30% to 60%. The same images converted into grayscale provide a higher accuracy ranging from 60% to 80%. On comparing Transym with Tesseract using the same test images, they noticed that Tesseract provided a better accuracy of 61% and 70% for colored and grayscale images, respectively, while Transym provided 47% accuracy in both cases. On comparing the execution time, they noticed that Tesseract is faster, averaging 1 and 0.82 s for colored and grayscale images, respectively, while Transym took 6.75 s, on average, to process a single image. The standard deviations for Tesseract were 34.21 and 24.64 for colored and grayscale images, respectively, while Transym recorded a standard deviation of 40.

Li *et al.* [4] proposed a new way to read irregular text in a natural scene. This kind of text is difficult to detect because of a large variance in text appearance like the curvature of the text, its orientation, and its distortion. This paper proposed an easy-to-implement system employing off-the-shelf neural network segments and word-level annotations. It consists of a 31-layer ResNet segment, an LSTM-based encoder–decoder component, and a 2D attention module. Here is the basic blueprint of the proposed model. It comprises two major parts: a ResNet convolution neural network (CNN) to extract features and a two-dimensional attention-based encoder/decoder. The network uses images as input, and the output is a series of characters. ResNet CNN: In the 31-layer of ResNet, for every residual block, if the input and output dimensions are dissimilar, a projection shortcut is used. This is done using 1×1 convolutions, and if they have similar dimensions, the identity shortcut is used. The resulting 2D feature maps will be used for two things. First, for extracting the holistic features of the entire image and, second, as the context for the 2D attention network. 2D attention-based encoder–decoder: The encoder is a two-layer LSTM model with 512 hidden layers separately. The output is a fixed-size representation of the image input data for decoding. The decoder is also an identical LSTM model which does not share parameters with the encoder. Finally, mathematical transformation computes the final output, which embeds the features into the output space of 94 types: 52 case-sensitive letters of the English alphabet (26 + 26), 10 digits, 31 punctuation marks, and the 'END' token. This model is verified to give the highest accuracy of all the other models regarding irregular text benchmarks and comparable accuracy for regular text. Future works aim to substitute the LSTM encoder–decoder with CNN for sequence modeling; the 2D attention section can be an individual case under graph neural networks.

The problem statement considered by Armengol-Estapé *et al.* is that large hospitals which have a lot of doctors who have to review the details of a large number of patients who have a long medical history have to put in an extended amount of time in doing something that is not the ideal use of their time and resources. There are other documents such as research, medical and biomedical literature, and chemical patents where it is critical to label the mentions of drugs in these records to get a faster inference on drug resistance, drug dosage recognition, period of medical therapy, allergies, etc. The paper seeks to provide an organized approach to recognizing the above-mentioned entities to make examining these records more accessible, faster, and more informative. The proposal involves advanced NER (NeuroNER; NER: named entity recognition) based on deep learning. This paper was done mainly keeping Spanish in mind, and hence the preprocessing was domain-specific and tools pertaining to the Spanish language have been used. This, however, can be extended to other languages as well by making some changes. The model mainly consists of three major modules: the POS features, the Gazetteer features, and the Affixes features. These three are language independent and can work on any language. Upon running the algorithm on the test set, an F1 score of 89.06 was recorded. Thus, extending the algorithm to other languages should also give a similar result as the main core functionality of the algorithm is language independent; however, there might be some changes due to a change in pre-processing.

Moving on to another work by Ting *et al.* [5] which focuses on human errors made in reading medical documents, the background of this work is based on the medication errors made by patients, pharmacists, and medicine buyers. This constitutes a major problem in the healthcare industry. This research utilizes a standard deep learning drug identification to understand how the identification confusion of the same type of images by humans arises and describe a technique to resolve them. The training phase uses the blister-packaged drugs' front or back side. About 250 types of images of blister-packaged drugs were obtained from an outpatient department; the deep learning network was trained and tested on these set of images. The model proposed in this paper makes use of CNN for feature extraction, but it was found that the basic CNN is not practical for complicated images, and hence R-CNN was used. The R-CNN was optimized to make it faster, and ultimately, the accuracy was significantly improved. It took 5 h and 34 min to train the front side model and 7 h and 42 min to train the back side of the model. For quantifying the result and to measure the accuracy of the model, F1 score was employed. It gives us a proper idea of the model. The result was as follows: the F1 score of the back side model was 95.99%, which was more promising than that of the front side model, which was 93.72%. Therefore, the back side model is more reliable when utilizing only one model is a choice. Ultimately, this model outperformed identification using computer vision-based methods and prevented medication errors that occurred by similar-looking blister packages. Integrating this system into pharmacies and hospitals can bring down the risk of handing out the wrong medication to patients.

The work by Sabu *et al.* [6] briefly describes various algorithms used to date for optical character recognition. In OCR, images or hand-written notes are transformed into a digital format. Moftah Elzobi's article presented a method for recognizing Arabic characters utilizing the Gabor wavelet transform and support vector machine. It is based on segmentation. Tasunva proposed a method to identify Bangla numerals using a binary pattern which improves the image quality. Then, the paper utilizes the KSC algorithm for slant correction and detection. Chamila used Tesseract algorithm to build and test Tamil character recognition. Various methods like character segmentation, namely, entity recognition, etc., were performed on the given dataset, and it was found that three fonts work best for Tamil. Ali Farhat built a model which automatically recognized quatari number plates. Every component involved were expressed in terms of vectors, and the whole model is built on MATLAB. The accuracy of the system was around 80.43%, with a noise removal rate of 72%. An OCR system was developed to identify Kannada digits and alphabets. Initially, skew detection, binarization, and noise removal were carried out, and structural and functional features were extracted from the feature extraction stage. The obtained data was split into four quadrants to identify the relationship between words. Wafa Quizer proposed a model using fuzzy logic to recognize characters on the license plate. Local image features were extracted using the SIFT technique, and noise removal was done using specialized segmentation techniques. The built model showed an accuracy rate of 82.8%. Abdullah-almamun proposed a method to use multi-layer perceptron for optical character recognition. The final accuracy for the model was around 90.53% and 80.43% for normal and sentential case characters, respectively.

Another approach can be seen in Shrivastava *et al.* This work proposes an artificial neural network-based model to recognize characters. The first step of the algorithm is to pre-process the data. The methods used for pre-processing are noise reduction and binarization. The main goal of binarization is to induce uniformity among all input images by converting black text on a white background. Feature vectors are input for the artificial neural networks (ANN); therefore, each character is segmented. The two phases are separating out lines and separating out characters. Different features have been used to recognize the characters in the algorithm. One of the algorithms is the sum of pixel where the sum of pixel along the row or column is used as a deciding factor. Other than this, symmetry is also used to differentiate characters—for example, the letters 8 and B can be differentiated by the corresponding axis they are placed in. If it is in the horizontal axis, it is B, and if it is vertical, it is 8. Another factor considered is the amount of area enclosed by the character as a closed letter—for example, characters like A, P, B, and D are all closed character, and if there was ambiguity, the amount of area can be considered to identify the character currently under observation. The ANN is trained with the help of the pre-processed text which comes as a result of the aforementioned processes. Inputs are represented as vectors and database templated using the feature extraction methods. The model is backpropagated to and fro to get a good result and to avoid the gradient descent problem; the iteration limit is set to 100. On the training set, the built model showed an accuracy rate of 100%, and in the untrained samples, it showed an accuracy rate of 85.53% on 10 fonts. The model can be still improved by using databases which offer a wide variety of fonts and by using better training algorithms for complex datasets in the future.

In the work proposed by Blanke *et al.* [7], the main aim was to develop an engine in order to support the easy customization of OCR using open-source technologies. As the main goal of OCR is towards large commercial collection, commercial OCR fails in the optimization process. Thus, the methodology presented in this paper paves a way for the user to integrate the best functionalities of the tool. Two case studies have been provided by the authors to show how this optimization works. High-quality, research-oriented digitization output and utility services were observed in the first one. The second case study shows the potential of OCR if it can be customized directly within a more extensive research infrastructure for history. In such a scenario, additional semantics can be added effortlessly to the workflow, drastically improving the research browse experience. The second case study serves as a good example to demonstrate how to use this OCR in order to maximize the accuracy. The paper gives an overview on how to combine the best features of various OCR engines and make the tool more flexible with respect to data mining and layout analysis. The main advantage is that no dedicated code is necessary to develop such a tool as it mainly involves combining the benefits of various components.

The work done by Hazra *et al.* [8] states the use of K-nearest neighbors algorithm for optical character recognition. The authors have explained about the various steps and pre-processing for the same. They have taken a training dataset which contains all possible characters in various shapes which is input to the model and processed. It is converted to a suitable size by flattening to make the model more effective for prediction. These images are extracted, and contours are identified and stored in the format of numpy datatype. Then, the training dataset is trained using OpenCV and KNN classifier. KNN is used for classification problems. In this algorithm, the input data is assigned a score of its possibility of being each of the input classes and then is classified based on the class which has the highest probability score. After the model has been trained, the input image is loaded in the format in which the model was trained, and the contours are identified by marking it on the image; using the KNN function, the character label with the highest probability score is assigned to it. The authors have also inferred via comparison that KNN algorithm gives better accuracy than the other optical character recognition models such as logistic regression, decision tree, and CART. They have also analyzed the performance of the algorithm on both MNIST and handwritten datasets and got commendable accuracy.

The work done by Karishma *et al.* has a comparison of various OCR steps, viz., HMM, neural networks, and character normalization. HMM is a double-feedforward neural network where each neuron is connected to both the forward layers and the backward layers and a set of scores and probability is attached. HMM learns through both forward processing and backward processing of the network. The neural network is a set of interconnected layers, which contain parameters which are tuned and trained according to the dataset, and predicts according to the input correctly. The advantage of the hidden Markov model over artificial neural networks is that HMM is more useful and gives better results for handwritten texts. The authors have explained the various stages of OCR using the hidden Markov model. Using HMM, we can estimate the chain of hidden states based on the viewing chain, and using algorithms such as the Viterbi algorithm or HMM counter-algorithms, one can get an accurate result. In character normalization, the input might not be in the proper format and has to be pre-processed to be sent for prediction. Thus, the size of the input is changed, and unnecessary portions are also eliminated. The OCR processing takes place in the following order—initial processing of the image, segmenting the image to locate the small units, distinguishing each token, and then prediction. The authors have used a contour algorithm at the edges of printed and handwritten characters. The contour algorithm helps produce an image or text vector when the symbol is first trained, which is used to compare the vector of the input element during the test or recognition stage. The contour algorithm depends on the sector pixel node algorithm, feature vector algorithm, node algorithm, and track node algorithm, but if the character is colored, this line algorithm will not produce the correct output; the symbols and character or input must be transformed to grayscale by utilizing the Otsu image threshold algorithm. Therefore, a methodology similar to the HMM counter-algorithm is employed for training and testing in the updated image to give a proper output for printed and handwritten letters in Hindi and English.

A new approach was proposed by Honey *et al.* Character recognition is challenging when one speaks of the record-keeping of all digital data forms that are continuously usable to perform various deceptive tasks. The problem is recognizing the letters of the different fonts in the written text. The authors have proposed a new approach to artificial neural networks for identifying characters in scanned documents and pictures. After processing the data with OCR and as it is digitized, it is editable, processed, and stored in a user-friendly computer system. The effectiveness of our program is gauged by evaluating the variance in the number of duplications and the variation in the number of characters. The suggested method produces a recognition rate of 98.89% for two different fonts (Latin Tahoma and Latin Arial) with a view of up to 90 characters simultaneously. The algorithm used by the authors is ANN. ANN contains a set of computational units spread across layers, each of which has a score which is fined-tuned while training so as to predict the image correctly when input data is fed.

17.2 Materials and Methods

This section explains the datasets, the methodology, and the components involved in the proposed system of identifying counterfeit drugs.

17.2.1 Data Description

The proposed system provides an on-the-spot validation of pharmaceutical drugs by extracting text present on the back-strip. The extracted data will have to be compared with accurate drug names, compositions, descriptions, and chemicals used so as to validate its authenticity. This is extremely data intensive as there are thousands of pharmaceutical drugs in existence at the moment. The dataset has been extracted from 1mg [9], India's biggest online pharmacy. The dataset includes the aforementioned parameters in addition to alternative drugs, side effects of each drug, storage procedures, general purposes, and the manufacturers' names. Records of all existing drugs are incorporated into the database to make the process versatile and beneficial to individuals.

17.2.2 Proposed Method

The proposed method introduces a novel multi-stage authentication mechanism for classifying pharmaceutical drugs as counterfeit or original. The block diagram of the proposed method is depicted in Figure 17.2. This system requires an image of the back-strip of the pharmaceutical drug as input. The preprocessing stage allows the input images to provide more pertinent data than the raw input images. Normalization is performed by altering the range of the intensity values of pixels and resizing the large input image; conversion to gray-scale is employed as the preprocessing technique in this work. The algorithm proposed in this work has four main stages of running the classification criteria. First, each input image is passed through a Tesseract engine for optical character recognition in stage I. This would facilitate text extraction from the image, line by line.

The output of stage I would involve a series of lines of text. Searching through each line to find a match in the database would be extremely time-consuming. The drug name will have to be identified from the set of words extracted.

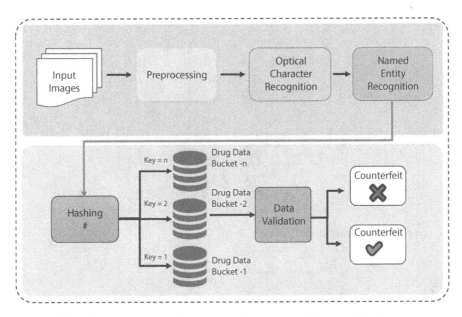

Figure 17.2 Workflow diagram of proposed system for pharmaceutical drug classification.

Stage II consists of a custom named entity recognizer which would enable the identification of the drug name so that the relevant information can be extracted from the database quickly.

Stage III involves searching the database through hashing techniques. The database will have records of thousands of medicines, thereby making sequential search an inefficient process. The drug name is passed through a hash function which returns the corresponding database bucket value. This would improve search time substantially as it would eliminate searching each record in the database sequentially.

Stage IV involves the comparison of the extracted data with the existing drug identity from the database. Parameters such as drug name, drug composition, drug description, chemicals used, manufacturer, and expiry date are validated to render a particular drug as real or counterfeit.

The proposed system consists of seven functional components: preprocessing, optical character recognition, named entity recognition, and hash function database search.

17.2.2.1 Preprocessing

Initially, the Input images require standardization for uniformity by the normalization process. This process utilizes the OpenCV library in Python. Then, the images are processed to remove unwanted distortions and noise from the image. It also enhances the image features to obtain optimum results in text recognition and extraction. It involves the following steps:

1. Resize the colored input images.
2. Removal of noise from the resultant image by applying the Non-local Means Denoising algorithm: This algorithm will replace each pixel value with the

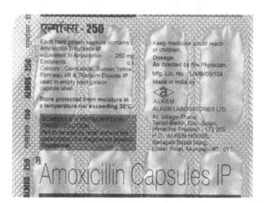

Figure 17.3 Input back-strip image before preprocessing.

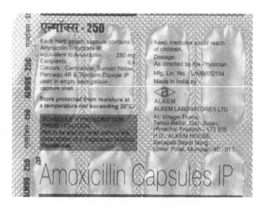

Figure 17.4 Input back-strip image after preprocessing.

average of other selected surrounding pixel values. This calculated average is for regions with patches near the current spot. Hence, this algorithm can yield fine textures, which might otherwise get blurred by other denoising algorithms.

3. Normalization of image: for improving the contrast in image segmentation.
4. Conversion of images to grayscale: to enhance feature extraction for the subsequent character recognition stage.

Figures 17.3 and 17.4 depict the images of the drugs before and after preprocessing, respectively.

17.2.2.2 Optical Character Recognition

Optical character recognition is the autonomous transformation of typed, handwritten, or printed text images into raw editable text data format by conducting image processing using machine learning algorithms. An optical character recognition model receives an image as it is input and gives the raw text data present in the image as its output. The OCR software converts the input image into grayscale for processing. It then scans the grayscale image and analyzes it for black and white areas.

The black regions are deemed as characters and needs to be identified, and the white regions are deemed as blank spaces. The black regions are then further processed to find the character, viz., alphabets, digits, etc., using different algorithms, but every OCR model targets one character or block and converts it to text at a time. The algorithms that are generally used for character identification are as follows:

- Pattern Recognition—where the model is fed different examples of texts which are used for comparison and text identification in the image.
- Feature Detection—Here the model applies rules regarding each character, and when the input character matches it, it classifies it accordingly—for example, the letter L could be stored as two perpendicular lines meeting each other. After classification, the character is converted to a machine-encoded ASCII format that can be used by the system for further editing.

For this system, Google's Tesseract has been used for performing OCR on the back-strip of pharmaceutical drugs. Tesseract is an optical character recognition engine released under Apache License by Hewlett Packard Enterprise. It can be used for performing OCR on over 100 languages and supports Unicode. The Tesseract engine can be integrated in almost every programming language for the purpose of OCR.

The Tesseract engine receives the input image of the medicine. The text lines in the input are split into different words according to the spacing and are chopped by character cells. It performs character recognition as a two-step process. In the first step, the model identifies the characters that are likely to be the input character and passes it to the adaptive classifier as training data.

Later, the adaptive classifier classifies the input character based on which it is most likely to be among the characters that is passed to the training data. Hence, Tesseract uses a two-stage feature detection for character recognition. In this system, the Tesseract engine extracts the drug's details (name, description, constituents, chemicals, manufacturing date, expiry date, and batch number) from the image of the medicine that is uploaded and passes the raw text output data to the named entity recognition model for further processing.

17.2.2.3 Named Entity Recognition

Named entity recognition (NER) is as a part of information extraction that aims to locate and identify various kinds of names present in the unstructured document into clear categories like names, locations, organization, quantities, timestamps, number, etc. An example for NER can be as follows:

- Pam bought 5000 shares of TESLA in 2019.
- [Pam] name bought [5000] number shares of [TESLA] ORG in [2019] year.

Some of the best NER platforms include GATE, OPENNLP, and SPaCy, and each of them supports more than 20 languages. The proposed system uses SpaCy and Python for NER. In a nutshell, it is a two-step process:

- Detect a named entity.
- Assign the recognized entity to a proper category.

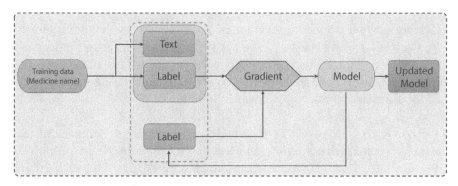

Figure 17.5 NER mechanism to identify drug names.

The first mainly involves detecting a set or a word that qualifies to be an entity. Every single word can be considered as a token. "ALMOX-500" is a single token that represents an entity called "medicine name". These entities are user-defined and solely depends on the training data and the relations (person, organization, date, medicine name) specified by the developer. The second step involves creating proper entity types and giving enough training data to the model so that the model can properly categorize the given word to the corresponding entity type—for example, the model will be able to classify the word "DIGENE" as "medicine name" and "Abbott" as "organization" based on the trained dataset. The NER process involved is summarized in Figure 17.5.

Training data: This consists all the medicine names with which the NER model will be trained to spot medicine names.
Label and Text: These are the input and output formats for the NER model. In other words, the medicine name can be said as the label for a word in the given text.
Model: The custom-built NER model with the help of the given training data.
Updated Model: Based on the value of the gradient, the model will be updated after every single epoch in order to maximize the accuracy.

17.2.2.4   Hash Functions

A hash function is a mathematical function that changes an input into a compressed numerical value. Hash functions can be provided inputs of various lengths, but the length of the result obtained is always fixed. The computation of a hash function h(x) is a quick operation. Hash functions are computationally hard to reverse. It is difficult to obtain an input value "x" from a hash value "z". These functions do not usually return the same hash for different inputs, although it is a possibility based on the type of function being performed. This property is also known as collision resistance. Hashing is a method used to retrieve required data from disks without having to use an index structure. These are used to retrieve items much faster than having to use its original value. These are employed for huge databases so that the sequential search of thousands or millions of records can be eliminated. Figure 17.6 depicts the database search mechanism using the hash function.

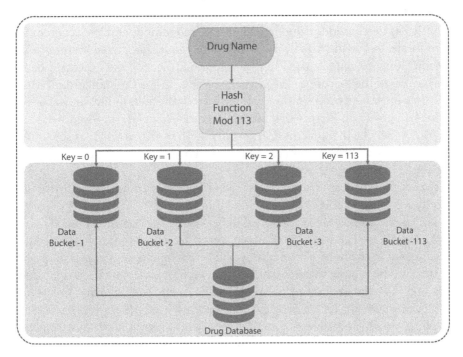

Figure 17.6 Hashing database search mechanism.

In the proposed system, a hash function is used to generate a numerical value for the input drug name. Next, a modulus operation is performed to shorten the value into an index through which particular data buckets can be accessed. Once a target index is matched, only drug names from within the matched buckets are compared. This reduces the overall search space substantially so that the access time is reduced. Through this technique, the large number of records in the database can be searched within a short period of time.

17.3   Results and Discussion

To demonstrate the proposed method's significance, evaluation of its performance through several measures is essential. First, normalization and resizing are preprocessing steps for improving the input image quality. The next step involves the conversion of images to grayscale so that the Tesseract engine provides a higher accuracy. It is noted that Tesseract has an accuracy rate of 61% and 87.78% for the colored and grayscale medicine images, respectively. The analyzed accuracy metrics for Tesseract is presented in Table 17.1.

Table 17.1 Tesseract accuracy metrics.

Image type	Precision	Recall	F-score
Coloured images	0.69	0.546	61
Greyscale images	0.922	0.839	87.78

Spacy NER has been used for the named entity recognition, and the accuracy result of our custom model is shown in Table 17.2. The NER model had taken 45 min to train the custom medicine name dataset used in our solution. To check the exactness of the built model, we have used the F-score as the primary metric, as it is the standard metric for systems based on named entity recognition. It is found that the built model shows the accuracy for medicine name with an F-score of 97.06%. The model displays an F-score of 92.05% for dates and 91.86% for the manufacturer, respectively. They are classified as separate entities to make the comparison process simpler. Thus, it can be inferred that our model gives good results for all the input images.

The accuracy of drug name recognition using SpaCy is compared with that of other models used as shown in Table 17.3.

As this is an application which is designed to be used by the common man, it is created in the form of a mobile application. Users can register and log in to the application, after which they are redirected to the home screen. They will be prompted to select an image from the gallery or turn on the camera to upload an image. Once an image has been uploaded, it will be sent via a HTTP post request to the server so that the steps involved in the proposed methodology can take place. If a drug is identified as "valid", the response is sent to the mobile application which generates a modal view with an animation to indicate success. The side effects of the drug are also listed for the user's perusal. If a drug is identified as "counterfeit", the response is sent to the mobile application which generates a modal view with an animation to indicate failure. The possible alternatives for the drug are listed so that users can consult with the doctors and other authorities and purchase them instead. Figure 17.7 depict the user interface of the resultant application.

Table 17.2 SpaCy accuracy metrics.

Entity	Total NE's in document	Total NE's in system	Correct NE's	Precision	Recall R	F-score
Drug Names	1380	1350	1325	0.9804	0.9601	97.06
Date	1425	1400	1375	1375	0.8742	92.05
Manufacturer	704	672	632	632	0.89770	91.86

Table 17.3 Comparison of NER accuracy with existing models.

Paper	Model	F-score
Exploring World Embedding for Drug Name Recognition [10]	Conditional Fields	77
	CRFD + Word2Vec k=50	80
Boosting drug named entity recognition using an aggregate classifier [11]	Perceptron	92.3
	MaxEntropy	95.1
Proposed Model	SpaCy NER	97.06

Figure 17.7 User interface of an application.

Artificial intelligence (AI) [12–15] has become a game-changer in a technological environment that is fast changing across a number of sectors [16]. The pharmaceutical industry has also adopted this ground-breaking technology to improve business processes and spur innovation. Organisations need to comprehend the dramatic influence AI [17, 18] may have on their sector given that the market for AI in pharma is expected to develop exponentially in the upcoming years. the top four applications of AI in the pharmaceutical industry and emphasise the advantages it provides to businesses [19] engaged in this industry are presented. With incomplete or faulty data used to train AI algorithms, misleading [20–23] information may propagate. Precision [24] is crucial to patient well-being in the healthcare industry; therefore, this is especially troublesome [25, 26]. The possibility of data breaches [27, 28] is one of the largest threats. Health care professionals become targets for hackers as they produce, receive, store, and transfer vast amounts of sensitive patient data. Anywhere along the pipeline of AI data, there are vulnerabilities [29, 30] that bad actors may and will exploit.

17.4   Conclusion

The application built will help millions of people around the world identify counterfeit pharmaceutical drugs. As and when more are identified, they can be reported so that necessary action can be taken by the authorities. It can also save many lives as fake drugs are a threat to an individual's health, especially elderly people and those suffering from existing ailments.

Identifying these drugs manually is a cumbersome task which most people would not do. Others would miss the subtle differences in the back-strips and packaging which make the medicine seem real. However, in reality, it may or may not be authentic. This is where our application comes into the picture. It offers a simple and seamless experience for users to upload images and receive the result. The application also offers appropriate animations to improve its usability.

References

1. Afroge, S., Ahmed, B., Mahmud, F., Optical character recognition using back propagation neural network. *2016 2nd International Conference on Electrical, Computer & Telecommunication Engineering (ICECTE)*, Rajshahi, Bangladesh, pp. 1–4, 2016, doi: 10.1109/ICECTE.2016.7879615.

2. Liu, X., DLI-IT: A deep learning approach to drug label identification through image and text embedding. *BMC Med. Inf. Decis. Making*, 20, 1–9, 2020.

3. Patel, C., Patel, A., Patel, D., Optical character recognition by open-source OCR tool tesseract: A case study. *Int. J. Comput. Appl.*, 55, 10, 50–56, 2012.

4. Li, H. *et al.*, Show, attend and read: A simple and strong baseline for irregular text recognition. *Proceedings of the AAAI Conference on Artificial Intelligence*, vol. 33. No. 01, 2019.

5. Ting, H.-W. *et al.*, A drug identification model developed using deep learning technologies: Experience of a medical center in Taiwan. *BMC Health Serv. Res.*, 20, 1–9, 2020.

6. Sabu, A.M. and Das, A.S., A survey on various optical character recognition techniques. *Conference on Emerging Devices and Smart Systems (ICEDSS)*, IEEE, 2018.

7. Blanke, T., Bryant, M., Hedges, M., Open-source optical character recognition for historical research. *J. Doc.*, 68, 5, 659–683, 2012.

8. Hazra, T.K., Singh, D.P., Daga, N., Optical character recognition using KNN on custom image dataset. *8th Annual Industrial Automation and Electromechanical Engineering Conference (IEMECON)*, Bangkok, Thailand, pp. 110–114, 2017, doi: 10.1109/IEMECON.2017.8079572.

9. https://www.1mg.com/.

10. Segura-Bedmar, I., Suárez-Paniagua, V., Martínez, P., Exploring word embedding for drug name recognition, in: *Proceedings of the Sixth International Workshop on Health Text Mining and Information Analysis*, September, pp. 64–72, 2015.

11. Korkontzelos, I., Piliouras, D., Dowsey, A.W., Ananiadou, S., Boosting drug named entity recognition using an aggregate classifier. *Artif. Intell. Med.*, 65, 2, 145–153, 2015.

12. Mahor, V., Bijrothiya, S., Rawat, R., Kumar, A., Garg, B., Pachlasiya, K., IoT and artificial intelligence techniques for public safety and security, in: *Smart Urban Computing Applications*, p. 111, 2023.

13. Mahor, V., Pachlasiya, K., Garg, B., Chouhan, M., Telang, S., Rawat, R., Mobile operating system (Android) vulnerability analysis using machine learning, in: *Proceedings of International Conference on Network Security and Blockchain Technology: ICNSBT 2021*, pp. 159–169, Springer Nature Singapore, Singapore, 2022, June.

14. Rawat, R., Garg, B., Pachlasiya, K., Mahor, V., Telang, S., Chouhan, M., Mishra, R., SCNTA: Monitoring of network availability and activity for identification of anomalies using machine learning approaches. *Int. J. Inf. Technol. Web Eng. (IJITWE)*, 17, 1, 1–19, 2022.

15. Rawat, R., Rimal, Y.N., William, P., Dahima, S., Gupta, S., Sankaran, K.S., Malware threat affecting financial organization analysis using machine learning approach. *Int. J. Inf. Technol. Web Eng. (IJITWE)*, 17, 1, 1–20, 2022.

16. Rawat, R., Mahor, V., Chouhan, M., Pachlasiya, K., Telang, S., Garg, B., Systematic literature review (SLR) on social media and the digital transformation of drug trafficking on darkweb, in: *International Conference on Network Security and Blockchain Technology*, pp. 181–205, Springer, Singapore, 2022.

17. Rawat, R., Ayodele Oki, O., Sankaran, S., Florez, H., Ajagbe, S.A., Techniques for predicting dark web events focused on the delivery of illicit products and ordered crime. *Int. J. Electr. Comput. Eng. (IJECE)*, 13, 5, 5354–5365, Oct. 2023, doi: 10.11591/ijece.v13i5.pp5354-5365.

18. Rawat, R., Garg, B., Mahor, V., Telang, S., Pachlasiya, K., Chouhan, M., Organ trafficking on the dark web—The data security and privacy concern in healthcare systems, in: *Internet of Healthcare Things: Machine Learning for Security and Privacy*, pp. 189–216, 2022.

19. Vyas, P., Vyas, G., Chauhan, A., Rawat, R., Telang, S., Gottumukkala, M., Anonymous trading on the dark online marketplace: An exploratory study, in: *Using Computational Intelligence for the Dark Web and Illicit Behavior Detection*, pp. 272–289, IGI Global, 2022.

20. Rawat, R., Oki, O.A., Sankaran, K.S., Olasupo, O., Ebong, G.N., Ajagbe, S.A., A new solution for cyber security in big data using machine learning approach, in: *Mobile Computing and Sustainable Informatics: Proceedings of ICMCSI 2023*, pp. 495–505, Springer Nature Singapore, Singapore, 2023.

21. Rawat, R., Chakrawarti, R.K., Raj, A., Mani, G., Chidambarathanu, K., Bhardwaj, R., Association rule learning for threat analysis using traffic analysis and packet filtering approach. *Int. J. Inf. Technol.*, 1–11, 2023.

22. Rawat, R., Logical concept mapping and social media analytics relating to cyber criminal activities for ontology creation. *Int. J. Inf. Technol.*, 15, 2, 893–903, 2023.

23. Rawat, R., Mahor, V., Álvarez, J.D., Ch, F., Cognitive systems for dark web cyber delinquent association malignant data crawling: A review, in: *Handbook of Research on War Policies, Strategies, and Cyber Wars*, pp. 45–63, 2023.

24. Rawat, R., Chakrawarti, R.K., Vyas, P., Gonzáles, J.L.A., Sikarwar, R., Bhardwaj, R., Intelligent fog computing surveillance system for crime and vulnerability identification and tracing. *Int. J. Inf. Secur. Priv. (IJISP)*, 17, 1, 1–25, 2023.

25. Rawat, R., Sowjanya, A.M., Patel, S.I., Jaiswal, V., Khan, I., Balaram, A. (Eds.), *Using Machine Intelligence: Autonomous Vehicles Volume 1*, John Wiley & Sons, 2022.

26. Rawat, R., Mahor, V., Díaz-Álvarez, J., Chávez, F., Rooted learning model at fog computing analysis for crime incident surveillance, in: *2022 International Conference on Smart Generation Computing, Communication and Networking (SMART GENCON)*, pp. 1–9, IEEE, 2022, December.

27. Rawat, R. and Shrivastav, S.K., SQL injection attack detection using SVM. *Int. J. Comput. Appl.*, 42, 13, 1–4, 2012.

28. Rawat, R., Bhardwaj, P., Kaur, U., Telang, S., Chouhan, M., Sankaran, K.S., *Smart vehicles for communication, volume 2*, John Wiley & Sons, 2023.

29. Mahor, V., Garg, B., Telang, S., Pachlasiya, K., Chouhan, M., Rawat, R., Cyber threat phylogeny assessment and vulnerabilities representation at thermal power station, in: *Proceedings of International Conference on Network Security and Blockchain Technology: ICNSBT 2021*, pp. 28–39, Springer Nature Singapore, Singapore, 2022, June.

30. Rawat, R., Gupta, S., Sivaranjani, S., Cu, O.K., Kuliha, M., Sankaran, K.S., Malevolent information crawling mechanism for forming structured illegal organisations in hidden networks. *Int. J. Cyber Warf. Terror. (IJCWT)*, 12, 1, 1–14, 2022.

Advanced Security Solutions for Conversational AI

Ranjana Sikarwar[1]*, Harish Kumar Shakya[1], Ajay Kumar[2] and Anjali Rawat[3]

[1]Department of Computer Science Engineering, Amity University Gwalior, Gwalior, India
[2]School of Computer Science and Engineering, Manipal University Jaipur, Jaipur, India
[3]Apostelle Overseas Education (AOE), Ujjain, India

Abstract

Conversational AI refers to technologies using machine learning and natural language processing to help simulate human interactions using chatbots or virtual agents which can understand and respond to the input text and speech. Conversational AI services have been used across various platforms nowadays to provide customer support for a better user experience. However, security issues are also an important concern for chatbots which hold the sensitive information of customers. Artificial intelligence is involved in the banking sector for the prevention of fraud and negative activities associated with financial transactions. Fraudulent activities can be either internal or external. Internal fraud may be committed by employees of the banks themselves through malevolent activities. Financial attacks on banks may take place externally also for money laundering or payments, etc. Fraud detection systems are used to identify, control, and block suspicious activities in the system. Anomaly detection is one of the crucial features of artificial intelligence used for the prevention of fraud and cyber-attacks.

Keywords: Chatbot, natural language processing, machine learning, SQL injection, vulnerabilities

18.1 Introduction

Conversational AI like chatbots, personal assistants, and voice recognition systems such as Alexa is used in commercial sectors to respond to customer queries as quickly as possible. A chatbot is any computer application developed to communicate with users visiting any website like amazon, Flipkart, etc. A wide variety of chatbots are available in the market nowadays like Siri, Alexa, and customer service chatbots. Chatbots provide a fast and accurate response to customer queries and contain the personal information of the customers, which is prone to attacks by hackers and malicious software. For answering customer queries in a fast and accurate way, companies have employed chatbots with automated response software on commercial and social media websites such as Facebook, Amazon, WhatsApp, etc. A chatbot is an abbreviation of the words chat and robot which uses artificial intelligence (AI) technologies to imitate interpersonal conversation. The first chatbot was created in the year 1966 and was limited to laboratory use only due to the lack of widespread

*Corresponding author: ranjana.sik@gmail.com

Romil Rawat, Rajesh Kumar Chakrawarti, Sanjaya Kumar Sarangi, Piyush Vyas, Mary Sowjanya Alamanda, Kotagiri Srividya and Krishnan Sakthidasan Sankaran (eds.) Conversational Artificial Intelligence, (387–302) © 2024 Scrivener Publishing LLC

network connectivity, high-performance equipment, etc. Chatbots are widely used in e-commerce-related services, Internet, financial, consulting, etc. Nowadays, chatbots are used mostly with social media or communication software. According to research reports, the global chatbot market will reach 1.23 billion US dollars in output value in 2025 [2]. There was a great need for banking and financial professionals to handle multiple customer inquiries because any financial personnel, doctors, consultants, or customer service representative can service only one customer at a time. A lot of training cost is required to train the financial personnel with professional knowledge. In recent years, many advanced countries use chatbots to assist customers and replace the work of professionals [3]. Chatbots are integrated into websites to function; thus, they depend on HTTPS and other protocols. Chatbots have database connectivity and, therefore, retrieve information through SQL queries. The use of personalized chatbots must ensure client data integrity and privacy. Authentication and authorization are also important security concerns for clients. Chatbot's working failure may produce vulnerabilities in the system and open it for attackers to target through SQL injection (SQLI) or cross-site scripting (XSS). The approach used for chatbot design focuses more on its functionality for natural language processing and answering user inquiries, not on its security. It is still an open issue for chatbot security, making them resistant to suspicious user inputs. Figure 18.1 shows the communication of a chatbot with a database system containing client information using the HTTPS protocol. While communicating with the user, the chatbot gathers as much information as possible about a particular client. Therefore, user authentication and data integrity must be ensured. Security leaks in the system can also allow vulnerabilities to trigger attacks—for example, malicious scripts can be executed on the client side or SQLI and XSS can be fired.

SQLI and XSS scripts are used to create test sets for chatbot security testing. These test sets are used to penetrate the chatbot system security with malicious and unsanitized input. XSS input contains JavaScript code and SQLI contains a list of SQL statements. Some approaches use Program O written in PHP and MYSQL databases for security testing [5]. A QED system is presented for testing against XSS and SQLI [9]. QED is meant for Java web application testing. Duchene *et al.* [7] present a testing tool for XSS that uses a black-box fuzzer with genetic algorithms. The work set comprises of an input flow of XSS attack vectors applying mutation and crossover operators. Bozie and Wotawa [10] used visual depictions of attacks against web applications. The attack patterns for XSS and SQLI were also specified. Chatbots are used in the education field, medical consultant systems, insurance services, and university admission services to provide counseling services.

18.1.1 Conversational AI Vulnerability

System defects are holes in a computer system that an attacker can use to bypass security measures. The system is exposed when it has obsolete device drivers, unsafe coding, a

Figure 18.1 Functionality of a chatbot system.

misconfigured firewall, and other issues. Human error is mostly to blame for system vulnerabilities [1]. You may use the security development lifecycle tool to prevent errors like these. The next paper focuses on the communication element and various elements of data manipulation because many chatbots store data in cloud-based services, which are well protected against threats and vulnerabilities. The use of chatbots in hacking has created a new problem. When business battles intensify, one strategy to damage an adversary's reputation in the sector is to use a chatbot. Microsoft [2] unveiled Tay, a chatbot designed to mimic and communicate with individuals at all times, in March 2016. Tay was a Twitter bot that was promoted as a conversational proficiency test. Microsoft claims [6] that Tay gets smarter the more you engage with it. The bot, though, was disappointed by showing itself to be a mistaken bot spouting terrible remarks like racism and anti-Semitism.

In encrypted texting, there are two realms. The safe transport of data, audio, and pictures to a server where the chatbot is kept is the first area of data transfer security. The second category is focused on the management, storage, and sharing of user data on the servers (backend). Both aliases span the duration of the user's realm. User communications are quite dangerous in the first domain. The next essay looks at ways to increase the security of a chatbot dialog. While many situations do not necessitate them, not all of them are often employed. If a business manages any user information, the bulk of the strategies described below must be used.

Sometimes it is not essential to confirm the digital credentials (authentication). When a user requests assistance, such as on a shopping website, verification is typically not required. In this case, connecting directly to the user's data or asking for their identity is not necessary for the operation [8]. When a user requests assistance and the chatbot uses their data, the situation is different. To guarantee that a user's login credentials are authentic and reliable, authentication and validation are necessary. The most typical credentials include a username, network interface, system ID, contact information, accreditation, passphrase, and other means of validation. The system receives the passcode and creates a secure authorization that is used throughout the user's transaction. The usage of tokens in messaging [11] online personal data exchange and archiving is never 100% safe. The user's approval of the bots while interacting with them would be authenticated by a personal authentication verification barrier (personal scan). Hence, if a user engaged with a malicious chatbot [10], the tailored scan would make sure that their credentials would not be used by fraudsters or other dishonest agents. It adds another layer of defense. It is a function that enables users to restrict information transmission to IP addresses on a white list. Moreover, the email accounts used to request the APIs will be shown. Users will get a warning if they attempt to send an SMS from a different IP address when API security is enabled.

End-to-end encryption is a type of encryption that allows only the people speaking to read each other's conversations. The conversation is encoded so as to protect the specific recipient of the article, and no one else can decode it. Data being communicated may be tampered with or faked by a third party. Thus, it is imperative to guarantee that the encryption process required to decode the conversation is in the hands of just the parties engaged. The user's device generates separate public and private keys. The RSA [3, 4] technique is one of the many protocols that are used to provide encryption. The public key is used to encrypt the communications, while the private key is used to decode them.

The public key can be used by anybody who sends a signal to the holder of the encryption key. Simply put, both ends of the chatbot can exchange the public key to secure communication. Techniques for identity control and safeguarding occasionally use encryption. It is vital to protect the encryption key; otherwise, a hacker will be able to decipher all communications delivered to this user. Conversational AI [6] and AI technologies are both a blessing and a burden in the digital age. Both protecting systems and breaking into them may be accomplished with it. Cybersecurity [7] will improve when firms use artificial intelligence more and more. AI can look into any situation, whereas humans can only do so to a limited extent due to their limited capacity.

18.2 Background

Reference [1] has presented an overview of cloud-based chatbot technologies, their programming, and the challenges faced by chatbot developments. The authors have discussed the programming challenges of handling natural language processing and machine learning in the design and development of chatbots. Also, the authors in reference [6] discussed the chatbot programming challenges. Examples of cloud-based chatbot services include the chatbot sector such as IBM Watson, Microsoft bot, AWS Lambda, Heroku, and many others. In, chatbots are used to assist tourists with limited time constraints. In [8], the authors have proposed a medical consultation system using chatbot technology for medical advice. The ability of a computer program to respond like humans in a conversation was studied in 1950 [4]. During examining this conversation, it was observed that the responses generated by the computer program were much like human responses. ELIZA, an intelligent computer program used for communication between humans and machines, was developed in the 1960s. ELIZA uses natural language processing. Artificial linguistic Internet computer entity (A.L.I.C.E.), another chatterbot like ELIZA, was developed later. The authors of reference [6] have studied the construction and design practices of two working chatbots that they have developed using programming languages like C++ and AIML, respectively. A chatbot provides services in many fields like education, the banking sector, medical consultation system, railway services, ontology, commercial websites, etc.

18.3 Components of Conversational AI

Conversational AI combines natural language processing (NLP) with machine learning to understand, process, and produce responses in a very natural way as humans do. Machine learning (ML) is a subfield of AI which consists of algorithms, features, and datasets that learn by experience continuously to make predictions by identifying matching patterns. NLP uses machine learning to analyze languages used in conversational AI. Deep learning methods will be used in the future to improve the NLP capabilities. The steps involved in NLP are input generation, input analysis, dialog management, and output response.

Input generation—Users provide input in the form of text or voice through a website or an app.

Input deciphering—Input is analyzed based on whether it is text-based or speech-based by conversational AI or automatic speech recognition (ASR) systems.

Dialogue management—Using dialog management, an AI-generated response is produced and presented in a human-understandable form.

Output response—AI-converted output is delivered as a response through text or speech synthesis to the user.

Machine learning is used to improve the application and process of communication between the user and conversational AI software or devices by learning from each interaction, adapting, and reacting accordingly.

18.4   Challenges with Conversational AI

Conversational AI applications use ASR systems, NLP, advanced dialog management system, and machine learning to process, learn and adapt to communication. There are some challenges faced by conversational AI, and more advanced and sophisticated technology is needed to overcome these challenges.

- Communication gap—Various factors such as language, accent, and dialect influence the working of the system conducting the conversation between a human and a machine. The pronunciation of words in different languages by people, fluency in English, and the choice of right words as abbreviations are sometimes challenging for AI to decipher. Thus, conversational AI applications must learn to cope with these differences.
- Security and privacy concerns—Conversational AI systems must secure the private and confidential information of the customers while interacting with them to protect them from fraudsters—for example, when a person verifies his/her identity by entering any security number, only a few digits should be asked to be entered in the system.
- Technology adoption—While conversational AI systems are easy to use, still some people found it a struggle to use the technology. People must learn to overcome the use of the latest applications. Companies have found some solutions to deal with these challenges. They embed the applications with a prompt to help customers with input choices. Systems offer prompts either verbally or through pop-up instruction bubbles.
- Use of advanced ASR systems in conversational AI—The use of high-quality automatic speech recognition systems enables conversational AI to interpret spoken language more correctly. Language experts and scientists must properly train these applications to ensure a successful customer experience.

Approaches to testing the system security

- Penetration testing—Done using ethical hacking by penetrating the system.
- API security testing—API security testing involves testing the endpoint application programming interface for security purposes to ensure basic security requirements like user access, encryption, and authentication issues.
- User behavioral analytics (UBA)—UBA studies human behaviors using different statistics and algorithms to predict abnormal behavior. UBA will be used as a tool to test the chatbot security systems.

Chatbot Security From Threats and Vulnerabilities

Chatbots can be secured using four ways, which include authentication, encryption, processes, protocols, and education.

End-to-end encryption—Whenever we chat on WhatsApp, it always shows "This chat is end-to-end encrypted", which means that only the sender and receiver can see the conversation and nobody else. It means that the conversation is encrypted and secure.

Authentication—Chatbots use a set of authentication processes to verify the user identity to ensure that a person is legitimate. It includes a set of steps to confirm user identity to access any website or portal. There are various types of authentications such as biometric authentication, two-factor authentication, userId, and authentication timeouts.

a. Biometric authentication—This type of authentication process uses body parts such as eyes, fingerprints, face, etc., to verify the identity of a person.
b. Two-factor authentication (2FA)—It requires two different forms of identification such as a password from the user or a personal identification number (PIN). To ensure secure access to something, a code is sent to the user's mobile as the second step of identity verification.
c. UserId—This is the oldest method of securing our identity by creating unique login credentials.
d. Authentication timeouts—This method can prevent the hackers who try to log in to the system from making multiple attempts. Only the right person that has the knowledge of the correct details can log in to a system.

Processes and protocols—HTTPS protocol is used with most websites to provide security. Transport layer and secure socket layer security are used to protect the encrypted connections.

- Education—Most cybercrimes take place by mistakes committed by naïve users or flawed systems. Thus, fundamental education of people on cybercrime activities by industry experts is necessary to conduct. A customer can be provided with a set of instructions to navigate through the system securely.
- Self-erasing messages—This feature is available on WhatsApp and Snapchat in which the messages are erased automatically after the conversation is over. Thus, nobody can recover them later.
- Web application firewall (WAF)—A WAF blocks suspected addresses and malicious activities, thus protecting the chatbots.

Different types of security measures can avoid security risks to customers.

Risks Associated With Chatbot Security

Chatbot security can be studied as threats and vulnerabilities. Vulnerabilities are the faults in the system or a state which increases the possibility of attacks by cybercriminals. The flaw in the system exposes it to attack or damage. Vulnerabilities are system problems that open the doors for threats to enter the system. Threats are one-time attacks that can steal data or modify it. Examples are malware attacks and distributed denial of service attacks. Unprotected chats may cause system vulnerabilities and may allow access to the database via chatbots. The Figure 18.2 shows about the Chatbot security specification. Different security

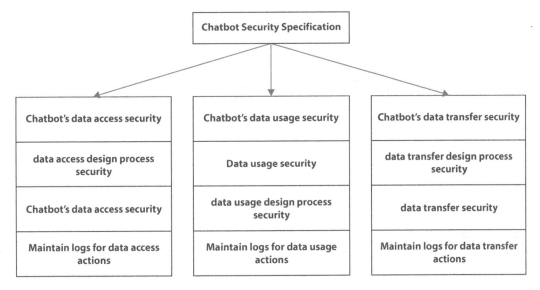

Figure 18.2 Chatbot security specification.

threats which can harm conversational AI are phishing attacks, whaling issues, ransomware and malware, team member impersonation, and bot repurposing. These attacks may occur on various modules of a chatbot architecture. A typical chatbot architecture has a client module, a communication module, a response generation module, and a database module. Each module is discussed below with its functioning and later followed by the type of adversarial attack on it with a solution.

- **Client module**—This is a user interaction platform such as an app or a website of a chatbot on the application side. Authentication and voice recognition systems are important.

Types of attacks
a. Unintended triggering attacks—Any adversary can talk to the personal assistant present at home through an infected IoT device remotely. The user's conversation may be recorded unintentionally, which may be confused with the wake-up phrases. Such activities may hinder the personal assistant's method of turning on and violate user privacy. A personal assistant can be activated remotely by the attacker. To detect whether a human is doing a conversation with the chatbot, Microsoft's Xiaoice is used. A human-to-bot classifier is used to detect the presence of humans in the room actually talking to the bot [10].
b. Access control attacks—As personal assistants are connected in some or another way to the IOT network and may follow the commands in case some malicious app on personal assistants tries to penetrate the security system of home. Such malicious application may control other devices to make sure of a coordinated attack. They can make an attack possible by finding a weakness in the permission system of an IOT network—for example, the malicious apps present on personal assistants may control

other devices in a home and manipulate them for an attack. Any malicious app can function as a home monitoring app and may control the security cameras to infiltrate and assure robbery at home. A temperature monitoring app may disturb the normally required temperature at home intentionally to harm the user or may open the doors and windows in the absence of humans. One solution to these access control attacks was given by Jia *et al.* [11] who developed a program to check the suspicious activity of apps. The main idea behind this program was to let users authorize each security-related action before it gets executed.

c. Faked acknowledgment—Many users know about how personal assistants operate and respond. However, there were some observations found by Zhang *et al.* [12] in their research findings like users usually switch from one task to another. The adversary can collect the user's personal information by introducing a malicious skill like an air ticket booking app, shopping app, or medical consultation app where the user's health information can be collected by the adversary. If the user does not switch off the personal assistants properly, then their personal conversation can also be recorded. These attacks by an adversary can be controlled by taking proper security measures for the developers to blacklist suspicious (distrustful) responses by personal assistants.

d. Faked voice samples—Usually, personal assistants respond to the voice sample of the user. The client module also has a voice recognition feature to communicate with the user. Hackers have been successful in fooling by imitating the voice of the user [13]. Attackers can craft the adversarial voice samples of the user in order to perform an attack. Two types of attack are often seen in this case: white box attack and black box attack. White box attacks assume to have some knowledge of the model, while black box attacks assume nothing about the model. The overall objective is to imitate the voice sample that the attacker is trying to invoke. Countermeasures have been proposed against this type of attack, like to control white box attacks by making the model secret. However, one cannot rely on keeping the model secret as black box attacks can still be active, so efforts are required to control the black box attacks as well. The adversary can practice or train the model many times through voice samples to correct the misunderstanding of the voice module.

- **Communication module**—This part of the system maintains a communication link between the client module and response generation module by transforming messages from one end to another and further between the response generation module and the database module.

Types of attacks
The function of the communication module is to transfer user messages through the client program to the response generation module and process data requests sent to the database module from the response module. Now, during the transfer of data requests from one module to another, the message may be intercepted,

stolen, or monitored by an eavesdropper. The different types of attacks on this module are DDoS attacks, man-in-the-middle attacks, or eavesdropping.

a.   Man-in-the-middle attack—Man-in-the-middle attacks can hear and harm the conversation between two users either by intercepting their messages and injecting their own malicious messages or by spamming malicious links during the conversation between client A and client B. Such attacks can provoke or agitate human users on social networking sites by creating misunderstandings through changes of opinion or views. Now, this is a challenge for developers to retain or secure the original message. The countermeasures against adversarial attacks are to adopt authentication and encryption methods to secure the communication between the client program and the response generation module.

b.   DDoS attacks—DDoS attacks hinder the natural conversation between a chatbot and the user by flooding the network with meaningless traffic or by sending server requests in bulk. Attackers conduct this attack by gathering a heavy amount of computing resources and flooding the server with too many requests, thus slowing down the response module. For conversational AI, attacks can be performed by a dialog agent through very long responses to a query. This type of attack may result in catastrophic damage for companies using chatbots. Feinstein *et al.* [14] have proposed statistical approaches to DDoS attacks in their research findings. Their idea is to measure the statistical properties of the network packets sent over the line.

c.   Eavesdropping—As the traffic in the communication module is fully secured by encryption algorithms, still the attackers can extract information from the communication module by tapping the line or eavesdropping. The different types of voice commands can be extracted; however, the data is encrypted. One such attack for extracting information was described by Kennedy *et al.* [15]. The voice command can be deduced by using packet size properties. Wireshark is a packet sniffer which sniffs for information using features like packet size or number of bytes transferred. Dyer *et al.* [16] proposed an approach as a countermeasure for packet sniffing in the network in which they aimed at fixed-size packet transfer to prevent hackers from discerning the packets' transfer pattern. This approach increases the overhead of conversational AIs. However, research is still going on with regards this challenge to protect user information sniffing on encrypted message transfer techniques.

- **Response module**—The part of the chatbot meant for generating a response for the user input message and understanding it. The task of this module is to understand the user input text and generate a proper response or reply to the user queries in an appropriate way.

    a.   Lack of domain knowledge attacks—Many conversational AIs are mostly perfect in answering all customer queries, but still they lack domain knowledge for customer queries. A hacker can perform brute-force attacks to find out such glitches or loopholes in the chatbots and can generate fraud responses for such domains. To counter these attacks, chatbots should be embedded with a classifier to differentiate between queries related to domain knowledge or out-of-domain knowledge. Zeng *et al.* [17] proposed a system to detect out-of-domain for understanding natural language in a dialog system.

b.   False information response—Conversational AI systems use natural language models which are basically dialog systems and generate novel responses. The conversation of a chatbot with a user is very natural and human-like as the dialog generation models used are trained on large-scale human conversation data. Adversaries can craft the input message in such a way that chatbots may answer with false information or use negative language to conduct an attack. Chatbots may also reply with offensive language in response to the input given by an attacker. Liu *et al.* [18] proposed a "reverse dialog generator" approach using reinforcement learning to defend against these attacks. This dialog defense generator can test the input sentence as to whether it is correct or not. This dialog system will check the input sentence for its correctness after training and will produce an output sentence. Another solution to address adversarial inputs is also to use the hate speech detector which can automatically filter out negative language or hateful words. However, this approach has its own limitations, so another approach is proposed which is more sophisticated and uses a neural network classifier to classify between hate speech and safe speech.

c.   Attacks on language models—Chatbots usually use language models to interpret user messages. These language models are used in various applications like sentiment analysis and hate speech detection and are found safer to be used in chatbots. The attackers can now craft adversarial language models using natural language processing systems to generate malicious output or may malfunction in many ways [19]. It is seen to be a very sophisticated attack because, at some point of triggers, chatbots may generate incorrect responses using offensive language. The security of the neural dialog model used in chatbots is a topic of great concern as neural language models are more vulnerable to attacks and can be forced to answer the way the attacker wants, which raises the security concern of chatbots. Thus, to protect against these attacks, developers must incorporate best practices in developing chatbots. The developers must verify correctly before they implement language models into chatbots. The regular update for this language model must also be monitored and verified.

d.   Reprogramming attacks—Different types of adversarial attacks are discussed in the literature, where the attacker intended to repurpose the machine learning model and considered both continuous and discrete input domains or spaces [24]. Here a neural network is repurposed to produce a different output as discussed by [25]. One example of an adversarial attack is discussed by the authors in which they repurposed the ImageNet model for the desired classification [26]. Examples of such adversarial attacks are predesigned inputs for a specific task so that the model functions in a completely different way and makes a mistake [27]. These attacks can be targeted or untargeted. An attacker can reprogram the response generation models to conduct another task instead of the original task to be performed by a chatbot. During reprogramming by an adversary, the model parameters are not modified. These attacks are more sophisticated and difficult to recognize as compared to standard adversarial attacks. The goal of these reprogramming attacks is to change the purpose of the model from the actual task that they are developed to perform. Adversarial reprogramming attacks simply repurpose the model for a different task. One countermeasure to these attacks is to expand the number of queries observed by the hacker to learn the model's pattern of classification.

- **Database module**—This module which is responsible for storing all the data pertinent to the conversation between a human user and chatbots may be in the form of text or images.

Attacks on the Database Module

Chatbots usually explore the database to generate any relevant information for user queries. Attacks on database modules may alter the user information, violate their privacy to manipulate useful data and information, and may coerce the chatbots for a changed behavior [21]—for example, a banking chatbot may reject/accept customer applications in the wrong way depending upon the changed information in the database module. Some of the attacks observed on database modules are SQL injection attacks as SQL is used to systematically store, update, and process data in a database, and another kind of attack uses knowledge graphs. Applications using SQL for database management are more vulnerable to SQL injection attacks. These attacks are found to harm web applications by penetrating the database and obtaining unrestricted access. This could be due to the improper validation of input data. Several solutions and guidelines are proposed by reference [22]. This may include user input encoding. There are various variants of injection attacks as discussed in [23]. To target web applications, SQL injection attacks are usually performed through HTTP Get or Post requests as discussed in [4]. An adversary can craft the input in order to force the database for unwanted or fake operations or outputs. Such attackers can either manipulate the information or get control over the sensitive information. These attacks are often seen to be triggered either through cookies or through server variables [20]. To provide defense against injection attacks, validation and cleaning of data or applying machine learning algorithms accompanied by static and dynamic analysis of data at regular intervals would be helpful. Knowledge graphs are a special database often used by chatbots to fetch information by reasoning and connecting with real-world situations. Usually, during the development process, these knowledge graphs are represented in a vector space.

The most important development is the possible use of real-time interactive experiences that are intended to control, compel, or convince people as a kind of targeted AI influence. Policymakers [28–31] have mainly ignored this problem in favour of typical privacy, prejudice, and surveillance problems. Policymakers need to understand that interactive influence campaigns may be implemented using Virtual Spokespeople (VSPs) [32, 33] driven by AI that appear, behave, and speak like actual users but are intended to promote the interests of outside parties. This "AI Manipulation Problem" is described in the framework of control theory in this research to help policymakers [34, 35] understand that rules are likely required to defend against closed-loop types of influence since it is specific to real-time interactive settings [36, 37]. Two human-computer interface (HCI) technologies have quickly entered the mainstream, attracting significant investments from big businesses. The first area of development is virtual and augmented worlds, sometimes known as The metaverse [38, 39]. The fundamental AI models that enable humans to freely connect with computers through natural dialogue [40] and [41] represent the second area of progress. This technology, also known as "Conversational This technology, also known as "conversational AI" [42, 43], has evolved quickly because of the use of Large Language Models (LLMs) [44]. Users will be able to interact with believable virtual characters based on the combination of these two professions. Although there will be numerous beneficial uses, there is a high risk of misuse [45, 46].

18.5   Conclusion

In this chapter, we have discussed conversational AI basics, types, definitions, and security issues. The components involved in conversational AI architecture and the challenging issues are also summarized in this article. The security issues of chatbots have also been analyzed with the objective of developing more secure systems for the next generation. The types of possible attacks, threats, and vulnerabilities performed on different modules are also discussed. It is imperative that conversational AI systems are tested fully before deployment, but still there are loopholes left in the system which invite threats.

References

1. Rahman, A.M., Mamun, A.A., Islam, A., Programming challenges of chatbot: Current and future prospective. *2017 IEEE Region 10 Humanitarian Technology Conference (R10-HTC)*, Dhaka, pp. 75–78, 2017.
2. Grand View Research, *Chatbot market size to reach $1.25 billion by 2025*, 2017, https:// www. grandviewresearch.com/press-release/global-chatbot-market.
3. Letheren, K. and Dootson, P., *Banking with a chatbot: A battle between convenience and security*, The Conversation, 2017.
4. Gentsch, P., Conversational AI: How (chat)bots will reshape the digital experience, in: *AI in Marketing, Sales, and Service*, Palgrave Macmillan, Cham, 2019.
5. Program O AI chatbot - the friendly open-source PHP, MySQL, AIML chatbot, https://www. program-o.com, accessed: 2018–02-04.

6. Rahman, A.M., Al Mamun, A., Islam, A., Programming challenges of chatbot: Current and future prospective. *Region 10 Humanitarian Technology Conference (R10-HTC)*, pp. 21–23, 2017.

7. Sano, A.V.D. *et al.*, The application of AGNES algorithm to optimize knowledge base for tourism chatbot. *2018 International Conference on Information Management and Technology (ICIMTech)*, IEEE, 2018.

8. Rosruen, N. and Samanchuen, T., Chatbot utilization for medical consultant system, in: *2018 3rd Technology Innovation Management and Engineering Science International Conference (TIMES-iCON)*, IEEE, 2018.

9. Martin, M. and Lam, M.S., Automatic generation of XSS and SQL injection attacks with goal-directed model checking, in: *17th USENIX Security Symposium*, 2008.

10. Lei, X., Tu, G.-H., Liu, A.X., Li, C.-Y., Xie, T., The insecurity of home digital voice assistants-vulnerabilities, attacks and countermeasures, in: *2018 IEEE Conference on Communications and Network Security (CNS)*, IEEE, pp. 1–9, 2018.

11. Jia, Y.J., Chen, Q.A., Wang, S., Rahmati, A., Fernandes, E., Mao, Z.M., Prakash, A., Contexlot: Towards providing contextual integrity to appified IoT platforms, in: *2017 NDSS Symposium*.

12. Zhang, N., Mi, X., Feng, X., Wang, X., Tian, Y., Qian, F., Dangerous skills: Understanding and mitigating security risks of voice-controlled third-party functions on virtual personal assistant systems, in: *2019 IEEE Symposium on Security and Privacy (SP)*, pp. 1381–1396, 2019.

13. Yuan, X., Chen, Y., Zhao, Y., Long, Y., Liu, X., Chen, K., Zhang, S., Huang, H., Wang, X., Gunter, C.A., Commander song: A systematic approach for practical adversarial voice recognition, in: *27th {USENIX} Security Symposium ({USENIX} Security 18)*, pp. 49–64, 2018.

14. Feinstein, L., Schnackenberg, D., Balupari, R., Kindred, D., Statistical approaches to DDoS attack detection and response, in: *Proceedings DARPA Information Survivability Conference and Exposition*, vol. 1, IEEE, pp. 303–314, 2003.

15. Kennedy, S., Li, H., Wang, C., Liu, H., Wang, B., Sun, W., I can hear your alexa: Voice command fingerprinting on smart home speakers, in: *2019 IEEE Conference on Communications and Network Security (CNS)*, IEEE, pp. 232–240, 2019.

16. Dyer, K.P., Coull, S.E., Ristenpart, T., Shrimpton, T., Peek-a-boo, i still see you: Why efficient traffic analysis countermeasures fail, in: *2012 IEEE Symposium on Security and Privacy*, pp. 332–346.

17. Zheng, Y., Chen, G., Huang, M., Out-of-domain detection for natural language understanding in dialog systems. *IEEE/ACM Trans. Audio Speech Lang. Process.*, 28, 1198–1209, 2020.

18. Liu, H., Derr, T., Liu, Z., Tang, J., Say what i want: Towards the dark side of neural dialogue models, arXiv preprint arXiv:1909.06044, 2019.

19. Zhang, X., Zhang, Z., Wang, T., Trojaning language models for fun and profit, arXiv preprint arXiv:2008.00312, 2020.

20. Halfond, W.G., Viegas, J., Orso, A. *et al.*, A classification of SQL-injection attacks and countermeasures, in: *Proceedings of the IEEE International Symposium on Secure Software Engineering*, vol. 1, IEEE, pp. 13–15, 2006.

21. Zhang, H., Zheng, T., Gao, J., Miao, C., Su, L., Li, Y., Ren, K., Data poisoning attack against knowledge graph embedding, in: *IJCAI*, 2019.

22. Howard, M. and LeBlanc, D., *Writing secure code*, second edition, Microsoft Press, Redmond, Washington, 2003.

23. Group, N.W., RFC 2616 – hypertext transfer protocol – HTTP/1.1. Request for comments, The Internet Society, 1999.

24. Szegedy, C., Zaremba, W., Sutskever, I., Bruna, J., Erhan, D., Goodfellow, I., Fergus, R., Intriguing properties of neural networks, in: *ICLR*, 2014.

25. Elsayed, G.F., Goodfellow, I.J., Sohl-Dickstein, J., Adversarial reprogramming of neural networks, in: *ICLR*, 2019.

26. Deng, J., Dong, W., Socher, R., Li, L.-J., Li, K., FeiFei, L., ImageNet: A large-scale hierarchical image database, in: *CVPR09*, 2009.

27. Goodfellow, I., Shlens, J., Szegedy, C., Explaining and harnessing adversarial examples, in: *International Conference on Learning Representations*, 2015.

28. Mahor, V., Bijrothiya, S., Rawat, R., Kumar, A., Garg, B., Pachlasiya, K., IoT and artificial intelligence techniques for public safety and security, in: *Smart Urban Computing Applications*, p. 111, 2023.

29. Mahor, V., Pachlasiya, K., Garg, B., Chouhan, M., Telang, S., Rawat, R., Mobile operating system (Android) vulnerability analysis using machine learning, in: *Proceedings of International Conference on Network Security and Blockchain Technology: ICNSBT 2021*, pp. 159–169, Springer Nature Singapore, Singapore, 2022, June.

30. Rawat, R., Garg, B., Pachlasiya, K., Mahor, V., Telang, S., Chouhan, M., Mishra, R., SCNTA: Monitoring of network availability and activity for identification of anomalies using machine learning approaches. *Int. J. Inf. Technol. Web Eng. (IJITWE)*, 17, 1, 1–19, 2022.

31. Rawat, R., Rimal, Y.N., William, P., Dahima, S., Gupta, S., Sankaran, K.S., Malware threat affecting financial organization analysis using machine learning approach. *Int. J. Inf. Technol. Web Eng. (IJITWE)*, 17, 1, 1–20, 2022.

32. Rawat, R., Mahor, V., Chouhan, M., Pachlasiya, K., Telang, S., Garg, B., Systematic literature review (SLR) on social media and the digital transformation of drug trafficking on darkweb, in: *International Conference on Network Security and Blockchain Technology*, pp. 181–205, Springer, Singapore, 2022.

33. Rawat, R., Ayodele Oki, O., Sankaran, S., Florez, H., Ajagbe, S.A., Techniques for predicting dark web events focused on the delivery of illicit products and ordered crime. *Int. J. Electr. Comput. Eng. (IJECE)*, 13, 5, 5354–5365, Oct. 2023, doi: 10.11591/ijece.v13i5.pp5354-5365.

34. Rawat, R., Garg, B., Mahor, V., Telang, S., Pachlasiya, K., Chouhan, M., Organ trafficking on the dark web—The data security and privacy concern in healthcare systems, in: *Internet of Healthcare Things: Machine Learning for Security and Privacy*, pp. 189–216, 2022.

35. Vyas, P., Vyas, G., Chauhan, A., Rawat, R., Telang, S., Gottumukkala, M., Anonymous trading on the dark online marketplace: An exploratory study, in: *Using Computational Intelligence for the Dark Web and Illicit Behavior Detection*, pp. 272–289, IGI Global, 2022.

36. Rawat, R., Oki, O.A., Sankaran, K.S., Olasupo, O., Ebong, G.N., Ajagbe, S.A., A new solution for cyber security in big data using machine learning approach, in: *Mobile Computing and Sustainable Informatics: Proceedings of ICMCSI 2023*, pp. 495–505, Springer Nature Singapore, Singapore, 2023.

37. Rawat, R., Chakrawarti, R.K., Raj, A., Mani, G., Chidambarathanu, K., Bhardwaj, R., Association rule learning for threat analysis using traffic analysis and packet filtering approach. *Int. J. Inf. Technol.*, 1–11, 2023.

38. Rawat, R., Logical concept mapping and social media analytics relating to cyber criminal activities for ontology creation. *Int. J. Inf. Technol.*, 15, 2, 893–903, 2023.

39. Rawat, R., Mahor, V., Álvarez, J.D., Ch, F., Cognitive systems for dark web cyber delinquent association malignant data crawling: A review, in: *Handbook of Research on War Policies, Strategies, and Cyber Wars*, pp. 45–63, 2023.

40. Rawat, R., Chakrawarti, R.K., Vyas, P., Gonzáles, J.L.A., Sikarwar, R., Bhardwaj, R., Intelligent fog computing surveillance system for crime and vulnerability identification and tracing. *Int. J. Inf. Secur. Priv. (IJISP)*, 17, 1, 1–25, 2023.

41. Rawat, R., Sowjanya, A.M., Patel, S.I., Jaiswal, V., Khan, I., Balaram, A. (Eds.), *Using Machine Intelligence: Autonomous Vehicles Volume 1*, John Wiley & Sons, 2022.

42. Rawat, R., Mahor, V., Díaz-Álvarez, J., Chávez, F., Rooted learning model at fog computing analysis for crime incident surveillance, in: *2022 International Conference on Smart Generation Computing, Communication and Networking (SMART GENCON)*, pp. 1–9, IEEE, 2022, December.

43. Rawat, R. and Shrivastav, S.K., SQL injection attack detection using SVM. *Int. J. Comput. Appl.*, *42*, 13, 1–4, 2012.

44. Rawat, R., Bhardwaj, P., Kaur, U., Telang, S., Chouhan, M., Sankaran, K.S., *Smart vehicles for communication, volume 2*, John Wiley & Sons, 2023.

45. Mahor, V., Garg, B., Telang, S., Pachlasiya, K., Chouhan, M., Rawat, R., Cyber threat phylogeny assessment and vulnerabilities representation at thermal power station, in: *Proceedings of International Conference on Network Security and Blockchain Technology: ICNSBT 2021*, pp. 28–39, Springer Nature Singapore, Singapore, 2022, June.

46. Rawat, R., Gupta, S., Sivaranjani, S., Cu, O.K., Kuliha, M., Sankaran, K.S., Malevolent information crawling mechanism for forming structured illegal organisations in hidden networks. *Int. J. Cyber Warf. Terror. (IJCWT)*, *12*, 1, 1–14, 2022.

Security Threats and Security Testing for Chatbots

Domenic T. Sanchez[1]* and Rodel S. Sartagoda[2]

[1]College of Education, Cebu Technological University-NEC, Cebu City, Philippines
[2]Department of Education - Cebu City Division, Guadalupe, Cebu City, Philippines

Abstract

Chatbots are vulnerable to vulnerabilities and attacks that are often utilized, such as cross-site scripting and SQL injections. As a result of these variables, it is quite probable that chatbots will also be the target of an attack. As a result of this, it is vital, while analyzing chatbots, to examine for problems about their level of security. The process of scanning and assessing vulnerabilities is a thorough analysis of computer networks and the components that make up such networks. By doing this study, we want to get a better understanding of the safety precautions that are now in place as well as the degree to which they are effective. The fundamental objective of penetration testing is to locate vulnerabilities in a protected setting so that they may be patched up before they are exploited by malicious actors (hackers, for example). In addition, doing penetration testing may be of use in determining how well the system can withstand genuine assaults. This article presents an investigation of vulnerability assessment and penetration testing for chatbots.

Keywords: Chatbot security, privacy, vulnerability assessment, penetration testing, vulnerabilities, attacks, threats

19.1 Introduction

Like any other kind of technology, there are potential drawbacks associated with using chatbots. Chatbots could first give the impression of being novel, but their construction really follows tried-and-true procedures. They are often included into the primary page of a website in a much different iteration. As a result, they communicate with one another using common protocols such as HTTP(S) and others. Since they are connected to databases, intelligent chatbots are able to conduct SQL searches when it comes to data. While working with bespoke chatbots, it is even more vital to safeguard the security of the client's data as well as their privacy and authentication. If a chatbot is unable to fulfill this responsibility, it might put the privacy of its users at risk and result in financial damages. Chatbots are susceptible to vulnerabilities and attacks that are often utilized, such as cross-site scripting (XSS) and SQL injections. As a result of these variables, it is quite probable that chatbots will

Corresponding author: domenic.sanchez@ctu.edu.ph

Romil Rawat, Rajesh Kumar Chakrawarti, Sanjaya Kumar Sarangi, Piyush Vyas, Mary Sowjanya Alamanda, Kotagiri Srividya and Krishnan Sakthidasan Sankaran (eds.) Conversational Artificial Intelligence, (303–318) © 2024 Scrivener Publishing LLC

also be the target of an attack (SQLI). As a result of this, it is vital, while analyzing chatbots, to examine for problems about their level of security [1].

In practice, however, it is sometimes difficult for network and system administrators to recognize security flaws, much alone locate the required patches or fixes to remedy such flaws. Finding out how much of a security breach important servers can endure is one of the steps involved in evaluating network security. The difficulty of this task adds to the already complicated nature of the situation that we are in. The response is dependent on a number of factors, such as the nature of the question, the current state of the network, the security policy of the network, the configuration of network devices like firewalls, routers, and switches, and the presence or absence of known vulnerabilities in the relevant protocols and systems. Investigations of this kind sometimes make use of a technique known as "penetration testing", which involves actively investigating a network and testing exploits that break into systems [2].

The process of scanning and assessing vulnerabilities is a thorough analysis of computer networks and the components that make up such networks. The goal of this inquiry is to ascertain the existence and the efficacy of defenses against unauthorized access. Network vulnerabilities and screening solutions are crucial because they maintain a record of known security gaps and detect potential threats before those vulnerabilities may be exploited by malicious software or hackers.

A system or application is put through a penetration test with the intention of replicating a real-world attack on it. This is accomplished by duplicating as many of the stages and variables as is humanly feasible. Testing for network vulnerability, often known as penetration testing, is a technique that evaluates the security of a network by emulating real attacks using known vulnerabilities in the underlying software and operating systems [3]. A penetration test is performed by an internal or external tester or auditor to uncover weak areas in a system (including but not limited to applications, hosts, and networks) that might be utilized by an attacker. These weak points could be exploited by an attacker. Because of these vulnerabilities, there is a chance that an adversary might get access to confidential information. An investigation of a target's information technology infrastructure, including the operating system (OS), communication channels, software, network devices, physical safeguards, and employee psychology, may be carried out by authorized information technology specialists using tactics similar to or identical to those used by a real attacker [4]. An operating system, communication channels, software, network devices, physical defenses, and even the mental health of the staff can all be evaluated during a penetration test, which, for those who are not familiar with the term, is a comprehensive analysis of the information technology systems of the target. This article presents an investigation of vulnerability assessment and penetration testing for chatbots.

19.2 Related Work

You got it right, Z. Oh, Li, *et al.* [5] described the process in detail. With this strategy, code inspection is used in order to find many faults that are occurring with the procedure. According to what is mentioned, the suggested approach is capable of locating each and every vulnerability in the NVD. Uwagboleet Al [6] was the one that devised the attack datasets. The categorization criteria are then used to sort the datasets into the appropriate categories. The use of this classifier helps to make the process of identifying vulnerabilities more straightforward.

In addition, Guojunet *et al.* [7] developed a web crawler for searching the Internet. This application organizes material on the web based on its similarities in an effort to improve web crawling. The methodology, known as term frequency-inverse document frequency (TF-IDF), serves as the basis for this procedure. Medeiros *et al.* [8] presented a technique for analyzing code that was given by the authors. These processes provide the groundwork for the notion of data mining. Adnan Masood and Jim Java [9] have developed innovative strategies for identifying vulnerabilities in web servers via their research.

Iberia Medeiros and NunoNeves have created a novel strategy for locating vulnerabilities in web applications. In addition to this, static analysis and data mining directly from the source code are used. Researchers Marcelo Invert Palma Salas, Paulo LiciodeGeus, and ElianeMartins [10] came to the conclusion that XML injection is a serious vulnerability in all web-based systems after conducting their examination. Even in the present day, XML injection issues continue to plague the vast majority of newly constructed online applications.

To demonstrate the extent to which online application security is included into mitigation measures, Madan *et al.* [11] conducted research on international standards such as ISO-27002, OWASP, COBIT, and PCI/DSS. The purpose of the research was to investigate potential means of protecting web applications against attacks based on injection. The developers claim that almost all international normative rules have a murky definition of what "acceptance" really entails. Despite this, the number of attacks is continuing to climb due to the vulnerabilities of code injection, which is a significant problem. In order to lessen the potential threat to people's safety, prompt action is required to notify engineers and customers about the problem and to encourage them to appropriately implement the rules.

During the whole of the product innovation life cycle, the writers Teodoro and Serrao [12] analyzed the function that value plays as well as the direct repercussions of a lack of protection. Even the most fundamental digital applications can benefit from the automated security tools and methodologies that have been developed by some programmers. These tools and methodologies can be used throughout the software development life cycle to further improve the quality of security offered by even the most fundamental digital applications. They also requested that all teams working to enhance networks give security the highest priority, ensure proper planning and understanding, classify risks, specify security specifications, model threats, carry out audits of architecture configuration, code in a secure manner, and evaluate the network's security after it has been transmitted.

Wang and Reiter [13] developed a method to protect a website against distributed denial of service attacks by making use of the structure of the website in conjunction with the most recent version of the Web Referral Architecture for Privileged Service (WRAPS). By the use of this approach, a legitimate consumer has the opportunity to swiftly and easily get a recommendation URL from a third-party source that has been authorized by the destination site. If the client uses that URL, they will have the option of visiting the website they are trying to reach in a manner that is less susceptible to distributed denial-of-service assaults. The user-facing code or the website's underlying structure would not need any modifications in order for the suggested paradigm to be implemented. Planning for the implementation of the WRAPS architecture was quite thorough. This example illustrates how WRAPS allows genuine users to connect to a site even while the site is under attack from a targeted flooding attack. Moreover, there is no effect on the edge switches that are provided by the site's Internet service provider as a result of this capability. While carrying out a logical attack against a web application, the attackers behind the attack will nearly always coordinate their approach. The established norms and policies are being undermined via the employment of a variety of different techniques. They are different from the typical online offers in a significant manner that sets them apart from others. Both the websites' business logic and the websites themselves run the risk of being exploited by malicious actors who want to advance their own agendas. Websites also run the risk of being utilized by such individuals to further those actors' own agendas.

Liu *et al.* [14] suggested SQL proxy-based blocker (SQLProb) as an alternative to the database driver in SDriver in order to prevent SQL infusion in web applications. This was done in an effort to prevent SQL injection. In order to ensure that the integrity of the question's syntax is maintained, the SQLProb will erase the client input data even if it has already been included into the question. The client's contributions are validated by the enhanced application of the calculation that was inherited by comparing them to the more significant ones. Since the SQLProb does not need any modifications to be made to the application or database, it is an all-encompassing discovery method that avoids the difficulties of polluting, learning, and instrumenting code. In addition, the information approval process does not need a certain level of education or metadata knowledge from applicants. The SQLProb will continue to perform as intended regardless of the programming language that was used to create your web application. Since the framework integrates the intermediate framework, more work must be done in order to secure a web project against SQL injection. This is because the framework integrates the intermediary framework. In a similar vein, it prohibits the use of queries that are correct from a grammatical standpoint but are potentially harmful from other perspectives and might result in SQL injection.

A comprehensive stream-based WS-Security handling framework was built by Gruschka and colleagues [15] to better equip administrators for processing and to strengthen defenses against different types of DoS attacks. The burden that is often associated with a susceptible implementation of WS-Security may be effectively managed by their engine. Its design was developed with the goal of bridging the gap between currently available web services and ones that are more reliable and efficient. To do this, it must permit a diverse array of application scenarios. These use cases include those involving any form of action, amount, or settlement level mark and encryption systems but are not restricted to just those use cases alone.

In order to assist us in gaining a deeper comprehension of the nature of web services metrics, Ladan divides them primarily into two categories: auxiliary metrics and quality metrics. The bulk of the web services metrics has been investigated by the author, who is a specialist in this field. A significant number of these characteristics, including as speed, dependability, scalability, durability, power, exception handling, correctness, openness, accessibility, interoperability, and security, do not meet the minimum requirements.

Hoquea *et al.* conducted an analysis of the activities as well as the potential implications or levels of damage. After that, the author separated the attacks into their respective subcategories. They established a standardized, scientific approach for identifying attack devices in order to better organize security professionals and make their work more efficient. They presented a comprehensive and well-structured analysis of current frameworks and technologies that might be of use to computer system attackers as well as computer system defenders.

In order to aid readers in better comprehending the different tools and frameworks, the writers have offered a review of the pros and downsides associated with each one.

In response to SQL injection and cross-site scripting, BinbinQu *et al.* [16] offered a full overview of the architecture of the framework. The key functionality of the website may be divided down into the following steps: first, utilizing static analysis to create a pollutant dependency diagram for the program; next, showing the diagram. The attack design and the limited state automata are both components of the verification process that determines whether or not the software provides a safe and robust processing of user input. They made use of a computerized recognition framework model that was dependent on loot examination.

19.3   Vulnerability Assessment Tools

The scanning and vulnerability assessment process is a rigorous investigation of computer networks and databases that exposes holes in the security of the system. It is critical to have solutions for network screening and vulnerability assessment because these solutions monitor any known security vulnerabilities and provide risk assessments far in advance of any attempts by bad software or hackers to exploit such gaps. These programs save data about vulnerabilities in networks and other types of systems. Before providing their conclusions, it will evaluate each deficit in the provided services of the target host range, categorize the severity of those deficiencies, and then offer those findings.

There are numerous kinds of these tools, but this study focuses primarily on three of them and they are as follows:

- Acunetix vulnerability scanner [17]
- Greenbone security manager/Open Vulnerability Assessment System (OpenVAS) [18]
- Zaproxy scanner by OWASP [19]
- Burpsuite by Portswigger

19.3.1   OpenVAS

OpenVAS is a vulnerability assessment system that is both open-source and free to use. It was formerly known as Greenbone Security Manager. OpenVAS will do a vulnerability assessment on both the network and the application, and then it will provide a report based on the results of the assessment.

As stated on the OpenVAS website, OpenVAS is a framework of several services and tools offering a vulnerability scanning and vulnerability management solution.

19.3.2   Acunetix Vulnerability Scanner

Acunetix was the initial web security analyzer on the sector and has been continuously improved since 2005. It is a sophisticated, customized tool created by cybersecurity testing experts.

Because of this specialization, it was possible to create a realistic alternative that is more efficient than most other proprietary tools. Acunetix vulnerability scanner is a comprehensive web application security screening solution that can be used independently or as part of a larger environment. It includes built-in known vulnerabilities detection and management as well as numerous functioning with economy software development tools. By incorporating Acunetix into your security plan, you can drastically enhance your security posture and completely eradicate many potential risks at a minimal price. The Figure 19.1 shows about Accunetix scanner scenario, the Figure 19.2 shows about the OWASP scanner and the Figure 19.3 displays about Burpsuite vulnerability scanner respectively.

19.3.3   Zaproxy by OWASP

The Open Web Application Security Project's (OWASP) Zed Attack Proxy (ZAP) is an easy-to-use integrated vulnerability assessment tool that may identify problems with website security. Everyone with an interest in security is welcome to use it despite the fact that it was developed specifically for researchers and professional testers who already have expertise with penetration testing.

Figure 19.1 Accunetix scanner.

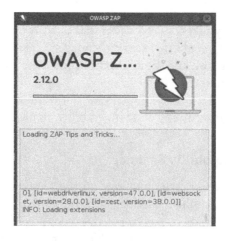

Figure 19.2 OWASP scanner.

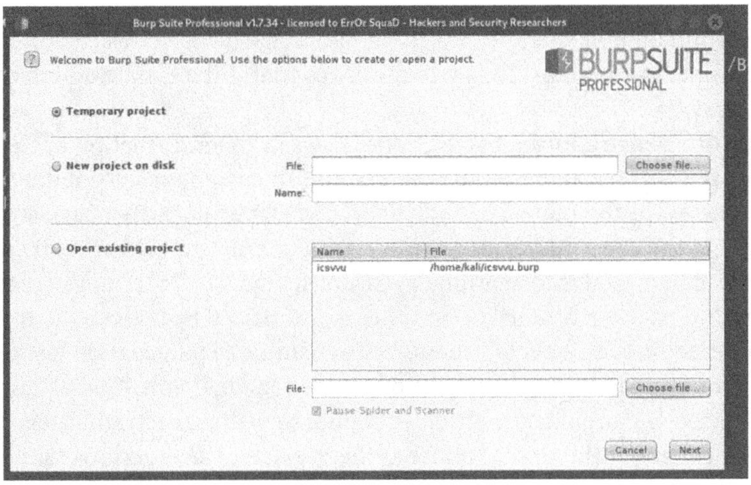

Figure 19.3 Burpsuite vulnerability scanner.

19.3.4   Burpsuite by Portswigger

Burpsuite is a vulnerability scanner that may be used to carry out automated web site scans, during which it can collect data and check the website in question for safety flaws. The improved crawling algorithm included in Burp Scanner is designed to function in a manner that is analogous to how an auditor would construct a model of the target. Handling the complexity of contemporary web applications as well as dynamic content, unreliable connections, and a significant portion of API specifications is one of its key aims. As a result, nearly no scan failures take place, yet the attack surface significantly expands. Burp Scanner is able to expose a broad range of flaws that are present in web apps thanks to the fact that it is regularly updated. Scan inspections may be carried out on an individual basis or in the context of a group, and each inspection can have its own distinct set of parameters preset for it.

19.4   Penetration Testing

The objective of a penetration test is to recreate the conditions of a real-world attack on a computer system or software program by mimicking as many of the variables as is practically achievable. The security of a network may be tested using a technique known as "penetration testing", which entails simulating assaults on the network and carrying them out in order to identify and exploit vulnerabilities in the underlying computer software and operating system. An internal or external tester or auditor will do a penetration test on a system in order to search for vulnerabilities in the system's security (any combination of application, host, or networks). Penetration testing is the process of evaluating the security of an organization's entire information technology infrastructure, including but not limited to the OS, communication channels, software, network devices, physical protections, and employee psychology, in the same manner that an actual attacker would but with the approval of the appropriate authorities and making use of the appropriate expertise.

The targeted outcome of the test and the authorization of the test by higher management are the primary distinguishing characteristics that differentiate a penetration tester from an adversary.

The purpose of a penetration test is to expose flaws in the information or network infrastructure, carry out a threat analysis, and then communicate the results of the test to higher management. Lastly, the top management will take whatever steps are necessary to close the security holes. On the other hand, an adversary will attempt to get through security measures in order to either steal information or disrupt services in order to gain access.

In contrast to an attacker, a penetration tester is authorized by management to examine a system for vulnerabilities and exploit them. Never conduct a penetration test on a network without the prior knowledge and consent of senior management. It is of utmost importance that you keep the organization that is conducting the penetration test informed of your progress throughout the testing phase as the trials may have serious repercussions for the system applications that are currently being tested. These repercussions may include system failure and network latency, both of which may render essential network or system devices inoperable.

A penetration test will expose any weaknesses that may exist in the information technology system of a company. The objective of a penetration test is to determine how realistic the possibility of an attack is. Inadequate and inaccurate setups, known and unknown equipment or software vulnerabilities, command and control flaws in the technique, or practical protection mechanisms are all being intensively examined at this time. It is possible to conduct tests on systems and networks in order to evaluate the efficiency of the security measures currently in place.

The fundamental objective of penetration testing is to locate vulnerabilities in a protected setting so that they may be patched up before they are exploited by malicious actors (hackers, for example). The National Institute of Standards and Technology (NIST) suggests that penetration testing might be helpful in determining how effectively a system can survive real-world assault patterns (800-115).

A metric for determining how challenging it would be for an adversary to effectively compromise the system. further safety measures in the form of enhanced systems for detection. The ability to perceive potential dangers and respond appropriately in protective situations.

19.4.1 Types of Penetration Test

The penetration test may be directed in a variety of ways, depending on the situation. The amount of knowledge that the tester has in relation to the systems that are being checked is the most critical differentiator. The three most prevalent kinds of testing are referred to, respectively, as black box testing, white box testing, and gray box testing.

19.4.1.1   Black Box Testing

Inadequate Exposure to Light Tests: You could also hear the term "penetration testing" used in connection with black-box testing from a greater distance. In the process of testing known as "black box testing", it is believed that the person conducting the test has no prior knowledge of the system that is being reviewed. Before continuing with the investigation, the tester has to establish the placement of the systems and their size. Black box testing simulates a real-world attack as if the testers had no prior knowledge of the architecture that is being evaluated by adhering to a predetermined test plan and employing a wide range of real-world attack techniques (such as social engineering, network inspection, remote access, Trojan horses, and so on). Black box testing is performed by following a predetermined test plan. As an example, it is possible that testers only have access to the website of the firm or to a portion of the network's IP addresses. As a direct result of this, testers make an effort to re-create every conceivable attack scenario, looking for both known and recently unknown vulnerabilities in the network's security. One of the primary goals of a black box pentest is to check the level of security that a company's network has and to determine what preventive actions should be taken against any possible risks. It should come as no surprise that the purpose of this form of examination is to provide the most accurate representation of a penetration test as is humanly feasible. This kind of attack has the distinct advantage of imitating a situation that is quite true to life. The following issues arise while doing a penetration test using a black box. There are certain situations in which it is impossible to optimize the amount of time spent testing. In addition, there may be difficulties with other components of the system that have not yet been rectified.

19.4.1.2   White Box Testing

White box testing is a kind of network security analysis in which the tester already has prior knowledge about the target system, such as its IP addresses and topology. White box testing is also known as an open box test. In this kind of testing, the testers take on the role of an attacker who has access to all of the necessary information about the system being tested, such as the operating system, the network, the runtime environment, and, in some cases, even the passwords. This kind of testing is particularly useful for identifying vulnerabilities in a system that could be exploited by a malicious actor. The tester is supplied with any and all information that can be reasonably acquired about the mechanism being tested so that they may become well versed in the mechanism and articulate the test in words that are as accurate as is feasible given the circumstances.

Yet there are a few negatives to consider: The assault is not realistic since the penetration tester is not in the same position as a hostile actor who is less well informed. The objective of white box testing is to simulate the behavior of an attacker who already has in-depth knowledge of the target organization's network architecture, such as an insider working for the target business. As a result, the primary goal of a white box pentest is to validate the safety of a business's network infrastructure and to successfully minimize risks from inside the organization, such as those posed by an upset employee or customer. Each approach has some advantages as well as disadvantages. When considering having a penetration test done, there is no one best option to choose between white box and black box testing. Both have their advantages and disadvantages. In each scenario, the approach that should be given the highest priority is the one that provides the foundational organizational structure with the greatest return on investment.

19.4.1.3   Gray Box Testing

If both kinds of penetration testing are performed at the same time, the collaborative approach generates data that is relevant from the external as well as the internal security point of view. This kind of testing is referred to as "gray box testing", and it is one sort of assessment. This strategy combines the ease of use of the two approaches that came before it, which is the fundamental benefit of using this approach. By the use of gray box security testing, potential vulnerabilities in an institution's design that may be used by an adversary are found. When money is a problem, gray box testing is preferred because it enables penetration testers to rapidly discover information that is often accessible in the institution's setup. This makes gray box testing an attractive option.

19.4.2   Penetration Testing Phases

The overall process of penetration testing is broken down into a number of separate steps that make up the individual phases. When taken together, the phases or stages that make up a comprehensive infiltration are as follows: Several strategies have adopted a variety of names for the various stages or phases of their processes, but, ultimately, their goals remain the same. In spite of the fact that various procedures may use distinct terminologies, the final result is always the same: an in-depth acquaintance with the various penetration testing methodologies. A testing approach consisting of four stages is recommended by the NIST (800-115).

19.4.2.1   Planning Process

In the planning phase, many tasks are completed, including the establishment of rules, the obtaining and documenting of management authorization, and the outlining of testing objectives. The findings of pentests often come out better when the test administrators devote more time and effort into the preparatory phase. At this juncture, there are no plans to do any genuine testing.

19.4.2.2   Discovery Phase

The discovery phase of the testing technique is comprised of two separate but equally important phases. In this first section, we will talk about the early steps of testing, which will include information gathering and scanning. These stages will be discussed in more detail later. The identification of network ports and services assists in the localization of potential targets. In addition to port scanning and service identification, numerous more approaches are used in order to get as much information as possible on a network in a single go. One may learn a host's name or IP address via a variety of ways, some of which include DNS queries, InterNIC (WHOIS) enquiries, and even listening in on conversations taking place over a network. If you attempt to seek up staff members using the website or database servers of the institution, you will be able to locate their names and email addresses. It is possible to discover system information such as labels and mentions via the use of NetBIOS enumeration, which is often carried out during the course of internal testing, as well as the Network Information System (NIS) (generally during internal tests).

Banner grabbing allows for the collection of a variety of data, including information on software and services (such as version numbers). By resorting to tactics such as garbage diving and physically strolling about the facility, it is possible to learn more about the computer that is the subject of the penetration test and get additional information that may be used during the test.

The second step in the discovery process is called attack surface analysis, and it involves defining the services, software, and system software of scanned hosts to vulnerability databases (which is a method that vulnerability scanners do automatically). This is done on the basis of the experts' own personal knowledge of vulnerabilities. Using either internal or external data sources, such as the National Vulnerability Database, testing teams made up of people are able to manually analyze possible hazards (NVD). While human approaches take longer, they have the potential to identify additional or unclear vulnerabilities that algorithmic scanners may miss.

19.4.2.3   Attack Phase

An attack must be carried out in a way that is useable for any penetration test to be considered successful. At the attack stage, your goal is to find a way to take advantage of the weaknesses you have found. In the event that the attack is successful, an exploited security vulnerability will be discovered, and steps will be identified to reduce the risk that will be caused by the exploit. After an exploit has been successfully carried out, an attacker will not often be provided the maximum possible degree of access to the target system. They may instead cause the targeted network's security to deteriorate or may direct testers to learn new information about the network and the possible flaws it may have. In this situation, more review and testing are necessary to determine the actual degree of threat that is presented to the network—for example, determining the types of information that can be added, deleted, or tampered with is one of the steps that must be taken. If the tester is unable to successfully exploit a specific vulnerability in the system, they may proceed to examine other vulnerabilities in the system. If testers are successful in circumventing security measures, they will be able to integrate supplementary tools into the system or network being tested in order to conduct a more thorough analysis of either. By using these technologies, one is able to not only get access to internal and external systems and resources but also gather information on the network or the organization itself. In order to determine how far an attacker may potentially go, a penetration test should evaluate and test a number of different ways. Although the security vulnerabilities discovery phase of testing just searches for the possibility of a weakness, the attack phase of testing actually exploits the vulnerability to demonstrate that it does, in fact, exist. The categories that are responsible for the great majority of vulnerabilities that are evaluated during penetration testing are discussed in the following subsections.

19.4.2.4   Reporting Phase

With the other three stages of the testing procedure, the phase that focuses on reporting results also takes place concurrently. At the phase of planning, we devise the method that will be used to carry out assessments. Written records are often kept, regardless of whether the process is in the discovery or attack stage, and periodic reports are given to the network administrator and/or supervisors. Typically, a report that details the security flaws, provides a grade, and offers advice on how to solve the concerns is not created until the very end of the process.

19.5   Vulnerabilities in Chatbot

SQL injection, cross-site scripting, slow HTTP denial of service attack, documentation file, and HTML form without CSRF protection are common vulnerabilities in chatbot. It is shown in Figure 19.4 below.

The term "SQL injection attack" refers to a form of "code injection attack" that makes use of the weaknesses exhibited by these interfaces. SQL injection allows attackers to get access to sensitive information, achieve a higher degree of privilege, modify data in the database, create a denial of service, and even remotely transmit and install malicious codes. All of these goals may be accomplished by an attacker. Blind SQL injection, injection based on query failures, injection through a saved procedure, and injection through a stored procedure are all examples of possible types of SQL injection.

Client Script, especially JavaScript, is a language that may be used to enhance websites and apps that run on the web. An adversary can take full control of a victim's session if the adversary inserts a malicious code into a request for a web page made by a user who is authorized to make the request. This form of attack is known as cross-site scripting since the malicious script came from another website and was injected into the target website (XSS). These assaults are carried out by taking advantage of vulnerabilities that are present in widely used Internet applications. In order for websites to be considered interactive, the input of the user is required. If the online program uses the input to build the answer web page, then it might be vulnerable to attack since the attacker would be able to exploit any flaws or vulnerabilities that may exist in the application's code. This is especially possible in the event that the application does not effectively sanitize the inputs, leaving them open to the possibility of being abused.

Because cross-site scripting [20] is a form of exploitation rather than just a vulnerability that may be exploited, phishing attacks, which are false attempts to obtain information, are

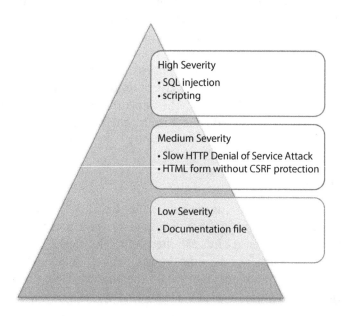

Figure 19.4 Vulnerabilities in chatbot.

very effective. During an attack of this kind, information is often gathered through the use of a hyperlink that contains malicious content. The web application, once it has received the data, will then construct an output page for the user, which will contain the malicious data that was given to it. If information that is stored in user cookies is revealed through an attack known as cross-site scripting, then there is a potential for a serious breach of security and confidentiality. An adversary now has the capability of stealing sensitive session data such as user IDs, passwords, and credit card numbers. By changing the user's settings in this manner, attackers have the ability to take control of the user's account, steal cookies, or install harmful advertisements. When other vulnerabilities are combined with cross-site scripting, it is possible for an arbitrary code to be executed on the machine of the victim. A cross-site scripting attack can be triggered in two different ways: by malicious pages or by parameter values. Cross-site scripting can be identified with a high degree of accuracy if the source of the attack, when it occurred, and the different kinds of signatures used are known. Cross-site scripting is a type of attack in which the attacker gets around security measures by exploiting a vulnerability in the scripting language that enables remote code execution. This type of attack is also known as XSS. A significant number of intrusion protection systems are incapable of detecting even the most fundamental types of assault, such as cross-site scripting. Many people who work in the security industry consider it to be only a moderate risk.

SQL injection [21] must exploit security vulnerabilities in the software. Attackers exploit the web servers' vulnerabilities and inject a malicious code to dodge login and gain unauthorized access to the database because the hacker's target is SQL servers that are running vulnerable database applications. It is generally launched by the botnets (infected computers with malicious software in the private networked), also called zombie army. If an attacker is successful, then he/she can remotely execute system commands, retrieve confidential data, manipulate the database contents, and also take control of the web server. The botnets are used in the form of thousands of bots that are equipped with an SQL injection kit to fire an SQL injection attack. SQL injection by botnets has infected millions of URLs at different web sites all around the world. In the cloud computing environment, retailers host their products and sell them online using SaaS applications.

The attacker [22–25] must convince the victim to provide malicious [26–28] input content or use an XSS vulnerability [29, 30]. The attacker [31, 32] embeds harmful code in a hyperlink that lures the victim [33, 34] into clicking in order to access the chatbot frontend. The webpage has harmful code inserted into it. Without the victim even realising it, it reads the victim's cookies and transmits them to the attacker. These cookies [35] and [36] can be used by the attacker to access the victim's account on the business website. By adding small, if possible, imperceptible modifications (noise) to the classifier input data, an adversarial [37, 38] approach seeks to uncover blind spots in the classifier [39, 40]. A well-known example is to introduce minute noise that is invisible to the human eye in order to misclassify a picture by an image classifier.

19.6   Conclusion

It is possible to compromise chatbots by using widespread vulnerabilities and exploits, such as cross-site scripting and SQL injections. In light of these considerations, it is possible that chatbots may also be the target of attacks one day. Thus, it is essential, while doing an analysis of chatbots, to look for vulnerabilities in their security measures. The process of vulnerability scanning and assessment entails conducting an exhaustive analysis of computer networks and the components that compose them. The purpose of this inquiry is to find defensive measures against unauthorized entrance and assess how effectively they operate. The fundamental objective of a penetration test is to uncover vulnerabilities in a system that an attacker might exploit in a controlled setting so that such vulnerabilities may be corrected before they are put into use. In addition, doing penetration testing may be of use in determining how well the system can withstand genuine assaults. The study on vulnerability assessment and penetration testing for chatbot is covered in this article.

References

1. Hill, J., Ford, W.R., Farreras, I.G., Real conversations with artificial intelligence: A comparison between human–human online conversations and human–chatbot conversations. *Comput. Hum. Behav.*, 49, 245–250, 2015.

2. Adiwardana, D., Luong, M.T., So David, R. *et al.*, Towards a human-like open-domain chatbot, 2020, arXiv preprint arXiv:2001.09977.

3. Nuruzzaman, M. and Hussain, O.K., A survey on chatbot implementation in customer service industry through deep neural networks. Paper Presented at: *Proceedings of the 2018 IEEE 15th International Conference on e-Business Engineering (ICEBE)*, China, IEEE, pp. 54–61, 2018.

4. Shi, W., Liu, D., Yang, J., Zhang, J., Wen, S., Su, J., Social Bots' sentiment engagement in health emergencies: A topic-based analysis of the COVID-19 pandemic discussions on twitter. *Int. J. Environ. Res. Public Health*, 17, 22, 8701, 2020.

5. Li, Z. *et al.*, VulPecker: An automated vulnerability detection system based on code similarity analysis. *ACM, Proc. of the 32 Annual Conference on Computer Security Applications*, p. 201213, 2016.

6. Uwagbole, S.O., Buchanan, W.J., Fan, L., Applied machine learning predictive analytics to SQL injection attack detection and prevention. *IEEE, Symposium on Integrated Network and Service Management (IM)*, IFIP/IEEE, pp. 1087–1090, 2017.

7. Guojun, Z. *et al.*, Design and application of intelligent dynamic crawler for web data mining, in: *Automation (YAC), 2017 32nd Youth Academic Annual Conference of Chinese Association*, IEEE, pp. 1098–1105, 2017.

8. Medeiros, I., Neves, N., Correia, M., Detecting and removing web application vulnerabilities with static analysis and data mining. *IEEE Trans. Reliab.*, 65, 1, 54–69, 2016.

9. Masood, A. and Java, J., Static analysis for web service security – Tools & techniques for a secure development life cycle. *International Symposium on Technologies for Homeland Security*, pp. 1–6, 2015.

10. Salas, M.I.P., de Geus, P.L., Martins, E., Security testing methodology for evaluation of web services robustness - case: XML injection. *IEEE World Congress on Services*, pp. 303–310, 2015.

11. Madan, S., Security standards perspective to fortify web database applications from code injection attacks. *International Conference on Intelligent Systems, Modelling and Simulation*, pp. 226–233, 2010.

12. Teodoro, N. and Serrao, C., Web application security: Improving critical web-based applications quality through in-depth security analysis, in: *International Conference on Information Society (i- Society)*, pp. 457–462, 2011.

13. Wang, X. and Reiter, M.K., Using web-referral architectures to mitigate denial-of-service threats. *J. IEEE Trans. Dependable Secure Comput.*, 7, 2, 203–216, 2010.

14. Liu, A., Yuan, Y., Wijesekera, D., Stavrou, A., SQLProb: A proxybased architecture towards preventing SQL injection attacks, in: *Proceedings ACM Symposium on Applied Computing (SAC'09)*, pp. 2054–2061, 2009.

15. Gruschka, N., Jensen, M., Lo Iacono, L., Luttenberger, Server-side streaming processing of WS-security. *IEEE Trans. Serv. Comput.*, 4, 4, 272–285, 2011.

16. Qu, B., Liang, B., Jiang, S., Ye, C., Design of automatic vulnerability detection system for web application program. *Proceeding of Fourth IEEE International Conference on Software Engineering and Service Science (ICSESS)*, pp. 89–92, 2013.

17. https://www.openvas.org/.

18. https://www.acunetix.com/vulnerability-scanner/.

19. https://www.zaproxy.org/.

20. Singh, M., Singh, P., Kumar, P., An analytical study on cross-site scripting. *2020 International Conference on Computer Science, Engineering and Applications (ICCSEA)*, Gunupur, India, pp. 1–6, 2020, doi: 10.1109/ICCSEA49143.2020.9132894.

21. Hlaing, Z.C.S.S. and Khaing, M., A detection and prevention technique on SQL injection attacks. *2020 IEEE Conference on Computer Applications (ICCA)*, Yangon, Myanmar, pp. 1–6, 2020, doi: 10.1109/ICCA49400.2020.9022833.

22. Mahor, V., Bijrothiya, S., Rawat, R., Kumar, A., Garg, B., Pachlasiya, K., IoT and artificial intelligence techniques for public safety and security, in: *Smart Urban Computing Applications*, p. 111, 2023.

23. Mahor, V., Pachlasiya, K., Garg, B., Chouhan, M., Telang, S., Rawat, R., Mobile operating system (Android) vulnerability analysis using machine learning, in: *Proceedings of International Conference on Network Security and Blockchain Technology: ICNSBT 2021*, pp. 159–169, Springer Nature Singapore, Singapore, 2022, June.

24. Rawat, R., Garg, B., Pachlasiya, K., Mahor, V., Telang, S., Chouhan, M., Mishra, R., SCNTA: Monitoring of network availability and activity for identification of anomalies using machine learning approaches. *Int. J. Inf. Technol. Web Eng. (IJITWE)*, 17, 1, 1–19, 2022.

25. Rawat, R., Rimal, Y.N., William, P., Dahima, S., Gupta, S., Sankaran, K.S., Malware threat affecting financial organization analysis using machine learning approach. *Int. J. Inf. Technol. Web Eng. (IJITWE)*, 17, 1, 1–20, 2022.

26. Rawat, R., Mahor, V., Chouhan, M., Pachlasiya, K., Telang, S., Garg, B., Systematic literature review (SLR) on social media and the digital transformation of drug trafficking on darkweb, in: *International Conference on Network Security and Blockchain Technology*, pp. 181–205, Springer, Singapore, 2022.

27. Rawat, R., Ayodele Oki, O., Sankaran, S., Florez, H., Ajagbe, S.A., Techniques for predicting dark web events focused on the delivery of illicit products and ordered crime. *Int. J. Electr. Comput. Eng. (IJECE)*, 13, 5, 5354–5365, Oct. 2023, doi: 10.11591/ijece.v13i5.pp5354-5365.

28. Rawat, R., Garg, B., Mahor, V., Telang, S., Pachlasiya, K., Chouhan, M., Organ trafficking on the dark web—The data security and privacy concern in healthcare systems, in: *Internet of Healthcare Things: Machine Learning for Security and Privacy*, pp. 189–216, 2022.

29. Vyas, P., Vyas, G., Chauhan, A., Rawat, R., Telang, S., Gottumukkala, M., Anonymous trading on the dark online marketplace: An exploratory study, in: *Using Computational Intelligence for the Dark Web and Illicit Behavior Detection*, pp. 272–289, IGI Global, 2022.

30. Rawat, R., Oki, O.A., Sankaran, K.S., Olasupo, O., Ebong, G.N., Ajagbe, S.A., A new solution for cyber security in big data using machine learning approach, in: *Mobile Computing and Sustainable Informatics: Proceedings of ICMCSI 2023*, pp. 495–505, Springer Nature Singapore, Singapore, 2023.

31. Rawat, R., Chakrawarti, R.K., Raj, A., Mani, G., Chidambarathanu, K., Bhardwaj, R., Association rule learning for threat analysis using traffic analysis and packet filtering approach. *Int. J. Inf. Technol.*, 1–11, 2023.

32. Rawat, R., Logical concept mapping and social media analytics relating to cyber criminal activities for ontology creation. *Int. J. Inf. Technol.*, 15, 2, 893–903, 2023.

33. Rawat, R., Mahor, V., Álvarez, J.D., Ch, F., Cognitive systems for dark web cyber delinquent association malignant data crawling: A review, in: *Handbook of Research on War Policies, Strategies, and Cyber Wars*, pp. 45–63, 2023.

34. Rawat, R., Chakrawarti, R.K., Vyas, P., Gonzáles, J.L.A., Sikarwar, R., Bhardwaj, R., Intelligent fog computing surveillance system for crime and vulnerability identification and tracing. *Int. J. Inf. Secur. Priv. (IJISP)*, 17, 1, 1–25, 2023.

35. Rawat, R., Sowjanya, A.M., Patel, S.I., Jaiswal, V., Khan, I., Balaram, A. (Eds.), *Using Machine Intelligence: Autonomous Vehicles Volume 1*, John Wiley & Sons, 2022.

36. Rawat, R., Mahor, V., Díaz-Álvarez, J., Chávez, F., Rooted learning model at fog computing analysis for crime incident surveillance, in: *2022 International Conference on Smart Generation Computing, Communication and Networking (SMART GENCON)*, pp. 1–9, IEEE, 2022, December.

37. Rawat, R. and Shrivastav, S.K., SQL injection attack detection using SVM. *Int. J. Comput. Appl.*, 42, 13, 1–4, 2012.

38. Rawat, R., Bhardwaj, P., Kaur, U., Telang, S., Chouhan, M., Sankaran, K.S., *Smart vehicles for communication, volume 2*, John Wiley & Sons, 2023.

39. Mahor, V., Garg, B., Telang, S., Pachlasiya, K., Chouhan, M., Rawat, R., Cyber threat phylogeny assessment and vulnerabilities representation at thermal power station, in: *Proceedings of International Conference on Network Security and Blockchain Technology: ICNSBT 2021*, pp. 28–39, Springer Nature Singapore, Singapore, 2022, June.

40. Rawat, R., Gupta, S., Sivaranjani, S., Cu, O.K., Kuliha, M., Sankaran, K.S., Malevolent information crawling mechanism for forming structured illegal organisations in hidden networks. *Int. J. Cyber Warf. Terror. (IJCWT)*, 12, 1, 1–14, 2022.

20

ChatBot-Based Next-Generation Intrusion Detection System

College of Management and Design, Ming Chi University of Technology, New Taipei City, Taiwan, Republic of China (ROC)

Abstract

An intrusion detection system, often known as IDS, is primarily used to gather and analyze data regarding security events that occur in computer systems and networks. Its subsequent purpose is to either prevent these events from happening or notify them to the administrator of the system. As a result of the increasing number of attacks carried out by attackers, the users' level of mistrust on the Internet has increased. Attacks that cause denial of service are a major violation of security. This article presents a particle swarm optimization and AdaBoost-based intrusion detection system. In this system, chatbot receives network traffic as input, and features of input dataset are selected using particle swarm optimization algorithm. A classification model is trained and tested. AdaBoost, KNN, and naïve Bayes algorithm are used to classify and detect malware-related records. NSL KDD dataset is used in the experimental work. PSO-AdaBoost achieves the highest accuracy, precision, and recall for intrusion detection and classification. The output of a chatbot is a language that is either normal or benign.

Keywords: Chatbot, intrusion detection, particle swarm optimization, feature selection, machine learning, AdaBoost

20.1   Introduction

Protecting sensitive data, ensuring the continued dependability of essential systems, and preventing unauthorized access to systems and data are the primary objectives of computer security [1]. An unwarranted entry into a computer system, network, or other service is referred to as an intrusion [2]. An intrusion might refer to any concerted attempt to achieve such access. An Intrusion Detection System, often known as an IDS, is primarily used to gather and analyze data regarding security events that occur in computer systems and networks. Its subsequent purpose is to either prevent these events from happening or notify them to the administrator of the system. As a result of the increasing number of attacks

Email: tzuchiachen1688@gmail.com; ORCID: 0000-0002-2942-7839

Romil Rawat, Rajesh Kumar Chakrawarti, Sanjaya Kumar Sarangi, Piyush Vyas, Mary Sowjanya Alamanda, Kotagiri Srividya and Krishnan Sakthidasan Sankaran (eds.) Conversational Artificial Intelligence, (319–334) © 2024 Scrivener Publishing LLC

carried out by attackers, users' level of mistrust on the Internet has increased. Attacks that cause denial of service are a major violation of security (DoS).

An intrusion detection system, also known as an IDS, is a type of network monitoring software that keeps tabs on and analyzes data from a company's computer networks and traffic in order to spot any signs of malicious incursion, regardless of whether it originates from the outside or from within the company's own walls. In most contexts, the term "burglar alarm" may be interchangeably used with "intrusion detection device"—for example, a potential thief is discouraged from stealing a car by the locking system.

However, if the lock on the vehicle is broken and the thief still attempts to take it, the burglar alarm will go off and the owner will be notified. In a similar manner, an intrusion detection system (IDS) serves as a warning in a computer system or network to notify and report on any potentially hazardous behavior.

There are a select few botnets that stand out from the others when it comes to performing distributed denial of service attacks. An attack that is known as a distributed denial of service, or DDoS, is one in which users from all over the world collaborate in an effort to flood a certain website or service with an excessive amount of traffic in order to disrupt its normal operation. Hackers may simply connect unprotected Internet of Things devices to a botnet and use them to launch attacks on other websites if they did not have the correct login and password combination.

Because of the infiltration, there is a possibility that the targeted system's availability, security, and privacy will all be compromised. When malevolent users gain access to a computer system, the system's defenses are immediately compromised. Network and host intrusions are the two most common kinds of security breaches. Any attempt to obtain unauthorized entrance into the system, modify or remove data, or render the host unreliable or unworkable is considered an intrusion. Threats such as Trojan horses, viruses, and worms together have the potential to compromise a system in a number of ways, including the unauthorized use of login credentials, the modification of sensitive files, the mutation of system call parameters, the elevation of privileges, and the manipulation of the file system.

A network intrusion occurs when malicious packets are allowed to enter a network for the purpose of launching a denial of service (DOS) attack or breaking into machines. An effort to prohibit authorized users from accessing their computers is an example of a denial-of-service attack, abbreviated as DoS. This category encompasses a wide variety of attacks, some of which include the "ping of death" (POD), an attack on land and water. In a cooperative environment, symptoms of an intrusion include strange results when implementing various user instructions, unanticipated system crashes, changes to the kernel's data structures, and abnormally poor network performance, such as when opening webpages or files. Other symptoms include changes to the kernel's data structures, such as the addition of new data fields. Computer systems have been safeguarded using intrusion prevention measures such as user authentication (passwords or biometrics), preventing programming errors, and encrypting critical data. This protection serves as the first line of defense against potential cyber attacks. For this reason, every computer system has to have an extra layer of defense in the form of intrusion detection so that it can protect itself from potential threats. The practice of maintaining a watchful eye on a system or network in order to identify any intrusions, suspicious actions, or tampering with data that has been saved is what this phrase refers to. The ability to detect intrusion is dependent on a few key components, including models that classify "legitimate" or "normal" behavior of resources—techniques that compare real system activities to the existing models and then differentiate "abnormal" or "invasive" behavior—and, of course, the resources themselves [3].

The three categories of "supervised", "unsupervised", and "semi-supervised" machine learning techniques are determined by using training data to differentiate between the candidates. Unsupervised learning is a kind of machine learning in which the input samples are not previously labeled with a preset class. This type of learning is also known as "learning in the dark". A dataset consisting of cases that have been given labels is required in order to conduct supervised learning. Although there is a large amount of network and host data, it would be prohibitively expensive to have it tagged by a professional. Semi-supervised learning methods may also make use of unlabeled instances in addition to the labeled ones that are often used in these methods. Semi-supervised learning methods need access to just a small number of labels in order to make effective use of the huge volumes of unlabeled data that are available. The test pattern is subsequently categorized by making use of the trained classifier or model that was developed, both of which take into consideration the features that were prioritized during the training process. Automatic learning methods make it possible for machine learning-based intrusion detection systems, also known as ML-IDSs, to quickly identify attacks with far less involvement from human operators. As a result of this, the approach is becoming more significant in the field of computer security. A dataset is essential for developing a classification model via the use of machine learning (ML) techniques. Constructing classifiers and testing them on a broad range of datasets is both possible and recommended. The KDD99 database, the DARPA 1998/1999 database, and the ISCX 2012 IDS dataset are some of the most well-known and frequently used datasets for intrusion detection [4].

This article presents a particle swarm optimization and AdaBoost-based intrusion detection system. In this system, features of input dataset are selected using particle swarm optimization algorithm. The classification model is trained and tested. AdaBoost, KNN, and naïve Bayes algorithm are used to classify and detect malware-related records. NSL KDD dataset is used in the experimental work. PSO-AdaBoost is achieving highest accuracy, precision, and recall for intrusion detection and classification.

20.2 Literature Survey

20.2.1 Review of Optimization Algorithms for IDS

The cloud-based intrusion detection model that Sun *et al.* developed makes use of an improved version of the back propagation (BP) algorithm [5]. This model is created by combining the BP algorithm's powers of doing local searches with the PSO algorithm's capabilities of performing global optimizations. We present a PSO method as a means of optimizing the value of the initial weight and threshold of BP within the context of the momentum and adaptive learning rate approach. This helps to ensure that the BP does not fall into a local optimum and that its speed of network convergence is increased to the greatest possible extent. The results of the studies demonstrate that the recommended model has a better average detection rate, and it is possible to use it in order to identify intrusions in the cloud.

Seth *et al.* have developed a method for the network intrusion detection system that makes use of key feature selection based on binary Grey Wolf Optimization (GWO) and a neural network classifier [6]. The installation of the IDS may be carried out at any important node in the network if desired. It is possible to utilize GWO to remove unnecessary features from the dataset, which, in turn, decreases the total size of the dataset, which in turn reduces the amount of time needed to train the classifier and the amount of space required to keep the dataset. When doing simulations using the NSL-KDD dataset, we discover that utilizing a more condensed feature set results in an improvement in the accuracy of the intrusion detection approach.

In 2016, Jaiswal *et al.* [7] developed an enhanced method of intrusion detection by using a data mining approach. The user's activities are monitored by the intrusion detection system, which then notifies the administrator of any potentially harmful behavior. In this experiment, we make use of the KDD Cup dataset to categorize the various forms of invasion, and we train a KNN classifier to find invaders by using the ACO method. The correctness of simulated data is evaluated, along with a performance statistic known as the false alarm rate (FAR). The outputs of this methodology are more exact when compared with the way that is being used at the moment.

Principal component analysis was used by Ahmad *et al.* [8] in order to limit down the characteristics that should be used. The features were first projected into an eigen space, and, after that, the ones whose deviations were found to be the greatest were selected for further study. It is possible that the features with the highest eigen value would not provide the classifier the best sensitivity, but those characteristics will still be employed anyhow (i.e., eigen values). It is not sufficient to just choose the features that have the highest eigen values; rather, an optimization technique is required to discover which features, after being transformed, retain the greatest number of their original properties. This is because there is an element of optimization involved in selecting the collection of converted characteristics that most effectively differentiates the object under consideration. Studies have been conducted using the evolutionary optimization approach known as the genetic algorithm (GA), with the goal of determining which characteristics may be optimized for greater differentiation. Another form of optimization, known as particle swarm optimization or PSO for short, draws its motivation from research on the behavior of animals and birds. PSO may be beneficial in some circumstances to a larger degree than GA, maybe in certain cases.

Tabatabaefar *et al.* [9] suggest the creation of two sets of antibodies, one positive and one negative, to identify normal and assault samples, respectively, in their proposal for an AIS-based intrusion detection system. These antibodies would be used to differentiate between the two types of samples. The ideas of positive selection and negative selection are used in this system, with the end goal of facilitating the production of primary detectors. As a consequence of this, training the more modern detectors with the more conventional PSO can result in a higher detection rate. Antibody radii are likewise constantly established by the algorithms that are responsible for their development and training. The results of a simulation indicate that the recently created approach obtains a true positive rate of 99.1% while only producing a false positive rate of 1.9% of the time.

By making use of the periodicity, unpredictability, and sensitivity of the chaos operator to the initial conditions, the authors Yang *et al.* [10] create an improved version of the particle swarm optimization IPSO technique. Particle swarm optimization (PSO) is used to optimize the value of the RBF kernel function parameter g as well as the penalty factor C.

This helps to increase convergence and accuracy. Experiments have demonstrated that the IPSO-SVM intrusion detection model is superior to both the PSO-SVM and the GA-SVM models in terms of its ability to identify intrusions. This argument is driven home by the higher performance of IPSO-superiority SVMs over both of these models.

Hosseini *et al.* [11] discuss the significance of a DoS attack intrusion detection system that is based on support vector regression and how it can be enhanced by combining two additional methods, such as an ant colony and a firefly. They explain how this can be accomplished. Hosseini and colleagues discuss, among other things, the significance of using an intrusion detection system for DoS attacks that is based on support vector regression (2015). The firefly technique utilizes a local search to move the ants, and its overall effectiveness may be enhanced by removing random variables from the equation. Utilizing the KDD Cup 99 evaluation framework allowed for the intrusion detection system to be put through its paces and given a thorough assessment. Only nine of the original 41 available homes have been selected as potential rentals by our team. The recommended approach achieves an accuracy of 99.57% and a detection error rate of only 0.0064%.

Kulshestha *et al.* [12] provide an innovative method that may be used to identify which feature subset and classifier performs the best with a particular dataset. If the issue was significant enough, it would be imperative to look for a remedy across a very wide scope of territory. When you take into consideration the assertion made before this one, it appears likely that this is the case. The search made use of a powerful meta-heuristic technique called the cuckoo search CS method in order to select a feature subset and classifier that minimizes the dimensionality of the feature vector as well as the rate of classification error. This was done in order to find the optimal solution. This was done so that we could determine which feature subset and classifier would be most effective for the task at hand. The validity and the accuracy of the CSFCS have been proven through the use of a large number of gold-standard datasets originating from a variety of fields. This challenge requires CS in the order to boost classification accuracy while using a smaller set of features, and it has been established that CSFCS is a flexible and realizable method for synthesizing CS. Hence, this task necessitates the use of CS. It has been established that CSFCS has the potential to be employed as a practical approach to the generation of CS. This is due to the fact that, in contrast to alternatives with more features, CSFCS may be simply modified to fulfil individualized needs.

20.2.2   Review of Classification Methods for IDS

To address both the unique characteristics of cloud computing and the unique security requirements of cloud computing, Zhao *et al.* [15] have developed a novel intrusion detection technique based on augmented K-means. This innovation can be used to create a clustering algorithm in addition to a distributed intrusion detection method. It can detect both known and unknown attacks against cloud infrastructures. The simulation results suggest that this approach could speed up intrusion detection while concurrently decreasing the rates of false positives and false negatives.

Chen *et al.* [14] introduced an approach that combines rough sets with data mining as a way to improve the detection efficacy of intrusion detection while simultaneously reducing the number of false alarms. This method was compared with established methods of intrusion detection. The first phase is the organization of the data that was gathered, followed by the normalization of the values of the collected variables, and then the processing of the nominal variables in a discrete way. In a manner similar to that in which the attributes of the property up and down approximation set may be employed in the Pawlak attribute weight rough set technique to conduct an attribute reduction on the final result set, the final result set will be described here. The generation of high-confidence association rules, which are then imported into the rule set once attribute reduction has been completed, is made possible thanks to this process. Experiments show that the detection technique that makes use of both rough sets and data mining results in an improvement of around 20% in terms of the efficiency of detection. The rate at which invasions are uncovered accelerates almost linearly in proportion to the overall number of invasions that have occurred.

Jing *et al.* [15] have developed and implemented similar approaches for detecting intrusions into a network. They do this by using a limited Boltzmann machine that is trained with the use of a relevant deep learning model. In this study, we analyzed past research in the area to determine whether or not it would be feasible to use deep learning to network IDS. The technology that is used to identify intrusions into networks is now undergoing development with the assistance of relevance depth learning in order to accomplish greater levels of detection accuracy. The findings of the simulation show that the approach to network intrusion detection that relies on relevance deep learning performs better, both in terms of the average detection rate and the average false detection rate for unknown intrusions and assaults. Specifically, the average detection rate for unknown intrusions and assaults is lower. The results of the experiments support the claims made about the resilience and effectiveness of the recently proposed approach.

Yuan *et al.* [16] used the two layers multi-class detection (TLMD) technique to detect intrusions in adaptive networks. It improves both the detection rate and the false alarm rate when used in conjunction with the C5.0 approach and the naive Bayes algorithm. The TLMD approach takes care of all the one-of-a-kind problems that arise in data mining. One of these problems is dealing with contiguous characteristics, which arises alongside the need to lessen noise in the training dataset. The procedure is capable of handling this intricate scenario. Based on the detection rate, accuracy, and false alarm rate on the KDD Cup99 benchmark dataset for intrusion detection, we evaluate the state-of-the-art algorithms against the recently created TLMD strategy. The novel TLMD technique appears to have a low false alarm rate and a high detection rate, even when applied to an unbalanced dataset. The dataset is unbalanced, but this still holds true. The conclusion is supported by all available evidence.

A risk-based warning prioritizing technique was employed by Chakir *et al.* [17] for the research that they conducted. The intensity of the warning may be determined by the model based on decision factors such as priority, reliability, and asset value indicators. This improves snort's ability to detect intrusions and presents the security administrator with only those alerts that pose a genuine risk, reducing both the number of false positives and the amount of time spent analyzing them. The goal is to determine the significance of individual IDS alerts in terms of the overall security of an information system. To conduct an evaluation of the model, we make use of the pattern-matching method and the KDD Cup 99 Dataset.

Gaikwad *et al.* [18] have developed a brand-new intrusion detection strategy by making use of a technique called ensemble machine learning. It is helpful to employ the Bagging approach of ensembles while developing IDS. This technique utilizes REP Tree as the foundation class. The accuracy of classification may be improved while simultaneously lowering the number of false positives if the proper attributes from the NSL KDD dataset are chosen. When evaluating the efficacy of the novel ensemble technique, classification accuracy, the amount of time spent developing the model, and the total number of false positives are taken into consideration. Experiments show that the Bagging ensemble achieves the maximum level of classification accuracy when working with a REP Tree base class. Creating the model in a shorter amount of time is one of the possible benefits that may be gained by using the bagging approach. The false positive rate that is generated by the ensemble approach is amazingly low in compared with that produced by other machine learning methods.

Research on a deep neural network intrusion detection system was carried out by Kim *et al.* [19] using the KDD Cup 99 dataset, which was produced by the whole AI community for use in the competition (DNN IDS). This was done due to the ever-changing nature of how network attacks are carried out. The data must first be prepared by undergoing transformation and normalization before it can be input into the DNN model. In the preprocessing step, the data is first cleaned and then processed. Then, in the stage called "learning model production", the DNN technique is used on the data to create the model. In the last step, the accuracy of the model is tested using the whole dataset from the KDD Cup 99. In the end, the accuracy, detection rate, and false alarm rate were calculated in order to determine the detection effectiveness of the DNN model, which has been demonstrated to deliver positive results in the field of intrusion detection. This was done so that the detection effectiveness could be determined.

20.3   Methodology

This section presents a particle swarm optimization and AdaBoost-based intrusion detection system. In this system, chatbot receives network traffic as input, and features of input dataset are selected using particle swarm optimization algorithm. The classification model is trained and tested. The Figure 20.1 shows about the Chatbot-based next generation intrusion detection system and the Figure 20.2 displays NSL KDD dataset distribution. AdaBoost, KNN, and naïve Bayes algorithm are used to classify and detect malware-related records. NSL KDD dataset is used in the experimental work. PSO-AdaBoost is achieving highest accuracy, precision, and recall for intrusion detection and classification. The output of chatbot is a language that is either normal or benign.

PSO [20] is an effective and efficient global optimization algorithm which is broadly utilized to pattern recognition and non-linear function optimization neural network training. During the process of searching for particles, it consecutively adjusts its location towards global optimum in accordance with two factors: the best position identified by itself is specified by Pi = (pi1, pi2, ..., piD) and that encountered by complete swarm (gbest) is denoted as Pg = (pg1, pg2, ..., pgD). Its velocity at t-th iteration is specified using V (t)I = (vi1, vi2, ..., viD). The position at the next iteration is evaluated in accordance with equations. If an element of velocities exceeds the threshold or it is set equal to the corresponding threshold, PSO computes from the scenario and utilizes it to solve the optimization crises.

Naive Bayes [21] classifiers are statistical classifiers that are based on Bayes theory with the assumption of class conditional independence. This assumption states that the impact

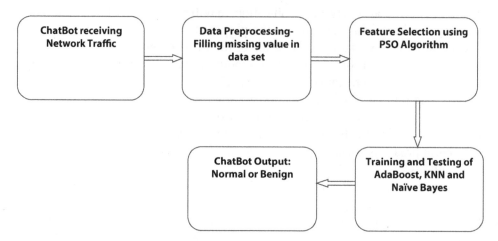

Figure 20.1 Chatbot-based next generation intrusion detection system.

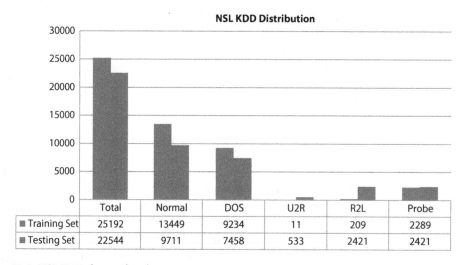

	Total	Normal	DOS	U2R	R2L	Probe
■ Training Set	25192	13449	9234	11	209	2289
■ Testing Set	22544	9711	7458	533	2421	2421

Figure 20.2 NSL KDD dataset distribution.

of a feature's value on the class supplied is unrelated to the feature values of other features. Naive Bayes classifiers are often used in machine learning and data mining applications. It does this by increasing categorization with the individual probabilities of each attribute–value combination, which is a probabilistic strategy. It is possible for the SL system to be used to successfully teach a wide variety of difficult real-world issues, particularly those that are amenable to computer-based diagnostic procedures. We do not need to create a whole covariance matrix in order to compute the variances of the characteristics for each class since they are conditionally independent of one another. In the naive Bayes classifier, P represents the probability, C' stands for the class variable, F stands for the feature variables, and the denominator does not depend on C' in any way. A Bayesian network, sometimes called a belief network, is a graphical representation (statistical model) that makes use of a directed acyclic graph to characterize a collection of random variables and their conditional relationships. This kind of network is also known as a belief network (DAG). To give you an example, it may show the probabilistic correlations between different diseases and the symptoms of such diseases. In order to determine the chance that a disease is present, a network is fed a list of symptoms, and then it does the calculation. Bayesian networks are directed acyclic graphs that include hypotheses expressed at their nodes. Bayesian networks contain latent variables, observable quantities, and unknown parameters. Edges link nodes that are not directly connected to variables that are conditionally independent of one another. Conditional dependencies are represented by edges, which connect nodes that are not directly connected to variables. Each node is linked to a probability function that, given a certain set of inputs, calculates the likelihood of the occurrence of its parent variables.

The K-nearest neighbors (KNN) classifier has been used in the organization of the data for a great number of investigations. In pattern recognition, a wide variety of algorithms are used to assist in the process of sorting and categorizing the data. KNN is a classification approach that is based on the distance between training samples. Learning by events is shown via the KNN algorithm. When a locally estimated function is used, the calculation is placed on hold until after the classification process is finished. The research group that was responsible for this study is referred to as [22]. KNN is the technique of categorizing that is the least complicated to apply when you do not know a lot about how your data is dispersed. In the process of pattern classification, the K-nearest neighbor approach is often used. The KNN method has been the subject of a number of studies that have shown outstanding results when applied to a variety of datasets.

When K is set to 1, the KNN rule is equivalent to the nearest neighbor rule in its most basic version. In order to use this technique, the samples first need to be organized into clusters according to the features they all have in common. You may make an educated estimate with the help of this method even if you are unsure how to categorize the people that are around your sample. Using a training set and a query sample may help you figure out how far away two different sets of data are from one another. Because of this, the identity of the unknown sample may be determined by contrasting it with the group to which it has been assigned.

AdaBoost is the name given to a unique gradient-boosting technique to binary classification that was developed by researchers at the University of Michigan. After the first tree decision tree has been constructed, its accuracy is evaluated in comparison to the benchmarks that have been established. This study will assess how effective the tree decision tree really is for the organization. This method creates a single comprehensive classification strategy by fusing together a number of distinct categorization algorithms. The first step is to construct a basic model with the training data serving as the input. The second step is to construct additional models to solve any problems that were found in the initial model. If all of the data in the training set can be successfully predicted, then the creation of the model is considered to be finished; otherwise, it will continue until the maximum number of models has been created. In order to develop the most effective classification system humanly feasible, each of the many different categorization models were integrated into one. When it comes to sensors that detect pedestrians, the AdaBoost sensor has garnered a lot of support from customers. Before the feature values are determined, the photos are partitioned into rectangular panes by the use of cropping. The numbering of the windows may be done in any order as long as it makes it simple to differentiate between cars and pedestrians. The exact same procedures are carried out, with the exception that the order in which the windows in the example image are chosen is changed this time. Aside from that, nothing has changed from before. It is conceivable to continue in this fashion until a cascade of classification criteria is established, with pedestrian windows being those that are not rejected by any of the models [19]. Proceeding in this manner is possible. This process may be repeated an unlimited number of times if necessary. In this scenario, the first model will exclude any windows that can be identified with absolute certainty as not being pedestrians. The second model will repeat this process for any windows that can be identified with just a moderate degree of uncertainty as not being pedestrians.

The naive Bayes method is a basic approach for choosing problem occurrence class labels from feature value vectors. This method is used in the process of creating classifier models. These classifiers are not trained with just one approach but rather by utilizing a broad variety of techniques that all have a base in common. If we just consider the class variable, it is not feasible to decide which quality is more important than the others [23].

Classifiers based on naive Bayes may be educated via the process of supervised learning for certain sorts of probability models. Dealing with the naive Bayes model does not need the use of Bayesian probability or any other Bayesian methods; the maximum likelihood technique for parameter approximation for naive Bayes models may be used instead. Naive Bayes classifiers are supervised learning algorithms that make use of the Bayes theorem in combination with the "naive" assumption that all pairs of attributes may be considered independent of one another.

20.4   Result Analysis

NSL KDD dataset [23] is used as an input dataset. This dataset consists of 125,973 instances and 41 features. In total, 20% of the NSLKDD dataset is training data (25,192 records), and the remaining 80% is testing data (100,781 records). A total of 12 features are selected using the PSO algorithm. The performance is shown in Figure 20.3, Figure 20.4, Figure 20.5, Figure 20.6, and Figure 20.7.

- **Accuracy**
  The proportion of all predictions that are predicted correctly (accurately) is referred to as accuracy.

$$Accuracy = (TP + TN) / (TP + TN + FP + FN)$$

- **Sensitivity**
  The proportion of positive cases projected as positive is known as sensitivity. It is also known as "recall".

$$Sensitivity = (TP) / (TP + FN)$$

- **Specificity**
  The proportion of actual negative cases projected as negative is known as sensitivity.

$$Specificity = (TN) / (TN + FP)$$

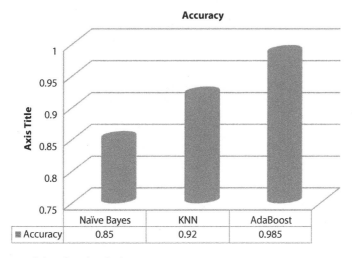

Figure 20.3 Accuracy of classifiers for chatbot IDS.

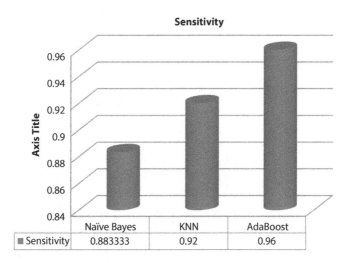

Figure 20.4 Sensitivity of classifiers for chatbot IDS.

Similarly, precision and recall are calculated as follows:

$$\text{Precision} = \text{TP}/ (\text{TP} + \text{FP})$$

$$\text{Recall} = \text{TP}/ (\text{TP} + \text{FN})$$

where
   TP = true positive
   TN = true negative
   FP = false positive
   FN = false negative

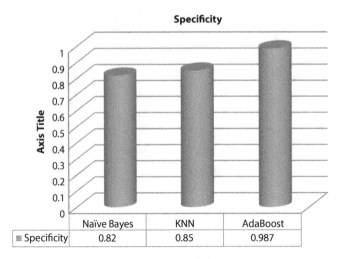

Figure 20.5 Specificity of classifiers for chatbot IDS.

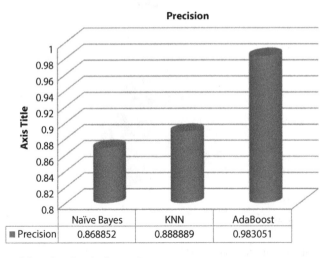

Figure 20.6 Precision of classifiers for chatbot IDS.

The accuracy of a classifier, which may be understood as the percentage of correct classifications that it creates, is the indication that is used most often in order to determine how successful it is. This metric is useful in comparing the different classifiers that are available. Even if it is essential to evaluate the fairness of classifiers, there are other factors that are often ignored. When a test is run on a particular population or collection of data linked to any ailment, there are a number of results that might possibly occur. These possibilities include true positives, false positives, true negatives, and false negatives. When determining the usefulness of the classifier, it is essential to be as objective as is humanly feasible, and the aforementioned metrics will be of great assistance in this endeavor.

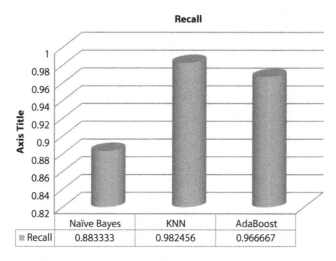

Figure 20.7 Recall of classifiers for chatbot IDS.

Threats [24–27], like malware and DDoS assaults [28–30], are one-time occurrences. Targeted incidents [31] that are tailored to your business run the risk of locking you out of your computer and demanding ransom. Alternately, hackers [32] and [33] can threaten to reveal (ostensibly protected) client information. Cracks in the system, known as vulnerabilities [34, 35], give hackers access to your system and jeopardise its security [36, 37]. Usually, they are brought on by shoddy programming, lax security [38, 39] measures, or human error. There is no system that is completely "hack-proof"; all systems contain weak points. However, chatbot security experts [40] are continually improving the system's protections to make sure that any gaps are immediately filled. Global technical progress has produced ground-breaking innovations like chatbot technology. Chatbots have been developed to serve as virtual advisers in a variety of fields, including banking, the financial industry, education, hospitality, and healthcare. Systems using chatbots were exposed to dangers and weaknesses. A chatbot might pose risks such as data theft, manipulation, and spoofing [41]. On the other side, a system becomes vulnerable when it is not properly maintained, has poor code, is not protected, or is susceptible to human error. In this sense, chatbot security [42] remains a significant issue that hasn't been entirely resolved.

20.5   Conclusion

The primary purpose of an intrusion detection system, which is more commonly referred to as an IDS, is to collect and analyze data regarding the many security events that take place in computer systems and networks. The next step that it is supposed to take is either to stop these events from taking place or to inform the administrator of the system about them. The amount of distrust that users have on the Internet has increased as a direct result of the growing number of attacks that have been carried out by attackers. Attacks that result in a denial of service are among the most serious kinds of security breaches. An intrusion detection system that is based on particle swarm optimization and AdaBoost is presented in this article. In this particular setup, the network traffic is used as input for the chatbot, and the particle swarm optimization technique is used to choose the features of the input dataset. Training and testing are being done on the classification model. In order to detect and categorize records that are related to malware, algorithms such as AdaBoost, KNN, and naive Bayes are utilized. During the experimental work, the NSL KDD dataset was utilized. When it comes to detection and classification of intrusions, PSO-AdaBoost is currently reaching the highest levels of accuracy, precision, and recall. The language that is produced by chatbot can be described as either typical or harmless.

References

1. Amendola, S., Lodato, R., Manzari, S., Occhiuzzi, C., Marrocco, G., RFID technology for IoT-based personal healthcare in smart spaces. *IEEE Internet Things J.*, 1, 2, 144–152, 2014.
2. Camara, C., Peris-Lopez, P., Tapiador, J.E., Security and privacy issues in implantable medical devices: A comprehensive survey. *J. Biomed. Inf.*, 55, 272–289, 2015.
3. Gope, P. and Hwang, T., BSN-care: A secure IoT-based modern healthcare system using body sensor network. *IEEE Sens. J.*, 16, 5, 1368–1376, 2016.
4. Raghuvanshi, A., Singh, U., Sajja, G., Pallathadka, H., Asenso, E., Kamal, M. *et al.*, Intrusion detection using machine learning for risk mitigation in IoT-enabled smart irrigation in smart farming. *J. Food Qual.*, 2022, 1–8, 2022, doi: 10.1155/2022/3955514.
5. Sun, H., Improved BP algorithm intrusion detection model based on KVM. *IEEE International Conference on Software Engineering and Service Science (ICSESS)*, pp. 442–445, 2016.
6. Seth, J.K. and Chandra, S., Intrusion detection based on key feature selection using binary GWO. *IEEE International Conference on Computing for Sustainable Global Development (INDIACom)*, pp. 3735–3740, 2016.
7. Jaiswal, S., Saxena, K., Mishra, A., Sahu, S.K., A KNN-ACO approach for intrusion detection using KDDCUP'99 dataset. *IEEE International Conference on Computing for Sustainable Global Development (INDIACom)*, pp. 628–633, 2016.
8. Ahmad, I. and Amin, F., Towards feature subset selection in intrusion detection. *IEEE Joint International Information Technology and Artificial Intelligence Conference*, pp. 68–73, 2014.
9. Tabatabaefar, M., Miriestahbanati, M., Grégoire, J.C., Network intrusion detection through artificial immune system. *IEEE International Systems Conference (SysCon)*, pp. 1–6, 2017.
10. Yang, Q., Fu, H., Zhu, T., An optimization method for parameters of SVM in network intrusion detection system. *IEEE International Conference on Distributed Computing in Sensor Systems (DCOSS)*, pp. 136–142, 2016.
11. Hosseini, Z.S., Chabok, S.J.S.M., Kamel, S.R., DOS intrusion attack detection by using of improved SVR. *IEEE International Congress on Technology, Communication and Knowledge (ICTCK)*, pp. 159–164, 2015.
12. Kulshestha, G., Agarwal, A., Mittal, A., Sahoo, A., Hybrid cuckoo search algorithm for simultaneous feature and classifier selection. *IEEE International Conference on Cognitive Computing and Information Processing (CCIP)*, pp. 1–6, 2015.
13. Zhao, X. and Zhang, W., An anomaly intrusion detection method based on improved K-means of cloud computing. *IEEE International Conference on Instrumentation & Measurement, Computer, Communication and Control (IMCCC)*, pp. 284–288, 2016.
14. Chen, C., Zhou, H., Wu, W., Shen, G., An intrusion detection method combined rough sets and data mining. *IEEE International Conference on Computer Science and Service System (CSSS)*, pp. 1091–1094, 2011.

15. Jing, L. and Bin, W., Network intrusion detection method based on relevance deep learning. *IEEE International Conference on Intelligent Transportation, Big Data & Smart City (ICITBS)*, pp. 237–240, 2016.

16. Yuan, Y., Huo, L., Hogrefe, D., Two layers multi-class detection method for network intrusion detection system. *IEEE Symposium on Computers and Communications (ISCC)*, pp. 767–772, 2017.

17. Chakir, E.M., Moughit, M., Khamlichi, Y.I., An efficient method for evaluating alerts of intrusion detection systems. *IEEE International Conference on Wireless Technologies, Embedded and Intelligent Systems (WITS)*, pp. 1–6, 2017.

18. Gaikwad, D.P. and Thool, R.C., Intrusion detection system using bagging ensemble method of machine learning. *IEEE International Conference on Computing Communication Control and Automation*, pp. 291–295, 2015.

19. Kim, J., Shin, N., Jo, S.Y., Kim, S.H., Method of intrusion detection using deep neural network. *IEEE International Conference on Big Data and Smart Computing (BigComp)*, pp. 313–316, 2017.

20. Vashishtha, J., Puri, V.H., Mukesh, Feature selection using PSO: A multi objective approach, in: *Machine Learning, Image Processing, Network Security and Data Sciences*. MIND 2020. Communications in Computer and Information Science, vol. 1241, A. Bhattacharjee, S. Borgohain, B. Soni, G. Verma, X. Z. Gao, (Eds.), Springer, Singapore, 2020.

21. Loor, M. and De Tré, G., Contextualizing naive bayes predictions, in: *Information Processing and Management of Uncertainty in Knowledge-Based Systems*. IPMU 2020.Communications in Computer and Information Science, vol. 1239, *et al.*, (Ed.), Springer, Cham, 2020.

22. Hatem, M.Q., Skin lesion classification system using a K-nearest neighbor algorithm. *Vis. Comput. Ind. Biomed. Art*, 5, 7, 2022, https://doi.org/10.1186/s42492-022-00103-6.

23. https://www.kaggle.com/datasets/hassan06/nslkdd

24. Mahor, V., Bijrothiya, S., Rawat, R., Kumar, A., Garg, B., Pachlasiya, K., IoT and artificial intelligence techniques for public safety and security, in: *Smart Urban Computing Applications*, p. 111, 2023.

25. Mahor, V., Pachlasiya, K., Garg, B., Chouhan, M., Telang, S., Rawat, R., Mobile operating system (Android) vulnerability analysis using machine learning, in: *Proceedings of International Conference on Network Security and Blockchain Technology: ICNSBT 2021*, pp. 159–169, Springer Nature Singapore, Singapore, 2022, June.

26. Rawat, R., Garg, B., Pachlasiya, K., Mahor, V., Telang, S., Chouhan, M., Mishra, R., SCNTA: Monitoring of network availability and activity for identification of anomalies using machine learning approaches. *Int. J. Inf. Technol. Web Eng. (IJITWE)*, 17, 1, 1–19, 2022.

27. Rawat, R., Rimal, Y.N., William, P., Dahima, S., Gupta, S., Sankaran, K.S., Malware threat affecting financial organization analysis using machine learning approach. *Int. J. Inf. Technol. Web Eng. (IJITWE)*, 17, 1, 1–20, 2022.

28. Rawat, R., Mahor, V., Chouhan, M., Pachlasiya, K., Telang, S., Garg, B., Systematic literature review (SLR) on social media and the digital transformation of drug trafficking on darkweb, in: *International Conference on Network Security and Blockchain Technology*, pp. 181–205, Springer, Singapore, 2022.

29. Rawat, R., Ayodele Oki, O., Sankaran, S., Florez, H., Ajagbe, S.A., Techniques for predicting dark web events focused on the delivery of illicit products and ordered crime. *Int. J. Electr. Comput. Eng. (IJECE)*, 13, 5, 5354–5365, Oct. 2023, doi: 10.11591/ijece.v13i5.pp5354-5365.

30. Rawat, R., Garg, B., Mahor, V., Telang, S., Pachlasiya, K., Chouhan, M., Organ trafficking on the dark web—The data security and privacy concern in healthcare systems, in: *Internet of Healthcare Things: Machine Learning for Security and Privacy*, pp. 189–216, 2022.

31. Vyas, P., Vyas, G., Chauhan, A., Rawat, R., Telang, S., Gottumukkala, M., Anonymous trading on the dark online marketplace: An exploratory study, in: *Using Computational Intelligence for the Dark Web and Illicit Behavior Detection*, pp. 272–289, IGI Global, 2022.

32. Rawat, R., Oki, O.A., Sankaran, K.S., Olasupo, O., Ebong, G.N., Ajagbe, S.A., A new solution for cyber security in big data using machine learning approach, in: *Mobile Computing and Sustainable Informatics: Proceedings of ICMCSI 2023*, pp. 495–505, Springer Nature Singapore, Singapore, 2023.

33. Rawat, R., Chakrawarti, R.K., Raj, A., Mani, G., Chidambarathanu, K., Bhardwaj, R., Association rule learning for threat analysis using traffic analysis and packet filtering approach. *Int. J. Inf. Technol.*, 1–11, 2023.

34. Rawat, R., Logical concept mapping and social media analytics relating to cyber criminal activities for ontology creation. *Int. J. Inf. Technol.*, 15, 2, 893–903, 2023.

35. Rawat, R., Mahor, V., Álvarez, J.D., Ch, F., Cognitive systems for dark web cyber delinquent association malignant data crawling: A review, in: *Handbook of Research on War Policies, Strategies, and Cyber Wars*, pp. 45–63, 2023.

36. Rawat, R., Chakrawarti, R.K., Vyas, P., Gonzáles, J.L.A., Sikarwar, R., Bhardwaj, R., Intelligent fog computing surveillance system for crime and vulnerability identification and tracing. *Int. J. Inf. Secur. Priv. (IJISP)*, 17, 1, 1–25, 2023.

37. Rawat, R., Sowjanya, A.M., Patel, S.I., Jaiswal, V., Khan, I., Balaram, A. (Eds.), *Using Machine Intelligence: Autonomous Vehicles Volume 1*, John Wiley & Sons, 2022.

38. Rawat, R., Mahor, V., Díaz-Álvarez, J., Chávez, F., Rooted learning model at fog computing analysis for crime incident surveillance, in: *2022 International Conference on Smart Generation Computing, Communication and Networking (SMART GENCON)*, pp. 1–9, IEEE, 2022, December.

39. Rawat, R. and Shrivastav, S.K., SQL injection attack detection using SVM. *Int. J. Comput. Appl.*, 42, 13, 1–4, 2012.

40. Rawat, R., Bhardwaj, P., Kaur, U., Telang, S., Chouhan, M., Sankaran, K.S., *Smart vehicles for communication, volume 2*, John Wiley & Sons, 2023.

41. Mahor, V., Garg, B., Telang, S., Pachlasiya, K., Chouhan, M., Rawat, R., Cyber threat phylogeny assessment and vulnerabilities representation at thermal power station, in: *Proceedings of International Conference on Network Security and Blockchain Technology: ICNSBT 2021*, pp. 28–39, Springer Nature Singapore, Singapore, 2022, June.

42. Rawat, R., Gupta, S., Sivaranjani, S., Cu, O.K., Kuliha, M., Sankaran, K.S., Malevolent information crawling mechanism for forming structured illegal organisations in hidden networks. *Int. J. Cyber Warf. Terror. (IJCWT)*, 12, 1, 1–14, 2022.

Conversational Chatbot With Object Recognition Using Deep Learning and Machine Learning

A. Mahesh Babu[1*], Malik Jawarneh[2], José Luis Arias-Gonzáles[3], Meenakshi[4], Kishori Kasat[5] and K.P. Yuvaraj[6]

[1]Computer Science and Engineering, Koneru Lakshmaiah Education Foundation, Hyderabad, India
[2]Faculty of Computing Sciences, Gulf College, Al-Khuwair, Oman
[3]Department of Business, University of British Columbia, Lima, Peru
[4]School of Journalism & Mass Communication, Apeejay Stya University Sohna Haryana, Gurugram, India
[5]Computer Studies Department, Symbiosis School for Liberal Arts, Symbiosis International (Deemed University), Pune, India
[6]Department of Mechanical Engineering, Sri Krishna College of Engineering and Technology, Coimbatore, India

Abstract

In the field of computer vision, the identification of an object offers evolving and challenging difficulties. Visual object identification is a common and automatic biological visual function for humans, but it is challenging for computers. Object recognition is a significant difficulty in computer vision because of the substantial diversity in images of objects in the same class under different viewing conditions. Object recognition has a wide range of uses, including in the fields of biometrics, defense, robotics, visual surveillance, and driving assistance. This article presents a chatbot framework for object detection. This proposed framework makes use of image processing and deep learning techniques. Three classification techniques—support vector machine, AdaBoost, and convolutional neural network (CNN)—are used in the proposed framework. COCO dataset is used to perform experiments. The experimental results have shown that the CNN algorithm is providing the best results in object detection.

Keywords: Chatbot, object recognition, deep learning, machine learning, natural language processing, accuracy, precision, recall

21.1 Introduction

The basic idea behind a chatbot is that it can hold a conversation with a human user (often via text messages) and appear as if it fully understands what is being said and can correctly respond. Computers talking to people has been around for as long as computer science has.

Corresponding author: mahiabhi@gmail.com

Romil Rawat, Rajesh Kumar Chakrawarti, Sanjaya Kumar Sarangi, Piyush Vyas, Mary Sowjanya Alamanda, Kotagiri Srividya and Krishnan Sakthidasan Sankaran (eds.) Conversational Artificial Intelligence, (335–352) © 2024 Scrivener Publishing LLC

In fact, in 1950, Alan Turing established a simple test now known as the Turing test [1], in which a human judge must determine whether or not the entity with which they are conversing via text is a computer program. However, the scope of this test is far beyond the typical application of chatbots, as the Turing test presupposes that one may have a conversation with the agent about any topic, but chatbots' domain knowledge is limited. This aids in the design of conversational agents because they do not have to have (possibly) limitless domain knowledge and may instead concentrate on aiding customers with very focused issues, like making a restaurant reservation.

In the field of computer vision, a developing and difficult issue to solve is the challenge of object recognition. Object recognition is a natural and undemanding aspect of the visual system of a human being; however, it is a significantly more challenging task for a computer. Computer vision has a huge challenge when attempting to recognize items since there is a large amount of diversity in the way that similar objects look in various photographs. It is a method for recognizing and localizing certain elements in images, such as people, automobiles, or structures, and it may be used in still or moving photographs. The photographs themselves include the elements that are considered to be of utmost significance by the object identification system [2]. A human being is capable of accurately recognizing an object despite the fact that it may appear in a wide range of shapes or despite considerable variations in the shape of the object. As a result, several groups of scientists examined various approaches of object identification in light of how people employ those methods. Because object identification is a challenging task for robots to do, there is opportunity for improvement in the development of a system that is not only efficient but also easy to understand [3].

Object recognition may be put to work in a broad range of fields, such as biometrics, the military, robotics, visual surveillance, and driving assistance, among others. The driver assistance system has features such as lane detection frameworks and obstacle recognition in front of the vehicle, whereas the surveillance system has features such as a warning framework for spotting a pedestrian in infrared camera pictures [4] and vehicle recognition in the actual driving environment. A number of circumstances, including but not limited to shifts in illumination, significant fluctuations in deformations, the presence of shadows, partial occlusion, and others, have the potential to impede recognition performance and cause issues. In light of this, an effective method for the identification of objects is now being explored. This chapter covers the principles of a variety of imaging modalities, including thermal imaging, object recognition, deep learning, and picture decomposition, among others.

The process of object recognition is comprised of several stages, the first of which is the acquisition of an image, followed by preprocessing, feature extraction, classifier prediction, and, finally, recognition. The object recognition architecture is broken down into its component parts and presented in Figure 21.1. The process of securing pictures by means of a camera or an already existing data collection and translating them into digital format is the initial stage of any object identification system. This stage is known as picture acquisition. The subsequent level is known as the preprocessing stage, and it is at this stage that the digital image is prepared for subsequent processing stages. Because of this, it is an essential component of any object identification system since it is responsible for preparing the input picture for the subsequent steps in the process [5].

The extraction of features is an essential phase since it is used to segment the picture and offer helpful data for a particular application. This process may be broken down into several substeps. At this point, we take a look at a feature set that may be used to zero down on the shape in the image for a more precise evaluation. This feature set has the potential to be employed in a number of different ways. Local and global characteristics are utilized, with the assistance of the classifier model, in order to discriminate between the various objects present in the image. The term "features" refers to several properties of the picture, such as its shape, size, color, and texture, among other things. The incoming image is parsed for its preliminary properties, and the mathematical shape features that it contains are employed to formulate a perception of the object. The last step is to train a classifier using the features that were retrieved and then to test those features using the sample picture to make sure that the classification is accurate.

The term "acquisition" refers to the initial step in the process of getting a digital picture. To begin the process of acquiring digital photographs, one must first decide what kind of data is needed as well as the recording method to make use of. Data may be collected in a number of ways, including shooting images in real time, utilizing previously collected benchmark datasets, etc. For the purpose of gathering real-time visual data, a number of sensors, such as thermal cameras, among others, are utilized.

Image preprocessing is a state of readiness for images which are frequently prepared by employing the image in the process that comes before their usage in model training and prediction. Changes may be made to the size, orientation, and color of the object, but this is not an exhaustive list of possible modifications. It is necessary to do pre-processing on image data before employing it as input into a model. For completely connected layers in convolutional neural networks, it is necessary, for instance, that all of the images be of the same size array. By applying preprocessing techniques to the photos themselves, the amount of time needed to train a model might potentially be reduced. When working with huge input photographs, lowering the size of such photos can dramatically speed up the training process without significantly affecting the performance of the model. To determine the pre-processing steps that will contribute the most to the successful execution of the model, it is vital to have a solid understanding of the problem, the data, and the surrounding environment.

Extraction of features is essential when it comes to determining the identity of a certain object. The patterns or traits that set an object out from others in an image are referred to as its features. Convolutional neural networks (CNNs) are superior to the traditional method of extracting features because of their powerful ability to obtain complex characteristics that typify the image in much more detail, their ability to learn from and improve upon these features, and their overall superiority. This enables CNNs to replace the conventional feature extraction approach. A significant amount of work has been completed up to this point. The deep CNN model takes into account the picture's region of interest when it is doing image feature matching. Even though recent developments in deep learning have made it possible to overcome challenges that were previously insurmountable, such as issues with scalability, rotation, distortion, etc., and push the boundaries of what was previously possible with traditional methods, this has not rendered computer vision approaches obsolete.

The process of methodically creating database-based classification models is referred to as "classifying", and a classifier is one such approach. As components of the models, we make use of support vector machines, naive Bayes classifiers, and deep neural networks.

A learning mechanism of some form is essential to the execution of any plan. It is important to determine the correspondence between the character set and the class label in order to find a classifier that works well with the data that has been provided. The output model has to perform a good job of properly predicting record class labels and initializing the data it receives from the input model. The construction of a model with a high rationalization ability, that is, a model that reliably predicts the class labels of previously unknown information, is the key objective of this learning process. This aim was established as the primary objective of this learning process.

Deep learning is the subfield of machine learning that delves most deeply into the subject matter. The creation of a multi-layered, abstracting framework that is also capable of being readily programmed is the primary objective of this branch of study. Automated feature extraction is employed, and no human participation is required in order to find the hidden relationship that exists across datasets. As a result of this, deep learning strategies produce higher results in comparison to more conventional learning approaches. Deep learning strategies have been implemented into human sensory systems. The implementation of an ANN has resulted in the creation of several deep learning architectures (ANN). The perceptron is the fundamental component of a neural network. It takes in a large number of inputs, performs an analysis of those inputs with the assistance of weighted summation, and then employs the outcome to feed into an activation function. This activation function then causes the repetition of an output [6]. A biased measure is first optimized during training, and then it is applied to a vector of weights that has the same size across all neurons. A training set, a test set, and a validation set are each constructed from the collected data.

21.2   Literature Survey

21.2.1   Object Recognition Using Deep Learning

R. Girshick and colleagues [7] came up with a recognition method that was not only versatile but also straightforward to implement. It involved two primary concepts: first, the application of high-capacity CNNs to region proposals in order to enclose and fragment objects and, second, the improvement of performance through the utilization of domain-specific fine-tuning in order to compensate for insufficiently labeled training data. The combination of the ideas represented by region proposals and convolutional neural networks is the inspiration for the naming of this technique, which is referred to as R-CNN. R-CNN performs noticeably better than the equivalent OverFeat detector when applied to the data from the 200-class ILSVRC2013 competition.

The network was outfitted with a spatial pyramid pooling strategy by K. He *et al.* [8] in order to produce a portrayal of a consistent length regardless of the size or scale of the picture. The performance of CNN-based techniques of picture classification was improved with the help of SPP-net. They demonstrate that applying SPP-net on the ImageNet 2012 dataset led to an improvement in the accuracy of a number of different CNNs. Considering the accuracy of a wide variety of different CNN architectures. In order to train detectors, SPP-net first computes a single set of feature maps for the whole picture and then utilizes those maps to produce representations of a defined length. When it came to processing test pictures, this approach was shown to be more effective in terms of time management than the R-CNN method.

R. Girshick and colleagues [9] suggest employing rapid R-CNN in order to speed up the process of finding items. It makes advantage of a few technological breakthroughs to speed up the training and testing processes while also increasing the accuracy of the detection. It trained the VGG16 network more rapidly than R-CNN and with greater accuracy and speed than SPPnet, all while surpassing SPPnet on the PASCAL VOC 2012 benchmark. Specifically, it trained the VGG16 network faster.

S. Ren *et al.* [10] presented a new variant of the RCNN known as Faster RCNN. This variant added a region proposal network (RPN) that shared convolutional properties with the recognition network. An RPN can predict objectness scores and object borders everywhere since it is a fully convolutional network. It was trained from the bottom up to produce region suggestions of a better quality, which Fast R-CNN then utilized to perform identifications. They were successful in developing a single network that derives its instructions from the RPN section by making use of the "attention" mechanism that is incorporated into the convolutional features of both the RPN and the Fast R-CNN.

W. Zhao *et al.* [11] introduced an object-based deep learning approach with the purpose of accurately defining the high-resolution picture without increasing the amount of human input required. In this method, high-resolution photo translation was made possible by integrating a deep feature learning strategy with an object-based categorization. Object-based categorization was also used. In particular, there are five distinct layers of structure that are investigated in terms of their high-level features. In addition, the object-based classification technique was used with the deep learning process in order to further enhance the classification accuracy, which ultimately resulted in a better degree of characterization precision.

R. Rothe and colleagues [12] proposed a system that could estimate a person's age from a single image of their face, and it did not include the use of facial landmarks in any way. Convolutional neural networks (CNNs) that had been pre-trained on ImageNet were utilized in order to successfully complete the two objectives. They saw the process of calculating a person's age as a classification issue that needed to be addressed, and they believed that this could be achieved by adding a softmax adjustment to the result that was projected. We are able to make an accurate prediction of a person's age by employing deep neural networks that have been trained on huge datasets, an expected value formulation, and a face template that has been carefully matched.

Conv-Deconv networks were proposed by L. Mou *et al.* [13] as a means of automatically learning the spectral and spatial characteristics of hyperspectral images without human intervention. Throughout the trial, it was discovered that this network was difficult to improve upon. This network design has been fine-tuned to handle the aforementioned problem by incorporating an unpooling operation with residual learning that may make use of retained indexes of max-pooling. This is one of the ways that the problem has been addressed. The higher effectiveness of our technique can be shown by comparing the outcomes of applying it to two hyper-spectral datasets that are utilized by a lot of people: Pavia University and Indian Pines.

Using the real-time identification framework YOLO9000, which was presented by J. Redmon *et al.* [14], it is possible to identify more than 9000 distinct article categories. There was no competition between the improved model Yolov2 and the faster RCNN with ResNet and SSD. At long last, there was a strategy for the group-based acquisition of skills in the areas of object recognition and classification. Using this strategy, they trained YOLO9000 in parallel on the COCO detection dataset as well as the ImageNet characterization dataset. Their approaches were put to the test by participating in the ImageNet detection challenge.

W. Liu and colleagues [15] introduced SSD, a technique for object identification that only makes use of a single deep network. It did this by taking each region of the feature map that included yield bounding boxes and turning it into a set of boxes of varied dimensions and orientations. It did this by combining the predictions obtained from a number of different feature maps with different resolutions, which enabled it to naturally cope with objects of variable sizes.

The application of EMD to hyperspectral images was demonstrated by B. Demir et al. [16] as a means to enhance the accuracy of classification achieved through the use of an SVM-based classifier. The initial image was disassembled with the assistance of EMD into a variety of individual IMFs as well as a residue in its final form. The classification accuracy of hyperspectral images was significantly improved as a result of its implementation as a spatially flexible decomposition for intrinsic properties. We used two different ways to improve the EMD-based hyperspectral image classification that we had previously developed. The initial step was to gather the IMFs for each hyperspectral band. After that, the aggregate of the lower-order IMFs was added to the SVM classifier as extra features. The next method, which utilized composite kernels, integrated the information that was contained in the first and second IMFs of each hyperspectral image in order to increase the accuracy of the SVM classification.

A. Pizurica and his colleagues [17] developed denoising algorithms for geographically adaptive, multivalued, and sub band-adaptive pictures. We looked at a number of different scenarios in which the signal presence probability was established on a per-subband basis, formed by a spatial relationship at the neighborhood level, and fine-tuned utilizing information from other image bands. All probabilities were computed utilizing a model of additive white Gaussian noise, a sub-band information that was free of noise, and a generalized Laplacian prior, all of which were used in conjunction with one another. As compared to Bayesian thresholding approaches, the performance of this sub-band-adaptive function was superior, as demonstrated by the findings, in terms of the mean squared error. In order to achieve the necessary outcomes, the spatially adaptive variation of this strategy performed far better than its comparable sophisticated competitors.

N. Golyandina et al. [18] investigated both the singular spectrum analysis and the subspace-based methods of signal processing. We talked about the typical and overt qualities of these strategies, as well as the many different types of issues that these approaches have the potential to tackle. During the building process, rates of error as well as assembly rates were analyzed.

Sharma et al. [19] employed the DWT to degrade the signal into its distinct components. This was accomplished by decomposing the signal. For studying the components of each sub-nonlinear band, the third-order cumulants (ToC) in higher dimensions were utilized for analysis. The information included in the higher dimensional space contains rehashed and repeated material because of the underlying nature of the many symmetries that are present in the ToC. Particle swarm optimization was utilized so that we could get rid of any unnecessary information. We use a deep learning approach that is based on long-term transitory memory in order to recover emotional fluctuations in the data that has been optimized.

An approach for characterization was described by Srirangam *et al.* [20], and it involved the use of both a deep convolutional neural network (CNN) and the Synchrosqueezing Transforms (SST). In order to conduct an analysis of the time-frequency lattices of the EEG data, both Fourier SST (FSST) and wavelet SST were utilized (WSST). We employed a two-dimensional deep CNN for the classification assignment that was given to us. The results revealed that, by utilizing this strategy, accuracy, responsiveness, and selectivity were significantly enhanced.

Chaudhary *et al.* [21] developed the 2D-FBSE-EWT method by employing the FBSE range between 0 and 1 order for the purpose of boundary detection. In the course of looking for gaps in the FBSE spectrum, it was also investigated at a number of other frequencies. In this particular experiment, we make use of three distinct frequency bands. These processes result in the image being segmented into smaller and smaller parts.

An application of the wavelet packet decomposition method within the context of the FourierBessel series expansion is what Chaudhary and colleagues [22] had in mind when they created the FBSED methodology. As a direct consequence of this, it was put to use deteriorating chest X-ray and computed tomography (CCTI and CXI) views into sub-band images (SBIs). Several CNN models that had been trained in the past were independently trained on the SBIs through the use of a transfer learning technique. It was discussed as though the CNN and SBI channels were a single entity when they were united. The deep properties of each channel were combined into a component vector after being pooled together.

21.2.2 Object Recognition in Real-Time Images

M. Irani *et al.* [23] provided an illustration of a unified technique that may be used to deal with the identification of mobile objects in scenes. It did this by dividing the difficulty of the task of recognizing moving objects into a number of distinct categories. The division described above was followed by a series of suggestions. The amount of difficulty required to execute these methods has increased over time, progressing from less complicated 2D methods to more intricate 3D approaches. Note that the computations needed to solve the issue at one complexity level become the basic preparation work for the arrangement at the following complexity level. This is a crucial point to keep in mind. These techniques were shown through the usage of actual photo sequences from the real world.

F. Xu *et al.* [24] exhibited a two-stage detection tracking system for recognizing and following pedestrians. The technology was shown by using a night vision camera that was mounted on a car. In order to recognize pedestrians, a support vector machine that had its size parameter changed was utilized, and in order to track their movements, a mix of Kalman filter prediction and mean shift tracking was utilized. From the module that was responsible for road detection, crucial information for the pedestrian validation was acquired, which assisted in strengthening the identification phase.

DECOLOR is an integrated framework that was utilized by X. Zhou *et al.* [25] to handle the challenges of non-rigid motion and changeable backgrounds. This resulted in a single optimization cycle that could be efficiently handled by an alternating algorithm. This cycle merged the process of identifying objects with the process of learning about the backgrounds of those objects. The connections that exist between DECOLOR and many other sparsity-based approaches have been outlined by us. In tests where real-world video sequences were used as the basis for comparison, DECOLOR emerged victorious.

Y. Chen and colleagues [26] developed an approach that is based on image matching and frame coupling as a way to handle the challenges associated with object recognition that are caused by both camera and subject motion. Initially, feature points were determined for each frame. The acquisition of motion boundaries would be possible as a result of this. We were able to dissociate sub-images from their parent frame by using the motion character-istics that were provided. In addition to this, the approach of searching for potential routes contributed significantly to an improvement in both the efficiency and the accuracy. In the end, an approach based on frame coupling was chosen as the most effective way to increase the accuracy of object detection.

Object detection has lately gained a great deal of attention as a result of the numerous possible applications it possesses. A presentation was given on the multiple-object iden-tification program that was created by S. Guennouni and colleagues [27]. Object iden-tification using a cascade of classifiers as an illustration of complexity-related factors In addition, the outcomes of profiling and adapting the application for use on an embedded platform were discussed and compared with the results obtained using more traditional computer systems. The operation of a real-time framework was monitored and controlled by this program.

A strategy that is computationally productive was described by Y. Wu *et al.* [28] in order to reliably and robustly detect moving objects in a photograph. In order to find a solution to this issue, we came up with a coarse-to-fine thresholding technique that is based on the tra-jectories that the particles take in a video sequence. At the beginning, we employed RSVD on a number of networks that were formed based on the collected particle trajectories in order to locate and single out the coarse foreground region. After this step, we were successful in recreating the motion of the background pixels in the rough foreground by employing a fast-painting approach. While separating the foreground features from the background, an adap-tive thresholding approach was applied, and it proved to be effective in a variety of different situations that involved moving objects. Once everything was said and done, the mean-shift segmentation approach provided an even finer level of precision for the identified foreground.

S. Mangale *et al.* [29] presented a proposal for target identification in thermal video that could be used for both single and multiple moving objects. After that, target segmentation using directed acyclic graph (DAG) [30] was carried out using the separated regions as input. After that, a scoring function was utilized to choose the particular object motion, and after that, DAG was implemented with a greater number of object suggestions based on the motion-dependent predictions of adjoining frames. Following the segmentation process, a method known as centroid-dependent object tracking was utilized on the videos in order to keep an eye on the aforementioned objects.

D. Heo *et al.* [31] provided evidence that ABMS may be utilized to bring the pedestrian into focus in response to shifting aspects of the weather. In order to identify pedestrians, the YOLO method was implemented. This method replaces the conventional classifier with a convolutional neural network for improved accuracy. Because it was anticipated in advance that a pedestrian would stand out more than the backdrop, YOLO was combined with an ABMS-created saliency feature map. With this method, a successful application was achieved using the thermal imaging dataset obtained by moving autos.

A. Neves *et al.* [32] reported on three different methods of face recognition that were based on the segmentation of pictures in order to get a binary image. Analyzing the contours that were produced after processing a binary image with an edge detection algorithm was the first approach for recognizing faces. This was done after the image had been converted to binary format. The last step was making use of a template matching method in order to find an image inside the binary picture that matched the form of a human head, and it was successful in locating the best option. In the third method, we apply a matching algorithm that compares the distance transform of the edge picture to the template. This is the way that we find to be the most successful. The data on the orientations of edges are pooled using this method, which helps to decrease the number of recognition failures.

The approach was created by A. Gomez and colleagues [33], and it is based on CNNs that are sufficiently tiny to function on a low-power, low-memory stage. The method can count the number of people in thermal photographs. The quick and precise CNN that delivered the error-free identification was educated using a library of 3,000 thermal images that were physically labelled.

Qi. Wang *et al.* [34] presented a deep neural network-based weakly supervised adversarial domain adaptation with the goal of improving segmentation performance in real-world contexts. Object identification and the accurate prediction of map segmentation were the two key focuses of the detection and segmentation (DS) model. An attempt was made by a pixel-level domain classifier (PDC) as well as an object-level domain classifier (ODC) to determine the properties of the image as well as to categories the objects included within it, respectively. In the context of our investigation, DS fulfilled the function of a generator, whereas PDC and ODC were considered to be discriminators.

N. Shahid *et al.* [35] disclosed a potent human detection approach in thermal imaging by integrating CNNs with background modeling. This combination produced excellent results. In order to represent the background, an improved running Gaussian average was utilized. Moreover, CNN-based classification was performed just for the foreground objects that were found, and this entire process was carried out in real time. In order to enhance the reliability of human identification, the use of morphological operators and ellipse testing has been approved for application in the process of extracting the area of interest. In a similar manner, three distinct CNN models were trained on real-time datasets by utilizing a variety of input sizes and voting strategies.

X. Wang and his colleagues [36] developed a loss function with the intention of bridging the gap that existed between the two classes. The moving elements of the movie supplied additional and crucial context, in comparison to the still image. Using a temporal connection between the photographs resulted in an improvement in the human detectability. When compared to the usage of a single image, the introduction of a sequence of images resulted in a significant improvement in human identification accuracy. The dataset from KAIST that was used for this investigation. In the past, human detection was accomplished with the assistance of three temporally stable CNN as well as a fundamental CNN.

M. Hasan and colleagues [37] examined the thermal IR hyperspectral emissivity of thirteen distinct plant species for their research. Convolutional neural networks, support vector machines, and artificial neural networks [38] were the three machine learning methodologies that were utilized in the process of classifying 13 plant species (CNN). We put each of the classifiers through a series of tests to determine how well they performed when given additional data to train on or larger objects to segment respectively. The performance of SVM was significantly enhanced by expanding the size of the training set. Although other machine learning algorithms reached a nearly flawless accuracy as well, CNN proved to be the most successful of the lot.

M. Ivasic-Kos *et al.* [39] aimed to solve the issues that arise when attempting to automate the detection of people in thermal images and videos. For the entirety of the recording process for the thermal videos, there were as many as three people present. These individuals were spaced away from the camera at varied distances. The nocturnal images, whether they are captured in rain, haze, or clear weather, are just as striking. The findings of human recognition on the thermal movies dataset were reported by making use of the YOLO network, which was trained on a section of the dataset. This component of the dataset was used to provide the results. The results of the experiments indicate that increasing the usage of thermal imaging for the purpose of identifying humans greatly improves the number of successful detections.

In particular, S. Zeng *et al.* [40] focused their attention on the recognition of signal lights and lane lines as ideal instances of semantic road segmentation and detection. It incorporated both the visual analysis approach as well as a sequence of deep learning-based algorithms for visual perception. Although while semantic segmentation and target identification have made significant strides in other settings, when applied to autonomous cars, these technologies were not yet at their full potential. In the end, a fusion network was designed specifically for autonomous driving scenarios that involve the detection of signal lights and the separation of lane lines.

21.3   Methodology

This section consists of three classification techniques—support vector machine, AdaBoost, and convolutional neural network.

The support vector machine is one method that has the potential to assist in pedestrian detection (SVM). Images are frequently presented in computer vision as a non-linear matrix made up of square pixel units. The returned characteristics of the target item are used as the basis for classification work to be carried out. It is possible to extract features from photographs by making use of tried-and-true techniques for the feature extraction process. In order to determine whether or not a picture contains pedestrians, support vector machines, often known as SVMs, along with other binary classifiers, are utilized. In order to accomplish this, an SVM first constructs a hyperplane between the non-linear data points of the images, and then assigns each point to one of two binary categories. It is possible to improve the accuracy of classification by increasing the distance that separates the hyperplane and the data point. In addition, the support vector machine, often known as SVM, may be used to pick out good qualities present in the photos [41].

AdaBoost is an alternate gradient-boosting method that was developed for binary classification by academics at the University of Michigan. Following the construction of the first tree decision tree, the effectiveness of the tree is evaluated for each training instance. In this approach, several distinct categorization systems, each of which provides a different level of precision, are integrated to produce a single, reliable solution. The training data are utilized in the construction of the first model, which is then iterated upon to correct any errors that the model may have produced. When either all of the feasible models have been constructed or when the data from the training set can be accurately predicted, it will be judged that the development of the model is complete. The process of merging all of the different classification models resulted in the development of the most effective categorization model. Many motorists choose to install the AdaBoost sensor in their vehicles so they can better identify pedestrians. The photos are cut up into rectangles, and the feature values are determined individually for each one of those rectangles. It is possible to distinguish pedestrians from other users of the road using virtually any configuration of marking the windows. The same approach is utilized, with the exception that the windows seen in the example image are chosen to be opened in a different order this time. Windows that are not considered to be pedestrians by the first model are discarded by the second model as being less obviously not pedestrians, and so on, until the only windows that are considered to be pedestrian windows are those that are not considered to be non-pedestrian windows by any of the models [42].

When applied to big datasets, the efficacy of machine learning algorithms is substantially reduced due to challenges such as underfitting, model complexity, and a lack of resource efficiency. The inefficiencies caused by these challenges reduce the effectiveness of the approaches. Deep learning networks, when applied to huge datasets, have the potential to yield new insights, allow for the creation of predictions, and enable the obtained information to be put to practical use. Computer models are now able to learn from both graphical and textual data thanks to the use of a technique known as "deep learning". As the amount of data available has increased, a great number of different deep learning architectures have been developed to offer superior performance in comparison to more conventional machine learning methods.

One of the most common and widely used implementations of deep neural network design [43] is the convolutional neural network, which is used in computer vision (CNN). The convolutional layer, the pooling layer, the activation layer, and the connected convolutional layer make up the layers that make up a convolutional neural network, also known as a CNN. A deep convolutional neural network, often known as a CNN, is able to carry out processes from beginning to end because to its many interconnected convolutional layers (Figure 21.1). The fundamental purpose of the convolutional layer is to do filtering. At the convolutional layer, we restricted the number of pixels that were allowed to pass through the filter to a very small fraction of the input picture (say, 3 x 3).

The values of the pixels are subjected to a "dot" operation, and the filter uses a predetermined weight to determine how much of an impact this operation will have on the final result. Because of this, the size of the image's data point matrices is decreased once the convolutional layer has been applied. The activation layer's matrix provides the network with nonlinearity and trains it by using back propagation with the matrices that are delivered to that layer. Pooling decreases the number of layers in samples, in addition to lowering the size of the filter matrix. This kind of layer is referred to as a max layer since it only selects one attribute from each category. In the linked layer, the output of the max layers is used to build a list of probabilities for various candidate labels. These probabilities are obtained

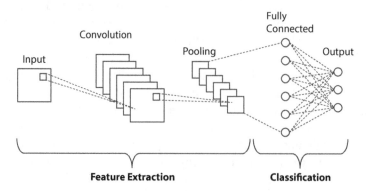

Figure 21.1 Convolutional neural network.

using the connected layer. The most probable result is taken into consideration when selecting a label.

21.4   Results and Discussion

Object Detection With the Use of COCO [44]: The phrase "common objects in context" is what the abbreviation "COCO" stands for. The goal of the COCO project was to compile natural images, which are defined as those that show everyday settings and provide additional context information. Daily scenes generally consist of a variety of elements, all of which need to be correctly categorized and labelled in order to convey information that is helpful to the reader. The COCO dataset was responsible for the labelling and segmentation of the things contained within the photos. Figures 21.2–21.6 show the results of an analysis of the techniques' performance using a variety of criteria.

A chatbot with keyword recognition employs natural language processing (NLP) [45–47] to assist its consumers [48]. Users can engage with this site by entering free text. Following

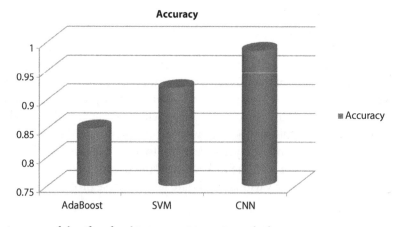

Figure 21.2 Accuracy of classifiers for object recognition using a chatbot.

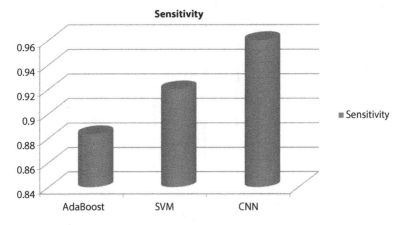

Figure 21.3 Sensitivity of classifiers for object recognition using a chatbot.

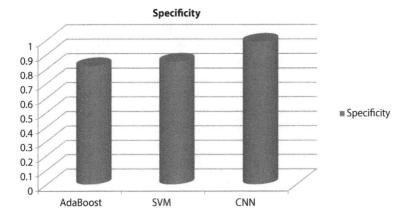

Figure 21.4 Specificity of classifiers for object recognition using a chatbot.

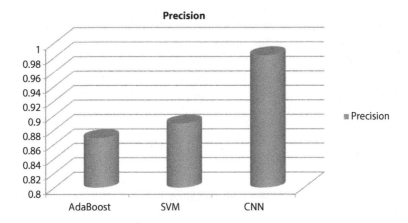

Figure 21.5 Precision of classifiers for object recognition using a chatbot.

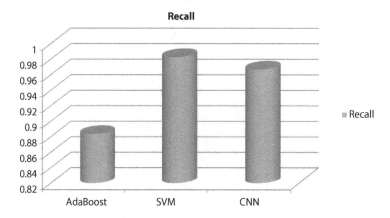

Figure 21.6 Recall of classifiers for object recognition using a chatbot.

a keyword-based analysis of the user's content, the chatbot responds with the most appropriate response. ControlNet and Stable Diffusion are just a few examples of Visual ChatGPT [49] and [50], which blend ChatGPT with VFMs. Because of its complex algorithms and cutting-edge deep learning methods, it can communicate with users in normal language and provide them with the information they need. With the aid of the visual foundation models, ChatGPT can also assess images or videos that users upload in order to understand the data and provide a more specialised solution. Millions of users were astounded by ChatGPT's capabilities when OpenAI [51–53] released its ground-breaking AI language model. However, for many people, curiosity rapidly gave way to sincere worry [54–56] about the tool's ability to advance the agendas of evil actors [57, 58]. In particular, ChatGPT creates additional entry points for hackers [59, 60] who may compromise sophisticated cybersecurity [61–63] tools. It's crucial that executives acknowledge the rising influence of AI and take appropriate action in a sector that is already suffering from a 42% global rise in data breaches.

21.5   Conclusion

This article outlines a chatbot architecture for the purpose of object detection. The image processing and deep learning methodologies are incorporated into the design of this suggested system. The suggested structure makes use of three different classification strategies: the support vector machine, the AdaBoost algorithm, and the convolutional neural network. Experiments are carried out with the help of the COCO data collection. The results of the experiments have demonstrated that the CNN algorithm yields the best results in terms of object detection.

References

1. Bansal, H. and Khan, R., A review paper on human computer interaction. *Int. J. Adv. Res. Comput. Sci. Software Eng.*, 8, 53, 2018.

2. Khanna, A., Pandey, B., Vashishta, K., Kalia, K., Bhale, P., Das, T., A study of today's A.I. through chatbots and rediscovery of machine intelligence. *Int. J. u- e-Serv. Sci. Technol.*, 8, 277–284, 2015.

3. Colace, F., De Santo, M., Lombardi, M., Pascale, F., Pietrosanto, A., Lemma, S., Chatbot for e-learning: A case of study. *Int. J. Mech. Eng. Robot. Res.*, 7, 528–533, 2018.

4. Ranoliya, B.R., Raghuwanshi, N., Singh, S., Chatbot for university related FAQs, in: *2017 International Conference on Advances in Computing, Communications and Informatics (ICACCI)*, Udupi, pp. 1525–1530, 2017.

5. Xu, A., Liu, Z., Guo, Y., Sinha, V., Akkiraju, R., A new chatbot for customer service on social media, in: *Proceedings of the 2017 CHI Conference on Human Factors in Computing Systems*, ACM, New York, pp. 3506–3510, 2017.

6. Akma, N., Hafiz, M., Zainal, A., Fairuz, M., Adnan, Z., Review of chatbots design techniques. *Int. J. Comput. Appl.*, 181, 7–10, 2018.

7. Girshick, R., Donahue, J., Darrell, T., Malik, J., Rich feature hierarchies for accurate object detection and semantic segmentation. *IEEE Conference on Computer Vision and Pattern Recognition*, IEEE, pp. 580–587, 2014.

8. He, K., Zhang, X., Ren, S., Sun, J., Spatial pyramid pooling in deep convolutional networks for visual recognition. *Proceeding in 13th European Conference on Computer Vision*, pp. 346–361, 2014.

9. Girshick, R., Fast R-CNN. *IEEE International Conference on Computer Vision*, IEEE, pp. 1440–1448, 2015.

10. Ren, S., He, K., Girshick, R., Sun, J., Faster R-CNN: Towards real-time object detection with region proposal networks. *IEEE Trans. Pattern Anal. Mach. Intell.*, 39, 6, 1137–1149, 2017.

11. Zhao, W., Du, S., Emery, W.I., Object based convolutional neural network for high resolution imagery classification. *IEEE J. Sel. Top. Appl. Earth Obs. Remote Sens.*, 10, 7, 3386–3396, 2017.

12. Rothe, R., Timofte, R., Goo, L.V., Deep expectation of real and apparent age from a single image without facial landmarks. *Int. J. Comput. Vision*, 126, 144–157, 2018.

13. Mau, L., Ghamisi, P., Zhu, X.X., Unsupervised spectral spatial feature learning via deep residual conv-deconv network for hyperspectral image classification. *IEEE Trans. Geosci. Remote Sens.*, 56, 1, 391–406, 2018.

14. Redmon, J., Divvala, S., Girshick, R., Farhadi, A., You only look once: Unified, real-time object detection. *IEEE Conference on Computer Vision and Pattern Recognition (CVPR)*, IEEE, pp. 779–788, 2016.

15. Liu, W., Anguelov, D., Erhan, D., Szegedy, C., Reed, S., Fu, C.Y., Berg, A.C., SSD: Single shot multibox detector. *IEEE European Conference on Computer Vision (ECCV)*. Lecture Notes in Computer Science, vol. 9905, Springer, Cham, pp. 21–37, 2016, IEEE.

16. Demir, B. and Erturk, S., Empirical mode decomposition of hyperspectral images for support vector machine classification. *IEEE Trans. Geosci. Remote Sens.*, 48, 11, 4071–4084, 2010.

17. Pizurica, A. and Philips, W., Estimating the probability of the presence of a signal of interest in multiresolution single & multiband image denoising. *IEEE Trans. Image Process.*, 15, 3, 654–665, 2006.

18. Golyandina, N., On the choice of parameters in singular spectrum analysis and related subspace-based methods. *Stat. Interface*, 3, 259–279, 2010.

19. Rahul, S., Ram Bilas, P., Pradip, S., Automated emotion recognition based on higher order statistics and deep learning algorithm. *Biomed. Signal Process. Control*, 58, 101867, 2020.

20. Madhavan, S., Tripathy, R.K., Pachori, R.B., Time-frequency domain deep convolutional neural network for the classification of focal and non-focal EEG signals. *IEEE Sens. J.*, 20, 6, 3078–3086, 2020.

21. Chaudhary, P.K. and Pachori, R.B., Automatic diagnosis of glaucoma using two dimensional Fourier-Bessel series expansion based empirical wavelet transform. *Biomed. Signal Process. Control*, 64, 1–17, 2021.

22. Chaudhary, P.K. and Pachori, R.B., FBSED based automatic diagnosis of COVID-19 using X-ray and CT images. *Comput. Biol. Med.*, 134, 104454, 2021.

23. Irani, M. and Anandan, P., A unified approach to moving object detection in 2D and 3D scenes. *IEEE Trans. Pattern Anal. Mach. Intell.*, 20, 6, 577–589, 1998.

24. Xu, F., Liu, X., FujiMura, K., Pedestrian detection and tracking with night vision. *IEEE Trans. Intell. Transp. Syst.*, 6, 1, 63–71, 2005.

25. Zhou, X., Yang, C., Yu, W., Moving object detection by detecting contiguous outliers in the low-rank representation. *IEEE Trans. Pattern Anal. Mach. Intell.*, 35, 3, 597–610, 2013.

26. Chen, Y., Zhang, R.H., Shang, L., A novel method of object detection from a moving camera based on image matching and frame coupling. *PLoS One*, 9, 10, 2014.

27. Guennouni, S., Ahaitouf, A., Mansouri, A.A., Comparative study of multiple object detection using haar-like feature selection and local binary patterns in several platforms. *Model. Simul. Eng.*, 2015, 1–8, 2015.

28. Wu, Y., He, X., Nguyen, T.Q., Moving object detection with a freely moving camera via background motion subtraction. *IEEE Trans. Circuits Syst. Video Technol.*, 27, 2, 236–248, 2017.

29. Mangale, S., Tambe, R., Khambete, M., Object detection and tracking in thermal video using directed acyclic graph (DAG). *ICTACT J. Image Video Process.*, 08, 01, 1566–1574, 2017.

30. Xue, Y., Ju, Z., Xiang, K., Chen, J., Liu, H., Multiple sensors based hand motion recognition using adaptive directed acyclic graph. *Appl. Sci.*, 7, 4, 358, 2017.

31. Heo, D., Lee, E., Ko, B.C., Pedestrian detection at night using deep neural networks and saliency maps. *Electron. Imaging*, 61, 6, 060403-1–060403-9, 2018.

32. Neves, A. and Ribeiro, R., Algorithms for face detection on infrared thermal images. *Int. J. Adv. Software*, 10, 499–512, 2018.

33. Gomez, A., Conti, F., Benini, L., Thermal image-based CNN's for ultra-low power people recognition. *Proc. 15th ACM Int. Conf. Comput. Frontiers*, May 2018, ACM, New York, USA, pp. 326–331.

34. Wang, Q., Gao, J., Li, X., Weakly supervised adversarial domain adaptation for semantic segmentation in urban scenes. *IEEE Trans. Image Process.*, 28, 9, 4376–4386, 2019.

35. Shahid, N., Yu, G.H., Trinh, T.D., Sin, D.S., Kim, J.Y., Real-time implementation of human detection in thermal imagery based on CNN. *J. Korean Inst. Inf. Technol.*, 17, 1, 107–121, 2019.

36. Wang, X. and Hosseinyalamdary, S., Human detection based on a sequence of thermal images using deep learning. *Int. Arch. Photogramm. Remote Sens. Spat. Inf. Sci.*, XLII-2/W13, 1–6, 2019.

37. Hasan, M., Ullah, S., Khan, M.J., Khurshid, K., Comparative analysis of SVM, ANN and CNN for classifying vegetation species using hyperspectral thermal infrared data. *Proceedings of the International Archives of the Photogrammetry, Remote Sensing & Spatial Information Sciences*, Enschede, The Netherlands, vol. XLII-2/W13, pp. 1861–1868, 2019.

38. Hirose, A., Complex-valued neural networks: Advances and applications. *IEEE Comput. Intell. Mag.*, Hoboken, NJ, USA. Wiley-IEEE Press, 8, 2, 77–79, 2013.

39. Ivasic-Kos, M., Kristo, M., Pobar, M., Human detection in thermal imaging using YOLO. *Proc. 5th Int. Conf. Comput. Technol. Appl. (ICCTA)*, New York, USA, pp. 20–24, 2019.

40. Shangsheng, Z., Jiangzhou, Z., Xiaobo, C., Yanqiang, L., Road information detection method based on deep learning. *6th International Conference on Electronic Technology and Information Science (ICETIS 2021)*, Journal of Physics: Conference Series, 8-10 January 2021, vol. 1827.

41. Rodríguez-Pérez, R. and Bajorath, J., Evolution of support vector machine and regression modeling in chemoinformatics and drug discovery. *J. Comput. Aided Mol. Des.*, 36, 355–362, 2022, https://doi.org/10.1007/s10822-022-00442-9.

42. Mitra, A., Jain, A., Kishore, A. *et al.*, A comparative study of demand forecasting models for a multi-channel retail company: A novel hybrid machine learning approach. *Oper. Res. Forum*, 3, 58, 2022, https://doi.org/10.1007/s43069-022-00166-4.

43. Durairaj, D.M. and Mohan, B.H.K., A convolutional neural network based approach to financial time series prediction. *Neural Comput. Appl.*, 34, 13319–13337, 2022, https://doi.org/10.1007/s00521-022-07143-2.

44. Lin, T.-Y., Maire, M., Belongie, S., Hays, J., Perona, P., Ramanan, D., Dollár, P., Zitnick, C.L., Microsoft COCO: Common objects in context, in: *ECCV*, vol. 2, 3, 2014.

45. Mahor, V., Bijrothiya, S., Rawat, R., Kumar, A., Garg, B., Pachlasiya, K., IoT and artificial intelligence techniques for public safety and security, in: *Smart Urban Computing Applications*, p. 111, 2023.

46. Mahor, V., Pachlasiya, K., Garg, B., Chouhan, M., Telang, S., Rawat, R., Mobile operating system (Android) vulnerability analysis using machine learning, in: *Proceedings of International Conference on Network Security and Blockchain Technology: ICNSBT 2021*, pp. 159–169, Springer Nature Singapore, Singapore, 2022, June.

47. Rawat, R., Garg, B., Pachlasiya, K., Mahor, V., Telang, S., Chouhan, M., Mishra, R., SCNTA: Monitoring of network availability and activity for identification of anomalies using machine learning approaches. *Int. J. Inf. Technol. Web Eng. (IJITWE)*, 17, 1, 1–19, 2022.

48. Rawat, R., Rimal, Y.N., William, P., Dahima, S., Gupta, S., Sankaran, K.S., Malware threat affecting financial organization analysis using machine learning approach. *Int. J. Inf. Technol. Web Eng. (IJITWE)*, 17, 1, 1–20, 2022.

49. Rawat, R., Mahor, V., Chouhan, M., Pachlasiya, K., Telang, S., Garg, B., Systematic literature review (SLR) on social media and the digital transformation of drug trafficking on darkweb, in: *International Conference on Network Security and Blockchain Technology*, pp. 181–205, Springer, Singapore, 2022.

50. Rawat, R., Ayodele Oki, O., Sankaran, S., Florez, H., Ajagbe, S.A., Techniques for predicting dark web events focused on the delivery of illicit products and ordered crime. *Int. J. Electr. Comput. Eng. (IJECE)*, 13, 5, 5354–5365, Oct. 2023, doi: 10.11591/ijece.v13i5.pp5354-5365.

51. Rawat, R., Garg, B., Mahor, V., Telang, S., Pachlasiya, K., Chouhan, M., Organ trafficking on the dark web—The data security and privacy concern in healthcare systems, in: *Internet of Healthcare Things: Machine Learning for Security and Privacy*, pp. 189–216, 2022.

52. Vyas, P., Vyas, G., Chauhan, A., Rawat, R., Telang, S., Gottumukkala, M., Anonymous trading on the dark online marketplace: An exploratory study, in: *Using Computational Intelligence for the Dark Web and Illicit Behavior Detection*, pp. 272–289, IGI Global, 2022.

53. Rawat, R., Oki, O.A., Sankaran, K.S., Olasupo, O., Ebong, G.N., Ajagbe, S.A., A new solution for cyber security in big data using machine learning approach, in: *Mobile Computing and Sustainable Informatics: Proceedings of ICMCSI 2023*, pp. 495–505, Springer Nature Singapore, Singapore, 2023.

54. Rawat, R., Chakrawarti, R.K., Raj, A., Mani, G., Chidambarathanu, K., Bhardwaj, R., Association rule learning for threat analysis using traffic analysis and packet filtering approach. *Int. J. Inf. Technol.*, 1–11, 2023.

55. Rawat, R., Logical concept mapping and social media analytics relating to cyber criminal activities for ontology creation. *Int. J. Inf. Technol.*, 15, 2, 893–903, 2023.

56. Rawat, R., Mahor, V., Álvarez, J.D., Ch, F., Cognitive systems for dark web cyber delinquent association malignant data crawling: A review, in: *Handbook of Research on War Policies, Strategies, and Cyber Wars*, pp. 45–63, 2023.

57. Rawat, R., Chakrawarti, R.K., Vyas, P., Gonzáles, J.L.A., Sikarwar, R., Bhardwaj, R., Intelligent fog computing surveillance system for crime and vulnerability identification and tracing. *Int. J. Inf. Secur. Priv. (IJISP)*, *17*, 1, 1–25, 2023.

58. Rawat, R., Sowjanya, A.M., Patel, S.I., Jaiswal, V., Khan, I., Balaram, A. (Eds.), *Using Machine Intelligence: Autonomous Vehicles Volume 1*, John Wiley & Sons, 2022.

59. Rawat, R., Mahor, V., Díaz-Álvarez, J., Chávez, F., Rooted learning model at fog computing analysis for crime incident surveillance, in: *2022 International Conference on Smart Generation Computing, Communication and Networking (SMART GENCON)*, pp. 1–9, IEEE, 2022, December.

60. Rawat, R. and Shrivastav, S.K., SQL injection attack detection using SVM. *Int. J. Comput. Appl.*, *42*, 13, 1–4, 2012.

61. Rawat, R., Bhardwaj, P., Kaur, U., Telang, S., Chouhan, M., Sankaran, K.S., *Smart vehicles for communication, volume 2*, John Wiley & Sons, 2023.

62. Mahor, V., Garg, B., Telang, S., Pachlasiya, K., Chouhan, M., Rawat, R., Cyber threat phylogeny assessment and vulnerabilities representation at thermal power station, in: *Proceedings of International Conference on Network Security and Blockchain Technology: ICNSBT 2021*, pp. 28–39, Springer Nature Singapore, Singapore, 2022, June.

63. Rawat, R., Gupta, S., Sivaranjani, S., Cu, O.K., Kuliha, M., Sankaran, K.S., Malevolent information crawling mechanism for forming structured illegal organisations in hidden networks. *Int. J. Cyber Warf. Terror. (IJCWT)*, *12*, 1, 1–14, 2022.

Automatic Speech Recognition Design Modeling

Babu Rao.K[1*], Bhargavi Mopuru[2], Malik Jawarneh[3], José Luis Arias-Gonzáles[4], Samuel-Soma M. Ajibade[5] and P. Prabhu[6]

[1]*Department of CSE, Koneru Lakshmaiah Education Foundation, Hyderabad, India*
[2]*Department of CSE, Koneru Lakshmaiah Education Foundation, Vaddeswaram, Guntur, India*
[3]*Faculty of Computing Sciences, Gulf College, Al-Khuwair, Oman*
[4]*University of British Columbia, Lima, Peru*
[5]*Department of Computer Engineering, Istanbul Ticaret University, Istanbul, Turkey*
[6]*Directorate of Distance Education, Alagappa University, Karaikudi, Tamilnadu, India*

Abstract

The term "automatic speech recognition" refers to the procedure by which an auditory signal of spoken words can be converted into text. Voice recognition is another term that may be used to describe this process in its simplest form. The challenging nature of automatic speech or voice recognition by a computer system can be attributed to a variety of contributing factors. Variation in the source, variation in the auditory surroundings, variation in the speaker's physical and emotional condition, variation in the speaking rate, and variance in the speaker's socio-linguistic background are all examples of these elements. This article presents a feature selection and machine learning-based automatic speech recognition system. Noise from speech is removed using least mean square adaptive algorithm. Then, feature selection is performed using Relied algorithm. It helps in improving the classification accuracy. Classification is performed using SVM-RBF, BPNN, and naïve Bayes algorithm.

Keywords: Speech recognition, feature selection, relief algorithm, LMS algorithm, SVM-RBF, accuracy

22.1 Introduction

Speech is by far the most common and effective means of communication between individuals, especially when it comes to the exchange of ideas and information. It will be important for machines to have the ability to automatically recognize spoken commands at some point in the future. Humans are dependent on computing equipment for a broad variety of tasks, some examples of which include directing applications, inputting data and storing it, generating documents, doing analysis, and retrieving information. In the business sector,

*Corresponding author: baburao.k@klh.edu.in

Romil Rawat, Rajesh Kumar Chakrawarti, Sanjaya Kumar Sarangi, Piyush Vyas, Mary Sowjanya Alamanda, Kotagiri Srividya and Krishnan Sakthidasan Sankaran (eds.) *Conversational Artificial Intelligence*, (353–368) © 2024 Scrivener Publishing LLC

this technology has found applications in a variety of domains, including business planning and scheduling, employee attendance tracking, electronic marketing and communication, and electronic resource management among others. Automatic speech or voice recognition refers to the process by which an auditory signal of speaking utterances may be transformed into text. This process can also be referred to simply as voice recognition. Automatic speech or voice recognition by a computer system is difficult because of a number of factors. These factors include variation in the source, variation in the acoustic environment, variation in the physical and emotional state of the speaker, variation in the speaking rate, and variation in the socio-linguistic background of the speaker. Spectrum analysis, which is also sometimes referred to as feature extraction, is the initial phase in automatic speech recognition systems. This is then followed by feature classification and feature matching. In the 1950s, researchers sought to construct a system for automatic speech recognition by directly converting audio impulses into a word sequence. Nevertheless, they were not successful in their efforts. In the 1970s, successful attempts at speech recognition were performed for the first time by using pattern matching algorithms [1].

Approaches to Automatic Speech Recognition

Speech recognition is the end result of the process in which the system makes a series of attempts to decode the signal based on the acoustic characteristics of the signal and phonetic units. Automated speech recognition may be performed using any one of the following three methods: the acoustic–phonetic approach, the pattern recognition method, or the artificial intelligence method [2].

i.   Acoustic–Phonetic Approach: The first step in the process is to determine the individual phonetic units. Phonetic units are so-called because these are the units whose primary definition comes from their aural properties. Even though the acoustic properties of a phonetic unit vary substantially from one speaker to another, the unit can still be recognized because of coarticulation. The procedure is broken down into two stages: the first stage, which involves segmentation and labeling, and the second stage, which involves speech recognition. It will begin by separating the signal into its component parts as the very first step. A label will be assigned to each phonetic unit, and that label will indicate the unit's sonic characteristics. At the second stage, signals are used to determine whether or not a particular string of phonetic labels represents a legitimate word. This determination is made in order to go on to the third stage. A speech analysis system begins by modeling the spectral features of the spoken stream in the initial phase of its operation. Spectrum analysis is comprised of a variety of different methods, including filter bank analysis and linear predictive coding. After that, a collection of features that have acoustic properties is created from the spectrum observations using feature detection. This collection of features is used to analyze the spectrum. During the stage that is dedicated to identifying features, we look for things like formants, pitch, voiced/unvoiced signal energy, nasality, and friction. In the third step, segmentation and labeling are utilized so that labels can be provided for each phonetic unit, and the stable areas may be brought to a conclusion.

ii. Pattern Recognition Approach: Instead of relying on the determination and segmentation of features, the technique uses a priori knowledge of speech patterns as its foundation. The two stages that make up this process are, first, the training of speech patterns and then the recognition of those patterns. In order to improve one's fluency in the use of spoken language, many training approaches are utilized. You may employ it to provide an accurate description of the acoustic features of a pattern. The term "pattern classification" is used to refer to this type of categorization. Pattern classification, when applied to the task of speech recognition, is dependent on a comparison phase that establishes direct similarities between the training patterns and the unidentified speech patterns. It does this by comparing patterns to previously unknown speech patterns in order to classify them. The quality of the output improves in proportion to the size of the training set that is being used. So, the effectiveness of a method for pattern recognition is contingent on the degree at which the recommended training plan is adhered to in an effective manner [3].

iii. Artificial Intelligence (AI) Approach: The acoustic–phonetic technique and pattern recognition are also elements of this approach. This tactic makes an effort to automate the recognition process in such a manner that it takes into consideration the natural talents of a person in a variety of domains, including visualization, analysis, and decision making. As a direct consequence of this, this technique is also put to use in order to compile and synthesize knowledge derived from different fields. The artificial intelligence works with acoustic knowledge, phonetic knowledge, lexical knowledge, syntactic knowledge, semantic knowledge, and pragmatic information once speech has been segmented and labeled [4].

This article presents a feature selection and machine learning-based automatic speech recognition system. Noise from speech is removed using least mean square adaptive algorithm. Then, feature selection is performed using Relied algorithm. It helps in improving the classification accuracy.

22.2 Literature Survey

22.2.1 Noise Reduction Algorithms for Speech Enhancement

The ordinary Wiener filter's lackluster performance inspired the development of the adaptive filter's innovative noise reduction capabilities. It is possible to make an approximation of the gradient vector using just a few pieces of information if this information is available. Iteratively shifting the weight vector in the opposite direction of the gradient vector is one application of the least mean square (LMS) adaptive technique. This is done with the goal of reducing the squared error as much as possible. It is not necessary for it to have knowledge of the frequency ratio between noise and speech.

The authors in [5] developed the Filtered-x LMS (FxLMS) adaptive noise reduction approach with the intention of mitigating the unfavorable impacts that are caused by the secondary pathway in ANM implementations. When the narrowband approach is used, rather than the wideband one, speech sounds are able to be cancelled out more efficiently, and the output signals have a greater quality overall. In contrast, it offers a mean square error that may be adjusted according to needs.

Block LMS is a technique that was suggested by Rahman *et al.* for the purpose of adaptive noise reduction. While using this strategy, the filter coefficients are modified only once for each data block. The demand for computers has thus decreased as a direct result of this. The technique with the steepest fall is the one that will bring you to your goal of minimizing the mean square error in a circumstance in which the whole of the signal is involved. In spite of the fact that it is anticipated that the LMS technique would be subject to a larger degree of fluctuation than this new strategy, it will yet be objective when it is in the steady state, yet this results in an issue that is referred to as the mean square error.

Normalized least mean square (NLMS)-based adaptive noise reduction is a strategy that was proposed by Huang *et al.* [6] to solve the trade-off between rapid convergence and moderate excess mean square error. They referred to this method as NLMS-based adaptive noise reduction. The mean square error and the expected amount of noise power in the system are taken into consideration when making adjustments to the step size. It is straightforward to put into action and has the potential to achieve fast convergence rates, great tracking, and little miss correction. In addition to that, a small mistake has been corrected. The challenge, on the other hand, is that doing so will result in a rise in the level of general ambient noise.

In this presentation, the results of an investigation that Vincent Wan [7] conducted on the use of support vector machines for speaker verification were discussed. He devised the essential ways for support vector machines (SVMs) to have the best possible performance in this context, which is required for the sequence discrimination method of speaker verification, which uses SVMs. Since the SVM considers the whole of the sequence to be a single vector, it is in a position to discriminate quite precisely between the various sequences. We demonstrate experimentally, with the help of the PloyVar speaker verification database, that state-of-the-art results can be obtained by training a SVM with a scorespace kernel and spherical normalization. This method is currently considered to be the most effective method available.

Thuong Le-Tien and Dinh Chien came up with a method that was based on wavelets and neural networks for detecting Vietnamese voices in robotic communications. When it comes to the Vietnamese language, speech synthesis and recognition systems have a long list of obstacles to overcome before they can become fully functional. Wavelet transformations were used to speech samples during processing in order to separate formants and pitch ranges. In addition, the neural networks and voice filaments were split apart so that pattern identification would be easier. We demonstrated that a robot could be operated in Vietnamese using just a few basic instructions in order to determine whether or not the way that was presented was effective.

Teddy Surya Gunawan and Eliathamby Arnbikairajah [8] employed a fractional bark gamma tone filter in conjunction with a short-term temporal masking threshold to noise ratio in order to enhance the quality of loud speech (MNR). The two strategies were combined into a single strategy. First, the noisy corrupted signal is segmented into a predetermined number of sub-bands with a fractional bark precision, and then the noise ratio is calculated with the use of a temporal masking threshold. The performance of the suggested method was evaluated and contrasted with that of conventional voice enhancement algorithms that are already in use. In order to accomplish this goal, we used a total of six unique forms of noise as well as three different signal-to-noise ratio (SNR) setups. The results of the tests revealed that the suggested method for voice augmentation was successful in a wide range of ambient noise circumstances.

Panu Somervuo and Teuvo Kohonen are the ones responsible for developing the algorithms SOM and LVQ, which are used for analyzing feature sequences of varied lengths and angular distortions [9]. Both of these approaches are used by practitioners of ML. The input distribution is projected onto a two-dimensional grid in a nonlinear fashion throughout the course of the self-organization process. The models that correspond to the grid points were acquired in the form of authentic feature vector sequences. We used a technique known as dynamic temporal warping (DTW) in order to determine the distances that existed between individual feature sequences. The DTW-LVQ achieved an error rate of 1.5% on the test set for speaker-independent isolated word recognition, while the DTWSOM was put to work in unsupervised clustering applications such as handwriting recognition. These two efforts at submitting an application were both successful.

Enginavci introduced a method in [10] that is capable of automatically recognizing Turkish words. Inside the system were implemented discrete wavelet neural networks that were based on adaptive entropy. Our model, which we call a discrete wavelet neural network, is composed of two parts. The first part is a discrete wavelet layer, which is used for adaptive feature extraction in the time–frequency domain. The second part is a multi-layer perceptron feedforward neural network layer, which is used for classification. These strata are next to one another; they are located on the same stratum. The performance of this technique in speech recognition was evaluated using noisy Turkish word signals from a total of 20 speakers (10 men and 10 women), indicating that it is effective. The test was conducted. There was a balanced representation of men and women among the presenters. It was discovered that 92.58% of the occurrences were accurately recognized, which is nearly unheard of.

Patil *et al.* [11] created the current speech augmentation system, which is based on an adaptive filtering approach that is implemented in digital filters. The step size is an essential component that must be taken into consideration in order to successfully execute the least mean square approach, which is what the adaptive filter accomplishes in order to get rid of noise. The least squares least absolute error technique will converge fast when the step size is increased; nevertheless, the steady-state mean square error will increase. This suggests that there is a limit to the SNR that can be enhanced with voice enhancement and the potential rate of convergence. Notwithstanding this limit, there is still room for improvement.

Shruthi and her coworkers presented research that aimed to improve both the intelligibility and overall quality of the human voice. The quality of the speech signals that have been gathered deteriorates in proportion to the amount of background noise. The process of enhancing the voice, which also reduces background noise, does not have any impact on the quality of the transmission. An adaptive Wiener filter is used in conjunction with two distinct methods of noise reduction, namely, two-step noise reduction and harmonic regeneration noise reduction, in order to cut down on the amount of background noise that is present in a speech signal. While setting the parameters of a filter, both the input and output SNRs are taken into consideration. If we examine the SNR values, we may be able to determine how well the filter performs its function.

Thakkar *et al.* provide in reference [12] the findings of a research that was conducted on adaptive noise canceling and its applications. Adaptive noise cancellation is a technique that may be used as an alternative in situations when one is attempting to estimate signals that have been corrupted by interference or additive noise. As there is no prioritizing of signal or noise estimates, it is possible to achieve high degrees of noise rejection, which would be difficult or impossible to do using standard techniques to signal processing. This is because there is no prioritizing of signal or noise estimates. Since there is no way to differentiate between the crucial signals and the background noise, this is the result. Adaptive noise cancellation is one approach that may be used in order to cut down on the amount of background noise that is included in a spoken signal.

In order to solve the problem of noise cancellation, Rahima *et al.* [13] focused their study on the ability to have hands-free conversations in loud environments. Very recently, forward and inverse Blind Source Separation structures have been proposed as a method for reducing ambient noise and increasing the quality of voice communication. This suggestion comes as a result of research that has been conducted in this area. As a result, the goal of this research is to develop a unique strategy that combines the dual backward structure with the Simple Fast Transversal Filter algorithm.

Ramli *et al.* [14] developed a way to decrease the effect that external noise has on a person's ability to understand what is being said over the phone in an attempt to improve the intelligibility of phone conversations. The method makes use of a two-sensor adaptive noise canceller, which has the capability of adjusting the filter it employs based on the particulars of the noise that is being processed. For determining whether or not the experiment was successful, the eigenvalue spread is computed using the autocorrelation of the noise input, which is then utilized to evaluate the outcome of the experiment. The intrinsic noise canceller that has been proposed uses an approach that is adaptive in order to eliminate noise from an input signal.

22.2.2 Speech Segmentation, Feature Extraction

Continuous speech may be successfully segmented into words or subwords in an efficient manner in a reasonably short period of time and with minimal amount of energy usage if a hybrid approach that is based on spectral centroid analysis is used. As a direct consequence of this, you may use this method to efficiently break up lengthy lengths of speech. The accuracy of its segmentation is far higher than that of other widely used approaches. The ability of short-term speech characteristics to differentiate between voiced and unvoiced speech components was described, along with a larger spectral centroid for voiced segments, the possibility that the movement of the centroid over time may disclose the underlying sound's rhythm and periodicity, and the ability of short-term speech characteristics to distinguish between voiced and unvoiced speech components. Inconsistent articulation, irregular word order, and varied pause durations are only some of the problems that may contribute to unsatisfactory results.

Wijoyo *et al.* [15] suggested the use of linear predictive coding (LPC) and artificial neural networks (ANNs) as a method for directing the mobility of a mobile robot. After taking continuous samples from the microphone, these continuous samples were then fed into the LPC and ANN algorithms to reduce the noise. A speaker-independent system capable of recognizing Tamil speech in closed captions has been developed by Radha and her colleagues [16]. The use of Hidden Markov Models (HMM) enabled us to extract features, develop an acoustic model, create a pronunciation dictionary, and create a language model, and we were successful in doing all of these things with an accuracy of 88% across 2,500 different words.

Hossan *et al.* [17] were the first to explain a method for collecting useful speech characteristics. They did this by making use of MelFrequency Cepstral Coefficients (MFCC) and their dynamic derivatives. When attempting to acquire meaningful speech characteristics, this strategy has now evolved into the industry standard. It is possible that the fact that the crucial frequency bandwidth of the human ear varies from listener to listener is what is responsible for its widespread usage. Calculating the MFCC coefficients requires, first, decorrelating the log energy outputs from a sequence of triangle filters that are linearly spaced on the Mel frequency scale. Temporal derivatives have also been added to the static speech features in order to complete them. The method has been altered, and as a result, it is now capable of capturing the transitional qualities of the speech signal in a more improved manner. The use of a feature vector in CSR modeling results in the generation of the MFCC.

A technique for the extraction of features, known as linear predictive coding or LPC for short, was developed by Sunny and colleagues [18]. The spoken signal is separated from the surrounding noise in order for it to function properly. In order to identify the resonance of the vocal tract, the signal waveform is analyzed using LPC. The linear predictive filter is a technique that can forecast the value of an incoming sample by utilizing the values of samples taken in the past as inputs. This approach is used to predict the value of a forthcoming sample. Because of its capacity to create a high-quality speech at a low bit rate and its ability to extract speech parameters like pitch, formants, and spectra, LPC is often employed as front-end processing in voice recognition systems. This is due to the fact that LPC can generate high-quality speech. In addition, for your perusal and consideration, an illuminating model for time-domain analysis of speech signals is presented here.

Unsupervised K-means clustering is a common method used in the practice of cluster analysis. The method that is being used here was created by Li *et al.* [19]. As a result of their primary purpose, which is to identify the parts of a dataset that are most like to one another, they are an important component of numerical data analysis. The significance of this, both geometrically and statistically, cannot be refuted. Before the relevant speech features can be labeled for the purpose of further modeling, they must first be categorized into groups based on the centroid positions of the groups to which they belong. During training, the nodes that were produced as a consequence of the clustering process are used in a manner similar to that of a codebook. Its user-friendly interface, outstanding efficiency, and low computational cost are some of the factors that have contributed to its broad acceptance and growing popularity. Even though the sizes of the clusters are all different, this makes it more probable that the clusters will all have the same dimensions.

The Fuzzy C-Means clustering methodology is the approach to soft clustering that has seen the most widespread use. This method was developed by Chattopadhyay and his colleagues [20]. When it comes to normalizing the data's original properties, this kind of unsupervised clustering outperforms other approaches that are currently available on the market. In order to solve a broad range of problems relating to geostatistical data analysis, a lot of people employ this method. The CSR system has grouped the data vectors in order to reduce the number of typos that are produced by the system on a regular basis.

Gaussian Mixture Models (GMMs) were used in Vyas's [21] approach, which he invented, in order to recognize individual phrases. With this configuration, everything depends on the person doing the talking. The goal of this method is to separate out each individual utterance of the numbers 0 through 9 that occur in the course of a spoken sequence. It is possible to get a high level of accuracy in speech recognition by using a statistical model that is derived from GMM. In addition to this, the structure is all-encompassing and can easily be enlarged such that it includes words with multiple syllables. GMM is not as successful as the other statistical models since it does not directly maximize the value of the training data that it uses. Mondher Frikha and Ahmed Ben Harnida conducted a research in which they compared the efficiency of ANN, hybrid HMM, and ANN Architectures with the purpose of achieving robust speech recognition [22].

The Elman Recurrent Neural Networks and the Multilayer Perceptron were the two varieties of neural networks that were investigated by the researchers. Hybrid connectionist–HMM systems were also investigated by the team. Using the TIMIT database and two perceptually driven characteristics, an analysis was carried out to determine the degree to which the suggested systems were successful in both clean and noisy environments (MFCC and PLP). After developing a wavelet-based denoising phase for the preprocessing stage, they put the systems through a durability test by adding different levels of additive noise and modifying the signal-to-noise ratio.

Hamdy K. Elminir and colleagues conducted a research on the subject of evaluation criteria for speech recognition. Throughout the course of their investigations, they put a wide variety of methods for feature extraction to the test and timed how long it took them to finish each stage [from training to feature extraction to principal component analysis (PCA) conversion and back again]. They compared and contrasted the feature extraction methods LPC, MFCC, and ZCPA for continuous speech in order to figure out which one was the most suited for the speech recognition process. This allowed them to choose the approach that would be used. Following reaching that verdict, they investigated the possibility of using PCA in order to get better results.

Research was carried out at Stanford University by Prasad and his colleagues employing artificial neural networks in order to build AVR for daily speech. The outcome is only described using the two options that were available, which were "yes" and "no". After the extraction of per-frame spectrum data by cepstral analysis, the data is then fed into a feed-forward neural network that has been trained by the process of back propagation with momentum. The network is educated to recognize input words and place them in the appropriate categories after identifying them. Words that are suitable for the input sequence are looked for with the assistance of a pattern search algorithm, which gets its information from the neural network. Because of the wide variety of voices being input, there is a decrease in both the amount of vocabulary and the network's stability.

Aranda *et al.* [23] developed a method for determining the identity of ambient sounds by using LPC-Cepstral coefficients for the purpose of characterization and a back propagation artificial neural network for the purpose of verification. Even though we were only using two feature vectors for the verification process, we still had a very successful outcome with a success rate of 96.66%. The lowest number of complaints received were about automobiles and trucks, followed by concerns about motorcycles and aeroplanes.

A speaker-independent system capable of recognizing Tamil speech in closed captions has been developed by Radha and her colleagues [16]. With the use of HMM, we were able to increase our accuracy across 2,500 words to 88%. This discovery was then used to lead the construction of a language model, a pronunciation dictionary, an acoustic model, and a collection of feature extractors. All of these were completed after the discovery was made.

The powerful voice recognition system proposed by Mahalakshmi *et al.* [24] was tested with MFCC, vector quantization, and HMM, and it successfully identified the speech 98% of the time. There are 10 different recordings of the same five words, each of which was made by one of four different people.

Choudhary *et al.* [25] described a system for completely automatic audio identification of Hindi words in context, encompassing both single and plural forms of the language. They were able to do this with the help of the Hidden Markov Model Toolbox. It has been determined that the MFCC-free dataset contains Hindi words and that the identification approach achieves a level of accuracy of 95% for single words and a level of accuracy of 90% for phrases and sentences.

Meng-Zhen Li and his colleagues [26] investigate five different strategies for reducing the dimensionality of data, including three dimensionality reduction methods, two clustering strategies, and an extraction method for high-dimensional super vectors. They provide the universal background model, which is a typical model that is based on the Gaussian mixture model. Dimensionality reduction may be accomplished using one of three techniques: PCA, spectral clustering, or multilayer bootstrap networks. K-means clustering and agglomerative hierarchical clustering are two methods that may be used to accomplish the same clustering objectives.

Using a GMM, Kalamani *et al.* [27] provide a method for continuous voice input recognition. One of the acoustic models that is used often in the industry of speech recognition is known as the GMM. For the purpose of assigning labels to recovered attributes in accordance with the voice input, this audio model makes use of the Fuzzy C-Means clustering preprocessing technique. The results of the simulation show that the proposed model may lower the bit error rate by as much as 2.5% when applied to a wide variety of clean speech signals, which can result in an increase in recognition accuracy of as much as 3.7% when compared to the models that are currently in use.

In their explanation, Rajendra Prasad *et al.* provide not just the theory that lies behind UBM but also an explicit technique of speech clustering that makes use of GMM. For the time being, the generalized method of moments is the most effective statistical model that can be used for the purpose of describing the speaker in a high-dimensional space. We create a two-dimensional map of the words that are used by each individual by using a technique known as PCA. Having stated that, the unsupervised classification of speakers via the use of Euclidean space is the aspect of speaker diarization that is considered to be the most important.

22.3   Methodology

In this section, Figure 22.1 represents a feature selection and machine learning-based automatic speech recognition system. Noise from speech is removed using least mean square adaptive algorithm. Then, feature selection is using Relied algorithm. It helps in improving the classification accuracy. Classification is using SVM-RBF, BPNN, and naïve Bayes algorithm.

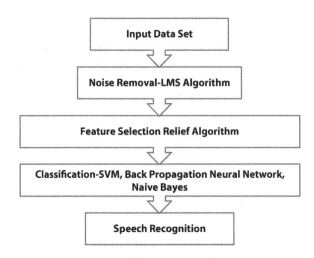

Figure 22.1 Automatic speech recognition using feature selection and machine learning.

The ordinary Wiener filter's lackluster performance inspired the development of the adaptive filter's innovative noise reduction capabilities. It is possible to make an approximation of the gradient vector using just a few pieces of information if this information is available. Iteratively shifting the weight vector in the opposite direction of the gradient vector is one application of the least mean square adaptive technique. This is done with the goal of reducing the squared error as much as possible. It is not necessary for it to have knowledge of the frequency ratio between noise and speech.

In 1992, Kira and Rendell [15] created the Relief algorithm as an instance-based learning technique in order to handle the challenges that are associated with binary classification. Individuals may use a filtering method to aid in the process of identifying correlations between features. Calculating feature statistics that take into account the dynamic relationship between the variables may be done with the help of nearest neighbors. Nonetheless, datasets with several classes or values that are missing do not lend themselves well to this strategy.

Machine learning technology based on computational learning theory, known as the SVM, has been developed. Finding the appropriate classification function for categorizing the training dataset is at the heart of SVM's quest for accuracy. SVM may be used to address classification problems such as density estimates and pattern recognition. The training data is first mapped nonlinearly into a higher dimension and then linearly separated [16]. The radial basis function (RBF) is the favored choice. SVM performs better with RBF mode.

Haykin and Anderson developed the back propagation method, which is one of the most widely used learning algorithms. Simple pattern recognition and mapping tasks may be accomplished using BPN, which is suitable. Back propagation is a learning process, not the network itself that takes examples as input and builds on them as output. In order to train the network to produce the correct output for every input pattern, algorithm examples of what the network must do will be provided. This modifies the weights of the network. A training pair is a pair consisting of an input and a target [17].

The theorem of Bayes provides the foundation for Bayesian classification. Simple bases, akin to the classification of end trees and chosen networks, are characterized by these naive Bayesian classification methods when applied to a big database. A subset of dependent characteristics can be represented using naive Bayes classification. P(x|c) is the posterior probability for each class in this technique. Predictions are made for each class with a higher likelihood.

$$P(c|x) = \frac{P(x|c)P(c)}{P(x)}$$ (22.1)

where $P(c|x)$ is the posterior probability of each class given diabetes × attribute
$P(x|c)$ is the likelihood value
$P(c)$ is the prior probability of diabetes class
P(x) is the prior probability of predictor
Each attribute conditionally forgives the subset class.

Naive Bayes uses a similar method to predict different types of probabilities based on various attributes.

22.4 Experimental Result Analysis

To examine the results of the framework, a series of experiments took place on speech audio dataset. A total of 100 audio speech are used. For training purposes, 80 samples are used as input. Noise is removed using LMS algorithm. The Relief algorithm is then used to choose features. It aids in the improvement of categorization accuracy. The SVM-RBF, BPNN, and naive Bayes algorithms are used for classification.

Five parameters—accuracy, sensitivity, specificity, precision, and recall—are used in the experimental analysis. The performance of machine learning algorithms on the basis of

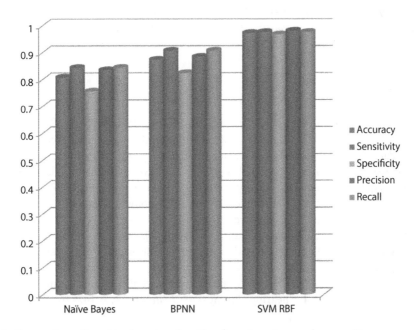

Figure 22.2 Comparison of machine learning algorithm for automatic speech recognition.

these five parameters is shown in Figure 22.2. SVM RBF is having better accuracy for the classification of glaucoma disease.

Static triggers, which are fixed patterns set in fixed locations, may be separated into two categories: dynamic triggers [28, 29], which have adjustable styles and placements and appear in different locations; Modern, state-of-the-art backdoor [30, 31] attack techniques rely too much on rigid, unchanging triggers (in terms of patterns and locations), which are unadaptable and quickly identified by defence systems. To achieve this straightforward one-to-one association discovered by the neural network model, they build a trigger with a static value and location matching a certain target label. When the static backdoor [32–34] attack [35, 36] approach is interfered with and restricted in real-world applications, it will perform much worse because of the repetitive attack [37–40] style. A dynamic trigger backdoor attack [41, 42] is more effective and adaptable to the real world than static triggers. However, there hasn't been much research done on backdoor assaults [43, 44] employing dynamic triggers in the audio domain yet. It highlights the need to develop dynamic backdoor [45, 46] assaults under more plausible circumstances.

22.5   Conclusion

Speech is by far the most common and effective way for people to talk to each other, especially when they want to share ideas and information. In the future, it will be important for machines to be able to automatically understand what people say to them. People use computers for a wide range of tasks, such as running programs, entering and storing data, making documents, analyzing data, and finding information. The purpose of this article is to provide an automatic speech recognition system that is based on feature selection and machine learning. The adaptive technique known as least mean square is utilized to reduce noise from voice. Thereafter, the Relied algorithm will take care of the feature selection. It contributes to the overall improvement of the categorization accuracy. SVM-RBF, BPNN, and the naive Bayes algorithm are used in the classification process, respectively.

References

1. Amodei, D., Ananthanarayanan, S., Anubhai, R., Bai, J., Battenberg, E., Case, C., Casper, J., Catanzaro, B., Cheng, Q., Chen, G. *et al.*, Deep speech 2: End-to-end speech recognition in English and Mandarin, in: *International Conference on Machine Learning*, PMLR, pp. 173–82, 2016.
2. Andrés-Ferrer, J., Albesano, D., Zhan, P., Vozila, P., Contextual density ratio for language model biasing of sequence to sequence ASR systems, in: *Proc. Interspeech*, pp. 2007–11, 2021.
3. Andrusenko, A., Laptev, A., Medennikov, I., Towards a competitive end-to-end speech recognition for CHiME-6 dinner party transcription, in: *Proc. Interspeech*, pp. 319–23, 2020.
4. Audhkhasi, K., Chen, T., Ramabhadran, B., Moreno, P.J., Mixture model attention: Flexible streaming and non-streaming automatic speech recognition, in: *Proc. Interspeech*, vol. 2021, pp. 1812–6, 2021.
5. Chi, H.-F., Gao, X.S., Soli, S., Alwan, A., Band-limited feedback cancellation with a modified filtered-X LMS algorithm for hearing aids. *Speech Commun.*, 39, 1, 147–161, 2003.

6. Huang, H.-C. and Lee, J., A new variable step-size NLMS algorithm and its performance analysis. *IEEE Trans. Signal Process. - TSP*, 60, 2055–2060, 2012, 10.1109/TSP.2011.2181505.

7. Wan, V. and William, C., Support vector machines for speaker verification and identification. *IEEE Workshop Neural Netw. Signal Process.*, vol. 2, pp. 775–784, 2000.

8. Gunawan, T. and Ambikairajah, E., Speech enhancement using temporal masking and fractional bark gammatone filters. *Australian International Conference on Speech Science & Technology*, 2004.

9. Somervuo, P. and Teuvo, K., Self-organizing maps and learning vector quantization for feature sequences. *Neural Process. Lett.*, 10, 151–159, 2004.

10. Polur, D.P. and Miller, G.E., Investigation of an HMM/ANN hybrid structure in pattern recognition application using cepstral analysis of dysarthric (distorted) speech signals. *Med. Eng. Phys.*, 28, 741–748, 2006.

11. Patidar, M., Patil, P.L., Bhalavi, A., Dubey, R., Efficient algorithm for speech enhancement using adaptive filter. *Int. J. Electr. Electron. Comput. Eng.*, 3, 1, 98–103, 2014.

12. Thakkar, V., Noise cancellation using least mean square algorithm. *IOSR J. Electron. Commun. Eng. (IOSR-JECE)*, 12, 5, 64–75, 2017.

13. Rahima, H., A dual backward adaptive algorithm for speech enhancement and acoustic noise reduction. *ICEMIS '18*, 2018.

14. Ramli, R., Abid Noor, A., Samad, S., Noise cancellation using selectable adaptive algorithm for speech in variable noise environment. *Int. J. Speech Technol.*, 20, 1–8, 2017.

15. Thiang, and Wijoyo, S., Speech recognition using linear predictive coding and artificial neural network for controlling movement of mobile robot. *International Conference on Information and Electronics Engineering*, vol. 6, pp. 179–183, 2011.

16. Vimala, C. and Radha, V., Speaker independent isolated speech recognition system for Tamil Language using HMM. *Proc. Eng.*, 30, 1097–1102, 2012.

17. Hossan, Md. A., Memon, S., Gregory, M., A novel approach for MFCC feature extraction, pp. 1–5, 2011.

18. Sunny, S., David, P.S., Jacob, K., Feature extraction methods based on linear predictive coding and wavelet packet decomposition for recognizing spoken words in Malayalam, pp. 27–30, 2012.

19. Li, X.-g., Yao, M.-f., Huang, W.-T., Speech recognition based on K-means clustering and neural network ensembles. *Proceedings - 2011 7th International Conference on Natural Computation*, vol. 2, ICNC, pp. 614–617, 2011.

20. Chattopadhyay, S., Pratihar, D., Sarkar, S., A comparative study of fuzzy c-means algorithm and entropy-based fuzzy clustering algorithms. *Comput. Inf.*, 30, 701–720, 2011.

21. Vyas, M., A gaussian mixture model based speech recognition system using Matlab. *Signal Image Process. : Int. J.*, 4, 109–118, 2013.

22. Masmoudi, S., Frikha, M., Chtourou, M., Hamida, A., Efficient MLP constructive training algorithm using a neuron recruiting approach for isolated word recognition system. *Int. J. Speech Technol.*, 14, 1–10, 2011.

23. Aranda-Uribe, O., Nakano-Miyatake, M., Perez-Meana, H., Environmental sounds recognition. *Telecommun. Radio Eng.*, 65, 271–279, 2006, 10.1615/TelecomRadEng.v65.i3.80.

24. Mahalakshmi, P., Muruganandam, M., Sharmila, A., Voice recognition security system using mel-frequency cepstrum coefficients. *Asian J. Pharm. Clin. Res.*, 9, 131, 2016.

25. Choudhary, A., Chauhan, M.R., Gupta, M.G., Automatic speech recognition system for isolated and connected words of Hindi language by using hidden Markov model toolkit (HTK), in: *Proceedings of International Conference on Emerging Trends in Engineering and Technology*, pp. 244–252, 2013.

26. Li, M.-Z. and Zhang, X.-L., An investigation of speaker clustering algorithms in adverse acoustic environments, pp. 1462–1466, 2018.

27. Kalamani, M., Krishnamoorthi, M., Valarmathi, R., Continuous speech recognition using Gaussian mixture model. *Int. J. Pure Appl. Math.*, 119, 16, 4513–4518, 2018.

28. Mahor, V., Bijrothiya, S., Rawat, R., Kumar, A., Garg, B., Pachlasiya, K., IoT and artificial intelligence techniques for public safety and security, in: *Smart Urban Computing Applications*, p. 111, 2023.

29. Mahor, V., Pachlasiya, K., Garg, B., Chouhan, M., Telang, S., Rawat, R., Mobile operating system (Android) vulnerability analysis using machine learning, in: *Proceedings of International Conference on Network Security and Blockchain Technology: ICNSBT 2021*, pp. 159–169, Springer Nature Singapore, Singapore, 2022, June.

30. Rawat, R., Garg, B., Pachlasiya, K., Mahor, V., Telang, S., Chouhan, M., Mishra, R., SCNTA: Monitoring of network availability and activity for identification of anomalies using machine learning approaches. *Int. J. Inf. Technol. Web Eng. (IJITWE)*, 17, 1, 1–19, 2022.

31. Rawat, R., Rimal, Y.N., William, P., Dahima, S., Gupta, S., Sankaran, K.S., Malware threat affecting financial organization analysis using machine learning approach. *Int. J. Inf. Technol. Web Eng. (IJITWE)*, 17, 1, 1–20, 2022.

32. Rawat, R., Mahor, V., Chouhan, M., Pachlasiya, K., Telang, S., Garg, B., Systematic literature review (SLR) on social media and the digital transformation of drug trafficking on darkweb, in: *International Conference on Network Security and Blockchain Technology*, pp. 181–205, Springer, Singapore, 2022.

33. Rawat, R., Ayodele Oki, O., Sankaran, S., Florez, H., Ajagbe, S.A., Techniques for predicting dark web events focused on the delivery of illicit products and ordered crime. *Int. J. Electr. Comput. Eng. (IJECE)*, 13, 5, 5354–5365, Oct. 2023, doi: 10.11591/ijece.v13i5.pp5354-5365.

34. Rawat, R., Garg, B., Mahor, V., Telang, S., Pachlasiya, K., Chouhan, M., Organ trafficking on the dark web—The data security and privacy concern in healthcare systems, in: *Internet of Healthcare Things: Machine Learning for Security and Privacy*, pp. 189–216, 2022.

35. Vyas, P., Vyas, G., Chauhan, A., Rawat, R., Telang, S., Gottumukkala, M., Anonymous trading on the dark online marketplace: An exploratory study, in: *Using Computational Intelligence for the Dark Web and Illicit Behavior Detection*, pp. 272–289, IGI Global, 2022.

36. Rawat, R., Oki, O.A., Sankaran, K.S., Olasupo, O., Ebong, G.N., Ajagbe, S.A., A new solution for cyber security in big data using machine learning approach, in: *Mobile Computing and Sustainable Informatics: Proceedings of ICMCSI 2023*, pp. 495–505, Springer Nature Singapore, Singapore, 2023.

37. Rawat, R., Chakrawarti, R.K., Raj, A., Mani, G., Chidambarathanu, K., Bhardwaj, R., Association rule learning for threat analysis using traffic analysis and packet filtering approach. *Int. J. Inf. Technol.*, 1–11, 2023.

38. Rawat, R., Logical concept mapping and social media analytics relating to cyber criminal activities for ontology creation. *Int. J. Inf. Technol.*, 15, 2, 893–903, 2023.

39. Rawat, R., Mahor, V., Álvarez, J.D., Ch, F., Cognitive systems for dark web cyber delinquent association malignant data crawling: A review, in: *Handbook of Research on War Policies, Strategies, and Cyber Wars*, pp. 45–63, 2023.

40. Rawat, R., Chakrawarti, R.K., Vyas, P., Gonzáles, J.L.A., Sikarwar, R., Bhardwaj, R., Intelligent fog computing surveillance system for crime and vulnerability identification and tracing. *Int. J. Inf. Secur. Priv. (IJISP)*, 17, 1, 1–25, 2023.

41. Rawat, R., Sowjanya, A.M., Patel, S.I., Jaiswal, V., Khan, I., Balaram, A. (Eds.), *Using Machine Intelligence: Autonomous Vehicles Volume 1*, John Wiley & Sons, 2022.

42. Rawat, R., Mahor, V., Díaz-Álvarez, J., Chávez, F., Rooted learning model at fog computing analysis for crime incident surveillance, in: *2022 International Conference on Smart Generation*

Computing, Communication and Networking (SMART GENCON), pp. 1–9, IEEE, 2022, December.

43. Rawat, R. and Shrivastav, S.K., SQL injection attack detection using SVM. *Int. J. Comput. Appl.*, *42*, 13, 1–4, 2012.

44. Rawat, R., Bhardwaj, P., Kaur, U., Telang, S., Chouhan, M., Sankaran, K.S., *Smart vehicles for communication, volume 2*, John Wiley & Sons, 2023.

45. Mahor, V., Garg, B., Telang, S., Pachlasiya, K., Chouhan, M., Rawat, R., Cyber threat phylogeny assessment and vulnerabilities representation at thermal power station, in: *Proceedings of International Conference on Network Security and Blockchain Technology: ICNSBT 2021*, pp. 28–39, Springer Nature Singapore, Singapore, 2022, June.

46. Rawat, R., Gupta, S., Sivaranjani, S., Cu, O.K., Kuliha, M., Sankaran, K.S., Malevolent information crawling mechanism for forming structured illegal organisations in hidden networks. *Int. J. Cyber Warf. Terror. (IJCWT)*, *12*, 1, 1–14, 2022.

The Future of Modern Transportation for Smart Cities Using Trackless Tram Networks

Samson Arun Raj A.[1]* **and Yogesh P.**[2]

[1]Department of Computer Science Engineering, Karunya Institute of Technology and Sciences, Coimbatore, Tamil Nadu, India
[2]Department of Information Science and Technology, College of Engineering, Guindy, Anna University, Chennai, India

Abstract

Intelligent transportation systems (ITSs) have provided various transportation services to air, rail, road, and sea-based systems in the transportation environment. ITS aims to deliver dependable data access, seamless Internet connectivity, emergency notifications, and other protocol information communicated via pole infrastructure-based roadside units (RSUs). However, as the change in the mode of communication and environmental situation increases drastically, the RSUs operate under a heavy burden to deliver the information on time. This paper proposes a programmable trackless tram-roadside unit (TRAM-RSU) framework in every RSU agent, also known as tram nodes, to communicate with vehicular nodes in the transportation environment. The TRAM-RSU framework has two functional subsystems: (1) network connectivity determines vehicular node physical characteristics and network connectivity status at various instants Ti. In addition, (2) the packet-label classifier is used to differentiate the incoming data packet service request based on their multiprotocol label switching header labels. The performance of the TRAM-RSU framework under various scenarios concerning its time instant Ti (in seconds) was experimented with quality of service, different arrival rates, and processing time analysis. The results indicate that the TRAM-RSU framework employs more transmission data rates due to its deployment and locality in the transportation environment.

Keywords: Data packet analysis, intelligent transportation system (ITS), multiprotocol label switching (MPLS), network measurement, queueing theory, tram-roadside unit (TRAM-RSU) framework

23.1 Introduction

An intelligent transportation system walks the modern era of providing travel, logistics, emergency, event notifications, electronic toll collections, and other general services communicated via infrastructure-based roadside unit (RSU) agents in the transportation

Corresponding author: samsonarun234@gmail.com

Romil Rawat, Rajesh Kumar Chakrawarti, Sanjaya Kumar Sarangi, Piyush Vyas, Mary Sowjanya Alamanda, Kotagiri Srividya and Krishnan Sakthidasan Sankaran (eds.) Conversational Artificial Intelligence, (369–384) © 2024 Scrivener Publishing LLC

environment [1]. The transportation environment is separated into multiple regions controlled by distributed RSU agents. Each RSU agent is assigned an AOR, including a collection of end-to-end transportation subunit teams, as discussed in [2, 3]. In addition, the RSU agents are given the necessary hardware and software to connect, communicate, process, and establish direct links with vehicular nodes to transmit messages. Furthermore, as vehicular nodes travel, the RSU agents provide a gateway for infotainment [1].

For the past two decades, most accidents have been caused by human mistakes, cooperative teamwork, and ineffective decision-making [4–10]. Furthermore, due to structural and other construction constraints, accepting request/response messages from the base control station or RSU agent to vehicular nodes is also challenging.

On movement, the vehicular nodes approach the intersection point to cross the lane/road, and they cannot self-schedule to move appropriately without proper guidance. A central intersection manager agent (IMA) acting as an RSU agent is constructed at each intersection point to avoid collision among the vehicular nodes. The vehicular node uses a real-time vehicle scheduling algorithm based on the information flow received via IMA to help in road conflicts [7]. Moreover, the authors of [11] have analyzed the overall performance outcome irrespective of the traffic density and vehicle locations communicated via multi-RSU agents. The authors of [12] have discussed rules to clarify the sequence of vehicular nodes to pass through an uncontrolled intersection. Such rules consume more time and resources when emergency vehicles such as ambulances and other subunits are stuck or delayed on their way to the destination, leading to heavy loss.

Inter-vehicle communication is essential for sharing data packets and must be done within a limited radio range on a self-organized ad hoc basis to explore the network connectivity behavior. To segregate the incoming flow of data traffic from the stakeholders, the authors of [5] have addressed the usage of classifying information clustering of incoming data packet requests. Organizing the information helps avoid task completion among the RSU agents by considering the mobility and quality of service metrics under the suitability value.

One of the most complex technical parts of the intelligent transportation system is congestion control. It degrades the quality of service data traffic its stakeholders receive. The authors of [7] examined two types of congestion, i.e., transient and persistent, causing the network performance towards packet loss and buffer overflow. Therefore, an effective queuing system is required to manage and identify the data packets in the transportation environment. Classifying data packets is the foundation for enabling many quality of service features to reduce packet drop probability and fast-forward data packets among the intermediate stakeholders. Thus, cluster-based RSU agents are needed in the transportation environment to resolve such complications among the stakeholders.

A. Problem Statement

The proposed TRAM-RSU framework is centered on tackling any of the following two fundamental challenges that frequently occur in intelligent transportation system applications:

- To address the network connectivity failures: In most cases, network connectivity is determined by the user's location and signaling strength. The proposed TRAM-RSU framework employs different physical and quality of service metrics characteristics from vehicular nodes to tackle this challenge.

- To solve the problem of RSU agents and vehicular node processing and transferring data packets: To discriminate, process, and provide the service on time, each RSU agent needs an effective MPLS label classification algorithm.

B. Contribution to Research Work

The contributions of the proposed TRAM-RSU framework are listed as follows:

- The network connectivity subsystem creates a reference matrix in which the communication connection stability is tested using physical and quality of service criteria to determine the network connectivity levels.
- An effective MPLS label classification technique invokes road-assisted service messages to differentiate incoming data packet requests. The performance of the packet-label classifier subsystem is also evaluated in terms of incoming data packets using the queuing approach that it provides.
- The TRAM-RSU architecture examines the performance metrics towards network connectivity levels (%), network load (bit/s), server utilization (%), and data packet analysis (packet/s) at various time instants Ti to compare the measured outcomes with other existing approaches.

23.2   Proposed System Architecture

The novelty of our research work is to make the roadside units mobile by introducing trackless trams as RSU agents, also known as tram nodes (TNs). These tram nodes are provided with a dedicated lane for movement along with vehicular nodes, as shown in Figure 23.1. Since the backbone network does not guarantee adequate ITS service, the chances of information flow and data packet requests cannot be predicted easily among/between the transportation stakeholders as the communication mode changes dynamically.

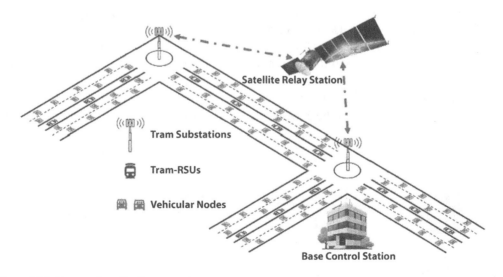

Figure 23.1 Proposed application scenario.

The idea of the proposed tram node was also inspired by an ongoing real-time project on intelligent transportation system (ITS) called "Perth-Trackless Tram" that started in Sydney, Australia, in March 2019 [13]. Our proposed model considers that the backbone network takes the burden to process, relay, and provide any additional changes to the existing tram node's programming. The tram substations act as docking stations for all the tram nodes moving in the transportation environment. This docking station takes the privilege of processing the information from the satellite's communication since the microwave's information needs to be formatted according to the user's service request.

Figure 23.2 depicts the information flow of data packets and the internal modules of the single TRAM-RSU system.

In the proposed work, the network connectivity subsystem aims to provide dynamic connectivity to all vehicular nodes seeking service. The network connectivity status among tram and vehicular nodes is measured every instant Ti and represented as a reference matrix. In the reference matrix, the first eight attributes determine the physical characteristics of the vehicular nodes with tram nodes at time Ti, from which the nine-attribute network connectivity status is computed in the reference matrix.

Overall, this reference matrix embraces 13 parameters to acquire a network connectivity status, of which four are used as a quality of service, i.e., data thought, data loss, delay, and network load are used to analyze the communication link stability. The computational modules present in the connectivity subsystem are also discussed as follows. The tram node knows who, where, and when to provide the necessary service upon these computations. Table 23.1 illustrates various vehicular nodes that enter/exit the transportation environment.

By distinguishing the stakeholder's request, the tram nodes in the packet-label classifier subsystem hope to give quick data access. The incoming data packets are discriminated against using MPLS header labels that follow differentiated service (DiffServ). The MPLS header used in the TRAM-RSU framework is a five-bit label holding 20 possible road-assisted service messages that stakeholders need to access in time. Finally, the service storage helps the requested entity discover and identify the services provided and are distributed across the tram network through many tram servers (nodes) to quickly access and avoid single-point failure in the entire ITS service system.

In this distributed architecture, the service storage of tram nodes registers themselves with their nearest base control stations or docking stations. A single docking station advertises the updated and available list of tram service storage under them to other docking stations. Therefore, it is enough for the requested entity to function like clients in sending their requests to their nearest tram servers or the docking stations instead of following the conventional flooding mechanism of service requests. Table 23.2 illustrates the notations used in the functional block of the TRAM-RSU framework as depicted in Figure 23.3.

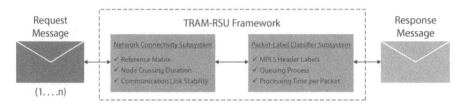

Figure 23.2 Internal modules of the single TRAM-RSU framework.

Table 23.1 Classification types of vehicular nodes.

Sl. no.	Vehicle types	Vehicle names	Priority level
1	A	Ambulance	1
2	B	Government	2
3	C	Patrols	3
4	D	Subunits	4
5	E	Commercial	5
6	F	Logistics	6
7	G	Bicycles	7

Table 23.2 List of notations used in the TRAM-RSU framework.

Symbols	Descriptions
ID_S	Node ID of the stakeholder
ID_N	Node ID of the neighboring stakeholder
TS_S	Time stamp of the stakeholder
TS_N	Time stamp of the neighboring stakeholder
LOC_S	Location of the stakeholder
LOC_N	Location of the neighboring stakeholder
$RVEL_{SN}$	Relative velocity between stakeholder and neighboring stakeholder
VEL_S	Velocity of stakeholder
VEL_N	The velocity of neighboring stakeholders
NCD	Node crossing duration
$\pm$	NCD duration (in a second)
°	Angle to pinpoint the direction of the stakeholder movement

23.3 Working Process of the TRAM-RSU Framework

The network connectivity subsystem's operation is divided into node initialization and CBM transmission. During the node initialization step, the docking stations, tram nodes, and vehicular nodes are initialized with specific functions to operate, process, and interact in the transportation environment. The docking stations are designed to serve as backbone communicators for all tram nodes, which require/need any latest updates regarding situation awareness, scalability of vehicular nodes entering/exiting the roads, or new directives

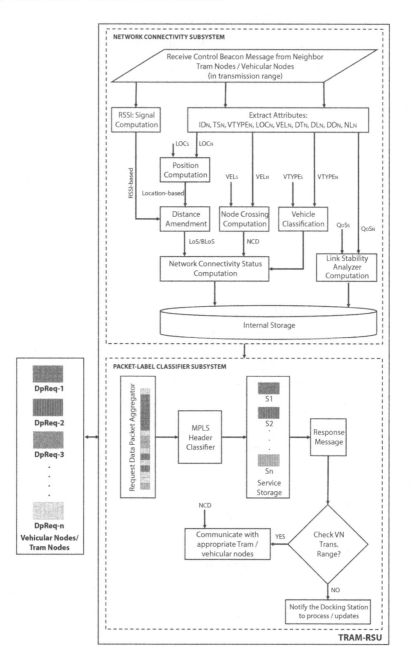

Figure 23.3 Network flow sub-system.

from BCS officials. On the other hand, the tram and vehicular nodes are designed and deployed to travel in a consistent direction and pace under the road pattern.

The following stage is CBM transmission, which establishes network connectivity between vehicular nodes and notifies them to operationalize the network. A control beacon message comprises two parameters: the related stakeholder's node ID and a timestamp. These attributes indicate that they request network connectivity for a specific service, as shown in Figure 23.4.

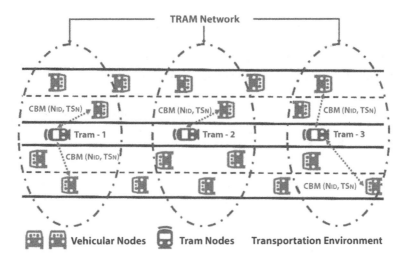

Figure 23.4 CBM transmission for connection request.

Based on our prior work [5], pseudocode 1 explains the operating mechanism of CBM transmission for network connectivity formation. In the TRAM-RSU framework, the same pseudocode is tested with diverse application scenarios for our network connectivity subsystem. The network connection and its accompanying network load are recognized and monitored in the reference matrix. The collection of notations used in pseudocode 1 is shown in Table 23.3.

Table 23.3 List of pseudocode 1 notations.

Notations	Descriptions
CBM_L	Control beacon messages, where $L = 1, 2, 3, \ldots n$
$CTNi$	Current tram node
TN_{DB}	Internal database of tram node
LOS_{TV}	Line-of-sight between tram and vehicular nodes
NCD_{TV}	Node crossing duration between tram and vehicular nodes
TN_i	Set of tram nodes
VN_i	Set of vehicular nodes
TN_{WP}	Set of waypoints for tram nodes
VN_{WP}	Set of waypoints for vehicular nodes
$TrDur_t$	Travel duration (maximum time limit)
T_i	Time instants in seconds, where $T_i = 60, 120, 180, \ldots n$

Pseudocode 1: Network Connectivity Establishment

Input: Transmission of control beacon message CBM_L
Output: Reference matrix construction of network connectivity among the stakeholders
1:   **BEGIN**
2:   **Initialize** TN_i, VN_j, TN_{WP}, VN_{WP}, CTN_i, CBM_L, $TrDur_t$, LOS_{TV}, NCD_{TV}, T_i
3:   $TN_i \leftarrow TN_1, TN_2, TN_3, \ldots TN_m$
4:   $VN_j \leftarrow VN_1, VN_2, VN_3, \ldots VN_n$
5:   $TN_{WP} \leftarrow$ Waypoints in (X_i, Y_i, Z_i) axis
6:   $VN_{WP} \leftarrow$ Waypoints in (X_j, Y_j, Z_j) axis
7:   **while** $(TrDur_t > T_i)$
8:   **for** $TrDur_t \leftarrow 1$ to T, do
9:   **for** $TN_i \leftarrow 1$ to m, do
10:   **for** $VN_j \leftarrow 1$ to n, do
11:   **Deploy** the node TN_i and VN_j in TN_{WP} and VN_{WP} coordinates
12:   Neighbor TN_i and $VN_j \leftarrow$ **Generate and Broadcast** CBM_L
13:   **Receive & Extract** Response CBM_L from vehicular nodes
14:   $CTN_i \leftarrow$ **Analyze** the CBM_L and **Construct** the reference matrix
15:   **If** Connectivity Level (Min. LOS_{TV} & Min. NCD_{TV}), **then**
16:   $CTN_i \leftarrow$ **return** High;
17:   **elseif** connectivity level (Avg. LOS_{TV} || Avg. NCD_{TV}), **then**
18:   $CTN_i \leftarrow$ **return** Medium;
19:   **else**
20:   $CTN_i \leftarrow$ **return** Low;
21:   **end if**
22:   Neighbor TN_i and $VN_j \leftarrow$ **Update** CTN_i in TN_{DB}
23:   **end for**
24:   **end for**
25:   **end for**
26:   **end while**
27:   **END**

The network connectivity subsystem builds the reference matrix at this point by detecting who (tram node) is connected to whom (vehicular nodes and other tram nodes) at each time instant Ti. The remaining eight criteria in the reference matrix measure the physical characteristics of the appropriate tram node concerning their stakeholders in the transportation environment. As illustrated in pseudocode 1, network connectivity is assessed based on physical traits and distance categories with a minimum node crossing duration (NCD) value. Finally, the link stability analyzer is considered and computed individually inside the subsystem depending on the number of control beacon messages exchanged. In the internal database of every tram node, the performance values of quality-of-service parameters toward the link stability analyzer are attached to the reference matrix to produce a reference network connectivity dataset.

In contrast, the packet-label classifier subsystem's operation stages are the request data packet aggregator, MPLS classifier, server access, and service transmission. In the first stage, the tram node uses a storage file, where the received data packet requests are aggregated from numerous stakeholders connected to instant Ti. The CBM transferred between the vehicle and tram nodes is an essential bit sequence combination; therefore, the file is only a few kilobytes. Following the aggregation process, the second stage, along with the queuing variables, is assessed to determine the priority level of the data packet request to which it needs to access the road-assisted service messages.

Pseudocode 2 outlines the functional approach for classifying data packet requests, as explained in detail in [5]. In the TRAM-RSU framework, the same pseudocode with an enhanced version of MPLS header classification is added inside the packet-label classifier subsystem. Table 23.4 illustrates the notations used in pseudocode 2.

The CTNi obtains the service information request using node ID, time stamp, and vehicle type. Then, all of these collected data are fed into the MPLS label classifier, which compares the original service information request to the MPLS labels built into the system. After authenticating the source and classifying the label, the data packet request is provided access to the service storage of the relevant CTNi to retrieve the needed service's response message.

The packet-label classifier subsystem uses the node crossing duration attribute obtained from its built-in database as a reference pointer to signal which stakeholder has the highest

Table 23.4 List of pseudocode 2 notations.

Notations	Descriptions
N_{ID}	Node ID
NCD	Node crossing duration
TS	Time stamp
DP_REQ_L	Data packet request from stakeholders
$MPLS_{Labels}$	Types of MPLS labels used for request classification
Lal_Classifier	Label classifier
Req_Type	Data packet request type
VTYPE	Vehicle type
SER_{Access}	Service access
$RM_{[0]}$	Invalid response
$RM_{[Ser\_Msg]}$	Service message
SER_{IR}	Service information request
SER_{STG}	Service storage
Dock	Docking station

Pseudocode 2: Classification of Data Packet Request from Stakeholders

Input: Transmission of data packet request (DP_REQ_L) to tram nodes
Output: Transmission of requested service to the appropriate stakeholder
1:   **BEGIN**
2:   **Initialize** CTNi, SER_{IR}, DP_REQ_L, Lal_Classifier, N_{ID}, TS, Req_Type, VTYPE, SER_{Access}, $RM_{[0]}$, $RM_{[Ser\_Msg]}$, SER_{STG}, Dock
3:        **Loop**
4:             CTNi ← **Aggregate:** DP_REQ_L [SER_{IR1}, SER_{IR2}, ..., SER_{IRn}]
5:             Lal_Classifier ← **Extract:** SER_{IR} [N_{ID}, TS, Req_Type, VTYPE]
6:             SER_{Access} ← **Lal_Classifier:** Compare (SER_{IR}, $MPLS_{Labels}$)
7:                  **Search** CTNi (SER_{STG}) ← SER_{Access}
8:                  **if** (SER_{IR} == SER_{STG}) **then**
9:                       CTNi ← **return** SER_{IR} ($RM_{[NID, TS, Req\_Type, VTYPE, Ser\_Msg]}$, NCD)
10:                  **elseif** (SER_{IR} != SER_{STG}) **then**
11:                       Dock ← **return** CTNi: Transmit SER_{IR}
12:                  **else**
13:                       CTNi ← **return** SER_{IR} ($RM_{[NID, TS, Req\_Type, VTYPE, 0]}$, NCD)
14:                  **end if**
15:             **Update** SER_{STG} ← CTNi (SER_{IR}, $RM_{[Ser\_Msg]}$ || $RM_{[0]}$)
16:        **End Loop**
17: **END**

---

priority to grant the service in time after the correct answer message to the desired service is acquired. Finally, as a future reference, the associated tram node (CTNi) updates its internal server service storage and alerts its nearby tram nodes to avoid redundant data transfer.

23.4   Experimental Analysis

The TRAM-RSU framework has been compared with existing methodologies [6, 14] for four performance indicators to instant data packet requests across vehicular nodes. Some of the comparison assessments performed against the proposed model are shown in Table 23.5.

Figure 23.5 shows the comparative performance metrics for monitoring the network connectivity levels against the TRAM-RSU framework at various time intervals, and the overall average is computed.

According to the evaluation and analysis, the network connectivity level is 21% low, 42% medium, and 37% high. Furthermore, it has been discovered that vehicular nodes with an intense network connection receive more service requests than those with the other two network connections. Fortunately, the TRAM-RSU paradigm ensures that all stakeholders in the transportation ecosystem have equal access to network connectivity. In addition to the tram networks, the network load for communication link consumption is calculated using other approaches, as shown in Figure 23.6.

Table 23.5 Existing schemes.

Sl. no.	References	Descriptions
1	[5]	Aerial RSU agents operating as intermediate buffers: These AIR-RSU frameworks use the same reference index as the proposed paradigm but with a different deployment motivation.
2	[14]	The RSU agents allocate a unique communication channel to connect and seek service. A queuing model also examines the data packet flow between intra- and inter-network stakeholders.
3	[15]	The ESRA-MD algorithm chooses the shortest route of sharing the service with minimum hop counts.
4	[16]	CIMST is a Delaunay Triangulation-based enhanced approach for improving connectivity (CIDT). It creates a Delaunay Triangulation of the independent network and adds new nodes to triangles chosen based on various parameters.
5	[17]	Connecting cars sends data to the nearest RSU via multi-hop routing over the shortest pathways, resulting in frequent communication failure. As a result, network connectivity varies and is assessed over time.

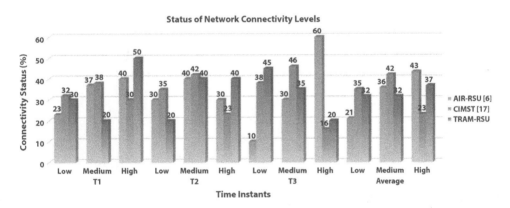

Figure 23.5 Network connectivity level analysis.

It is observed that the computation of network load is quite similar to the existing techniques reaching up to a data rate of 45.51 bit/s, distributing the network load evenly across all vehicular nodes wishing to access data service. However, as the trams and vehicular nodes are close, the network load rises to 96.64 and 148.48 bit/s, respectively. Similarly, the network load iteration is repeated 17 times, and the complete vehicular nodes are seen to run under a constant scalar amount of network load. However, our suggested model uses a ground-level rather than an aerial-based network service, so the network load is lower than the AIR-RSU [5] approach. Due to its proximity and fast movement speed, the TRAM-RSU framework uses more packet transmission with vehicular nodes in transportation.

Figure 23.7 shows the average tram server utilization using various approaches based on the stakeholder's two inbound arrival rates. Upon computation, we can observe that the

TRAM-RSU framework achieves a minimum of 10% to a maximum of 60% server utilization under the two arrival rates of data packet requests compared with the existing approaches.

Finally, the processing time analysis of each data packet request inside the tram server is calculated based on the queueing factors of the waiting time of the system and queue, as explained in detail in [5]. Upon measuring the waiting time, the tram nodes acquire a fixed duration to process and provide the response service message in time, as shown in Figure 23.8.

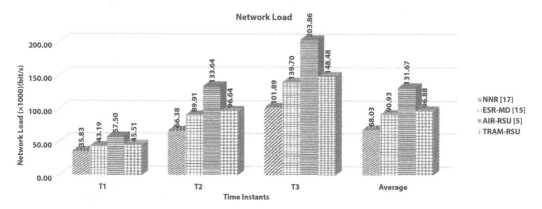

Figure 23.6 Network load analysis.

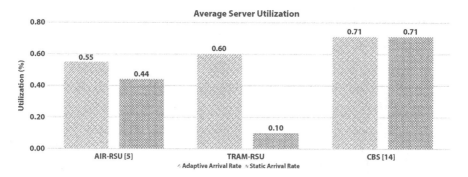

Figure 23.7 Average server utilization.

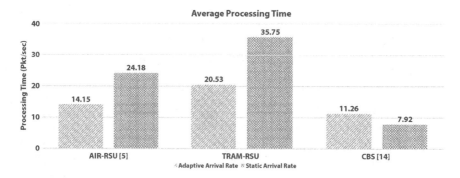

Figure 23.8 Average processing time analysis.

The computation presented above shows that the tram nodes achieve a minimum request processing duration of 21 to 36 s, giving an advantage over the existing methodologies. Thus, the less the data rate, the longer it takes to process the request. Hence, the TRAM-RSU framework's overall performance, strengths, and drawbacks in intelligent transportation system applications are recognized.

The significant requirement for cybersecurity [18–22] is one of the ITS's (Intelligent Transportation Systems) [23, 24] key distinguishing characteristics. Transportation safety, efficient road traffic, and entertainment are three categories into which ITS applications fall. Applications for improving road safety must adhere to strict real-time deadlines and have very high cybersecurity [25, 26] standards. Although infotainment apps and road traffic efficiency are not directly tied to the physical safety of road users, cybersecurity [27, 28] [29, 30] standards are nonetheless quite strict since a breach in any one of them might affect the effectiveness of the entire ITS. The Internet of Things (IoT) is the result of the fusion of a number of technologies, including wireless networks, control systems, real-time analytics, embedded systems [31, 32], and machine learning [33]. IoT refers to items that relate to the ideas of the intelligent home, intelligent healthcare system [34], intelligent city, and so on from the perspective of the customer. These regions share a lot of qualities and difficulties. It is typical for IoT sub-areas to share technology; however, this practise has to be carefully evaluated and investigated. Despite their commonalities, the requirements for communication range and bit rate, real-time operation, dependability, and security differ even within the same field. Intelligent Transportation Systems (ITS), a component of the smart city, are characterised by various IoT aspects [35, 36].

23.5   Summary

This paper proposes a programmable trackless tram-road side unit (TRAM-RSU) framework for every RSU agent with two functional subsystems: network connectivity and packet-label classifier subsystem. The network connectivity subsystem aims to continuously update the network connectivity status and analyze the requester's link stability. On the other hand, the packet-label classifier subsystem seeks to distinguish incoming data packet requests for road-assisted service messages based on their MPLS header labels.

According to the findings, the suggested TRAM-RSU framework delivers an average of 32% to 37% dynamic network connectivity with various network connections. In addition, the tram network estimates the overall network load for the communication links used to be up to 45.51 bit/s, delivering an equal amount of network load to all vehicular nodes wishing to access data service. Furthermore, whereas the adaptive arrival rate achieves 60% server utilization, the static arrival rate achieves only 10%, significantly lower than the other two approaches. Similarly, the TRAM-RSU framework's processing time analysis shows that it takes 21 to 36 s to process and communicate to the relevant vehicular node

The TRAM-RSU framework can be upgraded in the following areas for future enhancement: (1) the network connectivity subsystem can be trained to process and provide access to numerous data streams under a sustainable stakeholder network to avoid re-establishing the connection, and (2) the packet-label classifier subsystem can be trained to avoid unnecessary service requests, i.e., spam entering the packet-label classifier subsystem;

the tram nodes must be embedded in various authentication schemes and other fundamental exchange cryptography mechanisms.

References

1. Zhang, L., Liu, Y., Wang, Z., Guo, J., Huo, Y., Mobility and QoS oriented 802.11 p MAC scheme for vehicle-to-infrastructure communications. *Telecommun. Syst.*, 60, 1, 107–117, 2015, doi: 10.1007/s11235-014-9925-0.
2. Collision Avoidance System, Network information, Available from <https://www.revolvy.com/page/Collision-avoidance-system>.
3. Menouar, H., Guvenc, I., Akkaya, K., Uluagac, A.S., Kadri, A., Tuncer, A., UAV-enabled intelligent transportation systems for the smart city: Applications and challenges. *IEEE Commun. Mag.*, 55, 3, 22–28, March 2017, doi: 10.1109/MCOM.2017.1600238CM.
4. Airborne Wireless Network, Network information, Available from: <http://www.airbornewirelessnetwork.com/index.asp>.
5. Raj, and Palanichamy, Y., Packet classification based aerial intelligent relay-road side unit (AIR-RSU) framework for vehicular ad-hoc networks. *Peer-to-Peer Networking Appl.*, 14, 1132–1153, 2021, doi: 10.1007/s12083-021-01092-8.
6. Marinho, M.A.M., de Freitas, E.P., Lustosa da Costa, J.P.C., de Almeida, A.L.F., de Sousa, R.T., Using cooperative MIMO techniques and UAV relay networks to support connectivity in sparse Wireless Sensor Networks. *2013 International Conference on Computing, Management and Telecommunications (ComManTel)*, pp. 49–54, 2013, doi: 10.1109/ComManTel.2013.6482364.
7. Harigovindan, V.P., Babu, A.V., Jacob, L., Improving aggregate utility in IEEE 802.11p based vehicle-to-infrastructure networks. *Telecommun. Syst.*, 62, 2, 359–385, 2016.
8. Targe, P.A. and Satone, M.P., VANET based real-time intelligent transportation system. *Int. J. Comput. Appl.*, 145, 4, 34–38, 2016.
9. Tahmasebi, M. and Khayyambashi, M.R., An efficient model for vehicular cloud computing with prioritizing computing resources. *Peer-to-Peer Networking Appl.*, 12, 1466–1475, 2018, doi: 10.1007/ s12083-018-0677-6.
10. Raut, M. and Devane, S.R., Intelligent transportation system for smartcity using VANET. *2017 International Conference on Communication and Signal Processing (ICCSP)*, pp. 1602–1605, 2017, doi: 10.1109/ICCSP.2017.8286659.
11. Raj, and Palanichamy, Y., An aerial intelligent relay-road side unit (AIR-RSU) framework for modern intelligent transportation system. *Peer-to-Peer Networking Appl.*, 13, 965–986, 2020, doi: 10.1007/s12083-019-00860-x.
12. Chen, Du, X., Pei, Q., Jin, Y., Connectivity analysis for free-flow traffic in VANETs: A statistical approach. *Int. J. Distrib. Sens. Netw.*, Hindawi Publishing Corporation, 1–15, 2013, doi: 10.1155/2013/598946.
13. Perth-Trackless-Tram, Mobility system, Information Available from: <https://news.curtin.edu.au/stories/could-trackless-trams-replace-light-rail/>.
14. Zheng, Q., Zheng, K., Sun, L., Leung, V.C.M., Dynamic performance analysis of uplink transmission in cluster-based heterogeneous vehicular networks. *IEEE Trans. Veh. Technol.*, 64, 12, 5584–5595, Dec. 2015, doi: 10.1109/TVT.2015.2487682.
15. Al-Mayouf, Y.R.B., Ismail, M., Abdullah, N.F., Wahab, A.W.A., Mahdi, O.A., Khan, S., Choo, K.K.R., Efficient and stable routing algorithm based on user mobility and node density in urban vehicular network. *PLoS One*, 11, 11, 1–24, 2016.

16. Li, N. and Hou, J.C., Improving connectivity of wireless ad hoc networks. *The Second Annual International Conference on Mobile and Ubiquitous Systems: Networking and Services*, pp. 314–324, 2005, doi: 10.1109/MOBIQUITOUS.2005.32.

17. Das, and Misra, R., Improvised dynamic network connectivity model for Vehicular Ad-Hoc Networks (VANETs). *J. Network Comput. Appl.*, Elsevier, 122, 107–114, 2018.

18. Mahor, V., Bijrothiya, S., Rawat, R., Kumar, A., Garg, B., Pachlasiya, K., IoT and artificial intelligence techniques for public safety and security, in: *Smart Urban Computing Applications*, p. 111, 2023.

19. Mahor, V., Pachlasiya, K., Garg, B., Chouhan, M., Telang, S., Rawat, R., Mobile operating system (Android) vulnerability analysis using machine learning, in: *Proceedings of International Conference on Network Security and Blockchain Technology: ICNSBT 2021*, pp. 159–169, Springer Nature Singapore, Singapore, 2022, June.

20. Rawat, R., Garg, B., Pachlasiya, K., Mahor, V., Telang, S., Chouhan, M., Mishra, R., SCNTA: Monitoring of network availability and activity for identification of anomalies using machine learning approaches. *Int. J. Inf. Technol. Web Eng. (IJITWE)*, 17, 1, 1–19, 2022.

21. Rawat, R., Rimal, Y.N., William, P., Dahima, S., Gupta, S., Sankaran, K.S., Malware threat affecting financial organization analysis using machine learning approach. *Int. J. Inf. Technol. Web Eng. (IJITWE)*, 17, 1, 1–20, 2022.

22. Rawat, R., Mahor, V., Chouhan, M., Pachlasiya, K., Telang, S., Garg, B., Systematic literature review (SLR) on social media and the digital transformation of drug trafficking on darkweb, in: *International Conference on Network Security and Blockchain Technology*, pp. 181–205, Springer, Singapore, 2022.

23. Rawat, R., Ayodele Oki, O., Sankaran, S., Florez, H., Ajagbe, S.A., Techniques for predicting dark web events focused on the delivery of illicit products and ordered crime. *Int. J. Electr. Comput. Eng. (IJECE)*, 13, 5, 5354–5365, Oct. 2023, doi: 10.11591/ijece.v13i5.pp5354-5365.

24. Rawat, R., Garg, B., Mahor, V., Telang, S., Pachlasiya, K., Chouhan, M., Organ trafficking on the dark web—The data security and privacy concern in healthcare systems, in: *Internet of Healthcare Things: Machine Learning for Security and Privacy*, pp. 189–216, 2022.

25. Vyas, P., Vyas, G., Chauhan, A., Rawat, R., Telang, S., Gottumukkala, M., Anonymous trading on the dark online marketplace: An exploratory study, in: *Using Computational Intelligence for the Dark Web and Illicit Behavior Detection*, pp. 272–289, IGI Global, 2022.

26. Rawat, R., Oki, O.A., Sankaran, K.S., Olasupo, O., Ebong, G.N., Ajagbe, S.A., A new solution for cyber security in big data using machine learning approach, in: *Mobile Computing and Sustainable Informatics: Proceedings of ICMCSI 2023*, pp. 495–505, Springer Nature Singapore, Singapore, 2023.

27. Rawat, R., Chakrawarti, R.K., Raj, A., Mani, G., Chidambarathanu, K., Bhardwaj, R., Association rule learning for threat analysis using traffic analysis and packet filtering approach. *Int. J. Inf. Technol.*, 1–11, 2023.

28. Rawat, R., Logical concept mapping and social media analytics relating to cyber criminal activities for ontology creation. *Int. J. Inf. Technol.*, 15, 2, 893–903, 2023.

29. Rawat, R., Mahor, V., Álvarez, J.D., Ch, F., Cognitive systems for dark web cyber delinquent association malignant data crawling: A review, in: *Handbook of Research on War Policies, Strategies, and Cyber Wars*, pp. 45–63, 2023.

30. Rawat, R., Chakrawarti, R.K., Vyas, P., Gonzáles, J.L.A., Sikarwar, R., Bhardwaj, R., Intelligent fog computing surveillance system for crime and vulnerability identification and tracing. *Int. J. Inf. Secur. Priv. (IJISP)*, 17, 1, 1–25, 2023.

31. Rawat, R., Sowjanya, A.M., Patel, S.I., Jaiswal, V., Khan, I., Balaram, A. (Eds.), *Using Machine Intelligence: Autonomous Vehicles Volume 1*, John Wiley & Sons, 2022.

32. Rawat, R., Mahor, V., Díaz-Álvarez, J., Chávez, F., Rooted learning model at fog computing analysis for crime incident surveillance, in: *2022 International Conference on Smart Generation Computing, Communication and Networking (SMART GENCON)*, pp. 1–9, IEEE, 2022, December.

33. Rawat, R. and Shrivastav, S.K., SQL injection attack detection using SVM. *Int. J. Comput. Appl.*, *42*, 13, 1–4, 2012.

34. Rawat, R., Bhardwaj, P., Kaur, U., Telang, S., Chouhan, M., Sankaran, K.S., *Smart vehicles for communication, volume 2*, John Wiley & Sons, 2023.

35. Mahor, V., Garg, B., Telang, S., Pachlasiya, K., Chouhan, M., Rawat, R., Cyber threat phylogeny assessment and vulnerabilities representation at thermal power station, in: *Proceedings of International Conference on Network Security and Blockchain Technology: ICNSBT 2021*, pp. 28–39, Springer Nature Singapore, Singapore, 2022, June.

36. Rawat, R., Gupta, S., Sivaranjani, S., Cu, O.K., Kuliha, M., Sankaran, K.S., Malevolent information crawling mechanism for forming structured illegal organisations in hidden networks. *Int. J. Cyber Warf. Terror. (IJCWT)*, *12*, 1, 1–14, 2022.

Evaluating the Performance of Conversational AI Tools: A Comparative Analysis

Deepika Chauhan[1]*, Chaitanya Singh[2], Romil Rawat[3] and Manoj Dhawan[4]

[1]Computer Application Department, Silver Oak University, Ahmedabad, Gujarat, India
[2]Computer Engineering Department, Vidhyadeep University, Surat, Gujarat, India
[3]Department of Computer Science, Shri Vaishnav Vidyapeeth Vishwavidyalaya, Indore, India
[4]Department of Computer Science and Engineering, Avantika University, Ujjain, India

Abstract

In recent years, conversational AI has gained significant attention as a promising tool for enhancing various aspects of education and training. Despite the growing popularity of these tools, there is limited research that compares the efficacy of different conversational AI platforms. This study aims to address this gap by conducting a comparative analysis of leading conversational AI tools and evaluating their performance in terms of natural language processing (NLP) accuracy, personalization, interactivity, and overall user experience. The results of this study provide valuable insights into the strengths and limitations of different conversational AI tools and can help educators and trainers make informed decisions when selecting these tools for educational and training purposes. The findings also suggest areas for future research, such as improving NLP accuracy and personalization capabilities as well as exploring ethical considerations related to the use of conversational AI in education and training.

Keywords: Conversational AI, chatbots, ed-tech, virtual assistants, NLP, education

24.1 Introduction

Conversational AI tools have been gaining traction in recent years and have the potential to revolutionize the way we approach education. These tools leverage natural language processing, machine learning, and other artificial intelligence technologies to create conversational interactions between humans and machines. In education, conversational AI can provide personalized learning experiences, facilitate communication between teachers and students, and automate administrative tasks. As such, it is an exciting time for researchers to explore the possibilities of conversational AI in education. In this article, we will discuss the current state of conversational AI in education and highlight potential use cases for the future. We will also examine the challenges and limitations of conversational AI in

Corresponding author: chauhandeepika522@gmail.com

Romil Rawat, Rajesh Kumar Chakrawarti, Sanjaya Kumar Sarangi, Piyush Vyas, Mary Sowjanya Alamanda, Kotagiri Srividya and Krishnan Sakthidasan Sankaran (eds.) *Conversational Artificial Intelligence*, (385–410) © 2024 Scrivener Publishing LLC

education and discuss the ethical considerations that must be taken into account when developing and deploying these tools.

This literature review aims to provide an overview of the viewpoints of different authors on the use of conversational AI in education.

Ultimately, this article aims to provide insights into the benefits and limitations of conversational AI in education and to encourage further research in this exciting and rapidly evolving field.

24.2   Literature Review

Conversational AI tools are being increasingly used in the education sector to enhance learning experiences and provide personalized feedback to students. This literature review aims to provide an overview of the viewpoints of different authors on the use of conversational AI in education.

Ultimately, this article aims to provide insights into the benefits and limitations of conversational AI in education and to encourage further research in this exciting and rapidly evolving field.

According to Wang *et al.* (2020), conversational AI tools can provide personalized learning experiences by adapting to individual students' needs and preferences. These tools can use natural language processing to understand student queries and provide relevant feedback and guidance. Similarly, Chaffey *et al.* (2020) state that conversational AI tools can be used to provide personalized learning materials and track student progress, leading to improved learning outcomes.

Conversational AI tools can enhance cognitive engagement by providing interactive and conversational interfaces, according to Zhang and Zhang (2019). These interfaces can make learning more engaging and interactive for students, leading to increased motivation and learning outcomes. Similarly, Ramaswami and Sundararaman (2019) state that conversational AI tools can provide instant feedback and support to students, improving their engagement and performance.

Conversational AI tools can improve accessibility in education, particularly for students with disabilities, according to Sarwar *et al.* (2020). These tools can provide alternative forms of learning materials, such as audio and text-to-speech, which can support students with hearing or visual impairments. In addition, conversational AI tools can be used to support students who speak languages other than the primary language of instruction. According to Murugesan *et al.* (2020), one of the challenges of using conversational AI in education is the lack of sufficient data to train these tools, particularly in domains such as education where data privacy is a concern. Another challenge is the need for natural language processing capabilities, which can be challenging to implement accurately in education.

Higher education institutions are increasingly utilizing AI chatbots and virtual assistants to help students navigate their way through college. Popular AI chatbots such as Mongoose Harmony by Drift [1], Iggy and Pounce [2], Ems [2], Findo [2], Astro [2], Forksy [2], and Jobo [2] are all designed to provide assistance to college students. These AI chatbots can help students with searching for jobs, tracking food intake, communicating with health professionals, and much more. With the help of these AI chatbots and virtual assistants, college students can be better equipped to tackle their studies and make the most of their college experience. Squirrel AI, Duolingo, Woebot, Jill Watson, and Edly are some of the chatbots used in education. These chatbots use natural language processing to understand student queries and provide relevant responses, and studies have shown that they can improve learning outcomes, increase student engagement, and provide support for mental health and career guidance.

24.3   Methodology

Conversational AI tools are becoming increasingly popular due to their ability to interact with humans in natural language and their potential to automate customer service and support. Evaluating the performance of these tools is essential to ensure their efficiency and effectiveness in addressing user needs. The methodology that can be used to evaluate the performance of conversational AI tools is divided into six phases.

24.3.1   Methodology Phases

There are six phases involved in the process used for the evaluation. Figure 24.1 shows all the steps of the methodology.

24.3.1.1   Define the Evaluation Metrics

The first step in evaluating the performance of conversational AI tools is to define the metrics that will be used to measure their performance. These metrics should be specific, measurable, and relevant to the evaluation goals. Common evaluation metrics for conversational AI tools include accuracy, response time, user satisfaction, and task completion rate.

24.3.1.2   Prepare the Test Data and Scenarios

The next step is to prepare the test data and scenarios that will be used to evaluate the performance of the conversational AI tool. The test data should be representative of the types of inputs and queries that the tool is expected to handle. The test scenarios should cover a range of use cases and user interactions.

24.3.1.3   Select the Evaluation Methodology

There are various evaluation methodologies that can be used to evaluate the performance of conversational AI tools. Some of the commonly used methodologies include user studies, expert evaluations, and automated testing. The selection of the evaluation methodology will depend on the evaluation goals, resources, and constraints.

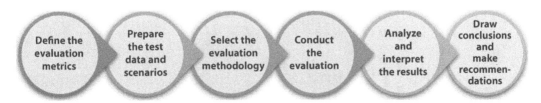

Figure 24.1 Methodology phases.

24.3.1.4 *Conduct the Evaluation*

Once the evaluation methodology has been selected, the evaluation can be conducted. The evaluation process will involve running the conversational AI tool through the test scenarios and measuring its performance against the defined metrics. The evaluation should be conducted in a controlled environment to ensure that the results are reliable and consistent.

24.3.1.5 *Analyze and Interpret the Results*

After the evaluation is complete, the results should be analyzed and interpreted. The analysis should include a comparison of the performance of the conversational AI tool against the defined metrics and the identification of any issues or areas for improvement. The interpretation should provide insights into the strengths and weaknesses of the tool and the potential implications for its use in the intended application domain.

24.3.1.6 *Draw Conclusions and Make Recommendations*

Based on the results of the evaluation and the analysis, conclusions can be drawn about the performance of the conversational AI tool. Recommendations can be made regarding improvements to the tool, changes to the evaluation methodology, or future research directions. The conclusions and recommendations should be communicated clearly and effectively to stakeholders.

24.3.2 Types of Evaluation Metrics Used for the Evaluation

To conduct this evaluation, we divided the evaluation metrics into four categories which are shown in Figure 24.2.

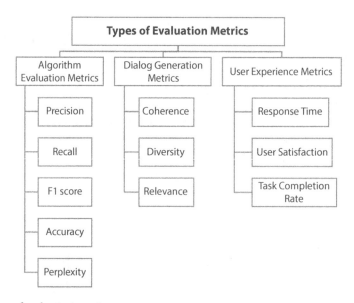

Figure 24.2 Types of evaluation metrics.

24.3.2.1   *Evaluation Metrics*

Evaluation metrics are used to measure the performance of conversational AI tools. The commonly used metrics include precision, recall, F1 score, accuracy, and perplexity. Precision measures the percentage of correct responses given by the AI tool, while recall measures the percentage of relevant responses provided. F1 score is the harmonic mean of precision and recall. Accuracy measures the percentage of correctly classified responses, while perplexity measures the effectiveness of the language model in predicting responses.

24.3.2.2   *Dialog Generation*

Dialog generation is a critical task in conversational AI. The performance of conversational AI tools in generating dialogs is evaluated using metrics such as coherence, relevance, and diversity. Coherence measures how well the responses of the AI tool are related to the user's previous message, while relevance measures the extent to which the AI tool addresses the user's query. Diversity measures the variety of responses generated by the AI tool.

24.3.2.3   *User Experience*

Evaluating the user experience is also essential in assessing the performance of conversational AI tools. User experience is evaluated using metrics such as response time, user satisfaction, and task completion rate. Response time measures how long it takes for the AI tool to respond to the user's query, while user satisfaction measures the extent to which the user is satisfied with the AI tool's response. Task completion rate measures the percentage of tasks completed successfully by the user with the help of the AI tool.

24.4   Result

In the modern age of technology, conversational AI tools are becoming increasingly popular in education settings. These tools can help instructors improve student engagement and provide information in a more efficient manner. With so many different tools available, it can be difficult to determine which is best suited for different contexts. This section will provide a comparative analysis of popular tools, helping instructors make more informed decisions on which is best suited for their educational setting. When it comes to conversational AI tools for educational applications, there are a number of great options available. It is important to consider a few essential factors such as the platform's scalability and flexibility, the ease of integration with existing systems, the accuracy of automated responses, the quality of customer support, and cost.

24.4.1   Platforms Used for the Implementation of Conversational AI Tools

24.4.1.1   *Amazon Lex*

Amazon Lex is part of the AWS portfolio. Lex offers an easy-to-use platform for building conversational interfaces and provides many features such as natural language understanding, automatic speech recognition, and text-to-speech. It is also highly customizable and scalable, so it can be adapted to the specific needs of an educational organization.

24.4.1.2   Google Dialog Flow

Google Dialog Flow is part of Google's AI suite. It is built to create chatbots for websites, mobile apps, and other messaging platforms. It is equipped with natural language understanding capabilities and integration with other Google products such as Google Cloud Speech-to-Text and Google Assistant. DialogFlow also supports a broad range of languages, so it can be easily tailored to the language needs of a particular school or university.

24.4.1.3   Microsoft's Bot Framework

Microsoft's Bot Framework is also a great option. This framework offers a comprehensive set of tools to create custom bots, and its conversational intelligence capabilities are powered by Microsoft's Cognitive Services. The Bot Framework can be used to create bots that can engage in conversations with students and teachers on any platform.

24.4.1.4   Wit.ai

Wit.ai is a natural language processing tool developed by Facebook. It enables users to quickly create natural language interfaces for educational applications. It provides an easy-to-understand interface and is perfect for novice developers. However, it is limited in its ability to understand complex conversations and has a small library of existing intents when compared to other tools.

24.4.1.5   Dialog Flow

Dialog Flow, previously known as Api.ai, is developed by Google. It enables developers to quickly build conversational applications. It provides an intuitive interface and is relatively easy to use for non-developers. It provides a wide range of machine learning capabilities, allowing it to understand more complex conversations than Wit.ai. It also has a larger library of existing intents. Figure 24.3 shows about the comparison of the platforms used for implementing conversational AI tools and Table 24.1 shows about the comparison of chatbot agents.

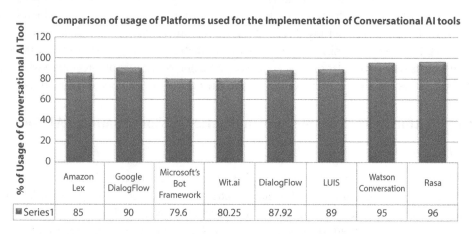

Figure 24.3 Comparison of the platforms used for implementing conversational AI tools.

Table 24.1 Comparison of chatbots/virtual assistant/conversational agent.

Features	GS	NDSR	IC	CGN	KNJ	QR	CT	M	AL	CLP	KA
Code-free development	✓					✓			✓	✓	
Live chat		✓	✓				✓		✓		
Chatbot (CB)/Web (W)/VA	CB	CB	CB	W	CB	W		VA			
Speech recognition		✓	✓		✓	✓		✓	✓	✓	✓
Intent recognition					✓				✓	✓	✓
Multi-language									✓	✓	✓
Pre-configured boat					✓				✓	✓	✓
Country								Poland			
Price (subscription-based: SB/Free: F)	SB	SB	SB	SB	SB	SB	SB				
Multi-channel communication			✓				✓				
NLP	✓	✓	✓	✓	✓				✓	✓	✓
Reporting/analytics	✓		✓		✓		✓		✓	✓	
Third party integration			✓					✓	✓		✓
Operating system supported							✓				
Manual questioning group	✓										
AI-enabled questioning group	✓		✓				✓		✓	✓	
Multiple modes of learning					✓		✓		✓	✓	
Accuracy		99									

(Continued)

Table 24.1 Comparison of chatbots/virtual assistant/conversational agent. (*Continued*)

Features	GS	NDSR	IC	CGN	KNJ	QR	CT	M	AL	CLP	KA
Administrative task							✔		✔	✔	
Recruitment process											
Self-learning			✔				✔	✔	✔	✔	✔
Higher education	✔	✔		✔			✔				
Professional education	✔	✔		✔			✔		✔	✔	✔
K-12 education				✔			✔	✔	✔	✔	
Customizable					✔						
Language learner					✔		✔		✔	✔	✔
Platform SP/TA/LA		ALL	ALL	ALL			ALL		ALL	ALL	ALL
Language of use								Polish			

GS, GradeScore; IC, Ivy Chatbot; CGN, Cognii; KNJ, Knowji, QR; Quirem CT, CenturyTech; M, Mika; AL, altitude learning; CLP, Carnegie Learning Platform; KA, Knewtons Alta; NDSR, nuances dragon speech recognition.

24.4.1.6   *LUIS*

LUIS (Language Understanding Intelligent Service) is developed by Microsoft. It enables developers to create natural language applications for various platforms. It provides an interactive interface and has powerful machine learning capabilities. Furthermore, it has a larger library of existing intents when compared to Wit.ai.

24.4.1.7   *Watson Conversation*

Watson Conversation is developed by IBM and is used to create chatbot applications. It has an easy-to-understand interface and powerful machine learning capabilities. It also has a larger library of existing intents when compared to Wit.ai.

24.4.1.8   *Rasa*

Rasa is an open-source framework for developing conversational AI. It is perfect for experienced developers and those who want to have more control over the development process. It provides powerful machine learning capabilities and has a large library of existing intents.

24.4.1.9   *Century Tech [9]*

When deciding which conversational AI tool is right for you, it is important to assess the needs and resources of your organization and consider the features and capabilities of the different options that are available.

24.4.2   Conversational AI Tools Used in Research

There are activities involved in the process of conducting research. Figure 24.4 presents the various AI tools used for research activities.

24.4.2.1   *Data Collection*

Conversational AI tools can be used for data collection in research activities—for example, chatbots can be used to conduct surveys, interviews, and focused group discussions, providing a more efficient and flexible method of data collection. These tools can also be used to collect data in real time, allowing researchers to collect more accurate and timely data.

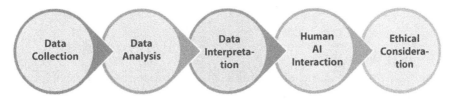

Figure 24.4 Conduct of a research activity.

24.4.2.1.1   Qualtrics

This is a platform that provides tools for online surveys and data collection, including the use of chatbots to enhance survey responses and engagement.

24.4.2.1.2   Amazon Mechanical Turk

This is a platform that provides access to a large pool of human workers who can be used to collect and label data and to evaluate chatbot performance as well as improve the response rates and quality of data collected.

24.4.2.1.3   SurveyMonkey

This is a platform that provides survey software and allows the use of chatbots to collect data more efficiently and accurately.

24.4.2.1.4   TypeForm

This is a conversational form builder that uses conversational AI to create engaging and interactive forms that can be used to collect data.

24.4.2.1.5   BotStar

This is a chatbot builder that can be used to create conversational bots to collect data in a conversational and engaging way.

24.4.2.1.6   Collect.Chat

This is a chatbot builder that can be used to create conversational surveys and feedback forms that can be used to collect data from users.

24.4.2.1.7   Microsoft Forms

This is a platform that provides survey software and allows the use of conversational AI to create engaging surveys to collect data from users.

24.4.2.2   Data Analysis

Conversational AI tools can be used for data analysis in research activities—for example, natural language processing algorithms can be used to analyze large volumes of text data, such as social media posts or customer reviews. These tools can identify patterns, sentiments, and themes in the data, providing insights into the research questions. Here are some conversational AI tools that can be used for data analysis, depending on the research goals and requirements.

24.4.2.2.1   IBM Watson

This is a suite of AI tools that includes natural language processing, machine learning, and chatbot creation capabilities, which can be used for data analysis and interpretation.

24.4.2.2.2   Google Cloud Natural Language
This is a platform that provides tools for natural language processing, sentiment analysis, and entity recognition, which can be used for data analysis.

24.4.2.2.3   Hugging Face
This is a platform that provides pre-trained models for natural language processing and chatbot development, which can be used for data analysis and interpretation.

24.4.2.2.4   Amazon Comprehend
This is a platform that provides tools for natural language processing, topic modeling, and entity recognition, which can be used for data analysis and interpretation.

24.4.2.2.5   Rapid Miner
This is a platform that provides tools for machine learning, data mining, and text analytics, which can be used for data analysis.

24.4.2.2.6   KNIME Analytics Platform
This is a platform that provides tools for data mining, machine learning, and natural language processing, which can be used for data analysis and interpretation.

24.4.2.2.7   IBM Watson
This is a suite of cognitive computing tools that include natural language processing, speech-to-text conversion, and chatbot creation capabilities, which can be used for data analysis and interpretation.

24.4.2.3   *Data Interpretation*

Conversational AI tools can be used for data interpretation in research activities—for example, chatbots can be used to interpret data by providing explanations or recommendations based on research findings. These tools can also be used to summarize research findings in a more accessible and engaging format, such as a chatbot interface.

24.4.2.3.1   Tableau
This is a data visualization platform that can be used to create interactive dashboards and visualizations that help to interpret and communicate data insights.

24.4.2.3.2   IBM Watson Studio
This is a cloud-based platform that provides tools for data analysis, machine learning, and data visualization, which can be used to interpret and communicate data insights.

24.4.2.3.3 Microsoft Power BI

This is a business analytics platform that can be used to create interactive dashboards and reports that help to interpret and communicate data insights.

24.4.2.3.4 QlikView

This is a data visualization platform that can be used to create interactive dashboards and visualizations that help to interpret and communicate data insights.

24.4.2.3.5 Google Data Studio

This is a free data visualization and reporting platform that can be used to create interactive dashboards and visualizations that help to interpret and communicate data insights.

24.4.2.3.6 Alteryx

This is a platform that provides tools for data blending, cleansing, and predictive analytics, which can be used to interpret and communicate data insights.

24.4.2.4 Human–AI Interaction

Conversational AI tools can be used for human–AI interaction in research activities—for example, chatbots can be used to facilitate communication and collaboration between researchers and participants, enhancing the quality and accuracy of research findings (Raza *et al.*, 2020). These tools can also be used to support participant engagement and motivation throughout the research process. Mentioned below are conversational AI tools that can be used for human–AI interaction, depending on the specific needs and use cases.

24.4.2.4.1 Dialogflow

This is a chatbot development platform that can be used to create conversational interfaces for applications, websites, and devices, allowing for a seamless interaction between humans and AI.

24.4.2.4.2 Microsoft Bot Framework

This is a platform that provides tools for building and deploying chatbots across multiple channels, allowing for natural language interaction between humans and AI.

24.4.2.4.3 Rasa

This is an open-source framework for building chatbots and AI assistants that can be customized to fit specific needs and use cases, providing a seamless interaction between humans and AI.

24.4.2.4.4 Amazon Lex

This is a platform that provides tools for building conversational interfaces for applications, websites, and devices using natural language processing and speech recognition, allowing for a seamless interaction between humans and AI.

24.4.2.4.5   Kore.ai

This is a chatbot development platform that can be used to create custom chatbots for various industries and use cases, allowing for a natural language interaction between humans and AI.

24.4.2.4.6   Tars

This is a chatbot development platform that can be used to create custom chatbots for lead generation, customer service, and other use cases, providing a seamless interaction between humans and AI.

24.4.2.5   *Ethical Considerations*

The use of conversational AI tools in research activities raises ethical considerations, such as privacy, informed consent, and transparency (Zarsky, 2016). Researchers should ensure that the use of these tools is in compliance with ethical guidelines and regulations and that participants are informed of the use of conversational AI tools in research. These are just a few examples of the many conversational AI tools and resources that can be used to address ethical considerations in AI development, depending on the specific needs and use cases.

24.4.2.5.1   IBM AI Fairness 360

This is a toolkit that can be used to detect and mitigate bias in AI models, promoting fairness, and ethical considerations in AI development.

24.4.2.5.2   TensorFlow Privacy

This is a framework that can be used to train machine learning models with privacy guarantees, addressing ethical considerations related to data privacy.

24.4.2.5.3   Fiddler

This is a AI explain ability platform that can be used to understand and interpret the behavior of AI models, promoting transparency and ethical considerations in AI development.

24.4.2.5.4   Open AI GPT-3

This is a language model that has been pre-trained on a large corpus of text, which can be fine-tuned to generate ethical and unbiased content, addressing ethical considerations related to language and content generation.

24.4.2.5.5   Google Responsible AI

This is a set of tools and resources that can be used to ensure that AI models are developed responsibly and ethically, promoting fairness and transparency in AI development.

24.4.2.5.6   Microsoft AI Ethics and Effects in Engineering and Research Committee

This is a committee established by Microsoft to address ethical considerations related to AI development, promoting responsible and ethical AI practices. Table 24.2 shows about the feature comparison of the smart invigilation tools used in education.

Table 24.2 Feature comparison of the smart invigilation tools used in education.

Tool name	Remote proctoring	Browser lockdown	ID verification	Secure delivery	Reporting and analytics	User friendly interface	Customization support	Ease of use	Content security	Exam administration support
Proctorio	★	★	★	★	★	★				
ExamSoft	★	★	★	★	★					
Respondus Monitor	★	★	★	★	★		★		★	
Honorlock	★	★	★	★	★		★			
ProctorU	★	★	★	★	★				★	
Kryterion Webassessor	★	★	★	★	★					
Bvirtual	★	★	★	★	★				★	
PSI Bridge	★	★	★	★	★				★	★
Talview	★				★				★	
Secure Exam Remote Proctor	★	★	★	★	★	★	★	★		

There are many conversational AI tools available for research, such as Landbot.io, Snaps, Liveperson, Ideta, Mindsay, Sparkcentral, SAP, Boost.ai, ChatBot, Clinc, HappyFox, Cognigy, and MobileMonkey [3]. You can also find and compare the top conversational AI platform software on Capterra [4], with their free and interactive tool. Additionally, there are many chatbot companies that help firms to save costs and improve customer experience using NLP and machine learning [5]. Examples of such companies include Codebots, Botpress, Dialog Flow, and Botfuel.

24.4.3   Smart Tutoring Systems

Smart tutoring systems are becoming increasingly popular in educational settings, as they offer a personalized, interactive experience for students of all ages and levels. Utilizing conversational AI, such systems can respond to student queries in an accurate, natural way, helping to guide them through their learning process. Conversational AI can be used to create a wide range of interactive content to support student learning—for example, AI chatbots can answer questions and provide feedback, explain concepts, and guide students through complex topics. AI-driven virtual tutors can also be used to simulate real-life teaching scenarios, allowing students to practice their skills in a safe and secure environment. Conversational AI can also be used to analyze student performance and provide personalized feedback. By collecting data from student interactions, AI systems can detect patterns in student responses and modify the content accordingly. This can help to identify areas of improvement and tailor the content to the individual student's needs.

24.4.3.1   Carnegie Learning

This is an AI-powered platform that provides personalized tutoring and adaptive learning for math education.

24.4.3.2   DreamBox Learning

This is an AI-powered platform that provides personalized tutoring and adaptive learning for K-8 math education.

24.4.3.3   Squirrel AI

This is an AI-powered platform that provides personalized tutoring and adaptive learning for K-12 education across multiple subjects.

24.4.3.4   Knewton

This is an AI-powered platform that provides personalized tutoring and adaptive learning for higher education across multiple subjects.

24.4.3.5   Duolingo

This is a language learning platform that uses AI to provide personalized tutoring and adaptive learning for language education.

24.4.3.6   Coursera

This is a platform that provides online courses and personalized tutoring using AI and machine learning technologies across multiple subjects and domains.

Using these tools, the AI can provide an interactive, personalized learning experience that is tailored to each student's individual needs. This helps to improve learning outcomes, increase engagement, and motivate students to stay on track with their studies.

24.4.4   Smart Invigilation

Smart invigilation is a technology that can help teachers monitor their students' online tests and exams. AI tools can play an important role in this process, helping teachers to identify suspicious activities and ensuring that tests are conducted fairly. AI-based software can detect facial recognition, keyboard strokes, and other activities to determine whether students are cheating or not. This helps teachers to ensure that students are not using external sources or technology to answer questions they may not know the answer to. AI tools can also detect suspicious patterns in a student's answers, such as multiple answers to the same question or the same pattern of answers to multiple questions. This helps teachers to identify if a student is plagiarizing or using a text-based cheating method. AI tools are also a great way to provide feedback to students. AI algorithms can be used to assess a student's answers and provide them with personalized feedback on how they can improve their answers. This helps to make the learning process more effective and rewarding for the students. Overall, AI tools can help teachers to monitor online exams and tests effectively and efficiently. This helps to ensure that students are following the rules and are not cheating. It also helps to make the learning process more engaging and rewarding for the students. Conversational AI tools are becoming increasingly popular for smart invigilation, allowing businesses to monitor exams and tests remotely. The most popular tools for this purpose include AlphaChat, HyroHyro, Meya, and EbiEbi [6], all of which are capable of understanding natural language and providing a reliable conversational interface. Activechat.ai is another popular tool which is specifically designed for subscription businesses and provides a live chat interface. Furthermore, Botpress , Rasa, Wit.ai, OpenDialog, and Botonic [7, 8] are also popular options. All of these tools allow businesses to automatically monitor exams and tests, making sure that the entire process is secure and accurate.

24.4.4.1   Proctorio

Proctorio is a remote invigilation platform that uses a combination of machine learning and human review to monitor students during online exams. It integrates with learning management systems like Canvas and Moodle and uses webcam and microphone feeds to capture audio and video of the exam session. Proctorio's AI algorithms flag potential incidents of cheating, and human reviewers then analyze these incidents to determine if there was any actual cheating.

24.4.4.2   *ExamSof*

ExamSoft is a secure exam platform that provides proctoring features like facial recognition and browser lockdown to prevent cheating during online exams. It also uses machine learning to flag potential incidents of cheating, and human reviewers analyze these incidents to determine if there was any actual cheating.

24.4.4.3   *Respondus Monitor*

Respondus Monitor is a remote invigilation tool that integrates with learning management systems like Blackboard and Canvas. It uses a webcam and microphone to monitor students during online exams and uses AI algorithms to flag potential incidents of cheating. Human reviewers then analyze these incidents to determine if there was any actual cheating.

24.4.4.4   *Honorlock*

Honorlock is a proctoring tool that uses AI and machine learning to detect potential incidents of cheating during online exams. It uses a webcam and microphone to monitor students during the exam and has features like ID verification, browser lockdown, and keystroke analysis to prevent cheating.

24.4.4.5   *ProctorU*

ProctorU is a remote invigilation platform that provides proctoring services for online exams. It uses a combination of AI and human review to monitor students during the exam and uses features like facial recognition, browser lockdown, and ID verification to prevent cheating.

24.4.4.6   *Kryterion Webassessor*

Kryterion Webassessor is an online assessment and certification platform that provides a secure testing environment for high-stake exams. It uses a combination of AI and human proctoring to monitor the test takers and prevent cheating during online exams. Kryterion Webassessor is used by a variety of organizations, including universities, certification bodies, and professional associations, to administer exams and assessments. The platform's focus on exam integrity and security makes it a popular choice for high-stake exams where cheating prevention is critical.

24.4.4.7   *Secure Exam Remote Proctor*

Secure Exam Remote Proctor (SERP) is an online exam proctoring tool that uses AI and machine learning algorithms to monitor the test takers during online exams. It provides a secure testing environment for remote exams and is used by educational institutions and certification providers.

24.4.4.8 Bvirtual

Bvirtual is a digital learning solutions company that offers a range of services to educational institutions and corporations. Their services include e-learning content development, learning management system implementation, and online exam proctoring. This online exam proctoring service is designed to ensure exam integrity during remote exams. It uses a combination of AI and human proctoring to monitor the test takers and prevent cheating. The platform offers several features to ensure exam integrity.

24.4.4.9 PSI Bridge

PSI Bridge offers a variety of tools for exam administrators, such as exam scheduling, test item banking, and automated scoring. The platform is also accessible through a web browser and supports a variety of question formats, including multiple choice, essay, and performance-based questions.

24.4.4.10 Talview

Talview is an AI-powered video interviewing and assessment platform designed for remote hiring and talent management. The platform leverages advanced technologies such as machine learning, natural language processing, and facial recognition to provide a seamless and efficient hiring process. Talview offers several features for recruiters and hiring managers, including the following:

24.4.4.10.1 Video Interviewing

Talview's video interviewing feature allows the candidates to record and submit their responses to pre-set interview questions. Recruiters and hiring managers can then review the videos at their convenience, reducing the need for scheduling and travel.

24.4.4.10.2 Automated Screening

The platform's AI-powered screening tool analyzes candidate responses to assess their skills and fit for the role.

24.4.4.10.3 Psychometric Assessments

Talview offers a variety of psychometric assessments to evaluate candidate traits such as personality, cognitive ability, and behavioral competencies.

In addition to these features, Talview's platform is designed to integrate with popular applicant tracking systems, making it easy to incorporate into existing recruitment workflows. Talview's focus on AI and automation has made it a popular choice for organizations seeking to streamline their recruitment process and reduce the time-to-hire. Its features and tools help to ensure fair and unbiased assessments, improving the quality of hires and driving business success. These tools and others like them are designed to provide a secure testing environment and prevent cheating during online exams. However, it is important to use them ethically and in compliance with privacy and data protection laws.

24.4.5 Conversational AI Tools Used for Autonomous Grading Systems

Conversational AI tools used for autonomous grading systems leverage natural language processing (NLP) and machine learning algorithms to automatically grade written assignments, essays, and other text-based assessments. These tools are designed to save time for instructors and provide students with quick feedback on their work.

24.4.5.1 Gradescope

Gradescope is an online platform that uses AI-powered image recognition and natural language processing to grade written assignments, including handwritten responses. It offers features such as rubric-based grading, automatic point allocation, and real-time feedback for students.

24.4.5.2 Turnitin

This is an online plagiarism checker that uses AI to identify similarities between submitted assignments and other sources on the Internet.

24.4.5.3 Coursera Auto-Grader

This is an automatic grading tool used in Coursera's online courses that can grade programming assignments in multiple programming languages.

24.4.5.4 Code Runner

This is an automatic grading tool for computer programming assignments that can grade code in various programming languages.

24.4.5.5 EdX

EdX is a Massive Open Online Course provider that uses AI-powered assessment tools to grade student work in online courses. Its platform offers features such as peer review, automated grading, and adaptive learning.

24.4.5.6 AI-Assisted Grading

This is a tool developed by Carnegie Mellon University that can grade short-answer questions and essays based on natural language processing techniques.

24.4.5.7 Light SIDE

This is an open-source natural language processing tool that can automatically grade short-answer questions and essays.

24.4.5.8   *Xceptiona lED*

This is an automatic grading tool for math and science assignments that uses machine learning to grade student work.

24.4.5.9   *Vantage Learning's MY Access*

This is an AI-powered writing evaluation tool that can grade student essays based on multiple factors such as grammar, style, and content.

24.4.5.10   *Gradescope for Programming*

This is an AI-powered grading tool designed for computer programming assignments that can grade and provide feedback on code submissions in a variety of programming languages.

24.4.5.11   *Grammarly*

Grammarly is an AI-powered writing assistant that uses machine learning algorithms to identify and correct errors in grammar, punctuation, and spelling. It provides feedback on written assignments and can be integrated into popular word processors and web browsers.

24.4.5.12   *Pearson*

Pearson is an educational technology company that offers AI-powered assessment tools for grading written assignments and essays. Its platform uses machine learning algorithms to analyze student writing for quality, originality, and content.

24.4.6   Conversational AI-Based Monitoring System Tools

Conversational AI tools used for autonomous monitoring systems are designed to monitor online activities, communications, and behavior in real time to identify potential security threats, fraud, or inappropriate behavior. These tools leverage NLP, machine learning, and predictive analytics to identify patterns and anomalies in data and detect potential risks. Some popular conversational AI tools used for autonomous monitoring systems are presented below.

24.4.6.1   *IBM Watson*

IBM Watson is an AI-powered system that uses NLP and machine learning to analyze large volumes of data in real time, including email, social media, and other online activities. Its platform offers features such as sentiment analysis, entity recognition, and anomaly detection to identify potential threats and risks.

24.4.6.2 Verint

Verint is an AI-powered surveillance and monitoring system that uses machine learning algorithms to analyze large volumes of data from multiple sources. Its platform offers features such as real-time monitoring, predictive analytics, and behavioral analysis to detect potential security threats and fraud.

24.4.6.3 Darktrace

Darktrace is an AI-powered cybersecurity platform that uses machine learning to analyze network traffic, user behavior, and device activity in real time. Its platform offers features such as threat detection, autonomous response, and forensic investigation to identify potential threats and respond to them in real time.

24.4.6.4 Cybereason

Cybereason is an AI-powered endpoint security platform that uses machine learning algorithms to detect and respond to potential threats in real time. Its platform offers features such as behavioral analysis, threat hunting, and incident response to identify and mitigate potential security risks.

24.4.6.5 Splunk

Splunk is an AI-powered security information and event management system that uses machine learning algorithms to analyze large volumes of data in real time. Its platform offers features such as threat detection, correlation analysis, and anomaly detection to identify potential security risks and respond to them in real time.

24.4.6.6 Microsoft Azure Monitor

This provides a chatbot interface that allows users to ask questions and get answers about their Azure resources.

24.4.6.7 OpsGenie

This is a tool that uses machine learning to monitor and respond to incidents in real time. It can also be integrated with various communication channels, such as email and SMS, to keep the users updated.

24.4.6.8 Botmetric

This is a tool that uses natural language processing to interpret user queries and provide relevant information about AWS infrastructure and services.

24.4.6.9 DataDog

This provides a conversational interface that allows users to ask questions about their infrastructure, metrics, and logs.

24.4.6.10 IBM Watson Assistant

This can be used to create chatbots that monitor various systems and processes, such as IT helpdesk, customer service, and marketing campaigns.

24.4.6.11 Hugging Face

This provides a platform for building and deploying conversational AI models, including chatbots and voice assistants.

24.4.6.12 Zabbix

This provides a chatbot interface that allows users to receive real-time alerts and updates about their infrastructure.

These conversational AI tools are used by organizations in various industries to monitor online activities and detect potential threats and risks. They help to ensure the safety and security of online communications and transactions and prevent fraud, cyber attacks, and other security breaches.

24.5 Discussion

The evaluation of conversational AI tools is crucial to determine their effectiveness and suitability for specific use cases. In this research article, we conducted a comparative analysis of several conversational AI tools to evaluate their performance in various domains. The purpose of this study was to provide insights into the strengths and limitations of different conversational AI tools and to guide the selection of appropriate tools for specific use cases. Our analysis was based on several criteria, including accuracy, speed, scalability, and user experience. We evaluated the performance of each tool in three domains: customer service, healthcare, and education. For each domain, we selected a set of tasks that are commonly performed using conversational AI tools, such as answering customer queries, diagnosing health conditions, and providing academic feedback. Our results showed that different conversational AI tools perform differently depending on the domain and task at hand. In the customer service domain, we found that tools such as Dialogflow and Microsoft Bot Framework performed well in terms of accuracy and speed while also providing a good user experience. However, these tools had limitations in terms of scalability and customization. In the education domain, we found that tools such as IBM Watson and Turnitin performed well in terms of accuracy and scalability and had the ability to provide personalized feedback to students. However, these tools had limitations in terms of user experience, as they required a high level of technical expertise to be used effectively.

Overall, our comparative analysis showed that there is no one-size-fits-all solution when it comes to conversational AI tools. Each tool has its strengths and limitations, and the choice of tool depends on the specific use case and requirements. Our study provides insights into the performance of different conversational AI tools in various domains and can be used as a guide for selecting appropriate tools for specific use cases. Evaluating the performance of conversational AI tools presents some challenges. One challenge is the lack of a standardized evaluation framework, making it difficult to compare the performance of different tools. Another challenge is the complexity of evaluating the user experience, as user preferences and expectations can vary widely.

The phoney [10–14] landing page that is frequently used in phishing [15–17] and man-in-the-middle (MitM) [18–21] attacks may also be included in these chatbot phishing emails [22, 23]. The correct language may be used by threat actors to generate socially engineered emails that are more convincing than those made by certain threat actors, even if chatbots do have restrictions and can indeed deny some requests to carry out such activities. Phishing emails [24] continue to be one of the most common ways for many threat actors [25] to gain initial access and conduct credential harvesting attacks [26]. Inaccurate spelling and punctuation are signs of a phishing attempt in an email. To make sophisticated, more convincing, and more human-like phishing emails into which threat actors may insert malware [27], chatbots have been utilised. The emails may be customised for certain businesses or organisations or represent more realistic attempts to get login information. Beyond emails, AI chatbots may produce communications that seem like scams [28] and contain fake gifts.

24.6   Conclusion

In conclusion, conversational AI tools have shown promising results in enhancing learning outcomes and engagement among students in education. These tools have the potential to personalize learning experiences, enhance cognitive engagement, and improve accessibility. However, challenges such as the lack of data and the need for natural language processing capabilities need to be addressed to improve the performance of conversational AI tools in education. Further research is required to develop and evaluate the effectiveness of these tools in different educational settings and for different types of learners.

References

1. Docken, C., Top 4 best chatbots for higher education 2023, o8.agency. Retrieved February 8, 2023, from https://www.o8.agency/blog/best-chatbots-higher-education.
2. Pappano, L., College chatbots, with names like iggy and pounce, are here to help, The New York Times, 2020, April 8, Retrieved February 8, 2023, from https://www.nytimes.com/2020/04/08/education/college-ai-chatbots-students.html.
3. Ramella, B., Top 13 conversational AI platforms & features compared, 2020, October 28, Cloud Communication Providers: User Reviews, Expert Guides. Retrieved February 8, 2023, from https://getvoip.com/blog/2020/10/28/conversational-ai-platforms/.

4. Best conversational AI platform software 2023: Reviews of the most popular tools & systems, Best Conversational AI Platform Software 2023 | Reviews of the Most Popular Tools & Systems, Retrieved February 8, 2023, from https://www.capterra.com/conversational-ai-platform-software/.

5. Dilmegani, C., 50+ chatbot companies to deploy conversational AI in 2023, AIMultiple, 2023, February 2, Retrieved February 8, 2023, from https://research.aimultiple.com/chatbot-companies/.

6. Top 16 conversational AI tools, Startup Stash, 2022, December 20, Retrieved February 8, 2023, from https://startupstash.com/conversational-ai-tools/.

7. Ghazanfar, Z., Top 7 tools for conversational AI in 2022, LinkedIn, 1659, December 10, Retrieved February 8, 2023, from https://www.linkedin.com/pulse/top-7-tools-conversational-ai-2022-zoya-ghazanfar?trk=pulse-article_more-articles_related-content-card.

8. Klaas, J., Conversational AI chatbot - 9 best software tools in 2022, alphachat, 2021, August 4, Retrieved February 8, 2023, from https://www.alphachat.ai/blog/conversational-ai-chatbot.

9. Online learning: English, Maths and Science, Century, 2023, Available at: https://www.century.tech/ (Accessed: February 24, 2023).

10. Mahor, V., Bijrothiya, S., Rawat, R., Kumar, A., Garg, B., Pachlasiya, K., IoT and artificial intelligence techniques for public safety and security, in: *Smart Urban Computing Applications*, p. 111, 2023.

11. Mahor, V., Pachlasiya, K., Garg, B., Chouhan, M., Telang, S., Rawat, R., Mobile operating system (Android) vulnerability analysis using machine learning, in: *Proceedings of International Conference on Network Security and Blockchain Technology: ICNSBT 2021*, pp. 159–169, Springer Nature Singapore, Singapore, 2022, June.

12. Rawat, R., Garg, B., Pachlasiya, K., Mahor, V., Telang, S., Chouhan, M., Mishra, R., SCNTA: Monitoring of network availability and activity for identification of anomalies using machine learning approaches. *Int. J. Inf. Technol. Web Eng. (IJITWE)*, 17, 1, 1–19, 2022.

13. Rawat, R., Rimal, Y.N., William, P., Dahima, S., Gupta, S., Sankaran, K.S., Malware threat affecting financial organization analysis using machine learning approach. *Int. J. Inf. Technol. Web Eng. (IJITWE)*, 17, 1, 1–20, 2022.

14. Rawat, R., Mahor, V., Chouhan, M., Pachlasiya, K., Telang, S., Garg, B., Systematic literature review (SLR) on social media and the digital transformation of drug trafficking on darkweb, in: *International Conference on Network Security and Blockchain Technology*, pp. 181–205, Springer, Singapore, 2022.

15. Rawat, R., Ayodele Oki, O., Sankaran, S., Florez, H., Ajagbe, S.A., Techniques for predicting dark web events focused on the delivery of illicit products and ordered crime. *Int. J. Electr. Comput. Eng. (IJECE)*, 13, 5, 5354–5365, Oct. 2023, doi: 10.11591/ijece.v13i5.pp5354-5365.

16. Rawat, R., Garg, B., Mahor, V., Telang, S., Pachlasiya, K., Chouhan, M., Organ trafficking on the dark web—The data security and privacy concern in healthcare systems, in: *Internet of Healthcare Things: Machine Learning for Security and Privacy*, pp. 189–216, 2022.

17. Vyas, P., Vyas, G., Chauhan, A., Rawat, R., Telang, S., Gottumukkala, M., Anonymous trading on the dark online marketplace: An exploratory study, in: *Using Computational Intelligence for the Dark Web and Illicit Behavior Detection*, pp. 272–289, IGI Global, 2022.

18. Rawat, R., Oki, O.A., Sankaran, K.S., Olasupo, O., Ebong, G.N., Ajagbe, S.A., A new solution for cyber security in big data using machine learning approach, in: *Mobile Computing and Sustainable Informatics: Proceedings of ICMCSI 2023*, pp. 495–505, Springer Nature Singapore, Singapore, 2023.

19. Rawat, R., Chakrawarti, R.K., Raj, A., Mani, G., Chidambarathanu, K., Bhardwaj, R., Association rule learning for threat analysis using traffic analysis and packet filtering approach. *Int. J. Inf. Technol.*, 1–11, 2023.

20. Rawat, R., Logical concept mapping and social media analytics relating to cyber criminal activities for ontology creation. *Int. J. Inf. Technol.*, *15*, 2, 893–903, 2023.

21. Rawat, R., Mahor, V., Álvarez, J.D., Ch, F., Cognitive systems for dark web cyber delinquent association malignant data crawling: A review, in: *Handbook of Research on War Policies, Strategies, and Cyber Wars*, pp. 45–63, 2023.

22. Rawat, R., Chakrawarti, R.K., Vyas, P., Gonzáles, J.L.A., Sikarwar, R., Bhardwaj, R., Intelligent fog computing surveillance system for crime and vulnerability identification and tracing. *Int. J. Inf. Secur. Priv. (IJISP)*, *17*, 1, 1–25, 2023.

23. Rawat, R., Sowjanya, A.M., Patel, S.I., Jaiswal, V., Khan, I., Balaram, A. (Eds.), *Using Machine Intelligence: Autonomous Vehicles Volume 1*, John Wiley & Sons, 2022.

24. Rawat, R., Mahor, V., Díaz-Álvarez, J., Chávez, F., Rooted learning model at fog computing analysis for crime incident surveillance, in: *2022 International Conference on Smart Generation Computing, Communication and Networking (SMART GENCON)*, 2022, December, pp. 1–9, IEEE.

25. Rawat, R. and Shrivastav, S.K., SQL injection attack detection using SVM. *Int. J. Comput. Appl.*, *42*, 13, 1–4, 2012.

26. Rawat, R., Bhardwaj, P., Kaur, U., Telang, S., Chouhan, M., Sankaran, K.S., *Smart vehicles for communication, volume 2*, John Wiley & Sons, 2023.

27. Mahor, V., Garg, B., Telang, S., Pachlasiya, K., Chouhan, M., Rawat, R., Cyber threat phylogeny assessment and vulnerabilities representation at thermal power station, in: *Proceedings of International Conference on Network Security and Blockchain Technology: ICNSBT 2021*, pp. 28–39, Springer Nature Singapore, Singapore, 2022, June.

28. Rawat, R., Gupta, S., Sivaranjani, S., Cu, O.K., Kuliha, M., Sankaran, K.S., Malevolent information crawling mechanism for forming structured illegal organisations in hidden networks. *Int. J. Cyber Warf. Terror. (IJCWT)*, *12*, 1, 1–14, 2022.

Conversational AI Applications in Ed-Tech Industry: An Analysis of Its Impact and Potential in Education

Deepika Chauhan[1]*, Chaitanya Singh[2], Romil Rawat[3] and Mukesh Chouhan

[1]Computer Application Department, Silver Oak University, Ahmedabad, Gujarata, India
[2]Computer Engineering Department, Vidhyadeep University, Surat, Gujarata, India
[3]Department of Computer Science, Shri Vaishnav Vidyapeeth Vishwavidyalaya, Indore, India
[4]HOD (Computer Science & Engineering), Government Polytechnic College, Sanawad, Khargone, India

Abstract

Conversational artificial intelligence (AI) has the potential to revolutionize the field of education. Its ability to understand natural language and engage in human-like conversations makes it a valuable tool for personalized learning and student engagement. This paper discusses the current state of conversational AI in education, including its use in tutoring systems, virtual learning assistants, and language learning applications. The research studies the effectiveness of conversational AI in improving student learning outcomes and engagement and highlights the potential challenges and limitations of this technology. Through this paper, we aim to provide an overview of the current research on the use of conversational AI in education and to offer insights into how this technology can be used to enhance student learning and engagement in the future.

Keywords: Conversational AI, chatbots, Ed-tech, virtual assistants, NLP, education

25.1 Introduction

Artificial intelligence (AI) adoption in organizations is growing rapidly. AI technology is acting as an umbrella for computer vision, robotics, natural language processing (NLP), and machine learning (ML). The tech jury report released in 2022 stated that AI-powered voice assistants will reach 8 billion by 2023 and global AI market reach will be 60$ billion by 2025 [1]. Digital momentum in education increases the need for AI integration in Ed-tech to improve remote learning experience, student support, virtual tutoring, mentoring, evaluation, feedback, and proctor examination. Conversational AI empowered humans for creating personalized, scalable, and emotionally resonant educational environments. Conversational AI includes virtual assistants, and chatbots, in turn, facilitated the rise in the smart learning management system (LMS), online class conduction, and

---

*Corresponding author: chauhandeepika522@gmail.com

Romil Rawat, Rajesh Kumar Chakrawarti, Sanjaya Kumar Sarangi, Piyush Vyas, Mary Sowjanya Alamanda, Kotagiri Srividya and Krishnan Sakthidasan Sankaran (eds.) Conversational Artificial Intelligence, (411–434) © 2024 Scrivener Publishing LLC

feedback. Education is one of the top five industries getting benefited with conversational AI. Conversational AI is a technology that enables conversation with humans in human-friendly language. Conversational AI incorporates NLP into technology like chatbot, voice assistant, and exam proctor to understand human speech or behavior and respond to their queries in a human-friendly manner. Figure 25.1 shows types of conversational AI.

Jian-Yun Nie, a leading researcher in the field of NLP, emphasized the need for conversational AI systems to understand the meaning and context of language, rather than just recognizing words and phrases [24]. Chaturvedi R, a professor of marketing and digital media, noted that conversational AI has the potential to revolutionize the way businesses interact with customers, providing more personalized and human-like experiences. Dan Roth, a computer science professor and researcher in NLP, stated that conversational AI has the potential to transform a wide range of industries, from customer service to healthcare, but that there is still much work to be done to develop systems that can handle more complex conversations. Jennifer Chu-Carroll, a researcher in the field of conversational AI, emphasized the importance of developing systems that can handle uncertainty and deal with the inherent ambiguity of human language. Deb Roy, a professor of media arts and sciences, noted that conversational AI has the potential to enhance human–computer interaction and improve the ways in which people access information and perform tasks. These perspectives demonstrate the diverse and rapidly evolving nature of the field of conversational AI in 2023. Figure 25.1 shows the timeline of the digital transformation of education system in a few years. Conversational AI has the potential to play a significant role in education. Figure 25.2 shows the various types of conversational AI mechanism used in education.

25.2 Conversational AI in Ed-Tech Overview

Conversational AI is a rapidly growing field that has garnered significant attention from researchers, practitioners, and industry experts. Different authors have different perspectives on what constitutes conversational AI, its applications, and its future. Below are some key perspectives from some of the leading experts in the field:

Shuai Wang and Wei Fan, authors of the book "Conversational AI: Techniques and Applications," define conversational AI as the application of AI technologies to NLP, speech recognition, and dialogue management to create human-like interaction between computers and humans. Fei Liu, a researcher in the field of conversational AI, emphasizes the importance of context in conversational AI, stating that systems need to understand the context of a conversation in order to respond appropriately. Vladimir Uskov, a professor

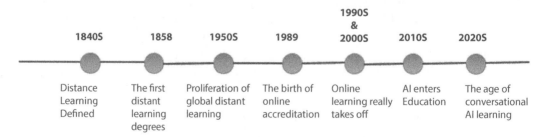

Figure 25.1 Timeline of digital education transformation.

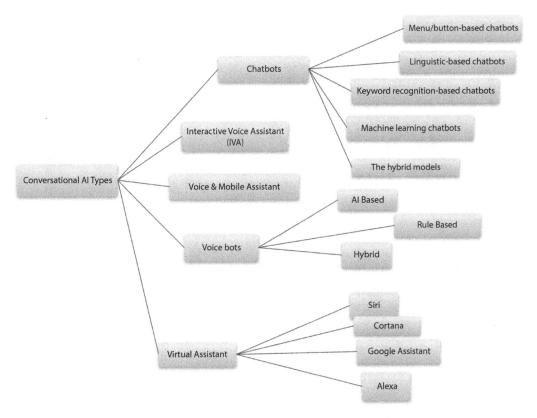

Figure 25.2 Types of conversational AI in education.

of computer science, highlights the importance of NLP and ML in conversational AI, stating that these technologies are critical to create systems that can understand and generate human-like language. Martin Hofmann, a researcher in the field of conversational AI, notes that there is a need for more research on the ethics and social implications of conversational AI, including privacy concerns, algorithmic bias, and the impact of these systems on employment. Eric J. Krupka, a researcher in the field of human–computer interaction, notes that conversational AI has the potential to enhance human–computer interaction and provide new opportunities for creating more natural and human-like interactions with technology. These perspectives demonstrate the diversity of thought in the field of conversational AI and highlight the need for ongoing research and development to understand the full potential and impact of these technologies.

Conversational AI tools are computer programs that use NLP and other AI techniques to enable human-like communication with users. These tools are used to improve customer service, automate repetitive tasks, and provide personalized experiences for users. However, it is important to note that the development and deployment of conversational AI is an ongoing process and new tools and applications are being developed all the time. Figure 25.3 demonstrates the direct interaction time of students, i.e., 49% can be improved to 80–90% by deploying conversational AI.

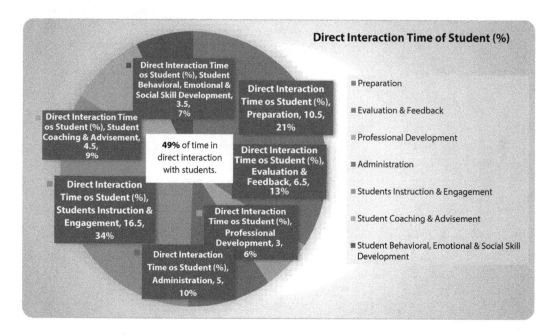

Figure 25.3 Activity composition of teachers' working hours.

25.3   Methodology

This study involves a review of existing literature on the use of conversational AI in Ed-Tech. This study is divided into three phases. The initial phase is the planning in which authors identify research gaps of the literature, formulation of research questions, finalization of databases for the search of literature, and determination of criteria for the inclusion and exclusion of research articles. The second phase is the research conduction phase in which different string combinations are used for the identification or selection of research articles for the analysis. The final phase of the process is the reporting phase in which results, analysis, and interpretations identified are presented.

25.3.1   Planning

25.3.1.1   Inclusion and Exclusion Criteria

Prior studies mentioned the methodology to be used for the inclusion and exclusion criteria. Below mentioned are the inclusion and exclusion criteria used for this study.
    The inclusion criteria:

1. Studies published in the English language.
2. Full-text journals or conference articles.
3. Studies on proposed frameworks and models related to this study.
4. Article and studies published before February 2023.

The exclusion criteria:

1. Eliminate duplicate studies.
2. Eliminate studies based on quality evaluation criteria.
3. Eliminate studies not addressing the research questions.
4. Eliminate studies in different languages.

25.3.1.2   Source of Information

This study requires a digital search of the existing literature in various available digital databases. Below mentioned are the databases used for the searching of literature.

1. IEEE digital
2. Science direct
3. Springer
4. PubMed
5. Taylor and Francis
6. Emeralds
7. Scopus

25.3.1.3   Search Procedure

In the search procedure, we used different keyword combinations. To conduct appropriate research, used keywords are "Conversational AI in education" OR "Chatbots in education" OR "Voice assistants in education" OR "Virtual agents in education" + "application" + "effectiveness" + "student engagement" + "future trends" + "privacy concerns." In this, manual and automatic search process is applied. In manual search, we use search different references of the articles. In automatic search, we use digital libraries (IEEE digital library, Science direct, Springer, PubMed, Taylor and Francis, Emeralds, and Scopus) to identify relevant studies for the article.

25.3.2   Conducting the Review

25.3.2.1   Search String

The search was based on the title, abstract, and keywords (title-abs-key). These defined words are combined in various ways for the accomplishment of the search. The search string is divided into three categories: conversational AI systems, AI, and education industry as shown in Table 25.1. Along with these search categories, we combined AND/OR operators to do search in a more meaningful manner. The review sought to collect all relevant articles, conference articles, book chapters, and case studies published in English from the tenure of 2018 to Feb 2023.

25.3.2.2   Data Extraction

Using inclusion, exclusion, and quality evaluation criteria, the quality research of the article was conducted. The data extraction process is shown in the Figure 25.1. This figure depicts the manual and automatic search process, selection process, and final dataset of selected articles. The extraction process begins with the formulation of the search string. The search string formulated was further used for the identification of relevant articles from various databases. The initial search yielded 1,806 articles, and 314 were downloaded. After the application of inclusion and exclusion criteria, articles were reduced to 30 indicated in the Table 25.1. These articles were then subjected to quality evaluation mentioned in the quality evaluation section. The Table 25.2 shows about database search, Table 25.3 highlights for quality evaluation criteria, Table 25.4 shows about selected article relevance with research question, Table 25.5 displays about quality evaluation result and Table 25.6 shows about platforms for conversational AI respectively.

Table 25.1 Search query.

S. no	Search category	Search query
1	Education Industry	"Education Industry" OR "Learning Industry" OR "Ed-Tech Industry" OR "Education Recommended System" OR" Teaching" OR "learning" OR "Student" OR "School" OR "Training" OR "Evaluation" OR "Intelligent Tutoring" OR "Mentoring" OR "Intelligent Feedback"
2	Conversational AI	"conversational AI" OR "spoken dialogue" OR "spoken dialog" OR "chat box" OR "conversational agent" OR "conversational system" OR "dialog system" OR "dialogue systems" OR "assistant technology" OR "relational agent" OR "chatbot" OR "digital agent" OR "digital assistant" OR "virtual assistant" OR "conversational user interface" OR "voice user interface" OR "Voice chat" OR "personal digital assistant" OR "virtual personal assistant" OR "PDA" OR "voice-based" OR "voice assistant" OR "Speech-based" OR "Interactive voice response" OR "personal assistant" OR "voice-driven" OR "voice interface"
3	Artificial Intelligence	"text to speech" OR "automatic Speech" OR "NLP" OR "Natural language understanding" OR "Voice recognition" OR "Speech recognition"
4	Combination	1 OR/AND 2 OR/AND 3

Table 25.2 Database search.

Database name	Related article	Full text download
IEEE digital	601	72
Science direct	450	60
Springer	200	48
Pubmed	15	10
Taylor and Francis	100	58
Emeralds	20	6
Scopus	420	60

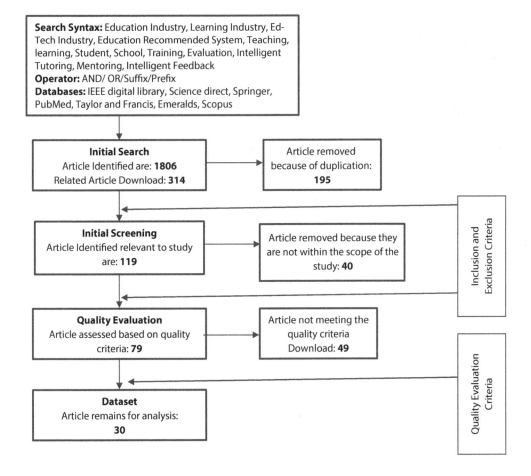

Table 25.3 Quality evaluation criteria.

Questions (QE)	Criteria
QE1	Are the aims and objectives clearly stated?
QE2	Are the proposed techniques well described?
QE3	Does the study meet the inclusion and exclusion criteria?
QE4	Whether the design followed well development principles and concepts.
QE5	Whether the study presents experimental or simulation-based performance evaluation or not.
QE6	Does the study efficiently compare the result set with the aim?
QE7	Is the paper published in a recognized source?
QE8	Does the database used for the study come from a recognized source?
QE9	Is the research process well documented?
QE10	Is the research reproducible?

Table 25.4 Selected article relevance with research question.

S. no	Article	Type	QE1	QE2	QE3	QE4	QE5	QE6	QE7
1	[1]	Journal	✓		✓	✓	✓	✓	
2	[2]	Journal	✓		✓	✓		✓	✓
3	[3]	Journal	✓	✓	✓	✓		✓	
4	[4]	Journal	✓	✓	✓	✓		✓	✓
5	[5]	Conference	✓	✓	✓	✓	✓	✓	✓
6	[6]	Conference		✓	✓	✓	✓		✓
7	[7]	Journal		✓	✓	✓	✓		✓
8	[8]	Journal		✓	✓	✓	✓		✓
9	[9]	Journal	✓	✓	✓		✓	✓	✓
10	[10]	Journal	✓	✓	✓	✓		✓	✓
11	[11]	Journal	✓	✓	✓	✓		✓	✓
12	[12]	Journal	✓	✓	✓	✓		✓	✓
13	[13]	Journal	✓	✓	✓	✓		✓	✓
14	[14]	Journal	✓	✓	✓	✓	✓	✓	

Table 25.5 Quality evaluation result.

Year	Type	Domains	Count of article
2022	Journal	Language Learning	[8]
2022	Conference	Language Learning	[9]
2019	Journal	Language Learning	[10]
2022	Journal	Language Learning	[12]
2022	Journal	Tutoring System	[11]
2021	Journal	K-12 Learning	[13]
2018	Journal	K-12 Learning	[14]
2018	Journal	K-12 Learning	[15]
2021	Journal	K-12 Learning	[16]
2020	Journal	Technical Education	[17]
2019	Journal	Technical Education	[18]
2016	Journal	Technical Education	[19]
2010	Journal	Technical Education	[21]
2021	Journal	Assessment System	[20]
2022	Journal	Online Learning	[21]
2022	Journal	Online Learning	[22]
2022	Journal	Professional Education	[23]

25.3.2.3   Quality Evaluation

According to authors Kitchenham and Charters [5], quality assessment was conducted using the checklist provided in the table as employed in similar studies. Publications that qualify 75% of the criteria mentioned in the checklist were considered for further evaluation in this study. The assessment was performed individually by the researchers using the QE criteria; the QE questions are measured with the scale of 1–4 (1: Not Good, 2: Average, 3: Good, and 4: Excellent). The evaluation was conducted by the two researchers. One researcher extracted the data, while the other double-checked it. Any conflict of opinion was discussed and resolved. Thirty publications were selected because they qualify the criteria >75%. Table 25.4 shows the quality assessment result.

25.3.3   Research Question Formulation

In this section, we formulate the research question that needs to be answered in the review reporting. These questions are formulated on the basis of discussion done by the experts in the field and analyzing the previous review papers to provide the detail review on this

Table 25.6 Details of platforms used for conversational AI.

Platform	K-12 education	Higher education	Technical education	Online education	Corporate training	Language learning	Special education
Chatbots	•	•	•	•	•	•	•
Mobile Applications	•	•	•	•	•	•	•
Virtual Assistants	•	•	•	•	•	•	•
Learning Management Systems (LMSs)	•	•	•	•		•	•
Web-Based Platforms	•	•	•	•	•	•	•
Social Media	•	•	•	•	•	•	•

technology. To conduct this review, we formulated six research questions (RQs). Below mentioned are the RQs to be answered in the review.

RQ1. What are the different streams in the Ed-tech Industry where conversational AI applications are used?

RQ2. What are the different platforms used in the Ed-tech Industry to operate conversational AI applications?

RQ3. What are the different roles played by conversational AI applications in the Ed-tech industry?

RQ4. What are the primary benefits of conversational AI applications in the Ed-tech Industry?

RQ5. What are the challenges faced in the implementation of conversational AI applications in the Ed-tech Industry that literature reviewed?

RQ6. What are the potential future areas of the Ed-tech industry that could be benefited via the applications of conversational AI applications?

25.3.4 Review Reporting

In this section, we provide the results obtained from the search process. This section presents the analysis of 30 publications retrieved documents that include conference papers and research articles that successfully qualify the evaluation criteria. The results of the search were presented in relation to the research questions.

25.3.4.1 RQ1. What are the Different Streams in the Ed-Tech Industry Where Conversational AI Applications are Used?

Conversational AI can be used in a variety of educational streams, including

K-12 Education: AI-powered virtual tutors, personalized learning, and interactive games can help students to learn in a more engaging and effective way.

Higher Education: AI-powered virtual assistants can help students with scheduling, course information, and answering questions.

Online Education: AI-powered virtual tutors, personalized learning, and virtual assistants can enhance the online learning experience [6].

Corporate Training: AI-powered virtual trainers can provide employees with personalized training and support in areas such as onboarding, product knowledge, and customer service.

Language Learning: AI-powered language tutors can provide real-time feedback and personalized instruction to help students improve their language skills.

Technical Education: AI-powered virtual tutors and trainers can help students to learn technical skills, such as coding and software development.

Special Education: AI-powered virtual tutors and assistants can help students with special needs, such as those with learning disabilities or visual impairments, to learn and achieve their full potential.

25.3.4.2 RQ2. What are the Different Platforms Used in the Ed-Tech Industry to Operate Conversational AI Applications?

The Ed-tech industry is leveraging conversational AI applications to provide personalized and effective learning experiences to students. The Figure 25.4 shows about adoption of AI-based systems in Education, Figure 25.5 displays for percentage of various platforms of CAI used in education domains, Figure 25.6 shows about role of conversational AI in education and Figure 25.7 highlights for benefits of conversational AI. Here are some of the platforms that are commonly used in the Ed-tech Industry to operate conversational AI applications:

1. **Chatbots:** Chatbots are computer programs that use NLP to simulate human-like conversations. Ed-tech companies use chatbots to engage with students, answer their queries, and provide personalized feedback.
2. **Virtual Assistants:** Virtual assistants are voice-enabled chatbots that use voice recognition technology to communicate with users. Ed-tech companies use virtual assistants to provide on-demand assistance to students, deliver personalized content, and track progress.
3. **Learning Management Systems (LMSs):** LMSs are a software application used to deliver educational courses and manage student records. Some LMSs have integrated conversational AI features, which can help students access course content, ask questions, and receive feedback.
4. **Mobile Apps:** Ed-tech companies use mobile apps to provide students with access to course content, interact with peers, and receive personalized feedback. Conversational AI can be integrated into mobile apps to provide a seamless user experience.
5. **Web-Based Platforms:** Web-based platforms are online platforms that provide students with access to educational content and interactive learning

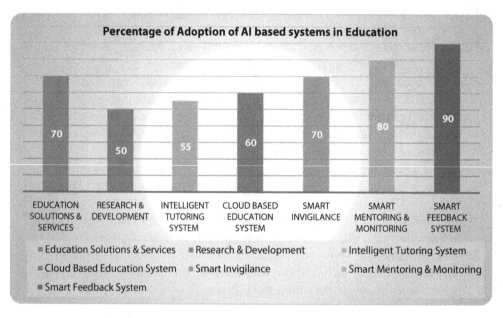

Figure 25.4 Adoption of AI-based systems in Education [2].

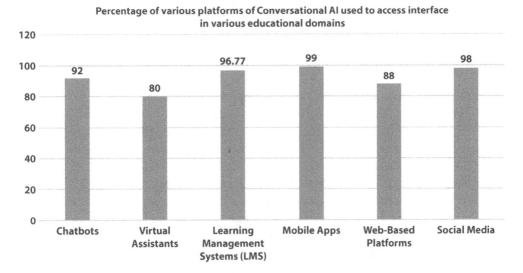

Figure 25.5 Percentage of various platforms of CAI used in education domains.

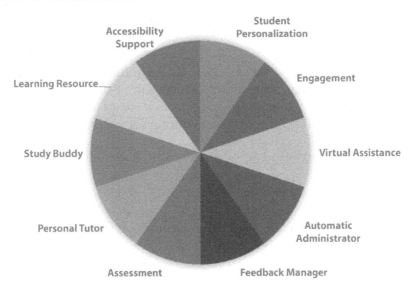

Figure 25.6 Role of conversational AI in education.

experiences. Conversational AI can be integrated into web-based platforms to provide students with personalized learning experiences.

6. **Social Media:** Social media platforms like Facebook, Instagram, and Twitter can be used to engage with students, deliver personalized content, and answer their queries. Conversational AI can be integrated into social media platforms to provide students with on-demand assistance.

Overall, the Ed-tech industry is continuously exploring new platforms and technologies to provide students with personalized and effective learning experiences using conversational AI applications.

25.3.4.3   RQ3. What are the Different Roles Played by Conversational AI Applications in the Ed-Tech Industry?

Conversational AI applications are playing an increasingly important role in the Ed-tech industry. Here are some of the different roles that these applications are playing:

1. **Student Personalization:** Conversational AI applications can use ML algorithms to analyze a student's learning patterns and provide personalized learning experiences. By understanding a student's strengths and weaknesses, these applications can adapt the curriculum to meet their needs and provide targeted feedback.

2. **Engagement:** Conversational AI applications can provide engaging learning experiences by using conversational interfaces. By engaging students in a conversational manner, these applications can keep students interested and motivated.

3. **Virtual Assistance:** Conversational AI applications can provide on-demand assistance to students, answering their questions and providing feedback in real time. This can help students stay on track and overcome challenges quickly.

4. **Automatic Administrator:** Conversational AI applications can automate administrative tasks, such as grading assignments, scheduling appointments, and sending reminders. This can save time for educators and allow them to focus on teaching.

5. **Feedback Manager:** Conversational AI applications can provide access to educational resources for students who may have difficulty accessing traditional learning environments. For example, students with disabilities can use conversational interfaces to access educational materials and interact with educators.

6. **Study Buddy:** Sometimes, students just need someone to study with. As a conversational agent, I can be that study buddy. I can help students stay on track with their studying, provide motivational support, and help them review material.

7. **Learning Resource:** Conversational agents can be an excellent resource for students to learn new information. As a conversational agent, I can provide students with explanations of complex concepts, offer practice problems and quizzes, and point them to additional resources to help them learn.

8. **Accessibility Support:** Conversational agents can provide support for students with disabilities or those who need additional accommodations. For example, a conversational agent can provide text-to-speech support, answer questions in sign language, or offer other forms of support that can help students with disabilities.

9. **Assessment:** Conversational AI applications can analyze a student's performance and provide detailed assessments of their skills and knowledge. This can help educators identify areas for improvement and provide targeted feedback.

10. **Personal Tutor:** As a conversational agent, I can act as a personal tutor for students. I can answer their questions, provide feedback, and offer personalized learning recommendations based on their performance and learning style.

Overall, conversational AI applications are playing a critical role in the Ed-tech industry by providing personalized, engaging, and accessible learning experiences for students. They are also helping educators to save time and improve the quality of their teaching.

25.3.4.4   RQ2. What are the Primary Benefits of the Conversational AI Applications in Ed-Tech Industry?

There are several benefits of conversational AI applications in the Ed-tech industry. Here are some of the primary benefits:

1. **Personalized Learning:** Conversational AI applications can provide personalized learning experiences by analyzing student data, identifying knowledge gaps, and adapting the curriculum to meet each student's needs. This can improve student engagement and lead to better learning outcomes.
2. **Real-time Feedback:** Conversational AI applications can provide real-time feedback to students, helping them to identify areas for improvement and address challenges quickly. This can help students to stay on track and achieve their learning goals more efficiently.
3. **24/7 Accessibility:** Conversational AI applications can be available 24/7, allowing students to access educational materials and receive assistance at

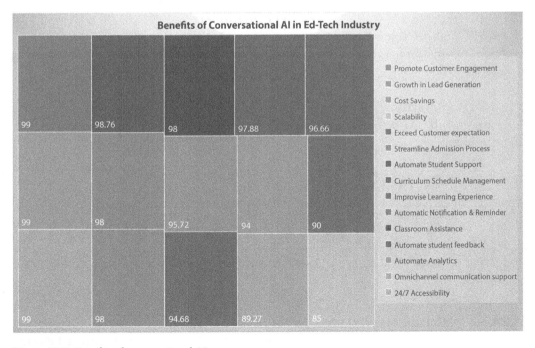

Figure 25.7 Benefits of conversational AI.

any time. This can be particularly useful for students who have busy schedules or are located in different time zones.

4. **Scalability:** Conversational AI applications can be easily scaled to accommodate large numbers of students, making it possible to provide personalized learning experiences to a large audience.

5. **Automation:** Conversational AI applications can automate administrative tasks, such as grading assignments and scheduling appointments. This can save time for educators and allow them to focus on teaching and interacting with students.

6. **Cost Savings:** Conversational AI applications can help to reduce the cost of education by automating administrative tasks, reducing the need for physical infrastructure, and improving the efficiency of the learning process.

25.3.4.5   *What are the Challenges Faced in the Implementation of Conversational AI Applications in the Ed-Tech Industry that Literature Reviewed?*

There are several challenges faced in implementing conversational AI in education, including.

25.3.4.5.1   Natural Language Understanding
The ability of the AI system to understand human language and interpret it accurately is a major challenge.

25.3.4.5.2   Personalization
The need for AI systems to be personalized to meet the individual needs and preferences of students.

25.3.4.5.3   Knowledge Representation
Representing educational content in a structured manner that can be easily understood and processed by AI systems.

25.3.4.5.4   Interactivity
Ensuring that the AI system is able to engage students in meaningful and interactive conversations.

25.3.4.5.5   Privacy and Security
Protecting student data and ensuring that the AI system complies with privacy regulations.

25.3.4.5.6   Integration with Existing Systems
Integrating conversational AI systems with existing education systems, such as LMSs, can be a challenge.

25.3.4.5.7   Ethical Considerations
Ensuring that the AI system operates in an ethical and transparent manner and that it does not perpetuate biases or discriminate against certain groups of students.

25.3.4.5.8 Regional Slangs & Jargon

The Regional Slangs and Jargon challenge in conversational AI in education is focused on creating AI systems that can understand and respond to regional slang and jargon that students may use in their conversations. In an educational setting, students may use colloquialisms, regional slang, or other jargon that can be difficult for the AI system to interpret accurately.

One of the key challenges in this area is that slang and jargon can be highly context-dependent, and the meaning may not be immediately clear to someone who is not familiar with the local culture or regional dialect. Additionally, slang and jargon can change rapidly over time, making it difficult for the AI system to keep up with the latest trends and expressions. To address the Regional Slangs and Jargon challenge, Conversational AI systems in education can use advanced NLP techniques and ML algorithms that are trained on a diverse range of regional language data. The system can also incorporate cultural and regional knowledge to better understand the context of the conversation and the meaning behind slang and jargon.

Additionally, the system can use multimodal inputs, such as video and audio, to better capture regional accents and dialects. The AI system can also incorporate personalized feedback and support that is tailored to the cultural and regional background of individual students. Overall, addressing the Regional Slangs and Jargon challenge is critical to create conversational AI systems that can provide effective communication and support for students across different regions and cultural backgrounds. As AI technology continues to evolve, we can expect to see even more innovative approaches to recognize and respond to regional slang and jargon in educational settings.

25.3.4.5.9 Training of AI Assistant

Training AI assistants for conversational AI is a challenging yet rewarding task. It requires an in-depth understanding of NLP and ML algorithms and techniques. To effectively train an AI assistant, developers must develop a library of conversational data that covers a wide range of topics and contexts, and use these data to train the AI system. Additionally, the AI assistant must be tested and evaluated regularly to ensure that it is functioning as expected and responding appropriately to user inputs. Finally, developers must also use reinforcement learning techniques to teach the AI assistant to respond more effectively to user inputs and make more accurate predictions.

25.3.4.5.10 Tracking & Optimization

Tracking & Optimization is a challenge in conversational AI in education where the AI system is required to track and optimize the learning process for individual students based on their interactions with the system. In an educational setting, conversational AI systems are used to provide personalized learning experiences for students, and to do that, it needs to track the progress of individual students, understand their strengths and weaknesses, and optimize the learning experience to meet their needs.

One of the key challenges in this area is that students may have different learning styles, interests, and abilities, which can make it difficult for a single conversational AI system to provide a personalized learning experience for all students. The AI system needs to be able to track the progress of individual students and optimize the learning experience to meet their unique needs.

Another challenge is that the data that the AI system collects from students may not always be accurate or complete. For example, students may provide incomplete or misleading answers to questions, or they may interact with the system in unexpected ways. This can make it difficult for the AI system to accurately track their progress and optimize the learning experience.

To address these challenges, conversational AI systems in education can use advanced ML algorithms and NLP techniques to analyze student data and provide personalized feedback and recommendations. The AI system can track the student's progress, identify knowledge gaps, and provide targeted learning materials and exercises to help the student improve.

Additionally, Conversational AI systems can incorporate adaptive learning techniques, where the system can adjust the learning experience based on the student's progress and feedback. The system can also use reinforcement learning to optimize the learning experience and make it more effective for individual students.

Overall, addressing the Tracking & Optimization challenge in conversational AI in education is critical to provide personalized and effective learning experiences for students. As AI technology continues to evolve, we can expect to see even more innovative approaches to track and optimize the learning process in education.

25.3.4.5.11   Simultaneous Conversation

Simultaneous conversation is a challenge in conversational AI where the AI system is required to process multiple streams of information at the same time in a conversation. In a natural conversation, people can speak and listen simultaneously, understand and interpret what is being said, and respond accordingly. However, for an AI system, it can be difficult to handle multiple streams of information at once and respond in real time.

For example, in a group conversation, different people may be speaking at the same time or interrupting each other, making it difficult for an AI system to keep track of the conversation and provide accurate responses. In addition, an AI system may need to process multiple types of information, such as text, audio, and visual cues, which can further complicate the simultaneous conversation challenge. One approach to addressing this challenge is to use advanced NLP techniques and ML algorithms to process and interpret multiple streams of information in real time. This can help the AI system to identify the most relevant information and respond appropriately, even in a complex conversational setting. Another approach is to use multiturn dialogues, where the AI system can track the context of the conversation and provide more accurate and personalized responses. Overall, addressing the simultaneous conversation challenge is critical for conversational AI systems to become more effective and provide more natural and seamless interactions with humans.

25.3.4.5.12   Conversation in Native Language

The Conversation in Native Language challenge in conversational AI in education is focused on creating AI systems that can understand and respond to students in their native language. In many educational settings, students may speak different languages or dialects, and the AI system needs to be able to communicate with them effectively in their preferred language. One of the key challenges in this area is that NLP technology and ML algorithms often require large amounts of training data to accurately understand and respond to language. This can make it difficult to create conversational AI systems that can handle a wide range of languages and dialects, especially for languages that are not as widely spoken or have limited available training data. Another challenge is that students may use informal or colloquial language, slang, or dialects that can be difficult for an AI system to interpret accurately. The system needs to be able to understand the context of the conversation and the student's intended meaning to provide accurate responses.

To address the Conversation in Native Language challenge, conversational AI systems in education can use advanced NLP techniques and ML algorithms that are trained on a diverse range of language data. The system can also incorporate language translation technology to facilitate communication between students who speak different languages.

Additionally, the system can use multimodal inputs, such as text, voice, and video, to improve the accuracy of language understanding and to provide more natural and effective interactions with students. The AI system can also leverage language models that are specifically designed for education to better understand the vocabulary and context of educational content. Overall, the Conversation in Native Language challenge is critical to create conversational AI systems that can effectively communicate with students in a wide range of languages and dialects and to provide more inclusive and accessible learning experiences for students around the world.

25.3.4.5.13   Students Emotion Understanding

The Students Emotion Understanding challenge in conversational AI in education is focused on creating AI systems that can understand and respond to the emotional states of students during interactions. In an educational setting, emotions can play a significant role in the learning process, and conversational AI systems need to be able to recognize and respond to the emotional states of students to provide effective feedback and support. One of the key challenges in this area is that emotions can be complex and difficult to interpret accurately, even for humans. Emotions can be expressed in many different ways, including tone of voice, body language, facial expressions, and the words that students use. Additionally, emotions can be influenced by many different factors, such as cultural background, personal experiences, and environmental factors.

25.3.4.6   *RQ3. What are the Potential Future Areas of the Ed-Tech Industry that Could be Benefited via the Applications of Conversational AI Applications?*

There are several potential areas within the Ed-tech industry that could benefit from the application of conversational AI. Here are a few examples:

Personalized Learning: Conversational AI can be used to create personalized learning experiences for students. By analyzing student performance data, conversational AI can identify areas of weakness and provide tailored learning materials to help students improve.

Student Support Services: Conversational AI can be used to provide student support services such as counseling and academic advising. By leveraging NLP and ML, conversational AI can engage in meaningful conversations with students, answer their questions, and provide them with the resources they need to succeed.

Language Learning: Conversational AI can be used to create immersive language learning experiences. By simulating real-world conversations, conversational AI can help students improve their language skills in a way that is engaging and interactive.

Assessment and Grading: Conversational AI can be used to grade assignments and provide feedback to students. By analyzing student responses and comparing them to model answers, conversational AI can provide immediate feedback to students, helping them identify areas of weakness and improve their performance.

Teacher Support: Conversational AI can be used to support teachers by automating routine tasks such as grading and lesson planning. This can free up teachers' time to focus on more meaningful tasks such as teaching and providing one-on-one support to students.

Overall, conversational AI has the potential to revolutionize the Ed-tech industry by creating more personalized and engaging learning experiences for students while also providing teachers and administrators with valuable insights into student performance and needs.

Because industry [25–28] deals with schooling and manages personal data [29, 30] for a substantial client base, many of whom may be under the age of 18, EdTech companies [31–33] must comprehend the cybersecurity [34–38] repercussions they face and design processes to minimise them. Institutions and organisations all across the world are using edtech to improve their services [39, 40]. But it's also crucial to understand that the swiftly developing EdTech industry [41] is vulnerable to certain security concerns that might be dangerous. Threat [42] Reports show a tendency to indicate that the education sector has been significantly impacted by cyberattacks [43]. The COVID-19 pandemic has heightened cyber dangers in this sector since remote learning has grown in popularity.

25.4   Conclusion, Limitation, and Future Work

Conversational AI has a vast scope in education, and it can be a game-changer for the industry. It can help create more engaging and personalized learning experiences for students while also providing valuable insights to teachers and administrators.

In conclusion, conversational AI has enormous potential in education and can revolutionize the way we teach and learn. By leveraging NLP, ML, and other AI technologies, Conversational AI can provide personalized and engaging learning experiences to students while also freeing up teachers and administrative staff to focus on more meaningful tasks. It can help create intelligent tutoring systems, virtual assistants, language learning programs, and more. Conversational AI can also help in grading and assessment, student support services, and administrative tasks. Furthermore, the adoption of conversational AI in education can lead to a more inclusive and accessible learning environment. Students who struggle with traditional classroom settings can benefit from personalized learning experiences provided by conversational AI. It can also help bridge the gap between students and teachers, providing instant feedback and guidance. As the field of conversational AI continues to evolve, we can expect to see more innovative applications of this technology in education. From K-12 to higher education, conversational AI has the potential to transform the way we learn and teach, making education more engaging, accessible, and effective.

While conversational AI has great potential in education, there are some limitations that need to be considered. One of the primary limitations of conversational AI in education is the lack of emotional intelligence. AI systems may struggle to understand the emotions and context of a conversation, which can hinder their ability to provide meaningful support to students. Another limitation is the issue of bias. AI systems are only as unbiased as the data they are trained on. If the data are biased, the AI system will be too. This can lead to unequal treatment of students, especially those from underrepresented backgrounds.

Additionally, conversational AI may not be effective in all educational contexts. For example, some students may prefer face-to-face interaction with their teachers or peers, and conversational AI may not be able to replicate that experience. Lastly, conversational AI systems require a significant amount of data to be trained effectively. This can be a challenge in smaller educational settings, where there may not be enough data to train the AI system. In summary, conversational AI has limitations that need to be considered when implementing it in education. While it has great potential, it is important to be aware of the potential biases, lack of emotional intelligence, and potential for ineffective learning experiences in some contexts. By being aware of these limitations, we can work to address them and create a more equitable and effective education system.

References

1. 101 Artificial intelligence statistics [updated for 2022], Techjury, 2022, November 26, https://techjury.net/blog/ai-statistics/.
2. Wadhwani, P. and Loomba, S., Artificial Intelligence (AI) in education market size by component (solution, service [professional service, managed service]), by deployment (on-premise, cloud), by technology (machine learning, deep earning, Natural Language Processing (NLP)), by application (learning platform & virtual facilitators, Intelligent Tutoring System (ITS), smart content, fraud & risk management), by end-use (higher education, K-12 education, corporate learning), COVID-19 impact analysis, regional outlook, growth potential, competitive market share & forecast, 2022 - 2030, Global Market Insights Inc., 2022, June 27, https://www.gminsights.com/industry-analysis/artificial-intelligence-ai-in-education-market.
3. 2023, Retrieved 6 January 2023, from https://yellow.ai/education-chatbot/.
4. Conversational AI, What is conversational AI?, Interactions, 2023, Retrieved 6 January 2023, from https://www.interactions.com/conversational-ai/.
5. Kitchenham, B. and Charters, S., Guidelines for performing systematic literature reviews in software engineering, 2007.
6. Chatterjee, J. and Dethlefs, N., This new conversational AI model can be your friend, philosopher, and guide ... and even your worst enemy. *Patterns*, 4, 1, 100676, 2023.
7. Zhang, D., Affective cognition of students' autonomous learning in College English teaching based on deep learning. *Front. Psychol.*, 12, 6601, 2022.
8. Zhai, C., Wibowo, S., Cowling, M., Work-in-progress—Embedding cross-cultural humorous and empathetic functions to facilitate language acquisition, in: *2022 8th International Conference of the Immersive Learning Research Network (iLRN)*, 2022, May, IEEE, pp. 1–4.
9. Xie, Y., Svikhnushina, E., Pu, P., A multi-turn emotionally engaging dialog model. *arXiv preprint arXiv:1908.07816.*, 2019.
10. Wu, C.H., Lin, H.C.K., Wang, T.H., Huang, T.H., Huang, Y.M., Affective mobile language tutoring system for supporting language learning. *Front. Psychol.*, 13, 833327, 2022.
11. Xie, Y., Liu, Y., Zhang, F., Zhou, P., Virtual reality-integrated immersion-based teaching to English language learning outcome. *Front. Psychol.*, 12, 767363, 2022.
12. Wang, Y., Grant, S., Grist, M., Enhancing the learning of multi-level undergraduate Chinese language with a 3D immersive experience-an exploratory study. *Comput. Assisted Lang. Learn.*, 34, 1-2, 114–132, 2021.
13. Weng, C., Otanga, S., Weng, A., Cox, J., Effects of interactivity in E-textbooks on 7th graders science learning and cognitive load. *Comput. Educ.*, 120, 172–184, 2018.

14. Wu, T.T. and Chen, A.C., Combining e-books with mind mapping in a reciprocal teaching strategy for a classical Chinese course. *Comput. Educ.*, *116*, 64–80, 2018.

15. Wang, Y., Grant, S., Grist, M., Enhancing the learning of multi-level undergraduate Chinese language with a 3D immersive experience-an exploratory study. *Comput. Assisted Lang. Learn.*, *34*, 1-2, 114–132, 2021.

16. Halabi, O., Immersive virtual reality to enforce teaching in engineering education. *Multimedia Tools Appl.*, *79*, 3-4, 2987–3004, 2020.

17. Seo, J.H., Bruner, M., Payne, A., Gober, N., McMullen, D., Chakravorty, D.K., Using virtual reality to enforce principles of cybersecurity. *J. Comput. Sci. Educ.*, *10*, 1, 2019.

18. Sochacka, N.W., Guyotte, K.W., Walther, J., Learning together: A collaborative autoethnographic exploration of STEAM (STEM+ the Arts) education. *J. Eng. Educ.*, *105*, 1, 15–42, 2016.

19. Cope, B., Kalantzis, M., Searsmith, D., Artificial intelligence for education: Knowledge and its assessment in AI-enabled learning ecologies. *Educ. Philos. Theory*, *53*, 12, 1229–1245, 2021.

20. Martínez, F., Herrero, L.C., De Pablo, S., Project-based learning and rubrics in the teaching of power supplies and photovoltaic electricity. *IEEE Trans. Educ.*, *54*, 1, 87–96, 2010.

21. Pogorskiy, E. and Beckmann, J.F., From procrastination to engagement? An experimental exploration of the effects of an adaptive virtual assistant on self-regulation in online learning. *Comput. Educ.: Artif. Intell.*, *4*, 100111, 2023.

22. Menictas, M., Rabbi, M., Klasnja, P., Murphy, S., Artificial intelligence decision-making in mobile health. *Biochemist*, *41*, 5, 20–24, 2019.

23. Blodgett, N.P., Howard, V.M., Phillips, B.C., Andolsek, K., Richard-Eaglin, A., Molloy, M.A., Developing virtual simulations to confront racism and bias in health professions education. *Clin. Simul. Nurs.*, *71*, 105–111, 2022.

24. Zhu, Y., Nie, J.Y., Zhou, K., Du, P., Dou, Z., Content selection network for document-grounded retrieval-based chatbots, in: *Advances in Information Retrieval: 43rd European Conference on IR Research, ECIR 2021, Virtual Event, March 28–April 1, 2021, Proceedings, Part I 43*, Springer International Publishing, pp. 755–769, 2021.

25. Mahor, V., Bijrothiya, S., Rawat, R., Kumar, A., Garg, B., Pachlasiya, K., IoT and artificial intelligence techniques for public safety and security, in: *Smart Urban Computing Applications*, p. 111, 2023.

26. Mahor, V., Pachlasiya, K., Garg, B., Chouhan, M., Telang, S., Rawat, R., Mobile operating system (Android) vulnerability analysis using machine learning, in: *Proceedings of International Conference on Network Security and Blockchain Technology: ICNSBT 2021*, pp. 159–169, Springer Nature Singapore, Singapore, 2022, June.

27. Rawat, R., Garg, B., Pachlasiya, K., Mahor, V., Telang, S., Chouhan, M., Mishra, R., SCNTA: Monitoring of network availability and activity for identification of anomalies using machine learning approaches. *Int. J. Inf. Technol. Web Eng. (IJITWE)*, *17*, 1, 1–19, 2022.

28. Rawat, R., Rimal, Y.N., William, P., Dahima, S., Gupta, S., Sankaran, K.S., Malware threat affecting financial organization analysis using machine learning approach. *Int. J. Inf. Technol. Web Eng. (IJITWE)*, *17*, 1, 1–20, 2022.

29. Rawat, R., Mahor, V., Chouhan, M., Pachlasiya, K., Telang, S., Garg, B., Systematic literature review (SLR) on social media and the digital transformation of drug trafficking on darkweb, in: *International Conference on Network Security and Blockchain Technology*, pp. 181–205, Springer, Singapore, 2022.

30. Rawat, R., Ayodele Oki, O., Sankaran, S., Florez, H., Ajagbe, S.A., Techniques for predicting dark web events focused on the delivery of illicit products and ordered crime. *Int. J. Electr. Comput. Eng. (IJECE)*, *13*, 5, 5354–5365, Oct. 2023, doi: 10.11591/ijece.v13i5.pp5354-5365.

31. Rawat, R., Garg, B., Mahor, V., Telang, S., Pachlasiya, K., Chouhan, M., Organ trafficking on the dark web—The data security and privacy concern in healthcare systems, in: *Internet of Healthcare Things: Machine Learning for Security and Privacy*, pp. 189–216, 2022.

32. Vyas, P., Vyas, G., Chauhan, A., Rawat, R., Telang, S., Gottumukkala, M., Anonymous trading on the dark online marketplace: An exploratory study, in: *Using Computational Intelligence for the Dark Web and Illicit Behavior Detection*, pp. 272–289, IGI Global, 2022.

33. Rawat, R., Oki, O.A., Sankaran, K.S., Olasupo, O., Ebong, G.N., Ajagbe, S.A., A new solution for cyber security in big data using machine learning approach, in: *Mobile Computing and Sustainable Informatics: Proceedings of ICMCSI 2023*, pp. 495–505, Springer Nature Singapore, Singapore, 2023.

34. Rawat, R., Chakrawarti, R.K., Raj, A., Mani, G., Chidambarathanu, K., Bhardwaj, R., Association rule learning for threat analysis using traffic analysis and packet filtering approach. *Int. J. Inf. Technol.*, 1–11, 2023.

35. Rawat, R., Logical concept mapping and social media analytics relating to cyber criminal activities for ontology creation. *Int. J. Inf. Technol.*, 15, 2, 893–903, 2023.

36. Rawat, R., Mahor, V., Álvarez, J.D., Ch, F., Cognitive systems for dark web cyber delinquent association malignant data crawling: A review, in: *Handbook of Research on War Policies, Strategies, and Cyber Wars*, pp. 45–63, 2023.

37. Rawat, R., Chakrawarti, R.K., Vyas, P., Gonzáles, J.L.A., Sikarwar, R., Bhardwaj, R., Intelligent fog computing surveillance system for crime and vulnerability identification and tracing. *Int. J. Inf. Secur. Priv. (IJISP)*, 17, 1, 1–25, 2023.

38. Rawat, R., Sowjanya, A.M., Patel, S.I., Jaiswal, V., Khan, I., Balaram, A. (Eds.), *Using Machine Intelligence: Autonomous Vehicles Volume 1*, John Wiley & Sons, 2022.

39. Rawat, R., Mahor, V., Díaz-Álvarez, J., Chávez, F., Rooted learning model at fog computing analysis for crime incident surveillance, in: *2022 International Conference on Smart Generation Computing, Communication and Networking (SMART GENCON)*, pp. 1–9, IEEE, 2022, December.

40. Rawat, R. and Shrivastav, S.K., SQL injection attack detection using SVM. *Int. J. Comput. Appl.*, 42, 13, 1–4, 2012.

41. Rawat, R., Bhardwaj, P., Kaur, U., Telang, S., Chouhan, M., Sankaran, K.S., *Smart vehicles for communication, volume 2*, John Wiley & Sons, 2023.

42. Mahor, V., Garg, B., Telang, S., Pachlasiya, K., Chouhan, M., Rawat, R., Cyber threat phylogeny assessment and vulnerabilities representation at thermal power station, in: *Proceedings of International Conference on Network Security and Blockchain Technology: ICNSBT 2021*, pp. 28–39, Springer Nature Singapore, Singapore, 2022, June.

43. Rawat, R., Gupta, S., Sivaranjani, S., Cu, O.K., Kuliha, M., Sankaran, K.S., Malevolent information crawling mechanism for forming structured illegal organisations in hidden networks. *Int. J. Cyber Warf. Terror. (IJCWT)*, 12, 1, 1–14, 2022.

Conversational AI: Introduction to Chatbot's Security Risks, Their Probable Solutions, and the Best Practices to Follow

Vivek Bhardwaj[1], Balwinder Kaur Dhaliwal[2], Sanjaya Kumar Sarangi[3], T.M. Thiyagu[4], Aruna Patidar[5] and Divyam Pithawa[6]*

[1]School of Computer Science and Engineering, Manipal University Jaipur, Jaipur India
[2]Department of Computer Science and Engineering, Lovely Professional University, Jalandhar, Punjab, India
[3]Coordinator and Adjunct Professor, Utkal University, Bhubaneswar, India
[4]Computer Science and Engineering, Karunya Institute of Technology and Sciences, Karunya Nagar, Coimbatore, Tamil Nadu, India
[5]Department of Information Technology, Shri Vaishnav Vidhyapeeth Vishwavidyalya, Indore, India
[6]Department of Computer Science Engineering, Shri Vaishnav Vidyapeeth Vishwavidyalaya, Indore, India

Abstract

Artificial intelligence (AI) of the conversational variety enables users to communicate with software programs in a manner similar to that of other people. AI that allows users to interact with chatbots or virtual agents is referred to as conversational AI. Using vast volumes of data, machine learning, and natural language processing, they recognize audio and text inputs and translate their contents into other languages to simulate human interactions.

Conversational AI Agents: Physical or virtual agents who can assist just about anyone from Mark Zuckerberg to a normal person like you and me in a variety of tasks ranging from a fully automated house like one of the Mark where Jarvis works based on the voice commands to telling today's weather to a normal person or even doing small talk. However, who doesn't love to have his/her house same as the Mark Zuckerberg's; where everything happens based on voice command? Just say something and consider it as done. But everything comes at a cost; in this case, convenience comes at a cost of privacy and various security risks (some are known, and some are still unknown). So, in this paper, we will discuss some of the security risks (threats and vulnerabilities) that a hacker or someone with malicious intentions could exploit to cause loss, damage, or destruction of an asset of the user or the organization along with probable solutions to the security vulnerabilities. We will also discuss the privacy laws made to protect the user's data and how the General Data Protection Regulation affects the chatbot and the process of data collected by various organizations. Lastly, we will discuss the best practices to follow to ensure chatbot's security.

Keywords: Chatbot, chatbot security, security risks, threats, vulnerabilities, artificial intelligence, natural language processing, conversational artificial intelligence

*Corresponding author: divyampithawa@gmail.com

Romil Rawat, Rajesh Kumar Chakrawarti, Sanjaya Kumar Sarangi, Piyush Vyas, Mary Sowjanya Alamanda, Kotagiri Srividya and Krishnan Sakthidasan Sankaran (eds.) Conversational Artificial Intelligence, (435–458) © 2024 Scrivener Publishing LLC

26.1   Introduction

Conversational artificial intelligence (AI) is a type of AI that lets people communicate with computers to ask questions, solve issues, or even simply strike up a conversation. Often, this technology takes the form of chatbots or virtual assistants. Every time it is used, the technology "learns" and improves. Via its interactions, it gathers data. As time passes, it uses that knowledge to advance itself and how it converses with clients and users.

Conversational AI combines machine learning (ML) and natural language processing (NLP). NLP activities engage in a continuous feedback loop with ML techniques to keep the AI systems updated. The fundamental building blocks of conversational AI enable it to absorb, comprehend, and provide replies intuitively.

Components of Conversational AI:

1. ML
2. NLP

We will discuss these components in detail in the coming section.

With the recent release of ChatGPT, a chatbot developed by the tech startup OpenAI that has won over investors, industry giants, and the general public with its human-like communication capabilities, conversational AI is currently notably in the spotlight.

In the meanwhile, during the past several years, the application of conversational AI has expanded significantly across numerous sectors. Moreover, industry research and consultancy firm Grand View Research predicts that by 2030, the worldwide conversational AI market would be valued at more than $41 billion [1].

As we've seen with cutting-edge new conversational AI systems like OpenAI's ChatGPT, Google's LaMDA, and others—some of which seem so convincingly human that they win prizes for it—that's less the case anymore. Today's chatbots are so advanced that they can handle anything from treating anxiety to defending a person in traffic court.

According to the size of the global chatbot industry (and the projected growth), chatbots have been around for a while and will continue to increase in importance. They haven't consistently lived up to customers' expectations or offered many great experiences in the past. However, improvements in conversational AI have changed how they may be employed in recent years. Due to the variety of uses chatbots have, they occasionally take on the role of collecting and safeguarding personal data.

As a result, they also attract a lot of hackers and unwanted cyberattacks. When the General Data Protection Regulation (GDPR) was implemented in Europe, it is more important than ever to ensure chatbot security. Statistics indicate that this technology will have a significant impact on our lives; thus, security testing has to be integrated into regular activities so that chatbots may be used with trust.

The fact that corporations may now have several concurrent one-on-one conversations utilizing conversational software explains why such worries tend to be more recent. Computers, which are now across the divide, have large, lengthy memory and a tendency to memorize everything. Consequently, the suspicion of data misuse becomes suddenly extremely tangible.

There are still a lot of unidentified dangers in the developing field of conversational AI technology that need to be found. Now, let's concentrate on a few security vulnerabilities that might be exploited by someone with bad intentions.

A few of the known vulnerabilities are

1. Cross-Site Scripting (XSS)
2. Structured Query Language (SQL) Injection
3. Denial of Service

The possible fixes for some of the known security flaws have also been discovered by several researchers and organizations.

A few of the solutions are

1. Defense against Cross-Site Scripting
2. Defense against SQL Injection
3. Defense against Denial of Service

We will discuss security risks, their probable solutions, and some of the emerging methods to ensure chatbot security.

We will also discuss the various privacy laws that are implemented by various governments to protect their citizen's data and privacy.

Various privacy laws include

1. GDPR
2. California Consumer Privacy Act (CCPA)
3. Children's Online Privacy Protection Act (COPPA)

and how the GDPR affects the chatbot and the process of data collected by various organizations and the best practices to follow in the coming sections.

Organization of Chapter

The rest of the chapter is outlined as follows. Section 26.2 is about related work. Section 26.3 shows the history and evolution of chatbots. Section 26.4 shows the components & concepts that make conversational AI possible. Section 26.5 shows the working of Conversational AI. Section 26.6 shows the reasons behind why companies are using chatbot. Section 26.7 shows about the plans for the future development of conversational AI. Section 26.8 shows about the security risks of conversational AI's chatbot. Section 26.9 shows about the probable solutions to the security vulnerability. Section 26.10 shows about the privacy laws for the security of conversational AI and chatbot. Section 26.11 shows about the chatbot and GDPR. Section 26.12 shows about the best practices to follow to ensure chatbot security, and finally, Section 26.13 concludes this chapter.

26.2   Related Work

The authors of this paper [2] review recently emerging neural techniques for conversational AI. Three categories were used to classify conversational systems: social bots, task-oriented dialogue agents, and question-answering agents. They reviewed the most recent neural techniques for each category, made a comparison with more conventional symbolic approaches, and then addressed the advancements they have achieved and issues they are now experiencing, using particular systems and models as case studies.

The study [8] examines the challenging landscape for the safety of end-to-end conversational AI and discusses recent and related work. It focuses on the safety problems in end-to-end conversational AI. Using the principles of value-sensitive design, they emphasized the conflicts between values, possible benefits, and potential drawbacks and provided a framework for deciding if and how to distribute these models.

The history, technology, and uses of natural dialog systems, or simply chatbots, are presented in this study [3]. Also, they created a generic architectural design that assembles essential information and highlights the vital considerations prior to system creation.

In order to create conversational agents responsibly, the authors of this research [4] highlighted certain growing ethical challenges and offered approaches for agent designers, developers, and owners to take.

This paper [5] discusses the most recent advancements in conversational AI architecture development, including ML, deep learning, natural language interface, and the development of highly accurate AI models. It also highlights the advantages these cutting-edge innovations have over their more established counterparts.

The overall design of contemporary chatbots and the primary platforms for their development, as well as a number of other chatbot-related topics, were given by the authors of this work [6].

The numerous facets of chatbots, such as security, privacy, data protection, and social factors, are the subject of this research [7]. Several methods are used to learn from a discussion that may include sensitive information. They talked about how chatbots handle such data and the conditions in which it may be used. A lot of chatbots work on social/messaging platforms, which each have its privacy policies. This essay tries to offer a thorough analysis of security issues in chatbot conversations. This article might start a debate by highlighting the issues with data storage and usage gathered through chatbot user communications and by suggesting some guidelines to safeguard users.

A study of the security and privacy flaws in the current conversation system was given by Winson Ye et al. [8]. They provide a definition of chatbot security as well as background information on the state of the art in the industry. Each element in a typical chatbot architecture—the client module, communication module, answer- generating module, and database module—is thoroughly described in this analysis' possible threats.

According to Josip Bozic et al. [9], chatbots use AI techniques to learn from previous communication interactions, to provide better and more personalized responses. As a result, because they are used as a component of web applications, they are susceptible to the same security attacks that are used against websites. Planning-based strategies can assist in intelligently identifying security leaks for typical attack scenarios. In this research, they provided a method for verifying the security of chatbots that are accessed through online apps by relying on AI planning.

Chatbots pose a new security risk and present significant security difficulties that must be resolved. The conditions for data utilization and how chatbots handle them are covered in this study [21]. Several chatbots use social/messaging platforms, which have their data usage policies. In order to give a thorough analysis of security issues in chatbot communication, this article will do so.

In this paper [22], the authors investigate how customers' reactions to highly customized chatbot advertising are impacted by regulatory attention and privacy concerns. According to research, customers who are more interested in promotions are more open to and favorably react to highly customized chatbot advertising. Consumers who are more concerned with the prevention, on the other hand, are more aware of the hazards involved and have negative attitudes regarding highly tailored chatbot advertising.

26.3   History and Evolution of Chatbots

Below is the history and evolution of the chatbot [10, 11] from the first ever ELIZA in 1966 to the currently very popular ChatGPT-3.

1966: At the Massachusetts Institute of Technology (MIT), Joseph Weizenbaum created ELIZA, the first chatbot. ELIZA was created to emulate the speech patterns of a therapist and was capable of having short talks with users. To imitate dialog, it employs pattern matching and substitution methods.

1972: American psychiatrist Kenneth Colby created PARRY. A natural language program called PARRY simulates the thoughts of a paranoid person. As a result, it consistently misinterprets other people's intentions. The first program to pass the Turing Test was Parry. A schizophrenic patient was portrayed by this program. It makes an effort to mimic the illness.

1988: Developer Rollo Carpenter designed the Jabberwacky chatbot. It attempted to entertain while simulating a real human discussion. The "contextual pattern matching" AI method is believed to be used by this chatbot.

1992: A chatbot named Dr. Sbaitso was developed by Creative Labs for MS-Dos. It is recognized as one of the earliest attempts to put AI into a chatbot and has completely voice-operated chat software. The computer program would address the user like they were speaking to a psychotherapist. The majority of its replies were along the lines of "Why do you feel that way?" rather than participating in sophisticated dialogues.

1995: A.L.I.C.E. (Artificial Linguistic Internet Computer Entity) construction was pioneered by Richard Wallace. Because it was the first program to run on a computer with the name Alice, it was once known as Alicebot. A.L.I.C.E. is a universal language-processing chatbot that carries on conversations via heuristic pattern matching.

2001: AOL IM and MSN Messenger both included the SmartChild chatbot, which had the ability to carry on lighthearted discussions and provide easy data access to various services. It served as Siri's forerunner in many aspects.

2010: Siri was formed by Apple for iOS. It has a natural language user interface and is both an intelligent personal assistant and a learning navigator. It set the stage for all subsequent AI bots and personal assistants (PAs). When transferred to them by the user, they were capable of responding to text, voice, pictures, and video. According to Apple, this will lead to a more successful consumer–digital assistant interaction.

2010: The Jeopardy game show features IBM's Watson, which is supported by 90 servers, and 21.6 TB of data defeats human champions.

2012: Google Now was launched at Google Inch. It sends queries to several web services to give information, provide suggestions, and complete tasks.

2014: Cortana made its debut during Microsoft's Build 2014 developer conference. Since then, both Windows 10 PCs and Windows Phone devices have smoothly incorporated it. This program has made use of relevant algorithms and voice recognition technologies to comprehend and execute speech instructions.

2014: Facebook introduces M to compete with Cortana and Siri. M is a virtual assistant that helps with tasks using ML.

2014: Amazon launched the intelligent personal assistant Alexa. It is now included in gadgets like the Amazon Echo, Echo Dot, Echo Show, and more.

2017: Google Assistant replaced Google Now.

2017: GPT-2, a sizable language model with the ability to produce text that resembles that of a human, is made available by OpenAI.

2022: Large-scale language model ChatGPT-3 was developed by OpenAI. In 2021, the OpenAI team established it. Its objective is to allow users to transform input into writing that seems human-like.

ChatGPT can be applied to a variety of tasks, such as conversation generation and language translation.

The model, which has been trained on a massive amount of data, may create text that is frequently hard to distinguish from language produced by a human.

26.4   Components & Concepts that Make Conversational AI Possible

Conversational AI combines ML and NLP. NLP performs a process in a continuous feedback loop with ML procedures to keep the AI systems updated. The essential components of conversational AI [12, 13] enable it to process, comprehend, and produce a response in a natural way.

Following are the few components that make conversational AI possible:

1. ML
2. NLP
3. Data

1. Machine Learning (ML)

A subfield of AI and computer science called ML focuses on using data and algorithms to simulate how people learn, gradually increasing the accuracy of the system.

ML, a branch of AI, makes use of a range of learning-driven techniques, features, and data sources. As the amount of input information increases, the AI platform machine gets better at spotting patterns and applying them to make predictions.

There are mainly three types of ML:

1. Supervised Machine Learning
2. Unsupervised Machine Learning
3. Reinforcement Learning

2. Natural Language Processing (NLP)

NLP is the approach currently utilized in conversational AI to analyze language with the use of machine learning. Before machine learning, language processing techniques went through stages of development in linguistics, computational linguistics, and statistical NLP. Future conversational AI systems will be better able to interpret natural language thanks to deep learning.

Input generation, input analysis, output generation, and reinforcement learning are the four stages that make up NLP. Unstructured data are transformed into a format that computers can understand, which is then examined to produce the proper answer. As they learn, underlying ML systems gradually increase the quality of their responses.

- **Input generation**: Users enter data via a website or an app, and the data can be speech- or text-based.
- **Input analysis**: Natural Language Understanding (NLU) will be utilized by the conversational AI solution app to interpret the content of the input and determine its intended purpose if it is text-based. However, if the input is voice-based, it will use Automatic Speech Recognition (ASR) and NLU to evaluate the data.
- **Dialogue management**: A answer is created at this point using Natural Language Generation (NLG), part of NLP.
- **Reinforcement learning**: Lastly, replies are improved in accuracy over time using ML algorithms.

3. Data

Contextual data about each user and training data from comparable discussions are essential for conversational AI to succeed. The AI may choose when and how to communicate based on demographics, user preferences, or conversation history.

While having a lot of data is necessary to train an ML model, having data that are accurate, exact, and relevant is just as crucial. The accuracy of any ML solution is directly influenced by the quality of the data. Inaccurately retrieved or collected data would render conversational AI ineffective.

Conversational AI can properly respond to any client requests or queries with good data quality, enhancing the user experience. Only high-quality data can the provide expected results.

26.5 Working of Conversational AI

Conversational AI responds instantly, but it goes through a number of steps to get the outcome. Let's now discuss the method by which conversational AI generates its output or how it works [14, 15].

The process is divided into four main steps:

1. Input Generation
2. Input Analysis
3. Output Generation
4. Reinforcement Learning

Let's discuss each step in detail:

1. Input Generation:

The first step is the input generation; it starts when the user provides some input query. The input could be through text or voice. An input can be an inquiry or statement.

2. Input Analysis:

As the user enters their query, the platform's machine learning layer employs NLU and NLP to deconstruct the text into more manageable chunks and, in the case of text input, extract meaning from the words.

The voice note is first subjected to ASR to separate the sound into a language the computer can comprehend if the user is utilizing voice input.

When a computer receives a text, AI in the decision engine analyzes the text to determine the query's purpose.

Conversational AI becomes the primary differentiation for businesses at this point. The AI's capacity to respond to questions including a variety of intents and utterances will rely on how effectively it is trained (which also depends on the quality of the dataset).

3. Output Generation

The AI will match the user's query with an appropriate response now that it has comprehended the question. It will answer the user via NLG.

The AI interacts with integrated systems to review the user's profile and prior interactions before producing the result. This provides a level of personalization to the response and aids in narrowing it down depending on client information.

When voice input is used, the AI's response is retranslated from text to speech. In real time, the user hears the Voice AI's speech answer.

4. Reinforcement Learning

At this point, a chatbot's conversational AI self-learning feature comes in. The AI is trained to improve its response in the subsequent contact based on how well received the answer was by the user.

By examining more user inputs and the most frequently requested questions, the AI learns. Over time, it learns how to improve its responses, leading to more accurate answers.

Businesses get a wealth of data from each encounter full of variances in intent and language that are used to train the AI further. The user's engagement with the machine improves over time as they start to get quicker and more accurate answers.

26.6   Reasons Behind why Companies are Using Chatbot

Chatbots can be used in a whole host of different ways.

The three primary functions of chatbots are [25]

1. Increase sales
2. Connect with customers
3. Better understanding of the customers

1. Increase sales:

Corporate leaders report that chatbots have, on average, improved sales by 67%, according to recent surveys [28], research, projections, and other quantitative assessments of the growth of AI.

The highest benefit was seen in the support and sales departments, with business executives saving an average of $300,000. The sales function is the most frequent use case for chatbots (41%), closely followed by support (37%) and marketing (17%). An average of 67% more sales were generated by chatbots, with 26% of all purchases beginning with a chatbot encounter; 35% of corporate executives claimed that chatbots aided in closing sales. Chatbots' most common automated jobs include directing website users, gathering data, and qualifying leads; Chatbots average a 4× increase in response times and 24% improvement in customer service satisfaction rankings.

2. Connect with customers:
The data are analyzed by an AI chatbot to provide consumers with a tailored experience. These chatbots do far more than merely respond to preprogrammed queries that every consumer would encounter in an identical manner.

Due to their adaptable design, these chatbots are quite simple to connect with various platforms, which raises consumer engagement. The consumer is content and delighted after such a quick and easy experience.

3. Better understanding of the customers:
Contrary to common assumptions, chatbots may deliver value-driven, contextual support that can help organizations tremendously. Contrary to popular belief, a chatbot's main advantage is only answering questions and providing customer care.

The data are used by an AI chatbot to provide consumers with a tailored experience. These chatbots do significantly more complex tasks than just responding to preprogrammed queries that each customer would encounter in the same way.

Businesses may examine how effectively the chatbot works in terms of successful business results, sales produced, and in-depth information on how customers interact with the company and what they are requesting with the use of chatbot analytics.

In addition, chatbots are adaptable and enable businesses to serve their customers across almost all platforms. Adopting a chatbot for use on different platforms and integrating them into current IT infrastructure can be very straightforward processes.

It highly depends on gathering and processing enormous volumes of data from user interactions.

Also, chatbots' simple-to-use instant messaging form makes it simple for customers and enterprises to share data quickly. Moreover, chatbots may readily include online analytics, which they most likely do, meaning that organizations may obtain a wealth of real-time data about consumers and leads via a chatbot.

A Typical Chat Session (what happens behind the scene of a chat session)
Before a chat session—A few chatbots can recognize user information including location, IP address, and company. In addition, data that are frequently recorded includes names, addresses, phone numbers, and email addresses. This varies from chatbot to chatbot, though.

During a chat session—Some residual consumer data can be retrieved after a user has engaged in an active conversation with a chatbot. Additionally, different kinds of data may be provided to the chat to address a request for the benefit of e-commerce or customer support operations.

After a chat session—In their application or website, the chatbot service will often have a section where users may access this information. Most often, these data can be integrated with Customer Relationship Management (CRM) or similar technologies. Very likely, sales reports and future plans would incorporate this data. This might imply that the user and lead-related data from the original website can be retrieved.

In essence, a chatbot has the ability to gather a wide range of customer data. Because of this, companies that use chatbots and companies that supply chatbots need to be familiar with the GDPR.

The natural or legal person, public authority, agency, etc., that chooses the goals and methods of the data is subject to duty, has less freedom to do as they like with these data, and must comply with the GDPR as of May 2018.

26.7   Plans for the Future Development of Conversational AI

Here are a few of the things that conversational AI may have in the future [16]:

1. Emotional Intelligence
2. AI Coaches for Different Industries
3. Better Positioning of Closed-Loop Systems
4. Discrimination-free Working of AI/ML
5. Contextual Awareness of AI Systems
6. Omnichannel Ecosystem Development
7. Multilingual AI Solution
8. Complex Conversation Handling

1. Emotional Intelligence
Several AI applications concentrate on managing tedious activities and assisting people in dealing with job pressure. The widespread growth of emotional intelligence to carry out creative, higher-order tasks, on the other hand, is anticipated to be the emphasis of the next evolutionary stage. Only 20% of respondents, according to a Verizon poll report, thought that emotional intelligence in AI was a crucial talent before the pandemic. The figure has increased to 69% in the post-pandemic period, showing the need for more conversational AI technology to be developed. As this aspect of AI is established, it will improve office environments and help strengthen the relationship between companies and their clients.

2. AI Coaches for Different Industries
Humans take pride in their work; however, the majority of the time, we require help. We make mistakes, forget things, and perform tasks improperly. It is anticipated that AI will be able to minimize or resolve many of these human problems.

Conversational AI platforms will be used by 70% of white-collar professionals every day, as projected by Gartner. Moreover, client interest in using chatbots and similar technology has increased by 160%. It simply serves to demonstrate how AI, based on previous data, can provide greater, error-free human connection. The workforce will be able to make better decisions and eliminate mistakes in routine jobs thanks to AI coaches or advisors.

3. Better Positioning of Closed-loop Systems

The consumer experience may be enhanced by AI bots by delivering a personalized touch in real time. The bots will offer immediate responses and quicker question resolution whenever a consumer wishes to know the status of his or her most recent inquiry. But what if the AI is not capable of providing the intended outcome?

This is the situation where closed-loop solutions are most necessary. These systems are anticipated to evolve into the new norm as AI technology advances. In order to grow wiser and more successful in obtaining a certain outcome, they can monitor, study, and learn from the interactions and usage patterns.

4. Discrimination-free Working of AI/ML

Today's society is increasingly reliant on AI and ML technology, particularly in high-stakes decision-making processes including loan judgments, job screenings, and sentencing in the criminal justice system. Avoiding the unfairness that AI and ML systems could introduce, which can result in biased judgments, is a major concern.

Numerous businesses are concerned about the bias and discrimination that AI and ML have brought about as a result of their development. For instance, it has been documented numerous instances where different image processing models wrongly categorized individuals depending on their skin tone. It is therefore anticipated that companies will continue to improve their software to reduce bias in their AI solutions.

5. Contextual Awareness of AI Systems

The capacity for AI systems and IT components to respond to requests based on their understanding of the context is known as contextual awareness. By comparing requests or issues to vast databases of layered neural knowledge, it aims to make AI more persuasive in the field of customer experience.

When using AI-powered solutions to service clients, contextual awareness is a key advantage. Advanced ML models make it possible for solutions to be aware of consumer attitudes, intent, and emotions.

6. Omnichannel Ecosystem Development

Nobody wants to repeat a question they asked a brand on one channel while speaking to a support agent on another. There will no longer be a single platform for moving the dialogues ahead with AI-backed assistants. To establish an omnichannel strategy for brands, it should instead be integrated across platforms.

In this approach, sales and support staff may build individualized experiences for each client by having a bird's-eye view of all available channels. To enhance customer dialogues, this may be paired with sentiment analysis and emotional intelligence.

7. Multilingual AI Solution

A multilingual chatbot or speech bot will be a huge tool for organizations looking to attract clients from linguistically varied regions or various countries. This will be especially helpful if the organization wants to expand its business in countries with sizable populations of non-English speakers. It is reasonable to expect that the targeted firms will find it simpler to employ AI products given that English is a widely recognized language. Yet, the bots must be set up to grasp regional languages to accomplish worldwide expansion and acceptance of conversational AI.

Chatbots that speak many languages will assist provide better service and answer client questions more quickly. Moreover, they can aid companies in identifying and converting new clients in regional marketplaces.

8. Complex Conversation Handling

The majority of conversational AI-based bots cannot answer complicated requests since they are built to address brief, basic questions. The customer experience is ineffective and sometimes annoying as a result of its failure to recognize various intentions in a single user command.

Future iterations of conversational AI are anticipated to manage a variety of client discussions more skillfully and accomplish several duties.

26.8   Security Risks of Conversational AI's Chatbot

Chatbot security risks [17] can be mainly divided into two broad categories:

1. Threats
2. Vulnerabilities

1. Threats

Threats are frequently described as potential ways to compromise a system. Events like spoofing, tampering, repudiation, information disclosure, denial of service, elevation of privileges, and many more might be considered threats.

Hackers may threaten to reveal information or trade confidential data on the dark web after an attack.

- **Spoofing**: Spoofing is a general word for the style of conduct in which a hacker poses as a reliable device or entity in order to manipulate you into acting in a way that is both harmful to you and advantageous to the hacker. When a person or machine falsely takes the name of another to gain an unwarranted edge, this is known as a spoofing attack.

  Spoofing often has two components: the actual spoof, such as a fake message or website, and the social engineering component, which persuades victims to act.
- **Tampering**: The purposeful manipulation of data through the use of authorized means. A hacker or other malicious user entering a website and changing, deleting, or gaining access to unauthorized files is known as "data tampering" in online applications. Via the use of a script attack, a hacker or malicious user might potentially interfere inadvertently by disguising their actions as user input from a website or a web link.
- **Denial of Service**: A malicious attempt to overburden and disable an online service is known as a denial-of-service (DoS) attack. In a DoS attack, a

malicious cyber threat actor tries to prevent legitimate users from accessing online accounts, websites, information systems, or other services that depend on the compromised computer or network by overloading them with traffic until they become unresponsive or crash outright.

- **Elevation of Privileges**: Exploiting a bug, a design fault, or a configuration overlook in an operating system or software program to obtain privileged access to resources that are usually forbidden from an application or users is known as privilege escalation.

2. Vulnerabilities

Vulnerabilities [18] are described as methods by which a system may be hacked that is not sufficiently mitigated. When a system is not effectively maintained, has a bad code, lacks security, or is the result of human mistakes, it becomes susceptible and subject to attack. Unencrypted communications, back-door access by hackers, lack of correct protocol, lack of security measures for workers, hosting platform difficulties, XSS, SQL Injection, and other vulnerabilities exist.

- **Unencrypted communications**: If the connection is unencrypted, an attacker in a position to access a valid user's network traffic might record and monitor their activities with the application and collect any information the user offers.
- **Back-door access by hackers**: Any methods through which high-level user access can be obtained by both authorized and unauthorized users while bypassing security measures to steal personal and financial data, install further malware, or hijack equipment.
- **Cross-Site Scripting (XSS)**: By inputting text that contains a malicious Javascript code, the XSS attack is carried out when the web browser executes the injected code. The attacker must deceive the victim into sending malicious input content in order to exploit an XSS vulnerability.
- **SQL Injection**: By using SQL Injection, the attacker deceives the chatbot's back end into thinking that the malicious content is a part of the information. When the attacker gets direct access to the chatbot, they can immediately exploit an SQL injection and do any sort of SQL (or no-SQL) query.

Chatbots are subject to two types of hacker attacks: technical and social engineering.

1. Technical attack: Attackers here can transform themselves into malicious bots that communicate with other bots. The goal is to find potential weaknesses in the target's profile that might be used later. It may ultimately result in data theft and the compromising of the entire system that safeguards the data.

2. Social Engineering attack: By leveraging the backup data of the potential targets of a social engineering attack, a malicious bot can mimic a legitimate user. Such information is gathered from a variety of places, including social networking sites and the dark web. Using a bot that offers these services, they may occasionally utilize both sources to obtain the data of another user.

26.9   Probable Solutions to the Security Vulnerabilities

Before making the chatbot available to the public, it is crucial to repair any security flaws because if a hacker takes advantage of them before they are fixed, it would cost the firm and its partners a huge loss. It not only damages the brand's reputation and market worth, but it also raises the possibility that client information and other crucial data may end up on the black web. So, it is important to rectify the flaws before making the chatbot available to the broader public. Also, it's critical to adhere to the best practices for chatbot security, which we'll cover in the section after this one.

Implementing Security Development Life Cycle (SDLC) activities into the development life cycle is the most efficient strategy to reduce vulnerabilities.

One of the most crucial areas in which a business should spend is security awareness, although security measures sometimes go ignored until an incident takes place.

A successful cyber-attack in 2017 had an average total cost of almost $5 million or $301 per employee.

Better to be safe than sorry!

Several of the well-known security flaws can be addressed via chatbots. A system's vulnerability is reduced by encryption and other security measures using relatively safe protocols.

A few security methods to protect against security vulnerabilities are

- **Defense against Cross-Site Scripting (XSS)**: By verifying and sanitizing user input, XSS vulnerabilities are simple to fight against.
- **Defense against SQL Injection**: The majority of the time, developers rely on their tokenizers and entity extractors to prevent injection attempts. Moreover, this vulnerability will often be closed by straightforward regular expression checks of user input.
- **Defense against DOS Attack**:
  o   Minimize the attack surface
  o   Find—and fix—known vulnerabilities that can facilitate DoS attacks
  o   Use a firewall

26.10   Privacy Laws for the Security of Conversational AI and Chatbot

Conversational AI systems must comply with various data protection regulations, such as

1. General Data Protection Regulation (GDPR)
2. CCPA
3. COPPA [24]:

1. General Data Protection Regulation (GDPR) [23]:
A regulation under EU law on data protection and privacy in the EU and the European Economic Area (EEA) is known as the General Data Protection Regulation (2016/679, or "GDPR"). Also, it talks about the transfer of personal data outside of the EEA and the EU. The main goals of the GDPR are to make it easier for multinational businesses to operate

legally and to provide individuals with more control and rights over their personal data. The regulation contains provisions and requirements relating to the processing of data of individuals who are located in the EEA and replaces the Data Protection Directive 95/46/ EC. It applies to any enterprise—regardless of its location and the citizenship or residence of the data subjects—that is processing the personal information of individuals inside the EEA.

2. California Consumer Privacy Act (CCPA)
The CCPA is a state law designed to strengthen consumers' rights to privacy and protection. On June 28, 2018, the California State Legislature approved it and Governor Jerry Brown signed it into law. This amended Part 4 of Division 3 of the California Civil Code. 1 The CCPA creates the California Privacy Protection Agency and allows customers more authority over the personal information that organizations gather about them. It also enables any Californian consumer to request access to all personal data that have been gathered on them.

3. Children's Online Privacy Protection Act (COPPA) [24]:
COPPA is a federal law of the United States that went into effect on April 21, 2000. It governs the online collection of personal data about children under the age of 13 by persons or entities subject to U.S. jurisdiction, including children outside the United States, if the website or service is based there. It explains what information a website operator must provide in a privacy policy, when and how to get verifiable authorization from a parent or guardian, and what duties an operator has to safeguard children's privacy and safety online, including limitations on marketing to those under the age of 13.

26.11   Chatbot and GDPR

As of May 25th, 2018, the GDPR became effective and was fully functioning. The new regulations strengthened the existing regulatory framework while bringing about a number of adjustments and improvements. Any website or mobile application that collects data from EU citizens is subject to the GDPR, which includes chatbots and voice assistants.

All businesses using customer data are required by the GDPR to have a clearly defined privacy policy that includes the following important details:

> What information is collected?
> Who is collecting it?
> Why is it being collected?
> How long will it be used for?
> Who will it be shared with?
> How can consumers withdraw from the agreement to give their data?

The following are the key regulations that chatbots should follow in order to comply with the GDPR [26]:

Principles:

- **Transparency:**
  Transparency demands that data controllers be transparent, truthful, and explicit about how they handle personal data.

  A fundamental tenet of the GDPR is transparency, which has an impact on many crucial areas. It mostly influences how companies deal with customers and grants them access to information. The details you provide the topic with must
  1. be intelligible and easily accessible,
  2. use clear language,
  3. be provided free of charge,
  4. in written form or by other means,
  5. contain all relevant information, and
  6. be provided by an appropriate measure and at an appropriate time.

- **Data minimization:**
  Data minimization requires data controllers to make sure that the processing of personal data is appropriate, pertinent, and restricted to what is required in connection to the processing purpose.

  Data minimization in the GDPR refers to taking reasonable measures to ensure that personal data are accurate, relevant, and limited to what is necessary concerning the purposes for which they are processed. This includes deleting most personal data and keeping only the minimum data needed to form a basic record of a person. Compliance with the GDPR's data minimization principle can benefit businesses by offering simple implementation solutions.

- **Purpose limitation:**
  Purpose limitation demands that personal data be acquired for clear, unambiguous, and legal objectives and not be handled further.

  The organization must be upfront about why it is gathering personal data and what it plans to do with it; adhere to documentation requirements to clearly state those purposes; adhere to transparency requirements to disclose those purposes to individuals; and ensure that any use or disclosure for a purpose other than the one that was initially specified is fair, legal, and transparent.

- **Storage limitation:**
  The GDPR's storage restriction principle states that personal data must only be retained in a form that makes it possible to identify data subjects for as long as is required to fulfill the purposes for which it is being processed.

Lawful basis for processing:

- **Consent:**
  It requires that all personal data be processed with the data subject's express consent, which can be revoked at any time.

- **Legitimate interest:**
  When data controllers have a genuine need and can demonstrate that the processing is required to fulfill it, they are one the situations in which they are exempt from needing consent.
- **Special category data:**
  A greater level of protection from controllers is necessary for some types of personal data (racial or ethnic origin, health data, political opinions, etc.).

Individual rights:

- **Right to be informed:**
  It enables people to see how their information is being used and allows individuals to know what is being done with their data.
- **Right of access:**
  Enables data subjects to request a copy of their data as well as information about the categories of data being processed, the reasons for which those data are being used, and the types of third parties who will receive the data.
- **Right to rectification:**
  Demands that data controllers correct or remove erroneous or outdated data.
- **Right to erasure:**
  The right to be forgone, often known as the obligation to delete, requires controllers to erase data in specific circumstances where there is no longer a justification for processing or when the data subject withdraws permission.

A chatbot cannot function without personalization, and personalization cannot occur without data. Hence, the bot performs better the more data it gathers, but businesses must also be mindful of the GDRP. So, the following set of questions [27] is for companies to use in determining if they are in compliance with the GDRP:

1. Am I a data controller or a data processor?
2. What kind of personal data do I collect?
3. Is the consent valid, and does it correspond to the purpose of the processing?
4. Have I provided appropriate information about the data processing and individual rights?
5. Have I implemented an adequate risk management system?
6. Are the third parties I work with GDPR compliant?
7. Am I able to demonstrate compliance with GDPR requirements?

26.12 Best Practices to Follow to Ensure Chatbot Security

Some of the best practices for ensuring the security of chatbots are listed below [19]:

1. End-to-End Encryption (E2EE)
2. User Identity Authentication and Authorization

3. Self-Destructive Messages
4. Secure Protocols
5. Education

Other emerging methods include

1. User Behavioral Analytics
2. Developments in AI

1. End-to-End Encryption

E2EE is crucial since it guarantees that the entire conversation will be encrypted. It is possible to tamper with and spoof data while they are in transit. Several protocols are available to offer encryption while addressing such problems.

Moreover, chatbots may link to platforms such as Facebook Messenger, Telegram, and Slack. The best E2E mitigation tactic is to only let chatbots connect to channels that support data encryption. Businesses are required by Article 32(a) of the GDPR to take efforts to pseudonymize and encrypt personal data. The good news is that due to regulations like the GDPR, more companies are taking data encryption seriously and offering chatbots more secure connection alternatives.

2. User Identity Authentication and Authorization

When a user is confirmed using legitimate and secure login information, such as a username and password, this is known as user authentication. The user's session is conducted using the secure authentication token received in return for the user's credentials.

It includes:

- Biometric authentication
- Two-factor authentication
- User ID
- Authentication timeouts

3. Self-Destructive Messages

When a certain amount of time has passed since the message was delivered, sensitive personally identifiable information will be removed. This form of security protection is necessary when communicating with financial institutions as well as their respective chatbots.

According to the GDPR Article 5(e), personal data should only be maintained as long as is required to meet the processing goals.

Having an "intent level" of privacy is another GDPR compliance need. The user can share personal data, but even from the back end, it won't be visible; just the user's intentions are recorded and maintained for auditing reasons.

4. Secure Protocols

The security and authenticity of information are guaranteed by the web protocol HTTPS. This protocol uses a Secure Sockets Layer- or Transport Layer Security-encrypted connection to send data over the Hypertext Transfer Protocol.

5. Education

One security flaw that is surprisingly hard to address is human mistakes. User behavior must be taken into consideration, particularly with commercial apps. Otherwise, the system has serious problems.

Although more users are beginning to understand the value of digital security, people continue to be the system's weakest link. The security of chatbots will remain a challenge as long as user mistake is a concern. This would require extensive education on the secure usage of digital technology like chatbots.

Nevertheless, problems don't simply come from customers. Employees are just as likely to make a mistake. Developers and IT professionals should teach the operators how to operate the system safely as part of the chatbot development plan to counter this risk.

Other Emerging Methods to Ensure Chatbot Security

In the near future, several cutting-edge breakthroughs in AI and behavior analytics are eager to play a significant role in safeguarding chatbots from threats and vulnerabilities [20].

These technologies include

1. User Behavioral Analytics

A cyber security technique called User Behavior Analytics (UBA) is used to spot targeted attacks, insider threats, and financial fraud. In order to find abnormalities that can point to possible hazards, it examines human behavior patterns and does observational analysis. UBA involves gathering information about the daily network events that users produce in order to identify harmful activity such as lateral movement and the usage of compromised credentials.

2. Developments in AI

Artificial technology is a double-edged sword that simultaneously has both advantages and dangers. Yet, if AI lives up to its potential, the systems will have an additional layer of security. The key reason for this is that it can detect security breaches and threats by wiping a lot of data for anomalies.

AI chatbots [29–33] like ChatGPT [34, 35] are praised for their capacity to completely change how people get information online. However, there are increasing worries over its possible application in cyberattacks [36, 37]. Experts have shown that AI chatbots can be programmed to produce malware, write attack [38–40] code, and create believable phishing lures [41, 42]. Despite having protections against producing cyberattack [43] tools, ChatGPT can nevertheless produce material that may be used as a phisher's bait. This is especially troubling given that social engineering was used in over 82% of cyber security [44, 45] incidents in the previous year. Chatbots powered by artificial intelligence (AI) have taken the globe by storm, and 2023 is going to be a big year for this technology. The launch of OpenAI's ChatGPT in the fourth quarter of 2022 has inspired a number of businesses, groups, and people to enter the market [46]. Even tech has weighed in on the debate about AI chatbots, underscoring the potential advantages and disadvantages of this technology [47]. Google has also unveiled Bard, its own AI chatbot.

26.13   Conclusion

Instead of just being useful assistants, users typically view chatbots as friendly companions. The majority of user requests (40%) are emotional rather than educational. Chatbots may now respond emotionally to customers because of the development of machine learning and sentiment analysis.

This alone creates a big risk for the chatbot company if the users' data and privacy are breached. So, it is extremely important for organizations to know the vulnerabilities in their chatbot and fix them before releasing it to the public.

So, in this paper, we have looked through the various security risks that a conversational AI chatbot may be having along with some of the probable solutions to those security risks. We have also discussed the best practices to follow to ensure chatbot security and the emerging methods like UBA and developments in AI.

Future research into testing various solutions for chatbot security should focus on establishing a clearer picture of how these methods protect the security risks and which method is best suited for each case; also, different communication protocols can be tested to find out those that are best suited for the organization. Further penetration testing can also be done to gain the perspective of a hacker to find new ways to hack a chatbot and mitigate those risks.

Acknowledgment

We are grateful to various folks for their advice and help during the period of finishing our research work. First and foremost, we would like to express our gratitude to Dr. Anand Rajavat, Head of the Department of Computer Science & Engineering at S.V.I.I.T., Indore, and Er. Romil Rawat, the research mentor, for their invaluable assistance and guidance. They also assisted us in discovering new technologies by sharing their technical knowledge. With his supervision, direction, and constructive criticism, he inspired us.

We also want to thank our director, Dr. Anand Rajavat, from the bottom of our hearts for all of his help.

We extend our heartfelt gratitude to the teaching and non-teaching personnel in the Computer Science & Engineering department at SVVV Indore for their kind cooperation and provision of the necessary information.

We appreciate the support and helpful suggestions provided by our parents, relatives, classmates, and friends during the research work. Last but not least, we wish to thank everyone who has contributed in any manner to our efforts. Being able to learn at SHRI VAISHNAV VIDYAPEETH VISHWAVIDYALAYA in Indore has been a blessing.

References

1. Artificial intelligence market size report, 2022-2030, 2023, January, Retrieved January 30, 2023, from https://www.grandviewresearch.com/industry-analysis/artificial-intelligence-ai-market.

2. Gao, J., Galley, M., Li, L., Neural approaches to conversational AI, in: *The 41st International ACM SIGIR Conference on Research & Development in Information Retrieval*, 2018, June, pp. 1371–1374.

3. Adamopoulou, E. and Moussiades, L., Chatbots: History, technology, and applications. *Mach. Learn. Appl.*, 2, 100006, 2020.

4. Ruane, E., Birhane, A., Ventresque, A., Conversational AI: Social and ethical considerations, in: *AICS*, 2019, December, pp. 104–115.

5. Kulkarni, P., Mahabaleshwarkar, A., Kulkarni, M., Sirsikar, N., Gadgil, K., Conversational AI: An overview of methodologies, applications & future scope, in: *2019 5th International Conference on Computing, Communication, Control And Automation (ICCUBEA)*, 2019, September, IEEE, pp. 1–7.

6. Adamopoulou, E. and Moussiades, L., An overview of chatbot technology, in: *Artificial Intelligence Applications and Innovations: 16th IFIP WG 12.5 International Conference, AIAI 2020, Neos Marmaras, Greece, June 5–7, 2020, Proceedings, Part II 16*, Springer International Publishing, pp. 373–383, 2020.

7. Hasal, M., Nowaková, J., Ahmed Saghair, K., Abdulla, H., Snášel, V., Ogiela, L., Chatbots: Security, privacy, data protection, and social aspects. *Concurrency Comput.: Pract. Exper.*, 33, 19, e6426, 2021.

8. Ye, W. and Li, Q., Chatbot security and privacy in the age of personal assistants, in: *2020 IEEE/ACM Symposium on Edge Computing (SEC)*, 2020, November, IEEE, pp. 388–393.

9. Bozic, J. and Wotawa, F., Planning-based security testing for chatbots. *Informacijska Družba-IS*, vol. 2018, p. 23, 2018.

10. Jacquet, F., A brief history of conversational AI, dzone, 2023, January 25, Retrieved February 5, 2023, from https://dzone.com/articles/Conversational-AI-a-Brief-Story.

11. I., The history of chatbots – from ELIZA to ChatGPT, 2022, March 15, AI-chatbot Software for Complex Requirements. Retrieved February 6, 2023, from https://onlim.com/en/the-history-of-chatbots/.

12. What is conversational AI, IBM, Retrieved February 7, 2023, from https://www.ibm.com/topics/conversational-ai.

13. Team, C. T., What is conversational AI? Definition, components, and benefits, CX Today, 2022, March 21, Retrieved February 7, 2023, from https://www.cxtoday.com/contact-centre/what-is-conversational-ai/.

14. Chotia, R., What is conversational AI? How it works?, 2022, June 29, with Examples & Use. Retrieved February 16, 2023, from https://verloop.io/blog/what-is-conversational-ai/.

15. Ambit, Conversational AI: What it is & how it works, Ambit, 2021, October 20, Retrieved February 16, 2023, from https://www.ambit.ai/resources/conversational-ai-what-it-is-how-it-works.

16. A., What is the future of conversational AI?, India, 2022, October 21, https://exotel.com/blog/future-of-conversational-ai/.

17. Chatbot Security, What you need to know, Retrieved February 19, 2023, from https://www.inform-comms.com/chatbot-security-what-you-need-to-know/.

18. Treml, F., Top 3 chatbot security vulnerabilities in 2022, DZone, 2022, January 21, Retrieved February 19, 2023, from https://dzone.com/articles/top-3-chatbot-security-vulnerabilities-in-2022.

19. Pinard, P., 4 Chatbot security measures you absolutely need to consider, 2019, February 25, Retrieved February 19, 2023, from https://dzone.com/articles/4-chatbots-security-measures-you-absolutely-need-t.

20. James, R., Are chatbots vulnerable? Best practices to ensure chatbots security, 2020, October 24, Retrieved February 19, 2023, from https://chatbotslife.com/are-chatbots-vulnerable-best-practices-to-ensure-chatbots-security-d301b9f6ce17.

21. Hasal, M., Nowaková, J., Ahmed Saghair, K., Abdulla, H., Snášel, V., Ogiela, L., Chatbots: Security, privacy, data protection, and social aspects. *Concurrency Comput.: Pract. Exper.*, 33, 19, e6426, 2021.

22. Kim, W., Ryoo, Y., Lee, S., Lee, J.A., Chatbot advertising as a double-edged sword: The roles of regulatory focus and privacy concerns. *J. Advert.*, 1–19, 2022.

23. Voigt, P. and Von dem Bussche, A., The EU general data protection regulation (GDPR), in: *A Practical Guide*, 1st Ed., vol. 10(3152676), pp. 10–5555, Springer International Publishing, Cham, 2017.

24. Ritvo, D., Bavitz, C., Gupta, R., Oberman, I., Privacy and children's data-an overview of the children's online privacy protection act and the family educational rights and privacy act. Berkman Center Research Publication, (23), 2013.

25. Charatan, H., Chatbots VS GDPR, 2019, Retrieved March 19, 2023, from https://chatamo.com/chatbots-vs-gdpr-interact/.

26. Sağlam, R.B. and Nurse, J.R., Is your chatbot GDPR compliant? Open issues in agent design, in: *Proceedings of the 2nd Conference on Conversational User Interfaces*, 2020, July, pp. 1–3.

27. Jaupi, A., GDPR and chatbots - a guide to compliance, 2018, September 5, Medium. Retrieved March 19, 2023, from https://medium.com/automated-conversations/gdpr-and-chatbots-a-guide-to-compliance-a23d37cb672b.

28. Yin, S., Intercom chatbot trends report, The Intercom Blog, Retrieved March 24, 2023, from https://www.intercom.com/blog/the-state-of-chatbots/.

29. Mahor, V., Bijrothiya, S., Rawat, R., Kumar, A., Garg, B., Pachlasiya, K., IoT and artificial intelligence techniques for public safety and security, in: *Smart Urban Computing Applications*, p. 111, 2023.

30. Mahor, V., Pachlasiya, K., Garg, B., Chouhan, M., Telang, S., Rawat, R., Mobile operating system (Android) vulnerability analysis using machine learning, in: *Proceedings of International Conference on Network Security and Blockchain Technology: ICNSBT 2021*, pp. 159–169, Springer Nature Singapore, Singapore, 2022, June.

31. Rawat, R., Garg, B., Pachlasiya, K., Mahor, V., Telang, S., Chouhan, M., Mishra, R., SCNTA: Monitoring of network availability and activity for identification of anomalies using machine learning approaches. *Int. J. Inf. Technol. Web Eng. (IJITWE)*, 17, 1, 1–19, 2022.

32. Rawat, R., Rimal, Y.N., William, P., Dahima, S., Gupta, S., Sankaran, K.S., Malware threat affecting financial organization analysis using machine learning approach. *Int. J. Inf. Technol. Web Eng. (IJITWE)*, 17, 1, 1–20, 2022.

33. Rawat, R., Mahor, V., Chouhan, M., Pachlasiya, K., Telang, S., Garg, B., Systematic literature review (SLR) on social media and the digital transformation of drug trafficking on darkweb, in: *International Conference on Network Security and Blockchain Technology*, pp. 181–205, Springer, Singapore, 2022.

34. Rawat, R., Ayodele Oki, O., Sankaran, S., Florez, H., Ajagbe, S.A., Techniques for predicting dark web events focused on the delivery of illicit products and ordered crime. *Int. J. Electr. Comput. Eng. (IJECE)*, 13, 5, 5354–5365, Oct. 2023, doi: 10.11591/ijece.v13i5.pp5354-5365.

35. Rawat, R., Garg, B., Mahor, V., Telang, S., Pachlasiya, K., Chouhan, M., Organ trafficking on the dark web—The data security and privacy concern in healthcare systems, in: *Internet of Healthcare Things: Machine Learning for Security and Privacy*, pp. 189–216, 2022.

36. Vyas, P., Vyas, G., Chauhan, A., Rawat, R., Telang, S., Gottumukkala, M., Anonymous trading on the dark online marketplace: An exploratory study, in: *Using Computational Intelligence for the Dark Web and Illicit Behavior Detection*, pp. 272–289, IGI Global, 2022.

37. Rawat, R., Oki, O.A., Sankaran, K.S., Olasupo, O., Ebong, G.N., Ajagbe, S.A., A new solution for cyber security in big data using machine learning approach, in: *Mobile Computing and*

Sustainable Informatics: Proceedings of ICMCSI 2023, pp. 495–505, Springer Nature Singapore, Singapore, 2023.

38. Rawat, R., Chakrawarti, R.K., Raj, A., Mani, G., Chidambarathanu, K., Bhardwaj, R., Association rule learning for threat analysis using traffic analysis and packet filtering approach. *Int. J. Inf. Technol.*, 1–11, 2023.

39. Rawat, R., Logical concept mapping and social media analytics relating to cyber criminal activities for ontology creation. *Int. J. Inf. Technol.*, 15, 2, 893–903, 2023.

40. Rawat, R., Mahor, V., Álvarez, J.D., Ch, F., Cognitive systems for dark web cyber delinquent association malignant data crawling: A review, in: *Handbook of Research on War Policies, Strategies, and Cyber Wars*, pp. 45–63, 2023.

41. Rawat, R., Chakrawarti, R.K., Vyas, P., Gonzáles, J.L.A., Sikarwar, R., Bhardwaj, R., Intelligent fog computing surveillance system for crime and vulnerability identification and tracing. *Int. J. Inf. Secur. Priv. (IJISP)*, 17, 1, 1–25, 2023.

42. Rawat, R., Sowjanya, A.M., Patel, S.I., Jaiswal, V., Khan, I., Balaram, A. (Eds.), *Using Machine Intelligence: Autonomous Vehicles Volume 1*, John Wiley & Sons, 2022.

43. Rawat, R., Mahor, V., Díaz-Álvarez, J., Chávez, F., Rooted learning model at fog computing analysis for crime incident surveillance, in: *2022 International Conference on Smart Generation Computing, Communication and Networking (SMART GENCON)*, pp. 1–9, IEEE, 2022, December.

44. Rawat, R. and Shrivastav, S.K., SQL injection attack detection using SVM. *Int. J. Comput. Appl.*, 42, 13, 1–4, 2012.

45. Rawat, R., Bhardwaj, P., Kaur, U., Telang, S., Chouhan, M., Sankaran, K.S., *Smart vehicles for communication, volume 2*, John Wiley & Sons, 2023.

46. Mahor, V., Garg, B., Telang, S., Pachlasiya, K., Chouhan, M., Rawat, R., Cyber threat phylogeny assessment and vulnerabilities representation at thermal power station, in: *Proceedings of International Conference on Network Security and Blockchain Technology: ICNSBT 2021*, pp. 28–39, Springer Nature Singapore, Singapore, 2022, June.

47. Rawat, R., Gupta, S., Sivaranjani, S., Cu, O.K., Kuliha, M., Sankaran, K.S., Malevolent information crawling mechanism for forming structured illegal organisations in hidden networks. *Int. J. Cyber Warf. Terror. (IJCWT)*, 12, 1, 1–14, 2022.

Recent Trends in Pattern Recognition, Challenges and Opportunities

S. Kannadhasan[1*] and R. Nagarajan[2]

[1]Department of Electronics and Communication Engineering, Cheran College of Engineering, Tamil Nadu, India
[2]Department of Electrical and Electronics Engineering, Gnanamani College of Technology, Tamil Nadu, India

Abstract

The process of identifying characters that have been subjected to a visible transformation is referred to as optical character identification (OCR). The OCR process allows for the conversion of a wide variety of texts, documents, and digital pictures into an American Standard Code for Information Interchange or another format that is modifiable by a computer. This enables the data to be edited or located. Current developments in pattern recognition have been demanded by a wide variety of applications, such as OCR, document categorization, and data mining, among others. OCR is an essential component of document scanners and plays an important role in the identification of characters and languages, as well as in the protection of financial identities. There are two distinct categories of OCR devices: online character recognition and offline character recognition. Online OCR is superior to offline OCR in terms of accuracy because it handles characters as they are written, bypassing the initial stage of character identification. Offline OCR can be broken down into two categories: printed OCR and handwritten OCR. The process of recording handwritten or typewritten characters into a binary or monochromatic picture, which is then processed by a computer in order to identify the text, is a common method for offline OCR. Scanned documents can now be transformed into text components that computers can recognize, making them more valuable than regular picture files. This was made possible by the introduction of OCR technology. In contrast to the traditional method of manually retyping data into an electronic database, OCR discovers an improved method of automatically inputting data into a database. The most common issue with OCR is the segmentation of associated characters or symbols. The accuracy of the OCR is inversely proportional to the original picture's pixel count.

Keywords: Conversional AI, chatbot, autobot and pattern recognition

*Corresponding author: kannadhasan.ece@gmail.com

Romil Rawat, Rajesh Kumar Chakrawarti, Sanjaya Kumar Sarangi, Piyush Vyas, Mary Sowjanya Alamanda, Kotagiri Srividya and Krishnan Sakthidasan Sankaran (eds.) Conversational Artificial Intelligence, (459–476) © 2024 Scrivener Publishing LLC

27.1 Introduction

A fascinating subfield of conversational artificial intelligence (AI) research, intelligent picture analysis is required for a number of the current research projects that need to be addressed. Learning models to recognize presegmented handwritten numerals is a subsection of the larger field of calligraphy number identification that has received a lot of research over the years. It is one of the most significant challenges facing researchers in the fields of data mining, machine learning, pattern recognition, and a wide variety of other implementations of AI in chatbots and autobots. Despite the fact that no identification program can match the level of intelligence possessed by humans, it has been demonstrated to be significantly quicker, which is an attractive feature. The primary use of machine learning techniques over the past 10 years has shown to be effective in creating decisive systems that compete with human performance and outperform manually written classical AI systems used in the early stages of OCR technology [1–3]. This has been demonstrated through the use of techniques that have shown to be effective in creating decisive systems that compete with human performance [1–3]. On the other hand, not every aspect of those particular models has been looked at in previous research. Specialists in the fields of machine learning and data mining have invested a significant amount of time and energy into the development of effective methods for deriving identification estimates from data. Handwritten digit communication has developed its own standard in the twenty-first century and is frequently used as a means of conversation as well as for keeping track of information that needs to be shared with others. In addition, handwritten digit communication has become increasingly popular in recent years. Because different groups may use a variety of penmanship techniques while still managing to sketch the same pattern of characters in their known script, identifying handwritten characters can be difficult due to the variety and deformation of the handwritten character set. This is one of the challenges that must be overcome in order to successfully identify handwritten characters.

One of the most challenging challenges in the field of numeral identification is trying to find the number that will lead to the recovery of the most distinguishing characteristics. Several different approaches to region selection are utilized [4–8] in the process of pattern identification in order to locate these types of regions. The numerous individual writing styles present the most significant barrier to the process of handwritten character identification. It is therefore necessary to have robust feature extraction in order to improve the efficiency of a handwritten character authentication system. Because it can be utilized in so many different fields, the study of handwritten number identification has attracted a lot of attention from researchers working in the field of pattern recognition systems. Character recognition systems have the potential to play a pivotal role in the future development of digital societies [9–11]. These systems work by digitizing existing paper records and analyzing the data they produce.

Keeping handwritten number records can be perplexing because there is no guarantee that the lines will be clear and uninterrupted. The utilization of a collection of number characteristics is the primary objective of feature extraction in digit identification. This is done with the intention of reducing the amount of redundant data and improving the word picture representation. It does this by removing the overwhelming majority of unstructured picture data and then analyzing what that data reveal about the image. In addition, the gradients do not always transition into one another smoothly like they do in written characters. Alterations can be made to the height of the characters as well as the direction they face, but they must be written on the grid in an upright or vertical position at all times. Because of this, it is possible to construct a system that is capable of detecting handwriting accurately by taking into account its constraints. The identification of handwritten characters can be challenging at times, which is especially problematic considering that the majority of people have difficulty deciphering their own handwriting. It is necessary for a writer to appear to have a restricted ability to write in order for their handwritten penmanship to be recognized. The software engineering instrument is presented first, followed by the technique that was utilized in order to carry out this research. Picture analysis and pattern recognition are extremely important components in the process of authenticating handwritten characters. Feature extraction methods can be categorized in a wide variety of different ways, including structural feature-based methods, statistical feature-based methods, and global transformation methods [12, 13]. The selection of data to be used in developing statistical techniques is an important step. It extracts information from the seemingly haphazard arrangement of pixels found in the image.

27.2 Optical Character Recognition

Research has been done on identifying characters based on their appearance. Perception, dividing the design, and placing the examples in sequence are the three primary stages of the example identification process. OCR frameworks are currently transforming a large number of reports—whether written letters in order or physically produced—into information that can be read by machines. This process occurs without any change, clamor, disparities in determination, or other factors. Offline character recognition and online character recognition are the two primary methods that are used for handwriting authentication in general. Offline handwriting recognition requires transforming text into a picture, which is then converted into letter characters that can be used in text-processing and computer programs. This process is carried out by converting text into a picture. Because different individuals have such a broad range of different writing styles, detecting calligraphy offline is a more challenging task.

On the other hand, online character authentication makes use of a data stream that is transmitted from a sensor while the user is writing. This allows the system to recognize characters as they are being written in real time. A pressure-sensitive or electromagnetic digitizing device is a standard component of the apparatus used for data collection. When a user writes on a device, the computer records and scrutinizes the sequence of movements made by the user's stylus by transforming those movements into an electronic signal sequence. The term "visual character identification" can refer to a number of different technologies, such as "artificial intelligence," "machine learning," "signal processing," "conversational AI," and "pattern recognition" (OCR). OCR, which stands for optical character recognition, is sometimes referred to as an offline character identification procedure. This is due to the fact that OCR analyses and recognizes still pictures of characters. It is the process of translating visible representations of handwritten text, printed text, or both into computer code using a non-variable mechanical or electrical translation process. The procedure of OCR involves a series of stages, including preprocessing, segmentation, feature extraction, classifications, and identification. The output from one level becomes the input for the stage that follows after it. The text that was written by hand is first digitized and then preprocessed to remove noise and difference. Offline handwriting recognition systems and pattern recognition are required for a wide variety of OCR applications. Some examples of these applications include letter organizing, bank processing, document digitization, and sending address verification. The process of transforming a paper-based, handwritten text into a shape that can be read on a computer is known as digitization. Each document consists of a single character only. Scanning a document results in the production of an electronic picture file format that is identical to the format of the document that was being scanned before it was scanned. In order to digitize the pictures, we employed a variety of devices, and once that process was complete, we moved on to the preparation phase. The recorded unprocessed picture undergoes a variety of manipulations as part of the preprocessing stage of the editing process. The picture is improved and made ready for partition as a result. The picture of the person in monochrome is adjusted so that it fits within the frame. After the disturbance in the picture was reduced, a vector image was created. After that, a more compacted version of the vector picture was created. The procedure of separation is the stage that bears the most weight. The process of segmentation can be completed by splitting a photograph up into its component characters.

It is significantly more difficult to separate handwriting texts into different zones (upper, middle, and lower zone) and characters when compared to printed texts in their conventional form. This is predominantly brought on by variations in the characters that make up paragraphs, lines, and words, in addition to offset, slant, height, and curvature. When the sections of two adjacent figures come into contact with or intersect with one another, the process of partition becomes more difficult. As a consequence of the changed characters in the top and bottom zones, the problem of contact or combining happens in a lot of games these days. An important element is classification. During this stage, we isolate particular aspects of the character. The success of each character authentication method is evaluated according to the retrieved characteristics. Using the characteristics that were extracted from the outgoing character, it ought to be feasible to assign a singular classification to the incoming one. To determine the feature set for a particular character, we made use of diagonal features, features that were based on joint and open end points, transition features, zoning features, directional features, features that were based on parabola curve fitting, and features that were based on power curve fitting.

Recently, the authentication of calligraphy has surfaced as one of the most interesting and difficult research subjects in the field of picture processing and pattern recognition. It represents a substantial improvement to an automated process and has the potential to enhance the relationship between humans and machines in a variety of contexts. A great number of studies have been focused on the development of novel methods and strategies that would accelerate the processing while simultaneously increasing identification precision. Offline and internet systems are the two most prevalent varieties of handwriting recognition software. During the offline authentication process, the writing is usually recorded visually by a camera, and the end result is presented as a photograph. The online method, on the other hand, also provides the order in which the writer struck, and the two-dimensional coordinates of successive locations are displayed as a function of time. Because the former provides information about time, it has been discovered that online techniques are more effective at recognizing handwritten patterns than their offline counterparts are. Neural networks have also been successfully implemented in offline systems, where they have been used to achieve comparable high levels of identification precision. Offline handwriting recognition systems are required for a variety of tasks, including the authentication of shipping addresses, the processing of bank documents, document digitization, and the organization of letters, as shown in Figure 27.1. As a consequence of this, offline handwriting identification remains an active area of research, and researchers are constantly looking into new methods to enhance detection precision. Pre-processing is the first step in each and every handwriting recognition system, which is followed by segmentation and feature extraction.

The term "preprocessing" refers to the steps that must be taken in order to transform the unprocessed picture into a form that is appropriate for segmentation. During the segmentation process, the original picture is broken down into individual characters, and then each character is enlarged to be m by n pixels so that it can be used by the training network. When it comes to achieving high levels of identification performance, the single most essential element is the method of feature extraction that is chosen to use. In the body of research that has been done, a great many different techniques for the separation of distinguishing characteristics of characters have been documented. Template matching, deformable templates, unitary image transforms, graph description, projection histograms, contour profiles, zoning, geometric moment invariants, Zernike moments, spline curve approximation, Fourier descriptors, gradient feature, and Gabor feature are some of the most popular techniques for feature extraction. Other popular techniques include Zernike moments, spline curve approximation, and Fourier descriptors. Jobs that require classification and identification make use of an artificial neural network at its heart. Neural networks have evolved as a rapid and trustworthy technique for categorization in offline identification systems, making it possible for them to achieve a high level of recognizing precision.

Methods of classification have been used since the 1990s in an effort to improve the handwritten character authentication process. These methods include artificial neural

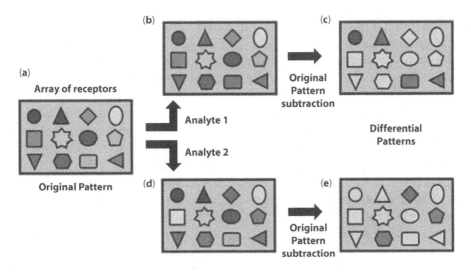

Figure 27.1 Pattern recognition.

networks (ANNs), kernel methods, such as support vector machines (SVMs), statistical strategies based on the Bayes decision formula, and multiple categorization combinations. ANNs are among the most popular of these methods.

27.3   Various Sectors of Pattern Recognition

Agriculture is responsible for a substantial share of the total production of the economy. Researchers collaborate with the breeding industry in order to fulfil an increasing demand, increase resistance to parasites and diseases, reduce negative effects on the environment (using less water and fertilizer, for example), and perpetuate essential characteristics. The objective is to develop agribusiness that is more environmentally friendly. If meticulous horticulture is utilized, it's possible that these requirements will be met. According to the scholarly literature on precision farming, the majority of efforts that have been put forth up until this point have been concentrated on the development and application of sensing technology rather than data processing methods that are specifically tailored to agricultural measures. To put this another way, rather than developing original frameworks or algorithms, most of the recent progress in cultivating conversational AI has relied heavily on pre-existing strategies found in software programs or modules. The study of pattern recognition draws from a wide range of academic disciplines, including mathematics, engineering, AI, computer science, psychology, and neurobiology, among others. In the subject of pattern identification, regularities in data are automatically recognized by computer programs, and these regularities are then used to carry out tasks such as data classification in order to complete these tasks.

Putting it more succinctly, categorization or categorizing is frequently achieved through the use of pattern recognition. People have been searching for answers to a broad variety of issues for a significant amount of time using analogical reasoning. When people are unable to recognize patterns, or when the process of recognizing needs to be mechanized and sped up, the use of computer-based automated pattern recognition systems is necessary. Pattern thinking employs the same strategy to solve problems arising in a variety of contexts by focusing on commonalities that are relevant to those contexts. The primary objective of pattern recognition is to locate and classify instances of similarity within the subject under investigation. Learning is either possible or not possible for the systems that recognize patterns. Monitored learning, on the other hand, refers to strategies that have been instructed, in contrast to unrestrained learning, which refers to methods that have not been taught. There is a wide variety of choices accessible when it comes to pattern recognition. When deciding which pattern to use, a pattern recognition algorithm ought to take into account the domain of application. It is not possible to use the same technique of pattern recognition across all of the regions. When it comes to most practical applications, the original input variables are frequently preprocessed so that, if necessary, they can be transformed into a new universe of variables. For the challenge of identifying numerals, for instance, the pictures of the digits are generally enlarged and transformed so that each number can be contained within a particular frame that has been established beforehand. A subsequent pattern recognition program will have a much simpler time differentiating between the various classes as a result of the uniform positioning and size of all of the digits. This is because the diversity that exists within each digit class is significantly reduced as a result of the uniform positioning and size of all of the digits. The information gathered from the worlds that are close by is used as a resource.

After that, the raw data are managed either to eliminate noise from the data or to extract a fascinating pattern from the background so that the pattern recognition system can use it as input. This is done so that the system can function properly. A measurable or observable aspect of the design is referred to as a feature. Features can be added or removed from a product. During the process of feature extraction, which also removes any unnecessary data, the pattern's distinguishing characteristics are reconstructed. The working time required for the authentication procedure will be cut down due to the elimination of material that serves no purpose. Comparable data processing approaches are used to determine pertinent characteristics. The combination of these essential characteristics results in the production of an object's personality, which can then be identified and categorized appropriately. There are many different methods for the extraction of features, such as the Fourier transform, the Radon transform, the Gabor Wavelets transform, the Fuzzy invariant transform, the principal component analysis (PCA), the semidefinite embedding, the multifactor dimensionality reduction, the multilinear subspace learning, the nonlinear dimensionality reduction, the isomap, the kernel PCA, and the multilinear PCA. The goal of variable selection is to improve the performance of predictors, make the delivery of predictors quicker and more reasonable, and achieve a greater level of comprehension regarding the foundational process that was responsible for the generation of the data. In order to acquire a section of the feature vector that is more discriminative or representational, the collection of features that was generated as a result of the feature extraction phase is processed through an additional filtration technique. The original characteristics are not altered in any way during this process; consequently, filtration is able to preserve the physical significance of the information. The training data set refers to the feature vector or subdivision that is made accessible at the conclusion of this portion of the process. By selecting characteristics, we are able to acquire a more in-depth comprehension of the subject matter, and by decreasing the number of models, we are able to save money.

Last but not least, the effectiveness of the technique for classifying things is enhanced by the characteristics of the feature selection. This strategy aims to lessen the negative effects of the multidimensional pandemic while also accelerating the process of reducing the number of dimensions. Dimensionality reduction and feature selection are two entirely different things. Feature selection methods and dimensionality reduction methods both aim to reduce the number of attributes present in a dataset; however, feature selection methods simply include and exclude qualities that are already present in the data, whereas dimensionality reduction methods create novel combinations of attributes. At the most basic level, a feature selection method can be segmented into covers, filters, and integration. For the purpose of determining score feature groups, Wrapper employs a projection algorithm. Before being evaluated on a reference collection, a model is first educated on the newly discovered subgroups. When calculating the score for that subcategory, the error rate of the model, which is also referred to simply as the model's error rate, is used. Wrapper methods

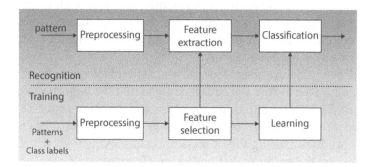

Figure 27.2 Pattern recognition processing.

generate the best performing feature set for that particular type of model; however, these methods are computationally demanding due to the fact that they train a new model for each subdivision. The Figure 27.2 shows about the pattern recognition processing.

Neural network image recognition is a brand new form of image recognition technology that was developed in combination with modern computer technology, image processing, AI, and the theory of pattern recognition. The technology of image identification has significant implications for the realm of computer vision and is deeply intertwined with social life. In order to identify a picture, you must first create a digital copy of its corresponding image by capturing it with an image capture tool. After that, you must identify the picture and gather additional information. This research introduces the Back Propagation (BP) neural network into the field of image identification. When combined with traditional digital image processing technology, the result is an effective technique for recognizing precise rectangular images. In order to meet the criteria for picture identification standards, the neural network must be able to function in real time, tolerate errors in compliance with those standards, have a high working speed, and be accurate when classifying data. This work first conducts an analysis of traditional image identification techniques in order to create a method for image processing that can be used for the study and advancement of picture segmentation. The analysis focuses on the traditional techniques' shortcomings as well as complex situations such as images in various states. By utilizing the technique of adaptable learning rate change, it is possible to simultaneously increase network productivity, increase the precision of picture identification, and decrease the number of network trainees as well as the amount of time spent training. This is accomplished by making use of the BP neural network's issues to determine the local minimum worth of those problems. To successfully reduce the network into a local minimum point and speed up training, the updated BP neural network method for rotational deformation picture placing and recognition will use a combination of additional momentum and an adjustable learning rate. This will be accomplished by successfully reducing the network into a local minimum point. An practice provided the opportunity to put the optimization strategy to the test, during which it demonstrated both its feasibility and its effectiveness. In addition to this, it was discovered that enhanced results could be achieved through the use of mathematics.

As a result of advances in technology and scientific knowledge, imaging has evolved in some respects. A picture needs to be digitized before it can be saved in the memory of a computer or on other types of media, such as a CD-ROM or a hard drive. Pixels, also known as picture elements, are the building blocks of digital images, which are two-dimensional pictures represented by a relatively small collection of digital values. You can scan your documents into digital format using either a scanner or a digital camera. After a photograph has been digitized, it can then be edited using a variety of different image altering techniques. The two primary functions of digital image processing are known as the enhancement of visual information for human comprehension and the processing of data pictures for the purposes of keeping, representing, and transmitting the data for independent machine consciousness. The goal of digital image processing is to identify an intensity distribution remnant in any given image and to convert three-dimensional pictures into two-dimensional image values that can be utilized to communicate quantifiable structure and characterize it. A few of the many processes that are used in digital image processing are digital improvement for enhanced visual perception, data organization and rectification, and computer-assisted target categories and characteristics. These are just a few of the many processes. It is necessary for the data to be provided and captured in a format that is suitable for storage on a computer disk or diskette in order for digital pictures to be produced using remote sensing. In order to alter digital photographs, you will need a computer system that is also referred to as an image analysis system and is equipped with the appropriate software as well as editing tools. There are many different software programs that have been developed particularly for the purpose of modifying and analyzing pictures acquired through remote sensing. These programs are generally available. The procedures of altering digital photographs have traditionally utilized a wide diversity of techniques or approaches. Image analysis grants access to a broad variety of conventional image processing techniques, including image preparation, image enhancement, image transformation, and image classification and analysis.

In the phase known as "preprocessing," which comes before an in-depth analysis of the data and the extraction of information, common steps include geometric modifications and spectrum adjustments. Changes to the data are made so that they more accurately reflect the radiation that was either released or reflected and was noticed by the sensor. Radiometric adjustments include removing unnecessary sensor or environmental noise, correcting for sensor anomalies, and changing the data to reflect the radiation in the correct manner. On the other hand, geometric adjustments involve rebirthing the data to actual world coordinates such as longitude and latitude on the earth's surface and correcting geometric mistakes brought on by sensor-earth geometry changes. These coordinates can be found on the surface of the planet. Procedures for altering pictures are conceptually comparable to those for enhancing images. In contrast to the widespread belief, picture-enhancement approaches are almost never applied to more than one data source at the same time. Whenever an image is altered, the combined processing of data coming from a wide variety of spectral regions is required. In order to combine and transform the different bands into new pictures that better emphasize or represent specific characteristics in the scene, arithmetic operations such as division, subtraction, addition, and multiplication are used. These operations are used in the process. PCA and band or spectrum distribution are two methods that are frequently used to better portray information in numerous photographs. Both of these methods can be broken down into several subcategories. Methods of picture classification and analysis are utilized in order to computationally categories and recognize photos contained within the data. Multichannel databases are utilized quite frequently for the purpose of classification. Using the statistical properties of the different brightness values, this technique assigns a particular topic or category to each picture as well as each pixel within the image.

The primary purpose of OCR is to categorize graphical patterns that are associated with alphanumeric or other characters and are generally found in digital images. Classification, segmentation, and feature extraction are the three stages that are involved in the OCR technique. According to what is written in the Matlab OCR code, each level is its own separate column. Scan the text from a particular piece of paper while simultaneously transforming the pictures into a language that the computer can understand. This activity belongs to the field of computer science and includes scanning the text. A person is able to digitize a book or notebook with the assistance of an OCR device, input the data into a computer, and then change the document using a word processor. OCR systems have a lot of potential because they allow users to utilize the processing capability of computers in order to retrieve written documents. This opens up a lot of possibilities. It is already used extensively, specifically in the legal industry, where investigations that used to take hours or days can now be completed in a matter of seconds thanks to the widespread adoption of this technology.

27.4   Applications of Natural Language Processing

Character identification is a relatively novel challenge, despite the fact that there are numerous commonly used digital image processing techniques and implementations that are capable of recognizing characters from pictures. It is of the utmost importance to select an appropriate method that is capable of rapidly adapting to a variety of pictures, regardless of how particular or complicated they may be. For the purposes of data visualization, analytical work, and the creation of new methods, the software known as MATLAB provides users with a comprehensive environment, as well as a broad variety of tools and methods. Image enhancement, deblurring, geographic customization, and analytic tools are all included in this application. In addition to this, it enables possible structural processes such as disintegration, reconstruction, and extension of the structure. Writing by hand is a skill that is now necessary in many parts of the world because it is so significantly used in a wide variety of contexts and applications. Before this technology was effectively implemented, we had to rely on handwriting notes, which increased the likelihood of making mistakes. It is challenging to store physical data, to retrieve it, and to rapidly analyze it. The data need to be revised on a frequent basis, and it requires effort to ensure that they are organized in the correct manner. We have been contending with substantial data loss for a very long time as a direct result of the antiquated technique of data storage that we have been using.

Because the administration, storage, and retrieval of data are simplified by contemporary technology, more and more people are preserving data on personal computers. Utilizing software that can recognize handwriting text is a prudent choice because it simplifies the process of saving data and retrieving information that has been previously saved. In addition to this, it strengthens the confidentiality of the information. In contrast to OCR scanners, which are an example of physical technology, Google Lens is an example of software that can recognize handwriting. Our research aims to develop a model based on deep learning that is capable of recognizing handwriting and converting it to speaking so that it can be utilized in the field of healthcare as well as personal care. Tensor Flow and OpenCV, in contrast to other techniques, come with pretrained models that can be used immediately to provide accurate results; as a result, we decided to use them to solve our problem because they both have this feature. These files, which are organized in their own distinct directories, can have data retrieved from them. When it comes to the development of the project, we rely almost exclusively on open-source frameworks. The natural language analysis was used as the foundation for the algorithms that we used [natural language processing (NLP)]. Data acquisition, processing, searching, and visualization are at the heart of this NLP system. After that, a character is fabricated using this information.

Humans are distinct from machines due to the fact that they possess human intelligence. They are capable of performing a significant number of activities that algorithms are unable to do on their own. One of these duties is determining whether or not the writing was composed by hand. In spite of the fact that a significant number of academics have focused a significant amount of their research over the course of the last few decades on the process of identifying handwritten text in documents, a variety of academics have in the past developed a number of automatic handwriting systems. However, research on the effectiveness of the identification method is currently being conducted. Due to the wide variety of handwriting styles, modern handwriting recognition systems frequently produce subpar results when tested with a variety of different instances of calligraphy. Reading calligraphy typically entails a multistep process, beginning with "preparation" and continuing on to "feature extraction," "categorization," and "postprocessing," among other stages. Feature extraction and classifier construction are, however, the two stages in any identification system that are considered to be the most important.

In spite of this, we still can't say for certain that the authentication issues with these programs have been resolved entirely. The development of an efficient and accurate handwritten text recognition system has been greatly aided by the application of the ANN, which has proven to be a lifesaver in this endeavor. Utilizing the ANN in the design of a system is quickly becoming one of the most well-liked approaches to training computers human-like abilities. Pattern recognition, object classification, data mining, and series forecast are all examples of problems that are especially amenable to being solved by neural networks, whose architecture is based on that of the human brain. Neural networks are particularly useful for tackling problems like these because they cannot be stated as a series of simple steps. It's possible that recognizing patterns is the most frequent use of neural networks, but there are many others. The neural network is fed the appropriate input vectors in addition to a predetermined group of target vectors (a vector containing pattern information). As input, one could make use of any kind of data, ranging from straightforward one-dimensional data to complex multidimensional data. Once the ANN has been trained using the appropriate data, it (like the human brain) can be put to use to discover patterns or groups that were not previously known to exist in previously unidentified data (new inputs).

The primary purpose of this research is to devise an effective handwritten character and number identification system for use with English symbols. As a result of the fact that handcrafted characters may incorporate the initial and miniature forms of English characters, this research is divided into 52 categories (26 for capital and 26 for tiny). It is important for the spectator to be aware that we did not investigate the identification of their English insignia.

Voice recognition, also known as Automatic Speech Recognition, is the process of utilizing computer software and a program to transform the sound of a person's voice into a series of words. Voice recognition is also sometimes referred to as speech recognition. Processing of speech is widely considered to be one of the most important subfields of signal processing. The goal of the speech recognition field is to create techniques for the entry of synthesized vocalizations. Early computer systems were restricted in terms of both their capabilities and their reach. Despite this, the field of automatically recognizing voices has made strides in recent years as a result of advancements in computer technology. As a result of developments in computer technology, it is now possible to keep large speech recognition databases up to date. Because language is the most fundamental method of communication, relationships between humans and machines in the native languages of the area should be planned for. Speech recognition software has only been developed for a handful of different languages. As a result, developing speech recognizers that are compatible with regional languages holds a lot of potential. The development of statistical models of speech has led to widespread applications in the field of sound recognition since these models have become more accurate. In many domains, including automatic call handling in telephone networks, data entry, voice transcription, query-based updated trip information and bookings, natural language understanding and interpreters. Furthermore, the use of automated speech recognition has led to a reduction in the amount of labor performed by humans. The use of speech recognition technology in telephone networks has led to significant efficiencies and improvements in the provision of assistant services.

This study places an emphasis not only on technological development but also on the foundational components that make up speech recognition systems. Recognizing characters that have been optically processed presents a challenge that can be overcome with OCR. Following the completion of the writing or printing process, the passive process of retinal authentication can then begin. In recent years, OCR for handwritten documents has become increasingly popular, and the study of handwritten character recognition has emerged as an important new academic field. Despite the fact that a great number of studies have been conducted on foreign scripts such as Chinese, Japanese, and Arabic characters, there have only been a very small number of studies done on handwritten character identification in Indian scripts. There is presently no foolproof technique for recognizing calligraphy in India due to the extensive character sets used by Indian languages, as well as the existence of characters that incorporate verbal modifications and composite characters within the Indian alphabet. Problems with letter identification can be categorized based on two different variables. The first stage will be determined by whether or not the material is printed, or whether it is written by hand. The second factor is determined by the method of recruitment, which may take place either online or offline.

It is generally agreed upon that the offline version of the handwritten text authentication technique does not perform as well as its digital counterpart does when used online. Characters are immediately recognized when you use character recognition software for the internet. Because they have access to chronological information, online systems are superior to their offline counterparts in terms of character identification. This enables online systems to skip the initial search period entirely. When offline character recognition is used, the handwriting or typewritten character is frequently digitized as a paper document and made available to the identification system as a binary or grayscale image. This is done because offline character recognition relies on the fact that paper documents are readily available. Because there is no way to regulate the medium or the instrument that is being utilized, offline character recognition is a significantly more challenging and demanding process. In the midst of the din and commotion of our modern "smart" lives, the establishment of a smart transportation management system that provides information on vehicle numbers for the purposes of follow-up, statistics, and monitoring is essential. Monitoring of vehicles, recognizing vehicles, and managing administrative tasks are all important aspects of today's traffic management systems. ALPR systems have a variety of uses in the fields of transportation and security, including the recovery of stolen vehicles, the collection of toll payments, the management of parking places, and the control of admission and departure points. The picture is captured by the ALPR device using a digital camera, and it is then subjected to pre-processing in order to get rid of any noise and prepare it for character segmentation and identification. The outcome of the method is the license number for the automobile, and the user may alter this number to fulfil any specific requirements they may have.

The mechanization of parking administration and security at marketplaces, universities, workplaces, and other locations is one of the consumer requests that this article addresses. The technology that has been developed has the potential to be used to automatically recognize a vehicle as it approaches a parking area or a toll location. A photograph of the automobile was utilized in the production of the license plate. Once the individual has recognized the signals, they will be able to utilize a simulated user interface in order to control the gadget. By presenting the date of the vehicle as it approaches, the Interface makes it possible for the user to monitor all vehicles that come into the building and keep track of them all. In the subject of pattern identification, regularities in data are automatically recognized by computer programs, and these regularities are then used to carry out tasks such as data classification in order to complete these tasks. The ultimate objective is to differentiate one class from the others by skillfully removing patterns that are determined by a set of predetermined criteria. The many applications of pattern recognition are depicted in Figure 27.3, which provides an example of this. Disease categorization, patient survival rate forecasting, biometric authentication, facial and eye recognition, genetic form discrimination, visual character recognition, material discrimination, speech recognition, and a host of other applications are a few examples of what can be done with this technology. When developing a pattern recognition system, the implementation region should be one of the primary considerations. It is both unexpected and fascinating to discover that computer identification systems, particularly those that learn from examples, are purportedly or almost completely based on a simulation of human perceptual and learning abilities. One of the reasons for this is that automatic systems can be utilized for a variety of tasks, and because of this, they

Figure 27.3 Applications of pattern recognition.

are often required to be quicker, bigger, and more reliable than they otherwise would be, which limits their flexibility.

We are not only capable of recognizing patterns, but we are also conscious of them, which enables us to recognize patterns. This makes us pattern recognizers. We have the ability to exercise control over it, communicate our findings to others, and explain the patterns to them. The process of being able to draw similarities between different objects or occurrences is referred to as generalization. Therefore, how the human mind moves from data to recollection and generalization is the central scientific topic of pattern recognition, and how this process can be incorporated into and taught to a computer is a task for its algorithms. Pattern recognition is a subfield of AI that aims to replicate human intelligence. Machine learning techniques allow for the identification of patterns to be carried out. These programs will classify data according to pre-existing knowledge or statistical information that is obtained from patterns and/or their representation, whichever comes first. The capacity to discover configurations of characteristics or data that disclose information about a particular system or data collection is what is meant by the term "pattern identification." In the field of data science, pattern recognition algorithms can be utilized to make predictions regarding the movements of time series data that are extremely probable to take place in the future. A pattern in a technological context could be, among an almost infinite number of other possibilities, particular clusters of behavior on a network that could indicate an attack; particular arrangements of features in images that identify objects; frequent combinations of words and phrases for NLP; or recurring patterns of data over time that can be used to predict trends. A straightforward public relations system is wholly dependent on data and is able to derive any conclusion or model from the data on its own, which enables it to accurately and swiftly discover patterns. The phases of preprocessing, feature extraction, and classification are the fundamental building blocks of any pattern recognition method.

Identifying patterns has been an ongoing project for a considerable amount of time. It encompasses a variety of strategies that encourage the development of a wide variety of applications in a variety of disciplines. Preprocessing, feature extraction, and classification are the three stages that are absolutely necessary for the pattern identification procedure. After the information has been obtained, it is subjected to a step known as preprocessing in order to get it ready for the subsequent subprocesses. The transformation of the information into a list of feature vectors that are designed to provide an accurate representation of the primary data is referred to as feature extraction. These characteristics are what the classification technique relies on to partition the data components into the many different problem categories. The goal of preprocessing is to separate the fascinating pattern from the background noise so that further analysis can be performed. It is utilized to cut down on differences and generate outcomes that are more dependable. In preprocessing, you should filter out some of the noise, compress the picture, and normalize it in order to correct the image for a variety of defects, such as radical variations in the direction and intensity of the light. For the purposes of agricultural applications, for instance, it is essential to segment the infected area of photographs of wounded plant specimens. When it comes to certain tasks, it is absolutely necessary to distinguish the interesting pattern from the background of a particular picture. In pattern recognition, a solution to the issue of the high complexity of the data collection is to employ the technique of feature extraction. The result will be the conversion of the entering data into a feature vector, which is a compacted representative collection of features. This will be the conclusion. When completing the work that is required, only the data that is absolutely essential should be taken from the input data. The full height input should not be used; rather, the smaller representation should be used. The retrieved features should be straightforward to calculate, robust, rotationally steady, and immune to changes and irregularities in the picture. The next step is to select, from the input region, the optimum characteristics group that has the potential to produce the greatest precision outcomes.

When it comes to pattern identification difficulties, there are two distinct types of characteristics that can be used. Statistics, mathematical or structural characteristics, and both have their own individual meanings in terms of the body's physiology. Another kind of characteristic has nothing to do with the body in any manner at all. In this context, the phrase "identifying characteristics" is applicable. One of the benefits of having physical characteristics is that they are not limited by inconsequential considerations. In spite of the fact that the mapping characteristics make the processing more complicated, they do have the benefit of making categorization easier because they define distinct boundaries between the different categories. The majority of strategies for selecting features involve performing a random survey over the complete region. Because the number of characteristics causes the area of the input space to increase at an exponential rate, heuristic techniques such as hill ascending are generally required to be used. Other techniques partition the feature space into subspaces that can be searched more efficiently. Filtering and wrapping are the two methods of feature selection that are used the most frequently. Filter algorithms choose the most advantageous characteristics based on previous data without taking into consideration the bias that may be introduced by a subsequent induction process. Because of this, the effectiveness of these strategies can be considered independent of the technique of classification or the criteria for mistakes. Most feature extraction approaches require supervision. For these methods, previous information and properly labelled teaching instances are required. Linear feature extraction and nonlinear feature extraction are the two primary types of directed techniques currently in use. Techniques such as PCA, linear discriminant analysis, projection pursuit, and independent component analysis are all examples of linear feature extraction methods. Multidimensional scaling, self-organizing map, kernel PCA, PCA network, nonlinear PCA, nonlinear auto-associative network, and a few other approaches are examples of non-linear feature extraction methods. During the classification process, the algorithm recognizes each pattern by making use of the characteristics that were collected in the previous phase. It then associates each pattern with the appropriate class. The volumes cover two distinct types of educational procedures in each of their sections.

Networks [14, 15] and organisations [16, 17] utilise sophisticated techniques to identify and respond to assaults [18, 19], and because of this, the response to an attack may be so powerful that criminals [20, 21] attempt to counter it with something even more powerful. Cybercriminals [22, 23] are becoming more sophisticated, and the potential for artificial intelligence (AI) assaults [24, 25] is growing. However, cybersecurity [26] is at a crucial crossroads, and the discipline has to concentrate its future research efforts on cyber-attack [27, 28] prediction systems that can foresee important situations and consequences rather than depending on defensive solutions and emphasising mitigation. Systems based on a thorough, predictive analysis of cyber risks [29–32] are required for computer systems all around the world.

27.5   Conclusion

Classifiers are a subtype of supervised learning, and as such, they comprise both information about each pattern group as well as a standard or measure for distinguishing them from one another. The goal of unsupervised learning is to discover fundamental patterns in the data, which can then be used to determine the appropriate output value for new data examples. This is accomplished by changing the system parameters based solely on the information received from the input, while being constrained by internal constraints that have been predetermined. For example, a face/non-face classification problem arises when determining whether or not a specific picture includes a countenance. This problem arises when attempting to classify images. Classes, also referred to as categories due to the fact that they are referred to in some contexts, are groups of patterns that share comparable feature values based on a measure. The method of learning that was applied in order to arrive at the outcome value in this stage is taken into consideration when classifying pattern recognition. At this point in the process, we are able to identify an object or a pattern by making use of the particular characteristics (features) collected in earlier phases. It is the process by which each input value of a feature vector is categorized into one of a number of different categories, and it is referred to as "feature vector categorization." During the pattern identification process, a wide variety of categorization approaches are utilized, each of which possesses its own unique set of capabilities and characteristics.

References

1. Naziya, S. and Deshmukh, R.R., Speech recognition system- a review. *IOSR J. Comput. Eng. (IOSR-JCE)*, 18, 4, 01–09, Jul.-Aug. 16.
2. Campbell, W.M., Sturim, D.E. *et al.*, The MIT- LL/IBM speaker recognition system using high performance reduced complexity recognition, MIT Lincoln Laboratory IBM, 2006.
3. Brady, K., Brandstein, M. *et al.*, An evaluation of audio-visual person recognition on the XM2VTS corpus using the Lausanne protocol, MIT Lincoln Laboratory, 244 Wood St., Lexington MA.
4. Kim, M.-H., Jang, D.-S., Yang, Y.-K., A robust-invariant pattern recognition model using fuzzy art. *Pattern Recognit.*, 34, 8, 1685–1696, 2001.
5. Vapnik, V.N., An overview of statistical learning theory. *IEEE Trans. Neural Networks*, 10, 5, 988–999, 1999.
6. Ruiz, L.R., Interactive pattern recognition applied to natural language processing, Thesis, 2010.
7. Cai, J. and Liu, Z.-Q., Pattern recognition using Markov random field models. *Pattern Recognit.*, 35, 3, 725–733, 002.
8. Girolami, M. and He, C., Probability density estimation from optimally condensed data samples. *IEEE Trans. Pattern Anal. Mach. Intell.*, 25, 10, 1253–1264, Oct. 2003.
9. Srivastava, S., Gupta, M.R., Frigyik, B.A., Bayesian quadratic discriminant analysis. *J. Mach. Learn. Res.*, 8, 1277–1305, 2007.
10. Saberi, M., Azadeh, A., Nourmohammadzadeh, A., Pazhoheshfar, P., Comparing performance and robustness of SVM and ANN for fault diagnosis in a centrifugal pump. *19th International Congress on Modelling and Simulation, Perth, Australia*, 12–16 December 2011.
11. Kannadhasan, S. and Suresh, R., EMD algorithm for robust image watermarking. *Recent Advances in Mechanical Engineering and Interdisciplinary Developments Organized by Ponjesly*

College of Engineering (ICRAMID 2014), Nagercoil, on 7-8 March 2014, Published *Adv. Mat. Res.*, 984-985, 1255–1260, 2014, ISSN No:1022-6680.

12. Watanabe, S., *Pattern recognition: Human and mechanical*, Wiley, New York, 1985.

13. Kannadhasan, S. and Rajesh Baba, M., A novel approach to detect text in various dynamic-color images. *Mathematics and its Applications Organized by University College of Engineering*, Anna University Villupuram (ICMAA 2014) on 15-17 December 2014, *Mach. Learn. Res.*, Sci. Publishing Group, 1, 1, 19–32, December 2016, doi: 10.11648/j.mlr.20160101.13.

14. Mahor, V., Bijrothiya, S., Rawat, R., Kumar, A., Garg, B., Pachlasiya, K., IoT and artificial intelligence techniques for public safety and security, in: *Smart Urban Computing Applications*, p. 111, 2023.

15. Mahor, V., Pachlasiya, K., Garg, B., Chouhan, M., Telang, S., Rawat, R., Mobile operating system (Android) vulnerability analysis using machine learning, in: *Proceedings of International Conference on Network Security and Blockchain Technology: ICNSBT 2021*, pp. 159–169, Springer Nature Singapore, Singapore, 2022, June

16. Rawat, R., Garg, B., Pachlasiya, K., Mahor, V., Telang, S., Chouhan, M., Mishra, R., SCNTA: Monitoring of network availability and activity for identification of anomalies using machine learning approaches. *Int. J. Inf. Technol. Web Eng. (IJITWE)*, 17, 1, 1–19, 2022.

17. Rawat, R., Rimal, Y.N., William, P., Dahima, S., Gupta, S., Sankaran, K.S., Malware threat affecting financial organization analysis using machine learning approach. *Int. J. Inf. Technol. Web Eng. (IJITWE)*, 17, 1, 1–20, 2022.

18. Rawat, R., Mahor, V., Chouhan, M., Pachlasiya, K., Telang, S., Garg, B., Systematic literature review (SLR) on social media and the digital transformation of drug trafficking on darkweb, in: *International Conference on Network Security and Blockchain Technology*, pp. 181–205, Springer, Singapore, 2022.

19. Rawat, R., Ayodele Oki, O., Sankaran, S., Florez, H., Ajagbe, S.A., Techniques for predicting dark web events focused on the delivery of illicit products and ordered crime. *Int. J. Electr. Comput. Eng. (IJECE)*, 13, 5, 5354–5365, Oct. 2023, doi: 10.11591/ijece.v13i5.pp5354-5365.

20. Rawat, R., Garg, B., Mahor, V., Telang, S., Pachlasiya, K., Chouhan, M., Organ trafficking on the dark web—The data security and privacy concern in healthcare systems, in: *Internet of Healthcare Things: Machine Learning for Security and Privacy*, pp. 189–216, 2022.

21. Vyas, P., Vyas, G., Chauhan, A., Rawat, R., Telang, S., Gottumukkala, M., Anonymous trading on the dark online marketplace: An exploratory study, in: *Using Computational Intelligence for the Dark Web and Illicit Behavior Detection*, pp. 272–289, IGI Global, 2022.

22. Rawat, R., Oki, O.A., Sankaran, K.S., Olasupo, O., Ebong, G.N., Ajagbe, S.A., A new solution for cyber security in big data using machine learning approach, in: *Mobile Computing and Sustainable Informatics: Proceedings of ICMCSI 2023*, pp. 495–505, Springer Nature Singapore, Singapore, 2023.

23. Rawat, R., Chakrawarti, R.K., Raj, A., Mani, G., Chidambarathanu, K., Bhardwaj, R., Association rule learning for threat analysis using traffic analysis and packet filtering approach. *Int. J. Inf. Technol.*, 1–11, 2023.

24. Rawat, R., Logical concept mapping and social media analytics relating to cyber criminal activities for ontology creation. *Int. J. Inf. Technol.*, 15, 2, 893–903, 2023.

25. Rawat, R., Mahor, V., Álvarez, J.D., Ch, F., Cognitive systems for dark web cyber delinquent association malignant data crawling: A review, in: *Handbook of Research on War Policies, Strategies, and Cyber Wars*, pp. 45–63, 2023.

26. Rawat, R., Chakrawarti, R.K., Vyas, P., Gonzáles, J.L.A., Sikarwar, R., Bhardwaj, R., Intelligent fog computing surveillance system for crime and vulnerability identification and tracing. *Int. J. Inf. Secur. Priv. (IJISP)*, 17, 1, 1–25, 2023.

27. Rawat, R., Sowjanya, A.M., Patel, S.I., Jaiswal, V., Khan, I., Balaram, A. (Eds.), *Using Machine Intelligence: Autonomous Vehicles Volume 1*, John Wiley & Sons, 2022.

28. Rawat, R., Mahor, V., Díaz-Álvarez, J., Chávez, F., Rooted learning model at fog computing analysis for crime incident surveillance, in: *2022 International Conference on Smart Generation Computing, Communication and Networking (SMART GENCON)*, pp. 1–9, IEEE, 2022, December.

29. Rawat, R. and Shrivastav, S.K., SQL injection attack detection using SVM. *Int. J. Comput. Appl.*, 42, 13, 1–4, 2012.

30. Rawat, R., Bhardwaj, P., Kaur, U., Telang, S., Chouhan, M., Sankaran, K.S., *Smart vehicles for communication, volume 2*, John Wiley & Sons, 2023.

31. Mahor, V., Garg, B., Telang, S., Pachlasiya, K., Chouhan, M., Rawat, R., Cyber threat phylogeny assessment and vulnerabilities representation at thermal power station, in: *Proceedings of International Conference on Network Security and Blockchain Technology: ICNSBT 2021*, pp. 28–39, Springer Nature Singapore, Singapore, 2022, June.

32. Rawat, R., Gupta, S., Sivaranjani, S., Cu, O.K., Kuliha, M., Sankaran, K.S., Malevolent information crawling mechanism for forming structured illegal organisations in hidden networks. *Int. J. Cyber Warf. Terror. (IJCWT)*, 12, 1, 1–14, 2022.

A Review of Renewable Energy Efficiency Technologies Toward Conversational AI

S. Kannadhasan[1]* and R. Nagarajan[2]

*[1]Department of Electronics and Communication Engineering,
Study World College of Engineering, Tamil Nadu, India*
*[2]Department of Electrical and Electronics Engineering, Gnanamani College of Technology,
Namakkal, Tamil Nadu, India*

Abstract

During the 1970s and the early 1980s, people gave a lot of attention to energy planning and how they could save energy. The oil supply was reduced as a result of the 1973 OPEC oil blockage and the 1979 Iranian hostage crisis, both of which contributed significantly to the sharp increase in oil prices. The increase in the price of petroleum led to an acceleration of the development of renewable energy sources in both the commercial and public sectors, such as solar, wind, geothermal, and methane. Nevertheless, as petroleum prices declined in the late 1980s, the nation's commitment to renewable energy began to fade. At a period when nonrenewable natural resources were selling for such low prices, neither the government nor the general public were prepared to invest in green energy initiatives and sources that were more expensive. There has been a recent uptick in interest in the field of energy, particularly renewable energy. This desire is not the result of quickly rising energy prices because nonrenewable energy sources such as petroleum are easily attainable and relatively inexpensive. Instead, concerns about the environment, particularly the combustion of fossil fuels, which many people believe to have a substantial impact on both acid rain and global warming, have sparked a revived interest in the topic as a whole. Awareness of America's growing dependence on foreign resources is another element that is helping to stimulate interest in issues pertaining to energy. This became abundantly clear during the conflict in the Persian Gulf. Concerns about energy strategy at the public level have a significant bearing on the business. Citizens and those in decision-making positions not only need to have a fundamental understanding of the various types of energy sources, but they also need to be able to analyse energy problems by applying fundamental economic concepts.

Keywords: Conversational AI, chatbot, autobot and energy AI

Corresponding author: kannadhasan.ece@gmail.com
S. Kannadhasan: ORCID: https://orcid.org/0000-0001-6443-9993
R. Nagarajan: ORCID: https://orcid.org/0000-0002-4990-5869

Romil Rawat, Rajesh Kumar Chakrawarti, Sanjaya Kumar Sarangi, Piyush Vyas, Mary Sowjanya Alamanda, Kotagiri Srividya and Krishnan Sakthidasan Sankaran (eds.) Conversational Artificial Intelligence, (477–494) © 2024 Scrivener Publishing LLC

28.1   Introduction

Vitality [1–3] can be defined as the capability to carry out responsibilities. The British thermal unit [4, 5], abbreviated "Btu," is the unit of measurement that is used to calculate how much heat is contained in various energy sources. One Btu is equal to the amount of thermal energy required to increase the temperature of one pound of water by one Fahrenheit degree Celsius. Btu is an infinitesimal quantity. One Btu [6, 7] of energy is generated, for instance, when a hardwood culinary match is allowed to burn to its completion without being extinguished. These fundamental kinds of energy can be broken down into two categories: renewable and nonrenewable [8, 9]. Energy sources are considered renewable if they can be readily replenished or if they cannot be depleted. A few examples of renewable energy sources are solar, wind, geothermal, and methane. The quantity of energy that comes from nonrenewable sources is limited. If we continue to use them, eventually, they will run out of energy for themselves. Examples of this include coal, natural gas, and various other solid substances. Due to the fact that electricity is a secondary energy source, it can only be manufactured using primary energy sources [10–12]. The generation of electricity in the United States is responsible for approximately 28% [12, 13] of the country's general primary energy consumption. The production of energy can be broken down into five primary categories: coal, nuclear power, electricity, and natural gas and petroleum. Electricity [14, 15], on the other hand, does not fit neatly into either the category of renewable or nonrenewable fundamental sources.

A rise in energy consumption has occurred concurrently with the expansion of both the business and the population in the United States [16, 17]. In spite of this, there have been significant leaps forward in terms of energy efficiency to accompany this development. For example, energy consumption in the United States increased by approximately 9% between 1973 and 1989, but the country's gross domestic product (the sum of all the products and services produced by the industry in a given year) increased by 46% during the same time period! The United States' energy production as a proportion of its gross national product has increased at least as quickly as in other industrialized countries. The steep rises in the price of natural oil that occurred in the 1970s were primarily responsible for this improvement in energy efficiency. Solar energy is transformed into usable forms by all forms of vegetation. The process of photosynthesis, which involves the combination of carbon dioxide, water, and various other elements to produce carbohydrates, is how plants store the energy they take in during the course of the day. Burning is the most prevalent method that is used to discharge energy that is stored in vegetation. Fermentation, bacterial decomposition, and conversion are three additional processes that are used, albeit much less frequently. Wood and agricultural products, solid waste, landfill emissions, and fuels derived from alcohol are the four primary categories of biomass. The vast majority of sustainable energy comes from wood, which accounts for approximately 90% of the total. Burning significant garbage produced by humans is a practice that dates back thousands of years and is still widely used today. It is an innovative approach to generate electricity by using garbage as fuel. Traditional coal-fired power stations are very similar in operation to their more modern counterparts, which generate steam by burning garbage instead of traditional coal. The production of electricity through the use of wood typically results in increased expenses; however, one significant benefit is that there is a reduction in the amount of waste that is dumped in landfills. There are some environmental concerns that are raised by waste-to-energy plants; however, considering how difficult it is to locate suitable disposal locations, these plants are beginning to appear more and more appealing. Sustainable energy has emerged as one of the most significant and promising facets of the international movement to protect the natural resources and pristine environment of the planet for the benefit of future generations. India has taken the initiative to head this project, which will demonstrate to other developing countries how to continue their economic and societal development without endangering the environment. Renewable energy is beginning to play a bigger part when it comes to improving electric power, increasing energy availability, decreasing India's dependence on fossil fuels, and advancing India's strategy for low-carbon development. All of these goals are being pursued by India.

Intended Nationally Determined Contribution (INDC) was a document that outlined India's post-2020 climate plans that was presented to the United Nations Framework Convention on Climate Change (UNFCCC) prior to the 21st Conference of the Parties (COP 21). In addition to its initial goal of adding 175 gigawatts (GW) of renewable power capacity by the year 2022, India's INDC establishes a new target to increase the country's proportion of constructed non-fossil energy capacity to 40% by the year 2030. This target is part of India's commitment to the UNFCCC. President Narendra Modi, the Prime Minister of India, gave a speech at the inaugural event of the Climate Action Conference on September 23, 2019, which took place at the same time as the United Nations General Assembly. Renewable energy is often referred to as "clean energy" due to the fact that it does not release any contaminants into the environment and is generated from naturally replenishable resources such as sunshine and wind. The quantities of non-renewable energy sources, such as coal, gas, and oil, are decreasing at an alarming rate, which is driving a greater shift toward the utilization of renewable energy sources. The production of green energy has increased all over the world as a result of a number of factors, including rising prices for fossil fuels, in particular for electricity and natural gas, concerns about the environment, the requirement for increased energy security, and increased investment in clean energy.

When compared to the 10 years that are typically required for conventional power projects, the time it takes to bring renewable energy projects into operation from the point at which they are first conceptualized is significantly shorter. In point of fact, the installation of solar power devices may take less than a year to complete. People living off the grid in India may also have access to energy choices that are more reasonable, and the use of renewable energy sources may offer up employment possibilities for local laborers, including opportunities for both professional and informal labor. When compared to conventional energy, renewable energy generates a substantially higher number of employment per unit of electricity generated. The overwhelming majority of these positions are located in the immediate area. Green energy, which has almost no fuel expenses and little impact on the atmosphere, has the potential to diminish the world's increasing dependence on foreign fossil fuels and their volatile values. Green energy also has fewer negative effects on the environment. India has committed, in accordance with its Globally Determined Obligations under the Paris Climate Agreement, to derive at least 40% of its total energy output capability from non-fossil fuel sources by the year 2030. This target will be met if India is successful in meeting its commitment. As of the 29th of February in the year 2020, the nation had an established renewable energy production of 132.45 GW, in addition to an additional 46.69 GW that was in various stages of implementation and 34.07 GW that was in various stages of procurement. The capacity of the nation's permanent non-fossil fuel sources had reached 139.22 GW as of the same date. As of the 29th of February in the year 2020, the overall possibility of generating electricity from non-fossil fuel sources and renewable energy sources combined was 369.41 GW, and the corresponding percentages of each were 35.85% and 37.68%.

When planning the use of renewable energy initiatives across the country, it is important to take into account the possibility of using a particular green energy source. Recent assertions made by Shri R. K. Singh, India's Minister of Electricity and New and Renewable Energy, indicate that by the year 2025, the country will have approximately 60% of its total energy. During a webinar that the Energy Resource Institute (TERI) hosted, he made this declaration in order to promote the reports that the organization authored titled "Renewable Power Pathways: Modelling the Integration of Wind and Solar in India by 2030" and "Bending the Curve: 2025 Forecasts for Electricity Demand by Sector and State in Light of the COVID Epidemic." Both of these reports can be found on the TERI website. According to the minister's projections, there will be 510 GW of accessible renewable energy by the year 2030, with 60 GW originating from water. Because of its technological advantage, India is in a position to provide investors with the boost they require while also encouraging the development of new technologies. Getting money at an affordable price for the prospective development of the industry is another significant challenge that must be overcome. This problem has been addressed by making inexpensive new project financing accessible for all upcoming initiatives, particularly small- and medium-sized businesses. Solar parks, solar roof tops, solar defense, solar schemes for power plants, solar pumps, and solar terraces have all been made possible thanks to the implementation of a number of significant programs and schemes.

The vast majority of the country's green energy projects that will be connected to the infrastructure are being developed by producers from the commercial sector. These producers were chosen through an open bidding procedure. The Indian Renewable Energy Development Agency (IREDA), a Non-Banking Financial Institution that is under the administrative control of the Ministry of New and Renewable Energy, raises money from both internal and external sources, such as bilateral and multilateral agencies, raising bonds from the international & domestic market, and borrowing from banks or financial institutions, in order to finance renewable energy and energy efficiency projects in the country. IREDA is an organization that is under the administrative control of the Ministry of New and Renewable Energy. Major banks and other financial organizations are also providing financing for green energy initiatives at interest rates that are lower than average thanks to the utilization of credit lines provided by the World Bank, the Asian Development Bank, and other similar organizations.

In addition to the categories that were already in place, the Reserve Bank of India has updated the requirements that apply to all authorized commercial institutions so that they now include environmentally friendly energy as one of the important areas. Tax breaks may be available to taxpayers who take out loans to finance the purchase of solar rooftop systems because these loans are considered a form of home improvement or mortgage debt. Under the automatic methodology, the green energy industry has been opened up to receiving 100% of foreign direct investment (FDI). The energy industry in India is undergoing transformation as a direct consequence of the growing contribution of renewable energy to the country's overall energy equilibrium. Finding the necessary financing to generate 175 GW of green energy by 2022, which is an innovative objective, is one of the primary obstacles that must be overcome in order to make such a change. Other obstacles include the fact that the difficulty that businesses in this sector have in securing private financing, in conjunction with the limited financial resources that are available, contributes to the escalation of the problem. In light of this, and looking at it from the vantage point of India, the current research provides a comprehensive overview of the difficulties that are associated with acquiring such funds. Our comprehension is enhanced as a result of the focus placed on the various new financial options for renewable energy sources, in addition to the challenges that these options entail. The conclusions shed a great deal of light on the situation. The present financial market in India is characterized by a number of challenges that make it difficult to finance renewable energy initiatives. These challenges include limited credit periods, expensive capital costs, a dearth of appropriate debt financing, and a number of other similar issues. In addition to the difficulties that are unique to the sustainable energy business, these problems also exist. Innovative strategies and financial instruments need to be put into practice for there to be any chance of success. Any nation's ability to realize its expansion objectives is directly tied to the state of its energy sector. The connection between energy and climate change has dominated the policy debate at a time when calls for wise energy sector reforms are being made to stop the imminent dangers of climate change. This has resulted in the importance of energy receiving a new boost at a time when these events have taken place. India, one of the countries with the highest rates of economic growth in the world, has recently gone through a period of time in which it has experienced significant changes to its energy systems and structures as a direct result of deliberate policy efforts designed to support renewable energy. This is in accordance with India's expanding sociopolitical significance on the international scene as a country that is increasingly leading the world's green energy policy, which is also supported by the fact that this is the case. India's decision to establish the International Solar Alliance (ISA) on December 1 in order to mobilize collaborative global efforts to address problems relating to climate change is a striking demonstration of the remarkable geopolitical significance of India's move. Given the steep rise in domestic energy demand caused by accelerated urbanization as a result of initiatives such as "Smart City Programs" and recent manufacturing efforts such as "Make in India," it is important for legislators to actively support renewable energy sources.

The government of India has established a national objective to provide all communities with electricity 24 hours a day by the year 2019, and it is anticipated that there will be an additional 600 million energy customers by the year 2040, which will result in a substantial increase in demand. According to recent studies, the nation's demand for electricity is expected to more than double by the year 2040, moving from its current capability of 300 GW to more than 1,000 GW. As a consequence of this, it will be difficult to accurately predict the path that the nation's energy sector will take in the future as it becomes less dangerous, more environmentally friendly, and more technologically advanced. The Indian electricity industry is continuing to be corrupted in a variety of ways, which presents a number of difficulties. The nation's electrical industry is still being negatively impacted by operational issues such as decreasing capacity factors, the financial uncertainty of the businesses that source power distribution, and infrastructure-related issues. These issues continue to have a negative impact. India is well known for being one of the world's energy poor regions due to the fact that its individual power availability is close to one-third of the global average and approximately 239 million people still do not have even the most rudimentary access to electricity. It would appear that a transformation to a low-carbon system that places a priority on renewable energy sources is possible, despite the existence of such abnormalities. Already, we can see the beginnings of how these changes will manifest themselves. For instance, the year 2017 was regarded as a watershed year in the history of the development of renewable energy in the country primarily because of two significant events: first, for the first time in India's history, the addition of renewable energy capacity has outpaced the addition of conventional capacity, and second, the year 2017 also witnessed an unprecedented decline in the price of renewable energy, in particular the price of solar energy. Combined, these two significant events contributed to the year 2017 being regarded as a watershed year in the history of However, transitioning to a source of electricity with lower carbon emissions is not an easy task. Producing sustainable energy faces a number of obstacles in the form of systematic, governmental, and societal roadblocks, despite the apparent promise that it holds. In spite of the fact that there is a crystal clear strategic policy emphasis on expanding green energy in the country, the vision remains cloudy as a result of the complicated political structure of the country as well as the variety of governmental institutions that regulate the energy sector. The organizational framework of the renewable energy industry in India also presents challenges for the sector as a whole. This is shown by the fact that the private sector is completely responsible for pushing the development of the green energy industry, in opposition to the conventional energy industry, where two-thirds of the capacity is directly owned by the federal and state governments.

28.2   Renewable Energy

Given the nation's emphasis on private-sector-driven and commercially oriented green energy development, one of the most significant challenges that the industry faces is locating the necessary financing, which is comprehensible given the nature of the sector. To be more specific, one of the major challenges that appears to stand in the way of accomplishing the audacious goal of adding 175 GW of green energy production by the year 2022 is the lack of affordable and sufficient financing. When it comes to the topic of purchasing environmentally friendly energy, one of the most important questions to ask is "where would all of these funds come from?" Growing renewable energy in India appears to be more difficult due to the fact that the country's business sector is more vulnerable to the accompanying risks and uncertainties.

In the framework of this discussion, the current research takes a critical look at India's support for renewable energy. This article's goals are to (1) provide readers with a comprehensive understanding of the structure and pattern of financing for green energy in India and (2) identify the primary roadblocks to obtaining the necessary funding for the sector. The purpose of this article is to provide readers with a thorough understanding of the structure and pattern of financing for green energy in India. This article contributes to the corpus of information about the financing of renewable energy sources by describing the strategies for funding renewable energy sources as well as the accompanying difficulties with reference to the environment in India. It is widely held that the global oil crisis that occurred in the late 1980s served as the impetus for India to accelerate the development of its renewable energy industry. Since then, the government of India has advanced the field of renewable energy by taking a number of significant measures in the areas of policy and legislation. In light of the fact that energy is statutorily designated as a parallel item, both the federal government and the governments of the provinces periodically produce successful policy initiatives with the intention of growing the green energy industry (entry 38 in the concurrent list). The most recent attempt by a government to transition to a greener energy system is the innovative energy strategy recently implemented by the Government of India. This strategy aims to generate 175 MW of renewable energy by the year 2022. Solar power has been given a significant position in the green energy inventory as a result of the particular policy declaration that was developed as part of the Jawaharlal Nehru National Solar Project (JNNSM). The emphasis placed on renewable energy is borne out by comparable policy-level initiatives, such as the deliverance of electricity availability 24 hours a day, 7 days a week across the entire country by the year 2019. This point is driven home even further by India's submission of its Globally Determined Contributions to the United Nations Framework Convention on Climate Change (INDCs).

The commitment made by nations around the world to acquire at least 40% of their energy from sustainable resources by the year 2040 is a powerful indication of the significance that policymakers attach to this topic. In addition, the present energy equilibrium of the country demonstrates how the federal government is shifting its emphasis on energy production with a growing percentage of nontraditional energy sources. The nation's overall competence is displayed and shown in [2, 4], broken down by source. According to the statistics that were presented earlier, which account for approximately 18% of the country's total capacity, or approximately 57,245 MW, the possibility of generating renewable energy has increased to a new high point. More than half of this total capacity is derived from the energy of the wind, while another 20% is derived from the energy of the sun, and the remaining 20% is derived from sources such as small water, methane, and waste-to-energy conversion. However, the most recent pattern reveals that solar energy is taking up an increasingly significant quantity of space in the collection of renewable energy sources. Green energy networks are very different from traditional electricity systems from a technological point of view. As a direct result of this, the two markets have distinctively dissimilar aspects of pricing. Green energy initiatives require a significant investment of capital but do not call for the use of any fuel, in contrast to conventional energy systems. The average monthly electricity costs are improved as a direct consequence of these one-time expenditures, which do not reoccur, because they are now more stable. Taking into account the technological facets of the sector, it is anticipated that approximately $189 billion in expenditures will be required in order to accomplish the ambitious goal of implementing 175 MW that has been established by the Government of India.

It would be interesting to learn more about how India's renewable energy industry is structured. In contrast to the conventional energy industry, the industrial sector is the primary force behind the growth of the green energy business. The sector is tasked with bringing in private funding at a rate and in a timeframe that are proportionate to the objectives and objectives of the policy. Given the constraints placed on the availability of public funds, this is of the utmost importance. Almost any quantity of state financing, no matter how insignificant, is almost always used as assistance money to encourage private capital to engage in the industry. It is predicated on the idea that the private sector has the ability to support the business, despite the fact that the government must first establish a favorable environment in order for the private sector to be able to do so. In the past quarter of a century, the ideas of sustainability and environmentally friendly energy sources have combined to become an essential component of modern life. These ideas are at the intersection of many different fields, including science, technology, culture, the economics, politics, and the environment. Both of these ideas have been proposed as potential solutions to the problems that are caused by human activities, which include the depletion of natural resources, the use of energy and water, and the emission of carbon emissions that contribute to climate change.

Researchers have been compelled to develop sources of sustainable and green fuels in order to guarantee energy consumption, safeguard the environment, and support regional development as a result of the energy crisis as well as other environmental, economic, political, market, and cultural problems. Processes that are more open and inclusive, which take into consideration the views, objectives, and perspectives of many different parties, have been linked to the acceptance of environmentally friendly energy sources that are both effective and feasible over time, particularly at the community level. Many different approaches have been used in the research that's been done on the challenges that come with sustainability and environmentally friendly energy. One of these is the practice of scenario preparation. Its goal is to improve responsiveness to a variety of variables while simultaneously reducing the amount of uncertainty that exists. Kowalski *et al.* reduce the amount of uncertainty in the process of energy development by combining scenario planning and multifactor analysis (also known as MCA), which is an approach in which a number of different stakeholders are included in the decision-making process and a wide variety of social, economic, environmental, and technical criteria are taken into consideration.

On the other hand, the connection between green energy initiatives and the overall sustainability of a particular community or system is given a lot of importance as a system that is sustainable as a technology. Sustainable sources of energy are frequently attributed with assuring the continued existence of certain regions by providing those regions with a diverse range of advantages, both social and environmental. When conducting these evaluations, the surveillance of data is the primary method for determining particular aspects of sustainability (ecological, societal, and economic), and the variable nature of sustainability is rarely taken into consideration. The problem of sustainability is a systemic one, not a technological or organizational one, despite the fact that this point is rarely brought up in the writing on environmentally friendly energy. When conducting an analysis of the sustainability of an energy system, a significant amount of attention is placed on the worth of comprehending the complexity of the system, adaptive management, and the adaptive capability in the effective implementation of sustainable energy technologies. The socioecological systems theory and the science of sustainability are utilized in order to accomplish this goal.

Multiple criteria decision-making, also known as MCDM, can be of assistance in accomplishing this goal, despite the complexity of sustainability and the requirement to provide a path toward the realization of a sustainable future. Because of the complexities involved in sustainability, decisions need to be made in a manner that is well organized, transparent, and trustworthy. Literature that is both theoretical and philosophical, as well as literature that is more functional, has been evaluated. This review aims to give examples of how various approaches and techniques have been applied to issues with sustainable and green energy sources, as well as a summary of some important MCDM methods and techniques that have been proposed over the course of time. This review also aims to give examples of how various approaches and techniques have been applied to issues with sustainable and green energy sources. The examples were selected in order to provide a comprehensive overview of all approaches and strategies that have been utilized in recent years in order to address issues pertaining to the environment, sustainability, and green energy. This article examines the primary benefits that can be gained from utilizing a variety of strategies and methods, as well as any potential drawbacks. Last but not least, the findings of this study suggest that a productive application of MCDM would be to make use of a variety of methods in order to address issues relating to green and sustainable forms of energy. Despite the fact that some earlier studies reviewed the significance of MCDM techniques like multiple criteria decision-making analysis in sustainable energy and sustainable energy planning, this kind of challenge has not been effectively addressed in MCDM review studies. The purpose of this paper is to conduct a literature review in order to identify the studies that have been published in reputable journals and have supplied practitioners and researchers who investigate issues relating to sustainable and renewable energy systems as well as MCDM and FMCDM techniques and approaches with the most important information. These studies have been selected based on the following criteria: (1) they have provided practitioners and researchers who investigate issues relating to sustainable and renewable energy systems. For this reason, a thorough search was conducted to discover MCDM and FMCDM in the research techniques, headlines, descriptions, and buzzwords of the articles that were found. This study makes an effort to chronicle the rapidly expanding interest in MCDM and FMCDM methods and approaches. Furthermore, it provides a current and up-to-date overview of the literature on sustainable and green energy systems, as well as on the applications of MCDM and its methodology. The use of a categorization system allowed for the creation of a reference collection that contains a total of 54 articles that have been published since 2003 in more than 30 publications. The articles are sorted into categories based on the research parameters, MCDM techniques and approaches, publication year, application regions, and the names of the magazines. The three contributions that this paper makes are the development of a classification system with a focus on practicality, a structural review of the literature to guide future research on sustainable and renewable energy systems, MCDM applications, and methodologies, and the identification of problems that require further study.

28.3   Energy Technologies

In addition to being analyzed from a fresh viewpoint, each of the articles is evaluated after being first sorted into one of two categories: green energy systems or sustainable energy systems. Because it contains the most significant publications in the fields of green and sustainable energy systems, Web of Science was the primary research database that we concentrated on. The assessment did not take into account things like graduate papers or master's theses, stories, magazines, or private writings of any kind. The original data used in this analysis came from 54 different referenced papers that have been published on the topic of renewable and environmentally friendly forms of energy since the year 2003. When making our selection of the 54 scholastic journal papers, we took into consideration the substantial majority of the international writings that dealt with the topics of MCDM as well as secure and environmentally friendly energy sources. Renewable Energy, Energy Policy, Applied Energy, Energy Conversion and Management, Energy Journal, Journal of Environmental

Management, Renewable and Sustainable Energy Reviews, Solar Energy, European Journal of Operational Research, Applied Soft Computing, Expert Systems with Applications, Journal of Cleaner Production, Energy and Buildings, etc., are some of the journals that are mentioned in this review. Other journals that are mentioned include Energy Journal, Journal of Environmental Management, Energy Conversion and Management, Energy Journal, Energy Policy, Applied Energy, Energy Journal, and Journal of Clean. Because the vast majority of research articles on sustainable and green energy systems, MCDM applications, and methods were published after 2003, we made an effort to evaluate the application of these methodologies in more recent years. As a direct consequence of this, this year was selected as the point of departure for the research. It is obvious that a number of the articles could not be acquired as a result of the restricted online database access point; consequently, these articles were not included in our investigation. Following the completion of a thorough perusal of each paper, a summary and any pertinent notes were attached. It is taken into consideration in this research if a paper thoroughly addresses the development and implementation of MCDM for the purpose of addressing problems associated with sustainability and green energy systems.

Because of the rapid rate at which natural resources are being depleted, there is an urgent requirement for the development of sustainable sources of energy in order to meet the ever-increasing demand for energy on a worldwide scale. The increasing problem of global warming is another important argument that supports the idea that we should reduce our dependence on natural fuels. The establishment of new electricity infrastructure in the future will be greatly reliant on technologies that can generate renewable energy. The production of electricity from natural energy sources such as wind, sunlight, micro-hydro, vegetation, ocean waves, geothermal, and storms is one of the sustainable energy methods. Other renewable energy methods include the fact that the benefits of the previously mentioned energy systems, which include supply security, reduced carbon pollution, improved power quality, reliability, and employment opportunities for the local people, are frequently what spur the acceptance of these energy systems. Considering the intermittent nature of renewable energy (RE) resources, blended combinations of two or more methods of power production along with storing may increase the effectiveness of the system. A hybrid renewable energy system (HRES) combines two or more forms of renewable energy with one or more conventional forms of energy (such as a gasoline or hydrocarbon engine) and storage in order to meet the demands of a specific location. When evaluating the effectiveness of hybrid systems, simulation tools are by far the most common and commonly used technique. Computer models can be utilized to evaluate the effectiveness and cost of energy generation across a variety of system designs. This allows for the selection of the most suitable design. For the purpose of constructing hybrid architectures, a wide variety of software development environments are available, including HOMER, HYBRID2, HOGA, and HYBRIDS.

The National Renewable Energy Laboratory is responsible for the development of the user-friendly HOMER software (Hybrid Optimization Model for Electric Renewables). Optimization is performed based on the Net Current Cost, and an analysis of the combined renewable energy system is carried out utilizing hourly models and environmental statistics. HOMER has seen significant application in a variety of different case studies. The Department of Electrical Engineering at the University of Zaragoza in Spain is responsible for the creation of the HOGA software, which is used for hybrid system modeling.

The training is carried out in 1-hour increments at a time. The Renewable Energy Research Laboratory (RERL) at the University of Massachusetts developed the hybrid system engineering software that is known as HYBRID. The game is played over the course of 10–60 minutes on each run. Hybrids is a piece of evaluation software and planning tool developed by Solaris Residences. The utility makes use of spreadsheets created in Microsoft Excel. In contrast to HOMER, HYBRIDS are only capable of imitating a single configuration at any given time. Although it is apparent that SMES is the most effective cutting-edge technology currently available, the fact that the coil makes use of superconductive wire also means that it is quite pricey. When there is insufficient technological assistance available, it is not recommended to use supercapacitors or hydrogen storage. The PHS system has a high initial investment, making it unsuitable for applications that require only a small amount of electricity. Although CAES is a comparatively inexpensive energy storage technology, the gadget must be installed in compressed-air storage caverns. All aspects, including the techniques, unit capacity and effectiveness, storing, and management of energy movement, have been investigated in great detail. The research also discusses difficulties and potential shifts in behavior in the near future. The supplied literature evaluation makes the construction and power management of HRES easier for students who are anxious to learn more about it. Technologies like wind power, solar power, and water power may be used as the primary types of sustainable energy to accomplish the goal of decarbonization in the energy business. On the other hand, conventional power plants are quite different from renewable energy facilities in a number of significant respects. The proportion of renewable energy sources has increased, which has brought about a variety of difficulties, in particular in the system that generates electricity. The objective of decarbonization may be achieved with the dependability of the power system, but this objective frequently encounters a number of obstacles and malfunctions that put the achievement of the target in jeopardy. Despite this, the writing still addresses the issues and possible technological solutions only very infrequently. The purpose of this research was to examine a variety of technological issues and potential solutions, with a particular emphasis on the field of electricity networks. The most essential elements that will need to be developed in the not-too-distant future are going to be the findings of the investigation into the solution matrix as well as the technological challenges connected to it.

The establishment of a system that incorporates a variety of environmentally friendly technology options might be helpful in finding solutions to problems. The potential of the developed technological solutions is anticipated to support and assist cost-effective energy in particular. Additionally, technically based solutions that were developed collaboratively may assist in resolving some of the issues. The classifications that were developed as part of this research are put to use in order to specify particular parameters and make the incorporation of renewable energy in the future more accessible. In order to provide a comprehensive overview of the numerous technological problems and solutions, the literature research carried out for this article was organized according to a number of categories. In the first group that was examined, the differences between methodical studies that focus specifically on technological issues and remedies and other emphases related to variable renewable energy (VRE) in specific locations, such as islands or towns, were investigated. These types of studies focus specifically on technological issues and remedies. The legislation or market share assessments are put into perspective by technical or practical solutions that are immediately connected to VRE. The last topic covered is the one that serves as the foundation for identifying technological issues and possible solutions. Eliminating uncertainty and locating obstacles can be accomplished through the use of future operations and technology studies. The dependence on fundamental technological procedures is to blame for this situation. Several studies have discovered that the outcome of VRE input can be improved by a succession of impacts that build upon one another. This is made feasible because there are no additional costs required to be incurred in order to circumvent the obstacles that must be overcome in order to incorporate renewable energy. The unpredictability of the challenge, when viewed from an economic point of view, carries a lower spot price due to the fact that it takes into consideration the perspectives of the community. Adjusting uncertainty based on numerous technological constraints, such as production, is insufficient because doing so could have unexpected consequences for the various stakeholders.

For instance, selecting a challenge is not a constraint imposed by either the organization or the government. As a direct result of this, it is very simple to disregard storage from a purely technological standpoint. In reality, the restructured organizations or companies are the strategies for the technological reorganization. It is also possible that this will increase the market percentage of different technological choices for electricity systems.

As a component of upcoming research procedures, the integration of questions and technological solutions gleaned and analyzed from a variety of literature sources, as well as comments gleaned from interviewees, will play a role. The nature of the issue at hand is difficult to pin down because the words that are being used to describe it do not correspond to its portrayal. The duties are initially organized in a lengthy form, and then, subsequent forms of organization, including recurrence, are applied. The technological solutions were gathered together on the basis of two criteria: first, they needed to be able to independently incorporate obstacles into VRE and individually handle one another's problems. These kinds of restrictions are absolutely necessary to stop the accumulation of subtechnologies that could be turned into technological solutions. The smart meter is an example of a subtechnology that has the potential to respond to inquiries as they are required. However, it is not capable of resolving the issues by itself even though they are directly related to VRE. It is essential to categorize reactions to requests for technological solutions, but this is not necessary in the case of smart meters. The responsibilities described earlier form the basis for the description of the technological choices for the second group. As a result of this, the distinctions between them might, in the end, make it possible to eliminate certain technological choices. The request–response situation exemplifies the primary objective of this technology, which is to reduce the amount of electricity consumed by particular gadgets during particular time intervals. On the other hand, due to the fact that numerous devices, such as heat pumps and electric warmers, operate in a wide diversity of settings, different technological techniques are unable to perform the same functions. Based on the numerous pieces of literature that were evaluated, this research investigates the problems as well as the technological solutions. A rundown of the various obstacles faced is part of the narrative that explains how all of these interconnected technological solutions were found. The list of difficulties that was presented previously will be improved with the assistance of studies and evaluations pertaining to difficulties associated with level-based classification and difficulties associated with general causes. The investigation into the connection between the problems and possible technological solutions revealed that they are irreconcilable with one another. As a direct result of this, the technique of analysis that was utilized in this investigation sought to identify the reasons, management tools, and general tools.

28.4 Conversational AI

The smart energy business in future smart communities is one of the most challenging subjects to research because of its complexity. Important issues relating to optimization, cleverly configurable networks, and these tasks are necessary, as are sophisticated analytical tools and processes made feasible by artificial intelligence (AI) and machine learning. These issues and tasks include the fact that given the impacts that climate change is having on the world and the fact that natural resources are running out, RE is an essential resource for prospective global development. The term "artificial intelligence" refers to the process of developing new guidelines for organizing activities in order to meet new requirements. It is necessary to enhance the construction of the energy infrastructure as well as the implementation and production of RE in order to surmount the numerous challenges that will prohibit the development and resilience of the industry. These challenges include the fact that in this study, we make use of recent advances that have been made in the implementation of AI technology in the real estate industry in the European Union (EU). In this regard, we looked at I the efficiency of the processes of the RE within the energy chain from Gross Inland Consumption to Final Energy Consumption, (ii) its implications on the structure of renewable energy by source (solar, wind, biomass, etc.), (iii) the labor productivity in the RE sector compared to the economy at large and its correlation with the investment level, and (iv) the implications of the adoption of AI for RE toward future smart cities. The establishment of a philosophical framework for comprehending the role that AI plays in Europe's renewable energy industry is the primary contribution that comes from this research. An additional innovative component that was added to this article is a discussion of the ramifications for upcoming research on smart cities and the direction that future research will take. dividing up a number of fascinating applications that span across multiple domains: AI and other technologies have a tremendous amount of potential because they enable and speed up the processing of enormous amounts of data, which can expand our knowledge, assist us in better comprehending and addressing environmental concerns, and help us better manage these issues. When data collected from Earth's surveillance systems are combined with AI, it may be possible to more effectively, swiftly, and efficiently observe environmental effects and patterns. In addition, new insights into the processes that are at the root of environmental impacts are gained, and existing forecasting capabilities are improved. Information that is helpful for environmental planning, decision-making, administration, and overseeing the implementation of environmental legislation will be produced by AI. The information that is generated by AI may also assist customers and businesses in modifying their behavior in order to be more environmentally responsible. The utilization of automated navigation systems as well as technology that permits anticipatory maintenance will eventually lead to an increase in the overall level of infrastructure security.

- There are a number of crucial areas in which an environmentally friendly transformation may also demonstrate the potential of AI. The primary goals of the Green Deal for the building sector, as well as the incorporation of green energy sources into power networks, have the potential to be assisted by AI used to track and control energy use. These goals and the incorporation of green energy sources are both a part of the Green Deal. It's possible that uses in agricultural land could enable more effective utilization of resources like water, herbicides, and fertilizers, thereby reducing the number of unfavorable effects on the environment. In principle, the transportation industry operates in the same manner: techniques based on AI are already being used to improve the planning of transportation systems and infrastructure, increase the efficiency of internal combustion engines, optimize the charging of electric vehicles, coordinate various modes of transportation, and manage and control railway systems. AI may also be put to use in use cases that support the cyclical economy. For example, AI may be used to improve the efficiency of eco-design or to support the investigation, categorization, division, and disassembly procedures that are necessary for the movement of materials throughout the economy. The use cases serve as representations of how AI can be applied to combat pollution, help in the transition to climate change, conserve species, and encourage environment preservation.

It is anticipated that artificial intelligence technologies, due to their growing significance and ubiquitous application of data, will substantially contribute to the energy consumption of information and communication technologies (ICTs) toward conversational AI models. It is estimated that by the year 2030, the amount of electricity used for the transportation of data in digital networks and other forms of technology will have increased to 13% from its present level of approximately 7%. It is predicted that ICT relating to conversational AI and chatbot technologies consumes 5%–9% of the total energy used in the globe, and it is possible that by 2030, that proportion will approach 20%. It is anticipated that by the year 2020, telecommunication and data facilities located all over the globe will be responsible for the production of between 1.1 and 1.3 Gt CO2eq worth of carbon. The amount that AI and smart chatbots will eventually contribute to carbon pollution is something that will depend on the energy efficiency of data centers as well as the amount of renewable energy that is used in such locations. During the process of creating AI, it is essential to prioritize the conservation of energy and other resources as a specialized area of development.

- Systemic effects, such as return effects, are the consequence of any change, whether intentional or accidental, in the behavior of customers, users, or suppliers. These effects, which may not have been anticipated and may even be in conflict with the objective of an application to minimize its impact on the environment, may be the result of the enigmatic dynamics that underlie the learning processes of AI systems. For example, devices that are supposed to automatically monitor and implement more effective ways of using energy may instead have the opposite impact, leading users to misuse them and lose control of their behavior. Assessing the potential impact of such impacts could be difficult. Nevertheless, as recent research demonstrates, such an evaluation is certainly a possibility to consider. It is possible that a greater comprehension of the patterns and processing techniques used by AI-based judgments could be beneficial to the process of creating appropriate regulatory measures. Therefore, the primary emphasis of environmental research and policy should be placed on conducting more in-depth analyses of the holistic impacts of AI. Examples of applications that, as a direct result of their intended use, contribute to the increase in greenhouse gas emissions and the destruction of the environment include the use of AI to unlock oil and gas deposits, as well as to explore and develop new areas for the extraction of fossil fuels. These applications are also responsible for other negative impacts that they have on the environment.

- The most recent proposal for a European "Artificial Intelligence Act" encourages an internal market within the EU for reliable, moral, and safe AI systems. Additionally, it offers a structure for governance and a method of enforcing it that is centered on the protection of fundamental rights and security. The policy will include an inventory of conversational AI that is prohibited, in addition to explicit recommendations for AI systems that pose substantial dangers to human health or safety or have a detrimental effect on fundamental rights. However, environmental concerns do not fall under this category unless there is a direct threat to human rights or interests posed by the consequences of unfavorable environmental effects. At this time, there is no governance structure that addresses issues of data governance, transparency, human supervision, and security, and that will also prevent negative effects on the environment. The report's primary recommendation is to undertake additional research and establish official policies and procedures for evaluating and controlling environmental dangers brought on by AI. This is the primary recommendation of the report. EU AI strategies and policies are already strongly concentrated on the objectives of the European Green Deal. This is particularly true of the European data strategy, which has plans for a distinctive "Common Europe Green Deal Data Space" and the initiative "GreenData4All." After the year 2020, the targeted programs, in particular the Digital Europe Programme (DEP), the Connecting Europe Facility (CEF2), Horizon Europe, and the Space Programme, have the goal of increasing investments in AI research, innovation, and adoption with an annual target of €20 billion coming from the public and private sectors.

- In the event that there is insufficient direction, it is possible that AI-based studies that have the potential to assist with the transition to a more sustainable economy will not be given priority if the economic return that is predicted for them is low. The instruments that are provided by the EU research programs are absolutely necessary for any prospective applications of AI in the environmental fields.

As governments [18, 19] increase their use of renewable energy sources and move away from fossil fuels [20, 21], there will likely be significant disruptions to the electrical system. In spite of the fact that renewable energy appears to be flourishing in this environment, grid stability issues will need to be resolved due to its intermittent nature. In order to incorporate renewable energy, the industry is also transitioning from a market [22, 23] based on commodity pricing to a market based on technical solutions. Accurate power generation and net load projections are increasingly necessary to maintain system stability, reduce carbon emissions, and make the most of renewable energy sources as the energy sector continues to use more variable generating sources. This could be only one of the numerous ways artificial intelligence (AI) [24–26] might be applied to change how the energy industry operates and improve system efficiency as a whole. The use of data [27, 28] and the potential for data breaches [29–31] are this technology's main flaws. Attacks [32, 33] on the supply chain pose a serious risk [34] to the energy industry. These assaults [35] take place when threat actors acquire access to a company's network via a vendor or supplier from a different business. Once they obtain access, they can steal confidential information, interfere with business operations [36], or even harm property.

28.5   Conclusion

The investigation of the fundamental causes that underlie particular issues and occurrences is yet another objective of this strategy. This technique locates, on micro-networks, groups of nodes that share failing patterns that can be applied to identify a variety of system issues and potential solutions. This technique is used to determine the increasing VRE entrance symptoms, which have been documented in a large number of scientific publications. The symptoms that were investigated point to a wide range of consequences that have a detrimental effect on the operational characteristics of the electricity system. After that, the indications of each particular VRE characteristic that is the source of the problem are used in order to pinpoint the problems that have been discovered in the literature. This study's research focuses on how variable VRE systems can be incorporated with contemporary electricity systems and technology in order to address problems. In addition to this, it discusses the role that power system technology plays in increasing VRE market share through the use of complicated integration. The concerns that were collected for this research originated from a variety of articles that discussed technological approaches to incorporating VRE. The most important challenge presented by this investigation is probably dependably incorporated by the difficulties that were brought about. The findings of the study have been augmented with information gleaned from discussions among technical experts, which has proven useful in previous research concerning technical questions and their obstacles.

References

1. Andersen, P.H., Mathews, J.A., Rask, M., Integrating private transport into renewable energy policy: The strategy of creating intelligent recharging grids for electric vehicles. *Energy Policy*, 37, 7, 2481–2486, 2009.
2. Asif, M. and Muneer, T., Energy supply, its demand and security issues for developed and emerging economies. *Renewable Sustainable Energy Rev.*, 11, 7, 1388–1413, 2007.
3. Benitez, L.E., Benitez, P.C., Van Kooten, G.C., The economics of wind power with energy storage. *Energy Econ.*, 30, 4, 1973–1989, 2008.
4. Bhattacharyya, S.C., *Energy Economics: Concepts, Issues, Markets and Governance*, Springer, 2011.
5. Blanco, M.I., The economics of wind energy. *Renewable Sustainable Energy Rev.*, 13, 6, 1372–1382, 2009.
6. Bodansky, D., Costs of electricity, in: *Nuclear Energy: Principles, Practices, and Prospects*, pp. 559–577, 2005, BP, (2012). BP Statistical Review of World Energy.
7. Branker, K., Pathak, M., Pearce, J., A review of solar photovoltaic levelized cost of electricity. *Renewable Sustainable Energy Rev.*, 15, 9, 4470–4482, 2011.

8. Chamorro, C.R., Mondéjar, M.E., Ramos, R., Segovia, J.J., Martín, M.C., Villamañán, M.A., World geothermal power production status: Energy, environmental and economic study of high enthalpy technologies. *Energy*, 42, 1, 10–18, 2012.

9. Christidis, A., Koch, C., Pottel, L., Tsatsaronis, G., The contribution of heat storage to the profitable operation of combined heat and power plants in liberalized electricity markets. *Energy*, 41, 1, 75–82, 2012.

10. Connolly, D., Lund, H., Finn, P., Mathiesen, B.V., Leahy, M., Practical operation strategies for pumped hydroelectric energy storage (PHES) utilising electricity price arbitrage. *Energy Policy*, 39, 7, 4189–4196, 2011.

11. Crawford, R., Life cycle energy and greenhouse emissions analysis of wind turbines and the effect of size on energy yield. *Renewable Sustainable Energy Rev.*, 13, 9, 2653–2660, 2009.

12. Kowalski, K., Stagl, S., Madlener, R., Omann, I., Sustainable energy futures: Methodological challenges in combining scenarios and participatory multi-criteria analysis. *Eur. J. Oper. Res.*, 197, 1063–1074, 2009.

13. Karger, C.R. and Hennings, W., Sustainability evaluation of decentralized electricity generation. *Renew. Sustain. Energy Rev.*, 13, 583–593, 2009.

14. Del Rio, P. and Burguillo, M., Assessing the impact of renewable energy deployment on local sustainability: Towards a theoretical framework. *Renew. Sustain. Energy Rev.*, 12, 1325–1344, 2008.

15. Kemp, R., Sustainable technologies do not exist, Available online: http://www.researchgate.net/profile/Rene_Kemp/publication/227351480_Sustainable_technologies_do_not_exist!/links/0a85e534ce87ce95cb000000.pdf (accessed on 13 October 2015).

16. Brent, A.C. and Rogers, D.E., Renewable rural electrification: Sustainability assessment of mini-hybrid off-grid technological systems in the African context. *Renew. Energy*, 35, 257–265, 2010.

17. Madlener, R., Antunes, C.H., Dias, L.C., Assessing the performance of biogas plants with multi-criteria and data envelopment analysis. *Eur. J. Oper. Res.*, 197, 1084–1094, 2009.

18. Mahor, V., Bijrothiya, S., Rawat, R., Kumar, A., Garg, B., Pachlasiya, K., IoT and artificial intelligence techniques for public safety and security, in: *Smart Urban Computing Applications*, p. 111, 2023.

19. Mahor, V., Pachlasiya, K., Garg, B., Chouhan, M., Telang, S., Rawat, R., Mobile operating system (Android) vulnerability analysis using machine learning, in: *Proceedings of International Conference on Network Security and Blockchain Technology: ICNSBT 2021*, pp. 159–169, Springer Nature Singapore, Singapore, 2022, June

20. Rawat, R., Garg, B., Pachlasiya, K., Mahor, V., Telang, S., Chouhan, M., Mishra, R., SCNTA: Monitoring of network availability and activity for identification of anomalies using machine learning approaches. *Int. J. Inf. Technol. Web Eng. (IJITWE)*, 17, 1, 1–19, 2022.

21. Rawat, R., Rimal, Y.N., William, P., Dahima, S., Gupta, S., Sankaran, K.S., Malware threat affecting financial organization analysis using machine learning approach. *Int. J. Inf. Technol. Web Eng. (IJITWE)*, 17, 1, 1–20, 2022.

22. Rawat, R., Mahor, V., Chouhan, M., Pachlasiya, K., Telang, S., Garg, B., Systematic literature review (SLR) on social media and the digital transformation of drug trafficking on darkweb, in: *International Conference on Network Security and Blockchain Technology*, pp. 181–205, Springer, Singapore, 2022.

23. Rawat, R., Ayodele Oki, O., Sankaran, S., Florez, H., Ajagbe, S.A., Techniques for predicting dark web events focused on the delivery of illicit products and ordered crime. *Int. J. Electr. Comput. Eng. (IJECE)*, 13, 5, 5354–5365, Oct. 2023, doi: 10.11591/ijece.v13i5.pp5354-5365.

24. Rawat, R., Garg, B., Mahor, V., Telang, S., Pachlasiya, K., Chouhan, M., Organ trafficking on the dark web—The data security and privacy concern in healthcare systems, in: *Internet of Healthcare Things: Machine Learning for Security and Privacy*, pp. 189–216, 2022.

25. Vyas, P., Vyas, G., Chauhan, A., Rawat, R., Telang, S., Gottumukkala, M., Anonymous trading on the dark online marketplace: An exploratory study, in: *Using Computational Intelligence for the Dark Web and Illicit Behavior Detection*, pp. 272–289, IGI Global, 2022.

26. Rawat, R., Oki, O.A., Sankaran, K.S., Olasupo, O., Ebong, G.N., Ajagbe, S.A., A new solution for cyber security in big data using machine learning approach, in: *Mobile Computing and Sustainable Informatics: Proceedings of ICMCSI 2023*, pp. 495–505, Springer Nature Singapore, Singapore, 2023.

27. Rawat, R., Chakrawarti, R.K., Raj, A., Mani, G., Chidambarathanu, K., Bhardwaj, R., Association rule learning for threat analysis using traffic analysis and packet filtering approach. *Int. J. Inf. Technol.*, 1–11, 2023.

28. Rawat, R., Logical concept mapping and social media analytics relating to cyber criminal activities for ontology creation. *Int. J. Inf. Technol.*, *15*, 2, 893–903, 2023.

29. Rawat, R., Mahor, V., Álvarez, J.D., Ch, F., Cognitive systems for dark web cyber delinquent association malignant data crawling: A review, in: *Handbook of Research on War Policies, Strategies, and Cyber Wars*, pp. 45–63, 2023.

30. Rawat, R., Chakrawarti, R.K., Vyas, P., Gonzáles, J.L.A., Sikarwar, R., Bhardwaj, R., Intelligent fog computing surveillance system for crime and vulnerability identification and tracing. *Int. J. Inf. Secur. Priv. (IJISP)*, *17*, 1, 1–25, 2023.

31. Rawat, R., Sowjanya, A.M., Patel, S.I., Jaiswal, V., Khan, I., Balaram, A. (Eds.), *Using Machine Intelligence: Autonomous Vehicles Volume 1*, John Wiley & Sons, 2022.

32. Rawat, R., Mahor, V., Díaz-Álvarez, J., Chávez, F., Rooted learning model at fog computing analysis for crime incident surveillance, in: *2022 International Conference on Smart Generation Computing, Communication and Networking (SMART GENCON)*, pp. 1–9, IEEE, 2022, December.

33. Rawat, R. and Shrivastav, S.K., SQL injection attack detection using SVM. *Int. J. Comput. Appl.*, *42*, 13, 1–4, 2012.

34. Rawat, R., Bhardwaj, P., Kaur, U., Telang, S., Chouhan, M., Sankaran, K.S., *Smart Vehicles for Communication, Volume 2*, John Wiley & Sons, 2023.

35. Mahor, V., Garg, B., Telang, S., Pachlasiya, K., Chouhan, M., Rawat, R., Cyber threat phylogeny assessment and vulnerabilities representation at thermal power station, in: *Proceedings of International Conference on Network Security and Blockchain Technology: ICNSBT 2021*, pp. 28–39, Springer Nature Singapore, Singapore, 2022, June.

36. Rawat, R., Gupta, S., Sivaranjani, S., Cu, O.K., Kuliha, M., Sankaran, K.S., Malevolent information crawling mechanism for forming structured illegal organisations in hidden networks. *Int. J. Cyber Warf. Terror. (IJCWT)*, *12*, 1, 1–14, 2022.

29

Messaging Apps Vulnerability Assessment Using Conversational AI

Tzu-Chia Chen

*College of Management and Design, Ming Chi University of Technology,
New Taipei City, Taiwan, ROC*

Abstract

In this day and age of smartphones and computers, the prevalence of mobile applications has skyrocketed. They have numerous applications, including but not limited to communication, social media, news, messaging, shopping, making payments, watching videos and transmissions, and engaging in online gaming. When it comes to mobile devices, Android is presently the operating system with the most users worldwide. The Android platform has emerged as the most popular mobile operating system, with an increasing number of applications developed especially for Android mobile devices. Simultaneously, there has been a rise in the number of incidents. Attackers exploit vulnerable areas in mobile apps to introduce potentially malicious code into the system and steal confidential data. When creating an app for a mobile device, it is critical to prioritize the security and protection of users' data. Only by thoroughly understanding the various vulnerabilities that could be introduced into their code can mobile app developers successfully fight potential security threats. This manuscript provides an in-depth study of vulnerability assessment and penetration testing in mobile applications. This manuscript also presents a mitigation plan for encountering vulnerabilities in mobile applications. A security framework is also proposed to enhance the security of mobile applications.

Keywords: Conversational AI, mobile applications, vulnerability detection, penetration testing, mitigation plan, security framework

29.1 Introduction

The popularity of mobile applications has skyrocketed in this day and age of smartphones and computers. They have a wide range of applications, some of which include but are not limited to the following: communication, social media, news, messaging, shopping, making payments, viewing videos and transmissions, and participating in online gaming. Android is currently the operating system (OS) that has the most users across the globe when it comes to mobile devices. The Android platform has emerged as the most popular mobile operating system, and the number of applications designed specifically for Android mobile

Email: ieeemtech4@gmail.com

Romil Rawat, Rajesh Kumar Chakrawarti, Sanjaya Kumar Sarangi, Piyush Vyas, Mary Sowjanya Alamanda, Kotagiri Srividya and Krishnan Sakthidasan Sankaran (eds.) Conversational Artificial Intelligence, (495–512) © 2024 Scrivener Publishing LLC

devices continues to expand. At the same time, there has been a concurrent increase in the number of incidents. Attackers take advantage of vulnerable areas in mobile applications in order to introduce potentially malicious code into the system and capture confidential information. When developing an app for a mobile device, it is absolutely necessary to place an emphasis on the safety and preservation of users' data. The only way for developers of mobile apps to successfully combat potential security threats is for them to have a thorough understanding of the various vulnerabilities that could be introduced into their code [1].

However, in practice, it is difficult for network and system administrators to detect security flaws, let alone locate the proper remedies or patches to mitigate those vulnerabilities. In fact, it is even more difficult to discover the appropriate remedies or patches. The evaluation of network security cannot be considered complete unless it is determined how much of a security breach important servers can tolerate. In addition to that, this is a difficult project. The answer is partially determined by aspects such as the design of the framework or the rule sets used in devices like firewalls, routers, and switches, as well as by deficiencies in protocols and systems. When doing this sort of investigation, penetration testing is often used [2]. During this testing, a network is actively examined, and attacks that may compromise systems are put through their paces.

Organizations focus a lot on data systems for critical functions such as educating children, acquiring knowledge, administrative structure, scientific studies, and knowledge transfer [1]. According to researchers, extensive dependence on computers as well as other techniques introduces a fresh set of security concerns. The security of networks and information systems is coming under more frequent attack from both within and outside the system, as well as from fraudulent activities that are supported by computers. There are now a significant number of dangers to information systems and the architecture of networked computer networks, both of which may compromise the dependability of the computers used in our educational institutions [3]. In light of this, it should come as no surprise that mobile applications need effective methods of risk management.

The number of people using web-based applications has significantly increased over the last several years. Utilizing just a web browser, we are able to connect with a server located anywhere in the world using web applications. As a direct consequence of this, it is now being utilized as an alternative to traditional desktop programs by businesses of all sizes throughout the world [4]. A web-based app is accessible from any device that is running any operating system. It is impossible to emphasize how much of a contribution a web appliance makes to a less formal way of life. Nowadays, web-based applications are preferred over desktop programs [5] because web-based apps do not require the installation of any additional software.

Because it is so versatile, it ought to function well on any device. Internet users have access to a wide variety of services, including those related to shopping, banking, social networking, television editing, maps, lexicons, search engines, and gaming, to name just a few. Utilization of these services by the general population is both effective and inexpensive. It can be done rapidly, at a low cost, and with little effort. In today's competitive market, web-based technologies are becoming the platform of choice for an increasing number of companies. Unfortunately, the use of many languages in these systems exposes them to a greater risk of suffering from a variety of possible vulnerabilities.

Network security may be breached in a variety of ways, including via hacking, virus attacks, pop-up ads, phishing, denial of service (DoS), and domain name service (DNS) spoofing. Some of these methods are more common than others [6]. The systems at universities may be vulnerable to direct assaults on networking equipment, advanced persistent threats, and cyberattacks in which hostile attackers gain access to restricted resources through network connections [7].

Administrators of computer networks and computer systems are tasked with the duty of protecting their respective systems and networks against threats originating both from the outside and from inside [8]. By taking advantage of loopholes in the network's security. Despite being authorized to access particular system resources or perform particular duties across the systems, a wide variety of users, such as students, university employees, administrators, contract employees, visitors, and guests, can cause the system administrator a wide variety of problems [9]. These users include students, university employees, administrators, contract employees, visitors, and guests.

Penetration testing, even though it is very successful, is difficult, time-consuming, and may potentially impair system operations. This article describes penetration testing as a method for evaluating the overall security of a campus network. This method has a minimal influence on the operations of the network and does not generate any more traffic on the network beyond what is required for testing the hosts' security.

For the purpose of identifying vulnerabilities in the computer networks used by educational institutions, this research makes use of the Acunetix Vulnerability Scanner, the Open Vulnerability Assessment System (OpenVAS), and the Zaproxy Scanner. Analyses are performed on the vulnerabilities discovered in a single commercial enterprise, one small institution, and one large institution, respectively. Risks have been recognized using this study, and a comparison of the efficacy of various scanners inside firms of diverse sizes has been completed. Every vulnerability has a severity rating associated with it. To determine whether an organization has vulnerable points of entry; penetration testing tools are used. Following this step, a plan is designed to remedy the vulnerabilities that were discovered and manage the risks that are linked to them. IT administrators working in educational institutions will have a greater capacity to respond effectively to risk as a direct consequence of the security architecture that was proposed in this research.

Information system security may be defined as the process of securing data and information systems against unauthorized access, use, disclosure, interruption, alteration, and destruction. This definition comes from the CIA's triad of cybersecurity, which was developed in 2002.

Any action performed to protect the confidentiality of digital data and the integrity of computer networks is referred to as "information system security." It is a set of processes and technologies that are meant to keep computers secure from damage, whether that threat comes from within the network or from outside the network. System security refers to the measures taken by companies, organizations, and other types of institutions to safeguard their information technology (IT) infrastructure, data, and other types of digital assets, as well as to assure the dependability and consistency of their business operations.

Methods of information security that are successful at their jobs manage a wide range of threats and halt them in their tracks inside a safe and secure data network. It is required to set up a variety of checks and balances at the technical, structural, managerial, and operational levels in order to secure the privacy of individuals, the validity of information, and the accessibility of that information. For the sake of maintaining secrecy, it is necessary to prevent information from getting into the wrong hands and to restrict who may access it.

Integrity refers to the protection of data from being altered in any way and the accurate permission of any data transfers that take place.

> Another way to think about security in computer networks is that we try to safeguard the services and data from security threats.

29.1.1   Nature of Information Security

According to researchers, regardless of how effective the security measures are, the impact on a person's ability to maintain their privacy may be devastating if non-technical issues are not considered throughout the process of implementing and using the system. For instance, even the most well-designed security measures may be rendered ineffective and even deadly if they are installed or used negligently, giving birth to a false sense of security in the process. This can also give rise to a false sense of safety. It is advised that knowledgeable architects, developers, and maintainers of security measures are vital to the successful application of such regulations to ensure that they are followed effectively. This includes every person who was involved as well as the actions taken to protect the mechanisms and procedures that were followed. One of the most important variables is an individual's capacity as well as their awareness of how to respond responsibly in a precarious circumstance. Even the most up-to-date control methods cannot guarantee the security of the data. The degree to which users understand and are willing to comply with the requirements of security measures is typically a critical factor in determining how successfully a system is secured [9].

29.1.2   Information Security Assessment

The process of determining whether or not an evaluated element (such as a host, framework, network, operation, or person) adequately achieves critical security objectives is known as information security assessment (or simply assessment) (NIST, 800-115). The remaining portion of NIST 800-115 provides an explanation of three separate evaluation methodologies that may be used to critically investigate cybersecurity: tests, whether they be diagnostic or evaluative, as well as interviews and interrogations.

29.1.2.1   Testing

Testing is performed to evaluate which of the real and predicted behaviors is more accurate when comparing and contrasting the two.

29.1.2.2   Checking

Checking, studying, assessing, inspecting, researching, or analyzing one or more assessment components to obtain insight, clear up misunderstandings, or collect information that cannot be refuted is the procedure that is referred to as the examination.

29.1.2.3   Interview

An interview is a means of establishing a discourse with individual individuals or groups inside an organization to enhance understanding, acquire explanation, or pinpoint.

Interviews may be conducted in person or over the phone. The results of these assessments are used to assess the measures taken for security in terms of their long-term efficacy.

This research applies technical evaluation techniques to identify, verify, and analyze security flaws to help academic institutions know and improve the security position of their networks and system infrastructure. Its goal is to assist institutions in confirming that their mechanisms are properly secured and identifying any organizational security standards that are not being met, in addition to other unpatched vulnerabilities that need to be resolved. This section gives a summary of infosec assessment procedures, specialized testing, and examination techniques in a broad sense.

29.1.3   Information Security Assessment Methodology

NIST 800-115 insists that it is convenient to use a repetitive and well-documented security evaluation method because:

- Uniformity and organized security testing can help reduce testing threats.
- Accelerate the transition of new assessment personnel.
- Clarify the bottlenecks and resource constraints associated with security evaluation.

The kind and frequency of vulnerability scanning are often constrained by the availability of resources like time, a technical team, equipment, and applications, which are constantly in short supply due to information security assessments. Examining the types of security tests and inspections that the company plans to do, creating an efficient strategy, specifying the resources that will be required, and adapting the review process to meet anticipated needs are all ways to combat the resource constraint.

There are clear points of transition amongst staff members in a well-structured information security assessment system. According to NIST 800-115, a phased approach should consist of at least the following steps:

- Planning
  Important steps in conducting a thorough and accurate security assessment include gathering the necessary data and deciding how that data will be analyzed. A security program should be treated like any other project, with a project delivery strategy that covers goals and outcomes, scope, requirements, objectives, constraints, performance metrics, assumptions, resources, timeframe, and deliverables.
- Execution
  The key objectives of the execution phase are to identify problems and verify them as necessary. Activities concerning the suggested assessment method and approach should be included at this stage. Key duties for this phase vary with the kind of assessment, but at the conclusion of it, evaluators will have identified weaknesses in the assessed system, network, or organization's process.
- Post-Execution
  The post-execution phase involves investigating existing security holes to ascertain their origins, designing preventative measures, and writing a comprehensive report. There are a wide variety of established approaches for evaluating data security.

Many well-established approaches exist for evaluating data security in its many forms. To evaluate the efficacy of the security measures described in NIST Special Publication 13 (SP) 800-53, for instance, NIST has established a methodology published in SP 800-53A, Guide for Assessing the Security Controls in Federal Information Systems. Another popular evaluation guide is the Open Source Security Testing Methodology Manual (OSSTMM). Organizations may utilize a wide range of assessment techniques since there are many factors to consider when planning and carrying out evaluations [10].

29.1.4   Information Security and Penetration Testing

The importance of information system security cannot be overstated. The overall security of an organization's IT infrastructure is evaluated during a penetration test. Penetration testing, as stated by McDermott (2000), is essential in the development of any safe system since it places an emphasis on not only the functionality but also the execution and structure of a system. The security infrastructure of any given data system may be evaluated with the use of penetration testing, which is an important security assessment approach.

29.2   Penetration Test

A penetration test involves simulating an attack on a specific system or application by performing a wide variety of activities and exploiting a wide range of vulnerabilities. Penetration testing is a method for evaluating network security by simulating attacks against it using flaws in the underlying operating system or application [4, 5]. An internal or external tester or auditor conducts a penetration test to look for security flaws in a system (any combination of applications, hosts, or networks) that an attacker may take advantage of. In other words, penetration testing is an audit of the entire IT infrastructure, including the OS, channels of communication, software, hardware, physical security, and user psychology, performed by authorized and competent IT professionals using techniques like or identical to those of an attacker [11].

29.2.1   Difference between a Penetration Tester and an Attacker

Two of the most important factors that differentiate a vulnerability tester from other potential dangers are the objective that they are working toward and the agreement of higher management.

Exploiting flaws in the information or network infrastructure, performing a threat analysis, and reporting their discoveries to higher management are the primary responsibilities of a penetration tester. After that, the executive management will make the necessary alterations to plug the security holes. On the other hand, an attacker will attempt to gain access to confidential information or cause a disturbance in service by taking advantage of any security flaws that may be present. Both goals can be achieved by exploiting any potential vulnerabilities.

In contrast to an attacker, a penetration tester has been given authorization from higher management to leverage security flaws in the system they are testing. Any and all vulnerability testing must be authorized by higher management and brought to their attention.

Because the trials may have serious consequences on the system applications that are being tested, such as system collapse and network latency, which may result in significant network or system devices going idle [12], it is essential to provide data to the staff of the organization that is conducting the penetration test throughout the testing period. This is because the trials may have serious consequences for the system applications that are being tested.

29.2.2   Objectives of Penetration Test

A comprehensive picture of the holes in the information technology security of an organization can be acquired through the use of a penetration test. A vulnerability test's primary objective is to ascertain how likely it is that an attack will occur. During the process, poor and inaccurate installations, known and undiscovered flaws in apparatus or software, command and control flaws in the procedure, and actual defense flaws are all actively investigated. It is possible that putting a device or network through evaluation will be helpful in determining how effective the security measures that are already in place.

The primary objective of penetration testing is to locate vulnerabilities in a protected setting so that they can be cleaned up before being used as entry points by malicious hackers. In addition, the National Institute of Standards and Technology (NIST) (800-115) recommends that penetration testing can help determine how well a system can respond to genuine assaults.

The most probable obstacle that an infiltrator would need to get past to successfully break into the system. Additional surveillance instruments that lessen the likelihood of susceptibility. Protections that can identify attacks and respond appropriately to them.

29.2.3   Penetration Testing Phases

There are various stages that make up the whole procedure of penetration testing. When combined, these steps or stages constitute a thorough infiltration. Various approaches have taken different names for different stages or phases, but they all aim to achieve the same thing. Although the procedure may not always utilize the same language, it does provide a comprehensive education in penetration testing methodologies. In NIST's recommended testing procedure (800-115), there are four phases.

29.2.3.1   Planning Process

During the preparation stage, you will establish parameters, obtain written permission from management, and describe the goals of your testing. A thorough amount of preparation is required in order to successfully carry out a pentest. At this moment, there no effort being put into conducting a significant investigation.

29.2.3.2   Discovery Phase

In the discovery part of the investigation, there are two different parts to consider. The testing technique is broken down in great detail in the first portion of the report, beginning with the collection and examination of intelligence. Finding prospective clients is made easier through the detection of network connections and services. In addition to monitoring ports and determining the identities of services, other methods, such as searching DNS servers and InterNIC registries (WHOIS), as well as eavesdropping on network traffic, can be utilized to collect data from multiple sources simultaneously. It is feasible to discover the identities of employees as well as their contact information by searching the organization's website or the computer systems. Network Information System (NIS) scanning and NetBIOS scanning are two methods that can be used to discover information such as label names and references. These scanning techniques are frequently carried out during internal evaluations (generally during internal tests).

You can acquire information about applications and services, including version numbers, using banners. Finding helpful information, such as paper credentials, that can be used during the pen testing process to gain access to the target computer can be obtained by rummaging through trash or simply walking around the building.

The second stage of discovery is called attack surface analysis, and it consists of matching the services, software, and system software of scanned hosts to vulnerability databases (a method that vulnerability scanners conduct automatically) and then basing their findings on their own personal knowledge of vulnerabilities. The evaluating team can conduct an accurate risk assessment by consulting either an internal or external database, such as the National Exposure Database (NVD). Human processes require more time, but they can find unusual or novel security flaws that automatic evaluators might overlook. These weaknesses could be exploited by malicious actors.

29.2.3.3   Attack Phase

The efficiency of a penetration test is directly proportional to the quality of the attack's execution. Hackers will attempt to take advantage of vulnerabilities that have already been discovered when they launch an assault. If an attack is successful, it confirms the existence of a security flaw and outlines the steps that need to be taken to address it. In some situations, the vulnerabilities that are being exploited are not providing the maximum amount of access that is feasible. The findings of these tests might improve the target network's level of security or give evaluators fresh perspectives on the functioning of the network and any vulnerabilities it might have. In the event that this happens, additional research and testing will be required to determine the real magnitude of the danger posed to the network. For example, it will be necessary to determine the various forms of data that could be changed, removed, or added. If the tester is unable to access the intended vulnerability in the system, they may continue their search for other weaknesses in the system. Pen testers may take advantage of security vulnerabilities in the system or network they are evaluating in order to introduce assessment tools to the system or network. These tools assist users in unearthing previously concealed information as well as resources that are contained within a network or organization. During a penetration test, there are a variety of approaches that need to be tried out and evaluated in order to determine the potential levels that an attacker could go to. The discovering phase of penetration testing consists of nothing more than a simple search for the possibility of a defect, whereas the assault phase exploits the vulnerability to determine whether or not it exists [13]. The bulk of vulnerabilities used in pen testing fall into the following categories, according to NIST 800-115:

> **Misconfigurations.** All too often, an exploit may be found in the system because of faulty security protocols or a default setting that allows for such a breach.

Flaws in the kernel. Security flaws in the kernel put the whole operating system at risk since it is at the core of the system and implements the security architecture.

Overflows in the buffer. Buffer overflows happen when programs do not adequately verify input for the correct length. Code may be injected into the system at any time and executed with the privileges of the currently executing application (often at the administrative level).

Inadequate input validation. While many applications claim to do so, many also fail to properly verify user input. A website that stores a user-provided value in a database management system is one example. A SQL injection attack may occur if a user inputs SQL queries in place of or in addition to the intended value and the Web page does not filter out the SQL queries.

Symbolic connections. An in-file reference to another file is called a symbolic link (symlink). Operating system software has the ability to modify a file's permissions. A user may utilize symlinks to manipulate or present crucial system files if these applications are run with administrative rights.

Attacks on file descriptors. File descriptors are numbers used by the operating system in place of filenames. The time for using certain file descriptors has passed. When privileged software mistakenly assigns a file descriptor, it leaves the file open to attack.

Conditions for the race. The privileged mode of operation of a program or process does not guarantee that no race situation will ever emerge. The user may even launch an attack while the application or activity is still in privileged mode in order to take advantage of those extra rights.

File and directory permissions are incorrect. File and directory permissions determine which users and programs may access certain files and directories. Inadequate approvals might open the door to a wide range of attacks, such as gaining access to sensitive information by reading or writing password files or adding untrusted sites to the trusted network.

29.2.3.4 Reporting Phase

The reporting level of the testing is presently taking place alongside the other three phases, which are occurring simultaneously. During the planning stage, one of the duties that needs to be completed is the creation of an assessment plan. During the investigation and assault stages, it is standard practice to make written notes and transmit frequent updates to the network administrator and/or supervisors. This should be done as often as possible. In many instances, documents detailing security defects, along with evaluations and recommendations for how to fix them, are not produced until the very end of the process. This is because creating such documents can take a significant amount of time.

29.3 Mobile App Security

A person may provide some degree of protection for himself against possible risks by securing himself. The meaning of this phrase is "protection from danger" or "damage avoided." It should be of people, communities, things, educational systems, ecosystems, or anything else that can be radically transformed by outside factors. It might be anything from people to communities to things to educational systems to ecosystems. Information technology security refers to the process of securing information and digital assets from unauthorized access, whether it is caused on purpose or by mistake. Protection is offered using security rules, programs, and information technology services to detect, halt, and deal with any potential threats [4].

Nowadays, almost all businesses and corporations totally depend on web appliances to communicate with consumers and sell products. Different tasks on a web site can be handled by different technologies. Websites are used to provide different types of services, and they are also directly connected with databases, so at that time, valuable assets targeted by the attacker, which directly affects the business strategy, causes losses, and crashes the system. Finding software-related bugs within web appliances is bad for the system. Normally, many web appliances have been developed only for competitive or functional reasons. With the help of such an application, we can have a better future [3]. The Figure 29.1 shows about the vulnerabilities discovered in mobile applications by OWASP.

29.3.1 Types of Attacks

- Passive Attack: In this attack, the attacker observes the contents of the message and the pattern of the message. It does not harm the system. Passive attacks never change the resources of system. But in this attack, the victim does not get informed about the attack. It is dangerous for confidentiality.
- Active Attack: In this attack, the attacker changes system resources and affects their operations. It involves modifications of messages, repudiation, replay attacks, and denial of service attacks.
- Distributed Attack: It is also called a cyber attack in which network resources are temporarily unavailable to the intended users.
- Phishing Attack: This type of attack is often used to steal sensitive data such as user names, passwords, and card information such as credit card details.
- Spyware Attack: This is malicious software that is installed on a device without the end user's knowledge. It steals sensitive data and internet usage data. It is specially designed to obtain sensitive data and damage the system without any knowledge.
- Insider Attack: An insider attack is an accidental attack. This type of attack is launched by internal users who are authorized to use the system. This attack mainly targets individuals within organizations.
- Wireless Attack: This type of attack means malicious action against any wireless technology or network. Denial of service, penetration, and sabotage are examples of this attack.
- Email Attack: This attack includes phishing, identity theft, viruses, and spam.
- Buffer Attack: When hackers intentionally hold extra data with specific instructions for actions, is called a buffer-overflow attack.
- Exploit Attack: When any attack takes advantage of vulnerabilities in the application, network or hardware, this type of attack is called an exploit attack.
- Spoof Attack: In this attack, a person is trying to gain access to the system by illegitimate means.

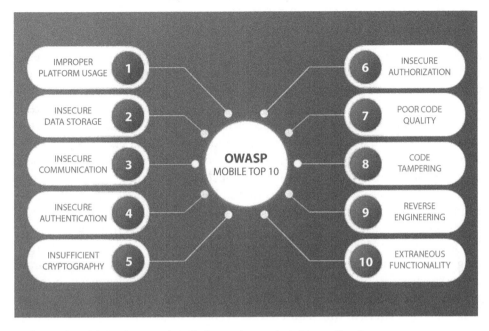

Figure 29.1 Vulnerabilities discovered, ranked according to their degree of seriousness.

29.4   Discovered Vulnerabilities in Mobile Applications

The efficiency of the scanning process was significantly improved by streamlining the process of data collecting and applying a vulnerability assessment method to hosts that were discovered. This was a huge assist in making the process more effective overall. Even though automated scanners are extensively used, many people still prefer to do tasks manually. It is vital to utilize both human and automated scanning methodologies, however, to have a complete understanding of the vulnerabilities that may have led to the system or network being hacked. Assume that the systems or networks being evaluated are part of a massive network that contains hundreds of different systems. Making an effort to do this task by hand would be a waste of time and resources. Because employing conventional ways to get a faultless scan takes more time, automated scanners were used instead throughout this step of the process.

Acunetix [14], Zaproxy [15], and OpenVAS [16] are the programs that we have decided to use as algorithmic evaluators and security vulnerability detectors, respectively. In the lab, smartphone applications were put through their paces using instruments from Acunetix, Zaproxy, and OpenVAS. For purposes of safety, no information about the visitors, including their identities, will be disclosed.

29.5   Mitigation Strategies Against Cross-Site Scripting and SQL Attacks

This section presents mitigation strategies for cross-site scripting and SQL attacks.

29.5.1   Cross-Site Scripting Mitigation Strategies

Because cross-site scripting [17] is a form of exploitation rather than just a vulnerability that may be exploited, phishing attacks, which are false attempts to obtain information, are very effective. During an attack of this kind, information is often gathered through the use of a hyperlink that contains malicious content. The web application, once it has received the data, will then construct an output page for the user, which will contain the malicious data that was given to it. If information that is stored in user cookies is revealed through an attack known as cross-site scripting, then there is a potential for a serious breach of security and confidentiality. An adversary now has the capability of stealing sensitive session data such as user IDs, passwords, and credit card numbers. By changing the user's settings in this manner, attackers can take control of the user's account, steal cookies, or install harmful advertisements. When other vulnerabilities are combined with cross-site scripting, it is possible for arbitrary code to be executed on the victim's machine of the victim. A cross-site scripting attack can be triggered in two different ways: by malicious pages or by parameter values. Cross-site scripting can be identified with a high degree of accuracy if the source of the attack, when it occurred, and the different kinds of signatures used are known. Cross-site scripting is a type of attack in which the attacker gets around security measures by exploiting a vulnerability in the scripting language that enables remote code execution. This type of attack is also known as XSS. A significant number of intrusion protection systems are incapable of detecting even the most fundamental types of assault, such as cross-site scripting. Many people who work in the security industry consider it to be only a moderate risk.

It is standard practice to translate user input into HTML before it is shown on the server. This is done so that a cross-site scripting attack can be carried out. Methods for preventing scripting that occurs between sites are discussed further down:

- Input Validation: Before making use of the input data, it is common practice to investigate whether or not it is a legitimate source.
- HTTP Cookies: A cookie is sent to the client as part of the HTTP response header so that it may help avoid attacks that use cross-site scripting. If a cookie has these characteristics, then scripting cannot be used to access the cookie.
- HTML Encoding: When you utilize encoding, also known as an HTML quotation, all users will get non-alphanumeric characters in their HTML output that cannot be understood as HTML.
- Intrusion detection system monitoring: The intrusion detection technique is one way that may be used for monitoring and managing the many safety elements that are included in a system. An intrusion detection system (IDS) will gather and examine the data from all connections, both incoming and outgoing, to a Web application in order to look for any indications of an incursion. The two most prevalent types of security breaches are known as misuse-based intrusions and unusual events. The objective of the attackers, who are known as masqueraders, is to compromise the web system by putting malicious script into the database of the system to make changes to the confidential information in some manner.
- URL analysis: This method accepts the URL request Ui as an argument, and it then provides either a successful or unsuccessful answer with the request status Si. First, the URL of the ith user is acknowledged and processed for

the projected session ID to be validated. After that, the session ID that was projected is employed in a process of validation. In the event that the request is granted, the information is sent to the server, and the user is given credit for initiating the request. If this is not the case, both the URL request and the status of the request are rejected.

- Hash verification: Each user of the online application is required to have the extension for the web browser installed in their respective web browser. In the moments leading up to the launch, it examines the validity of the application signatures. Pseudocode is used to explain the process of web content verification. The public key for the website is stored in the verification certificate of the server that houses the web application.

29.5.2 SQL Injection Attack Mitigation Strategies

SQL injection [18] necessitates the use of software vulnerabilities that have not been addressed. Because hackers focus on SQL servers that are running vulnerable database applications, they take advantage of the vulnerabilities of the servers and install malicious code to circumvent authentication and get unauthorized access to the database. Botnets, often known as private networks of computers that have been infiltrated, are typically the ones responsible for initiating these kinds of assaults. In the event that the attacker is successful, they will be able to gain control of the web server, execute instructions on the system, access sensitive information, update data in the database, and do a number of other malicious actions. These botnets are made up of thousands of infected machines that are all poised and ready to launch an attack using SQL injection. SQL injection attacks carried out by botnets have resulted in the compromise of millions of URLs across a wide variety of websites all over the world. Businesses that are conducted online often make use of platforms that are based on software as a service (SaaS) and store their inventory in the cloud.

29.6 Mobile Application Security Framework

This section presents a security framework to enhance the security of mobile applications. This framework consists of three phases, as shown in the Figure 29.2.

During the phase of vulnerability identification and evaluation, every significant vulnerability in the network of the educational institute is identified. In this step, we will also evaluate the severity of each vulnerability that has been found. Testing for breaches in security is the second step. In this step, penetration testing is carried out to validate the vulnerabilities discovered in the previous phase. The existence of vulnerabilities in any organization's network can be verified through penetration testing. This testing works by simulating the actions of skilled cybercriminals who test the access control of a target website on purpose to locate and exploit any vulnerabilities they find there. The cross-scripting site assaults and the SQL injection attacks that were found and confirmed in phases 1 and 2, respectively, are the focus of phase three's presentation of a corrective mitigation strategy to counteract them.

When scanning the host networks, a vulnerability assessment technique is put into action. The algorithmic scanning and security vulnerability scanners that were selected are

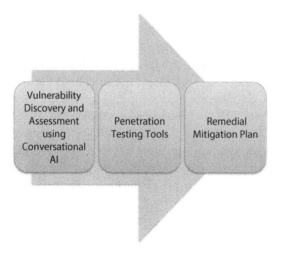

Figure 29.2 Mobile application security framework.

referred to as Acunetix, and Zaproxy. The scanners described above were put to use to discover not only which hosts and utilities were susceptible to attack but also which operating systems and services were active on the target hosts. In the course of the experimental study, Acunetix, Zaproxy, and OpenVAS scanners were used to examine both of the host networks. The educational institutions located in northern India own and operate these host networks. For reasons relating to security, the identities of any and all hosts will not be provided here.

The various forms of warnings that were discovered during active scanning are depicted in Figure 5.4. The level of severity that was discovered in the scanning of the web application is depicted in Figure 29.3. It is very obvious that a high or medium degree of severity best describes the 59% of warnings that have been issued. As a result, we may draw the conclusion that the level of severity in the networks of educational institutions has reached

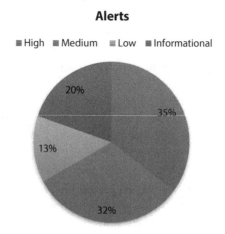

Figure 29.3 Risk level in mobile applications.

an alarming level. In this first investigation, a total of 160 warnings were discovered, all of which carried varying degrees of risk, including high risk, medium risk, and low risk, respectively.

Penetration testing is conducted using the Metasploit Framework. Penetration testing is conducted to confirm the vulnerabilities identified in Phase 1. By imitating the activities of malevolent hackers who are attempting to obtain unauthorized access to a system, penetration testing validates the existence of vulnerabilities in the system's security. It has been discovered that a cross-site scripting and SQL assault could be launched against the network that is used at the university. Phase three presents a remedial mitigation plan to encounter cross-scripting site and SQL injection attacks.

Not just WhatsApp [19, 20] is vulnerable [21, 22] to hackers [23–26]; nearly anything linked to the internet is. Following reports that malware had targeted the chat network [27], experts are emphasising this point. The newspaper published information on the flaw in the most widely used messaging system in the world, which purportedly made it possible for an Israeli business to download malware onto both Android and iPhone devices. According to reports, the security flaw might have been leveraged to listen in on calls made using the app. A technique called end-to-end encryption (E2EE) [28–32] is used to shield data in transit from snoopers, outsiders, and server breaches [33, 34]. The number of online communications has exponentially increased in recent years, and E2EE has been widely adopted in IoT, email, and messaging applications. The work being done seeks to develop an instant messaging client for end users that offers E2EE service for media file transmission, calls, and messages. The app now uses Signal encryption technology [35], has over 500 million users, and is free. Key terminology has been established to offer context, and based on information that is readily accessible to the public, the application's underlying schema has been described. Frameworks for threat [36, 37] modelling have been used to find weaknesses in the application and its environment.

29.7 Conclusion

The Android platform has emerged as the most popular mobile operating system, with an increasing number of applications developed specifically for Android mobile devices. This has led to Android becoming the most widely used mobile operating system. At the same time, there has been an increase in the total number of incidents. Attackers take advantage of weak spots in mobile applications in order to pilfer sensitive data and introduce potentially harmful code into the system. It is essential to place a high priority on the security and preservation of users' data whenever an application is being developed for a mobile device. Mobile app developers can only effectively combat potential security risks if they have an in-depth comprehension of the various vulnerabilities that could be introduced into their code. This manuscript offers a comprehensive look at checking for vulnerabilities and unauthorized access in mobile applications. In addition to that, a mitigation strategy for dealing with vulnerabilities in mobile applications is presented in this manuscript. In addition, a security framework is suggested as a means of improving the safety of mobile applications.

References

1. Raghuvanshi, A., Singh, U., Joshi, C., A review of various security and privacy innovations for IoT applications in healthcare, in: *Advanced Healthcare Systems*, pp. 43–58, 2022, doi: 10.1002/9781119769293.ch4.
2. Prabhakar, S., Network security in digitalization: Attacks and defence. *Int. J. Res. Comput. Appl. Robot.*, 5, 46–52, 2017.
3. Conti, M., Dragoni, N., Lesyk, V., A survey of man in the middle attacks. *IEEE Commun. Surv. Tutor.*, 18, 2027–2051, 2016, doi: 10.1109/COMST.2016.2548426.
4. Raghuvanshi, A., Singh, U.K., Bulla, C., Saxena, M., Abadar, K., An investigation on detection of vulnerabilities in Internet of Things. *Eur. J. Mol. Clin. Med.*, 07, 10, 3289–3299, 2020.
5. Li, Z. *et al.*, VulPecker: An automated vulnerability detection system based on code similarity analysis. *ACM, Proc. of the 32 Annual Conference on Computer Security Applications*, p. 201213, 2016.
6. Raghuvanshi, A., Singh, U., Kassanuk, T., Phasinam, K., Internet of Things: Security vulnerabilities and countermeasures. *ECS Trans.*, 107, 1, 15043–15052, 2022, Available: 10.1149/10701.15043ecst.
7. Masood, A. and Java, J., Static analysis for web service security – tools & techniques for a secure development life cycle. *International Symposium on Technologies for Homeland Security*, pp. 1–6, 2015.
8. Salas, M.I.P., de Geus, P.L., Martins, E., Security testing methodology for evaluation of web services robustness - case: XML injection. *IEEE World Congress on Services*, pp. 303–310, 2015.
9. Madan, S., Security standards perspective to fortify web database applications from code injection attacks. *International Conference on Intelligent Systems, Modelling and Simulation*, pp. 226–233, 2010.
10. Liu, A., Yuan, Y., Wijesekera, D., Stavrou, A., SQLProb: A proxy based architecture towards preventing SQL injection attacks, in: *Proceedings ACM Symposium on Applied Computing (SAC'09)*, pp. 2054–2061, 2009.
11. Gruschka, N., Jensen, M., Lo Iacono, L., Luttenberger, Server-side streaming processing of WS-security. *IEEE Trans. Serv. Comput.*, 4, 4, 272–285, 2011.
12. Ladan, M.I., Web services metrics: A survey and a classification. *J. Commun. Comput.*, 9, 7, 824–829, 2012.
13. Qu, B., Liang, B., Jiang, S., Ye, C., Design of automatic vulnerability detection system for web application program. *Proceeding of Fourth IEEE International Conference on Software Engineering and Service Science (ICSESS)*, pp. 89–92, 2013.
14. https://www.openvas.org/.
15. https://www.acunetix.com/vulnerability-scanner/.
16. https://www.zaproxy.org/.
17. Singh, M., Singh, P., Kumar, P., An analytical study on cross-site scripting. *2020 International Conference on Computer Science, Engineering and Applications (ICCSEA)*, Gunupur, India, pp. 1–6, 2020, doi: 10.1109/ICCSEA49143.2020.9132894.
18. Hlaing, Z.C.S.S. and Khaing, M., A detection and prevention technique on SQL injection attacks. *2020 IEEE Conference on Computer Applications (ICCA)*, Yangon, Myanmar, pp. 1–6, 2020, doi: 10.1109/ICCA49400.2020.9022833.
19. Mahor, V., Bijrothiya, S., Rawat, R., Kumar, A., Garg, B., Pachlasiya, K., IoT and artificial intelligence techniques for public safety and security, in: *Smart Urban Computing Applications*, p. 111, 2023.

20. Mahor, V., Pachlasiya, K., Garg, B., Chouhan, M., Telang, S., Rawat, R., Mobile operating system (Android) vulnerability analysis using machine learning, in: *Proceedings of International Conference on Network Security and Blockchain Technology: ICNSBT 2021*, pp. 159–169, Springer Nature Singapore, Singapore, 2022, June.

21. Rawat, R., Garg, B., Pachlasiya, K., Mahor, V., Telang, S., Chouhan, M., Mishra, R., SCNTA: Monitoring of network availability and activity for identification of anomalies using machine learning approaches. *Int. J. Inf. Technol. Web Eng. (IJITWE)*, 17, 1, 1–19, 2022.

22. Rawat, R., Rimal, Y.N., William, P., Dahima, S., Gupta, S., Sankaran, K.S., Malware threat affecting financial organization analysis using machine learning approach. *Int. J. Inf. Technol. Web Eng. (IJITWE)*, 17, 1, 1–20, 2022.

23. Rawat, R., Mahor, V., Chouhan, M., Pachlasiya, K., Telang, S., Garg, B., Systematic literature review (SLR) on social media and the digital transformation of drug trafficking on darkweb, in: *International Conference on Network Security and Blockchain Technology*, pp. 181–205, Springer, Singapore, 2022.

24. Rawat, R., Ayodele Oki, O., Sankaran, S., Florez, H., Ajagbe, S.A., Techniques for predicting dark web events focused on the delivery of illicit products and ordered crime. *Int. J. Electr. Comput. Eng. (IJECE)*, 13, 5, 5354–5365, Oct. 2023, doi: 10.11591/ijece.v13i5.pp5354-5365.

25. Rawat, R., Garg, B., Mahor, V., Telang, S., Pachlasiya, K., Chouhan, M., Organ trafficking on the dark web—The data security and privacy concern in healthcare systems, in: *Internet of Healthcare Things: Machine Learning for Security and Privacy*, pp. 189–216, 2022.

26. Vyas, P., Vyas, G., Chauhan, A., Rawat, R., Telang, S., Gottumukkala, M., Anonymous trading on the dark online marketplace: An exploratory study, in: *Using Computational Intelligence for the Dark Web and Illicit Behavior Detection*, pp. 272–289, IGI Global, 2022.

27. Rawat, R., Oki, O.A., Sankaran, K.S., Olasupo, O., Ebong, G.N., Ajagbe, S.A., A new solution for cyber security in big data using machine learning approach, in: *Mobile Computing and Sustainable Informatics: Proceedings of ICMCSI 2023*, pp. 495–505, Springer Nature Singapore, Singapore, 2023.

28. Rawat, R., Chakrawarti, R.K., Raj, A., Mani, G., Chidambarathanu, K., Bhardwaj, R., Association rule learning for threat analysis using traffic analysis and packet filtering approach. *Int. J. Inf. Technol.*, 1–11, 2023.

29. Rawat, R., Logical concept mapping and social media analytics relating to cyber criminal activities for ontology creation. *Int. J. Inf. Technol.*, 15, 2, 893–903, 2023.

30. Rawat, R., Mahor, V., Álvarez, J.D., Ch, F., Cognitive systems for dark web cyber delinquent association malignant data crawling: A review, in: *Handbook of Research on War Policies, Strategies, and Cyber Wars*, pp. 45–63, 2023.

31. Rawat, R., Chakrawarti, R.K., Vyas, P., Gonzáles, J.L.A., Sikarwar, R., Bhardwaj, R., Intelligent fog computing surveillance system for crime and vulnerability identification and tracing. *Int. J. Inf. Secur. Priv. (IJISP)*, 17, 1, 1–25, 2023.

32. Rawat, R., Sowjanya, A.M., Patel, S.I., Jaiswal, V., Khan, I., Balaram, A. (Eds.), *Using Machine Intelligence: Autonomous Vehicles Volume 1*, John Wiley & Sons, 2022.

33. Rawat, R., Mahor, V., Díaz-Álvarez, J., Chávez, F., Rooted learning model at fog computing analysis for crime incident surveillance, in: *2022 International Conference on Smart Generation Computing, Communication and Networking (SMART GENCON)*, pp. 1–9, IEEE, 2022, December.

34. Rawat, R. and Shrivastav, S.K., SQL injection attack detection using SVM. *Int. J. Comput. Appl.*, 42, 13, 1–4, 2012.

35. Rawat, R., Bhardwaj, P., Kaur, U., Telang, S., Chouhan, M., Sankaran, K.S., *Smart vehicles for communication, volume 2*, John Wiley & Sons, 2023.

36. Mahor, V., Garg, B., Telang, S., Pachlasiya, K., Chouhan, M., Rawat, R., Cyber threat phylogeny assessment and vulnerabilities representation at thermal power station, in: *Proceedings of International Conference on Network Security and Blockchain Technology: ICNSBT 2021*, pp. 28–39, Springer Nature Singapore, Singapore, 2022, June.

37. Rawat, R., Gupta, S., Sivaranjani, S., Cu, O.K., Kuliha, M., Sankaran, K.S., Malevolent information crawling mechanism for forming structured illegal organisations in hidden networks. *Int. J. Cyber Warf. Terror. (IJCWT)*, *12*, 1, 1–14, 2022.

Conversational AI Threat Identification at Industrial Internet of Things

Boussaadi Smail[1], Meenakshi[2], José Luis Arias-Gonzáles[3], Malik Jawarneh[4], P. Venkata Hari Prasad[5] and Harikumar Pallathadka[6*]

[1]Research Center on Scientific and Technical Information (DTISI), CERIST, Algiers, Algeria
[2]Apeejay STYA University Sohna Haryana, India
[3]University of British Columbia, Lima, Peru
[4]Faculty of Computing Sciences, Gulf College, Al-Khuwair, Oman
[5]Department of Computer Science and Engineering, Koneru Lakshmaiah Education Foundation, Vaddeswaram, India
[6]Manipur International University, Manipur, India

Abstract

Industrial internet of things (IIoT) is bringing about the next industrial revolution, and its use in business has made it easier for people to do business from anywhere and at any time. Through machine automation and robotics, IIOT has helped the manufacturing industry. Also, most data processing and computing services in the internet of things (IoT) ecosystem are done in the cloud. Because of this, the service-oriented architecture also uses the cloud to virtualize its usefulness service-oriented architecture (SOA). So, IoT helps us get to Industry 4.0, which is the next generation of business and manufacturing. Also, when IoT and cloud computing are used with existing industry infrastructure, they help the robust data system make new products and get good results in real time. Along with this growth, security problems are also getting worse and worse. Researchers are paying attention to how quickly cyberattacks on IoT are growing. In the IoT ecosystem, security is much more complex and needs to cover many different areas, such as data security, the availability of data and services, access control, and the security of physical devices. IoT ecosystems can be set up as either open or closed ecosystems, so more research is needed for security deployments in both areas. Artificial intelligence and machine learning are important for attack detection and providing security solutions in IIoT. This manuscript provides an investigation of various security issues and security attacks in IIoT. A detailed study is conducted to identify all existing attacks in IIoT. These attacks are categorized on the basis of layers of IoT architecture.

Keywords: Conversational AI, machine learning, threat identification, industrial internet of things, security, privacy, IoT architecture

Corresponding author: ieeemtech8@gmail.com

Romil Rawat, Rajesh Kumar Chakrawarti, Sanjaya Kumar Sarangi, Piyush Vyas, Mary Sowjanya Alamanda, Kotagiri Srividya and Krishnan Sakthidasan Sankaran (eds.) Conversational Artificial Intelligence, (513–532) © 2024 Scrivener Publishing LLC

30.1   Introduction

The rise of the internet of things (IoT) [1] has accelerated the transition of businesses and governments all over the globe toward web-based information systems as their primary mode of operation (IoT). It is possible for services to be automatically exchanged with one another. The IoT has found significant applications in a variety of disciplines, including medicine, the management of resources, education, and the processing of information, among many others. Concerns regarding network security have expanded at a pace that is proportional to the exponential growth of the network. Because of the rapidly growing number of cyberattacks launched against the IoT, researchers are giving closer attention to it.

The IoT in commercial settings ushers in a new age of connectivity that enables conducting business whenever, wherever, and from virtually any location. The IIoT has been helpful to the manufacturing sector by utilizing automated machinery and robotics [2]. In addition, the cloud is utilized extensively within the IoT environment for the purpose of performing functions related to data processing and computation. Consequently, companies make use of cloud computing in order to practically improve the efficiency of their SOAs [3]. Consequently, the IoT contributes to the actualization of Industry 4.0, the next-generational business and manufacturing system [4]. In addition, the implementation of IoT and cloud computing within an already-established industry infrastructure helps to facilitate the production of cutting-edge output in addition to beneficial real-time results [5] for the solid data system.

The Internet of Things, also known as IoT, is a worldwide network that connects all of the intelligent devices in the world in an attempt to provide its users with cutting-edge intelligent services. The original Internet has been upgraded to become the IoT, which is an abbreviation of the acronym. It is a network that links together various appliances, such as refrigerators, lights, ventilation, and other devices that can be linked to the Internet via the Internet Protocol (IP). This type of network can also connect to other networks. Devices that are part of the IoT have increased intelligence and responsiveness as a result of the incorporation of sensors, actuators, electrical components, network connectedness, and other similar features. It keeps an eye on the environment and sends the information it gathers to a remote computer so that it can be processed and analyzed. It is then able to make a decision regarding the action that it will take in reaction to that decision [6].

The IoT is anticipated to experience phenomenal expansion during the upcoming fourth wave of the industrial revolution. The IoT is no longer only applicable in extremely technologically advanced homes. The IoT encompasses absolutely everything that can be connected to the internet, from manufacturing plants to vehicle networks, utility companies to healthcare facilities, and everything in between. The IoT is experiencing growth at the same time that an unprecedented increase in the quantity of electronic devices is taking place. According to reports from 2015, the amount of connected IoT devices reached 25 billion. On the other hand, it is anticipated that there will be 50 billion IoT-connected devices in use by the year 2020. It is anticipated that 125 billion devices will be connected to the IoT environment around the world by the year 2030. Each of these devices will provide outstanding services to the customers who use them. Alongside this meteoric growth, the number of cyberattacks had also dramatically increased [6].

Every IoT node that makes up the enormous IoT network is a resource-constrained device that has restricted computational power, memory, and the ability to communicate with other nodes. In addition to this, the majority of the machinery is used in an area that is neither guarded nor regulated in any way. Because of these vulnerabilities, it is possible for malicious actors to conduct questionable operations on them. As a result, the ecosystem supporting IoT devices depends significantly on the implementation of security and privacy precautions. There are only a few security requirements that need to be satisfied in order to ensure the safety of the IoT infrastructure. These requirements include things like confidentiality, availability, and integrity, among others. In order to satisfy these requirements, numerous academics have proposed a variety of solutions. Nevertheless, there are issues with the majority of the approaches.

Real-time application domains that are included in the generalized IoT network architecture include things like smart health monitoring systems, smart house monitoring systems, and weather tracking systems, among others. One thing that all of them have in common is that they make use of a variety of different kinds of smart devices or devices that are incorporated with the IoT, wherein each smart device serves either as a sensor to collect data in real time from the IoT application world or as an actuator to take some kind of action based on the processed information gathered by other sensors. The former collects data from the IoT application world; the latter takes action based on the information. The communications between all of the smart devices and the cloud data center, which is where the information that has been collected can be processed and used to influence subsequent decisions, are mediated by a gateway node, also known as a gateway server (GS). People in remote locations frequently make an effort to establish communication with the GS in order to retrieve data that were previously saved or to access particular real-time data from connected devices.

According to the review of relevant literature, the environment of the IoT is composed of three fundamental components: end-users or customers who are on the receiving end of services provided by the IoT; end-sensor nodes; and the computer that functions as a gateway for those services. Every component of the IoT has a continuous conversation with every other component based on the requirements of each component to deliver services to the world. This point of interaction is the target of the overwhelming majority of assaults that are made in an effort to take control of the system. In addition to employing a robust dada encryption method, one of the most important things that can be done to ensure the safety of the IoT network is to implement a robust identification method, which, prior to the establishment of any contact, is capable of verifying the identities of legitimate communicators [2].

All of the detecting devices will, at regular intervals, be required to transmit their most recent data to the central computer. Before any communication can take place between 1) an IoT user and the gateway server, 2) an IoT end-node and the gateway server, 3) an IoT user and an IoT node, and 4) an IoT node and an IoT node, there must be a safe and effective authentication process in place. According to the LoRaWAN architecture, all of the devices that make up the Internet of Things have the ability to communicate with the gateway server, which is a component of the network server.

The overwhelming majority of networks that make up the IoT are designed to function in settings that do not require human supervision. This places them in a permanent state of risk of being physically harmed. If a potential threat were to acquire the long-term secret as well as the short-term secret of the identification credential, then they would be in a position to take control of the communication. On the other hand, this is something that is very challenging to forecast. The gateway server is the node in an IoT environment that has the highest degree of dependability. If the gateway server is hidden away in a secure location, it will be resistant to any kind of physical capture attack that might be launched against it. A bigger IoT framework might contain more than one real-time application for the IoT. "Smart" environments are now available to us in many aspects of life, including healthcare, public transportation, shopping, and parking, among other areas [4].

During the course of the past 10 years, the IoT has progressed from an exploratory stage into a stage of change. On the other hand, a large number of IoT businesses have already established themselves and are working to expand the product lines that they offer in this market. In one of their articles, Gartner argues that the IoT should no longer be considered an initiative and that businesses should instead focus on achieving operational excellence and achieving their business objectives. An ever-increasing number of specialized applications and devices have emerged as a direct result of the IoT's growing level of acceptance. The increased rate of development in fields like smart homes, cities, healthcare, agribusiness, and businesses raises concerns about the ecosystem's overall safety.

The ever-evolving character of the devices that make up the IoT ecosystem has also contributed to an increase in security concerns. There are many different aspects of IoT security that need to be taken into consideration, including data security, availability of data and services, access management, and physical device security. When deploying security measures for the IoT ecosystem, companies need to take into account both open and restricted ecosystem deployment choices. Since the beginning of this decade, the IoT has been one of the most talked-about topics.

The way that the business and technology operate in the modern day is entirely different. Along with the many benefits that have surfaced, there have also been a number of challenges. This has a broad variety of benefits and drawbacks, ranging from the fact that it is user-friendly to concerns over one's privacy and security. The sophisticated and user-friendly management of the IoT has received a significant boost from the application of machine learning and artificial intelligence [3] techniques. Many writers have contributed to the body of literature by conducting research on the IoT ecosystem and publishing their findings on its design, challenges, and potential solutions for both individuals and businesses [4, 5]. In this chapter, a comprehensive literature review of the ecosystem of the internet of things is introduced. First, we take a look at the many different IoT networks that are currently available, and then, we move on to discuss the various ways in which these networks can be connected to one another and put into effect. Following that, we will discuss precisely what a software-defined network is, how it operates, and the different varieties that are available.

30.2   IoT Layered Architecture

There is no standard architecture for IoT infrastructure. Based on the business requirement, the number of layers of IoT architecture are defined. The Figure 30.1 shows about the IoT architecture. Basically, there are four layers.

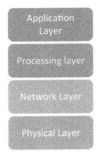

Figure 30.1 IoT architecture.

- The perception layer or physical layer: The fundamental components that make up this layer are the things that can be seen and touched. In this future, every object will already have built-in electrical components such as sensors, actuators, and network connectivity. It then transmits the information that it has gathered in real time from its surroundings to a computer that is located in the cloud. Not only that, but at some point, it must also respond in a predetermined fashion in response to the data that have been analyzed. This must happen in response to the data. It acts as a connection between the actual world and the virtual one that we inhabit online.
- The network layer: The fundamental components of this layer are predominately composed of the visible and the tactile aspects. In the not-too-distant future, it will be the norm for every material object to incorporate electrical components such as sensors, actuators, and network access. The information that it gathers about its immediate surroundings is immediately transmitted to a computer located elsewhere. As soon as the data are analyzed, it needs to respond in a manner that was previously determined. Because of the evidence, you are obligated to take this action. It creates a connection between our actual lives and the virtual realms that we inhabit on the internet.
- The processing layer: This building is capable of handling any and all types of manufacturing work imaginable. This layer is responsible for the processing, analysis, and storage of large quantities of data that have been transferred from the network layer. It retrieves the primary data from duplicate data sets, thereby putting an end to the problem of having an excessive quantity of data.
- The application layer: Customers are able to take advantage of the intelligent and individualized features offered by the system. There is no one method that is applicable to everything and can be used in any situation. At this stage, a variety of approaches are utilized in order to carry out extensive service provision.

Each individual component in this infrastructure fulfills a specific role that is critical to the effective operation of the IoT as a whole. The IoT may be vulnerable at any one of its levels. Each day brings a brand-new threat to national security. The security infrastructure of the IoT ecosystem is the subject of multiple ongoing studies. It is recommended that layered architectures be used depending on the requirements of the application and the necessary degree of protection. Recent research proposed the existence of 10 different architectural levels. In addition to these four levels, there are a further six that collaborate to ensure complete safety throughout the entirety of the system. These six levels are as follows: the tracking layer, the preprocessing layer, the temporary storage layer, the security layer, and the service management layer.

30.3   Security Issues in IoT

Conventional information technology infrastructure is where new dangers that are arising in the IoT environment have their origins. The protection of information, networks, and personal data, as well as the management of distributed denial-of-service (DoS) attacks and other forms of assaults, are all examples of such challenges. The principal security goals of confidentiality, integrity, and availability should each be addressed by the IoT ecosystem using a design that incorporates multiple layers.

These three goals need to be accomplished in order to make the IoT network secure in the same way that certain requirements need to be met in order to guarantee the data security in an IT environment. As has been established, the three foundations upon which security is based are availability, integrity, and confidentiality of the information. The protection of data confidentiality ensures that only authorized parties have access to the data and prevents any parties that are not authorized from getting access to the data. Through the use of cryptography, information can be rendered unreadable in its original, plaintext version. Access control is helpful in putting in place the authentication and authorization procedures that are necessary for using a resource. When data are said to have integrity, it means that it has not been corrupted in any manner during the production, processing, or storage of the data. Hashing and checksums are two methods that can be utilized to keep the integrity intact [7, 8]. Some instances of secure hashing functions include MD5, SHA-1, SHA-2, and LANMAN. In order for a security system to be effective, it is necessary for it to ensure that authorized users will always have access to the data or infrastructure that is being safeguarded. In the event that there is a problem, the availability of the system is ensured by a backup, sites that are redundant, and recovery techniques that have been carefully considered.

However, the security problems that are afflicting the IoT environment are not the same as those that are plaguing the traditional IT infrastructure. The majority of the supporting infrastructure of the IoT ecosystem, on the other hand, is ubiquitous. This provides a snapshot of the entire ecosystem and sheds light on the technologies and components at play at each level. In a similar vein, it details the issues that may arise in the future in addition to the possible solutions to those issues. The final portion provides an overview of the layer-specific security objective that has been met. The difficulty of securing the IoT network is proportional to the complexity of the network itself. Even a comparatively minor security hole can have significant repercussions for the ecosystem as a whole if it is allowed to persist. That is why it is of the utmost importance to eradicate security flaws at each and every level. Every one of the three layers that make up an IoT network possesses a unique set of characteristics [9].

Author describes the IoT as a developing worldwide internet-based specialized innovation that enables commodity trading and initiatives in global inventory network systems.

This is done in order to facilitate global inventory network systems. The interconnected structure of the internet environment has an effect on the partners' ability to maintain their privacy and safety online. The aforementioned research [10] addresses a number of problems, some of which are foreseen developments, conventional IoT engineering, distinguishing characteristics, and potential future applications. This investigation looks into some of the most significant challenges facing the development of the IoT. The authors describe the various research challenges in their own distinctive formats. In many instances, researchers identify questions that have not been addressed and suggest new avenues of investigation. When attempting to incorporate the IoT with preexisting systems, you run into complications due to the fact that the IoT must deal with a diverse set of products.

Author [11] presents the concept of the IoT, in which overall physical entities are differentiated and configured in a bonding manner. The IoT brings up a number of valid concerns with regard to individuals' right to privacy and safety. This document provides a concise summary of the challenges associated with securing the IoT. The article [12] discusses the security and protection aspects of the IoT, as well as the numerous security threats that currently exist across all layers of the IoT. Therefore, funding for research is required to guarantee the safety and accessibility of this technology for customers, with a particular emphasis on the protection and security of IoT devices.

Research [13] that examines the structure of a three-tiered system and provides solutions to those challenges by incorporating key advancements sheds light on some of the obstacles that must be overcome in order to ensure the safety of the IoT. Specifically described are the well-being estimates that are associated with the discernment layer. These estimates encompass things like mandatory services and algorithms, a security guidance protocol, an innovation in data combination, a validation system, and a system for restricting access. Concerns regarding the security of the IoT are outlined in [14], including issues pertaining to anonymity, dependability, and usability. People are brought into harmony with the always-on world of the internet through the implementation of a lawful access control mechanism. It leads to improved conditions in which any vehicle can ask for oil to fill its tank and any refrigerator can ask for milk without being interrupted. These conditions are made possible as a result of this improvement. Along these lines, we can fashion a universe that satisfies everyone's desire for stylistic appeal while also providing a solid foundation for their lives.

The studies that are described in [15] demonstrate the unique causes, intriguing properties, and strengths of the distributed approach. The primary objective of this line of investigation is to disseminate a comprehensive analysis of the benefits and security challenges presented by the most effective strategy for the IoT.

The authors of [16] provide a summary of the methods that are used to guarantee the safety of IoT gadgets when utilizing cutting-edge matrix-based applications. The information and communication domain, the network domain, and the problem domains of the human field are all covered in this discussion. In a recent study [17], the new initiatives for the security and protection of the IoT are dissected in reverse order. The advantages that cutting-edge technologies such as blockchain and Software-Defined Networking (SDN) offer to the environment of the IoT can be summed up in two words: adaptability and flexibility.

The research presented in reference [18] provides a comprehensive overview of the work that is currently being done to ensure the safety of the IoT ecosystem, with a particular concentration on cutting-edge IoT security risks and vulnerabilities. It contains a scientific analysis of the various dangers that could affect operations, apparatus, and communication. Threats to the security of the IoT are also investigated in this research. The research that is described in [19] offers a comprehensive analysis of the current state of the art in IoT security, covering topics such as the most recent vulnerabilities and dangers. The entirety of the existing dangers to system security, including those posed by its operation, architecture, and correspondence, have been analyzed using technical means and incorporated into the system. This research also examines the potential dangers posed to the IoT by the breach of its security.

In their research, the authors [20] emphasize the primary research challenges and current IoT security arrangements, point out the open issues, and make a few recommendations for further research. It contains more recent sources, and it examines every possible vulnerability in a comprehensive manner. The writers of [21] discuss the significance of existing IP-based cyberspace safety conventions as well as the limitations of these conventions, as well as other safety conventions that are utilized in remote sensor systems and that may be applicable to the IoT.

30.4   Literature Survey of Various Attacks on Industrial Internet of Things

Radio frequency identification (RFID) tags may be easily accessed by unauthorized users because there are not enough powerful authentication methods [22–24]. Criminals who operate online might put the information they steal to inappropriate use in the completion of their crimes. Any user who is granted access to a wireless detecting network has the potential to launch an attack against that network, regardless of whether or not they intend to do so. Because of this, it is susceptible to cyberattacks.

It is feasible to replicate RFID tags with sufficient accuracy. This intelligence can be obtained by an adversary through a variety of methods, such as environmental observation and reverse engineering [22–25]. RFID detectors, for example, are unable to differentiate between the tag and the tag, which has resulted in concessions being made in earlier work.

The intruder may listen in on conversations that are taking place between the sensing device and the router, particularly if those conversations take place wirelessly. An antenna is able to pick up the signals that are transmitted by authentic RFID tags and scanners [26]. For instance, a person who is not authorized to use the microphone could potentially eavesdrop on the conversation that is taking place between the reader and the tag [27].

Radio frequency (RF) waves are transmitted out of the system in order to prevent the scanners from picking up the actual tag [28]. RFID tags are used by invaders because this technology enables them to disable reader connections with all other tags in the region [29]. An attack of this nature could put at risk the capability of the system to track the consciousness levels of other individuals.

If a tag can successfully imitate an already-existing legitimate tag without being discovered to be doing so, then that tag is considered to be valid. If a watcher is fooled by the hoax, they will be dealt with in the same manner as the genuine tag would be. In previous studies [27], obtaining the same level of authorization as the genuine tag required access as well as an in-depth understanding of the protocols and automation. An adversary needs access to a communication channel that is analogous to that of a genuine tag in order to successfully replicate the communications of a genuine tag. When an assault technique known as spoofing is used, it is possible for packets to be lost while they are being transmitted [29]. Additionally, as a result of this attack, nodes will be forced to resend data, which has the potential to substantially increase the amount of traffic that is moving across the network.

The functionality of the gadget as well as the visual layer node can only be preserved by the energy that comes from the battery. It is necessary for the device to go into a "sleep mode" when it is not being used so that power can be conserved and the device's lifespan can be extended. By continuously sending control data to the node, the goal of this attack is to trick it into believing everything is fine when, in reality, the system is not under anyone's control [22].

The spike in traffic that results from a DoS assault can easily cause a network to become overwhelmed [29, 30]. A breach of this kind has the potential to use up all of the resources of a network, rendering them inaccessible to users. If the data are not safeguarded, the confidentiality of an even greater amount of the user's personal information is put at risk. It is also possible that a very large number of computers are used as the attachment platform for the distributed denial-of-service (DDoS) attack. This would make it possible to launch simultaneous attacks against numerous targets.

In the event of a Sybil attack, it is possible for a device node to escape redundancy by maintaining multiple identities for victim nodes. The attack is rendered pointless because the victim node is now able to execute the same action repeatedly [31]. Due to the fact that the attacker is able to assume numerous identities, it is possible for the target node in the wireless network to be duped into rerouting the data through a node that is further away. This is due to the fact that a threat can conceal themselves under a variety of guises in order to trick defenders Wireless Sensor Network (WSN).

The node is being utilized by the adversaries as a conduit in order to collect data from other nodes in the surrounding area [32]. This kind of assault can take the form of, for instance, a sinkhole impact. On August 8th, a device and its associated data were both tainted by the actions of an unauthorized third party. An adversary utilizing WSN has the potential to obtain sporadic access to the sensor data and steal information from the network if a node in the network is compromised.

Sniffer devices and software were utilized by the attackers prior to the theft of sensitive data [24]. This was done so that the attackers could learn as much as possible about the network that was being targeted. Intruders can figure out the transmission pattern and the load by monitoring and analyzing the data packets [32]. This is feasible because it is possible for them to determine the transmission pattern. When conducting an analysis, including more files in the example data set typically results in the discovery of additional information. These approaches, in a more generalized form, could be used to break encryption on transmitted packets. Even the route that the signal took to get to its destination can be analyzed. There are three distinct approaches to collecting data from WSN, and they are all centered on monitoring traffic in some way. The activity of an intruder while they are on the network can then be used to identify the network. It's also possible for an attacker to find wireless access points on their own, which brings us to our second concern: an intruder might be able to do this application program (APs). Eavesdropping on the communication process is the adversary's final option for figuring out the protocol style if they have exhausted all other options.

The assailants are eavesdropping on the conversation of the targets in order to gain further insight into their intended actions. The consistent exchange of information between a large number of communication partners is one more factor that contributes to the difficulty of communication services. This kind of attack is also feasible with RFID technology, specifically whenever there is contact between a reader and a tag. Both the front-end and the back-end computer resources, such as those used in reader-to-tag processing, are utilized by the assault [25]. As an illustration, take into consideration the amount of energy that is spent on the reader-to-tag processing. In addition to the benefits described above, the transmission of wireless signals also provides users with access to various types of material.

The attacker in a man in the middle attack targets two networks while also behaving as if they are part of just one. It has been proven that the criminal hid a legitimate node that is connected to two nodes that belong to victims. Two of the nodes have been compromised, and the process of accumulating them results in a marginal degree of annoyance.

The objective of a code injection attack is to take advantage of software vulnerabilities in order to inject malicious code into the device that is the target of the assault. By inserting malicious code into a program, it is possible to pilfer information, obtain administrative access, or even spread worms [16, 33]. Shell injection and HyperText Markup Language (HTML) script injection are two common forms of cyber attack. If an assault of this kind was successful, it might compromise the users' privacy and bring the system to a halt.

An overflow of data or code into a buffer can be caused by a buffer flow attack, which takes advantage of a vulnerability in the software. For the purpose of storing data and commands, a wide variety of software and hardware make use of a variety of different memory architectures. When significant amounts of data are frequently added to a field, the sequence in the field may overflow, causing the field to become unusable. This could have been caused by someone who is actively working to hurt you. Data corruption (when the series invades another data buffer's field), the execution of malicious code (when the series prohibits, for example, a code segment from being executed), and the loss of software control flow are all possible side effects that could occur. The stack overflow attack, the memory buffer overflow attack, the string assault attack, the integer overflow attack, and the double free attack are all common attack techniques [27, 34].

An attack that involves the management of protected information presents a risk to the privacy of the customer [35]. This is due to the fact that it enables unauthorized parties to view or make changes to the customer's personal information. The majority of attacks of this kind can be tracked back to flaws in the manner in which the model authorization was implemented. There is evidence that hackers are taking advantage of security loopholes in the authorization to control programs of smart homes, which can lead to theft as well as malfunctions in the house. When problems of this nature occur, there may be a breach of security. Previous research [36] concentrated almost entirely on analyzing how SmartApps and SmartDevices carried out their functions. It is important to keep in mind that the primary contributors to the data protection issue are smart applications and smart gadgets. The information that is sent to SmartApps from SmartDevices can arrive in the form of events, and the apps can then use these data to carry out a variety of functions. On the other hand, in the absence of adequate event security, this may lead to leaks of the event, which would be extremely detrimental to the consumer. Because the data of users are not sufficiently protected, the personally identifiable information of users may also be at risk. It was recommended that a strategy to protect sensitive data by anticipating the flow of data should be put into action in order to address the issues that were described above.

Phishers will often make believe that they are legitimate businesses or individuals so that they can steal private information such as passwords and credit card details [37]. The majority of these attacks are carried out through spam emails, with the hacker getting access to the victim's personal details even before the recipient has opened the message that they have received.

A stringent identification process is the only way to ensure that the data of users as well as their security requirements are met within the IoT. At this point in time, it is not possible to conduct more stringent testing of modern verification techniques [38]. After being installed, the programs had the potential to carry out activities such as downloading malicious payloads and enabling attackers to remotely monitor a computer [36]. However, the authorization infrastructure still has some areas of improvement to make. Even though it is missing some of its essential components, the device is still able to obtain access to confidential information. In addition, the permission source, which is the standard practice, presents a challenge. If the vulnerability was successfully exploited, an attacker with unauthorized access to files and directories could use it to create attacks of varying degrees of severity. This is because the vulnerability could be used to craft attacks. There are known vulnerabilities in the smart card's remote authentication that could be leveraged in certain application scenarios to steal data or modify them. These scenarios have been the subject of previous research. Due to the fact that the smart house does not have a security system that is completely foolproof, it is also possible for an intruder to perform criminal acts such as opening the door.

When it comes to resolving security issues such as authentication and authorization, cloud-based servers adhere to the guidelines provided by online browsers [39]. eXtensible Markup Language (XML) identifiers, on the other hand, are not something that can be generated by computers on their own. Attackers can avoid going through the normal login procedure and still obtain unauthorized access if they exploit this vulnerability. It is possible for web-based cloud services to generate metadata that contains a significant amount of cloud-related content and service deployments. This metadata can be accessed through a search engine. If attackers were able to acquire access to these data, cloud systems would be vulnerable to compromise [39].

It is possible to exploit software with poor design by inserting Structured Query Language (SQL) commands into incoming data in an effort to initiate attacks of this kind [40]. An attacker has the ability to access, change, and delete data by using SQL commands. SQL searches are frequently used by attackers. This method may be helpful to the intruder in getting access to private information; however, it does so at the expense of compromising the security of the database as a whole. When contrasted with the data that were actually collected, the data that were displayed here reveals significant new insights into SQL injection attacks that were carried out against web applications.

30.5 Various Attacks in Industrial Internet of Things

30.5.1 Perception Layer Attacks

This layer mainly depends on sensor/actuators, which are embedded physical devices that have a limited set of capabilities (such as a lack of processing power and memory backup). Because of these limitations, the actual hardware that makes up the IoT network is exposed to a wide variety of potentially harmful conditions, which has a knock-on effect on the privacy of the data, as well as its veracity and security. The terminals serve as the major entry points for communication with the IoT. It is necessary to have a trustworthy authentication system in place, preferably one that is able to maintain the confidentiality and safety of sensitive information in order to prevent unauthorized access. In the next section, we will discuss a number of significant risks that are posed by the object layer as well as the physical layer.

- **Node capture:** Using this tactic, the attacker has a considerable advantage in the network once they have control of the seized node. This form of assault may easily target sensor nodes and devices that are not secured in any way. When anything like this occurs, the security of the device has been compromised because an adversary interfered with either the device's software or its physical components.
- **Firmware Attack:** In this scenario, attackers would breach a device connected to the IoT by installing malicious software to it, and then, they would take remote control of the gadget.
- **Tag cloning:** In this scenario, the attacker steals information by copying or otherwise manipulating an RFID tag. The real tag is replaced with this false one, and the intruder then makes off with the goods.
- **Unauthorized access to the tags:** Within an RFID system, the personally identifiable information of users is susceptible to being altered and, in some instances, deleted.
- **Side-Channel attack:** If the culprit has access to the system, it is also conceivable for them to carry out this kind of assault against encrypted devices.
- **Battery drainage attack:** The attacker will eventually drain the battery by continuously communicating with a single node using legitimate messages.
- **Eavesdropping:** Due to the fact that the RFID technology is wireless, there is a possibility that some sensitive data may be hacked. The person listening in on this conversation has some understanding of the data that are being sent from the base station to the IoT nodes. An individual who is listening in on a conversation archives the knowledge so that they may use it in a later attack. In the context of the IoT, an adversary may take information on energy use from a smart meter. He takes advantage of the scenario to steal since he is certain that no one will be home while the noise level is low.
- **Node cloning:** When an insider attacker has access, cloning of IoT sensor nodes most often happens throughout the development, production, and operation stages of the process.
- **RF jamming:** When a DoS attack is carried out against an RFID system, the RF signal that is used for communication is disrupted by the introduction of noise. Assaults that force IoT devices to reject service to authorized users are a danger to the IoT since these types of attacks are caused by jamming.
- **Gaining unauthorized access to the device:** Some developers, encode admin user name, password, and insecure Application Programming Interface (APIs) with devices that are left intentionally for future attacks.
- **Spoofing:** After successfully compromising a node, an attacker will go on to the end device or end gateway as their next objective.

30.5.2   Network Layer Attacks

Through the network layer, the application layer and perception layer may communicate with one another. It may be handy for rerouting data and doing subanalysis. The following is a list of the basic types of attacks that may be made in this layer:

- **Man-in-the-Middle (MITM):** An unattractive method of transmitting data packets is developed by the attacker. The adversary in this most comprehensive kind of attack observes communications between endpoints and the hub and then makes inferences about what the data represent based on what they see. After an adversary has successfully listened in on a discussion and taken notes, he may easily add his own information to the line.
- **Sinkhole attack:** In a sinkhole attack, the attacker node functions as a mirror, providing the other nodes with access to the phony routing information that it has. Because of this, it ends up being a traffic magnet for the whole network. This might be exploited by an adversary in order to fool a machine into accessing a malicious website.
- **Traffic Analysis Attack:** In this kind of cyberattack, the attacker monitors and evaluates the manner in which the IoT components of the target system interact with one another.
- **Black hole:** Before returning the essential data packets to their original source node, the malicious node poses as the recipient of a reply message and either steals or deletes the packets containing the data. At this stage, the node that is attacking the other node must demonstrate that it is, in fact, the node from where the path leading to the target node begins that is the shortest. As a consequence of this, the malicious node, also known as a black hole, consumes all of the resources that are accessible.
- **Hello flood:** Congestion on the network might be caused by a rogue node that acts as a parent node and sends out strong Hello packets to all of the other nodes in the network. In order for the flood node to be able to send out a large number of bogus data packets, it must first establish connectivity with all of the other nodes in the network. It is impossible to determine where these false packets are coming from and stop them from putting the network to a halt.
- **Worm hole:** If a rogue node generates a shorter alternative route, it may be possible to deceive the routing system. During a wormhole attack, the attacker node takes data packets from one location on the network and sends them to a different, more distant location on the network. A basic start-up technique.
- **Sybil:** The attacker splits a single node into a large number of separate identities by forking it. Congestion on the network is caused by users who are masquerading as someone else on the network. When targeting a device connected to the IoT in this manner, the attacker takes on the persona of a legitimate user. However, this requires the deployment of phony identities, which compromises the reliability of the IoT.

- **Gray hole:** It is similar to black hole attack but drop only selected packets.
- **Denial of sleep attack:** Sending spam request continuously and trying to reduce the lifetime of nodes by making them asleep for a long time.
- **Distributed Denial of Service (DDoS) attack:** Multiple affected devices or multiple attackers send malicious traffic to their target node.
- **Denial of Service (DoS) attack:** The attacker infiltrates to the network by flooding disruptive packets and trying to spoil the real communication system.
- **Replay Attack:** In order to deplete the resources of the sensor, the attacker will first steal the message and then continually send it back to the sensor.
- **Routing threats:** The attacker creates a loop in routing path; as a result, it increases the end-to-end delay.

30.5.3   Application Layer Attacks

Various application layer attacks are listed as follows:

- **Malicious code:** Malicious software code that was purposefully installed in order to cause damage. When an attacker targets an IoT network, they will choose the system configuration in order to get skewed or inaccurate data from the network. As a direct consequence of this, the safety of the network may be compromised.
- **Cross site scripting:** Client-side script is inserted by the attacker in order to change application content and make use of real-time data for malicious purposes.
- **Denial of Service attack/DDOS:** The large volumes of spam that were sent out by the attacker have caused the communication network to become overloaded. This is the most significant cause for worry about the possibility for harm to the IoT. In this kind of attack, the target network is brought down by an onslaught of requests that have no discernible purpose. The proper node in the network is unable to respond to the inquiry because it consumes up too many network resources. The Teardrop and Ping of Death attacks are two examples of the types of DoS attacks that exploit vulnerabilities in the Transmission Control Protocol (TCP)/IP protocols.
- **Insider attack:** To sniff the personal information, this attack is organized by an authorized user.
- **Exhaustion attack:** To make the data processing of the IoT network busy, generally, this attack happens. It is an aftereffect of any attack.
- **Malware:** It is an attack on the confidentiality of the user personal data as an application of viruses, worms, etc.
- **Logic attack:** There are some loopholes in business logic through improper coding, encryption, etc., that can be used by the attacker.
- **Zero-Day attack:** Here, the attacker uses the software security weakness to attack the system.
- **Phishing attacks:** Obtaining confidential information using dishonest means of electronic communication.

30.6   Recent Attacks on Industrial IoT

The control mechanisms for gasoline pipelines in the United States were compromised by ransomware. The Colonial Pipeline Company immediately terminated service as a preventative measure against the occurrence of additional chain reactions. The criminals made off with approximately 100 Gb of data after breaking one passcode and getting access to it. As a direct consequence of this, the price of the deciphering tool was determined to be 75 Bitcoin, which is equivalent to approximately $5 million. After the pipeline broke, there was a serious shortage of fuel at airports and gas stations, which resulted in the cancellation of flights and a mad rush to fill up vehicles. This caused flight cancellations.

A DDoS attack was launched against the Polish aviation carrier. One strategy for breaching the security of a computer network is to flood it with so much information that it becomes inoperable. Due to the fact that it took the security expert at Warsaw Chopin Airport 5 hours to correct the problem, 10 flights had to be canceled, and an additional 15 were delayed.

The intrusion known as Stuxnet, which was discovered for the first time in 2010 and targeted supervisory control and data acquisition (SCADA) systems, is generally regarded as the most complex breach in the history of computer security. Malware was able to circumvent air-gapped networks and cause damage to nuclear centrifuges at Iranian enrichment facilities because it exploited four unpatched zero-day vulnerabilities in Microsoft that allowed for self-replication and privilege escalation. These vulnerabilities were exploited by exploiting four unpatched zero-day vulnerabilities in Microsoft. These vulnerabilities served as entry locations for the virus. Centrifuges used in uranium enrichment facilities were made vulnerable by the malware known as Stuxnet, which slowed the speed at which the blades rotated. Because of the vibrations and distortions caused by significant and unexpected variations in their speed, 1,000 centrifuges were rendered useless, which, in turn, decreased the amount of enriched uranium that was produced.

Hackers used the BlackEnergy virus to break into the computer systems of three companies that distribute electricity in Ukraine during a cyberattack that took place in December of 2015. The incident occurred in Ukraine. Because of this, the power to approximately 225,000 homes and businesses was turned off for anywhere from 1 to 6 hours at a time.

Hackers operating at the German Steel Plant resorted to social engineering tactics like spear phishing in order to break into the mill's management systems and take control of the facility. It was done inadvertently, but it ended up causing the furnace to shut down, which, in turn, led to substantial structural damage being done to the steel mill.

In the hands of a determined adversary, a hack on crucial infrastructure can have catastrophic results, as these examples demonstrate. These exploits could either lessen the system's capacity to run the program or disclose the inner workings of the program. Both of these outcomes are possible.

Devices that have been compromised as a result of the exploitation of zero-day vulnerabilities or vulnerabilities that have been disclosed but not patched may suddenly stop functioning, exhibit strange behavior, or be used to initiate DDoS attacks. In addition, the attackers gained access to the victim computers by exploiting a wide variety of security flaws that were present in the software as well as the hardware that was being utilized.

Vulnerability management, also known by its acronym VM, is an essential component of any system security management strategy that has as its overarching objective the reduction of the harm that is caused by assaults that are successful.

The goal of artificial intelligence (AI) [41–45] is to enable computers to reason similarly to humans. This change will hasten the digital revolution in several sectors [46, 47]. The planet may become autonomous by linking things like people, animals, plants, machinery, appliances, dirt, stones, lakes, construction sites, and anything else that comes to mind. We require both a data analysis (DA) [48, 49] module in the system and a machine learning (ML) [50, 51] module that mimics human learning in order to make the environment and its physical objects truly autonomous. While DA would evaluate and analyse all the data that is collected over time to figure out historical trends and be more efficient and effective, ML would develop strategies to assist learning in various components and devices of the network to make them automated and self-standing. As a result of this expanding tendency, attempts are currently being undertaken to integrate ML [52–54] and DA [55] into the smart systems' embedded systems [56] and sensors [57]. The science underlying AI is really fascinating, and what it will eventually become compels us to reevaluate everything we believe to be true about what life and work are all about. Given how quickly ML and DA are advancing AI, it is important to talk about future trends, obstacles, and dangers [58, 59].

30.7   Conclusion

The ioT is accelerating our progress toward Industry 4.0, the next generation of business and manufacturing. In addition, the IoT and cloud computing help the robust data system create new products and get good results in real time when they are used in conjunction with existing industry infrastructure. Alongside this development, there has also been an increase in the severity of the security issues. Researchers are keeping an eye on how rapidly there are more and more cyberattacks on the IoT. Security in the IoT ecosystem is much more complicated and needs to encompass a wide variety of domains, including data security, the availability of data and services, access control, and the security of physical devices. These are just some of the domains that need to be protected. Because IoT ecosystems can be organized as either open or closed ecosystems, additional research is required for the implementation of security measures in both of these categories. When it comes to providing security solutions and detecting attacks in the IIoT, artificial intelligence and machine learning are extremely essential components. This manuscript presents an investigation of several different security problems as well as security attacks that are prevalent in the IIoT. An in-depth study is being carried out to determine all of the threats that currently exist in the IIoT. The layers of IoT infrastructure serve as a categorization scheme for these kinds of assaults.

References

1. Raghuvanshi, A., Singh, U., Joshi, C., A review of various security and privacy innovations for IoT applications in healthcare, in: *Advanced Healthcare Systems*, pp. 43–58, 2022, doi: 10.1002/9781119769293.ch4.

2. Singh, U.K., Panse, P., Saxena, M., A taxonomy of various building blocks of Internet of Things. *Int. J. Future Gener. Commun. Netw.*, 13, 4, 4397–4404, 2020.

3. Bulla, C., Saxena, M., Abadar, K., An investigation on detection of vulnerabilities in Internet of Things. *Eur. J. Mol. Clin. Med.*, 07, 10, 3289–3299, 2020.

4. Raghuvanshi, A., Singh, U., Kassanuk, T., Phasinam, K., Internet of Things: Security vulnerabilities and countermeasures. *ECS Trans.*, 107, 1, 15043–15052, 2022, Available: 10.1149/10701.15043ecst.

5. Singh, U., Sajja, G., Pallathadka, H., Asenso, E., Kamal, M. *et al.*, Intrusion detection using machine learning for risk mitigation in IoT-enabled smart irrigation in smart farming. *J. Food Qual.*, 2022, 1–8, 2022, doi: 10.1155/2022/3955514.

6. Raghuvanshi, A., Singh, U.K., Panse, P., Saxena, M., Veluri, R.K., Internet of Things: Taxonomy of various attacks. *Eur. J. Mol. Clin. Med.*, 7, 10, 3853–3864, 2020.

7. Cherdantseva, Y., Burnap, P., Blyth, A., Eden, P., Jones, K., Soulsby, H., Stoddart, K., A review of cyber security risk assessment methods for scada systems. *Comput. Secur.*, 56, 1–27, 2016.

8. Chinese-MSS, CNNVD, 2021, http://www.cnnvd.org.cn/. last accessed 01-09-2021.

9. Cinque, M., Cotroneo, D., Pecchia, A., Event logs for the analysis of software failures: A rule-based approach. *IEEE Trans. Software Eng.*, 39, 6, 806–821, 2013.

10. Coffey, K., Smith, R., Maglaras, L., Janicke, H., Vulnerability analysis of network scanning on scada systems. *Secur. Commun. Netw.*, 2018, 3794603, 2018.

11. Denis, M., Zena, C., Hayajneh, T., Penetration testing: Concepts, attack methods, and defense strategies, in: *2016 IEEE Long Island Systems, Applications and Technology Conference (LISAT)*, pp. 1–6, 9, 25, 26, 27, 74, 2016.

12. Dhirani, L.L., Armstrong, E., Newe, T., Industrial IoT, cyber threats, and standards landscape: Evaluation and roadmap. *Sensors*, 21, 11, 5, 2021.

13. Dobrovoljc, A., Trček, D., Likar, B., Predicting exploitations of information systems vulnerabilities through attackers' characteristics. *IEEE Access*, 5, 26063–26075, 2017.

14. Fovino, I.N., Carcano, A., Masera, M., Trombetta, A., Design and implementation of a secure modbus protocol, in: *Critical Infrastructure Protection*, p. 62, 2009.

15. Frei, S., May, M., Fiedler, U., Plattner, B., Large-scale vulnerability analysis, in: *Proceedings of the 2006 SIGCOMM Workshop on Large-Scale Attack Defense, LSAD '06*, vol. 22, Association for Computing Machinery, New York, NY, USA, pp. 131–138, 2006.

16. Frei, S., Tellenbach, B., Plattner, B., *0-day Patch Exposing Vendors (In)Security Performance*, p. 22, 2008.

17. Fruhwirth, C. and Mannisto, T., Improving CVSS-based vulnerability prioritization and response with context information, in: *2009 3rd International Symposium on Empirical Software Engineering and Measurement*, pp. 535–544, 2009, 30, 71, 128.

18. Keshav Kolla, S.S.V., Lourenço, D.M., Kumar, A.A., Plapper, P., Retrofitting of legacy machines in the context of industrial Internet of Things (IIoT). *Proc. Comput. Sci.*, 200, 62–70, 2022, 3rd International Conference on Industry 4.0 and Smart Manufacturing. 12.

19. Koroniotis, N., Moustafa, N., Turnbull, B., Schiliro, F., Gauravaram, P., Janicke, H., A deep learning-based penetration testing framework for vulnerability identification in Internet of Things environments, 2021.

20. Lee, R.M., Assante, M.J., Conway, T., German steel mill cyber attack. *Industrial Control Systems*, pp. 1–15, 2014.

21. Nerwich, M., Gauravaram, P., Paik, H.-y., Nepal, S., Vulnerability database as a service for IoT, in: *Applications and Techniques in Information Security*, L. Batina, and G. Li (Eds.), pp. 95–107, Springer Singapore, Singapore, 2020.

22. Liu, W., Study and application on the architecture and key technologies for IoT, in: *Proceeding of 2011 International Conference on Multimedia Technology (ICMT)*, pp. 747–751, 2011.

23. Farooq, M.U., Waseem, M., Khairi, A., Mazhar, S., A critical analysis on the security concerns of Internet of Things (IoT). *Int. J. Comput. Appl.*, 111, 7, 2015.

24. Khan, R., Khan, S., Zaheer, R., Khan, S., Future internet: The Internet of Things architecture, possible applications and key challenges, in: *2012 10th International Conference on Frontiers of Information Technology (FIT)*, IEEE, pp. 257–260, 2012.

25. Welch, D. and Lathrop, S., Wireless security threat taxonomy, in: *2003 IEEE Systems, Man and Cybernetics Society and Information Assurance Workshop*, IEEE, pp. 76–83, 2003.

26. Ding, Z.-h., Li, J.-t., Feng, B., A taxonomy model of RFID security threats, in: *2008 11th IEEE International Conference on Communication Technology*, ICCT 2008. IEEE, pp. 765–768, 2008.

27. Yampolskiy, M., Horvath, P., Koutsoukos, X.D., Xue, Y., Sztipanovits, J., Taxonomy for description of cross-domain attacks on CPS, in: *Proceedings of the 2nd ACM International Conference on High Confidence Networked Systems*, ACM, pp. 135–142, 2013.

28. Mitrokotsa, A., Rieback, M.R., Tanenbaum, A.S., Classification of RFID attacks. *Gen*, 15693, 14443, 2010.

29. Khoo, B., RFID as an enabler of the Internet of Things: Issues of security and privacy, in: *2011 International Conference on Internet of Things (ithings/CPSCom) and 4th International Conference on Cyber, Physical and Social Computing*, IEEE, 2011.

30. Sastry, A.S., Sulthana, S., Vagdevi, S., Security threats in wireless sensor networks in each layer. *Int. J. Adv. Netw. Appl.*, 4, 4, 1657, 2013.

31. Zhang, W. and Qu, B., Security architecture of the Internet of Things oriented to perceptual layer. *Int. J. Comput. Consumer Control (IJ3C)*, 2, 2, 37–45, 2013.

32. Ahmed, N., Kanhere, S.S., Jha, S., The holes problem in wireless sensor networks: A survey. *ACM SIGMOBILE Mob. Comput. Commun. Rev.*, 9, 2, 4–18, 2005.

33. Cho, J.-S., Yeo, S.-S., Kim, S.K., Securing against brute-force attack: A hash-based RFID mutual authentication protocol using a secret value. *Comput. Commun.*, 34, 3, 391–397, 2011.

34. Mattern, F. and Floerkemeier, C., From the internet of computers to the Internet of Things, in: *From Active Data Management to Event Based Systems and More*, pp. 242–259, 2010.

35. Zhu, B., Joseph, A., Sastry, S., A taxonomy of cyber attacks on SCADA systems, in: *Internet of Things (Ithings/CPSCom), 2011 International Conference on and 4th International Conference on Cyber, Physical and Social Computing*, IEEE, pp. 380–388, 2011.

36. Jia, Y.J., Chen, Q.A., Wang, S., Rahmati, A., Fernandes, E., Mao, Z.M., Prakash, A., Unviersity, S.J., ContexIoT: Towards providing contextual integrity to appified IoT platforms, in: *Proceedings of the 21st Network and Distributed System Security Symposium (NDSS'17)*, 2017.

37. Fernandes, E., Jung, J., Prakash, A., Security analysis of emerging smart home applications, in: *2016 IEEE Symposium on Security and Privacy (SP)*, IEEE, pp. 636–654, 2016.

38. Thakur, B.S. and Chaudhary, S., Content sniffing attack detection in client and server side: A survey. *Int. J. Adv. Comput. Res.*, 3, 2, 7, 2013.

39. Bugiel, S., Heuser, S., Sadeghi, A.-R., Flexible and fine-grained mandatory access control on Android for diverse security and privacy policies, in: *USENIX Security Symposium*, pp. 131–146, 2013.

40. Jensen, M., Schwenk, J., Gruschka, N., Iacono, L.L., On technical security issues in cloud computing, in: *2009 IEEE International Conference on Cloud Computing. CLOUD'09*, IEEE, pp. 109–116, 2009.

41. Mahor, V., Bijrothiya, S., Rawat, R., Kumar, A., Garg, B., Pachlasiya, K., IoT and artificial intelligence techniques for public safety and security, in: *Smart Urban Computing Applications*, p. 111, 2023.

42. Mahor, V., Pachlasiya, K., Garg, B., Chouhan, M., Telang, S., Rawat, R., Mobile operating system (Android) vulnerability analysis using machine learning, in: *Proceedings of International*

Conference on Network Security and Blockchain Technology: ICNSBT 2021, pp. 159–169, Springer Nature Singapore, Singapore, 2022, June.

43. Rawat, R., Garg, B., Pachlasiya, K., Mahor, V., Telang, S., Chouhan, M., Mishra, R., SCNTA: Monitoring of network availability and activity for identification of anomalies using machine learning approaches. *Int. J. Inf. Technol. Web Eng. (IJITWE)*, 17, 1, 1–19, 2022.

44. Rawat, R., Rimal, Y.N., William, P., Dahima, S., Gupta, S., Sankaran, K.S., Malware threat affecting financial organization analysis using machine learning approach. *Int. J. Inf. Technol. Web Eng. (IJITWE)*, 17, 1, 1–20, 2022.

45. Rawat, R., Mahor, V., Chouhan, M., Pachlasiya, K., Telang, S., Garg, B., Systematic literature review (SLR) on social media and the digital transformation of drug trafficking on darkweb, in: *International Conference on Network Security and Blockchain Technology*, pp. 181–205, Springer, Singapore, 2022.

46. Rawat, R., Ayodele Oki, O., Sankaran, S., Florez, H., Ajagbe, S.A., Techniques for predicting dark web events focused on the delivery of illicit products and ordered crime. *Int. J. Electr. Comput. Eng. (IJECE)*, 13, 5, 5354–5365, Oct. 2023, doi: 10.11591/ijece.v13i5.pp5354-5365.

47. Rawat, R., Garg, B., Mahor, V., Telang, S., Pachlasiya, K., Chouhan, M., Organ trafficking on the dark web—The data security and privacy concern in healthcare systems, in: *Internet of Healthcare Things: Machine Learning for Security and Privacy*, pp. 189–216, 2022.

48. Vyas, P., Vyas, G., Chauhan, A., Rawat, R., Telang, S., Gottumukkala, M., Anonymous trading on the dark online marketplace: An exploratory study, in: *Using Computational Intelligence for the Dark Web and Illicit Behavior Detection*, pp. 272–289, IGI Global, 2022.

49. Rawat, R., Oki, O.A., Sankaran, K.S., Olasupo, O., Ebong, G.N., Ajagbe, S.A., A new solution for cyber security in big data using machine learning approach, in: *Mobile Computing and Sustainable Informatics: Proceedings of ICMCSI 2023*, pp. 495–505, Springer Nature Singapore, Singapore, 2023.

50. Rawat, R., Chakrawarti, R.K., Raj, A., Mani, G., Chidambarathanu, K., Bhardwaj, R., Association rule learning for threat analysis using traffic analysis and packet filtering approach. *Int. J. Inf. Technol.*, 1–11, 2023.

51. Rawat, R., Logical concept mapping and social media analytics relating to cyber criminal activities for ontology creation. *Int. J. Inf. Technol.*, 15, 2, 893–903, 2023.

52. Rawat, R., Mahor, V., Álvarez, J.D., Ch, F., Cognitive systems for dark web cyber delinquent association malignant data crawling: A review, in: *Handbook of Research on War Policies, Strategies, and Cyber Wars*, pp. 45–63, 2023.

53. Rawat, R., Chakrawarti, R.K., Vyas, P., Gonzáles, J.L.A., Sikarwar, R., Bhardwaj, R., Intelligent fog computing surveillance system for crime and vulnerability identification and tracing. *Int. J. Inf. Secur. Priv. (IJISP)*, 17, 1, 1–25, 2023.

54. Rawat, R., Sowjanya, A.M., Patel, S.I., Jaiswal, V., Khan, I., Balaram, A. (Eds.), *Using Machine Intelligence: Autonomous Vehicles Volume 1*, John Wiley & Sons, 2022.

55. Rawat, R., Mahor, V., Díaz-Álvarez, J., Chávez, F., Rooted learning model at fog computing analysis for crime incident surveillance, in: *2022 International Conference on Smart Generation Computing, Communication and Networking (SMART GENCON)*, pp. 1–9, IEEE, 2022, December.

56. Rawat, R. and Shrivastav, S.K., SQL injection attack detection using SVM. *Int. J. Comput. Appl.*, 42, 13, 1–4, 2012.

57. Rawat, R., Bhardwaj, P., Kaur, U., Telang, S., Chouhan, M., Sankaran, K.S., *Smart vehicles for communication, volume 2*, John Wiley & Sons, 2023.

58. Mahor, V., Garg, B., Telang, S., Pachlasiya, K., Chouhan, M., Rawat, R., Cyber threat phylogeny assessment and vulnerabilities representation at thermal power station, in: *Proceedings of*

International Conference on Network Security and Blockchain Technology: ICNSBT 2021, pp. 28–39, Springer Nature Singapore, Singapore, 2022, June.

59. Rawat, R., Gupta, S., Sivaranjani, S., Cu, O.K., Kuliha, M., Sankaran, K.S., Malevolent information crawling mechanism for forming structured illegal organisations in hidden networks. *Int. J. Cyber Warf. Terror. (IJCWT)*, *12*, 1, 1–14, 2022.

Conversational AI—A State-of-the-Art Review

Vivek Bhardwaj[1], Mukesh Kumar[2], Divyani Joshi[3], Ankita Chourasia[4], Bhushan Bawaskar[5]*
and Shashank Sharma[5]

[1]School of Computer Science and Engineering, Manipal University Jaipur, Jaipur, India
[2]School of Computer Applications, Lovely Professional University, Phagwara, Punjab, India
[3]Department of Computer Science and Engineering, IPS Academy, Indore, India
[4]Department of Computer Science and Engineering, Medi-Caps University, Indore, India
*[5]Department of Computer Science Engineering, Shri Vaishnav Vidyapeeth Vishwavidyalaya,
Indore, India*

Abstract

Conversational artificial intelligence (AI), also known as a chatbot or virtual assistant, has become increasingly popular in recent years. The technology allows machines to communicate with humans in natural language, providing a seamless user experience. This paper provides an overview of conversational AI, including its history, applications, and technical aspects. We also discuss the challenges and opportunities of conversational AI, such as natural language understanding, ethical considerations, and personalized experiences. Finally, we explore the future of conversational AI and its potential impact on society. Conversational AI will completely change the way we interact with machines, and this paper aims to provide a comprehensive understanding of this exciting technology.

Keywords: Conversational AI, artificial intelligence, machine learning, natural language processing, natural language understanding, dialogue management, cognitive search, regulatory landscape

31.1 Introduction

Conversational artificial intelligence (AI) [1] refers to chatbots and virtual agents, which interact with with and take suggestions from them. They reply in real time with accurate and correct data; they use machine learning (ML) and natural language processing (NLP) to help imitate human interactions, recognize speech and text inputs, and translate their meanings across various languages.

Conversational AI mainly uses NLP [2] with ML. NLP courses flow in a constant feedback look with ML to constantly improvise the algorithms. Conversational AI understands and generates answers in a more understanding and natural way.

**Corresponding author*: bhusan.bawaskar@gmail.com

Romil Rawat, Rajesh Kumar Chakrawarti, Sanjaya Kumar Sarangi, Piyush Vyas, Mary Sowjanya Alamanda, Kotagiri Srividya and Krishnan Sakthidasan Sankaran (eds.) Conversational Artificial Intelligence, (533–556) © 2024 Scrivener Publishing LLC

ML comes under AI [2]. ML is made of algorithms, datasets, and features that continuously improve themselves and become a better version of themselves with time. The more input data are provided, the more they train and the better they can recognize patterns. Recognizing patterns helps them to make faster and more accurate predictions.

NLP [3] is a branch of AI that provides the ability for computers to understand text and voice messages easily and comfortably. NLP understands human thinking and the human language and converts the information in such a way that the computer/machine can understand it. Shortly, it is guaranteed that deep learning will improve the NLP capabilities of conversational AI to the next level. Figure 31.1 shows the Natural Language Question Flow.

NLP plays an important role in conversational AI by performing

1. Speech recognition
2. Intent recognition
3. Natural language generation (NLG)
4. Sentiment analysis
5. Name entity recognition

Overall, NLP is very much essential for creating conversational AI [3, 4] systems that can identify and respond to natural language queries in such a way that feels natural and human-like. As NLP technology continues to improve, conversational AI systems are likely to become even more sophisticated and effective at understanding and responding to user queries.

In conversational AI, NLP converts unstructured data into structured data so that the computer can understand it easily, and then, ML helps to generate a quality response in a short amount of time.

NLP uses four steps to generate a response:

- **Input generation:** In input generation, the input provided by the user is in the form of text or voice.
- **Input analysis:** In this, for a text-based input, conversational AI uses natural language understanding (NLU) to recognize the meaning of the input and derive its intention and for a voice-based input; it uses a combination of automatic speech recognition [5] and NLU to analyze the data.

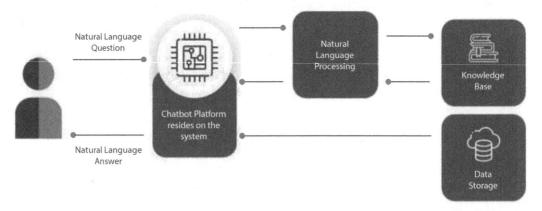

Figure 31.1 Natural language question flow.

- **Dialog management:** In dialog management, the application uses NLG, a subpart of NLP, to formulate a response.
- **Reinforcement learning:** In the last step, machine learning algorithms refine the output over time to ensure accuracy and correctness.

According to statistics by 2030, researchers [6] have predicted that the global conversational AI market size is projected to reach $32.62 billion. Conversational agent interaction is increased by as much as 250% in multiple industries since the pandemic. Companies that are using AI for digital marketing worldwide have seen their share skyrocket, from 29% in 2018 to 84% in 2020.

Almost all adult voice assistant users are using conversational AI tech on a smartphone (91.0% in 2022).

Experts suggest that AI-based chatbots will continue to enhance and transform consumer experiences for companies of all shapes and sizes. Conversational-based AI chatbots will become foundational for all kinds of employee interaction, experience management, and future automation.

Since customer and employee experiences have become important for business growth, many companies have started investing heavily in discovering new ways of providing an extraordinary customer experience at every step. This investment [7] leads to less frustrated customers, faster issue resolution, and increased business value. Figure 31.2 shows the NLP paradigm.

Conversational AI is widely used in this modern technology [8, 9] because

- It saves time.
- Increased accessibility.
- Helps in making decisions.
- No language barrier.

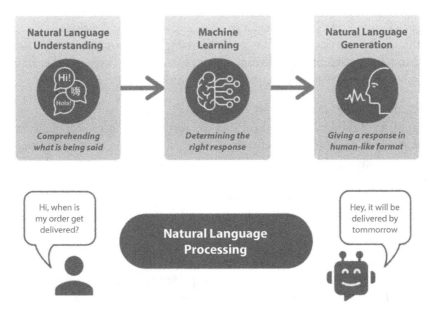

Figure 31.2 Natural language processing paradigm.

31.1.1   History of Conversational AI

The concept of conversational AI can be traced back to the 1960s when computer scientist Joseph Weinbaum [10, 11] developed ELIZA, a program that could mimic a psychotherapist. ELIZA used pattern matching and simple rules to respond to user inputs in a way that made it seem like the program was engaging in conversation. ELIZA was the first chatbot built in the year 1966. ELIZA's communication ability was very minimal, but it was a crucial step in the field of conversational AI. ELIZA was the building stone for the field of conversational AI.

In the 1970s, researchers began exploring more sophisticated NLP techniques for conversational AI. However, progress was slow due to the limited computing power available at the time.

The development of the internet in the 1990s paved the way for new applications of conversational AI, such as chatbots for customer support. However, these early chatbots were often limited in their capabilities and could only respond to simple, scripted queries.

The rise of machine learning and cloud computing in the early 2000s led to a new wave of advances in conversational AI. With access to more computing power and data, researchers were able to develop more sophisticated NLP techniques and create chatbots that could learn from user interactions.

In recent years, conversational AI has become increasingly common in a wide range of applications, from customer support to healthcare. Virtual assistants [12] like Amazon's Alexa and Google Assistant are now commonplace in many homes, and chatbots are used by businesses to provide round-the-clock customer support. Looking to the future, the development of conversational AI is expected to continue at a rapid pace, with more sophisticated NLP techniques and more personalized, context-aware responses becoming the norm.

31.1.2   Evolution of Conversational AI

The 1960s–1980s: The birth of conversational AI

The concept of conversational AI began in the 1960s with the development of ELIZA, a program that could mimic a psychotherapist by using pattern matching and simple rules to respond to user inputs. In the following decades, researchers continued to explore NLP techniques, but progress was slow due to limited computing power.

The 1990s–2000s: The rise of chatbots [13]

The development of the internet in the 1990s paved the way for new applications of conversational AI, such as chatbots for customer support. However, these early chatbots were often limited in their capabilities and could only respond to simple, scripted queries.

The rise of ML and cloud computing in the early 2000s led to a new wave of advances in conversational AI. With access to more computing power and data, researchers were able to develop more sophisticated NLP techniques and create chatbots that could learn from user interactions.

The 2010s: The emergence of virtual assistants [14]

In the 2010s, conversational AI took a major leap forward with the emergence of virtual assistants like Apple's Siri and Amazon's Alexa. These assistants were able to perform a wide range of tasks, from setting reminders to controlling smart home devices and could respond to a wide range of natural language queries.

Today: Conversational AI becomes ubiquitous

Today, conversational AI is ubiquitous, with chatbots and virtual assistants playing an increasingly important role in a wide range of industries. Healthcare providers use chatbots to triage patient inquiries, financial institutions use them to provide customer support, and retailers use them to assist with online purchases. Additionally, advances in NLP and ML are making conversational AI more sophisticated and context-aware, enabling more personalized and effective interactions.

Some Applications of Conversational AI are [15]

1. **Customer Service:** Conversational AI can be used to provide customers with 24/7 support via chatbots. Chatbots can quickly and efficiently handle common customer queries, freeing up customer service representatives to focus on more complex issues.

2. **Sales and Marketing:** Conversational AI can be used to engage with potential customers through chatbots, virtual assistants, and voice assistants. This can help to increase sales and conversions.

3. **Healthcare:** Conversational AI can be used to provide patients with virtual consultations, triage services, and health advice. This can help to improve access to healthcare services and reduce the burden on healthcare professionals [16].

4. **Education:** Conversational AI can be used to provide personalized learning experiences to students. Virtual tutors and language learning chatbots are examples of conversational AI applications in education.

5. **Finance:** Conversational AI can be used to provide customers with financial advice and support. Chatbots can help customers to manage their finances, track their spending, and make investment decisions.

6. **Hospitality:** Conversational AI can be used to improve the guest's experience and improve relationships with them in hotels and resorts. Chatbots can be used to handle guest requests, provide recommendations, and answer common questions.

7. **Human Resources:** Conversational AI can be used to streamline Heuristic Research (HR) processes such as recruitment, onboarding, and performance management. Chatbots can be used to answer employee queries and provide support.

8. **E-commerce:** Conversational AI can be used in e-commerce to help customers find products, answer their questions about products and services, and facilitate the purchase process. This can improve customer satisfaction and increase sales.

9. **Travel and Tourism [17]:** Conversational AI can be used to provide travel recommendations, suggest itineraries, and help customers book travel accommodations. Chatbots can also be used to answer common questions about travel requirements, such as visa and passport requirements.

10. **Gaming:** Conversational AI can be used to provide a more interactive gaming experience. Virtual assistants can help players navigate through games, provide hints and tips, and even engage in conversations with players to create a more immersive experience.

11. **Insurance:** Conversational AI can be used in the insurance industry to help customers file claims, get quotes, and manage policies. Chatbots can also provide customers with information about policy coverage and assist with the claims process.

12. **Real Estate:** Conversational AI can be used in the real estate industry to help customers find properties, answer questions about properties, and even schedule virtual tours. Virtual assistants can also be used to provide information about neighborhoods and the home-buying process.

13. **Automotive:** Conversational AI can be used in the automotive industry to help customers find and purchase cars, schedule maintenance appointments, and answer questions about vehicle features and specifications.

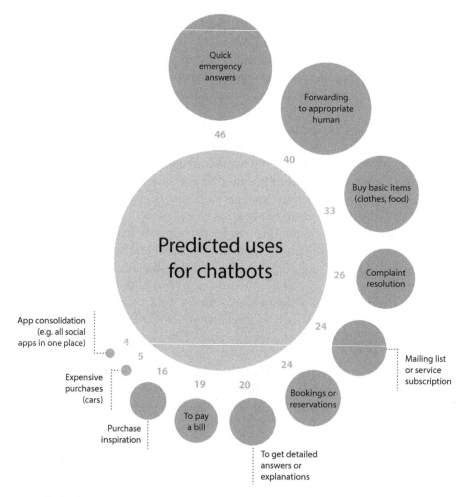

Figure 31.3 Chatbot processing paradigm.

14. **Government:** Conversational AI can be used in government services to improve citizen engagement, assist with application processes, and provide information about government policies and services.
15. **Legal:** Conversational AI can be used in the legal industry to assist with legal research, answer questions about legal documents and processes, and even provide basic legal advice.
16. **Agriculture and farming:** Conversational AI can be used to monitor crop growth and provide farmers with real-time insights and recommendations on how to optimize their yields.
17. **Security and surveillance:** Conversational AI can be used to power security and surveillance systems that can detect and respond to threats in real time.
18. **Public transportation:** Conversational AI can be used to create virtual assistants that help commuters navigate public transportation systems, find routes, and provide real-time updates on delays or disruptions.
19. **Language learning:** Conversational AI can be used to create language learning applications that provide users with natural language interactions and personalized feedback.
20. **Personal finance management:** Conversational AI can be used to create personal finance management tools that help users manage their finances, create budgets, and track expenses. Figure 31.3 shows the chatbot processing paradigm.

Some Conversational AI Tools [18, 19]

There are many conversational AI tools available in the market, ranging from open-source platforms to enterprise-level solutions. Here are some popular conversational AI tools:

1. **Dialogflow:** Google's Dialogflow is a popular platform for creating chatbots and voice assistants. It offers NLP capabilities and supports multiple languages.
2. **IBM Watson Assistant:** IBM Watson Assistant is an enterprise-level platform for building chatbots and virtual assistants. It uses NLU to understand user queries and offers a range of integrations with other enterprise applications.
3. **Amazon Lex:** Amazon Lex is a cloud-based service that allows developers to build chatbots and voice assistants powered by Amazon's Alexa technology. It offers advanced NLU capabilities and can integrate with other Amazon services like AWS Lambda and Amazon S3.
4. **Botpress:** Botpress is an open-source platform for building chatbots. It offers a range of prebuilt templates and integrations with other tools like Slack and Facebook Messenger.
5. **Rasa:** Rasa is an open-source platform for building chatbots and voice assistants. It offers NLU capabilities and can be customized to fit specific use cases.
6. **Microsoft Bot Framework:** Microsoft Bot Framework is a platform for building chatbots that can integrate with Microsoft services like Azure and Teams. It offers NLU capabilities and supports multiple languages.
7. **Wit.ai:** Wit.ai is a natural language processing platform that allows developers to build chatbots and voice assistants. It offers a range of integrations with other tools like Facebook Messenger and Twilio.

8. **Kore.ai:** A platform for building intelligent chatbots and virtual assistants that integrates with enterprise systems.
9. **Ada:** A chatbot platform that uses AI and NLP to improve customer service and support.
10. **Tars:** A drag-and-drop chatbot builder that allows nontechnical users to create and deploy chatbots for their businesses.
11. **Landbot:** A no-code chatbot builder that allows businesses to create conversational workflows for lead generation and customer engagement.
12. **Flow.ai:** A chatbot-building ML and NLP to create intelligent conversational interfaces.
13. **Chatfuel:** A platform for building chatbots on Facebook Messenger that uses a drag-and-drop interface and no coding is required.
14. **ManyChat:** A tool for building Facebook Messenger chatbots that integrates with popular marketing and sales tools.
15. **SnatchBot:** A chatbot-building platform that creates and deploys chatbots across multiple channels including websites, mobile apps, and messaging platforms.
16. **Zoho SalesIQ:** A live chat and chatbot tool for businesses that integrates with popular customer relationship management tools.
17. **KAI:** KAI is a conversational AI tool that allows businesses to create chatbots and other conversational interfaces that can be used for customer service support, sales assistance, and other functions.
18. **Flow.ai:** Flow.ai is a conversational AI tool that allows businesses to create chatbots and other conversational interfaces that can be integrated with Facebook Messenger, Slack, and other messaging platforms.
19. **Bold360:** Bold360 is a conversational AI tool that allows businesses to create chatbots and other conversational interfaces that can be used for customer service support, sales assistance, and other functions.
20. **BotStar:** BotStar is a conversational AI tool that allows businesses to create chatbots and other conversational interfaces that can be integrated with Facebook Messenger, Slack, and other messaging platforms.

These are just a few examples of the many conversational AI tools available in the market. The choice of tool will depend on the specific requirements of the project and the level of customization required.

Terms related to conversational AI [20, 21]:

a. Dialog Management:
Dialog management is a fundamental component of conversational AI systems that involves managing the conversation flow between a user and the AI agent. It is responsible for understanding the user's intent, extracting relevant information, and generating appropriate responses. Dialog management is often implemented using a state machine or a decision tree to map out the conversation flow.

Effective dialog management requires a range of techniques such as intent recognition, context management, slot filling, and response generation. These techniques ensure that the AI agent can understand and respond accurately and appropriately to user requests.

Dialog management has significant implications for a wide range of applications, including customer service, healthcare, education, and entertainment. Research in dialog management is focused on developing new techniques and algorithms for improving the accuracy, speed, and effectiveness of conversational AI systems.

The goal of dialog management research is to provide new methods and algorithms that will increase the precision, efficiency, and efficacy of conversational AI systems.

Techniques for effective dialog management

For conversational AI systems to provide correct and pertinent replies to user queries, dialog management must be effective. In dialog management, the following strategies are frequently applied:

- **Intent Recognition:** Understanding the user's intention or the goal of the communication is known as intent recognition. It entails figuring out what the user wants to accomplish and what they are requesting. NLP methods, ML algorithms, and rule-based strategies can all be used to recognize the intent.
- **Context Management:** Monitoring the conversation's context is part of context management. It involves being aware of the user's prior encounters, how the discussion is going right now, and any pertinent background knowledge. A dialog history can be kept up to date to help with context management, or context-aware methods like memory networks can be used.
- **Slot Filling:** Extracting pertinent data from user input is required for slot filling. It entails locating crucial details like names, dates, and locations. ML algorithms or pattern matching methods can both be used for slot filling.
- **Response Generation:** Answer generation is the process of coming up with the best possible answers depending on the user's input and the context of the present dialogue. NLG methods like template-based approaches, rule-based approaches, or machine learning algorithms like sequence-to-sequence models can all be used to generate responses.
- Integration of these strategies is necessary for effective dialog management to guarantee that the AI agent can comprehend user requests and react properly and appropriately. A variety of strategies, including rule-based systems, state machines, and reinforcement learning algorithms, can be used to achieve dialog management.

The goal of dialog management research is to provide new methods and algorithms that will increase the precision and efficiency of conversational AI systems. Dialog management has been improved because of recent developments in ML techniques like deep learning and reinforcement learning. The processing of complicated user requests, dealing with confusing user input, and enhancing the general effectiveness and scalability of dialog management systems are some of the issues that still need to be resolved.

In conclusion, developing conversational AI systems that can have tailored and interesting dialogs with people requires excellent dialog management. In many different fields, including healthcare, education customer service, and government, the creation of intelligent conversational bots will depend heavily on advances in dialog management research.

b. Multimodal Conversational AI:

Building conversational bots using a variety of modes, including speech, writing, and pictures, is known as multimodal conversational AI. This strategy makes it possible for users and computers to communicate more organically and straightforwardly. Due to the growing accessibility of multimodal data and the quick development of ML algorithms, multimodal chat AI has attracted a lot of interest lately.

The advantages and disadvantages of multimodal conversational AI will be discussed in this study paper, along with methods for merging various modes, creating efficient dialog management schemes, and assessing the effectiveness of multimodal conversational agents.

The study will also examine contemporary multimodal conversational AI uses in several industries, including healthcare, education, and amusement.

All things considered, multimodal conversational AI has the potential to revolutionize how we engage with computers and open up new possibilities for engaging and customized experiences. It is anticipated that studies in this area will continue to progress quickly and produce new developments in human–machine communication.

Advantages of multimodal conversational AI

Compared to conventional single-modal talking systems, multimodal conversational AI has several benefits, such as

1. **Enhanced User Experience:** Multimodal conversational AI enables more instinctive and natural interactions between users and computers. Users can interact more successfully and plainly by combining different modalities, such as speech, writing, and images.
2. A more precise understanding of user purpose is possible thanks to multimodal conversational AI, which takes into account a variety of data points. The agent may be able to comprehend the user's intended meaning better by merging voice and gesture detection, for instance.
3. **Robustness:** By minimizing the effects of mistakes in any one mode, multimodal conversational AI can make the system more robust. For instance, the system can still comprehend the user's input if voice recognition is unsuccessful by using text or gesture detection.
4. **Personalization:** By taking into account multiple sources of information like user past, tastes, and circumstances, multimodal conversational AI enables more personalized encounters with users.
5. **Accessibility:** By offering a variety of speech modes, multimodal conversational AI can increase accessibility for people with impairments, such as those who are deaf or hard of hearing.

6. The user experience could be greatly enhanced by multimodal conversational AI, which could also lead to more personalized and interesting encounters with computers. It is anticipated that research in this field will continue to progress quickly, resulting in new advancements in human–machine communication.

c. Contextual Understanding:

An AI system's contextual understanding refers to its capacity to grasp the subtleties and intricacies of a particular situation and to act properly in light of that knowledge. To comprehend the context in which the data are being given, the system must be able to evaluate information from a variety of sources, including text, auditory, visual, and other sensor data.

Modern AI systems must have contextual knowledge because it enables more natural and intuitive interactions between computers and people. Machines can better interpret and react to user requests by knowing the context of a discussion or circumstance, resulting in more effective and efficient interactions.

The application of contextual knowledge to computer vision is another illustration of its significance. An AI system can better comprehend the meaning of the data and make more accurate forecasts based on that knowledge by analyzing visual data in the context of its environment. Using contextual understanding, an AI system, for instance, can recognize the various items in a scenario, such as personnel, tools, and materials, and forecast their movements and interactions.

Overall, contextual understanding is a key element of contemporary AI systems, and continuing research in this field is anticipated to result in new advancements in human–machine interaction and allow machines to respond to user queries even more individually and effectively.

Challenges in Conversational AI

1. **Context Understanding:** Understanding the context of a conversation is crucial to providing relevant and helpful responses. However, context understanding is difficult, and AI systems can struggle to grasp the nuances of a conversation.
2. **Personalization:** Users expect personalized interactions with conversational AI systems, but achieving this requires access to user data and advanced ML algorithms.
3. **Handling Complex Queries:** Conversational AI systems need to be able to handle complex queries and provide accurate responses. This requires advanced NLP and ML capabilities.
4. **Multilingual Support:** Supporting multiple languages is important for global companies, but it can be challenging to develop and maintain conversational AI systems that can handle multiple languages.
5. **User Engagement:** Keeping users engaged in a conversation with a chatbot or virtual assistant can be difficult. Conversational AI systems need to be

designed to understand the user's intent and provide relevant responses that keep the conversation flowing.

6. **Error Handling:** Conversational AI systems need to be able to handle errors and provide meaningful feedback to users when errors occur.

7. **Integration with Existing Systems:** Integrating conversational AI systems with existing enterprise systems can be complex and challenging, requiring significant IT resources.

8. **Data Security and Privacy:** Conversational AI systems collect and store large amounts of user data, raising concerns about data security and privacy. Developers need to implement appropriate security measures to protect user data.

9. **Bias and Fairness:** Conversational AI systems can be biased based on the data they are trained on, leading to unfair or inappropriate responses. Developers need to take steps to reduce bias and ensure that conversational AI systems are fair and unbiased.

10. **Ethical Concerns:** Conversational AI raises ethical concerns related to privacy, data collection, and transparency. Developers need to be aware of these concerns and design conversational AI systems that are ethical and transparent.

Techniques

NLP, ML, and knowledge modeling methods must be combined to create conversational AI systems that can comprehend and react to context. The following are some of the main methods for creating talking AI systems that are context-aware:

NLP in context: Context-aware talking intelligence systems rely heavily on NLP. By examining the conversation's context, which includes the user's prior encounters with the system, the conversation's tone, and any other pertinent factors, contextual NLP techniques enable AI systems to comprehend the purpose behind a user's request.

Machine learning: AI systems can learn from previous interactions and adjust to new situations thanks to ML methods. For instance, to find trends and connections between various kinds of inputs and outputs, ML algorithms can be taught on huge datasets of conversation transcripts.

Knowledge representation: Techniques for knowledge representation are used to help AI systems comprehend the connections between various bits of information and to make decisions about complex situations. This includes methods like ontologies, which give information a means to be structurally organized and represented.

User modeling: By using user modeling methods, AI systems can tailor their responses to each user's unique tastes and behavior.

Context-aware reasoning: AI systems can reason about complex situations and make choices based on the context of the situation by using context-aware reasoning methods. Rule-based reasoning and probability reasoning are examples of such methods.

By utilizing these methods, AI researchers and developers can create talking AI systems that are context-aware and can comprehend and react more naturally and intuitively to the subtleties of human interactions. It is anticipated that ongoing study in this field will further improve the precision and efficacy of these systems, allowing them to manage increasingly complex duties and offer users even more individualized experiences.

31.2 Related Work

Conversational AI has been a rapidly evolving field in recent years, with many exciting developments in NLU, dialog generation, and evaluation. Recent papers have explored a wide range of topics, including transfer learning for conversational modeling, persona-based neural conversational models, and training and training personalized dialogue agents. Other researchers have proposed novel approaches for dialogue generation, such as using adversarial training or incorporating emotion detection. While these approaches have shown promising results, there are still many challenges in this field such as robustness to noise, handling of out-of-domain queries, and evaluation metrics. Table 31.1 shows the literature review of existing techniques.

31.3 Problem Statement

Conversational AI has completely changed how companies communicate with their consumers. Building conversational bots that can converse with people are not natural and fluidly difficult. The ability to correctly understand and react to complex customer requests is one of the major issues in this area. For instance, a conversational assistant should be able to comprehend the user's purpose, context, and tastes to give an appropriate and accurate answer when the user requests the location of a local Italian eatery that also accepts vegans. To enhance user experience and happiness, conversational AI systems that can correctly comprehend and react to user requests must be built.

Table 31.1 Literature review of existing techniques.

S. no.	Title	Authors	Year of publication
1	"BERT: Pre-training of Deep Bidirectional Transformers for Language Understanding."	Jacob Devlin, Ming-Wei Chang, Kenton Lee, and Kristina Toutanova	2018
2	OpenDialKG: Explainable Conversational Reasoning with Attention-based Walks over Knowledge Graphs	Seungwhan Moon, Pararth Shah, Anuj Kumar, and Rajen Subba	2019
3	Effective Analysis of Chatbot Frameworks: RASA and Dialogflow	Shalini Singh and Satwinder Singh	2022
4	"Chitty-Chitty-Chatbot": Deep Learning for Conversational AI	Rui Yan	2018
5	Conversational AI: Social and Ethical Considerations	Elayne Ruane, Abeba Birhane, and Anthony Ventresque	2019

The following are problems that have been identified:

1. **Lack of empathy and emotional intelligence in conversational AI:** While conversational AI has advanced significantly in recent years, one area where it still falls short is in its ability to empathize with and understand human emotions. This can be a major drawback when it comes to applications like mental health chatbots or customer service bots.

2. **Dealing with non-textual input:** Conversational AI systems are primarily designed to handle text-based input, but there are many situations where users may want to communicate through voice, images, or other forms of non-textual input. Developing systems that can effectively interpret and respond to these inputs presents a significant challenge.

3. **Handling complex queries:** Conversational AI systems are often designed to respond to specific types of queries or commands, but what happens when a user asks a complex question or makes a request that the system is not equipped to handle? Developing systems that can effectively handle these types of scenarios is an ongoing challenge.

4. **Dealing with multiparty conversations:** Most conversational AI systems are designed to handle one-on-one conversations, but what happens when there are multiple parties involved? Developing systems that effectively manage and mediate multiparty conversations is a complex and ongoing challenge.

5. **Enhancing creativity and imagination:** Conversational AI systems can enhance their engagement with users by incorporating creativity and imagination into their responses, such as generating original content or storytelling.

31.4   Proposed Methodology

The suggested approach is to make full use of the capabilities of NLP and ML techniques to overcome the difficulties of developing conversational AI systems that can effectively interpret and respond to user requests. In particular, the conversational agent can be created by combining NLP methods like sentiment analysis, entity extraction, and intent detection with ML models like deep learning and reinforcement learning algorithms.

To increase the conversational agent's precision and capacity for complicated user requests, massive datasets of conversational data can also be used for training. Additionally, adding user feedback and regularly updating the system with fresh data can improve the user experience overall while also enhancing the efficiency of the conversational agent.

The proposed solution's ultimate goal is to create conversational AI systems that can have conversations that are similar to those between humans and enhance customer engagement and satisfaction.

1. Lack of empathy and emotional intelligence:

One possible technical remedy is to use sentiment analysis algorithms and ML techniques to identify and react to human emotions in real time to resolve the absence of empathy and emotional intelligence in conversational AI.

The following actions could be done to put this approach into practice:

- **Data collection:** Compile a sizable database of human-to-human text-based exchanges and the associated emotional states (e.g., happy, sad, and frustrated).
- Using ML methods like deep learning and NLP trains a sentiment analysis model on the dataset to identify and categorize feelings in text-based data.
- **Integration with conversational AI:** By incorporating the mood analysis model into the conversational AI system, users' mental states can be recognized and addressed in real time.
- Create a collection of emotional responses that the conversational AI system can use to react to users most suitably based on their emotional state. As an illustration, if a user complains, the system might answer with a note that shows sympathy and offers help.
- Allow the system to learn and adjust to users' emotional responses constantly over time by using reinforcement learning or other ML methods. This will increase the system's emotional intelligence.
- The conversational AI system can become more sympathetic and receptive to users' emotional requirements by incorporating sentiment analysis and emotional responses, improving the user experience.

2. Dealing with non-textual input:

Using multimedia processing methods to assess and understand non-textual inputs like images, videos, and voice inputs is one possible technical answer to the problem of coping with non-textual input in conversational AI.

The following actions could be done to put this approach into practice:

- **Data gathering:** Compile a sizable dataset of non-text inputs, such as pictures, videos, and audio files, along with the accompanying text-based titles or descriptions.
- Using methods like computer vision, voice recognition, and audio processing to identify pertinent features and decipher non-textual inputs, train a multimedia processing model on the dataset.
- **Integration with conversational AI:** By integrating the multimedia processing model with the conversational AI system, it will be possible for it to comprehend and evaluate human input that is not text-based.
- The conversational AI system can answer users based on their non-textual inputs by using a set of responses that you create. For instance, the system may respond to a user who uploads an image of a product with details about that product or similar products.
- Allow the system to learn and adapt continuously to users' non-textual inputs over time, utilizing ML techniques to increase accuracy and efficiency.
- The conversational AI system can be made more adept at accepting non-textual inputs by including multimedia processing techniques, leading to a more adaptable and useful user experience.

3. Handling complex queries:

Using NLU and information retrieval (IR) techniques to effectively read and reply to complex user inquiries is one potential technical answer to the problem of processing complex queries in conversational AI.

The following actions could be taken to put this approach into practice:

- **Data collection:** Compile a sizable database of intricate user inquiries and the text-based answers or actions that correlate to them. Gather a complicated, varied set of user questions that cover a wide variety of topics. To guarantee that the NLU and IR models can correctly read a wide range of inputs, the queries should be as diverse as feasible.
- Compile a collection of text-based responses or actions for each inquiry. The answers must be thorough, accurate, and pertinent to the question. They must also cover a wide range of potential solutions. Gather any pertinent contextual information that may be required in addition to the questions and answers to correctly comprehend the inquiry.
- **NLU Model:** Train an NLU model on the dataset, using techniques such as deep learning and NLP to accurately interpret complex user queries.
- **IR Model:** Train an IR model on the dataset, using techniques such as vector space models and query expansion to retrieve relevant responses or actions based on user queries.
- **Annotations:** It could be essential to add extra information to the data by way of labels that describe the type of query or the inquiry's purpose. This can help to increase the NLU and IR models' accuracy and help the system comprehend and respond to more complicated user questions.

4. Dealing with multiparty conversations:

Using dialog management systems that can accommodate numerous speakers and keep track of the conversation's status is one possible technical answer to the problem of handling multiparty talks in conversational AI.

The following actions could be taken to put this approach into practice:

- Compile a sizable collection of multiparty interactions and the text-based exchanges that go with them.
- **Dialog Management Model:** Train a dialog management model on the dataset, using techniques such as reinforcement learning or rule-based systems to manage the flow of conversation and track the state of the dialogue.
- Create a speaker identification model to identify the participants in the conversation and to distinguish between each speaker's contributions.
- Using dialog management systems that can accommodate numerous speakers and keep track of the conversation's status is one possible technical answer to the problem of handling multiparty talks in conversational AI. The following actions could be taken to put this approach into practice:

- Compile a sizable collection of multiparty interactions and the text-based exchanges that go with them.
- Train a dialog management model on the dataset using methods like reinforcement learning or rule-based systems to control the direction of talk and monitor the dialog's status.
- Create a speaker identification model to identify the participants in the conversation and to distinguish between each speaker's contributions.

5. Enhancing Creativity and Imagination:

One possible technical approach is to use generative models, such as neural language models, to produce imaginative and creative responses in conversational AI.

The following actions could be taken to put this approach into practice:

- **Data Gathering:** Compile a sizable body of imaginative and creative text-based material, such as poems, novels, and other literary works.
- **Language Model:** Train a neural language model, such as a generative adversarial network or a variational autoencoder, on the dataset, using techniques such as unsupervised learning to generate novel and imaginative responses.
- **Integration with Conversational AI:** Integrate the language model with the conversational AI system, enabling it to generate creative and imaginative responses to user queries or prompts.
- **Continuous Learning:** Enable the system to continuously learn and adapt to new data over time, using techniques such as reinforcement learning or active learning to improve its creativity and imagination.

31.5   Regulatory Landscape of Conversational AI

The regulatory landscape for conversational AI is still evolving and varies across different countries and regions. However, there are some key regulations and guidelines that developers and businesses should be aware of:

1. **GDPR (General Data Protection Regulation):** The GDPR is a regulation in the European Union that governs data privacy and protection. It applies to any organization that processes the personal data of EU citizens, which includes conversational AI systems that collect user data.
2. **CCPA (California Consumer Privacy Act):** The CCPA is a regulation in California, United States that grants California residents certain privacy rights concerning their personal information. It applies to any organization that processes the personal data of California residents, including conversational AI systems.
3. **HIPAA (Health Insurance Portability and Accountability Act):** HIPAA is a US federal law that regulates the use and disclosure of protected health information. It applies to healthcare organizations that collect and store personal

health information, including conversational AI systems that interact with patients.

4. **Accessibility Guidelines:** Many countries have guidelines and regulations for accessibility to ensure that people with disabilities have equal access to technology. Conversational AI systems need to be designed to meet these guidelines to ensure that everyone can access and use them.

5. **Transparency and Accountability Guidelines:** Various guidelines and regulations have been developed to ensure that conversational AI systems are transparent, accountable, and ethical. These guidelines include the IEEE P7000 series, the AI Ethics Guidelines developed by the European Commission, and the Principles for Accountable Algorithms developed by the Berkman Klein Center for Internet & Society.

6. **Industry-Specific Regulations:** Conversational AI systems may be subject to industry-specific regulations, such as financial regulations, healthcare regulations, or telecommunications regulations.

7. **ePrivacy Directive:** The ePrivacy Directive is a regulation in the European Union that governs the use of electronic communications. It applies to any organization that processes electronic communications data, which include conversational AI systems.

8. **Children's Online Privacy Protection Act (COPPA):** COPPA is a US federal law that regulates the collection of personal information from children under the age of 13. It applies to any organization that operates a website or online service that collects personal information from children, including conversational AI systems.

9. **European Electronic Communications Code (EECC):** The EECC is a regulation in the European Union that aims to harmonize electronic communications across the EU. It applies to any organization that provides electronic communications services, including conversational AI systems.

10. **Federal Trade Commission Act (FTC Act):** The FTC Act is a US federal law that prohibits unfair or deceptive practices in commerce. It applies to any organization that engages in commerce, including those that develop and operate conversational AI systems.

Businesses and developers need to be aware of these regulations and guidelines to ensure that their conversational AI systems are compliant and ethical. As the technology continues to evolve, new regulations and guidelines will likely be introduced to address emerging challenges and concerns.

31.6   Future Works

Contextual Information Incorporation: Contextual factors like the user's position, the time of day, or recent actions can have an impact on a conversation. Future studies could investigate how to improve the relevance and responsiveness of talking AI models by incorporating environmental information.

Integrating Multiple Modalities: Conversational AI has mainly concentrated on text-based conversation, but other modalities, like speech, pictures, or video, may one day be included. Future research could investigate how to combine various modes to improve the conversation's depth and expressiveness.

Explainable Conversational AI: As conversational AI spreads, it's critical to make sure users are aware of how these programs function and how they make choices. Future research could look into how to make conversational AI clearer and more understandable, as well as how to factor user tastes and input into decision-making.

Conversational AI systems that can switch between languages and manage code-switching in the same conversation are still needed, even though there are presently many different languages accessible for conversational AI systems. Research in the future might concentrate on creating more sophisticated language models and language translation tools that can support international interactions.

Approaches involving a human in the process could be used to enhance the precision and caliber of talking AI systems. Future studies might concentrate on formulating strategies for adding human input to the system to boost performance.

The goal is to use human input to enhance the precision and caliber of the system's answers, particularly when the system is unsure or runs into a problem that it is unable to resolve on its own.

The learning phase and the feedback phase are the two stages that usually make up the Human-in-the-Loop Overview (HITL) method. The conversational AI system is taught on a collection of human interactions during the learning phase. ML algorithms are used to spot trends and create a model of how to react to various inputs. However, even the most advanced models occasionally run into challenges that they are unable to resolve on their own, such as comprehending sarcasm or an allusion to a particular cultural event.

With titles on the Dark Web [22–26] like How to Breach ChatGPT and ChatGPT [27, 28] as a Phishing [29, 30] Tool, the hacker [31, 32] community is eager to use AI. These kinds of searches demonstrate that cybercriminals [33–35] are seeking opportunities to utilise and abuse these technologies to defraud or compromise internet users. With the use of strong AI, it does raise questions about the possibility that these criminals [36] may perpetrate fraud, such as romance scams [37], and concurrently target several victims. Hackers may now use artificial intelligence to create more convincing frauds, which makes it possible for them to be employed in phishing scams. Phishing assaults are frequently identifiable by their poor usage of language, spelling, and arrangement of sentences. However, AI may make this obsolete; therefore, it's critical to verify any sender's address and search for errors in links or domain names. to you. Customers [38] are promptly paid for the items in their virtual shopping cart as they leave the store and given a digital receipt. As customers browse the aisles, the AI keeps note of the items they select. The information it gathers includes not only the choices made by the customer but also their browsing habits and needs. Since there is a lot of data, the corporation can quickly chart it and provide each customer with a customised menu of choices. The use of personal information by AI systems goes much beyond this apparent value. AI chatbots [39] adhere to policies that include access control, data anonymization, end-to-end encryption, and compliance transparency, among others. This does not, however, exclude the prospect of harm to data privacy [40].

31.7   Conclusion

The sophistication of today's interactive AI systems is rising as a result of advancements in ML and NLP. These systems, which can comprehend and produce natural language, have a variety of uses, such as personal assistants and customer support, among others.

Deep learning, a branch of ML that employs artificial neural networks to mimic the learning process of the human brain, is one of the main technologies underlying these systems. Deep learning algorithms can be used to train models that can identify patterns and make predictions by learning from vast amounts of data.

Deep learning is frequently used in conversational AI to teach language models that can comprehend and produce natural language. These models can learn the conventions and patterns of human language because they have been trained on vast datasets of text-based material, including emails, news articles, and social media posts.

The language model can produce natural language responses to user prompts or inquiries once it has been trained. The system takes the user input and uses the language model to generate a response that is appropriate for the context and intent of the query.

Conversational AI systems frequently integrate additional technologies, such as sentiment analysis and entity recognition, to enhance the precision and relevance of these answers. Sentiment analysis helps the system produce appropriate responses that take into consideration the user's attitude or mood by helping it comprehend the emotional tone of user queries. On the other hand, entity identification is used to recognize and extract important data from user queries, including names, dates, and locations.

In general, conversational AI systems are sophisticated, complicated technologies that can comprehend and produce natural language. These systems are improving in accuracy and efficacy by utilizing the most recent developments in deep learning and natural language processing, and they are likely to play a larger role in a broad range of applications in the future.

References

1. What is conversational AI?, IBM, www.ibm.com/topics/conversational-ai.
2. What is machine learning?, IBM, www.ibm.com/in-en/topics/machine-learning.
3. What is natural language processing?, IBM, www.ibm.com/in-en/topics/natural-language-processing.
4. Wu, C.-S., Madotto, A., Hosseini-Asl, E., Xiong, C., Socher, R., Fung, P., Transferable multi-domain state generator for task-oriented dialogue systems, in: *arXiv [cs.CL]*, 2019, http://arxiv.org/abs/1905.08743.
5. Wang, X., Shi, W., Kim, R., Oh, Y., Yang, S., Zhang, J., Yu, Z., Persuasion for good: Towards a personalized persuasive dialogue system for social good, in: *arXiv [cs.CL]*, 2019, http://arxiv.org/abs/1906.06725.
6. Sankar, C., Subramanian, S., Pal, C., Chandar, S., Bengio, Y., Do neural dialog systems use the conversation history effectively? An empirical study, in: *arXiv [cs.CL]*, 2019, http://arxiv.org/abs/1906.01603.
7. Ghandeharioun, A., Shen, J.H., Jaques, N., Ferguson, C., Jones, N., Lapedriza, A., Picard, R., Approximating interactive human evaluation with self-play for open-domain dialog systems, in: *arXiv [cs.CL]*, 2019, http://arxiv.org/abs/1906.09308.

8. Gao, X., Lee, S., Zhang, Y., Brockett, C., Galley, M., Gao, J., Dolan, B., Jointly optimizing diversity and relevance in neural response generation, in: *arXiv [cs.CL]*, 2019, http://arxiv.org/abs/1902.11205.

9. Dinan, E., Humeau, S., Chintagunta, B., Weston, J., Build it break it fix it for dialogue safety: Robustness from adversarial human attack, in: *arXiv [cs.CL]*, 2019, http://arxiv.org/abs/1908.06083.

10. Rawat, R., Logical concept mapping and social media analytics relating to cyber criminal activities for ontology creation. *Int. J. Inf. Technol.*, 15, 2, 893–903, 2023.

11. Rawat, R., Mahor, V., Álvarez, J.D., Ch, F., Cognitive systems for dark web cyber delinquent association malignant data crawling: A review, in: *Handbook of Research on War Policies, Strategies, and Cyber Wars*, pp. 45–63, 2023.

12. Rawat, R., Chakrawarti, R.K., Vyas, P., Gonzáles, J.L.A., Sikarwar, R., Bhardwaj, R., Intelligent fog computing surveillance system for crime and vulnerability identification and tracing. *Int. J. Inf. Secur. Priv. (IJISP)*, 17, 1, 1–25, 2023.

13. Mahor, V., Bijrothiya, S., Rawat, R., Kumar, A., Garg, B., Pachlasiya, K., IoT and artificial intelligence techniques for public safety and security, in: *Smart Urban Computing Applications*, p. 111, 2023.

14. Mahor, V., Pachlasiya, K., Garg, B., Chouhan, M., Telang, S., Rawat, R., Mobile operating system (android) vulnerability analysis using machine learning, in: *Proceedings of International Conference on Network Security and Blockchain Technology: ICNSBT 2021*, 2022, June, Springer Nature Singapore, Singapore, pp. 159–169.

15. Mahor, V., Garg, B., Telang, S., Pachlasiya, K., Chouhan, M., Rawat, R., Cyber threat phylogeny assessment and vulnerabilities representation at thermal power station, in: *Proceedings of International Conference on Network Security and Blockchain Technology: ICNSBT 2021*, 2022, June, Springer Nature Singapore, Singapore, pp. 28–39.

16. Rawat, R., Gupta, S., Sivaranjani, S., Cu, O.K., Kuliha, M., Sankaran, K.S., Malevolent information crawling mechanism for forming structured illegal organisations in hidden networks. *Int. J. Cyber Warf. Terror. (IJCWT)*, 12, 1, 1–14, 2022.

17. Rawat, R., Rimal, Y.N., William, P., Dahima, S., Gupta, S., Sankaran, K.S., Malware threat affecting financial organization analysis using machine learning approach. *Int. J. Inf. Technol. Web Eng. (IJITWE)*, 17, 1, 1–20, 2022.

18. Rawat, R., Mahor, V., Chouhan, M., Pachlasiya, K., Telang, S., Garg, B., Systematic literature review (SLR) on social media and the digital transformation of drug trafficking on darkweb, in: *International Conference on Network Security and Blockchain Technology*, Springer, Singapore, pp. 181–205, 2022.

19. Cheng, H., Fang, H., Ostendorf, M., A dynamic speaker model for conversational interactions. *Proceedings of the 2019 Conference of the North*, 2019.

20. Byrne, B., Krishnamoorthi, K., Sankar, C., Neelakantan, A., Goodrich, B., Duckworth, D., Yavuz, S., Dubey, A., Kim, K.-Y., Cedilnik, A., Taskmaster-1: Toward a realistic and diverse dialog dataset. *Proceedings of the 2019 Conference on Empirical Methods in Natural Language Processing and the 9th International Joint Conference on Natural Language Processing (EMNLP-IJCNLP)*, 2019.

21. Gopalakrishnan, K., Hedayatnia, B., Chen, Q., Gottardi, A., Kwatra, S., Venkatesh, A., Gabriel, R., Hakkani-Tür, D., Topical chat: Towards knowledge-grounded open-domain conversations. *Interspeech 2019*, 2019.

22. Mahor, V., Bijrothiya, S., Rawat, R., Kumar, A., Garg, B., Pachlasiya, K., IoT and artificial intelligence techniques for public safety and security, in: *Smart Urban Computing Applications*, p. 111, 2023.

23. Mahor, V., Pachlasiya, K., Garg, B., Chouhan, M., Telang, S., Rawat, R., Mobile operating system (Android) vulnerability analysis using machine learning, in: *Proceedings of International Conference on Network Security and Blockchain Technology: ICNSBT 2021*, pp. 159–169, Springer Nature Singapore, Singapore, 2022, June.

24. Rawat, R., Garg, B., Pachlasiya, K., Mahor, V., Telang, S., Chouhan, M., Mishra, R., SCNTA: Monitoring of network availability and activity for identification of anomalies using machine learning approaches. *Int. J. Inf. Technol. Web Eng. (IJITWE)*, 17, 1, 1–19, 2022.

25. Rawat, R., Rimal, Y.N., William, P., Dahima, S., Gupta, S., Sankaran, K.S., Malware threat affecting financial organization analysis using machine learning approach. *Int. J. Inf. Technol. Web Eng. (IJITWE)*, 17, 1, 1–20, 2022.

26. Rawat, R., Mahor, V., Chouhan, M., Pachlasiya, K., Telang, S., Garg, B., Systematic literature review (SLR) on social media and the digital transformation of drug trafficking on darkweb, in: *International Conference on Network Security and Blockchain Technology*, pp. 181–205, Springer, Singapore, 2022.

27. Rawat, R., Ayodele Oki, O., Sankaran, S., Florez, H., Ajagbe, S.A., Techniques for predicting dark web events focused on the delivery of illicit products and ordered crime. *Int. J. Electr. Comput. Eng. (IJECE)*, 13, 5, 5354–5365, Oct. 2023, doi: 10.11591/ijece.v13i5.pp5354-5365.

28. Rawat, R., Garg, B., Mahor, V., Telang, S., Pachlasiya, K., Chouhan, M., Organ trafficking on the dark web—The data security and privacy concern in healthcare systems, in: *Internet of Healthcare Things: Machine Learning for Security and Privacy*, pp. 189–216, 2022.

29. Vyas, P., Vyas, G., Chauhan, A., Rawat, R., Telang, S., Gottumukkala, M., Anonymous trading on the dark online marketplace: An exploratory study, in: *Using Computational Intelligence for the Dark Web and Illicit Behavior Detection*, pp. 272–289, IGI Global, 2022.

30. Rawat, R., Oki, O.A., Sankaran, K.S., Olasupo, O., Ebong, G.N., Ajagbe, S.A., A new solution for cyber security in big data using machine learning approach, in: *Mobile Computing and Sustainable Informatics: Proceedings of ICMCSI 2023*, pp. 495–505, Springer Nature Singapore, Singapore, 2023.

31. Rawat, R., Chakrawarti, R.K., Raj, A., Mani, G., Chidambarathanu, K., Bhardwaj, R., Association rule learning for threat analysis using traffic analysis and packet filtering approach. *Int. J. Inf. Technol.*, 1–11, 2023.

32. Rawat, R., Logical concept mapping and social media analytics relating to cyber criminal activities for ontology creation. *Int. J. Inf. Technol.*, 15, 2, 893–903, 2023.

33. Rawat, R., Mahor, V., Álvarez, J.D., Ch, F., Cognitive systems for dark web cyber delinquent association malignant data crawling: A review, in: *Handbook of Research on War Policies, Strategies, and Cyber Wars*, pp. 45–63, 2023.

34. Rawat, R., Chakrawarti, R.K., Vyas, P., Gonzáles, J.L.A., Sikarwar, R., Bhardwaj, R., Intelligent fog computing surveillance system for crime and vulnerability identification and tracing. *Int. J. Inf. Secur. Priv. (IJISP)*, 17, 1, 1–25, 2023.

35. Rawat, R., Sowjanya, A.M., Patel, S.I., Jaiswal, V., Khan, I., Balaram, A. (Eds.), *Using Machine Intelligence: Autonomous Vehicles Volume 1*, John Wiley & Sons, 2022.

36. Rawat, R., Mahor, V., Díaz-Álvarez, J., Chávez, F., Rooted learning model at fog computing analysis for crime incident surveillance, in: *2022 International Conference on Smart Generation Computing, Communication and Networking (SMART GENCON)*, pp. 1–9, IEEE, 2022, December.

37. Rawat, R. and Shrivastav, S.K., SQL injection attack detection using SVM. *Int. J. Comput. Appl.*, 42, 13, 1–4, 2012.

38. Rawat, R., Bhardwaj, P., Kaur, U., Telang, S., Chouhan, M., Sankaran, K.S., *Smart vehicles for communication, volume 2*, John Wiley & Sons, 2023.

39. Mahor, V., Garg, B., Telang, S., Pachlasiya, K., Chouhan, M., Rawat, R., Cyber threat phylogeny assessment and vulnerabilities representation at thermal power station, in: *Proceedings of International Conference on Network Security and Blockchain Technology: ICNSBT 2021*, pp. 28–39, Springer Nature Singapore, Singapore, 2022, June.

40. Rawat, R., Gupta, S., Sivaranjani, S., Cu, O.K., Kuliha, M., Sankaran, K.S., Malevolent information crawling mechanism for forming structured illegal organisations in hidden networks. *Int. J. Cyber Warf. Terror. (IJCWT)*, *12*, 1, 1–14, 2022.

Risks for Conversational AI Security

Vivek Bhardwaj[1], Safdar Sardar Khan[2], Gurpreet Singh[3], Sunil Patil[4],
Devendra Kuril[5] and Sarthak Nahar[6]*

[1]School of Computer Science and Engineering, Manipal University Jaipur, Jaipur, India
[2]Department of Computer Science and Engineering, Medi-Caps University, Indore, India
[3]Department of Computer Science and Engineering, Lovely Professional University, Jalandhar,
Punjab, India
[4]Department of Computer Science and Engineering, Vedica Institute of Technology,
RKDF University Bhopal, Bhopal, India
[5]Department of Information Technology, Shri Vaishnav Vidyapeeth Vishwavidyalaya, Indore, India
[6]Department of Computer Science Engineering, Shri Vaishnav Vidyapeeth Vishwavidyalaya Indore,
Indore, India

Abstract

Conversational artificial intelligence (AI) systems have become increasingly popular, and their integration into various industries has grown significantly. With the advent of advanced technologies like machine learning and natural language processing, conversational AI has become capable of performing complex tasks, including processing customer requests, providing recommendations, and facilitating transactions. However, these systems are also vulnerable to various security risks that can expose sensitive data and compromise the privacy of users. This paper provides a comprehensive review of the risks associated with conversational AI security, including attacks such as phishing, malware injection, and voice cloning. The paper also discusses the potential impact of these attacks on businesses and end-users and proposes strategies to mitigate these risks [1].

Conversational AI is a rapidly growing field, with a wide range of applications such as customer service, personal assistants, and healthcare. However, with the increasing use of conversational AI, there are also growing concerns about the security risks associated with these systems. This research paper aims to explore the risks associated with conversational AI security, including privacy breaches, data leakage, and manipulation of conversational agents. This paper also discusses the current state of research in this area and proposes recommendations for improving conversational AI security. Conversational AI has gained significant popularity in recent years due to its ability to enable natural and seamless interactions between humans and machines. However, with the increasing use of conversational AI, the risks for security have also increased. The risks for conversational AI security include both technical and non-technical threats that can compromise the confidentiality, integrity, and availability of sensitive information. This paper provides an overview of the risks associated with conversational AI security, including threats such as data breaches, malicious attacks, impersonation attacks, and social engineering attacks. It also discusses the measures that can be taken to mitigate these risks, including implementing secure authentication mechanisms, using encryption,

*Corresponding author: sarthaknahar123@gmail.com

Romil Rawat, Rajesh Kumar Chakrawarti, Sanjaya Kumar Sarangi, Piyush Vyas, Mary Sowjanya Alamanda, Kotagiri Srividya and Krishnan Sakthidasan Sankaran (eds.) Conversational Artificial Intelligence, (557–588) © 2024 Scrivener Publishing LLC

monitoring user behavior, and adopting a risk management approach. Ultimately, understanding the risks for conversational AI security is crucial for organizations to develop effective security strategies and protect their sensitive information from potential threats.

Keywords: Conversational AI, natural language processing, machine learning (ML), Chatbots, virtual assistants, voice assistants

32.1 Introduction

Natural language processing (NLP) and machine learning (ML) are combined in conversational artificial intelligence (AI). To keep the AI algorithms up to date, these NLP operations interact with ML processes in a continual feedback loop. The fundamental elements of conversational AI enable it to process, comprehend, and produce responses in a natural manner.

An area of AI called ML consists of algorithms, features, and data sets that constantly get better with use. The AI platform machine gets better at identifying patterns and employs them to create predictions as the input increases.

Conversational AI currently uses NLP to analyze language with the use of ML. Before ML, linguistics, computational linguistics, and statistical NLP were the stages in the development of language processing techniques. Deep learning will enhance conversational AI's capacity for natural language understanding (NLU) in the future [2].

NLP consists of four steps: Input generation, input analysis, output generation, and reinforcement learning. Unstructured data are transformed into a format that can be read by a computer, which is then analyzed to generate an appropriate response. Underlying ML algorithms improve response quality over time as it learns. These four NLP steps can be broken down further below:

- Input generation: Using a website or an app, users can offer input in the form of text or voice.
- Analysis of the input: If the input is text-based, the conversational AI solution app will utilize NLU to interpret the input's meaning and determine its intended purpose. However, if the input is speech-based, it will use automatic speech recognition (ASR) and NLU to interpret the data.
- Conversation management: A response is created at this stage using Natural Language Generation (NLG), a part of NLP.
- Reinforcement learning: To assure accuracy, ML algorithms continuously improve replies.

Conversational AI security refers to the measures taken to protect the privacy, confidentiality, and integrity of data and interactions between users and conversational AI systems. As conversational AI systems become more prevalent, they can potentially become targets for malicious attacks, such as identity theft, fraud, or unauthorized access to sensitive information. Therefore, ensuring the security of these systems is of utmost importance.

Conversational AI, also known as chatbots, virtual assistants, or voice assistants, is a rapidly growing technology that enables human-like interactions between users and machines. As conversational AI becomes more prevalent in our daily lives, it is important to be aware of the potential security risks associated with these systems.

One major risk for conversational AI security is the potential for hackers to exploit vulnerabilities in the system. These vulnerabilities could be in the software, hardware, or network infrastructure used to run the conversational AI. Hackers could use these vulnerabilities to gain unauthorized access to the system, steal sensitive data, or even take control of the conversational AI to carry out malicious activities.

Another risk is the potential for conversational AI to be used to spread misinformation or propaganda. Because conversational AI can be programmed to mimic human speech patterns and behaviors, they can be used to spread fake news, conspiracy theories, and other forms of disinformation. This can have serious consequences for individuals, organizations, and society as a whole.

Privacy is also a concern when it comes to conversational AI security. Conversational AI systems often collect and store sensitive information, such as personal data, financial information, and health records. If these systems are not properly secured, this information could be vulnerable to unauthorized access, theft, or misuse.

Finally, there is a risk of bias in conversational AI systems. Because these systems are trained on large datasets, they can inherit biases from the data they are trained on. This can result in discriminatory behavior toward certain groups of people or perpetuate existing societal biases.

The research work on Risks for Conversational AI Security explores the potential security risks associated with conversational AI systems. With the increasing popularity of virtual assistants, chatbots, and other conversational AI applications, it is important to identify and mitigate the potential security threats that these systems may pose.

The research work aims to identify and classify the various types of security risks that may arise in conversational AI systems, including but not limited to authentication and authorization issues, privacy and data protection concerns, and malicious attacks such as phishing and social engineering. The work also focuses on analyzing the underlying vulnerabilities and weaknesses that can be exploited by malicious actors and proposes solutions to mitigate these risks.

The study examines existing security measures and protocols in place for conversational AI systems and identifies areas where improvements can be made. The work also highlights the importance of user education and awareness, as users can inadvertently expose themselves to security risks by disclosing sensitive information or engaging with malicious actors.

Overall, the research work aims to provide a comprehensive overview of the security risks associated with conversational AI systems and proposes recommendations for developers, organizations, and users to ensure the safe and secure use of these technologies.

Overall, it is important to consider these risks and take steps to mitigate them in order to ensure the security and reliability of conversational AI systems.

Organization of Chapter
The rest of the chapter is outlined as follows. Section 32.2 discusses related work, Section 32.3 presents a history and evolution of conversational AI security, Section 32.4 discusses the components and concepts that makes conversational AI security, Section 32.5 presents working of conversational AI Security, Section 32.6 discusses the risks for conversational AI security, Section 32.7 presents solutions for conversational AI security, and Section 32.8 wraps up this chapter.

32.2   Related Work

There is a growing body of research on the risks associated with conversational AI security. Some examples of related research work include

"Attacks and Defenses for Deep Learning-based Conversational Agents" by Samira Shekhar and colleagues (2018): This paper describes various attacks that can be launched against conversational AI systems, such as input manipulation, model poisoning, and adversarial examples. The authors also propose several defenses to mitigate these risks [3].

"Towards Evaluating the Robustness of Neural Networks" by Nicholas Carlini and David Wagner (2017): This paper explores the vulnerability of neural networks to adversarial attacks, which can be used to deceive conversational AI systems. The authors propose a method for evaluating the robustness of neural networks and demonstrate its effectiveness on conversational AI models [4].

"Security and Privacy Challenges in the Internet of Things" by Pradeep Kumar and colleagues (2020): This paper discusses the security and privacy challenges associated with the internet of things (IoT), which includes conversational AI systems. The authors identify several potential risks, such as data breaches, unauthorized access, and malware attacks [5].

"A Survey of Conversational AI: Foundations, Recent Advances, and Emerging Applications" by Jie Hou and colleagues (2021): This paper provides a comprehensive survey of conversational AI, including its security risks and challenges. The authors highlight the importance of security in conversational AI systems and provide an overview of existing security solutions [6].

"A Survey on Security and Privacy Issues in Conversational AI" by V. Chandrasekaran, S. Yang, and S. S. Iyengar (2020): This paper provides a comprehensive survey of security and privacy issues in conversational AI. It covers topics such as data privacy, authentication, access control, and threat modeling [7].

"Adversarial Attacks on Conversational AI Systems: A Survey" by Y. Chen, H. Wang, and X. Zhang (2020): This paper surveys adversarial attacks on conversational AI systems, including attacks on speech recognition, NLP, and dialog management.

"Conversational AI: Review and Research Directions" by J. Xu, Y. Zhang, and Y. Wang (2020): This paper reviews recent developments in conversational AI and identifies research directions for improving its security, including developing new security models and frameworks [8].

"Security and Privacy in Conversational AI: Challenges and Opportunities" by S. Zou, M. Zhang, and L. Gao (2021): This paper discusses security and privacy challenges in conversational AI and proposes potential solutions, including encryption, authentication, and access control mechanisms.

Overall, these and other related research works highlight the need for increased attention to security risks in conversational AI systems and the development of effective defenses to mitigate these risks.

32.3   History and Evolution of Conversational AI Security

Conversational AI refers to the technology that enables machines to communicate with humans in natural language. Conversational AI has become increasingly popular in recent years with the rise of voice assistants, chatbots, and other similar technologies. However, with the increased use of conversational AI, there is also an increased need for security measures to protect the privacy of users and prevent malicious attacks.

The history of conversational AI security can be traced back to the early days of chatbots. Initially, chatbots were created to mimic human-like conversations and provide customer support. However, as chatbots became more sophisticated, they were also used for more nefarious purposes such as phishing and social engineering attacks.

As a result, security measures were developed to protect users from these types of attacks. For example, one common approach is to use ML algorithms to detect patterns in user input and identify potential security threats. Additionally, authentication measures, such as two-factor authentication, are used to verify the identity of users before allowing them to access sensitive information.

With the rise of voice assistants, such as Amazon Alexa and Google Assistant, new security challenges have emerged. These devices are always listening and can potentially record sensitive conversations. To address these concerns, many devices have built-in privacy features such as mute buttons and the ability to delete recordings.

Another security concern with conversational AI is the potential for bias. Since these systems are trained on large datasets, they may inadvertently pick up biases that can lead to discriminatory behavior. To address this issue, many researchers are working on developing more ethical and transparent algorithms that can detect and correct bias.

Overall, the evaluation of conversational AI security is an ongoing process. As technology advances, so do the security threats. Therefore, it is important to continuously assess and improve the security measures in place to protect users from potential attacks.

One approach to evaluating the security of conversational AI is through penetration testing. Penetration testing involves simulating a cyberattack to identify vulnerabilities in the system. This type of testing can help developers identify and address potential security threats before they are exploited by malicious actors.

Another approach is to use threat modeling, which involves identifying potential security threats and developing strategies to mitigate them. This process involves considering the various ways in which an attacker could potentially exploit the system and developing defenses against those attacks.

In addition to these technical evaluations, it is also important to consider the ethical implications of conversational AI security. As these systems become more widespread, they will have a significant impact on society. Therefore, it is important to consider how the use of conversational AI could potentially harm vulnerable populations and to develop strategies to mitigate those risks.

In conclusion, the history and evaluation of conversational AI security is an ongoing process. As the technology continues to advance, so do the security threats. It is important to continuously assess and improve the security measures in place to protect users from potential attacks. Additionally, ethical considerations should be taken into account to ensure that the use of conversational AI does not harm vulnerable populations.

32.4 Components and Concepts that Make Coversational AI Security

Conversational AI, also known as chatbots or virtual assistants, has become increasingly popular in recent years due to the advancements in NLP and ML. However, as conversational

AI becomes more pervasive, it is crucial to ensure that these systems are secure and protect users' data and privacy. In this article, we will discuss the components and concepts that make conversational AI security possible.

32.4.1   Authentication and Authorization

One of the most critical components of conversational AI security is authentication and authorization. Authentication ensures that the user accessing the chatbot is indeed who they claim to be. Authorization verifies that the user has the appropriate level of access to perform the requested action. Implementing strong authentication and authorization mechanisms will help prevent unauthorized access to sensitive information.

Authentication is the process of verifying the identity of a user or device. This is typically done using a username and password combination, but there are other authentication methods available such as biometric authentication (fingerprint or face recognition), two-factor authentication, or multifactor authentication. The goal of authentication is to ensure that only authorized users or devices can access the system or data.

Authorization is the process of determining what level of access a user or device has to a system, application, or data. This is typically done by assigning roles or permissions to users or devices. For example, an administrator may have full access to a system, while a regular user may only have access to certain parts of the system. Authorization helps in ensuring that users or devices have access only to the resources that they need to perform their tasks.

32.4.1.1   Authentication and Authorization Working Together

Authentication and authorization work together to ensure the security of a system or application. Before a user or device is granted access to a system or data, they must first be authenticated to ensure that they are who they claim to be. Once authenticated, the system then checks the user's or device's authorization level to determine what level of access they have to the system or data.

For example, when a user logs into a website using a username and password, the system first authenticates the user's credentials. Once the user is authenticated, the system then checks the user's authorization level to determine what actions they are authorized to perform on the website. If the user has administrator privileges, they may have access to all the features of the website, while a regular user may only have access to certain parts of the website.

32.4.1.2   Benefits of Authentication and Authorization

Authentication and authorization provide several benefits to a system or application, including

Increased Security:
Authentication and authorization ensure that only authorized users or devices can access the system or data. This helps in preventing unauthorized access and data breaches.

Improved Compliance:
Many regulations and standards, such as the Payment Card Industry Data Security Standard (PCI DSS) and Health Insurance Portability and Accountability Act (HIPAA), require organizations to implement strong authentication and authorization controls to protect sensitive data.

Enhanced User Experience:
Authentication and authorization can be used to personalize the user experience by providing access to only the resources that are relevant to the user.

32.4.2   Encryption

Encryption is the process of converting data into a secure format that cannot be easily understood by unauthorized parties. Conversational AI systems must use encryption to protect sensitive information such as user credentials, payment information, and other personally identifiable information (PII).

Encryption is a crucial aspect of conversational AI security. Conversational AI systems process and store a vast amount of sensitive information, including personal and financial data, and encryption is used to protect this information from unauthorized access or tampering.

Conversational AI systems use encryption to protect sensitive data in the following areas:

Data in Transit:
When conversational AI systems communicate with users, the data are transmitted over the internet, which makes it vulnerable to interception or eavesdropping. Encryption is used to protect the data in transit and ensure that it is only accessible to authorized parties.

Data at Rest:
Conversational AI systems store user data, such as chat logs, preferences, and account information, in databases or cloud storage systems. Encryption is used to protect the data at rest and ensure that it is only accessible to authorized parties.

Machine Learning Models:
Conversational AI systems use ML models to recognize and interpret user input and generate responses. These models are trained on large datasets of user interactions, which may contain sensitive information. Encryption is used to protect the ML models and ensure that the data used to train them are secure.

Encryption Techniques in Conversational AI

Symmetric Encryption:
Symmetric encryption uses a single key to encrypt and decrypt data. The same key is used to encrypt the data at the sender's end and decrypt it at the receiver's end. Symmetric encryption is fast and efficient but requires a secure key exchange process to ensure that the key is only accessible to authorized parties.

Asymmetric Encryption:
Asymmetric encryption uses a pair of keys, one public and one private, to encrypt and decrypt data. The public key is widely distributed and used to encrypt the data, while the private key is kept secure and used to decrypt the data. Asymmetric encryption is slower than symmetric encryption but provides better security and eliminates the need for a secure key exchange process.

Hashing:
Hashing is a one-way encryption technique that converts data into a fixed-length string of characters. Hashing is commonly used to store passwords securely, where the hashed password is stored instead of the plaintext password. Hashing is irreversible, and the same input always produces the same output.

Encryption Standards in Conversational AI
Several encryption standards are commonly used in conversational AI systems, including

Transport Layer Security (TLS):
TLS is a protocol that provides encryption and authentication for internet communications. TLS is commonly used to encrypt data in transit between conversational AI systems and users.

Advanced Encryption Standard (AES):
The AES is a symmetric encryption algorithm that is widely used in conversational AI systems to encrypt data at rest. AES provides a high level of security and is considered one of the most secure encryption algorithms.

Secure Hash Algorithm (SHA):
The SHA is a hashing algorithm that is widely used to store passwords securely in conversational AI systems. The SHA produces a fixed-length hash that is irreversible and provides a high level of security.

32.4.3   Privacy

Privacy is a critical concept in conversational AI security. Conversational AI systems must ensure that users' data are protected and only used for authorized purposes. This means that the system must be transparent about what data are being collected, how they are being used, and who has access to it. Additionally, conversational AI systems must comply with data privacy regulations such as General Data Protection Regulation (GDPR), California Consumer Privacy Act (CCPA), and HIPAA.

Conversational AI systems face several privacy challenges, including

User Consent:
Users must provide consent for conversational AI systems to collect, process, and store their personal data. Consent must be explicit, informed, and freely given, and users should be informed about how their data will be used.

Data Storage:
Conversational AI systems store user data, such as chat logs, preferences, and account information, in databases or cloud storage systems. The data must be stored securely and protected from unauthorized access or disclosure.

Data Sharing:
Conversational AI systems may share user data with third-party services or partners. Data sharing must be transparent and in compliance with data protection regulations.

Data Anonymization:
Conversational AI systems must ensure that the personal data collected from users is anonymized, pseudonymized, or de-identified to protect user privacy.

Privacy Measures in Conversational AI
To address the privacy challenges, conversational AI systems implement various privacy measures, such as

Data Minimization:
Conversational AI systems collect only the necessary data required to provide the requested services, and the data are deleted when they are no longer needed.

Data Encryption:
Conversational AI systems encrypt personal data in transit and at rest to protect them from unauthorized access or disclosure.

User Authentication:
Conversational AI systems authenticate users to ensure that only authorized parties access personal data.

Privacy Policies:
Conversational AI systems provide clear and concise privacy policies that inform users about how their data are collected, processed, and shared.

Data Access Controls:
Conversational AI systems implement access controls to restrict access to personal data to authorized parties only.

Anonymization and Pseudonymization:
Conversational AI systems anonymize, pseudonymize, or de-identify personal data to protect user privacy.

Privacy Regulations in Conversational AI
Conversational AI systems must comply with various data protection regulations, such as

General Data Protection Regulation (GDPR):
GDPR is a European Union regulation that governs the processing of personal data of EU citizens. GDPR requires that organizations obtain explicit and informed consent from users before collecting their personal data and implement measures to protect the data.

California Consumer Privacy Act (CCPA):
CCPA is a California state law that gives California residents the right to know what personal data are collected about them and the right to request that the data be deleted.

Children's Online Privacy Protection Act (COPPA):
COPPA is a US federal law that regulates the collection of personal data from children under 13 years old. COPPA requires that organizations obtain verifiable parental consent before collecting personal data from children.

32.4.4 Trust

Trust is an essential concept in conversational AI security. Users must trust that the conversational AI system is secure and will protect their data and privacy. To build trust, conversational AI systems must be transparent about their security measures and provide clear information about how users can protect themselves.

Trust Challenges in Conversational AI

Conversational AI systems face several trust challenges, including

Accuracy:

Conversational AI systems must provide accurate and relevant responses to user queries. If the system provides inaccurate or irrelevant responses, users may lose trust in the system.

Transparency:

Conversational AI systems must be transparent in how they collect, process, and use user data. If users feel that their data are being misused or mishandled, they may lose trust in the system.

Bias:

Conversational AI systems can be biased if they are trained on biased data. If users perceive bias in the system's responses, they may lose trust in the system.

Security:

Conversational AI systems must be secure and protect user data from unauthorized access or disclosure. If users feel that their data are not secure, they may lose trust in the system.

Trust Measures in Conversational AI

To address the trust challenges, conversational AI systems implement various trust measures, such as

Accuracy Monitoring:

Conversational AI systems monitor the accuracy of their responses and adjust their algorithms to provide more accurate responses.

User Feedback:

Conversational AI systems collect user feedback to improve their accuracy and relevance.

Data Transparency:

Conversational AI systems provide clear and concise privacy policies that inform users about how their data are collected, processed, and shared.

Bias Mitigation:

Conversational AI systems use techniques such as data cleaning and algorithmic fairness to reduce bias in their responses.

Security Measures:
Conversational AI systems implement security measures such as data encryption and access controls to protect user data.

Explainability:
Conversational AI systems provide explanations for their responses to help users understand how the system arrived at its conclusions.

Human Oversight:
Conversational AI systems may have human agents available to assist with complex or sensitive issues, providing users with the assurance that their queries are being handled appropriately.

32.4.5 Threat Detection and Response

Threat detection and response are critical components of conversational AI security. Conversational AI systems must be able to detect and respond to security threats quickly. This means that the system must be able to monitor for suspicious activity and respond appropriately when a threat is detected.

Threat detection in conversational AI involves monitoring the system for suspicious activity that may indicate a security threat. The following are some of the techniques used for threat detection in conversational AI:

Behavioral analysis:
Behavioral analysis involves analyzing user behavior to detect anomalies that may indicate a security threat. For example, if a user suddenly starts asking for sensitive information that they had not asked for before, this may indicate that the user's account has been compromised.

Anomaly detection:
Anomaly detection involves identifying deviations from expected patterns of behavior. For example, if a conversational AI system suddenly starts generating a large number of errors, this may indicate a security threat.

Signature-based detection:
Signature-based detection involves comparing incoming requests against known patterns of malicious activity. For example, if a request matches a known pattern of a Structured Query Language (SQL) injection attack, it may be flagged as a potential security threat.

Machine learning-based detection:
Machine learning–based detection involves training ML models to identify patterns of behavior associated with security threats. For example, ML models can be trained to detect patterns of behavior associated with account takeover attacks.

Threat Response in Conversational AI
Threat response in conversational AI involves taking action to mitigate security threats once they have been detected. The following are some of the techniques used for threat response in conversational AI:

Access control:

Access control involves limiting access to sensitive data or features of the system to authorized users. For example, if an account has been compromised, access to sensitive data may be restricted until the account is secured.

User authentication:

User authentication involves verifying the identity of users before allowing them access to sensitive data or features of the system. For example, two-factor authentication can be used to ensure that only authorized users can access sensitive data.

Incident response:

Incident response involves following established protocols to address security incidents. For example, if a security breach is detected, an incident response team may be activated to investigate the breach, contain the damage, and restore normal operations.

Threat mitigation:

Threat mitigation involves taking steps to reduce the impact of a security threat. For example, if a conversational AI system is under a denial-of-service (DoS) attack, traffic may be redirected to other servers to maintain system availability.

32.4.6 Compliance

Conversational AI systems must comply with relevant security standards and regulations. Compliance ensures that the system meets a minimum level of security and data privacy requirements. Compliance also ensures that the system can be audited and tested for security vulnerabilities regularly.

Compliance is a critical aspect of conversational AI, as it ensures that the use of the technology is in accordance with legal and regulatory requirements. Failure to comply with applicable regulations can result in significant legal and financial consequences, as well as damage to reputation. Therefore, it is important for organizations that use conversational AI to ensure that they are in compliance with relevant laws and regulations.

Here are some of the compliance considerations for conversational AI:

Data privacy:

Conversational AI systems often collect and process personal data, which is subject to data privacy regulations such as the GDPR and the CCPA. Organizations that use conversational AI must ensure that they are complying with these regulations by obtaining consent from users before collecting their personal data, implementing appropriate security measures to protect the data, and providing users with the ability to access, correct, or delete their personal data.

Accessibility:

Conversational AI systems must be accessible to all users, including those with disabilities. Organizations must comply with accessibility standards such as the Web Content Accessibility Guidelines to ensure that their conversational AI systems can be used by everyone.

Ethical considerations:

Conversational AI systems must be developed and deployed in an ethical manner. Organizations must consider ethical issues such as bias, transparency, and accountability when designing and implementing conversational AI systems. For example, they must ensure that the systems do not discriminate against certain groups of users and that they are transparent about how they process user data.

Security:
Conversational AI systems must be secure to protect user data and maintain system integrity. Organizations must comply with security regulations such as the PCI DSS and the HIPAA to ensure that their conversational AI systems are secure.

Intellectual property:
Conversational AI systems may use intellectual property such as trademarks, copyrights, and patents. Organizations must ensure that they have the necessary permissions and licenses to use such intellectual property.

To ensure compliance with relevant laws and regulations, organizations that use conversational AI should

- Conduct a compliance audit to identify the applicable regulations and assess their compliance with them.
- Develop policies and procedures that outline how they will comply with the regulations.
- Train employees on compliance requirements and how to adhere to them.
- Conduct regular compliance assessments to ensure that they are complying with the regulations.
- Work with legal and compliance experts to ensure that their conversational AI systems comply with all relevant laws and regulations.

32.4.7   Testing and Auditing

Testing and auditing are critical components of conversational AI security. Conversational AI systems must be tested regularly for security vulnerabilities and weaknesses. Additionally, the system must be audited to ensure that it complies with relevant security standards and regulations.

Testing in conversational AI involves evaluating the functionality, accuracy, and effectiveness of the conversational agent. The goal of testing is to identify any issues or errors in the agent's performance and to ensure that it performs as intended. Testing can be performed at different stages of the development lifecycle, such as during development, before deployment, and after deployment.

Types of Testing in Conversational AI

Functional Testing:
This type of testing evaluates the conversational agent's functionality and ensures that it performs as intended. It involves testing the agent's ability to recognize and interpret user input, generate appropriate responses, and handle exceptions and errors.

Performance Testing:
This type of testing evaluates the conversational agent's performance under different conditions, such as varying levels of user traffic and load. It involves testing the agent's response time, scalability, and resource utilization.

Security Testing:
This type of testing evaluates the conversational agent's security posture and ensures that it is resistant to attacks, such as malware, phishing, and social engineering. It involves testing the agent's data handling, access controls, and authentication mechanisms.

Usability Testing:
This type of testing evaluates the conversational agent's user experience and ensures that it is intuitive, user-friendly, and accessible. It involves testing the agent's user interface, navigation, and feedback mechanisms.

Auditing in conversational AI involves reviewing and evaluating the conversational agent's compliance with relevant standards, regulations, and policies. The goal of auditing is to ensure that the conversational agent meets the legal and ethical requirements for data privacy, security, and accuracy. Auditing can be performed by internal or external auditors and can cover different areas, such as data privacy, security, and compliance.

Types of Auditing in Conversational AI

Data Privacy Auditing:
This type of auditing evaluates the conversational agent's compliance with data privacy regulations, such as the GDPR and CCPA. It involves reviewing the agent's data handling policies, data retention policies, and data sharing policies.

Security Auditing:
This type of auditing evaluates the conversational agent's compliance with security regulations, such as the National Institute of Standards and Technology (NIST) Cybersecurity Framework and International Organization for Standardization (ISO) 27001. It involves reviewing the agent's access controls, authentication mechanisms, and data protection mechanisms.

Compliance Auditing:
This type of auditing evaluates the conversational agent's compliance with relevant industry standards and policies, such as the PCI DSS and HIPAA. It involves reviewing the agent's processes, policies, and procedures to ensure that they meet the required standards.

Benefits of Testing and Auditing in Conversational AI
Testing and auditing provide several benefits to the development and deployment of conversational AI systems, including

Improved Accuracy:
Testing and auditing can help identify and correct errors and issues in the conversational agent's performance, resulting in higher accuracy and effectiveness.

Enhanced Security:
Testing and auditing can help identify and mitigate security risks, such as vulnerabilities and attacks, ensuring that the conversational agent is secure and resilient.

Increased Compliance:
Testing and auditing can help ensure that the conversational agent is compliant with relevant standards, regulations, and policies, reducing the risk of legal and ethical violations.

Improved User Experience:
Testing and auditing can help ensure that the conversational agent provides a positive user experience, resulting in higher user engagement and satisfaction.

32.4.8   Continuous Improvement

Finally, continuous improvement is essential in conversational AI security. The threat landscape is constantly evolving, and conversational AI systems must be able to adapt and improve their security measures accordingly. This means that the system must be regularly updated to address new security threats and vulnerabilities.

Continuous improvement is a crucial aspect of conversational AI development that ensures that conversational agents become more efficient, accurate, and effective over time. Conversational AI refers to the technology that enables computers to understand, interpret, and respond to human language. These conversational agents can be used for various purposes, such as customer service, personal assistants, or virtual assistants.

Continuous improvement in conversational AI involves the following key steps:

Data Collection:
The first step in continuous improvement is to collect data from user interactions with the conversational agent. These data include the conversation logs, user feedback, and contextual data.

Data Analysis:
The collected data are analyzed to identify patterns and trends in user behavior, such as frequently asked questions, misunderstood intents, or misinterpretations. This analysis helps in identifying areas for improvement in the conversational agent.

Model Training:
Based on the data analysis, the conversational agent's underlying model is trained to improve its accuracy and effectiveness in handling user interactions. This training can involve various techniques, such as ML, NLP, or reinforcement learning.

Testing and Evaluation:
The updated conversational agent is tested to ensure that it performs better than the previous version. User feedback and engagement metrics are used to evaluate the conversational agent's performance.

Deployment:
The updated conversational agent is deployed to production once it is deemed to be performing better than the previous version.

Continuous Monitoring:
Once the conversational agent is deployed, it is continuously monitored to identify any issues that may arise. This monitoring can involve both manual and automated techniques, such as user feedback analysis, quality assurance testing, or anomaly detection.

Iteration:
Based on the monitoring results, the conversational agent is iterated again to improve its performance, and the cycle of continuous improvement continues.

Benefits of Continuous Improvement in Conversational AI
Continuous improvement in conversational AI provides several benefits, including

Improved User Experience:
By continuously improving the conversational agent's accuracy and effectiveness, users are more likely to have a positive experience when interacting with the agent, which can improve user engagement and satisfaction.

Increased Efficiency:
Continuous improvement can lead to a reduction in the time and resources required to handle user interactions, as the conversational agent becomes better at handling common user requests.

Higher Accuracy:
By continuously training and updating the model, the conversational agent's accuracy can be improved, resulting in fewer errors and misunderstandings.

Competitive Advantage:
By continuously improving the conversational agent's performance, organizations can stay ahead of the competition and provide a better customer experience.

In conclusion, conversational AI systems must incorporate several components and concepts to ensure security. Authentication and authorization, encryption, privacy, trust, threat detection and response, compliance, testing and auditing, and continuous improvement are all critical components of conversational AI security. By incorporating these components and concepts, conversational AI systems can protect users' data and privacy and build trust with users.

32.5   Working of Conversational AI Security

Conversational AI refers to the technology that enables machines to understand, interpret, and respond to human language. It is becoming increasingly popular with the widespread adoption of virtual assistants and chatbots in various industries, including customer service, healthcare, finance, and education. However, with the increase in the use of conversational AI, security concerns have also arisen. In this article, we will discuss the working of conversational AI security.

Conversational AI Security

Conversational AI security refers to the measures and techniques used to protect conversational AI systems from cyber threats. These threats can be in the form of unauthorized access, data breaches, fraud, and malicious attacks. Conversational AI systems that are not properly secured can be vulnerable to these threats, which can lead to serious consequences for businesses and individuals.

Working of Conversational AI Security

The working of conversational AI security involves several steps and processes that aim to ensure the confidentiality, integrity, and availability of conversational AI systems. Let's discuss each of these steps in detail:

32.5.1   Threat Modeling

The first step in securing conversational AI systems is to identify the potential threats and risks. Threat modeling involves analyzing the system architecture, design, and functionalities to identify potential vulnerabilities that could be exploited by cybercriminals. This step helps in developing a comprehensive security strategy that can mitigate these risks.

Threat modeling is a process of identifying and evaluating potential threats to a system, application, or organization. The purpose of threat modeling is to identify potential vulnerabilities and risks and to determine the best way to mitigate them. Threat modeling is an essential component of a comprehensive security strategy and is used by organizations to ensure the security of their systems and data.

Threat modeling involves the following steps:

Identify the System or Application:
The first step in threat modeling is to identify the system or application that needs to be protected. This could be a software application, a network, or an entire organization.

Create a Data Flow Diagram:
A data flow diagram is a visual representation of the system or application, which illustrates how data flows through the system. This helps in identifying potential points of entry for attackers.

Identify Threats:
In this step, potential threats are identified based on the data flow diagram. These could include insider attacks, external attacks, data breaches, or other types of attacks.

Evaluate the Threats:
Once the threats are identified, they are evaluated to determine the likelihood of occurrence and the potential impact on the system or organization.

Prioritize Threats:
Based on the evaluation of threats, they are prioritized according to their severity and potential impact. This helps in determining which threats need to be addressed first.

Develop Mitigation Strategies:
Mitigation strategies are developed to address the identified threats. These could include implementing security controls, upgrading software, or modifying business processes.

Review and Update:
Threat modeling is an ongoing process, and it is important to review and update the threat model regularly to ensure that it remains relevant and effective.

Threat modeling is an essential component of a comprehensive security strategy. It helps in identifying potential threats and vulnerabilities and provides a roadmap for implementing effective mitigation strategies. By using threat modeling, organizations can ensure that their systems and data are protected against potential security threats.

Authentication and Authorization
Authentication and authorization are two important security measures that help in controlling access to conversational AI systems. Authentication involves verifying the identity of users before granting access to the system. Authorization, on the other hand, involves determining the level of access that users have to the system. These measures ensure that only authorized users can access and use the conversational AI system.

32.5.2 Data Encryption

Data encryption is the process of converting sensitive data into an unreadable format that can only be decrypted with a secret key. This technique is used to protect the confidentiality of data that are transmitted between the user and the conversational AI system. By encrypting the data, it becomes difficult for cybercriminals to intercept and steal the data.

Data encryption in conversational AI can be achieved through various encryption techniques, such as symmetric encryption, asymmetric encryption, and hashing.

Symmetric encryption uses a single key for both encryption and decryption. This means that the same key is used to encrypt the data on the sender's side and decrypt it on the receiver's side. Symmetric encryption is fast and efficient, but it requires the key to be kept secret to ensure security.

Asymmetric encryption, also known as public-key encryption, uses two keys: a public key and a private key. The public key is used to encrypt the data, while the private key is used to decrypt it. Asymmetric encryption is slower than symmetric encryption, but it is more secure because the private key is kept secret and not shared with anyone.

Hashing is a one-way encryption technique that converts data into a fixed-length string of characters. The resulting string, known as a hash, is unique to the original data and cannot be used to reconstruct the data. Hashing is commonly used for password storage, where the password is hashed and stored in a database, and then, the hash is compared to the user's input to verify the password without actually storing the password itself.

To implement data encryption in conversational AI, the following steps can be taken:

- Identify the data that need to be encrypted, such as user input, conversation history, and personal information.

- Choose an appropriate encryption technique, such as symmetric encryption, asymmetric encryption, or hashing, depending on the type of data and the level of security required.
- Generate encryption keys and store them securely. Symmetric encryption requires a single secret key, while asymmetric encryption requires a public key and a private key. The keys must be kept secret and protected from unauthorized access.
- Encrypt the data before storing it in a database or transmitting it over the network. The data must be decrypted using the same key or keys to be readable.
- Monitor the encryption process to ensure that it is working correctly and that there are no vulnerabilities or weaknesses that could be exploited by attackers.
- Regularly review and update the encryption process to ensure that it is up to date with the latest security standards and best practices.

32.5.3   Secure Communication

Secure communication refers to the use of secure protocols and encryption algorithms to protect the data that are transmitted between the user and the conversational AI system. These protocols and algorithms ensure that the data are transmitted over a secure channel and cannot be intercepted or modified by unauthorized entities.

Secure communication in conversational AI can be achieved through various mechanisms such as Transport Layer Security (TLS), Secure Sockets Layer (SSL), and virtual private networks (VPNs).

TLS and SSL are cryptographic protocols that provide secure communication over the internet. These protocols use a combination of symmetric and asymmetric encryption to ensure confidentiality, integrity, and authenticity of the data transmitted between the user and the system. TLS and SSL are widely used in web applications and messaging platforms, including conversational AI systems, to protect against eavesdropping, man-in-the-middle attacks, and other security threats.

VPNs provide a secure and private network connection between the user and the system. VPNs use encryption and tunneling techniques to ensure secure communication over the internet. VPNs are commonly used in remote work scenarios and can also be used in conversational AI systems to ensure secure communication between the user and the system.

To ensure secure communication in conversational AI systems, the following steps can be taken:

- Implement TLS or SSL protocols to ensure secure communication between the user and the system. This includes using strong encryption algorithms, secure key exchange mechanisms, and digital certificates to ensure authenticity and integrity.
- Use VPNs to establish a secure and private network connection between the user and the system. This includes ensuring that the VPN connection is properly configured and that the encryption algorithms used are strong and up to date.

- Monitor and log network traffic to detect any anomalies or suspicious activity that could indicate a security threat. This includes setting up intrusion detection and prevention systems to prevent and mitigate security breaches.
- Train users on security best practices and awareness to ensure that they are aware of the risks and threats associated with conversational AI systems. This includes providing guidelines on password management, data protection, and safe browsing practices.
- Regularly update and patch the system to ensure that it is up to date with the latest security standards and best practices. This includes conducting regular vulnerability scans and penetration testing to identify and address any security vulnerabilities.

32.5.4   Bot Detection

Bot detection is the process of identifying and blocking malicious bots that attempt to exploit vulnerabilities in conversational AI systems. These bots can be used to steal sensitive data or launch attacks on the system. Bot detection techniques involve analyzing user behavior patterns to identify bots and blocking them from accessing the system.

Bot detection is an essential aspect of conversational AI security. Bots, also known as chatbots or virtual assistants, are programmed to interact with humans through chat interfaces. However, some bots are malicious and can be used to perform automated attacks such as spamming, phishing, and credential stuffing. Therefore, it is important to detect and mitigate bot attacks in conversational AI systems.

Bot detection in conversational AI can be achieved through various methods such as

CAPTCHA:
CAPTCHA (Completely Automated Public Turing test to tell Computers and Humans Apart) is a challenge-response test that is designed to determine whether the user is human or not. CAPTCHAs can be used in conversational AI systems to prevent automated bot attacks by requiring users to solve a puzzle or answer a question.

Behavioral analysis:
Behavioral analysis involves analyzing user behavior patterns to identify whether the user is human or a bot. Behavioral analysis can be used to detect anomalies such as high-speed typing, copy-pasting, and rapid responses, which are typical of bot activity.

Machine learning:
ML algorithms can be used to detect bot activity in conversational AI systems. These algorithms can be trained to identify patterns and characteristics of bot behavior based on historical data. ML algorithms can also be used to detect and prevent bot attacks in real time.

User verification:
User verification involves verifying the user's identity before allowing access to the system. This can be achieved through various mechanisms such as biometric authentication, two-factor authentication, and email or phone verification.

IP blocking:
Internet Protocol (IP) blocking involves blocking IP addresses that are associated with bot activity. This can be achieved by using IP reputation services that identify and blacklist IP addresses that are known to be associated with bot activity.

32.5.5 Continuous Monitoring

Continuous monitoring involves monitoring the system for any suspicious activity or behavior that could indicate a security breach. This step helps in identifying and responding to security incidents in a timely manner, minimizing the damage caused by cyber-attacks.

Continuous monitoring is a crucial component of conversational AI security that involves the ongoing observation and analysis of system activity to detect and respond to security threats in real time. With conversational AI systems becoming increasingly complex and sophisticated, continuous monitoring is necessary to ensure that security controls are functioning effectively and to identify any potential security incidents.

Continuous monitoring in conversational AI involves the following steps:

Monitoring System Activity:
The first step in continuous monitoring is to collect and analyze system logs and network traffic to identify any unusual activity or potential security incidents. This includes monitoring user interactions with the conversational AI system, as well as any backend processes or systems that support the system.

Threat Detection:
Once the system activity has been monitored and analyzed, the next step is to identify potential security threats or vulnerabilities. This involves using ML algorithms and other analytics tools to analyze system logs and network traffic for anomalies and indicators of compromise.

Incident Response:
When a potential security incident is identified, it is essential to respond quickly and effectively to contain the incident and minimize its impact. This involves following a predefined incident response plan that includes processes for identifying the source of the incident, containing the incident, and remediating any damage or vulnerabilities that were exploited.

Continuous Improvement:
Continuous monitoring also involves regularly reviewing and updating security controls to ensure that they are effective and up to date. This includes reviewing system logs and network traffic to identify areas of weakness or potential vulnerabilities and implementing new security controls or measures to address them.

Some best practices for continuous monitoring in conversational AI systems include

- Implementing security information and event management tools to collect and analyze system logs and network traffic.

- Using ML and other analytics tools to identify potential security threats and vulnerabilities.
- Establishing predefined incident response plans to quickly respond to security incidents.
- Regularly reviewing and updating security controls to address new threats and vulnerabilities.
- Conducting regular vulnerability assessments and penetration testing to identify and address potential weaknesses in the system.

32.5.6   Regular Updates and Patching

Regular updates and patching are essential for maintaining the security of conversational AI systems. These updates include security patches and bug fixes that address known vulnerabilities in the system. Regular updates ensure that the system is protected against the latest security threats.

Conversational AI systems are complex software systems that require regular updates and patches to ensure that they are functioning correctly and securely. These updates and patches can include security updates, bug fixes, and new features. Regular updates and patches help to address security vulnerabilities and protect against the latest security threats.

To ensure that conversational AI systems are regularly updated and patched, the following steps can be taken:

- Monitor and track updates and patches from vendors and software providers. This includes regularly reviewing release notes and security bulletins to identify any security vulnerabilities that need to be addressed.
- Prioritize updates and patches based on the severity of the security vulnerability and the potential impact on the system. This includes determining the criticality of the update and the potential risks associated with not applying the patch.
- Test updates and patches in a staging environment before deploying them to the production environment. This includes testing the updates and patches to ensure that they do not introduce new vulnerabilities or cause any performance issues.
- Schedule regular maintenance windows to apply updates and patches. This includes planning downtime for the system to apply updates and patches and communicating the downtime to users and stakeholders.
- Automate the update and patching process to streamline the process and reduce the risk of human error. This includes setting up automated tools to download, test, and deploy updates and patches.

32.6   Risk for Conversational AI Security

32.6.1   Data Privacy

Conversational AI systems collect vast amounts of data from users, including personal information such as names, addresses, and credit card details. These data can be used for malicious purposes if it falls into the wrong hands, such as identity theft or financial fraud. Conversational AI systems must ensure that all user data are properly encrypted, and access to this data is restricted only to authorized individuals.

Data privacy is a critical aspect of conversational AI security. Conversational AI systems, such as chatbots, virtual assistants, and voice assistants, rely on large amounts of personal data to provide personalized and contextually relevant responses. However, the collection and use of these data can also pose significant risks to users' privacy.

To ensure data privacy in conversational AI security, several best practices should be followed:

Data encryption:
Conversational AI systems should use encryption techniques to protect the data transmitted between the user and the system. This ensures that even if the data are intercepted, they cannot be read or used by unauthorized parties.

Data anonymization:
Whenever possible, conversational AI systems should anonymize user data to protect users' identities. This means removing or masking identifying information from data sets so that it cannot be traced back to specific individuals.

Data minimization:
Conversational AI systems should only collect and use the data necessary to provide the requested service. Unnecessary data should not be collected, stored, or used.

User consent:
Users should be informed of the data collected and used by the conversational AI system, and their consent should be obtained before collecting and using their data.

Data storage:
Conversational AI systems should securely store user data and ensure that it is not accessible by unauthorized parties.

Regular audits:
Regular audits should be conducted to ensure that data privacy practices are being followed and that there are no security vulnerabilities in the system.

By following these best practices, conversational AI systems can provide personalized and contextually relevant responses while also protecting users' privacy and security.

32.6.2 Malicious Attacks

Conversational AI systems are vulnerable to a range of malicious attacks, including DoS attacks, man-in-the-middle attacks, and phishing attacks. These attacks can compromise the integrity of the system and steal user data or perform unauthorized actions. Conversational AI systems must be designed with security in mind, and regular security audits should be conducted to identify and mitigate potential vulnerabilities.

However, malicious actors can exploit vulnerabilities in conversational AI systems to gain unauthorized access to sensitive information, inject malicious code, or manipulate the system to behave in unexpected ways. Some common types of malicious attacks on conversational AI systems include

Spoofing attacks:
These attacks involve impersonating a legitimate user to gain access to the system. For example, an attacker could use a fake identity to trick a chatbot into disclosing confidential information.

Injection attacks:
These attacks involve injecting malicious code into the conversation. For example, an attacker could use an SQL injection attack to gain unauthorized access to a database.

Evasion attacks:
These attacks involve exploiting weaknesses in the system's NLP algorithms to bypass security measures. For example, an attacker could use misspellings or slang to confuse the system and evade detection.

To protect against these types of attacks, conversational AI systems must be designed with security in mind. This includes implementing measures such as user authentication, encryption, and input validation to prevent malicious actors from gaining unauthorized access or injecting malicious code. Additionally, ML models used in conversational AI systems should be trained on a diverse range of data to avoid bias and ensure that the system can handle unexpected input. Regular security audits and testing can also help identify and address vulnerabilities before they can be exploited by attackers.

32.6.3   Misuse of User Data

Conversational AI systems are often used to collect data from users for marketing or advertising purposes. However, these data can be misused if it is sold to third-party companies without user consent or used to create targeted advertising campaigns that infringe on user privacy. Conversational AI systems must be transparent about their data collection practices, and users must be given the option to opt out of data collection altogether.

Misuse of user data is a significant concern in conversational AI security. Conversational AI systems can collect a vast amount of user data, including personal and sensitive information, to improve the accuracy and effectiveness of their responses. However, if these data fall into the wrong hands, they can be used for malicious purposes, such as identity theft or fraud.

32.6.4   Social Engineering

Conversational AI systems are vulnerable to social engineering attacks, in which an attacker manipulates a user into revealing sensitive information or performing unauthorized actions. These attacks can be difficult to detect, as they rely on the user's trust in the system. Conversational AI systems must be designed to recognize and respond to suspicious behavior, and users should be educated on how to recognize and avoid social engineering attacks.

In the context of conversational AI systems, social engineering attacks can take various forms, including

Phishing attacks:
These attacks involve sending fraudulent messages or emails that appear to be from a trusted source, such as a chatbot or virtual assistant. The message might ask the user to provide sensitive information, such as login credentials or personal data.

Impersonation attacks:
These attacks involve impersonating a trusted entity, such as a company or individual, to trick the user into revealing sensitive information or performing an action. For example, an attacker could impersonate a customer support representative to gain access to a user's account.

Manipulation attacks:
These attacks involve manipulating the user's emotions or behavior to extract sensitive information or perform an action. For example, an attacker could use social engineering techniques to convince a user to disable security features or install malware.

32.7   Solutions for Conversational AI Security

32.7.1   Encryption and Access Control

Conversational AI systems must ensure that all user data are properly encrypted and access to this data is restricted only to authorized individuals. This can be achieved through the use of strong encryption algorithms and access control mechanisms, such as two-factor authentication.

To ensure that conversational AI systems are secure, both encryption and access control mechanisms should be implemented. These can include

- TLS or SSL encryption for data transmission
- Encryption of stored user data at rest
- Authentication mechanisms to restrict access to the AI system, such as username/password or multifactor authentication
- Role-based access control (RBAC) to restrict access to specific functionality within the AI system based on the user's role or permissions
- Logging and auditing to monitor access to the AI system and data and to detect any unauthorized access or activity
- By implementing these measures, conversational AI systems can help ensure the privacy and security of user data and prevent unauthorized access or disclosure of sensitive information.

32.7.2   Regular Security Audits

Conversational AI systems must undergo regular security audits to identify and mitigate potential vulnerabilities. This can be done by conducting penetration testing, vulnerability assessments, and code reviews on a regular basis.

Conversational AI security audits should be performed on a regular basis by a qualified security professional. The frequency of the audits will depend on the level of risk and the complexity of the system but typically should be performed at least annually or whenever there are significant changes to the system.

During a security audit, the following areas should be reviewed:

Access control:
Review the access controls in place to ensure that only authorized individuals have access to the system and its data. This includes reviewing authentication mechanisms, RBAC, and other access control measures.

Encryption:
Review the encryption mechanisms in place to ensure that all sensitive data are properly encrypted both at rest and in transit.

Threat modeling:
Conduct a threat modeling exercise to identify potential attack vectors and vulnerabilities in the system.

Logging and monitoring:
Review the system's logging and monitoring mechanisms to ensure that they are adequate for detecting and responding to security incidents.

Incident response:
Review the system's incident response plan to ensure that it is up to date and includes procedures for responding to security incidents.

Third-party security:
Review the security of any third-party services or components used by the conversational AI system.

Compliance:
Review the system's compliance with relevant security standards and regulations, such as the GDPR and the HIPAA.

Once the security audit is complete, a report should be generated that summarizes the findings and provides recommendations for addressing any vulnerabilities or weaknesses in the system. These recommendations should be prioritized based on their severity and addressed in a timely manner.

By conducting regular security audits, conversational AI systems can help ensure that they are secure and that they are protecting user data and privacy.

32.7.3   Transparent Data Collection Practices

Conversational AI systems must be transparent about their data collection practices, and users must be given the option to opt out of data collection altogether. This can be achieved through the use of clear and concise privacy policies and user agreements.

To implement transparent data collection practices, conversational AI systems should

Provide clear and concise privacy policies:
Users should be able to easily understand what data are being collected and how it will be used. The privacy policy should be prominently displayed and easily accessible from the conversational interface.

Obtain user consent:
Users should be asked to provide their consent for data collection before any data are collected. This consent should be explicit and should clearly indicate what data are being collected and how they will be used.

Minimize data collection:
Conversational AI systems should only collect data that are necessary for the system to function properly. Unnecessary data should not be collected.

Securely store data:
All user data should be securely stored and encrypted both at rest and in transit. Access to the data should be restricted to authorized personnel only.

Allow users to control their data:
Users should have the ability to view and manage their personal data. This can include the ability to delete their data or opt out of data collection altogether.

Regularly review data collection practices:
Data collection practices should be regularly reviewed to ensure that they remain necessary and that they are aligned with user expectations.

Train personnel on data privacy and security:
Personnel who handle user data should be trained on data privacy and security best practices to ensure that they are handling user data responsibly.
   By implementing transparent data collection practices, conversational AI systems can build trust with users and ensure that they are handling user data responsibly. This can help prevent data breaches, protect user privacy, and promote a positive user experience.

32.7.4   Suspicious Behavior Detection

Conversational AI systems must be designed to recognize and respond to suspicious behavior, such as requests for sensitive information or unusual patterns of activity. This can be achieved through the use of ML algorithms that analyze user behavior and identify potential threats.
   To detect suspicious behavior in conversational AI systems, the following measures should be taken:

Real-time monitoring:
Conversational AI systems should be monitored in real time to identify any unusual or suspicious activity. This may include monitoring user interactions, system logs, and network traffic.

Machine learning algorithms:
ML algorithms can be trained to detect and identify patterns of suspicious behavior. These algorithms can learn from past incidents and adapt to new threats as they emerge.

Anomaly detection:
Anomaly detection techniques can be used to identify behavior that is outside the normal range of activity. This can include identifying users who are accessing the system from unusual locations or at unusual times of day.

User authentication and authorization:
Strong user authentication and authorization measures can help prevent unauthorized access to the system. This can include multifactor authentication, role-based access control, and session management.

Threat intelligence:
Threat intelligence feeds can be used to stay up to date on the latest threats and attack vectors. This information can be used to proactively identify and mitigate potential security risks.

Incident response plan:
Conversational AI systems should have a documented incident response plan in place to respond to suspicious behavior. This plan should include procedures for investigating and containing security incidents, as well as notifying users and law enforcement if necessary.

By implementing these measures, conversational AI systems can effectively detect and respond to suspicious behavior. This can help prevent data breaches, protect user privacy, and ensure the overall security of the system.

Because conversational AI [9, 10] is evolving so quickly, new rules and legislation are required to protect consumer data. Not only does new AI legislation need to be created, but the laws regulating data privacy [11, 12] and other technology-related crimes also need to be updated in order to increase the severity of the punishments. A workable legal framework may impose strict and visible compliance measures on AI programmers, including monitoring, harsh access limits, regular security checks, high-level encryption [13, 14], and many layers of access authorization, similar to the situation with health information protection. Additionally, it could require the use of secure vaults and minimal storage requirements, much like the Indian Aadhaar data rules, which preserve information. In the absence of a clear legal personhood for an AI bot, responsibility for carelessness in failing to maintain security [15–17] would naturally pass onto the programmer and the organisation collecting and exploiting the data, in addition to the responsibility of the individuals responsible for the breach [18–20], if any. The traditional issue of being unable to determine the AI bot's [21, 22] responsibility owing to the uncertainty surrounding its legal personhood just adds to the myriad issues already present. The issue of who should be held accountable for the AI's failure to protect [23, 24] the data it uses because it acted beyond the parameters of its programming requires an answer. Vicarious responsibility, or its equivalent, strict liability, which places the guilt on the programmer as they were the ones who created the AI [25], is a strategy that has several drawbacks [26, 27].

32.8   Conclusion

Conversational AI is a powerful tool that can transform the way humans interact with machines. However, the use of conversational AI also introduces new risks for security, including attacks on the NLP model, data breaches, and privacy violations. To mitigate these risks, multiple security measures should be employed, including the use of multiple NLP models, anomaly detection techniques, data encryption, and access controls. Additionally, transparent information should be provided to users on the data collected and how they are used. By addressing these risks, conversational AI can be used safely and effectively in a variety of applications. After conducting research on the risks for conversational AI security, several key conclusions can be drawn. Firstly, conversational AI systems pose significant privacy risks due to the collection and storage of sensitive user data. Secondly, these systems may be vulnerable to attacks by malicious actors who seek to exploit vulnerabilities in the system for their own gain.

Additionally, the use of conversational AI systems in high-stakes contexts such as healthcare or finance may pose additional risks to users. It is essential to address these risks through the development of robust security measures and ongoing monitoring and maintenance of conversational AI systems. Further research is needed to fully understand the nature and extent of these risks, as well as to develop effective strategies for mitigating them. Overall, the risks associated with conversational AI security should not be overlooked, and organizations and developers must take proactive steps to ensure the safety and security of users.

Conversational AI systems have transformed the way businesses interact with their customers and provide services. However, these systems are also vulnerable to security risks that can compromise the privacy of users and expose sensitive data. As the use of conversational AI continues to grow, it is essential to address these risks and implement effective strategies to mitigate them. By doing so, we can ensure that conversational AI remains a safe and valuable tool for businesses and end-users alike.

Acknowledgement

In this research work to review the Risk for Conversational AI Security.

We are grateful to various folks for their advice and help during the period of finishing our research work. First and foremost, we would like to express our gratitude to Dr. Anand Rajavat, Head of the Department of Computer Science & Engineering at S.V.I.I.T., Indore, for their invaluable assistance and guidance. With his supervision, direction, and constructive criticism, he inspired us. We also want to thank our director, Dr. Anand Rajavat, from the bottom of our hearts for all of his help. We extend our heartfelt gratitude to the teaching and non-teaching personnel in the Computer Science & Engineering department at SVVV Indore for their kind cooperation and provision of the necessary information. We appreciate the support and helpful suggestions provided by our parents, relatives, classmates, and friends during the project. Last but not least, we wish to thank everyone who has contributed in any manner to our efforts. Being able to learn at Shri Vaishnav Vidyapeeth Vishwavidyalaya in Indore has been a blessing.

References

1. Team, L., What is conversational AI?, LivePerson, https://www.liveperson.com/conversational-ai/.
2. Boonstra, L., Introduction to conversational AI, in: *The Definitive Guide to Conversational AI with Dialogflow and Google Cloud: Build Advanced Enterprise Chatbots, Voice, and Telephony Agents on Google Cloud*, pp. 1–27, Apress, Berkeley, CA, 2021.
3. Shekhar, S., Troncoso, C., Hubaux, J.P., Attacks and defenses for deep learning-based conversational agents: A survey. *IEEE Trans. Emerging Top. Comput. Intell.*, 3, 5, 416–431, 2018.
4. Carlini, N. and Wagner, D., Towards evaluating the robustness of neural networks, in: *Proceedings of the 2017 IEEE Symposium on Security and Privacy*, San Jose, CA, USA, May 2017, pp. 39–57, doi: 10.1109/SP.2017.17.
5. Kumar, P., Lee, J., Kim, H., Security and privacy challenges in the Internet of Things, 2020.
6. Hou, J., Wang, X., Zhang, Y., Yang, Y., Huang, X., Liu, Q., A survey of conversational AI: Foundations, recent advances, and emerging applications. *IEEE Trans. Neural Networks Learn. Syst.*, 32, 9, 3635–3659, 2021, doi: 10.1109/TNNLS.2021.3055874.
7. Chandrasekaran, V., Yang, S., Iyengar, S.S., A survey on security and privacy issues in conversational AI. *IEEE Access*, 8, 165123–165145, 2020, DOI: 10.1109/ACCESS.2020.3026929.
8. Xu, J., Zhang, Y., Wang, Y., Conversational AI: Review and research directions. *IEEE Access*, 8, 179020–179037, 2020, doi: 10.1109/access.2020.3023391.
9. Mahor, V., Bijrothiya, S., Rawat, R., Kumar, A., Garg, B., Pachlasiya, K., IoT and artificial intelligence techniques for public safety and security, in: *Smart Urban Computing Applications*, p. 111, 2023.
10. Mahor, V., Pachlasiya, K., Garg, B., Chouhan, M., Telang, S., Rawat, R., Mobile operating system (Android) vulnerability analysis using machine learning, in: *Proceedings of International Conference on Network Security and Blockchain Technology: ICNSBT 2021*, pp. 159–169, Springer Nature Singapore, Singapore, 2022, June.
11. Rawat, R., Garg, B., Pachlasiya, K., Mahor, V., Telang, S., Chouhan, M., Mishra, R., SCNTA: Monitoring of network availability and activity for identification of anomalies using machine learning approaches. *Int. J. Inf. Technol. Web Eng. (IJITWE)*, 17, 1, 1–19, 2022.
12. Rawat, R., Rimal, Y.N., William, P., Dahima, S., Gupta, S., Sankaran, K.S., Malware threat affecting financial organization analysis using machine learning approach. *Int. J. Inf. Technol. Web Eng. (IJITWE)*, 17, 1, 1–20, 2022.
13. Rawat, R., Mahor, V., Chouhan, M., Pachlasiya, K., Telang, S., Garg, B., Systematic literature review (SLR) on social media and the digital transformation of drug trafficking on darkweb, in: *International Conference on Network Security and Blockchain Technology*, pp. 181–205, Springer, Singapore, 2022.
14. Rawat, R., Ayodele Oki, O., Sankaran, S., Florez, H., Ajagbe, S.A., Techniques for predicting dark web events focused on the delivery of illicit products and ordered crime. *Int. J. Electr. Comput. Eng. (IJECE)*, 13, 5, 5354–5365, Oct. 2023, doi: 10.11591/ijece.v13i5.pp5354-5365.
15. Rawat, R., Garg, B., Mahor, V., Telang, S., Pachlasiya, K., Chouhan, M., Organ trafficking on the dark web—The data security and privacy concern in healthcare systems, in: *Internet of Healthcare Things: Machine Learning for Security and Privacy*, pp. 189–216, 2022.
16. Vyas, P., Vyas, G., Chauhan, A., Rawat, R., Telang, S., Gottumukkala, M., Anonymous trading on the dark online marketplace: An exploratory study, in: *Using Computational Intelligence for the Dark Web and Illicit Behavior Detection*, pp. 272–289, IGI Global, 2022.
17. Rawat, R., Oki, O.A., Sankaran, K.S., Olasupo, O., Ebong, G.N., Ajagbe, S.A., A new solution for cyber security in big data using machine learning approach, in: *Mobile Computing and*

Sustainable Informatics: Proceedings of ICMCSI 2023, pp. 495–505, Springer Nature Singapore, Singapore, 2023.

18. Rawat, R., Chakrawarti, R.K., Raj, A., Mani, G., Chidambarathanu, K., Bhardwaj, R., Association rule learning for threat analysis using traffic analysis and packet filtering approach. *Int. J. Inf. Technol.*, 1–11, 2023.

19. Rawat, R., Logical concept mapping and social media analytics relating to cyber criminal activities for ontology creation. *Int. J. Inf. Technol.*, *15*, 2, 893–903, 2023.

20. Rawat, R., Mahor, V., Álvarez, J.D., Ch, F., Cognitive systems for dark web cyber delinquent association malignant data crawling: A review, in: *Handbook of Research on War Policies, Strategies, and Cyber Wars*, pp. 45–63, 2023.

21. Rawat, R., Chakrawarti, R.K., Vyas, P., Gonzáles, J.L.A., Sikarwar, R., Bhardwaj, R., Intelligent fog computing surveillance system for crime and vulnerability identification and tracing. *Int. J. Inf. Secur. Priv. (IJISP)*, *17*, 1, 1–25, 2023.

22. Rawat, R., Sowjanya, A.M., Patel, S.I., Jaiswal, V., Khan, I., Balaram, A. (Eds.), *Using Machine Intelligence: Autonomous Vehicles Volume 1*, John Wiley & Sons, 2022.

23. Rawat, R., Mahor, V., Díaz-Álvarez, J., Chávez, F., Rooted learning model at fog computing analysis for crime incident surveillance, in: *2022 International Conference on Smart Generation Computing, Communication and Networking (SMART GENCON)*, pp. 1–9, IEEE, 2022, December.

24. Rawat, R. and Shrivastav, S.K., SQL injection attack detection using SVM. *Int. J. Comput. Appl.*, *42*, 13, 1–4, 2012.

25. Rawat, R., Bhardwaj, P., Kaur, U., Telang, S., Chouhan, M., Sankaran, K.S., *Smart vehicles for communication, volume 2*, John Wiley & Sons, 2023.

26. Mahor, V., Garg, B., Telang, S., Pachlasiya, K., Chouhan, M., Rawat, R., Cyber threat phylogeny assessment and vulnerabilities representation at thermal power station, in: *Proceedings of International Conference on Network Security and Blockchain Technology: ICNSBT 2021*, pp. 28–39, Springer Nature Singapore, Singapore, 2022, June.

27. Rawat, R., Gupta, S., Sivaranjani, S., Cu, O.K., Kuliha, M., Sankaran, K.S., Malevolent information crawling mechanism for forming structured illegal organisations in hidden networks. *Int. J. Cyber Warf. Terror. (IJCWT)*, *12*, 1, 1–14, 2022.

Artificial Intelligence for Financial Inclusion in India

Samir Xavier Bhawnra and K.B. Singh*

Department of Commerce and Financial Studies, Central University of Jharkhand, Brambe, India

Abstract

Many countries are adopting financial inclusion as a sustainable development goal by incorporating policy-based changes in the banking and financial sectors. New technologies are being adopted to reach universal financial inclusion. In India, *Pradhan Mantri Jan Dhan Yojana* (which holds the world record for the highest number of bank accounts opened in a week) and Direct Benefit Transfer (the world's biggest cash and benefit transfer) and, in recent years, the development of digital infrastructure are examples of important policy interventions by the Indian government for inclusive finance. The objective of this chapter is to explore the application of technology, especially AI, in the banking sector for the purpose of financial inclusion in India and to mention some of the examples of commercial banks in India where AI is being used for the purpose of financial inclusion. There are four areas of the banking and financial sectors where artificial intelligence (AI)-based technology is being adopted. These areas are risk management; personal financial management—the credit score of the customer and the choice of financial products; conversational interfaces—chatbots; and machine vision or voice recognition—facial recognition, voice assistants, biometric identification, and eKYC. The chapter concludes that AI technology can enhance financial inclusion by cutting costs, breaking geographical barriers, and boosting the competition among banks.

Keywords: Financial inclusion, artificial intelligence, chatbots, eKYC, banking, fintech

33.1 Introduction

According to recent World Bank data (2017), 1.7 billion adults do not own a formal bank account. The other half of the unbanked population consists of women, poor households in villages, and those who are excluded from the active economic workforce. Such large unbanked populations have difficulties accessing banking and financial services. According to the World Bank, the first and most important step for financial inclusion is to own a transaction account. A transaction account helps the customers save, send money, and receive payments. The World Bank has defined financial inclusion as a situation where "individuals and businesses have access to useful and affordable financial products and services that meet their needs—transactions, payments, savings, credit, and

Corresponding author: kbsingh.cuj@gmail.com

Romil Rawat, Rajesh Kumar Chakrawarti, Sanjaya Kumar Sarangi, Piyush Vyas, Mary Sowjanya Alamanda, Kotagiri Srividya and Krishnan Sakthidasan Sankaran (eds.) Conversational Artificial Intelligence, (589–606) © 2024 Scrivener Publishing LLC

insurance—delivered in a responsible and sustainable way." Expansion of bank branches is important to access such formal banking services. According to World Bank data from 2019, there are 11.51 commercial bank branches worldwide for every 1 lakh adults. The bank branch penetration in the developed countries is higher than in the developing countries of South Asia. For example, in the United States, there are 30.46 and in Australia, 26.43 bank branches for every 1 lakh adults, which is higher than the bank branch penetration in South Asian developing countries.

According to Khan (2012), in addition to financial inclusion, there is also the Financial Inclusion Index. The purpose of the Financial Inclusion Index is to measure and assess the degree of financial inclusion in a nation. There are three fundamental components to calculate the Financial Inclusion Index: banking penetration, the availability of banking services, and the use of the banking system. The first indicator is banking penetration, which is calculated as the proportion of people with bank accounts to the overall population of a nation. Owning at least one bank account is a requirement for financial penetration. The second parameter, the accessibility of banking services (including physical branches, banking correspondents, and ATMs), identifies the number of bank outlets per 1,000 people that provide financial services. The third parameter, banking administration usage, which goes beyond the simple opening of records, is assessed based on outstanding deposits and credits, which is the usage of a bank account.

Further, the United Nations is working on 17 SDGs (sustainable development goals). Seven of the 17 SDGs are directly related to inclusive finance. The UN emphasizes that opportunity should be created for everyone to avail loans and borrowing, invest in remunerative avenues of banks, have access to insurance, save money in banks for education and health purposes, and avoid uncertain financial jolts.

33.1.1   Financial Inclusion in India

The meaning and concept of financial inclusion in a country like India have gained importance since the 2005–2006 annual policy statement of the Reserve Bank of India (RBI). The RBI, the central bank of India, headed by C. Rangarajan (2008), has defined financial inclusion as "the process of ensuring access to financial services and timely and adequate credit where needed by vulnerable groups such as weaker sections and low-income groups at an affordable cost." Process, access, time, credit, and cost are the important dimensions of inclusive finance for the Rangarajan committee. Since then, a lot of steps have been taken to meet the goal of inclusive finance in the country. Initiatives of "no frill accounts," later named Basic Savings Bank Deposit accounts (BSBD accounts), modification in KYC norms, launching of General Credit Cards (GCC), use of regional dialects in the banking sector, introduction of financial education in 2006, and introduction of the idea of business correspondents (BCs) and business facilitators (BFs) with the purpose of giving banking services at the doorstep of the customers are some of the important steps taken for the purpose of financial inclusion.

However, credit availability through the formal banking system was one of the key concepts of this definition given by Rangarajan. Rajan has broadened this understanding of financial inclusion. Rajan (2017) emphasized that financial inclusion is not merely credit for business purposes (as earlier mentioned by C. Rangarajan), but also credit for health-care emergencies, school, and college fees. Financial inclusion should be an avenue for savings to earn interest and an easy and safe mode for payments and remittances. Inclusive finance also includes insurance and pensions, and in addition to these, financial literacy, and consumer protection. Thus, Rajan has brought all aspects of economic life under the umbrella of financial inclusion. Since then, a lot of innovation has been taking place to make use of fintech in the banking sector.

33.1.2   Growth of Financial Inclusion in India

India has progressed significantly in all spheres of financial inclusion in the past five years. A lot of policy-based efforts have been made to give greater access to basic transaction accounts. There is a growth in the number of banking outlets in villages from 5.98 lakh in March 2017 to 12.95 lakh in December 2020, and the majority (95.5%) of these are branch-less BC (business correspondent) modes. The data shows that about 649 million BSBD accounts (basic saving banking deposit accounts) will have been opened in the country by December 2020; this is a growth of about 8% over the previous year. The following Table 33.1 shows the growth of BSBD accounts in the country from 2017 to 2020. The Table 33.1 shows about the Basic Saving Banking Deposit account (BSBD account) and Table 33.2 highlights for Top reasons banks use Artificial Intelligence.

Pradhan Matri Jan Dhan Yojana (PMJDY) was launched in 2014. Since then, it has contributed a lot to financial inclusion for the financially weaker groups in the country. The data for March 2021 shows that about 67% of PMJDY account holders were from villages and semi-urban regions, and the rest (33%) were from cities. A total of 31.10 crore, or 73.02% of PMDJY account holders, have been issued with RuPay debit cards to provide banking operations. The public sector banks are responsible for 79.06%, the RRB for 17.98%, and the private sector banks for 2.95% of the total PMJDY bank accounts in the country. Figure 33.1 below shows

Table 33.1 Basic Saving Banking Deposit account (BSBD account).

	Particulars	March 2017	March 2018	March 2019	March 2020
1	Banking Outlets in Villages (Total)	5,47,233	5,18,742	5,41,129	5,99,217
2	(BSBDAs)—Open total (No. in Million)	533	536	574	600
3	No. of BSBDA per Branch	4,994	4,862	4,858	4,784
4	BSBDA through BCs (No. in Million)	280	289	319	339
5	Number of BSBDA per BC	512	557	590	626

Source: 2021–22 Trend Report on Financial Inclusion; Bankers Institute of Rural Development, Lucknow.

Table 33.2 Top reasons banks use Artificial Intelligence.

Data analysis and insights	Increased productivity	Cost benefits/savings
60%	59%	54%

Source: The exploding use of AI in the banking sector by Biswadeep Ghosh Hazra; https://www.linkedin.com/pulse/exploding-use-ai-banking-sector-biswadeep-ghosh-hazra.

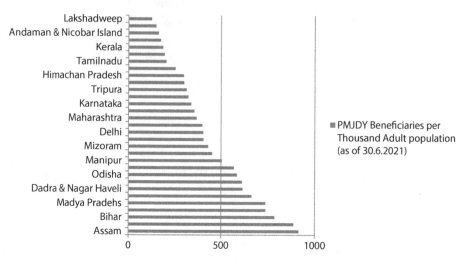

Figure 33.1 Source: 2021–22 Trend Report on Financial Inclusion; Bankers Institute of Rural Development, Lucknow.

three important points: one Assam has the highest (915) basic account per thousand adult population and Lakshadweep the lowest (125), while India has 510 basic bank accounts per thousand adult population. Figure 33.1 exhibits the Indian state population that has opened a basic bank account per thousand adult populations.

Further, the government has been working to offer microinsurance. *Pradhan Mantri Jeevan Jyoti Bima Yojana* (PMJJBY) and *Pradhan Mantri Suraksha Bima Yojana* (PMSBY) are the microinsurance schemes brought by the government. A total of 10.27 crore account holders are included in PMJJBY and 23.26 crore account holders in PMSBY.

In addition, there is the *Pradhan Mantri Mudra Yojana* (PMMY) scheme meant for microcredit for the people. As of March 2021, the PMMY scheme had provided credit assistance totaling Rs. 15.52 lakh crore to 29.55 crore microborrowers. Further, there is direct benefit transfer (DBT) for 311 government schemes.

33.1.3   Direct Benefit Transfer

The International Monetary Fund (IMF) has referred to India's direct benefit transfer (DBT) program's implementation as a "logistical wonder" for successfully reaching hundreds of millions of people. This program is a classic example of how technology can help reach millions of citizens who are at the bottom of the pyramid. Cash amounts were transferred using the digital payments technology vehicle, the public financial management system (PFMS), under central schemes (CS) and centrally sponsored schemes (CSS). Beneficiary account validation systems, a strong payment and reconciliation platform integrated with RBI, NPCI, public and private sector banks, regional rural banks, and cooperative banks (core banking solutions of banks, settlement systems of RBI, and Aadhaar Payment Bridge of NPCI), among others, are essential to the implementation of DBT schemes. With the use of digital currency transfers, India was able to support 69% of urban households and a staggering 85% of rural households with food or cash.

In a direct benefit transfer scheme, the government sends its benefits, such as subsidies, pensions, scholarships, insurance, etc., directly to the bank account of the concerned beneficiary. The JAM (Jan-Dhan Bank Account, Aadhaar and Mobile) link has become an efficient means to transfer government benefits to the beneficiaries. Some of the advantages provided to the nation's poor under the Direct Benefit Transfer project include *Pratyaksh Hanstantrit Labh* (PAHAL-cooking gas subsidy), wages for MGNREGA workers, money for relief, and the *Pradhan Mantri Garib Kalyan Yojana* (PMGKY) to fight against COVID pandemics.

Organization of Chapter

The rest of the chapter has been outlined as follows. In Section 33.2, we present the digitalization of the banking sector, which has paved the way for the usage of AI in financial inclusion. Here we discuss the digital financial inclusion journey in India and some remarkable recent technological developments in the Indian banking sector, such as the linkage of Aadhaar for digital banking, the Unified Payments Interface (UPI), and RuPay. In Section 33.3, we present the technology acceptance model. In Section 33.4, the discussion mainly focuses on artificial intelligence, where the use of AI in financial inclusion and banking has been presented. We also highlight the success of JAM and eKYC adopted for financial inclusion. Finally, in Section 33.5, we conclude the chapter by presenting a snapshot illustrating the adoption of conversational AI by major banks in India.

33.2 Digitalization of Banking Sector Paving Way for AI in Financial Inclusion

33.2.1 Digital Financial Inclusion Journey

The Pradhan Mantri Jan Dhan Yojana (PMJDY) has facilitated the opening of new bank accounts for economically disadvantaged and marginalized individuals. By providing access to formal banking institutions, PMJDY has enabled these individuals to receive direct benefit transfers (DBT) from the government and other financial services. Additionally, PMJDY has facilitated the provision of remittances, credit, insurance, and pensions, and has also encouraged the development of FinTech products to reach a vast consumer base in India.

The expansion of digital financial inclusion in India has been affected by significant innovation in both the public and private sectors. The government has taken some significant steps for the innovation and expansion of technology in the banking and finance sectors. For example, steps towards growing internet coverage and smartphone penetration have given a boost to digital banking. The bank accounts of an individual have been linked to biometric identification (through Aadhaar) and mobile phone numbers. This initiative has marked a big shift from the traditional banking system. Further, by giving licenses to mobile network operators (MNOs), the government has created a new tier of financial institutions. FinTechs are permitted to provide banking services under the Payment Bank License. Microfinance institutions (MFIs) are encouraged to leverage technology to align with the market and as an incentive for their growth into small finance banks. The development of digital banking infrastructure is important for private companies to carry on business. The digital banking infrastructures for digital identification and payment technology are Aadhar and Aadhar-based identification and KYC measures, RuPay, and UPI. These digital infrastructures also help private companies carry forward the goal of financial inclusion in the country.

33.2.2   Importance of Aadhaar for Digital Banking

In India, since 2014, the Pradhan Mantri Jan Dhan Yojana has been one of the important pillars of financial inclusion. Then, Aadhaar is the second important component of the JAM trinity. Aadhaar, the national ID scheme issued by UIDAI with a unique biometric-linked 12-digit identification, has become one of the most important documents for proof of identity. The unique identification authority of India (UIDAI) is a statutory authority established by the Government of India. UIDAI was created to issue Unique Identification numbers (UIDs), named "Aadhaar," to all residents of India. The importance of Aadhaar has grown with its use in PMJDY as a minimum document needed to verify the proof of identity of a customer desiring to open a bank account. Its importance could be noticed from the data that shows that between 2016–17 and 2017–18, the number of e-KYC verifications through Aadhaar grew from 48 million to 138 million. As of 2018, more than 83% of active PMJDY accounts—excluding the accounts from the states of Assam, Meghalaya, and Jammu and Kashmir—had been linked with Aadhaar. This highlights the important role that Aadhaar has played in facilitating digital financial inclusion in the country. The linking of a persons' mobile phone number with their Aadhaar number and their bank account completes the JAM trinity. This is the foundation of digital infrastructure. The JAM trinity covers the identification and e-KYC of a customer and provides a broader range of personalized digital financial services. The India Stack has observed the use of application programming interface (APIs). Through this, customers can store their documents as proof of identity (e.g., Aadhaar) and consent (e.g., e-signature) digitally in a digital locker. This initiative has created an opportunity for financial service providers to deliver services digitally, even at remote locations at a low cost. This infrastructure, too, has helped the growth of digital banking in the country.

33.2.3   Unified Payments Interface (UPI)

The National Payments Council of India (NPCI) launched the Unified Payments Interface (UPI) in April 2016. UPI is a system that powers multiple bank accounts into a single mobile application, merging several banking features, seamless fund routing, and merchant payments into one hood. It has played a significant role in promoting digital payments in India since 2014. UPI offers a low-cost, high-volume payment interoperability solution that enables users to make payments directly from their bank accounts by using only a virtual payment address (VPA) linked to the recipient's bank account and phone number. As of July 2021, UPI registered 432.5 million transactions, the highest in the world, that accounted for ₹567,345 million, with the highest average daily transaction of approximately 100 million, which is double the amount from July 2020. UPI enabled 2,348 transactions every second in 2022.

33.2.4   RuPay

Customers who had recently opened PMJDY bank accounts were given RuPay debit cards that could be used to make ATM withdrawals and POS (point of sale) payments. As a domestic alternative to Visa and MasterCard, RuPay was first introduced by the NPCI in 2012 as an open-loop, interoperable, all-purpose payment system. Approximately 79% of the 330 million individuals with PMJDY plan bank accounts also have a RuPay card.

33.3   Technology Acceptance Model

One of the well-known approaches to embracing and utilizing technology that Davis (1989) first suggested is the technology acceptance model (TAM). As it illustrates the causal relationships between expectations (the utility of a system and ease of use) and behaviors, actions, and the actual use of the system, TAM portrays the behavioral intents of future users when employing a technical creation. The TAM also contends that external influences influence purpose and actual usage through indirect effects on perceived utility and ease of use. Variables favorably affect the attitude toward adoption. Perceived usefulness, according to the TAM, is the extent to which a person thinks that utilizing a specific technology will improve his or her ability to accomplish their work. TAM is a concise model that is generalizable. Many studies offered evidence in support (Adams, Nelson, & Todd, 1992; Taylor & Todd, 1995). According to several studies on TAM, plans to adopt new technology are predicated on having a favorable attitude toward it. The standard TAM, which is widely accepted in the banking sector, asserts a considerably positive link between users' attitudes about a specific technology and their adoption intentions. To explain the influence of variables on consumer behavior and intentions, Rustam and Aimon (2020) made a proposal. The degree to which innovation is viewed as not being difficult to comprehend, use, or function was initially confirmed by Rogers and Cartano (1962). According to Venkatesh and Davis (2000), perceived ease of use is not a reliable indicator of perceived usefulness in terms of a user's attitude towards adopting new technology. Yet, when the frequency of use rose, the perceived ease of use became more significant (Venkatesh & Davis, 2000). Over the past ten years, numerous empirical studies on the adoption of IT have demonstrated how perceived utility can influence user intentions (Hong & Zhu, 2006; Ng & Kwok, 2017). Users choose to use a service based on its perceived utility when they believe the financial inclusion onboarding mechanism will have a beneficial effect. The following Figure 33.2 shows about the technology acceptance model (TAM) and well describes the technology acceptance model and the Figure 33.3 highlights for Aadhaar E-KYC API Specification-Version 2.0; source—UIDAI-May 2016.

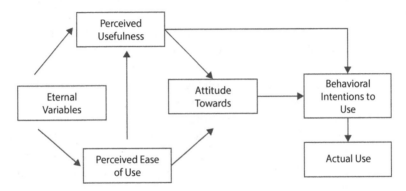

Figure 33.2 Technology acceptance model (TAM).

33.4   AI and Use of AI in Financial Inclusion

33.4.1   Advent of AI Banking in India

According to Sangani's (2017), with reference to Accenture Banking Technology Vision 2017, most bankers worldwide (78%) and in India (87%) believe that AI technology will facilitate the creation of user interfaces that are simpler to use. This initiative will lead to a more human-like customer experience. Additionally, the report states that 79% of bankers globally and almost 87% of bankers in India anticipate that AI technology will transform how banks gather information and engage with customers. Aurora asserts that AI is not a new concept in India, as certain research institutions and universities have been utilizing various AI technologies for social transformation for many years. With the availability of more affordable and accessible enabling technologies, AI is now becoming more widespread, and both large companies and startups are exploring its potential uses. The author suggests that research indicates that the implementation of AI has the potential to contribute almost $1 trillion to the Indian economy by 2035.

33.4.2   Artificial Intelligence (AI)

The term "artificial intelligence" was coined in 1956 by John McCarthy. FSB (2017) describes AI as "the study and advancement of computer systems that have the ability to perform tasks that typically necessitate human intelligence."

Kaplan (2016) defined AI as "the ability to draw suitable conclusions rapidly from limited data, making effective generalizations, which is the crux of intelligence. The more expansive the range of applications and the faster the conclusions are made with minimal data, the more intelligent the behavior is perceived to be." According to Hall and Pesenti (2017), there are three specific areas within the UK finance industry where AI is being implemented: personalized financial planning, the detection of fraud and anti-money laundering efforts, and the automation of various financial processes. Milojević and Redzepagic (2021) have conducted research on the growing utilization of artificial intelligence in the banking sector, specifically as it pertains to risk management. Their analysis sought to identify the potential benefits and challenges associated with implementing AI and machine learning in this context, particularly with regards to credit risk management. The authors concluded that the use of AI, machine learning, deep learning, and big data analytics has the potential to improve risk management across multiple areas, including credit, market, liquidity, and operational risks.

Further, machine learning (ML), robotic process automation (RPA), predictive analytics, and artificial intelligence (AI) are all components of artificial intelligence (AI).

a. Artificial intelligence—Artificial intelligence is the imitation of human intellect by computer systems, to put it simply.
b. Machine learning—Machine learning is a subset of artificial intelligence. It involves algorithms that allow computers or machines to learn and improve their ability to solve complex problems by analyzing their previous data and learning from mistakes. The process relies heavily on identifying patterns within the data to make better decisions when presented

with new information. The goal is to provide the most effective and efficient solution possible.

c. Robotic process automation—Robotic process automation (RPA) is a technique that utilizes the capabilities of artificial intelligence (AI) and machine learning (ML) to handle large amounts of data and automate repetitive tasks, resulting in reduced human effort and time consumption. RPA can be categorized into three types: probots, knowbots, and chatbots.

Thus, banks and other organizations are utilizing AI and other complementary technologies to enhance their efficiency by saving time. Below are some of the ways in which AI is used in a bank:

33.4.3 Function of AI in Banking Sector

Artificial intelligence (AI) is improving and becoming smarter for the use of both companies and customers. The implementation and use of AI are spreading in various sectors. One of the industries that has been quick to adopt AI technology is the banking industry. The banking industry is investigating the potential applications of AI technologies.

Some examples of AI in the banking industry include the use of chatbots for customer service, personalizing services for each customer, and even installing an AI robot for self-service at banks. In addition to these, the bank is studying the viability and effectiveness of AI in the back office, as well as the possibility of reducing fraud and other security threats.

According to the ASSOCHAM and PWC (2021) report, the Fintech market in India was estimated to be worth INR 1,920.16 billion in 2019 and is anticipated to grow to INR 6,207.41 billion by 2025, growing at a compound annual growth rate (CAGR) of 22.7% between 2020 and 2025.

The Indian Fintech sector has been completely changed by recent reforms. For example, the Indian government is also making efforts to transform the Fintech sector and lay the groundwork for digital payments. The finance minister proposed to allocate INR 1,500 Cr to promote digital transactions in the nation in the Union Budget 2021 speech. This move aims to promote digital payment methods. High levels of equity and venture funding in open API platforms like Aadhar, the Open Credit Enablement Network (OCEN), the Unified Payments Interface (UPI), and the Bharat Bill Payment System (BBPS); in the area of cutting-edge technologies like AI, ML, and IoT; and in the area of strong payments and acceptance infrastructure are the main drivers of the Fintech boom.

33.4.4 The Main Purpose of Using AI in Banking

There are different purposes for which AI is used. One of the purposes of adopting AI is to speed up the time it would take a human to process a certain amount of data and information and to produce precise results at a lower cost. AI is becoming a favorite technology in the banking sector. By lowering banking costs, the application of technology not only supports company automation but also boosts customer acquisition and money transfers.

According to Ris, Stankovic, and Zoran (2020), financial inclusion can be achieved by owning a bank account, and advancements in AI and blockchain technology can facilitate banking services at the doorstep. The use of AI and machine learning algorithms can help with documentation requirements. The use of artificial intelligence in the banking system has been successful in areas such as custom management services, credit information services, frequently asked questions (FAQ) services, and financial assistance services, among others. AI is being applied in various fields such as cybersecurity, risk management, fraud management, sales, internal audit, financial assistance, asset management, loan management, and customer management to improve the overall performance of the banking system.

Customers can now access banking services without having to physically visit a bank. By visiting the bank's website, customers can interact with a pre-programmed chatbot that can gather the necessary data and ask questions to determine whether the customer meets the eligibility criteria. If the customer's issue can be resolved using the chatbot algorithm, the chatbot will provide instructions to guide the customer to a solution. However, if the customer's problem cannot be solved using the chatbot algorithm, the chatbot will direct the customer to visit a nearby branch for assistance.

33.4.5   Adoption of AI for Financial Inclusion

Many countries have taken the issue of financial inclusion very seriously and brought about a lot of changes in their economic and financial policies. Today, there are a greater number of bank branch penetrations than a decade ago. A lot of serious banking and policy changes have taken place to ensure universal access to banking and financial services. Despite these efforts, banking and financial services are not accessible to many populations. Therefore, there is a genuine question as to how to create a situation of universal and inclusive finance for all.

The rise of ownership of mobile phones and growth in information and communication technologies (ICTs) has given hope of successful artificial intelligence-based financial inclusion. There are some countries in the world where AI-based financial inclusion has already been implemented, e.g., in African countries. FIBER—Financial Inclusion on Business Runways (2018) has mentioned four areas of the banking sector where AI-based technology is adopted: personal financial management, credit risk assessments, conversational interfaces, and machine vision or voice recognition. These four areas are explained below.

A. **Personal Financial Management:** Abe AI of the US provides a conversational AI platform to financial institutions. It has formed a partnership with **Absa Bank**. Absa Bank is a subsidiary bank of Barclays in South Africa. This bank is engaged in the work of personal financial management; it helps in the financial decision-making process of the customers by providing them with some important strategies. Further, the Abe AI solution uses several ML financial algorithms for determining customers' future transactions, encourages savings, and, if needed, provides credit to the customers and foretells their cash flows.

B. **Credit Risk Assessments:** Artificial intelligence technology for credit risk assessment is used by Kenya's Branch and Tala companies. Both are digital financial service platforms. These companies use credit assessments to offer credit directly to individual customers with the help of mobile phones. Further, Aella Credit of Nigeria and Lulalend of South Africa provide funds for the SMEs. These companies assess the credit worthiness of these SMEs with the help of AI. Aella Credit, with the help of mobile phones, provides machine learning (ML)-based evaluation of risk in business-to-business and business-to-customer service models. Aella Credit and Lulalend are examples of companies that use behavioral data from phones. These behavioral data include details of the device, details of call logs, and details of social media used by the customers. These companies also study the number of times given to make a purchase by customers and their financial transactions. These companies also offer small loans to consumers.

C. **Conversational Interfaces:** Many Fintech companies are developing ML (machine learning) models to enhance interactions with customers and serve them best according to their different needs. For example, the Fintech companies interact with the customers by responding to their inquiries, which helps the customers make greater usage of their products and thus usher in financial wellness for them. Chatbot is an AI-based conversational interface technology. It can interact with customers to solve their problems. It can also reduce operating costs and boost returns. Some of the examples of these chatbot applications at an international level are described below.

   i. **DataProphet:** It is a South African AI company. It provides business-to-business consulting and artificial intelligence solutions to companies. The Dataprophet company is engaged with insurance institutions and manages customer queries with the help of chatbots. Dataprophet has concluded that customer service is one of the largest costs in any insurance company, and therefore, these companies should adopt strategies to reduce the cost related to customers' queries. The chatbot cannot just reduce operating costs but also serve many customers. DataProphet supports the idea that customers get financial services on a low touch basis and realize savings for the companies. The company is continuously evolving some new avenues for customers to access with the help of text, web, or other channels.

   ii. **FinChatBot:** It is another South African-based company that is bringing an equivalent chatbot system from DataProphet to support insurance customers. FinChatBot is developing a platform for customers to interact with chatbots with some basic questions on insurance products and services and the process related to getting them. Further, the company is also using ML for conversational flow by constructing sequences of questions and styles of chat according to the needs and segments of customers.

33.4.6   Use of AI for Financial Inclusion

Customers can open accounts or deposit cash through their mobile phones. They can transfer funds through blockchain in only 10 min, which is faster than traditional methods in developing nations. Financial institutions save on costs because blockchain payments do not need to go through national payment systems, eliminating the need for physical branches. Individuals and small businesses can add funds in fiat currency, which shifts volatility risk to financial intermediaries. These intermediaries often use bitcoin as a "vehicle currency" to avoid exposure to virtual currency volatility.

Further, AI can be used in the following ways for financial inclusion: AI can be utilized to generate the credit history of customers by collecting information from various sources, such as Aadhar linked data, GPS data, handset details, insurance, etc. HDFC was the first to introduce a chatbot to serve as a relationship manager, and AI-trained robots can function as financial advisors. Finally, AI can also assist in financial literacy programs, specifically lifestyle-based banking. Banks can use data from government schemes that incentivize the use of Pradhan Mantri Jan Dhan accounts and analyze it through an AI engine to determine the best products to offer customers.

33.4.7   Financial Inclusion With the Help of e-KYC

The process of KYC (know your customer) has become crucial for financial institutions worldwide as a preventive measure against financial fraud, terrorist funding, and money laundering. It involves obtaining essential identity and address information about customers. However, the industry encounters a significant challenge when increasing monitoring efforts, which is the vast amount of data, its speed of generation, and the complexity resulting from various non-standard formats.

Know Your Customer, or KYC, is an important tool in India for confirming each customer's proof of identity and address to conduct any financial transaction through banking institutions. Since 2004, the RBI has prohibited individuals from opening bank A/C, trading A/C, or demat A/C without fulfilling the KYC procedure. There are two types of KYC: in-person based KYC is where a person must visit a KYC kiosk in person and authenticate his identity; on the other hand, Aadhar-based KYC is internet-based KYC.

Fulfilling the goal of financial inclusion for all eKYC will be a great help. In India, eKYC is based on unique 12-digit Aadhar card information provided by the customer to UIDAI. Any authorized financial institution may obtain a customer's Aadhar card information and use it to find the customer's information using the eKYC Application Programming Interface (API). Data flow for the e-KYC API according to the Aadhar e-KYC API Specification, Version 2.0: The data flow of a typical e-KYC API request is as follows, going from left to right and back:

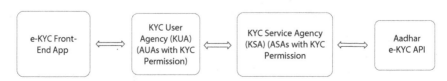

Figure 33.3 Aadhaar E-KYC API Specification-Version 2.0; source—UIDAI-May 2016.

e-KYC can be completed in two ways: biometric-based and OTP-based. In biometric-based transactions, the customer must present his 12-digit Aadhaar identification number together with biometrics. A scan of the fingerprints or iris will be done as part of the authentication procedure for the customer. In OTP-based e-KYC, the customer must also present the Aadhaar number. An OTP will be dispatched to the registered mobile phone of the customer, and then the eKYC will be completed. Further, eKYC could be done by QR Code Scan, mAadhar App, or paperless offline KYC. Initially, the software professionals working in the technology domain were the target group of UIDAI for the eKYC service. However, this could be applicable in the banking sector for the purpose of financial inclusion, as it could help in cost cutting and reaching many target groups. The eKYC could remove the barriers of geographical isolation.

Further, mobile banking, approved by the RBI under the Payment and Settlement Systems Act of 2007 is another initiative that can give greater access to financial inclusion. The RBI has given approval to 80 banks for the purpose of mobile banking services. The acceptance of mobile banking can bring greater access to financial inclusion by breaking the barriers of cost and geographical distance.

The way clients engage with banks and financial [22] services in the new digital [23–26] world is changing thanks to conversational AI, which is the next big thing. By 2023, "more than 80% of businesses [27, 28] want to deploy a chatbot." This fact amply demonstrates the world's drastic transition to a more digitalized economy, where chatbots and voicebots [29, 30] are fundamentally altering the consumer experience landscape. The essence has already been deduced by top businesses [31], and they have created Conversational AI-based solutions that can provide outstanding customer experiences. Financial [32, 33] institutions may now offer highly individualised client experiences that are readily automated across the web [34, 35], audio, messaging platforms, and mobile devices thanks to conversational AI, which is gaining popularity. The interaction between employees and the financial institution of their company has also undergone a fundamental transformation as a result of conversational AI [36, 37] and voice-based digital [38, 39] assistant technologies. Employees may now be ramped up more rapidly thanks to automated workflows and quicker inquiry resolution. Additionally, voice-activated bots may simply and effectively communicate information about their daily activities and other pertinent information. AI-powered technologies might be used by cybercriminals [40] to attack financial institutions and steal confidential information or cash. In addition, if AI systems are not properly guarded and monitored, they may be influenced or compromised, which might have disastrous effects.

33.5 Conclusion

Artificial intelligence (AI) can show human traits of thinking, learning, and self-revision. These features of AI have made the hope of universal financial inclusion a reality. Speed, security, cost-effectiveness, and customization of banking products are some of the important features of AI-based financial inclusion. These features prompt the banking operation to go beyond the boundaries of a brick-and-mortar setup. As of the present situation, the banking industry is implementing AI-based technology to carry out tasks in four different areas: credit risk assessments, personal financial management, conversational interfaces, and machine vision or voice recognition. With the help of AI, the banks can focus on the personal finances of the customer, e.g., the choice of a product, saving, taking an overdraft, and cash flows. The machine vision or voice recognition feature of AI can be used for facial recognition, voice assistant, biometric identifications, and document digitalization by banks. Chatbot—the AI-based conversational interface technology—can interact with the customers and give augmentation to greater usage of products and financial wellness. Chatbots can also solve the customer's problem and thus reduce operating costs and boost returns for the banks. Along with mobile banking, the adoption of AI for eKYC—Know Your Customer—can be a greater milestone to achieve the target of inclusive finance in India.

Snapshot: Adoption of Conversational AI by Major Banks in India

SIA (State Bank of India Intelligent Assistant), the chatbot of SBI: The State Bank of India (SBI) is the largest public-sector bank in India. It has focused its AI application for both the staff and the customers. However, SIA is a chatbot from the customer's perspective. It is loaded with answers based on frequently asked questions from customers. This AI-enabled chatbot can address the customer's inquiries promptly. It can assist the customers with routine tasks of the bank, just as the bank representative can. Payjo, the developer of SIA, claims that SIA has answered millions of questions from many customers since its launch. As per Payjo's claim of Payjo, SIA has the capacity to handle 10,000 queries per second, or 864 million per day. SBI claims that SIA improves over time by constantly learning from each interaction. In the present situation, SIA can respond to questions about banking products and services.

EVA (Electronic Virtual Assistant) of HDFC Bank: HDFC Bank has created an AI-based chatbot, Eva. It is developed by Senseforth AI Research based in Bangalore. Eva the chatbot has the capacity to take in knowledge from multiple sources and provide correct answers in less than 0.4 s. Since its launch, Eva has received thousands of queries from customers and answered them. Since its launch in 2017, as per the information, Eva has attended to more than 2.7 million customer queries. It has interacted with more than 530,000 unique users and conducted 1.2 million chats. The customers do not have to spend time searching, browsing, and calling; they can directly get information about the bank's products and services. Further, it has the capacity for continuous improvement in interactions with customers. Moreover, Eva could handle real banking transactions with its customers. HDFC is also developing IRA (Intelligent Robotic Assistant) for in-store robotic applications to help guide customers or visitors. However, there is a need for more research and development in this area.

Robotic Software of ICICI Bank: ICICI Bank has developed "robotic software" that focuses on automating workplace tasks. This technology automates time-consuming, repetitive, and high-volume business chores by mimicking human behavior. Robotic software has improved accuracy to 100%; at the same time, it has cut response time to customers by up to 60%. The result is that it has achieved sharp growth in the productivity and efficiency of banks. Additionally, it has allowed bank staff to concentrate more on tasks that are value-added and directly concerned with customers. The "software robots" can carry out a variety of tasks, such as gathering and analyzing data from computer systems. Among other tasks, the software robots can automate text mining, account reconciliations, and processing foreign exchange rates. Additionally, software robotics with AI features have the capability for voice and facial recognition as well as the ability to handle natural language.

iPal Chatbot of ICICI Bank: The iPal chatbot of ICICI Bank communicates with clients. According to the claim, the chatbot can respond to millions of inquiries with an accuracy rate of 90%. The iPal services are classified into three main groups, the majority of which are recorded in the iMobile app.

Category 1: This category includes frequently asks questions and offers simple structured answers that could be asked of a bank executive. The bot gives the correct answers, and it improves performance as it interacts with customers.

Category 2: This category incorporates financial dealings. A customer could transfer funds, pay bills, or recharge mobile phone.

Category 3: This category involves helping customers discover new features. It helps with how to perform a task, for example, how to reset an ATM pin. This category is higher level, where a customer can interact with an AI as he or she would with a bank executive. Further, the bank is developing to assimilate iPal with voice assistants such as Cortana, Siri, and Assistant. The bank is exploring its ability to interface with multiple voice assistants.

AI & NLP (Natural Language Processing)-Enabled App of Axis Bank: Axis Bank launched an AI & NLP (Natural Language Processing) enabled app for conversational banking to help consumers with financial and non-financial transactions. AI and NLP can answer frequently asked questions from customers. It can get in touch with the bank to provide loans and other products to the customers. The result of the implementation of AI and NLP is that it has reduced the turnaround time (TAT) across more than 125 processes and improved cognitive automation across 90 processes. The latter were basically repetitive manual tasks. The bank has completed robotic process automation (RPA) for most of the processes, including account maintenance and servicing, loan disbursements, bulk transaction processes, and ATM support. The implementation of RPA has brought a lot of reduction in the total time taken to do a banking activity. For example, for the opening of savings accounts, turnaround time has been reduced by 90%; for current accounts, TAT has been reduced by 92%; and for other processes, it has been reduced from 50% to 80%.

Canara Bank: Canara Bank has introduced humanoid robots named Mitra and Candi at some of its branches. Mitra, created by Invento Robotics in Bengaluru, is a symbol of collaboration in AI between India and China and is named after the Vedic god of friendship. Soft Bank Robotics from Japan has also contributed to the initiative with Candi, another humanoid robot. These robots are currently located in the Karnataka capital and have different functions. Mitra greets customers in Kannada and assists them in navigating the bank's headquarters on JC Road, while Candi answers 215 preset questions in English at the financial institution's circle office on MG Road.

References

1. Adams, D.A., Nelson, R.R., Todd, P.A., Perceived usefulness, ease of use, and usage of information technology: A replication. *MIS Q.*, 16, 2, 227–247, 1992.
2. ASSOCHAM, Financial inclusion & future of financial services in India vision 2030, The Associated Chambers of Commerce and Industry of India (ASSOCHAM), September 2022.
3. Davis, F.D., Perceived usefulness, perceived ease of use, and user acceptance of information technology. *MIS Q.*, 13, 3, 319–340, 1989.
4. FIBER (Financial Inclusion on Business Runways), Artificial intelligence: Practical superpowers the case for AI in financial services in Africa, 2018.
5. Hall, W. and Pesenti, J., Growing the artificial intelligence industry in the UK, working paper, 2017, Available at: https://www.gov.uk/government/publications/growing-the-artifcialin-telligence-industry-intheuk. https://www.gov.uk/government/uploads/system/uploads/attachment_data/le/652097/Growing_the_artificial_intelligence_industry_in_the_UK.pdf.
6. Khan, H.R., Issues and challenges in financial inclusion–policies, partnerships, processes & products, https://www.bis.org/review/r120802f.pdf.
7. Hong, W. and Zhu, K., Migrating to internet-based e-commerce: Factors affecting e-commerce adoption and migration at the firm level. *Inf. Manage.*, 43, 2, 204–221, 2006.
8. Kaplan, J., *Artificial intelligence: What everyone needs to know*, Oxford University Press, 2016.
9. Milojević, N. and Redzepagic, S., Prospects of artificial intelligence and machine learning application in banking risk management. *J. Cent. Bank. Theory Pract.*, 3, 41–57, 2021, Received: 04 July 2020; accepted: 27 November 2020.
10. Ng, A.W. and Kwok, B.K.B., Emergence of Fintech and cybersecurity in a global financial centre. *J. Financ. Regul. Compliance*, 25, 4, 422–434, 2017.
11. Pradhan Mantri Jan-Dhan Yojana, Continuation of Pradhan Mantri Jan Dhan Yojana (PMJDY), https://www.aspirationaldistricts.in/wp-content/uploads/2019/02/PM-Jandhan-Yojana.pdf.
12. PWC and Assocham, FinTech for the underserved: Future of FinTech and payments to drive financial inclusiveness, 2021, Published on September 2021. https://www.pwc.in/assets/pdfs/consulting/financial-services/fintech/publications/fintech-for-the-underserved.pdf.
13. Raja, R.G., *I do what i do*, Harper Business, India, 2017.
14. Rangarajan, C., Report of the committee on financial inclusion, January 2008, https://www.findevgateway.org/sites/default/files/publications/files/mfg-en-paper-report-of-the-committee-on-financial-inclusion-jan-2008.pdf (accessed on 01-12-2022).
15. Ris, K., Stankovic, Z., Avramovic, Z., Implications of implementation of artificial intelligence in the banking business with correlation to the human factor. Scientific Research Publishing; *J. Comput. Commun.*, 8, 130–144, 2020, https://www.scirp.org/journal/jcc ISSN Online: 2327-5227 ISSN Print: 2327-5219. https://www.scirp.org/pdf/jcc_2020112615471696.pdf.
16. Rogers, E.M. and Cartano, D.G., Methods of measuring opinion leadership. *Public Opin. Q.*, 26, 3, 435–441, 1962.
17. Rustam, D. and Aimon, H., The analysis of poverty and unemployment in West Sumatra. Paper presented at the *4th Padang International Conference on Education, Economics, Business and Accounting (PICEEBA-2 2019)*, 2020, doi: https://dx.doi.org/10.2991/aebmr.k.200305.070.
18. Sangani, P., AI to present huge opportunity for banks to transform customer experience. Accenture; The Economic Times, 2017, Published on March 29 2017. https://economictimes.indiatimes.com/industry/banking/finance/ai-to-present-huge-opportunity-for-banks-to-transform-customer-experience-accenture/articleshow/57888265.cms?from=mdr.
19. Taylor, S. and Todd, P.A., Understanding information technology usage: A test of competing models. *Inf. Syst. Res.*, 6, 2, 144–176, 1995.

20. The World Bank, Financial inclusion: Financial inclusion is a key enabler to reducing poverty and boosting prosperity, March 29, 2022, https://www.worldbank.org/en/topic/financialinclusion/overview (accessed on 10-12-2022).
21. Venkatesh, V. and Davis, F.D., A theoretical extension of the technology acceptance model: Four longitudinal field studies. *Manage. Sci.*, 46, 2, 186–204, 2000.
22. Mahor, V., Bijrothiya, S., Rawat, R., Kumar, A., Garg, B., Pachlasiya, K., IoT and artificial intelligence techniques for public safety and security, in: *Smart Urban Computing Applications*, p. 111, 2023.
23. Mahor, V., Pachlasiya, K., Garg, B., Chouhan, M., Telang, S., Rawat, R., Mobile operating system (Android) vulnerability analysis using machine learning, in: *Proceedings of International Conference on Network Security and Blockchain Technology: ICNSBT 2021*, pp. 159–169, Springer Nature Singapore, Singapore, 2022, June.
24. Rawat, R., Garg, B., Pachlasiya, K., Mahor, V., Telang, S., Chouhan, M., Mishra, R., SCNTA: Monitoring of network availability and activity for identification of anomalies using machine learning approaches. *Int. J. Inf. Technol. Web Eng. (IJITWE)*, 17, 1, 1–19, 2022.
25. Rawat, R., Rimal, Y.N., William, P., Dahima, S., Gupta, S., Sankaran, K.S., Malware threat affecting financial organization analysis using machine learning approach. *Int. J. Inf. Technol. Web Eng. (IJITWE)*, 17, 1, 1–20, 2022.
26. Rawat, R., Mahor, V., Chouhan, M., Pachlasiya, K., Telang, S., Garg, B., Systematic literature review (SLR) on social media and the digital transformation of drug trafficking on darkweb, in: *International Conference on Network Security and Blockchain Technology*, pp. 181–205, Springer, Singapore, 2022.
27. Rawat, R., Ayodele Oki, O., Sankaran, S., Florez, H., Ajagbe, S.A., Techniques for predicting dark web events focused on the delivery of illicit products and ordered crime. *Int. J. Electr. Comput. Eng. (IJECE)*, 13, 5, 5354–5365, Oct. 2023, doi: 10.11591/ijece.v13i5.pp5354-5365.
28. Rawat, R., Garg, B., Mahor, V., Telang, S., Pachlasiya, K., Chouhan, M., Organ trafficking on the dark web—The data security and privacy concern in healthcare systems, in: *Internet of Healthcare Things: Machine Learning for Security and Privacy*, pp. 189–216, 2022.
29. Vyas, P., Vyas, G., Chauhan, A., Rawat, R., Telang, S., Gottumukkala, M., Anonymous trading on the dark online marketplace: An exploratory study, in: *Using Computational Intelligence for the Dark Web and Illicit Behavior Detection*, pp. 272–289, IGI Global, 2022.
30. Rawat, R., Oki, O.A., Sankaran, K.S., Olasupo, O., Ebong, G.N., Ajagbe, S.A., A new solution for cyber security in big data using machine learning approach, in: *Mobile Computing and Sustainable Informatics: Proceedings of ICMCSI 2023*, pp. 495–505, Springer Nature Singapore, Singapore, 2023.
31. Rawat, R., Chakrawarti, R.K., Raj, A., Mani, G., Chidambarathanu, K., Bhardwaj, R., Association rule learning for threat analysis using traffic analysis and packet filtering approach. *Int. J. Inf. Technol.*, 1–11, 2023.
32. Rawat, R., Logical concept mapping and social media analytics relating to cyber criminal activities for ontology creation. *Int. J. Inf. Technol.*, 15, 2, 893–903, 2023.
33. Rawat, R., Mahor, V., Álvarez, J.D., Ch, F., Cognitive systems for dark web cyber delinquent association malignant data crawling: A review, in: *Handbook of Research on War Policies, Strategies, and Cyber Wars*, pp. 45–63, 2023.
34. Rawat, R., Chakrawarti, R.K., Vyas, P., Gonzáles, J.L.A., Sikarwar, R., Bhardwaj, R., Intelligent fog computing surveillance system for crime and vulnerability identification and tracing. *Int. J. Inf. Secur. Priv. (IJISP)*, 17, 1, 1–25, 2023.
35. Rawat, R., Sowjanya, A.M., Patel, S.I., Jaiswal, V., Khan, I., Balaram, A. (Eds.), *Using Machine Intelligence: Autonomous Vehicles Volume 1*, John Wiley & Sons, 2022.

36. Rawat, R., Mahor, V., Díaz-Álvarez, J., Chávez, F., Rooted learning model at fog computing analysis for crime incident surveillance, in: *2022 International Conference on Smart Generation Computing, Communication and Networking (SMART GENCON)*, pp. 1–9, IEEE, 2022, December.

37. Rawat, R. and Shrivastav, S.K., SQL injection attack detection using SVM. *Int. J. Comput. Appl.*, 42, 13, 1–4, 2012.

38. Rawat, R., Bhardwaj, P., Kaur, U., Telang, S., Chouhan, M., Sankaran, K.S., *Smart vehicles for communication, volume 2*, John Wiley & Sons, 2023.

39. Mahor, V., Garg, B., Telang, S., Pachlasiya, K., Chouhan, M., Rawat, R., Cyber threat phylogeny assessment and vulnerabilities representation at thermal power station, in: *Proceedings of International Conference on Network Security and Blockchain Technology: ICNSBT 2021*, pp. 28–39, Springer Nature Singapore, Singapore, 2022, June.

40. Rawat, R., Gupta, S., Sivaranjani, S., Cu, O.K., Kuliha, M., Sankaran, K.S., Malevolent information crawling mechanism for forming structured illegal organisations in hidden networks. *Int. J. Cyber Warf. Terror. (IJCWT)*, 12, 1, 1–14, 2022.

Revolutionizing Government Operations: The Impact of Artificial Intelligence in Public Administration

Aman Kumar Mishra¹*, Amit Kumar Tyagi², Sathian Dananjayan¹, Anand Rajavat³, Hitesh Rawat⁴ and Anjali Rawat⁵

¹School of Computer Science and Engineering, Vellore Institute of Technology, Chennai, Tamil Nadu, India
²Department of Fashion Technology, National Institute of Fashion Technology, New Delhi, Delhi, India
³Department of Computer Science Engineering Director, Shri Vaishnav Institute of Information Technology, Shri Vaishnav Vidyapeeth Vishwavidyalaya, Indore, India
⁴Faculty at Management Department, Sri Aurobindo Institute of Technology and Management, Indore, India
⁵Apostelle Overseas Education (AOE), Ujjain, India

Abstract

The incorporation of artificial intelligence (AI) into public administration has seen a significant increase in recent years as governments strive to enhance their operational efficiency and improve the quality of services offered to citizens. This study aims to examine the ways in which AI can be utilized in public administration, contributing to the ongoing discussion about the potential applications and benefits of AI in this field. The paper will also explore best practices and case studies of AI implementation in good governance, both in India and internationally. The integration of AI in public administration can lead to significant improvements in efficiency, transparency, and accountability. For example, AI-powered chatbots can automate routine tasks, such as answering citizens' inquiries, which will help public servants concentrate on more complex tasks. Artificial intelligence-based decision-making tools have the potential to assist governments in making data-driven decisions by processing vast amounts of information and detecting patterns and tendencies. This contribution to decision-making processes can improve the accuracy and efficiency of government decisions. However, the integration of AI into public administration also raises significant ethical considerations. There are worries about the possibility of bias in AI-powered decision-making, particularly in areas that are highly sensitive, such as criminal justice and social welfare. Furthermore, the utilization of AI raises questions about its impact on employment, as automation may result in job loss and the need for public servants to acquire new abilities and training. In conclusion, this research paper aims to provide a comprehensive overview of the use of AI in public administration, highlighting its potential benefits, challenges, and ethical considerations. The paper also identifies opportunities for

*Corresponding author: amankr.mishra2020@vitstudent.ac.in
Amit Kumar Tyagi: ORCID: 0000-0003-2657-8700

Romil Rawat, Rajesh Kumar Chakrawarti, Sanjaya Kumar Sarangi, Piyush Vyas, Mary Sowjanya Alamanda, Kotagiri Srividya and Krishnan Sakthidasan Sankaran (eds.) *Conversational Artificial Intelligence*, (607–634) © 2024 Scrivener Publishing LLC

further research and development in this field and its implications for the future of public administration and governance.

Keywords: Artificial intelligence, E-government, predictive analytics, automated decision making, chatbots, digital transformation

34.1   Introduction

The use of artificial intelligence (AI) holds the potential to revolutionize the way public administration is carried out, with applications ranging from automating bureaucratic processes to improving service delivery. With the increasing availability of data and the advancement of technology, governments globally are investigating the potential benefits of AI for enhancing the efficiency, transparency, and accountability of public administration operations. However, the adoption of AI in government operations also presents significant ethical challenges and considerations.

The purpose of this research is to assess the present state of AI within public administration, including its possible uses, advantages, and difficulties, as well as the ethical considerations that must be addressed. The paper will also explore best practices and case studies of AI implementation in government, both nationally and internationally. Now, we need to explain the first few government operations in detail:

Government operation: This refers to the activities and functions of government entities at various levels (federal, state, and local) that are necessary for the effective governance of a country or region. These operations can include everything from managing budgets and collecting taxes to providing essential public services such as healthcare, education, and law enforcement. Government operations can be divided into several key areas, including:

- Administration and management: These include managing government employees, developing policies and regulations, and overseeing the operations of government agencies.
- Finance and budgeting: These involve managing government finances, including collecting taxes, creating budgets, and managing public debt.
- Public services: This includes providing essential services such as healthcare, education, transportation, and law enforcement.
- Infrastructure: This includes managing public infrastructure such as roads, bridges, water systems, and public buildings.
- National defense: This includes maintaining a military and protecting the country from external threats.

Note that effective government operations are essential for the functioning of a society, and they require a skilled workforce, robust information technology systems, and sound financial management practices. Now, we will explain the basics of Artificial Intelligence in detail.

Artificial Intelligence: Artificial Intelligence (AI) refers to the ability of machines to perform tasks that normally require human intelligence, such as recognizing speech, making decisions, and solving problems. AI technologies are typically based on complex algorithms that can learn from data and improve their performance over time. There are various types of AI, including:

- Machine learning: This is a type of AI that allows machines to learn from data and improve their performance over time without being explicitly programmed.

- Neural networks: These are a type of machine learning algorithm inspired by the structure and function of the human brain.
- Natural language processing (NLP): This is a type of AI that enables machines to understand and interpret human language.
- Robotics: This is a field of AI that focuses on the development of robots that can perform tasks autonomously.

AI has many practical applications, including in healthcare, finance, transportation, and entertainment. For example, AI can help doctors diagnose diseases more accurately and develop personalized treatment plans; help financial analysts identify investment opportunities; and help self-driving cars navigate roads safely.

However, AI also raises ethical and societal concerns, such as the potential for bias in decision-making algorithms, the impact on employment and the workforce, and the potential for AI to be used for malicious purposes. As AI continues to develop, it will be important for policymakers, researchers, and the public to work together to ensure that these technologies are used ethically and responsibly.

Type of AI:

There are mainly three types of Artificial Intelligence (AI):

- Artificial Narrow Intelligence (ANI) or Weak AI: ANI is a type of AI that is designed to perform a specific task or solve a specific problem. ANI systems are limited in their abilities and cannot perform tasks outside their specific domain.
- Artificial General Intelligence (AGI) or Strong AI: AGI refers to AI systems that can perform any intellectual task that a human being can perform. AGI is a hypothetical form of AI that does not exist yet, but it is a goal that some researchers are working towards.
- Artificial Super Intelligence (ASI): ASI refers to AI systems that are vastly more intelligent than humans in every conceivable way. ASI is also a hypothetical form of AI that does not exist yet, but it is a topic of speculation and concern in the field of AI research and philosophy.

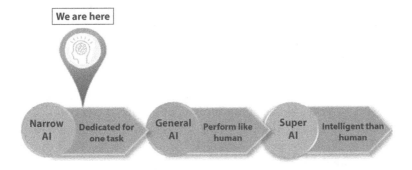

Other types of AI are:

XAI: XAI stands for Explainable Artificial Intelligence. It refers to the ability of an AI system to explain its decision-making process and provide clear and understandable reasons for why it made a particular decision or took a specific action. In recent years, there has been growing concern about the lack of transparency and accountability in AI systems, especially in high-stakes applications such as healthcare, finance, and criminal justice. XAI aims to address these concerns by making AI more transparent, interpretable, and accountable. XAI techniques include methods such as rule-based systems, decision trees, and model interpretability methods such as LIME (Local Interpretable Model-Agnostic Explanations) and SHAP (Shapley Additive Explanations). These techniques allow users to understand how AI systems work and make informed decisions based on their outputs.

Conversational AI: Conversational AI is a type of artificial intelligence that enables computers to understand and respond to natural language input from humans in a conversation. It involves the use of machine learning, natural language processing (NLP), and other AI techniques to build systems that can understand and generate human-like responses. Conversational AI is used in a variety of applications, such as chatbots, virtual assistants, and voice assistants. Chatbots are computer programs that can simulate human conversation and are often used in customer service and support, while virtual assistants and voice assistants like Amazon Alexa and Google Assistant are designed to interact with users through spoken language. To create a conversational AI system, developers typically use machine learning algorithms to train models on large datasets of text and speech. These models learn to recognize patterns in language and can generate responses based on the input they receive. Natural language understanding (NLU) techniques are used to help the system understand the meaning of the input, and natural language generation (NLG) techniques are used to generate human-like responses. Conversational AI is a rapidly growing field, and it has the potential to revolutionize the way people interact with technology in a more natural and intuitive way.

Hence, after explaining a few essential terms about government operations and AI, we can easily understand its role in the respective sectors. The utilization of AI in public administration has the possibility of optimizing routine processes by automating them. This can include using AI-powered chatbots to address citizens' inquiries and provide 24/7 access to information and services without the need for human involvement. Furthermore, AI-based decision-making tools can aid governments in making well-informed decisions through the analysis of vast amounts of data, leading to the detection of patterns and trends. Note that AI can be helpful in improving service delivery by as identifying and addressing citizens' needs and priorities. For example, AI-powered predictive analytics can be used to identify at-risk individuals and provide targeted services, such as health care or social support. AI can also improve the performance of public sector services, such as by optimizing the scheduling of public transportation or identifying and addressing maintenance issues in public infrastructure.

However, the implementation of AI in public administration also presents significant ethical considerations. There are worries regarding potential bias in AI-powered decision-making, particularly in delicate areas such as criminal justice and social welfare. There are also concerns about the effect of AI on employment, as automation could result in job losses and require public servants to acquire new skills and undergo training. Another important challenge for the implementation of AI in public administration is the availability and quality of data. Governments must guarantee the accuracy, impartiality, and representativeness of the data utilized to train AI systems in accordance with the population they serve. Additionally, governments must ensure that the data is protected from breaches and misuse and that citizens' privacy rights are respected.

Addressing these ethical considerations and challenges necessitates the creation of straightforward and transparent policies and guidelines by governments for the application of AI in public administration. This includes developing a framework for the ethical use of AI as well as establishing mechanisms for monitoring and evaluating the performance of AI systems. In conclusion, the purpose of this research paper is to provide a comprehensive overview of the implementation of AI in public administration, highlighting its potential benefits, challenges, and ethical considerations. The paper also identifies opportunities for further research and development in this field and its ramifications for the future of public administration and governance. The paper will examine existing case studies and best practices of AI implementation in government, both in the United States and internationally, to provide a clearer picture of the current scenario and future possibilities. The research will also aim to provide recommendations for governments and policymakers on how to effectively integrate AI into public administration and address the challenges and ethical considerations that arise.

34.2   Methodology

The study is focused on AI technologies. The study's goal is to employ AI to promote economic growth and enhance public administration. The goal of this study is to pinpoint potential advances that could aid in the creation, application, and utilization of AI. To accomplish these objectives, the following actions should be taken:

- List the various AI technologies and their uses.
- The market for AI technologies should be studied.
- A thorough examination of the evolution of AI technologies and different definitional philosophies.
- Research the use of AI technology and its effects in various nations, such as the Russian Federation.
- Identify the support structure for AI development, application, and use to reach the widest possible audience in the nation and get opinions prior to any government decision being made.

Theoretical procedures, including analysis, synthesis, abstraction, observation, and generalization, provide the foundation of the research's methodology. This essay draws on a variety of sources, including federal legislation, Russian Federation government resolutions, strategic planning documents, and other legal and regulatory frameworks.

34.3   The Origin and Development of AI Technology and Current Methodologies in the Field

Artificial intelligence (AI) is a technology that has been under development for several decades, with roots dating back to the 1950s. The origin of AI can be traced to the pioneering work of figures such as Alan Turing, who put forth the idea of a machine capable of exhibiting human-like thinking. However, it was not until the advent of modern computing technology that the development of AI truly began to take off. Note that in the initial stage of AI development, the emphasis was on developing machines that exhibit "intelligence" by executing specific functions such as playing chess or solving mathematical equations.

These initial AI systems were designed using rule-based and expert systems, which enabled them to make decisions based on a pre-established set of rules. However, the limited adaptability of these systems to new circumstances was a hindrance to their broader application.

In the late 1980s and early 1990s, the field of AI began to evolve with the introduction of machine learning (ML) algorithms. Machine learning, a subfield of AI, enables systems to continuously improve their performance through experience without the need for explicit programming. This marked a significant shift in the field of AI, as it allowed for the development of systems that could learn and adapt to new situations. Another recent development in the field of AI is the rise of reinforcement learning (RL), a type of ML that allows systems to learn by trial and error, much like a child learning to walk. Reinforcement learning has led to significant advancements in areas such as game play and autonomous systems. In recent years, AI has been used to solve real-world problems in various industries, including healthcare, finance, transportation, and retail. AI-powered systems are emerging as a boon in natural language processing, image and speech recognition, and predictive analytics. AI-powered chatbots are being used to automate customer service, and AI-powered decision-making tools are being taken into consideration to predict patterns and trends in large amounts of data.

AI is also being used in the field of self-driving cars, where it is used to process sensor data and make decisions about the car's movement. In the healthcare sector, AI-powered systems are used for tasks such as image analysis and drug discovery. AI is also being used in the field of finance to detect fraud and analyze financial data.

However, AI is not without its challenges. The biggest challenge faced in the AI field is the problem of biased. While training data is bias, the systems will also be biased. AI systems fit the data they are trained on, which leads to discriminatory or unfair decision-making, particularly when it comes to sensitive issues such as criminal justice and welfare. Another major challenge in the field of AI is explainability. In a complex AI system, it is difficult to know how the system is making decisions, which makes it difficult for the user difficult to trust the decisions made by AI systems and ensure that they are fair and ethical. Finally, there are concerns about the impact of AI on the workforce, as automation may lead to job losses and the need for new skills and training for workers. In conclusion, AI is a rapidly evolving technology with a long history. Today, AI is being used to solve real-world problems in various industries, and its potential to transform the way we live and work is undeniable. However, there are also challenges to be addressed.

34.4   Artificial Intelligence in Indian Governance

This part of the paper examines the utilization and patterns of AI in the Indian government by pinpointing crucial applications and developments.

34.4.1   Law Enforcement

In India, the adoption of AI technology for law enforcement is still in its early stages. Nevertheless, there are various AI solutions, such as facial recognition, speech recognition, drones, robocops, and autonomous patrol vehicles, that hold potential for utilization in this field.

34.4.1.1   Facial and Speech Recognition

Facial recognition and speech recognition are two areas in which AI can have a significant impact on Indian governance and law enforcement. India is yet to fully embrace AI technology in the realm of law enforcement. Despite this, there are several AI innovations, including facial recognition, speech recognition, drones, robocops, and self-driving patrol cars, that hold promise for use in this area.

Facial recognition utilizes AI algorithms to perform an analysis of facial images and compare them with a pre-existing database of individuals for identification purposes. In law enforcement, facial recognition technology can be used for tasks such as identifying suspects, monitoring public spaces, and tracking missing persons. For example, facial recognition technology can be used to scan surveillance footage to identify suspects in criminal cases or to match images of missing persons to images in a database of known individuals.

Similarly, speech recognition technology uses AI algorithms to analyze speech and convert it into text. In law enforcement, speech recognition technology could be used for tasks such as transcribing interviews, monitoring phone calls, and automating routine tasks. For instance, speech recognition technology can be used to transcribe interviews with witnesses and suspects or to automatically transcribe phone calls to identify key words or phrases. One of the main benefits of facial recognition and speech recognition technology in law enforcement is the ability to automate routine tasks and improve the efficiency and effectiveness of law enforcement operations. An example of AI technology usage is facial recognition, which can streamline the identification of suspects in criminal cases by reducing manual searches and increasing the efficiency and precision of investigations. Additionally, speech recognition technology can automate the transcription of interviews and phone calls, lowering the requirement for manual transcription and enhancing the accuracy of records. Another benefit of these technologies is their ability to improve public safety. For example, facial recognition technology can be used to monitor public spaces and identify potential security threats, such as individuals on a watchlist or known criminals. Similarly, speech recognition technology can be used to monitor phone calls and identify potential threats, such as calls related to terrorism or organized crime.

However, the use of facial recognition and speech recognition technology in law enforcement also raises important ethical considerations. For example, concerns have been raised about the potential for bias in these technologies, particularly when it comes to sensitive issues such as race and ethnicity. Additionally, there are concerns about the impact of these technologies on privacy and civil liberties, as well as the potential for them to be used for surveillance and control. A major challenge in utilizing AI technology for law enforcement is the quality and availability of data. Governments need to guarantee that the data used for training these systems is precise, neutral, and reflective of the population they serve. It is also crucial for governments to take measures to protect the data from breaches and improper use while also preserving citizens' privacy rights. To address these challenges and ethical considerations, it is important for governments to develop clear and transparent policies and guidelines for the use of these technologies in law enforcement. This includes developing a framework for the ethical use of these technologies as well as establishing mechanisms for monitoring and evaluating their performance. Additionally, it is important for governments to engage with stakeholders, such as civil society organizations and the private sector, to ensure that the use of these technologies in law enforcement is aligned with the needs and values of the population it serves.

In conclusion, this research paper has explored the ways in which facial recognition and speech recognition technology can be used in Indian governance for law enforcement. Law enforcement operations and public safety can be enhanced through the implementation of cutting-edge technologies, which promise increased efficiency and efficacy. However, the use of these technologies also raises important ethical considerations and challenges, which must be addressed through clear and transparent policies and guidelines. The paper also identifies opportunities for further research and development in this field and its implications for the future of law enforcement in India.

34.4.1.2   *Predictive Analytics*

Law enforcement operations and public safety can be enhanced through the implementation of cutting-edge technologies, which promise increased efficiency and efficacy. One of the key applications of predictive analysis in Indian governance and law enforcement is crime forecasting. This involves using historical crime data to predict the likelihood of future criminal activity in a specific area. Law enforcement operations and public safety can be enhanced through the implementation of cutting-edge technologies, which promise increased efficiency and efficacy. Predictive analysis can also be used to identify patterns and trends in specific types of crime, such as drug trafficking or organized crime, which can help law enforcement agencies target their efforts more effectively. Another potential application of predictive analysis in Indian governance for law enforcement is the optimization of police resources. Predictive analysis can be used to identify the areas where crime is most likely to occur as well as the times of day when crime is most likely to occur. This can help law enforcement agencies optimize the deployment of patrol routes and surveillance cameras, as well as identify areas where additional resources may be needed.

Predictive analysis can also be used to identify potential suspects in criminal cases. This can be done by analyzing data such as social media, credit card transactions, and phone records to identify individuals who are most likely to be involved in criminal activity. This can help law enforcement agencies target their investigations more effectively as well as identify potential suspects who may not have been flagged by traditional methods. However, the use of predictive analysis in Indian governance and law enforcement also raises important ethical considerations. For example, concerns have been raised about the potential for bias in predictive algorithms, particularly when it comes to sensitive issues such as race and ethnicity. Additionally, there are concerns about the impact of predictive analysis on privacy and civil liberties, as well as the potential for predictive analysis to be used for surveillance and control. Another important challenge for the implementation of predictive analysis in Indian governance and law enforcement is the availability and quality of data. It is crucial for governments to guarantee that predictive algorithms are trained with precise, impartial, and representative data for the populations they serve. Additionally, governments must ensure that the data is protected from breaches and misuse and that citizens' privacy rights are respected.

To overcome these challenges and ethical considerations, it is necessary for governments to develop clear and transparent policies and guidelines for the use of predictive analysis in Indian governance and law enforcement. This includes developing a framework for the ethical use of predictive analysis as well as establishing mechanisms for monitoring and evaluating the performance of predictive algorithms. Additionally, it is important for governments to engage with stakeholders, such as civil society organizations and the private sector, to ensure that the use of predictive analysis in Indian governance for law enforcement is aligned with the needs and values of the population it serves. In conclusion, this research paper has explored the ways in which predictive analysis can be used in Indian governance and law enforcement. Predictive analysis has the potential to improve efficiency and effectiveness.

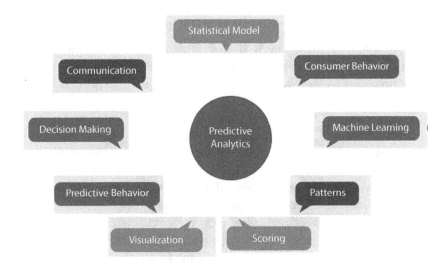

Different Aspects of Predictive Analysis

34.4.1.3   Robo-Cops

The use of AI-powered "Robo-Cops" in Indian governance for law enforcement has the potential to revolutionize the way in which investigations are conducted and crimes are solved. These systems, also known as autonomous robots, can be used for tasks such as monitoring public spaces, identifying suspects, and assisting in investigations. One of the main potential benefits of Robo-Cops in law enforcement is their ability to monitor public spaces and identify potential criminal activity. These systems can be equipped with a variety of sensors, such as cameras, microphones, and thermal imaging, which can be used to scan areas for suspicious activity. Robo-Cops equipped with machine learning algorithms can detect patterns and trends in criminal behavior, such as recognizing individuals with a history of criminal involvement or predicting crime-prone areas. Another potential application of Robo-Cops in law enforcement is in the area of crowd control. These systems can be used to monitor large crowds, such as at public events or protests, and identify potential security threats, such as individuals who are carrying weapons or acting in a suspicious manner. Additionally, Robo-Cops can be equipped with non-lethal weapons, such as pepper spray or tasers, which can be used to control crowds and maintain public order. Note that Robo-Cops can also be used to assist in investigations. For example, they can be used to scan crime scenes and collect evidence such as fingerprints, DNA, and ballistics. They can also be used to analyze surveillance footage and social media to identify suspects and track their movements. Additionally, Robo-Cops can be used to interview witnesses and suspects using natural language processing and speech recognition technology.

34.4.2   Education

Artificial intelligence is predominantly applied in decision-making, student services, individualized learning, and monitoring of student progress.

34.4.2.1   *Decision Making*

The utilization of Artificial Intelligence (AI) holds the promise to transform the way decisions are made within the realm of Indian educational governance. From streamlining administrative processes to improving student outcomes, the use of AI in education can lead to significant improvements in the education system. In this research paper, we will explore the ways in which AI can be used in Indian governance for decision-making in education, including its potential applications and benefits, as well as the challenges and ethical considerations that must be considered. One of the significant benefits of incorporating AI in the educational field is its capability to tailor the learning experience to each student's unique needs. By leveraging AI technology, educational systems can process data on student outcomes such as exam results, participation, and assignment completion to determine the student's strengths and areas requiring improvement. This can help educators tailor instruction and resources to meet the unique needs of individual students. Additionally, AI-powered systems can be used to provide real-time feedback to students, helping them identify areas for improvement and stay on track to achieve their goals. Another boon of AI in education is in teacher training and professional development. AI-powered systems can be used to analyze data on teacher performance, such as observations and evaluations, to identify areas of strength and weakness. This can help educators tailor training and support to meet the unique needs of individual teachers. Additionally, AI-powered systems can be used to provide real-time feedback to teachers, helping them to improve their instruction and stay on track to achieve their goals.

AI can also be used in the field of education to improve administrative processes such as student and teacher scheduling and resource allocation. AI algorithms can help optimize these processes, making them more cost-effective, efficient, and accurate. Additionally, AI can be utilized to analyze data from student assessments to help educators and administrators identify areas for improvement and inform decision-making on curriculum development. However, the implementation of AI in the educational sector also raises significant ethical questions. There are apprehensions regarding the possibility of prejudice in decision-making through AI, especially with regards to delicate matters such as student achievement and teacher appraisal. There are also concerns regarding the effects of AI on privacy rights and individual freedoms, along with the possibility of its use for monitoring and control purposes. A crucial challenge faced in the integration of AI in education lies in the adequacy and excellence of data. Governments are responsible for guaranteeing that the data employed to train AI models is precise, impartial, and reflects the population being served. Furthermore, the government must take measures to secure the data from unauthorized access and exploitation while also safeguarding citizens' privacy rights.

To overcome these difficulties and ethical concerns, it is imperative for governments to formulate unambiguous and open policies and directions for the utilization of AI in education. This encompasses constructing a system for the ethical usage of AI and creating methods for assessing and scrutinizing the operation of AI systems. Furthermore, it is vital for governments to involve key players, including educators, students, and parents, to guarantee that the implementation of AI in education aligns with the requirements and beliefs of the population being served.

In conclusion, this research paper has explored the ways in which AI can be used in Indian governance for decision-making in education. AI has the potential to improve student outcomes and administrative processes in the education system. However, the integration of AI in the educational sector also raises significant ethical issues and obstacles, which must be tackled through the establishment of transparent and unambiguous policies and directives. The paper also identifies opportunities for further research and development in this field and their implications for the future of education in India.

34.4.2.2 *Personalized Learning*

The implementation of Artificial Intelligence in the Indian education system has the potential to bring about a transformative change by offering a tailored educational experience to each student. One significant advantage of AI in education is its ability to adjust to the specific requirements of each student, providing a personalized learning journey. By using data on a student's performance, learning style, and preferences, AI algorithms can create customized lesson plans and educational materials that are tailored to their specific needs. One example of how AI can be used in Indian governance for personalized learning is through the use of AI-powered learning management systems. These systems can analyze student data and provide teachers with insights into which students are struggling with certain concepts and which students are excelling. This information can then be used to create customized lesson plans and educational materials that are tailored to the specific needs of each student.

Another way AI can be used in Indian governance for personalized learning is through virtual tutors and AI-powered chatbots. These tools can provide students with instant feedback and assistance on their homework and assignments, allowing them to get the help they need when they need it. Additionally, virtual tutors can be used to provide students with extra practice and support in areas where they are struggling. AI can also be used in Indian governance for personalized learning using adaptive learning software. These programs use data on a student's performance and learning style to adjust the difficulty level and pacing of the material, ensuring that each student is challenged at the appropriate level.

The use of AI in education can also help increase access to education in India, particularly in rural and remote areas. By using AI-powered learning management systems and virtual tutors, students in these areas can receive the same quality of education as their peers in urban areas, regardless of their location. Moreover, AI can also be used to help identify students who may be at risk of falling behind or dropping out of school. By analyzing data on a student's attendance, performance, and behavior, AI algorithms can identify students who may be at risk and provide them with the support they need to stay on track. In conclusion, the utilization of AI technology holds tremendous promise for transforming the way education is imparted in India by enabling the provision of customized learning journeys for students. By using data on a student's performance, learning style, and preferences, AI algorithms can create customized lesson plans and educational materials that are tailored to their specific needs. Additionally, AI can also be used to increase access to education in remote and rural areas and help identify students who may be at risk of falling behind or dropping out of school. However, it should be noted that AI is a tool, and its effectiveness depends on how it is implemented and used. Therefore, it is necessary to make sure that the deployment of AI in education is aligned with the overall goals of education and guided by the principles of equity and accessibility.

34.4.2.3   Student Services

Artificial Intelligence (AI) can be used in Indian governance for student services in education in several ways. One of the key advantages of incorporating AI in educational support systems is its capability to streamline repetitive tasks through automation, allowing educators and administrators to focus on more important tasks such as providing personalized support and guidance to students.

One way AI can be used in Indian governance for student services is through AI-powered chatbots. Chatbots can be used to provide students with instant assistance and support on a wide range of topics, such as course registration, financial aid, and academic advising. Another benefit is that chatbots can be designed to comprehend student questions in several languages, facilitating access to information and assistance for students who may not have English as their primary language.

Another way AI can be used in Indian governance for student services is by using AI-powered student tracking systems. These systems can collect and analyze data on a student's performance, attendance, and behavior, providing educators and administrators with valuable insights into a student's progress and potential areas of concern. This information can then be used to provide targeted support and interventions to help students succeed.

In the Indian governmental context, AI can also be leveraged in student services through the implementation of virtual and augmented reality technologies. VR and AR can provide students with immersive and interactive educational experiences, promoting deeper comprehension and engagement with course content. Additionally, VR and AR can also be used to provide students with virtual field trips, simulations, and other hands-on learning experiences that can enhance their education.

Moreover, AI can be used to help identify students who may be at risk of falling behind or dropping out of school. By analyzing data on a student's attendance, performance, and behavior, AI algorithms can identify students who may be at risk and provide them with the support they need to stay on track. This can include early warning systems that alert educators and administrators to potential issues, as well as targeted interventions such as tutoring and mentoring programs. In conclusion, AI has the potential to revolutionize student services in Indian education by automating routine tasks, providing students with instant assistance and support, and providing educators and administrators with valuable insights into student progress. By using AI-powered chatbots, student tracking systems, VR and AR technologies, and early warning systems, it is possible to provide students with the support they need to succeed and improve their overall educational experience. However, as with any new technology, it is necessary to ensure that the use of Artificial Intelligence in student services aligns with the overall goals of education and is guided by the principles of equity and accessibility.

34.4.2.4   Student Progress Monitoring

Artificial Intelligence (AI) can be used in Indian governance for student progress monitoring in education in several ways. One significant advantage of incorporating AI in student performance tracking is its ability to process vast amounts of data quickly and accurately, thus providing educational leaders and administrators with valuable perspectives on student advancement and potential issues of concern. One way AI can be used in Indian governance for student progress monitoring is through the use of AI-powered student tracking systems. These systems can collect and analyze data on a student's performance, attendance, and behavior, providing educators and administrators with valuable insights into a student's progress and potential areas of concern. This information can then be used to provide targeted support and interventions to help students succeed. Another way AI can be used in Indian governance for student progress monitoring is through the use of AI-powered learning analytics. These analytics can be used to track student progress in real-time, providing educators and administrators with immediate feedback on student performance. Additionally, these analytics can be used to identify patterns in student performance that may indicate potential areas of concern, such as a lack of engagement or difficulty with certain concepts.

In the Indian government sector, AI can also be employed for student performance monitoring through the utilization of natural language processing and machine learning algorithms. NLP algorithms can be used to analyze student written work, providing teachers with insights into students' understanding and comprehension of course material. ML algorithms can be used to analyze student data, providing educators with insights into student performance and helping them identify areas of concern.

Moreover, AI can be used to help identify students who may be at risk of falling behind or dropping out of school. By analyzing data on a student's attendance, performance, and behavior, AI algorithms can identify students who may be at risk and provide them with the support they need to stay on track. This can include early warning systems that alert educators and administrators to potential issues, as well as targeted interventions such as tutoring and mentoring programs. In conclusion, AI can be used in Indian governance for student progress monitoring in education by analyzing large amounts of data quickly and accurately, providing educators and administrators with valuable insights into student progress and potential areas of concern. By using AI-powered student tracking systems, learning analytics, NLP and ML algorithms, and early warning systems, it is possible to provide students with the support they need to succeed and improve their overall educational experience. However, it is necessary to note that AI is a tool, and its effectiveness depends on how it is implemented and used. Therefore, it is significant to ensure that the use of Artificial Intelligence in student progress monitoring is aligned with the overall goals of education and guided by the principles of equity and accessibility. Additionally, it is crucial to consider the ethical and privacy concerns that come with collecting and using student data and to ensure that such data is handled responsibly and in compliance with regulations and laws.

Different uses of AI in the field of education

34.4.3   Defense

In the realm of defense, artificial intelligence is widely utilized for purposes such as surveillance and reconnaissance, risk assessment, cyber security, and the development of intelligent weapons and robotic soldiers.

34.4.3.1   Intelligence, Surveillance, and Reconnaissance

Artificial Intelligence (AI) can be used in Indian governance for Intelligence, Surveillance, and Reconnaissance (ISR) in defense in several ways. One of the significant advantages of implementing AI in Intelligence, Surveillance, and Reconnaissance (ISR) is its capability of processing vast amounts of information efficiently and with precision, thereby furnishing defense authorities with crucial intelligence and insights. One way AI can be used in Indian governance for ISR in defense is through the use of AI-powered image and video analysis. These systems can be used to automatically analyze video and images from cameras, drones, and other sources, providing defense officials with valuable intelligence on potential threats. Moreover, AI-powered systems can be leveraged to automatically detect and distinguish targets of significance, such as vehicles and individuals. Another way AI can be used in Indian governance for ISR in defense is through the use of AI-powered signal processing and analysis. These systems can be used to automatically analyze signals from radar, electronic warfare systems, and other sources, providing defense officials with valuable intelligence on potential threats. Additionally, these systems can be used to automatically detect and track potential targets, such as aircraft or missiles.

In Indian governance, AI can also play a role in Intelligence, Surveillance, and Reconnaissance (ISR) within the defense sector by incorporating techniques such as Natural Language Processing (NLP) and Machine Learning (ML). NLP algorithms enable automatic analysis of text-based information, including social media posts and news articles, to provide defense authorities with significant intelligence related to potential threats. ML algorithms can be utilized to process substantial amounts of data, such as satellite imagery, thereby supplying defense officials with valuable insights and intelligence. Additionally, AI can assist in detecting patterns and variations in data that may signify potential hazards. By analyzing data from multiple sources, such as satellite imagery, social media posts, and news articles, AI algorithms can identify patterns and anomalies that may indicate potential threats, such as the buildup of military equipment or signs of unrest. In conclusion, AI can be used in Indian governance for ISR in defense by analyzing large amounts of data quickly and accurately, providing defense officials with valuable insights and intelligence. The enhancement of Intelligence, Surveillance, and Reconnaissance (ISR) operations can be achieved by incorporating AI-based techniques, such as image and video analysis, signal processing and analysis, Natural Language Processing (NLP), Machine Learning (ML) algorithms, and anomaly detection. Nevertheless, it is essential to recognize that AI is a mere tool, and its performance is contingent upon its implementation and utilization. As a result, it is critical to ensure that AI's application in ISR aligns with broader defense and security objectives and adheres to ethical and privacy principles. Additionally, it is crucial to have a robust governance structure and to ensure that the data is handled responsibly and in compliance with regulations and laws.

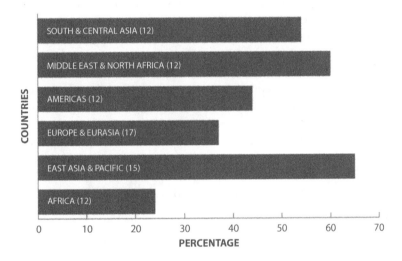

Percentage of countries by region adopting AI Surveillance

34.4.3.2   Robot Soldiers

Artificial Intelligence (AI) can be used in Indian governance for robot soldiers in defense in several ways. One of the key advantages of AI in robotic soldiers is its capability to act independently and execute tasks autonomously, thereby mitigating the requirement for human soldiers in hazardous circumstances. One way AI can be used in Indian governance for robot soldiers in defense is through the use of AI-powered navigation and mobility systems. These systems can be used to guide robot soldiers through difficult terrain and obstacle-filled environments, allowing them to navigate and move more efficiently and effectively than human soldiers. Additionally, these systems can also be used to avoid hazards and obstacles, such as mines or booby traps. Another way AI can be used in Indian governance for robot soldiers in defense is through the use of AI-powered target acquisition and tracking systems. These systems can be used to automatically detect and track potential targets, such as enemy vehicles or individuals, providing robot soldiers with the information they need to engage and eliminate threats. Additionally, these systems can also be used to auto-matically engage targets, reducing the need for human soldiers to make quick decisions in high-stress situations.

In Indian governance, AI can also play a role in the development of robotic soldiers for defense purposes, utilizing techniques such as Natural Language Processing (NLP) and Machine Learning (ML). NLP algorithms can be used to enable robot soldiers to under-stand and respond to natural language commands, making it easier for human soldiers to control and direct the robots. ML algorithms can be used to enable robot soldiers to learn and adapt to new situations, improving their overall performance and effectiveness. Moreover, AI can be used to help identify patterns and anomalies in data that may indicate potential threats. By analyzing data from multiple sources, such as sensor data, surveillance footage, and other intelligence, AI algorithms can identify patterns and anomalies that may indicate potential threats. This can help improve the situational awareness of robot soldiers and allow them to react more quickly and effectively to potential threats.

In conclusion, AI can be used in Indian governance for robot soldiers in defense by making decisions and performing tasks autonomously, reducing the need for human sol-diers in dangerous situations. By using AI-powered navigation and mobility systems, target acquisition and tracking systems, NLP and ML algorithms, and anomaly detection, it is possible to improve the efficiency and effectiveness of robot soldiers. However, it is import-ant to note that AI is a tool, and its effectiveness depends on how it is implemented and used. Hence, it is crucial to ensure that the implementation of AI in robotic soldiers aligns with the broader objectives of defense and security and adheres to ethical and privacy stan-dards. Additionally, it is crucial to have a robust governance structure and to ensure that the data is handled responsibly and in compliance with regulations and laws. Furthermore, it is important to consider the legal, moral, and ethical implications of using autonomous weapons in warfare.

34.4.3.3   Cyber Defense

Artificial Intelligence (AI) can be used in Indian governance for cyber defense in several ways. One of the key advantages of AI in the domain of cyber defense is its capability to ana-lyze vast amounts of data rapidly and accurately, furnishing defense officials with valuable intelligence regarding potential cyber threats and weaknesses. One way AI can be used in Indian governance for cyber defense is through the use of AI-powered intrusion detection systems. These systems can be used to automatically detect and identify potential cyber-attacks, such as malware or phishing attempts, providing defense officials with valuable information on potential threats. Additionally, these systems can also be used to automat-ically respond to cyber-attacks, reducing the need for human intervention in high-stress situations. Another way AI can be used in Indian governance for cyber defense is by using AI-powered vulnerability management systems. These systems can be used to automati-cally identify and prioritize vulnerabilities in computer networks and systems, providing defense officials with the information they need to take action to address potential threats. Additionally, these systems can also be used to automatically apply security updates and patches, reducing the risk of successful cyber-attacks.

In Indian governance, AI can also be employed in the field of cyber defense through the utilization of Natural Language Processing (NLP) and Machine Learning (ML) algorithms.

NLP algorithms can be used to automatically analyze text-based data, such as social media posts or news articles, providing defense officials with valuable intelligence on potential cyber threats. ML algorithms can be used to analyze large amounts of data, such as network traffic or system logs, providing defense officials with valuable insights into potential cyber-attacks and vulnerabilities. Additionally, AI can be utilized to detect patterns and unusual behavior in data, which could signify potential cyber threats. By analyzing data from multiple sources, such as network traffic, system logs, and social media posts, AI algorithms can identify patterns and anomalies that may indicate potential cyber-attacks, such as a sudden increase in network traffic from a particular IP address or an unusual number of login attempts.

In conclusion, AI can be used in Indian governance for cyber defense by analyzing large amounts of data quickly and accurately, providing defense officials with valuable insights into potential cyber threats and vulnerabilities. The deployment of AI-powered intrusion detection systems, vulnerability management systems, NLP, ML algorithms, and anomaly detection offers the possibility of enhancing the efficiency and effectiveness of cyber defense operations. However, it must be acknowledged that AI operates as a tool, and its success is contingent upon its implementation and usage. Thus, it is vital to guarantee that the implementation of AI in cyber defense is aligned with the overall goals of defense and security and adheres to ethical and privacy standards. Additionally, it is crucial to have a robust governance structure and to ensure that the data is handled responsibly and in compliance with regulations and laws. Furthermore, it is important to keep in mind that AI can be used by cyber attackers as well; therefore, it is essential to stay aware of the potential for AI-based cyber threats and to develop countermeasures accordingly.

34.4.3.4 *Intelligent Weapon Systems*

The integration of AI has the capability to have a transformative impact on government operations, including in the realm of defense. In India, AI holds the possibility of elevating the country's armaments and strengthening its overall defense capacities through its utilization in various forms. One of the primary applications of AI in the defense sector involves the advancement of smart weapon systems. These systems can be designed to be highly autonomous, able to make decisions and take actions without human intervention. This can include things like target identification, tracking, and engagement. AI-powered systems can also be used to improve the accuracy and effectiveness of weapons as well as reduce the risk of collateral damage. Another potential application of AI in defense is in the area of surveillance and reconnaissance. AI-powered systems can be used to process and analyze vast amounts of data from sensors and cameras, making it possible to detect and track potential threats more quickly and accurately. This can include things like identifying suspicious activity, tracking the movement of enemy forces, and monitoring the battlefield in real-time.

AI can also be used in defense logistics and supply chain management. AI-powered systems can be used to optimize the logistics of military operations, including the movement of troops and equipment. This can include things like predicting the need for supplies and equipment, scheduling the movement of troops and equipment, and identifying the best routes for transport. In addition, AI can also be leveraged to enhance the planning and decision-making processes in defense operations. By utilizing AI technology, an increased amount of data, such as weather patterns, terrain, and adversary force movements, can be analyzed and processed efficiently. This can help military commanders make more informed decisions about the deployment of troops and the use of weapons. Overall, AI has the potential to greatly enhance India's defense capabilities by improving the intelligence, efficiency and effectiveness of weapon systems, logistics, and operations planning. However, there are also potential dangers associated with AI-based technology. These dangers include the possibility of system malfunction, or cyber-attacks, which may result in unintended outcomes. Additionally, the use of AI in defense raises ethical and legal issues, such as the potential for AI to make decisions that violate international laws or human rights.

In conclusion, the use of AI has the possibility of transforming the functioning of India's defense system, including in the fields of intelligent weapons systems, surveillance and reconnaissance, decision-making, logistics, and supply chain management. Nevertheless, it is crucial for the Indian government to consider the potential drawbacks and difficulties linked with AI utilization in defense and to establish specific rules and regulations to oversee its use.

34.5 Discharge of Government Functions

The Government of India is making efforts to incorporate AI into the delivery of public services to citizens.

34.5.1 Citizen/Government Interface/E-Governance

AI has the potential to transform the way governmental functions are performed, particularly in the realm of citizen-government interaction and electronic governance. In India, AI can be used in several ways to improve the country's e-governance and overall government functioning. The implementation of AI-powered chatbots and virtual assistants can play a significant role in enhancing the efficiency of e-governance. These systems can be designed to interact with citizens in natural language, providing them with information and assistance on a wide range of government services. This can include things like passport application status, tax filing, and other services. AI-powered chatbots can also be used to answer frequently asked questions and provide guidance on government policies and procedures. AI can also play a crucial role in the analysis of government data and decision-making by utilizing its algorithms to process large amounts of information from various departments and identify patterns and trends that can inform decision-making. This can include things like identifying areas with high levels of poverty, tracking the effectiveness of government programs and policies, and identifying potential fraud and corruption.

AI can also enhance the efficiency of government service delivery by automating application and request processing using AI-powered systems. This helps reduce the amount of time and effort required by citizens to access government services. This can include things like automating the approval of permits and licenses and the processing of benefit claims. In addition, AI can also be used in e-governance for citizen engagement and participation. AI-powered systems can be used to identify and analyze citizen feedback, providing government officials with insights into citizens' needs and preferences. This can help government officials make more informed decisions about policies and programs. In conclusion, the application of AI in Indian governance has the potential to transform its processes, particularly in the domains of citizen-government communication, the provision of services, and decision-making. Nevertheless, it is imperative for the Indian government to meticulously evaluate the risks and obstacles associated with using AI in e-governance and establish concise regulations and guidelines for its utilization. Additionally, the government should focus on building trust among citizens in the use of AI in governance by providing transparency, explainability, and accountability for AI systems.

34.5.1.1 Agriculture

The integration of Artificial Intelligence (AI) has the potential to transform the way government tasks in the agricultural sector of India are carried out. By leveraging AI technologies, the government can improve the efficiency, effectiveness, and transparency of its agricultural policies and programs. One potential application of AI in Indian governance for agriculture is precision farming. Precision farming systems powered by AI have the capability to process significant amounts of data related to weather, soil status, and crop development, thereby providing farmers with up-to-date advice on how to improve their crop output. For example, precision farming systems can use satellite imagery to identify areas of a field that are suffering from drought or disease and then provide farmers with specific recommendations on how to address these issues. Another application of AI in Indian governance for agriculture is crop monitoring and disease detection. AI-powered systems can use image recognition and machine learning algorithms to identify and track the growth of different crops. Additionally, these systems can be trained to detect signs of disease or pest infestation in crops, which can help farmers take prompt action to prevent crop loss.

AI can also be used to improve the efficiency and transparency of government programs and policies related to agriculture. For example, the utilization of AI can analyze data related to crop yields and prices to recognize trends and patterns, thus serving as a basis for government policies concerning subsidies and price support. Additionally, AI can be used to automate the process of distributing subsidies and benefits to farmers, which can reduce the chances of fraud and corruption. Furthermore, AI can also be used to enhance the decision-making capabilities of government officials responsible for agricultural policy. AI-powered systems can analyze large amounts of data on weather patterns, crop yields, and market prices to provide officials with real-time insights on the state of the agricultural sector. These insights can help officials make more informed decisions on policies related to agriculture. In conclusion, the integration of Artificial Intelligence (AI) has the capability to transform the execution of government operations in the agricultural sector of India. By leveraging AI technologies, the government can improve the efficiency, effectiveness, and transparency of its agricultural policies and programs. AI applications such as precision farming, crop monitoring, disease detection, and decision-making capabilities can provide significant benefits to farmers, government officials, and the agricultural sector.

34.5.1.2 Categorization and Arrangement of Documents

The implementation of Artificial Intelligence (AI) has the potential to alter the way government tasks are performed in the realm of document management. By leveraging AI technologies, the government can improve the efficiency, accuracy, and security of its document management processes. An example of AI implementation in Indian governance for document management is document categorization. Utilizing natural language processing (NLP) and machine learning algorithms, AI-based systems can categorize and classify documents automatically based on their content, enhancing the efficiency of document management procedures by eliminating manual categorization and sorting of documents. Additionally, AI-powered document categorization systems can be trained to recognize specific keywords and phrases, which can help ensure that sensitive and confidential documents are properly classified and protected. Another application of AI in Indian governance for document management is document arrangement. AI-powered systems can use NLP and machine learning algorithms to automatically arrange documents in a logical and coherent manner. This can greatly improve the efficiency of document management processes, as it eliminates the need for manual sorting and arrangement of documents. Additionally, AI-powered document arrangement systems can be trained to recognize specific keywords and phrases, which can help ensure that related documents are grouped together. AI can also be used to improve the security of government documents. AI-powered systems can use image recognition and machine learning algorithms to detect and prevent unauthorized access to sensitive and confidential documents. Additionally, AI-powered document security systems can be trained to detect and prevent attempts to alter or forge documents.

Furthermore, AI can also be used to improve the accessibility of government documents. AI-powered systems can use NLP and machine learning algorithms to automatically generate summaries of documents, which can make it easier for government officials and citizens to access and understand important information. Additionally, AI-powered document accessibility systems can be trained to recognize specific keywords and phrases, which can help ensure that relevant documents are easily found.

In conclusion, Artificial Intelligence (AI) has the potential to transform the approach to document management in government operations. Through the integration of AI technologies, the government can enhance the efficiency, precision, and security of its document management processes. AI applications such as document categorization, document arrangement, document security, and document accessibility can provide significant benefits to government officials, citizens, and the government.

34.6 Challenges

Although AI has immense potential for development within governance, there are specific socio-economic, technological, and regulatory realities in India that present unique challenges that must be acknowledged and resolved while shaping policy and implementing the technology.

34.6.1 Improved Capacity And Enhanced Understanding of Emerging Technologies

Artificial intelligence (AI) holds significant potential for improving the capacity and understanding of emerging technologies for use in public administration. However, there are several challenges that need to be addressed for AI to be effectively implemented in public administration. One major challenge is the lack of data and information infrastructure to support AI applications. For AI systems to function effectively, they require large amounts of data to be trained and to improve their decision-making capabilities. However, many government organizations do not have the necessary data infrastructure in place to support AI applications. Another challenge is the lack of technical expertise in government organizations. The deployment and maintenance of AI necessitate a high degree of technical proficiency, yet numerous government organizations lack the necessary personnel with the appropriate skills and experience. The third challenge is the risk of bias in AI systems, which poses a significant challenge in their deployment. The quality of AI systems is dependent on the data they are trained on, and any biases present in this data will be reflected in the AI system's outputs. This can result in unjust and discriminatory decisions, particularly in crucial areas such as recruitment, financing, and the administration of criminal justice. The fourth hindrance to the proliferation of AI is the absence of proper administration and regulations. Given the growing utilization of AI in government operations, it is imperative to establish governance and regulations to guarantee the ethical usage of AI systems in compliance with legal and regulatory requirements. The fifth obstacle in the development of AI is the scarcity of transparency and comprehensibility in AI systems. The difficulty in comprehending the decision-making processes of AI systems hampers trust in their decisions, and this can hinder the implementation of AI in public administration.

In conclusion, while AI has the power to improve the capacity and understanding of emerging technologies for use in public administration, there are several challenges that need to be addressed to ensure that AI is effectively implemented in public administration. These include a lack of data and information infrastructure, a lack of technical expertise, a risk of bias, a lack of governance and regulation, and a lack of transparency and explainability.

34.6.2 Infrastructure

Infrastructure is a critical challenge for the effective use of artificial intelligence (AI) in public administration. Without proper infrastructure, the implementation and maintenance of AI systems can be difficult and costly. A significant challenge in the field of AI is the absence of adequate data infrastructure. To enhance the decision-making ability of AI systems, significant amounts of data are necessary for training purposes. However, many government organizations do not have the necessary data infrastructure in place to support AI applications. This includes the lack of data standardization, data quality control, and data accessibility. Another challenge is the lack of computing infrastructure. AI systems require significant computational power to function effectively. This encompasses the requirement for robust computing systems, such as GPUs, and the utilization of cloud computing services. A third obstacle is the lack of communication infrastructure. AI systems often require real-time communication between different components, such as sensors, cameras, and other devices. This can be challenging in government organizations, where communication infrastructure is often outdated or inadequate. The fourth hindrance is the lack of security infrastructure. AI systems are vulnerable to cyber-attacks and data breaches, which can compromise sensitive information. This necessitates the deployment of strong security measures, such as encryption, firewalls, and intrusion detection systems.

In conclusion, the absence of infrastructure, including data, computing, communication, and security, presents a crucial challenge for the efficient application of AI in public administration. To harness the full potential of AI in government operations, organizations must make investments in the necessary infrastructure to support AI system deployment and upkeep.

34.6.3   Trust

Trust is a crucial hindrance to the efficient utilization of AI in public administration. Without trust in AI systems, it can be difficult to gain acceptance and adoption of these systems within government organizations and among citizens. A major challenge in the use of AI in public administration is the lack of transparency and interpretability in AI systems. This makes it challenging for humans to comprehend the decision-making processes of AI systems, leading to mistrust in their decisions. The lack of understanding can hinder the acceptance of AI in government operations, with government officials and the public being wary of relying on decisions made by systems that are not transparent.

Another hindrance to the implementation of AI in public administration is the threat of bias in AI systems. The quality of AI systems is dependent on the data used for training, and if the data holds biases, the AI systems will exhibit the same biases. This can result in discriminatory and unjust decisions, especially in fields such as hiring, lending, and criminal justice, eroding the trust of citizens in AI systems and obstructing government organizations from achieving acceptance and implementation of these systems. A third challenge in the adoption of AI systems is the shortage of accountability and governance. The absence of proper administration and regulation makes it challenging to hold AI systems responsible for their decisions, which can lead to mistrust among citizens who are uncertain of the entity responsible for these decisions. A fourth challenge is the lack of trust in the organizations responsible for the AI systems. If citizens do not trust the government organizations responsible for the development and deployment of AI systems, they may be very less likely to trust the systems themselves.

In conclusion, trust constitutes a crucial hindrance to the efficient implementation of AI in public administration. The lack of transparency and explainability of AI systems, the risk of bias, the lack of accountability and governance, and the lack of trust in the organizations responsible for the AI systems can greatly impede the acceptance and adoption of these systems within government organizations and among citizens. Addressing these challenges and building trust in AI systems will be essential for the successful application of AI in public-based services.

34.6.4   Funding

Funding is a critical challenge for the effective implementation of AI in public administration. Without adequate funding, government organizations may struggle to implement and maintain AI systems, which can impede the realization of the possible benefits of Artificial Intelligence in public administration. One major challenge is the lack of funding for the development and research of AI systems. Developing and deploying new AI systems can be a costly and time-consuming process, and government organizations may struggle to secure adequate funding for these efforts. This can impede the development of new AI systems as well as the implementation of existing ones.

Another challenge is the lack of funding for data infrastructure. AI systems require large amounts of data to function effectively, and government organizations may struggle to secure adequate funding for the necessary data infrastructure. This includes the lack of funding for data standardization, data quality control, and data accessibility.

A third challenge is the lack of funding for computing infrastructure. AI systems require significant computational power to function effectively, and government organizations may struggle to secure adequate funding for the necessary computing infrastructure. "The requirement for advanced computing systems like GPUs and cloud computing services has become increasingly crucial." A fourth challenge is the lack of funding for security infrastructure. AI systems are vulnerable to cyber-attacks and data breaches, which can compromise sensitive information. "Securing these systems necessitates the application of sturdy security protocols like encryption, firewalls, and intrusion detection systems. However, government organizations may encounter difficulties in procuring sufficient funding for these measures."

In conclusion, funding is a critical challenge for the effective implementation of AI in public-based services. The lack of funding for research and development, data infrastructure, computing infrastructure, and security infrastructure can greatly impede the implementation and maintenance of AI systems. Securing sufficient financing is crucial for government entities to attain the advantages of AI implementation in public sector administration. This requirement must be met to ensure the successful implementation of AI in public administration.

34.6.5 Privacy and Security

Privacy and security are critical challenges for the effective use of artificial intelligence (AI) in public administration. Without proper privacy and security measures in place, the deployment of AI technology can pose substantial threats to the confidentiality of citizens' personal data and the stability of government procedures. One major challenge is the risk of data breaches and cyber-attacks. AI systems handle large amounts of sensitive personal information, and if this information is not properly protected, it can be vulnerable to data breaches and cyber-attacks. This can compromise citizens' personal information and lead to a loss of trust in government organizations and AI systems. Another challenge is the risk of bias in AI systems. The efficacy of AI systems is contingent upon the quality of the data they are trained on. If the training data encompasses biases, the AI system will perpetuate these biases and result in unfair and discriminatory decisions in areas such as employment, lending, and criminal justice. This can undermine public trust in AI systems, hindering their widespread adoption and implementation by government organizations. Another challenge faced by AI is the lack of transparency and interpretability in decision-making processes. The difficulty for humans to comprehend the mechanisms by which AI systems arrive at decisions creates a barrier to trust and undermines confidence in these systems. This presents a hindrance to the incorporation of AI in government operations, as both public officials and citizens may be reticent to depend on decisions made by opaque and unexplainable AI systems. And the fourth challenge facing the adoption and deployment of AI systems is the absence of effective governance and regulation. This presents a formidable obstacle to ensuring that these systems operate in an ethical manner and align with prevailing laws and regulations. The absence of clear governance and regulation can also erode public trust in AI systems, as the responsibility for their actions remains unclear.

In conclusion, it is crucial to address the privacy and security challenges for AI to be utilized effectively in the realm of public administration. The risk of data breaches and cyber-attacks, the risk of bias, the lack of transparency and explainability, and the lack of governance and regulation can greatly impede the acceptance and adoption of these systems within government organizations and among citizens. It is imperative to tackle these challenges and guarantee the protection of citizens' personal information for AI to successfully be integrated into public administration.

34.6.6 Transparency

Transparency presents a significant challenge in the effective deployment of artificial intelligence (AI) within the realm of public administration. Without transparency in AI systems, it can be difficult to gain acceptance and adoption of these systems within government organizations and among citizens.

One major challenge is the lack of explainability of AI systems. It is difficult for humans to understand how AI systems make decisions, which makes it difficult to trust their decisions. This lack of transparency can impede the acceptance of AI in public administration, as both government officials and citizens may hesitate to rely on decisions made by AI systems whose workings remain opaque to them. Another hindrance to the effective deployment of AI in public administration is the transparency of the data used to train AI systems. The absence of transparency in this regard makes it challenging to detect and correct biases in the data, thereby compromising the reliability of AI systems. This can lead to unfair and discriminatory decisions, particularly in areas such as hiring, lending, and criminal justice. This can erode trust in AI systems among citizens, making it difficult for government organizations to gain acceptance and adoption of these systems.

A third challenge is the lack of transparency in the algorithms used by AI systems. If the algorithms used by AI systems are not transparent, it can be difficult to detect and address biases in the algorithms. This can lead to unfair and discriminatory decisions, particularly in areas such as hiring, lending, and criminal justice. This can erode trust in AI systems among citizens, making it difficult for government organizations to gain acceptance and adoption of these systems. A fourth challenge faced in the use of AI in public administration is the transparency of the decision-making process of AI systems. The lack of visibility into how and why decisions are made can make it challenging for both government officials and citizens to comprehend the functioning of AI systems. This, in turn, can erode public trust in these systems, as the responsibility for their decisions remains unclear. In conclusion, transparency plays a crucial role in the successful deployment of AI in public administration. The absence of transparency in the AI's algorithms, the data used for training, and the decision-making process can significantly hinder the widespread adoption and usage of AI by both government organizations and citizens. Addressing these challenges and ensuring transparency in AI systems will be essential for the successful implementation of AI in public administration.

By utilising data-based inspection [1], combating [2] disinformation and cyberattacks [3, 4], and ensuring access to quality information, democracy might be strengthened. AI might also promote openness and diversity, for instance, by reducing the likelihood of bias in hiring choices by substituting analytical data. As enormous data [5, 6] sets could be processed more quickly, prisoner flight risks could be assessed more precisely, and crime or even terrorist [7–9] attacks might be foreseen and averted, AI is expected to be employed more in crime prevention and the criminal justice system. Online platforms currently employ it to identify and respond to undesirable and illegal [10, 11] online activity. When it comes to the military [12], AI might be employed for critical system targeting in cyberwarfare [13–15] as well as defensive and attack techniques in hacking and phishing. Conversational AI may benefit individuals through better health care, safer vehicles and other forms of transportation, and individualised, less expensive, and more durable goods and services. Additionally, it may make information, education, and training more accessible. The COVID-19 [16] outbreak made the necessity for distant learning even more crucial. Additionally, AI may increase workplace safety by using robots to do hazardous tasks and by creating new employment opportunities as AI-driven sectors develop and adapt. AI can help businesses create a new generation of goods and services, even in industries like green and circular economies, equipment, farming, healthcare [17], fashion, and tourism [18], where European firms already have dominant positions. Sales [19] may increase, equipment maintenance may improve, manufacturing productivity and quality may increase, customer service may be enhanced, and energy may be saved.

34.7 Conclusion

In conclusion, the integration of Artificial Intelligence (AI) in public administration holds the promise of transforming government operations and services, making them more efficient, effective, and transparent. However, there are several challenges that need to be addressed for AI to be effectively implemented in public administration. These include a lack of data and information infrastructure, a lack of technical expertise, a risk of bias, a lack of governance and regulation, a lack of transparency and explainability, privacy and security, and funding. To effectively use AI in public administration, it is important to invest in data infrastructure and build technical expertise in government organizations. This includes investing in data standardization, data quality control, and data accessibility, as well as providing training and development opportunities for government employees and hiring employees with the necessary technical skills and experience.

Addressing the risk of bias in AI systems is also crucial for ensuring that the decisions made by these systems are fair and unbiased. This can be done by carefully selecting and preprocessing data to minimize bias, as well as regularly monitoring and testing AI systems to detect and address bias. Additionally, interpretable models can be used to ensure transparency and explainability of the decision-making process.

Implementing governance and regulation for AI systems is crucial to ensuring their ethical usage and compliance with laws and regulations. This can be achieved by formulating policies and ethical guidelines for AI in public administration and maintaining adherence to relevant laws and regulations. Note that ensuring the transparency and explainability of AI systems and ensuring the privacy and security of citizens' personal information are also crucial steps for gaining the trust and acceptance of citizens and government officials. This can be achieved by providing clear explanations of how AI systems make decisions and what data they use, as well as by implementing robust security measures to protect sensitive information. Finally, funding is a critical challenge that needs to be addressed in order for government organizations to effectively implement and maintain AI systems. Government organizations need to secure adequate funding for research and development, data infrastructure, computing infrastructure, security infrastructure, and other necessary resources.

Overall, addressing these challenges and investing in the necessary infrastructure and expertise will be essential for the successful implementation of AI in public administration. By effectively using AI, government organizations can improve the efficiency, effectiveness, and transparency of their operations, leading to better outcomes for citizens and society.

References

1. Mahor, V., Bijrothiya, S., Rawat, R., Kumar, A., Garg, B., Pachlasiya, K., IoT and artificial intelligence techniques for public safety and security, in: *Smart Urban Computing Applications*, p. 111, 2023.
2. Mahor, V., Pachlasiya, K., Garg, B., Chouhan, M., Telang, S., Rawat, R., Mobile operating system (Android) vulnerability analysis using machine learning, in: *Proceedings of International Conference on Network Security and Blockchain Technology: ICNSBT 2021*, pp. 159–169, Springer Nature Singapore, Singapore, 2022, June.
3. Rawat, R., Garg, B., Pachlasiya, K., Mahor, V., Telang, S., Chouhan, M., Mishra, R., SCNTA: Monitoring of network availability and activity for identification of anomalies using machine learning approaches. *Int. J. Inf. Technol. Web Eng. (IJITWE)*, 17, 1, 1–19, 2022.
4. Rawat, R., Rimal, Y.N., William, P., Dahima, S., Gupta, S., Sankaran, K.S., Malware threat affecting financial organization analysis using machine learning approach. *Int. J. Inf. Technol. Web Eng. (IJITWE)*, 17, 1, 1–20, 2022.
5. Rawat, R., Mahor, V., Chouhan, M., Pachlasiya, K., Telang, S., Garg, B., Systematic literature review (SLR) on social media and the digital transformation of drug trafficking on darkweb, in: *International Conference on Network Security and Blockchain Technology*, pp. 181–205, Springer, Singapore, 2022.
6. Rawat, R., Ayodele Oki, O., Sankaran, S., Florez, H., Ajagbe, S.A., Techniques for predicting dark web events focused on the delivery of illicit products and ordered crime. *Int. J. Electr. Comput. Eng. (IJECE)*, 13, 5, 5354–5365, Oct. 2023, doi: 10.11591/ijece.v13i5.pp5354-5365.
7. Rawat, R., Garg, B., Mahor, V., Telang, S., Pachlasiya, K., Chouhan, M., Organ trafficking on the dark web—The data security and privacy concern in healthcare systems, in: *Internet of Healthcare Things: Machine Learning for Security and Privacy*, pp. 189–216, 2022.
8. Vyas P., Vyas, G., Chauhan, A., Rawat, R., Telang, S., Gottumukkala, M., Anonymous trading on the dark online marketplace: An exploratory study, in: *Using Computational Intelligence for the Dark Web and Illicit Behavior Detection*, pp. 272–289, IGI Global, 2022.
9. Rawat, R., Oki, O.A., Sankaran, K.S., Olasupo, O., Ebong, G.N., Ajagbe, S.A., A new solution for cyber security in big data using machine learning approach, in: *Mobile Computing and Sustainable Informatics: Proceedings of ICMCSI 2023*, pp. 495–505, Springer Nature Singapore, Singapore, 2023.
10. Rawat, R., Chakrawarti, R.K., Raj, A., Mani, G., Chidambarathanu, K., Bhardwaj, R., Association rule learning for threat analysis using traffic analysis and packet filtering approach. *Int. J. Inf. Technol.*, 1–11, 2023.
11. Rawat, R., Logical concept mapping and social media analytics relating to cyber criminal activities for ontology creation. *Int. J. Inf. Technol.*, 15, 2, 893–903, 2023.
12. Rawat, R., Mahor, V., Álvarez, J.D., Ch, F., Cognitive systems for dark web cyber delinquent association malignant data crawling: A review, in: *Handbook of Research on War Policies, Strategies, and Cyber Wars*, pp. 45–63, 2023.
13. Rawat, R., Chakrawarti, R.K., Vyas, P., Gonzáles, J.L.A., Sikarwar, R., Bhardwaj, R., Intelligent fog computing surveillance system for crime and vulnerability identification and tracing. *Int. J. Inf. Secur. Priv. (IJISP)*, 17, 1, 1–25, 2023.

14. Rawat, R., Sowjanya, A.M., Patel, S.I., Jaiswal, V., Khan, I., Balaram, A. (Eds.), *Using Machine Intelligence: Autonomous Vehicles Volume 1*, John Wiley & Sons, 2022.
15. Rawat, R., Mahor, V., Díaz-Álvarez, J., Chávez, F., Rooted learning model at fog computing analysis for crime incident surveillance, in: *2022 International Conference on Smart Generation Computing, Communication and Networking (SMART GENCON)*, pp. 1–9, IEEE, 2022, December.
16. Rawat, R. and Shrivastav, S.K., SQL injection attack detection using SVM. *Int. J. Comput. Appl.*, 42, 13, 1–4, 2012.
17. Rawat, R., Bhardwaj, P., Kaur, U., Telang, S., Chouhan, M., Sankaran, K.S., *Smart vehicles for communication, volume 2*, John Wiley & Sons, 2023.
18. Mahor, V., Garg, B., Telang, S., Pachlasiya, K., Chouhan, M., Rawat, R., Cyber threat phylogeny assessment and vulnerabilities representation at thermal power station, in: *Proceedings of International Conference on Network Security and Blockchain Technology: ICNSBT 2021*, pp. 28–39, Springer Nature Singapore, Singapore, 2022, June.
19. Rawat, R., Gupta, S., Sivaranjani, S., Cu, O.K., Kuliha, M., Sankaran, K.S., Malevolent information crawling mechanism for forming structured illegal organisations in hidden networks. *Int. J. Cyber Warf. Terror. (IJCWT)*, 12, 1, 1–14, 2022.

Bibliography

Ahn, M.J. and Chen, Y.-C., Digital transformation toward AI-augmented public administration: The perception of government employees and the willingness to use AI in government. *Gov. Inf. Q.*, 39, 2, 101664, 2022.
Wirtz, B.W., Weyerer, J.C., Sturm, B.J., The dark sides of artificial intelligence: An integrated AI governance framework for public administration. *Int. J. Public Adm.*, 43, 9, 818–29, 2020 Jul 3.
Agarwal, P.K., Public administration challenges in the world of AI and bots. *Public Adm. Rev.*, 78, 6, 917–921, 2018.
Loi, M. and Spielkamp, M., Towards accountability in the use of artificial intelligence for public administrations, in: *Proceedings of the 2021 AAAI/ACM Conference on AI, Ethics, and Society*, pp. 757–766, 2021.
Misuraca, G., van Noordt, C., Boukli, A., The use of AI in public services: Results from a preliminary mapping across the EU, in: *Proceedings of the 13th International Conference on Theory and Practice of Electronic Governance*, pp. 90–99, 2020.
van Noordt, C., Medaglia, R., Misuraca, G., Stimulating the uptake of AI in public administrations: Overview and comparison of AI Strategies of European Member States, EGOV-CeDEM-ePart, pp. 269–278, 2020.
van Noordt, C., Conceptual challenges of researching artificial intelligence in public administrations, in: *DG. O 2022: The 23rd Annual International Conference on Digital Government Research*, pp. 183–190, 2022.
Ebers, M. and Tupay, P.K., The promise and perils of AI and ML in public administration, in: *Artificial Intelligence and Machine Learning Powered Public Service Delivery in Estonia*, pp. 7–33, Springer, Cham, 2023.
da Costa Alexandre, A. and Pereira, L.M., European Union fosters ethical AI in the public administration, in: *International Conference on Disruptive Technologies, Tech Ethics and Artificial Intelligence*, Springer, Cham, pp. 103–113, 2023.
Mikhail, B., Aleksei, M., Ekaterina, S., On the way to legal framework for AI in public sector, in: *Proceedings of the 11th International Conference on Theory and Practice of Electronic Governance*, pp. 682–684, 2018.

Wong, J., Morgan, D., Straub, V., Hashem, Y., Bright, J., Key challenges for the participatory governance of AI in public administration, 2022.

Busuioc, M., Accountable artificial intelligence: Holding algorithms to account. *Public Adm. Rev.*, 81, 5, 825–836, 2021.

Cheng, Y.D., Pandey, S., Hall, J., Introduction to the virtual issue: Advancing public policy research through the lens of public administration, 2022.

Bundin, M., Martynov, A., Aliev, Y., Kutuev, E., Legal aspects of the use of AI in public sector, in: *International Conference on Digital Transformation and Global Society*, Springer, Cham, pp. 171–180, 2018.

Alon-Barkat, S. and Busuioc, M., Human–AI interactions in public sector decision making: "Automation bias" and "selective adherence" to algorithmic advice. *J. Public Adm. Res. Theory*, 33, 1, 153–169, 2023.

Ojo, A., Mellouli, S., Zeleti, F.A., A realist perspective on AI-era public management, in: *Proceedings of the 20th Annual International Conference on Digital Government Research*, pp. 159–170, 2019.

Zheng, D., Chen, J., Huang, L., Zhang, C., E-government adoption in public administration organizations: Integrating institutional theory perspective and resource-based view. *Eur. J. Inf. Syst.*, 22, 2, 221–234, 2013.

Kuziemski, M. and Misuraca, G., AI governance in the public sector: Three tales from the frontiers of automated decision-making in democratic settings. *Telecomm. Policy*, 44, 6, 101976, 2020.

Aoki, N., An experimental study of public trust in AI chatbots in the public sector. *Gov. Inf. Q.*, 37, 4, 101490, 2020.

Klijn, E.-H., Complexity theory and public administration: What's new? Key concepts in complexity theory compared to their counterparts in public administration research. *Public Manage. Rev.*, 10, 3, 299–317, 2008.

Vandenabeele, W., Toward a public administration theory of public service motivation: An institutional approach. *Public Manage. Rev.*, 9, 4, 545–556, 2007.

Madhav, A.V.S. and Tyagi, A.K., The world with future technologies (post-COVID-19): Open issues, challenges, and the road ahead, in: *Intelligent Interactive Multimedia Systems for e-Healthcare Applications*, A.K. Tyagi, A. Abraham, A. Kaklauskas (Eds.), Springer, Singapore, 2022, https://doi.org/10.1007/978-981-16-6542-4_22.

Mishra, S. and Tyagi, A.K., The role of machine learning techniques in Internet of Things-based cloud applications, in: *Artificial Intelligence-Based Internet of Things Systems. Internet of Things (Technology, Communications and Computing)*, S. Pal, D. De, R. Buyya (Eds.), Springer, Cham, 2022, https://doi.org/10.1007/978-3-030-87059-1_4.

George, T.T. and Tyagi, A.K., Reliable edge computing architectures for crowdsensing applications. *2022 International Conference on Computer Communication and Informatics (ICCCI)*, pp. 1–6, 2022, doi: 10.1109/ICCCI54379.2022.9740791.

Conversational AI and Cloud Platform: An Investigation of Security and Privacy

V. Durga Prasad Jasti[1]*, Devabalan Pounraj[2], Malik Jawarneh[3], Meenakshi[4], P. Venkata Hari Prasad[5] and Samrat Ray[6]

[1]CSE Department, VR Siddhartha Engineering College, Vijayawada, India
[2]Department of Computer Science and Engineering, BVC Engineering College (Autonomous), Andhrapradesh, India
[3]Faculty of Computing Sciences, Gulf College, Al-Khuwair, Oman
[4]Apeejay Stya University, Sohna, Haryana, India
[5]Department of Computer Science and Engineering Koneru Lakshmaiah Education Foundation, Vijayvada, India
[6]SBES, Pune, India

Abstract

The term "conversational AI" refers to a system that can accurately imitate natural discourse. This is made possible by natural language processing (NLP), a subfield of artificial intelligence that examines how computers learn to comprehend and evaluate human speech. Natural language processing, also known as NLP, is a technique that interprets both written and spoken language in order to generate relevant and appropriate responses to questions or comments. Cloud-dependent chatbots are prevalent in many real-world applications. This manuscript explores various security and privacy concerns in conversational AI and cloud platforms. This article also describes attacks against the cloud and chatbots.

Keywords: Conversational AI, cloud platform, security, privacy, attacks, Chatbots

35.1 Introduction

Within the domain of artificial intelligence (AI), the term "conversational AI" refers to a system that is capable of imitating natural speech in an accurate manner. This is made possible by natural language processing, or NLP, which is a subsection of artificial intelligence that studies how computers learn to understand and evaluate human speech [1]. Natural language processing, also referred to as NLP, is a technique that deciphers both written and spoken language to generate responses that are relevant and appropriate to inquiries or comments [2]. During the teaching process of conversational AI systems, both text and speech recordings

*Corresponding author: prasadjasti2018@gmail.com

Romil Rawat, Rajesh Kumar Chakrawarti, Sanjaya Kumar Sarangi, Piyush Vyas, Mary Sowjanya Alamanda, Kotagiri Srividya and Krishnan Sakthidasan Sankaran (eds.) Conversational Artificial Intelligence, (635–654) © 2024 Scrivener Publishing LLC

are utilized. This information is utilized in the process of training the system to understand human communication and respond in an appropriate manner to it [3]. The accumulated knowledge of the system then makes it possible to have a natural conversation with other individuals. The more it engages with the outside world, the more it learns, and the more effectively it can respond to challenges [4, 5]. Figure 35.1 shows the workings of chatbots.

In recent years, cloud computing has emerged as one of the most promising technologies, with the potential to completely overhaul the conventional approach to computing. Cloud computing has the potential to completely overhaul the traditional approach to computing. It signifies a significant shift in the utilization and acquisition of hardware, software, and other forms of information technology (IT). Businesses and government organizations that are looking for more effective methods of handling data and a more comprehensive strategy for determining the impact of outsourcing can benefit from the profits made from using cloud storage services. The pay-as-you-go model of cloud computing is readily apparent in this new age of responsiveness, speed, and ability in the provision of information technology services [6].

The following is an excerpt from the National Institute of Standards and Technology's [7] description of the five major characteristics that designate a cloud-based system as a broad paradigm delivering paid on-demand services. This should help you get a bearing on the most fundamental concepts and information pertaining to the cloud. These major features are described below:

- **On demand self-service:** This permits customers to attain assets without of human involvement. It signifies the norm of autonomic computing.
- **Broad network access:** This characteristic is sustained by means of customary protocols via the Internet.
- **Shared resources:** Resource pooling is allowed based on the multi-tenant model among several users. It is constructed using virtualization methods

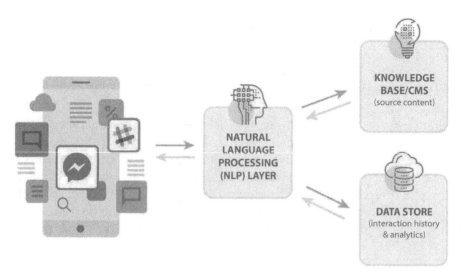

Figure 35.1 Working of Chatbot.

where numerous OS co-exist on the same physical appliance. Security concerns arise because there is no physical contour in a multi-tenant environment.

- **Elasticity:** The assets can be vigorously delivered or freed on demand and in any measure. This property demonstrates the stability of resources. Scalability and reliability are vital key aspects of the resource elasticity of a cloud system.
- **Metered service:** The CSP observes and governs the resources utilized by the cloud customers; delivers appropriate reports according to the category of service; and prices the consumers on a pay-as-you-go scheme. Therefore, the validation and the responsibility necessities are obligated to be deliberated as noteworthy needs.
- **No upfront investment:** The resources are provided to the customer from the cloud pool of resources conferred on him.
- **Small operational price:** Assets can be simply assigned and released on request (supplies resources conferring the highest load and releases when service demand is small).
- **High scalability:** It allows you to massively scale bandwidth and storage space.
- **Modest access:** Internet links provided to web-based services through a set of equipment.
- **Decreased occupational menaces:** Better expertise provided by the infrastructure provider lends itself to improved management of risks.

This manuscript explores various security and privacy concerns in conversational AI and cloud platforms. This article also describes attacks against the cloud and chatbots.

35.2 Cloud Architecture

A cloud engineer's duties include the preparation of both the hardware and software components of a cloud architecture. Cloud architecture refers to the system design that is involved in the intricate process of delivering cloud computing services. This generally includes a large number of distinct cloud components talking to one another through application programming interfaces (APIs), which are most frequently online services. This philosophy is strikingly similar to that of the UNIX operating system, which promotes the practice of downloading and running as many distinct kinds of software as is practically feasible. The infrastructure of cloud computing is composed of a wide variety of distinct components that have only a tenuous connection to one another. The general infrastructure of the cloud can be split in two different ways [8]. In most cases, each end is connected to the other via the internet. The subsequent Figure 35.2 illustrates the vision of cloud computing architecture.

The user experience is what is meant to be referred to as the "front end" of a cloud computing infrastructure. It contains the requests and application programming interfaces (APIs) necessary to communicate with the cloud computing infrastructure. Take the example of the computer browser for clarification. A reference is made to the cloud as the backbone of the system. Included in this package is everything that is required to offer cloud computing services. Massive quantities of data, along with other conveniences and security measures, dissemination methods, processors, and so on, can be housed there.

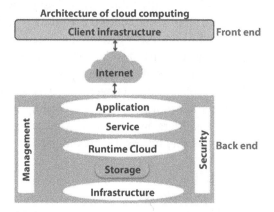

Figure 35.2 Cloud computing architecture.

Cloud infrastructure comprises the following entities:

- **Hypervisor:** It is a low-level package that permits the allocation of physical instances of cloud resources among numerous occupants.
- **Management Software:** It supports the preservation and organization of the structure.
- **Deployment Software:** It is comforting to organize and assimilate the program on the cloud.
- **Network:** It is the main constituent and permits linking services over the net.
- **Server:** The server assists in calculating the asset distribution in addition to observing the resources, granting safety, etc.
- **Storage:** The cloud retains manifold copies of storage. If any of the stowage possession flops, at that time it can be replaced with another one, which makes cloud computing more consistent.

35.2.1   Cloud Components

In a modest intellect, a cloud computing system consists of numerous components: clients, the datacenter, and distributed servers, each playing a precise part in conveying a useful cloud-based application [9].

35.2.1.1   Clients

Clients are devices like laptops, tablet computers, and mobile phones that the clients employ to store their data on the cloud. Clients are usually of three sorts:

- **Mobile:** Mobile devices include personal digital assistants or smartphones.
- **Thin Clients:** the nodes have no inbuilt hard drives and allow the server to perform all the computations and then show the outcome.
- **Thick clients:** They link to the cloud through a web browser like Yahoo or Firefox.

Thin clients are attractive as a suitable key, as they include benefits like lower hardware and IT costs, greater secure, minimum electricity consumption, and easy replacement.

35.2.1.2 Datacenter

A group of servers to which the application is subscribed comprises a datacenter. In virtualizing servers, the software can be mounted, permitting numerous instances of virtual servers to be executed on a single physical server.

35.2.1.3 Distributed Servers

The servers can be geographically stored at disparate locations. But they still act as if they are working next to each other, thereby providing more flexibility and security options.

35.2.2 Cloud Deployment Models

As an amalgamation of hardware and software assets, NIST [9] mentioned that cloud infrastructure delivers the features needed to maintain cloud service models.

They are described as follows:

35.2.2.1 Public Cloud

Cloud computing can be defined as "resources vigorously supplied on a self-serve basis accomplished over the internet, by virtue of web-based applications or services, originating at an off-site, third-party supplier who allocates collateral and reckons on the utility model." This is the conventional description of cloud computing. Clients of public clouds are viewed as untrustworthy because anonymous third parties grant them access to private data that they should not have access to. Salesforce Chatter, Gmail, and Dropbox are just a few examples of popular public software-as-a-service offerings. Force.com and Google App Engine are two examples of well-known public platforms that provide application hosting services. Amazon Web Services and Microsoft Azure are the two most widely used public IaaS choices currently available.

Advantages:
Below are the strengths of organizing public cloud archetypal:

- **Cost Remunerative:** The sharing of resources among numerous consumers makes it inexpensive.
- **Consistency:** The public cloud hires a huge quantity of assets from diverse places. If some of the resources fail, it hires a different one.
- **Litheness:** They can effortlessly assimilate with a private cloud, offering clients a malleable methodology.
- **Site Liberation:** The Internet supports site liberation.
- **Viability Style Estimation:** As constructed on the pay-per-use archetypal, assets are available every time the client requires them.
- **High Scalability:** Being accessible on request, resources can be allocated and de-allocated according to needs.

Drawbacks:
Listed below are some shortcomings of the public cloud:

- **Less safe:** As information is accommodated off-site and assets are mutually pooled, they do not guarantee a greater level of safety.
- **Less arduous:** It is relatively customizable in a smaller amount than a private cloud.

35.2.2.2   Private Cloud

The use of private networks, which enable a greater degree of control over the data as well as the level of service and protection, is encouraged. An organization may commission the construction of a private cloud from a cloud service provider (CSP) or business of equivalent standing. Both the on-premise data center managed by the administration and the off-premise facility managed by a third-party service provider (CSP) are viable options for housing the infrastructure. Both the on-premise data center managed by the administration and the off-premise facility managed by a CSP are able to implement their own surveillance and security measures as required [8].

Profits:
Mentioned below are the gains of deploying a private cloud:

- **Enhanced Safety and Confidentiality:** The resources being available to a limited number of clients ensure high security.
- **Extra Control:** As resources are accessed only within an institution, there is more control over resources.
- **Price and Energy Proficiency:** The private cloud assets are less cost-efficient but offer high efficiency as compared to public clouds.

Weaknesses:
Here are the drawbacks of the private cloud archetypal:

- **Limited Region of Process:** The private cloud is merely reachable nearby and is challenging to organize universally.
- **Increased Expenditure:** Buying new hardware is a costly deal.
- **Restricted Scalability:** Scalability is limited to the capability of in-house hosted assets.
- **Supplementary Skills:** Skilled expertise is required for private cloud deployment.

35.2.2.3   Community Cloud

Instead of joining a single company, they provide assistance to a collection of cloud consumers who have similar concerns regarding things like the objectives of their projects, the level of security, and their confidentiality. Patrons can include professors, students, and faculty advisers at a university, for example, because all of these groups make use of the various academic support services that are provided by the organization.

Advantages:
Several aids to deploying cloud as a community cloud model are:

- o **Expenditure Operative:** The community cloud incurs a low cost.
- o **Sharing among Organizations:** Cloud resources and capabilities are shared among several organizations.
- o **Safety measures:** The community cloud is relatively safer than the public cloud but less secure than the private cloud.

Contentions:

- The storage of information at a single place in the community must be done carefully.
- Allocation of tasks in governance, security, and cost among organizations is hard to manage.

35.2.2.4   Hybrid Cloud

It syndicates inherent and outer clouds (public, private, and/or community). A public cloud achieves non-critical jobs, and precarious actions are accomplished through a private cloud.

Assistances
Some of the advantages of deploying a hybrid cloud model as listed below:

- **Scalability:** It provides the combined traits of public and private clouds.
- **Elasticity:** It delivers scalable public assets.
- **Expenditure Proficiency:** Public clouds generate more revenue operative than private clouds. Thus, hybrid clouds can be less costly.
- **Safety measures:** The private cloud in the hybrid cloud confirms greater safety.

Demerits

- **Networking Concerns:** The amalgamation of public and private clouds makes networking complex.
- **Security Agreement:** The security policies of the organization must be obeyed.
- **Organization Dependence:** Redundancy among data centers arises because of internal clouds.

In a hybrid cloud, a segment of the service structure executes in the private cloud (e.g., core applications and sensitive data), while the non-core applications run in the public cloud, which are less sensitive applications and data that are in-house in nature.

35.2.3   The Cloud Computing Stack as Cloud Services

There are three different standard distribution models provided by the CSPs, and each one is determined by the degree of abstraction offered by the supplier as well as the prototypicality of the service being provided. The following illustration illustrates the three primary layers that comprise the technology stack, along with a description of how the higher layers can leverage the capabilities of the lower levels to accomplish their own objectives [10].

They are described as follows:

35.2.3.1   Software as a Service (SaaS)

Users now have the option of leasing services from CSPs through predefined interfaces as an alternative to purchasing, downloading, and operating software. Because the applications are stored off-site, the customer is exempt from being responsible for their upkeep and assistance. Along with the management of the fundamental infrastructure and any user-facing applications, the preservation of data, the sharing of data, and the management of access are all responsibilities that fall under the purview of the cloud service provider. Examples of software that is provided on a cloud-based service include Google Docs, SalesForce CRM, and Mobile MC.

It has many benefits:

i.   Permits groups to outsource the web hosting and supervision of services to the CSPs, thereby decreasing prices related to licensing, employees, and infrastructure.
ii.   The supervision of a SaaS function is reinforced by the vendors. Yet, they are not completely customized.
iii. SaaS allows for the maximum the sharing of resources among multiple customers by utilizing the same physical structure.

Traits of SaaS
Some important features of SaaS encompass:

I.   Net access to the business software programs.
II.   Users are not required to address software program enhancements and patches.
III. APIs permit integration among several chunks of software.
IV.   Software is controlled from a single site.
V.   Software provided in a "one-to-many" version.

35.2.3.2   Platform as a Service (PaaS)

It does this by providing computational resources that can be used as a platform for describing requirements and delineating desires in a collection of computer languages that are made possible by the CSP. The user is responsible for managing requests and potentially establishing an application hosting setting [9]. This responsibility also includes establishing an application hosting setting. The Core Service Provider (CSP) is the entity that is accountable for supervising and regulating the core infrastructure, which may consist of the network, computers, operating systems, or files [9]. The Google App Engine and the Microsoft Azure cloud platforms are two examples of well-known situations.

The significant advantages of PaaS are

I.   The low cost incurred in the rapid propagation of software applications.
II. Software vendors are allowed to limit the use, control, prohibit replicating, and disseminate their software by controlling the versions of their software.
III. Single developers and emerging companies are allowed to organize network-centered applications, deprived of the price and intricacy of purchasing and setting up services.

Traits of PaaS
Some basic characteristics of PaaS encompass:

I.   The services required to create an application development process in the same cohesive production milieu.
II. Web-based client interface creation tools assist in making, altering, checking, and deploying distinct user interface situations.
III. The multi-tenant architecture where more than one concurrent user utilizes the identical development software.
IV. Equipment to address billing and subscription control.

35.2.3.3   Infrastructure as a Service (IaaS)

It is the paradigm of the basic minimal service, supplying customers with computation, storage, networks, and so on that can be extended and controlled. Users are the ones who are ultimately accountable for the safety of their cloud-based data and applications; cloud service providers (CSPs) only play a supporting role in this regard. Rackspace, Amazon S3, and SQL Azure are some examples.
The advantages of IaaS are:

i.   It allows the purchase and payment of an amount of infrastructure required at a specific time.
ii. It scales and adopts the infrastructure on demand to fulfill ability needs almost at real-time speed.

Features of IaaS
IaaS is broadly recognized to fulfill the following:

- Resources are disseminated as a service.
- Dynamic scaling is permitted.
- The utility pricing model is variable.
- Several clients operate on a single portion of the hardware.

PaaS may not be as well-known as SaaS, but it is quickly becoming one of the most popular aspects of cloud computing. This is due to the fact that PaaS combines the ease of use of SaaS with the strength of IaaS.

When clients transition to using IaaS, they are granted complete control over the manner in which the applications contained within their virtual machines are executed. Users have administrative access to the fundamental infrastructure of a platform that is provided as a service, but they still retain control over the applications and services that they have created for themselves. Users of a SaaS model have restricted access to the fundamental apps and resources, and administration of those apps and resources is also restricted.

35.3   Literature Survey

According to Tebaa *et al.* (2014), the security of one's company's data should be the primary concern of any business that is considering making the move to the cloud. HE prevents the cloud service provider from being in a position where it is unable to carry out activities on protected data in this manner. Users would receive calculated results that are comparable to what HE would have generated if it had been applied directly to unstructured data. These results would be given to users as part of the output of the computing process. Ronald Rivest, Leonard Adleman, and Michel Dertozos were the ones who first introduced it to the public in 1978. Pascal Paillier hypothesized the existence of a brand-new encryption technique for additive HE in 1999. An additive homomorphism was constructed by basing its construction on the "Decisional Composite Residuosity Assumption," also known as the DCRA. In 2005, Dan Bonch, Jin Goh, and Kobi constrained multiplication to a single operation. Based on their findings, they hypothesized that it would be feasible to create cryptography with demonstrated levels of security. The author saw that HE-based cloud computing security is gaining momentum and that future work will concentrate on evaluating and enhancing existing cryptosystems to enable computers to carry out a variety of activities that have been requested by customers [10].

The ubiquitous use of cloud computing can be attributed to the flexibility and accessibility of the technology, as stated by Aljafer *et al.* (2014). However, refuge risks present a significant challenge to the promotion and development of a secure system for the storage, dissemination, and retrieval of data. In this article, various strategies for protecting the storage of data in the cloud, such as AES, HE, ABE, proxy encryption, HIBE, and IBBE, were contrasted and compared, as were their advantages and disadvantages. Based on the comparative chart, fully homomorphic encryption (HE) and hierarchical attribute-based encryption (HABE) were deduced to be the most effective methods for the protection of sensitive data [11].

Benzeki *et al.* (2016) disclosed why homomorphic encryption was considered suitable for the storage of documents in the cloud and stated a number of concerns that are associated with this decision. It was described how homomorphic encryption could be used for a variety of purposes in addition to safeguarding confidential information during communication, such as examining protected data, performing computations over encrypted information, and other activities. It was recommended that a multi-cloud architecture be utilized for the purpose of managing protected data. This architecture would consist of a 'N' number of geographically dispersed computers that would redistribute the data and, in the process, achieve completely homomorphic encryption, or come as close as possible to achieving this goal. We were able to enhance the system's security in two different ways by utilizing the Data Partitioning Algorithm (DPA), which involved distributing the data across a number of different cloud providers. The first way was to reduce the risk of data intrusions, and the second way was to increase the number of concurrent dispensations used when performing homomorphic encryption. The following work would focus on putting the recommended design into action and evaluating its efficacy and safety in order to demonstrate that it is feasible [12].

According to Kayed *et al.* (2015), the act of outsourcing data to the cloud makes it difficult to establish a virtual boundary and boundaries around the team. The report analyzed the different approaches to data partitioning that are currently in use, discussing their benefits and drawbacks as well as the levels of protection they offered. There were multiple aspects of cloud data security objectives that were addressed, including confidentiality, integrity, and availability. In a multi-tenant implementation, the three primary methods for data administration that were considered were distinct databases, collective databases with scattered schemes, and common databases with shared structures. Each of these three approaches has its own set of benefits and drawbacks in terms of the amount of data sharing that is possible, the level of security that is provided, and the amount of space that is required to store the data. The increased data security dangers that come along with multi-tenancy were also mentioned, even though better resource utilization and quicker adaptability were cited as benefits of multi-tenancy. For subsequent variations of the work described, it was recommended that an improved data segmentation technique that was both more durable and efficient be developed [13].

The research that was carried out by Tari (2015) looked into the difficulties, elucidations, and constraints that are associated with cloud security. The author made a correlation between the protection of private data and having people who are authenticated. According to the findings of the report, closing any vulnerabilities in the system's security is necessary to guarantee the trustworthiness of cloud computing operations. Due to the fact that both the client and the server use the same underlying infrastructure, it is imperative that both of these components have adequate security to prevent unauthorized access. The availability of the server, providing services to multiple tenants, keeping data, managing access, and ensuring identification protection were all topics of discussion. Homomorphic encryption, trustworthy identity management, distributed access control, and a number of other possibilities are some of the choices that have been recommended [14].

According to Hayward (2015), cloud computing has been utilized for the purpose of data storage; however, the preservation of data continues to be the primary concern. For this reason, an explanation was given regarding the technique of completely homomorphic encryption. On the other hand, HE had trouble getting up to maximum speed. Because of this, one strategy that can be utilized to improve productivity is processing in parallel. The operations on the HE-encrypted data were carried out simultaneously, and the data that was produced as a result was split up and disseminated across a number of processing processors. HE conducted an analysis of the amount of time the engine (PE) was actually functioning, and then the engine was installed on a private computer. It was hypothesized that the results of the experiment would increase productivity more than what could be accomplished through the use of a singular model computation on its own. It was decided to develop a client–server architecture. In the testing environment, the spread strategy delivered faster results in terms of performance [15] than the single-mode configuration did.

Information transmission has become a desirable service as a result of the effectiveness and expense reductions made possible by cloud computing, as Li *et al.* (2018) pointed out.

This is due to the fact that cloud computing makes it feasible. The use of attribute-based encryption allowed for access management to be provided by cloud computing (ABE). The most significant discovery made in this study was the utilization of offline and online ABE for the purpose of ensuring the integrity of attribute-based data interchange (ABDS). The generation of an immediate cipher-text was the end product of using the chameleon hash function. After conducting a thorough investigation into its operations, the ABDS system's viability and safety were both verified to have been established. One possible advancement that could take place in the not-too-distant future [16] involves the elimination of direct traits in the information interchange process for customers with asset restrictions who use the cloud.

An innovative strategy for cloud security was presented for the first time by Liu *et al.* (2018) in the form of an effective and distributable cloud storage gateway that acts as a mediator between end users and private cloud service providers. The reduction of data and the simplification of protocol updates offered by a cloud storage interface were highlighted as two of the many helpful features that were mentioned. The High Available Cloud Storage Gateway (HASG) architecture, which can be used to store information and data independently, is one of the most helpful improvements to the document and is regarded as one of its most important contributions. Because of the amount of accessible network throughput, the agent was chosen to be utilized in the connection between the gateway and the cloud storage. A microdata upgrading technique that would result in the introduction of identical divisions was proposed [17] as an alternative to the more common practice of completely substituting data whenever it is adjusted.

Fabian *et al.* brought to light the significance of utilizing large amounts of data by medical service providers (2014). In the article, a technique was described for maintaining confidentiality while transferring large amounts of medical data between different businesses using multiple online storage locations. For user identification and key exchange, the design relied on an attribute-based encryption approach. This was necessary because the data was partitioned across numerous computers. Multi-cloud proxies were utilized so that compressed medical data could be distributed to and retrieved from many computers at the same time. In order to determine the characteristics of a medical document and the role-based input criteria, we utilized ABE. The analysis of the findings from a number of different experiments revealed that the technique is both practically viable and produces outcomes that are satisfactory. It was mentioned that future work will be done to evaluate cross-enterprise elements of key management and role-based access control (RBAC) strategy administration, in addition to numerous improvements to the multi-cloud proxy [18].

According to Varghese and Buyya's explanation, there has been a change in the environment of cloud computing (2017). This analysis presented a prospective path for cloud computing's development in the future. Alterations in the construction of clouds, such as the proliferation of multi-clouds, micro-clouds, and cloudlets, as well as ad hoc clouds and diversified clouds, were a topic of conversation. A fresh multi-tier cloud architecture was mulled over as a potential replacement for the more traditional two-tier approach. Following are some of the potential community applications and areas of investigation that could be influenced by cloud computing: The future study avenues that ought to be encouraged have been enumerated [19], and they include ones that contribute to increased security, the expression of distributed applications, efficient administration strategies, and the dependability of cloud computing systems.

Cigoj and Blazic were the ones who made the observation regarding the investigation of clarifications to security concerns (2015). This article demonstrates that the single sign-on (SSO) strategy works across numerous platforms for cloud customers. Additionally, this approach is verified and supported by the authors of this article. Handling confidential data in a way that is rapid, simple, and safe could be made feasible through the use of once-and-for-all individual authentication. OpenStack and VMware working together to create a hybrid cloud led to the creation of a multiplatform cloud authentication system (MUPASS). The method that was developed made it possible to improved data protection and monitor records of user activity. Users were given the choice to register themselves or make use of the OAuth internet interface. The forthcoming development work for MUPASS will include the addition of new features that will be made possible by the advancement of cloud systems [20].

Zissis and Lekkas *et al.* (2012) both anticipated that cloud computing would become increasingly popular and usher in a new era of computing. On the other hand, there have been concerns raised regarding the protection of the area as well as potential dangers. In this article, the commonalities and distinctions between grid computing and cloud computing, as well as their essential qualities, dissemination techniques, and service models, were addressed. The dissemination strategy that is used is what determines the level of trustworthiness that can be attached to the cloud's generated data and requests. The article recommended using TTP to enable confidence by using cryptography in order to guarantee the CIA of information and transactions. This was done in order to guarantee the CIA. TTP has been described as the perfect cloud infrastructure for establishing protected communications because of its ability to enable security. Threats to security, including those to privacy and confidentiality, the veracity of data, and the availability of the system, were dealt with. The importance of customizing security measures for each individual user was discussed [21]. This topic was approached from the perspectives of service level, users, security-requirements, and hazards.

According to Jaiswal and Gupta (2017), there has been a significant increase in the rate of security risks, which cannot be ignored. This has delayed the widespread adoption of cloud-based services because the risks cannot be disregarded. The author came up with the idea for the security index as a means to evaluate the risk that could be caused by prospective dangers. A need-gathering exercise, a ranking of security requirements based on a risk inquiry system, and an evaluation of a few established cloud-based storage arrangements were among the accomplishments made by this study. The cloud-based storage system that is currently in use was analyzed, and the technique that was recommended for preserving the model was broken down in detail. During the course of the development process, insufficiently explaining and managing the safety requirements led to the identification of potential threats. Case studies were supposed to be investigated as an additional component of the proposal model for the purpose of designing and assessing a method that is secure and adaptable [22].

35.4   Security in Conversational AI and Cloud Computing

One description of security describes it as "the quality or state of being safe from hazards." Protecting the sufferer from any harm that could be caused, whether on purpose or inadvertently, is a necessary step in this process. It is necessary to have a security system that has multiple levels in order to protect not only the company's tangible assets but also its intellectual property and the employees who work there. According to Whitman and Mattord's point of view, it is necessary for organizations to have a defense strategy for the future.

1. **Physical security:** It is mandatory for safeguarding against illegal access and misuse of information and objects.
2. **Personnel security:** It is necessary to grant the person or collection of users authorization of access.
3. **Operational security:** It is vital to shield the data of a particular task or a sequence of actions or procedures.
4. **Communication security:** It is required to safeguard communication media, technology, and content from unauthorized access.
5. **Network security:** It is essential to preserve network mechanisms, links, and the content they handle.
6. **Information security:** It is a prerequisite to guard the confidentiality, integrity, and availability of data resources, whether in stowage, handling, or communication.

35.4.1   Importance of Security in Cloud Computing

Computing in the cloud presents an innovative and user-friendly method for controlling user access and streamlining administrative responsibilities; however, the widespread acceptance of this method is in jeopardy due to a number of concerns and complaints. The customization, accessibility, and convenience offered by cloud computing are accompanied by a plethora of security concerns. The need for security in a cloud platform is established by the data available in Figure 35.3.

The preservation of personal information can have far-reaching effects. Information security is characterized by a number of characteristics, including confidentiality, stability,

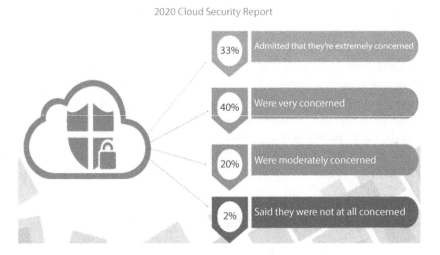

Figure 35.3 Cloud security report by BitGlass Agency.

and availability. Customers should proceed with prudence when evaluating the risks associated with data breaches because it is disconcerting to consider that a third party will be responsible for overseeing confidential information.

35.4.2   Security Principles

There are six chief security requirements, as elaborated in [23].

i.   **Identification:** Does authentication and corroboration of cloud clients and then verifies the consent of access.
ii.   **Authorization:** Access for management and opportunity processes in the cloud is provided.
iii.   **Confidentiality:** This is the main requirement for outsourcing data to be stored in the cloud.
iv.   **Integrity:** To guarantee the truthfulness and reliability of information.
v.   **Nonrepudiation:** It can be guaranteed through sanctuary practices and token allotment.
vi.   **Availability:** It is an essential parameter when taking into consideration the delivery form and choosing the service type.

35.4.3   Cloud Computing and Conversational AI Security Issues

Next, we list the security issues [24] occurring in cloud computing and chatbot:

1.   **Trust:** An efficient security policy is mandatory to diminish the danger of information loss or manipulation.
2.   **Confidentiality:** Storing information on remote servers may lead to a breach of confidentiality.
3.   **Privacy:** It mentions the readiness of a client to reveal his data. Any illegal access to the user's confidential information may lead to safety issues.
4.   **Integrity:** It is to safeguard the correctness and reliability of information. Thus, protection against internal attacks is mandatory.
5.   **Consistency and accessibility:** The reliability of CSP diminishes in cases of data leakage.
6.   **Verification and authorization:** To inhibit illegal entry, the software is compulsory exterior the administration's firewall.
7.   **Information Damage:** Prohibiting or altering of data deficient in any standby might lead to information harm.
8.   **Easy Accessibility of the Cloud:** A simple registration procedure might open chances to access services for devious minds.
9.   **Extended feasibility:** In case of any failure of any CSP, what are the provisions offered to the clients so that they don't have to suffer and there is no loss to their data.
10.   **Data seizure:** In case of any violation of rules and laws, the data can be seized by any foreign country.

11. **Policy integration:** Policy integration issues can arise while using a varied number of tools deployed on many servers.
12. **Audit:** Because a huge amount of data is stored in the cloud, it becomes difficult for the cloud service provider to trace and then audit all the records.
13. **Virtualization:** Data and applications being managed and supervised by a single cloud service provider may result in several security-related risks.

35.4.4   Security Attacks in Chatbot and Cloud Platform

Although cloud service providers offer tremendous benefits to users, security attacks [24] may still occur in the cloud computing environment, which may cause users to hesitate to trust the service providers. The following are some of the most prominent concerns related to cloud security.

1. **Authentication attack:** Due to the feeble verification scheme used in machines, they become highly prone to attacks on the server.
2. **MIM attack:** This kind of assault happens when an invader tries to obstruct and places himself amid two clients in a communication way, harming the organization by altering or intercepting data and adding false information.
3. **Denial of service attacks:** The shared nature of resources in the cloud makes the cloud system very vulnerable to this attack. We cannot access a particular site because of the overload on the server. A scenario when such an attack occurred was in 2009, when Twitter suffered from a DoS attack.
4. **Side Channel attacks:** Security can be violated by inserting a wicked VM into to the intended CSP and subsequently causing harm through it.
5. **Network security:** Due to unsafe SSL trust and session supervision flaws, network safety can be affected by network infiltration and packet scrutiny.
6. **Web Application Security:** There are many factors causing this type of attack. Cross-site scripting, unrestricted URLs, and an unsafe transport layer are some of the reasons behind this attack.

AI [25, 26] might also promote openness and diversity, for instance, by reducing the likelihood of bias in hiring choices by substituting analytical data. As enormous data sets could be processed more quickly, prisoner flight risks [27, 28] could be assessed more precisely, and crime [29, 30] or even terrorist attacks might be foreseen and averted, AI is expected to be employed more in crime prevention and the criminal justice system. Bad actors [31] have been able to adapt and create new attack techniques with the aid of generative AI, keeping them one step ahead of cybersecurity defences [32, 33]. Cybercriminals [34] may target a wider spectrum of prospective victims by using AI to automate assaults [35], scan attack surfaces [36], and create material that appeals to diverse demographics and geographic locations [37]. The technique was used by cybercriminals [38, 39] to produce convincing phishing emails [40]. Attackers may create highly personalised emails and SMS [41] messages using AI, increasing the likelihood that their targets will be duped. Cybersecurity [42] is changing as a result of generative AI, which benefits both attackers and defenders [43]. AI is being used by cybercriminals to carry outcomplex, original, large-scale assaults.

Additionally, the threat intelligence platform Recorded Future's business networks, government agencies, and vital infrastructure are all being protected by defenders using the same technology.

35.5 Conclusion

A computer program that can mimic human communication in a realistic manner is referred to as having "conversational AI." Natural language processing (NLP), a subcategory of artificial intelligence that studies how computers learn to understand and evaluate human communication, is what makes this possible. NLP is the discipline that makes this feasible. The method that is referred to by its acronym, natural language processing, or NLP, is a process that analyzes not only written but also spoken language in order to generate responses that are pertinent and appropriate to inquiries or comments. Chatbots that are contingent on the cloud are becoming increasingly common in a variety of real-world applications. This manuscript investigates a variety of potential threats to users' personal information posed by conversational AI and cloud platforms. Additionally, assaults against the cloud and chatbots are discussed in this article.

References

1. Rahman, A.M., Mamun, A.A., Islam, A., Programming challenges of chatbot: Current and future prospective. *2017 IEEE Region 10 Humanitarian Technology Conference (R10-HTC),* Dhaka, pp. 75–78, 2017.
2. Molnár, G. and Szüts, Z., The role of chatbots in formal education. *2018 IEEE 16th International Symposium on Intelligent Systems and Informatics (SISY),* Subotica, pp. 000197–000202, 2018.
3. AgusSantoso, H. *et al.,* Dinus Intelligent Assistance (DINA) chatbot for university admission services. *2018 International Seminar on Application for Technology of Information and Communication,* Semarang, pp. 417–423, 2018.
4. Rosruen, N. and Samanchuen, T., Chatbot utilization for medical consultant system. *2018 3rd Technology Innovation Management and Engineering Science International Conference (TIMES-iCON),* Bangkok, Thailand, pp. 1–5, 2018.
5. Raghuvanshi, A., Singh, U.K., Bulla, C., Saxena, M., Abadar, K., An investigation on detection of vulnerabilities in Internet of Things. *Eur. J. Mol. Clin. Med.,* 07, 10, 3289–3299, 2020.
6. Leong, P.H., Goh, O.S., Kumar, Y.J., MedKiosk: An embodied conversational intelligence via deep learning. *2017 13th International Conference on Natural Computation, Fuzzy Systems and Knowledge Discovery (ICNC-FSKD),* Guilin, pp. 394–399, 2017.
7. Peter, M. and Tim, G., The NIST definition of cloud computing. *Natl. Inst. Stand. Technol.,* 53, 6, 50, 2009.
8. Zhang, Q., Cheng, L., Boutaba, R., Cloud computing: State-of-the-art and research challenges. *J. Internet Serv. Appl.,* 1, 7–18, 2010.
9. Wang, C., Wang, Q., Ren, K., Cao, N., Lou, W., Toward secure and dependable storage services in cloud computing. *IEEE Trans. Serv. Comput.,* 5, 2, 220–232, April-June 2012, doi: 10.1109/TSC.2011.24.

10. Tebaa, M. and El Hajji, S., From single to multi-clouds computing privacy and fault tolerance. *IERI Proc.*, 10, 112–118, 2014.
11. Aljafer, A.K., Malik, Z., Alodib, M., Rezgui, A., A brief overview and an experimental evaluation of data confidentiality measures on the cloud. *J. Innov. Digit. Ecosyst.*, 1, 1–2, 1–11, 2014.
12. Benzekki, K., El, A., El, A., A secure cloud computing architecture using homomorphic encryption. *Int. J. Adv. Comput. Sci. Appl.*, 7, 2, 293–298, 2016.
13. Kayed, A., Abd, E., Latif, A., Badawi, A., Survey on enhancing the data security of the cloud computing environment by using data segregation technique. *IJRRAS*, 23, 2, 136–143, 2015.
14. Tari, Z., Security and privacy in cloud computing. *IEEE Cloud Comput.*, 1, 1, 54–57, 2014.
15. Hayward, R., Parallelizing fully homomorphic encryption for a cloud environment. *J. Appl. Res. Technol.*, 13, 245–252, ScienceDirect, 2015.
16. Li, J., Zhang, Y., Chen, X., Xiang, Y., Secure attribute-based data sharing for resource-limited users in cloud computing. *Comput. Secur.*, 72, 1–12, ISSN 0167-4048, 2018.
17. Liu, S., Zhang, C., Chen, Y., HASG: Security and efficient frame for accessing cloud storage. *China Commun.*, 15, 1, 86–94, Jan 2018, doi: 10.1109/CC.2018.8290808.
18. Fabian, B., Ermakova, T., Junghanns, P., Collaborative and secure sharing of healthcare data in multi-clouds. *Inf. Syst.*, 48, 132–150, 2015.
19. Varghese, B. and Buyya, R., Next generation cloud computing: New trends and research directions. *Future Gener. Comput. Syst.*, 79, 849–861, 2018.
20. Cigoj, P. and Blažič, B.J., An authentication and authorization solution for a multiplatform cloud environment. *Inf. Secur. J.*, 24, 4–6, 146–156, 2015.
21. Zissis, D. and Lekkas, D., Addressing cloud computing security issues. *Future Gener. Comput. Syst.*, 28, 3, 583–592, 2012.
22. Jaiswal, S. and Gupta, D., Engineering and validating security to make cloud secure. *Int. J. Syst. Assur. Eng. Manage.*, 8, 2, 1419–1441, 2017, doi: 10.1007/s13198-017-0612-x.
23. Raghuvanshi, A., Singh, U.K., Panse, P., Saxena, M., Veluri, R.K., Internet of Things: Taxonomy of various attacks. *Eur. J. Mol. Clin. Med.*, 7, 10, 3853–3864, 2020.
24. Raghuvanshi, A., Singh, U., Kassanuk, T., Phasinam, K., Internet of Things: Security vulnerabilities and countermeasures. *ECS Trans.*, 107, 1, 15043–15052, 2022, Available: 10.1149/10701.15043ecst.
25. Mahor, V., Bijrothiya, S., Rawat, R., Kumar, A., Garg, B., Pachlasiya, K., IoT and artificial intelligence techniques for public safety and security, in: *Smart Urban Computing Applications*, p. 111, 2023.
26. Mahor, V., Pachlasiya, K., Garg, B., Chouhan, M., Telang, S., Rawat, R., Mobile operating system (Android) vulnerability analysis using machine learning, in: *Proceedings of International Conference on Network Security and Blockchain Technology: ICNSBT 2021*, 2022, June, Springer Nature Singapore, Singapore, pp. 159–169.
27. Rawat, R., Garg, B., Pachlasiya, K., Mahor, V., Telang, S., Chouhan, M., Mishra, R., SCNTA: Monitoring of network availability and activity for identification of anomalies using machine learning approaches. *Int. J. Inf. Technol. Web Eng. (IJITWE)*, 17, 1, 1–19, 2022.
28. Rawat, R., Rimal, Y.N., William, P., Dahima, S., Gupta, S., Sankaran, K.S., Malware threat affecting financial organization analysis using machine learning approach. *Int. J. Inf. Technol. Web Eng. (IJITWE)*, 17, 1, 1–20, 2022.
29. Rawat, R., Mahor, V., Chouhan, M., Pachlasiya, K., Telang, S., Garg, B., Systematic literature review (SLR) on social media and the digital transformation of drug trafficking on darkweb, in: *International Conference on Network Security and Blockchain Technology*, Springer, Singapore, pp. 181–205, 2022.

30. Rawat, R., Ayodele Oki, O., Sankaran, S., Florez, H., Ajagbe, S.A., Techniques for predicting dark web events focused on the delivery of illicit products and ordered crime. *Int. J. Electr. Comput. Eng. (IJECE)*, 13, 5, 5354–5365, Oct. 2023, doi: 10.11591/ijece.v13i5.pp5354-5365.

31. Rawat, R., Garg, B., Mahor, V., Telang, S., Pachlasiya, K., Chouhan, M., Organ trafficking on the dark web—The data security and privacy concern in healthcare systems, in: *Internet of Healthcare Things: Machine Learning for Security and Privacy*, pp. 189–216, 2022.

32. Vyas, P., Vyas, G., Chauhan, A., Rawat, R., Telang, S., Gottumukkala, M., Anonymous trading on the dark online marketplace: An exploratory study, in: *Using Computational Intelligence for the Dark Web and Illicit Behavior Detection*, pp. 272–289, IGI Global, 2022.

33. Rawat, R., Oki, O.A., Sankaran, K.S., Olasupo, O., Ebong, G.N., Ajagbe, S.A., A new solution for cyber security in big data using machine learning approach, in: *Mobile Computing and Sustainable Informatics: Proceedings of ICMCSI 2023*, Springer Nature Singapore, Singapore, pp. 495–505, 2023.

34. Rawat, R., Chakrawarti, R.K., Raj, A., Mani, G., Chidambarathanu, K., Bhardwaj, R., Association rule learning for threat analysis using traffic analysis and packet filtering approach. *Int. J. Inf. Technol.*, 1–11, 2023.

35. Rawat, R., Logical concept mapping and social media analytics relating to cyber criminal activities for ontology creation. *Int. J. Inf. Technol.*, 15, 2, 893–903, 2023.

36. Rawat, R., Mahor, V., Álvarez, J.D., Ch, F., Cognitive systems for dark web cyber delinquent association malignant data crawling: A review, in: *Handbook of Research on War Policies, Strategies, and Cyber Wars*, pp. 45–63, 2023.

37. Rawat, R., Chakrawarti, R.K., Vyas, P., Gonzáles, J.L.A., Sikarwar, R., Bhardwaj, R., Intelligent fog computing surveillance system for crime and vulnerability identification and tracing. *Int. J. Inf. Secur. Priv. (IJISP)*, 17, 1, 1–25, 2023.

38. Rawat, R., Sowjanya, A.M., Patel, S.I., Jaiswal, V., Khan, I., Balaram, A. (Eds.), *Using Machine Intelligence: Autonomous Vehicles Volume 1*, John Wiley & Sons, 2022.

39. Rawat, R., Mahor, V., Díaz-Álvarez, J., Chávez, F., Rooted learning model at fog computing analysis for crime incident surveillance, in: *2022 International Conference on Smart Generation Computing, Communication and Networking (SMART GENCON)*, 2022, December, pp. 1–9, IEEE.

40. Rawat, R. and Shrivastav, S.K., SQL injection attack detection using SVM. *Int. J. Comput. Appl.*, 42, 13, 1–4, 2012.

41. Rawat, R., Bhardwaj, P., Kaur, U., Telang, S., Chouhan, M., Sankaran, K.S., *Smart vehicles for communication, volume 2*, John Wiley & Sons, 2023.

42. Mahor, V., Garg, B., Telang, S., Pachlasiya, K., Chouhan, M., Rawat, R., Cyber threat phylogeny assessment and vulnerabilities representation at thermal power station, in: *Proceedings of International Conference on Network Security and Blockchain Technology: ICNSBT 2021*, 2022, June, Springer Nature Singapore, Singapore, pp. 28–39.

43. Rawat, R., Gupta, S., Sivaranjani, S., Cu, O.K., Kuliha, M., Sankaran, K.S., Malevolent information crawling mechanism for forming structured illegal organisations in hidden networks. *Int. J. Cyber Warf. Terror. (IJCWT)*, 12, 1, 1–14, 2022.

Chatbot vs Intelligent Virtual Assistance (IVA)

Ajit Noonia[1], Rijvan Beg[2], Aruna Patidar[3], Bhushan Bawaskar[4], Shashank Sharma[4]* and Hitesh Rawat[5]

[1]*School of Computer Science and Engineering, Manipal University Jaipur, Jaipur, India*
[2]*Department of Computer Science and Engineering, Maulana Azad National Institute of Technology (MANIT), Bhopal, India*
[3]*Department of Information Technology, Shri Vaishnav Vidhyapeeth Vishwavidyalya, Indore, India*
[4]*Department of Computer Science Engineering, Shri Vaishnav Vidyapeeth Vishwavidyalaya, Indore, India*
[5]*Faculty at Management Department, Sri Aurobindo Institute of Technology and Management, Indore, India*

Abstract

Chatbots and intelligent virtual assistants are two AI-powered technologies that have gained increasing attention in recent years due to their potential to enhance the user experience and improve business efficiency. While both technologies aim to provide personalized and context-aware assistance to users, they differ in terms of their design, features, and capabilities.

This research paper presents a comparative analysis of chatbots and intelligent virtual assistants, examining their effectiveness in different contexts and applications. We conducted a systematic literature review of studies that compare chatbots and intelligent virtual assistants and identified the key differences between the two technologies. Our findings show that chatbots are typically rule-based and use predefined responses, whereas intelligent virtual assistants use machine learning and natural language processing to provide more personalized and context-aware responses.

We also found that the success of both technologies depends on their ability to provide a seamless and natural conversational experience for users, and that the design and implementation of chatbots and intelligent virtual assistants play a crucial role in their effectiveness. Overall, this research paper provides a comprehensive understanding of the strengths and limitations of chatbots and intelligent virtual assistants and offers insights into their effective use in different industries and applications.

Keywords: Chatbot, intelligent virtual assistance, artificial intelligence, natural language processing, machine learning

36.1 Introduction

Chatbot is a program that uses artificial intelligence (AI), machine learning (ML), and natural language processing (NLP) to understand user problems and their queries and generate an

---

Corresponding author: shashankprsharma@gmail.com

Romil Rawat, Rajesh Kumar Chakrawarti, Sanjaya Kumar Sarangi, Piyush Vyas, Mary Sowjanya Alamanda, Kotagiri Srividya and Krishnan Sakthidasan Sankaran (eds.) Conversational Artificial Intelligence, (655–674) © 2024 Scrivener Publishing LLC

accurate and correct response to them. They use natural language processing (NLP) and machine learning (ML) algorithms to understand and respond to user queries conversationally. Chatbots can be integrated into messaging platforms, websites, mobile apps, and other digital channels to provide automated customer support, assistance, and information to users. Some chatbots are rule-based, meaning they use pre-defined scripts and decision trees to respond to user queries, while others use ML algorithms to learn from past interactions and improve their responses over time. Chatbots are widely used in customer service, e-commerce, healthcare, finance, and other industries to improve customer engagement and streamline business processes.

Chatbots can be classified into different categories based on their functionality and design. Some types of chatbots are:

- Scripted chatbots: These chatbots follow a pre-defined script and provide answers to specific questions asked by the user. They are often used for basic customer support or information retrieval tasks.
- AI-powered chatbots: These chatbots use natural language processing (NLP) and machine learning (ML) algorithms to learn from user interactions and provide more personalized and context-aware responses. They can easily handle complex queries and provide a human-like communication experience.
- Transactional chatbots: These chatbots are designed to handle specific transactions, such as booking a flight or ordering food. They often integrate with third-party APIs to provide a seamless transactional experience.

Some types of chatbots are:

- Voice bots
- Hybrid chatbots
- Social messaging chatbots
- Menu-based chatbots
- Skill chatbots
- Keyword-based chatbots.

These are just a few examples of the types of chatbots that exist. As technology continues to evolve, we can expect to see even more specialized and sophisticated chatbots in different industries and domains. Figure 36.1 shows the variety of functions that you can use in a chatbot.

Chatbots can be implemented using different technologies and platforms, such as Facebook Messenger, WhatsApp, Slack, or custom chatbot frameworks. They can also be integrated with other AI technologies, such as speech recognition or image recognition, to provide a more comprehensive user experience.

The benefits of chatbots include 24/7 availability, instant response times, reduced response times, cost savings, and improved customer engagement. However, they also have some limitations, such as limited domain knowledge, an inability to handle complex tasks, and a lack of emotional intelligence. As such, it is important to carefully design and implement chatbots to ensure that they meet user needs and provide a positive user experience.

One of the key advantages of chatbots is their ability to automate routine tasks and reduce the workload of human customer support representatives. This can result in significant cost savings for businesses and faster response times for users. In addition, chatbots can be programmed to handle multiple conversations simultaneously, which can further improve efficiency and scalability.

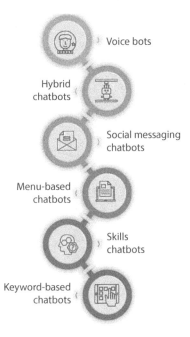

Voice bots

Hybrid chatbots

Social messaging chatbots

Menu-based chatbots

Skills chatbots

Keyword-based chatbots

Figure 36.1 There is a variety of functions that you can use in a chatbot.

Another benefit of chatbots is their ability to improve customer engagement and satisfaction. By providing personalized and context-aware responses to user queries, chatbots can create a more positive user experience and increase customer loyalty. Chatbots can also be used to collect feedback and data from users, which can be used to improve business processes and products.

However, chatbots also have some limitations and challenges. One of the main challenges is ensuring that chatbots can understand and respond to a wide range of user queries and preferences. This requires sophisticated natural language processing algorithms and the ability to learn from past interactions. In addition, chatbots need to be designed to handle unexpected or ambiguous queries and provide appropriate error messages when they are unable to provide a satisfactory response.

Another challenge with chatbots is maintaining user trust and confidence [1]. If a chatbot provides incorrect or misleading information or is unable to handle a user's request, this can lead to frustration and mistrust. As such, it is important to design chatbots that are transparent about their limitations and capabilities and to provide clear communication channels for users to escalate issues or provide feedback.

Overall, chatbots are a powerful tool for improving customer engagement and streamlining business processes. However, their success depends on careful design and implementation, as well as ongoing monitoring and improvement to ensure that they are meeting user needs and providing a positive user experience. Figure 36.2 shows a rule-based chatbot working according to a set of predefined rules.

Application of Chatbot [2, 3]:

- Customer service: Chatbots can be used to provide 24/7 customer service support, handle inquiries, and resolve issues.

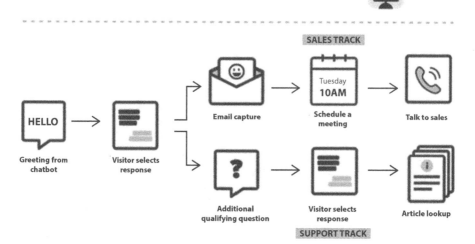

Figure 36.2 A rule-based chatbot working by a set of predefined rules.

- E-commerce: Chatbots can be used to assist with online shopping by providing product recommendations and assisting with the checkout process.
- Healthcare: Chatbots can be used to assist with healthcare-related tasks, such as scheduling appointments, providing health advice, and reminding patients to take medication.
- Banking: Chatbots can be used to assist with banking-related tasks, such as checking account balances, transferring funds, and applying for loans.
- Travel and tourism: Chatbots can be used to assist with travel-related tasks, such as booking flights and hotels, providing travel recommendations, and answering queries.
- Education: Chatbots can be used to assist with educational tasks such as providing tutoring services, answering questions, and grading assignments.
- Human resources: Chatbots can be used to assist with HR-related tasks, such as scheduling interviews, providing job recommendations, and answering questions about employee benefits.
- Insurance: Chatbots can be used to assist with insurance-related tasks such as filing claims, answering questions about coverage, and providing quotes.
- Entertainment: Chatbots can be used to provide entertainment services such as playing games, telling jokes, and providing personalized recommendations for movies and TV shows.
- Real estate: Chatbots can be used to assist with real estate-related tasks, such as property searches, scheduling viewings, and providing information about listings.

An intelligent virtual assistant (IVA) [4] is a software program that uses artificial intelligence (AI) technologies, such as natural language processing (NLP) and machine learning (ML), to provide personalized assistance and support to users. IVAs can interact with users through multiple channels, including voice, text, and chat interfaces, and can be integrated with a variety of devices and platforms, such as smartphones, smart speakers, and web browsers.

IVAs are designed to provide a more human-like and natural interaction with users than traditional chatbots or automated customer support systems. They can understand and interpret user requests and provide context-aware responses based on their understanding of the user's preferences, past behavior, and other contextual factors. IVAs can also learn and adapt to user behavior over time, improving the accuracy and relevance of their responses.

IVAs are used in a variety of industries, including healthcare, finance, retail, and customer service, to provide personalized assistance and support to users. For example, an IVA in healthcare might be used to provide patients with personalized health advice, medication reminders, and appointment scheduling. In finance, an IVA might be used to help customers with account management, investment advice, and financial planning. In customer service, an IVA might be used to provide instant support and assistance to users, helping to resolve issues and answer questions in real time.

Overall, IVAs are a powerful tool for improving user engagement and satisfaction, reducing response times, and streamlining business processes. However, like chatbots, IVAs require careful design and implementation to ensure that they meet user needs and provide a positive user experience.

IVAs can be classified into different categories based on their functionality and design. Some common types of IVAs include:

Personal assistants: These IVAs [5, 6] are designed to provide personalized assistance to individuals, such as scheduling appointments, setting reminders, and providing recommendations based on the user's preferences and past behavior.

Customer service assistants: These IVAs are used to provide instant support and assistance to customers, helping to resolve issues and answer questions in real time. They can handle a wide range of queries and are often integrated with customer service platforms, such as chat systems and ticketing systems.

Enterprise assistants: These IVAs are used to improve business processes and productivity within organizations. They can help employees with tasks such as scheduling meetings, accessing company information, and completing administrative tasks.

IVAs can be implemented using a variety of AI technologies and platforms, such as Amazon Alexa, Google Assistant, and Microsoft Cortana. They can also be customized and integrated with other software systems to provide a seamless user experience. IVAs can be trained and optimized using machine learning algorithms to improve their accuracy and relevance over time.

One of the key advantages of IVAs is their ability to provide personalized assistance and support to users. By understanding and interpreting user requests and preferences, IVAs can provide more accurate and relevant responses, leading to a more positive user experience. In addition, IVAs can automate routine tasks and processes, reducing the workload of human employees and improving efficiency and productivity.

However, IVAs also have some limitations and challenges. One of the main challenges is ensuring that IVAs can understand and interpret user requests accurately and provide appropriate responses. This requires sophisticated natural language processing algorithms and the ability to learn and adapt to user behavior over time. In addition, IVAs need to be designed to handle unexpected or ambiguous queries and provide appropriate error messages when they are unable to provide a satisfactory response.

Another challenge with IVAs is maintaining user trust and confidence. If an IVA provides incorrect or misleading information or is unable to handle a user's request, this can lead to frustration and mistrust. As such, it is important to design IVAs that are transparent about their limitations and capabilities and to provide clear communication channels for users to escalate issues or provide feedback.

Overall, IVAs are a powerful tool for improving user engagement and streamlining business processes. However, their success depends on careful design and implementation, as well as ongoing monitoring and improvement to ensure that they are meeting user needs and providing a positive user experience.

Applications of Intelligent Virtual Assistance [7]:

- > Personalized customer service: IVAs can be used to provide personalized customer service by understanding customers' preferences, purchase history, and behavior to provide personalized recommendations and resolve issues.
- > Healthcare: IVAs can be used to provide healthcare-related services, such as triaging patients, scheduling appointments, providing medication reminders, and answering health-related queries.
- > Banking and finance: IVAs can be used to assist with banking and finance-related tasks, such as helping customers with account management, providing financial advice, and processing transactions.
- > Sales and marketing: IVAs can be used to enhance sales and marketing efforts by engaging with customers, providing product recommendations, and answering questions about products and services.
- > Human resources: IVAs can be used to assist with human resources-related tasks, such as onboarding new employees, providing training, and answering questions about company policies.
- > Education: IVAs can be used to assist with educational tasks such as providing personalized learning experiences, answering questions, and providing tutoring services.
- > Travel and hospitality: IVAs can be used to assist with travel and hospitality-related tasks, such as booking reservations, providing travel recommendations, and assisting with customer service issues.
- > Insurance: IVAs can be used to assist with insurance-related tasks, such as processing claims, answering questions about coverage, and providing quotes.
- > Government services: IVAs can be used to assist with government services, such as answering questions about government programs and providing assistance with tax filings.
- > Manufacturing: IVAs can be used to assist with manufacturing-related tasks, such as providing production processes, scheduling maintenance, and providing troubleshooting support.

Type of Intelligent Virtual Assistance [8, 9]:

- Personal IVA: These IVAs are designed to assist individuals with personal tasks such as scheduling appointments, setting reminders, and making phone calls.
- Enterprise IVA: These IVAs are designed to assist businesses with customer service, HR, and other enterprise-related tasks.

- Healthcare IVA: These IVAs are designed to assist patients with healthcare-related queries, such as medication reminders, symptom checking, and appointment scheduling.
- Financial IVA: These IVAs are designed to assist customers with financial queries, such as account management, bill payments, and investment advice.
- Retail IVA: These IVAs are designed to assist customers with shopping queries, such as product recommendations, order tracking, and returns.
- Travel IVA: These IVAs are designed to assist customers with travel-related queries, such as flight bookings, hotel reservations, and travel itineraries.
- Education IVA: These IVAs are designed to assist students and educators with educational tasks such as homework help, lesson planning, and course registration.
- Government IVA: These IVAs are designed to assist citizens with government-related queries, such as tax information, public services, and emergency response.
- Smart home IVA: These IVAs are designed to assist homeowners with home automation and smart home devices, such as controlling lights, thermostats, and security systems.
- Automotive IVA: These IVAs are designed to assist drivers with in-car infotainment and navigation systems, such as providing directions, playing music, and answering queries.
- Legal IVA: These IVAs are designed to assist lawyers and legal professionals with legal research, document drafting, and case management.
- Marketing IVA: These IVAs are designed to assist marketers with marketing-related tasks such as lead generation, customer segmentation, and campaign optimization.
- Gaming IVA: These IVAs are designed to enhance the gaming experience by providing personalized recommendations, game tips, and in-game assistance.
- Real estate IVA: These IVAs are designed to assist with real estate-related tasks, such as property searches, mortgage applications, and property management.
- Fitness IVA: These IVAs are designed to assist with fitness-related tasks, such as creating workout plans, tracking fitness goals, and providing health advice.

Key Difference between Chatbot and Intelligent Virtual Assistance [10–12]

- Scope: Chatbots are typically designed for a narrow scope of tasks, while IVAs are designed to handle more complex tasks across multiple domains.
- Intelligence: IVAs use advanced natural language processing and machine learning algorithms to provide personalized responses, while chatbots may rely on pre-programmed responses.
- Integration: IVAs are often integrated with backend systems and data sources, while chatbots may operate independently.
- Flexibility: IVAs are designed to be more flexible than chatbots, able to handle a wider range of inputs and respond to changing situations.
- Personalization: IVAs are designed to provide personalized assistance to users, while chatbots may provide a more generic response.

- ▶ Complexity: IVAs are designed to handle complex tasks that may require multiple steps and decision-making, while chatbots may be limited in their ability to handle more complex tasks.
- ▶ Proactivity: IVAs are often proactive, offering suggestions and recommendations to users based on their behavior and preferences, while chatbots may be more reactive.
- ▶ Natural language understanding: IVAs are better equipped to understand natural language and context, while chatbots may struggle with complex language and nuances.
- ▶ Human-like interaction: IVAs are designed to provide a more human-like interaction, using natural language and empathy to engage with users, while chatbots may be more robotic and less personable.
- ▶ Customer engagement: IVAs are designed to enhance customer engagement and satisfaction, while chatbots may be more focused on providing a functional service.
- ▶ Multi-modal interaction: IVAs can handle multi-modal interactions, such as voice, text, and touch, while chatbots are often limited to text-based interactions.
- ▶ Contextual awareness: IVAs can maintain context across multiple interactions and understand the user's intent and preferences, while chatbots may not be able to maintain context as well.
- ▶ Decision-making: IVAs are designed to make decisions based on user data and behavior, while chatbots may not have the ability to make decisions on their own.
- ▶ Problem-solving: IVAs are equipped to solve complex problems and provide recommendations based on user data, while chatbots may be limited in their ability to provide in-depth solutions.
- ▶ Integration with other technologies: IVAs can be integrated with other technologies, such as machine learning and artificial intelligence, to enhance their capabilities, while chatbots may not have the same level of integration with other technologies.

36.2   Related Work [13]

The field of conversational agents has seen significant advancements in recent years, particularly in the areas of chatbots and intelligent virtual assistants (IVAs). Chatbots are computer programs designed to simulate conversation with human users, while IVAs are more sophisticated systems that can understand natural language queries and provide personalized assistance.

Several studies have compared the performance of chatbots and IVAs in different contexts, such as customer service, healthcare, and education. While chatbots are often limited to providing scripted responses, IVAs can use machine learning and artificial intelligence algorithms to learn from user interactions and provide more personalized and contextualized assistance.

One study found that IVAs outperformed chatbots in terms of user satisfaction and task completion rates in a customer service setting. Another study found that IVAs were more effective than chatbots in supporting student learning in an educational context.

However, despite the advantages of IVAs, they are often more expensive and time-consuming to develop and maintain than chatbots. Additionally, the effectiveness of both chatbots and IVAs is highly dependent on their design, implementation, and integration with existing systems.

Overall, the literature suggests that both chatbots and IVAs have their unique strengths and weaknesses, and the choice between them depends on the specific use case and the resources available for development and deployment.

Another important consideration when comparing chatbots and IVAs is the level of human involvement required to maintain and improve their performance. Chatbots are often designed to be fully automated and require minimal human intervention, while IVAs may require more human oversight and training [14] to ensure accurate and personalized assistance.

In terms of technical capabilities, IVAs are often equipped with natural language processing (NLP) [15] and machine learning algorithms that allow them to understand and interpret user queries in a more sophisticated manner than chatbots. IVAs can also integrate with other systems and databases to provide personalized recommendations and insights based on user data.

On the other hand, chatbots are often more straightforward to implement, making them a popular choice for businesses and organizations looking to quickly deploy conversational agents without significant investment in resources and infrastructure.

Overall, the choice between chatbots and IVAs ultimately depends on the specific use case and the desired level of sophistication and personalization required for the conversational agent. While IVAs may offer more advanced features and capabilities, chatbots can be a more cost-effective and efficient option for certain applications. Table 36.1 shows the technique comparisons.

Table 36.1 Technique comparisons.

S. no.	Title	Author	Date
1	A comparison of Chatbots and Intelligent Virtual Assistance in customer service	Kim	2018
2	A survey of Intelligent Virtual Assistance and Chatbots in healthcare	Nguyen	2020
3	Comparing the effectiveness of IVA and Chatbot in Financial services	Chen [1]	2018
4	Comparison of Chatbots and IVA in educational settings	Smith [2]	2020
5	A systematic review of Chatbots and IVA in various domains	Kumar [3]	2019

36.3   Problem Statement

The rapid growth of chatbot and intelligent virtual assistance (IVA) technologies has led to widespread adoption in various industries for enhancing customer experiences and improving operational efficiency. However, there is a lack of clarity on the differences between chatbots and IVAs, their respective strengths and limitations, and their effectiveness in different applications. This lack of clarity can make it challenging for organizations to make informed decisions on the adoption of these technologies and to design effective solutions for their specific needs. Thus, this research paper aims to address this gap by conducting a systematic review of the existing literature on chatbots and IVA and performing a comparative analysis of their features, limitations, and effectiveness in enhancing customer experience in different industries. The proposed research will help organizations better understand the differences between chatbots and IVAs and make informed decisions on their adoption and use.

Despite the growing popularity of chatbots and intelligent virtual assistance (IVA) technologies, there is still a lack of consensus on their definitions, features, and applications. This lack of clarity can create confusion for organizations seeking to implement these technologies and hinder their ability to realize their full potential benefits. Additionally, there is limited research on the comparative effectiveness of chatbots and IVAs in different industries and use cases. Therefore, the purpose of this research paper is to provide a comprehensive review of the literature on chatbots and IVAs, including their definitions, features, and applications, as well as a comparative analysis of their effectiveness in improving customer experience in various industries. The proposed research will provide valuable insights into the differences between chatbots and IVAs, and help organizations make more informed decisions on their implementation and use.

Some Problems are:

1. Organizations across various industries are adopting chatbots and intelligent virtual assistance (IVA) technologies to improve customer service, reduce costs, and enhance the customer experience. However, there is a lack of clarity on the differences between these two technologies, their respective strengths and limitations, and their effectiveness in various applications.

2. While chatbots and intelligent virtual assistance (IVA) have become increasingly popular in various industries, there is a lack of consensus on the best practices for designing and implementing these technologies. As a result, many organizations struggle to achieve the desired outcomes from their chatbot and IVA initiatives.

3. Lack of clarity: As the field of AI and NLP continues to evolve, there is often a lack of clarity in the definitions and features of chatbots and intelligent virtual assistance. This can lead to confusion and inconsistencies in their applications and evaluation.

4. Data privacy and security: As chatbots and IVAs are designed to interact with users and collect personal data, there are concerns regarding data privacy and security. It is important to ensure that these technologies comply with regulations such as GDPR and CCPA and that user data is protected from misuse or breaches.

5. Integration and compatibility: Chatbots and IVA are often deployed in conjunction with other systems, such as CRM or ERP. However, compatibility issues can arise between different software and hardware systems, which can limit the effectiveness of these technologies.
6. User acceptance: Chatbots and IVA are still relatively new technologies, and some users may be hesitant to interact with them. Factors such as ease of use, trustworthiness, and effectiveness can impact user acceptance and adoption.
7. Ethical considerations: The use of chatbot and IVAs raises ethical concerns related to issues such as bias, transparency, and accountability. It is important to consider the ethical implications of these technologies in the design and deployment processes.

36.4 Proposed Methodology

1. This research paper aims to address the lack of clarity on chatbots and IVAs by comparing their features, limitations, and effectiveness in enhancing customer experiences in different industries. The proposed solution is to conduct a systematic review of the existing literature on chatbots and IVAs and to perform a comparative analysis of their use in various applications.

   The study will involve a comprehensive literature search of academic journals, conference proceedings, and industry reports. Relevant studies will be analyzed and synthesized to identify common themes, trends, and gaps in the literature. A comparative analysis will then be conducted to compare and contrast the features, limitations, and effectiveness of chatbots and IVAs in different industries, such as healthcare, e-commerce, and banking.

   The proposed solution aims to provide a comprehensive understanding of the differences between chatbots and IVAs, their respective strengths and limitations, and their effectiveness in various applications. The findings of the study will help organizations make informed decisions on the adoption of chatbot and IVA technologies and guide future research and development in the field.

2. The objective of this research paper is to identify the best practices for designing and implementing chatbots and IVA technologies. The proposed solution is to conduct a qualitative case study analysis of successful chatbot and IVA implementations in various industries.

   The study will involve a multi-case analysis of organizations that have successfully implemented chatbot and IVA technologies. Data will be collected through interviews with key stakeholders, observation of chatbot and IVA interactions, and review of relevant documentation. The collected data will be analyzed using qualitative analysis methods to identify the best practices for designing and implementing chatbot and IVA technologies.

   The proposed solution aims to provide practical insights and recommendations for organizations that are considering or currently implementing chatbot and IVA technologies. By identifying the best practices for chatbot and IVA implementation, the study can help organizations avoid common pitfalls and increase the likelihood of success. The findings of the study can also guide future research and development in the field and contribute to the overall understanding of chatbot and IVA technologies.

3. Clearly define and compare the features and capabilities of chatbots and IVAs in terms of their natural language processing (NLP), machine learning (ML), and cognitive computing abilities. This will help clarify their respective strengths and limitations and facilitate more accurate comparisons.

4. Develop and implement strong data privacy and security policies and protocols that are compliant with relevant regulations such as GDPR and CCPA. This includes securing user data through encryption, anonymization, and other best practices, as well as providing transparency and user control over data collection and use.

5. Identify compatibility issues between chatbots, IVAs, and other software/ hardware systems and propose solutions for ensuring seamless integration and compatibility.

6. Investigate user attitudes towards chatbot and IVA technologies and propose design principles that enhance user experience, trust, and adoption.

7. Analyze the ethical implications of chatbot and IVA technologies and propose ethical guidelines and best practices for ensuring fairness, transparency, and accountability.

36.5   Regulatory Landscape

- Data protection and privacy: Chatbot and IVA interactions often involve the processing of personal data, which is regulated by data protection and privacy laws such as the General Data Protection Regulation (GDPR) in the European Union, the California Consumer Privacy Act (CCPA) in the United States, and the Personal Data Protection Act (PDPA) in Singapore. Organizations must ensure that their chatbot and IVA technologies comply with these regulations and that users' data is handled securely.

- Advertising and marketing: Chatbots and IVA technologies are often used for advertising and marketing purposes, which may be subject to industry-specific regulations. For example, in the United States, the Federal Trade Commission (FTC) has issued guidelines on how chatbots and IVA technologies can be used for advertising and marketing without misleading consumers.

- Financial services: In the financial services industry, chatbot and IVA technologies may be subject to regulations such as the Payment Services Directive (PSD2) in the European Union and the Consumer Financial Protection Bureau (CFPB) regulations in the United States. Organizations using chatbots and IVA technologies in this industry must ensure compliance with these regulations.

- Healthcare: In the healthcare industry, chatbots and IVA technologies may be subject to regulations such as the Health Insurance Portability and Accountability Act (HIPAA) in the United States, which regulates the privacy and security of patients' personal health information. Organizations using chatbots and IVA technologies in healthcare must ensure compliance with these regulations.

- Intellectual property: Chatbots and IVA technologies may be subject to intellectual property laws, such as patents and trademarks. Organizations using chatbots and IVA technologies must ensure that they are not infringing on any existing patents or trademarks.

- Telecommunications: In some countries, chatbot and IVA technologies may be subject to telecommunications regulations, which govern the use of voice and messaging services. For example, in the United States, the Federal Communications Commission (FCC) regulates the use of voice services, including chatbots and IVA technologies.

- Accessibility: Chatbot and IVA technologies may be subject to accessibility regulations that require them to be accessible to individuals with disabilities. For example, in the United States, the Americans with Disabilities Act (ADA) requires that public accommodations, including websites and mobile apps, be accessible to individuals with disabilities.

- Consumer protection: Chatbots and IVA technologies may be subject to consumer protection laws that prohibit unfair and deceptive practices. For example, in the United States, the FTC enforces consumer protection laws and has acted against companies using chatbots and IVA technologies to deceive consumers.

- Employment and labor law: In some industries, chatbot and IVA technologies may be used to interact with employees, which may be subject to employment and labor laws. For example, in the United States, the National Labor Relations Act (NLRA) protects employees' rights to engage in protected concerted activity, which may include communicating with chatbots and IVA technologies.

- International trade: Organizations using chatbot and IVA technologies for international trade must ensure compliance with international trade regulations and export control laws, such as the International Traffic in Arms Regulations (ITAR) in the United States, which regulate the export of defense articles and services.

36.6   Future Works

- Integration of chatbot and IVA: One possible direction for future work is to investigate ways to integrate chatbot and IVA technologies. This could involve combining the strengths of each technology to create a more comprehensive and versatile virtual assistant that can handle a wider range of tasks and interact with users in a more natural and intuitive manner.

- Natural language processing: Advances in natural language processing (NLP) technology could be leveraged to improve the ability of chatbots and IVA technologies to understand and respond to user requests. Future research could explore ways to enhance NLP algorithms, such as incorporating machine learning and deep learning techniques to improve accuracy and efficiency.

- Personalization: Another potential direction for future work is to develop chatbot and IVA technologies that are more personalized to individual users. This could involve using data analytics and machine learning to learn more about each user's preferences, habits, and behavior patterns, allowing the virtual assistant to tailor its responses and recommendations accordingly.

- Multimodal interactions: Future research could also explore ways to enable chatbot and IVA technologies to interact with users using multiple modalities, such as voice, text, and images. This could enhance the user experience by allowing users to communicate in the way that feels most natural and intuitive to them.

- Ethical considerations: As chatbot and IVA technologies become more prevalent and sophisticated, there is a need to consider the ethical implications of their use. Future work could explore ways to ensure that these technologies are used in a responsible and ethical manner, such as by addressing issues of bias, privacy, and transparency.

- Contextual understanding: Future research could explore ways to improve chatbot and IVA technologies' ability to understand the context of user requests. This could involve developing algorithms that can analyze and interpret user data, such as location, time, and past interactions, to provide more relevant and personalized responses.

- Emotion recognition: Emotion recognition technology is becoming increasingly sophisticated and could be leveraged to enhance chatbot and IVA interactions. Future research could explore ways to incorporate emotion recognition algorithms to enable virtual assistants to recognize and respond to users' emotional states.

- Collaboration with humans: Another possible direction for future work is to investigate ways to enable chatbot and IVA technologies to collaborate with humans in real-time. This could involve developing hybrid models that combine human and machine intelligence to solve complex problems and provide more comprehensive support.

- Evaluation and metrics: As chatbot and IVA technologies continue to evolve, there is a need to develop standard metrics and evaluation methods to assess their performance and effectiveness. Future research could explore ways to develop robust evaluation methods that can measure the impact of chatbot and IVA technologies on user satisfaction, productivity, and other key metrics.

- User experience design: One area of future research could focus on improving the user experience of chatbots and IVA technologies. This could involve exploring ways to make the interactions with these virtual assistants more engaging, intuitive, and personalized.

- Security and privacy: As chatbot and IVA technologies become more prevalent, there is a need to ensure that they are secure and protect users' privacy. Future work could explore ways to enhance the security of these technologies, such as by incorporating encryption and multi-factor authentication, and to ensure that they comply with relevant privacy laws and regulations.

- Scalability: As the use of chatbot and IVA technologies grows, it becomes important to ensure that they can scale effectively to meet increasing demand. Future research could explore ways to improve the scalability of these technologies, such as using cloud-based infrastructure and automation tools.
- Industry-specific applications: Chatbot and IVA technologies have numerous potential applications in a variety of industries, such as healthcare, finance, and education. Future work could focus on exploring the use of these technologies in specific industries and identifying the unique challenges and opportunities associated with each.
- Human-in-the-loop: Despite the advances in chatbot and IVA technologies, there are still many scenarios where human intervention is necessary. Future research could explore ways to integrate human experts into the chatbot and IVA workflows, either by incorporating human oversight or by providing users with the option to interact with a live agent if necessary.
- Hybrid approaches: As chatbots and IVAs have different strengths and weaknesses, future research could explore the use of hybrid approaches that combine the best aspects of both technologies. For example, chatbots could be used for initial interactions and simple tasks, while IVAs could be used for more complex interactions.
- Multilingual support: As businesses become increasingly global, there is a growing need for chatbots and IVAs to support multiple languages. Future research could explore ways to improve the accuracy and naturalness of interactions in different languages and develop tools and techniques to facilitate multilingual support.
- Ethical considerations: As chatbots and IVAs become more ubiquitous, there is a growing need to address ethical concerns such as privacy, security, and bias. Future research could explore ways to ensure that these technologies are developed and deployed in an ethical and equitable way.
- Integration with other technologies: Chatbots and IVAs can be integrated with a range of other technologies, such as artificial intelligence, natural language processing, and machine learning. Future research could explore how these technologies can be combined to create more powerful and effective virtual assistants.
- User experience design: As chatbots and IVAs become more prevalent, there is a growing need to design user experiences that are engaging, intuitive, and satisfying. Future research could explore ways to improve the design of chatbots and IVAs to enhance the user experience and develop metrics to measure the effectiveness of these designs.

A chatbot, [16, 17] often known as an intelligent VA (Virtual Assistant) [18, 19], is just a piece of software that mimics human communication. This communication might take place verbally or in writing. Natural language processing (NLP) [20–22], is used by these automated VA programmes to converse with consumers like a real person would. Cyberattacks [23–26] on these automated systems have increased because of the growing trend of organisations using VAs. Let's take a broader view of this: the whole point of using chatbots is to offer efficient, personalised customer care that is available around the clock.

Although AI [27] has the ability to assist in thwarting these new dangers [28], it also carries a number of concerns. For instance, computers with powerful processing power [29, 30] might break into systems more quickly and successfully than people. We must make sure AI is deployed defensively and with a clear grasp of who is in control in order to combat [31] these dangers. It's critical for politicians, judges, and other decision-makers [32] to comprehend AI and its ramifications as the technology becomes more deeply ingrained in society. In order to successfully navigate the future of AI in threat [33, 34] hunting and beyond, it will be essential to forge strong partnerships between technical experts and politicians.

36.7   Conclusion

The use of virtual assistants, whether in the form of chatbots or intelligent virtual assistants (IVAs), has gained significant traction in recent years, providing users with a range of benefits such as increased convenience, faster response times, and improved customer service. However, as the technology continues to evolve and become more sophisticated, there are still many challenges to be addressed, such as improving the accuracy and naturalness of interactions, ensuring privacy and security, and addressing ethical concerns.

In this paper, we compared chatbot and IVA technologies in terms of their features, capabilities, and applications. While chatbots are typically better suited for handling simple, rule-based tasks, IVAs are designed to handle more complex, dynamic interactions that require more advanced AI capabilities. We also discussed the regulatory landscape for chatbots and IVAs, highlighting the need to ensure compliance with relevant privacy and security laws.

Overall, the development of chatbot and IVA technologies is still in its early stages, and there is significant room for further research and development. Future work could focus on integrating these technologies, enhancing the user experience, improving scalability, and addressing ethical concerns. By addressing these challenges, virtual assistants have the potential to revolutionize the way we interact with technology and provide significant benefits to businesses and consumers alike.

The emergence of chatbots and IVAs has disrupted traditional ways of customer service delivery, providing an opportunity for organizations to increase efficiency and productivity and reduce costs. However, it is important for businesses to carefully consider which technology is best suited for their needs, considering factors such as the complexity of interactions, the level of personalization required, and the user demographic.

While chatbots and IVAs have already been adopted by various industries, there is still significant potential for their use in many more areas. For example, chatbots could be used in the education sector to provide personalized learning experiences, while IVAs could be used to improve patient care in the healthcare sector.

The field of chatbot and IVA development is rapidly evolving, with new technologies and tools being developed all the time. As a result, it is important for researchers and practitioners to stay up-to-date with the latest trends and best practices in this field to maximize the benefits of these technologies.

Finally, it is important to note that chatbots and IVAs are not a replacement for human interaction but rather an augmentation of it. While these technologies can help streamline interactions and improve efficiency, there will always be situations where a human touch is necessary. Therefore, it is important to strike a balance between automated and human interactions to achieve the best results.

References

1. Wahde, M. and Virgolin, M., Conversational agents: Theory and applications, Feb. 07, 2022, doi: 10.1142/9789811246050_0012.
2. Ekbal, A., Towards building an affect-aware dialogue agent with deep neural networks. *CSIT*, 8, 2, 249–255, Jun. 2020, doi: 10.1007/s40012-020-00304-5.
3. Inam, I.A., Azeta, A.A., Daramola, O., Comparative analysis and review of interactive voice response systems, in: *2017 Conference on Information Communication Technology and Society (ICTAS)*, Mar. 2017, pp. 1–6, doi: 10.1109/ICTAS.2017.7920660.
4. Følstad, A. and Brandtzæg, P.B., Chatbots and the new world of HCI. *Interactions*, 24, 4, 38–42, Jun. 2017, doi: 10.1145/3085558.
5. What is AI? / Basic questions, http://jmc.stanford.edu/artificial-intelligence/what-is-ai/index.html.
6. Conversational AI is reshaping the human-machine interaction, Deloitte China | Innovation, Deloitte China, https://www2.deloitte.com/cn/en/pages/innovation/articles/innovation-con-versational-ai-is-reshaping-the-human-machine-interaction.html.
7. Molnár, G. and Szüts, Z., The role of chatbots in formal education, in: *2018 IEEE 16th International Symposium on Intelligent Systems and Informatics (SISY)*, Sep. 2018, pp. 000197–000202, doi: 10.1109/SISY.2018.8524609.
8. Adiwardana, D. et al., Towards a human-like open-domain chatbot, arXiv, Feb. 27, 2020, doi: 10.48550/arXiv.2001.09977.
9. Shuster, K. et al., BlenderBot 3: A deployed conversational agent that continually learns to responsibly engage, arXiv, Aug. 10, 2022, doi: 10.48550/arXiv.2208.03188.
10. Navigli, R., Natural language understanding: Instructions for (present and future) use, in: *Proceedings of the Twenty-Seventh International Joint Conference on Artificial Intelligence*, Stockholm, Sweden, Jul. 2018, pp. 5697–5702, doi: 10.24963/ijcai.2018/812.
11. Dong, C. *et al.*, A survey of natural language generation. *ACM Comput. Surv.*, 55, 8, 173:1–173:38, Dec. 2022, doi: 10.1145/3554727.
12. Anand, D., The review of natural language processing (technology to communicate and understand the contents through human languages). *AIP Conf. Proc.*, 2555, 1, 050015, Oct. 2022, doi: 10.1063/5.0109799.
13. Bocklisch, T., Faulkner, J., Pawlowski, N., Nichol, A., Rasa: Open source language understanding and dialogue management, arXiv, Dec. 15, 2017, doi: 10.48550/arXiv.1712.05181.
14. Bunk, T., Varshneya, D., Vlasov, V., Nichol, A., DIET: Lightweight language understanding for dialogue systems, arXiv, May 11, 2020. [Online]. Available: http://arxiv.org/abs/2004.09936.
15. Floridi, L. and Chiriatti, M., GPT-3: Its nature, scope, limits, and consequences. *Minds Mach.*, 30, 4, 681–694, Dec. 2020, doi: 10.1007/s11023-020-09548-1.
16. Mahor, V., Bijrothiya, S., Rawat, R., Kumar, A., Garg, B., Pachlasiya, K., IoT and artificial intelligence techniques for public safety and security, in: *Smart Urban Computing Applications*, p. 111, 2023.
17. Mahor, V., Pachlasiya, K., Garg, B., Chouhan, M., Telang, S., Rawat, R., Mobile operating system (Android) vulnerability analysis using machine learning, in: *Proceedings of International Conference on Network Security and Blockchain Technology: ICNSBT 2021*, 2022, June, Springer Nature Singapore, Singapore, pp. 159–169.

18. Rawat, R., Garg, B., Pachlasiya, K., Mahor, V., Telang, S., Chouhan, M., Mishra, R., SCNTA: Monitoring of network availability and activity for identification of anomalies using machine learning approaches. *Int. J. Inf. Technol. Web Eng. (IJITWE)*, 17, 1, 1–19, 2022.

19. Rawat, R., Rimal, Y.N., William, P., Dahima, S., Gupta, S., Sankaran, K.S., Malware threat affecting financial organization analysis using machine learning approach. *Int. J. Inf. Technol. Web Eng. (IJITWE)*, 17, 1, 1–20, 2022.

20. Rawat, R., Mahor, V., Chouhan, M., Pachlasiya, K., Telang, S., Garg, B., Systematic literature review (SLR) on social media and the digital transformation of drug trafficking on darkweb, in: *International Conference on Network Security and Blockchain Technology*, Springer, Singapore, pp. 181–205, 2022.

21. Rawat, R., Ayodele Oki, O., Sankaran, S., Florez, H., Ajagbe, S.A., Techniques for predicting dark web events focused on the delivery of illicit products and ordered crime. *Int. J. Electr. Comput. Eng. (IJECE)*, 13, 5, 5354–5365, Oct. 2023, doi: 10.11591/ijece.v13i5.pp5354-5365.

22. Rawat, R., Garg, B., Mahor, V., Telang, S., Pachlasiya, K., Chouhan, M., Organ trafficking on the dark web—The data security and privacy concern in healthcare systems, in: *Internet of Healthcare Things: Machine Learning for Security and Privacy*, pp. 189–216, 2022.

23. Vyas, P., Vyas, G., Chauhan, A., Rawat, R., Telang, S., Gottumukkala, M., Anonymous trading on the dark online marketplace: An exploratory study, in: *Using Computational Intelligence for the Dark Web and Illicit Behavior Detection*, pp. 272–289, IGI Global, 2022.

24. Rawat, R., Oki, O.A., Sankaran, K.S., Olasupo, O., Ebong, G.N., Ajagbe, S.A., A new solution for cyber security in big data using machine learning approach, in: *Mobile Computing and Sustainable Informatics: Proceedings of ICMCSI 2023*, Springer Nature Singapore, Singapore, pp. 495–505, 2023.

25. Rawat, R., Chakrawarti, R.K., Raj, A., Mani, G., Chidambarathanu, K., Bhardwaj, R., Association rule learning for threat analysis using traffic analysis and packet filtering approach. *Int. J. Inf. Technol.*, 1–11, 2023.

26. Rawat, R., Logical concept mapping and social media analytics relating to cyber criminal activities for ontology creation. *Int. J. Inf. Technol.*, 15, 2, 893–903, 2023.

27. Rawat, R., Mahor, V., Álvarez, J.D., Ch, F., Cognitive systems for dark web cyber delinquent association malignant data crawling: A review, in: *Handbook of Research on War Policies, Strategies, and Cyber Wars*, pp. 45–63, 2023.

28. Rawat, R., Chakrawarti, R.K., Vyas, P., Gonzáles, J.L.A., Sikarwar, R., Bhardwaj, R., Intelligent fog computing surveillance system for crime and vulnerability identification and tracing. *Int. J. Inf. Secur. Priv. (IJISP)*, 17, 1, 1–25, 2023.

29. Rawat, R., Sowjanya, A.M., Patel, S.I., Jaiswal, V., Khan, I., Balaram, A. (Eds.), *Using Machine Intelligence: Autonomous Vehicles Volume 1*, John Wiley & Sons, 2022.

30. Rawat, R., Mahor, V., Díaz-Álvarez, J., Chávez, F., Rooted learning model at fog computing analysis for crime incident surveillance, in: *2022 International Conference on Smart Generation Computing, Communication and Networking (SMART GENCON)*, 2022, December, pp. 1–9, IEEE.

31. Rawat, R. and Shrivastav, S.K., SQL injection attack detection using SVM. *Int. J. Comput. Appl.*, 42, 13, 1–4, 2012.

32. Rawat, R., Bhardwaj, P., Kaur, U., Telang, S., Chouhan, M., Sankaran, K.S., *Smart vehicles for communication, volume 2*, John Wiley & Sons, 2023.

33. Mahor, V., Garg, B., Telang, S., Pachlasiya, K., Chouhan, M., Rawat, R., Cyber threat phylogeny assessment and vulnerabilities representation at thermal power station, in: *Proceedings of International Conference on Network Security and Blockchain Technology: ICNSBT 2021*, 2022, June, Springer Nature Singapore, Singapore, pp. 28–39.

34. Rawat, R., Gupta, S., Sivaranjani, S., Cu, O.K., Kuliha, M., Sankaran, K.S., Malevolent information crawling mechanism for forming structured illegal organisations in hidden networks. *Int. J. Cyber Warf. Terror. (IJCWT)*, *12*, 1, 1–14, 2022.

Digital Forensics with Emerging Technologies: Vision and Research Potential for Future

Anand Kumar Mishra[1], V. Hemamalini[2] and Amit Kumar Tyagi[3]*

[1]*Computer Science and Engineering, NIIT University, Neemrana, Rajasthan, India*
[2]*Department of Networking and Communications, School of Computing, SRM Institute of Science and Technology, Chennai, India*
[3]*Department of Fashion Technology, National Institute of Fashion Technology, New Delhi, Delhi, India*

Abstract

Digital forensics is a crucial aspect of modern-day investigations (using emerging technologies), with the increasing use of digital devices and technology in everyday life. The integration of artificial intelligence (AI), blockchain, and the Internet of Things (IoT) (as examples of emerging technologies) can revolutionize the field of digital forensics, enhancing the effectiveness and efficiency of investigations. This paper explores the opportunities and challenges of AI, blockchain, and IoT-enabled technology for digital forensics. It discusses how these technologies can be utilized to analyze digital evidence, track and trace the origin of data, and enhance the security and integrity of digital evidence. The paper also examines the issues and challenges that need to be addressed to enable the adoption of these technologies in digital forensics, such as the need for standards, interoperability, and legal and ethical considerations. The paper provides examples of successful applications of AI, blockchain, and IoT in digital forensics, such as the use of AI algorithms to analyze large volumes of data, the use of blockchain to provide secure and transparent storage and sharing of digital evidence, and the use of IoT devices to capture and analyze digital evidence in real-time. In summary, the paper argues that AI, blockchain, and IoT-enabled technology can significantly enhance the capabilities of digital forensics, providing opportunities for more efficient and effective investigations. However, it emphasizes the need for a thoughtful and strategic approach to the adoption of these technologies based on a deep understanding of user needs, ethical considerations, and regulatory requirements.

Keywords: Artificial intelligence, blockchain, Internet of Things, digital forensics, smart era

37.1 Introduction

In the current world, blockchain, the Internet of Things (IoTs), and AI are a few of the major technologies that have rapidly advanced and are emerging technologies that are poised

Corresponding author: amitkrtyagi025@gmail.com; ORCID: https://orcid.org/0000-0003-2657-8700

Romil Rawat, Rajesh Kumar Chakrawarti, Sanjaya Kumar Sarangi, Piyush Vyas, Mary Sowjanya Alamanda, Kotagiri Srividya and Krishnan Sakthidasan Sankaran (eds.) Conversational Artificial Intelligence, (675–698) © 2024 Scrivener Publishing LLC

to revolutionize many areas of modern life, including digital forensics. Digital forensics involves the collection, analysis, and interpretation of electronic data in the context of legal investigations or other types of incidents. The combination of AI, blockchain, and IoT offers several advantages in this field. AI can be used to quickly process large amounts of data and identify patterns that might be missed by human analysts. Blockchain can provide an immutable record of digital transactions and other activities, making it harder for criminals to cover their tracks. Moreover, IoT devices can generate vast amounts of data that can be analyzed to uncover evidence or clues. However, there are also challenges associated with these technologies, including issues related to privacy, security, and data management. For example, the use of AI in digital forensics raises questions about bias and transparency, while blockchain and IoT both require robust security measures to prevent unauthorized access or manipulation of data. Despite these challenges, the potential benefits of using AI, blockchain, and IoT in digital forensics are significant. As these technologies continue to evolve, it is likely that they will play an increasingly important role in investigations and legal proceedings related to digital crimes and other incidents. Now we will discuss each emerging technology in detail.

- AI

Artificial intelligence (AI) is a concept that falls under the broad umbrella of computer science, with a special focus on curating intellectual devices and systems that can carry out chores that would generally require human interference. These include speech recognition, decision-making, etc. AI systems are designed to simulate human intelligence, including reasoning, learning, problem-solving, perception, and natural language processing. They are created utilizing a variety of methods, including computer vision, deep learning, natural language processing, and machine learning. One of the primary goals of AI is to create machines that can think, reason, and learn like humans and perform tasks that would otherwise be difficult or impossible for humans to perform. AI systems can be found in a wide range of applications, including self-driving cars, virtual assistants, recommendation systems, and medical diagnosis tools.

There are various sorts of AI systems, such as narrow AI systems that are created to complete tasks and general AI systems that are created to do any intellectual work that a human can complete. While there are many potential benefits to AI, there are also concerns about its impact on jobs, privacy, and society.

- Blockchain Technology

Blockchain technology is a distributed ledger system with the potential to transform numerous industries. It makes it possible to conduct secure and open transactions without using middlemen, making it a viable option for a variety of applications. With the rise of cryptocurrencies such as bitcoin and ethereum in recent years, blockchain technology has seen widespread use in the financial industry. In summary, blockchain is a distributed ledger system that is decentralized and allows for secure transactions without the involvement of third parties like banks, governments, or other centralized authorities. The system is composed of a network of nodes that verify and keep track of transactions, creating a tamper-proof and immutable record that can be shared across the network. Cryptocurrencies like bitcoin and ethereum, which employ blockchain technology to enable peer-to-peer transactions without the need for a central authority, are among the most well-known implementations of the technology. However, blockchain technology has potential applications beyond just cryptocurrency. It can be utilized, for instance, in voting procedures, supply chain management, and digital identity verification. Smart contracts, which are self-executing contracts with the terms of the agreement between buyer and seller being directly put into lines of code, can also be created using blockchain technology.

In summary, blockchain technology has the potential to disrupt various industries by providing secure and transparent transactions, reducing the need for intermediaries, and increasing efficiency and cost savings. However, there are also challenges to be addressed, such as scalability, interoperability, and regulatory issues.

- IoT

The Internet of Things (IoT) is a network of actual physical objects, or "things," that are connected to the internet and equipped with sensors, connections, electronics, and software. The IoT includes devices such as smart home appliances, wearables, industrial machinery, medical equipment, and more. The concept of IoT is based on the idea that any physical object can be connected to the internet and communicate with other connected devices. This connectivity allows for a wide range of applications, from monitoring and controlling devices remotely to collecting data for analysis and optimization.

IoT technology is made up of several components, including sensors that collect data from the physical world, processors that analyze the data, and communication technologies that enable the devices to exchange information over the internet. IoT devices can be connected through wired or wireless networks, and the data they generate can be stored in the cloud or processed locally.

The potential applications of IoT are vast, from improving efficiency in manufacturing and supply chains to enhancing healthcare through remote patient monitoring. As more devices are connected to the internet, the amount of data generated by the IoT is expected to grow exponentially, creating new opportunities for innovation and improving the way we live and work.

- Cloud Computing

Computational services, which include servers, software, databases, etc., are what cloud computing is all about, and it works on a pay-as-you go basis. In other words, it is a way to access computing resources on-demand rather than having to buy and manage physical hardware and software. Cloud computing is characterized by its flexibility, scalability, and cost-effectiveness. Instead of investing in expensive hardware and software, companies can simply rent resources from cloud service providers and only pay for what they use. This enables businesses to quickly scale up or down their computing resources as needed without incurring the high costs associated with traditional IT infrastructure.

Software as a service (SaaS), platform as a service (PaaS), and infrastructure as a service (IaaS) are the three main types of cloud services. IaaS offers virtualized computing resources, such as servers and storage, while PaaS offers a platform for developing and deploying applications. SaaS offers software applications through the internet. In recent years, cloud computing has grown in popularity, and the three biggest cloud service providers are Amazon Web Services, Microsoft Azure, and Google Cloud Platform. It has revolutionized the way businesses operate by providing them with flexible and cost-effective access to powerful computing resources, enabling them to focus on their core business activities rather than IT infrastructure management.

- AI-based blockchain technology

AI and blockchain technology are two of the most significant technical advances of our time. AI refers to robots' ability to learn and accomplish activities that would normally require human intellect, whereas a distributed ledger system called blockchain technology enables secure and open transactions. The marriage of AI and blockchain technology has the potential to provide tremendous synergy, allowing for the development of decentralized, autonomous systems with enhanced decision-making skills. Among the potential uses of AI-based blockchain technology are [1]:

- Supply Chain Management: AI algorithms can be used to track and analyze data from every stage of the supply chain, while blockchain technology can ensure secure and transparent record-keeping.
- Financial Services: AI algorithms can be used to identify patterns in financial data and make predictions, while blockchain technology can ensure secure and transparent transactions.
- Healthcare: AI algorithms can be used to analyze patient data and make personalized treatment recommendations, while blockchain technology can ensure secure and transparent record-keeping.
- Identity Verification: AI algorithms can be used to analyze biometric data and other identifying information, while blockchain technology can ensure secure and transparent identity verification.

In summary, the combination of AI and blockchain technology has the potential to create innovative solutions to some of the most pressing challenges of our time, such as supply chain transparency, financial inclusion, and healthcare access.

- Blockchain-based IoT devices

Blockchain-based IoT devices are devices that utilize blockchain technology to enhance their security and functionality. Blockchain technology is a decentralized, irreversible ledger that is utilized to record and verify transactions in IoT (Internet of Things) devices, which are connected gadgets that communicate with one another through the internet. When these two technologies are combined, they create a secure and transparent system for data exchange and communication between IoT devices. One of the main benefits of using blockchain technology in IoT devices is the increased security it provides. With traditional centralized systems, data is stored on a single server, making it vulnerable to hacking and data breaches. However, with blockchain technology, data is stored on a distributed network of nodes, making it much more difficult for hackers to compromise the system. In addition to security, blockchain technology also allows for more efficient and transparent communication between IoT devices. By using a decentralized ledger, transactions can be verified and recorded in real-time without the need for intermediaries or middlemen. This can greatly improve the efficiency and speed of communication between IoT devices while also providing greater transparency and accountability [2]. In summary, the combination of blockchain technology and IoT devices has the potential to revolutionize many industries, from healthcare and logistics to energy and manufacturing. By creating a more secure, efficient, and transparent system for communication and data exchange, these technologies can help businesses and organizations streamline their operations and improve their bottom line.

- AI, blockchain, and IoT-based technology
Three quickly developing technologies—artificial intelligence (AI), blockchain, and the Internet of Things (IoT)—have the potential to change businesses and enhance our daily lives.

- Artificial intelligence (AI) is the capacity of machines to carry out operations that ordinarily require human intelligence, such as speech recognition, data interpretation, and decision-making. AI can be applied in many fields, such as healthcare, finance, and transportation, to automate processes and improve efficiency.
- Blockchain is a decentralized digital record that eliminates the need for a middleman and enables safe and transparent transactions. Although it is frequently connected to cryptocurrencies like bitcoin, it is also applicable to other fields, including supply chain management and voting systems.
- The Internet of Things (IoT) is a network of physical objects, including computers, mobile phones, and home appliances, that can exchange and gather data. IoT has the potential to improve many aspects of our lives, such as energy efficiency, healthcare, and home automation.

Together, these technologies can be used to create innovative solutions that can help solve complex problems and create new opportunities for businesses and individuals alike [2]. For example, AI and IoT can be used to create smart homes that can automatically adjust temperature and lighting based on the occupants' preferences, while blockchain can be used to ensure secure and transparent transactions for buying and selling energy credits between homeowners.

- Forensics
Forensics is the scientific study and application of evidence in criminal investigations and legal proceedings. Forensic science involves the collection, analysis, and interpretation of physical and digital evidence to provide evidence in a court of law. There are many different fields within forensic science, including DNA analysis, ballistics, toxicology, and digital forensics. In each field, forensic scientists use specialized techniques and tools to analyze evidence and draw conclusions that can be used to solve crimes and prosecute criminals. Forensic evidence can take many forms, such as bloodstains, fingerprints, hair, fibers,

and digital data. Forensic scientists must be meticulous in their work and follow strict protocols to ensure that evidence is collected and analyzed correctly, as even small mistakes can compromise the integrity of the evidence and render it inadmissible in court. Forensic science plays a crucial role in modern criminal investigations, helping to identify suspects, reconstruct crime scenes, and establish timelines of events. It is also used to exonerate innocent people who have been wrongly accused of crimes.

- Digital Forensics

To investigate and resolve crimes or other situations, the process of locating and analyzing electronic evidence is known as "digital forensics." This field involves using scientific methods and techniques to extract and interpret data from digital devices such as computers, mobile phones, and other electronic storage devices. The goal of digital forensics is to gather and analyze evidence from digital devices to establish facts and help solve a crime or incident. This evidence can include data stored on hard drives, memory cards, and other electronic devices, as well as network logs, email records, and other digital communications. Various scenarios, such as criminal investigations, civil lawsuits, and corporate investigations, use digital forensics. It is also used by government agencies, law enforcement, and other organizations to protect against cybercrime and other digital threats. Digital forensics involves a range of techniques, including forensic imaging, data recovery, and data analysis. It requires specialized training and expertise and involves following a strict chain of custody to ensure that the evidence gathered is admissible in court. In summary, digital forensics plays an important role in modern law enforcement and investigations and is an essential tool for uncovering and prosecuting digital crimes.

37.2   Background Work

Randa Kamal investigates IoT forensics, which is the method for quickly and securely conducting digital forensic investigations in an IoT environment. IoT device development is advancing quickly, which has many advantages but also raises new security and forensic issues. One of the most recent suggestions for improving IoT forensics is the use of blockchain technology. Blockchain ensures data integrity, immutability, scalability, and security when utilized in digital forensics. This article offers a comprehensive analysis of IoT security and forensics in relation to blockchain technology. It starts off with a thorough discussion of IoT security as well as the need for blockchain principles and IoT forensics. The issues associated with IoT security and forensics using blockchain are then examined.

According to Alex Akinbi, digital forensic examiners and stakeholders have substantial challenges when examining Internet of Things (IoT) environments because of the varied nature of IoT infrastructure. Among these challenges is maintaining the integrity of forensic evidence that is collected and stored during an investigation. They also struggle to ensure the investigating process's transparency, which includes the evidence trail and chain of custody. Recently, several safe evidence models built on blockchain that are suited for IoT forensic investigations have been introduced. These proof-of-concept models secure the evidence chain of custody and uphold the privacy, integrity, provenance, traceability, and verification of the evidence gathered and stored during the investigation process by utilizing the inherent properties of blockchain.

Gulshan Kumar analyzes the importance of digital forensics on the Internet of Things (IoT) paradigm owing to its heterogeneity and lack of openness in evidence processing. Moreover, cross-border legality impedes the process of dealing with cloud forensic difficulties. To enable distributed computing, decentralization, and transparency in the forensic analysis of digital evidence from a cross-border perspective, an IoT forensic framework must be created. The Internet-of-Forensics (IoF) solution that has been proposed considers a blockchain-specific IoT infrastructure for digital forensics. By uniting all stakeholders (such as heterogeneous devices and cloud service providers) in a single framework, it provides a comprehensive image of the investigation process. Using a blockchain-based case chain, it manages the investigative process, including the chain of custody and the evidence chain.

Guangjun Liang specializes in IoT forensics research. The definition of IoT forensics is provided by contrasting it with traditional digital forensics (DF). Since the notion of IoT forensics was presented in 2013, we have methodically sifted through the study results and provided a generic IoT forensics model. Following an examination of blockchain technology and its integration into the IoT forensics framework, a blockchain-based IoT forensics architecture was developed. Additionally available is an alliance chain IoT forensics system. From the viewpoints of the data provider and the data visitor, the procedure for evidence storage and forensics in the IoT system is described. Finally, we demonstrate an experiment in IoT forensics analysis using an example from manned aerial vehicle (UAV) forensics.

Imran Ahmed investigates how the system uses blockchain technology to promote diverse applications by providing digital analytics and storing data in decentralized cloud repositories. Furthermore, the layer-based design enables a long-term incentive structure, which may help ensure safe and protected smart city applications. We examined the improved solutions, summarizing the essential elements that may be used to create various artificial intelligence and blockchain-based systems. We also highlighted the difficulties that remain unresolved as well as our future research objectives, which can provide new concepts and future recommendations for sustainable IoT applications.

Abdullah Ayub Khan analyzes these issues and provides an innovative and safe architecture for distributed SMEs with a standardized process hierarchy/lifecycle based on collaborative blockchain, the Internet of Things (IoT), and artificial intelligence (AI) using machine learning algorithms (ML). "B-SMEs" is a blockchain that provides services to cross-chain platforms and has an IoT-enabled permissionless network topology. B-SMEs also address simple stakeholder authentication problems. For this, three different chain codes are employed [3]. Prior to being recorded on the blockchain's immutable storage, it administers the registration of participating SMEs, daily information management and communication between nodes, and the analysis of partnership exchange-related transaction data. Utilizing AI-enabled machine learning-based artificial neural networks is intended to manage and optimize the volume of SME transactions that occur daily so that the proposed B-SMEs use less computational resources, network bandwidth, and preservation-related issues throughout the entire process of SME service delivery.

Sukhpal Singh Gill's research on modern society depends heavily on cloud computing since it makes a wide range of applications possible, from social media to infrastructure. To represent society's engagement with and reliance on automated computer systems, such a system must be able to handle varying loads and evolving use while still upholding Quality of Service (QoS) standards. These systems are made possible by a collection of theoretical technologies that have been combined to meet the needs of new computer applications. Important technologies that enable potential applications in the future must be identified to understand the present and future issues with such a system. The goal of this study is to determine how three emerging paradigms—blockchain, the Internet of Things, and artificial intelligence—will impact cloud computing platforms in the future. Additionally, we identify several technologies that are powering these paradigms and invite experts from around the world to discuss the status of cloud computing and its potential in the future. Finally, we proposed a conceptual framework for cloud futurology to look at how future paradigms and technologies will affect the development of cloud computing.

Ranu Tyagi investigates how autonomously linked vehicles are changing the automobile industry's vision and business model. This trend is anticipated to have an influence on other connected businesses and their business models, such as automobile insurance firms, Tier-II car manufacturers, and automotive maintenance service providers [4]. In an era of increasing digitization and automation, the expanding number of connected cars will necessitate new policy development by the government on privacy and security problems. Standards for linked automobiles are being developed by organizations such as 3GPP and IEEE. We nevertheless address privacy and security issues with a blockchain-based intelligent digital forensics solution for autonomous connected cars (ACVs) in a linked smart world embracing artificial intelligence because AI and ML will play a significant role in 5G networks and beyond.

To examine digital forensic data on the IoT ecosystem, P. Mohamed Shakeel recommended the blockchain-assisted shared audit framework (BSAF). The proposed method was developed to locate the source or reason behind data scavenging attacks on virtualized resources (VR). The suggested solution makes use of blockchain technology for access records and control administration. Access log data is analyzed for adversary event consistency using cross-validation and logistic regression (LR) machine learning. A cross-validation filter is used to remove an adversary event that LR has identified to preserve the accuracy of data analysis for varying user densities and VRs. The experimental findings demonstrate the consistency of the suggested strategy by enhancing data processing and decreasing analysis time and adversarial event rate.

37.3   Digital Twin Technology—An Era of Emerging Technology

One of the rising technologies that revolves around the curation of virtual modes of physical resources and assets such as buildings, machines, products, etc. to simulate their performance and behavior patterns in real time is referred to as a "digital twin." The concept of digital twin technology has been around for several years, but recent advancements in technology have made it more accessible and affordable for businesses and organizations.

The idea behind digital twin technology is to create a virtual model of a physical asset, such as a building, machine, or product, and use data from sensors, cameras, and other sources to simulate its behavior and performance in real-time. This technology enables organizations to monitor, analyze, and optimize their assets' performance, identify potential issues before they occur, and improve their overall efficiency and effectiveness.

Digital twin technology is being used in several industries, including manufacturing, healthcare, transportation, and construction. In manufacturing, digital twin technology is used to simulate the production process and optimize the performance of machines and equipment. In healthcare, digital twins are being used to simulate the human body and identify potential health issues before they occur. In transportation, digital twin technology is being used to simulate traffic patterns and optimize routes for vehicles.

The benefits of digital twin technology are many. It provides organizations with a more comprehensive understanding of their assets, enables them to identify potential issues before they occur, and allows them to make data-driven decisions that can improve their overall performance and efficiency. However, the adoption of digital twin technology also requires significant investments in technology and infrastructure, as well as a skilled workforce and training.

In summary, digital twin technology (DTT) is an exciting and promising era of emerging technology that has the potential to transform various industries and create new opportunities for businesses and organizations. Its adoption requires a coordinated effort from various stakeholders, including technology companies, academia, and policymakers, to ensure its proper implementation and maximize its benefits.

37.4   Security

Security is a critical aspect of any technology, particularly in the era of emerging technologies such as artificial intelligence, the Internet of Things, blockchain, and digital twin technology. As more devices become connected to the internet, the risk of cyber threats and attacks also increases. Ensuring the security of emerging technologies requires a multi-layered approach that includes encryption, authentication, access control, and data protection. Organizations must also establish clear security policies and guidelines, train their workforce to identify and mitigate security threats, and regularly audit and update their security measures to ensure their effectiveness. One of the key challenges in securing emerging technologies is the lack of standardization and interoperability across different devices and systems. Developing standards and guidelines is necessary to ensure the interoperability and security of emerging technologies and promote their widespread adoption. Moreover, emerging technologies themselves can also be used to enhance security. For example, artificial intelligence can be used to detect and respond to cyber threats in real-time, while blockchain technology can provide a tamper-proof and secure method for storing and sharing data. In summary, security is a critical aspect of any emerging technology, and it requires a coordinated effort from various stakeholders, including technology companies, policymakers, and end-users, to ensure its effectiveness. With proper planning, implementation, and training, emerging technologies can provide a more secure and reliable foundation for the digital economy.

37.4.1 Types of Security

There are several types of security that are relevant in the context of technology:

- Physical security: This refers to the protection of physical assets, such as hardware and devices, from theft, damage, or unauthorized access. Physical security measures include security cameras, access control systems, and biometric authentication.
- Network security: This is a reference to safeguarding computer networks from unauthorized usage, access, or manipulation. Firewalls, intrusion detection and prevention systems, and VPNs are examples of network security mechanisms.
- Data security: Data protection here refers to preventing unauthorized access, use, or disclosure. Encryption, access limits, and data backup and recovery are examples of data security procedures.
- Application security: This refers to the protection of software applications from security threats such as malware, viruses, and other malicious attacks. Application security measures include security testing, code reviews, and vulnerability assessments.
- Cloud security: This refers to the protection of cloud-based services, such as software as a service (SaaS), platform as a service (PaaS), and infrastructure as a service (IaaS), from security threats. Cloud security measures include encryption, access controls, and data backup and recovery.
- Cybersecurity: This refers to the protection of computer systems, networks, and data from digital attacks, such as hacking, phishing, and ransomware. Cybersecurity measures include network security, data security, and application security.

In summary, ensuring the security of technology requires a multi-layered approach that addresses various types of security threats and vulnerabilities.

37.5 Digital Forensics Characteristics

Digital forensics has several characteristics that set it apart from other forms of investigation and analysis. Here are some of the key characteristics of digital forensics:

- Electronic data: Digital forensics involves the investigation of electronic data, which can include data stored on computers, mobile devices, and other digital media.
- Volatility: Digital data is volatile and can be easily modified or deleted, so it is important to preserve and analyze it quickly to ensure its integrity.
- Complexity: Digital forensics involves complex processes and techniques, including data recovery, decryption, and analysis of large amounts of data.
- Use of specialized tools: Digital forensics requires specialized tools and software to extract and analyze data from digital devices.

- Chain of custody: Digital forensics requires a strict chain of custody to ensure that the evidence gathered is admissible in court.
- Cross-disciplinary: Digital forensics requires expertise in computer science, law, and other fields and often involves collaboration between different experts.
- Continuous learning: Digital forensics requires continuous learning and updating of skills as new technologies and techniques are constantly emerging.

In summary, digital forensics requires specialized knowledge, skills, and tools to investigate and analyze electronic data and is a critical component of modern law enforcement and investigations.

37.6 Computer Forensics

Computer forensics is a branch of digital forensics that involves the collection, preservation, analysis, and presentation of electronic data that can be used as evidence in a legal investigation or a civil dispute. The purpose of computer forensics is to recover, identify, analyze, and preserve electronic data that may be stored on computers, mobile devices, servers, or other electronic storage devices [5].

The process of computer forensics involves a variety of techniques and tools that are used to recover data from electronic devices, including file carving, disk imaging, data analysis, and data recovery. Computer forensics experts are often called upon to investigate cases of cybercrime, intellectual property theft, corporate espionage, and other types of digital wrongdoing [6].

To be successful in the field of computer forensics, individuals must have a strong knowledge of computer systems, software applications, and networking technologies, as well as an understanding of legal procedures and practices. They must also be able to work with a variety of digital tools and software applications to collect, analyze, and present electronic data in a clear and concise manner.

37.7 Tool Required for Digital Forensics

Digital forensics is a branch of forensic science that involves the collection, preservation, analysis, and presentation of electronic evidence in a court of law. The field of digital forensics relies on a range of specialized tools and techniques to perform its investigations. Here are some of the essential tools required for digital forensics:

- Imaging Software: This is used to create a bit-for-bit copy of a digital storage device, such as a hard drive or memory card, in a forensically sound manner.
- Forensic Analysis Software: This type of software is used to analyze and interpret the data collected during an investigation, such as email messages, documents, and other types of files.
- Network Analysis Tools: These tools are used to investigate network traffic, including examining data packets to identify communication patterns, anomalies, and security breaches.

- Password Recovery Tools: These tools are used to recover passwords or other authentication credentials, which may be necessary to access encrypted or password-protected files or devices.
- Mobile Forensics Tools: These tools are used to investigate mobile devices, such as smartphones and tablets, including their data, messaging, and communication history.
- Memory Analysis Tools: These tools are used to investigate the volatile memory of a computer or mobile device, including the data that is stored in RAM.
- Steganography Detection Tools: These tools are used to detect hidden or encrypted data within files, images, or other digital media.
- Hashing Tools: These tools are used to calculate and verify the digital signature of a file or a piece of data, ensuring its integrity and authenticity.
- Live Response Tools: These tools are used to perform forensic analysis on a live system without disrupting or altering its current state.
- Reporting Tools: These tools are used to generate detailed reports that document the findings of a digital forensic investigation.

37.8   Importance of Computer and Digital Forensics in Smart Era

Computer and digital forensics are crucial in the smart era as they enable investigators to analyze and collect digital evidence from a wide range of digital devices and systems. With the increasing use of smart technologies such as smartphones, laptops, tablets, smartwatches, and IoT devices, the importance of digital forensics has grown significantly. Digital forensics involves the identification, preservation, analysis, and presentation of digital evidence. This evidence can be critical in legal proceedings and can help identify and prosecute cybercriminals. Digital forensics is also important for businesses and organizations, as it helps them prevent and detect cyber-attacks, data breaches, and other security incidents. In the smart era, digital forensics is used to investigate a wide range of crimes, including cybercrime, intellectual property theft, fraud, and terrorism [7]. Digital forensics is also used to recover data from damaged or corrupted digital devices, which is essential for businesses and individuals who rely on digital data for their operations. In conclusion, the importance of digital forensics in the smart era cannot be overstated. It is a critical tool for investigating and preventing cybercrime, protecting businesses and organizations from data breaches and security incidents, and ensuring that justice is served in legal proceedings.

37.9   Methods/Algorithms for Digital Forensics in Smart Era

Digital forensics in the smart era refers to the techniques and tools used to investigate and analyze digital devices and data that are connected to the internet and have smart capabilities. Some methods and algorithms commonly used in digital forensics in the smart era include:

- Memory forensics: This involves analyzing the memory of a device to identify any running processes, open files, and other data that may be relevant to an investigation.

- Network forensics: This involves analyzing network traffic to identify any suspicious or malicious activity. This can include examining network logs, packet captures, and other data to determine the source of an attack or intrusion.
- File carving: This involves searching for and extracting data fragments from unallocated disk space, temporary files, and other areas of a device's storage. This can be useful for recovering deleted or hidden files as well as identifying evidence of malicious activity.
- Malware analysis: This involves analyzing malware to understand its behavior and identify any indicators of compromise. This can include static analysis (examining the code and structure of the malware) and dynamic analysis (running the malware in a controlled environment to observe its behavior).
- Digital footprint analysis: This involves examining a person's digital footprint (i.e., their online activity and presence) to identify any relevant information that may be useful in an investigation.
- Data recovery: This involves using specialized tools and techniques to recover data from damaged or corrupted devices. This can be useful for recovering data that has been accidentally or intentionally deleted, as well as identifying evidence of malicious activity.
- Forensic analysis of IoT devices: This involves analyzing the data and communication protocols used by smart devices such as home automation systems, wearables, and other IoT devices. This can help identify evidence of malicious activity, such as unauthorized access or data exfiltration.

In summary, the methods and algorithms used in digital forensics in the smart era are constantly evolving as technology advances and new threats emerge. It is important for forensic investigators to stay up-to-date with the latest techniques and tools to ensure that they can effectively investigate and analyze digital evidence in the smart era.

37.10   Popular Tools Available for Digital Forensics

Digital forensics is the process of investigating and analyzing digital devices or electronic data to gather evidence for a criminal or civil investigation. There are several tools available for digital forensics that can assist forensic investigators in collecting, analyzing, and preserving electronic data. Some of the most popular digital forensics tools include:

- EnCase: EnCase is a popular digital forensics tool used to collect and analyze data from electronic devices, including computers, smartphones, and other digital devices. It allows investigators to conduct a comprehensive analysis of data by providing advanced features like file carving, keyword searching, and hash value computation.
- FTK Imager: FTK Imager is a forensic imaging tool used to capture data from a live system or forensic image. It can capture data in a variety of formats, including dd, E01, and AFF. It also allows forensic investigators to perform basic analysis of captured data.

- Autopsy: Autopsy is an open-source digital forensics tool that allows investigators to analyze data from computers and mobile devices. It has a user-friendly interface that makes it easy to use, and it provides advanced features like timeline analysis, keyword searching, and file carving.
- Volatility: Volatility is an open-source memory forensics tool used to analyze volatile memory data from a live system or forensic image. It can be used to extract information like running processes, network connections, and registry keys from memory.
- Wireshark: Wireshark is a popular network analysis tool used to capture and analyze network traffic. It can be used to capture packets and analyze them to extract information like network traffic patterns, network protocols, and packet contents.
- Oxygen Forensic Detective: Oxygen Forensic Detective is a commercial digital forensics tool used to analyze data from mobile devices like smartphones and tablets. It provides advanced features like logical and physical data extraction, password cracking, and cloud data extraction.

These are just a few of the many digital forensics' tools available. Forensic investigators use a combination of these tools and other specialized tools to conduct a comprehensive analysis of digital devices and electronic data.

37.11   Popular Issues Towards Using AI–Blockchain–IoT in Digital Forensics

The use of AI, blockchain, and IoT in digital forensics has the potential to revolutionize the field by enhancing the efficiency, accuracy, and reliability of investigations. However, there are also some concerns and challenges that need to be addressed, including:

- Privacy concerns: The use of these technologies may involve the collection and analysis of large amounts of data, raising concerns about privacy and data protection.
- Ethical considerations: The use of AI and IoT in digital forensics may raise ethical questions about the appropriate use of technology and its potential impact on human rights.
- Legal issues: The use of these technologies may pose legal challenges related to its admissibility of evidence, the chain of custody, and the potential for manipulation of data.
- Technical challenges: The implementation of these technologies may require specialized technical expertise, which may be lacking in many organizations.
- Interoperability: The integration of AI, blockchain, and IoT systems may require a high level of interoperability, which can be difficult to achieve due to differences in technical standards and protocols.

- Trust: The use of blockchain and AI technologies in digital forensics requires a high degree of trust in the accuracy and reliability of the data and algorithms being used.
- Cost: The adoption of these technologies may require significant financial resources, which may be a barrier for many organizations, especially smaller ones.

In summary, while the use of AI, blockchain, and IoT in digital forensics has the potential to improve the efficiency and accuracy of investigations, there are also significant challenges that need to be addressed to ensure that these technologies are used ethically, legally, and effectively [8].

37.12   Future Research Opportunities Using AI-Blockchain-IoT in Digital Forensics

The intersection of AI, blockchain, and IoT presents several exciting research opportunities in digital forensics. Here are a few potential areas of study:

- AI-assisted digital forensics: Artificial intelligence can assist investigators in identifying patterns and anomalies in large data sets. Using machine learning algorithms, AI can identify patterns that may be overlooked by human investigators, leading to more accurate and efficient forensic investigations.
- Blockchain-enabled digital forensics: Blockchain technology can be used to establish a tamper-evident chain of custody for digital evidence, ensuring that data cannot be altered or deleted without detection. By utilizing blockchain, investigators can ensure that digital evidence is admissible in court and maintain the integrity of the evidence.
- IoT device forensics: As the number of IoT devices continues to grow, so does the potential for these devices to be involved in criminal activity. Researchers can investigate the types of digital evidence that can be obtained from IoT devices and develop methodologies for analyzing the data.
- Privacy and security in AI–blockchain–IoT systems: The use of AI, blockchain, and IoT in digital forensics raises concerns about privacy and security. Researchers can investigate the risks associated with these technologies and develop methods for mitigating those risks.
- Hybrid AI–blockchain–IoT systems: Researchers can explore the potential benefits of combining AI, blockchain, and IoT technologies to create hybrid systems for digital forensics. These systems could leverage the strengths of each technology to create more robust and effective forensic tools.

In summary, the integration of AI, blockchain, and IoT presents many exciting research opportunities in the field of digital forensics. By exploring these areas, researchers can develop new methods and tools for more accurate and efficient forensic investigations [9].

37.12.1   Other Future Works

In this section, we will discuss a few interesting future works with respect to AI/ML, blockchain, etc. Machine learning (ML) adoption in blockchain-based smart applications can bring several benefits. Here are some potential advantages:

- Improved Security: Blockchain technology is known for its secure and immutable nature. By integrating ML algorithms, blockchain-based smart applications can enhance their security by detecting and preventing potential threats, such as fraud and cyber-attacks.
- Decentralization: Decentralized applications (DApps) built on blockchain technology offer several advantages, such as increased transparency and security. By incorporating ML algorithms, these DApps can be further enhanced to provide better decision-making capabilities, more accurate predictions, and increased automation.
- Data Privacy: ML models require large amounts of data to train effectively. However, privacy concerns can arise when sensitive data is shared or stored. By leveraging blockchain technology, data can be stored and shared securely, providing greater protection against data breaches and unauthorized access.
- Trust and Transparency: ML algorithms can be complex and difficult to interpret. By integrating blockchain technology, the decision-making process of

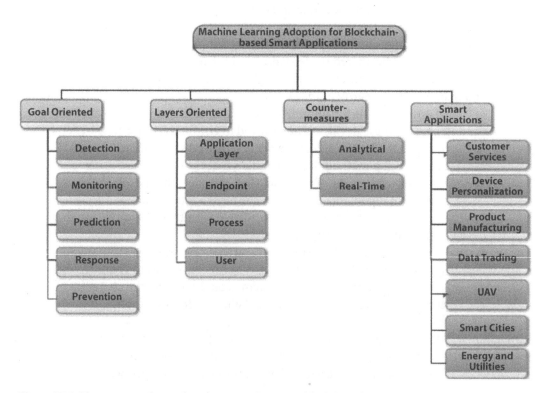

Figure 37.1 The taxonomy for machine learning adoption in blockchain-based smart applications.

these algorithms can be made more transparent and trustworthy, providing greater accountability and reducing the risk of bias.

- Smart Contracts: Smart contracts are self-executing agreements that can be used to automate business processes. By incorporating ML algorithms into smart contracts, these agreements can be made more intelligent, enabling them to analyze data, make predictions, and adjust terms and conditions automatically.

In summary, the integration of ML in blockchain-based smart applications holds great promise. However, it is important to carefully consider the potential risks and limitations, such as the complexity of integrating these technologies, the need for large amounts of data, and the potential for bias in ML models (refer to Figure 37.1).

37.12.2 Future of Blockchain

In the coming years, we can expect blockchain to be used in areas such as finance, healthcare, supply chain management, and more. With its decentralized and immutable nature, blockchain has the potential to enhance transparency, security, and efficiency across many different domains. One of the biggest advantages of blockchain is its ability to enable secure and transparent transactions without the need for intermediaries. This can reduce costs and increase speed, which can be particularly beneficial in industries such as finance and supply chain management. Additionally, blockchain can help improve data privacy and security, as all transactions are recorded on a decentralized ledger that cannot be altered. Note that blockchain technology also has the potential to enable new business models and revenue streams. For example, the use of smart contracts can enable automatic and self-executing agreements between parties, which can significantly streamline processes and reduce the need for manual intervention. However, there are still challenges and concerns that need to be addressed in the future of blockchain, such as scalability, interoperability, and regulatory compliance. As blockchain continues to grow and evolve, it will be important to address these challenges to ensure that its benefits can be fully realized. In summary, the future of blockchain is promising, and it has the potential to transform many aspects of our lives. As the technology continues to mature and develop, we can expect to see even more innovative and impactful use cases emerge.

37.12.3 Future of Artificial Intelligence

The future of AI (artificial intelligence) is likely to be characterized by even more advanced and sophisticated technologies that have the potential to revolutionize virtually every industry and aspect of human life. In the coming years, we can expect AI to become even more ubiquitous, integrated, and accessible across a wide range of devices and platforms, including smartphones, wearables, smart homes, autonomous vehicles, and more. We can also expect AI to play an increasingly important role in areas such as healthcare, finance, logistics, and education, helping to improve efficiency, accuracy, and decision-making. However, with these advancements come challenges and concerns. There is a need to ensure that AI is developed and used in an ethical and responsible way, that it does not perpetuate biases or discrimination, and that it is not used for harmful purposes. Additionally, there may be concerns about the impact of AI on employment, privacy, and security. In summary, the future of AI is exciting and promising, but it is important to approach its development and use with caution and careful consideration of the potential risks and benefits.

37.12.4   Future of Internet of Things

The future of the IoT (Internet of Things) is expected to be characterized by even more connected and intelligent devices that can communicate with each other and with humans in real-time. In the coming years, we can expect the IoT to continue to grow and expand across a wide range of industries and applications, including smart homes, smart cities, healthcare, agriculture, transportation, and more. With the help of IoT, we can expect to see more efficient and sustainable solutions that can improve our quality of life and address complex problems. One of the biggest advantages of the IoT is the ability to collect and analyze vast amounts of data in real-time. This will enable more precise and accurate decision-making as well as the development of more personalized and adaptive solutions. For example, in healthcare, IoT can be used to monitor patients remotely, detect early warning signs of illness, and provide personalized treatment recommendations. However, the growth of the IoT also raises concerns about data privacy and security. With more devices connected to the internet, there is a greater risk of cyber-attacks and data breaches. It is therefore important to ensure that appropriate security measures are in place to protect against these risks. In summary, the future of IoT is exciting, and it has the potential to transform many aspects of our lives. However, it is important to approach its development and use in a responsible and ethical manner to ensure that its benefits are maximized while minimizing any potential risks.

37.12.5   Future of AI/ML–Blockchain–IoT Based Smart Devices in Digital Forensics

Digital forensics could change in several ways if blockchain, artificial intelligence/machine learning (AI/ML), and Internet of Things (IoT)-based smart devices are combined as follows:

- Increased Data Analysis: AI/ML algorithms can be used to analyze large amounts of data collected from IoT devices, such as smartphones, smart homes, and wearable devices. This can help forensic investigators identify patterns and detect anomalies more efficiently.
- Improved Evidence Integrity: Blockchain technology can be used to ensure the integrity of digital evidence, providing a tamper-proof record of any changes or modifications made to the data.
- Real-time Monitoring: IoT devices can be used to monitor and collect data in real-time, enabling forensic investigators to quickly respond to incidents and analyze data as it is generated.
- Faster Investigations: The integration of AI/ML algorithms and blockchain technology can help automate the digital forensic investigation process, reducing the time and resources required for manual analysis.
- Enhanced Security: By leveraging blockchain and IoT technologies, the security of digital devices and data can be improved, reducing the risk of data breaches and cyber-attacks.
- Increased Efficiency: The combination of these technologies can help streamline the digital forensic investigation process, enabling investigators to identify and analyze data more quickly and accurately.

In summary, the future of digital forensics with AI/ML–blockchain–IoT-based smart devices is promising, and the integration of these technologies has the potential to transform the field in several ways. However, it is important to consider the potential risks and limitations associated with these technologies, such as the potential for bias in AI/ML algorithms and the need for robust cybersecurity measures.

37.13   Limitations AI/ML–Blockchain–IoT-Based Smart Devices in Digital Forensics

AI/ML-based smart devices in digital forensics face several limitations, such as:

- Lack of standardization: The lack of standardization in data formats and protocols across different smart devices makes it challenging to collect and analyze data from these devices.
- Privacy concerns: Smart devices collect a vast amount of data that may contain personal information, and privacy concerns arise when this data is accessed by forensic investigators.
- Complexity: The complex nature of smart devices and the vast amount of data they generate make it challenging for forensic investigators to analyze the data accurately and efficiently.
- Data encryption: Smart devices often use encryption to protect data, making it difficult for forensic investigators to access and analyze the data.
- Rapid technological advancements: Smart device technology is rapidly evolving, and forensic investigators may struggle to keep up with the latest advancements in technology.
- Lack of interoperability: Smart devices often use different communication protocols and data formats, making it challenging to integrate them into a unified forensic investigation framework.
- Storage capacity: Smart devices often have limited storage capacity, which can result in the loss of critical data during forensic investigations.

When it comes to blockchain-based smart devices, the limitations include:

- Limited access to data: Blockchain-based smart devices use distributed ledger technology, which means that data is distributed across multiple nodes. This can make it challenging for forensic investigators to access all the data required for a complete investigation.
- Immutable data: The data stored in a blockchain is immutable, meaning that it cannot be altered or deleted. This can make it difficult to remove sensitive information or data that is no longer required for the investigation.
- Limited scope: Blockchain-based smart devices are currently limited in scope and do not yet cover a wide range of digital devices.

Finally, when it comes to IoT-based smart devices, the limitations include:

- Lack of standardization: Like AI/ML-based smart devices, IoT-based smart devices lack standardization in data formats and communication protocols, making it difficult to collect and analyze data.
- Limited processing power: IoT-based smart devices often have limited processing power, making it challenging to perform complex analysis on the data they generate.
- Security concerns: IoT-based smart devices are often vulnerable to cyber-attacks, which can compromise the integrity of the data shared in the network.
- Privacy Concerns: IoT-based smart devices are often vulnerable to cyber-attacks and may use or sell this stored data to an unauthorized or other third party.

Hence, as limitations, there will be security, privacy, scalability, and trust issues with respect to blockchain, IoT, and AI/ML in the required cyber-attack detection sectors [10–14].

The chatbot ChatGPT [15, 16], newly published by OpenAI [17, 18], can interpret and produce natural language, react to queries, follow discussions, and provide natural language answers. Compared to conventional chatbots [19, 20], ChatGPT may provide replies that seem considerably more conversational and natural. This is due to the system's extensive training on natural language data, which enables it to produce replies that sound more human. The ChatGPT can also determine the conversation's context and offer more logical replies. A user-friendly convergence ecosystem called an AI speaker [21, 22] was developed by fusing cloud computing and the Internet of Things (IoT). The cloud-based AI speaker ecosystem manages operations and offers Q&A services via an AI-enabled speaker ecosystem. In contrast to standard IoT [23, 24] devices, an AI speaker plays a crucial role as a system that manages multiple IoT devices while collaborating with mobile devices. The Q&A features and management of an IoT device family both emphasise the requirement for digital forensic [25, 26] study. Globally, the market for AI speakers is expanding quickly; 25% of people in developed countries will use AI assistants [27, 28] to help them with a variety of operational tasks." The appealing AI speaker ecosystem [29, 30] has been established or connected by every major IT business [31], so the penetration rate will keep rising consistently. As a result, AI speakers are becoming increasingly significant in the field of digital forensics [32, 33]. The number of customers and service providers has expanded as a result of market development, and as a result, so have the vendors who provide the ecosystem.

37.14   Conclusion

The convergence of artificial intelligence (AI), blockchain, and the Internet of Things (IoT) has brought significant opportunities to the field of digital forensics. These technologies have the potential to enhance the efficiency and effectiveness of digital forensic investigations and provide more robust and reliable evidence in court. However, the adoption of these technologies in digital forensics also brings several challenges and issues. One of the key challenges is the lack of standardization in the use of AI, blockchain, and IoT in digital forensics. The development of standards and guidelines is necessary to ensure the interoperability of these technologies and promote their widespread adoption. Another challenge is the potential for biases in AI algorithms and the need for transparency and accountability in their use. Moreover, the integration of these technologies also requires significant investments in terms of infrastructure, training, and a skilled workforce. The development of legal frameworks and ethical considerations is also critical to addressing the challenges and issues associated with the adoption of these technologies in digital forensics. In summary, the convergence of AI, blockchain, and IoT has significant potential to transform the field of digital forensics, but their adoption requires a coordinated effort from various stakeholders, including law enforcement agencies, technology companies, academia, and policymakers. With proper planning, standardization, and ethical considerations, these technologies can enhance the capabilities of digital forensics and provide more reliable evidence in court.

References

1. Karger, E., Combining blockchain and artificial intelligence - literature review and state of the art. *International Conference on Information Systems*, 2020.
2. Habib, G., Sharma, S., Ibrahim, S., Blockchain technology: Benefits, challenges, applications, and integration of blockchain technology with cloud computing, in: *Blockchain Security in Cloud Computing*, 2022.
3. Khan, A.A., Laghari, A.A., Li, P. *et al.*, The collaborative role of blockchain, artificial intelligence, and industrial Internet of Things in digitalization of small and medium-size enterprises. *Sci. Rep.*, 13, 1656, 2023.
4. Tyagi, R., Sharma, S., Mohan, S., Blockchain enabled intelligent digital forensics system for autonomous connected vehicles. *International Conference on Communication, Computing and Internet of Things (IC3IoT)*, 2022.
5. Daniel, L.E. and Daniel, L.E., Digital forensics: The subdisciplines, in: *Digital Forensics for Legal Professionals*, pp. 17–23, 2012.
6. Hamad, N. and Eleyan, D., Digital forensics tools used in cybercrime investigation – comparative analysis, in: *Architecture & Technology*, 2022.
7. Day, C. and Vacca, J.R., Intrusion prevention and detection systems, in: *Computer and Information Security Handbook*, Third Edition, Chapter 72, pp. 1011–1025, 2013.
8. Atlam, H.F., Alenezi, A., Alassafi, M.O., Security, cybercrime and digital forensics for IoT, in: *Principles of Internet of Things (IoT) Ecosystem*, Chapter 22, pp. 551–577, 2020.
9. Lakshmana Kumar, R., Khan, F., Kadry, S., Rho, S., A survey on blockchain for industrial Internet of Things. *Alexandria Eng. J.*, 61, 8, 6001–6022, 2022.
10. Tyagi, A.K., Dananjayan, S., Agarwal, D., Thariq Ahmed, H.F., Blockchain—Internet of Things applications: Opportunities and challenges for industry 4.0 and society 5.0. *Sensors*, 23, 2, 947, 2023, https://doi.org/10.3390/s23020947.
11. Mishra, S. and Tyagi, A.K., The role of machine learning techniques in Internet of Things-based cloud applications, in: *Artificial Intelligence-based Internet of Things Systems*, S. Pal, D. De, R. Buyya (Eds.), Internet of Things (Technology, Communications and Computing). Springer, Cham, 2022, https://doi.org/10.1007/978-3-030-87059-1_4.
12. Deshmukh, Sreenath, N., Tyagi, A.K., Jathar, S., Internet of Things based smart environment: Threat analysis, open issues, and a way forward to future. *2022 International Conference on Computer Communication and Informatics (ICCCI)*, pp. 1–6, 2022, doi: 10.1109/ICCCI54379.2022.9740741.

13. Deshmukh, Sreenath, N., Tyagi, A.K., Eswara Abhichandan, U.V., Blockchain enabled cyber security: A comprehensive survey. *2022 International Conference on Computer Communication and Informatics (ICCCI)*, pp. 1–6, 2022, doi: 10.1109/ICCCI54379.2022.9740843.

14. Tyagi, K., Agarwal, D., Sreenath, N., SecVT: Securing the vehicles of tomorrow using blockchain technology. *2022 International Conference on Computer Communication and Informatics (ICCCI)*, pp. 1–6, 2022, doi: 10.1109/ICCCI54379.2022.9740965.

15. Mahor, V., Bijrothiya, S., Rawat, R., Kumar, A., Garg, B., Pachlasiya, K., IoT and artificial intelligence techniques for public safety and security, in: *Smart Urban Computing Applications*, p. 111, 2023.

16. Mahor, V., Pachlasiya, K., Garg, B., Chouhan, M., Telang, S., Rawat, R., Mobile operating system (Android) vulnerability analysis using machine learning, in: *Proceedings of International Conference on Network Security and Blockchain Technology: ICNSBT 2021*, 2022, June, Springer Nature Singapore, Singapore, pp. 159–169.

17. Rawat, R., Garg, B., Pachlasiya, K., Mahor, V., Telang, S., Chouhan, M., Mishra, R., SCNTA: Monitoring of network availability and activity for identification of anomalies using machine learning approaches. *Int. J. Inf. Technol. Web Eng. (IJITWE)*, 17, 1, 1–19, 2022.

18. Rawat, R., Rimal, Y.N., William, P., Dahima, S., Gupta, S., Sankaran, K.S., Malware threat affecting financial organization analysis using machine learning approach. *Int. J. Inf. Technol. Web Eng. (IJITWE)*, 17, 1, 1–20, 2022.

19. Rawat, R., Mahor, V., Chouhan, M., Pachlasiya, K., Telang, S., Garg, B., Systematic literature review (SLR) on social media and the digital transformation of drug trafficking on darkweb, in: *International Conference on Network Security and Blockchain Technology*, Springer, Singapore, pp. 181–205, 2022.

20. Rawat, R., Ayodele Oki, O., Sankaran, S., Florez, H., Ajagbe, S.A., Techniques for predicting dark web events focused on the delivery of illicit products and ordered crime. *Int. J. Electr. Comput. Eng. (IJECE)*, 13, 5, 5354–5365, Oct. 2023, doi: 10.11591/ijece.v13i5.pp5354-5365.

21. Rawat, R., Garg, B., Mahor, V., Telang, S., Pachlasiya, K., Chouhan, M., Organ trafficking on the dark web—The data security and privacy concern in healthcare systems, in: *Internet of Healthcare Things: Machine Learning for Security and Privacy*, pp. 189–216, 2022.

22. Vyas, P., Vyas, G., Chauhan, A., Rawat, R., Telang, S., Gottumukkala, M., Anonymous trading on the dark online marketplace: An exploratory study, in: *Using Computational Intelligence for the Dark Web and Illicit Behavior Detection*, pp. 272–289, IGI Global, 2022.

23. Rawat, R., Oki, O.A., Sankaran, K.S., Olasupo, O., Ebong, G.N., Ajagbe, S.A., A new solution for cyber security in big data using machine learning approach, in: *Mobile Computing and Sustainable Informatics: Proceedings of ICMCSI 2023*, Springer Nature Singapore, Singapore, pp. 495–505, 2023.

24. Rawat, R., Chakrawarti, R.K., Raj, A., Mani, G., Chidambarathanu, K., Bhardwaj, R., Association rule learning for threat analysis using traffic analysis and packet filtering approach. *Int. J. Inf. Technol.*, 1–11, 2023.

25. Rawat, R., Logical concept mapping and social media analytics relating to cyber criminal activities for ontology creation. *Int. J. Inf. Technol.*, 15, 2, 893–903, 2023.

26. Rawat, R., Mahor, V., Álvarez, J.D., Ch, F., Cognitive systems for dark web cyber delinquent association malignant data crawling: A review, in: *Handbook of Research on War Policies, Strategies, and Cyber Wars*, pp. 45–63, 2023.

27. Rawat, R., Chakrawarti, R.K., Vyas, P., Gonzáles, J.L.A., Sikarwar, R., Bhardwaj, R., Intelligent fog computing surveillance system for crime and vulnerability identification and tracing. *Int. J. Inf. Secur. Priv. (IJISP)*, 17, 1, 1–25, 2023.

28. Rawat, R., Sowjanya, A.M., Patel, S.I., Jaiswal, V., Khan, I., Balaram, A. (Eds.), *Using Machine Intelligence: Autonomous Vehicles Volume 1*, John Wiley & Sons, 2022.

29. Rawat, R., Mahor, V., Díaz-Álvarez, J., Chávez, F., Rooted learning model at fog computing analysis for crime incident surveillance, in: *2022 International Conference on Smart Generation Computing, Communication and Networking (SMART GENCON)*, 2022, December, pp. 1–9, IEEE.

30. Rawat, R. and Shrivastav, S.K., SQL injection attack detection using SVM. *Int. J. Comput. Appl.*, *42*, 13, 1–4, 2012.

31. Rawat, R., Bhardwaj, P., Kaur, U., Telang, S., Chouhan, M., Sankaran, K.S., *Smart vehicles for communication, volume 2*, John Wiley & Sons, 2023.

32. Mahor, V., Garg, B., Telang, S., Pachlasiya, K., Chouhan, M., Rawat, R., Cyber threat phylogeny assessment and vulnerabilities representation at thermal power station, in: *Proceedings of International Conference on Network Security and Blockchain Technology: ICNSBT 2021*, 2022, June, Springer Nature Singapore, Singapore, pp. 28–39.

33. Rawat, R., Gupta, S., Sivaranjani, S., Cu, O.K., Kuliha, M., Sankaran, K.S., Malevolent information crawling mechanism for forming structured illegal organisations in hidden networks. *Int. J. Cyber Warf. Terror. (IJCWT)*, *12*, 1, 1–14, 2022.

Leveraging Natural Language Processing in Conversational AI Agents to Improve Healthcare Security

Jami Venkata Suman¹*, Farooq Sunar Mahammad², M. Sunil Kumar³, B. Sai Chandana⁴, and Sankararao Majji⁵

¹Department of ECE, GMR Institute of Technology, Rajam, Andhra Pradesh, India
²Department of Computer Science Engineering, Santhiram Engineering College Nandyal, Nandyal, Andhra Pradesh, India
³Department of Computer Science and Engineering, School of Computing, Mohan Babu University (erstwhile Sree Vidyanikethan Engineering College), Tirupathi, AP, India
⁴School of Computer Science and Engineering, VIT-AP University, Amaravathi, India
⁵Department of ECE, GRIET, Hyderabad, India

Abstract

While the widespread adoption of healthcare information technology has many positive outcomes, it has also presented new obstacles for protecting patient information. Natural language processing (NLP)-enabled conversational artificial intelligence (AI) agents are becoming increasingly useful in the healthcare industry as a means to improve both patient encounters and administrative workflows. Due to its sensitive nature, healthcare data must be protected by strict security procedures. This research delves into NLP in conversational AI agents' potential for enhancing healthcare's security infrastructure. We talk about how entity recognition, sentiment analysis, and anomaly detection are just some of the NLP-driven tactics that may be used to strengthen healthcare data security. Furthermore, we evaluate preexisting security architectures and suggest novel methods to better protect the privacy and safety of patients' information during conversations. Healthcare institutions may improve the quality and safety of healthcare services in the digital age by employing NLP capabilities to strike a balance between personalized patient involvement and tight security regulations.

Keywords: Natural language processing, artificial intelligence, healthcare services

*Corresponding author: venkatasuman.j@gmrit.edu.in

Romil Rawat, Rajesh Kumar Chakrawarti, Sanjaya Kumar Sarangi, Piyush Vyas, Mary Sowjanya Alamanda, Kotagiri Srividya and Krishnan Sakthidasan Sankaran (eds.) Conversational Artificial Intelligence, (699–712) © 2024 Scrivener Publishing LLC

38.1 Introduction

Patient care, operational efficiency, and medical research have all benefited greatly from the recent blending of cutting-edge technology with the healthcare industry [1]. A key component of this digital transformation is the introduction of conversational artificial intelligence (AI) agents, which are complex digital beings made to carry on conversations in natural language with users in the roles of patients, clinicians, and administrators. These AI assistants have shown tremendous promise in improving doctor–patient communication, easing administrative processes, and disseminating up-to-date health data [2]. There is, however, a growing cause for alarm as healthcare systems adopt these AI-driven conversational platforms, and that is the need to bolster security measures to protect the personal and confidential health information that is shared inside these conversations. Due to the sensitive nature of patients' medical records, the healthcare industry is increasingly struggling to protect their privacy. This problem becomes even more complicated when conversational AI bots become more widely used. Conversations with these entities can be complex and sophisticated, going beyond the typical one-way flow of information [3]. Therefore, conventional methods of protection cannot guarantee the privacy, security, and veracity of medical records.

In light of this critical need, natural language processing (NLP) appears as a powerful tool within the context of conversational AI agents, with the potential to improve healthcare security [4]. Thanks to NLP, these bots can now understand, generate, and interpret human language, allowing them to have conversations that make sense in their given circumstances [5]. Healthcare businesses can use NLP to strike a balance between patient convenience and data security. This work sets out to investigate the significant part that natural language processing plays in improving the safety profile of healthcare conversational AI agents [6]. It explores the complexities of AI-driven discussions and the promise of natural language processing to solve healthcare data security problems [7]. This study seeks to shed light on the complementary nature of NLP and healthcare security enhancement by a detailed analysis of relevant NLP techniques, security frameworks, and practical implementations. Figure 38.1 shows the applications of NLP [1, 2].

Figure 38.1 Applications of NLP [1, 2].

Natural language processing is a flexible technology that can understand and synthesize human language, allowing it to find use in a wide variety of contexts [8]. Sentiment analysis is one of NLP's most recognized uses; by analyzing text data from sources like social media, customer reviews, and polls, NLP can determine whether responses were favorable, negative, or neutral. This enables companies to collect user feedback, track how customers feel about their brand, and base strategic decisions on that feedback [9]. Furthermore, systems that translate between languages, such as Google Translate, are made possible by natural language processing. These innovations have completely changed the way people throughout the world connect with one another, facilitating international partnerships and eliminating language obstacles [10]. Chatbots and virtual assistants, such as Siri and Alexa, also make use of NLP to interpret user questions and respond with relevant information or carry out activities by using the user's natural language [11–15]. Voice assistants, transcription services, and smart gadgets controlled by voice all benefit from natural language processing's ability to convert spoken language into textual form. Another intriguing use case is text summarizing, where NLP is used to automatically generate brief summaries of extensive texts. Articles, papers, and news pieces can all have their information extracted more quickly and easily using this feature [16]. In information extraction, NLP is essential due to its capacity to extract structured information from unstructured text [17].

Document classification is another area where the technology shows its potential since it allows for more streamlined filing and searching. Important for uses like information retrieval and data analysis, named entity recognition (NER) classifies items like individuals, companies, and dates referenced in text [18]. OpenAI's GPT is a prime example of an NLP model's text generation capabilities, demonstrating its ability to produce coherent, contextually appropriate text for a wide range of uses, from content production to code development. Clinical notes can be mined for medical insights using NLP, which can also be used to measure patient sentiment, aid in diagnosis, streamline record maintenance, and improve patient care [19]. To better understand market patterns and investor sentiment, financial research can benefit from NLP's ability to interpret financial reports, news stories, and social media data. The legal industry makes use of NLP for tasks such as contract analysis, document summarization, and risk assessment. Language-learning apps, computerized grading systems, and personalized educational chatbots are just a few examples of how NLP improves the classroom experience [16–20]. Natural language processing is used by content recommendation systems to learn about individual users so that they can provide tailored recommendations for media and merchandise. In addition to its use in research and keeping tabs on people's mental health, NLP-powered emotion detection has applications in customer service and business analysis [17, 18]. Only a small portion of NLP's potential is reflected in these varied uses.

Organization of the Chapter

In the following sections, we will explore the various ways in which NLP is used by conversational AI agents, explain how NLP can be used to strengthen security procedures, and introduce some fresh ideas for incorporating NLP into these systems. After finishing this guide, you should have a firm grasp on the revolutionary power of NLP to strengthen health data privacy, paving the way for a safe, patient-centered, and tech-enabled healthcare future.

38.2   Natural Language Process in Healthcare

So that analytics systems can make sense of it, NLP analyzes unstructured data from various sources (such as EMRs, literature, and social media) (Figure 38.2). Health systems can use the data for patient classification, insight extraction, and summary purposes once NLP has transformed the language into structured data [19]. Medical doctors, nurses, pharmacists, and even hospital administrators all make use of medical NLP in their daily work. As a result, they are able to minimize administrative costs, boost predictive analytics, and streamline workflows. In particular, NLP in healthcare can save doctors time by automatically extracting information from patient records. They can now swiftly find crucial data that would have required more time and effort if searched manually [18–20]. For better decision-making assistance and data mining for population health insights, natural language processing in healthcare has also been utilized to automate the summarizing of clinical notes. As a result of its usefulness in so many areas of healthcare, the NLP system is now widely used in clinical workflow optimization and trial matching. Learning how to read and write in medical notation is crucial for any career in the medical field. This facilitates the transmission of critical health information and the upkeep of precise records, allowing for the optimal treatment of patients. However, it is essential to keep in mind that physicians inside healthcare companies do not "speak the same way" and that their notes and reports will likely be viewed by coworkers, patients, and even computers in violation of the organization's privacy policy [18]. It is crucial that, when creating and managing notes, you avoid using any non-standard terminology. Most healthcare NLP engines are designed to work with a wide range of medical notation systems. However, NLP coding algorithms and other medical note readers sometimes get thrown off by the usage of odd acronyms. Improving healthcare data through natural language processing has been difficult. Users will learn to ignore the intelligence, and the system as a whole will be less productive if the NLP system output presents too many proposed conclusions in the electronic health record that are artificial and inaccurate [19]. Data findings with the least noise and the strongest signal regarding what healthcare professionals need to perform should be prioritized in NLP software for healthcare. There are certain things that healthcare companies can do to boost the performance of their AI and NLP systems. They need to start by creating high-quality data sets for use in model training [20]. Professionals in the medical field can build more robust models, ready to handle real-world scenarios, by using complete and precise training data. Second, healthcare systems should conduct surveys of patients and healthcare providers to better understand the language preferences of their intended audience. This paves the way

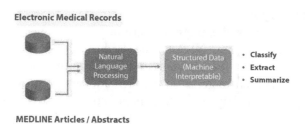

Figure 38.2 NLP process in healthcare.

for the creation of more user-friendly systems that can adapt to the specific ways in which people interact with healthcare providers. Figure 38.2 shows the NLP process in healthcare.

During the lengthy ICD-10 discussion process, computer-assisted coding built on natural language processing was seen as a potential panacea for the challenges of providing adequate detail and specificity in clinical documentation. NLP can and is being utilized for clinical decision support, which is of particular relevance right now, especially to clinicians in need of point-of-care solutions for highly complex patient problems [13]. IBM Watson, the industry's most well-known example of a machine learning NLP whiz kid, has been making headlines in recent months thanks to its prodigious appetite for academic literature and its expanding expertise in clinical decision support (CDS) for precision medicine and cancer care [14]. In 2014, before IBM established its Watson Health division, the Jeopardy!-winning supercomputer collaborated with EHR developer Epic and the Carillion Clinic in Virginia to examine how NLP and machine learning could be used to flag patients with a heart disease. Important clinical information was not the only thing the system highlighted. It also found social and behavioral elements mentioned in the clinical report but not included in the EHR's predefined categories. In total, 8,500 patients at a high risk of developing congestive heart failure within a year were effectively identified by the pilot study [15]. In just 6 weeks, Watson processed 13 million records and was 85% accurate in identifying patients.

Recently, Watson has taken on tougher problems, like cancer and sophisticated genomics, which require even more extensive data sets. Work with some of the largest clinical and cancer care providers in the country, as well as a new partnership with the New York Genome Center, have all helped to prepare the cognitive computing superstar for a future in CDS. "Cancer is a natural choice to focus on, because of the number of patients and the available proof points in the space," said Vanessa Michelini, distinguished engineer and master inventor at IBM Watson Health, who heads up the genomics group. "There's this explosion of data, not just genomic data but all sorts of data, in the healthcare space, and the industry needs to find the best ways to extract what's relevant and bring it together to help clinicians make the best decisions for patients," says one expert [16]. She also noted that 140,000 scholarly articles were published in 2014 alone about cancer diagnosis and therapy.

38.3   Role of Conversational AI in Healthcare

Chatbots play a crucial role in the healthcare industry by facilitating communication between patients, doctors, and insurance companies with minimal human intervention. Automating mundane tasks can help providers save time and money without negatively impacting the quality of care they deliver to patients. However, the fundamental goal of conversational AI in healthcare is to make vital information accessible whenever and wherever it is needed. There are a number of issues plaguing the healthcare sector at the moment, including a lack of available workers, a growing demand for high-quality services, and the need to integrate new technologies with older infrastructure. Artificial intelligence chatbots have the potential to ease the workload of healthcare providers while also facilitating patient–provider communication and speeding up the delivery of care [17]. According to Gartner, by 2020, almost 25% of companies will utilize chatbots as their primary channel for customer assistance. Conversational AI can offer strategic insights to improve patients' experiences, which is especially important since data and analytics play more important roles in helping businesses optimize their processes. When it comes to healthcare, conversational chatbots have an essential advantage over traditional chatbots: they can have discussions with humanlike empathy. There is also less of a learning curve than with mobile apps, which can need users to do things like download and enter passwords. Figure 38.3 shows the applications of conversational AI in healthcare.

Conversational AI allows healthcare providers to better meet the requirements of their patients. The five most common applications of artificially intelligent chatbots in healthcare are as follows:

A. Automating appointment scheduling and reminders

When patients do not show up for their scheduled visits, it causes healthcare providers to lose money and waste resources. Conversational chatbots streamline the appointment-making process for patients by providing an easy-to-use chat interface. In addition, they can send timely reminders, which decreases the number of no-shows and so saves time and money. Because patients commonly schedule appointments far in advance, it is not uncommon for them to need to be rescheduled. However, many people find it inconvenient to contact their doctor's office to reschedule an existing appointment. It can be difficult to reschedule an appointment to a time that is more convenient and to remember the new date. Chatbots make it simple for patients and their carers to reschedule or cancel appointments. Patients also need not worry about forgetting their appointments thanks to automated reminders.

B. Medication assistance and prescription refill tracking

By establishing reminders for when prescriptions need be restocked, conversational chatbots can streamline the process of seeking refills. Patients can check the status of their current and former prescriptions, place new orders with their pharmacy, and be informed of when their medications will arrive. Patients can keep track of their medicine supplies and consumption with the help of conversational AI. Chatbots can also be a great resource for learning about drug interactions and adverse effects.

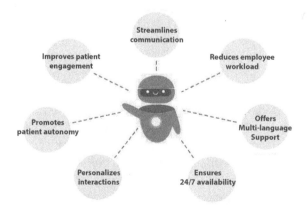

Figure 38.3 Applications of conversational AI in healthcare.

C. Informational queries

Medical chatbots powered by AI can ensure that the right people receive the right data at the right time. Patients often have immediate concerns regarding their healthcare, pharmacy, insurance, etc. When it comes to choosing a healthcare provider, chatbots can act as a one-stop shop for patients to obtain all the information they need—for example, a healthcare chatbot can quickly respond to questions like finding a nearby healthcare practitioner or learning about diagnostic procedures and protocols to follow during hospital visits. Because of their natural conversational flow, AI chatbots are a great resource for patient engagement and education. In addition, people are able to take a more active role in their treatment because of the accessibility of information. Managing medical expenses and insurance claims may be a tedious ordeal. Patients can get help from chatbots with billing and claims processes. Conversational chatbots powered by artificial intelligence can offer individualized guidance by asking a sequence of questions designed to elicit information about the user's symptoms. Patients can evaluate the severity of their symptoms and make an informed decision about whether or not to seek professional help when they have access to curated information and individualized recommendations. Chatbots facilitate virtual triage and help cut down on unneeded hospital visits, which benefits both patients and healthcare providers by saving time and resources.

D. Discreet mental health support

The stigma that exists in our culture around mental health disorders might discourage many people from seeking treatment. The stigma associated with discussing mental health issues might make it difficult to get help. Powerful NLP capabilities allow chatbots to accurately interpret user intent and provide lifelike dialogues. Talking to someone who would not judge them can be helpful for many people's mental health. Using conversational messaging with the highest sensitivity, chatbots that deal with mental health conversations can be a source of emotional support and are available around the clock. In addition, conversational chatbots can help raise awareness of mental health by giving immediate and individualized support to people struggling with disorders like sadness and anxiety.

E. Health and wellness management

Patients can benefit greatly from the chatbots' wealth of information, especially as more attention is paid to patients' overall health. Patients and caregivers can benefit from conversational chatbots that provide information on healthy eating, exercise, and rest. Patients can also benefit from their virtual coaches' ability to provide individualized guidance in adopting healthier living habits.

38.4   NLP-Driven Security Measures

Rule-based NLP, statistical NLP, and neural NLP are the three primary types of popular NLP methods, and they each have their own unique qualities. We then introduce representative algorithms for each of the three classes and examine their relative merits and shortcomings. Dedicated research by domain experts can improve the accuracy of rule-based NLP techniques like pattern matching [18] and parsing. In addition, rule-based NLP methods have a low learning curve. However, given the fluidity and complexity of human language, rules are typically insufficient to address all circumstances. In addition, rule-based NLP is limited in its potential for widespread use since it necessitates knowledge of both computer science and linguistics to build effective rules that work with human language. Although rule-based methods are still occasionally employed for improved preprocessing, they are generally regarded archaic in the academic community. Statistical natural language processing is more effective and reliable than rule-based NLP. However, it is limited in its ability to fully leverage available data and provide sufficient accuracy in complicated applications because it takes domain expertise to develop handcrafted features. Unlike rule-based NLP, which is opaque and difficult to read, statistical NLP is transparent and easy to understand because of its direct feature design [19]. In addition, statistical NLP is more effective than neural NLP because it does not require extensive computing resources or a large-scale dataset. In addition, there are notable distinctions between the features of many sample statistical NLP models including bag-of-words, TF-IDF, and n-gram. While bag-of-words is simple to construct, it fails to take into account other factors such as the relative importance of words and their placement inside a phrase.

The demand for artificial intelligence in healthcare has been motivated by developments in computational and data sciences as well as engineering improvements in medical equipment [20]. This might significantly alter the face of healthcare as we know it. To mimic human intelligence, AI makes use of sophisticated computer programs and algorithms. Computer algorithms are used to process complex data, allowing for inferences and conclusions to be drawn without the need for human intervention. AI is having an ever-increasing impact on all facets of society, and the healthcare industry is no exception. Large-scale deployments of AI in healthcare have been occurring in recent years in an effort to enhance healthcare delivery generally. There is currently no agreement on how to categorize the uses of AI in the healthcare industry. When discussing the implementation of AI in healthcare, however, we rely on the categorization of the applications outlined therein. Expert systems, machine learning, natural language processing, automated planning and scheduling, and image and signal processing are all examples of how artificial intelligence is used in the healthcare industry and are separated out in [15]. Artificially intelligent systems that have been "trained" with real-world examples to carry out complex tasks are called "expert systems". Figure 38.4 shows the architecture of NLP-data driven architecture.

Using supervised learning, unsupervised learning, and reinforcement learning, machine learning applies algorithms to recognize and learn from data patterns [18]. Using an algorithm to recognize significant words and phrases in natural language, natural language processing allows AI to be used to ascertain the meaning of a text [18]. A developing area of AI use in healthcare, automated planning and scheduling focuses on the coordination and prioritization of tasks needed to achieve an objective [18]. In addition, artificial intelligence is used in image and signal processing to hone data that has been gleaned from an actual physical occurrence (pictures and signals) [18]. All of these programs share a common goal: to improve healthcare decisions by making use of the huge amounts of data being created in the industry. Disease surveillance, decision support systems, fraud detection, and improved privacy and security are only few of the applications of collected data from healthcare workers [10]. In reality, for reasons of security, the Norwegian healthcare sector code of conduct mandates the proper preservation and safeguarding of healthcare information system access logs [16]. Electronic health records (EHR) and network activity leave trails

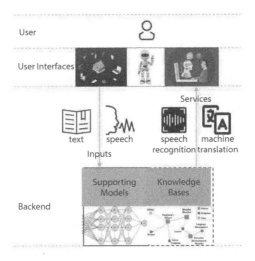

Figure 38.4 Architecture of NLP-data-driven architecture.

that can be tracked and used to create individual profiles for healthcare workers [16]. The EHR and other networks used by healthcare professionals create trails of activity that can be logged and pieced together to provide individual profiles [16]. Thus, such records can be mined using the appropriate AI approaches to identify the distinctive security procedures employed by healthcare personnel. These results will help management make decisions about the most effective incentives for encouraging patients to practice more safety-conscious caregiving.

An innovative approach to bolstering data security and privacy in a variety of settings is to implement security mechanisms that are driven by NLP. Organizations can improve their threat detection processes, enhance their access controls, and boost their overall cybersecurity standards by leveraging NLP approaches. The benefits of NLP-driven security solutions become clear upon closer inspection. First, these safeguards are exceptional at identifying outliers and stopping intrusions. NLP algorithms enable the proactive identification of potential security breaches or suspicious activity inside textual data by examining language patterns and finding deviations from established norms. This allows businesses to react quickly to new security risks. Furthermore, contextual permission is where NLP-driven security solutions really shine. Access privileges are determined by natural language processing systems based on their understanding of the context and intent of interactions. The risk of data leakage is reduced thanks to this contextual approach, which assigns users different levels of access depending on their jobs and the severity of the information being sought.

The use of natural language processing algorithms has also proven useful in the detection and redaction of sensitive material. In order to prevent accidental data leaks and increase confidentiality, these safeguards allow for the automated detection and masking of sensitive content inside text. In addition, NLP-driven models aid in the fight against fraud and phishing. These systems are able to spot questionable material, warn users, and prevent further security breaches by evaluating it for language patterns typically associated with phishing attempts. Behavioral biometrics add an extra layer of protection. Individuals' distinct linguistic habits allow NLP-based systems to profile users and spot impersonation and other forms of anomaly. The capabilities of NLP can also be used to improve multi-factor authentication by utilizing language patterns and conversational history as extra layers of verification. Furthermore, by processing huge amounts of textual data from many sources, NLP can help with contextual threat intelligence. By enabling NLP-driven security systems to extract insights from unstructured data, companies will have a better chance of receiving contextualized threat intelligence, improving their preparedness for new security threats. Systems driven by natural language processing are increasingly being used for real-time monitoring and incident response, where they scan conversations in progress for indicators of security or policy violations.

38.5   Integrating NLP With Security Framework

In the field of natural language processing, methods can be categorized as either symbolic or statistical. According to a recent review [7], symbolic approaches are the most commonly used in clinical NLP, primarily because dictionary or rule-based methodologies are adequate to address the information needs of many clinical applications. While statistical NLP necessitates the time-consuming creation of a tagged example set [8, 9], the narrow margin for mistake in clinical applications is another factor to think about. Accuracy tuning in symbolic systems is open and manageable with the addition of new resources (such as words or filters). Authoring interpretable rules reduces the effort in huge data annotation, which is especially helpful in clinical use cases where expert time is limited and the objectives to extract are well defined within a self-contained application. Correcting mistakes in statistical systems is more challenging without the use of symbolic approaches like post-processing rules. When using symbolic NLP, it is easy to correct mistakes like misidentifying the state code "CA" as cancer by adding contextual rules (like "look ahead for zip code" or "look behind for city name"). To resolve this issue in statistical NLP systems would require extensive time investment in the creation of training annotations, feature engineering, and retraining. When it comes to healthcare AI applications as a whole, NLP is typically used as a means of information extraction rather than as a complete stand-alone solution [10, 11]. This means that NLP output is usually incorporated into a larger input set or used to systematically extract training target values for subsequent AI models. Figure 38.5 shows the integration of NLP tasks.

Developing more sophisticated and all-encompassing NLP applications requires a systematic strategy like the integration of different NLP activities. Merging NLP tasks can produce more sophisticated and accurate results since they involve a wider set of processes targeted at understanding and interpreting human language. The revolutionary potential of NLP is best shown when exploring how various NLP activities may be easily coupled to produce robust applications. NER and relation extraction are two examples of methods that have been integrated. Relation extraction creates connections between the entities that NER finds, such as names, dates, and locations. By combining them, programs may do more than simply recognize entities; they can also comprehend the relationships between them. Knowledge graph construction, sentiment analysis, and information retrieval are just few of the areas where this combination shines. Similarly, sentiment analysis and aspect-based sentiment analysis have been combined. Aspect-based sentiment analysis goes deeper than simple sentiment analysis by measuring how readers feel about various entities or parts of

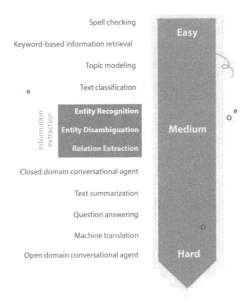

Figure 38.5 Integration of NLP tasks.

a text. Applications that do both of these functions can provide more nuanced insights into the sentiments expressed towards various parts of the text, thus enhancing the reader's ability to comprehend the full range of the author's intended meaning.

Another helpful strategy is to combine text classification with document summarization. Document summarizing creates succinct summaries, whereas text categorization places content into predetermined categories.

38.6   Conclusion

Finally, conversational AI agents that make use of NLP approaches show a lot of potential for improving both the patient experience and healthcare safety. NLP-driven solutions offer a promising way to meet the difficult concerns of data security and privacy in today's increasingly digital healthcare systems. Healthcare organizations can proactively identify possible security threats and prevent unauthorized access to critical patient information by deploying powerful NLP algorithms like entity recognition, sentiment analysis, and anomaly detection. A strong defense against ever-evolving cyber threats also requires the creation of novel security frameworks that integrate NLP capabilities with known security protocols. These systems need to be flexible enough to respond to ever-changing security threats so that sensitive patient information is always safe during phone calls. The implementation of NLP-based security measures is vital in establishing trust between patients and healthcare providers as the use of conversational AI agents spreads since it will help patients feel more at ease about the safety of their private health data. To ensure efficacy and legality, however, the installation of NLP-driven security innovations should be paired with rigorous testing, validation, and compliance with regulatory standards. In order to develop complete solutions that put patients' needs first, it will be necessary for teams of specialists in NLP, cybersecurity, and healthcare to work together. In conclusion, a game-changing opportunity to significantly improve healthcare security is presented by the convergence of natural language processing and conversational AI technologies. Healthcare organizations can strike a better balance between patient-centric care and strict security protocols with the use of NLP, thereby improving the quality, accessibility, and trustworthiness of healthcare in the current era.

References

1. Choi, E., Bahadori, M.T., Searles, E., Coffey, C., Thompson, M., Bost, J., Stewart, W.F., Developing and evaluating a deep learning model to predict postoperative opioid use. *JAMA Surg.*, 157, 5, 414–421, 2022.

2. Miotto, R., Li, L., Kidd, B.A., Dudley, J.T., Deep patient: An unsupervised representation to predict the future of patients from the electronic health records. *Sci. Rep.*, 6, 26094, 2022.

3. Heo, J. and Lee, S.W., Towards reliable explainability in medical NLP, 2023. arXiv preprint arXiv:2302.02835.

4. Ghorbani, A. and Zou, J., Interpretation of natural language processing models in clinical applications. *JAMA*, 327, 6, 571–572, 2022.

5. Amin, W., Al-Azawi, R., Ghaly, F., Alshaikh, F.S., A comprehensive survey on Arabic natural language processing for health care. *Artif. Intell. Med.*, 123, 102090, 2022.

6. Ogrin, M., Steenkamp, J., Hartvigsen, G., Detecting critical care events through distributed word embeddings. *J. Biomed. Inf.*, 124, 103900, 2023.

7. Raghu, A., Abbeel, P., Irvin, J., Rajpurkar, P., Lungren, M.P., Large-scale evaluation of anonymization techniques for clinical notes. *J. Biomed. Inf.*, 128, 103800, 2022.

8. Shooshan, S.E. and Crandall, A.S., Identifying potential drug-drug interactions with NLP and machine learning in EHR data. *J. Biomed. Inf.*, 132, 103714, 2023.

9. Kavuluru, R. and Rios, A., Using NLP to support Healthcare Providers' involvement in medication-related conversations on Twitter. *J. Biomed. Inf.*, 136, 103796, 2022.

10. Kahen, R.E., Bakken, S., Sarwar, S., Pfaff, T., Use of machine learning and natural language processing to inform nurse staffing ratios. *West. J. Nurs. Res.*, 2022. 19394592211024403.

11. Kuang, J., Xie, J., Lu, J., Zhang, C., Cancer-specific symptom extraction from free-text electronic medical records with semi-supervised learning. *J. Biomed. Inf.*, 134, 103673, 2023.

12. Sanan, P., Schier, J.G., Smith, T.P., Combining machine learning and natural language processing to enhance pharmacovigilance in medical devices. *J. Biomed. Inf.*, 134, 103729, 2023.

13. Zhang, J. and Fung, G., Machine learning and natural language processing for early detection of mental health disorders in healthcare, in: *Machine Learning and Natural Language Processing for Mental Health*, pp. 23–39, Springer, 2022.

14. Haug, P.J., Ferraro, J.P., Wu, W., Desai, A.S., A natural language processing approach for improving the identifiability of blood transfusion reactions in electronic health records. *JAMA Surg.*, 157, 1, 65–71, 2022.

15. Zheng, G., Duvall, S., Chapman, W., Crowley, R.S., Natural language processing for identifying adverse drug events, in: *Pharmacovigilance*, pp. 123–143, Springer, 2022.

16. Patel, M.K., Raman, S.R., Camp, M.S., Combining natural language processing and machine learning for accurate identification of patients for clinical trials. *J. Biomed. Inf.*, 137, 103769, 2023.

17. Westergaard, M.L. and Kankar, P.K., A review of NLP methods in mental health research. *IEEE J. Biomed. Health Inform.*, 26, 6, 1687–1694, 2022.

18. Krittanawong, C. and Zhang, H., Natural language processing in cardiovascular medicine. *J. Am. Coll. Cardiol.*, 81, 13, 1517–1526, 2023.
19. Tapiador, J.E. and Farré, J., Natural language processing and machine learning in a comprehensive system for automated suicide risk assessment: New horizons in psychoinformatics. *J. Affect. Disord.*, 296, 118–128, 2022.
20. Posada, J.D. and Yala, A., Pioneering the application of natural language processing to radiology. *J. Magn. Reson. Imaging*, 57, 1, 9–17, 2023.

NLP-Driven Chatbots: Applications and Implications in Conversational AI

A. Mary Sowjanya[1*] and Kotagiri Srividya[2]

¹Dept. of CS&SE, College of Engineering, Andhra University, Visakhapatnam, AP, India
²Department of AI&ML, GMR Institute of Technology, Rajam, AP, India

Abstract
The emergence of natural language processing (NLP) technologies has revolutionized the field of conversational AI, giving rise to sophisticated chatbot systems that simulate human-like interactions. This paper delves into the diverse applications and profound implications of NLP-driven chatbots in the realm of conversational AI. We explore how these chatbots have been harnessed across various sectors, including customer service, healthcare, e-commerce, and education, to enhance user experiences, automate tasks, and provide real-time assistance. Furthermore, we investigate the ethical and societal implications that arise with the increasing integration of NLP-driven chatbots in our daily lives, addressing concerns related to privacy, data security, algorithmic bias, and the potential displacement of human roles. Through an in-depth analysis, we highlight the transformative potential of NLP-driven chatbots, emphasizing the need for a balanced approach that leverages their benefits while mitigating potential drawbacks. This paper contributes to a comprehensive understanding of the landscape surrounding NLP-driven chatbots, offering insights into their evolving applications and the imperative considerations for a responsible and effective deployment in the field of conversational AI.

Keywords: Chatbots, natural language processing, NLP-driven chatbots, conversational AI

39.1 Introduction

Artificial intelligence (AI) technology enables the creation of computer programs that mimic human intelligence while solving problems. When it comes to AI, chatbots are taken very seriously as a medium through which information can be provided to users and activities can be completed with the help of AI [1]. We have not yet fully evaluated and utilized the potential of such systems. Almost all dialogue bots take user questions in the form of text written in natural language and return the optimal response in written or spoken form [2]. This procedure is repeated until the end of the discussion [3]. The interaction between people and chatbots is represented graphically in Figure 39.1. A chatbot's capacity to carry on a conversation with the user in either text or speech

---

Corresponding author: dr.amsowjanya@andhrauniversity.edu.in

Romil Rawat, Rajesh Kumar Chakrawarti, Sanjaya Kumar Sarangi, Piyush Vyas, Mary Sowjanya Alamanda, Kotagiri Srividya and Krishnan Sakthidasan Sankaran (eds.) Conversational Artificial Intelligence, (713–726) © 2024 Scrivener Publishing LLC

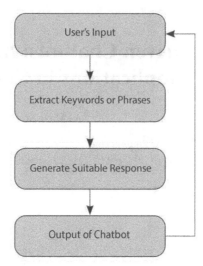

Figure 39.1 Conversational AI-based process flow for chatbots.

without interruption is crucial [4]. Only if the chatbot can interpret the user's intent and supply a relevant response will this be possible. Knowledge bases, interpretation software, and the actual chat engine are the three basic components of a chatbot [5]. The knowledge base is the repository of the system's intelligence; it is made up of search terms and the accompanying answers. Knowledge bases are typically implemented using a combination of data files, text files, database files, and XML files [6]. Figure 39.1 shows the conversational AI-based process flow for chatbots.

The interpreter software has two ancillary modules, an analyzer and a generator, that let it communicate with the user. The analyzer takes human-provided text as input and evaluates it based on its syntax and semantics. Normalization techniques such as pattern fitting, substitution, and phrase splitting are among those employed by this pre-processor [7]. The conversation engine compares the pre-processed output of the analyzer with the information in the knowledge base, using methods such as pattern matching, sentence reconstruction, indexing, etc., to determine the appropriate response [8]. The chat engine's response is processed by the generator, which then produces a grammatically correct sentence. The usual parts of a chatbot and their connections are shown in Figure 39.2.

Conversational AI has entered a new phase thanks to the rapid development of natural language processing (NLP) technology, which has profoundly altered the ways in which humans engage with machines [9]. Thanks to recent developments in machine learning and language comprehension, chatbots powered by NLP have emerged as important instruments in molding this new environment. These smart chatbots can both comprehend and produce natural-sounding dialogue, making it difficult to discern whether you are talking to a real person or a computer. The use cases and consequences of NLP-driven chatbots in the field of conversational artificial intelligence are investigated in depth in this research study [10]. Chatbots, which combine natural language processing methods with software development methodologies, have proliferated across industries and are reshaping everything from customer service to business operations to consumer engagement. NLP-driven

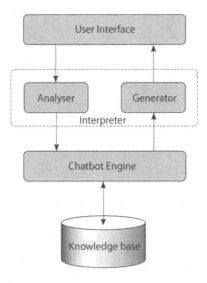

Figure 39.2 Architecture of a chatbot.

chatbots have proven their capacity to provide real-time assistance, automate processes, and increase engagement across a wide range of use cases, from personalized customer service interactions to healthcare diagnostics to e-commerce recommendations to educational support. Rapid adoption of natural language processing-driven chatbots, however, brings with it a number of ethical, cultural, and practical difficulties [11]. Important considerations about the ethical use of these technologies arise in the context of concerns about privacy, data security, algorithmic fairness, and the potential displacement of human positions in the workforce. To ensure the successful and ethical integration of NLP-driven chatbots into our daily lives, it is crucial to strike a balance between maximizing their benefits and resolving these problems. This study paper attempts to provide a thorough grasp of the complex terrain of NLP-driven chatbots through a methodical examination of real-world applications, ethical frameworks, and future trends [12]. We hope to contribute to an informed discussion on the role of NLP-driven chatbots in determining the future of conversational AI by diving into both their transformative potential and the difficult considerations they bring out. The major objective is to conduct an in-depth analysis of NLP-driven chatbots in conversational AI and their potential applications and ramifications [13]. To do so, we must first investigate the many applications of chatbots and identify the social and moral issues that arise from their widespread use. The purpose of this essay is to offer a balanced perspective on the topic, covering the advantages and disadvantages of chatbots powered by NLP.

Organization of the Chapter
The rest of the chapter is outlined as follows: Section 39.2 shows the types of chatbots and the architecture of chatbots, Section 39.3 shows the NLP-driven chatbot technology and its applications, Section 39.4 outlines the chatbot software for an automated system, and, finally, Section 39.5 concludes this chapter.

39.2   Related Work

A conversation framework for chatbots is the backbone for coordinating user–chatbot interactions. This methodical technique is meant to guarantee consistent, well-organized, and meaningful exchanges [14]. The framework consists of numerous central features that serve as a road map for any given dialogue. The discussion is set in motion by the user's initial command. NLP methods that are state-of-the-art are then applied to the input, whether it be text or speech [15]. Tokenization is one of these methods; it breaks down the input into manageable chunks, while part-of-speech tagging identifies the grammatical functions of individual words. Sentiment analysis provides insights into the user's emotional tone, while named entity recognition (NER) helps extract relevant entities like dates or locations [16]. An essential step is intent recognition, which entails understanding the user's true motivation for providing input. The system uses machine learning models to categorize the inputs into known purposes and then uses entity extraction to isolate information that is crucial to understanding the recognized intent [17]. The dialogue is enriched even further thanks to context management, which remembers previous exchanges. To guarantee contextual consistency and coherence, dialogue state tracking stores all previous inputs, responses, and entities. Figure 39.3 shows the chatbot framework based on conversations.

The chatbot then constructs replies in light of the inferred intent and the retained context. Different methods, from simple rule-based processes to complex natural language generation models, are used in answer generation to create natural-sounding, relevant responses [18]. User-friendly forms are used to deliver these answers, which may include text, audio, graphics, or interactive features. Learning and change are essential to the survival of the conversation framework. The chatbot gets smarter over time thanks to input from its users and machine learning models that learn from their experiences. The effectiveness and popularity of the chatbot are both boosted by this adaptive learning loop [19]. The framework's distinguishing characteristic is its ability to handle interactions with multiple turn-based stages. Users and chatbots have ongoing conversations; thus, it is important for the framework to keep track of the conversation history and context in order to facilitate fluent and meaningful exchanges on both sides. User engagement tactics give online interactions a more personal feel [20]. Follow-up inquiries, ideas, and even a little humor can go a long way toward improving the user experience and making encounters more pleasurable

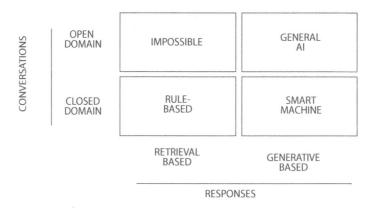

Figure 39.3 Chatbot framework based on conversations.

overall. When the user's goal is accomplished or a logical break in the dialogue occurs, the chat ends [21]. This final step can include farewell messages or additional support options to help users leave on a good note. Essentially, a chatbot conversation framework combines NLP developments, machine learning approaches, and user-centric design concepts to orchestrate interactions that are not only effective and context-aware but also infused with the spirit of genuine conversation [22]. This architecture is state-of-the-art because it allows chatbots to improve their abilities to interact with, assist, and comprehend consumers over time.

A. Types of chatbots

Chatbot systems come in various types, each differing in complexity, capabilities, and the technologies they leverage [23]. These types can be classified based on their sophistication and the depth of their interactions with users. Here different types of chatbot systems according to their complexities will be explained:

- Rule-based chatbots: Rule-based chatbots, also known as scripted chatbots, are the simplest type. They operate on predefined rules and scripts. These chatbots can respond to specific keywords or patterns in user inputs. Rule-based chatbots are ideal for handling straightforward tasks and providing basic information. However, they lack the ability to understand context or engage in nuanced conversations.
- Menu-driven chatbots: Menu-driven chatbots present users with predefined options in the form of menus. Users select options using buttons or text commands, and the chatbot responds accordingly. While these chatbots provide a structured interaction flow, they can be limited in handling open-ended queries or complex conversations.
- Retrieval-based chatbots: Retrieval-based chatbots use predefined responses stored in a database. They match user inputs to the closest predefined response based on keywords or patterns. These chatbots can handle a wider range of queries compared to rule-based or menu-driven systems, but they still lack true understanding of language semantics and context.
- Generative chatbots: Generative chatbots employ more advanced techniques, such as machine learning and NLP, to create responses from scratch. They can generate human-like text based on the patterns and context in the input. Generative chatbots can provide more contextually relevant responses and handle more complex queries, making them suitable for a broader array of applications.
- AI-powered chatbots: AI-powered chatbots, also referred to as context-aware or NLP-driven chatbots, are the most sophisticated type. They utilize deep learning and NLP techniques to understand user intent and context. These chatbots can engage in natural conversations, comprehend nuances, and provide more accurate and human-like responses. They can also learn from user interactions and improve over time.
- Virtual assistants: Virtual assistants are a subset of AI-powered chatbots that are designed to perform tasks and engage in more extensive interactions. They can execute commands, schedule appointments, make reservations, and perform a wide range of tasks beyond simple information retrieval.

Virtual assistants like Siri, Google Assistant, and Amazon Alexa fall into this category.

- Hybrid chatbots: Hybrid chatbots combine different approaches to achieve a balance between complexity and efficiency. They might use rule-based logic for simple tasks, retrieval-based methods for common queries, and generative responses for more unique interactions. This approach aims to leverage the strengths of different techniques to provide a versatile and effective chatbot experience.

In conclusion, the complexity of chatbot systems varies significantly, ranging from simple rule-based systems to highly sophisticated AI-powered virtual assistants. The choice of the type of chatbot depends on the specific requirements of the application, the desired level of interaction, and the technologies available for implementation.

B. Architecture of NLP-based chatbots

The core of a chatbot's functionality is its architecture, which includes a complex framework for facilitating user–chatbot interaction. This design is built on a foundation of layered components, all of which work together to ensure fluent communication [24]. The user interface layer, located at the forefront of the architecture, is where users will input their questions or orders. A chat window, message platform, or mobile app could all serve as potential manifestations of this interface, which is where users first interact with the chatbot. The chatbot's brains are the NLP layer, which processes human language [25]. This layer parses user inputs, determining their meaning and intent based on techniques such as tokenization, part-of-speech tagging, named entity recognition, intent recognition, and sentiment analysis. The component known as the knowledge base or database stores all of the collected data [26]. The chatbot can draw on the stored structured data, programmed responses, and knowledge graphs to offer appropriate and accurate responses. Both retrieval-based and generative chatbots rely heavily on this pool of knowledge. The dialogue is managed by a layer called "dialogue management." In this setting, past contacts are recorded and maintained for future reference [27]. This layer makes sure the chatbot is having meaningful conversations that make sense in its context. The information, intent, and context that have been analyzed are then used by the response generation layer to produce appropriate responses. These responses could be predefined based on criteria or dynamically created utilizing sophisticated machine learning and natural language processing models, depending on the type of chatbot. The architecture relies heavily on the success of the user context management system [28]. It is crucial for the chatbot to grasp the ongoing conversation in order to provide relevant responses and a natural conversational flow. By connecting to third-party APIs, chatbots can gain access to up-to-the-minute information and data. Because of their connectedness, they can provide timely and relevant responses to user inquiries, especially about external aspects like weather forecasts and product availability [29]. Finally, the chatbot's capacity to evolve over time is encapsulated in the learning and improvement feature. Machine learning techniques allow the chatbot to continuously improve its responses and performance as users interact with it and provide feedback, leading to a more efficient and user-centric experience [30]. The architecture of chatbots is, in essence, a complex orchestration of layers, all of which work together to allow the chatbot to understand human inputs, remember their context, and respond appropriately. Chatbots are set to provide increasingly sophisticated and natural conversational interactions as their

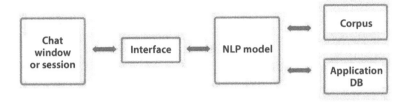

Figure 39.4 General architecture of NLP-driven chatbots.

underlying architecture adapts to new technologies. Figure 39.4 shows the general architecture of NLP-driven chatbots.

39.3   NLP-Driven Chatbot Technologies

Using a technique called deep learning, NLP enables the computer (a chatbot in this case) to interpret the user's input and provide a meaningful response. The user's inquiry (utterance) is parsed by the NLP engine, which uses natural language understanding to determine the user's intended action. The machine then communicates back to the user in a human-comprehensible language through natural language generation (NLG) [31]. Chatbots that use NLP interpret and generate human language using a complex procedure. A chatbot performs a number of analyses on the user's input before responding to them, whether that input is textual or verbal. Tokenization, where the input is broken down into smaller parts called tokens, and part-of-speech tagging are both a part of this preliminary analysis. Sentiment analysis evaluates the user's mood, whereas named entity recognition adds further context to the dialogue by detecting elements like names and locations [32]. The chatbot uses methods such as purpose classification and entity extraction to deduce the user's intent after processing the input. Conversational context must be preserved at all times, and dialogue state tracking is the means through which this is accomplished. The chatbot then provides a response using language generation algorithms, making sure the language is natural and the content is relevant to the conversation. The completed response is then displayed to the user, and the chatbot continues to get better through learning and adaption. The chatbot's responses and understanding of context can always be improved through further engagement with the user. Simply said, NLP-based chatbots are the pinnacle of user–machine communication because they expertly combine linguistic analysis, machine learning, and contextual awareness to enable natural and coherent conversations. Figure 39.5 shows the working process of NLP-based chatbots.

The new generation of chatbots represents a paradigm shift, harnessing the power of NLP to create intelligent virtual agents that continuously evolve in sophistication. These NLP-powered chatbots exhibit a unique ability to accumulate knowledge over conversations, progressively enhancing their capabilities. A cornerstone of their operation is the dialogue management component, which is responsible for tracking conversation context and session continuity, thus ensuring seamless interactions from beginning to end. A defining feature of these advanced chatbots is their seamless transition from AI to human interaction, known as human handoff. This ensures that, when necessary, the conversation

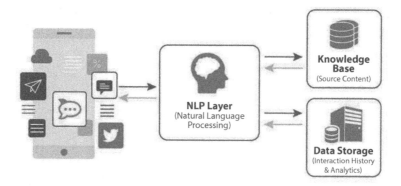

Figure 39.5 Working process of NLP-based chatbots.

is seamlessly transferred to a human agent, guaranteeing a smooth customer experience. Integral to the functionality of these NLP-powered chatbots is the integration of business logic, which aligns their behavior with the specific requirements and processes of the company they serve. Rapid iteration is another crucial aspect, enabling the swift development and deployment of bot solutions that not only are efficient but also adapt to emerging challenges. The significance of training and iteration cannot be overstated. Continuous refinement through systematic training and feedback mechanisms helps the chatbot understand customer intents better, drawing insights from real-world conversations across various channels. Underpinning these capabilities is the foundation of natural language processing, wherein the chatbot processes user utterances to determine intent, identify relevant entities, and maintain context throughout the session. Utterances, intents, entities, context, and session are the keys that empower the chatbot's understanding of user input and drive meaningful interactions. Simplicity is the guiding principle for setting up these virtual agents. The goal is to provide the necessary functionality without unnecessary complexity. This approach ensures optimal user engagement while leaving room for future enhancements or additions as needs evolve. As NLP-powered chatbots continue to refine their abilities and expand their applications, they redefine the landscape of customer interactions and pave the way for more intuitive and efficient customer service experiences.

Delving into the intricate workings of today's AI chatbots unveils a comprehensive process involving five pivotal stages that collectively enable these systems to comprehensively understand and respond to user input. These steps—encompassing tokenizing, normalizing, entity recognition, dependency parsing, and generation–form the backbone of the chatbot's operational framework, transforming raw text into meaningful interactions. Kicking off with tokenizing, the chatbot dissects the input text into smaller fragments known as tokens while simultaneously removing punctuation. This segmentation serves as the foundation for subsequent analysis. Normalizing follows suit as the chatbot eliminates extraneous details and standardizes words, often converting them to lowercase, streamlining the information for easier processing. In the phase of entity recognition, the chatbot capitalizes on the normalized text to discern the type of entities being referred to. Whether identifying locations like "North America," quantifying percentages like "67%," or recognizing organizations like "Google," this step provides context to the conversation. Proceeding to dependency parsing, the chatbot ascertains the grammatical roles of each word within the sentence, distinguishing between nouns, verbs, adjectives, and objects. This dissection enhances the bot's understanding of sentence structure and semantics. The culminating step is generation, wherein the chatbot employs the information gathered in the preceding stages to craft potential responses. Multiple response options are generated and subsequently evaluated, with the most fitting and contextually relevant response being selected for transmission to the user. Collectively, these five steps showcase the intricate intricacies involved in the AI chatbot's journey from reading and interpreting user input to formulating and delivering meaningful and coherent responses.

39.4   Chatbot Software for Automated Systems

It takes a well-orchestrated sequence of steps to turn the idea of an intelligent conversational agent into a fully effective chatbot software for an automated system. In the first stage, called "requirement gathering and analysis," stakeholders and potential end-users work together to establish the chatbot's precise goals. The next step is to create a design and architectural plan that details the chatbot's functionality, platform support, and integration points as well as the user interaction flow and interface design. An essential step in making the chatbot understandable to humans is the incorporation of NLP technologies. Tokenization, sentiment analysis, and intent identification are just few of the components that go into making a chatbot intelligent. At the same time, a database of often-asked questions and answers and other information the chatbot will need to function is being compiled. After an architecture has been established, the next step is development and implementation, during which time the chatbot software is built using the relevant programming languages and frameworks. We implement natural language processing algorithms, dialogue management logic, response generating mechanisms, and connections with external services to ensure that conversations make sense and are relevant to the user's context. The chatbot's ability to maintain knowledge of ongoing discussions is improved by the use of context management and state tracking. Designing intuitive interfaces *via* which people can communicate with the chatbot is of paramount importance. With this end in mind, designers of web-based chat windows, mobile apps, and integrations with messaging networks craft their products. The chatbot is put through rigorous testing and quality assurance to find and fix any technological problems, and further testing of its usability and functionality guarantees that it will function as intended. During this stage, the chatbot is trained and fine-tuned to improve its functionality. If machine learning models are used, they are educated with pertinent information to improve precision. Users' actions and comments are used to fine-tune the natural language processing modules and the algorithms that generate responses. After all the necessary setup is complete, the application is deployed to the user's choice of platform and integrated into the automated system, paving the way for seamless communication with third-party APIs and services. After that, training and documentation are made available to users so that they can interact with the chatbot effectively, and efforts are made to continually monitor and develop the chatbot's performance and the quality of the user experience. Figure 39.6 shows the process of a chatbot software for an automated system.

Establishing a bridge between chatbot theory and implementation is crucial. Major aspects of bot creation and development are being overlooked by the current study.

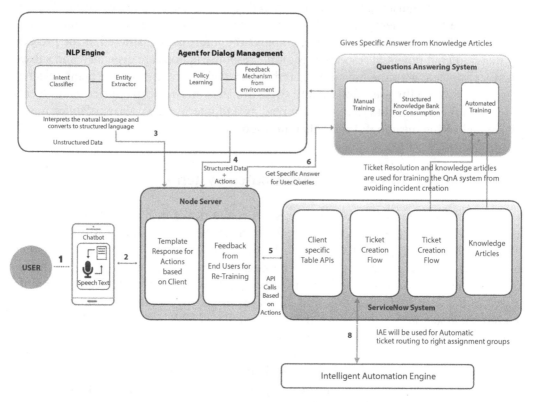

Figure 39.6 Process of chatbot software for an automated system.

Personality of chatbots, response flexibility, interaction simplicity, task and duty specification, empathy and emotional state, and user boredom, to name a few, are some of the significant topics. There is a lot of work involved in finding the proper piece of information because this field of study is continually developing. Designing a chatbot for a niche market requires sticking to a process flow and figuring out what features it needs. In Figure 39.7, we outline the process that must be followed to create a functional chatbot.

Conversational AI will soon replace many current technologies. They will be helpful in finding the most relevant information for your needs. We present a scenario explaining how a developer might follow the pipeline above to construct a chatbot using a validated approach to further illustrate what are the necessary steps to take while designing and developing such a system. Think about hiring chatbot developer Matthew to help you stay on track with your healthy eating habits. Mathew wants to create a chatbot system that is intuitive and efficient and that can effectively reply to consumer inquiries. Following the

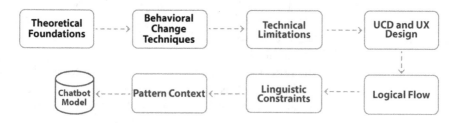

Figure 39.7 Future trends of a NLP-driven chatbot software.

chatbot system pipeline, he plans to address the areas of behavior, theory, and technology specified therein. Theoretical underpinnings of the chatbot system design (like theory to motivate veggie eating) are the first thing Mathew looks into. The next step is to learn the theory behind user motivation, the bot's ability to effectively intervene, and the users' ability to maintain their commitment to the process over time. Mathew must now make a choice from the various theoretical frameworks at his disposal. After deciding on a theoretical model to follow, Mathew must research the behavior modification strategy needed to create the bot and reach the specified objective (for instance, a plan to encourage vegetable consumption). UX design is the next phase, and while it may appear simple, especially for chatbots, it can quickly become a formidable challenge for Mathew. Mathew has to use a user experience design principle that is more suitable for chatbot software. When designing the chat's user interface, he must make trade-offs between features (such as letting users type or giving them buttons to report their daily dietary actions). Mathew must now analyze and require the technical tools and models he must use to power the bot with AI and decide the necessary intelligent behavior the bot must carry out after he has decided the theory and technique to implement the theory and design the initial command user interface (CUI). To program the chatbot's varied behaviors, Mathew must select to employ whether a rule-based or AI-based method. He can also use existing platforms to implement additional behavior-oriented features (like sentiment analysis and intend detection). Finally, he will need to carefully construct the pattern that best suits the chatbot's personality and language as well as the context of the interaction.

39.5   Conclusion

In conclusion, the rapid development of NLP-driven chatbots has shown their significant potential to transform the landscape of conversational AI in many fields. Access to information and services has been greatly improved, while customer interactions have been transformed, all thanks to these smart systems. Their capacity to comprehend and produce natural-sounding language paves the way for better user experiences and more effective workflows. The widespread use of natural language processing-powered chatbots, however, raises a number of important ethical and cultural concerns. To make sure that the rollout of these chatbots is in line with ethical principles and regulatory frameworks, concerns about privacy, data security, fairness, and responsibility must be addressed. In addition, the displacement of human roles brings up concerns about the future of work and the function of automation in society. As we move forward, it will be essential to find a happy medium between making full use of NLP-driven chatbots and preventing their misuse. For conversational AI to undergo a constructive shift, it is crucial that researchers, developers, governments, and stakeholders work together to promote responsible innovation. Achieving a successful, equitable, and ethical use of NLP-driven chatbots requires keeping an eye on the advantages and disadvantages of this technology. Conversational AI's NLP-driven chatbots are still in the early stages of their development, and their influence on human–machine interaction is only just beginning to be seen. We may fully utilize the promise of NLP-driven chatbots while maintaining a peaceful coexistence between human and automated conversational agents if we navigate this environment with awareness, sensitivity, and dedication to responsible growth.

References

1. Alawad, M. *et al.*, Privacy-preserving deep learning NLP models for cancer registries. *IEEE Trans. Emerg. Topics Comput.*, 9, 3, 1219–1230, 1 July-Sept. 2021, doi: 10.1109/TETC.2020.2983404.

2. Ding, J. and Li, S., A low-latency and low-cost montgomery modular multiplier based on NLP multiplication. *IEEE Trans. Circuits Syst. II: Express Br.*, 67, 7, 1319–1323, July 2020, doi: 10.1109/TCSII.2019.2932328.

3. Singh, S. and Mahmood, A., The NLP cookbook: Modern recipes for transformer based deep learning architectures. *IEEE Access*, 9, 68675–68702, 2021, doi: 10.1109/ACCESS.2021.3077350.

4. Patil, R., Boit, S., Gudivada, V., Nandigam, J., A survey of text representation and embedding techniques in NLP. *IEEE Access*, 11, 36120–36146, 2023, doi: 10.1109/ACCESS.2023.3266377.

5. Breve, B., Cimino, G., Deufemia, V., Identifying security and privacy violation rules in trigger-action IoT platforms with NLP models. *IEEE Internet Things J.*, 10, 6, 5607–5622, 15 March15, 2023, doi: 10.1109/JIOT.2022.3222615.

6. Tambe, T. *et al.*, A 16-nm SoC for noise-robust speech and NLP edge AI inference with bayesian sound source separation and attention-based DNNs. *IEEE J. Solid-State Circuits*, 58, 2, 569–581, Feb. 2023, doi: 10.1109/JSSC.2022.3179303.

7. Amosa, T.I., Izhar, L.I.B., Sebastian, P., Ismail, I.B., Ibrahim, O., Ayinla, S.L., Clinical errors from acronym use in electronic health record: A review of NLP-based disambiguation techniques. *IEEE Access*, 11, 59297–59316, 2023, doi: 10.1109/ACCESS.2023.3284682.

8. Sonbol, R., Rebdawi, G., Ghneim, N., The use of NLP-based text representation techniques to support requirement engineering tasks: A systematic mapping review. *IEEE Access*, 10, 62811–62830, 2022, doi: 10.1109/ACCESS.2022.3182372.

9. Li, Z. *et al.*, A unified understanding of deep NLP models for text classification. *IEEE Trans. Vis. Comput. Graph.*, 28, 12, 4980–4994, 1 Dec. 2022, doi: 10.1109/TVCG.2022.3184186.

10. Houssein, E.H., Mohamed, R.E., Ali, A.A., Machine learning techniques for biomedical natural language processing: A comprehensive review. *IEEE Access*, 9, 140628–140653, 2021, doi: 10.1109/ACCESS.2021.3119621.

11. Liu, F., Huang, H., Yang, Z., Hao, Z., Wang, J., Search-based algorithm with scatter search strategy for automated test case generation of NLP toolkit. *IEEE Trans. Emerg. Top. Comput. Intell.*, 5, 3, 491–503, June 2021, doi: 10.1109/TETCI.2019.2914280.

12. Bahja, M. and Safdar, G.A., Unlink the link between COVID-19 and 5G networks: An NLP and SNA based approach. *IEEE Access*, 8, 209127–209137, 2020, doi: 10.1109/ACCESS.2020.3039168.

13. Nawaz, H.S., Shi, Z., Gan, Y., Hirpa, A., Dong, J., Zheng, H., Temporal moment localization via natural language by utilizing video question answers as a special variant and bypassing NLP for corpora. *IEEE Trans. Circuits Syst. Video Technol.*, 32, 9, 6174–6185, Sept. 2022, doi: 10.1109/TCSVT.2022.3162650.

14. Sánchez-Adame, L.M., Mendoza, S., Urquiza, J., Rodríguez, J., Meneses-Viveros, A., Towards a set of heuristics for evaluating chatbots. *IEEE Lat. Am. Trans.*, 19, 12, 2037–2045, Dec. 2021, doi: 10.1109/TLA.2021.9480145.

15. Daniel, G., Cabot, J., Deruelle, L., Derras, M., Xatkit: A multimodal low-code chatbot development framework. *IEEE Access*, 8, 15332–15346, 2020, doi: 10.1109/ACCESS.2020.2966919.

16. Ren, R., Pérez-soler, S., Castro, J.W., Dieste, O., Acuña, S.T., Using the SOCIO chatbot for UML modeling: A second family of experiments on usability in academic settings. *IEEE Access*, 10, 130542–130562, 2022, doi: 10.1109/ACCESS.2022.3228772.

17. Santos, G.A., de Andrade, G.G., Silva, G.R.S., Duarte, F.C.M., Costa, J.P.J.D., de Sousa, R.T., A conversation-driven approach for chatbot management. *IEEE Access*, 10, 8474–8486, 2022, doi: 10.1109/ACCESS.2022.3143323.

18. Chakraborty, S. *et al.*, An AI-based medical chatbot model for infectious disease prediction. *IEEE Access*, 10, 128469–128483, 2022, doi: 10.1109/ACCESS.2022.3227208.

19. Medeiros, L., Bosse, T., Gerritsen, C., Can a chatbot comfort humans? Studying the impact of a supportive chatbot on users' self-perceived stress. *IEEE Trans. Hum.-Mach. Syst.*, 52, 3, 343–353, June 2022, doi: 10.1109/THMS.2021.3113643.

20. Abdellatif, A., Badran, K., Costa, D.E., Shihab, E., A comparison of natural language understanding platforms for chatbots in software engineering. *IEEE Trans. Software Eng.*, 48, 8, 3087–3102, 1 Aug. 2022, doi: 10.1109/TSE.2021.3078384.

21. Ren, R., Castro, J.W., Santos, A., Dieste, O., Acuña, S.T., Using the SOCIO chatbot for UML modelling: A family of experiments. *IEEE Trans. Software Eng.*, 49, 1, 364–383, 1 Jan. 2023, doi: 10.1109/TSE.2022.3150720.

22. Wu, E.H.-K., Lin, C.-H., Ou, Y.-Y., Liu, C.-Z., Wang, W.-K., Chao, C.-Y., Advantages and constraints of a hybrid model K-12 E-Learning assistant chatbot. *IEEE Access*, 8, 77788–77801, 2020, doi: 10.1109/ACCESS.2020.2988252.

23. Cai, W., Jin, Y., Chen, L., Task-oriented user evaluation on critiquing-based recommendation chatbots. *IEEE Trans. Hum.-Mach. Syst.*, 52, 3, 354–366, June 2022, doi: 10.1109/THMS.2021.3131674.

24. Zhang, L., Yang, Y., Zhou, J., Chen, C., He, L., Retrieval-polished response generation for chatbot. *IEEE Access*, 8, 123882–123890, 2020, doi: 10.1109/ACCESS.2020.3004152.

25. Srivastava, B., Rossi, F., Usmani, S., Bernagozzi, M., Personalized chatbot trustworthiness ratings. *IEEE Trans. Technol. Soc.*, 1, 4, 184–192, Dec. 2020, doi: 10.1109/TTS.2020.3023919.

26. Ait-Mlouk, A. and Jiang, L., KBot: A knowledge graph based chatBot for natural language understanding over linked data. *IEEE Access*, 8, 149220–149230, 2020, doi: 10.1109/ACCESS.2020.3016142.

27. Miklosik, A., Evans, N., Qureshi, A.M.A., The use of chatbots in digital business transformation: A systematic literature review. *IEEE Access*, 9, 106530–106539, 2021, doi: 10.1109/ACCESS.2021.3100885.

28. Chen, T.-Y., Chiu, Y.-C., Bi, N., Tsai, R.T.-H., Multi-modal chatbot in intelligent manufacturing. *IEEE Access*, 9, 82118–82129, 2021, doi: 10.1109/ACCESS.2021.3083518.

29. García-Méndez, S., De Arriba-Pérez, F., González-Castaño, F.J., Regueiro-Janeiro, J.A., Gil-Castiñeira, F., Entertainment chatbot for the digital inclusion of elderly people without abstraction capabilities. *IEEE Access*, 9, 75878–75891, 2021, doi: 10.1109/ACCESS.2021.3080837.

30. Rajkumar, R. and Ganapathy, V., Bio-inspiring learning style chatbot inventory using brain computing interface to increase the efficiency of E-Learning. *IEEE Access*, 8, 67377–67395, 2020, doi: 10.1109/ACCESS.2020.2984591.

31. Martínez-Gárate, Á. A., Aguilar-Calderón, J.A., Tripp-Barba, C., Zaldívar-Colado, A., Model-driven approaches for conversational agents development: A systematic mapping study. *IEEE Access*, 11, 73088–73103, 2023, doi: 10.1109/ACCESS.2023.3293849.

32. Gao, Y., Tong, W., Wu, E.Q., Chen, W., Zhu, G., Wang, F.-Y., Chat with ChatGPT on interactive engines for intelligent driving. *IEEE Trans. Intell. Veh.*, 8, 3, 2034–2036, March 2023, doi: 10.1109/TIV.2023.3252571.

About the Editors

Romil Rawat, PhD, is an assistant professor at Shri Vaishnav Vidyapeeth Vishwavidyalaya, Indore. With over 12 years of teaching experience, he has published numerous papers in scholarly journals and conferences. He has also published book chapters and is a board member on two scientific journals. He has received several research grants and has hosted research events, workshops, and training programs. He also has several patents to his credit.

Rajesh Kumar Chakrawarti, PhD, is a professor and the Dean of the Department of Computer Science & Engineering, Sushila Devi Bansal College, Bansal Group of Institutions, India. He has over 20 years of industry and academic experience and has published over 100 research papers and chapters in books.

Sanjaya Kumar Sarangi, PhD, is an adjunct professor and coordinator at Utkal University, Coordinator and Adjunct Professor, Utkal University, Bhubaneswar, India. He has over 23 years of academic experience and has authored textbooks, book chapters, and papers for journals and conferences. He has been a visiting doctoral fellow at the University of California, USA, and he has more than 30 patents to his credit.

Piyush Vyas, PhD, is an assistant professor of computer information systems at Texas A&M University Central-Texas, USA. He has published numerous journal and conference articles in scholarly journals and conferences.

Mary Sowjanya Alamanda, PhD, is an associate professor in the Department of Computer Science and Systems Engineering at Andhra University College of Engineering, Visakhapatnam, India. She has four patents to her credit and has published more than 80 research publications in scholarly journals and conferences.

Kotagiri Srividya, PhD, is an associate professor and Head of the Department of Computer Science at the GMR Institute of Technology, Rajam, India. He has 18 years of teaching experience.

K. Sakthidasan Sankaran, is a professor in the Department of Electronics and Communication Engineering at Hindustan Institute of Technology and Science, India. He is a reviewer and an editorial board member for several scholarly journals, and he has published more than 70 papers. He also has three books to his credit.

Index

Page numbers followed by f and t indicate figures and tables, respectively.

Also of Interest

From the same editors

QUANTUM COMPUTING IN CYBERSECURITY, Edited by Romil Rawat, Rajesh Kumar Chakrawarti, Sanjaya Kumar Sarangi, Jaideep Patel, and Vivek Bhardwaj, ISBN: 9781394166336. This cutting-edge new volume provides a comprehensive exploration of emerging technologies and trends in quantum computing and how it is used in cybersecurity, covering everything from artificial intelligence to how quantum computing can be used to secure networks and prevent cyber crime.

ROBOTIC PROCESS AUTOMATION, Edited by Romil Rawat, Rajesh Kumar Chakrawarti, Sanjaya Kumar Sarangi, Rahul Choudhary, Anand Singh Gadwal, and Vivek Bhardwaj. ISBN: 9781394166183. Presenting the latest technologies and practices in this ever-changing field, this groundbreaking new volume covers the theoretical challenges and practical solutions for using robotics across a variety of industries, encompassing many disciplines, including mathematics, computer science, electrical engineering, information technology, mechatronics, electronics, bioengineering, and command and software engineering.

AUTONOMOUS VEHICLES VOLUME 1: Using Machine Intelligence, Edited by Romil Rawat, A. Mary Sowjanya, Syed Imran Patel, Varshali Jaiswal, Imran Khan, and Allam Balaram. ISBN: 9781119871958. Addressing the current challenges, approaches and applications relating to autonomous vehicles, this groundbreaking new volume presents the research and techniques in this growing area, using Internet of Things, Machine Learning, Deep Learning, and Artificial Intelligence.

AUTONOMOUS VEHICLES VOLUME 2: Smart Vehicles for Communication, Edited by Romil Rawat, Purvee Bhardwaj, Upinder Kaur, Shrikant Telang, Mukesh Chouhan, and K. Sakthidasan Sankaran, ISBN: 9781394152254. The companion to *Autonomous Vehicles Volume 1: Using Machine Intelligence*, this second volume in the two-volume set covers intelligent techniques utilized for designing, controlling and managing vehicular systems based on advanced algorithms of computing like machine learning, artificial Intelligence, data analytics, and Internet of Things with prediction approaches to avoid accidental damages, security threats, and theft.

Check out these other related titles from Scrivener Publishing

CONVERGENCE OF CLOUD WITH AI FOR BIG DATA ANALYTICS: Foundations and Innovation, Edited by Danda B. Rawat, Lalit K Awasthi, Valentina Emilia Balas, Mohit Kumar and Jitendra Kumar Samriya, ISBN: 9781119904885. This book covers the foundations and applications of cloud computing, AI, and Big Data and analyses their convergence for improved development and services.

SWARM INTELLIGENCE: An Approach from Natural to Artificial, By Kuldeep Singh Kaswan, Jagjit Singh Dhatterwal and Avadhesh Kumar, ISBN: 9781119865063. This important authored book presents valuable new insights by exploring the boundaries shared by cognitive science, social psychology, artificial life, artificial intelligence, and evolutionary computation by applying these insights to solving complex engineering problems.

FACTORIES OF THE FUTURE: Technological Advances in the Manufacturing Industry, Edited by Chandan Deep Singh and Harleen Kaur, ISBN: 9781119864943. The book provides insight into various technologies adopted and to be adopted in the future by industries and measures the impact of these technologies on manufacturing performance and their sustainability.

AI AND IOT-BASED INTELLIGENT AUTOMATION IN ROBOTICS, Edited by Ashutosh Kumar Dubey, Abhishek Kumar, S. Rakesh Kumar, N. Gayathri, Prasenjit Das, ISBN: 9781119711209. The 24 chapters in this book provide a deep overview of robotics and the application of AI and IoT in robotics across several industries such as healthcare, defense. education, etc.

SMART GRIDS AND INTERNET OF THINGS, Edited by Sanjeevikumar Padmanaban, Jens Bo Holm-Nielsen, Rajesh Kumar Dhanaraj, Malathy Sathyamoorthy, and Balamurugan Balusamy, ISBN: 9781119812449. Written and edited by a team of international professionals, this groundbreaking new volume covers the latest technologies in automation, tracking, energy distribution and consumption of Internet of Things (IoT) devices with smart grids.